Table of Contents

Introduction

Nearly all of us have to work during our lives. We reach adulthood and seek employment, and then we work for the next 30 to 50 years. Work is our primary means of livelihood. It serves an important economic function in the global world of commerce. It creates opportunities for social interactions and friendships. And it provides the products and services that sustain and improve our standard of living.

This text is all about work and the systems by which it is accomplished. The text also examines the principles and programs that allow work to be performed most efficiently and safely, and it discusses the techniques used to measure and manage work. The common denominator in the analysis, design, and measurement of work is time. For many reasons that are enumerated in this chapter time is important in work. In general, it is desirable to accomplish a given task in the shortest possible time.

Work systems constitute the central theme in the discipline of industrial engineering. Each engineering discipline is concerned with its own type of technical system. The correlations are listed in Table 1 for the major engineering disciplines. In most cases, each engineering field has expanded to include several related kinds of systems, and these additional systems are also listed in the table. Their addition has been a natural evolutionary process that has paralleled the development of new technologies. For industrial engineering, the additional subjects include operations research, ergonomics, discrete event simulation, and information systems. We can reasonably argue that all of these fields are related to the study of systems that perform work.

In this chapter, we define (1) work itself, (2) work systems, (3) jobs and occupations, and (4) productivity. In Section 5, we discuss the variety of topics covered in this text and the way in which the topics are organized. All of these topics are concerned with work in one way or another. Some familiar quotations and sayings about work and jobs are presented in Table 2 for the reader's amusement. Work has been the object

TABLE 1 Engineering Disciplines and the Types of Systems They Design and Analyze

Engineering Discipline	Type of System	New Systems and Subjects
Aeronautical engineering	Airplanes	Aerospace systems, missile systems
Chemical engineering	Chemical systems, chemical processing systems	Processing of integrated circuits, process control, polymer science, biotechnology
Civil engineering	Structural systems (e.g., bridges, buildings, roads)	Environmental systems, transportation systems, fluid systems
Electrical engineering	Electrical systems, power generation systems	Computer systems, integrated circuits, control systems
Industrial engineering	Work systems	Operations research, ergonomics, simulation, information systems
Mechanical engineering	Mechanical systems, thermal systems	Control systems, computer-aided design, micro-electro-mechanical systems
Metallurgical engineering[a]	Metals systems	Ceramics, polymers, composites, electron microscopy

[a]The name *materials science and engineering* has largely replaced *metallurgical engineering.*

TABLE 2 Notable Observations About Work and Jobs

I do not like work even when someone else does it. (Mark Twain)
All work and no play make Jack a dull boy—to everyone but his employer.
Man may work from sun to sun, but a woman's work is never done.
A woman's work is never done, especially the part she asks her husband to do.
The people who claim that brain work is harder than physical work are generally brain workers.
Many thousands of people are already working a four-day week; the trouble is it takes them five days to do it.
Hard work never hurt anyone who hired someone else to do it.
Hard work pays off in the future; laziness pays off now.
Some people are so eager for success that they are even willing to work for it.
It isn't the hours you put into your work that count, it's the work you put into the hours.
What will happen to work when the trend toward longer education meets the trend toward earlier retirement?
Genius is one percent inspiration and ninety-nine percent perspiration. (Thomas A. Edison)
The difference between a job and a career is the difference between 40 and 60 hours a week. (Robert Frost)
The softer the job, the harder it is to get.
The best man for the job is often a woman.
Two can live as cheaply as one—if they both have good jobs.

Source: Compiled from J. Bartlett, *Familiar Quotations*, 14th ed., E. M. Beck, ed. (Boston: Little, Brown, 1968); E. Esar, *20,000 Quips and Quotes*, (New York: Barnes and Noble, 1995); and other sources.

of study for many years, and some of the more significant findings and personalities that have contributed to this field are described in Historical Note 1.

HISTORICAL NOTE 1 THE STUDY OF WORK

There is evidence that the study of work and some of the basic principles about work originated in ancient times [1]. The Babylonians used the principle of a ***minimum wage*** around 1950 B.C. The Chinese organized work according to the principle of ***labor specialization*** around 1644 B.C. The ancient Romans used a primitive form of ***factory system*** for the production of armaments, textiles, and pottery. They also perfected the military organizational structure, which is the basis for today's ***line and staff organization*** of work.

The ***Industrial Revolution*** started in England around 1770 with the invention of several new machines used in the production of textiles,[1] ***James Watt***'s steam engine, and ***Henry Maudslay***'s screw-cutting lathe. These inventions resulted in fundamental changes in the way work was organized and accomplished: (1) the transfer of skill from workers to machines, (2) the start of the machine tool industry, based on Maudslay's lathe and other new types of metal-cutting machines that allowed parts to be produced more quickly and accurately than the prior handicraft methods, and (3) the introduction of the factory system in textile production and other industries, which used large numbers of unskilled workers (including women and children) who labored long hours for low pay. The factory system employed the specialization of labor principle.

While England was leading the Industrial Revolution, the important concept of ***interchangeable parts manufacture*** was being introduced in the United States. Much credit for this concept is given to ***Eli Whitney*** (1765–1825), although others had recognized its importance [7]. In 1797, Whitney negotiated a contract to produce 10,000 muskets for the U.S. government. The traditional way of making guns at the time was to custom-fabricate each part for a particular gun and then hand-fit the parts together by filing. Each musket was therefore unique. Whitney believed that the components could be made accurately enough to permit parts assembly without fitting. After several years of development in his Connecticut factory, he was able to demonstrate the principle before government officials, including Thomas Jefferson. His achievement was made possible by the special machine tools, fixtures, and gauges that he had developed. Interchangeable parts manufacture required many years of refinement in the early and mid-1800s before becoming a practical reality, but it revolutionized work methods used in manufacturing. It is a prerequisite for mass production of assembled products.

The mid- and late 1800s and early 1900s witnessed the introduction of several consumer products, including the sewing machine, bicycle, and automobile. In order to meet the mass demand for these products, more efficient production methods were required. Some historians identify developments during this period as the Second

[1]The machines included (1) James Hargreaves's Spinning Jenny, patented in 1770; (2) Richard Arkwright's Water Frame, developed in 1771; (3) Samuel Crompton's Mule-Spinner, developed around 1779; and (4) Edmund Cartwright's Power Loom, patented in 1785. Historians sometimes include James Kay's Flying Shuttle introduced in 1733 in the list of great inventions of the Industrial Revolution.

Industrial Revolution, characterized in terms of its effects on work systems by the following: (1) mass production, (2) assembly lines, and (3) scientific management.

Mass production was primarily an American phenomenon. Its motivation was the mass market that existed in the United States, where the population in 1900 was 76 million and growing and by 1920 exceeded 106 million. Such a large population, larger than any western European country, created a demand for large numbers of products. Mass production provided those products. Certainly one of the important technologies of mass production was the moving ***assembly line***, introduced by ***Henry Ford*** (1863–1947) in 1913 at his Highland Park plant. The assembly line was a new form of work system and made possible the mass production of complex consumer products. Use of assembly line methods permitted Ford to sell a Model T automobile for less than $500 in 1916, thus making ownership of cars feasible for a large segment of the American population.

The ***scientific management*** movement started in the late 1800s in the United States in response to the need to plan and control the activities of growing numbers of production workers. The most important members of this movement were Frederick W. Taylor, Frank Gilbreth, and Lillian Gilbreth. The principal approaches of scientific management were the following: (1) motion study, aimed at finding the best method to perform a given task and eliminating delays; (2) time study to establish work standards for a job; (3) extensive use of standards in industry; (4) the piece rate system and similar labor incentive plans; and (5) use of data collection, record keeping, and cost accounting in factory operations. These approaches, while revolutionary at the time they were first implemented, are fundamental and indispensable techniques used today in business and industry for work management.

Frederick W. Taylor (1856–1915) is known as the "father of scientific management" for his application of systematic approaches to the study and improvement of work. His findings and writings have influenced factory management in virtually every industrialized country in the world, especially the United States. It can be argued that much of the mass production power of the United States in the twentieth century is due to the scientific management principles espoused by Taylor.

Born in Philadelphia into an upper middle class family, Taylor attended the local Germantown Academy and then Phillips Exeter Academy in New Hampshire. His father's wish was for young Taylor to pursue a legal career. However, after passing the entrance tests for Harvard University, poor eyesight forced him to abandon those plans.[2] Instead, he became an apprentice patternmaker and machinist in 1874. In 1878, he became an employee at the Midvale Steel Company in Philadelphia and during the next 12 years progressed from machine shop worker to gang boss, foreman, and master mechanic. In 1883, he earned a mechanical engineering degree from Stevens Institute of Technology through part-time study and was promoted to chief engineer at the company.

[2]Taylor's poor eyesight was apparently caused by too much nighttime study at Phillips Exeter. He was at the top of his class at the Academy. There is some speculation that young Taylor did not want to follow his father's profession as a lawyer. He preferred to follow his own career path. His eyesight was largely recovered by 1875.

Taylor introduced time study at Midvale Steel sometime between 1881 and 1883 while he was foreman of the machine shop. By 1883, a given task had been divided into work elements, and the timing of each element and then summing the times had been found to be more useful than timing the whole task. Taylor's belief was that by studying each element, wasted motions could be eliminated and efficiency could thereby be improved in every step of an operation. While at Midvale, Taylor also conducted metal-cutting experiments on the company's products, which included military cannons and locomotive wheels. The experiments resulted in significant improvements in productivity in the plant. However, not all of Taylor's proposals about work were successful. A notable example was his idea to separate the shop foreman's job into eight specialized functions. The resulting structure is called a functional organization.

Taylor left Midvale Steel in 1889. From 1890 to 1893, he served as general manager of a company that processed wood pulp. He then became a management consultant from 1893 to 1901. During this latter period, his most important engagement was with the Bethlehem Iron Works (predecessor to the Bethlehem Steel Company) between 1898 and 1901. Two famous experiments were conducted at Bethlehem: (1) the shoveling experiment and (2) pig iron handling.

In the ***shoveling experiment***, Taylor observed that each yard worker brought his own shovel to work, and the shovels were all different sizes. The workers were required to shovel various materials in the yard, such as ashes, coal, and iron ore. Because the densities of these materials differed, it meant that the weight per shovelful varied significantly. Through experimentation with the workers, he determined that different-sized shovels should be used for the different materials. His conclusion was that the appropriate shovel size was one in which the load was 21 pounds. This load weight maximized the amount of work that could be accomplished each day by a worker and minimized the costs to the company.

In the study of ***pig iron handling***,[3] Taylor believed that the yard workers who loaded pig iron from the storage yard into freight cars were not using the best method. The workers seemed to work too hard and then had to rest for too long to recover from the exertion. Their daily wage was $1.15 (in 1898) and they averaged 12.5 tons per day. Taylor confronted one of the men named Schmidt and offered him the opportunity to earn $1.85 per day if he followed Taylor's instructions on how to perform the work. The instruction consisted of improvements in the way the pig iron was picked up, carried, and dropped off, combined with more frequent but shorter rest breaks. Enticed by the opportunity to earn more money, Schmidt agreed.[4] By using the improved method, Schmidt was able to consistently load 47 tons per day. Other workers were eager to sign on for the higher pay.

[3]Pig iron is the iron tapped from a blast furnace. It contains impurities and must be subsequently refined to make cast iron and steel.

[4]In fact, Taylor dreamed up the name Schmidt. The worker's real name was Henry Knolle. Opponents of Taylor and scientific management circulated reports in 1910 that Schmidt had died from overworking to achieve the 47 tons per day. The truth is that Henry Knolle lived on until 1925, dying at the age of 54.

In 1901, Taylor retired to his estate in Philadelphia but continued to promote the emerging field of scientific management through lectures and publications such as ***Shop Management*** (1903), ***On the Art of Cutting Metals*** (1906), and ***Principles of Scientific Management*** (1911). Perhaps Frederick W. Taylor's most important contribution in the improvement of work was his successful promotion and promulgation of the field of scientific management during the period of his retirement.

Frank Gilbreth (1868–1924) is noted for his pioneering efforts in analyzing and simplifying manual work. He was associated with the scientific management movement in the late 1800s and early 1900s, in particular for his achievements in motion study. He is sometimes referred to as the "father of motion study." Two of his important theories about work were (1) that all work was composed of 17 basic motion elements that he called "therbligs" and (2) the principle that there is "one best method" to perform a given task.

As a young man, Gilbreth had planned to attend college but was forced to get a job due to his father's untimely death. He started as a bricklayer's apprentice in 1885 at age 17. On his first day at work, Gilbreth noticed that the bricklayer assigned to teach him laid bricks in three different ways, one in normal working, a second when working fast, and a third when instructing Gilbreth. He also noticed that other bricklayers used other methods, all of which seemed to be different. It occurred to Gilbreth that there should be one best way to accomplish bricklaying, and all bricklayers should use that one best method. Gilbreth analyzed the work elements that were required in bricklaying, attempting to simplify the task and eliminate wasted motions. He was able to develop a method that reduced the number of steps required to lay one brick by about 70 percent. He participated in the development of a bricklayer's scaffold that could be adjusted in height so the worker would have bricks and mortar at the same elevation level as he was working rather than be required to stoop to ground level to retrieve these materials. The movable scaffold is still used today.

By age 26, Gilbreth decided to go into business for himself and became a widely recognized building contractor in New York City. One of the reasons for his success was the capability of his crews to complete a project quickly, a result of his interest in time and motion study. He was able to apply the principles of time and motion study to the labor of construction workers and other industrial employees so as to increase their efficiency and output. Ultimately, he would become one of the leading public speakers for Taylor's scientific management movement.

In 1904, Gilbreth married Lillian Moller, a teacher and psychologist who collaborated in his research on motion study, contributing an emphasis on the human and social attributes of work. In 1911, Gilbreth published ***Motion Study***, a book that documented many of their research findings. Around 1915, they founded the management consulting firm of Frank B. Gilbreth, Inc. When Frank died prematurely in 1924, Lillian assumed the presidency of the firm and carried on his work as a researcher and advocate of motion and time study. She became a noted educator, author, engineer, and consultant in her own right.

Lillian Gilbreth (1878–1972) was the oldest of nine children. She earned bachelor's and master's degrees at the University of California, Berkeley. During her marriage to Frank, she became the mother of 12 children and earned a doctorate at Brown

University in 1915, a rare achievement for a woman at the time. Her other accomplishments were equally noteworthy. With her husband, she co-authored four books: ***A Primer of Scientific Management*** (1914), ***Fatigue Study*** (1916), ***Applied Motion Study*** (1917), and ***Motion Study for the Handicapped*** (1917). On her own, she wrote ***The Psychology of Management*** (1914) and several other books after Frank's death. She also held faculty positions at Purdue University (1935–1948) and several other universities. Among the many honors and awards she received during her lifetime, one of the most significant was her election to the National Academy of Engineering. She was the first woman ever to be elected to the NAE. With good reason, she has been called the "First Lady of Engineering."

The story of how Frank and Lillian Gilbreth practiced efficiency and motion study in their own home was humorously documented by two of their 12 children in 1949 with the publication of ***Cheaper by the Dozen***. It was made into a motion picture in 1950.

1 THE NATURE OF WORK

For our purposes, ***work*** is defined as an activity in which a person exerts physical and mental effort to accomplish a given task or perform a duty. The task or duty has some useful objective. It may involve one or more steps in making a product or delivering a service. The worker performing the task must apply certain skills and knowledge to complete the task or duty successfully. There is usually a commercial value in the work activity, and the worker is compensated for performing it. By commercial value, we mean that the task or duty contributes to the buying and selling of something (e.g., a product or service), which ultimately provides the means of paying for the work. Work is also performed in government, but its value is surely measured on a scale other than commercial.

In physics, ***work*** is defined as the displacement (distance) that an object moves in a certain direction multiplied by the force acting on the object in the same direction. Thus, physical work is measured in units of newton-meters (N-m) in the International System of Units (metric system) or foot-pounds (ft-lb) in U.S. customary units. This definition can be reconciled with our labor-oriented work definition by imagining a material handling worker pushing a cart across a warehouse floor by exerting a force against the cart to move it a certain distance. However, human work includes many activities other than the muscular application of forces to move objects. Nearly all human work activities include both physical and mental exertions by the worker. In some cases, the physical component dominates the activity, while in others the mental component is more important. In virtually all work situations, the activity cannot be performed unless the worker applies some combination of physical and cognitive effort.

1.1 The Pyramidal Structure of Work

Work consists of tasks. A ***task*** is an amount of work that is assigned to a worker or for which a worker is responsible. The task can be repetitive (as in a repetitive operation in mass production) or nonrepetitive (performed periodically, infrequently, or only once). A task can be divided into its constituent activities, which form the pyramidal structure

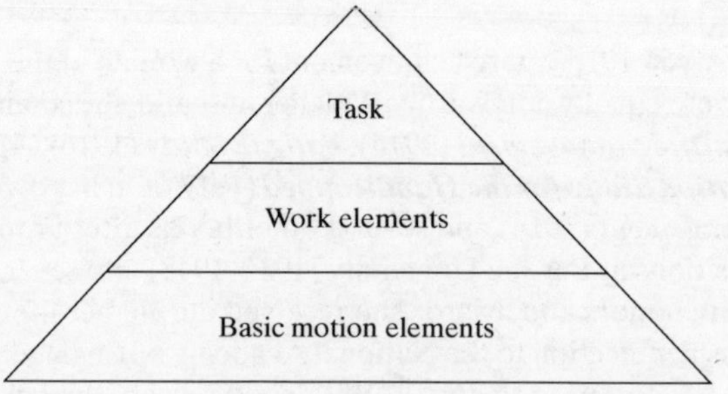

Figure 1 The pyramidal structure of a task. Each task consists of multiple work elements, which in turn consist of multiple basic motion elements.

shown in Figure 1. Each task consists of several work elements, and each work element consists of basic motion elements. ***Basic motion elements*** are actuations of the limbs and other body parts while engaged in performing the task. These basic motion elements include reaching for an object, grasping an object, or moving an object. Other basic motions include walking and eye movement (e.g., eye focusing, reading). Multiple basic motion elements are generally required to perform a ***work element***, which is defined as a series of work activities that are logically grouped together because they have a unified function within the task. For example, a typical assembly work element consists of reaching for a part, grasping it, and attaching it to a base part, perhaps using one or more fasteners (e.g., screws, bolts, and nuts). Many such work elements make up the total work content of assembling all of the components to the base part. Work elements usually take six seconds or longer, while a basic motion element may take less than a second. The entire task may take 30 seconds to several minutes if it is a repetitive task, while nonrepetitive tasks may require a much longer time to complete.

Just as a task can be divided into its component activities (work elements each consisting of multiple basic motion elements), the typical job of a worker is likely to consist of more than one task. Thus the job adds a next higher level to the existing pyramid. Furthermore, a worker's career is likely to consist of more than one job, as he or she changes employers and/or advances through several jobs with a single employer during a lifetime of working. Accordingly, one might envision the ultimate work pyramid as consisting of the five levels shown in Figure 2.

1.2 Importance of Time

In nearly all human endeavors, "time is of the essence." In sports, time is often the major factor in deciding the outcome of a contest. The fastest time wins the race. In games that use time periods, the victor must score the winning points within the limits of those periods. In other aspects of life, time is also important. Students must be in class on time. They must complete an hour quiz in 50 minutes (or other designated time limit). Medical patients must schedule appointments with their doctors at specific times. When we drive to a given

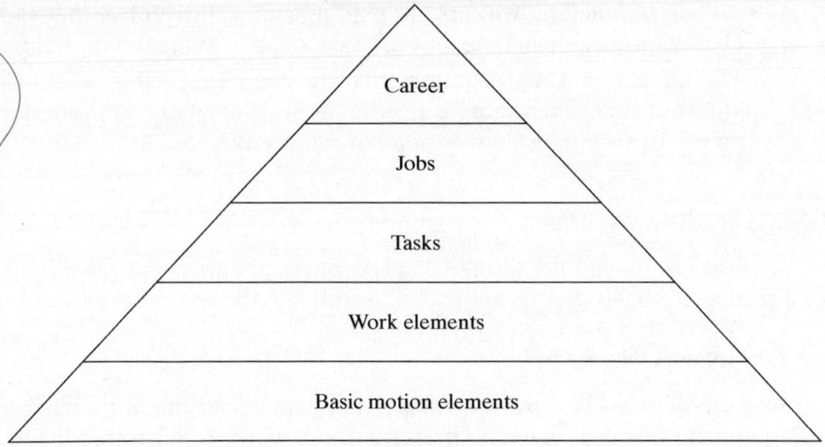

Figure 2 The pyramidal structure of work.

destination, whether it is a long vacation trip or a nearby shopping expedition, we select the route that will get us there in the shortest possible time. Why waste time and gasoline?

Time is important in business and industry, as the following examples demonstrate:

- *New product introduction.* The manufacturer introducing a new product to the market in the shortest time is usually the one rewarded with the most profits.
- *Product cost.* In many cases, the number of labor hours required to produce a product represents a significant portion of total manufacturing cost, which determines the price of the product. Companies that can reduce the time to make a product can sell it at a more competitive price.
- *Delivery time.* Along with cost and quality, delivery time is a key criterion in vendor selection by many companies. The supplier that can deliver its products in the shortest time is often the one selected by the customer.
- *Overnight delivery.* The success of overnight delivery offered by parcel transport companies (e.g., UPS, Fed Ex) illustrates the growing commercial importance of time.
- *Competitive bidding.* In many competitive bidding situations, proposals must be submitted by a specified date and time. Late proposals will be disregarded.
- *Production scheduling.* The production schedule in a manufacturing plant is based on dates and times.

Time is important in work. The many reasons why this is so include the following:

- The most frequently used measure of work is time. How many minutes or hours are required to perform a given task?
- Most workers are paid according to the amount of time they work. They earn an hourly wage rate or a salary that is paid on a weekly, biweekly, or monthly basis.
- Workers must arrive at work on time. If a worker is a member of a work team, his or her absence or tardiness may handicap the rest of the team.

- When production workers are paid on an incentive plan, they earn their bonuses based on how much time they can save relative to the standard time for a given task.
- Labor and staffing requirements are computed using workloads measured in units of time. For example, how many workers will be required during a 40-hour week to accomplish a workload of 600 hours?

2 DEFINING WORK SYSTEMS

A work system can be defined as (1) a physical entity and (2) a field of professional practice. Both definitions are useful in studying the way work is accomplished.

2.1 Physical Work Systems

As a physical entity, a ***work system*** is a system consisting of humans, information, and equipment that is designed to perform useful work, as illustrated in Figure 3. The result of the useful work is a contribution to the production of a product or the delivery of a service. Examples of work systems include the following:

- A worker operating a production machine in a factory
- An assembly line consisting of a dozen workers at separate workstations along a moving conveyor
- A robotic spot welding line in an automobile final assembly plant performing spot welding operations on sheet metal car bodies
- A freight train transporting 60 intermodal container cars from Los Angeles to Chicago
- A parcel service agent driving a delivery truck to make customer deliveries in a local area
- A receptionist in an office directing visitors to personnel in the office and answering incoming telephone calls

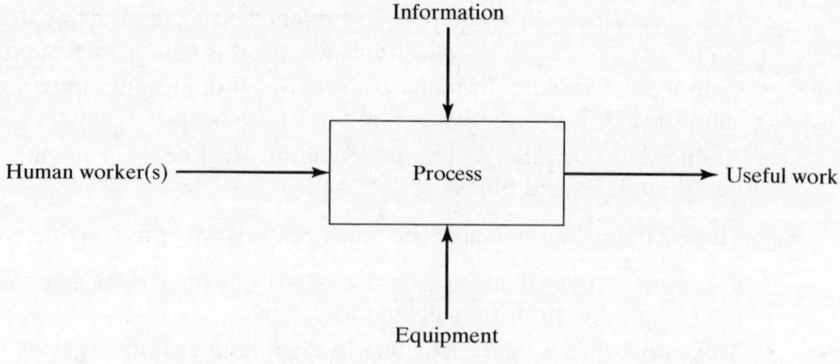

Figure 3 A work system consists of human workers, information, and equipment designed to accomplish useful work by means of a process.

- A designer working at a computer-aided design (CAD) station to design a new product
- A construction project consisting of a work crew building a highway bridge

As our list indicates, a work system can include one or more human workers. It can also include automated systems that operate for extended periods of time without human attention. Sooner or later, automated systems require the attention of human workers for purposes of maintenance or reprogramming or other reasons. The information associated with the work system may consist simply of a worker's knowledge required to perform an operation, or it may involve the use of databases and programs that must be accessed using computer systems. The equipment in a work system may be a single machine tool operated by one worker or a collection of automated machines that operate under computer control in a coordinated fashion.

2.2 Work Systems as a Field of Professional Practice

As a field of professional practice, ***work systems*** includes (1) work methods, (2) work measurement, and (3) work management.[5] The term ***work science*** is often used for this professional practice. The field of ***work methods*** consists of the analysis and design of tasks and jobs involving human work activity. Terms related to work methods include ***operations analysis*** and ***methods engineering***. The term ***motion study*** is also used, but its scope is usually limited to the physical motions, tools, and workplace layout used by a worker to perform a task. The other terms are less restrictive and include the analysis and design of complex processes consisting of material and information flows through multiple operations.

Work measurement is the analysis of a task to determine the time that should be allowed for a qualified worker to perform the task. The time thus determined is called the ***standard time***. Among its many applications, the standard time can be used to compute product costs, assess worker performance, and determine worker requirements (e.g., how many workers are needed to accomplish a given workload). Because of its emphasis on time, work measurement is often referred to as time study. However, in the modern context, ***time study*** has a broader meaning that includes work situations in which an operation is performed by automated equipment, and it is desired to determine the cycle time for the operation. Thus, time study covers any and all work situations in which it is necessary to determine how long it takes to accomplish a given unit of work, whether the work unit is concerned with the production of a product or the delivery of a service. Time is important because it equates to money ("time is money," as the saying goes), and money is a limited resource that must be well managed in any organization.

Work management refers to the various organizational and administrative functions that must be accomplished to achieve high productivity of the work system and effective supervision of workers. Work management includes functions such as (1) organizing workers to perform the specialized tasks that constitute the workload in each

[5]The title of this text emphasizes the two definitions: (1) work systems as physical entities and (2) work systems as a field of professional practice.

department of the company or other organization, (2) motivating workers to perform the tasks, (3) evaluating the jobs in the organization so that each worker is paid an appropriate wage or salary commensurate with the type of work performed, (4) appraising the performance of workers to reward better-performing workers appropriately, and (5) compensating workers using a rational payment system for the work they perform.

3 TYPES OF OCCUPATIONS

The Bureau of Labor Statistics of the U.S. Department of Labor identifies 821 occupations in its Standard Occupational Classification (SOC). The SOC covers virtually every type of work performed for pay or profit in the United States, and organizes these occupations into 23 major groups, based on type of work and/or industry sector. The categories are listed in Table 3. Representative positions and job titles are also given.

Rather than use the 23 categories in the SOC system, it is convenient for our purposes to group occupations into the following four broad categories that reflect the work content and function of the jobs rather than type of work and industry sector:

- *Production workers*, in which the work involves making products.
- *Logistics workers*, in which the work involves moving materials, products, or people.
- *Service workers*, in which the work involves one or more of the following functions: (1) providing a service, (2) applying existing information and knowledge, and (3) communicating.
- *Knowledge workers*, in which the work involves one or more of the following functions: (1) creating new knowledge, (2) solving problems, and (3) managing.

These categories are correlated with the types of work systems used in business, industry, and government. Production workers have jobs in production systems (manufacturing, construction), logistics workers are employed in logistics systems (transportation, material handling), service workers work in service operations (retail, government, health care), and knowledge workers are involved in knowledge-oriented activities (creative work, probiem solving, management).

The characteristics and representative job titles of the four categories are summarized in Table 4. We see that production and logistics workers engage in mostly physical labor, while service and knowledge workers perform duties that require mostly cognitive activities. Overlaps exist. Production and logistics workers must utilize their brains in their jobs, while the work of service and knowledge workers usually includes physical activities.

A key feature among the four categories is worker discretion [17], which refers to the necessity to make responsible decisions and exercise judgment in carrying out the duties of the position. Jobs that are highly standardized and routine require minimum worker discretion, while jobs in which workers must adapt their behavior in response to variations in the work situation require high discretion. As indicated in Table 4, production and logistics workers are required to use limited or moderate discretion in performing their duties, while service and knowledge workers must exercise much greater discretion in their jobs. In production and logistics operations, the objective is to complete

TABLE 3 Major Occupation Categories of the U.S. Department of Labor Standard Occupational Classification

SOC #	Occupation Category	Representative Positions and Job Titles
11	Management Occupations	Chief executive officer, construction manager, funeral director, hotel manager, postmaster, plant manager, sales manager, school principal
13	Business and Financial Operations Occupations	Accountant, auditor, claims adjuster, cost estimator, financial analyst, loan officer, purchasing agent, tax collector
15	Computer and Mathematical Occupations	Actuary, computer programmer, systems analyst, database administrator, mathematical analyst, software engineer, statistician
17	Architecture and Engineering Occupations	Architect, drafter, engineering technician, engineers (e.g., civil, electrical, industrial, mechanical), landscape architect, surveyor
19	Life, Physical, and Social Science Occupations	Agricultural scientist, astronomer, chemist, economist, geoscientist, materials scientist, physicist, psychologist, sociologist
21	Community and Social Services Occupations	Clergy, family therapist, marriage counselor, high school counselor, mental health worker, probation officer, social worker
23	Legal occupations	Court reporter, judge, law clerk, lawyer, legal assistant, magistrate, paralegal, title examiner
25	Education, Training, and Library Occupations	College professor, elementary school teacher, high school teacher, kindergarten teacher, librarian, special educator, teacher assistant
27	Arts, Design, Entertainment, Sports and Media Occupations	Actor, artist, athlete, coach, composer, dancer, fashion designer, movie director, musician, news reporter, referee, singer
29	Healthcare Practitioners and Technical Occupations	Chiropractor, clinical technician, dental hygienist, dentist, paramedic, pharmacist, physician, psychiatrist, nurse, therapist, veterinarian
31	Healthcare Support Occupations	Dental assistant, medical assistant, nursing aide, orderly, pharmacy aid, physical therapist, veterinary assistant
33	Protective Services Occupations	Bailiff, detective, firefighter, fire inspector, game warden, jailer, police officer, private investigator, security guard
35	Food Preparation and Serving Occupations	Bartender, chef, cook, dishwasher, dining room host/hostess, fast food worker, food preparation worker, waiter, waitress
37	Building and Grounds Cleaning and Maintenance	Groundskeeper, grounds maintenance worker, housekeeping cleaner, janitor, landscape worker, maid, pest control worker, tree trimmer
39	Personal Care and Service Related Occupations	Animal trainer, barber, bellhop, concierge, cosmetologist, fitness trainer, flight attendant, funeral attendant, hairdresser, usher
41	Sales and Related Occupations	Cashier, salesperson, insurance agent, model, real estate broker, sales engineer, sales representative, telemarketer, travel agent
43	Office and Administrative Support Occupations	Bank teller, bill collector, bookkeeper, hotel desk clerk, office manager, receptionist, police dispatcher, secretary, stock clerk
45	Farming, Fishing, and Forestry Occupations	Agricultural inspector, animal breeder, farm worker, fishing worker, forest and conservation worker, hunter, logging worker, ranch hand
47	Construction and Extraction Occupations	Bricklayer, building inspector, carpenter, cement mason, construction laborer, electrician, oil drill operator, painter, plumber, roofer
49	Installation, Maintenance, and Repair Occupations	Aircraft mechanic, automotive mechanic, home appliance repairer, locksmith, office machine repairer, security system installer
51	Production Occupations	Assembly worker, bookbinder, food processing worker, foundry mold maker, machinist, sewing machine operator, welder
53	Transportation and Material Moving Occupations	Aircraft pilot, bus driver, crane operator, garbage collector, material handling worker, sailor, ship captain, truck driver
55	Military Specific Occupations	Air crew member, infantry soldier, military officer, radar technician, sonar technician, special forces commando

Source: From the Bureau of Labor Statistics, www.bls.gov/soc.

TABLE 4 Comparison of Work Characteristics of Four Categories of Workers

Worker Category	Production Workers	Logistics Workers	Service Workers	Knowledge Workers
Basic functions	Make products	Move materials, products, or people	Provide service Apply information and knowledge Communicate	Create knowledge Solve problems Manage and coordinate
Type of work	Mostly physical	Mostly physical	Mostly cognitive	Mostly cognitive
Worker discretion	Limited	Limited to moderate	Moderate to broad	Broad
Equipment required for basic work	Machinery systems (production tools and machines)	Machinery systems (transportation, material handling)	Computer systems Communication systems	Computer systems Information resources
Industry and professional examples	Manufacturing Construction Agriculture Power generation	Transportation Distribution Material handling Storage	Banking Government service Health care Retail	Management Designing Legal Education Consulting
Representative positions and job titles	Laborer Machine operator Assembly worker Machinist Quality inspector Construction worker	Truck driver Airplane pilot Ship captain Material handler Order picker Shipping clerk	Bank teller Police officer Nurse Physical trainer Salesperson Foreman	Manager Physician Designer Researcher Lawyer Teacher

Source: Adapted from a figure in [17].

TABLE 5 Characteristics of Jobs Requiring Low and High Worker Discretion

Characteristics of Jobs Requiring Low Discretion	Characteristics of Jobs Requiring High Discretion
The work is performed at one location.	Workers determine where they will do their jobs.
Almost any able-bodied person could perform the work if provided with basic training.	The work depends heavily on technical knowledge and prior experience.
The work is dominated by machinery operation, routine procedures, or predetermined activities.	Workers manage their own schedules and the processes used to perform their jobs.
The methods, techniques, and materials are specified.	Workers determine the methods, techniques, and materials they use in their jobs.
The work requires interactions with the same people every day.	Workers must deal with different types of people in their daily work activities.
Work performance is measured primarily in quantitative terms.	Work performance is measured primarily in qualitative terms.

Source: Adapted from [17].

the work precisely as specified and with minimum variation. In service and knowledge operations, the objective is to deal in a discretionary way with situations and people that are inherently variable. Typical characteristics associated with jobs requiring low discretion and jobs requiring high discretion are listed in Table 5.

The relative proportions of workers in various occupational categories are given in Table 6, based on data in an article by Bailey and Barley [2]. The table covers most of the twentieth century for the United States, and indicates trends in the labor force

TABLE 6 Relative Percentages of Occupations in the U.S. Workforce: 1900–1998

Occupational Category	Percentage in 1900	1950	1998	Net Percentage Change 1900–1998
Production and logistics workers:				
Farmworkers	38	12	3	−35
Craft and similar	11	14	11	0
Operatives and laborers	25	26	13	−12
Total production and logistics workers	74[a]	52[a]	27	−47
Service and knowledge workers:				
Service	9	11	16	+7
Sales workers	5	7	11	+6
Clerical and similar	3	12	17	+14
Professional and technical	4	8	18	+14
Managerial and administrative	6	9	11	+5
Total service and knowledge workers	27[a]	47[a]	73	+47

Source: Adapted from [2].

[a]Totals do not add to 100% due to round-off errors.

during this period in which the total U.S. population grew from 76 million to approximately 280 million. The data published in [2] are organized into eight occupational categories, which we have grouped into two major categories, consistent with the worker classification in this text: (1) production and logistics workers and (2) service and knowledge workers. At the beginning of the twentieth century, nearly three-quarters of U.S. workers were employed in farming, skilled trades, factories, and manual labor, which we have grouped as production and logistics workers. Only one-quarter was employed as service and knowledge workers. One hundred years later, the proportions had reversed. Today, most occupations fall within the category of service and knowledge work.

4 PRODUCTIVITY

Productivity is defined as the level of output of a given process relative to the level of input. The term *process* can refer to an individual production or service operation, or it can be used in the context of a national economy. Productivity is an important metric in work systems because improving productivity is the means by which worker compensation can be increased without increasing the costs of the products and services they produce. This leads to more products and services at lower prices for consumers, which improves the standard of living for all. In this section we define labor productivity and examine the theoretical basis for increasing productivity.

4.1 Labor Productivity

The most common productivity measure is ***labor productivity***, defined by the following ratio:

$$LPR = \frac{WU}{LH} \tag{1}$$

where LPR = labor productivity ratio, WU = work units of output, and LH = labor hours of input. The definition of output work units depends on the process under consideration. For example, in the steel industry, tons of steel is the common measure. In the automobile industry, the number of cars produced is the appropriate output measure. In both industries, it is important to know how many labor hours are required to produce one unit of output. This measure can be used to compare the labor efficiencies of different companies in a given industry, or to compare the same industries among different nations. Obviously, fewer labor hours are better and mean higher productivity. A company or a country that can produce the same output with fewer input labor hours not only has a higher productivity; it also has a competitive advantage in the global economy.

Although labor productivity is a commonly used measure, labor itself does not contribute much to improving productivity. More important factors in determining and improving productivity are capital and technology. ***Capital*** refers to the substitution of machines for human labor; for example, investing in an automated production machine to replace a manually operated machine. The automated machine can probably operate at a higher production rate, so even if a worker is still needed to monitor the operation, productivity has been increased. If the worker is no longer needed at the machine, then labor productivity has been increased even more. ***Technology*** refers to a fundamental change in the way some activity or function is accomplished. It is more than simply using a machine in place of a human worker. It is using a brand new type of machine to replace the previous type. Some examples of how new technologies have made dramatic improvements in productivity are listed in Table 7.

Admittedly, the distinctions between capital improvements and technology improvements are sometimes subtle, because new technologies almost always require capital investments. Anyway, arguing about these differences and subtleties is not as important as recognizing that the important gains in productivity are generally made by the introduction of capital and technology in a work process, rather than by attempting to extract more work in less time from workers. By investing in capital and technology to increase the rate of output work units and/or reduce input labor hours, the labor productivity ratio is increased.

TABLE 7 Examples of Technology Changes that Dramatically Improved Productivity

Old Technology	New Technology	Improvement
Horse-drawn carts	Railroad trains	Substitution of steam power for horse power, use of multiple carts (passenger or freight cars)
Steam locomotive	Diesel locomotive	Substitution of diesel power technology for steam power technology
Telephone operator	Dial phone	Dial technology allowed "clicks" of the dial to be used to operate telephone switching systems
Dial phone	Touch-tone phone	Substitution of tone frequencies in place of "clicks" to operate telephone switching systems for faster dialing
Manually operated milling machine	Numerical control milling machine	Substitution of coded numerical instructions to operate the milling machine rather than a skilled machinist
DC3 passenger airplane (1930s)	Boeing 747 passenger airplane (1980s)	Substitution of jet propulsion for piston engine for higher speed, larger aircraft for more passenger miles

Measuring productivity is not as easy as it seems. Although the labor productivity ratio defined by equation (1) appears simple and straightforward, the following problems are often encountered in its measurement and use:

- *Nonhomogeneous output units.* The output work units are not necessarily homogeneous. For example, using the annual production of automobiles as the output measure does not account for differences in models, vehicle sizes, and prices. An expensive luxury model is likely to require more labor hours of assembly time than an inexpensive compact car.
- *Multiple input factors.* As previously indicated, labor is not the only input factor in determining productivity. In addition to capital and technology, other input factors may include materials and energy. For example, in the production of aluminum, electric power and the raw material bauxite are much more important than labor as inputs to the process.[6]
- *Price and cost changes.* The prices of output work units and the costs of input factors (labor, materials, power) change over time, often unpredictably. A company may improve productivity, but if the prices of its products decrease due to market forces, the company could find itself in severe financial difficulty. The steel industry in the United States during the late 1990s and early 2000s provides a perfect example of this case.
- *Product mix changes.* Product mix refers to the relative proportions of products that a company sells. If the mix of expensive and inexpensive products changes from year to year, an annual comparison based on the labor productivity ratio is less meaningful.

An alternative productivity measure is the labor productivity index that compares the output/input ratio from one year to the next. The productivity index is defined as follows:

$$LPI = \frac{LPR_t}{LPR_b} \tag{2}$$

where LPI = labor productivity index, LPR_t = labor productivity ratio during some time period of interest, and LPR_b = labor productivity ratio during some defined base period.

Example 1 Productivity Measurement

During the base year in a small steel mill, 326,000 tons of steel were produced using 203,000 labor hours. In the next year, the output was 341,000 tons using 246,000 labor hours. Determine (a) the labor productivity ratio for the base year, (b) the labor productivity ratio for the second year, and (c) the labor productivity index for the second year.

Solution **(a)** In the base year, $LPR = \frac{326{,}000}{203{,}000} = 1.606$ tons per labor hour.

(b) In the second year, $LPR = \frac{341{,}000}{246{,}000} = 1.386$ tons per labor hour.

[6]Bauxite is the principal ore used to produce aluminum. It consists largely of hydrated aluminum oxide ($Al_2O_3H_2O$).

(c) The productivity index for the second year is $LPI = \dfrac{1.386}{1.606} = 0.863$.

Comment: No matter how it is measured, productivity went down in the second year. ■

4.2 Productive Work Content

Work is usually not performed in the most efficient way possible. A given task performed by a worker can be considered to consist of (1) the basic productive work content and (2) excess nonproductive activities. In general, the task is associated with the production of a product or the delivery of a service. The ***basic productive work content*** is the theoretical minimum amount of work required to accomplish the task, where the amount of work is expressed in terms of time. Thus, the time required to perform the basic productive work content is the theoretical minimum. It cannot be further reduced. The basic productive work content time is a theoretical concept implying optimal conditions that rarely, if ever, are achieved in practice. Nevertheless, it is an optimum worth seeking.

The ***excess nonproductive activities*** in the task are the extra physical and mental actions performed by the worker that do not add any value to the task, nor do they facilitate the productive work content that does add value. The excess nonproductive activities take time. They add to the basic productive work content time to make up the total time needed to perform the task. The excess nonproductive activities can be classified into three categories, as illustrated in the time line in Figure 4:

- Excess activities caused by poor design of the product or service
- Excess activities caused by inefficient methods, poor work layout, and interruptions
- Excess activities caused by the human factor

Some examples of the three categories of nonproductive activities are listed in Table 8. As several of these examples indicate, nonproductive activities do not necessarily occur during every cycle of the task. For example, industrial accidents occur infrequently in most work situations. However, over the long run, their effects extract a heavy toll on productive work content.

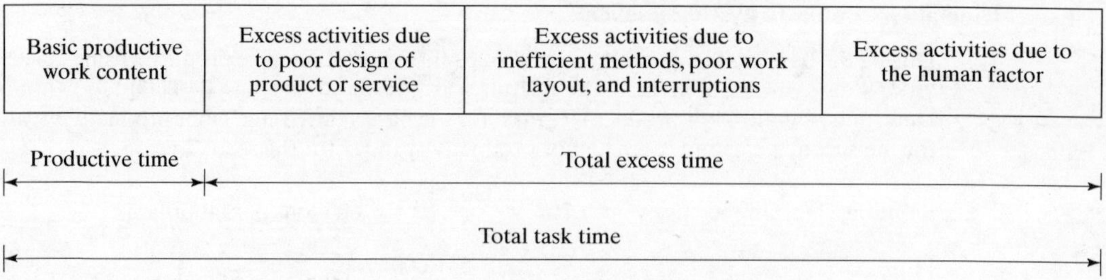

Figure 4 Total task time consists of basic productive work content and nonproductive activities.

TABLE 8 Examples of Excess Nonproductive Activities that Add to Total Task Time

Category of Activity	Examples
Poor design of the product or service	Products designed with more parts than necessary, so that excess assembly time is required
	Product proliferation (e.g., more choices for the customer than necessary)
	Frequent product design changes, causing changes in tooling, methods, and layout
	Waste of materials (e.g., machining from bar stock rather than machining from a forging or casting)
	Quality standards that are more stringent than necessary, requiring excess processing time
Inefficient methods, poor work layout, and interruptions	Inefficient plant layout that requires excess movement of materials
	Inefficient workplace layout that requires excess hand, arm, and body motions
	Inefficient methods that waste time
	Wasted space (e.g., using valuable floor space to store materials instead of storing vertically in racks)
	Inefficient material handling (e.g., using manual methods to move materials rather than mechanized methods)
	Long setup times between batches of work
	Frequent breakdowns of equipment
	Workers waiting for work
The human factor	Absenteeism and tardiness
	Workers spending too much time socializing
	Workers deliberately working slowly
	Inadequate training of workers
	Industrial accidents
	Hazardous materials that cause occupational illnesses

Source: Adapted from [9].

The concepts of basic productive work content and excess nonproductive activities are applicable not only to individual tasks but also to the entire work sequence required to manufacture a product or provide a service. There are value-adding activities and non-value-adding activities in virtually all work systems. An important objective in the design of a work system is to minimize the non-value-adding activities so that only productive work is accomplished. This objective is achieved through the use of methods engineering, operations analysis, work measurement, and other topics discussed in this text.

REFERENCES

[1] Amrine, H. T., J. A. Ritchey, and C. L. Moodie. *Manufacturing Organization and Management.* 5th ed. Englewood Cliffs, NJ: Prentice Hall, 1987.

[2] Bailey, D. E., and S. R. Barley. "Return to Work: Toward Post-Industrial Engineering." *IIE Transactions* 37 (2005): 737–52.

[3] Brogan, J. "Distinguishing Functions." *Industrial Engineer* (April 2003): 32–34.

[4] Chase, R. B., and N. J. Aquilano. *Production and Operations Management: A Life Cycle Approach*. 5th ed. Homewood, IL: Irwin, 1989.

[5] Groover, M. P. *Automation, Production Systems, and Computer Integrated Manufacturing*. 2nd ed. Upper Saddle River, NJ: Prentice Hall, 2001.

[6] Hicks, P. E. *Industrial Engineering and Management*. 2nd ed. New York: McGraw-Hill, 1994.

[7] Hounshell, D. A. *From the American System to Mass Production, 1800–1932*, Baltimore, MD: Johns Hopkins University Press, 1984.

[8] Jay, T. A. *Time Study*. Poole, England: Blandford Press, 1981.

[9] Kanawaty, G., ed. *Introduction to Work Study*. 4th ed. Geneva, Switzerland: Industrial Labour Office, 1992.

[10] Karger, D. W., and F. H. Bayha. *Engineered Work Measurement*. 4th ed. New York: Industrial Press, 1987.

[11] Konz, S., and S. Johnson. *Work Design, Industrial Ergonomics*. 5th ed. Scottsdale, AZ: Holcomb Hathaway Publishers, 2000.

[12] McGinnis, L. "A Brave New Education." *IIE Solutions* (December 2002): 27–32.

[13] Monks, J. G. *Operations Management, Theory and Problems*. New York: McGraw-Hill, 1977.

[14] Moore, F. G. *Manufacturing Management*. 3rd ed. Homewood, IL: Irwin, 1961.

[15] Nadler, G. *Work Design*. Homewood, IL: Irwin, 1963.

[16] Owens, R. N. *Management of Industrial Enterprises*. 4th ed. Homewood, IL: Irwin, 1961.

[17] Pepitone, J. S. "A Case for Humaneering." *IIE Solutions* (May 2002): 39–44.

[18] Russell, R. S., and B. W. Taylor III. *Operations Management*. 4th ed. Upper Saddle River, NJ: Prentice Hall, 2003.

[19] Theriault, P. *Work Simplification*. Norcross, GA: Engineering and Management Press, Institute of Industrial Engineers, 1996.

[20] Wredge, C. D., and R. G. Greenwood. *Frederick W. Taylor: The Father of Scientific Management: Myth and Reality*. Burr Ridge, IL: Irwin Professional Publishing, 1991.

REVIEW QUESTIONS

1 Define work.
2 What are basic motion elements? Give some examples.
3 What is a work element?
4 Why is time important in work?
5 Define work system as a physical entity.
6 Define work system as a field of professional practice.
7 What are some of the functions included within the scope of work management?
8 Name the four broad categories of worker occupations.
9 Define productivity.
10 Labor is one input factor that determines productivity. What are two other factors that are more important than labor in improving productivity? Define each of these two additional input factors.
11 What is the difference between the labor productivity ratio and the labor productivity index?
12 A given task performed by a worker can be considered to consist of the basic productive work content and excess nonproductive activities. (a) What is meant by the term *basic productive work content*? (b) What is meant by the term *excess nonproductive activities*?
13 What are the three categories of excess nonproductive activities, as they are defined in the text?

PROBLEMS

1 A work group of 5 workers in a certain month produced 500 units of output working 8 hr/day for 22 days in the month. (a) What productivity measures could be used for this situation, and what are the values of their respective productivity ratios? (b) Suppose that in the next month, the same work group produced 600 units but there were only 20 workdays in the month. Using the same productivity measures as before, determine the productivity index using the prior month as a base.
2 A work group of 10 workers in a certain month produced 7200 units of output working 8 hr/day for 22 days in the month. Determine the labor productivity ratio using (a) units of output per worker-hour and (b) units of output per worker-month. (c) Suppose that in the next month, the same work group produced 6800 units but there were only 20 workdays in the month. For each productivity measure as in (a) and (b), determine the productivity index for the next month using the prior month as a base.
3 A work group of 20 workers in a certain month produced 8600 units of output working 8 hr/day for 21 days. (a) What is the labor productivity ratio for this month? (b) In the next month, the same work group produced 8000 units but there were 22 workdays in the month and the size of the work group was reduced to 14 workers. What is the labor productivity ratio for this second month? (c) What is the productivity index using the first month as a base?
4 There are 20 forging presses in the forge shop of a small company. The shop produces batches of forgings requiring a setup time of 3.0 hours for each production batch. Average standard time for each part in a batch is 45 seconds, and there are an average of 600 parts in a batch. The plant workforce consists of two workers per press, two foremen, plus three clerical support staff. (a) Determine how many forged parts can be produced in 1 month, if there are 8 hours worked per day and an average of 21 days per month at one shift per day. (b) What is the labor productivity ratio of the forge shop, expressed as parts per worker-hour?

5 A farmer's market is considering the addition of bar code scanners at their check-out counters, which would use the UPC marked on all grocery packaging. Currently, the check-out clerk keypunches the price of each item into the register during check-out. Observations indicate that an average of 50 items are checked out per customer. The clerk currently takes 7 seconds per item to keypunch the register and move the item along the check-out table. On average it takes 25 seconds to total the bill, accept money from the customer, and make change. It then takes 4 seconds per item for the clerk to bag the customer's order. Finally, about 5 seconds are lost to transition to the next customer. Bar code scanners would eliminate the need to keypunch each price, and the time per item would be reduced to 3 seconds with the bar code scanner. (a) What is the hourly throughput rate (number of customers checked out per hour) under the current check-out procedure? (b) What would be the estimated hourly throughput rate if bar code scanners were used? (c) If separate baggers were used instead of requiring the check-out clerk to perform bagging in addition to check-out, what would be hourly throughput rate? Assume that bar code scanners are used by the clerk. (d) Determine the productivity index for each of the two cases in (b) and (c), using (a) as the basis of comparison and hourly customers checked out per labor hour as the measure of productivity.

Manual Work and Worker–Machine Systems

There are various types of work systems used in production, services, offices, projects, and other work situations. All of these work systems utilize the physical and mental capabilities of humans. In terms of the human participation in the tasks performed, work systems can be classified into the three basic categories depicted in Figure 1: (a) manual work systems, (b) worker–machine systems, and (c) automated systems. A ***manual work system*** consists of a worker performing one or more tasks without the aid of powered tools. The tasks commonly require the use of hand tools (e.g., hammers, screwdrivers, shovels). In a ***worker–machine system***, a human worker operates powered equipment (e.g., a machine tool). An ***automated work system*** is one in which a process is performed by a machine without the direct participation of a human worker.

As indicated in Figure 1, the work accomplished by a work system is almost always acted upon some object, called the ***work unit***. The state of the work unit is advanced in some way through the process performed on it. In production, the work may alter the geometry of a work part. In logistics, the work may involve transporting

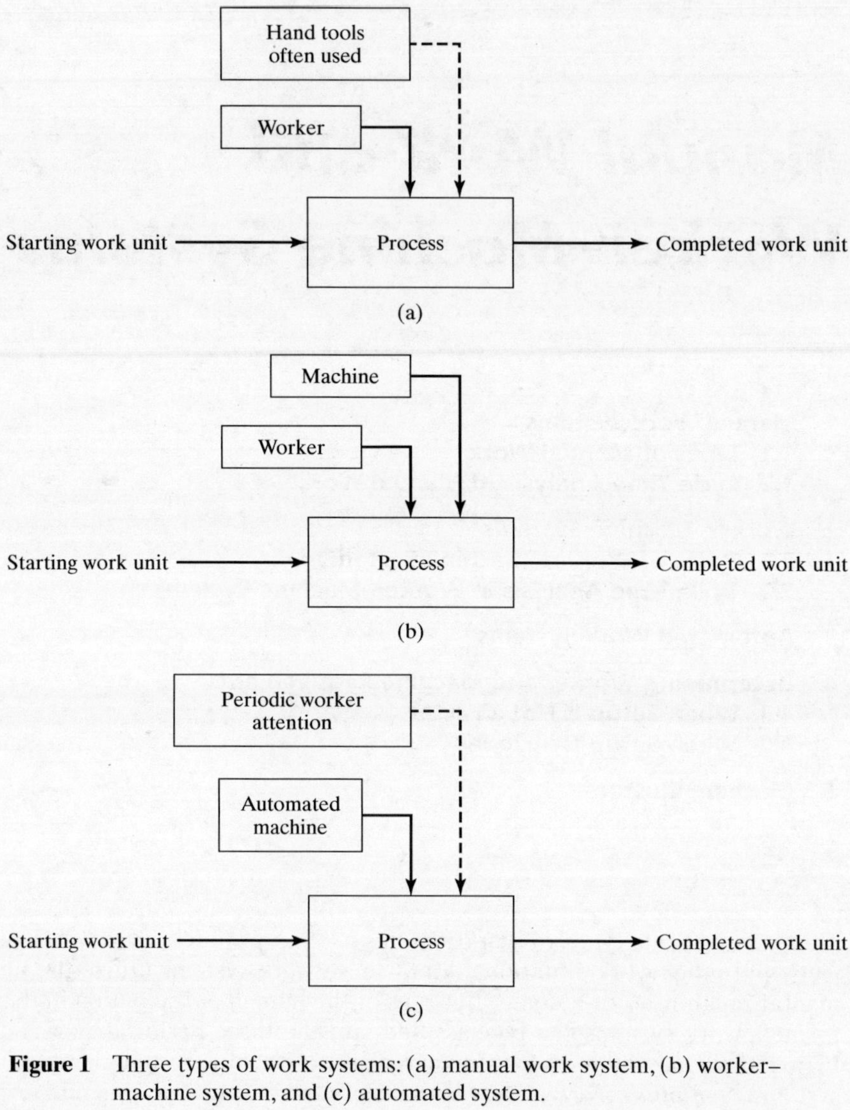

Figure 1 Three types of work systems: (a) manual work system, (b) worker–machine system, and (c) automated system.

material from a warehouse to a customer. In service work, a sales prospect is transformed into a paying customer by a persuasive salesperson. In knowledge work, a designer takes a product concept and converts it into specifications and engineering drawings.

In this chapter, we discuss the three categories of work systems. These systems are associated mostly with work that is performed by production and logistics workers. The emphasis in our coverage is on unit operations—tasks and processes that are treated as being independent of other work activities in a given facility or work site.

1 MANUAL WORK SYSTEMS

Manual work is the most basic form of work, engaging the human body to accomplish some physical task without an external source of power. Hand tools are often used to facilitate the task, but the power to operate them derives from the strength and stamina of a human worker. With or without hand tools, the worker must expend physical energy to accomplish the task. In addition, other human faculties are required, such as hand-eye coordination and mental effort. Our coverage of manual work includes two sections: (1) types of manual work and (2) cycle time analysis of manual work.

1.1 Types of Manual Work

Two forms of manual work can be distinguished: (1) pure manual work and (2) manual work using hand tools. ***Pure manual work*** involves only the physical and mental capabilities of the human worker, and no machines, tools, or other implements are employed in performing the task. Examples of pure manual work include the following:

- A material-handling worker moving cartons from the floor onto a conveyor in a warehouse
- Workers loading furniture into a moving van from a house without the use of dollies or other wheeled platforms
- A dealer at a casino table dealing cards
- An office worker filing documents in a file cabinet
- An assembly worker snap-fitting two parts together
- An assembly worker assembling two sheet metal parts with a bolt and nut by hand (tightening is done later using appropriate hand or power tools).

Note that the common characteristic in these examples is that they consist of moving things. Performing manual work without tools almost always involves the movement and handling of objects. Even assembly tasks include moving the parts in order to join them.

Manual tasks are commonly augmented by the use of hand tools. The ability to design and use tools is one of the attributes that distinguish humans from other species on earth. A ***tool*** is a device or implement for making changes to some object (e.g., the work unit), such as cutting, grinding, striking, squeezing, or other process. Instruments used for measurement are also included in the category of tools, even though no physical change in the object results directly from their use. A ***hand tool*** is a small tool that is operated by the strength and skill of the human user. When using hand tools, a ***workholder*** is sometimes employed to grasp the work unit and position it securely during processing. Examples of manual tasks involving the use of hand tools include the following:

- A machinist using a file to round the edges of a rectangular part that has just been milled
- An assembly worker using a screwdriver to tighten a screw
- A painter using a paintbrush to paint the trim around a doorway
- A sculptor using a carving knife to carve a wooden statue
- A grass-cutter using a rake to collect the grass clippings after mowing
- A quality control inspector using a micrometer to measure the diameter of a shaft
- A material-handling worker using a dolly to move cartons in a warehouse
- An office worker using a pen to handwrite entries into a ledger.

1.2 Cycle Time Analysis of Manual Work

Manual tasks usually consist of a work cycle that is repeated with some degree of similarity, and each cycle usually corresponds to the processing of one work unit. When a painter is hired to paint the wooden trim around the doorways in a new house, the painting cycle is repeated for each doorway. If the doorways are all the same size, and the wood trim is identical for all doors, then the painting cycle should exhibit a high degree of similarity. If there are differences in the doorways, then the painting cycles will be less similar.

If the work cycle is relatively short, and there is a high degree of similarity from one cycle to the next, we refer to the work as ***repetitive***. If the work cycle takes a long time and the cycles are not similar, the work is ***nonrepetitive***.[1] In either case, the task can be divided into work elements that consist of logical groupings of motions performed by the worker. The cycle time T_c is therefore the sum of the work element times

$$T_c = \sum_{k=1}^{n_e} T_{ek} \tag{1}$$

where T_{ek} = time of work element k, where k is used to identify the work elements, min; and n_e = number of work elements into which the cycle is divided. Our focus in this section is on repetitive work. Consider the following example of a pure manual task.

Example 1 A Repetitive Manual Task

An assembly worker performs a repetitive manual task consisting of inserting 8 plastic pegs into 8 holes in a flat wooden board. A slight interference fit is involved in each insertion. The worker holds the board in one hand and picks up the pegs from a tray with the other hand and inserts them into the holes, one peg at a time. The workplace layout is shown in Figure 2 (a), and the sequence of work elements is given in the table below. Can the work method be improved in order to reduce the cycle time?

[1]There is no clear boundary between repetitive and nonrepetitive work. When referring to repetitive work cycles, we usually mean a cycle time of a few minutes or less, and the motion patterns are intended to be identical for every cycle, so that cycle-to-cycle variations in time and work content tend to be random.

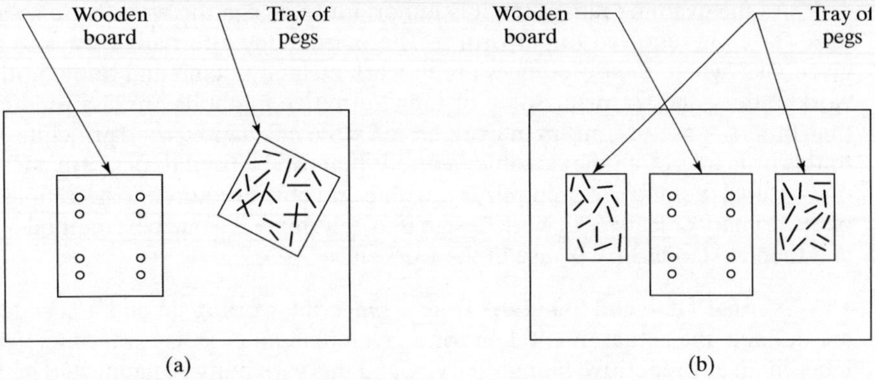

Figure 2 Workplace layout for assembly task in Example 1: (a) before methods improvement and (b) after methods improvement.

Sequence	Work Element Description	Work Element Time, T_{ek} (min)
1	Worker picks up board with one hand and holds it.	0.08
2	Worker picks peg from tray and inserts it into hole in board.	0.06
3	Worker picks second peg and inserts it into hole in board.	0.06
4	Worker picks third peg and inserts it into hole in board.	0.06
5	Worker picks fourth peg and inserts it into hole in board.	0.06
6	Worker picks fifth peg and inserts it into hole in board.	0.06
7	Worker picks sixth peg and inserts it into hole in board.	0.06
8	Worker picks seventh peg and inserts it into hole in board.	0.06
9	Worker picks eighth peg and inserts it into hole in board.	0.06
10	Worker lays assembled board into tote pan.	0.06
Total work cycle time		0.62

Solution: An opportunity for improvement lies in using a work-holding device to hold and position the board while the worker uses both hands simultaneously to insert the pegs. Two trays filled with pegs will be used, one for each hand. Instead of picking the pegs out of the tray one peg at a time, each hand will grab four pegs in order to minimize the number of times the worker's hands must reach to the trays. The revised workplace layout is shown in Figure 2 (b), and the revised sequence of work elements is presented in the table below. The cycle time is reduced from 0.62 min to 0.37 min, a reduction of 40%, which corresponds to an increase in production rate of almost 68%.

Sequence	Work Element Description	Work Element Time, T_{ek} (min)
1	Worker picks up board and positions it in workholder.	0.12
2	Worker picks 4 pegs each with both hands from 2 trays and inserts them into 8 holes in board.	0.15
3	Worker removes board from workholder and places in tote pan.	0.10
Total work cycle time		0.37

■

As the example illustrates, it is important to design the work cycle so as to minimize the time required to perform it. There are many alternative ways to perform a given task, where the differences are in work elements, hand and body motions, tools, workholders, and so forth. Some of the alternative methods are less time-consuming than others. A useful concept in work design is the ***one best method*** principle. According to this principle, of all the possible methods that can be used to perform a task, there is one optimal method that minimizes the time and effort required to accomplish it. [2] One of the primary objectives in work design is to determine the one best method for the task, and then to standardize its use in the workplace.

Normal Time and Standard Time. Once the work cycle and associated method are defined, the actual time taken for a given manual cycle is a variable. Variability is inherent in any repetitive human activity, and this variability is manifested in the time to perform the activity. Reasons for variations in work cycle times include the following:

- Differences in worker performance from one cycle to the next
- Variations in hand and body motions
- Worker blunders and bungles
- Variations in the starting work units
- Inclusion of extra elements that are not performed every cycle
- Differences in the physical and cognitive attributes among workers performing the task
- Variations in the methods used by different workers to perform the task
- The learning curve phenomenon.

Topping the list is worker ***performance***, which can be defined simply as the pace or relative speed with which the worker does the task. As worker performance increases, the time to accomplish the work cycle decreases. From the employer's viewpoint, it is desirable for the worker to work at a high level of performance. The question is: what is a reasonable performance or pace to expect from a worker in accomplishing a given task? To answer the question, let us introduce the concept of normal performance. ***Normal performance*** (or ***normal pace***) means a pace of working that can be maintained by a properly trained average worker throughout an entire work shift without deleterious short-term or long-term effects on the worker's health or physical well-being. The work shift is usually assumed to be eight hours, during which periodic rest breaks are allowed. Normal performance refers to the pace of the worker while actually working. When a worker works at a normal performance level, we say he or she is working at 100% performance. A faster pace than normal is greater than 100% and a slower pace is less than 100%. A common benchmark of normal performance is walking on level ground at three miles per hour.

The term ***standard performance*** is often used in place of normal performance. They both refer to the same pace while working, but standard performance acknowledges that periodic rest breaks are included in the work shift. For example, a healthy human

[2]The one best method should also satisfy other criteria in addition to minimizing the work cycle time, such as ensuring a safe and convenient workplace for the worker, and producing a work unit of high quality.

can walk at a pace of three miles per hour for an hour or two. However, walking for a solid eight hours without ever stopping for a rest break would be physically wearing. Accordingly, normal performance and standard performance both mean walking three miles per hour during an eight-hour period, but the walker could stop for a rest a few times and take a lunch break during the eight hours.

When a work cycle is performed at 100% performance, the time taken is called the ***normal time*** for the cycle. If worker performance is greater than 100%, then the time required to complete the cycle will be less than the normal time; and when worker performance is less than 100 percent, the time taken will be greater than the normal time. The actual time to perform the work cycle is a function of the worker's performance as indicated in the equation

$$T_c = \frac{T_n}{P_w} \tag{2}$$

where T_c = actual cycle time, min; T_n = normal time for the work cycle, min; and P_w = pace or performance of the worker, expressed as a decimal fraction (e.g., 100% = 1.0).

Example 2 Normal Performance

A man walks in the early morning for health and fitness. His usual route is 1.85 miles long. The route has minimal elevation changes. A typical time to walk the 1.85 miles is 30 min. Using the benchmark of 3 miles/hr as normal performance, determine (a) how long the route would take at normal performance and (b) the man's performance when he completes the route in 30 min.

Solution: **(a)** At 3 miles/hr, 1.85 miles can be covered in 1.85/3.0 = 0.6167 hr or 37 min.

(b) If the man takes 30 min to complete the walk, then his performance can be determined by dividing the normal time by the actual time, by rearranging equation (2). Thus,

$$P_w = 37/30 = 1.233 \text{ or } 123.3\%$$

Alternative Solution: For part (b), we could determine the man's velocity and compare it to the benchmark of 3.0 miles/hr in order to determine his performance. If the man completes 1.85 miles in 30 min, then his walking velocity is 1.85 miles divided by 0.5 hr, which equals 3.7 miles/hr.

$$P_w = 3.7/3.0 = 1.233 \text{ or } 123.3\%$$

■

Workers are allowed periodic rest breaks (e.g., coffee breaks) during their work shift. A typical work shift is eight hours (e.g., 8:00 A.M. to 5:00 P.M. with an hour from noon to 1:00 P.M. for lunch). The shift usually includes a rest break in the morning and another in the afternoon. Unlike the lunch period, these rest breaks are normally included within the eight-hour time of the shift. The employer allows these breaks because it has been found that the overall productivity of the worker during the shift is greater if rest breaks are provided. More work is accomplished by the end of the day and fewer mistakes are made if the worker can take time out periodically from the normal work routine. In addition to the rest breaks, the worker is likely to have other interruptions during the shift, such as equipment breakdowns (if the manual task is somehow dependent on equipment), receiving instructions from the foreman, personal telephone calls, and so on. As a result of all of these factors, the total time actually worked during the shift will be less than the full eight hours, in all likelihood.

To account for these delays and rest breaks, an ***allowance*** is added to the normal time in order to determine an "allowed time" for the worker to perform the task throughout the shift. More commonly known as the ***standard time***, it is defined as follows:

$$T_{std} = T_n(1 + A_{pfd}) \tag{3}$$

where T_{std} = standard time, min; T_n = normal time, min; and A_{pfd} = allowance factor, usually expressed as a percentage but used in equation (3) as a decimal fraction. The allowance is commonly called the personal time, fatigue, and delay allowance (abbreviated ***PFD allowance***), and it is figured in such a way that, if the worker works at 100 percent performance during the portion of the shift that he or she is working, the amount of work accomplished will be eight hours' worth.

Manual work cycles often include ***irregular work elements***, which are elements performed with a frequency of less than once per cycle. Examples of irregular work elements include periodic changing of tools (e.g., changing a knife blade) and replacing tote pans of parts when the containers become full. In determining a standard time for the cycle, the irregular element times are prorated in the regular cycle time. The following examples illustrate these concepts and definitions.

Example 3 Determining Standard Time and Standard Output

The normal time to perform the regular work cycle for a certain manual operation is 3.23 min. In addition, an irregular work element whose normal time is 1.25 min must be performed every 5 cycles. The PFD allowance factor is 15%. Determine (a) the standard time and (b) how many work units are produced if the worker's performance in an 8-hour shift is standard.

Solution: **(a)** The normal time for the work cycle includes the irregular element prorated according to its frequency:

$$T_n = 3.23 + \frac{1.25}{5} = 3.23 + 0.25 = 3.48 \text{ min}$$

The standard time is $T_{std} = T_n(1 + A_{pfd}) = 3.48(1 + 0.15) = 4.00$ min.

(b) The number of work units produced at standard performance in an 8-hour shift is the clock time of the shift divided by the standard time:

$$Q_{std} = \frac{8.0(60)}{4.00} = 120 \text{ work units}$$

■

Example 4 Determining Lost Time Due to the Allowance Factor

Determine the anticipated amount of time lost per 8-hour shift when an allowance factor of 15% is used, as in the previous example.

Solution: Given that $A_{pfd} = 0.15$, the anticipated amount of time lost per 8-hour shift is determined as follows:

$$8.0 \text{ hr} = (\text{actual time worked})(1 + 0.15)$$

$$\text{Actual time worked} = \frac{8.0}{1.15} = 6.956 \text{ hr}$$

$$\text{Time lost} = 8.0 - 6.956 = 1.044 \text{ hr}$$

This is the anticipated daily amount of time lost due to personal time, fatigue, and delays corresponding to a 15% PFD allowance factor. ■

Example 5 Production Rate When Worker Performance Exceeds 100%

Now that the standard is set ($T_{std} = 4.00$ min), and given the data from the previous examples, how many work units would be produced if the worker's average performance during an 8-hour shift were 125% and the hours actually worked were exactly 6.956 hr, which corresponds to the 15% allowance factor.

Solution: Based on the normal time $T_n = 3.48$ min, the actual cycle time with a worker performance of 125% is

$$T_c = \frac{3.48}{1.25} = 2.78 \text{ min}$$

Assuming one work unit is produced each cycle, the corresponding daily production rate (symbolized by R_p) is

$$R_p = \frac{6.956(60)}{2.78} = 150 \text{ work units}$$

Note that 150 units = 125% of 120 units at 100% performance. ■

Standard Hours and Worker Efficiency. Two common measures used in industry to assess a worker's productivity are standard hours and worker efficiency. The ***standard hours*** represents the amount of work actually accomplished by the worker during a given period (e.g., shift, week), expressed in terms of time. In its simplest form, it is the quantity of work units produced during the period multiplied by the standard time per work unit; that is,

$$H_{std} = QT_{std} \tag{4}$$

where H_{std} = standard hours accomplished, hr; Q = quantity of work units completed during the period, pc; and T_{std} = standard time per work unit, hr/pc. If the time standard

T_{std} is expressed in min/pc, then conversion of units is required to obtain standard hours H_{std}. When a worker works at a performance level greater than 100% and his or her actual time worked during the shift is consistent with or greater than what is provided by the allowance factor, then the number of standard hours accomplished will be greater than the number of hours in the shift.

Worker efficiency is the amount of work accomplished during the shift expressed as a proportion of the shift hours. In equation form,

$$E_w = \frac{H_{std}}{H_{sh}} \tag{5}$$

where E_w = worker efficiency, normally expressed as a percentage; H_{std} = number of standard hours of work accomplished during the shift, hr; and H_{sh} = number of shift hours (e.g., 8 hr).

Example 6 Standard Hours and Worker Efficiency

For the worker performance of 125% in the previous example (T_{std} = 4.00 min), determine (a) number of standard hours produced and (b) worker efficiency.

Solution: **(a)** H_{std} = 150(4.0 min) = 600 min = 10.0 hr

(b) E_w = (10.0 hr)/(8.0 hr) = 1.25 = 125% ■

In Example 5 and 6, the worker's efficiency and performance level are equal for two reasons: (1) the number of hours actually worked is exactly consistent with the 15% allowance factor, and (2) the entire work cycle consists exclusively of manual labor and is therefore entirely operator-controlled. In the absence of either or both of these conditions, worker efficiency will not equal worker performance level (except by coincidence, when certain combinations of values offset each other). In reality, the number of hours actually worked by a worker in an 8-hour shift varies each day, depending on the amount of time lost due to personal reasons, rest breaks, and delays. Worker performance and worker efficiency are different if the time lost is different from what is accounted for by the PFD allowance factor, as the following example illustrates.

Example 7 Standard Hours and Worker Efficiency as Affected by Hours Actually Worked

Suppose the worker's pace in the task is 125%, but the actual hours worked is 7.42 hr. Determine (a) the number of pieces produced, (b) the number of standard hours accomplished, and (c) the worker's efficiency.

Solution: **(a)** The actual cycle time at 125% performance is 2.78 min, as calculated in Example 5. The number of work units produced in 7.42 hr is

$$Q = \frac{7.42(60)}{2.78} = 160 \text{ units}$$

(b) H_{std} = 160(4.0 min) = 640 min = 10.67 hr

(c) E_w = 10.67/8.0 = 1.333 = 133.3% ■

Worker efficiency is commonly used to evaluate workers in industry. In many incentive wage payment plans, the worker's earnings are based on his or her efficiency or the number of standard hours accomplished. Worker efficiency and standard hours are easily computed, because the number of hours in the shift and the standard time are known, and the number of work units produced can be readily counted. The two measures are basically equivalent, because either one can be derived from the other. One might think that worker performance would also be a useful measure; however, it is more difficult to assess because it requires data on the amount of time actually worked by the worker during the shift. This varies from day to day because the interruptions and delays vary from day to day. Some method of continuously observing the worker would be required. Aside from the cost, the worker would likely find such observation objectionable. In addition, the effect of worker performance is reduced when machine time is included in the work cycle, as we see in Section 2.

2 WORKER–MACHINE SYSTEMS

When a worker operates powered equipment, we refer to the arrangement as a ***worker–machine system***. It is one of the most widely used work systems. Worker–machine systems include combinations of one or more workers and one or more pieces of equipment. The workers and machines are combined to accomplish a desired output. Examples of worker–machine systems include the following:

- A skilled machinist operating an engine lathe in a tool room to fabricate a component (the work unit) for a custom-designed product. The machinist must exercise considerable skill in controlling the feed, speed, and tool position while operating the lathe.
- A construction worker operating a backhoe at a construction site. The worker must continuously operate the machine, using the various levers that control the different hydraulically operated mechanisms.
- A truck driver driving an 18-wheel tractor-trailer on an interstate highway. The driver must constantly be alert while operating the vehicle.
- A factory worker loading and unloading parts at a machine tool. The machine tool operates on semiautomatic cycle to process the parts. At the end of each work cycle, the worker unloads the completed part. Machine processing time is about 3 min. While the machine performs its process, the worker is idle. Loading and unloading the machine takes about 30 sec.
- A crew of workers operating a rolling mill that converts hot steel slabs into flat plates. Each worker has an assigned function. The most important job is the rolling mill operator who must coordinate the gap size (i.e., distance between opposing rolls) and the passing of the slab back and forth between the rolls. Each pass reduces the thickness of the starting slab until the specified thickness has been achieved.
- A secretary using a personal computer with word processor in an office typing pool.
- A clerical worker in a billing center entering data based on checks received by mail from customers into account records on a networked personal computer.
- An industrial engineer creating the design of a plant layout on a computer-aided design (CAD) workstation.

TABLE 1 Relative Strengths and Attributes of Humans and Machines

Relative Strengths of Humans	Relative Strengths of Machines
Sense unexpected stimuli	Perform repetitive tasks consistently
Develop new solutions to problems	Store large amounts of data
Cope with abstract problems	Retrieve data from memory reliably
Adapt to change	Perform multiple tasks at the same time
Generalize from observations	Apply high forces and power
Learn from experience	Perform simple computations quickly
Make difficult decisions based on incomplete data	Make routine decisions quickly

Source: [2].

Although the last three examples relate to service and knowledge work rather than production and logistics work, they also illustrate the widespread use of worker–machine systems. In these latter examples, the machine is a computer.

In a worker–machine system, the worker and the machine both contribute their own strengths and capabilities to the combination, and the result is synergistic. The relative strengths and attributes of humans and machines are presented in Table 1, and the worker–machine system should be designed to exploit these relative strengths.

2.1 Types of Worker–Machine Systems

It is instructive to distinguish the various categories and arrangements of worker–machine systems, some of which are suggested by our list of examples. In this section, we discuss the following classifications: (1) types of powered machinery used in the system, (2) numbers of workers and machines in the system, and (3) level of operator attention required to run the machinery.

Types of Powered Machinery. Powered machinery is distinguished from hand tools by the fact that a source of power other than human (or animal) strength is used to operate it. Common power sources are electric, pneumatic, hydraulic, and fossil fuel motors (e.g., gasoline, propane). In most cases, the power source is converted to mechanical energy to process the work unit. Powered machinery can be classified into three categories, summarized in Figure 3: (1) portable power tools, (2) mobile powered equipment, and (3) stationary powered machines.

Portable power tools are light enough in weight that they can be carried by the worker from one location to another and manipulated by hand. Examples include portable power drills, rotary saws, chain saws, and electric hedge trimmers. Common power sources are electric, pneumatic, and gasoline.

Mobile powered equipment can be divided into three categories: (1) transportation equipment, (2) transportable and mobile during operation, and (3) transportable and stationary during operation. They are generally heavy pieces of equipment and cannot be classified as power hand tools. Transportation equipment is a large category that includes cars, taxicabs, buses, trucks, trains, airplanes, boats, and ships. This powered machinery is designed to carry materials and/or people. Equipment in category (2), transportable

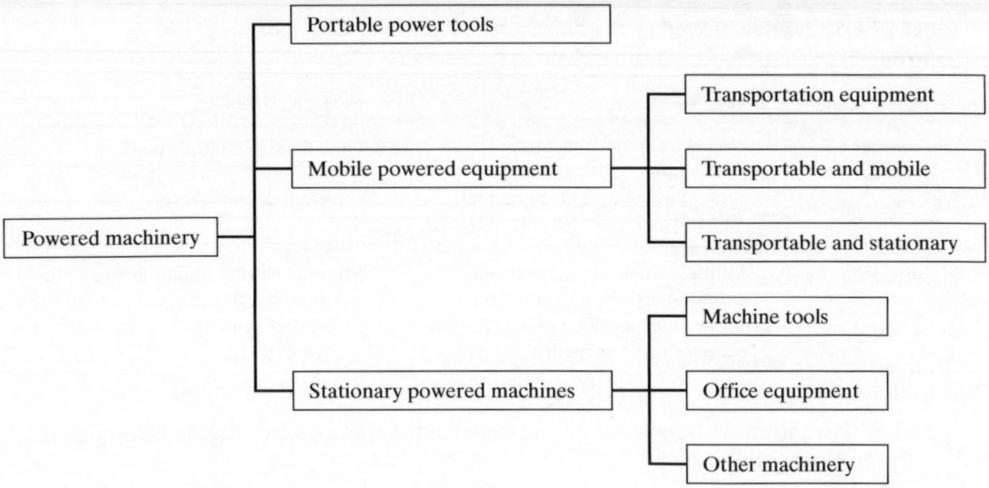

Figure 3 Classification of powered machinery in worker–machine systems.

and mobile during operation, consists of equipment that can move under its own power but can also be moved by transportation equipment (e.g., tractor and flatbed). Examples include construction equipment (e.g., bulldozers, backhoes), agricultural and lawn-keeping (e.g., small tractors, lawn mowers), and material-handling equipment (e.g., forklift trucks). The third category, transportable and stationary during operation, is equipment that can be transported by highway truck but it performs its function in a stationary location once it is moved (e.g., electric power generator, large power saws used at construction sites). The typical power sources are fossil fuels.

Stationary powered machines stand on the floor or ground and cannot be moved while they are operating, and they are not normally moved between operations. Electricity is the usual power source. We can classify stationary power tools into the following categories: (1) machine tools, (2) office equipment, and (3) other. A ***machine tool*** is a stationary power-driven machine that shapes or forms parts. Machine tools are normally associated with factory production operations such as machining (e.g., turning, drilling, milling), shearing (e.g., blanking, hole-punching), and squeezing (e.g., forging, extrusion). Office equipment (second category) includes personal computers, photocopiers, telephones, fax machines, design workstations, and other equipment and systems normally found in an office facility. The "other" types of equipment (third category) are a miscellaneous group that includes machinery not fitting into the other two categories. Examples include furnaces, ovens, cash registers, and sewing machines.

Numbers of Workers and Machines. Another means of classifying worker–machine systems is according to whether there are one or more workers and one or more machines. This provides four categories, as indicated in Table 2.

TABLE 2 Classification of Worker–Machine Systems According to Number of Machines and Workers

	One Machine	Multiple Machines
One worker	One worker–one machine. **Examples**: (1) A worker loading and unloading a machine tool, (2) a truck driver driving a tractor trailer.	One worker–multiple machines **Example**: A worker tending several production machines.
Multiple workers	Multiple workers–one machine. **Examples**: (1) Several workers operating a rolling mill, (2) a crew on a ship or airplane.	Multiple worker–multiple machines. **Example**: An emergency repair crew responding to machine breakdowns in a factory.

For the case of one worker and one machine, good work design attempts to achieve the following objectives:

- Design the controls of the machine to be logical and easy to operate for the worker.
- Design the work sequence so that as much of the worker's task as possible can be accomplished while the machine is operating, thereby minimizing worker idle time.
- Minimize the idle times of both the worker and the machine.
- Design the task and the machine to be safe for the worker. If the task is inherently hazardous to the worker, then an automated work system should be considered.

The same design objectives are applicable when the work system consists of multiple workers and/or multiple machines. An additional objective is to optimize the number of workers or machines in the system according to some appropriate economic objective. For example, if one worker is assigned to attend to multiple machines, how many machines should be assigned to that worker so as to avoid machine idle time?

Level of Operator Attention Required. Another way to distinguish among worker–machine systems is by the level of attention required by the worker(s). In this classification, we have the four categories described in Table 3. Full-time attention means that the worker must devote virtually 100% of his or her time to the operation of the equipment during the performance of the task.

2.2 Cycle Time Analysis in Worker–Machine Systems

In terms of cycle time analysis, worker–machine systems fall into two categories: (1) systems in which the machine time depends on operator control, and (2) systems in which the machine time is constant and independent of operator control, and the work cycle is repetitive. In the first category, in which machine time depends on operator control, the task can be either (1) repetitive or (2) nonrepetitive. The following examples illustrate repetitive tasks with cycle times that depend on the pace and skill with which the operator applies the powered equipment:

- A typist typing a list of names and telephone numbers on a conventional electric typewriter

TABLE 3 Levels of Operator Attention in Worker–Machine Systems

Category	Description	Examples
Full-time attention	Worker is engaged 100% of the time in operating the equipment. The task can be (1) repetitive and cyclical or (2) nonrepetitive.	Worker operating a drop forge hammer (repetitive and cyclical). Worker on an assembly line whose task time equal to available service time (repetitive and cyclical). Truck driver driving an 18-wheeler (nonrepetitive). Worker mowing the lawn (nonrepetitive).
Part-time attention during each work cycle	Worker is engaged less than 100% of the time in operating the equipment. Task is repetitive and cyclical.	Worker loading and/or unloading production machine each cycle. Machine processes work units on mechanized or semiautomatic cycle. Worker is idle during machine cycle.
Periodic attention with regular servicing	Worker must service machine at regular intervals that are greater than one work cycle	Crane operator in steel mill moving molten steel ingots after each heat cycle. The operator must spend most of his time waiting for the next heat. Worker loading and/or unloading an automated production machine every 20 cycles. The machine operates on automatic cycle for the 20 cycles, but its storage capacity is limited to 20 work units.
Periodic attention with random servicing	Worker must service machine at random intervals that average more than one work cycle	Maintenance worker repairing production equipment when it malfunctions at random times. Firefighters responding to alarms that occur at random times.

- A metal trades worker operating a power buffer to buff the surface of a metal part
- A carpenter using a power saw to cut standard lengths of lumber
- A forklift driver moving pallet loads from the truck dock to the storage racks in a warehouse.

In these cases when the work cycle is repetitive but the cycle time is not constant, the analysis methods in Section 1.2 can be used.

Examples of worker–machine systems that operate on a nonrepetitive work cycle include the following:

- A trucker driving a tractor-trailer on an interstate highway
- A construction worker operating a backhoe
- A farmer operating a threshing machine to separate seeds from crop
- A carpenter using portable power tools to build a deck on a newly constructed house.

These nonrepetitive work situations do not consist of a regular work cycle that is repeated over and over. The time to accomplish the work depends on the skill and work ethic of the persons performing the tasks. Estimates or historical records based on previous similar jobs are often used to determine how long the work should take to complete.

In this section, we focus attention on the second category of worker–machine system, in which machine time is constant and does not depend on operator control, and the work cycle is repetitive. Two cases are discussed: (1) cycle times with no overlap between worker and machine and (2) worker–machine systems with internal work elements.

Cycle Times with No Overlap Between Worker and Machine. In a worker–machine system, the work elements include one or more actions and/or operations performed by the machine. If there is no overlap in work elements between the worker and the machine, then the normal time for the cycle is simply the sum of their respective normal times:

$$T_n = T_{nw} + T_m \tag{6}$$

where T_{nw} = normal time for the worker-controlled portion of the cycle, min; and T_m = machine cycle time (assumed constant).

To determine the standard time for the cycle, a machine allowance is sometimes added to the machine time. If we include such an allowance factor in the standard time calculation, we have

$$T_{std} = T_{nw}(1 + A_{pfd}) + T_m(1 + A_m) \tag{7}$$

where T_{nw} = normal time of the worker, min; T_m = constant time for the machine cycle, min; A_m = machine allowance factor, used in the equation as a decimal fraction; and the other terms have the same meaning as before.

A typical value used by companies for the machine allowance factor is $A_m = 30\%$. This tends to help workers achieve higher worker efficiencies, which is especially important if the worker is paid on an incentive basis. Workers might prefer to work on an entirely manual cycle if the machine allowance were not provided. On the other hand, some companies do not see the need to use a machine allowance, in which case $A_m = 0$. An argument for $A_m = 0$ is that the worker is idle during the machine cycle, and so does not have to expend any effort during this portion of the work cycle. Other companies simply set the A_m value to be the same as A_{pfd}. The following examples show how the value of A_m affects the standard time and worker efficiency.

Example 8 Effect of Machine Allowance on Standard Time

In the operation of a worker–machine system, the work cycle consists of several manual work elements (operator-controlled) and one machine element performed under semiautomatic control. One workpiece is produced each cycle. The manual work elements total a normal time of 1.0 min and the semiautomatic machine cycle is a constant 2.0 min. The PFD allowance factor A_{pfd} is 15%. Determine the standard time using (a) $A_m = 0$ and (b) $A_m = 30\%$.

Solution: The normal time for the work cycle is the normal time for the worker-controlled elements plus the machine cycle time:

$$T_n = 1.0 + 2.0 = 3.0 \text{ min}$$

(a) With a machine allowance of 0, the standard time is calculated as

$$T_{std} = 1.0(1 + 0.15) + 2.0 = 3.15 \text{ min}$$

(b) With a machine allowance of 30%, the standard time is

$$T_{std} = 1.0(1 + 0.15) + 2.0(1 + 0.30) = 1.15 + 2.60 = 3.75 \text{ min}$$ ■

Example 9 Effect of Machine Allowance on Worker Efficiency

Based on the standard times computed in (a) and (b) of the previous example, determine the worker efficiencies for two cases if 150 units are produced in one 8-hour shift.

Solution: **(a)** If T_{std} = 3.15 min, the number of standard hours accomplished is

$$H_{std} = 150(3.15) = 472.5 \text{ min} = 7.875 \text{ hr}$$

$$\text{Worker efficiency } E_w = 7.875/8.0 = 0.984 = 98.4\%$$

(b) If T_{std} = 3.75 min, the number of standard hours accomplished is

$$H_{std} = 150(3.75) = 562.5 \text{ min} = 9.375 \text{ hr}$$

$$\text{Worker efficiency } E_w = 9.375/8.0 = 1.172 = 117.2\%$$ ■

When the work cycle includes a machine cycle and the machine time is a constant, then operator performance has no effect on this machine element. The only way the worker's pace can affect the work cycle time is during those elements that are operator-controlled. The operator may be idle during the machine element, as in Examples 8 and 9, unless the work sequence can be designed to include operator work elements that are performed while the machine is running.

Worker–Machine Systems with Internal Work Elements. In the operation of a worker–machine system, it is important to distinguish between the operator's work elements that are performed in sequence with the machine's work elements and those that are performed simultaneously with the machine elements. Operator elements that are performed sequentially are called ***external work elements*** while those that are performed simultaneously with the machine cycle are called ***internal work elements***. The distinction is important because it is desirable to construct the work cycle sequence so that as many of the operator elements as possible are performed as internal elements. This tends to minimize the cycle time, as illustrated by the following example.

Example 10 Internal Versus External Work Elements in Cycle Time Analysis

The work cycle in a worker–machine system consists of the elements and associated times given in the table below. All of the operator's work elements are external to the machine time. Can some of the worker's elements be made internal to the machine cycle, and if so, what is the expected cycle time for the operation?

Sequence	Work Element Description	Worker Time (min)	Machine Time (min)
1	Worker walks to tote pan containing raw stock	0.13	(idle)
2	Worker picks up raw workpart and transports to machine	0.23	(idle)
3	Worker loads part into machine and engages machine semiautomatic cycle	0.12	(idle)
4	Machine semiautomatic cycle	(idle)	0.75
5	Worker unloads finished part from machine	0.10	(idle)
6	Worker transports finished part and deposits into tote pan	0.15	(idle)
Totals		0.73	0.75

Solution: Since all of the work elements in the cycle are sequential, the total cycle time is the sum of the worker elements and the machine element:

$$T_c = 0.73 + 0.75 = 1.48 \text{ min.}$$

The worker is idle during the entire machine semiautomatic cycle. It should be possible to imbed elements 1, 2, and 6 as internal elements that are performed while the machine is running on a semiautomatic cycle. Using the times from the preceding table, the resulting work cycle can be organized as follows:

Sequence	Work Element Description	Worker Time (min)	Machine Time (min)
1	Worker unloads finished part from machine	0.10	(idle)
2	Worker loads part into machine and engages semiautomatic machine cycle	0.12	(idle)
3	Machine semiautomatic cycle		0.75
4	Worker transports finished part and deposits it into tote pan, walks to tote pan containing raw stock, and picks up raw workpart and transports it to machine. (This element is internal to the machine semiautomatic cycle.)	0.15 + 0.13 + 0.23 = 0.51	
Totals		0.73	0.75

Although the total times for the worker and the machine are the same as before, element 4 in the revised cycle (which consists of elements 1, 2, and 6 from the original work cycle) is performed simultaneously with the machine time, resulting in the following new cycle time:

$$T_c = 0.10 + 0.12 + 0.75 = 0.97 \text{ min}$$

This represents a 34% reduction in cycle time, which translates into a 53% increase in production rate.

■

When internal elements are present in the work cycle, it must then be determined whether the machine cycle time or the sum of the worker's internal elements take longer. To determine the normal time for the cycle,

$$T_n = T_{nw} + \text{Max}\{T_{nwi}, T_m\} \tag{8}$$

where T_{nw} = normal time for the worker's external elements, min; T_{nwi} = normal time for the worker's internal elements, min; and T_m = machine cycle time. The standard time for the cycle is given by

$$T_{std} = T_{nw}(1 + A_{pfd}) + \text{Max}\,\{T_{nwi}(1 + A_{pfd}),\, T_m(1 + A_m)\} \tag{9}$$

where A_{pfd} and A_m are the worker's allowance factor and the machine allowance factor, respectively. Finally, the actual cycle time depends on the worker's performance level, applied to the normalized times as

$$T_c = \frac{T_{nw}}{P_w} + \text{Max}\left(\frac{T_{nwi}}{P_w},\, T_m\right) \tag{10}$$

where P_w is the worker performance level during the cycle, expressed as a decimal fraction; and the other symbols mean the same as before. We assume in equation (10) that the worker's performance level is the same on the external and internal elements. If these P_w values are different, then the computations must reflect these differences.

3 AUTOMATED WORK SYSTEMS

Automation is the technology by which a process or procedure is accomplished without human assistance. It is implemented using a program of instructions combined with a control system that executes the instructions. Power is required to drive the process and to operate the program and control system.

There is not always a clear distinction between worker–machine systems and automated systems, because many worker–machine systems operate with some degree of automation. Let us distinguish between two forms of automation: semiautomated and fully automated. A ***semiautomated machine*** performs a portion of the work cycle under some form of program control, and a human worker tends to the machine for the remainder of the cycle, by loading and unloading it, or performing some other task during each cycle. An example of this category is an automated lathe controlled for most of the work cycle by the part program but requiring a worker to unload the finished part and load the next workpiece at the end of each machine cycle. In these cases, the worker must attend to the machine during every cycle. This type of operation has the same characteristics as a worker–machine system that requires the part-time attention of the worker during each work cycle (Table 3). Its cycle time analysis is discussed in Section 2.2.

The continuous presence of the operator during the cycle may not always be required. If the automatic machine cycle takes, say, 10 min while the part unloading and loading portion of the work cycle takes only 30 sec, then there may be an opportunity for one worker to tend more than one machine. We analyze this possibility in Section 5.

A ***fully automated machine*** is distinguished from its semiautomated cousin by the capacity to operate for extended periods of time with no human attention. By extended periods of time, we mean longer than one work cycle. A worker is not required to be present during each cycle. Instead, the worker may need to tend the machine every tenth cycle, or every hundredth cycle. An example of this type of operation is found in many injection molding plants, where the molding machines run on automatic cycle, but periodically the molded parts at the machine must be collected by a worker. This case is identified in Table 3 as periodic attention with regular servicing.

Certain fully automated processes require one or more workers to be present to continuously monitor the operation and make sure that it performs according to the intended specifications. Examples of these kinds of automated processes are found at chemical-processing facilities, oil refineries, and nuclear power plants. The workers do not actively participate in the process except to make occasional adjustments in the equipment settings, to perform periodic maintenance, and to spring into action if something goes wrong.

4 DETERMINING WORKER AND MACHINE REQUIREMENTS

One of the problems faced by any organization is determining the appropriate staffing levels. How many workers are required to achieve the organization's work objectives? If too few workers are assigned to perform a given amount of work, then the work cannot be completed on time, and customer service suffers. If too many workers are assigned, then payroll costs are higher than needed, and productivity suffers. Determining the number of workers or worker–machine systems that will be required to accomplish a specified amount of work is the problem we address in this section. The basic approach consists of two steps:

1. Determine the total workload that must be accomplished in a certain period (hour, week, month, year), where ***workload*** is defined as the total hours required to complete a given amount of work or to produce a given number of work units scheduled during the period.
2. Divide the workload by the available time per worker, where ***available time*** is defined as the number of hours in the same period available from one worker or worker–machine system.

Let us consider two general cases: (1) when setup time is not a factor and (2) when setup time must be included in the determination.

4.1 When Setup Is Not a Factor

Workload is figured as the quantity of work units to be produced during the period of interest multiplied by the time (hours) required for each work unit. The time required for each work unit is the work cycle time in most cases, so that workload is given by

$$WL = QT_c \tag{11}$$

where WL = workload scheduled for a given period, hr of work/period (e.g., hr/wk); Q = quantity to be produced during the period, pc/period (e.g., pc/wk); and T_c = work cycle time required per work unit, hr/pc. Normally, the work cycle time T_c would be the standard time T_{std} for the task, and so the workload is the number of standard hours scheduled during the period.

If the workload includes multiple part or product styles that can all be produced by the same worker or work system during the period of interest, then the following summation is used:

$$WL = \sum_j Q_j T_{cj} \tag{12}$$

where Q_j = quantity of part or product style j produced during the period, pc; T_{cj} = cycle time of part or product style j, hr/pc; and the summation includes all of the parts or products to be made during the period. In step (2) the workload is divided by the hours available of one worker in the same time period; that is,

$$w = \frac{WL}{AT} \quad \text{or} \quad n = \frac{WL}{AT} \tag{13}$$

where w = number of workers, n = number of workstations (e.g., worker–machine systems); and AT = available time of one worker in the period, hr/period/worker. We can understand the use of these equations with a simple example, and then consider some of the complications.

Example 11 Determining Worker Requirements

A total of 800 shafts must be produced in the lathe section of a machine shop during a particular week. Each shaft is identical and requires a standard time T_{std} = 11.5 min (machining time plus worker time). All of the lathes in the department are equivalent in terms of their capability to produce the shaft in the specified cycle time. How many lathes and lathe operators must be devoted to shaft production during the given week, if there are 40 hours of available time on each lathe.

Solution: The workload consists of 800 shafts at 11.5 min per shaft.

$$WL = 800\,(11.5\text{ min}) = 9200\text{ min} = 153.33\text{ hr}$$

The time available per lathe during the week is AT = 40 hr.

$$w = n = \frac{153.33}{40} = 3.83\text{ lathe operators and }3.83\text{ lathes}$$

This calculated value would probably be rounded up to four lathes and operators that are assigned to the production of shafts during the given week. ■

There are several factors present in most work systems that make the computation of the number of workers somewhat more complicated than suggested by Example 11. These factors influence either the workload or the amount of time available per worker during the period of interest. There are three principal factors that affect workload during a given period:

- *Worker efficiency.* Workload varies when the worker performs either above or below standard performance for a given manual task.
- *Defect rate.* The output of the work system may not be 100% good quality. Defective units may be produced at a certain fraction defect rate that must be accounted for by increasing the total number of units processed.
- *Learning curve phenomenon.* As the worker becomes more familiar with a repetitive task, the time to accomplish each cycle tends to decrease.

Worker efficiency is defined in Section 1.2 and equation (5) as the amount of work accomplished during a shift expressed as a proportion of the shift hours. It is the workload actually completed by a worker in a given time period divided by the workload that would be completed at standard performance. An efficiency greater than 1.00 reduces the workload, while an efficiency less than 1.00 increases the workload. Many companies establish their time standards for tasks so that most workers are able to exceed standard performance. In this case, worker efficiency will be greater than 100% on average, and the company should take this into account in determining workloads.

Defect rate is the fraction of parts produced that are defective. A defect rate greater than zero increases the quantity of work units that must be processed in order to yield the desired quantity. If a process is known to produce parts at a certain average scrap rate, then the starting quantity should be increased to compensate for the defective parts that will be made. The relationship between the starting quantity and the final quantity produced is

$$Q = Q_o(1-q) \tag{14}$$

where Q = quantity of good units made in the process; Q_o = original or starting quantity; and q = fraction defect rate. Thus, if we want to produce Q good units, we must process a total of Q_o starting units, which is

$$Q_o = \frac{Q}{(1-q)} \tag{15}$$

The combined effect of worker efficiency and fraction defect rate is given in the following equation, which amends the workload formula, equation (11):

$$WL = \frac{QT_{std}}{E_w(1-q)} \tag{16}$$

where E_w = worker efficiency, expressed as a decimal fraction; and q = fraction defect rate.

As learning occurs in repetitive manual work, worker efficiency increases and the cycle time decreases, so that the workload is gradually reduced as the job progresses. An attempt is made in most companies to take the learning curve into account when determining workloads.

An important factor that affects the available time per worker or per worker–machine system is availability. ***Availability*** is a common measure of reliability for equipment and is defined as the proportion of time the equipment is available to run relative to the total time it could be used. It is the proportion of time that the equipment is not malfunctioning or broken down. Availability is especially applicable for mechanized or automated equipment. As availability decreases, the available time of the equipment is reduced. The available time becomes the actual shift time in the period multiplied by availability. In equation form,

$$AT = H_{sh}A \tag{17}$$

where AT = available time, hr/worker; H_{sh} = shift hours during the period, hr.; and A = availability, expressed as a decimal fraction.

Example 12 Effect of Worker Efficiency, Defect Rate, and Availability on Worker Requirements

Suppose in Example 11 that the anticipated availability of the lathes is 95%. The expected worker efficiency during production = 110%. The fraction defect rate for lathe work of this type is 3%. Other data from Example 11 are applicable. How many lathes are required during the 40-hour week, given this additional information?

Solution: The total workload for the 800 parts is equation (16):

$$WL = \frac{800(11.5/60)}{(1.10)(1-0.03)} = 143.7 \text{ hr}$$

The available time is affected by the 95% availability:

$$AT = 40(0.95) = 38 \text{ hr/machine}$$

$$n = \frac{143.7}{38} = 3.78 \text{ lathes and lathe operators}$$

This should be rounded up to four lathes, unless the remaining time on the fourth lathe can be used for other production.

■

4.2 When Setup Time Is Included

Setup time is associated with batch processing. Briefly, ***batch processing*** refers to operations in which work units are processed in groups (i.e., batches). In most cases, the equipment must be changed over between batches, and the time lost for the changeover is called the ***setup time***. Setup time is required because the tooling and fixturing must be changed to accommodate the next work unit type, and the machine settings must be adjusted. Time is lost during setup because no work units are produced (except perhaps a few trial units to check out the new setup). Yet setup consumes available time at a machine. In this section, we examine two alternative cases in which setup time must be accounted for: (1) the number of setups is known and (2) the number of setups is unknown.

Number of Setups Is Known. In batch production, we know how many batches must be produced in a given period. Since there is one setup associated with each batch, we therefore know how many setups must be made. Accordingly, the setup workload can be computed as the sum of the setup times for all batches. The following example illustrates this case, as well as some other variations.

Example 13 Determining Worker Requirements When Number of Setups Is Known

This is another variation of Example 11. A total of 800 shafts must be produced in the lathe section of the machine shop during a particular week. The shafts are of 16 different types, each type being produced in its own batch. Average batch size is 50 parts. Each batch requires a setup and the average setup time is 3.5 hr. The average machine cycle time to produce a shaft T_c is 11.5 min. Assume that the fraction defect rate is 3%, and worker efficiency is 100%. Availability is assumed to be 100% during setup but only 95% during a production run. How many lathes are required during the week?

Solution: In this case we know how many setups are required during the week because we know that 16 batches will be produced. We can determine the following workload for the 16 setups and the workload for 16 production batches:

$$WL = 16(3.5) + \frac{16(50)(11.5/60)}{(0.97)} = 56 + 158.076 = 214.08 \text{ hr}$$

Since machine availability differs between setup and run time, we must figure worker requirements for each separately. For setup, $AT = 40(1.0) = 40$ hr/machine, but for run time, $AT = 40(0.95) = 38$ hr. These two values must be allocated respectively to the two terms of the workload. The number of lathes and operators is calculated as

$$n = \frac{56}{40} + \frac{158.076}{38} = 1.40 + 4.16 = 5.56$$

which would be rounded up to six machines and operators. Note that the rounding up should occur after adding the machine fractions; otherwise there is a risk of overestimating machine requirements.

■

In this example there is a separation of tasks between two or more types of work (in this problem, setup and run are two separate types of work), so we must be careful to use the various factors only where they apply. For example, fraction defect rate does not apply to setup time. Availability is also assumed not to apply to setup (how can the machine break down if it is not running?). Also, worker efficiencies might differ between setup and run. Accordingly, it is appropriate to compute the number of equivalent machines (and/or workers) for setup separately from the number for production.

Number of Setups Is Unknown. In this case, each worker–machine system that will be used to meet production requirements must be set up at the beginning of its respective production run, but we do not know how many machines there will be. Accordingly, we must express the total workload for setup time as a function of the number of machines. This case is illustrated by the following example.

Example 14 Including Setup Time When Each Machine Must Be Set Up Once

In another variation of Example 11, suppose that a setup is required for each lathe that is used to satisfy the production requirements. The lathe setup for this type of part takes 3.5 hr. Assume that fraction defect rate is 3%, worker efficiency is 100%, and availability is 100%. How many lathes and lathe operators are required during the week?

Solution: The fraction defect rate applies to the production workload but not to the setup workload. Thus workload consists of two terms, as follows:

$$WL = \frac{800(11.5/60)}{(1-0.03)} + 3.5\,n = 158.076 + 3.5\,n$$

For $A = 1.0$,

$$AT = 40(1.0) = 40 \text{ hr of available time per lathe}$$

Dividing WL by AT, we have

$$n = \frac{158.076 + 3.5n}{40} = 3.95 + 0.0875\,n$$

Solving, $n = 4.33$ lathes and lathe operators, which must be rounded up to five lathes and associated workers.

Comment: It is inefficient to devote five lathes and operators for the 40-hour week, because the lathes will not be fully utilized. Given this unfortunate result, it might be preferable to offer overtime to the workers on four of the lathes. How much overtime (represented by OT) above the regular 40 hours will be required?

$$OT = \left(3.5 + \frac{158.076}{4}\right) - 40 = (3.5 + 39.52) - 40 = 3.02 \text{ hr}$$

This is a total of 4 (3.02 hr) = 12.08 hr for the four machine operators. ■

5 MACHINE CLUSTERS

When the machine in a worker–machine system does not require the continuous attention of a worker during its machine cycle (i.e., no internal work elements), an opportunity exists to assign more than one machine to the worker. We refer to this kind of work organization as a ***machine cluster***—a collection of two or more machines producing parts or products with identical cycle times and serviced by one worker (the servicing is usually loading and/or unloading parts).

Several conditions must be satisfied in order to organize a collection of machines into a machine cluster: (1) the machine cycle is long relative to the service portion of the cycle that requires the worker's attention; (2) the machine cycle time is the same for all machines; (3) the machines that the worker services are located in close enough proximity to allow time to walk between them; and (4) the work rules of the plant permit a worker to service more than one machine.

Consider a collection of single workstations, all producing the same parts and operating with the same machine cycle time. Each machine operates for a certain portion of the total cycle under its own control T_m (machine cycle), and then it requires servicing by the worker, which takes time T_s. Thus, assuming the worker is always available when servicing is needed so that the machine is never idle, the total cycle time of a machine is $T_c = T_m + T_s$. If more than one machine is assigned to the worker, a certain amount of time will be lost because of walking from one machine to the next, referred to here as the ***repositioning time***, which is represented by T_r. The time required for the operator to service one machine is therefore $T_s + T_r$, and the time to service n machines is $n(T_s + T_r)$. For the system to be perfectly balanced in terms of worker time and machine cycle time,

$$n(T_s + T_r) = T_m + T_s$$

We can determine from this the number of machines that should be assigned to one worker by solving for n:

$$n = \frac{T_m + T_s}{T_s + T_r} \tag{18}$$

where n = number of machines; T_m = machine cycle time, min; T_s = worker service time per machine, min; T_r = worker repositioning time between machines, min.

It is likely that the calculated value of n will not be an integer, which means that the worker time in the cycle—that is, $n(T_s + T_r)$—cannot be perfectly balanced with the cycle time T_c of the machines. However, the actual number of machines in the cluster must be an integer, so either the worker or the machines will experience some idle time. The number of machines will either be the integer that is greater than n from equation (18) or it will be the integer that is less than n. Let us identify these two integers as n_1 and n_2. We can determine which of the alternatives is preferable by introducing cost factors into the analysis. Let C_L = the labor cost rate and C_m = machine cost rate (certain overhead costs may be applicable to these rates). The decision will be based on the cost per work unit produced by the system.

Case 1: If we use n_1 = maximum integer $\leq n$, then the worker will have idle time and the cycle time of the machine cluster will be the cycle time of the machines $T_c = T_m + T_s$. Assuming 1 work unit is produced by each machine during a cycle, we have the following cost:

$$C_{pc}(n_1) = \left(\frac{C_L}{n_1} + C_m\right)(T_m + T_s) \tag{19}$$

where $C_{pc}(n_1)$ = cost per work unit, \$/pc; C_L = labor cost rate, \$/min; C_m = cost rate per machine, \$/min; and $(T_m + T_s)$ is expressed in min.

Case 2: If we use n_2 = minimum integer $> n$, then the machines will have idle time, and the cycle time of the machine cluster will be the time it takes for the worker to service the n_2 machines, which is $n_2(T_s + T_r)$. The corresponding cost per piece is given by

$$C_{pc}(n_2) = (C_L + C_m n_2)(T_s + T_r) \tag{20}$$

The selection of n_1 or n_2 is based on whichever case results in the lower value of cost per work unit.

In the absence of cost data needed to make these calculations, the author's view is that it is generally preferable to assign machines to a worker so that the worker has some idle time and the machines are utilized 100%. The reason for this is that the total hourly cost rate of n production machines is usually greater than the labor rate of one worker. Therefore, machine idle time costs more than worker idle time. The corresponding number of machines to assign the worker is therefore given by

$$n_1 = \text{maximum integer} \leq \frac{T_m + T_s}{T_s + T_r} \tag{21}$$

Example 15 How Many Machines for One Worker?

A machine shop contains many semiautomated lathes that operate on a machining cycle under part program control. A significant number of these machines produce the same part, whose cycle time = 2.75 min. One worker is required to perform unloading and loading of parts at the end of each machining cycle. This process takes 25 sec. Determine how many machines one worker can service if it takes an average of 20 sec to walk between the machines and no machine idle time is allowed.

Solution: Given that $T_m = 2.75$ min, $T_s = 25$ sec $= 0.4167$ min, and $T_w = 20$ sec $= 0.3333$ min, equation (21) can be used to obtain n_1:

$$n_1 = \text{maximum integer} \leq \frac{2.75 + 0.4167}{0.4167 + 0.3333} = \frac{3.1667}{0.75} = 4.22 = 4 \text{ machines}$$

Each worker can be assigned four machines. With a machine cycle $T_c = 3.1667$ min, the worker will spend 4(0.4167) = 1.667 min servicing the machines and 4(0.3333) = 1.333 min walking between machines, and the worker's idle time during the cycle will be 0.167 min (10 sec). ■

Note the regularity of the worker's schedule in this example. If we imagine the four machines to be laid out on the four corners of a square, the worker services each machine and then proceeds clockwise to the machine in the next corner. Each cycle, servicing, and walking take 3.0 min, with a slack time of 10 sec left over. If this kind of regularity characterizes the operations of a cluster of mechanized or semiautomatic machines, then the preceding analysis can be applied to determine the number of machines to assign to one worker. On the other hand, if servicing is required at random and unpredictable intervals by each machine, then it is likely that there will be periods when several machines require servicing simultaneously, thus overloading the capabilities of the human worker. In addition, at other times during the shift, the worker will have no machines to service and will therefore be idle.

REFERENCES

[1] Barnes, R. M. *Motion and Time Study: Design and Measurement of Work*. 7th ed. New York: Wiley, 1980.

[2] Groover, M. P. *Automation, Production Systems, and Computer Integrated Manufacturing*. 2nd ed. Upper Saddle River, NJ: Prentice Hall, 2001.

[3] Mundel, M. E., and D. L. Danner. *Motion and Time Study: Improving Productivity*. 7th ed., Englewood Cliffs, NJ: Prentice Hall, 1994.

REVIEW QUESTIONS

1 In terms of human participation, what are the three basic categories of work systems?

2 What is the general characteristic that is common to nearly all pure manual work?

3 What is the one best method principle?

4 What is meant by the term *normal performance*?

5 What is meant by the term *normal time* for a task?

6 What does PFD stand for? What is the purpose of the PFD allowance in determining the standard time for a task?

7 What is an irregular work element?

8 Define the meaning of worker efficiency.

9 What is a worker–machine system?

10 What are the three main categories of powered machinery in worker–machine systems?

11 Define machine tool.

12 Cycle times in worker–machine systems divide into two categories: (1) machine time depends on operator and (2) machine time is constant and repetitive. Give an example of each category.

13 What is the difference between an external work element and an internal work element in a worker–machine cycle?

14 What are the factors that affect the workload calculation when determining worker requirements?

15 What does availability mean?

16 What is a machine cluster?

PROBLEMS

Cycle Time Analysis of Manual Work

1 If the normal time is 1.30 min for a repetitive task that produces one work unit per cycle, and the company uses a PFD allowance factor of 12%, determine (a) the standard time for the task and (b) how many work units are produced in an 8-hour shift at standard performance.

2 The normal time for a repetitive task that produces two work units per cycle is 3.0 min. The plant uses a PFD allowance factor of 15%. Determine (a) the standard time per piece and (b) how many work units are produced in an 8-hour shift at standard performance.

3 The normal time to perform a certain manual work cycle is 3.47 min. In addition, an irregular work element whose normal time is 3.70 min must be performed every 10 cycles. One work unit is produced each cycle. The PFD allowance factor is 14%. Determine (a) the standard time per piece and (b) how many work units are produced during an 8-hour shift at 100% performance, and the worker works exactly 7.018 hr, which corresponds to the 14% allowance factor. (c) If the worker's pace is 120% and he works 7.2 hours during the regular shift, how many units are produced?

4 The normal time to perform a repetitive manual assembly task is 4.25 min. In addition, an irregular work element whose normal time is 1.75 min must be performed every 8 cycles. Two work units are produced each cycle. The PFD allowance factor is 16%. Determine (a) the standard time per piece and (b) how many work units are produced in an 8-hour shift at standard performance. (c) Determine the anticipated amount of time worked and the amount of time lost per 8-hour shift that corresponds to the PFD allowance factor of 16%.

5 The standard time for a manual material-handling work cycle is 2.58 min per piece. The PFD allowance factor used to set the standard was 13%. During a particular 8-hour shift of interest, it is known that the worker lost a total of 53 min due to personal time, rest breaks, and delays. On that same day, the worker completed 214 work units. Determine (a) the number of standard hours accomplished, (b) worker efficiency, and (c) the worker's performance level expressed as a percentage.

6 A worker performs a repetitive assembly task at a workbench to assemble products. Each product consists of 25 components. Various hand tools are used in the task. The standard time for the work cycle is 7.45 min, based on using a PFD allowance factor of 15%. If the worker completes 75 product units during an 8-hour shift, determine (a) the number of standard hours accomplished and (b) worker efficiency. (c) If the worker took only one rest break, lasting 13 min, and experienced no other interruptions during the 8 hours of shift time, determine her worker performance.

Cycle Time Analysis in Worker–Machine Systems

7 The normal time of the work cycle in a worker–machine system is 5.39 min. The operator-controlled portion of the cycle is 0.84 min. One work unit is produced each cycle. The machine cycle time is constant. (a) Using a PFD allowance factor of 16% and a machine allowance factor of 30%, determine the standard time for the work cycle. (b) If a worker assigned to this task completes 85 units during an 8-hour shift, what is the worker's efficiency? (c) If it is known that a total of 42 min was lost during the 8-hour clock time due to personal needs and delays, what was the worker's performance on the portion of the cycle he controlled?

8 A worker is responsible for loading and unloading a production machine. The load/unload elements in the repetitive work cycle have a normal time of only 24 sec, and the machine cycle time is 2.83 min. One part is produced each cycle. Every sixth cycle, the operator must replace the tote pans of parts, which takes 2.40 min (normal time). For setting the standard time, the PFD allowance factor is 15% and the machine allowance factor is 15%. Determine the standard time under the following alternative assumptions: (a) the irregular element is performed as an external element and (b) the irregular element is performed as an internal element. (c) Determine the corresponding standard daily production quantities (8-hour shift) for each of these time standards.

9 The work cycle in a worker–machine system consists of (1) external manual work elements with a total normal time of 0.42 min, (2) a machine cycle with a machine time of 1.12 min, and (3) internal manual elements with a total normal time of 1.04 min. (a) Determine the standard time for the cycle, using a PFD allowance factor of 15% and a machine allowance factor of 30%. (b) How many work units are produced daily (8-hour shift) at standard performance?

10 Solve the previous problem but assume that the machine allowance factor is 0%.

11 The normal time for a work cycle in a worker–machine system is 6.27 min. For setting the standard time, the PFD allowance factor is 12% and the machine allowance factor is 25%. The work cycle includes manual elements totaling a normal time of 5.92 min, all but 0.65 min of which are performed as internal elements. Determine (a) the standard time for the cycle and (b) the daily output at standard performance. (c) During an 8-hour shift, the worker lost 39 min due to personal time, rest breaks, and delays, and she produced 72 pieces. What was the worker's pace on the operator-controlled portion of the shift?

12 Solve the previous problem but assume that the machine allowance factor is 0%.

Determining Worker and Work Cell Requirements

13 A total of 1000 units of a certain product must be completed by the end of the current week. It is now late Monday afternoon, so only four days (8-hour shifts) are left. The standard time for producing each unit of the product (all manual operations) is 11.65 min. How many workers will be required to complete this production order if it is assumed that worker efficiency will be 115%?

14 Future production requirements in the turret lathe department must be satisfied through the acquisition of several new machines and the hiring of new operators, the exact number to be determined. There are three new parts that will be produced. Part A has annual quantities of 20,000 units; part B, 32,000 units; and part C, 47,000 units. Corresponding standard times for these parts are 7.3 min, 4.9 min, and 8.4 min, respectively. The department will operate one 8-hour shift for 250 days/yr. The machines are expected to be 98% reliable, and the anticipated scrap rate is 4%. Worker efficiency is expected to be 100%. How many new turret lathes and operators are required to meet these production requirements?

15 A new stamping plant must supply an automotive final assembly plant with stampings, and the number of new stamping presses must be determined. Each press will be operated by one worker. The plant will operate one 8-hour shift per day, five days per week, 50 weeks per year. The plant must produce a total of 20,000,000 stampings annually. However, 400 different stamping designs are required, in batch sizes of 5000 each, so each batch will be produced 10 times per year to minimize build-up of inventory. Each stamping takes 6 sec on average to produce. Scrap rate averages 2% in this type of production. Before each batch, the press must be set up, with a standard time per setup of 3.0 hours. Presses are 95% reliable (availability = 95%) during production and 100% reliable during setup. Worker efficiency is expected to be 100%. How many new stamping presses and operators will be required?

16 Solve the previous problem, except the plant will operate two 8-hour shifts instead of one. (a) How much money would be saved if each press has an investment and installation cost of $250,000. (b) If each worker's wage rate is $15.00/hr, how much money would be saved by operating two 8-hour shifts per day rather than one 8-hour shift?

17 Specialized processing equipment is required for a new type of integrated circuit to be produced by an electronics manufacturing company. The process is used on silicon wafers. The standard time for this process is 10.6 min per wafer. Scrap rate is 15%. A total of 125,000 wafers will be processed each year. The process will be operated 24 hours per day, 365 days per year. Data provided by the manufacturer of the processing equipment indicate that the availability is 93%. Each machine is operated by one worker, and worker efficiency is 100%. No setups are required for the machine. How many pieces of processing equipment will be needed to satisfy production requirements?

18 The standard time to produce a certain part in a worker–machine system is 9.0 min. A rush order has been received to supply 1000 units of the part within five working days (40 hours). How many worker–machine systems must be diverted from other production to satisfy this order? Each machine must be set up at the beginning of production of parts for the order, and the setup time per machine is 5.0 hours. Fraction defect rate is 5%, and worker efficiency is 100%. Availability is expected to be 98% during setup and production. How many machines and machine operators are required during the week?

19 A small company that specializes in converting pickup trucks into rear-cabin vehicles has just received a long-term contract and must expand. Heretofore, the conversion jobs were customized and performed in a garage. Now a larger building must be occupied, and the operations must be managed more like a production plant. Three models will be produced: A, B, and C. Annual quantities for the three models are as follows: A, 700; B, 400; and C, 250. Conversion times are as follows: A, 20 hr; B, 30 hr; and C, 40 hr. Defect rates are as follows: A, 11%; B, 7%; and C, 8%. Work teams of three workers each will accomplish the conversions. Each work team will require a space of 350 ft^2 in the plant. Reliability (availability) and worker efficiency of the work teams are expected to be 95% and 90%, respectively. Although the defect rates are given, no truck is permitted to leave the plant with any quality defects. Accordingly, all of the defects must be corrected, and the average time to correct the defect is 25% of the initial conversion time. The same work teams will accomplish this rework. (a) If the plant is run as a one-shift (2000 hr/yr) operation, how many work teams will be required? (b) If the total floor space in the building must include additional space for aisles and offices and the allowance that is added to the working space is 30%, what is the total area of the building?

20 It has just been learned that a Boeing 747 transporting garments made in China crashed in the Pacific Ocean during its flight to Los Angeles. Although the crew was saved, all cargo was lost, including 3000 garments that must be delivered in one week. The garment company must produce the order at its Los Angeles plant to satisfy delivery obligations. The number of workers must be determined and workspace must be allocated in the plant for this emergency job. Standard time to produce one garment is 6.50 min. The garments are then 100% inspected at a standard time of 0.75 min per unit. The scrap rate in production is 7%. However, all defective garments can be corrected through rework. Standard time for rework is 5.0 min per unit reworked. It is not necessary to reinspect the garments after rework. Worker efficiency is 120% during production and 100% during inspection and rework. The same production workers do the rework, but inspectors are a different job class. How many workers and how many inspectors are required to produce the required batch of 3000 garments in the regular 40-hour work week?

21 In the previous problem, suppose it turns out that only five workers are available to accomplish the production and rework, and because they must work overtime, worker efficiency will be reduced to 110% in production and 90% in rework. If they work 6 days/wk for one week, how many hours per day must they work to produce the 3000 garments?

Machine Clusters

22 The CNC grinding section has a large number of machines devoted to grinding of shafts for the automotive industry. The machine cycle takes 3.6 min to grind the shaft. At the end of this cycle, an operator must be present to unload and load parts, which takes 40 sec. (a) Determine how many grinding machines the worker can service if it takes 20 sec to walk between the machines and no machine idle time is allowed. (b) How many seconds during the work cycle is the worker idle? (c) What is the hourly production rate of this machine cluster?

23 The screw machine department has a large number of machines devoted to the production of a certain component that is in high demand for the personal computer industry. The semiautomatic cycle for this component is 4.2 min per piece. At the end of the machining cycle, an operator must unload the finished part and load raw stock for the next part. This servicing time takes 21 sec and the walking time between machines is estimated at 24 sec. (a) Determine how many screw machines one worker can service if no idle machine time is allowed. (b) How many seconds during the work cycle is the worker idle? (c) What is the hourly production rate of this machine cluster if one part is produced per machine each cycle?

24 A worker is currently responsible for tending two machines in a certain production cell. The service time per machine is 0.35 min and the time to walk between machines is 0.15 min. The machine automatic cycle time is 1.90 min. If the worker's hourly rate is $12/hr and the hourly rate for each machine is $18/hr, determine (a) the current hourly rate for the cell, and (b) the current cost per unit of product, given that two units are produced by each machine during each machine cycle. (c) What is the percentage of idle time for the worker? (d) What is the optimum number of machines that should be used in the cell, if minimum cost per unit of product is the decision criterion?

25 In a worker–machine cell, the appropriate number of production machines to assign to the worker is to be determined. Let n = the number of machines. Each production machine is identical and has an automatic processing time $T_m = 4.0$ min to produce one piece. Servicing time $T_s = 12$ sec for each machine. The full cycle time for each machine in the cell is $T_c = T_s + T_m$. The walk time (repositioning time) for the worker is given by $T_r = 5 + 3n$, where T_r is in seconds. T_r increases with n because the distance between machines increases with more machines. (a) Determine the maximum number of machines in the cell if no machine idle time is allowed. For your answer, compute (b) the cycle time, (c) the worker idle time expressed as a percentage of the cycle time, and (d) the production rate of the machine cluster.

26 The injection-molding department contains a large number of molding machines, all of which are automated. They can run continuously for multiple molding cycles without the attention of a human operator by allowing the molded parts to fall into tote pans beneath the machines. However, the tote pans must be periodically emptied by a worker who must attend the machine to perform this task. Each machine can run continuously for approximately 20 min between tote pan changes. A time of 2.0 min is allowed for a worker to tend a given machine. The time to walk between machines increases with the number of machines tended by a worker. In measurements by the time study department, the walking time between two machines in close proximity is about 15 sec. This walking time increases by 15 sec for each new machine added to the worker's tour. Determine (a) how many injection-molding machines one worker can service if no idle machine time is allowed, and (b) how many seconds during the work cycle the worker is idle.

Work Flow and Batch Processing

Production of a product or delivery of a service usually requires more than one unit operation. Multiple operations are typically needed. They are performed sequentially, usually by multiple workers at multiple workstations. Often, the workstations are located separately, which means that the work units must be moved from one operation to the next in the sequence. In many cases, the most practical way to accomplish the processing is to perform each unit operation on batches of work units. Thus we have the following topics to discuss in this chapter:

- *Sequential operations,* which refers to the series of separate processing steps that are performed on each work unit
- *Work flow,* which is concerned with the physical movement or transportation of work units through the sequence of unit operations (the unit operations might be thought of as interruptions in the work flow)
- *Batch processing,* which consists of the processing of work units in finite quantities or amounts, called *batches*.

The first section of the chapter discusses sequential operations and work flow, while the second section covers batch processing and the economic order quantity model. We then examine the issue of defects in sequential operations and batch processing. The final section in this chapter is concerned with work cells, a possible alternative to batch processing, and worker teams who staff the cell. This chapter is important because sequential operations, work flow, batch processing, work cells, and worker teams are so widely used in production, logistics, and service operations. Applications can also be found in office work and knowledge work.

1 SEQUENTIAL OPERATIONS AND WORK FLOW

The term ***sequential operations*** refers to a work system in which multiple processing steps are accomplished in order to complete a work unit, and the processing steps are performed sequentially (rather than simultaneously). The work units may be materials, parts, products, or people. In sequential operations, there are usually limitations on the order in which the operations can be performed, called ***precedence constraints***. Some operations must be completed before others can be started. For example, a hole must be drilled before it can be tapped to cut the threads. The internal components of a product must be assembled to the base part before the cover is attached. Passengers must be checked in and then processed through security at the airport before being allowed to board an aircraft. A surgery patient must be anesthetized before the scalpel is used. There are many examples of sequential operations in production, logistics, service operations, and knowledge work.

Sequential operations usually mean that the work units are processed at different locations. In a manufacturing plant (production work), different locations refer to the locations of the various processing machines and workstations used in the sequence. In a distribution center (logistics work), the various locations include the unloading dock, receiving stations, storage racks, and loading docks through which a product is moved inside the facility before being shipped to the retail store. In a hospital (service work), a surgery patient is first admitted and then moved to a waiting room before arriving in the operating room for the procedure. Because different locations are usually involved in sequential operations, the work units must be transported between the locations. The term ***work flow*** refers to this physical movement of work units in sequential processing. Associated with the physical flow is an information flow to monitor and control the movements of work units.

1.1 Work Flow Patterns

The work flow through a sequence of operations can follow different paths. Two basic types of work flow patterns can be distinguished: (1) pure sequential and (2) mixed sequential. In a ***pure sequential pattern***, all work units follow the same exact sequence of workstations and operations. There is no variation in the processing sequence. In a ***mixed sequential pattern***, there are variations in the work flow for different work units. The different work units are processed through different stations. The two types are depicted in Figure 1. The diagram is called a ***network diagram***, which is used here to show the flow of work units through a series of operations.

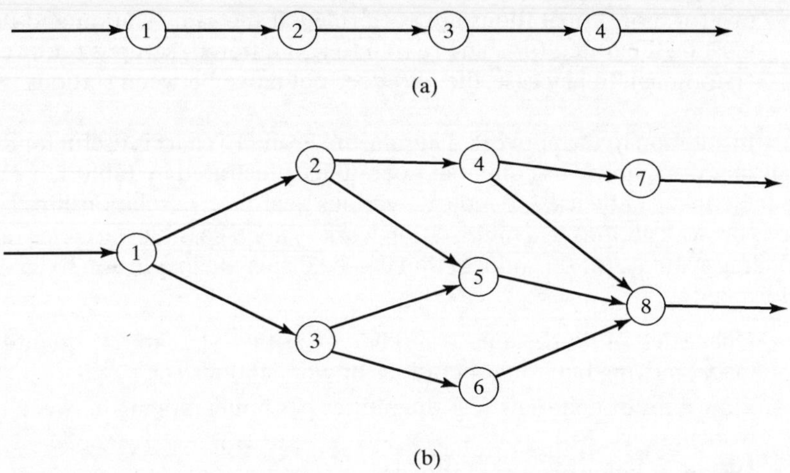

Figure 1 Network diagrams representing (a) pure sequential work flow and (b) mixed sequential work flow.

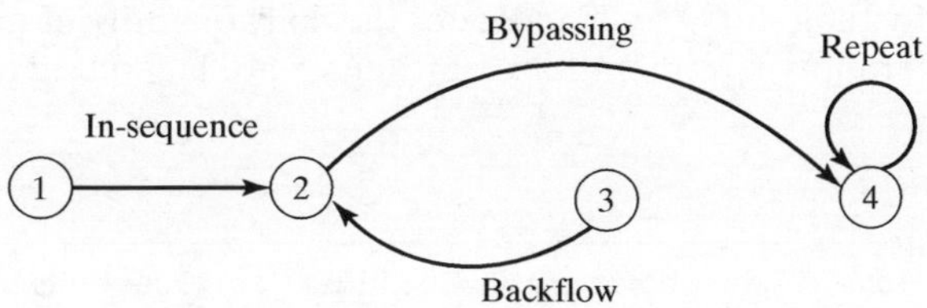

Figure 2 Four types of movements in a sequential work flow: in-sequence, bypassing, backflow, and repeat operation.

The nodes (circles) represent operations and the arrows indicate the direction of work flow.

Several types of movements experienced by different work units can be distinguished in a sequential work flow. As illustrated in Figure 2, there are four types of moves:

- *In-sequence.* A transport of the work unit from the current operation (workstation) to the neighboring operation immediately downstream. It is a move in the forward direction in the sequence.
- *Bypassing.* A move in the forward direction but beyond the neighboring workstation by two or more stations ahead of the current station.
- *Backflow.* A move of the work unit in the backward direction by one or more stations.
- *Repeat operation.* An operation that is repeated at the same workstation. This might imply that several attempts are required to complete the operation, or that

two (or more) operations are performed at the same station and the operations must be separated for some reason (e.g., a different setup is required for the two operations). In any case, the part does not move between stations.

In addition to the network diagram, the From-To chart is useful for displaying and analyzing work flows in sequential operations. Illustrated in Table 1, a ***From-To chart*** is a table that can be used to indicate various quantitative relationships between operations or workstations in a multistation work system. Possible variables (and the corresponding symbols for the values) that can be displayed in a From-To chart include the following:

- Quantities of work units (or other measures of material quantity, e.g., pallet loads) moving between operations or workstations (Q_{ij})
- Flow rates of materials (e.g., quantities per hour) moving between operations or workstations (R_{fij})
- Distances between workstations (L_{ij})
- Combinations of these values (e.g., $R_{fij}L_{ij}$)

The subscripts used in Q_{ij}, R_{fij}, and L_{ij} indicate the "from" and "to" operations involved. For example, Q_{ij} indicates quantities of work units moving from operation i to operation j. In Table 1, $Q_{12} = 40$ indicates the daily quantity of units moving from operation 1 to operation 2. If operations 1 through 5 are laid out in an in-line arrangement,

TABLE 1 From-To Chart Showing Daily Quantities Q_{ij} of Work Units Moving Between Five Workstations

		To operation j				
		1	2	3	4	5
	1	—	40		15	
	2		—	30		
From operation i	3		10	—	20	
	4				25	50
	5					—

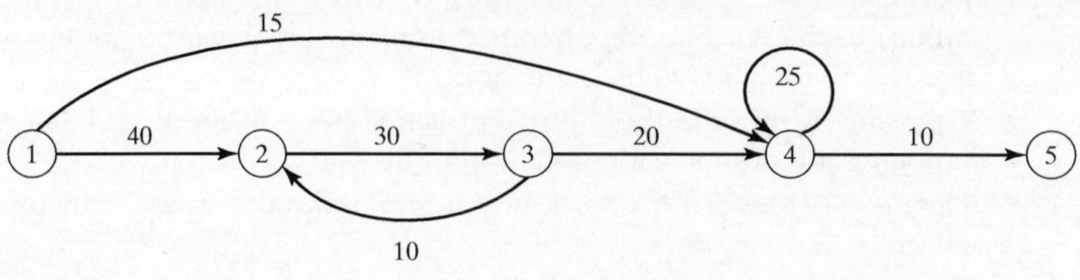

Figure 3 Network diagram of the data in the From-To chart of Table 1.

as shown in Figure 3, then we can make the following interpretations with respect to our previous definitions of the four types of moves:

- Repeat operations are represented by values along the main diagonal—that is, Q_{11}, Q_{22}, Q_{33}, Q_{44}, and Q_{55}. For example, $Q_{44} = 25$ is a repeat operation.
- In-sequence moves are indicated by values immediately above the main diagonal—that is, Q_{12}, Q_{23}, Q_{34}, and Q_{45}. For example $Q_{12} = 40$, $Q_{23} = 30$, $Q_{34} = 20$, and $Q_{45} = 50$ are all in-sequence moves.
- Bypassing moves are indicated by values located above the in-sequence moves—that is, Q_{13}, Q_{14}, Q_{15}, Q_{24}, Q_{25}, and Q_{35}. For example, $Q_{14} = 15$ is a bypassing move.
- Backflow moves are indicated by values below the main diagonal—that is, Q_{21}, Q_{31}, Q_{41}, Q_{51}, Q_{32}, Q_{42}, Q_{52}, Q_{43}, Q_{53}, and Q_{54}. For example, $Q_{32} = 10$ is a backflow move.

1.2 Bottlenecks in Sequential Operations

In a work system consisting of a sequence of processing operations, the overall production rate of the system is limited by the slowest operation in the sequence. That is,

$$R_{ps} = \text{Min}\{R_{pi}\} \text{ for } i = 1, 2, \ldots, n \tag{1}$$

where R_{ps} = overall production rate of the system, pc/hr; R_{pi} = production rate of operation i, pc/hr; and n = the number of operations in the sequence. Because the overall production rate is limited by the slowest operation, it is called the ***bottleneck*** operation.

Ultimately, the slowest process limits the output of the other operations in the sequence. It may be technologically possible to run the other operations faster, at least those that are upstream from the bottleneck, but this would only cause an accumulation of parts in front of the bottleneck. Accumulating work-in-process inventory before the bottleneck station makes no sense, except on a temporary basis. In the long run, the upstream operations must produce at a rate that is no greater than the bottleneck operation. The upstream operations are said to be blocked. ***Blocking*** means that the production rate(s) of one or more upstream operations are limited by the rate of a downstream operation.

The downstream operations can work no faster than the rate at which the bottleneck feeds work units to them. The operations downstream from the bottleneck are said to be starved for work. ***Starving*** means that the production rate(s) of one or more downstream operations are limited by the rate of an upstream operation (e.g., the bottleneck).

The reasons why one workstation is the slowest are usually due to (1) technological factors, (2) work allocation decisions, and (3) ergonomic limitations. ***Technological factors*** include limits on the speed of the equipment in the workstation—for example, the upper limit on the rotational speed of the motor that drives the machine at the workstation. Also included in this category are equipment breakdowns representing reliability problems. ***Work allocation decisions*** refer to the ways in which the total work content in the sequence is divided among the workstations. For instance, should the drilling operation included in the sequence be performed at the milling station, or should it be performed at a separate drilling station? Work allocation decisions are often influenced by technological factors. For example, the drilling operation cannot be performed at the milling station because that machine does not have a feed capability for drilling.

Ergonomic limitations are the physical (and mental) restrictions of the human worker at the workstation. How much time should the worker be allowed to manually load and unload a work unit into the machine? We cannot expect the worker to accomplish loading and unloading at a pace so fast that it leads to physiological injury.

2 BATCH PROCESSING

Work units are often processed in batches. ***Batch processing*** consists of the processing of work units—materials, products, information, or people, depending on the nature of the processes—in finite quantities or amounts. Batch processing is common in many production, logistics, and service operations. In low and medium quantity production, it is common to process parts in batches. Passengers who travel by airplane are transported in batches. Freight is moved in batch loads by truck or railway train. Teachers grade reports and exams one at a time in batches. Personal laundry is washed as a batch in a washing machine.

Batch processing is accomplished in either of two ways: (1) ***sequential batch processing***, in which the members of the batch are processed one after the other; and (2) ***simultaneous batch processing***, in which the members of the batch are processed all at the same time. Both types of processing are represented in our preceding list of examples. Table 2 presents more examples illustrating the two categories.

2.1 The Pros and Cons of Batch Processing

Batch processing is discontinuous because there are interruptions between the batches. The interruptions represent times when the equipment is not being productive, which adversely affects productivity. In production, the machine tool must be changed over for the next part style. In air travel, the airplane must remain at the terminal to discharge passengers, be cleaned and refueled, and load passengers for the next flight. In book publishing, the plates on the printing presses must be changed for the next book.

When viewed as an operation sequence, delays occur between processing steps because multiple batches are competing for the same equipment. Queues of batches

TABLE 2 Examples of Sequential and Simultaneous Batch Processing

Sequential Batch Processing	Simultaneous Batch Processing
Production machining operations. Other examples include sheet metal stamping, injection molding, casting, welding, and powder-metal pressing.	Production electroplating operations. Other examples include many chemical batch processes and powder-metal sintering.
Batch assembly	Passenger air travel
Book publishing	Cargo transportation
Payroll checks	Entertainment in movie theaters
Grading of student papers	Laundry

form in front of workstations, resulting in long lead-times to complete the work units and the accumulation of large quantities or amounts of work units in the sequential processing system. In production this accumulation of inventory is called ***work-in-process*** (WIP). Neither long lead-times nor high work-in-process are desirable. Yet these are typical characteristics of batch processing.

Despite the disadvantages cited above, batch production is nevertheless widely used for the following reasons:

- *Work unit differences.* There are differences in work units between batches, and it is necessary to make changes in the methods, tooling, and equipment to accommodate the differences.
- *Equipment limitations.* The size capacity of the equipment restricts the amount of material or quantity of work units that can be processed at one time (e.g., the equipment capacity imposes an upper limit on the batch size).
- *Material limitations.* The material in the operation must be processed as a unit, and that unit will be later divided into multiple work units (e.g., the processing of silicon wafers into individual integrated circuit chips).

Batch processing is widely used in production operations. It is probably the most common form of production. In ***batch production***, a batch of one type of part (or product) is completed, and then the work system is changed over to produce a batch of a different type of part, and then another, and so on. The changeover takes time, because the physical setup for the second product is different from the first. Tooling has to be changed, equipment settings must be adjusted, and workers need to familiarize themselves with the new part or product. This setup time is lost production time, which is a disadvantage of batch production. Thus, a work system used for batch production experiences a sequence of setups followed by production runs, as illustrated in Figure 4.

While the work system is producing, its production rate is greater than the demand rate for the current product type. This has two effects. First, it means that the same work system can be shared among multiple products, which has economic benefits in terms of equipment investment. Second, it means that the units in a batch of items must be held in inventory for extended periods of time, while demand gradually reduces the stock level down to the point at which another production run will be made. This is the typical ***make-to-stock*** situation, in which items are manufactured to replenish inventory

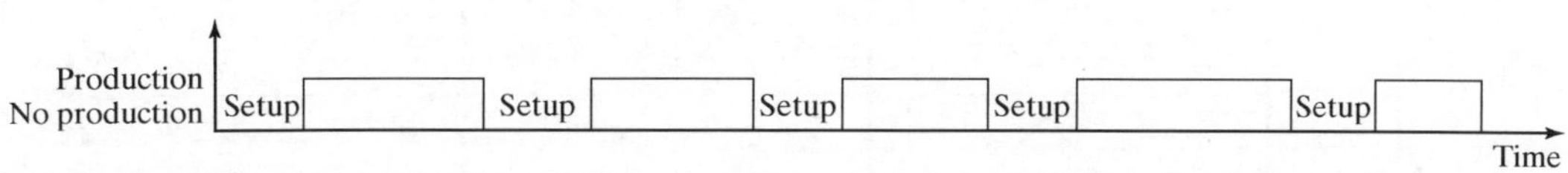

Figure 4 The alternating cycles of setup and production run experienced by a work system engaged in batch production.

that has been gradually depleted by demand. An important question arises in make-to-stock situations and in batch production: How many units should be produced in a given batch? The answer involves achieving a balance between inventory costs and setup costs. Holding items in inventory is an expense in the form of storage costs and investment interest. And each time the work system must be changed over, the resulting downtime is also an expense. From the viewpoint of items that are produced in batches and carried in inventory, the sudden increase and gradual depletion causes the inventory level over time to have the sawtooth appearance shown in Figure 5.

2.2 Economic Order Quantity Model

A total cost equation can be derived for the sum of carrying cost and setup cost for the inventory model in Figure 5. The figure assumes that demand rate is constant, so that inventory is gradually depleted over time and then quickly replenished to some maximum level determined by the order quantity. Because of the triangular shape of inventory cycle, the average inventory level is one-half the maximum level Q in our figure, and this average is multiplied by the inventory carrying cost per item. The annual setup cost is determined as the number of setups per year multiplied by the cost per setup. The total annual inventory cost is therefore given by

$$TIC = \frac{C_h Q}{2} + \frac{C_{su} D_a}{Q} \tag{2}$$

where TIC = total annual inventory cost (holding cost plus ordering cost), \$/yr; Q = order quantity, pc/order; C_h = inventory carrying or holding cost, \$/pc/yr; C_{su} = setup cost and/or ordering cost for an order, \$/setup or \$/order; and D_a = annual demand for the item, pc/yr. In the second term on the right-hand side of the equation, the ratio D_a/Q is

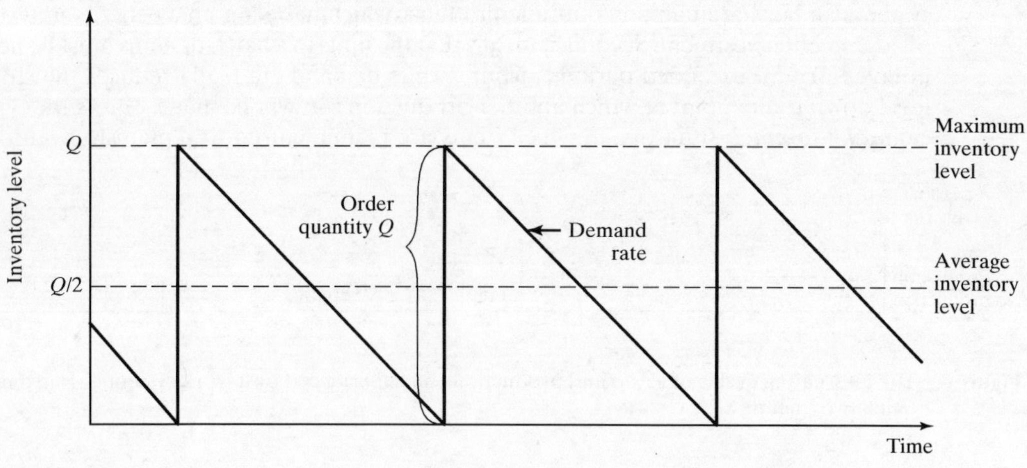

Figure 5 Model of inventory level over time in the typical make-to-stock situation.

the number of orders or batches produced per year; it therefore gives the number of setups per year.

The holding cost C_h consists of two main components, investment cost and storage cost. Both are related to the time that the inventory spends in the warehouse or factory. The investment cost results from the money the company must invest in inventory before it is sold to customers. This inventory investment cost can be calculated as the interest rate paid by the company, i (expressed as a fraction), multiplied by the value of the inventory.

Storage cost occurs because the inventory takes up space that must be paid for. The amount of the cost is generally related to the size of the part and how much space it occupies. As an approximation, it can be related to the value or cost of the item stored. For our purposes, this is the most convenient method of valuating the storage cost of an item. By this method, the storage cost equals the cost of the inventory multiplied by the storage rate, s. The term s is the storage cost as a fraction of the value of the item in inventory.

Combining interest rate and storage rate into one factor, we have $h = i + s$, where h is the holding cost rate. Like i and s, it is a fraction that is multiplied by the cost of the item to evaluate the cost of holding the items in inventory. Accordingly, holding cost can be expressed as

$$C_h = h\, C_{pc} \tag{3}$$

where C_h = holding (carrying) cost, \$/pc/yr; C_{pc} = unit cost of the item, \$/pc; and h = holding cost rate, rate/yr.

Setup cost includes the cost of idle production equipment during the changeover time between batches. The costs of labor performing the setup changes might also be added in. Thus,

$$C_{su} = T_{su} C_{dt} \tag{4}$$

where C_{su} = setup cost, \$/setup or \$/order; T_{su} = setup or changeover time between batches, hr/setup or hr/order; and C_{dt} = cost rate of machine downtime during the changeover, \$/hr. In cases where parts are ordered from an outside vendor, the price quoted by the vendor usually includes a setup cost, either directly or in the form of quantity discounts. C_{su} should also include the internal costs of placing the order to the vendor.

Equation (2) excludes the actual annual cost of part production. If this cost is included, then annual total cost is given by the following equation:

$$TC = D_a C_{pc} + \frac{C_h Q}{2} + \frac{C_{su} D_a}{Q} \tag{5}$$

where $D_a C_{pc}$ = annual demand (pc/yr) multiplied by cost per item (\$/pc).

If the derivative is taken with respect to Q in either equation (2) or (5), the economic order quantity (EOQ) formula is obtained by setting the derivative equal to zero and solving for Q. This batch size minimizes the sum of carrying costs and setup costs:

$$Q = EOQ = \sqrt{\frac{2D_a C_{su}}{C_h}} \tag{6}$$

where EOQ = economic order quantity (number of parts to be produced per batch), pc/batch or pc/order; and the other terms have been defined previously.

Example 1 Economic Order Quantity Formula

The annual demand for a certain item made-to-stock is 15,000 pc/yr. One unit of the item costs \$20.00 and the holding cost rate is 18%/yr. Setup time to produce a batch is 5 hr. The cost of equipment downtime plus labor is \$150/hr. Determine the economic order quantity (EOQ) and the total inventory cost for this case.

Solution: Setup cost $C_{su} = 5 \times \$150 = \$750$. Holding cost per unit $= 0.18 \times \$20.00 = \$3.60$. Using these values and the annual demand rate in the EOQ formula, we have

$$EOQ = \sqrt{\frac{2(15000)(750)}{3.60}} = 2500 \text{ units}$$

Total inventory cost is given by the TIC equation:

$$TIC = 0.5(3.60)(2500) + 750(15{,}000/2500) = \$9000$$

Including the actual production costs in the annual total and using equation (5), we have:

$$TC = 15{,}000(20) + 9000 = \$309{,}000$$

■

The EOQ formula has been widely used for determining so-called optimum batch sizes in production. More sophisticated forms of equations (2) and (5) have appeared in the literature—for example, models that take production rate into account to yield alternative EOQ equations [7]. Equation (6) is the most general form and is quite adequate for most real-life situations. The difficulty in applying the EOQ formula is in obtaining accurate values of the parameters in the equation—namely, (1) setup cost and (2) inventory carrying costs. These cost factors are usually difficult to evaluate; yet they have an important impact on the calculated economic batch size.

There is no disputing the mathematical accuracy of the EOQ equation. Given specific values of annual demand (D_a), setup cost (C_{su}), and carrying cost (C_h), equation (6) computes the lowest cost batch size to whatever level of precision the user desires. The trouble is that the user may be lulled into a false sense of security by the knowledge that no matter how much it costs to change the setup, the EOQ formula always calculates the optimum batch size for that setup cost. For many years in U.S. industry, this belief tended to encourage long production runs by manufacturing managers. The thought process went something like this: "If the setup cost increases, we just increase the batch size, because the EOQ formula always tells us the optimum production quantity."

Users of the EOQ equation must not lose sight of the total inventory cost equation, equation (2), from which EOQ is derived. Examining the TIC equation, a cost conscious production manager would quickly conclude that total inventory cost can be reduced by decreasing the values of holding cost (C_h) and setup cost (C_{su}). The production manager may not be able to exert much influence on holding cost, because it is determined largely by prevailing interest rates. However, methods can be developed to reduce setup cost by reducing the time required to accomplish the changeover of a production machine. Reducing setup times is an important focus in lean production.

3 DEFECTS IN SEQUENTIAL OPERATIONS AND BATCH PROCESSING

In a sequence of operations, defective units may be produced in any or all of the operations. The defect rate must be considered in determining the quantity of good units produced. This is the issue we consider in this section. Figure 6 depicts a unit operation in which incoming work units are processed to yield good products and defects. The starting quantity or batch size of raw material to be processed is Q_o, the fraction defect rate produced by the operation is q, yielding good units of quantity Q and defects numbering D. The relationships among the variables in a unit operation are defined as follows:

$$Q = Q_o(1-q) \tag{7}$$

and

$$D = Q_o q \tag{8}$$

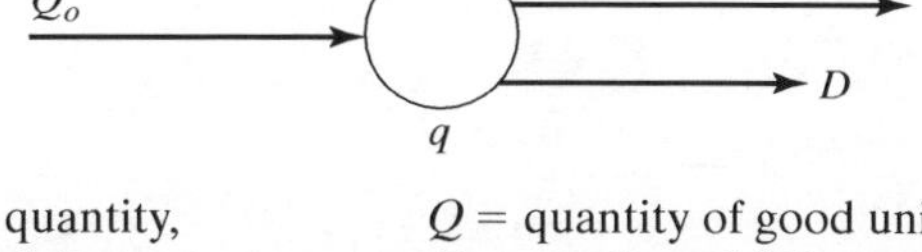

Q_o = starting quantity, Q = quantity of good units produced, and
q = fraction defect rate, D = number of defects produced.

Figure 6 The unit operation in which incoming work units are processed to yield good products and defects.

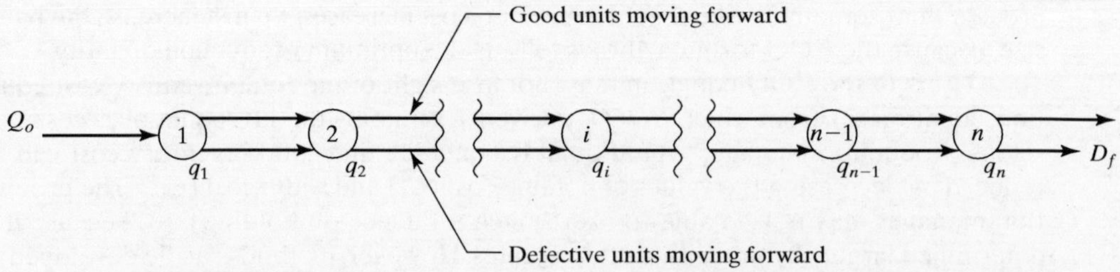

Q_o = starting quantity, Q_f = quantity of good units produced, and
q_i = fraction defect rate in operation i, D_f = number of defects produced.

Figure 7 A sequence of unit operations where each operation has a certain fraction defect rate.

A sequence of unit operations is portrayed in Figure 7. Each operation or workstation has a certain fraction defect rate q_i, so the final quantity of defect-free units exiting the sequence is given by

$$Q_f = Q_o(1 - q_1)(1 - q_2)\ldots(1 - q_i)\ldots(1 - q_n) \tag{9}$$

where Q_f = final quantity of good units produced by the sequence of n operations and Q_o = the starting quantity. The ratio of good units produced to starting units in a sequence of operations is called the ***yield***.

$$Y = \frac{Q_f}{Q_o} = (1 - q_1)(1 - q_2)\ldots(1 - q_i)\ldots(1 - q_n) \tag{10}$$

where Y = yield, usually expressed as a percentage. The yield metric can be applied to a sequence of operations or to an individual process in the sequence. The number of defects in the final batch is given by

$$D_f = Q_o\{1 - (1 - q_1)(1 - q_2)\ldots(1 - q_i)\ldots(1 - q_n)\} \tag{11}$$

where D_f = number of defects in the final batch. If all q_i are equal, then the two equations reduce to

$$Q_f = Q_o(1 - q)^n \tag{12}$$

and

$$D_f = Q_o\{1 - (1 - q)^n\} \tag{13}$$

where q = fraction defect rate of each operation in the sequence.

Example 2 The Compounding Effect of Defect Rate in Sequential Operations

A starting batch of 1000 work units is processed through 10 operations, each of which has a fraction defect rate of 5%. Determine (a) how many good parts and defects are produced by the first operation, (b) how many good parts and defects are in the final batch, and (c) the yield of the first operation and the yield of the operation sequence.

Solution **(a)** For the first operation,

$$Q = 1000(1 - 0.05) = 950 \text{ good units}$$

and

$$D = 1000(0.05) = 50 \text{ defects}$$

(b) For the 10 sequential operations,

$$Q_f = 1000(1 - 0.05)^{10} = 1000(0.95)^{10} = 1000(0.5987) = 599 \text{ good units}$$

and

$$D_f = 1000(1 - 0.5987) = 1000(0.4013) = 401 \text{ defects}$$

(c) The yield of the first process is $Y_1 = 950/1000 = 95\%$. The yield of the process sequence is $Y = 0.5987 = 59.87\%$. ■

The binomial expansion can be used to determine the allocation of defects associated with each operation or workstation i. Given that q_i equals probability of a defect being produced in operation i, let p_i equal the probability of a good unit being produced in the sequence; thus $p_i + q_i = 1$. Expanding this for n operations, we have

$$\prod_{i=1}^{n} (p_i + q_i) = 1 \tag{14}$$

To illustrate, consider the case of two operations in sequence ($n = 2$). The binomial expansion yields the expression

$$(p_1 + q_1)(p_2 + q_2) = p_1p_2 + p_1q_2 + p_2q_1 + q_1q_2$$

where p_1p_2 = proportion of defect-free parts; p_1q_2 = proportion of parts that have no defects from operation 1 but a defect from operation 2; p_2q_1 = proportion of parts that have no defects from operation 2 but a defect from operation 1; and q_1q_2 = proportion of parts that have both types of defect.

As the number of operations in the sequence increases, the number of terms in the binomial expansion increases exponentially in proportion to 2^n, where n equals the number of operations. Thus for 10 operations in sequence, the number of terms is 1024, all but one representing various combinations of processing defects. The one term representing the proportion of good units is the yield, given by equation (10).

4 WORK CELLS AND WORKER TEAMS

A ***work cell*** is a group of workstations dedicated to the processing of a range of work units within a given type. The processing is typically performed as a sequence of operations. In production, where work cells are often employed, the work units are parts, and the range of parts is called a ***part family***. The members of the part family possess similarities that permit them to be processed by the work cell. The processing of part families is associated with an approach to manufacturing called ***group technology***, in which similar parts are identified and grouped together to take advantage of their similarities in design and production.

Work cells can often be used to mitigate some of the disadvantages of batch processing. Instead of processing each of the various part types in batches, the work units are processed individually and continuously, without the need for time-consuming changeovers between part types. This is made possible by (1) the similarity of parts within a part family and (2) the adaptability and flexibility of the workers and equipment in the cell that can accommodate the moderate differences among part family members. In a work cell, the operations are integrated to facilitate the flow of work from one workstation to the next, so that lead time and work-in-process are minimized.

4.1 Work Cell Layouts and Material Handling

Because the range of parts or products in a work cell is limited, the processing (or assembly) of work units consists of operations that are similar but not identical. Thus, although the layout of the cell is fixed, the operations and their sequence are not. We are dealing with a mixed sequential work flow system (Section 1.1). The workstations in the cell are usually arranged to facilitate the flow of work from one operation to the next. In some cases, the stations are connected by a mechanized material-handling system. In other cases the work is carried from station to station by hand.

Work cells can be distinguished according to the following factors: (1) number of workstations in the cell, (2) material-handling method, and (3) layout of the cell. They can also be distinguished by the way in which the workers are organized into worker teams. We discuss worker teams in Section 4.3.

The number of workstations in a cell can range from two to about a dozen. There are no hard limits on the upper end of the range. However, one of the advantages of a work cell is that it promotes teamwork and a sense of mission among its workers, and this advantage tends to be diminished if the cell becomes too large. If the number of workstations is very large (e.g., several dozen to several hundred), then the work is more likely to be organized as a manual assembly line.

The material-handling method in a work cell can be manual or mechanized. Manual material handling consists of the workers in a cell moving the work units between stations. This is appropriate when one worker performs all of the operations to complete a given work unit, so it is logical for the worker to carry the units through the sequence of stations, stopping at those stations where processing is required. Manual handling can also be used when workers are assigned to specific workstations. Either the station operators themselves are responsible for moving the work units forward, or designated material-handling workers are assigned to move the units between stations. Manual work cells are often organized into a U-shaped layout, as shown in Figure 8. This arrangement has been found to promote teamwork among the workers. It also allows for variations in operation sequence among different part or product styles.

Mechanized handling is usually achieved by means of a powered conveyor, such as a belt conveyor. A variety of layouts are possible in work cells with mechanized handling, including in-line, U-shaped, loop, and rectangular, as shown in Figure 9. In an in-line layout, the workstations are arranged in a straight line, as in Figure 9 (a). This layout type is appropriate when all work units are processed in the same basic operation

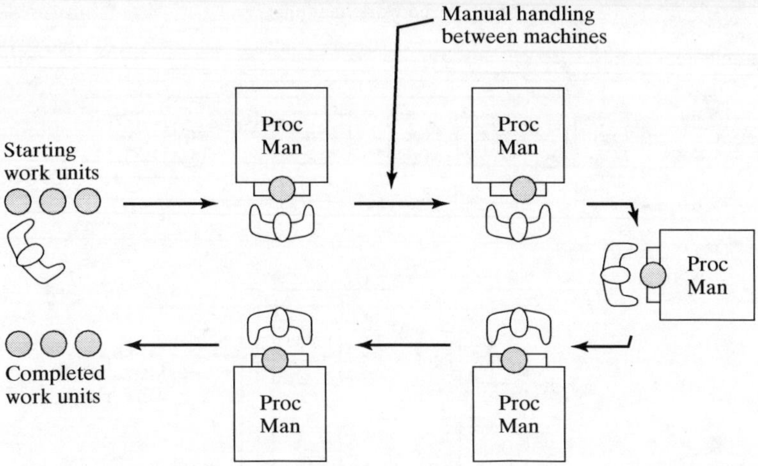

Proc = processing operation (e.g., mill, drill), Man = manual operator, arrows indicate predominant work flow.

Figure 8 U-shaped work cell with manual handling between stations.

sequence. It does not facilitate variations in work sequence as readily as other layout configurations. The U-shaped layout, Figure 9 (b), is an adaptation of the in-line type that allows some flexibility in processing sequence. If the work units move through the system attached to work carriers, then some means of returning the carriers to the beginning of the sequence is required. Loop and rectangular layouts accommodate this return requirement, as seen in Figure 9 (c) and (d).

4.2 Determining the Operation Sequence in a Work Cell

Techniques are available for determining the most appropriate sequence of workstations in a work cell. Let us introduce a simple yet effective method described in Hollier [4] that uses data contained in From-To charts and is intended to arrange the stations in an order that maximizes the proportion of forward moves (in-sequence and bypassing moves) within the cell. The Hollier algorithm can be outlined as follows:

1. *Develop the From-To chart from part routing data.* The data contained in the From-To chart indicates numbers of part moves between the workstations (or machines) in the cell. Moves into and out of the cell are not included in the chart.
2. *Determine the From-To ratio for each workstation.* This is accomplished by summing up all of the "From" and "To" trips for each workstation. The From sum for a station is determined by adding the entries in the corresponding row, and the To sum is determined by adding the entries in the corresponding column. For each station, the From-To ratio is calculated by taking the From sum for each station and dividing by the respective To sum.
3. *Arrange workstations in order of decreasing From-To ratio.* Stations with high From-To ratios distribute work to other stations in the cell but receive work from few of them. Conversely, stations with low From-To ratios receive more work than

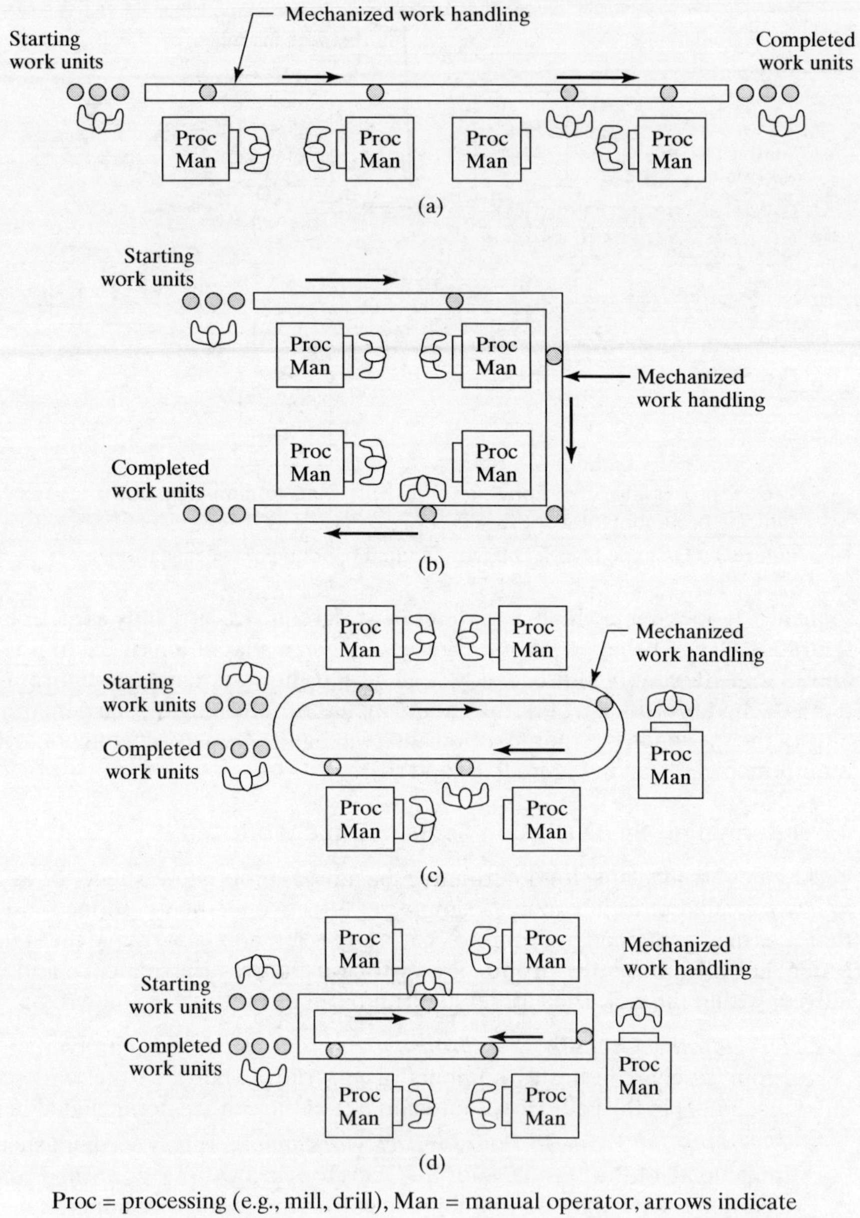

Proc = processing (e.g., mill, drill), Man = manual operator, arrows indicate predominant work flow.

Figure 9 Alternative layouts in work cells with mechanized material handling: (a) in-line, (b) U-shaped, (c) loop, and (d) rectangular.

TABLE 3 From-To Chart for Example 3

To:	1	2	3	4
From: 1	0	5	0	25
2	30	0	0	15
3	10	40	0	0
4	10	0	0	0

TABLE 4 From-To Sums and Ratios for Example 3

To:	1	2	3	4	**From Sums**	**From-To Ratios**
From: 1	0	5	0	25	**30**	**0.60**
2	30	0	0	15	**45**	**1.0**
3	10	40	0	0	**50**	**∞**
4	10	0	0	0	**10**	**0.25**
To Sums	**50**	**45**	**0**	**40**	**135**	

they distribute. Therefore, stations are arranged in order of descending From-To ratio; that is, stations with high ratios are placed at the beginning of the work flow, and stations with low ratios are placed at the end of the work flow. In case of a tie, the workstation with the higher From value is placed ahead of the station with a lower value.

Example 3 Work Cell Station Sequence

Four workstations, 1, 2, 3, and 4, have been assigned to a work cell. An analysis of 50 parts processed in these stations has been summarized in the From-To chart of Table 3. Additional information is that 50 parts enter the cell at station 3, 20 parts leave after processing at station 1, and 30 parts leave after station 4. Determine a logical workstation arrangement using the Hollier algorithm.

Solution: Table 3 is repeated in Table 4 along with the From-To sums. The From-To ratios are given in the last column on the right. Arranging the stations in order of descending From-To ratio, the cell is sequenced as follows:

$$3 \rightarrow 2 \rightarrow 1 \rightarrow 4$$

■

It is helpful to use a network diagram (Figure 10) to conceptualize the work flow in the cell. The work flow consists of mostly in-sequence moves; however, there is some bypassing and backflow of parts that must be considered in the design of any material-handling system that might be used in the cell. A powered conveyor would be appropriate for the forward flow between machines, with manual handling for the back flow.

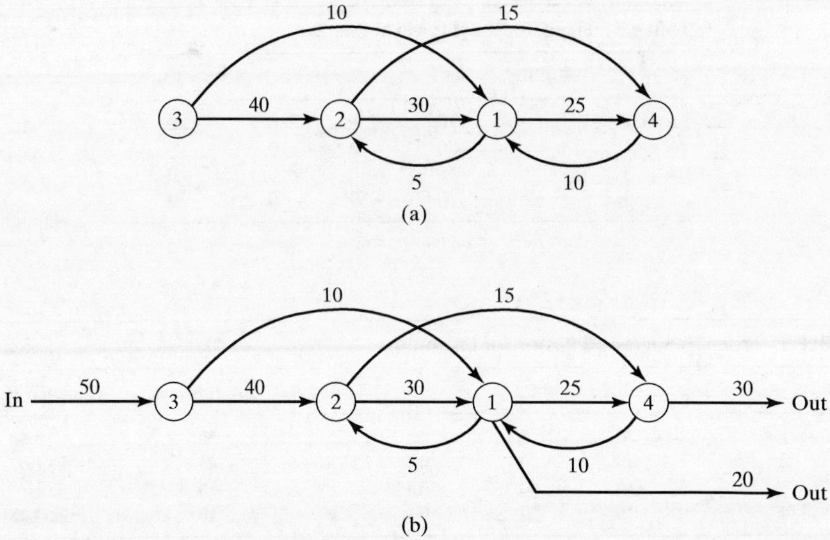

Figure 10 Network diagram for the work cell station sequence in Example 3: (a) internal work flow given in Table 3 and (b) work flow including work units into and out of the cell.

Several performance measures can be used to compare alternative solutions to the machine sequencing problem. The measures are based on the types of moves defined in Section 1:

1. *Percentage of in-sequence moves*, computed by adding all of the values representing in-sequence moves and dividing by the total number of moves.
2. *Percentage of bypassing moves*, found by adding all of the values representing bypassing moves and dividing by the total number of moves.
3. *Percentage of backflow moves*, determined by summing all of the values representing backflow moves and dividing by the total number of moves.
4. *Percentage of repeated operations*, which is the sum of all repeated operations divided by the total number of moves.

It is desirable for the layout arrangement to have high proportions of in-sequence and bypassing moves since these both represent forward work flow (in-sequence moves are more desirable than bypassing moves). The layout should minimize the percentage of backflow moves. The percentage of repeated operations will have the same value for all solutions.

Example 4 Performance Measures for Example 3

Compute (a) the percentage of in-sequence moves, (b) the percentage of bypassing moves, and (c) the percentage of backflow moves for the solution in Example 3.

Solution: From Figure 10, the total number of moves is 135 (totaling either the From sums or the To sums).

(a) The number of in-sequence moves = 40 + 30 + 25 = 95; percentage of in-sequence moves = 95/135 = 0.704 = 70.4%.

(b) The number of bypassing moves = 10 + 15 = 25; percentage of bypassing moves = 25/135 = 0.185 = 18.5%.

(c) The number of backflow moves = 5 + 10 = 15; percentage of backflow moves = 15/135 = 0.111 = 11.1%.

There are no repeated operations, so all of the part moves between workstations are accounted for by the three measures in (a), (b), and (c). ■

4.3 Worker Teams

Worker teams are closely associated with the operation of work cells. A ***worker team*** is a group of employees who work together to achieve common objectives. In the case of a work cell, the common objectives of the team are to (1) meet the production or service schedule, (2) achieve high quality in the goods or services provided by the cell, and (3) make the operation of the cell as efficient as possible. These objectives are achieved by means of ***teamwork***, in which the collective skills and efforts of the team members exceed the sum of their individual skills and efforts. Teamwork provides a synergistic effect that would not be realized by each member working independently.

Production Work Teams. Our primary interest is in production work teams, which are generally limited in size to between five and 15 workers, and the team has a defined level of authority for operating the work cell (or other organizational unit) for which it is responsible. Production work teams represent an attempt to instill a sense of teamwork in a production department, office, or other work unit. Accordingly, the membership of the team consists of the regular workers in the unit. The purpose of organizing them as a team is to improve the morale and efficiency of the work unit. Work teams can be organized and operated in various ways, the differences being in the level of autonomy given to them. At one end of the spectrum are ***work-unit teams*** that have little autonomy and are basically a unit in the traditional hierarchical structure of the organization. They operate with a foreman or manager who supervises the team members. At the other extreme are ***self-managed work teams*** that enjoy significant autonomy. They not only perform the work of the unit, they also plan and manage it. Self-managed work teams manifest a high level of worker involvement and empowerment. Team leaders are elected by the membership, and the position is often rotated among the members.

An evolutionary process often occurs between the two forms, with work-unit teams gradually transforming themselves into self-managed teams over the course of several years under the guidance and encouragement of management. The final form of the self-managed work team is one in which the regular management and administrative duties in a traditional organization are assumed by the team leadership, at least within their own working units. The function of company management evolves from commanding the work units under the former hierarchical structure to coordinating their activities in the new worker team organization.

One of the important keys to success for production work teams is ***cross-training***, in which workers become trained in more than one job in the work cell. Although each individual brings unique knowledge, skills, and abilities to the team's activities, having more than one team member know each job mitigates problems of absences and allows for job rotations to increase work variety and employee satisfaction. Workers are often rewarded in proportion to their versatility in acquiring multiple task skills.

Other Types of Worker Teams. There are several other types of worker teams, each suited to different objectives that the sponsoring organization is attempting to achieve. These objectives may be temporary and short term (e.g., solving a problem or completing a project) or continuous and long term (e.g., production work teams). Here we discuss three principal categories, classified according to function and/or objective: (1) project teams, (2) cross-functional teams, and (3) improvement teams.

Project teams are organized for the purpose of expeditiously completing a given project. They are commonly associated with construction projects (e.g., buildings, bridges, roads), but other project areas include new product design, research, and software development. Like production work teams, the team membership consists of the workers responsible for doing the work. However, whereas production is continuous and ongoing, projects are completed one at a time and have a predictable life cycle.

Cross-functional teams are distinguished by the fact that their members are drawn from different functional departments in the organization. Upper management is responsible for identifying the problem area to be addressed and selecting the appropriate team members who are qualified to solve it. The purpose of organizing a cross-functional team is to bring a diversity of knowledge and backgrounds together and to overcome functional boundaries. Examples of cross-functional teams include (1) ***concurrent engineering teams***, which are involved in the development and design of a new product; (2) ***task forces***, which are constituted to deal with an urgent problem or immediate commercial opportunity confronting the organization; and (3) ***crisis management teams***, which are a form of task force intended to cope with a particular crisis or disaster faced by the organization, such as the loss of key personnel (e.g., the unexpected death of the chief executive officer), floods and hurricanes, terrorist attacks, and liability lawsuits.

Improvement teams are organized to improve the operations of a department or process. The focus of the improvement may be on product quality, productivity and process efficiency, job design and ergonomics, safety, or some other aspect of the department. Improvement teams are usually temporary; they are instituted to address a particular problem area (e.g., product quality), and once that problem is solved, the team is disbanded.

REFERENCES

[1] Besterfield, D. H., C. Besterfield-Michna, G. H. Besterfield, and M. Besterfield-Sacre. *Total Quality Management*. 3rd ed. Upper Saddle River, NJ: Prentice Hall, 2003.

[2] Goetsch, D. L., and S. B. Davis. *Quality Management: Introduction to Total Quality Management for Production, Processing, and Services*. 4th ed. Upper Saddle River, NJ: Prentice Hall, 2003.

[3] Groover, M. P. *Automation, Production Systems, and Computer Integrated Manufacturing.* 2nd ed. Upper Saddle River, NJ: Prentice Hall, 2001.

[4] Hollier, R. H. "The Layout of Multi-Product Lines." *International Journal of Production Research* 2 (1963): 47–57.

[5] McGinnis, L. "A Brave New Education." *IIE Solutions* (December 2002): 27–32.

[6] Medsker, G. J., and M. A. Campion. "Job and Team Design." Chapter 33 in *Handbook of Industrial Engineering.* 3rd ed., edited by G. Salvendy. New York: Wiley and Institute of Industrial Engineers, Norcross, GA, 2001, pp. 868–98.

[7] Sipper, D., and R. L. Buffin. *Production: Planning, Control, and Integration.* New York: McGraw-Hill, 1997.

REVIEW QUESTIONS

1 What does sequential operations mean?

2 What is a precedence constraint in sequential operations?

3 What is the difference between pure sequential work flow and mixed sequential work flow?

4 Name and define the four types of part moves between workstations in sequential operations.

5 What is a From-To chart?

6 What is a bottleneck in sequential operations?

7 What do the terms *starving* and *blocking* mean in terms of sequential operations?

8 What does the term *batch processing* mean?

9 What are some of the disadvantages of batch processing?

10 Given the disadvantages of batch production, what are the reasons why it is so widely used in industry?

11 What are the two cost terms in the economic order quantity model?

12 Write the equation that describes the relationship between the starting quantity of work units Q_o, the completed quantity Q, and the fraction defect rate q of the operation processing the work units.

13 What is a work cell?

14 What is a worker team?

15 Define teamwork.

16 What is the difference between a work-unit team and a self-managed work team?

17 What is cross-training and what is its value in a worker team?

18 Name some examples of cross-functional teams.

PROBLEMS

Workflow Structures

1 Four parts (A, B, C, and D) are processed through a sequence of four operations (1, 2, 3, and 4). Not all parts are processed in all operations. Part A, which has weekly quantities of 70 units, is processed through operations 1, 2, and 3 in that order. Part B, which has weekly quantities of 90 units, is processed through operations 2, 4, and 1 in that order. Part C, which has weekly quantities of 65 units, is processed through operations 3, 2, and 4 in that order. Finally, part D, which has weekly quantities of 100 units, is processed through operations

2, 1, and 4 in that order. (a) Draw the network diagram and (b) prepare the From-To table for this work system.

2 Five parts (A, B, C, D, and E) are processed through a sequence of five operations (1, 2, 3, 4, and 5). Not all parts are processed in all operations. Part A, which has daily quantities of 50 units, is processed through operations 1, 3, 5, and 1 in that order. Part B, which has daily quantities of 70 units, is processed through operations 2, 4, and 5 in that order. Part C, which has daily quantities of 25 units, is processed through operations 3, 2, and 4 in that order. Part D, which has daily quantities of 10 units, is processed through operations 1, 2, 4, and 5 in that order. Finally, part E, which has daily quantities of 15 units, is processed through operations 3, 1, and 2 in that order. (a) Draw the network diagram and (b) prepare the From-To table for this work system.

Bottleneck Operations

3 A factory produces cardboard boxes. The production sequence consists of three operations: (1) cutting, (2) indenting, and (3) printing. There are three automated machines in the factory, one for each operation. The machines are 100% reliable and the scrap rate in each operation is zero. In the cutting operation, large rolls of cardboard are fed into the cutting machine, which cuts the cardboard into blanks. Each large roll contains enough material for 4000 blanks. Production time is 0.03 min/blank during a production run, but it takes 25 min to change rolls and cutting dies between runs. In the indenting operation, indentation lines are pressed into printed blanks that allow the blanks to later be bent into boxes. Indenting is performed at an average time of 2.5 sec/blank. Batches from the previous cutting operation are subdivided into two smaller batches with different indenting lines, so that starting batch size in indenting is 2000 blanks. The time needed to change dies between batches on the indenting machine is 30 min. In printing, the blanks are printed with labels for a particular customer. Starting batch size in printing is 2000 blanks (these are the same batches as in indenting). The production rate is 30 blanks/min. Between batches, changeover of the printing plates is required, which takes 40 min. What is the maximum possible output of this factory during a 40-hour week, in printed and indented blanks/week. Assumptions: (1) steady state operation and (2) there is work-in-process between operations 1 and 2 and between 2 and 3, so that blocking and starving of operations is negligible.

4 Solve the previous problem but assume that the reliability of the cutting machine is 80% (availability or uptime proportion is 80%), the reliability of the indenting machine is 95%, and the reliability of the printing machine is 85%. These reliability factors apply only when the machines are producing, not during setup or changeovers.

5 A factory produces one product, with 1 unit of raw material required for each unit of product. Two processes are required to produce the product: process 1, which feeds into process 2. A total of five identical machines are available in the plant that can be set up to perform either process. Once set up, each machine will be dedicated to perform that process. For each machine that is set up for process 1, production rate is 12 units/hr. For each machine that is set up for process 2, production rate is 18 units/hr. Both processes produce 100% good units (fraction defect rate = 0). A work-in-process buffer is provided between the two processes to avoid starving and blocking of machines. The factory operates 40 hr/week. (a) In order to maximize factory production, how many machines should be set up for process 1 and how many for process 2? (b) What is the factory's maximum possible weekly production rate of good product units?

6 A factory is dedicated to the production of one product, with 1 unit of raw material required for each unit of product. Two processes are required to produce the product: process 1, which feeds into process 2. A total of eight identical machines are available in the plant that can be set up to perform either process. Once set up, each machine will be dedicated to that process. For each machine that is set up for process 1, the production rate is 10 units/hr. For each machine that is set up for process 2, the production rate is 6 units/hr. Both processes produce 100% good units (fraction defect rate = 0). A work-in-process buffer is provided between the two processes to avoid starving and blocking of machines. The factory operates 40 hr/week. (a) In order to maximize factory production, how many machines should be set up for process 1 and how many for process 2? (b) What is the factory's maximum possible weekly production rate of good product units?

7 There are 20 automatic turning machines in the lathe department. Batches of parts are machined in the department. Each batch consists of setup and run. Batch size is 100 parts. The standard time to set up a machine for each batch is 5.0 hr. Four setup workers perform the setups. They each work 40 hr/week. Once a machine is set up, it runs automatically, with no worker attention until the batch is completed. Cycle time to machine each part is 9.0 min; thus it takes 15 hr of run time to produce a batch. Assume all machines are perfectly reliable. (a) What is the production output of the lathe department in 40 hr of operation per week? (b) How many machines are idle (not in use or being set up between production runs) on average at any moment?

Batch Processing and Economic Order Quantities

8 The annual demand for a certain item is 22,500 pc/yr. One unit of the product costs $35.00, and the holding cost rate is 15%/yr. Setup time to produce a batch is 3.25 hr. The cost of equipment downtime during setup plus associated labor is $200/hr. Determine the economic order quantity and the total inventory cost for this case.

9 A stamping plant supplies sheet metal parts to a final assembly plant in the automotive industry. Annual demand for a typical part is 150,000 pc. Average cost per piece is $20; holding cost is 25%; changeover (setup) time for the presses is 5 hr; and cost of downtime for changing over a press is $200/hr. Compute the economic batch size and the total annual inventory cost for the data.

10 Demand for a certain product is 25,000 units/yr. Unit cost is $10.00. Holding cost rate is 30%/yr. Changeover (setup) time between products is 10.0 hr, and downtime cost during changeover is $150/hr. Determine (a) economic order quantity, (b) total inventory costs, and (c) total inventory cost per year as a proportion of total production costs.

11 Last year, the annual demand for a certain piece of merchandise that is inventoried at a department store warehouse was 13,688 units. The annual demand is expected to increase 10% in the next year. One unit of the product costs $8.75, and the selling price is $19.95. The holding cost rate is 15%/yr. The cost to place an order for the merchandise is figured at $65. Determine the economic order quantity and the total inventory cost for this case.

12 A part is produced in batches containing 3000 pc in each batch. Annual demand is 60,000 pc, and piece cost is $5.00. The setup time to run a batch is 3.0 hr, the cost of downtime on the affected equipment is figured at $200/hr, and the annual holding cost rate is 30%. What would the annual savings be if the product were produced in the economic order quantity?

13 A certain machine tool is used to produce several components for one assembled product. To keep in-process inventories low, a batch size of 100 units is produced for each component.

Demand for the product is 3000 units/yr. Production downtime costs an estimated \$150/hr. All parts produced on the machine tool are approximately \$9.00/unit. The holding cost rate is 30%/yr. In how many minutes must the changeover between batches be accomplished so that 100 units is the economic order quantity?

14 The annual demand for a certain part is 10,000 units. At present the setup time on the machine tool that makes this part is 5.0 hr. The cost of downtime on this machine is \$200/hr. Annual holding cost per part is \$1.50. Determine (a) EOQ and (b) total inventory costs for this data. Also, determine (c) EOQ and (d) total inventory costs if the changeover time could be reduced to 6 min.

15 A variety of assembled products is made in batches on a manual assembly line. Every time a different product is produced, the line must be changed over, which causes lost production time. The assembled product of interest here has an annual demand of 12,000 units. The changeover time to set up the line for this product is 6.0 hr. The company figures that the hourly rate for lost production time on the line due to changeovers is \$500/hr. Annual holding cost for the product is \$7.00/product. The product is currently made in batches of 1000 units for shipment each month to the wholesale distributor. (a) Determine the total annual inventory cost for this product in batch sizes of 1000 units. (b) Determine the economic batch quantity for this product. (c) How often would shipments be made using this EOQ? (d) How much would the company save in annual inventory costs, if it produced batches equal to the EOQ rather than 1000 units?

Fraction Defect Rate

16 A starting batch of 5000 work units is processed through 8 sequential operations, each of which has a fraction defect rate of 3%. (a) How many good parts and (b) how many defects are in the final batch? (c) What is the yield of the operation sequence?

17 A starting batch of 10,000 parts is processed through 6 sequential operations. Operations 1 and 2 each have a fraction defect rate of 4%, operations 3, 4, and 5 each have a fraction defect rate of 6%, and operation 6 has a fraction defect rate of 10%. (a) How many good parts and (b) how many defects are in the final batch? (c) What is the yield of the operation sequence?

18 A total of 1000 good units must be produced by a sequence of 10 operations, each of which has fraction defect rate of 6%. (a) How many units must be in the starting batch in order to produce this required quantity? (b) What is the yield of the operation sequence?

19 A starting batch of 20,000 work units is processed through 7 sequential operations. Operations 1, 2, and 3 each have a fraction defect rate of 5%, and operations 4, 5, and 6 each have a fraction defect rate of 4%. The fraction defect rate of operation 7 is unknown. If a final batch contains a total of 5328 defects, determine the fraction defect rate of operation 7.

20 Three sequential operations are required for a certain automotive component. The defect rates are 4% for operation 1, 5% for operation 2, and 10% for operation 3. Operations 2 and 3 can be performed on units that are already defective. Assume that 25,000 starting parts are processed through the sequence. (a) How many units are expected to be defect-free? (b) How many units are expected to have exactly one defect? (c) How many units are expected to have all three defects?

21 Solve Problem 3 but assume that there is a 10% scrap rate in printing (operation 3).

22 A starting batch of 10,000 workparts is processed through three sequential operations: 1 then 2 then 3. Operation 1 sometimes produces parts with defect type 1 at a rate of 5%;

operation 2 sometimes produces parts with defect type 2 at a rate of 8%; and operation 3 sometimes produces parts with defect type 3 at a rate of 10%. Assume that the defects occur randomly and that all 10,000 parts are processed through all three operations. (a) How many are expected to be defect free? (b) How many are expected to have all three defects? (c) How many are expected to have exactly one defect?

23 A factory is dedicated to the production of one product. One unit of raw material is required for each unit of product. Two processes are required to produce the product: process 1, which feeds into process 2. A total of eight identical machines are available in the plant that can be set up to perform either process. Once set up, each machine will be dedicated to the performance of that process. For each machine set up, the production rate is 10 units/hr for process 1, production rate = 6 units/hr for process 2. Process 1 produces only good units, but process 2 has a scrap rate of 20%. A work-in-process buffer is allowed between the two processes so that process 2 will not be starved for work. The factory operates 40 hr/wk. (a) In order to maximize factory production, how many machines should be set up for process 1 and for process 2? (b) What is the factory's maximum possible weekly production rate of good product units? (c) How many starting units of raw material are needed each week to attain this production rate?

24 Two sheet metal parts, A and B, are produced separately, each requiring two press-working operations. Part A is routed through operations 1 and 2, and part B is routed through operations 3 and 4. The two parts are then joined in a welding step (operation 5), and the assembly is routed to an electroplating operation (operation 6). The six operations have the following fraction defect rates: $q_1 = 0.05, q_2 = 0.15, q_3 = 0.10, q_4 = 0.20, q_5 = 0.13, q_6 = 0.08$. If the desired final quantity of assemblies is 100,000 units, how many starting units of parts A and B will be required? There is no inspection or separation of defective units until after the final process, so defective units and good units are processed together through all production processes.

25 Two subassemblies, A and B, are processed separately, each requiring two finishing operations. A is routed through operations 1 and 2, and B is routed through operations 3 and 4. The two subassemblies are then joined in an assembly operation (operation 5). The five operations have the following fraction defect rates: $q_1 = 0.03$, $q_2 = 0.08$, $q_3 = 0.05$, $q_4 = 0.09$, $q_5 = 0.01$. If the desired final quantity of completed assemblies is 10,000 units, how many starting units of A and B will be required? There is no inspection or separation of defective units until after the final operation, so defective units and good units are processed together through all processing and assembly steps.

Work Cells and Worker Teams

26 For Problem 1, (a) use the Hollier algorithm to determine the most logical in-line sequence of workstations in the work system, and (b) compute the percentages of in-sequence, backflow, and bypassing moves for the sequence.

27 For Problem 2, (a) use the Hollier method to find the most logical in-line sequence of workstations in the work system, and (b) compute the percentages of in-sequence, backflow, and bypassing moves for the sequence.

28 Four workstations (1, 2, 3, and 4) used to produce a family of similar parts are to be arranged into an in-line layout. The daily flow of parts between workstations is as follows: 10 parts from stations 1 to 2, 40 parts from stations 1 to 4, 50 parts from stations 3 to 1, 20 parts from stations 3 to 4, and 50 parts from stations 4 to 2. (a) Use the Hollier algorithm to determine the most logical sequence of stations in the work system. (b) Draw the network diagram for the system. (c) Compute the percentages of in-sequence, bypassing, and backflow moves for the sequence.

29 Four workstations (1, 2, 3, and 4) are used to produce similar parts. The stations are to be arranged into a work cell with an in-line layout. The daily flow of parts between workstations is as follows: 15 parts from stations 2 to 4, 60 parts from stations 3 to 2, 35 parts from stations 2 to 1, 20 parts from stations 4 to 3, and 30 parts from stations 4 to 2. (a) Use the Hollier algorithm to determine the most logical sequence of stations in the work system. (b) Draw the network diagram for the system. (c) Compute the percentages of in-sequence, bypassing, and backflow moves for the sequence.

30 Five workstations (1, 2, 3, 4, and 5) that produce about 10 similar parts must be arranged into an in-line layout. The daily flow of parts between workstations is as follows: 20 parts from stations 1 to 2, 30 parts from stations 1 to 3, 25 parts from stations 3 to 4, 20 parts from stations 5 to 4, 10 parts from 5 to 2, and 35 parts from stations 4 to 2. (a) Use the Hollier algorithm to determine the most logical sequence of stations in the work system. (b) Draw the network diagram for the system. (c) Compute the percentages of in-sequence, bypassing, and backflow moves for the sequence.

31 Five workstations (1, 2, 3, 4, and 5) that produce about 10 similar parts must be arranged into an in-line layout. The daily flow of parts between workstations is as follows: 40 parts from stations 5 to 2, 35 parts from stations 5 to 3, 20 parts from stations 3 to 1, 25 parts from stations 1 to 4, 60 parts from 3 to 2, 15 parts from stations 2 to 5, and 30 parts from stations 4 to 2. (a) Use the Hollier algorithm to determine the most logical sequence of stations in the work system. (b) Draw the network diagram for the system. (c) Compute the percentages of in-sequence, bypassing, and backflow moves for the sequence.

32 A team approach is to be used in an assembly cell; each team will consist of w workers, all working together to assemble the same product. The total work content time per product is T_{wc} and so the cycle time T_c to complete a unit is ideally T_{wc} divided by w. However, congestion occurs as the number of workers in the cell increases; the workers get in each other's way, and this degrades the cycle time. Thus a better model of cycle time is $T_c = T_{wc}/w + wF_cT_{wc}$, where T_c = production cycle time, min; F_c = the congestion factor (a constant of proportionality); and other terms are defined above. If T_{wc} = 45 min and F_c = 0.02, and it is desired to maximize the production rate of the cell, determine (a) the optimum number of workers w and (b) the corresponding production rate. The number of workers must be an integer.

Manual Assembly Lines

Manual assembly lines are work systems consisting of multiple workers who are organized to produce a single product or a limited range of products. They are usually associated with the mass production of assembled products such as automobiles, appliances, and other consumer products for which demand is high. The assembly workers perform various tasks at workstations that are physically located along the line-of-flow of the product as it is being made. In assembly lines, the workers usually accomplish their tasks on work units that are moved by a powered conveyor. In addition, some of the workstations may be equipped with portable powered tools for the assembly operations. Factors favoring the use of manual assembly lines include the following:

- Demand for the product is high or medium.
- The products made on the line are identical or similar.
- The total work required to assemble the product can be divided into small work elements.

TABLE 1 Products Usually Made on Manual Assembly Lines

Audio equipment	Lamps	Stoves
Automobiles	Luggage	Telephones
Cameras	Microwave ovens	Toasters, toaster ovens
Cooking ranges	Personal computers and printers, monitors, scanners, etc.	Trucks, light and heavy
Dishwashers		Videocassette players
Dryers (laundry)	Power tools (drills, saws, etc.)	Washing machines (laundry)
Electric motors	Pumps	
Furniture	Refrigerators	

- It is technologically impossible or economically infeasible to automate the assembly operations.

Table 1 provides a list of products characterized by these factors that are usually made on manual assembly lines.

Several reasons can be given to explain why manual assembly lines are so productive compared to alternative methods in which multiple workers each perform all of the tasks to assemble the products:

- *Specialization of labor.* When a large job is divided into small tasks and each task is assigned to one worker, the worker becomes highly proficient at performing the single task. Each worker becomes a specialist. One of the major explanations of specialization of labor is the ***learning curve***.
- *Interchangeable parts.* This means that each component is manufactured to sufficiently close tolerances that any part of a certain type can be selected at random for assembly with its mating component. Without interchangeable parts, assembly would require filing and fitting of mating components, rendering assembly line methods impractical.
- *Work flow.* In the context of assembly line technology, work flow means that each work unit should move steadily along the line and travel minimum distances between stations.
- *Line pacing.* Workers on an assembly line are usually required to complete their assigned tasks on each product unit within a certain cycle time, which paces the line to maintain a specified production rate. Pacing is generally implemented by means of a mechanized conveyor.

1 FUNDAMENTALS OF MANUAL ASSEMBLY LINES

A ***manual assembly line*** is a production line that consists of a sequence of workstations where assembly tasks are performed by human workers, as depicted in Figure 1. Products are assembled as they move along the line. At each station, a portion of the total work is performed on each unit. The common practice is to "launch" base parts onto the beginning of the line at regular intervals. Each base part travels through successive stations and workers add components that progressively build the product. A mechanized material transport system is typically used to move the base part along the line as it is gradually transformed into the final product. However, in some manual lines the product is manually passed from

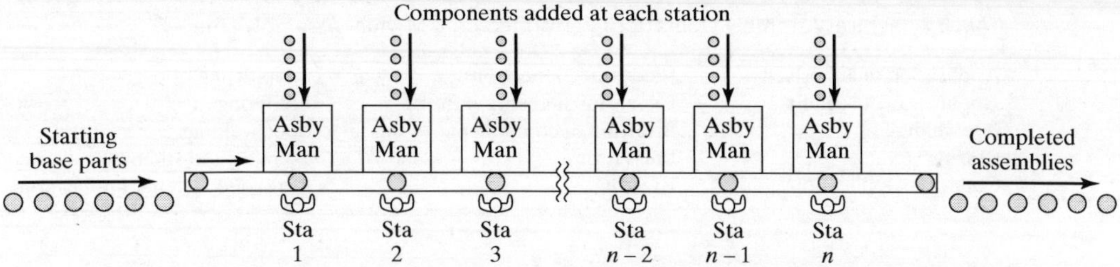

Asby = assembly, Man = manual, Sta = workstation, n = number of stations on the line

Figure 1 Configuration of a manual assembly line.

station to station. The production rate of an assembly line is determined by its slowest station. Stations capable of working faster are ultimately limited by the slowest station.

Manual assembly line technology has made a significant contribution to the development of American industry in the twentieth century (Historical Note 1). It remains an important work system throughout the world for producing assembled products in large quantities.

HISTORICAL NOTE 1 ORIGINS OF THE MANUAL ASSEMBLY LINE

The origins of the manual assembly line can be traced to the meat industry in Chicago and Cincinnati. In the mid- and late 1800s, meat-packing plants used unpowered overhead conveyors to move the slaughtered stock from one worker to the next. These unpowered conveyors were later replaced by power-driven chain conveyors to create "disassembly lines," which were the predecessor of the assembly line. The work organization permitted meat cutters to concentrate on single tasks (specialization of labor).

American automotive industrialist Henry Ford had observed these meat-packing operations. In 1913, he and his engineering colleagues designed an assembly line in Highland Park, Michigan, to produce magneto flywheels. Productivity increased fourfold. Flushed by success, Ford applied assembly line techniques to chassis fabrication. Using chain-driven conveyors and workstations arranged for the convenience and comfort of his assembly line workers, productivity was increased by a factor of eight, compared to previous single-station assembly methods. These and other improvements resulted in dramatic reductions in the price of the Model T Ford, which was the main product of the Ford Motor Company at the time. American consumers could now afford an automobile because of Ford's achievement in cost reduction. This stimulated further development and the use of production line techniques, including automated transport lines. It also forced Ford's competitors and suppliers to imitate his methods, and the manual assembly line became intrinsic to American industry.

1.1 Assembly Workstations

A ***workstation*** on a manual assembly line is a designated location along the work flow path at which one or more work elements are performed by one or more workers. The work elements represent small portions of the total work that must be accomplished to

TABLE 2 Typical Assembly Operations Performed on a Manual Assembly Line

Application of adhesive	Electrical connections	Snap fitting of parts
Application of sealants	Expansion and shrink fitting	Soldering
Arc welding	Insertion of components	Spot-welding
Brazing	Press fitting	Stapling and stitching
Cotter pin applications	Riveting	Threaded fastener applications

assemble the product. Typical assembly operations performed at stations on a manual assembly line are listed in Table 2. A given workstation also includes the tools (hand tools or powered tools) required to perform the task assigned to the station.

Some workstations are designed for workers to stand, while others allow workers to sit. When the workers stand, they can move about the station area to perform their assigned tasks. This is common for assembly of large products such as cars, trucks, and major appliances. The typical case is when the product is moved by a conveyor at constant velocity through the station. The worker begins the assembly task near the upstream side of the station and moves along with the work unit until the task is completed, then walks back to the next work unit and repeats the cycle. For smaller assembled products (such as small appliances, electronic devices, and subassemblies used on larger products), the workstations are usually designed to allow the workers to sit while they perform their tasks. This is more comfortable and less fatiguing for the worker and is generally more conducive to precision and accuracy in the assembly task.

Manual assembly lines that produce large items (e.g., cars, trucks) may have more than one worker per station. The ***manning level*** of workstation i, symbolized M_i, is the number of workers assigned to that station; where $i = 1, 2, \ldots, n$; and n = number of workstations on the line. The generic case is one worker: $M_i = 1$. In cases where the product is large, such as a car or a truck, multiple workers are often assigned to one station, so that $M_i > 1$. Multiple manning conserves valuable floor space in the factory and reduces line length and throughput time because fewer stations are required. The average manning level of a manual assembly line is simply the total number of workers on the line divided by the number of stations; that is,

$$M = \frac{w}{n} \tag{1}$$

where M = average manning level of the line, workers/station; w = number of workers on the line; and n = number of stations on the line. This seemingly simple ratio is complicated by the fact that manual assembly lines often include more workers than those assigned to stations, so that M is not a simple average of M_i values. These additional workers, called ***utility workers***, are not assigned to specific workstations; instead they are responsible for functions such as (1) helping workers who fall behind, (2) relieving workers for personal breaks, and (3) maintenance and repair duties. Including the utility workers in the worker count, we have

$$M = \frac{w_u + \sum_{i=1}^{n} w_i}{n} \tag{2}$$

where w_u = number of utility workers assigned to the system and w_i = number of workers assigned specifically to station i for $i = 1, 2, \ldots, n$. The parameter w_i is almost always an integer, except for the unusual case where a worker is shared between two adjacent stations.

1.2 Work Transport Systems

There are two basic ways to accomplish the movement of work units along a manual assembly line: (1) manually or (2) by a mechanized system. Both methods provide the fixed routing (pure sequential work flow) that is characteristic of production lines.

Manual Methods of Work Transport. In manual work transport, the units of product are passed from station to station by hand. Two problems result from this mode of operation: starving and blocking. When ***starving*** occurs, the assembly operator has completed the assigned task on the current work unit, but the next unit has not yet arrived at the station. The worker is thus starved for work. When ***blocking*** occurs, the operator has completed the assigned task on the current work unit but cannot pass the unit to the downstream station because that worker is not yet ready to receive it. The operator is therefore blocked from working.

To mitigate the effects of these problems, storage buffers are sometimes used between stations. In some cases, the work units made at each station are collected in batches and then moved to the next station. In other cases, work units are moved individually along a flat table or unpowered conveyor. When the task is finished at each station, the worker simply pushes the unit toward the downstream station. Space is often allowed for one or more work units in front of each workstation. This provides an available supply of work for the station, as well as room for completed units from the upstream station. Hence, starving and blocking are minimized. The trouble with this method of operation is that it can result in significant work-in-process, which is economically undesirable. Also, workers are unpaced in lines that rely on manual transport methods, and production rates tend to be lower.

Mechanized Work Transport. Powered conveyors and other types of mechanized material-handling equipment are widely used to move units along a manual assembly line. These systems can be designed to provide paced or unpaced operation of the line. There are three major categories of work transport systems in production lines: (a) continuous transport, (b) synchronous transport, and (c) asynchronous transport.

A ***continuous transport system*** uses a continuously moving conveyor that operates at constant velocity. This method is common on manual assembly lines. The conveyor usually runs the entire length of the line. However, if the line is very long, such as the case of an automobile final assembly plant, it is divided into segments with a separate conveyor for each segment.

Continuous transport can be implemented in two ways: (1) work units are fixed to the conveyor, and (2) work units are removable from the conveyor. In the first case, the product is large and heavy (e.g., automobile, washing machine) and cannot be removed from the conveyor. The worker must therefore walk along with the product at the speed of the conveyor in order to accomplish the assigned task.

In the case where work units are small and lightweight, they can be removed from the conveyor for the physical convenience of the operator at each station. Another convenience for the worker is that the assigned task at the station does not need to be completed within a fixed cycle time. Flexibility allows each worker to deal with technical problems that may be encountered with a particular work unit. However, on average, each worker must maintain a production rate equal to that of the rest of the line. Otherwise, the line will produce ***incomplete units***, which occurs when parts that were supposed to be added at a station are not added because the worker runs out of time.

In ***synchronous transport systems***, all work units are moved simultaneously between stations with a quick, discontinuous motion, and then positioned at their respective stations. This type of system is also known as ***intermittent transport***, which describes the motion experienced by the work units. Synchronous transport is not common for manual lines, due to the requirement that the task must be completed within a certain time limit. This can result in incomplete units and excessive stress on the assembly workers. Despite its disadvantages for manual assembly lines, synchronous transport is often ideal for automated production lines.

In an ***asynchronous transport system***, a work unit leaves a given station when the assigned task has been completed and the worker releases the unit. Work units move independently, rather than synchronously. At any moment, some units are moving between workstations while others are positioned at stations. With asynchronous transport systems, small queues of work units are permitted to form in front of each station. This tends to be forgiving of variations in worker task times.

1.3 Coping with Product Variety

Because human workers are flexible in terms of the variety of tasks they can perform, manual assembly lines can be designed to deal with differences in assembled products. Three types of assembly line can be distinguished: (1) single model, (2) batch model, and (3) mixed model.

A ***single model line*** produces many units of one product, and there is no variation in the product. Every work unit is identical, and so the task performed at each station is the same for all product units. This line type is intended for products with high demand.

Batch model and mixed model lines are designed to produce two or more models, but different approaches are used to cope with the model variations. As its name suggests, a ***batch model line*** produces each model in batches. Workstations are set up to produce the required quantity of the first model, then the stations are reconfigured to produce the next model, and so on. Products are often assembled in batches when demand for each product is medium. It is generally more economical to use one assembly line to produce several products in batches than to build a separate line for each different model.

When we state that the workstations are set up, we are referring to the assignment of tasks to each station on the line, including the special tools needed to perform the tasks, and the physical layout of the station. The models made on the line are usually similar, and the tasks to make them are therefore similar. However, differences exist among models so that a different sequence of tasks is usually required, and tools used at a given workstation for the last model might not be the same as those required for the next model. One model may take more total time than another, requiring the line to be operated at a slower pace. Worker retraining or new equipment may be needed to produce each new model. For these kinds of reasons, changes in the station setup are required before production of the next model can begin. These changeovers result in lost production time on a batch model line.

A ***mixed model line*** also produces more than one model; however, the models are not produced in batches. Instead, they are made simultaneously on the same line. While one model is being worked on at one station, a different model is being made at the next station. Each station is equipped to perform the variety of tasks needed to produce any model that moves through it. Many consumer products are assembled on mixed model lines. Examples are automobiles and major appliances, which are characterized by model variations, differences in available options, and even brand name differences in some cases.

The advantages of a mixed model line over a batch model line include the following: (1) no production time is lost when changing over between models; (2) high inventories typical of batch production are avoided; and (3) production rates of different models can be adjusted as product demand changes. On the other hand, the problem of assigning tasks to workstations so that they all share an equal workload is more complex on a mixed model line. Scheduling (determining the sequence of models) and logistics (getting the right parts to each workstation for the model currently at that station) are more difficult in this type of line.

2 ANALYSIS OF SINGLE MODEL ASSEMBLY LINES

The relationships developed in this section and the algorithms described in the following section are applicable to single model assembly lines. With a little modification, the same relationships and algorithms can be applied to batch model and mixed model assembly lines.

The assembly line must be designed to achieve a production rate R_p sufficient to satisfy demand for the product. Product demand is often expressed as an annual quantity, which can be reduced to an hourly rate. Management must decide how many shifts per week the line will operate and how many hours per shift. Assuming that the plant operates 50 weeks per year, the required hourly production rate is given by

$$R_p = \frac{D_a}{50 S_w H_{sh}} \tag{3}$$

where R_p = average production rate, units/hr; D_a = annual demand for the single product to be made on the line, units/yr; S_w = number of shifts/wk; and H_{sh} = hr/shift. If the line operates 52 weeks rather than 50, then $R_p = D_a/52 S_w H_{sh}$. If a time period other than a year is used for product demand, then the equation can be adjusted by using consistent time units in the numerator and denominator.

This production rate must be converted to a cycle time T_c, which is the time interval at which the line will be operated. The cycle time must take into account the reality that some production time will be lost due to occasional equipment failures, power outages, lack of a certain component needed in assembly, quality problems, labor problems, and other reasons. As a consequence of these losses, the line will be up and operating only a certain proportion of time out of the total shift time available; this uptime proportion is referred to as the ***line efficiency***. The cycle time can be determined as

$$T_c = \frac{60E}{R_p} \tag{4}$$

where T_c = cycle time of the line, min/cycle; R_p = required production rate, as determined from equation (3), units/hr; the constant 60 converts the hourly production rate to a cycle time in minutes; and E = line efficiency, the proportion of shift time that the line is up and operating. Typical values of E for a manual assembly line are in the range 0.90 to 0.98. The cycle time T_c establishes the ideal cycle rate for the line:

$$R_c = \frac{60}{T_c} \tag{5}$$

where R_c = cycle rate for the line, cycles/hr; and T_c is in min/cycle, as in equation (4). This rate R_c must be greater than the required production rate R_p because the line efficiency E is less than 100%. R_p and R_c are related to E as follows:

$$E = \frac{R_p}{R_c} \tag{6}$$

An assembled product requires a certain total amount of time to build, called the ***work content time*** T_{wc}. This is the total time of all work elements that must be performed to make one unit of the product. It represents the total amount of work that is accomplished on the product by the assembly line. It is useful to compute a theoretical minimum number of workers that will be required on the assembly line to produce a product with known T_{wc} and specified production rate R_p. The approach is basically the same as the one used to compute the number of workers required to achieve a specified workload. Making use of equation in the footnote below, we determine the number of workers on the production line:

$$w = \frac{WL}{AT} \tag{7}$$

where w = number of workers on the line; WL = workload to be accomplished in a given time period; and AT = available time in the period. The time period of interest will be 60 min. The ***workload*** in that period is the hourly production rate multiplied by the work content time of the product; that is,

$$WL = R_p T_{wc} \tag{8}$$

where R_p = production rate, pc/hr; and T_{wc} = work content time, min/pc.

* $w = \dfrac{WL}{AT}$ or $n = \dfrac{WL}{AT}$

Equation (4) can be rearranged to the form $R_p = 60E/T_c$. Substituting this into equation (8), we have

$$WL = \frac{60ET_{wc}}{T_c}$$

The available time AT is 1 hr (60 min) multiplied by the proportion uptime on the line; that is,

$$AT = 60E$$

Substituting these terms for WL and AT into equation (7), the equation reduces to the ratio T_{wc}/T_c. Since the number of workers must be an integer, we can state

$$w^* = \text{Minimum Integer} \geq \frac{T_{wc}}{T_c} \quad (9)$$

where w^* = theoretical minimum number of workers. If we assume one worker per station ($M_i = 1$ for all $i, i = 1, 2, \ldots, n$; and the number of utility workers $w_u = 0$), then this ratio also gives the theoretical minimum number of workstations on the line.

Achieving this minimum value in practice is very unlikely. Equation (9) ignores two factors that exist in a real assembly line and tend to increase the number of workers above the theoretical minimum value:

- *Repositioning losses.* Some time will be lost at each station for repositioning of the work unit or the worker. Thus, the time available per worker to perform assembly is less than T_c.
- *The line balancing problem.* It is virtually impossible to divide the work content time evenly among all workstations. Some stations are bound to have an amount of work that requires less time than T_c. This tends to increase the number of workers.

The following sections will focus on repositioning losses and imperfect balancing. We will consider the simplest case where one worker is assigned to each station ($M_i = 1$). Thus, when we refer to a certain station, we are referring to the worker at that station, and vice versa.

2.1 Repositioning Losses

Repositioning losses on a production line occur because some time is required each cycle to reposition the worker, or the work unit, or both. For example, on a continuous transport line with work units attached to the conveyor and moving at a constant speed, time is required for the worker to walk from the unit just completed to the upstream unit entering the station. In other conveyorized systems, time is required to remove the work unit from the conveyor and position it at the station for the worker to perform his or her task on it. In all manual assembly lines, there is some lost time for repositioning.

We will define T_r as the time required each cycle to reposition the worker or the work unit or both. In our subsequent analysis, we assume that T_r is the same for all workers, although repositioning times may actually vary among stations.

The repositioning time T_r must be subtracted from the cycle time T_c to obtain the available time remaining to perform the actual assembly task at each workstation. Let us refer to the time to perform the assigned task at each station as the ***service time***. It is symbolized T_{si}, where i is used to identify station i, $i = 1, 2, \ldots, n$. Service times will vary among stations because the total work content cannot be allocated evenly among them. Some stations will have more work than others. There will be at least one station at which T_{si} is maximum. This is sometimes referred to as the ***bottleneck station*** because it establishes the cycle time for the entire line. This maximum service time can be no greater than the difference between the cycle time T_c and the repositioning time T_r; that is,

$$\text{Max}\{T_{si}\} \leq T_c - T_r \qquad \text{for } i = 1, 2, \ldots n \tag{10}$$

where $\text{Max}\{T_{si}\}$ = maximum service time among all stations, min/cycle; T_c = cycle time for the assembly line from equation (4), min/cycle; and T_r = repositioning time (assumed the same for all stations), min/cycle. For simplicity of notation, let us use T_s to denote this maximum allowable service time; that is,

$$T_s = \text{Max}\{T_{si}\} \leq T_c - T_r \tag{11}$$

At all stations where T_{si} is less than T_s, workers will be idle for a portion of the cycle, as portrayed in Figure 2. When the maximum service time does not consume the entire available time $T_c - T_r$ (that is, when $T_s < T_c - T_r$), then this means that the line could be

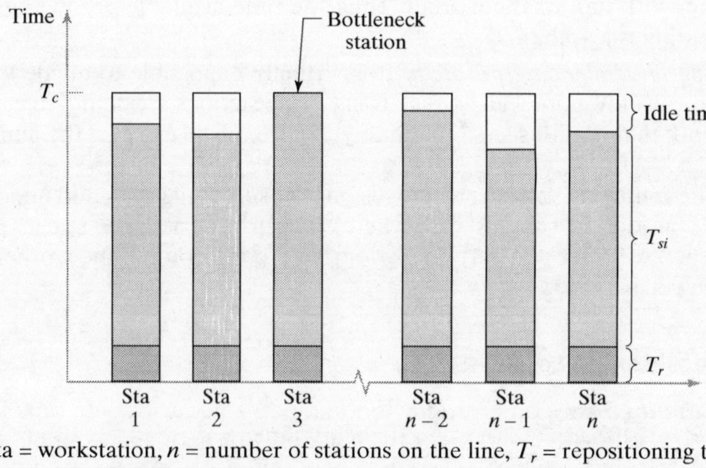

Sta = workstation, n = number of stations on the line, T_r = repositioning time, T_{si} = service time, T_c = cycle time

Figure 2 Components of cycle time at several stations on a manual assembly line. At the slowest station, the bottleneck station, idle time is zero; at other stations idle time exists.

operated at a faster pace than T_c from equation (4). In this case, the cycle time T_c is usually reduced so that $T_c = T_s + T_r$; this allows the production rate to be increased slightly.

Repositioning losses reduce the amount of time that can be devoted to productive assembly work on the line. These losses can be expressed in terms of an efficiency factor as follows:

$$E_r = \frac{T_s}{T_c} = \frac{T_c - T_r}{T_c} \tag{12}$$

where E_r = ***repositioning efficiency***, and the other terms are defined above.

2.2 The Line Balancing Problem

The work content performed on an assembly line consists of many separate and distinct work elements. Invariably, the sequence in which these elements can be performed is restricted, at least to some extent. And the line must operate at a specified production rate, which reduces to a required cycle time as defined by equation (4). Given these conditions, the line balancing problem is concerned with assigning the individual work elements to workstations so that all workers have an equal amount of work while simultaneously achieving the specified production rate of the line. We discuss the terminology of the line balancing problem in this section and present some of the algorithms to solve it in Section 3.

Minimum Rational Work Elements. A ***minimum rational work element*** is a work element that has a specific limited objective on the assembly line, such as adding a component to the base part, joining two components, or performing some other small portion of the total work content. A minimum rational work element cannot be subdivided any further without loss of practicality. For example, fastening two parts together with a bolt and nut would be defined as a minimum rational work element. It makes no sense to divide this element into smaller units of work. The sum of the work element times is equal to the work content time; that is,

$$T_{wc} = \sum_{k=1}^{n_e} T_{ek} \tag{13}$$

where T_{ek} = time to perform work element k, min; and n_e = number of work elements into which the work content is divided; that is, $k = 1, 2, \ldots, n_e$.

In line balancing, we make the following assumptions about work element times: (1) element times are constant values, and (2) T_{ek} values are additive; that is, the time to perform two or more work elements in sequence is the sum of the individual element times. In fact, we know these assumptions are not quite true. Work element times are variable, leading to the problem of task time variability. And there is often motion economy that can be achieved by combining two or more work elements, thus violating the additivity assumption. Nevertheless, these assumptions are made to allow solution of the line balancing problem.

The task time at station i, or service time as we are calling it, T_{si}, is composed of the work element times that have been assigned to that station; that is,

$$T_{si} = \sum_{k \in i} T_{ek} \tag{14}$$

An underlying assumption in this equation is that each T_{ek} is less than the maximum service time T_s.

Different work elements require different times, and when the elements are grouped into logical tasks and assigned to workers, the station service times T_{si} are likely not to be equal. Thus, simply because of the variation among work element times, some workers will be assigned more work, while others will be assigned less. Although service times vary from station to station, they must add up to the work content time:

$$T_{wc} = \sum_{i=1}^{n} T_{si} \tag{15}$$

Precedence Constraints. In addition to the variations in element times that make it difficult to obtain equal service times for all stations, there are restrictions on the order in which the work elements can be performed. Some elements must be done before others. For example, to create a threaded hole, the hole must be drilled before it can be tapped. A machine screw that will use the tapped hole to attach a mating component cannot be fastened before the hole has been drilled and tapped. These technological requirements on the work sequence are called ***precedence constraints***. As we shall see, they complicate the line balancing problem.

Precedence constraints can be presented graphically in the form of a ***precedence diagram***, which indicates the sequence in which the work elements must be performed. Work elements are symbolized by nodes, and the precedence requirements are indicated by arrows connecting the nodes. The sequence proceeds from left to right. Figure 3

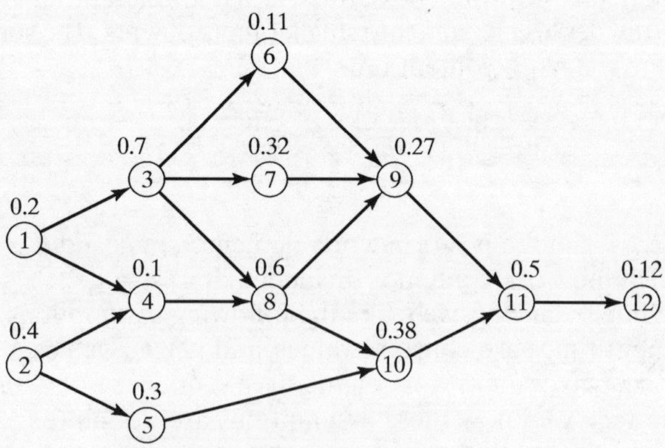

Figure 3 Precedence diagram for Example 1. Nodes represent work elements, and arrows indicate the sequence in which the elements must be done. Element times are shown above each node.

presents the precedence diagram for the following example, which illustrates the terminology and some of the equations presented here.

Example 1 A Problem for Line Balancing

A small electrical appliance is to be produced on a single model assembly line. The work content of assembling the product has been reduced to the work elements listed in Table 3. The table also lists the standard times that have been established for each element, as well as the precedence order in which they must be performed. The line is to be balanced for an annual demand of 100,000 units/yr. The line will operate 50 wk/yr, 5 shifts/wk, and 7.5 hr/shift. Manning level will be 1 worker/station. Previous experience suggests that the uptime efficiency for the line will be 96%, and repositioning time lost per cycle will be 0.08 min. Determine (a) total work content time T_{wc}, (b) required hourly production rate R_p to achieve the annual demand, (c) cycle time T_c, (d) theoretical minimum number of workers required on the line, and (e) service time T_s to which the line must be balanced.

TABLE 3 Work Elements for Example 1

No.	Work Element Description	T_{ek} (min)	Must Be Preceded by
1	Place frame in workholder and clamp	0.2	—
2	Assemble plug, grommet to power cord	0.4	—
3	Assemble brackets to frame	0.7	1
4	Wire power cord to motor	0.1	1,2
5	Wire power cord to switch	0.3	2
6	Assemble mechanism plate to bracket	0.11	3
7	Assemble blade to bracket	0.32	3
8	Assemble motor to brackets	0.6	3,4
9	Align blade and attach to motor	0.27	6,7,8
10	Assemble switch to motor bracket	0.38	5,8
11	Attach cover, inspect, and test	0.5	9,10
12	Place in tote pan for packing	0.12	11

Solution **(a)** The total work content time is the sum of the work element times in Table 3.

$$T_{wc} = 4.0 \text{ min}$$

(b) Given the annual demand, the hourly production rate is

$$R_p = \frac{100{,}000}{50(5)(7.5)} = 53.33 \text{ units/hr}$$

(c) The corresponding cycle time T_c with an uptime efficiency of 96% is

$$T_c = \frac{60(0.96)}{53.33} = 1.08 \text{ min}$$

(d) The minimum number of workers is given by equation (9):

$$w^* = \left(\text{Min Int} \geq \frac{4.0}{1.08} = 3.7\right) = 4 \text{ workers}$$

(e) The available service time against which the line must be balanced is

$$T_s = 1.08 - 0.08 = 1.00 \text{ min}$$ ■

Measures of Line Balance Efficiency. Owing to the differences in minimum rational work element times and the precedence constraints among the elements, it is virtually impossible to obtain a perfect line balance. Measures must be defined to indicate how good a given line balancing solution is. One possible measure is ***balance efficiency***, which is the work content time divided by the total available service time on the line:

$$E_b = \frac{T_{wc}}{wT_s} \tag{16}$$

where E_b = balance efficiency, often expressed as a percentage; T_s = the maximum available service time on the line (Max$\{T_{si}\}$), min/cycle; and w = number of workers. The denominator in equation (16) gives the total service time available on the line to devote to the assembly of one product unit. The closer the values of T_{wc} and wT_s, the less idle time on the line. E_b is therefore a measure of how good the line balancing solution is. A perfect line balance yields a value of $E_b = 1.00$. Typical line balancing efficiencies in industry range between 0.90 and 0.95.

The complement of balance efficiency is ***balance delay***, which indicates the amount of time lost due to imperfect balancing as a ratio to the total time available; that is,

$$d = \frac{(wT_s - T_{wc})}{wT_s} \tag{17}$$

where d = balance delay; and the other terms have the same meaning as before. A balance delay of zero indicates perfect balance. Note that $E_b + d = 1$.

Worker Requirements. In our discussion of the assembly line relationships, we have identified three factors that reduce the productivity of a manual assembly line. They can all be expressed as efficiencies:

1. *Line efficiency*, the proportion of uptime on line E, as defined in equation (6).
2. *Repositioning efficiency*, E_r, as defined in equation (12).
3. *Balancing efficiency*, E_b, as defined in equation (16).

Together, they constitute the overall labor efficiency on the assembly line, defined as

$$\text{Labor efficiency on the assembly line} = EE_rE_b \tag{18}$$

Using this measure of labor efficiency, we can calculate a more realistic value for the number of workers on the assembly line, based on equation (9):

$$w = \text{Minimum Integer} \geq \frac{R_pT_{wc}}{60EE_rE_b} = \frac{T_{wc}}{E_rE_bT_c} = \frac{T_{wc}}{E_bT_s} \tag{19}$$

where w = number of workers required on the line; R_p = hourly production rate, units/hr; T_{wc} = work content time per product to be accomplished on the line, min/unit. The trouble with this relationship is that it is difficult to determine values for E, E_r, and E_b before the line is built and operated. Nevertheless, the equation provides an accurate model of the parameters that affect the number of workers required to accomplish a given workload on a single model assembly line.

2.3 Workstation Considerations

Let us attach a quantitative definition to some of the assembly line parameters discussed in Section 1.1. A workstation is a position along the assembly line where one or more workers perform assembly tasks. If the manning level is one for all stations ($M_i = 1.0$ for $i = 1, 2, \ldots, n$) then the number of stations is equal to the number of workers. In general, for any value of M for the line,

$$n = \frac{w}{M} \tag{20}$$

A workstation has a length dimension L_{si}, where i denotes station i. The total length of the assembly line is the sum of the station lengths:

$$L = \sum_{i=1}^{n} L_{si} \tag{21}$$

where L = length of the assembly line, m (ft); and L_{si} = length of station i, m (ft). In the case when all L_{si} are equal,

$$L = nL_s \tag{22}$$

where L_s = station length, m (ft).

A common transport system used on manual assembly lines is a constant speed conveyor. Let us consider this case in developing the following relationships. Base parts are launched onto the beginning of the line at constant time intervals equal to the cycle time T_c. This provides a constant feed rate of base parts, and if the base parts remain fixed to the conveyor during their assembly, this feed rate will be maintained throughout the line. The feed rate is simply the reciprocal of the cycle time:

$$f_p = \frac{1}{T_c} \tag{23}$$

where f_p = feed rate on the line, products/min. A constant feed rate on a constant speed conveyor provides a center-to-center distance between base parts given by

$$s_p = \frac{v_c}{f_p} = v_c T_c \tag{24}$$

where s_p = center-to-center spacing between base parts, m/part (ft/part); and v_c = velocity of the conveyor, m/min (ft/min).

In general, it is desirable to allow a worker more time to complete the assigned task than what is provided by the cycle time, so that if a particular work unit takes longer than the average, the worker can still complete the task. In the long run, the worker must keep pace with the cycle time, but he or she may fall behind for an individual work unit. Achieving this time allowance is called ***pacing with margin***, a desirable way to operate the line so as to achieve the desired production rate and at the same time provide for some product-to-product variation in task times at workstations. One way to achieve pacing with margin in a continuous transport system is to provide a tolerance time that is greater than the cycle time. ***Tolerance time*** is defined as the time a work unit spends inside the boundaries of the workstation. It is determined by the length of the station and the conveyor velocity, as follows:

$$T_t = \frac{L_s}{v_c} \tag{25}$$

where T_t = tolerance time, min/part, assuming that all station lengths are equal. If stations have different lengths, identified by L_{si}, then the tolerance times will differ proportionally, since v_c is constant. Thus, providing a tolerance time greater than the cycle time is achieved by making the station length greater than the distance traveled by a work unit during T_c.

The total elapsed time a work unit spends on the assembly line can be determined simply as the length of the line divided by the conveyor velocity. It is also equal to the tolerance time multiplied by the number of stations. Expressing these relationships in equation form, we have

$$ET = \frac{L}{v_c} = nT_t \tag{26}$$

where ET = elapsed time a work unit (specifically, the base part) spends on the conveyor during its assembly, min.

3 LINE BALANCING ALGORITHMS

The objective in line balancing is to distribute the total workload on the assembly line as evenly as possible among the workers. This objective can be expressed mathematically in two alternative but equivalent forms:

$$\text{Minimize } (wT_s - T_{wc}) \qquad \text{or} \qquad \text{Minimize } \sum_{i=1}^{w}(T_s - T_{si}) \tag{27}$$

subject to: (1) $\sum_{k \in i} T_{ek} \leq T_s$ and (2) all precedence requirements are obeyed.

In this section we consider several algorithms to solve the line balancing problem, using the data of Example 1 to illustrate (1) the largest candidate rule, (2) the Kilbridge and Wester method, and (3) the ranked positional weights method. These methods are heuristic, meaning they are based on common sense and experimentation rather than mathematical optimization. In each of the algorithms, we assume that the manning level

TABLE 4 Work Elements Arranged According to T_{ek} Value for the Largest Candidate Rule

Work Element	T_{ek} (min)	Preceded by
3	0.7	1
8	0.6	3,4
11	0.5	9,10
2	0.4	—
10	0.38	5,8
7	0.32	3
5	0.3	2
9	0.27	6,7,8
1	0.2	—
12	0.12	11
6	0.11	3
4	0.1	1,2

is one, so when we identify station *i*, we are also identifying the worker at station *i*. Computer programs based on these and other algorithms have been written to solve large-scale assembly line problems.

3.1 Largest Candidate Rule

According to the largest candidate rule, work elements are arranged in descending order based on their T_{ek} values, as in Table 4. Given this list, the algorithm consists of the following steps:

1. Assign elements to the worker at the first workstation by starting at the top of the list and selecting the first element that satisfies precedence requirements and does not cause the total sum of T_{ek} at that station to exceed the allowable T_s; when an element is selected for assignment to the station, start back at the top of the list for subsequent assignments.
2. When no more elements can be assigned without exceeding T_s, then proceed to the next station.
3. Repeat steps 1 and 2 for the other stations in turn until all elements have been assigned.

Example 2 Largest Candidate Rule

Apply the largest candidate rule to the problem in Example 1.

Solution: Work elements are arranged in descending order in Table 4, and the algorithm is carried out as presented in Table 5. Five workers and stations are required in the solution. Balance efficiency is computed as:

$$E_b = \frac{4.0}{5(1.0)} = 0.80$$

Balance delay $d = 0.20$. The line balancing solution is presented in Figure 4.

TABLE 5 Work Elements Assigned to Stations According to the Largest Candidate Rule

Station	Work Element	T_{ek} (min)	Station Time (min)
1	2	0.4	
	5	0.3	
	1	0.2	
	4	0.1	1.0
2	3	0.7	
	6	0.11	0.81
3	8	0.6	
	10	0.38	0.98
4	7	0.32	
	9	0.27	0.59
5	11	0.5	
	12	0.12	0.62

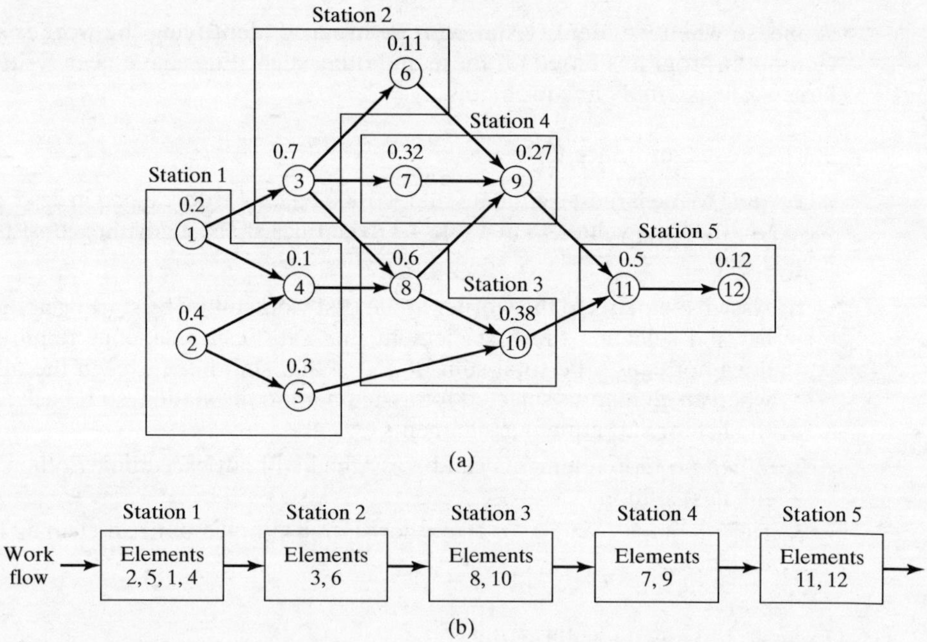

Figure 4 Solution for Example 2, which indicates (a) assignment of elements according to the largest candidate rule, and (b) physical sequence of stations with assigned work elements. ■

3.2 Kilbridge and Wester Method

The Kilbridge and Wester method [3] has received considerable attention since its introduction in 1961, and it has been applied with apparent success to several complicated line balancing problems in industry [4]. It is a heuristic procedure that selects work

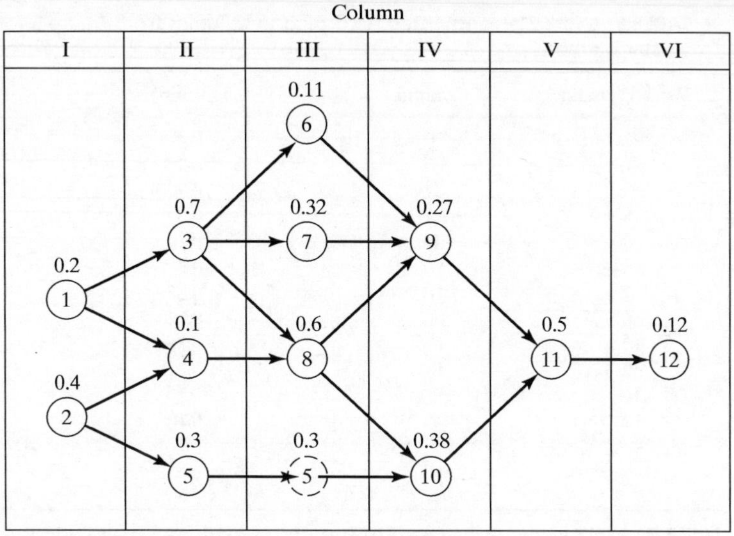

Figure 5 Work elements in example problem arranged into columns for the Kilbridge and Wester method.

elements for assignment to stations according to their position in the precedence diagram. This overcomes one of the difficulties with the largest candidate rule in which an element may be selected because of a high T_e value but irrespective of its position in the precedence diagram. In general, the Kilbridge and Wester method provides a superior line balance solution than the largest candidate rule (although this is not the case for our example problem).

In the Kilbridge and Wester method, work elements in the precedence diagram are arranged into columns, as shown in Figure 5. The elements can then be organized into a list according to their columns, with the elements in the first column listed first. We have developed such a list of elements for our example problem in Table 6. If a given element can be located in more than one column, then list all of the columns for that element, as we have done in the case of element 5. In our list, we have added the feature that elements in a given column are presented in the order of their T_{ek} value; that is, we have applied the largest candidate rule within each column. This is helpful when assigning elements to stations, because it ensures that the larger elements are selected first, thus increasing our chances of making the sum of T_{ek} in each station closer to the allowable T_s limit. Once the list is established, the same three-step procedure is used as before.

Example 3 Kilbridge and Wester method

Apply the Kilbridge and Wester method to the problem in Example 1.

Solution: Work elements are arranged in order of columns shown in Table 6. The Kilbridge and Wester solution is presented in Table 7. Five workers are again required and the balance efficiency is once more $E_b = 0.80$. Note that although the balance efficiency is the same as in the largest candidate rule, the allocation of work elements to stations is different.

TABLE 6 Work Elements Listed According to Columns from Figure 5 for the Kilbridge and Wester Method

Work Element	Column	T_{ek} (min)	Preceded by
2	I	0.4	—
1	I	0.2	—
3	II	0.7	1
5	II, III	0.3	2
4	II	0.1	1, 2
8	III	0.6	3,4
7	III	0.32	3
6	III	0.11	3
10	IV	0.38	5,8
9	IV	0.27	6, 7, 8
11	V	0.5	9, 10
12	VI	0.12	11

TABLE 7 Work Elements Assigned to Stations According to the Kilbridge and Wester Method

Station	Work Element	Column	T_{ek} (min)	Station Time (min)
1	2	I	0.4	
	1	I	0.2	
	5	II	0.3	
	4	II	0.1	1.0
2	3	II	0.7	
	6	III	0.11	0.81
3	8	III	0.6	
	7	III	0.32	0.92
4	10	IV	0.38	
	9	IV	0.27	0.65
5	11	V	0.5	
	12	VI	0.12	0.62

■

3.3 Ranked Positional Weights Method

The ranked positional weights method was introduced by Helgeson and Birne [2], and it is sometimes identified by their names. In this method, a ranked positional weight value (call it *RPW* for short) is computed for each element. The *RPW* takes into account both the T_{ek} value and its position in the precedence diagram. Specifically, RPW_k is calculated by summing T_{ek} and all other times for elements that follow T_{ek} in the arrow chain of the precedence diagram. Elements are compiled into a list according to their *RPW* value, and the algorithm proceeds using the same three steps as before.

Example 4 Ranked Positional Weights Method

Apply the ranked positional weights method to the problem in Example 1.

TABLE 8 Elements and Their Ranked Positional Weight (*RPW*)

Work Element	*RPW*	T_{ek} (min)	Preceded by
1	3.30	0.2	—
3	3.00	0.7	1
2	2.67	0.4	—
4	1.97	0.1	1, 2
8	1.87	0.6	3, 4
5	1.30	0.3	2
7	1.21	0.32	3
6	1.00	0.11	3
10	1.00	0.38	5, 8
9	0.89	0.27	6, 7, 8
11	0.62	0.5	9, 10
12	0.12	0.12	11

TABLE 9 Work Elements Assigned to Stations According to *RPW* Method

Station	Work Element	T_{ek} (min)	Station Time (min)
1	1	0.2	
	3	0.7	0.90
2	2	0.4	
	4	0.1	
	5	0.3	
	6	0.11	0.91
3	8	0.6	
	7	0.32	0.92
4	10	0.38	
	9	0.27	0.65
5	11	0.5	
	12	0.12	0.62

Solution: The *RPW* must be calculated for each element. To illustrate,

$$RPW_{11} = 0.5 + 0.12 = 0.62$$

$$RPW_8 = 0.6 + 0.27 + 0.38 + 0.5 + 0.12 = 1.87$$

Work elements are listed according to *RPW* value in Table 8. Assignment of elements to stations proceeds with the solution presented in Table 9. Note that the largest T_s value is 0.92 min. This can be exploited by operating the line at this faster rate, with the result that line balance efficiency is improved and the production rate is increased.

$$E_b = \frac{4.0}{5(.92)} = 0.87$$

The cycle time is $T_c = T_s + T_r = 0.92 + 0.08 = 1.00$; therefore,

$$R_c = \frac{60}{1.0} = 60 \text{ cycles/hr, and from equation (4.6), } R_p = 60 \times 0.96 = 57.6 \text{ units/hr}$$ ■

This is a better solution than the previous line balancing methods provided. It turns out that the performance of a given line balancing algorithm depends on the problem to be solved. Some line balancing methods work better on some problems, while other methods work better on other problems.

4 OTHER CONSIDERATIONS IN ASSEMBLY LINE DESIGN

The line balancing algorithms described in Section 3 are precise computational procedures that allocate work elements to stations based on deterministic quantitative data. However, there may be other opportunities for improvement in the design and operation of a manual assembly line, some of which may increase line performance beyond what the balancing algorithms provide. Some of the considerations are as follows:

- *Methods analysis.* Methods analysis involves the study of human work activity to seek out ways in which the activity can be done with less effort, in less time, and with greater effect. This analysis is an obvious step in the design of a manual assembly line, since the work elements need to be defined in order to balance the line. In addition, methods analysis can be used after the line is running to examine workstations that are bottlenecks. The analysis may result in improved hand and body motions, better workplace layout, design of special tools to facilitate manual work elements, or even changes in the product design for easier assembly.
- *Utility workers.* We have previously mentioned utility workers in our discussion of manning levels. Utility workers can be used to relieve congestion at stations that are temporarily overloaded.
- *Preassembly of components.* To reduce the total amount of work done on the regular assembly line, certain subassemblies can be prepared off-line, either by another assembly cell in the plant or by purchasing them from an outside vendor that specializes in the type of processes required. Although it may seem like simply a means of moving the work from one location to another, there are some good reasons for organizing assembly operations in this manner: (1) the required process may be difficult to implement on the regular assembly line, (2) task time variability (e.g., for adjustments or fitting) for the associated assembly operations may result in a longer overall cycle time if done on the regular line, and (3) an assembly cell set up in the plant or a vendor with certain special capabilities to perform the work may be able to achieve higher quality.
- *Storage buffers between stations.* A storage buffer is a location in the production line where work units are temporarily stored. There are several reasons to include one or more storage buffers in a production line: (1) to accumulate work units between two stages of the line when their production rates are different; (2) to smooth production between stations with large task time variations; and (3) to permit continued operation of certain sections of the line when other sections are temporarily down for service or repair. The use of storage buffers generally improves the performance of the line operation.
- *Parallel workstations.* Parallel stations are sometimes used to balance a production line. Their most obvious application is where a particular station has an unusually

long task time that would cause the production rate of the line to be less than required to satisfy product demand. In this case, two stations operating in parallel with both performing the same long task may eliminate the bottleneck.

5 ALTERNATIVE ASSEMBLY SYSTEMS

The well-defined pace of a manual assembly line has merit from the viewpoint of maximizing production rate. However, assembly line workers often complain about the monotony of the repetitive tasks they must perform and the unrelenting pace they must maintain when a moving conveyor is used. Poor quality workmanship, sabotage of the line equipment, and other problems have occurred on high production assembly lines. To address these issues, alternative assembly systems are available in which either the work is made less monotonous and repetitious by enlarging the scope of the tasks performed, or the work is automated. The alternative work systems include (1) single-station manual assembly cells, and (2) assembly cells based on worker teams.

A ***single-station manual assembly cell*** consists of a single workplace in which the assembly work is accomplished on the product or on some major subassembly of the product. This method is generally used on products that are complex and produced in small quantities, sometimes one-of-a-kind. The workplace may utilize one or more workers, depending on the size of the product and the required production rate. Custom-engineered products such as machine tools, industrial equipment, and prototype models of complex products (e.g., aircraft, appliances, cars) make use of a single manual station to perform the assembly work on the product.

Assembly by worker teams involves the use of multiple workers assigned to a common assembly task. The pace of the work is controlled largely by the workers themselves rather than by a pacing mechanism such as a powered conveyor moving at a constant speed. Team assembly can be implemented in several ways. A single-station manual assembly cell in which there are multiple workers is a form of worker team. The assembly tasks performed by each worker are generally less repetitious and broader in scope than the corresponding work on an assembly line.

Reported benefits of worker team assembly systems compared to conventional assembly line include greater worker satisfaction, better product quality, increased capability to accommodate model variations, and greater ability to cope with problems that require more time rather than stopping the entire production line. The principal disadvantage is that these team systems are not capable of the high production rates characteristic of a conventional assembly line.

REFERENCES

[1] Groover, M. P. *Automation, Production Systems, and Computer Integrated Manufacturing*. 2nd ed. Upper Saddle River, NJ: Prentice Hall, 2001.

[2] Helgeson, W. B., and D. P. Birnie. "Assembly Line Balancing Using Ranked Positional Weight Technique." *Journal of Industrial Engineering* 12, no. 6 (1961): 394–98.

[3] Kilbridge, M., and L. Wester. "A Heuristic Method of Assembly Line Balancing." *Journal of Industrial Engineering* 12, no. 6 (1961): 292–98.

[4] Prenting, T. O., and N. T. Thomopoulos. *Humanism and Technology in Assembly Systems*. Rochelle Park, NJ: Hayden Book Company, 1974.

[5] Wild, R. *Mass Production Management*. London: Wiley 1972.

REVIEW QUESTIONS

1 What is a manual assembly line?

2 What are the factors that favor the use of manual assembly lines?

3 What are the reasons why manual assembly lines are so productive compared to alternative methods of assembly?

4 What does the term *manning level* mean in the context of a manual assembly line?

5 What are utility workers on a manual assembly line?

6 What is *starving* on a manual assembly line?

7 What is *blocking* on a manual assembly line?

8 What are the three major categories of work transport in mechanized production lines?

9 What are the two types of line that can be designed to cope with product variety? What is the difference between them?

10 What does *work content time* mean?

11 What are repositioning losses as they are explained in the text?

12 What is the line balancing problem in the design of a manual assembly line?

13 What is a minimum rational work element in the context of manual assembly lines?

14 What is a precedence constraint in the context of manual assembly lines?

15 What are the three types of efficiency that must be considered in designing and operating a manual assembly line?

16 What does *tolerance time* mean?

17 Name the three line balancing algorithms described in the text.

18 What are some of the methods by which assembly line balancing efficiency can be improved that are outside the scope of the line balancing algorithms?

PROBLEMS

Manual Assembly Lines

1 Determine (a) the required hourly production rate and (b) the cycle time for a manual assembly line that will be used to produce a product with a work content time of 75 min and an annual demand of 150,000 units, if the plant operates 50 wk/yr, 5 days/wk, and 8 hr/day. It is anticipated that the line efficiency will be 94%.

2 A manual assembly line has 25 workstations and the manning level is 1.0. The work content time to assemble the product is 29.5 min. Production rate of the line is 40 units/hr. The proportion uptime is 96% and the repositioning time is 9 sec. Determine the balance delay on the line.

3 A manual assembly line is being planned for an assembled product whose work content time is 47.2 min. The line will be operated 2000 hr/yr. The annual demand anticipated for the product is 100,000 units. Based on previous assembly lines used by the company, the proportion of uptime on the line is expected to be 94%, the line balancing efficiency will be 92%, and the repositioning time lost each cycle will be 6 sec. The line will be designed with 1 worker/station. Determine (a) the required hourly production rate of the line, (b) the cycle time, (c) the ideal minimum number of workers required, and (d) the actual number of workers required based on the efficiencies given.

4 A manual assembly line is being planned for an assembled product whose annual demand is expected to be 175,000 units/yr. The line will be operated two shifts (4000 hr/yr). Work content time of the product is 53.7 min. For planning purposes, the following line parameter values will be used: uptime efficiency = 96%, balancing efficiency = 94%, and repositioning time = 8 sec. Determine (a) the required hourly production rate of the line, (b) the cycle time, (c) the ideal minimum number of workers required, and (d) the actual number of workers required based on the efficiencies given.

5 The required production rate for a certain product is 45 units/hr. Its work content time is 71.5 min. The production line for this product includes 5 automated workstations. Because the automated stations are not entirely reliable, the overall line efficiency is expected to be only 88%. All of the other stations will have one worker each. It is anticipated that 6% of each cycle will be lost due to worker repositioning. Balance delay is expected to be 7%. Determine (a) cycle time, (b) number of workers, (c) number of workstations, (d) average manning level on the line, including the automated stations, and (e) labor efficiency on the line.

6 A manual assembly line is being designed for a product whose annual demand is 100,000 units. The line will operate 50 wk/yr, 5 shifts/wk, and 8 hr/shift. Work units will be attached to a continuously moving conveyor. Work content time is 42.0 min. Assume line efficiency is 0.95, balancing efficiency is 0.93 or slightly less, repositioning time is 6 sec, and manning level is 1.4. Determine (a) average hourly production rate to meet demand and (b) number of workers required. (c) If each station on the line is 3 m long, what is the total length of the assembly line?

7 The work content for a product assembled on a manual production line is 48 min. The work is transported using a continuous overhead conveyor that operates at a speed of 5 ft/min. There are 24 workstations on the line, one-third of which have two workers; the remaining stations each have one worker. Repositioning time per worker is 9 sec, and uptime efficiency of the line is 95%. (a) What is the maximum possible hourly production rate if the line is assumed to be perfectly balanced? (b) If the actual production rate is only 92% of the maximum possible rate determined in part (a), what is the balance delay on the line? (c) If the line is designed so that the tolerance time is 1.3 times the cycle time, what is the total length of the production line? (d) What is the elapsed time a product spends on the line?

8 A manual assembly line must be designed for a product with annual demand of 150,000 units. The line will operate 50 wk/yr, 10 shifts/wk, and 7.5 hr/shift. Work units will be attached to a continuously moving conveyor. Work content time is 58.0 min. Assume line efficiency is 0.95, balancing efficiency is 0.93, and repositioning time is 8 sec. Determine (a) hourly production rate to meet demand, and (b) number of workers required.

9 The total work content for a product assembled on a manual production line is 33.0 min, and the production rate of the line must be 47 units/hr. Work units are attached to a moving conveyor whose speed is 7.5 ft/min. Repositioning time per worker is 6 sec, and uptime efficiency of the line is 94%. Owing to imperfect line balancing, the number of workers needed on the line must be two more workers than the number required for perfect balance. Assume the manning level is 1.6. (a) How many workers are required on the line? (b) How many workstations will be in the line? (c) What is the balance delay for this line? (d) If the workstations are arranged in a line, and the length of each station is 11 ft, what is the tolerance time in each station? (e) What is the elapsed time a work unit spends on the line?

10 The production rate for a certain assembled product is 45 units/hr. The total assembly work content time is 33 min of direct manual labor. The line operates at 95% uptime. Ten workstations have two workers on opposite sides of the line so that both sides of the product can be worked on simultaneously. The remaining stations have one worker. Repositioning time lost by each worker is 10 sec/cycle. It is known that the number of workers on the line is three more than the number required for perfect balance. Determine (a) number of workers, (b) number of workstations, (c) the balance delay, and (d) manning level.

11 A powered overhead conveyor is used to carry washing machine base parts along a manual assembly line. The spacing between base parts is 2.5 m and the speed of the conveyor is 1.2 m/min. The length of each workstation is 3.1 m. The line has 30 stations and 42 workers. Determine (a) cycle time, (b) feed rate, (c) tolerance time, and (d) elapsed time a washing machine base part spends on the line.

12 An automobile final assembly plant is being planned for an annual production of 150,000 cars. The plant will operate one shift, 250 days per year, but the duration of the shift (hr/shift) is to be determined. The plant will be divided into three departments: (1) body shop, (2) paint shop, and (c) general assembly. The body shop welds the car bodies, and the paint shop coats the welded car bodies. Both of these departments are highly automated. The general assembly department has no automation, but a moving conveyor is used to transport the cars through the manual workstations. A total of 14.0 hours of direct labor (work content time) are accomplished in general assembly. Based on previous lines installed by the company, it is anticipated that the following design parameters will apply to the general assembly department: line efficiency = 95%, balance efficiency = 94%, repositioning time = 0.10 min, and manning level = 2.5. If the plant must produce 60 cars per hour, determine the following for the general assembly department: (a) number of hours the shift must operate, (b) number of workers required, and (c) number of workstations.

13 In the previous problem, each workstation in the general assembly department will be 6.0 m long, and the tolerance time will be equal to the cycle time. Determine (a) speed of the moving conveyor, (b) center-to-center spacing of car bodies on the line, (c) total length of the line in general assembly, and (d) elapsed time a work unit spends in the department.

14 The production rate for a certain assembled product is 48 units/hr. The assembly work content time is 36.3 min of direct labor. Twelve of the workstations have two workers on opposite sides of the product, and the remaining stations have one worker each. Repositioning time lost per cycle is 0.10 min. The uptime efficiency of the line is 96%. It is known that the number of workers on the line is three more than the number required for perfect balance. Determine (a) number of workers, (b) number of workstations, (c) balance efficiency, (d) average manning level, and (e) overall labor efficiency on the line.

15 The work content time for an appliance product on a manual production line is 90.4 min. The required production rate is 45 units/hr. Work units are attached to a moving overhead conveyor whose speed is 2.5 m/min. Repositioning time per cycle is 9 sec, uptime efficiency is 96%, and manning level is 1.4. Because of imperfect line balancing, the number of workers needed on the line will be 5% more than the number required for perfect balance. The workstations are arranged in one long straight line, and the length of each station is 3.6 m. Determine (a) balance efficiency, (b) total length of the line, and (c) elapsed time a unit spends on the line.

Assembly Line Balancing

16 The letters in the table below represent work elements in an assembly precedence diagram. (a) Construct the precedence diagram and (b) determine the total work content time. (c) Use the largest candidate rule to assign work elements to stations using a service time (T_s) of 1.5 min, and (d) compute the balance delay for your solution.

Work element or tasks	A	B	C	D	E	F	G	H	I	J
Time (min)	0.5	0.3	0.8	1.1	0.6	0.2	0.7	1.0	0.9	0.4
Preceding	—	A	A	A	B, C	D	E	F	F	G, H, I

17 Solve the previous problem but use the Kilbridge and Wester method in part (c).

18 Solve the previous problem but use the ranked positional weights method in part (c).

19 The table below defines the precedence relationships and element times for a new assembled product. (a) Construct the precedence diagram for this job. (b) If the ideal cycle time is 1.1 min and the repositioning time is 0.1 min, what is the theoretical minimum number of workstations required to minimize the balance delay under the assumption that there will be one worker per station? (c) Using the largest candidate rule, assign work elements to stations. (d) Compute the balance delay for your solution.

Work Element	T_e (min)	Immediate Predecessors
1	0.5	—
2	0.3	1
3	0.8	1
4	0.2	2
5	0.1	2
6	0.6	3
7	0.4	4, 5
8	0.5	3, 5
9	0.3	7, 8
10	0.6	6, 9

20 Solve the previous problem but use the Kilbridge and Wester method in part (c).

21 Solve the previous problem but use the ranked positional weights method in part (c).

22 The table below lists the work elements (in minutes) to be performed on an assembly line and the precedence requirements that must be satisfied. Annual demand for the product will be 60,000 units. The line will operate one shift (2000 hr/yr). Expected line efficiency (proportion uptime) is 95%. Repositioning time per cycle is 6 sec. Manning level is 1.0 for all stations. The products will be moved through the line by conveyor at a speed of 4 ft/min. All stations are of equal length, which is 10 ft. Determine (a) theoretical minimum number of workers, (b) actual number of workers, based on previous experience with similar lines in which the highest possible balance efficiency is 93%, (c) tolerance time, and (d) elapsed time a product spends on the line from when it is first launched at the front of the first station until it is finally removed after the last station. (e) Construct the precedence diagram and (f) solve the line balancing problem using the Kilbridge and Wester method.

Work element	1	2	3	4	5	6	7	8	9	10	11	12	13
Time (min)	0.5	0.3	0.8	1.1	0.6	0.2	0.7	1.0	1.2	0.4	0.9	0.1	1.3
Preceded by	—	—	1	1, 2	2	3	4	5	5	6	7	8, 9	10, 11, 12

23 A manual assembly line is being planned to produce a small consumer appliance. The work elements, element times, and precedence constraints are indicated in the table below. The workers will work for 420 min/shift and must produce 350 units/day. A mechanized conveyor, moving at a speed of 1.4 m/min will transport work units through stations. Manning level is 1.0, and repositioning time is 0.1 min. Because worker service time at each station is variable, it has been decided to use a tolerance time that is 1.5 times the cycle time. (a) Determine the ideal minimum number of workers. (b) Use the largest candidate rule to solve the line balancing problem. (c) For your line balancing solution, compute the balancing efficiency. Determine (d) spacing between work units on the line and (e) required length of each workstation to satisfy the specifications of the line.

Work Element	T_e (min)	Immediate Predecessors
1	0.4	—
2	0.5	1
3	0.2	1
4	0.6	—
5	0.25	2
6	0.3	3
7	0.37	4
8	0.15	4
9	0.41	5
10	0.2	6, 7
11	0.3	8
12	0.33	9, 10
13	0.4	11
14	0.62	12, 13

24 Solve the previous problem but use the Kilbridge and Wester method in part (b).

25 Solve the previous problem but use the ranked positional weights method in part (b).

Logistics Operations

The term ***work flow*** refers to the physical movement of materials, parts, and products as they are being processed through a sequence of operations. Work flow is an important activity within the broader subject of ***logistics***, which is concerned with all of the activities involved in acquiring, transporting, storing, and delivering materials and products to customers. The purpose of this chapter is to provide an introduction to the subject of logistics and in particular the kinds of operations that are performed in logistics work. Logistics workers are one of the four basic categories of occupations identified. Logistics workers move things. They are the human components of a logistics system, and a logistics system is a work system.

This chapter is organized into four sections. The first provides a general overview of the subject of logistics. Sections 2 and 3 address two important categories of logistics operations: transportation and material handling. Transportation includes the operations of the trucking industry, railroads, and airlines. Material-handling operations include the movement and storage of materials that take place within a given facility such as a factory or warehouse. Section 4 presents a quantitative analysis of material-handling operations.

1 INTRODUCTION TO LOGISTICS

The subject of ***logistics*** has its origins in military science, where it is defined as the procurement, transportation, and maintenance of military supplies, equipment, and personnel. Armies must be supplied in order to successfully wage war. Today, logistics has a broader scope that includes the same basic supply functions applied to business and industry. Thus, ***business logistics*** is concerned with the acquisition, movement, storage, and distribution of materials and products, as well as the planning and control of these operations in order to satisfy customer demand. In an industrialized nation such as the United States, business logistics is one of the two basic components of the commercial infrastructure that is required to get products to markets; the other component is the collection of producers and suppliers of the products.

Logistics operations can be divided into two basic categories: external logistics and internal logistics. ***External logistics*** is concerned with ***transportation*** and related activities that occur outside of a facility. In general, these activities involve the movement of materials between different geographical locations (e.g., between cities or countries). The five traditional modes of transportation are rail, truck, air, ship, and pipeline. External logistics also includes the transportation of people (e.g, air travel). ***Internal logistics*** involves the handling of materials inside a given facility. The more popular term for internal logistics is ***material handling***, which can be defined as the movement and storage of materials during manufacturing and distribution.[1] As the definition indicates, the two most significant operational aspects of material handling are transport and storage. The transport function in material handling involves the movement of materials within a facility such as a manufacturing plant, whereas material storage consists of storing materials within a facility such as a warehouse. Internal logistics also includes the movement of people (e.g., moving patients in a hospital).

The vast majority of logistics workers are employed in transportation and material handling and the information processing services required to support these operations. Some of the occupations and job titles are identified in Table 1 for the three operational areas of transportation, material transport within a facility, and material storage.

1.1 Objectives in Logistics

The basic objectives in business logistics are to (1) provide a specified level of customer service and (2) deliver that level of service at the lowest possible cost. ***Customer service*** refers to the timely and accurate delivery of items ordered by customers. It includes

[1]The Material Handling Industry of America (MHIA), the trade association for material handling companies that do business in North America, defines material handling as "the movement, storage, protection and control of materials throughout the manufacturing and distribution process including their consumption and disposal."

TABLE 1 Occupations and Job Titles in the Three Categories of Logistics Operations

Transportation Operations	Material Transport Within a Facility	Material Storage
Airline pilot	Airport baggage handler	Crane operator in a mechanized storage/retrieval system
Air traffic controller	Conveyor operator	Inventory control manager
Bus driver	Crane operator	Order picker
Parcel service dispatcher	Forklift truck dispatcher	Shipping clerk
Railroad train conductor	Forklift truck operator	Tool crib stores clerk
Ship captain	Material handler	Wholesale stock clerk
Teamster (truck driver)	Stevedore	

being responsive to customers' needs with regard to the logistics service. Logistical customer service is defined by factors such as the following:

- *Accuracy.* Accuracy in logistics means delivering exactly what the customer ordered, in terms of the items specified and the quantities of those items.
- *Availability.* Availability in logistics means having items in inventory when the customer needs them. Better availability is usually achieved by increasing the inventory level in a store or warehouse. Higher inventory levels reduce the risk of stock-outs.
- *Orders shipped complete.* Related to availability, this measure indicates the proportion of orders in which every item in the customer order is included in the shipment to the customer, and there are no back-orders.
- *Speed of delivery.* This refers to the time between when the customer order is received and when the shipment arrives at the customer location. Fast-food restaurants specialize in speedy delivery.
- *Returns and error recovery.* Returns and error recovery are concerned with activities that occur after the delivery. How effectively and efficiently does a supplier deal with errors, such as missing or incorrect items in the order, or situations in which the customer wants to return the items?

In general, increased customer service is achieved only at higher cost. The objective in logistics is to provide a specified level of service at minimum cost. Thus, the logistics provider must establish a policy regarding the level of customer service to provide. Should the policy of a discount department store be to guarantee availability for every item, which means a very high inventory level? Or should a certain stock-out frequency be tolerated to achieve savings in inventory carrying costs.

Once the service level has been specified, the objective is to minimize the ***total logistics cost***, which includes capital costs and operating costs. Capital costs are investments in facilities, transportation equipment, material-handling equipment, and storage equipment. Operating costs consist of expenses such as labor, power and fuel for equipment, and warehouse rental. Capital costs are treated as fixed costs, while operating costs are considered to be variable costs.

1.2 The Logistics System

To achieve a specified level of service at minimum total cost, the logistics provider must integrate and coordinate the operations of the multiple components of the logistics system. The following system components are involved: [2]

- *Facilities.* The facilities component consists of the production plants and warehouses where the materials and products are produced and stored. Decisions about the locations and capacities of these facilities have an important effect on customer service and total logistics cost.
- *Inventory.* The inventory component is composed of the raw materials, work-in-process, and finished products in the logistics system. Thus, it includes all inventories located in the production plants and warehouses as well as inventory in transit (e.g., inventory on board a slow-moving river barge).
- *Transportation and material handling.* This component provides the means by which inventory is moved between and within facilities in the supply chain. It includes the equipment used for transporting, material handling, and storage of inventory.
- *Information system.* Information provides the means to integrate and coordinate other components. The information system refers to the collection and processing of data related to facilities, inventory, transportation, and other logistics activities such as order processing, order tracking, and procurement.
- *Logistics workers.* Logistics workers are the employees who operate and coordinate the other components of the logistics system. They make the system work.

There are trade-offs among the components of the logistics system. In the facilities component, the logistician must weigh the customer service value of a greater number of geographically dispersed warehouses against the greater cost of maintaining those warehouses and the inventory in them. A similar trade-off exists in the inventory component. More inventory means better customer service, but the investment in more inventory increases operating costs. In the transportation component, certain modes of transport are faster (e.g., air transport), thus providing greater speed of delivery, but they cost more. Other modes are slower (e.g., rail transport), thus reducing customer service, but they are less expensive. In the information systems component, investing in a computer program to monitor trends in customer demand may provide the information necessary to allow inventory levels and transportation costs to be reduced.

Supply Chains. The term supply chain is often associated with logistics. For our purposes, the terms *supply chain* and *logistics system* are synonymous. A ***supply chain*** is the set of activities that is concerned with the flow of materials and products from raw materials through production and distribution of finished goods to customers. It is called a "chain" because it consists of many links and connections that lie between the original supplier of the starting raw material and the product sold to the final consumer.

[2]The source for this list is [3], which lists four components: (1) facilities, (2) inventory, (3) transportation, and (4) information. We have taken liberties by combining material handling with transportation and by adding logistics workers to the list.

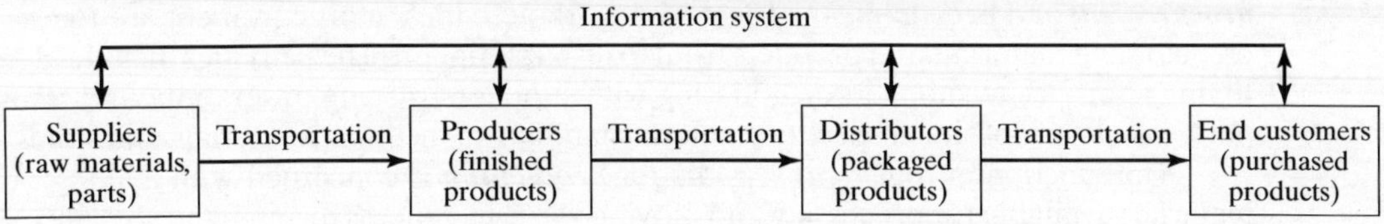

Figure 1 Block diagram of a supply chain.

A typical sequence is illustrated in Figure 1. The physical flow is from suppliers to producers to distributors to final customers. The transportation infrastructure and information system are the means by which the flow is accomplished, coordinated, and integrated. Each block might represent multiple supplier-customer transactions. Also, a given company might own more than one block. For example, Dell Computer produces and sends its products directly to customers (producer and distributor). General Motors makes parts, assembles cars, and distributes them to dealers (supplier, producer, and distributor). The planning, coordination, and administration of the flow of materials and products in the supply chain is called ***supply chain management***. By our reasoning, ***logistics management*** means the same thing.

Functional Areas and Associated Work Activities in Logistics. Logistics operations and the associated work activities can be divided into three functional areas [2]: (1) procurement, (2) logistical support for production, and (3) distribution. The relationships among these areas are portrayed in Figure 2. The work activities in the three functional areas include various combinations of physical labor and information processing. The physical labor correlates with the physical movement of materials, work-in-process, and finished products, while the information processing provides planning, coordination, and control of the physical movement.

The ***procurement*** function is concerned with the acquisition and movement of materials from suppliers to manufacturing plants that produce parts or assemble products. Procurement may include the temporary storage of materials in warehouses to conform to production schedules or to take advantage of quantity discounts from suppliers. Procurement also includes the acquisition and transportation of materials or products to retail or wholesale establishments. Various terms are used for the procurement function and the workers responsible for the function in different types of organizations. In manufacturing, the term ***purchasing*** is common, and the responsible company official is the ***purchasing agent***. In retail or wholesale operations, ***buying*** is the common term, and the company agent is called the ***buyer***. In government operations, the terms are

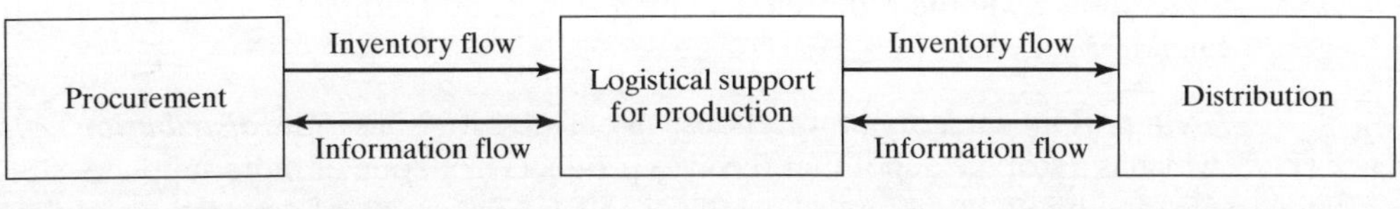

Figure 2 Three functional areas in logistics operations.

procurement and ***procurement officer***. The work activities in procurement are focused on obtaining materials and products from external suppliers. The activities include identifying appropriate suppliers, negotiating with suppliers, placing orders, inbound transportation, receiving and inspection, material handling of incoming materials, and storage.

The function of ***logistical support for production*** is concerned with making raw materials available for processing and moving work-in-process through the sequence of operations between and within production facilities. The key activities are transport and storage of work-in-process between operations. These activities include both external logistics (transportation between facilities) and internal logistics (material handling within facilities). Scheduling is a critical aspect of this logistical support function. The starting materials and/or work-in-process must be available when the production equipment is ready to begin processing. Accordingly, participation of logistical support personnel in developing the master production schedule is critical.

Physical distribution is concerned with moving finished goods to customers. The physical distribution system can be thought of as a channel that links suppliers, producers, wholesalers, and retailers with their respective final customers. Depending on its effectiveness, the distribution channel provides availability of products to customers. Work activities in physical distribution include order receipt and processing, planning of finished inventories, outbound transportation, material handling, and storage of finished goods.

1.3 Warehousing

A ***warehouse*** is a facility for storing materials, merchandise, and other items. Warehouses are widely used by companies to facilitate the three functions in logistics: storing raw materials in the procurement process, maintaining work-in-process for production support, and making finished goods available for distribution. Storage is only one of the activities that occur in a warehouse. The following four activities are involved in warehousing:

1. *Receive*. Receiving consists of the activities associated with handling and controlling incoming materials to the facility. It includes unloading the materials from the carrier vehicle (e.g., truck, rail car), inspecting and verifying the materials as to quantity and quality, and recording the receipt.
2. *Store*. The store function involves putting the received materials into storage and recording their respective locations.
3. *Pick*. The more complete term is ***order picking***, which refers to the retrieval of materials from their storage locations in response to customer orders.
4. *Ship*. The ship function includes packaging the materials for shipment to the customer, preparing the required documentation, and loading the materials into the carrier.

An important category of warehouse in business logistics is the ***distribution center*** (DC), which is a storage depot that receives products from one or more suppliers, stores the items for a limited time, and ships the products to a variety of destinations, typically wholesale or retail outlets. The operations of a DC are illustrated in Figure 3 for the case

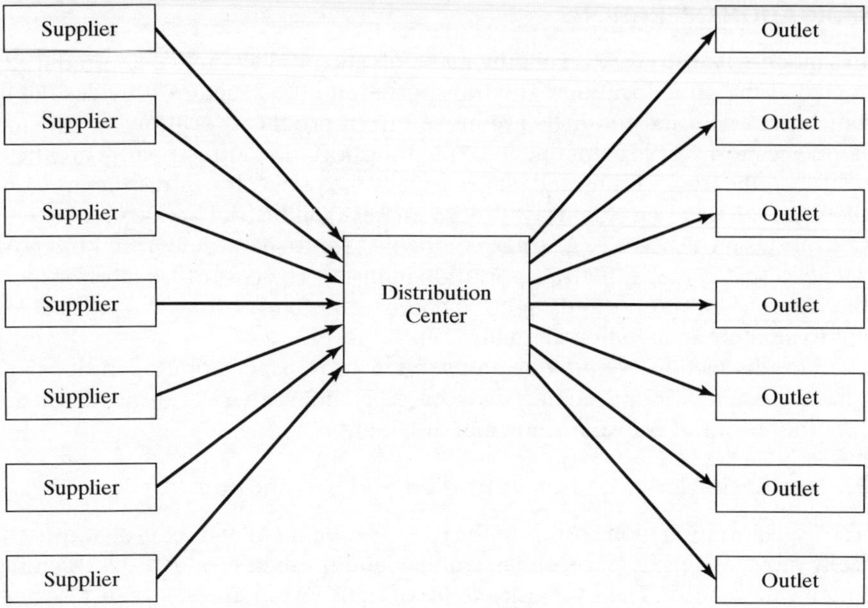

Figure 3 Typical operations of a distribution center.

when there are multiple suppliers and multiple outlets. A different combination of products is shipped to each outlet according to customer demand at that location.

Warehousing can be a very labor-intensive activity. Several improvements have been made over the past few decades to increase efficiency and save labor costs in warehouse operations. These improvements include the following:

- *Automated and mechanized storage systems.* These systems reduce labor costs and increase the rate of storing and order picking operations. The various types of storage systems are discussed in Section 3.2.
- *Cross-docking.* This is a warehousing operation in which shipments are received from suppliers, and the items are sorted and shipped to their respective destinations without being placed into storage. Cross-docking eliminates the store and pick steps in the preceding list of warehousing functions, thus saving the costs associated with those steps.
- *Warehouse management systems.* A warehouse management system (WMS) automates many of the day-to-day operations of a warehouse or distribution center. It maintains inventory records and the changes in inventory resulting from incoming and outgoing shipments. Other functions include managing transportation operations (e.g., selection of carriers), optimizing storage locations for various categories of stock (e.g., placement of high sales volume items close to loading and shipping docks to minimize storing and picking times), and reporting labor performance.

2 TRANSPORTATION OPERATIONS

In a modern industrialized economy, materials and products are rarely produced and consumed at the same locations. The transportation infrastructure provides the means by which materials and products are moved from producer locations to consumer locations. The most visible components of the transportation infrastructure are the transport vehicles—the trucks, trains, and planes seen by the public. The infrastructure also includes the rights-of-way (e.g., highways, tracks, airways), industrial organizations that provide transportation services (e.g., truck companies, railroads, airlines), and the government agencies that oversee the transportation industry. The cost of freight transportation in the United States represents approximately 6% of gross domestic product [3]. That is approximately $500 billion annually [12].

In this section, we provide an overview of transportation operations in logistics. The discussion is organized into two topics: (1) the five basic transportation modes and (2) other forms of transportation and distribution.

2.1 Five Basic Modes of Transportation and Distribution

The transportation mode refers to the type of equipment and right-of-way used to physically move materials, parts, subassemblies, and finished products over significant geographical distances. The five basic modes of transportation are (1) rail, (2) truck, (3) air, (4) waterway, and (5) pipeline. The relative importance of the five modes in the U.S. economy is illustrated in Table 2.

The company that provides the transportation service is called a ***carrier***. Some of the carrier companies usually associated with each transportation mode are identified in Table 3. The company (or other organization) that engages the services of a carrier to transport materials is called the ***shipper***. And the recipient of the shipped materials is called the ***consignee***. The three parties may be separate business entities. Business integrations are also common; for example, Wal-Mart operates its own truck fleet to deliver merchandise between its distribution centers and retail stores.

Rail Transport. The main economic advantage of rail transportation is its capability to efficiently move large tonnage over long mileage. The disadvantage is that rail is a relatively slow freight mover. Prime applications of rail transport are commodities such as raw materials located away from waterways (e.g., coal, ore, lumber), agricultural products, and low-value manufactured goods (e.g., paper, wood products). Railway freight

TABLE 2 The Five Basic Transportation Modes

Mode	Intercity Tonnage (millions of tons)	Intercity Ton-Miles (billions of ton-miles)	Freight Expense (billions of $)	Revenue per Ton-Mile (cents per ton-mile)
Rail	1972	1421	35	2.4
Truck	3745	1051	402	9.1 (TL), 26.1 (LTL)[a]
Air	16	14	23	56.3
Waterway	1005	473	25	0.7
Pipeline	1142	628 (oil)	9	1.4

Source: [3].

[a]TL means a full truckload was delivered; LTL means less than a full truckload was delivered.

TABLE 3 Companies and Applications of Each of the Five Basic Transportation Modes

Mode	Companies
Rail	Burlington Northern Santa Fe, CSX, Norfolk Southern, Union Pacific
Truck	CNF, Ryder System, J. B. Hunt Transport Services, Yellow Roadway
Air	American Air Lines, Northwest Air Lines, Southwest Air Lines, United Parcel Service (UPS)
Waterway	American President Lines, Evergreen Group, Maersk Sealand
Pipeline[a]	Kinder Morgan Energy, Plains All American Pipeline, Trans-Alaska Pipeline, Western Gas Resources

[a]In addition, oil companies own significant pipelines in addition to the pipeline companies identified in the table.

also includes intermodal operations, in which truck trailers and containers are moved over long distances by rail and then delivered locally by motor tractor. Today, intermodal operations account for more than half of total rail traffic in the United States.

Certain inefficiencies are inherent in rail operations, such as the idle time of freight cars in rail yards, terminal time for loading and unloading freight cars, and delays of trains due to track congestion. Changes in work rules have reduced some of the costly labor inefficiencies that have plagued the railroad industry during its long history. For example, when diesel-powered locomotives were replacing steam locomotives during the 1950s, the railway unions resisted the elimination of firemen in the engine cab. The job of the firemen was to shovel coal from the tender into the locomotive's steam boiler. This job had no purpose in a diesel locomotive, and yet the unions insisted that the position be retained. New labor agreements have reduced or eliminated these kinds of wasteful workforce requirements to contain the variable operating costs of rail transportation. Other efficiency improvements in rail operations include the following:

- Consolidation of a large number of independent railroad companies into the four major companies listed in Table 3
- Abandoning railway lines that are unprofitable
- Unit trains, which are trains that transport a single bulk commodity such as coal or grain and travel directly from source to destination without being built up or broken down in rail yards
- Double-stack railcars, which are designed to carry two levels of containers for intermodal operations
- Trilevel automobile cars, which are oversized freight cars capable of carrying large numbers of automobiles and light trucks.

Although the railroads are not a growth industry today, they have managed to retain their share of the transportation market by reducing costs through improvements and innovations such as those listed above.

Trucking Operations. Truck transportation has expanded significantly since World War II in the United States, largely at the expense of rail transport. Deregulation of the trucking industry by the passage of the Motor-Carrier Act of 1980 has helped to encourage competition and improve efficiencies in trucking operations. As indicated in Table 2, intercity tonnage movement by truck is far higher than by any other transportation mode. Ton-mileage is less than by rail because the average distances are less by truck. Motor-carrier service is suited to high-value finished products and semifinished items (e.g., parts and subassemblies) that are transported over short or medium distances (e.g., several hundred miles). Important examples are the movement of merchandise between distribution centers and retail stores, and the delivery of components and subassemblies to final assembly plants in the automotive industry. In these applications, truck transportation has the following advantages over railroads: (1) door-to-door delivery, (2) service availability and frequency, and (3) speed of delivery.

Trucking operations can be divided into two major industry segments: truckload and less-than-truckload. The ***truckload*** (TL) category refers to the transportation of loads over 15,000 lb. In general, these truckloads move directly from the shipper to the destination without intermediate stops for load consolidation. In effect, the shipper pays for the entire truck rig (tractor and trailer), regardless of the amount shipped, and the transportation charge is based on distance moved. It is to the shipper's advantage to fill the truck to its capacity if possible. The ***less-than-truckload*** (LTL) segment consists of loads that are less than 15,000 lb, and stops are usually made along the way. Intermediate stops are necessary in LTL operations to pick up and drop off other loads and for combining loads at consolidation terminals. Because of these stops, delivery times are usually longer for LTL than for TL deliveries. LTL rates are generally much higher per ton-mile than for TL because of the additional consolidation and administrative expenses involved in LTL deliveries. However, the pricing is designed so that if a shipper deals in smaller load sizes, it is cheaper to use an LTL carrier than to pay the TL rate for an entire rig.

The improvements in trucking operations that have taken place in recent years include the following:

- More efficient scheduling of truck movements (e.g., carrying loads both ways rather than making a delivery and then returning empty)
- Optimized routing of trucks in LTL operations
- Mechanized handling equipment at consolidation terminals in place of human labor
- Tandem trailers, in which one tractor pulls two or three trailers
- Intermodal operations, which involve transportation of trailers by a combination of truck and rail.

The motor-carrier industry has established itself as a leading freight transportation service because of its advantages of availability, flexibility, and short delivery times over short and medium distances.

Air Transport. Although passengers are the most visible customers in air travel, the major airlines also provide freight service. In addition, parcel delivery companies such as UPS and FedEx specialize in the movement and handling of packages, including large containerized loads (e.g., 500 lb). Air transport is suited to the delivery of high-value items that need to be shipped long distances and time is an important factor. The significant advantage of air transport in these types of applications is speed of delivery. The disadvantage is that airfreight rates are much higher per ton-mile than any other transport mode. In addition, it should be noted that door-to-door delivery time in air transport consists not only of the actual air travel time between airports but also the local delivery times between (1) the shipper and the airport and (2) the airport and the consignee. Air passengers experience similar time delays at the beginning and end of a flight. When these local delivery times are taken into account, air transport often loses its speed advantage to motor carrier when distances are less than about 500 miles.

The control of air transport operating costs focuses on the efficient and effective use of resources—specifically, equipment, labor, and fuel. Airlines strive to keep their planes in the air as much of the time as possible and to fully utilize the space onboard. The success of these attempts is subject to the vagaries of market competition. On the one hand, there are many airlines available in most markets, and air passengers are always trying to find the minimum airfare. On the other hand, the cost of fuel rises and falls due to the forces of supply and demand, and the airlines need fuel at whatever the price to operate their planes. Operational approaches used by the airlines in the face of these challenges include the following:

- Strategic planning of routes and schedules (in light of what the competitors are doing or are expected to do)
- Optimizing the assignment of planes in the fleet (e.g., most airlines have planes of various capacities) to different routes
- Optimizing the number and locations of hubs
- Scheduling of crews to achieve adequate coverage while minimizing excess labor costs (e.g., overtime)
- Optimizing aircraft maintenance schedules

The primary business of most airlines is passenger service. Their freight transport operations might be considered a niche market. Air transport accounts for only about 1% of total ton-mileage.

Water Transport. The use of waterways for transportation dates from ancient times. It is the dominant mode of freight transportation in global trade and is used for all varieties of materials and products. Many of the products are moved in containers using container ships. Within a given country, water transport is obviously limited by rights-of-way that are defined by the waterways. In the United States, these include the major rivers and canals, the Great Lakes, and the coastal waters (e.g., Atlantic and Pacific Oceans, Gulf of Mexico). Types of vessels include flat barges towed by tugboats (for rivers and canals) and deep-water ships (for coastal waters and the Great Lakes). For domestic transport, the waterways are used for very large shipments and when time is not a factor. Applications include basic bulk commodities such as coal, ore, cement, and certain agricultural products. Water transport is the slowest and lowest cost of the five transportation modes.[3] The origination and destination points of deliveries must be at terminal facilities that are located along the waterways; otherwise, supplemental transport is necessary by rail or truck.

Some of the technologies that have improved water transportation include containerized cargo, mechanized equipment to speed loading and unloading in ports, satellite

[3]In some applications, pipeline transport is slower than water transport.

navigation (of primary importance in oceangoing vessels), autopilot technology, sonar and radar, and improvements in ice-breaking equipment (for vessels operating during the winter in northern regions).

Pipelines. Applications of pipelines are limited to the transport of gases, liquids, and slurries in large volumes. Hence, materials suited to pipeline transport include natural gas, water, crude petroleum and petroleum products, and sewage. There are over 200,000 miles of pipeline operating in the domestic United States. Movement of material through pipelines is slow, in some cases slower than water transport. For example, the flow velocity of petroleum in the 800 mile-long Trans-Alaska Pipeline is about 4 miles per hour. Yet the flow rate is approximately one million barrels per day (2001 average) through the 48-inch diameter tube. The material moves 24 hours per day and is not affected by weather conditions that might plague the four other transportation modes. Pipeline delivery is therefore very dependable. In addition, there are no empty containers or vessels that need to be returned for reuse as in the other modes.[4]

2.2 Other Forms of Transportation and Distribution

In addition to the five basic transportation modes, other means of transport are available to deliver and distribute materials and products. These additional means include combinations of the five basic modes, several specialized services, and the Internet.

Intermodal Operations. Intermodal operations involve the use of more than one transportation mode to move materials and products between suppliers and customers. The use of intermodal services has grown substantially in recent decades, driven by increases in global trade and facilitated by the convenience of containers for freight movement. Common forms of intermodal transportation include the following:

- *Rail and truck.* Also known as ***piggyback***, this is the most widely used intermodal combination. The two basic types are highway truck trailer on flatcar (TOFC) and container on flatcar (COFC). Together they constitute more than half of all railcar loadings in the United States. Most containers are standardized at 8 ft by 8 ft in cross section by either 20 ft or 40 ft in length. Truck trailers have a similar cross section but can be up to 53 ft in length.
- *Containership.* Much international trade is accomplished today using oceangoing vessels equipped to transport containers. This mode is highly suited to products of medium and high value. Loading and unloading of the containers at ports is performed using large cranes that transfer the entire box from ship to shore. This compares to the former means of handling each crate or pallet load separately at much greater expense in time and labor.
- *Truck and ship.* Also identified by the term ***fishyback***, this combination is similar to containerships, except that truck trailers are hauled instead of containers.
- *Train ship.* This combination involves the transport of railcars by ship or barge.

[4]Good scheduling can reduce the number of carriers, cars, or vessels returned empty in these other modes, but in pipeline operations, return of empty containers is not an issue. There are no containers in pipeline operations.

Freight charges for intermodal transportation are usually between those of the modes that are involved. For example, rail and truck intermodal freight costs less than truck but more than rail, but it provides door-to-door service that cannot usually be provided by rail alone over distances that are generally too long for truck alone.

Parcel Delivery Services. Companies such as United Parcel Service (UPS), FedEx, and the U.S. Postal Service (USPS) are examples of parcel delivery services. Their transport services are unique in that they deliver small packages (ranging up to about 150 lb), rather than much larger shipment sizes for each customer. For this service they charge a premium price. These companies can also provide fast transport (e.g., overnight delivery) for an even higher price if the customer desires. As commerce over the Internet has increased, demand for parcel delivery services has grown in parallel, driven by companies such as Dell Computer and Amazon.com that ship their products directly to individual customers.

The operations of the parcel delivery companies are basically intermodal, because they employ combinations of air, truck, and rail transportation. To pick up and drop off packages, local delivery trucks are used (e.g., the familiar brown UPS truck). For long haul transport, rail is used for packages that do not require timely delivery, and air transport is used for shipments that are time-sensitive. For intermediate distances, highway tractor-trailer transport is used. Because of the tremendous number of combinations of origination and destination points in parcel delivery operations, the companies must ship packages through sortation centers. The sortation hubs, as they are sometimes called, perform two basic functions: (1) incoming items are consolidated for transport to common destinations and (2) incoming consolidated shipments are broken down for local delivery of individual packages.

Transportation Agencies. Several types of agencies provide specialized transportation services by being intermediaries between shippers and carrier companies. Their services are analogous to those of wholesalers in the distribution of physical products between suppliers and retail outlets. The transportation agencies purchase transportation services from common carriers at high-volume, low-cost rates and then sell the services to small-lot shippers at prices that are less than what the same carriers would charge those shippers. In order to obtain the favorable transportation rates from carriers, the agencies consolidate the small lots into large shipment sizes (e.g., full truckloads). The agencies' profits are made on the difference between the rates they pay the common carriers and the rates they collect from the shippers for small shipment sizes. In general, the agencies do not own any transportation equipment, except perhaps for local delivery trucks if they provide a local pick-up and/or delivery service.

Included in this category of transportation agencies are ***freight forwarders***, which are companies that consolidate the small shipments of multiple customers into a large shipment and then transport it by common carrier (e.g., rail, truck, air). Upon arrival at the destination, the large load is then separated into the original small shipments for delivery to the final customer.

Internet and Similar Communication-Based Distribution Modes. All of the preceding transportation methods are concerned with the movement and distribution of physical products. However, of increasing importance in the global economy and information age is the distribution of products and services that are exclusively informational and possess no physical form. Entertainment products are a good example. Radio and television shows have an information content that provides enjoyment and/or education. Their electronic distribution is to mass audiences, so that everyone receives the same show on the same station or channel, and the cost of producing and distributing the show is born by advertisers. In addition to these mass markets, informational products and services are also sent to individual customers over new electronic distribution channels such as the Internet. Unlike radio and TV, individual customers purchase the product (or service) and payment is directly between buyer and seller. The transaction is often accomplished entirely over the Internet or other communication-based medium. The product is transmitted electronically, usually in digitized form, and the customer's credit card account is debited in a similar manner. Examples of this form of product and service distribution include the following:

- *Airline tickets.* Electronic ticketing of passengers has become common. Instead of issuing a paper ticket and mailing it to the customer, the passenger's flight information is logged into the airline's database. Even the boarding pass can be transmitted to the customer through the Internet for printing.
- *Digital distribution of music.* Apple iTunes are delivered to customers on demand for a price per recording.
- *Satellite radio.* Satellite radio is based on the premise that listeners are willing to pay a monthly fee for good programming and no commercial interruptions. The two leading companies at time of writing are XM and Sirius.
- *Video-on-demand.* Pay-for-TV has been around a long time, but new features include pause, rewind, fast-forward, and other conveniences traditionally available only on a videocassette or DVD player.
- *High-speed Internet access.* A monthly fee buys the customer unlimited access to all of the information contained on the Internet.

The use of the Internet and other communication-based systems for the distribution of information and entertainment products is expected to grow in the future.

3 MATERIAL HANDLING

Whereas transportation operations occur between facilities that are geographically separated (external logistics), material handling occurs inside of a facility (internal logistics). The handling of materials must be performed safely, efficiently, at low cost, in a timely manner, accurately (the right materials in the right quantities to the right locations), and without damage to the materials. Material handling is an important yet often overlooked issue in industry. According to a survey reported in [14],[5] material handling

[5]The results of the survey were published in E. H. Frazelle, "Material Handling: A Technology for Industrial Competitiveness," *Material Handling Research Center Technical Report*, Georgia Institute of Technology, Atlanta, April 1986.

accounts for 25% of the employees, 55% of factory space, and 87% of production time in a typical industrial facility. These proportions vary, depending on type of production and degree of automation in the material-handling function.

Many material-handling tasks are accomplished manually, with workers moving boxes, containers, and other items without the aid of equipment. However, a great variety of material-handling equipment is commercially available to reduce the physical labor and associated safety risks to the workers. Material-handling equipment can be classified into four major categories:

- *Material transport equipment* that is used to move materials inside a factory, warehouse, or other facility. The category includes industrial trucks, automated guided vehicles, monorails and other rail-guided vehicles, conveyors, cranes, and hoists.
- *Storage systems* that are used to temporarily store raw materials, work-in-process, final products, and other items in factories and warehouses. Storage systems include traditional storage equipment, such as racks and shelves, and automated equipment, such as automated storage/retrieval systems.
- *Unitizing equipment* that includes the pallets and containers used to hold materials, as well as equipment for loading and unloading the pallets and containers.
- *Identification and tracking systems* that use bar codes and other technologies to identify materials and keep track of their locations and movements.

3.1 Material Transport Equipment

Material transport equipment can be divided into the following five categories, illustrated in Figure 4: (1) industrial trucks, (2) automated guided vehicles, (3) monorails and other rail-guided vehicles, (4) conveyors, and (5) cranes and hoists. In Section 4, we consider quantitative techniques by which material transport systems composed of this equipment can be analyzed.

Industrial Trucks. Industrial trucks are classified as nonpowered and powered. The nonpowered types are often referred to as hand trucks because human workers push or pull them by hand. The amounts and quantities of materials that can be moved and the distances involved are relatively low when this type of equipment is used.

Powered trucks are self-propelled vehicles capable of transporting larger loads over greater distances than hand trucks. They are steered by a human driver. There are three common types of powered trucks used in factories and warehouses, illustrated in Figure 5:

- *Walkie trucks*, Figure 5 (a), are battery-powered vehicles equipped with wheeled forks to insert into pallet openings but with no provision for a worker to ride on the vehicle. A worker steers the truck using a control handle at the front of the vehicle. The speed of a walkie truck is limited to the normal walking speed of an average human worker.
- *Forklift trucks*, Figure 5 (b), include a cab for the worker to sit or stand in and drive the vehicle. The various types of forklift truck applications has resulted in a variety of vehicle configurations and features. These include trucks with high reach

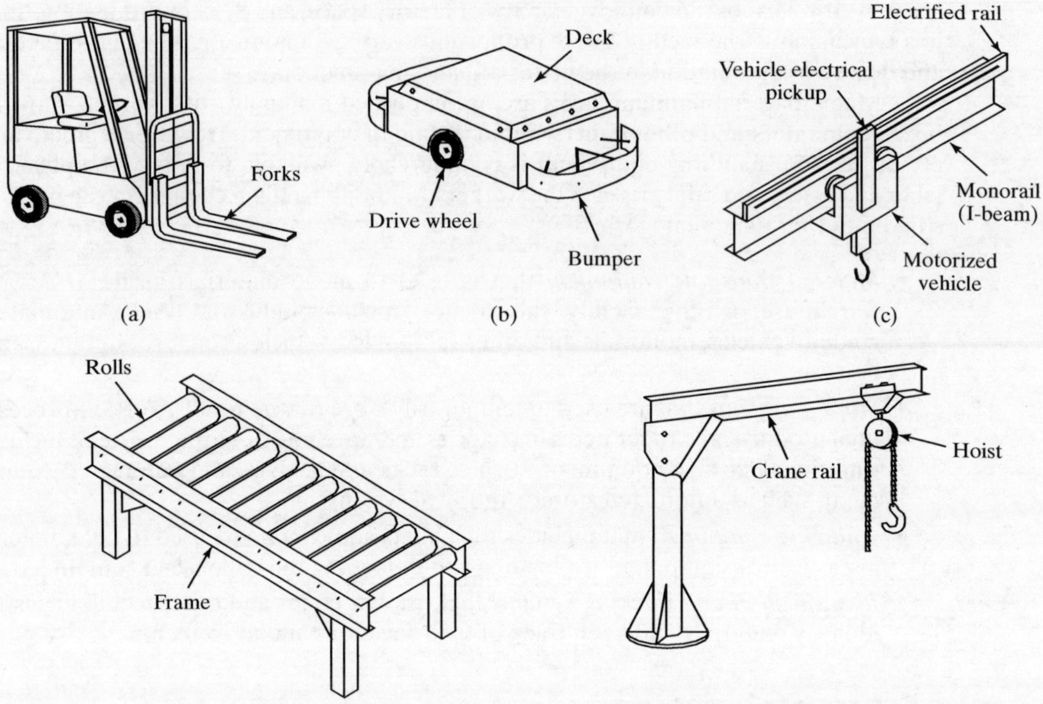

Figure 4 Examples of the five basic types of material-handling equipment: (a) forklift truck, an industrial truck, (b) unit load automated guided vehicle, (c) monorail, (d) roller conveyor, and (e) a jib crane with hoist.

capacities for accessing pallet loads on high rack systems and trucks capable of operating in narrow aisles of high-density storage racks.

- *Towing tractors*, Figure 5 (c), are designed to pull one or more trailing carts on the relatively smooth floor surfaces in factories and warehouses. They are generally used for moving large amounts of materials over long distances. Tow tractors also find significant applications in air transport operations for moving baggage and airfreight in airports.

Forklift trucks are widely used in industry, owing to the very common use of pallets and similar unit load containers for moving and storing materials. Except for materials that are moved in bulk form (e.g., coal, sand, many chemicals, lumber), most materials are shipped and stored in pallet loads. The forks of the forklift truck can be adjusted (in width) to accommodate the variety of pallet sizes used commercially.

Automated Guided Vehicle Systems. Automated guided vehicles are basically industrial trucks capable of operating without human drivers. An ***automated guided vehicle system*** (AGVS) is a material-handling system that uses independently operated,

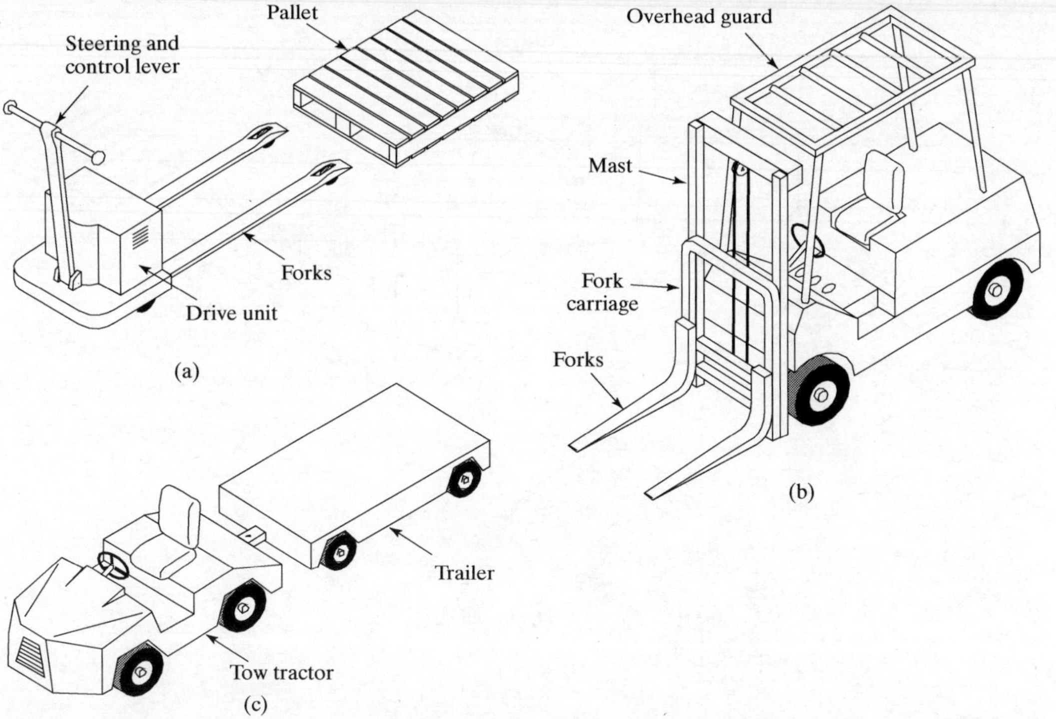

Figure 5 Three principal types of powered trucks: (a) walkie truck, (b) forklift truck, and (c) towing tractor.

self-propelled vehicles guided along defined pathways on the facility floor. The vehicles are powered by onboard batteries that allow many hours of operation (8 to 16 hours is typical) between recharging. A distinguishing feature of an AGVS, compared to rail-guided vehicle systems and most conveyor systems, is that the pathways are unobtrusive. The traditional AGV guidance system is based on guide wires buried in the floor that emit a magnetic signal and can be tracked by the vehicle. More modern technologies include laser guidance and global navigation. There are three common types of automated guided vehicles, illustrated in Figure 6:

- *Driverless trains* consist of a towing vehicle (the AGV) that pulls one or more trailer carts to form a train. A common application is moving heavy payloads over large distances in warehouses or factories.
- *Pallet trucks* are used to move palletized loads along predetermined routes in factories, warehouses, and distribution centers. In the typical application, the vehicle is backed into the loaded pallet by a human worker who steers the truck and uses its forks to elevate the load slightly. Then the worker drives the pallet truck to the guide path, programs its destination, and the vehicle proceeds automatically to the destination for unloading.

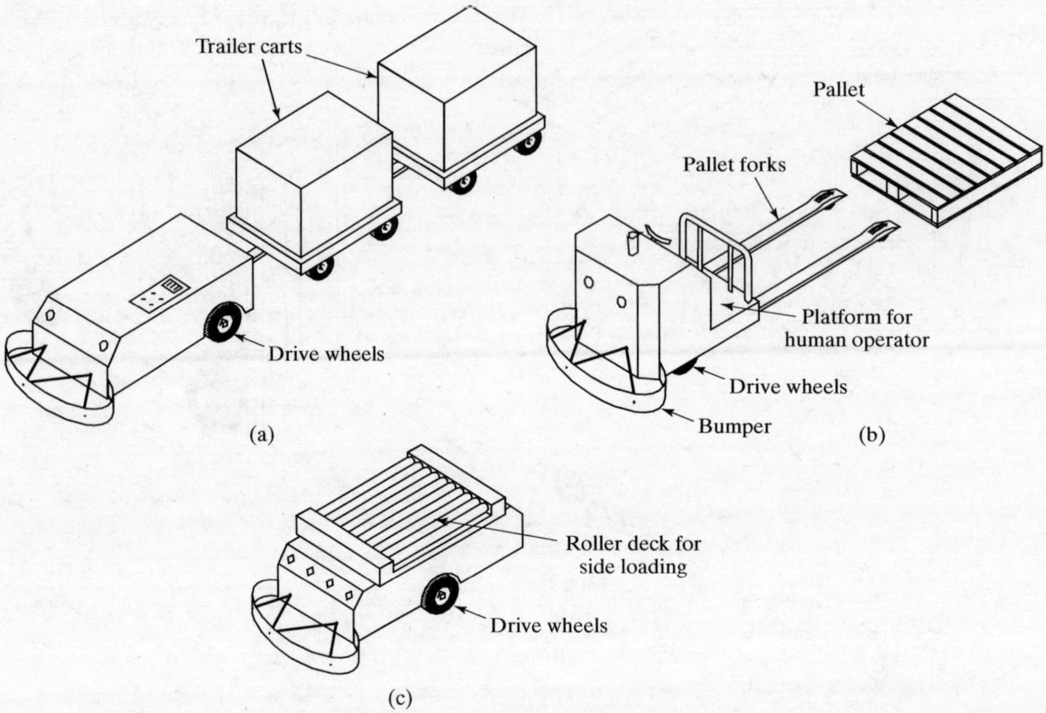

Figure 6 Three types of automated guided vehicles: (a) driverless train, (b) pallet truck, and (c) unit load AGV.

- *Unit load AGVs* are used to move unit loads from one station to another in factories, warehouses, and distribution centers. They are often equipped for automatic loading and unloading of pallets or tote pans by means of powered rollers, moving belts, mechanized lift platforms, or other devices built into the vehicle deck.

Other applications of automated guided vehicle systems include *office mail delivery* and *hospital material transport*. Hospital guided vehicles transport meal trays, linen, medical and laboratory supplies, and other materials between various departments in the building. These transports typically require movement of vehicles between different floors in the hospital, and hospital AGV systems have the capability to summon and use elevators for this purpose.

Monorails and Other Rail-Guided Vehicles. The third category of material transport equipment consists of motorized vehicles that are guided by a fixed rail system. The rail system consists of either one rail (called a ***monorail***) or two parallel rails (similar to railway tracks). Monorails in factories and warehouses are typically suspended overhead from the ceiling. In rail-guided vehicle systems using parallel fixed rails, the tracks generally protrude up from the floor. In either case, the presence of a fixed-rail pathway distinguishes these systems from automated guided vehicle systems. As with AGVs, the vehicles operate asynchronously and are driven by an onboard electric motor. But unlike AGVs, which are powered by their own onboard batteries, rail-guided vehicles pick up electrical power from an electrified rail (similar to an urban rapid transit rail system). This relieves the vehicle from periodic recharging of its battery; however, the electrified rail system introduces a safety hazard not present in an AGVS.

Routing variations are possible in rail-guided vehicle systems through the use of switches, turntables, and other special track sections. This permits different loads to travel different routes, similar to an AGVS. Rail-guided systems are generally considered to be more versatile than conveyor systems but less versatile than automated guided vehicle systems.

Conveyor Systems. Conveyors are used when materials must be moved in relatively large amounts or quantities between specific locations over a fixed path. The fixed path is implemented by a track system that may be in-the-floor, above-the-floor, or overhead. Conveyors divide into two basic categories: (1) powered and (2) nonpowered. In ***powered conveyors,*** the power mechanism for transporting materials is contained in the fixed path, using chains, belts, rotating rolls, or other mechanical devices to propel loads along the path. Basically, the pathway moves. Powered conveyors are commonly used in automated material transport systems in manufacturing plants, warehouses, and distribution centers. In ***nonpowered conveyors***, materials are moved either manually by human workers who push the loads along the fixed path or by gravity from a higher elevation to a lower elevation.

A variety of conveyor equipment is commercially available. Some of the common types of conveyors are illustrated in Figure 7.

- *Roller conveyors* have rolls on which the loads ride. The pathway consists of a series of rollers that are perpendicular to the direction of travel. Flat pallets or tote pans carrying unit loads are moved forward by the rotating rollers. Roller conveyors can either be powered or nonpowered.
- *Skate-wheel conveyors* are similar in operation to roller conveyors. Instead of rollers, they use skate wheels rotating on shafts connected to a frame to roll pallets or tote pans or other flat-bottom containers along the pathway.
- *Belt conveyors* consist of a continuous loop so that half its length is used for delivering materials, and the other half is the return run. At one end of the loop is a drive roll that powers the belt.
- *In-floor towline conveyors* use four-wheel carts powered by moving chains or cables located in trenches in the floor. The chain or cable is called a towline. Pathways for the conveyor system are defined by the trench and cable, and the cable is driven as a powered pulley system. Steel pins or gripper mechanisms are used to engage and disengage the carts from the moving chain or cable.
- *Overhead trolley conveyor*, consists of multiple trolleys, usually equally spaced along a fixed overhead track. A ***trolley*** is a wheeled carriage from which loads can be suspended. The trolleys are connected together and moved along the track by means of a chain or cable that forms a complete loop. Suspended from the trolleys are hooks, baskets, or other containers to carry loads.

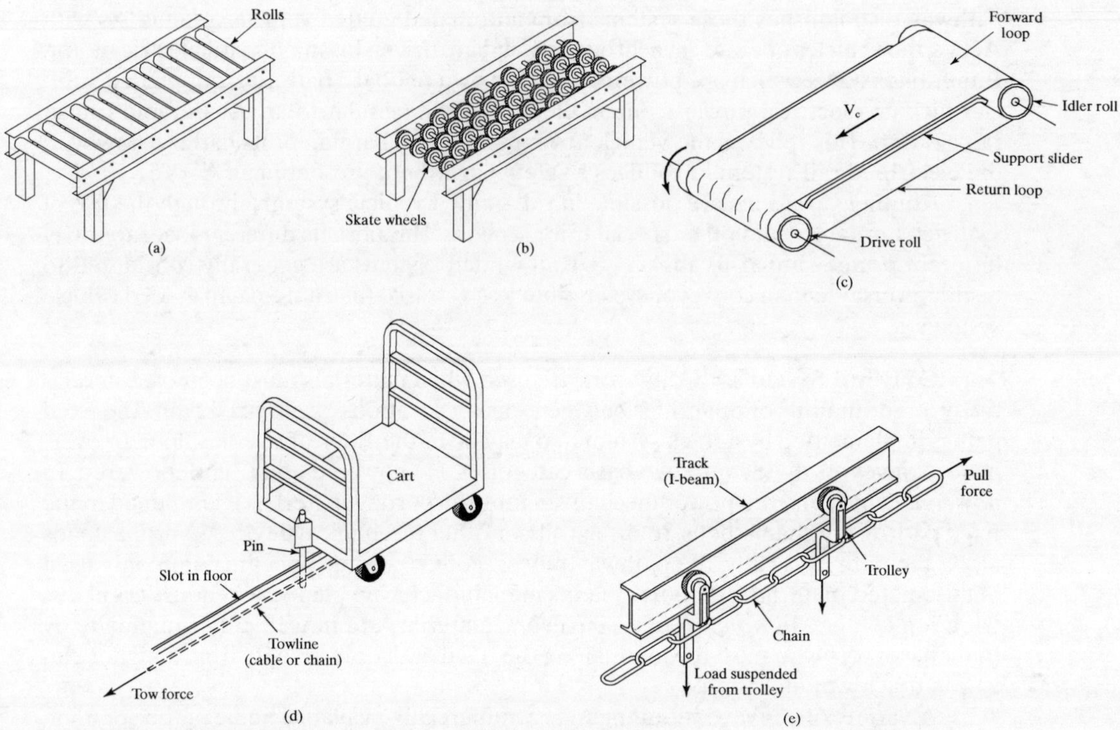

Figure 7 Conveyor types: (a) roller conveyor, (b) skate wheel conveyor, (c) belt conveyor, (d) in-floor towline conveyor, and (e) overhead trolley conveyor.

Cranes and Hoists. Cranes are used for horizontal movement of materials in a facility, and hoists are used for vertical lifting. A crane invariably includes a hoist; thus the hoist component of the crane lifts the load and the crane transports the load horizontally to the desired destination. This class of material-handling equipment includes cranes capable of lifting and moving very heavy loads, in some cases over 100 tons.

A ***hoist*** consists of one or more fixed pulleys, one or more moving pulleys, and a rope, cable, or chain strung between the pulleys. A hook or other means for attaching the load is connected to the moving pulley(s). The number of pulleys in the hoist determines its mechanical advantage, which is the ratio of the load weight to the force required to lift the weight. The force to operate the hoist is applied either manually or by electric or pneumatic motor.

Cranes include a variety of material-handling equipment designed for moving heavy loads using one or more overhead beams for support. One or more hoists are mounted to a trolley that rides on the overhead beam. The following are three types of cranes used in production and warehousing operations:

- *Bridge cranes* consist of one or two horizontal girders or beams suspended between fixed rails on either end that are connected to the structure of the building, as shown in Figure 8 (a). The hoist trolley can be moved along the length of the

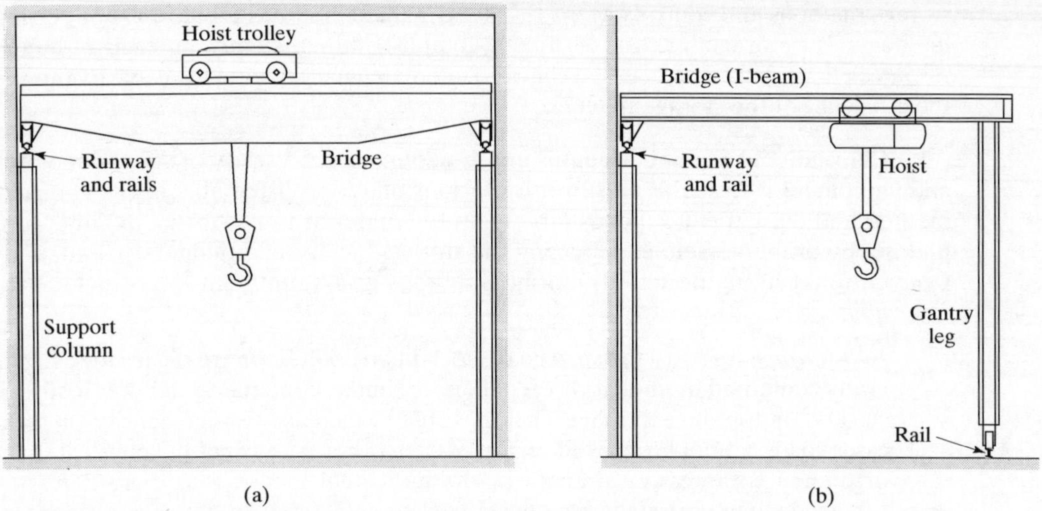

Figure 8 Two types of cranes: (a) bridge crane and (b) half gantry crane.

bridge, and the bridge can be moved the length of the rails in the building to provide horizontal motion (x- and y-axes of the building), and the hoist provides vertical motion (z-axis). Applications include heavy machinery fabrication, steel and other metal mills, and power generating stations.

- *Gantry cranes* are distinguished from bridge cranes by the presence of one or two vertical legs that support the horizontal bridge. A ***double gantry crane*** has two legs. A ***half gantry crane***, Figure 8 (b), has a single leg on one end of the bridge, and the other end is supported by a rail mounted on the wall or other structural member of a building.
- *Jib cranes* consist of a hoist supported on a horizontal beam that is cantilevered from a vertical column or wall support, as illustrated earlier in Figure 4 (e). The horizontal beam is pivoted about the vertical axis to provide a horizontal sweep for the crane. The beam also serves as the track for the hoist trolley to provide radial travel along the beam. Thus, the horizontal area included by a jib crane is circular or semicircular.

3.2 Storage Systems

The function of a material storage system is to store materials for a period of time and to permit retrieval of those materials when required. Storage systems are used in warehouses, distribution centers, wholesale dealerships, retail stores, and factories. They are important components in the logistics system that moves materials and products from suppliers to customers. Although it is generally desirable to reduce the storage of materials, it seems nevertheless unavoidable that most commercial items spend at least some time in storage. These items include raw materials, purchased parts, work-in-process, finished products, tooling, spare parts, and refuse. In offices, stored materials include paper, office supplies, records, and files. The different categories of materials require different storage methods and controls. Many firms use manual methods for storing and retrieving items. The storage function is often accomplished inefficiently, in terms of human resources, floor space, and material control. Automated methods are available to improve the efficiency of the storage function.

Conventional Storage Methods and Equipment. A variety of storage methods and equipment is available to store the various materials listed above. The choice of method and equipment depends largely on the material to be stored, the operating philosophy of the personnel managing the storage facility, and budgetary limitations. Conventional (nonautomated) storage methods and equipment types include the following:

- *Bulk storage* refers to the storage of stock in an open floor area. The stock is generally contained in unit loads on pallets or similar containers, and unit loads are stacked on top of each other when possible to increase storage density (in some cases, loads cannot be stacked on top of each other because of the physical shape or limited compressive strength of the individual loads). Maximum density is achieved when unit loads are placed next to each other in both floor directions throughout the storage area. However, this provides very poor access to internal loads for retrieval. To increase accessibility, unit loads can be organized into rows and blocks to create natural aisles. The block widths can be planned to provide an appropriate balance between density and accessibility. Although bulk storage requires no specific storage equipment, material transport vehicles must be used to put unit loads into storage and to retrieve them. Forklift trucks are typically used for this purpose.
- *Rack systems* provide a means of stacking loads vertically without the need for the loads themselves to provide support. Rack systems are widely used in warehouses and distribution centers. One of the most common rack systems is the ***pallet rack***, consisting of a frame that includes horizontal load-supporting beams, as shown in Figure 9. Pallet loads are stored on these horizontal beams.
- *Shelving* represents one of the most common storage equipment types. A ***shelf*** is a horizontal platform, supported by a wall or frame, upon which materials are stored. Steel shelving sections are manufactured in standard sizes, to permit the user to customize the storage facility.
- *Drawer storage* is used to alleviate the problem of finding items in shelving that is either far above or below eye level for the storage attendant. Each drawer in such a unit pulls out to allow its entire contents to be readily seen. Modular drawer storage cabinets are available with a variety of drawer depths for different item sizes and are widely used for storage of small tools, parts, and maintenance items. File cabinets are another form of drawer storage widely used in offices.

Automated Storage Systems. The conventional storage equipment described above requires a human worker to access the items in storage. Mechanized and automated storage systems are available to reduce or eliminate the human resources required to operate the system. The level of automation varies. In less automated systems, a human operator participates in each storage/retrieval transaction. In highly automated systems,

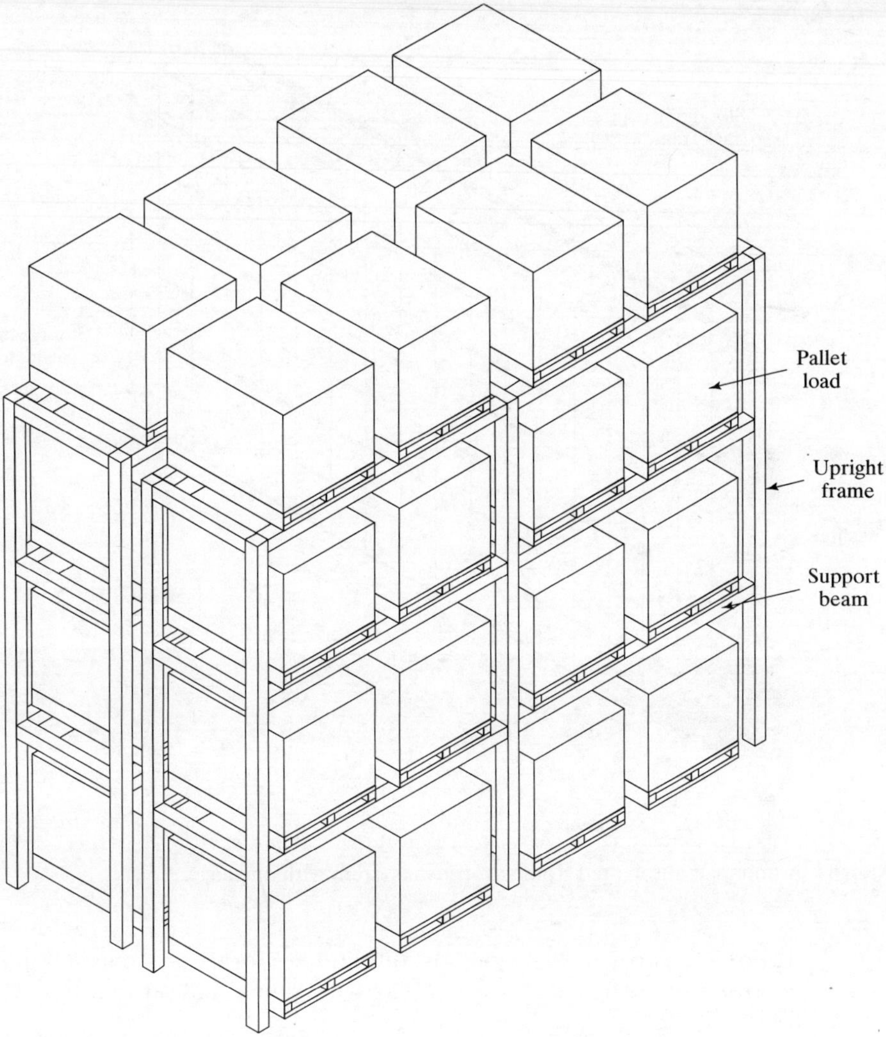

Figure 9 Pallet rack system for storage of unit loads on pallets.

loads are entered and retrieved under computer control, with little or no human involvement. There are several reasons for automating the storage function: (1) increase storage capacity, (2) increase storage density, (3) recover factory floor space presently used for storing work-in-process, (4) improve security and reduce pilferage, (5) reduce labor cost and/or increase labor productivity, (6) improve safety, (7) improve control over inventories, (8) improve stock rotation, (9) improve customer service, and (10) increase throughput.

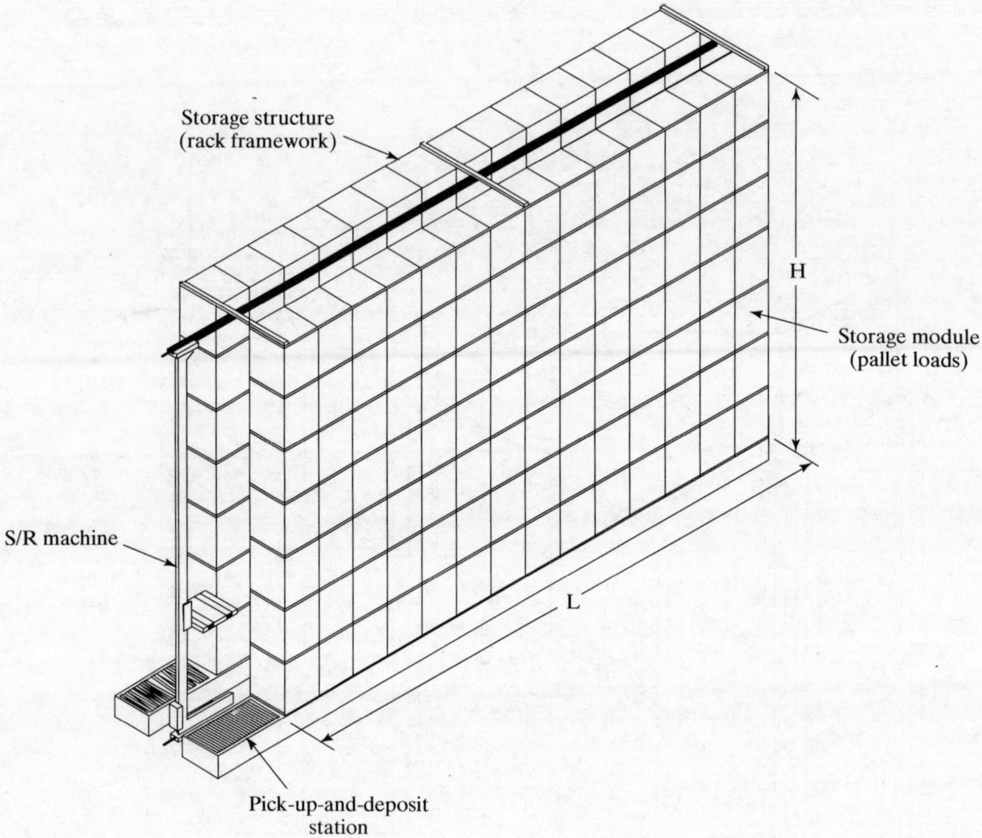

Figure 10 A unit load automated storage/retrieval system with one aisle.

There are two general types of automated storage systems: (1) automated storage/retrieval systems and (2) carousel storage systems. These are illustrated in Figures 10 and 11.

An ***automated storage/retrieval system*** (AS/RS) is a storage system that consists of one or more storage aisles, each serviced by a storage/retrieval (S/R) machine (also known as a crane). Such a system performs storage and retrieval operations under a defined degree of automation. The aisles have storage racks for holding the stored materials. The S/R machines move horizontally and vertically to deliver and retrieve materials within the storage racks. Each AS/RS aisle has one or more input/output stations where materials are delivered into and moved out of storage. The input/output stations are called pickup-and-deposit (P&D) stations in AS/RS terminology. P&D stations can be manually operated or interfaced to some form of automated handling system such as a conveyor or an AGVS. The most common type of AS/RS is the unit load AS/RS illustrated in Figure 10, which is designed to handle unit loads stored on pallets or other standard containers.

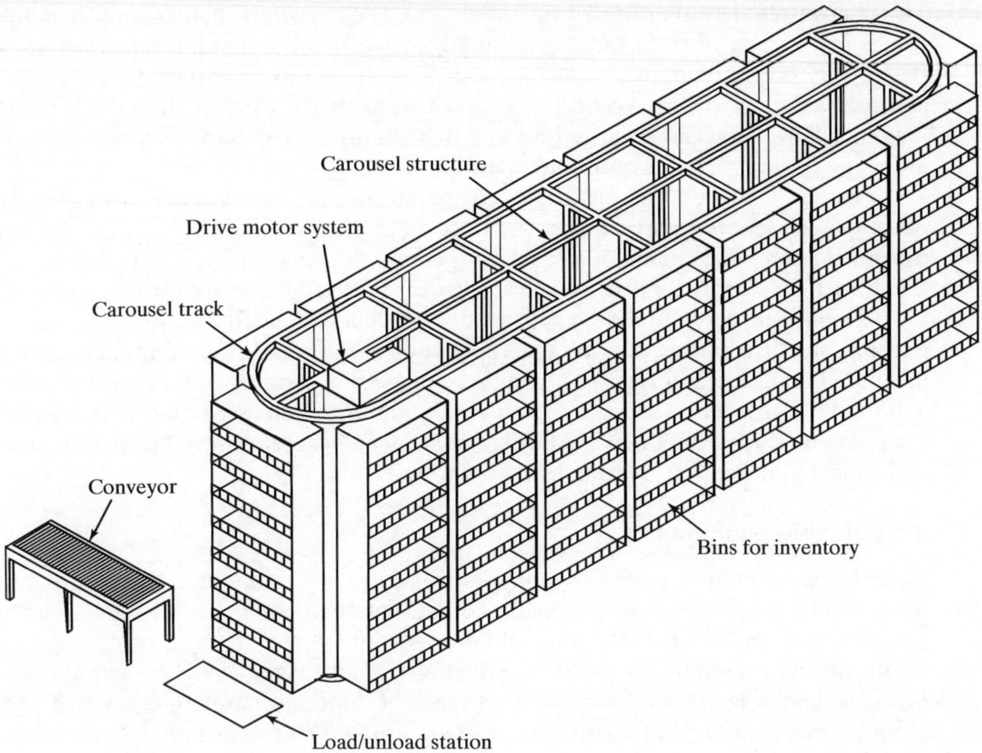

Figure 11 A horizontal carousel storage system.

A wide range of automation is found in commercial AS/R systems. At the most sophisticated level, the operations are totally automated, computer controlled, and fully integrated with factory and/or warehouse operations. At the other extreme, human workers operate the equipment and perform the storage/retrieval transactions by riding in the crane. Automated storage/retrieval systems are custom-designed for each application, although the designs are based on standard modular components available from each respective AS/RS supplier.

A ***carousel storage system*** consists of a series of bins or baskets suspended from an overhead chain conveyor that revolves around a long oval rail system, as depicted in Figure 11. The purpose of the chain conveyor is to position bins at a load/unload station at the end of the oval. The operation is similar to the powered overhead rack system used by dry cleaners to deliver finished garments to the front of the store. Most carousels are operated by human workers located at the load/unload station. The worker activates the powered carousel to deliver a desired bin to the station. One or more parts are removed from or added to the bin, and then the cycle is repeated. Automatic loading and unloading is available on some carousel storage systems, allowing it to be interfaced with automated handling systems without the need for human participation in the load/unload operations.

Carousels are either horizontal or vertical. The horizontal configuration in Figure comes in a variety of sizes, ranging in length between about 3 m (10 ft) and 30 m (100 ft). Carousels at the upper end of the range have higher storage density, but the average access time is longer. Accordingly, most carousels are 10 m to 16 m (30 ft to 50 ft) long to achieve a proper balance between these competing objectives. The storage bins are made of steel wire for optimum operator visibility.

Vertical carousels are constructed to operate around a vertical conveyor loop. They occupy much less floor space than the horizontal configuration but require sufficient overhead space. The ceiling of the building limits the height of vertical carousels, and therefore their storage capacity is typically lower than for the average horizontal carousel.

Applications of automated storage systems are associated with production, warehousing, and distribution operations. Application areas for AS/R systems and carousels include (1) unit load storage and handling for AS/RS installations, (2) order picking, and (3) work-in-process storage. Carousel systems are often associated with ***kitting***, an operation in which components to be used in an assembly are retrieved from the carousel and collected into a "kit" for the assembly worker.

3.3 Unitizing Equipment

Unitizing equipment refers to (1) containers used to hold individual items during handling and (2) equipment used to load and package the containers. Containers include pallets, boxes, baskets, barrels, pails, and drums, some of which are shown in Figure 12. Of the available containers, pallets are the most widely used, owing to their versatility, low cost, and compatibility with various types of material-handling equipment. Most factories, warehouses, and distribution centers use forklift trucks to move materials on pallets. Although seemingly mundane, this type of equipment is very important for moving materials efficiently as a unit load rather than as individual items. A given facility must often standardize on a specific type and size of container if it utilizes automatic transport and/or storage equipment to handle the loads.

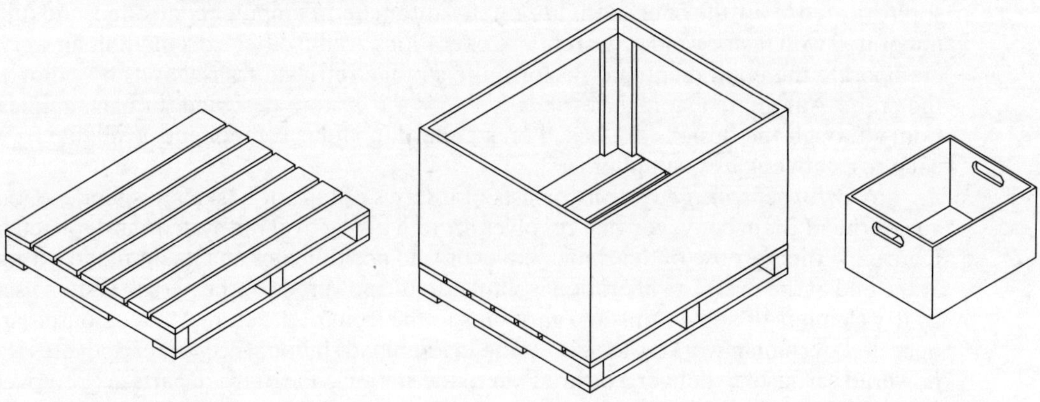

(a) (b) (c)

Figure 12 Examples of unit load containers for material handling: (a) wooden pallet, (b) pallet box, and (c) tote box.

The second category of unitizing equipment is loading and packaging equipment, which includes ***palletizers*** designed to automatically load cartons or other items onto pallets and shrink-wrap plastic film around them for shipping. Other wrapping and packaging machines are also included in this equipment category, as are ***depalletizers*** designed to unload cartons from pallets.

Unitizing equipment exploits the ***unit load principle***, one of the most important and widely applied in material handling. A ***unit load*** is simply the mass that is to be moved or otherwise handled at one time. Such a load may consist of only one part; it may consist of a container loaded with multiple parts; or it may consist of a pallet loaded with multiple containers of parts. In general, the unit load should be as large as is practical for the material-handling system that will move or store it, subject to considerations of safety, convenience, and access to the materials making up the unit load. This principle is widely applied in the trucking, rail freight, airfreight, and cargo ship industries, where it is referred to as the ***consolidation principle***. Palletized unit loads are collected into truckloads or containers, which then become unit loads themselves. These truckloads and containers are then aggregated once again on freight trains or cargo ships, in effect becoming even larger unit loads.

3.4 Identification and Tracking Systems

Material handling must include a means of keeping track of the materials being moved or stored. This is usually done by affixing some kind of label to the item, carton, or unit load that uniquely identifies it. The most common label used today consists of bar codes that can be read quickly and automatically by bar code scanners. This is the same basic technology used by grocery stores and retail merchandisers. Other types of labels include magnetic stripes and radio frequency tags that can encode more data than bar codes. The term ***automatic identification and data capture*** (AIDC) refers to these technologies that provide direct entry of data into a computer or other microprocessor controlled system without using a keyboard (or pen and pencil). Many of these technologies require no human involvement in the data capture and entry process. Automatic identification systems are being used increasingly to collect data in material handling and other applications, including shipping and receiving, storage, sortation, order picking, monitoring the status of work-in-process in a factory, retail sales and inventory control, mail and parcel handling, patient identification in hospitals, and check processing in banks.

The alternative to automatic data capture is manual collection and entry of data. This often involves recording the data on paper and later entering it into the computer by means of a keyboard. There are several drawbacks to this method. The first is that human errors occur in both data collection and keyboard entry when performed manually. The average error rate of manual keyboard entry is one error per 300 characters. The error rate in bar code technology is about 10,000 times lower than manual keyboard data entry. The second drawback is the time factor. When manual methods are used, there is a time delay that occurs during the period when the activities and events are being processed and when the data on status are entered into the computer. In addition, manual methods are themselves inherently more time consuming than automated methods. Automatic identification methods are capable of reading hundreds of characters per second. Finally, there is the cost of labor incurred when the full-time attention of human workers is required in manual data collection and entry. These drawbacks are virtually eliminated when automatic identification and data capture are used. With AIDC, the data on activities, events, and conditions are acquired at the location and time of their occurrence and entered into the computer immediately.

Some of the automated identification applications require workers to participate in the data collection procedure, usually to operate the identification equipment in the application. These techniques are therefore semiautomated rather than automated methods. Other applications accomplish the identification with no human participation. The same basic sensor technologies may be used in both cases. For example, certain types of bar code scanners are operated by humans while others work automatically.

4 QUANTITATIVE ANALYSIS OF MATERIAL-HANDLING OPERATIONS

Mathematical equations can be developed to model the operations of the material transport systems discussed in Section 3.1. Our coverage of these models consists of (1) analysis of vehicle-based transport systems and (2) analysis of conveyor systems. We should also mention that the From-To charts and network diagrams are very helpful for visualizing the movement of materials.

4.1 Analysis of Vehicle-Based Material Transport Systems

The equipment used in vehicle-based material transport systems includes industrial trucks (both hand trucks and powered trucks), automated guided vehicles, monorails and other rail-guided vehicles, certain types of conveyor systems (e.g., in-floor towline conveyors), and certain crane operations. We assume that the vehicle operates at a constant velocity throughout its operation, and ignore effects of acceleration, deceleration, and other speed differences that might depend on whether the vehicle is traveling loaded or empty. The time for a typical delivery cycle in the operation of a vehicle-based transport system consists of (1) loading at the pickup station, (2) travel time to the drop-off station, (3) unloading at the drop-off station, and (4) empty travel time of the vehicle between deliveries. The total cycle time per delivery per vehicle is given by

$$T_c = T_L + \frac{L_d}{v_c} + T_U + \frac{L_e}{v_c} \tag{1}$$

where T_c = delivery cycle time, min/delivery; T_L = time to load at load station, min; L_d = distance the vehicle travels between load and unload station, m (ft); v_c = carrier (AGV) velocity, m/min (ft/min); T_U = time to unload at unload station, min; and L_e = distance the vehicle travels empty until the start of the next delivery cycle, m (ft).

T_c calculated by equation (1) must be considered an ideal value, because it ignores any time losses due to reliability problems, traffic congestion, and other factors that might slow down a delivery. In addition, not all delivery cycles are the same. Originations and destinations may be different from one delivery to the next, which will affect the L_d and L_e terms in the equation. Accordingly, these terms are considered to be average values for the population of loaded and empty distances traveled by the vehicle during the course of a shift or other period of analysis.

The delivery cycle time can be used to determine certain parameters of interest in the vehicle-based transport system. Let us use T_c to determine the rate of deliveries per vehicle and the number of vehicles required to satisfy a specified total delivery requirement. The hourly rate of deliveries per vehicle is 60 min divided by the delivery cycle time T_c, adjusting for any time losses during the hour. The possible time losses include (1) availability, (2) traffic congestion, and (3) worker efficiency of drivers in the case of manually operated trucks. ***Availability*** (symbolized A) is the proportion of total shift time that the vehicle is operational and not broken down or being repaired.

To deal with traffic congestion, let us define the ***traffic factor*** F_t as a parameter for estimating the effect of these time losses on system performance. Sources of inefficiency accounted for by the traffic factor include waiting at intersections, blocking of vehicles, and waiting in a queue at load/unload stations. If there is no congestion, then $F_t = 1.0$. As the number of vehicles in the system increases relative to the size of the layout, congestion tends to increase, and the value of the traffic factor decreases. Typical values of traffic factor for an AGVS range between 0.85 and 1.0 [5].

For systems based on hand trucks and powered trucks operated by human workers, performance is very dependent on the work efficiency of the operators who drive the trucks. ***Worker efficiency*** is defined as the actual work rate of the human operator relative to work rate expected under standard or normal performance. Our symbol for worker efficiency is E_w.

With these factors defined, we can now express the available time per hour per vehicle as 60 min adjusted by A, F_t, and E_w. That is,

$$AT = 60AF_tE_w \tag{2}$$

where AT = available time, min/hr/vehicle; A = availability; F_t = traffic factor; and E_w = worker efficiency. The parameters A, F_t, and E_w do not take into account poor vehicle routing, poor guide path layout in an AGVS, or poor management of the vehicles in the system. These factors should be minimized, but if present they are accounted for in the values of L_d and L_e.

We can now write equations for the two parameters of interest. The rate of deliveries per vehicle is given by

$$R_{dv} = \frac{AT}{T_c} \tag{3}$$

where R_{dv} = hourly delivery rate per vehicle, delivery/hr/vehicle; T_c = delivery cycle time computed by equation (1), min/delivery; and AT = available time in 1 hr with adjustments for time losses, min/hr.

The total number of vehicles (trucks, AGVs, trolleys, carts, etc.) needed to satisfy a specified total delivery schedule R_f in the system can be estimated by first calculating the total workload required and then dividing by the available time per vehicle. Workload is defined as the total amount of work, expressed in terms of time, that must be accomplished by the material transport system in an hour. This can be expressed as

$$WL = R_fT_c \tag{4}$$

where WL = workload, min/hr; R_f = specified flow rate (total deliveries per hour) for the system, delivery/hr; and T_c = delivery cycle time, min/delivery. The number of vehicles required to accomplish this workload can be written as

$$n_c = \frac{WL}{AT} \tag{5}$$

where n_c = number of carriers (e.g., trucks, AGVs) required; WL = workload, min/hr; and AT = available time per vehicle, min/hr/vehicle. It can be shown that equation (5) reduces to

$$n_c = \frac{R_f}{R_{dv}} \tag{6}$$

where n_c = number of carriers required;
R_f = total delivery requirements, deliveries/hr; and R_{dv} = delivery rate per vehicle, delivery/hr/vehicle. Although the traffic factor accounts for delays experienced by the vehicles, it does not include delays encountered by a load/unload station that must wait for the arrival of a vehicle. Owing to the random nature of the load/unload demands, workstations are likely to experience waiting time while vehicles are busy with other deliveries. The preceding equations do not consider this idle time or its impact on operating cost. If station idle time is to be minimized, then more vehicles may be needed than the number indicated by equations (5) or (6).

Example 1 Determining Number of Vehicles in a Vehicle-based Material-Handling System

The hourly delivery requirements among the four production departments in a factory are listed in the From-To table below. Forklift trucks are used to make the deliveries. All entries in the chart above the main diagonal represent loaded transports, while the single entry below the diagonal represents empty moves. The value in front of the slash indicates the number of moves per hour, while the value following the slash is the average distance traveled (meters) in the move. Loading time in a department is 0.50 min, and unloading time is 0.40 min. Average vehicle velocity is 80 m/min, availability is 0.95, traffic factor is 0.90, and operator efficiency is assumed to be 1.0. Determine (a) travel distances loaded and empty, (b) ideal delivery cycle time, and (c) number of vehicles required to satisfy the delivery demand.

To	1	2	3	4
From 1	—	12/200		4/120
2		—	7/160	5/300
3			—	7/140
4	16/150			—

Solution **(a)** The value of L_d is determined as a weighted average of the individual move distances for the loaded transports.

$$L_d = \frac{12(200) + 4(120) + 7(160) + 5(300) + 7(140)}{12 + 4 + 7 + 5 + 7} = \frac{6480}{35} = 185.2 \text{ m}$$

We see that the total delivery requirements (the denominator in the preceding equation) is $R_f = 35$ deliveries per hour. The value of L_e must be determined as an average per delivery, so the denominator has the same value as for L_d.

$$L_e = \frac{16(150)}{35} = 68.6 \text{ m}$$

(b) Ideal cycle time per delivery per vehicle is given by equation (1).

$$T_c = 0.50 + \frac{185.2}{80} + 0.40 + \frac{68.6}{80} = 4.07 \text{ min}$$

(c) To determine the number of vehicles required to make 35 deliveries/hr, we compute the workload of the AGVS and the available time/hr/vehicle.

$$WL = 35(4.07) = 142.5 \text{ min/hr}$$

$$AT = 60(0.95)(0.90)(1.0) = 51.3 \text{ min/hr/vehicle}$$

Therefore, the number of vehicles required is

$$n_c = \frac{142.5}{51.3} = 2.78 \text{ vehicles}$$

This value should be rounded up to $n_c = 3$ vehicles since the number of vehicles must be an integer. ■

Determining L_e, the average distance a vehicle travels empty for a delivery cycle, can be complicated. First, note in our example that we computed L_e using the total number of deliveries as the denominator. The average is based not on the number of empty moves but on the number of deliveries. Second, the average empty travel distance depends on the dispatching and scheduling methods used to decide how a vehicle should proceed from its last drop-off location to its next pickup location. The From-To chart in Example 1 indicates that there are only 16 moves out of 35 deliveries that the vehicle is forced to travel empty. These are return trips from department 4 to department 1. All of the other moves (the remaining 19 out of 35) involve no empty travel. The forklift drops off a pallet load and immediately picks up another pallet load in the same department for the next delivery.

Ideally, L_e should be reduced to zero. It is highly desirable to minimize the average distance a vehicle travels empty through good dispatching and scheduling of the vehicles. Our mathematical model of vehicle-based transport systems indicates that the delivery cycle time will be reduced if L_e is minimized, and this will have a beneficial effect on the delivery rate and the number of vehicles required.

4.2 Analysis of Conveyor Systems

Conveyor systems can be classified as (1) single direction and (2) continuous loop. ***Single direction conveyors*** are used to transport loads one way from origination point to destination point, as depicted in Figure 13 (a). These systems are appropriate when there is no need to move loads in both directions or to return containers or carriers from the unloading stations back to the loading stations. Single direction powered conveyors include roller and belt types. In addition, gravity conveyors operate in one direction.

Continuous loop conveyors form a complete circuit, as shown in Figure 13 (b). An overhead trolley conveyor is an example of this conveyor type. However, any conveyor type can be configured as a loop, even those that are identified above as single

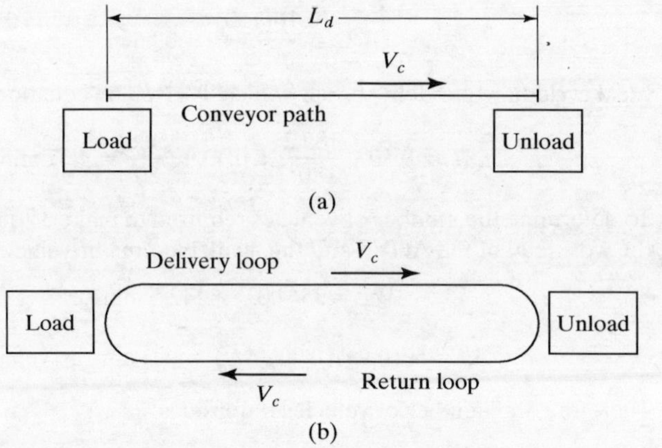

Figure 13 Conveyor system classifications: (a) single direction and (b) continuous loop.

direction conveyors, simply by connecting several single direction conveyor sections into a closed loop. A continuous loop system allows materials to be moved between any two stations along the pathway. Continuous loop conveyors are used when loads are moved in carriers (e.g., hooks, baskets) between load and unload stations and the carriers are affixed to the conveyor loop. In this design, the empty carriers are automatically returned from the unload station back to the load station.

Analysis of Single Direction Conveyors. Consider the case of a single direction powered conveyor with one load station at the upstream end and one unload station at the downstream end, as in Figure 13 (a). Materials are loaded at one end and unloaded at the other. The materials may be parts, cartons, pallet loads, or other unit loads. Assuming the conveyor operates at a constant speed, the time required to move materials from load station to unload station is given by

$$T_d = \frac{L_d}{v_c} \tag{7}$$

where T_d = delivery time, min; L_d = length of conveyor between load and unload stations, m (ft); and v_c = conveyor velocity, m/min (ft/min).

The flow rate of materials on the conveyor is determined by the rate of loading at the load station. The loading rate is limited by the reciprocal of the time required to load the materials. Given the conveyor speed, the loading rate establishes the spacing of materials on the conveyor. Summarizing these relationships,

$$R_f = R_L = \frac{v_c}{s_c} \le \frac{1}{T_L} \tag{8}$$

where R_f = material flow rate, parts/min; R_L = loading rate, parts/min; s_c = center-to-center spacing of materials on the conveyor, m/part (ft/part); and T_L = loading time, min/part. One might be tempted to think that the loading rate R_L is the reciprocal of the loading time T_L. However, R_L should be consistent with the flow rate requirement R_f, while T_L is determined by ergonomic factors. The worker who loads the conveyor may be capable of performing the loading task at a faster rate than R_f. On the other hand, the flow rate requirement cannot be faster than it is humanly possible to perform the loading task.

An additional requirement on loading and unloading is that the time required to unload the conveyor must be equal to or less than the loading time. That is,

$$T_U \leq T_L \tag{9}$$

where T_U = unloading time, min/part. If unloading requires more time than loading, then loads not removed at the unload station will accumulate or be dumped onto the floor at the downstream end of the conveyor.

We are using parts as the material in equations (8) and (9), but the relationships can be adapted to loads consisting of multiple parts. Let n_p = the number of parts contained in a carrier that is being transported as a unit load on the carrier. Then equation (8) can be recast as

$$R_f = \frac{n_p v_c}{s_c} \leq \frac{1}{T_L} \tag{10}$$

where R_f = flow rate, parts/min; n_p = number of parts per carrier; s_c = center-to-center spacing of carriers on the conveyor, m/carrier (ft/carrier); and T_L = loading time per carrier, min/carrier. The flow rate of parts transported by the conveyor is potentially much greater in this case.[6] However, loading time is still a limitation, and T_L may consist of not only the time to load the carrier onto the conveyor but also the time to load parts into the carrier. The preceding equations must be interpreted and perhaps adjusted for a given application.

Example 2 Single Direction Conveyor

A roller conveyor follows a pathway 35 m long between a parts production department and an assembly department. Conveyor velocity is 40 m/min. Parts are loaded into large tote pans that are then placed onto the conveyor at the load station in the production department. Two workers operate the loading station. The first worker loads parts into tote pans, which takes 25 sec. Each tote pan holds 20 parts. The parts production rate is consistent with this 25 sec cycle. The second worker loads tote pans onto the conveyor, which takes 10 sec. Determine (a) the spacing between tote pans along the conveyor, (b) the maximum possible flow rate in parts/min, and (c) the maximum allowable time to unload the tote pan in the assembly department.

Solution **(a)** Spacing between tote pans on the conveyor is determined by the loading time. It takes only 10 sec to load a tote pan onto the conveyor, but 25 sec are required to load parts into the tote pan. Therefore, the loading cycle is limited by this 25 sec. At a conveyor speed of 40 m/min, the spacing will be

$$s_c = (25/60 \text{ min})(40 \text{ m/min}) = 16.67 \text{ m}$$

[6]Equation (10) illustrates the Unit Load Principle, discussed in Section 3.3.

(b) Flow rate is given by equation (10):

$$R_f = \frac{20(40)}{16.67} = 48 \text{ parts/min}$$

This is consistent with the parts loading rate of 20 parts in 25 sec, which is 0.8 parts/sec or 48 parts/min.

(c) The maximum allowable time to unload a tote pan must be consistent with the flow rate of tote pans on the conveyor, which in turn depends on the loading time. The loading time is one tote pan every 25 sec, so

$$T_U \leq 25 \text{ sec}$$

■

Analysis of Continuous Loop Conveyors. Consider a continuous loop conveyor such as an overhead trolley in which the pathway is formed by an endless chain moving around a track loop, and carriers are suspended from the track and pulled by the chain. The conveyor moves parts in the carriers between a load station and an unload station. The complete loop is divided into two sections: a delivery (forward) loop in which the carriers are loaded, and a return loop in which the carriers travel empty, as shown in Figure 13 (b). The length of the delivery loop is L_d, and the length of the return loop is L_e. The total length of the conveyor is therefore $L = L_d + L_e$. The total time required to travel the complete loop is

$$T_c = \frac{L}{v_c} \tag{11}$$

where T_c = total cycle time, min; and v_c = speed of the conveyor chain, m/min (ft/min). The time a load spends in the forward loop is

$$T_d = \frac{L_d}{v_c} \tag{12}$$

where T_d is the delivery time on the forward loop, min.

Carriers are equally spaced along the chain at a distance s_c apart. Thus the total number of carriers in the loop is given by

$$n_c = \frac{L}{s_c} \tag{13}$$

where n_c = number of carriers; L = total length of the conveyor loop, m (ft); and s_c = center-to-center distance between carriers, m/carrier (ft/carrier). The value of n_c must be an integer, and therefore L and s_c must be consistent with that requirement.

Each carrier is capable of holding n_p parts on the delivery loop and it holds no parts on the return trip. Since only those carriers on the forward loop contain parts, the maximum number of parts in the system at any one time is given by

$$\text{Total parts in system} = \frac{n_p n_c L_d}{L} \tag{14}$$

As in the single direction conveyor, the maximum flow rate between load and unload stations is

$$R_f = \frac{n_p v_c}{s_c}$$

where R_f = parts/min. Again this rate must be consistent with limitations on the time it takes to load and unload the conveyor.

REFERENCES

[1] Ballou, R. H. *Business Logistics Management.* 4th ed. Upper Saddle River, NJ: Prentice Hall, 1999.

[2] Bowersox, D. J., and D. J. Closs. *Logistical Management: The Integrated Supply Chain Process.* New York: McGraw-Hill, 1996.

[3] Chopra, S., and P. Meindl. *Supply Chain Management.* 2nd ed. Upper Saddle River, NJ: Prentice Hall, 2004.

[4] Coyle, J. J., E. J. Bardi, and C. J. Langley Jr. *The Management of Business Logistics*, 7th ed. Mason, OH: South-Western, 2003.

[5] Fitzgerald, K. R. "How to Estimate the Number of AGVs You Need." *Modern Materials Handling* (October 1985): 79.

[6] Groover, M. P. *Automation, Production Systems, and Computer Integrated Manufacturing.* 2nd ed. Upper Saddle River, NJ: Prentice Hall, 2001.

[7] Kulwiec, R. A. "Basic Material Handling Concepts." Pp. 3–18 in *Materials Handling Handbook*, 2nd ed., edited by R. A. Kulwiec. New York: Wiley, 1985.

[8] Kulwiec, R. A., ed. *Materials Handling Handbook.* 2nd ed. New York: Wiley, 1985.

[9] Lane, D. A. "Material Handling." Pp. 10. 31–10. 56 in *Maynard's Industrial Engineering Handbook*, 5th ed. edited by K. Zandin. New York: McGraw-Hill, 2001.

[10] Material Handling Industry, *Annual Report.* Charlotte, NC, 2003.

[11] Saenz, N. "Which Way to Convey." *IIE Solutions* (July 2002): 35–42.

[12] Russell, R. S., and B. W. Taylor III. *Operations Management.* 4th ed. Upper Saddle River, NJ: Prentice Hall, 2003.

[13] College Industry Council on Material Handling Education. *The Ten Principles of Material Handling.* Charlotte, NC: Material Handling Institute, 1997.

[14] Tompkins, J. A., J. A. White, Y. A. Bozer, and J. M. A. Tanchoco. *Facilities Planning.* 3rd ed. New York: Wiley, 2003.

REVIEW QUESTIONS

1 What is business logistics?

2 What is the difference between external logistics and internal logistics?

3 What are the basic objectives in business logistics?

4 Identify the five components of the logistics system.

5 With what is the procurement function in logistics concerned?

6 What are the four warehousing functions?

7 What is cross-docking?
8 Name the five basic transportation modes.
9 What are the general characteristics of freight that is suited to rail transport? Give examples of this freight.
10 What are the general characteristics of freight that is suited to truck transport? Give examples of this freight.
11 What are the advantages of truck transport over rail transport when the applications are appropriate for trucking?
12 What are the general characteristics of freight that is suited to air transport?
13 What are the applications of pipelines?
14 What are intermodal operations?
15 What are freight forwarders?
16 Give some examples of the distribution of information and entertainment products by means of the Internet and similar communication-based distribution modes.
17 Define material handling.
18 What are the four major categories of material-handling equipment?
19 What are the five basic types of material transport equipment?
20 Why are forklift trucks so widely used in industry?
21 What is an automated guided vehicle system? Define the term.
22 How is a monorail different from an automated guided vehicle? Identify two differences.
23 Conveyors can be classified as powered and nonpowered. What is the feature about powered conveyors that distinguishes them from rail-guided vehicles and automated guided vehicles?
24 Name some of the major types of powered and nonpowered conveyors.
25 What are the four conventional (nonautomated) storage methods and equipment types?
26 What are the two basic types of automated storage systems?
27 What are some of the reasons that companies automate the storage function?
28 What is a carousel storage system?
29 What is unitizing equipment? Define what the term means.
30 What are the three drawbacks in manual data collection and entry that automatic identification and data capture systems tend to eliminate?
31 What is the unit load principle in material handling?

PROBLEMS

Analysis of Vehicle-based Material Handling Systems

1 A fleet of forklift trucks has an average travel distance per delivery of 600 ft loaded and an average empty travel distance of 500 ft. The fleet must make a total of 55 deliveries/hr. Load and unload times are each 0.4 min and the speed of the vehicles is 400 ft/min. The traffic factor for the system is 0.93. Availability is 1.0 and worker efficiency is assumed to be 100%. Determine (a) ideal cycle time per delivery, (b) the resulting average number of deliveries per hour that a forklift truck can make, and (c) how many trucks are required to accomplish the specified number of deliveries per hour.

2 An automated guided vehicle system has an average travel distance per delivery of 250 m and an average empty travel distance of 200 m. Loading time is 0.4 min, unloading time is 0.35 min, and the speed of the AGV is 1 m/s. The traffic factor is 0.9, and availability is 1.0. How many vehicles are needed to satisfy a delivery requirement of 40 deliveries/hr?

3 Four forklift trucks are used to deliver pallet loads of parts between work cells in a factory. Average travel distance loaded is 300 ft and the travel distance empty is estimated to be the same. The trucks are driven at an average speed of 4 miles/hr when loaded and 4.5 miles/hr when empty. Terminal time per delivery averages 1.0 min (loading time = 0.5 min and unloading time = 0.5 min). Availability is 1.0 and worker efficiency is assumed to be 100%. If the traffic factor is assumed to be 0.90, what is the maximum hourly delivery rate of the four trucks?

4 Hourly delivery requirements among four departments in a factory are listed in the From-To table below. Forklift trucks are used to make the deliveries. All entries in the chart are loaded transports. The deliveries can be scheduled so there are no empty moves. All loads enter and exit the factory through Department 1. In the table below, the values in front of the slash indicate the number of moves per hour, and the values following the slash represent the average distance traveled (ft) in the move. Loading time in a department is 0.40 min, and unloading time in a department is 0.30 min. Average vehicle velocity is 300 ft/min, availability is 0.96, traffic factor is 0.94, and operator efficiency is assumed to be 1.0. Determine (a) travel distances loaded and empty, (b) ideal delivery cycle time, and (c) number of vehicles required to satisfy the delivery demand.

To	1	2	3	4
From 1	—	15/350	10/500	
2		—	3/300	12/600
3			—	13/400
4	25/250			—

5 Solve the preceding problem but assume that all loads enter the factory through department 1 and exit the factory through department 4. Therefore, there is no need to transport the 25 loads from department 4 back to department 1. However, the forklift trucks must still return from department 4 to department 1 so that they can make deliveries that originate at department 1. This means that 25 empty moves must be made from department 4 to department 1. The distance remains the same 250 ft.

6 A proposed AGVS will operate between points A and B. In a given hour, 6 loads must be delivered from A to B, and 4 loads must be delivered from B to A. The AGVS layout will be a simple oval loop, with a travel distance between A and B of 500 m in either direction. The traffic factor is therefore 1.0, availability is 1.0, and vehicle speed is 50 m/min. The time to load is 1.0 min and to unload is 1.0 min. Determine the required minimum number of vehicles that will satisfy these delivery requirements. Indicate the assumptions concerning vehicle operation under which this minimum number will be achieved.

7 An AGVS has three load/unload stations (numbered 1, 2, and 3) that form the corners of an equilateral triangle whose sides are each 1000 m long. The hourly rate of loads carried between stations is as follows: 20 loads from station 1 to station 2, 20 loads from station 2 to station 3, and 15 loads from station 3 to station 1. The From-To chart requires that the vehicles always move in one direction around the triangle (from 1 to 2 to 3 to 1 . . .), so the traffic factor is assumed to be 1.0. Vehicle speed is 60 m/min. A total of 1.0 min is required for handling time per delivery (0.5 min for loading and 0.5 min for unloading). The AGVs must be scheduled as efficiently as possible, but the delivery requirements make it impossible to avoid some empty traveling by the vehicles. Assume that availability is 100%. Determine (a) average delivery cycle time of a vehicle and (b) how many vehicles are needed to meet the hourly delivery schedule.

8 An AGVS is being proposed to deliver parts between 22 workstations in a factory. Loads must be moved from each station about once every 30 min; the delivery rate is thus 44 loads per hour. Average travel distance loaded is estimated to be 200 ft and travel distance empty is estimated to be 250 ft. Vehicles move at a speed of 150 ft/min. Total handling time per delivery is 1.2 min (load = 0.6 minute and unload = 0.6 minute). Availability is 1.0. Traffic factor F_t becomes increasingly significant as the number of vehicles n_c increases. This relationship can be modeled as $F_t = 1.0 - 0.04(n_c - 1)$ for n_c = Integer > 0. Determine the minimum number of vehicles needed in the factory to meet the flow rate requirement.

9 An AGV driverless train system is being planned for a warehouse. Each train will consist of the towing vehicle plus three pulled carts. Train velocity is 200 ft/min. Only the pulled carts carry loads, one load per cart. The average loaded travel-distance per delivery cycle is 2500 ft and empty travel distance is the same. The anticipated traffic factor is 0.95 and availability is 0.98. The load handling time per train per delivery is expected to be 7.5 min. If the requirements on the AGVS are 20 loads per hour, determine the number of trains required.

10 The From-To chart below indicates the number of loads moved per 8-hr day (before the slash) and the distances in feet (after the slash) between departments in a factory. Forklift trucks are used to transport loads between departments. Average truck speed is 300 ft/min (loaded) and 400 ft/min (empty). Load handling time per delivery is 1.0 min, and anticipated traffic factor is 0.95. Availability is 0.97 and worker efficiency is assumed to be 100%. Determine the number of trucks required under each of the following assumptions: (a) trucks never travel empty; and (b) trucks travel empty a distance equal to their loaded distance.

To Dept.		1	2	3	4	5
From Dept.	1	—	70/600	50/500	40/300	
	2		—		65/400	
	3			—		75/250
	4				—	60/350
	5					—

11 Riding lawnmowers are assembled on a production line at the rate of 45/hr. The products are moved along the conveyorized line on work carriers (one lawnmower per carrier). At the end of the line, the finished products are removed from the carriers, which are then removed from the line and delivered back to the front of the line so they can be reused. Automated guided vehicles are used to transport the work carriers to the front of the line, a distance of 750 ft. Return trip distance (empty) to the end of the line is 800 ft. Each AGV carries four work carriers and travels at a speed of 165 ft/min (either loaded or empty). The work carriers form queues at each end of the line, so that neither the production line nor the AGVs are ever starved for work carriers. Time to load each work carrier onto an AGV is 0.3 min; time to release a loaded AGV and move an empty AGV into position for loading at the end of the line is 0.4 min. The same times apply for work carrier handling and release/positioning at the unload station located at the front of the production line. The traffic factor is 1.0 since the route is a simple loop. Availability is 95%. How many vehicles are needed to operate the AGV system?

12 A rail-guided vehicle system is being planned as part of an assembly work cell. Delivery requirements (loads/hr, before the slash) and distances (ft, after the slash) are indicated in the From-To chart below. In operation, a base part is loaded at station 1 and travels either through stations 2 and 3 or through stations 4 and 5, where components are assembled to the base part. From stations 3 or 5, the product moves to station 6 for removal from the system. Vehicles remain with the products as they move through the station sequences; thus no loading and unloading of parts occurs at stations 2, 3, 4, and 5. After unloading at station 6, the vehicles then return to station 1 for reloading. The speed of each rail-guided vehicle is 120 ft/min. Assembly cycle times at stations 2 and 3 are 5.0 min each (10 min total), and at stations 4 and 5 they are 6.0 min each (12 min total). Load and unload times at stations 1 and 6 respectively are each 0.75 min. The traffic factor is 0.95. How many vehicles are required to operate the assembly work cell?

To:		1	2	3	4	5	6
From:	1	—	20/45		16/55		
	2		—	20/50			
	3			—			20/30
	4				—	16/60	
	5					—	16/35
	6	36/150					—

Analysis of Conveyor Systems

13 A roller conveyor is 250 ft long and its velocity is 80 ft/min. It is used to move pallets between load and unload stations. Each pallet carries 10 parts. Cycle time to load a pallet is 0.25 min and one worker at the load station is able to load pallets at the rate of 4/min. It takes 0.20 min to unload at the unload station. Determine (a) the center-to-center distance between pallets, (b) the number of pallets on the conveyor at one time, and (c) the hourly flow rate of parts.

14 A roller conveyor moves tote pans at 200 ft/min between a load station and an unload station, a distance of 250 ft. The time to load parts into a tote pan at the load station is 0.05 min/part. Each tote pan holds 12 parts. In addition, it takes 0.15 min to load a tote pan onto the conveyor. One worker is assigned to loading the parts and then loading the tote pan onto the conveyor. Determine (a) the spacing between tote pan centers flowing in the conveyor system, and (b) the flow rate of parts on the conveyor system. (c) Consider the effect of the unit load principle. Suppose the tote pans were smaller and could hold only one part rather than 12. Determine the flow rate in this case if it takes 0.10 min to load a tote pan onto the conveyor (instead of 0.15 min for the larger tote pan), and it takes the same 0.05 min to load the part into the tote pan.

15 An overhead trolley conveyor forms a continuous closed loop. The delivery loop has a length of 150 m and the return loop is 120 m. All parts loaded at the load station are unloaded at the unload station. Each work carrier on the conveyor can hold one part and the carriers are separated by 5 m. Conveyor speed is 1.10 m/s. Determine (a) maximum number of parts in the conveyor system, (b) parts flow rate, and (c) maximum loading and unloading times that are compatible with the operation of the conveyor system.

16 A closed loop overhead conveyor must be designed to deliver parts from a load station to an unload station. The specified flow rate of parts between the two stations is 320 parts/hr.

The conveyor has carriers spaced at a center-to-center distance that is to be determined. Each carrier holds one part. Forward and return loops are each 75 m. Conveyor speed is 0.6 m/s. Minimum feasible times to load and unload parts at the respective stations is 0.16 min for each. Does the system achieve the specified flow rate? If so, what are appropriate values for the number of carriers and the spacing between carriers?

Service Operations and Office Work

One hundred years ago, most workers were employed to perform jobs consisting primarily of manual labor. These jobs were in the manufacturing, construction, agriculture, and mining industries. Today, about 70% of the U.S. economy is driven by the service sector, which includes banking, education, government, insurance, health and medical, and retail trade. The 70% also includes the transportation industry. Even when logistics workers are excluded, the fact is that a majority of U.S. workers are employed in service operations. Service operations are performed by service workers and knowledge workers. Service operations are often accomplished in offices, and we include office work as the second major topic in this chapter.

1 SERVICE OPERATIONS

Service operations provide a service to a client or customer, contrasted with production operations, which provide a product. The major service industries, called the tertiary industries in economic classifications, are listed in Table 1. Our primary concern is on the types of work and work systems that are associated with the service industries, but let us begin our coverage with some general observations about service operations.

1.1 The Nature of Services

A product is tangible, consumed or used by the customer who purchases it. A service is intangible, experienced in some form by a customer. To produce a product, it is possible to determine with great accuracy how much time will be required for each of the operations needed to make the parts and assemble them. To provide a service it is not possible in many cases to predict in advance how much time will be required to complete a service of a given type. For example, how long will it take for an automobile mechanic to diagnose an engine problem and then complete the repairs and adjustments? How long will it take an obstetrician to deliver a woman's baby in a hospital maternity ward? How long will it take for a mechanical engineer to design a new machinery component?

To deliver a service, the customer almost always comes in contact with the service provider. With a product, the customer is unlikely to ever come into contact with the original manufacturer. An automobile is a good example here. When we buy a car, we have contact with the car dealer, not the car company that made the car. The car dealer is a service provider. These and other comparisons between products and services are summarized in Table 2.

The customer judges the quality of a service, just as the customer judges the quality of a product. Accordingly, service quality is an issue that the service provider must address in order to be successful. If the customer has a poor service experience, repeat business is unlikely. Service quality is usually judged according to customer expectations. A customer eating out at McDonald's will not have the same expectations when dining at a fine restaurant. In addition to customer expectations, other factors determine service quality:

- *Customer interaction.* This refers to the interaction between the customer and the service provider during the customer contact portion of the service. How well did the customer get along with the car salesperson?
- *"Quality of workmanship" provided.* Did the customer get a good haircut?
- *Waiting time.* How long did the customer have to wait before the service started?
- *Service time.* How much time did it take for the service to be completed, once it was started?

As Table 1 indicates, a wide variety of services are performed. In fact, our list is incomplete, because it only includes industries whose main business function is providing a service. Service operations and providers can be divided into three main categories:[1]

- *Service organizations.* These are the companies and institutions whose primary purpose is to provide a service to its customers. The customers are external to the service organization. The organizations listed in Table 1 are service organizations.

[1]The classification presented here is similar to one published in [1].

TABLE 1 Service Industries and Companies[a]

Industry	Examples of Companies or Other Organizations
Advertising	Omnicom Group, Interpublic Group
Automotive Retailing and Services	AutoNation, United Auto Group, Sonic Automotive, Asbury Automotive Group, Group I Automotive
Banking	Citigroup, Bank of America, J. P. Morgan Chase, Wells Fargo, Wachovia, Bank One Corp., FleetBoston, U.S. Bancorp
Communications	*Telephone*: Verizon Communications, AT&T, Sprint, Bell South *Cable TV*: Comcast, RCN, Cablevision Systems
Education	*Higher education*: Swarthmore College, Lehigh University, Penn State University *Other*: high schools, middle schools, grammar schools, training institutes
Entertainment	AOL Time Warner, Walt Disney, Viacom, Metro-Goldwyn-Mayer
Financial Services	*Diversified financial services*: General Electric, Fannie Mae, American Express *Securities*: Morgan Stanley, Merrill Lynch, Charles Schwab *Accounting firms*: Ernst & Young, Deloitte & Touche, KPMG *Other*: Automatic Data Processing, H&R Block
Government	Federal, state, county, and local governments, prisons
Health Care and Medical	*Companies*: United Health Group, Cigna, Aetna, Health Net, *Hospitals*: Johns Hopkins Hospital, Hahnemann Hospital, Mayo Clinic *Other*: doctors and dentists offices, physical therapists, fitness clubs
Hotel	Marriott International, Hilton Hotels, Hyatt Regency Hotels, Ritz Carlton
Information	Public libraries, museums
Insurance	*Life and health*: New York Life, TIAA-CREF, Northwestern Mutual *Property and casualty*: State Farm Insurance, Allstate Insurance
Legal	Law offices
Mail and Package Delivery	U.S. Postal Service, United Parcel Service, FedEx, Airborne Express
Personal Services	Barbers, hairdressers, limousine services, funeral homes
Real Estate	Century 21, RE/MAX, Better Homes & Gardens
Repair and Maintenance	Car dealers, appliance repair companies, computer repair services, plumbers, electricians, custodial and janitorial services, lawn and garden services
Restaurant and Food Services	*Fast foods*: McDonald's, Burger King, Domino's, Wendy's International *Restaurants*: Olive Garden, Denny's, Bennigan's, Outback Steakhouse, Perkins Restaurant
Retail Trade	*General merchandisers*: Wal-Mart Stores, Target, Sears Roebuck, J. C. Penney *Drug merchandisers*: Walgreen, CVS, Rite Aid *Grocery*: Kroger, Safeway, Weis Markets, Shop Rite, Giant, Wegman's *Specialty merchandisers*: Home Depot, Borders, Staples, Circuit City, Amazon.com *Other*: car and truck dealers, farm equipment dealers, machinery and equipment dealers
Temporary Help	Manpower, Kelly Services
Tourism and Travel	*Cruise lines*: Princess, Carnival, Holland America *Resorts and casinos*: Park Place Entertainment, Harrah's, Trump Hotels and Casinos
Waste Management	Waste Management, Allied Waste Industries, Browning Ferris Industries
Wholesale Trade	*Diversified*: Genuine Parts, W.W. Grainer, Fisher Scientific, Reliance Steel and Aluminum *Food and grocery*: Sysco, Supervalu, Fleming *Electronics and office equipment*: Ingram Micro, Tech Data

Source: This list is based largely on the Fortune 500 list published in April each year by *Fortune* magazine.

[a]Transportation services have been excluded.

TABLE 2 Comparisons Between Products and Services

Comparison Feature	Products	Services
Tangible or intangible	Tangible	Intangible
Variability	Minimum variations in manufactured products	Significant variations are possible in the delivery of a given service
Time to complete	Constant and usually known with accuracy and precision	Variable and not known in advance, although average time may be known
How customer interacts	Products are consumed or used	Services are experienced
Customer contact	No (there are exceptions)	Yes (there are exceptions)

- *Internal services.* These are service operations performed for customers that are inside the company, and the services support the business of the larger organization. Depending on the types of organization, the services are likely to include data processing, accounting, plant engineering, custodial services, and equipment maintenance. Note that these internal services are often the same as those provided by service companies. For example, most medium and large companies have an internal accounting department, yet they also retain an outside accounting firm to certify their financial statements.
- *Product companies that also provide services.* These are companies whose main business is producing and selling products, but they must also provide a service in order to support that main business. For example, Microsoft's main business is selling software, either directly to customers or indirectly as installed software on personal computers purchased by customers. Microsoft maintains a telephone help center to assist customers who encounter problems with its software products.

Some service operations can be scheduled while others occur randomly. A ***scheduled service operation*** is one in which the starting time of the service is known in advance. It may not be possible to determine in advance how long the service will take, but knowing the starting time is helpful in planning staff requirements and scheduling staff hours. Examples of scheduled services include airline passenger service, doctor and dental office appointments, college courses,[2] and mail pickup at a given public mailbox. A ***random service operation*** is one in which the services are not scheduled, and the customers arrive at random times during the available hours when the service is offered. The service operations of hospital emergency rooms, retail stores, and fast food restaurants are examples of random servicing. The service provider may be able to predict arrival patterns based on previous experience (e.g., McDonald's is busier at noon than at 3:00 P.M.), but no exact schedule can be determined.

Another difference among service providers is whether the service occurs at the provider's location or the customer's location. The two cases have been called (1) ***facilities-based services***, where the customer must be at the provider's facility for

[2]It is not possible to predict how many students will register for a given course, and it is not possible to predict how many students will show up for a given class, but at least we can schedule when the course will be offered.

the service to be rendered, and (2) ***field-based services***, where the delivery of the service occurs at the customer's location [1]. Examples of each case are listed in Table 3.

1.2 Service Work

The difference between facilities-based and field-based services is highly correlated with the level of contact between the customer and the service provider. ***Level of customer contact*** refers to the proportion of time that the customer is involved relative to the total time to provide the service. In ***high-contact services***, the customer is involved a high proportion of the service time, and this is generally associated with facilities-based services. Examples include restaurants, hairdressers, dental offices, and prisons. The service worker must use his or her own discretion in dealing with and relating to the customer. Each service is different in this respect, because each customer is different. In ***low-contact services***, there is little direct contact between the customer and the service provider. This is most likely to correlate with field-based services. Examples include postal and parcel delivery, news associations such as Associated Press, and many government services (e.g., fire departments, planning commissions, county offices, tax collectors). Between the two extremes there is a range of ***medium-contact services***, such as police departments, law firms, banks, and automotive repair centers. Some of the important implications of customer contact level on the design of service work and the selection of workers can be summarized as follows [1]:

- In high-contact, random service operations, it is more difficult to plan staffing requirements because the duration of the service time of each customer is not known in advance, and the times and numbers of arrivals are not known in advance. This is not as much of a problem in low-contact service operations, because the service is not performed in the presence of the customer, so the service provider has more control over scheduling.
- With low-contact services, it is possible to analyze the work process, make methods improvements, and achieve efficiencies that are normally associated with factory production operations. In fact, low-contact service operations can often be organized in much the same way as a production process. Such improvements are more difficult with high-contact services due to the close coupling of the service procedure and the customer.
- Different types of workers are required for high-contact services than for low-contact services. For services with high customer contact, workers should have good

TABLE 3 Examples of Facilities-based and Field-based Services

Facilities-based Services	Field-based Services
Bank	Custodial and janitorial services
Restaurant, hotel, casino, movie theater	Temporary manpower services
Retail trade, excluding mail order services	Large household appliance repairs
Hairdresser's shop, barbershop	Waste management (garbage collection services)
Automotive repair shop	Telecommunication (telephone services)
Transportation of passengers (not freight)	Cable TV provider
Doctor's office, dental office	Plumber (repairs)

interpersonal skills and a sense of public relations on behalf of the organization. For low-contact services, technical and analytical skills are more important.

- When a service consists of both high-contact and low-contact components, there is an opportunity to divide the service work accordingly. Division of labor can be implemented by the service organization, with a different group of workers performing the high-contact component of the service, and another group performing the low-contact component. Many service departments of automobile dealers are organized this way. The people at the front counter write up the maintenance and repair orders with the customer, and the repair mechanics perform the work in the garage that is out of sight to the customer.

In general, the work performed in service operations tends to emphasize mental activities and communication skills rather than manual labor and physical endurance. Manual labor is most often performed in factories, warehouses, construction sites, and similar settings. By contrast, service work is usually performed in retail stores, offices, and other facilities that are usually characterized by cleaner and more pleasant working environments, especially in facilities-based services. If the common denominator in manual labor is the processing and flow of materials, then the common denominator in service work is the processing and flow of information. Managing the customer experience is also an important component in service delivery. Other comparisons between manual work and service work are summarized in Table 4.

It would be an oversimplification to suggest that the two categories of work, manual and service, consist of activities and requirements that are mutually exclusive. The fact is that manual work usually requires some mental activity and problem-solving skills. For example, a machine operator in a factory must exercise judgment to assess whether the quality of the parts being produced is satisfactory or whether the machine is operating properly. The worker must take some form of corrective action when things go wrong. He or she must figure out what to do when a problem occurs, even if figuring out what to do is as simple as calling the supervisor. Similarly, service work often requires physical labor and manual dexterity, at least some of the time. An office worker must perform physical work when putting a file folder into a file drawer or carrying a stack of forms to another office two floors above. Virtually all work situations require a combination of physical and mental activities to perform the job. The proportions vary from job to job.

TABLE 4 Comparison of Manual Work and Service Work

Comparison Factor	Manual Work	Service Work
Processing and flow of work:	Materials	Information, customer experience
Worker attributes:	Physical strength and endurance, manual dexterity, ability to learn a physical task	Mental acuity, communication skills, problem-solving skills, ability to learn a task involving information
Worker moniker:	Blue-collar worker	White-collar worker
Industry categories:	Primary and secondary industries	Tertiary industries
Where the work is performed:	Factories, warehouses, distribution centers, farms, mines, construction sites	Banks, schools, government offices, retail and grocery stores, restaurants, airports, hospitals, hotels, various types of offices

1.3 Standards and Staffing for Service Work

In general, determining time standards for service work is not as straightforward as it is for repetitive production work involving physical labor. Analysis techniques for determining staffing requirements for manual work and worker-machine systems that involve repetitive work cycles typically found in production work are based on the availability of time standards for the tasks performed. The time required to perform a given manual task can be determined with considerable precision because the method and other attributes of the repetitive work cycle have been standardized.

The following reasons explain why setting standards and determining staffing levels are more difficult for service operations:

- *Variable service.* Services of a given type vary, and therefore the time to provide the service varies. Even services that are provided on a repetitive basis are variable. For example, the time for a car salesman to sell a car to a prospective buyer is highly variable. In some cases, several hours may be invested to sell the car. In other cases, the car is sold in much less than an hour. Oftentimes, the salesman invests several hours, but the outcome of the effort is no sale.
- *Random arrivals.* In many service operations, customers arrive at random intervals, making it difficult to predict workloads and determine appropriate staffing levels.
- *Customer contact.* The level of customer contact affects the service time. In general, services characterized by a high level of customer contact tend to be more variable, because the customer's presence affects the time to complete the service.
- *Intangible work units.* The work units in service work are intangible and sometimes difficult to define, and therefore the problem of defining a standard method and standard time is difficult.
- *Undefined service.* Service work may consist of a variety of tasks whose exact details are not known in advance, and therefore a standard method cannot be specified. An example is nonroutine automotive repair work, such as work requiring diagnostics analysis (e.g., fixing a rattle in the car door). Service work of this kind is often charged simply by the time it takes a worker to complete a job, usually at an hourly rate.
- *Intermittent services.* Some services are delivered on an ongoing and intermittent basis. There is a continuing relationship between the service provider and the customer, but the interactions do not occur continuously. An example is an investor's account executive at a stockbroker. The investor and the account executive have a continuing relationship that requires only occasional contact, usually by telephone, to buy or sell securities. Standards in this kind of work are impractical.
- *Creative work.* In service work that requires creativity, the work cannot be directly measured. Therefore, time standards for creative work are not practical. The results of the work are usually measurable, but not the work itself. Evaluation of knowledge workers is therefore best assessed by the quality of what they produce, not by the methods of working.

Despite these reasons, good management of service operations requires both the efficient utilization of labor resources as well as the delivery of a quality service that meets or exceeds customer expectations. In the simplest case, the service manager has knowledge of the following two parameters regarding the work to be done and the resources for doing it: (1) some measure of the workload to be accomplished by the organization, and (2) the capacity of each service worker to contribute to the completion of that workload. If these two parameters can be expressed in terms of time, then staffing requirements can be estimated using the same basic equation:

$$w = \frac{WL}{AT} \tag{1}$$

where w = number of service workers required, WL = workload to be accomplished during a given period (e.g., hour, day, week), expressed in units of time (e.g., hours of work per hour), and AT = the available time of a service worker, expressed in the same units as the workload.

Example 1 Camera Repair Service

A camera repair plant receives broken cameras from customers through its dealership network. The broken cameras arrive by parcel delivery, and when repaired, they are returned to the dealerships by parcel delivery. The dealer includes an explanation of the malfunction with each camera returned for repair. The repair procedure followed by each repairperson is to read the explanation, decide what repairs are needed, make the repairs, and test the camera before turning it over to the shipping department for return to the originating dealer. There are three camera models involved, and several different malfunctions are associated with each model. Any repairperson can repair any of the models. Data have been compiled to determine the average repair time for each model, which is given in the table below. The average weekly number of cameras for each model returned to the plant for repairs are also shown. Each repairperson works on repairs for 6.5 hours per day, 5 days per week. How many repairpersons are required in the plant to service the repair workload?

	Basic Model	Deluxe Model	Super Model
Mean repair time, min	24	32	39
Cameras returned per week	173	148	94

Solution: We first compute the weekly workload:

$$WL = 173(24) + 148(32) + 94(39) = 12{,}554 \text{ min} = 209.2 \text{ hr/week}$$

The available time per week per repairperson is given by

$$AT = 5(6.5) = 32.5 \text{ hr/week per repairperson}$$

The number of workers required is therefore

$$w = \frac{209.2}{32.5} = 6.4, \text{ rounded up to } 7$$ ■

The best chance for using equation (1) is when the service work is somewhat repetitive and routine, such as in our example. Other examples of this kind of work include routine office work (e.g., typing, photocopying), order picking in a warehouse, and making parcel deliveries in a local metropolitan area. Estimating staff requirements is much more difficult for service work that is nonrepetitive, creative (e.g., the work of knowledge workers), and/or requires a high degree of worker discretion. Table 5 presents a number of examples of how standards are defined in various service operations.

The manager of a service operation is always faced with the challenge of finding the appropriate balance between achieving good customer service (which usually requires a greater number of available service workers) and keeping wage costs as low as possible (which means fewer service workers). A good example is the operations of a telephone call center, where customers call into the center for service (e.g., to answer questions

TABLE 5 Examples of Standards used in Service Work

Service Worker and Definition of Work Standard
Hospital nurse. The standard for a nurse is defined in terms of the number of patients for which the nurse is responsible. The standard varies depending on the type of ward. For a general medical/surgical ward, the number may be around seven or eight. For an intensive care unit, each nurse may be responsible for only three patients, because they require much more care and attention.
Salesperson. In many sales operations, quotas are used to provide standards or targets for sales staff. In some cases, the quota may be used for incentive purposes. For example, if the salesperson achieves the quota, a bonus is paid.
Server in a restaurant. Servers in traditional restaurants are assigned tables, which in effect determine the number of customers that are assigned to the server. The allocation method is highly variable, because often the restaurant manager does not know how many customers will show up on a given day or time. Also, the number of customers that sit at any given table varies. The result is that on a given evening, the server may be overworked or underworked. The level of work activity also translates back to the kitchen.
Repair and maintenance worker. Repair and maintenance work often divides into two categories: emergency work and preventive maintenance. Emergency work is unpredictable and time standards for it are difficult to set. The repair worker must drop everything and attend to the machine that has just broken down. Regular (preventive) maintenance can usually be scheduled using estimated times for each unit of work that is to be completed.
Pharmacist. Pharmacists at the local stores of large drug merchandisers (e.g., Walgreens, CVS) are expected to fill prescriptions at a certain rate. A typical standard used by these companies is 20 prescriptions per hour.
Dental hygienist in a dentist's office. The dentist sets the standard by deciding on how much time should be devoted to each patient and then the office support staff schedules the appointments accordingly. Forty-five minutes to an hour is typical.
Dentist. A dentist's time is valuable. Dentists want to schedule appointments so as to maximize the utility of their time. Different categories of dental work require different times. A simple filling may take 30 to 45 minutes. Bridgework and crowns are much more time consuming. Knowing the type of work that will be done for a given patient allows the office support staff to schedule patient appointments so as to minimize gaps in the schedule.
Caseworker (e.g., social service worker, probation officer, public defender). This service work is assigned to a caseworker as a caseload. Details of each case differ, and each case requires attention over an extended period of time (e.g., months). Although a similar service is provided for each case, the singular details of the case as well as the cognitive nature of the work make it impractical to define a standard method. The standard for casework is defined in terms of the number of cases per caseworker. It is generally a tight standard (i.e., a large caseload). When the caseload is too large, the resulting attention to each case is less than desirable, sometimes with dire consequences.
College faculty. The work standard for college faculty is usually defined in terms of the number of courses taught per semester. A typical course load is three courses per semester. There are factors that often alter this workload. For example, a large number of students in a course increases the amount of grading and student-faculty interaction that is required, so the load may be reduced to two courses per semester. In addition, faculties at leading universities are expected to engage in research and scholarly work, and this requirement justifies a reduction in course load.

about their bills or bank statements, to provide help in solving computer software problems, to change long distance telephone providers). With too few technicians answering the calls, customers experience long waiting times before their queries are answered. Adding more technicians reduces the average customer waiting time, but at greater labor cost for the calling center.

2 OFFICE WORK

Although the service industries include a wide variety of activities, many service operations are accomplished in offices, either in direct contact with the customer or behind the scenes supporting the service delivery. Despite the differences in the services, there are common aspects in the nature of the office work that is required to provide the service. In this section, we examine these commonalities.

An ***office*** is a place where the business-oriented activities of an organization are transacted and/or its services are rendered. The office is where the information-processing and related activities of the organization are accomplished. ***Office work*** is concerned with business functions such as design, sales, accounting, scheduling, and administration. Office work usually involves tasks associated with the receipt or collection of information received from various sources and its transformation into information of greater value and/or refinement that can be distributed to and used by various customers, employees, and other stakeholders of the organization. Office work also includes the storage of this information, and it may include the creation of information (e.g., designing a product) for subsequent processing within the organization. Office work has changed dramatically over the past 100 years, influenced by a variety of technological innovations that includes computers, photocopiers, fax machines, and the Internet.

2.1 Office Activities and Applications

Activities performed during office work should be distinguished from office applications [3]. ***Office activities*** are the physical and mental actions performed by an office worker while carrying out an assigned task. Activities include typing or keying, filing papers, participating in meetings, and telephoning. A more complete list of office activities is presented in Table 6. Note that the list includes activities with various proportions of mental and physical effort. Reading and decision-making contain a high proportion of mental exertion but very little physical work, while filing papers and mail handling have a higher physical content. Of course, activities performed in offices include more general actions such as talking, walking, and waiting.

Office applications are related to the business functions of the organization and are oriented toward end results and accomplishments. They include reports, proposals, accounts payable, and inventory control. Office applications often require multiple activities for their completion. For example, preparing a report requires typing or keying, proofreading, and photocopying. A more complete list of office applications is presented in Table 7. Routine applications such as accounts payable or accounts receivable are sometimes referred to as ***business processes***. Of course, different applications and business processes occur in different types of offices. The office applications in a doctor's office are different from those in a production-scheduling department.

TABLE 6 Examples of Office Activities

Analysis (e.g., analysis of data)	Making telephone calls
Answering telephone calls	Participating in meetings
Calculating	Photocopying
Collating and sorting	Proofreading or checking (e.g., a document)
Decision-making	Reading
Drawing or sketching	Thinking
Drawing conclusions or inferences	Typing or keying (e.g., personal computer)
Filing papers	Writing (with pen or pencil)
Mail handling	

Source: Based on lists in [2] and [3].

TABLE 7 Examples of Office Applications

Accounts payable	Presentations
Accounts receivable	Price lists
Bills or material (parts list for products)	Production scheduling
Engineering drawing preparation	Proposals (e.g., proposal to a customer)
Inventory lists	Purchase orders
Invoices	Reports (e.g., research report)
Payroll	Sales forecasts

Source: [3].

2.2 Creative Work Versus Routine Work

In terms of intellectual requirements and degree of difficulty, a range of work is performed in offices. Let us use the words "creative" and "routine" to describe the two extremes of the range.[3] Between the two extremes lies a continuum of work activities whose content is both creative and routine in varying proportions. ***Creative work*** tends to be intellectually more difficult and requires special skills and knowledge that may take years of education and/or experience to acquire. Creative work involves learning, analysis, decision-making, and problem solving. And the decisions and problems tend to be unique and individual. For example, designing a machine that has never been built before requires creativity and engineering knowledge about machinery.

By contrast, ***routine work*** tends to be repetitive and less difficult. The educational requirements to perform routine work are not as demanding as they are for creative work. Training is required, but not necessarily a college degree or professional training (e.g., medical school, graduate studies). Routine work consists of procedures that are replicated closely for every task of a certain type. If the procedures are performed in large volumes, there may be opportunities for automating the work (Section 2.4). The characteristics and typical activities of routine and creative office work are compared in Table 8.

[3]The terms "creative" and "routine" were suggested by [3].

TABLE 8 Comparison of Routine and Creative Office Work

	Routine Office Work	Combination of Routine and Creative	Creative Office Work
Characteristics:	Easy Less education required Repetitive Predictable Defined procedures		Difficult More education required Nonrepetitive Problem solving Unique problems
Office activities:	Filing papers Carrying things Collating and sorting Mail handling Photocopying Typing or keying	Answering telephone calls Making telephone calls Participating in meetings Reading Writing	Analysis Calculating Decision-making Drawing conclusions or inferences Drawing or sketching Proofreading or checking Thinking

2.3 Knowledge Workers and Support Personnel

Office workers are often organized as a department or work group that is supervised by a single manager. The reason for organizing the workers in this way is because they share a common purpose or function in the organization, and there is a need to communicate with each other in accomplishing their function. Certain members of the group have skills and areas of expertise that are different from but complementary to the skills and expertise of other members, so that the collective knowledge of the group can effectively serve the larger organization.

The workers in a department or work group can be classified into two general categories: knowledge workers and support personnel. The ***knowledge workers*** are the office workers who accomplish the creative information-processing activities and applications in offices. They are the white-collar professionals such as managers, lawyers, engineers, designers, researchers, and technical specialists. Two types of knowledge workers can be distinguished: managerial and nonmanagerial. Table 9 presents a list of knowledge worker titles for the two categories.

TABLE 9 Typical Titles of Knowledge Workers Who Work in Offices

Managerial Titles		NonManagerial Titles	
Chief executive officer	Principal (school)	Engineer	Research scientist
President	Provost (university)	Senior engineer	Professor
Vice president	Dean (college)	Lawyer	Editor
Manager	Department chairperson	Doctor	Chemist
Superintendent (schools)	(academic department)	Dentist	Sales/marketing analyst

Knowledge is more than information. ***Information*** is data that has acquired relevance and meaning by virtue of the context in which it exists and the way in which it is organized. Information requires human interpretation. ***Knowledge*** is information that has been learned and synthesized with other information in the human brain. Possession of knowledge is a human capability. It requires understanding and comprehension that cannot be readily captured in a computer database. A computer database contains data that can be presented as information for interpretation by knowledge workers.

As the name suggests, ***support personnel*** provide administrative and staff assistance for the office, usually reporting to the department manager but serving the needs of the knowledge worker staff. Support personnel perform the routine tasks in the office, thus allowing the knowledge workers to perform the more creative and professional work. A more complete list of support personnel titles is presented in Table 10.

Knowledge work is different from the routine office work usually performed by support staff or the physical work performed in production and logistics. Whereas routine office work and manual labor can be subjected to analysis, mechanization, and automation to improve operational efficiency, knowledge work depends on uniquely human traits that cannot be automated.[4] These human traits include creative abilities, discretion, and self-pacing. Creative abilities are required to do creative work. Discretion is required because the knowledge worker must decide how to approach a given problem or task, what methods to use, and how to adapt to new discoveries during the creative process. The knowledge worker works at his or her own pace; there is no machine operating at a constant cycle time that regulates the worker's pace.

In some offices, the support personnel outnumber the knowledge workers. For example, in the private practice of a physician or dentist, the number of support personnel assisting the doctor during office hours may range from two to five. The president of a corporation is likely to have a large office staff of support personnel, not including vice presidents reporting to the president. In other types of offices, the professional staff outnumbers the support staff. Examples include engineering offices, college academic departments, research laboratories, design studios, and other offices that accomplish creative or knowledge-oriented work and therefore require a large number of professional staff. The ratios in these cases may be five-to-one or more.

TABLE 10 Typical Titles of Support Personnel Who Work in Offices

Administrative assistant	Data entry operator	Secretary
Administrative associate	Editorial assistant	Stenographer
Bookkeeper	Equipment technician	Telephone operator
Clerical worker	Receptionist	Typist

[4]Readers familiar with artificial intelligence and expert systems may challenge this statement. The author's view is that expert systems have been applied to situations in which a body of information related to a specific field or discipline has been reduced to a set of rules and formulas that can be used for diagnostic or predictive purposes. For example, diagnosing diseases in medical science or developing process plans for manufacturing plants are representative of expert systems applications. In effect, the expert system is performing a routine work process (albeit a complicated one) by comparing the known facts about the case (e.g., medical patient or part design) against the body of available information on the subject to compute an answer (e.g., diagnosis or process plan).

Determining the appropriate ratio depends on how much of the office workload requires the special skills, knowledge, and credentials of the knowledge workers and how much of the workload does not have this requirement and therefore can be delegated to the support staff. For the knowledge workers in an office, the proportion of creative work should be high and the proportion of routine work should be low. For support staff, the proportion of routine work should be high and the proportion of creative work should be low. Knowledge workers are paid at a much higher rate than support personnel, usually by a factor of two or more, sometimes much more. They are paid more because they are creative. They do not justify their higher salaries when they spend their time performing routine tasks that should be delegated to support staff. The ideal allocation of workloads between knowledge workers and support staff is depicted in Figure 1.

Although the ideal allocation of routine and creative work is indicated in Figure 1, it must be acknowledged that virtually all jobs contain both creative work and routine work in various proportions. The results of a 1988 study reported in [3] indicate that the proportions of routine and creative work among knowledge workers and support personnel were as shown in Figure 2.[5] The fact is that a large proportion of a knowledge worker's workday can be spent performing routine work. Table 11 lists many of the reasons and excuses given by professionals for why they perform routine work.

When support staff is called upon to perform creative work, the reactions are mixed. Some feel stressed at being required to work above their level of competence. They are being taken advantage of. Others welcome the challenge and extra responsibility, perhaps sensing an opportunity to upgrade their skills and advance their careers in the organization. Similarly, when knowledge workers are required to perform routine tasks, the feelings are mixed. Some feel that they are working below their job description, and that their skills, knowledge, and education are not being used to the fullest.

	Routine work	Creative work
Knowledge workers	0%	100%
Support staff	100%	0%

Figure 1 Ideal allocation of workloads between knowledge workers and support staff.

	Routine work	Creative work
Knowledge workers	63%	37%
Support staff	93%	7%

Figure 2 Allocation of workloads between knowledge workers and support staff as indicated in a 1988 study reported in [3].

[5]Although a 1988 study may seem out of date, it should be noted that much of the office automation brought about by the introduction of photocopiers and personal computers (PCs) had already occurred by 1988.

TABLE 11 Reasons and Excuses Why Professionals (Knowledge Workers) Perform Routine Tasks

The work is easier. It is more comfortable. As the saying goes, "Thinking is hard; that's why so few people do it."
Managers can measure results of routine tasks. The results of creative tasks are often more difficult to measure.
Managers can predict the time required for routine tasks. It is more difficult to predict the time required for creative tasks.
Support personnel are not available to delegate the work to them.
Support personnel are only assigned to managers and not available to regular professional staff. Therefore, the regular professional staff must do the routine work themselves.
Support personnel do not do their jobs adequately, so it is easier for the knowledge workers to do the work themselves.
Support personnel are not trained properly, so it is easier for the knowledge workers to do the work themselves.

Source: Based largely on [3].

Others take comfort in the routine work. After all, it is easier, and they are still getting paid their high salaries. For that very reason, it is costly to the organization for knowledge workers to do routine work.

Staffing levels in offices can be determined by knowing or estimating the total workload that the office must accomplish, and then apportioning the workload according to its creative and routine contents. The following example illustrates the approach.

Example 2 Office Staffing Levels

An engineering consulting firm has 15 engineers and one staff support person, all of whom work in one office complex. The firm is forced to turn away work because the engineers currently have more work than they can handle. An analysis by the managing partner shows that 33% of the working time of the engineers involves routine tasks that could be done by support staff. The main reason the engineers perform this routine work is because the single staff support person in the firm is already overloaded. Determine (a) how many more staff personnel the firm should hire and (b) by what percentage could the firm's revenues be increased by freeing the engineers of the routine work.

Solution **(a)** Assuming that each engineer works an 8-hour day, and that the 33% is evenly distributed among the 15 engineers, the total amount of routine work done by the engineers is computed as follows:

$$\text{Total routine workload of engineers} = 0.33(15)(8) = 39.6 \text{ hr of routine work/day}$$

Assuming each additional staff support person works 8 hours, the number of additional support people that should be hired is 39.6/8 = 4.95, which would be rounded up to five new support personnel.

(b) Given that 33% of the engineers' time is lost to routine work, this leaves 67% of their time that is devoted to creative work. If all of their routine work is delegated to support staff, so that 100% of their time involves creative work, then the firm's revenues could increase by 1.00/0.67 − 1 = 0.493 = 49.3%. ■

A factor that negatively impacts productivity in office operations is the typical unpaced nature of office work. By contrast, factory work is often paced by the automatic cycle of the production machine or the speed of the assembly line conveyor.

The worker is forced to maintain a pace that is consistent with the rhythm of the equipment. Office work has no analogous mechanized pacing. As a result, office workers typically spend less time performing the work of the organization and more time engaged in non-productive activities, such as rest breaks, coffee breaks, snack breaks, smoke breaks,[6] personal time (e.g., paying personal bills), talking, waiting (e.g., for elevators), attending meetings (which may or may not be productive), and socializing. Consequently, the proportion of time spent actually accomplishing productive work may be only 5.5 hours out of an 8-hour shift [3]. This constitutes an allowance factor of 45% compared to a typical allowance factor of 15% in factory production work.

2.4 Office Automation and Augmentation

One usually associates automation with production operations, where the quantities are high and the parts or products are identical. However, automation can also be applied to office work. The introduction of the computer as a widely used business machine in the 1950s, and more particularly the introduction of the personal computer in the 1980s, has resulted in significant changes in the way office work is performed. ***Office automation*** is the term used to describe these and other changes in which computers and other business machines automate much of the routine and repetitive work that is accomplished in offices. Given our definition of office work as information-processing activities concerned with the business functions of an organization, then a significant part of office automation consists of the computerization of these information-processing activities. The various business tools and technologies for implementing office automation are still evolving, and they will continue to do so as computer technology continues to advance. At this point in time, the characteristics of a modern office automation system can be described as follows:

- Office automation involves the convergence and integration of three traditional office technologies: (1) ***office machine*** technology, which included typewriters, adding machines, dictation machines, and photocopiers; (2) ***data processing*** technology, which includes computers, data storage devices, printers, and other output devices; and (3) ***communication*** technologies, which includes telephones and teletype machines.[7]
- Office automation consists of hardware and software. The hardware includes personal computers, telephones, photocopiers, and scanners. The software includes word processors, spreadsheets, and other business-related software.
- Office automation systems operate in a network environment, which includes the capability to share information within the organization and to access information and accomplish business transactions on the Internet.

[6]Most offices are designated as "smoke-free workplaces," so workers who smoke must do so outside the building, which prolongs the break.

[7]Many of the traditional machines identified in this list of office technologies have virtually disappeared from the office scene and been replaced by newer technologies. Two examples: (1) Typewriters have been largely replaced by personal computers with word processing software. They are still used but usually for odd jobs and filling out paper forms. (2) Teletype machines have been replaced by fax machines and electronic mail (e-mail).

- The purpose of office automation is to assist office workers in accomplishing their information-processing activities and applications (Tables 6 and 7)—that is, creating, processing, storing, retrieving, and communicating information.

Computerization has significantly improved the efficiency of office applications that are routine and accomplished in high volumes. These applications include payroll, production scheduling, inventory control, material requirements planning, and sales forecasting. Computerization has also been of tremendous value in implementing database applications, in which large amounts of data must be stored, maintained, and made accessible to large numbers of users. Examples of these database applications include accounting, employee records, airline flight scheduling, product catalogs, and product design (e.g., bills of material, design drawings that have been developed using computer-aided design systems).

In addition to high-volume tasks and database applications, which are classified as routine office work, computerization has also been effective in assisting the knowledge worker who performs creative work. This is sometimes called ***office augmentation***, which refers to the use of computer systems to enhance the abilities of a worker in low-volume creative work, such as designing a product or writing a proposal. Whereas office automation is concerned with making a process more efficient, less time-consuming, and less costly, office augmentation is concerned with increasing the effectiveness of the process, the convenience of the worker, and the quality of the result. Office augmentation is achieved by providing the worker with tools that allow quicker access to information that is needed, more convenient communication with colleagues and coworkers, and improved procedures for performing the creative work required in the process. Figure 3 summarizes the characteristics of computer automation and computer augmentation.

A good example to help distinguish computer automation from computer augmentation is the difference in the way different types of workers use a personal computer equipped with word processing software. When a secretary is given a handwritten document to enter into the computer, the secretary types the document, which is stored electronically in the computer's hard drive or other storage medium. The work of the

Computer application:	Automation	Augmentation
Type of work:	Routine work	Creative work
Type of office worker:	Support personnel	Knowledge workers
Attributes:	High efficiency Less time consuming Less costly	High effectiveness Convenience to worker High quality results
Office application examples:	High-volume tasks Database applications	Designing products Creating new text

Figure 3 Automation and augmentation for routine and creative work.

secretary in this situation is routine. But when a newspaper reporter composes an article on a word processor, creative work is being accomplished. The secretary and the reporter have access to the same word processing features (spellchecker, grammar check, dictionary), but their use of the tool is quite different. The computer has increased the effectiveness of the reporter's creative task, while it has only increased the efficiency of the secretary's routine task. Some examples of computer augmentation in office and professional work are presented in Table 12.

TABLE 12 Examples of Computer Augmentation in Performing Creative Work.

Design engineer working at a computer-aided design (CAD) workstation designing a product. Specialized CAD software is available for mechanical design, architectural design, electrical and electronics design, and other design fields.
Writer or author using word processor software on a personal computer (PC) to develop the text for an article or book. Typesetting for the publication can be prepared directly from the computer file.
College professor using slide preparation software (e.g., Microsoft PowerPoint) on a PC to prepare slides for a class.
Commercial artist working at a computer graphics terminal preparing line drawings for an engineering textbook.
Lawyer preparing a legal document on a word processor by starting with a standard document and making alterations to suit the specific needs of a client.
Research program administrator using specialized spreadsheet software to prepare the budget for a proposal on a PC.
Process planner preparing the route sheet (manufacturing process plan) for a part using specialized process planning software on a PC.
Time study engineer using specialized work measurement software on a PC to prepare the time standard and method description for a manual assembly operation.

REFERENCES

[1] Chase, R., N. Aquilano, and R. Jacobs. *Operations Management for Competitive Advantage*. New York: McGraw-Hill, 2001.

[2] Galitz, W. O. *Humanizing Office Automation*. Wellesley, MA: QED Information Sciences, 1984.

[3] Larson, R. W., and D. J. Zimney. *The White-Collar Shuffle: Who Does What in Today's Computerized Workplace*. New York: AMACOM, American Management Association, 1990.

[4] Lee, J. "Knowledge Management: The Intellectual Revolution." *IIE Solutions* (October 2000):34–37.

[5] Mundel, M. E. *The White-Collar Knowledge Worker*. Norcross, GA Asian Productivity Organization, 1989.

[6] Odgers, P., and B. L. Keeling. *Administrative Office Management*. 12th ed. Cincinnati, OH: South-Western Educational Publishing, Thomson Learning, 2000.

[7] Pepitone, J. S. "A Case for Humaneering." *IIE Solutions* (May 2002): 39–44.

[8] Pepitone, J. S. "Humaneered Work Systems." Paper presented at the 12th World Productivity Congress, November 30, 2000.

[9] Quibble, Z. K. *Administrative Office Management*. 7th ed. Upper Saddle River, NJ: Prentice Hall, 2001.

[10] Website: www.bls.gov

[11] Website: www.ulrichwerner.com/ba303/documents/42.html

[12] Whitehead, E. "Paper Chase." *Work Study* 50, no. 6 (2001).

REVIEW QUESTIONS

1 What are some of the factors that distinguish services from products?

2 Identify the factors by which the quality of a service is judged by a customer.

3 Service operations and organizations can be divided into three major categories. Name those categories.

4 What is the difference between a facilities-based service and a field-based service?

5 Give some examples of high-contact services and of low-contact services.

6 What are the differences in worker attributes between high-contact services and low-contact services?

7 What are some of the differences between manual work and service work?

8 In general, determining time standards for service work is more difficult than for repetitive production work. Why?

9 Define what an office is.

10 Define office work.

11 What is the difference between office activities and office applications?

12 Identify some of the differences between creative office work and routine office work.

13 What are the differences between office knowledge workers and office support personnel?

14 Define office automation.

15 Office automation reflects the convergence and integration of three traditional office technologies. Name the three technologies and identify some of the equipment in each technology.

16 Define office augmentation.

PROBLEMS

1 A small appliance manufacturer is planning to open a repair facility that would receive broken appliances from customers and repair them. Customers would send their broken appliances to the facility, and when repaired, they would be returned directly to the customer. There are five different appliance models that would be repaired, identified here as A, B, C, D, and E. The industrial engineering department has provided estimates of the average time to repair each model. These mean times are, respectively, 23 min, 42 min, 19 min, 27 min, and 35 min. The management wants to staff the facility in anticipation of a weekly return rate of 100 appliances per week for models A, B, and C, and a weekly return rate of 150 appliances for models D and E. The facility will operate one shift five days per week, but it is anticipated that each repairperson will spend an average of only 6.0 hours per day repairing appliances. How many repairpersons will be required for the facility?

2 The Best Eastern Hotel chain is opening a new luxury hotel in Atlantic City, and its maid staff requirements must be determined. The new hotel will have 250 rooms. The occupancy rate is expected to be 75% during the week (five nights) and 95% on weekends (two nights). Each maid will be responsible for cleaning 12 rooms per day (approximately 35 min per room). Their day begins at 7:00 A.M., and the cleaning of all rooms must be completed by 3:00 P.M. each day. One hour is allowed out of their day for lunch and breaks, so the actual time worked is 7.0 hours. Maids will work five days per week on a revolving schedule to balance weekday and weekend duties. Given an absentee rate of 5% that must be included in the determination, how many cleaning maids must be hired by the new hotel?

3 A new metropolitan hospital will have 500 beds, and nursing staff requirements must be determined. The occupancy rate (ratio of patients to beds) is expected to be 85% on average. For temporary peaks above 85%, the hospital plans to use overtime to cope with the extra workload. The hospital must have a nursing staff for all three shifts, but the number of patients per nurse is different for different shifts. For the first and second shift (6 A.M. to 10 P.M.), the ratio will be 8 patients per nurse. For the third shift (10 P.M. to 6 A.M.), the ratio will be 12 patients per nurse. Each nurse would work a regular 40 hours per week in shifts of 8 hours. (a) How many staff nurses (not counting supervisors) must be hired by the new hospital, if the anticipated nurse absentee rate (due mostly to illness) is 6%, which must be factored into the calculation? (b) How many nurses would work each shift during any given 24-hour period?

4 An accounting firm has 22 accountants and two staff support personnel. The firm has trouble handling all of its workload, especially around tax time each year, because the accountants currently have more work than they can accomplish. The president of the firm has studied the work content of the various jobs done by the firm and has determined that 27% of job activities performed by the accountants are routine work that could be done by support staff. The reason the accountants perform this routine work is because the two staff support people are already overloaded. Assume a 40-hour workweek. Determine (a) how many more staff personnel the firm should hire and (b) by what percentage could the firm's revenues be increased by freeing the accountants of the routine work.

Projects and Project Management

Work systems perform ***operations work***, which consists mostly of repetitive activities. In this chapter, we consider ***project work***, in which the activities are usually nonrepetitive. A ***project*** is a temporary undertaking directed at accomplishing some major output, usually requiring substantial resources and significant time to complete. In general, each project is unique. It is done only once. The major output of the project might be a large construction job, a military weapons system, a new product design, or the development of a new medicine. The resources in a project consist of people and equipment. In some cases, thousands of workers are required. Although we have called it a temporary undertaking, some projects take decades to complete.[1] The cost to fund a project can run into billions of dollars.

A project is a work system. It consists of a series of related activities, some of which can be done simultaneously while others must be performed sequentially. Each activity is usually a significant effort in its own right, consisting of multiple tasks, and requiring many people and much time. Because a project is usually large and expensive, it should

[1]For example, the Panama Canal, constructed in the early part of the twentieth century, required more than 75,000 workers and more than 10 years to complete.

have specific objectives regarding performance, cost, time, and scope (PCTS objectives). Cost refers to the budget that is established for the project. Time refers to the planned schedule. Performance refers to the progress of the work and how the various measures of cost, time, and scope compare with the plan at any point during project execution. Performance is also concerned with the quality of the product that results from the project. Scope is concerned with defining the tasks that will and will not be done during the project. ***Project management*** (PM) consists of planning, scheduling, organizing, monitoring, and controlling the activities of a project so that the PCTS objectives are achieved to the satisfaction of the customer or sponsor. The overall responsibility for managing a given project is assigned to an individual who is designated as the ***project manager***.

1 PROJECTS

As our introduction states, a project is temporary, its output is unique, it requires substantial resources, consists of multiple tasks, and takes significant time to finish. Let us elaborate on those characteristics that are common to all projects:

- A project is ***temporary***. A given project is intended to satisfy a defined need. Once that need is satisfied, then the project is completed, and the resources required for it are disbanded or reassigned to other activities. A project should have a single beginning point and a single endpoint in time. The beginning represents the launching of the initial tasks, and the endpoint represents the delivery of the project's outcome to the customer or sponsor.
- Its ***output is unique***. Each project is done only one time. There may be similarities to other projects (e.g., construction projects), but the details are different because the circumstances surrounding each endeavor are rarely or never the same.
- ***Substantial resources*** are usually required, both human and nonhuman. A variety of worker skills and knowledge as well as equipment is needed. The different resources must be coordinated.
- A project consists of ***multiple tasks***. Some of the tasks must be accomplished before others can be started. Completion of each task is required in order to complete the project. There are resource and time considerations in each task. The different tasks must be scheduled and managed.
- A project requires ***significant time*** to complete. A major development project can consume years, but it ultimately comes to an end. The end comes when the objectives of the project are accomplished, or when it is decided that the objectives cannot be achieved, or when the reason for doing the project no longer exists.

A project must be distinguished from the output or product that results from it. If a bridge is built, the bridge is the output, and the project is the planning, design, and construction of the bridge. If a new generation of automobile is designed, the automobile is the product, and the project is the variety of design activities that are accomplished to bring it to market. If a new military weapon system is developed, the weapon system is the product, and the project consists of the research, testing, design, and fabrication work required to create it. The project and the product are not synonymous.

The term *program* is often used in the context of projects and project management. In the hierarchy of project activity levels, a program is considered to be the highest level. An extremely large and expensive undertaking, consisting of several major development efforts and expected to take many years to complete, would be called a ***program***. The major development efforts in a program are designated as projects. The group of projects under a program would be coordinated to achieve benefits not possible if the projects were managed separately. Development of the Polaris missile system in the 1950s was called a program. The projects required to complete the program included the development of the submarine, the missile, and other systems and technologies required for them to work together. A program is driven by the strategic goals of the organization sponsoring it.

A project consists of multiple tasks. In some cases, hundreds of unique tasks can be identified in a project, forming a pyramidal hierarchy of upper-level subprojects consisting of middle-level tasks and lower-level work packages. A typical hierarchy consists of six levels, as illustrated in Figure 1. Each level is subdivided into smaller work activities below until it makes no sense to subdivide further. As many as 20 levels may be defined in a very large project or program [4].

A project has a life cycle. The life cycle consists of a series of phases, each phase bringing the project closer to completion and usually concluding with the achievement of a major deliverable. The phases vary for different application areas (e.g., construction, new car design, software development, biotechnology research) and even for projects within a single application area. Different work packages in the work breakdown structure are associated with different phases of the project. Those responsible for accomplishing the work packages are also associated with different phases. For example, an electrician working on a building project would be involved in the execution phase (construction) but not in the architectural design (planning). A typical project life cycle consists of five phases (based mostly on [4] and [5]):

1. *Concept and feasibility phase.* This is a preliminary phase in which the concept and feasibility of the project outcome are evaluated. The relevance of the project to the strategic goals of the organization is assessed. Tactical decisions about technologies, styles, and research directions are often made. Market surveys, feasibility studies, or research proposals may be required, depending on the application area. The deliverable at the end of this phase is a decision to proceed or not to proceed with the project. The project manager is likely to be appointed during this initial phase.

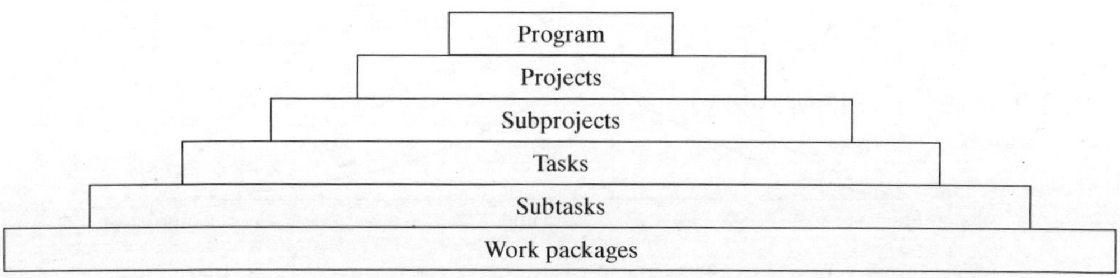

Figure 1 Hierarchy of program and project levels.

2. *Definition phase.* This is the problem definition step in the project. In a construction project, the definition phase would involve the architectural design of the structure. In a new product development project, the preliminary design or prototype of the product may be delivered. In some projects, problem definition may be part of the concept and feasibility phase.
3. *Planning phase.* The detailed planning of the project itself is accomplished during this phase. A breakdown of the work activities is developed, and the schedule for the work activities is laid out. Risks associated with the project are evaluated, and measures are devised to address those risks. The deliverable at the end of this phase is approval of the plan. Contracts to outside vendors are awarded.
4. *Execution phase.* The actual work on the project is done during this phase. The majority of the time and cost of the project is consumed during execution. The progress of the work is monitored against the schedule, and corrective action is taken to deal with any exceptions. Additional resources must be allocated to tasks that are behind schedule or re-allocated from other tasks. If the corrective action does not bring progress back into agreement with the schedule, then the schedule must be revised. The deliverable at the end of the execution phase is that the project is essentially completed.
5. *Closeout.* This final phase involves turning over the outcome or product of the project to the customer or sponsor. In addition, it is useful to conduct a review of the project to determine lessons learned that might be applied to future projects.

The phases suggested here are shown on a time plot in Figure 2. The level of planning effort is high in the beginning phases of a project, and the majority of the cost and staffing of the project are expended during the execution phase. As the project draws closer to closeout, the level of expenditures generally begins to diminish, as indicated in the figure. The control of total expenditures in a project often depends on how effective the up-front planning is. On this note, let us turn our attention to the topic of project management, an important component of which is planning.

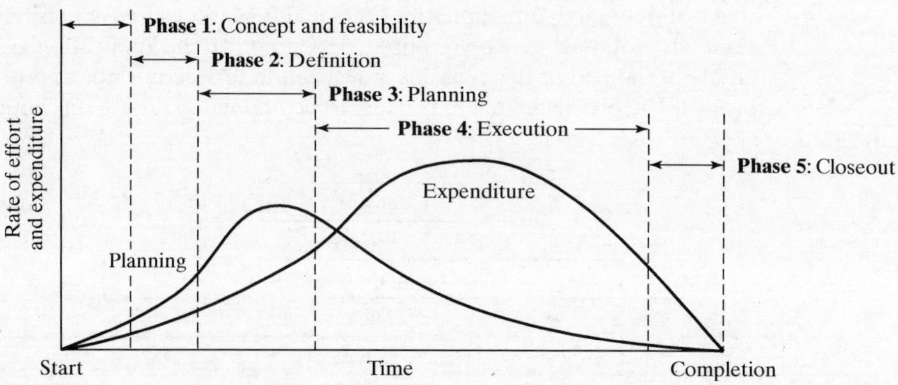

Figure 2 Typical project life cycle, showing five phases and the level of planning effort and project expenditure level throughout the project.

2 PROJECT MANAGEMENT

Project management (PM) shares much in common with operations management. Both are concerned with functions such as planning, organizing, staffing, coordinating, executing, monitoring, and controlling the enterprise being managed in order to achieve organizational objectives. Project management differs from operations management in that the enterprise being managed is temporary rather than ongoing. In PM, once the objectives are achieved and the project is completed (or otherwise terminated), the management effort is dispersed. In the current section, we discuss the following aspects of project management: (1) project teams, (2) project planning, and (3) project control.[2]

2.1 Project Teams

Management of a project is accomplished through the use of a project team. In many cases, the team is dedicated full time (or nearly so) to the project, at least during the phase or phases in which their services are required. Construction projects usually have this kind of organization. Skilled workers (e.g., concrete workers, carpenters, electricians, plumbers) are hired full-time at the construction site during the phases of the project when their trades are needed. An advantage of this project structure is that the team's composition can be designed to precisely fit the needs of the project, and the specialized resources (human and otherwise) can be applied to the project exactly when they are needed. A disadvantage for the workers is the risk that there may be a delay (time off without pay) until their services are needed on the next project.

A project team is usually ***cross-functional***, meaning that its members are selected from a variety of departments within the organization. Some of the members may even be from outside the organization. For example, the membership of a new product design team is likely to consist not only of design engineers but also representatives from manufacturing, sales and marketing, quality control, and other departments in the company. In some product design teams, customers and suppliers may be included as members, as they represent a unique perspective not likely to exist within the company itself.

Managing the project and the team members assigned to it is the responsibility of the ***project manager***. Challenges facing the project manager are different from those of an operations manager. If the team is cross-functional, then its members have different educations, skills, and experiences. The diversity represented in the project team is likely to be more of a management challenge than what is usually experienced in one department of a line organization. Another issue faced by the project manager is greater risk. There is more security in operations management simply because it is concerned with the continuation of an ongoing activity. A project is unique and temporary, and there is uncertainty in its outcome.

The project team often overlaps with the traditional organizational structure. When team members have functional or operational responsibilities at the same time they are participating in the project, the arrangement is called a ***matrix structure***. The term *matrix* derives from the fact that the organizational structure is two-dimensional. Superimposed on the traditional vertical structure that is designed to serve the operational needs of

[2]The Project Management Institute, located in Newtown Square, Pennsylvania, is the largest professional organization dedicated to the field of project management. Its Web site is www.pmi.org.

the organization is a horizontal structure that is intended to satisfy the objectives of the project. Participation in a project team is usually a temporary assignment for a team member, because the project itself is temporary. When the project is completed, the members resume their regular jobs or are assigned to other projects. While members of the team, their participation on the project may be full-time or part-time. If full-time, they are loaned by their home departments to participate in the project, and the home departments must somehow figure out how to operate without them. If part-time, the employees must find a suitable balance between their duties to the traditional organization and their obligations to the project. Serving part-time in a matrix organizational structure can sometimes be a problem because the employee must report to two supervisors, the project manager and the home department supervisor.

2.2 Project Planning

Project planning is concerned with the development of a formal document (i.e., the project plan) that will be used to direct the execution and control of the project. The project plan describes the objectives and deliverables of the project (its outcome and scope), the work to be accomplished, its cost, and its time frame. The principal uses of the project plan are to (1) document the assumptions and decisions underlying the plan, (2) facilitate communication among those who are involved in the project or have an interest in it, and (3) document the performance, cost, time, and scope (PCTS) objectives of the project [5].

Details of the work to be accomplished in the project plan are captured in a ***work breakdown structure*** (WBS), which defines and organizes the project into increasingly more detailed task descriptions in each descending level of the project hierarchy (Figure 1). The lowest level items in the WBS are typically called *work packages*. The WBS identifies the relationships among the various work packages and how they fit together into each higher level. The required workload, time, and cost can be estimated for each work package more easily and accurately than for the higher levels.

The work breakdown structure does not indicate the sequence in which the work packages are to be performed. This is done in ***project scheduling***—the component of project planning that is concerned with (1) estimating the times required for the work packages in the WBS, (2) determining the sequence of the work packages, and (3) planning the dates for performing them and the dates for meeting milestones in the project. The dates can then be compared to the overall completion date specified for the project. If the schedule does not achieve the specified completion date, then adjustments must be made in the project schedule, or agreement must be reached with the project sponsor on a later completion date. Adjustments in the schedule are usually made by increasing the resources available to those activities that are deemed critical in the project, the objective being to reduce the time to complete these activities. Techniques used in project scheduling include Gantt charts and critical path scheduling methods. These tools are described in Section 3.

Activity times should be estimated by those individuals on the project team who are most familiar with the type of work involved. Time estimates are usually based on one or more of the following [5]: (1) expert judgment guided by historical data, (2) actual times taken by previous activities that were similar, and (3) quantity of work units to be completed, multiplied by their corresponding standard times (if the nature of the activity lends itself to this kind of analysis). Contingencies are often added to the estimated times in recognition of the uncertainty involved in the activity.

2.3 Project Control

Once project planning has been completed and the required approvals are given to proceed, then the project execution phase begins. The actual work on the project commences. During the execution phase, the emphasis in project management shifts to project control. ***Project control*** is concerned with (1) monitoring the progress of the work activities, (2) comparing the progress with the project schedule, and (3) taking corrective action when activities are found to be behind schedule. Project control considers not only the time aspects of the project but also performance, cost, and scope (the PCTS objectives).

Techniques used in project control include performance reviews, variance analysis, earned value analysis, and trend analysis [5]. ***Performance reviews*** are project management meetings that are held periodically to assess and communicate the status and progress of the project. The meetings often include presentations on the results of the other control techniques: variance analysis, earned value analysis, and trend analysis.

In ***variance analysis***, the actual progress at a given point in the schedule is compared with the planned progress at that point. Schedule and cost are the most common measures considered in variance analysis, but other measures may also be included, such as quality, risk, or scope. When a variance is identified, its cause must be determined, and decisions must be made on how to respond to it. The possible responses are [4]: (1) cancel the project, an action taken only when a project is determined to no longer be viable; (2) ignore the variance, when its effect does not seriously impact progress; (3) take corrective action, such as increasing the resources available to the activity that is in variance; or (4) revise the plan to accommodate the variance.

Earned value analysis is a technique that integrates the performance measures of cost, time, and scope as a function of time. It is most easily conceptualized in the form of a graphical plot, as shown in Figure 3. The plot shows the budgeted cumulative cost throughout the project schedule and its actual cost for work completed at a given point in time during the schedule. By comparing the budgeted cost and actual cost, a sense of the project's status can be immediately and visually assessed. Earned value analysis is often associated with variance analysis because it indicates variances from the schedule.

Trend analysis is concerned with the assessment of the various performance measures as a function of time into the project to identify whether performance is improving or worsening. Trend analysis may help to identify certain activities in the project that are at risk of falling behind schedule or overrunning the budget.

3 PROJECT SCHEDULING TECHNIQUES

Project planning and control is usually implemented using project scheduling techniques such as Gantt charts and network diagrams. Two types of network diagrams are covered: critical path method (CPM) and program evaluation and review technique (PERT).

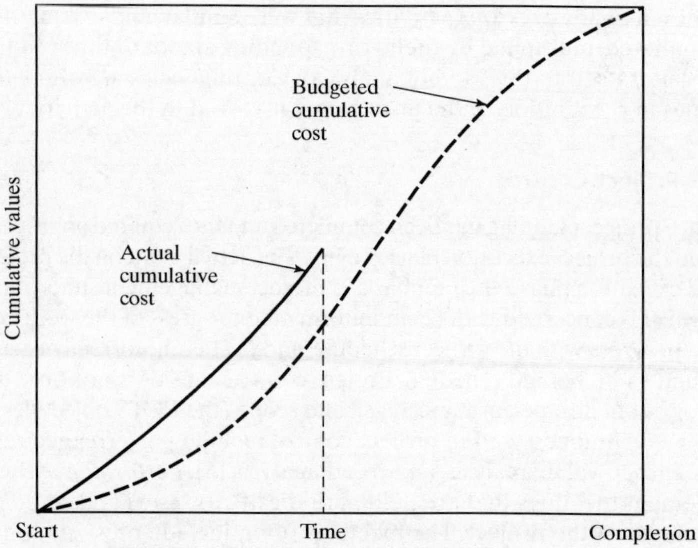

Figure 3 Typical plot used in earned value analysis, showing the budgeted cumulative cost of a project and the actual cumulative cost for work completed.

3.1 Gantt Charts

A ***Gantt chart*** is a graphical display of scheduled project activities on a time axis. As illustrated in Figure 4, project activities are listed along the vertical axis, and their time durations are shown as horizontal bars with starting and ending dates scaled on the time axis. The project manager can utilize a Gantt chart to monitor the status of the project's activities. Figure 4 (a) shows the planned schedule for a hypothetical project, and (b) shows the status at some point after project execution has commenced, providing a visual comparison between scheduled and actual accomplishments.

In a conventional Gantt chart, precedence can usually be inferred from the relative starting and ending points of the activities. When activities have starting points corresponding with the ending times of other activities, it is assumed that there is a precedence relationship between them. For example, we must infer that activity 3 in Figure 4 (a) must be completed before activities 4, 5, 6, and 7 can begin. Unfortunately, the precedence relationships among the activities are not always clearly indicated in this form of Gantt chart. However, arrows can be added to clarify the precedence relationships, as shown in Figure 5. The network scheduling techniques discussed in Sections 3.2 and 3.3 identify the precedence relationships more clearly, but they do not show the timing relationships as well as a Gantt chart.

The Gantt chart is a widely used tool not only in project scheduling but in production scheduling as well. Its name is based on its inventor, Henry Gantt, one of the pioneers in scientific management (Historical Note 1).

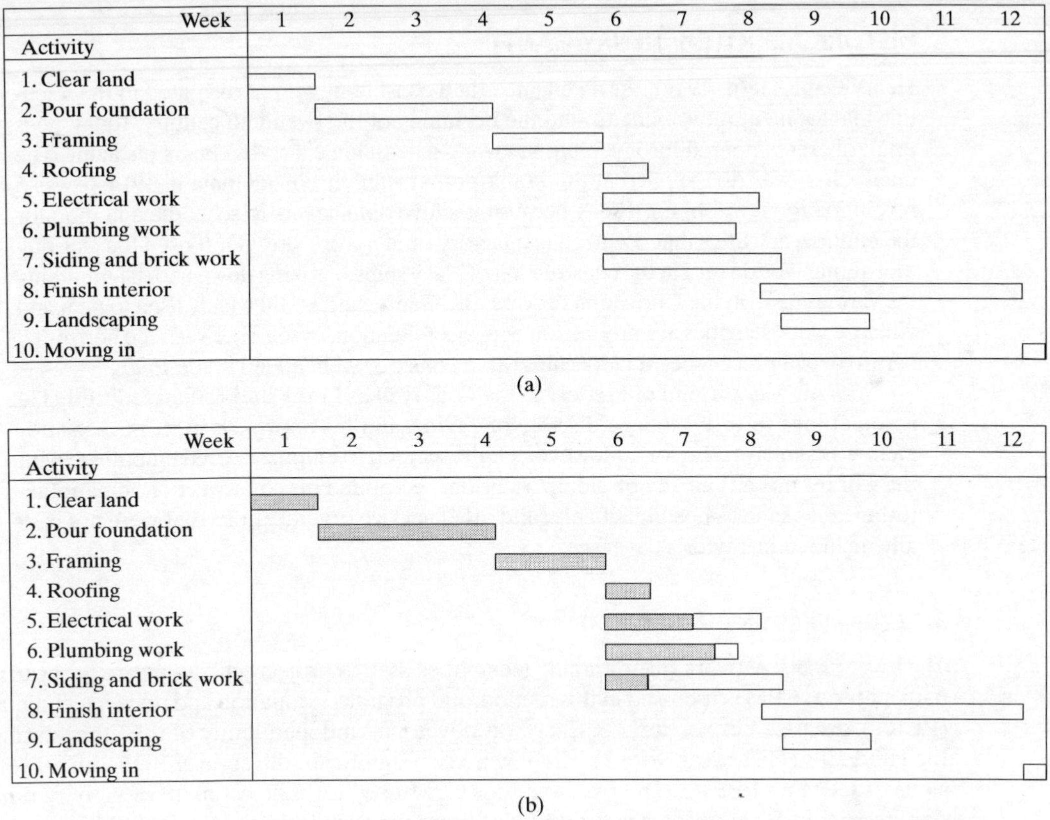

Figure 4 Gantt chart for a construction project: (a) planned schedule of activities and (b) actual work accomplished at some point during week 7.

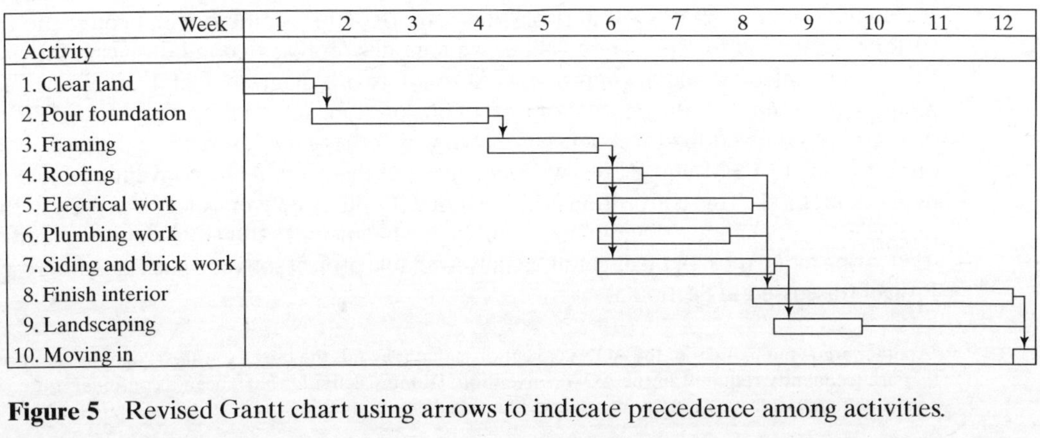

Figure 5 Revised Gantt chart using arrows to indicate precedence among activities.

HISTORICAL NOTE 1 HENRY GANTT

Henry Gantt (1861–1919) was an engineer and consultant who participated in the scientific management movement around the beginning of the twentieth century. Today, he is primarily remembered for inventing the work-scheduling chart that bears his name. The Gantt chart was first applied at the Frankford Arsenal in Philadelphia in 1914. It was a revolutionary new tool for its day because it allowed managers to schedule and monitor the multiple activities that occurred in a factory or at a work site. Gantt used the charting tool during World War I in the construction of Navy ships, breaking down and diagramming the various tasks in the fabrication process. The Gantt chart is still widely used to plan and visualize work activities in a production or project situation. Arrows between the horizontal bars to depict precedence relationships (as in Figure 5) were added in the 1990s.

Gantt was a friend of Frederick Taylor as well as Frank and Lillian Gilbreth. He is sometimes referred to as a disciple of Taylor, and his approach in work measurement was similar to Taylor's. However, Gantt seemed to emphasize and empathize with the worker more than Taylor did. In addition, he applied his concepts to nonmanufacturing areas such as hospitals, banks, and other service organizations that were not usually included in Taylor's coverage.

3.2 Critical Path Method (CPM)

The two primary network diagramming techniques used in project scheduling are the critical path method (CPM), discussed in this section, and program evaluation and review technique (PERT), discussed in Section 3.3. Each was developed independently of the other during the late 1950s (Historical Note 2). There were two significant differences in the initial versions of CPM and PERT. The first was that CPM used a single estimate of activity time duration, while PERT used a distribution of times for each activity. Hence, CPM is considered to be a deterministic network method while PERT is a probabilistic method. The second difference was related to the convention used to construct the network diagram, which consists of nodes and arrows as indicated in Figure 6. In CPM, nodes represent activities in the project, and arrows indicate precedence among the activities—that is, which activities must be completed before other activities can be started. Today we refer to this convention as an ***activity-on-node*** (AON) network diagram. By contrast, the original convention in PERT used arrows to represent activities while nodes represented milestones in the project. This is called an ***activity-on-arrow*** (AOA) network diagram. PERT milestones are points in time denoting the end and/or start of one or more activities. The arrows in a PERT diagram also showed the precedence order in which the activities must be performed. In our coverage of CPM and PERT, we have adopted the same AON convention for both network methods. This convention is consistent with other network diagrams used in this text (e.g., the precedence diagram in assembly line balancing). AON is also the convention used in one of the most popular commercially available project software packages: Microsoft Project (discussed in Section 5).[3]

[3]Another argument in favor of the AON convention is that it avoids the use of so-called "dummy" activities that are frequently required in the AOA convention. Dummy activities have been a continual source of confusion to my students over the many years I have been teaching PERT.

HISTORICAL NOTE 2 CPM AND PERT

CPM and PERT were each developed during the late 1950s in response to problems associated with the scheduling of projects. In 1956, a research effort was undertaken by the DuPont Company in collaboration with Remington-Rand Corporation to develop a computerized system for planning, scheduling, and controlling DuPont's engineering projects, in particular its plant construction and maintenance operations. The network technique developed from this effort was the ***critical path method*** (CPM).

Around the same time that CPM was being developed, the U.S. Navy was working on a research program to develop a nuclear submarine capable of firing ballistic missiles while submerged. Called the Polaris Missile Program, it was the first weapon system of its kind, requiring solutions to many formidable technical problems. To schedule and manage the Polaris missile development program, the navy sponsored a research team consisting of its own Special Projects Office, Lockheed Corporation (a defense contractor), and Booz Allen Hamilton (a consulting firm) to develop a network scheduling technique. The technique was called ***program evaluation and review technique*** (PERT). The Polaris Missile Program was managed using 23 PERT networks consisting of a total of 3000 activities.

The Polaris submarine-launched missile system was initially deployed in 1960 and remained operational until around 1978. In 1971, the navy began replacing its Polaris missile with the newer Poseidon missile system.

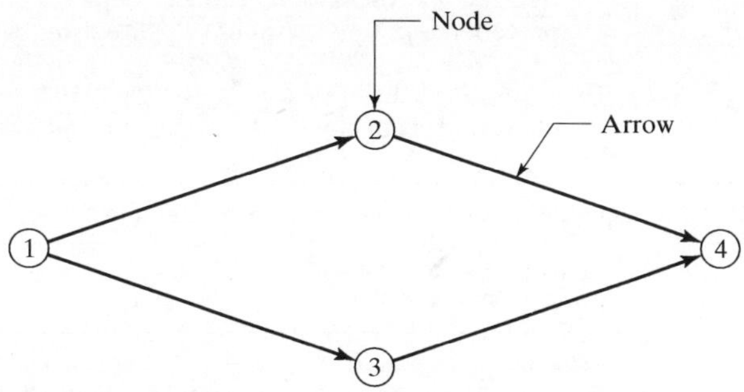

Figure 6 Network components used in CPM and PERT diagrams. In CPM, the nodes represent activities while arrows indicate precedence. In the original PERT network, the arrows represented activities as well as precedence while nodes represented milestones in the project.

We consider the critical path method first because it is the simpler of the two network techniques. It uses a single time estimate for each activity, whereas PERT uses several time estimates that form a probability distribution. The objectives in both CPM and PERT are to schedule the sequence of work activities in the project and to determine the total time the project will take. The total time duration is the longest sequence of activities in the network (the longest path through the network diagram) and is called the ***critical path***. Expressing this mathematically, CP represents the critical path through the network from the first node to the last node. Then the total project time duration is given by

$$T_{cp} = \sum_{i \in CP} T_{ai} \tag{1}$$

where T_{cp} = total project time (time along the critical path), and T_{ai} = activity time for activity i, and the summation of activity times is carried out only along the critical path.

The critical path method might be best explained in the context of a hypothetical construction project consisting of multiple activities that must be completed. The project is described in the following example.

Example 1 A Construction Project and CPM

A construction project involves the building of a house. The actual construction work consists of the ten activities briefly described in Table 1. The table also presents the estimated time duration for each activity (in units of days) and the order in which the activities must be performed, indicated in the column labeled immediate predecessor(s). (a) Construct the CPM network diagram for the project and (b) identify the critical path in the network and determine the total time duration of the project.

Solution **(a)** The CPM network diagram for the project is illustrated in Figure 7, using the AON convention (nodes depict activities and arrows indicate precedence). Activity times (T_{ai}) are listed above each node.

(b) There are a total of four paths (sequences of activities) in the diagram, identified according to the nodes through which they pass. The four paths,

TABLE 1 Activities in Construction Project of Example 1

Activity i	Activity Time Estimate T_{ai}	Immediate Predecessors	Description
1	5 days	—	Clear land and excavate property
2	14 days	1	Pour foundation and allow time for curing
3	8 days	2	Frame house
4	3 days	3	Roofing work
5	10 days	3	Electrical and heating work
6	9 days	3	Plumbing work
7	11 days	3	Siding and brickwork
8	22 days	4, 5, 6	Finish interior (drywall, moldings, painting, etc.)
9	6 days	7	Landscaping work
10	2 days	8, 9	Move in

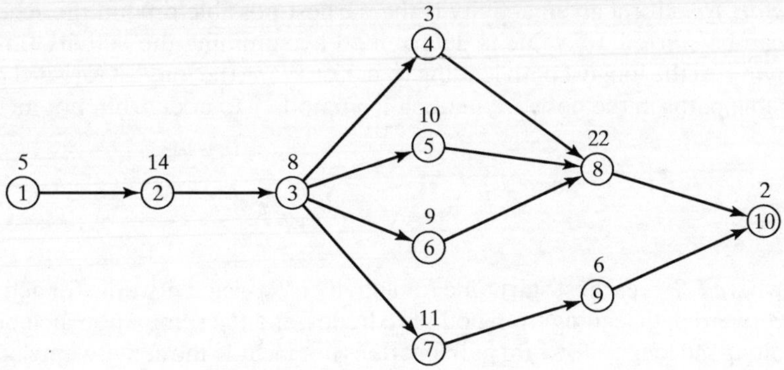

Figure 7 CPM network diagram for Example 1.

labeled A, B, C, and D, and their respective sums of activity times are as follows:

Path	Path Activities	Activity Times (days)	Sum of Activity Times (days)
A	1-2-3-4-8-10	5 + 14 + 8 + 3 + 22 + 2	54
B	1-2-3-5-8-10	5 + 14 + 8 + 10 + 22 + 2	61
C	1-2-3-6-8-10	5 + 14 + 8 + 9 + 22 + 2	60
D	1-2-3-7-9-10	5 + 14 + 8 + 11 + 6 + 2	46

The critical path is the path with the largest sum of activity times. This is path B passing through activities 1-2-3-5-8-10, and its duration is 61 days (T_{cp} = 61 days). ■

Given that the critical path through the network in our example is 61 days, then the other paths through the network contain scheduling flexibility. In other words, the activities in the other paths do not have to be started immediately after their immediate predecessors have been completed. These paths include ***slack time***—the amount of extra time that an activity can be postponed without delaying any of the subsequent activities or jeopardizing the completion time of the entire project. Slack time is useful to the project manager because it might permit resources presently assigned to activities with slack to be reallocated to other activities, if only on a temporary basis. There are several reasons why the other activities might require more resources: (1) the activities lie on the critical path, (2) the time estimates for these activities are now considered to be too optimistic, and (3) delays have occurred in certain paths in the network, causing the activities on those paths to become more critical than previously thought.

Path A in Example 1 has a total slack time of 7 days (61 days – 54 days), but that does not mean that every activity along path A can be postponed by 7 days. Because of the precedence interrelationships among activities in a critical path network, the slack time must be analyzed for every activity in the network, including the activities along the critical path. The first step in the analysis is to make a ***forward pass*** through the network (starting with the first node and proceeding to the last node). During the forward pass, the earliest start time and earliest finish time are determined for each activity. The ***earliest***

start time for a given activity is the earliest possible time in the schedule that activity i can be started. Its value is determined by summing the activity times of the activities lying on the longest path leading to it. Let FP_i = the longest forward path among all possible paths in the network leading from node 1 to node i, but not including node i. Then

$$ES_i = \sum_{j \in FP_i} T_{aj} \tag{2}$$

where ES_i = earliest start time for activity i, T_{aj} = activity time for activity j, FP_i = longest forward path leading from node 1 to node i, and the summation includes the activity times along the longest forward path but does not include the activity time of node i. The ***earliest finish time*** for a given activity is its earliest start time plus its activity time. That is,

$$EF_i = ES_i + T_{ai} \tag{3}$$

where EF_i = earliest finish time, and T_{ai} = activity time for activity i.

Example 2 Earliest Start Times and Finish Times

Determine the earliest start times and finish times for the activities in Example 1.

Solution: Starting from node 1 and making a forward pass through the network, equations (2) and (3) are applied to determine ES_i and EF_i values. The results are shown in Table 2.

TABLE 2 Earliest Start Times and Finish Times in Example 2

Activity i	Longest Forward Path FP_i	$ES_i = \sum_{j \in FP_i} T_{aj}$ (days)	T_{ai}(days)	EF_i (days) $= ES_i + T_{ai}$
1	—	0	5	5
2	1	5	14	19
3	1-2	5+14 = 19	8	27
4	1-2-3	5+14+8 = 27	3	30
5	1-2-3	5+14+8 = 27	10	37
6	1-2-3	5+14+8 = 27	9	36
7	1-2-3	5+14+8 = 27	11	38
8	1-2-3-5	5+14+8+10 = 37	22	59
9	1-2-3-7	5+14+8+11 = 38	6	44
10	1-2-3-5-8	5+14+8+10+22 = 59	2	61

■

The second step in the analysis is to make a ***backward pass*** through the network (starting with the last node and proceeding backward to the first node). During the backward pass, the latest finish time and latest start time are determined for each node. The ***latest finish time*** is the latest time that an activity must be completed in order to finish the overall project on schedule. For the last activity in the network diagram, and for our purposes here, we will set it equal to the total project time T_{cp}. This is the same value as the EF time for the last activity determined in the forward pass analysis.[4] For other activities in the network, the latest finish time is determined by subtracting from T_{cp} the activity time along the longest path leading backward from the last node. Let BP_i = the longest path among all possible paths from the last node to node i, not including node i. Then

$$LF_i = T_{cp} - \sum_{j \in BP_i} T_{aj} \tag{4}$$

where LF_i = latest finish time for activity i, T_{aj} = activity time for activity j, BP_i = longest path leading from the last node to node i, and the summation includes the activity times along the longest backward path but does not include the activity time of node i. The ***latest start time*** is the latest time that an activity must be started in order to complete the project on schedule. It is determined for a given activity as its latest finish time minus its activity time. That is,

$$LS_i = LF_i - T_{ai} \tag{5}$$

where LS_i = latest start time, and T_{ai} = activity time for activity i.

Example 3 Latest Finish Times and Start Times

Determine the latest finish times and latest start times for the activities in Example 1 using a total project time T_{cp} of 61 days.

Solution: Starting from node 10 and using a backward pass through the network, equations (4) and (5) are used to determine LF_i and LS_i values. The results are shown in Table 3. ■

TABLE 3 Latest Finish Times and Start Times in Example 3

Activity i	Longest Backward Path BP_i	$\sum_{j \in BP_i} T_{aj}$ (days)	LF_i(days) = $61 - \sum_{j \in BP_i} T_{aj}$	T_{ai} (days)	LS_i (days) = $LF_i - T_{ai}$
10	—	0	61	2	59
9	10	2	59	6	53
8	10	2	59	22	37
7	10-9	2+6 = 8	53	11	42
6	10-8	2+22 = 24	37	9	28
5	10-8	2+22 = 24	37	10	27
4	10-8	2+22 = 24	37	3	34
3	10-8-5	2+22+10 = 34	27	8	19
2	10-8-5-3	2+22+10+8 = 42	19	14	5
1	10-8-5-3-2	2+22+10+8+14 = 56	5	5	0

■

[4]There are sometimes reasons why the total project time T_{cp} would not be used in the backward pass through the network. For example, the contract may specify a project completion time that is different from the total time along the critical path, in which case the analysis of slack time would be based on this other date.

The third step in the analysis of the network is to determine the slack for each activity. Recall that the slack time for an activity is the amount of time that the activity can be delayed without delaying any of the subsequent activities in the project. It can also be interpreted as the amount of extra time available to perform the activity. The slack time for an activity can be determined as either the difference between the latest and earliest start times or the difference between the latest and earliest finish times. That is,

$$S_i = LS_i - ES_i = LF_i - EF_i \tag{6}$$

where S_i = slack time for activity i; the other terms have been previously defined.

Example 4 Slack Times

Determine the slack time for each activity in the construction project in the previous examples.

Solution: Using the calculated values of ES_i and EF_i from Example 2 and the values of LS_i and LF_i from Example 3, the slack time is computed for each activity in Table 4. The values are also displayed in Figure 8.

TABLE 4 Slack Times in Example 4

Activity i	LS_i	ES_i	LF_i	EF_i	S_i
1	0	0	5	5	0
2	5	5	19	19	0
3	19	19	27	27	0
4	34	27	37	30	7
5	27	27	37	37	0
6	28	27	37	36	1
7	42	27	53	38	15
8	37	37	59	59	0
9	53	38	59	44	15
10	59	59	61	61	0

■

Note that the activities along the critical path (activities 1-2-3-5-8-10, as determined in Example 1) have zero slack. These activities must start on schedule and be completed within their respective activity times in order to complete the overall project on time. Activities not lying on the critical path have positive slack, meaning that they could be delayed by an amount of time equal to the slack without delaying the project completion date. For instance, activities 4 and 6 could be delayed by 7 days and 1 day, respectively. Activities 7 and 9 both have the same slack value of 15 days. The interpretation of these slack values is slightly different than for activities 4 and 6. The slack for activities 7 and 9 is called ***shared slack***, which means they can jointly be delayed by a total of 15 days, but they cannot each be delayed by 15 days (because that would mean a total delay of 30 days).

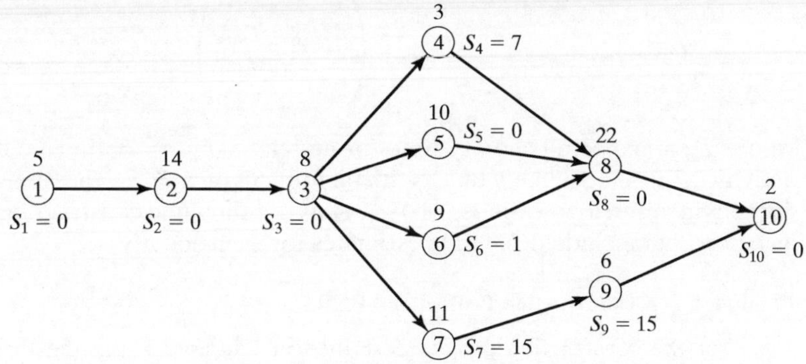

Figure 8 The CPM network diagram for the example construction project with values of slack displayed for each activity. The nodes in the critical path are highlighted.

3.3 Program Evaluation and Review Technique (PERT)

The critical path method uses a single time estimate for each activity. The estimate is based on the judgment of the person making it. Because projects tend to be unique and their activities are therefore unique, it must be acknowledged that uncertainty exists in any estimated times that are based on judgment. PERT deals with this uncertainty by using three time values for each activity. While the three time values are themselves estimates, subject to the same frailties of judgment as before, PERT provides a means for assessing the effects of uncertainty on the project schedule, and that is more than what can be done using CPM.

Three time estimates are used to form a beta probability distribution for each activity in the network. The beta distribution is a continuous function of its variable (in our case, activity time is the continuous variable of interest). The distribution is approximately bell-shaped, but the shape can be skewed to the right or left, depending on the relative values of the three time estimates.

The three time estimates for each activity are the optimistic or minimum time (T_{min}), the most likely time (T_{ml}), and the pessimistic or maximum time (T_{max}). The optimistic time is the estimate that would apply if everything went well during the activity, and completion occurred in the minimum possible time. The most likely time is the estimate that would apply if everything went as expected during the activity. The pessimistic time represents a worst-case scenario in which everything went wrong during the activity and it required a maximum time to complete.

The mean and variance of the activity time in the beta distribution can be computed from the three estimates as follows:

$$T_{ai} = \frac{T_{min} + 4T_{ml} + T_{max}}{6} \tag{7}$$

$$\sigma_i^2 = \left(\frac{T_{max} - T_{min}}{6} \right)^2 \tag{8}$$

where T_{ai} = expected activity time for activity i, T_{min} = optimistic time estimate for activity i, T_{ml} = most likely time estimate for activity i, T_{max} = pessimistic time estimate for activity i, and σ_i^2= variance of T_{ai}. Let us use the same construction project example as before, but include three time estimates for each activity.

Example 5 A Construction Project and PERT

For the construction project described in Example 1, use the three time estimates (T_{min} = most optimistic, T_{ml} = most likely, and T_{max}= most pessimistic) given in Table 5 to compute the activity times and their variances for each of the ten activities shown.

Solution: Using equations (7) and (8) to compute the expected activity times and their variances, we have the results shown in Table 6.

TABLE 5 Construction Project in Example 5

Activity i	Immediate Predecessors	T_{min} (days)	T_{ml} (days)	T_{max} (days)
1	—	3	5	7
2	1	12	14	16
3	2	5	8	11
4	3	2	3	4
5	3	7	9	17
6	3	6	9	12
7	3	8	11	14
8	4, 5, 6	14	23	26
9	7	3	6	9
10	8, 9	1	2	3

TABLE 6 Values of Expected Activity Times and Their Variances in Example 5

Activity i	T_{ai}(days)	σ^2 (days)^2
1	5	0.44
2	14	0.44
3	8	1.00
4	3	0.11
5	10	2.78
6	9	1.00
7	11	1.00
8	22	4.00
9	6	1.00
10	2	0.11

■

Note that the expected activity times have the same values we used in our previous CPM network, and therefore the critical path has the same duration of 61 days that we determined in Example 1. What is new here is that we have a probability distribution for each activity time. Therefore, the 61 days along the critical path represents an expected or mean value rather than a single estimated value, as in CPM. Also, this mean project time has a variance that can be used to assess the probabilities of completing the project in a shorter or longer time than the expected 61 days.

In PERT, we assume that the activity time distributions are statistically independent. According to the central limit theorem in probability theory, the sum of the means of the independent activity time distributions along the critical path approximates the mean of a normal distribution, whose variance is the sum of the variances along the same critical path. The approximation improves as the number of activities increases, but the activity time distributions do not have to be normal themselves. The fact that the activity times are beta distributions does not reduce the validity of using the central limit theorem in PERT analysis. The distribution of T_{cp} would appear as in Figure 9.

To determine the probability of completing a project within a given time period, we make use of the standard normal distribution. The standard normal variate z is computed as follows:

$$z = \frac{x - \mu}{\sigma}$$

where x = desired or proposed completion time of the project, μ = mean or expected time along the critical path T_{cp}, and σ = standard deviation of T_{cp} (the square root of the variance σ^2). The probability corresponding to the value of z can be determined from a table of the standard normal distribution.

Example 6 Probability Analysis in PERT

Determine the probability of completing the construction project discussed in the previous examples within the following proposed completion times: (a) 61 days, (b) 59 days, and (c) 65 days.

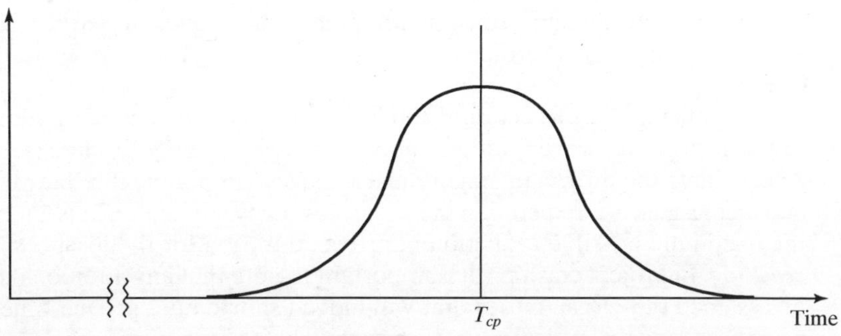

Figure 9 Normal distribution of project completion time T_{cp}.

Solution: First of all, the sum of the variances along the critical path is $\sigma^2 = 0.44 + 0.44 + 1.00 + 2.78 + 4.00 + 0.11 = 8.77$. The standard deviation of T_{cp} is $\sigma = \sqrt{8.77} = 2.96$ (days).

(a) The proposed 61 days is the expected completion time for the project. The probability of completing the project in 61 or fewer days is therefore 0.50 (50%).

(b) The proposed 59 days is less than the expected completion time. The probability of completing the project in 59 or fewer days is less than 0.50.

$$z = \frac{59 - 61}{2.96} = -0.68$$

The corresponding probability is 0.25 (25%).

(c) The proposed 65 days is greater than the expected completion time. The probability of completing the project in 65 or fewer days is greater than 0.50.

$$z = \frac{65 - 61}{2.96} = 1.35$$

The corresponding probability is 0.91 (91%). ■

4 PROJECT CRASHING

Sometimes there are reasons for wanting to complete a project in less time than the completion time indicated by the critical path. These reasons include the following:

- A scheduled deadline that is sooner than the critical path completion time must be met.
- There is a desire to earn incentives that are included in the contract for finishing early.
- Penalties that are included in the contract for finishing late must be avoided.
- The benefits of the project outcome must be achieved sooner; for example, if the project is a production plant, the sooner it is finished, the sooner it will begin making products to generate cash flow for the owner organization.
- The indirect costs associated with the resources used on the project (e.g. personnel, equipment, utilities, investment interest, and so forth) must be reduced; the sooner the current project is completed, the sooner these resources can be put to work on the next project.

Reducing the project duration is accomplished by devoting additional resources to the project. However, adding more resources is likely to increase the project cost. Accordingly, the project manager must achieve a proper balance between reducing time and increasing cost. Expediting the project by analyzing the various alternatives to obtain the maximum possible reduction in project duration for the least cost is called ***project crashing***. In project crashing, it is important to note that any additional resources should be assigned only to activities that will indeed shorten the project time, and this means activities along the critical path. There would be no reduction in the overall project duration if activities not on the critical path were expedited. On the other hand, reducing the time along the critical path can sometimes have the effect of turning other paths in the network into critical paths.

The cost of a given project activity typically increases as the time to accomplish it is reduced. The relationship is depicted in Figure 10. Completing the activity in the normal time has a normal cost associated with it. The normal time is T_{ai} computed by equation (7), and the associated cost is C_{ai}. If the completion time is expedited, its cost is greater, as indicated by EC_{ai} (expedited cost) and ET_{ai} (expedited time). The values of C_{ai}, ET_{ai}, and EC_{ai} are estimated values, just as the original values of normal activity time (T_{ai}) were estimated in our previous analysis of the network in Section 3. The reasons why the expedited cost is greater are due to overtime for the workers (at time-and-a-half wage rate), less efficient use of resources, learning curve effects (more workers each having less time to learn their tasks), and various other factors.

For analysis purposes, it is useful to know the rate of increase in the cost of the expedited activity. The cost rate (e.g., cost per day, week, month, or whatever time units are used in the CPM/PERT network) is determined as the total cost increase due to expediting the activity divided by the reduction in time spent on the activity. The relationship between cost increase and time reduction is assumed to be linear. Referring to Figure 10,

$$CR_i = \frac{EC_{ai} - C_{ai}}{T_{ai} - ET_{ai}} \tag{9}$$

where CR_i = cost rate of expediting activity i, EC_{ai} = cost of expedited activity i, C_{ai} = normal cost of activity i, T_{ai} = normal time of activity i, and ET_{ai} = expedited time of activity i. Once these cost rates are evaluated for each activity, a comparison is made among the activities along the critical path to find which activity can be expedited for the lowest cost. Let us use our construction example to illustrate the cost analysis.

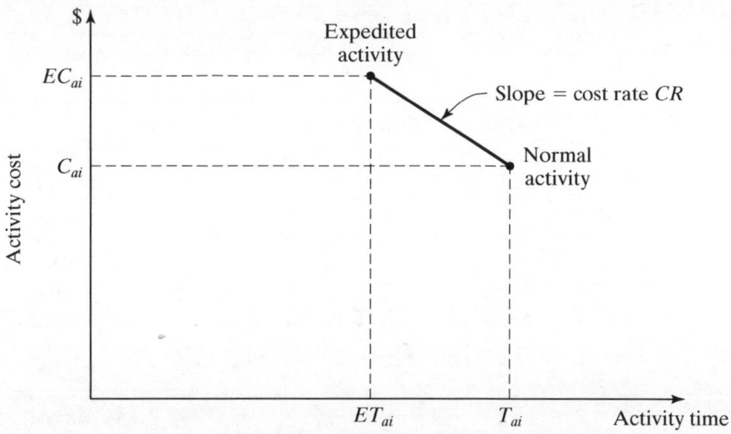

Figure 10 The typical relationship between cost and time when an activity is expedited.

Example 7 Cost Analysis of Expediting the Construction Project

The normal time, expedited time, normal cost, and expedited cost of the 10 activities in the construction project are listed in Table 7. The goal is to complete the project in 60 days, which is one day less than the schedule project duration indicated by the critical path. (a) Determine which activity or activities should be expedited so as to minimize the cost of reducing the project duration. Also calculate (b) the normal total cost of the project and (c) the expedited total cost of the project.

Solution **(a)** To determine which activity or activities should be expedited so as to minimize the cost of reducing the project duration, the cost rate CR_i must be computed for each activity using equation (9). The results of the computations are shown in Table 8, with the activities along the critical path shaded in gray. Note that activity 6 has the lowest cost to expedite of all activities in the network, with $CR_6 = \$300$. However, it is not along the critical path, so expediting activity 6 would have no effect on the overall project duration. The lowest cost activity to expedite on the critical path is activity 5, with $CR_5 = \$400$. Accordingly, this is the activity that should be expedited to minimize the cost of reducing the project schedule by one week.

TABLE 7 Cost Data for Example 7

Activity i	T_{ai}(days)	ET_{ai}(days)	C_{ai}($)	EC_{ai}($)
1	5	4	4,500	5,500
2	14	12	7,400	8,700
3	8	6	5,000	6,500
4	3	2	3,000	3,600
5	10	7	6,600	7,800
6	9	7	4,700	5,300
7	11	8	7,300	9,400
8	22	16	12,400	15,400
9	6	5	4,800	5,350
10	2	1	1,200	2,000

TABLE 8 Cost Rate Values for Example 7

Activity i	T_{ai}(days)	ET_{ai}(days)	C_{ai}($)	EC_{ai}($)	CR_i($)
1	5	4	4,500	5,500	1,000
2	14	12	7,400	8,700	650
3	8	6	5,000	6,500	750
4	3	2	3,000	3,600	600
5	10	7	6,600	7,800	400
6	9	7	4,700	5,300	300
7	11	8	7,300	9,400	700
8	22	16	12,400	15,400	500
9	6	5	4,800	5,350	550
10	2	1	1,200	2,000	800
	Total normal cost (ΣNC_i)		$56,900		

(b) The normal cost of the project is the sum of the normal costs of all 10 activities (the fourth column in the table):

$$TC = \sum_{i=1}^{n} C_{ai} \quad (10)$$

where TC = normal total cost of the project, n = number of activities in the project, and the summation is over all n activities. For our problem,

$$TC = \$56,900$$

(c) The expedited cost of the project is the normal total cost of the project plus the cost of expediting activity 5. The total expedited cost is \$56,900 + \$400 = \$57,300. ■

Example 8 Further Expediting the Project

Determine (a) which activities should be expedited if it is desired to reduce the overall project duration to 59 days and (b) the total cost of the project when it is completed in this time.

Solution **(a)** In the preceding example, expediting activity 5 by one day reduces the overall duration of the project from 61 days to 60 days. This results in a tie between two paths in the network: the original critical path (1-2-3-5-8-10) and the previous noncritical path (1-2-3-6-8-10), whose sum of activity times is 60 days. Now both paths are critical paths. To further reduce the duration of the project, both paths must be considered. Comparing the activities along these two critical paths, the lowest cost occurs if activity 8 is reduced by one day, with CR_8 = \$500. The closest competing alternative solution is to expedite two activities, 5 and 6, with a total cost of \$400 + \$300 = \$700.

(b) The total cost of the project when it is completed in 59 days is the total project cost at 60 days from the previous example plus the added cost of expediting one more day to reduce the total duration to 59 days. The total expedited cost is \$57,300 + \$500 = \$57,800. ■

5 SOFTWARE FOR PROJECTS

There are approximately 250 software products available to perform various functions related to project management.[5] One of the leading packages is Microsoft Project.[6] Microsoft Project has data entry features that should make users of other Microsoft products (e.g., Word, Excel) feel quite at home. At the start, the user clicks "New" under "File" for a new project analysis. This opens a "Project Information" window where the user enters a project start date. A project end date can also be entered, but this is optional. On the left side of the screen, the user lists the work activities, called "Task Names" in MS Project, providing brief descriptions (similar to our listing of construction activities in Example 1). The activities are numbered at the far left of the screen (similar to line

[5]As reported on the Web site of the Project Management Center at www.infogoal.com/pmc/pmcswr.htm.

[6]It is no surprise that Microsoft Project is Windows-based, as are about 80 PM software products. Approximately 140 PM software packages are Web-based, and the remaining 30 or so are based on platforms such as Mac, Unix, and Linux.

entries in Excel). The user enters other data about each activity, such as the duration of the activity and its immediate predecessors. Given the start date for the project, MS Project automatically computes the start date and finish date for each activity based on its duration and predecessors. MS Project generates a Gantt chart for the project as activities are entered, representing each activity by a bar opposite its description. The length of each bar corresponds to the activity duration, and the precedence order is indicated by arrows between the bars (similar to our Figure 5). The calendar used in MS Project accounts for weekends, so the workweek is Monday through Friday. Options are available to change this weekly calendar.

MS Project uses the activity-on-node (AON) convention for network diagrams, the same convention we have adopted in this chapter.[7] A network diagram button is available, so the user can view the AON network diagram for the project. The critical path through the network is highlighted in red on the monitor screen and in color printouts. Each node (activity) in the network is a rectangle listing data about the activity (description, number, duration, start date, and finish date).

REFERENCES

[1] Belack, C. N. "Computer-Aided Project Management." Pp. 1252–62 in *Handbook of Industrial Engineering*, 3rd ed., edited by G. Salvendy. New York: Wiley and Institute of Industrial Engineers, Norcross, GA, 2001.

[2] Golany, B., and A. Shtub. "Work Breakdown Structure." Pp.1263–80 in *Handbook of Industrial Engineering*, 3rd ed., edited by G. Salvendy. New York: Wiley and Institute of Industrial Engineers, Norcross, GA, 2001.

[3] Hicks, P. E. *Industrial Engineering and Management*. 2nd ed. New York: McGraw-Hill, 1994.

[4] Lewis, J. P. *Fundamentals of Project Management*. 2nd ed. New York: AMACOM (American Management Association), 2002.

[5] Project Management Institute, *A Guide to the Project Management Body of Knowledge* (PMBOK® Guide), 2000 ed. Project Management Institute, Newtown Square, PA: 2000.

[6] Russell, R. S., and B. W. Taylor III. *Operations Management*. 4th ed. Upper Saddle River, NJ: Prentice Hall, 2003.

[7] Shtub, A., "Project Management Cycle: Process Used to Manage Project (Steps to Go Through)." Pp. 1241–51 in *Handbook of Industrial Engineering*, 3rd ed., edited by G. Salvendy. New York: Wiley and Institute of Industrial Engineers, Norcross, GA, 2001.

[8] Webster, F. M., "Project Management," Pp. 17.161–17.196 in *Maynard's Industrial Engineering Handbook*, 5th ed., edited by K. B. Zandin. New York: McGraw-Hill, 2001.

REVIEW QUESTIONS

1 What is a project?

2 Define project management.

3 What is the difference between a project and a program?

4 Identify and briefly describe the five typical phases in a project life cycle.

5 What is the difference between project management and operations management?

[7]Other PM software packages use the activity-on-arrow (AOA) convention or can be adapted to either AON or AOA conventions.

6 Project teams are usually cross-functional. What does cross-functional mean?
7 What is a matrix organizational structure and why is it often applicable in project teams?
8 What is project planning?
9 What are the three principal uses of the project plan?
10 What is the work breakdown structure in project planning?
11 What is project scheduling and what is accomplished by it?
12 What is project control concerned with?
13 What are the three project scheduling techniques discussed in the text?
14 What is a Gantt chart?
15 Describe what is meant by the AON and AOA conventions for diagramming networks?
16 What are the general objectives in both CPM and PERT?
17 What is the critical path in a CPM or PERT network diagram?
18 What is meant by the term slack time in a CPM or PERT network?
19 What is the basic difference between PERT and CPM?
20 What is project crashing?

PROBLEMS

Gantt Charts

1 A planned project contains the activities shown in the table below, along with their required completion times and precedence. (a) Construct the Gantt chart for the project. (b) Determine the critical path and the estimated time to complete the project.

	Activity					
	1	2	3	4	5	6
Activity time (weeks)	3	8	5	4	6	3
Immediate predecessor	—	1	1	2, 3	3	4, 5

2 A planned project contains the activities shown in the table below, along with their required completion times and precedence. (a) Construct the Gantt chart for the project. (b) Determine the critical path and the estimated time to complete the project.

	Activity								
	1	2	3	4	5	6	7	8	9
Activity time (days)	1	4	3	7	5	2	6	9	4
Immediate predecessor	—	1	1	1	2	3, 4	5, 6	4	7, 8

Critical Path Method (CPM)

3 A planned construction project contains the activities shown in the table below, along with their required completion times and precedence. (a) Draw the CPM network diagram for

the project, labeling all activities and times. (b) Perform a forward pass and backward pass through the network to determine the critical path, the expected duration of the project, and the slack time for each activity.

	Activity					
	1	2	3	4	5	6
Activity time (weeks)	3	8	5	4	6	
Immediate predecessor	—	1	1	2, 3	3	4, 5

4 The table below lists the time estimates and immediate predecessor(s) for each activity in a product marketing project that is to be scheduled using CPM. Similar projects for other products have been accomplished in the past, so the activity times are fairly certain. (a) Draw the CPM network diagram for the project, labeling all activities and times. (b) Perform a forward pass and backward pass through the network to determine the critical path, the expected duration of the project, and the slack time for each activity.

	Activity								
	1	2	3	4	5	6	7	8	9
Activity time (days)	1	4	3	7	5	2	6	9	4
Immediate predecessor	—	1	1	1	2	3, 4	5, 6	4	7, 8

5 Solve the preceding problem but use an estimated activity time of 4 days instead of 2 days for activity 6.

6 A product development project is planned to contain the activities shown in the table below, along with their required completion times and precedence. (a) Draw the CPM network diagram for the project, labeling all activities and times. (b) Perform a forward pass and backward pass through the network to determine the critical path, the expected duration of the project, and the slack time for each activity.

	Activity									
	1	2	3	4	5	6	7	8	9	10
Activity time (weeks)	2	5	4	2	7	5	8	4	3	1
Immediate predecessor	—	1	1	2	2, 3	3	4	5	5, 6	7, 8, 9

Program Evaluation and Review Technique (PERT)

7 The table below lists three time estimates and the immediate predecessor(s) for each activity in a construction project that is to be scheduled using PERT. The three time estimates (in weeks) are in the order: optimistic time, most likely time, and pessimistic time. (a) Draw the PERT network diagram for the project, labeling all activities and times. (b) Perform a forward pass and backward pass through the network to determine the critical path, the expected duration of the project, and the slack time for each activity. (c) What is the probability that the project will be completed within 22 weeks?

	Activity							
	1	2	3	4	5	6	7	8
Time estimates (weeks)	1, 2, 3	3, 5, 7	5, 7, 9	5, 7, 12	1, 2, 3	2, 3, 4	7, 9, 11	1, 3, 8
Immediate predecessor	—	1	1	2	3	4, 5	3	6, 7

8 The table below lists the activity times and precedence requirements for the activities required to complete a new equipment installation project in a factory. Three time estimates (in weeks) are given for each activity: optimistic time, most likely time, and pessimistic time. (a) Draw the PERT network diagram for the project, labeling all activities and times. (b) Perform a forward pass and backward pass through the network to determine the critical path, the expected duration of the project, and the slack time for each activity. (c) What is the probability that the project will be completed one week or more before the expected completion time?

Activity	Optimistic Time (weeks)	Most Likely Time (weeks)	Pessimistic Time (weeks)	Immediate Predecessor
1	0	0	0	—
2	3	4	5	1
3	4	6	8	1
4	2	3	4	2
5	4	5	8	3
6	5	7	9	3
7	6	8	10	4
8	2	3	4	5
9	4	8	12	5
10	1	2	3	6
11	3	6	9	7, 8
12	2	4	6	9, 10
13	0	0	0	11, 12

9 The Industrial Engineering Department at Ivy University is moving from its old building to a new building. The move must be completed within the 17-day period between semesters. A list of tasks (activities) has been prepared. The activities and precedence requirements are presented in the table below. Three time estimates (in weeks) are given for each activity: optimistic time, most likely time, and pessimistic time. (a) Draw the PERT network diagram for the project, labeling all activities and times. (b) Perform a forward pass and backward pass through the network to determine the critical path, the expected duration of the project, and the slack time for each activity. (c) What is the probability that the project will be completed in 17 days? (d) Allowing for lost days due to snow emergencies, what is the probability that the project will be completed in 15 days?

Activity	Activity Description	Immediate Predecessor	Optimistic Time (days)	Most Likely Time (days)	Pessimistic Time (days)
1	Initiate move	—	0	0	0
2	Prepare new building space	1	3	5	6
3	Pack faculty files and books	1	3	4	5
4	Disconnect computers	1	1	1	2
5	Disconnect lab equipment	1	3	6	9
6	Movers move files and books	2, 3	2	3	6
7	Movers move furniture	4, 6	1	2	3
8	Riggers move lab equipment	5	2	4	6
9	Movers move computers	4	1	1	2
10	Install computers, telephones	9	2	5	8
11	Install lab equipment	8	3	4	7
12	Faculty set up new offices	7, 10	3	5	9
13	Department ready	11, 12	0	0	0

10 A company specializing in custom-engineered equipment is planning to submit a proposal to the National Aeronautics and Space Administration (NASA) to build an assembled component for a new space station that NASA plans to launch into orbit approximately 20 months from now. The winning proposal will be selected on the basis of both cost and timely delivery. Also, there will be a penalty clause in the NASA contract for late delivery. The company has developed the schedule of activities that are required to produce the assembled component. The activities and precedence requirements are presented in the table below. Three time estimates (in weeks) are given for each activity: optimistic time, most likely time, and pessimistic time. (a) Draw the PERT network diagram for the project, labeling all activities and times. (b) Perform a forward pass and backward pass through the network to determine the critical path, the expected duration of the project, and the slack time for each activity. (c) What completion time should the company specify in its proposal in order to be 95% sure that it will complete the project on time?

Activity	a	b	c	d	e	f	g	h	i	j
Immediate predecessor	—	a	a	a	b	c, d	d	e, f	f, g	h, i
Optimistic time (weeks)	5	15	8	7	10	20	17	5	7	10
Most likely time (weeks)	8	24	16	10	14	26	23	9	10	12
Pessimistic time (weeks)	11	39	24	19	24	32	35	13	13	20

11 Nanosoft Corporation is planning a major new software product designed around several integrated modules. Work activities related to the development of the modules are listed below together with estimated activity times (in weeks) and standard deviations (in weeks) that indicate the uncertainty in the given activity time. Activities "s" and "t" represent the start and termination (completion) of the project, but they have no time values. (a) Draw the PERT network diagram for the project, labeling all activities and times. (b) Perform a forward pass and backward pass through the network to determine the critical path, the expected duration of the project, and the slack time for each activity. (c) What is the probability that the activity can be finished within 24 weeks?

Activity	s	a	b	c	d	e	f	g	h	i	t
Immediate predecessor	—	s	s	s	a	b	b	c	d, e	f, g	h, i
Estimated activity time	0	10	8	6	9	4	5	8	3	11	0
Standard deviation	0	2.0	1.6	1.2	1.8	0.8	1.0	1.4	0.6	2.2	0

12 The table below lists the code letters of activities for a project to establish a telephone calling center. Also included are expected activity times (in days), their variances, and their precedence requirements. Activity "s" represents the start of the project, but it has no time value. (a) Draw the PERT network diagram, labeling all activities and times. (b) Perform a forward pass and backward pass through the network to determine the critical path, the expected duration of the project, and the slack time for each activity. (c) What is the probability that the activity can be finished within 28 weeks?

Activity	s	a	b	c	d	e	f	g	h	i	j
Immediate predecessor	—	s	s	a	a	b	b	c	d, e	f	g, h, i
Estimated activity time	0	7	10	8	5	9	6	11	4	11	3
Variance	0	2.1	3.0	2.4	1.5	2.7	1.8	3.3	1.2	3.3	0.9

Case Problem: PERT

13 The Mall-Mart department store chain is planning to construct a new warehouse to reduce the company's inventory storage problems. Most of the work will be performed by the company's own construction division, but certain portions of the project, such as electrical and plumbing work, will be subcontracted. You have been retained as a consultant to develop the PERT network diagram to assist in the planning and administrative control of the project. Before beginning on the PERT network, you called a meeting with the general foreman, estimator, and chief engineer, all from the company's construction division. Together, you have prepared a list of the various steps required to accomplish the project, as well as time estimates needed to carry out these steps. The time estimates include an optimistic time, a most likely time, and a pessimistic time. This list appears as Exhibit A below. In addition to determining the list of activities, the estimator and foreman also discussed in some detail how these activities should be sequenced. During the discussion, you took down the notes shown in Exhibit B. Your assignment: (a) Draw the PERT network diagram, labeling all activities and times (using the letter labels in Exhibit A). (b) Perform a forward pass and backward pass through the network to determine the critical path, the expected duration of the project, and the slack time for each activity. (c) What is the most likely time estimate for the project, and what is the probability of completing it within this time period? (d) It is anticipated that management will establish a scheduled completion date of 110 working days from the time your report is presented to them. What is the probability that the project will be completed within this schedule?

Exhibit A: Activities required to complete warehouse project (times are given in working days only, days/week)

Activity Code	Activity Description	Optimistic Time (days)	Most likely Time (days)	Pessimistic Time (days)
a	Obtain management approval	2	5	8
b	Subcontractor negotiations	1	3	7
c	Initial grading, excavation	5	7	9
d	Procure structural steel	10	15	20
e	Procure concrete for foundation	1	3	5
f	Procure exterior windows, doors	5	7	11
g	Procure wall and roof supplies	1	3	5
h	Pour building footings, allow time for curing	12	13	14
i	Erect formwork for foundation	3	4	5
j	Pour foundation concrete, allow time for curing	12	15	18
k	Erect steel framework	8	11	14

(Continued)

Activity Code	Activity Description	Optimistic Time (days)	Most likely Time (days)	Pessimistic Time (days)
l	Pour floor slab and lay floor	5	9	13
m	Erect exterior walls	11	14	17
n	Pour roof slab	9	12	15
0	Lay roofing	2	3	8
p	Electrical work (subcontracted)	8	10	14
q	Plumbing (subcontracted)	7	10	13
r	Install insulation	6	8	12
s	Install inside walls	7	9	11
t	Paint interior	3	5	9
u	Install fuel tank and heating	8	10	16
v	Excavate and lay sewage drain	5	8	11
w	Driveway and parking lot	9	12	15
x	Backfill building, final grade	6	8	10
y	Clean up building and grounds	2	2	2
z	Obtain job acceptance	3	5	9

Exhibit B: Notes taken during discussion on activity sequencing

Corporate management approval must be obtained before any work or procurement of supplies can begin. Procurement of materials and subcontractor negotiations can begin as soon as approval is obtained.
Grading can begin as soon as subcontractor negotiations are completed.
Footings must be poured after excavation and before any foundation formwork.
Foundation can be poured after concrete is received and formwork has been erected.
Floor slab can be poured at completion of foundation pouring. Extra time must be allowed in floor slab work for safety reasons so that this work does not interfere with framework construction.
When structural steel is received and foundation has been poured, steel framework can be erected.
Exterior walls can be installed following steel framework and arrival of windows, doors, and wall supplies.
Exterior walls must be erected before electrical and plumbing work is performed.
Roof can be poured after steel framework is up. Roof slab must precede roofing installation.
Insulation must be installed before interior walls are attached. Insulation can be started after all electrical and plumbing work.
Interior painting must be preceded by installation of interior walls.
The sewage drain, driveway, and parking lot can be started as soon as the exterior walls are up.
Backfilling around the building and final grading of the property can be performed after the sewage drain, driveway, and parking lot are completed.
Installation of fuel oil tank and heating system must be started after the foundation has been poured. This work must be completed before interior walls are put up.
Clean up can be started after flooring, roofing, painting, and final grading are completed.
Clean up is the final work before job acceptance.

Project Crashing

14 The project detailed in the table below is contracted for delivery in 11 weeks, with a penalty clause requiring the contractor to pay a penalty of $5000 for each week late. The project must therefore be expedited. The possible reductions and associated costs are shown in the table. Times in the table are given in weeks. Only activity 5 can be expedited two weeks. Activities 1 and 9 cannot be expedited. The other activities can be expedited one week. (a) Draw the CPM network and identify the critical path. How many weeks will the project require under normal operations? What is the total project cost with penalty included? (b) How could the project time be reduced to 12 weeks and what is the total project cost including penalty? (c) How could the project time be reduced to 11 weeks and what is the total project cost? (d) What is the lowest cost decision, 12 weeks or 11 weeks?

Activity	Immediate Predecessor	Normal Time	Expedited Time	Normal Cost ($)	Expedited Cost ($)
1	—	0	0	0	0
2	1	4	3	5,000	6,900
3	1	2	2	3,000	3,000
4	2	5	4	7,000	9,200
5	3	6	4	9,000	13,000
6	3	4	3	6,000	7,800
7	4, 5	3	2	4,000	6,500
8	6	5	4	8,000	11,000
9	7, 8	1	1	500	500

15 The table below lists the activities required to complete an equipment installation project. Also included are expected (normal) activity times and variances, precedence requirements, normal costs at expected times, and the cost to expedite by 1 week. Any activity can only be expedited by 1 week maximum. Activity times (in weeks) and variances are computed using most likely, optimistic, and pessimistic times. Activity "s" represents the start of the project, but it has no time or cost value. (a) Draw the network diagram, labeling all activities and times. What is the expected duration of the project? (b) What is the probability the project can be finished within 30 weeks? How much would it cost and which activities would you expedite to reduce the expected duration of the project by (c) 1 week? (d) 2 weeks?

Activity	Immediate Predecessor	Expected Activity Time (weeks)	Variance of Activity Time	Normal Cost ($)	Cost to Expedite by 1 week($)
s	—	0	0	0	0
a	s	5	1	5000	1500
b	s	3	1	3000	2000
c	s	7	2	7000	1000
d	a	4	1	3000	1300
e	b	2	1	2000	3000
f	c	5	2	5000	1600
g	d	6	2	6000	1100
h	f	4	1	4000	1400
i	e, g, h,	7	3	7000	1000
j	f, i	6	2	6000	1200

16 The table below lists the activities required to complete a construction project. Also included are activity times (in weeks) and standard deviations (in weeks), precedence requirements, normal costs at expected times, and the cost to expedite by 1 week. Any activity can only be expedited by 1 week maximum. Activities "s" and "t" represent the start and termination (completion) of the project, but they have no time or cost values. (a) Draw the network diagram, labeling all activities and times. What is the expected duration of the project? (b) How much would it cost and which activity(ies) should be expedited to reduce the expected duration of the project to 23 weeks?

Activity	Immediate Predecessor	Expected Time (weeks)	Standard Deviation	Normal Cost ($)	Cost to Expedite by 1 week($)
s	—	0	0	0	0
a	s	10	2.0	10,000	2000
b	s	8	1.6	8,000	1600
c	s	6	1.2	6,000	1200
d	a	9	1.8	9,000	1800
e	b	4	0.8	4,000	800
f	b	5	1.0	5,000	1000
g	c	8	1.4	7,000	1400
h	d, e	3	0.6	3,000	600
i	f, g	11	2.2	11,000	2100
t	h, i	0	0	0	0

17 The table below lists the activities required to complete a certain project. Also included are activity times and variances, precedence requirements, normal costs at expected times, and the cost to expedite by 1 week. Any activity can be expedited by only 1 week maximum. (a) Draw the network diagram, labeling all activities and times. What is the expected duration of the project? (b) Which activity(ies) should be expedited to reduce the expected duration of the project to 28 weeks and how much would it cost to expedite this (these) activity(ies)?

Activity	Expected Time (weeks)	Variance	Normal Cost ($)	Cost to Expedite by 1 week ($)	Immediate Predecessor
a	7	2.1	14,000	2800	—
b	10	3.0	20,000	4000	—
c	8	2.4	16,000	3200	a
d	5	1.5	10,000	2000	a
e	9	2.7	18,000	3600	b
f	6	1.8	12,000	2400	b
g	11	3.3	24,000	4800	c
h	4	1.2	8,000	1600	d, e
i	11	3.3	22,000	4400	f
j	3	0.9	6,000	1200	g, h, i

Introduction to Methods Engineering and Operations Analysis

The techniques discussed in this chapter have the following basic objectives:

- To analyze existing work systems
- To make improvements in existing work systems
- To design new work systems
- To plan the facilities in which the work systems operate

Most of the techniques that we discuss are traditional industrial engineering "tools of the trade." Methods engineering is often associated with work measurement. The two areas are often referred to collectively as "motion and time study." Many of the motion and time study techniques can be traced to the origins of industrial engineering, when it was referred to as the "scientific management movement." The techniques have been used to analyze, design, and measure work for many decades.

Methods engineering is a broader term than motion study. The scope of this field has expanded well beyond its original focus on human body motions to perform physical labor. We define ***methods engineering*** as the analysis and design of work methods and systems, including the tooling, equipment, technologies, workplace layout, plant layout, and environment used in these methods and systems.[1] Other names have sometimes been used to indicate the same basic approaches of methods engineering. These other names include ***work study***, ***work simplification***, ***methods study***, ***process re-engineering***, and ***business process re-engineering***.

The traditional objectives in methods engineering, whatever the name for this improvement activity, are the following:

- To increase productivity and efficiency
- To reduce cycle time
- To reduce product cost
- To reduce labor content

In addition, other objectives are frequently defined for process improvement efforts. Some of these additional objectives have a more contemporary appeal in today's society. They include the following:

- To improve customer satisfaction
- To improve product and/or service quality
- To reduce lead times and improve work flow
- To increase work system flexibility
- To improve worker safety
- To apply more ergonomic work methods
- To enhance the environment (both inside and outside the facility)

A term closely related to methods engineering is ***operations analysis***, defined as the study of an operation or group of related operations for the purpose of analyzing their efficiency and effectiveness so that improvements can be developed relative to specified objectives.[2] The specified objectives are basically the same as in methods engineering: to increase productivity, reduce time and cost, and improve safety and quality. Thus, methods engineering and operations analysis are very similar terms, except that methods engineering places more emphasis on design. Both terms are widely used in industrial engineering and this is why both names are included in our chapter title.

[1]The definition of methods engineering developed by the Work Measurement and Methods Standards Subcommittee [ANSI Standard Z94.11-1989] is the following: "That aspect of industrial engineering concerned with the analysis and design of work methods and systems, including the technological selection of operations or processes, specification of equipment type and location, design of manual and worker-machine tasks. May include the design of controls to insure proper level of output, inventory, quality, and cost."

[2]The definition of operations analysis developed by the Work Measurement and Methods Standards Subcommittee [ANSI Standard Z94.11-1989] is the following: "A study of an operation or scenes of operations involving people, equipment, and processes for the purpose of investigating the effectiveness of specific operations or groups so that improvements can be developed which will raise productivity, reduce costs, improve quality, reduce accident hazards, and attain other desired objectives."

1 EVOLUTION AND SCOPE OF METHODS ENGINEERING

The initial research in the area of methods engineering by Frank Gilbreth in 1885 dealt with the motions performed by workers in bricklaying. Motion study was truly an appropriate term for Gilbreth's research. The study of manual physical labor in manufacturing and construction was the primary concern of the scientific management movement in the late nineteenth and early twentieth centuries, and motion study was one of the two principal techniques used by the practitioners in that movement (the other, of course, was time study). Today, methods engineering is being applied in many other areas of work, including indirect labor, logistics, service operations, office work, and plant layout design. As these other areas have grown in importance in the economies of industrialized nations, methods engineering has been applied to analyze, improve, and design the work methods.

In terms of the problems that are addressed, methods engineering can be divided into two areas: (1) methods analysis and (2) methods design. ***Methods analysis*** is concerned with the study of an existing method or process, usually by breaking it down into the work elements or basic operations that comprise it.[3] By examining the details of the elements or operations, a systematic search can be carried out to find ways to improve the method or process. The systematic search often consists of checklists of questions and suggestions that offer opportunities for improvement. There are several objectives of using checklists in methods analysis:

- To *eliminate* unnecessary and non-value-adding elements or operations from the larger method or process
- To *combine* multiple elements or operations by performing them at one location and/or simultaneously
- To *rearrange* the elements or operations into a more logical sequence and work flow
- To *simplify* the remaining elements or operations so they can be accomplished more quickly and with minimum effort.

In addition to studying an existing method or process, methods analysis can also be used to analyze a proposed new method for possible improvements. In this regard the two areas of methods analysis and methods design overlap each other.

Methods design is concerned with either of the following situations: (1) the design of a new method or process or (2) the redesign of an existing method or process based on a preceding methods analysis. The design of a new method or process occurs when a new product or service is introduced and/or a new facility or equipment is installed, and there is no existing precedent for the operation. In this case, the method or process must be designed from scratch. This can often be accomplished by referring to best current practice for similar operations and attempting to improve on the current work design. In other cases, an original work design must be developed, including the basic operations,

[3]The definition of methods analysis developed by the Work Measurement and Methods Standards Subcommittee [ANSI Standard Z94.11-1989] is the following: "That part of methods engineering normally involving an examination and analysis of an operation or a work cycle broken down into its constituent parts for the purpose of improvement, elimination of unnecessary steps, and/or establishing and recording in detail a proposed method of performance."

methods, equipment, special tooling, workplace layout, and plant layout. As in other areas of design, guidelines are available, such as the principles of motion economy and the plant layout planning approach, and these can be applied in solving the design problem.

Methods engineering studies have traditionally been the province and responsibility of industrial engineers. Today, methods analysis and design are no longer accomplished exclusively by industrial engineers. They are accomplished, with greater or lesser effectiveness, by a variety of individuals, departments, and teams. The workers themselves often participate in the development and improvement of their own work methods, under the assumption that they know their jobs better than anyone else. Industrial engineers often participate in these improvement activities, serving an important role as technical consultant and mentor.

2 HOW TO APPLY METHODS ENGINEERING

In this section we present a systematic approach that can be used to accomplish a methods engineering study. We then survey the tools and techniques used in such a study. Finally, we present a procedure for selecting among alternative possible solutions to a methods engineering problem.

2.1 Systematic Approach in Methods Engineering

An underlying assumption in methods engineering is that a systematic approach is more likely to yield operational improvements than an undisciplined approach. Our systematic approach to problem solving in methods engineering has its basis in the ***scientific method*** used in science, research and development, engineering design, and other problem areas. The systematic approach in methods engineering consists of the steps described below.

Step 1: Define the Problem and Objectives. The problem is the reason for needing a systematic approach to determine its solution. The problem in a methods engineering study may be low productivity, high cost, inefficient methods, or the need for a new method or a new operation. The objective is the desired improvement or new methods design that would result from the methods engineering project. Possible objectives are to increase productivity, reduce labor content and cost, improve safety, or develop a new method or new operation. These are the typical objectives discussed in our chapter introduction. The problem definition and objectives must be specific to the problem under investigation, although there may be similarities with other problems.

Step 2: Analyze the Problem. This step consists of data collection and analysis activities that are most appropriate for the type of problem being studied. The kinds of activities often used in this step include the following:

- Identify the basic function of the operation.
- Gather background information.
- Observe the existing process or observe similar processes if the problem involves a new work design.

- Collect data on the existing operation and document the details in a format that lends itself to examination.
- Conduct experiments on the process.
- Develop a mathematical model of the process or utilize an existing mathematical model such as those on work systems and how they work.
- Perform a computer simulation of the process.
- Use charting techniques.

A survey of the analysis techniques used in step 2 is provided in Section 2.2.

Step 3: Formulate Alternatives. There are always multiple ways to perform a task or accomplish a process, some of which are more efficient and effective than others. Only by enumerating the alternative ways and comparing them can the most efficient and effective method or process be determined.[4] However, the purpose of this step in the problem-solving approach is not to identify the best alternative but to formulate all of the alternatives that are feasible.[5]

Step 4: Evaluate Alternatives and Select the Best. This step consists of a methodical assessment of the alternatives and the selection of the best solution among them, based on the original definition of the problem and objectives. The selection procedure described in Section 2.3 is useful in this step of the methods engineering approach.

Step 5: Implement the Best Method. Implementation means installing the selected solution: introducing the changes proposed in the existing method or operation, or instituting the new method or process. This may involve pilot studies or trials of the new or revised method preliminary to online implementation and application of the method. Implementation also includes complete documentation of the new or revised method and replacement of the previous documentation in the case of a revised method. Unless the old documentation is replaced, the old method may remain as the official method until a new methods engineering study is performed sometime in the future (thus reinventing the wheel).

Step 6: Audit the Study. It is desirable to perform an audit or follow-up on the methods engineering project. How successful was the project in terms of the original problem definition and objectives? What were the implementation issues? What should be done differently in the next methods engineering study? For an organization committed to continuous improvement, answers to these kinds of questions help to fine-tune its problem-solving and decision-making skills.

[4]In the scientific method as applied to research, the alternatives are typically the different proposed theories to explain the observed phenomenon. Ultimately, one theory is selected as the most reasonable in terms of explaining the phenomenon.

[5]Even the infeasible solutions should probably be included in the list. Sometimes the alternatives that initially seem infeasible turn out to be quite doable after all. What made them seem unacceptable on first consideration were artificial or false constraints that proved not to be constraints upon closer scrutiny.

2.2 The Techniques of Methods Engineering

A variety of techniques are available for operations analysis. The techniques are most closely associated with the analysis step in methods engineering, although they may also be applicable in some of the other steps as well. As a starting point, we have the basic data collection and analysis techniques discussed in Section 3. These are graphical and statistical methods for gathering, plotting, and displaying data. They include histograms and *x-y* plots as well as other charts and diagrams.

Beyond the basic data collection and analysis techniques, which are applicable in many disciplines other than methods engineering, there are the specialized analysis techniques more closely associated with operations analysis and industrial engineering. They are described briefly in the following sections.

Charting and Diagramming Techniques. There are many charting techniques available for collecting, displaying, and analyzing data on a given work system or operation sequence of interest. They can be classified into the following categories:

- *Network diagrams.* These are used for analyzing work flow, assembly line balancing, and project scheduling. Special algorithms are often available to analyze these network diagrams.
- *Traditional industrial engineering charting techniques.* These are used to symbolize and summarize the details of an existing operation or sequence of operations. The traditional charting techniques can be used to analyze the activities of one human worker, groups of workers, worker-machine systems, materials, parts, and products.
- *Block diagrams and process maps.* These diagrams represent alternative ways of depicting processes. They are sometimes used in place of the traditional IE charting techniques.

Motion Study and Work Design. This area of methods engineering is concerned with the study of the basic motions of a human worker while performing a given task. The basic motions include ***reach*** (using the hand to reach for an object), ***grasp*** (grasping the object), ***move*** (moving the object), and ***release*** (releasing it). All manual tasks performed at a single workplace are composed of these basic motions. There are 17 basic motion elements, most of which involve movements of the arm and hand. By studying the basic motions in the work method used by a worker, unnecessary motions can be eliminated, or some of the motion elements can be combined (for example, using both hands to simultaneously perform motions rather than one arm doing everything), or the method can be otherwise simplified.

Over many years, the study of basic motions in manual operations has resulted in the development of certain principles on how to perform work. Commonly called the ***principles of motion economy***, they provide guidelines for work design in three categories: (1) use of the human body in developing the standard method, (2) workplace layout, and (3) design of the tooling and equipment used in the task. Many of the principles are simple and obvious; for example, "design the work so that both hands are fully utilized." Yet simple work design principles such as these are often neglected in many manual operations performed throughout the world. By having these guidelines available, work methods can be designed to be safer, faster, more efficient, and less fatiguing.

Facility Layout Planning. A facility (e.g., factory, office building, warehouse, hospital) is a fixed asset of the organization that owns (or rents) it. ***Facility layout*** refers to the size and shape of a facility, the arrangement of the different functions and/or departments in it, and the way the equipment is positioned. The layout plays a significant role in determining the overall efficiency of the operations accomplished in the facility. Facility layout planning represents an important problem area in industrial engineering, and we discuss the techniques for solving it within the scope of methods engineering. The problem area includes designing a new facility, installing new equipment, retiring old equipment, and expanding (or contracting) an existing facility.

Plant layout planning and design are best accomplished using a systematic approach, similar to the systematic approach in methods engineering. As in other problem areas in methods engineering, there are tools available to use in a plant layout design project. The approach is called "systematic layout planning," developed by Richard Muther [13].

Work Measurement Techniques. Several of the work measurement techniques can also be used in methods engineering. We mention two that seem most relevant for studying and analyzing operations and methods: predetermined motion time systems and work sampling.

A ***predetermined motion time system*** (PMTS) is a database of basic motion elements and their associated normal time values, and it includes procedures for applying the database to analyze manual tasks and establish standard times for the tasks. The principal application of a PMTS is to determine standard times. However, some systems also include tools for analyzing methods and motions in the task, which is a methods engineering function.

Work sampling is a statistical technique for determining the proportions of time spent by workers or machines in various categories of activity. It can be applied to determine machine utilization, worker utilization, and the average time spent performing various types of activities. As such it can be a useful tool in methods engineering for identifying areas that need attention. For example, if a work sampling study finds that workers in a facility spend large amounts of their time waiting for work, then this is a management problem that should be addressed.

New Approaches in Methods Engineering. Nearly all of the preceding techniques have been used for many decades, some even longer.[6] More recently, alternative approaches for improving production and service operations have evolved from these traditional techniques. These alternative approaches include lean production (based on

[6]An example: Frank Gilbreth's interest in motion study dates from 1885; his book, *Motion Study*, was published in 1911.

the famed Toyota Production System), total quality management, and Six Sigma.

It is the view of this author that most of the tools used in these more recent approaches are basically adaptations and modifications of good industrial engineering techniques and principles. Not to demean their importance, they are often used with good effect to identify and solve problems and to make improvements. And they sometimes successfully serve the function of providing a rallying point for motivating workers who might not be motivated by something called motion and time study. Their objectives are generally the same as the objectives of methods engineering.

2.3 Selecting Among Alternative Improvement Proposals

Evaluating the alternative improvement proposals and selecting the best among them (step 4 in the systematic methods engineering approach) can be a difficult process in methods engineering. As always, it is helpful to use a systematic procedure to decide which improvement proposal(s) should be selected. The procedure recommended here is most applicable when the selection is to be made among specific proposals—for example, alternative process designs or different equipment proposals from vendors. The alternatives have been developed to address a specified problem or a need of the customer organization. Each proposed solution has its relative strengths and weaknesses, and the selection procedure must weigh the pros and cons in a fair and logical way. The procedure is explained as follows.[7]

Prior to the development of proposals, a list of technical features and functional specifications for the given application must be prepared by the customer organization. This is an essential part of the problem definition step (step 1) in the methods engineering approach. The operations analyst(s) or equipment vendors will use this list as the basis for formulating alternative solutions and proposals (step 3 in the systematic approach). The same list will be used by the customer organization to evaluate the proposals. The features and specifications should be divided into two categories:

1. *Must features.* These are the features and specifications that the proposal must satisfy. If these are not satisfied, then the proposal is not suitable for the application.
2. *Desirable features.* These are features and specifications that are not necessarily required to satisfy the application, but they are desirable.

After all of the proposals have been submitted, the evaluation process begins. The tabular format shown in Table 1, sometimes referred to as a ***criteria matrix***, is used. First, the proposals are evaluated against the must features. A candidate proposal must satisfy all of the must features or it is dropped from further consideration.

[7]Although we are presenting this selection procedure as a decision-making tool in methods engineering, its applications are much broader and more diverse. For example, it can be used for selecting which new car to buy, deciding which job offer to accept (assuming there is more than one offer), or even choosing a prospective spouse.

TABLE 1 Evaluation of Alternative Industrial Robots for a Welding Application in Example 1

	Industrial Robot Candidates			
	Model A	Model B	Model C	Model D
Must features:				
Continuous path control	OK	OK	OK	OK
Six-axis robot arm	OK	OK	Not OK	OK
Walkthrough programming	OK	OK	OK	OK
Desirable features:				
Ease of programming (0–9)	6	4		6
Capability to edit program (0–5)	4	2		5
Multipass features (0–4)	2	2		2
Work volume (0–9)	5	8		6
Repeatability (0–5)	5	2		4
Lowest price (0–5)	4	5		3
Delivery (0–3)	1	1		3
Evaluation of vendor (0–9)	6	5		8
Totals:	33	29		37

Source: [6].

Next, the proposals are compared against each of the desirable features. For each feature, a rating score is given to each candidate to indicate how well it satisfies that feature. No doubt there will be differences in the relative importance of the different features, and this is taken into account by assigning a maximum possible point score to each desirable feature. For example, if a particular feature is judged to be twice as important as another, then the more important feature is assigned a maximum score of, say, 10 points, while the less important feature is given a maximum of 5 points. These maximum point scores are judgment calls made by the methods engineer or by the collective wisdom of the project team doing the selection. Scoring each proposal on each feature is also a judgment call based on the relative merits of each candidate.

Finally, for the proposals that still remain after elimination of those that failed one or more of the must features, the scores of each proposal are tallied and the proposal with the highest total score is selected as the winner.

Of course, economics must play a role in the selection process. One might be inclined to simply choose the low cost bidder. However, that is often a mistake. Cost is rarely the only factor in implementing a new process, purchasing a piece of equipment, or making other investment decisions. The cost factor can be included as one of the desirable features in the list and given an appropriate weighting score to reflect its importance. The following example illustrates the use of this procedure to select a robot for a welding application.

Example 1 Selecting a Welding Robot[8]

Four industrial robots were being considered to satisfy an arc-welding application at the company. They are identified in Table 1 as Models A, B, C, and D. As suggested in the selection

[8]This example is based on an industrial case study in which the author participated. The case study was first reported in [7]. The company remains anonymous.

procedure, the features and specifications are divided into two categories: "must" and "desirable." The must features were considered essential for the application. The desirable features were assigned maximum point scores as shown in the table. The entries in the table for each robot indicate how that candidate was scored in each of the features. Note that one of the features was price, but it was not considered to be the most important feature.

Conclusion. First, model C was eliminated from consideration because it did not satisfy one of the "must" features. For the three remaining models, model D was selected because it had the highest point score among the desirable features. ■

3 BASIC DATA COLLECTION AND ANALYSIS TECHNIQUES

The data collection and analysis techniques discussed in this section are used by scientists, engineers, mathematicians, and statisticians. Most of them are statistical charting tools used to record and/or exhibit data so that it can be interpreted more readily. The techniques also have value for analysis. When used to measure and analyze production and service operations, these statistical tools are often associated with a field known as ***statistical process control*** (SPC).[9] Statistical process control and other quality-oriented programs are discussed in Chapter 21. In these programs, worker teams are organized to study operational problems. To enable the teams to be more effective, they are trained in the use of these basic tools. Thus, industrial engineers are not the exclusive users of these techniques in operations analysis. Instead, IEs must often serve as team leaders, training instructors, and expert consultants for the worker teams who carry out the studies.

Histograms. A ***histogram*** is a statistical graph consisting of bars representing different values or ranges of values, in which the length of each bar is proportional to the frequency or relative frequency of the value or range, as shown in Figure 1. Also known as a bar chart, it is a graphical display of the ***frequency distribution*** of the numerical data. What makes the histogram such a useful statistical tool is that it enables the analyst to quickly visualize the features of a complete set of data. These features include (1) the shape of the distribution, (2) any central tendency exhibited by the distribution, (3) approximations of the mean and mode of the distribution, and (4) the amount of scatter or spread in the data.

Example 2 Frequency Distribution and Histogram

Part dimension data from a manufacturing process are displayed in the frequency distribution of Table 2. The data are the dimensional values of individual parts taken from the process, while the process is running normally. Plot the data as a histogram and draw inferences from the graph.

Solution: The frequency distribution in Table 2 is displayed graphically in the histogram of Figure 1. We can see that the distribution is normal (in all likelihood), and that the mean is

[9]Although we are giving due recognition to the field of statistical process control, it should also be noted that many of these basic tools have been taught for many years in industrial engineering courses and used by practicing industrial engineers to study problems in methods engineering and operations analysis.

TABLE 2 Frequency Distribution of Part Dimension Data

Range of Dimension	Frequency	Relative Frequency	Cumulative Relative Frequency
$1.975 \leq x < 1.980$	1	0.01	0.01
$1.980 \leq x < 1.985$	3	0.03	0.04
$1.985 \leq x < 1.990$	5	0.05	0.09
$1.990 \leq x < 1.995$	13	0.13	0.22
$1.995 \leq x < 2.000$	29	0.29	0.51
$2.000 \leq x < 2.005$	27	0.27	0.78
$2.005 \leq x < 2.010$	15	0.15	0.93
$2.010 \leq x < 2.015$	4	0.04	0.97
$2.015 \leq x < 2.020$	2	0.02	0.99
$2.020 \leq x < 2.025$	1	0.01	1.00

around 2.00. We can approximate the standard deviation to be the range of the values (2.025–1.975) divided by 6, based on the fact that nearly the entire distribution (99.73%) is contained within $\pm 3\sigma$ of the mean value. This gives a σ value of around 0.008. ■

Pareto Charts. A ***Pareto chart*** is a special form of histogram, illustrated in Figure 2, in which attribute data are arranged according to some criteria such as cost or value. When appropriately used, it provides a graphical display of the tendency for a small proportion of a given population to be more valuable than the much larger majority. This tendency is sometimes referred to as ***Pareto's law***, which can be succinctly stated:

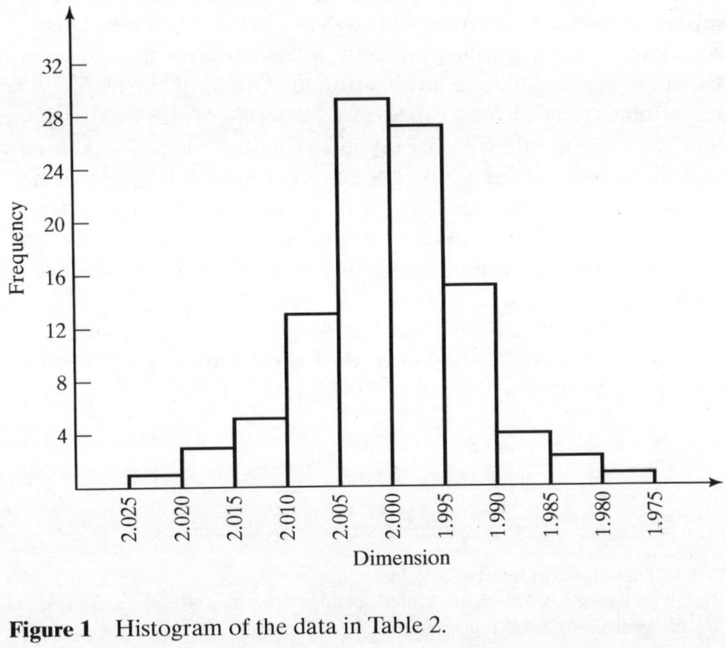

Figure 1 Histogram of the data in Table 2.

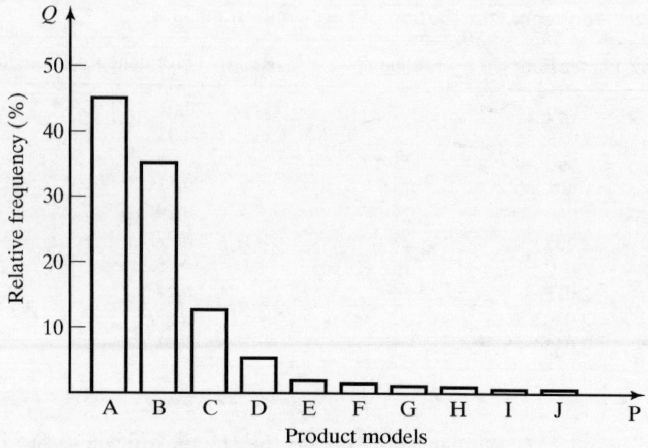

Figure 2 Typical (hypothetical) Pareto distribution of a factory's production output. Although there are ten models produced, two of the models account for 80% of the total units. This chart is sometimes referred to as a *P-Q* chart, where *P* = products and *Q* = quantity of production.

"the vital few and the trivial many."[10] The "law" was identified by Vilfredo Pareto (1848–1923), an Italian economist and sociologist who studied the distribution of wealth in Italy and found that most of it was held by a small percentage of the population.

Pareto's law applies not only to the distribution of wealth, but to many other distributions as well. The law is often identified as the 80%–20% rule (although exact percentages may differ from 80 and 20): 80% of the wealth of a nation is in the hands of 20% of its people; 80% of inventory value is accounted for by 20% of the items in inventory; 80% of sales revenues are generated by 20% of the customers; and 80% of a factory's production output is concentrated in only 20% of its product models (as in Figure 2). A Pareto chart identifies the proportion of the population that is the most important, and the focus in any improvement study or project should be on that proportion.

A Pareto distribution can also be plotted as a cumulative frequency distribution, as shown in Figure 3 for the same data shown in Figure 2. The Pareto cumulative distribution can be modeled by the following equation:[11]

$$y=\frac{(1+A)\,x}{A+x} \quad \text{for} \quad 0 \le y \le 1 \quad \text{and} \quad 0 \le x \le 1 \qquad (1)$$

[10]The statement is attributed to J. M Juran [8].

[11]Based on Bender, P., "Mathematical Modeling of the 20/80 Rule: Theory and Practice," *Journal of Business Logistics*, Vol. 2, No. 2, 1981, pp 139–157.

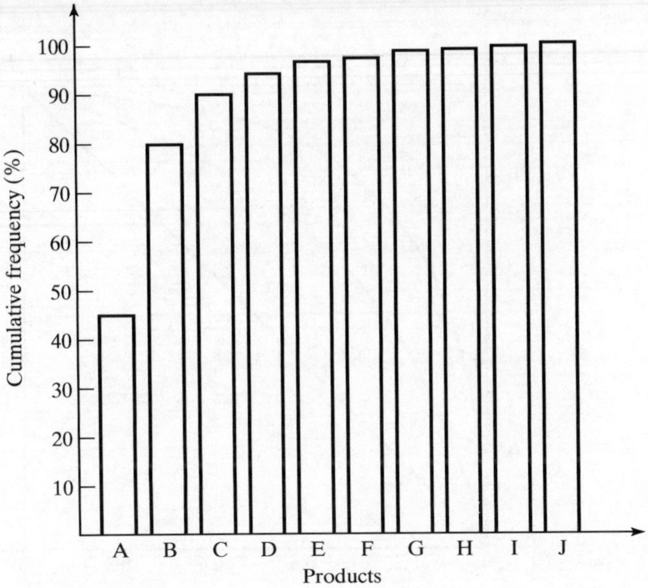

Figure 3 Pareto chart plotted as a cumulative frequency distribution for the same data shown in Figure 2.

where y = cumulative fraction of the value variable (e.g., wealth, inventory value, sales revenue), x = cumulative fraction of the item variable (e.g., population, inventory items, customers), and A is a constant that determines the shape of the distribution. Values of A between zero and infinity provide shapes that possess the Pareto characteristic, as shown in Figure 4. When $A = 0$, the equation reduces to $y = 1$ for all x, and when $A = \infty$, the equation becomes $y = x$.

To determine the appropriate value of A for a given situation or set of data, equation (1) can be rearranged to solve for A as a function of x and y, as follows:

$$A = \frac{x(1-y)}{y-x} \qquad (2)$$

where x and y are the cumulative frequencies of the two variables at a given point in the distribution. The following example illustrates the approach.

Example 3 Pareto Cumulative Distribution

It is known that 20% of the total inventory items in a company's warehouse accounts for 80% of the value of the inventory. (a) Determine the parameter A in the Pareto cumulative distribution equation. (b) Given that the relationship is valid for the remaining inventory, how much of the inventory value is accounted for by 50% of the items?

Solution **(a)** To find A, we use equation (2) given that $x = 0.20$ and $y = 0.80$ (20% of the items, 80% of the value).

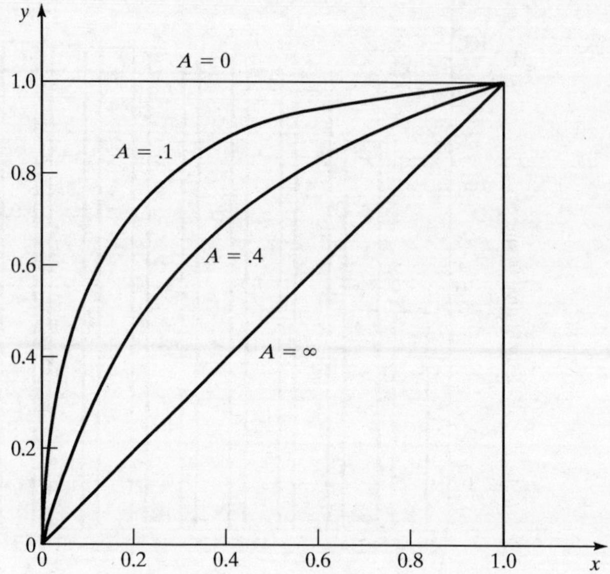

Figure 4 Shape of plots of equation (1) for several values of A.

$$A = \frac{0.20(1 - 0.80)}{0.80 - 0.20} = 0.06667$$

(b) Now that we know the value of A, the following Pareto cumulative distribution equation can be used:

$$y = \frac{(1.06667)x}{0.06667 + x}$$

For $x = 0.50$, the equation can be used to calculate y:

$$y = \frac{(1.06667)(0.50)}{0.06667 + 0.50} = 0.941$$

We expect that 50% of the items in inventory account for 94.1% of the value of the inventory. ■

Pie Charts. A ***pie chart*** is a circular (pie-shaped) display that is sliced by radii into segments whose relative areas are proportional to the magnitudes or frequencies of the data categories comprising the total circle. The visual effect is similar to a Pareto chart, in the sense that the important categories can be immediately recognized because of their relative sizes. Multiple pie charts can be displayed side by side to indicate not only the relative category sizes within a circle but also the relative sizes of the circles. Figure 5 shows two consecutive years of company sales, indicating how sales increased the second year and how the increase was distributed among types of customers.

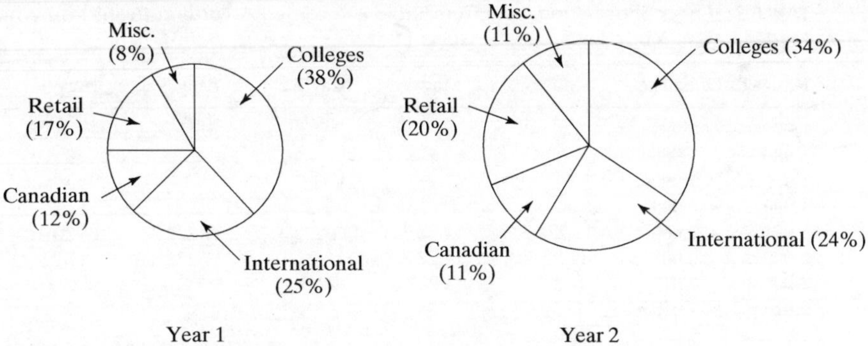

Figure 5 Pie charts showing two annual sales revenues and the customer distributions for the two years. Sales in year 2 increased 43% over year 1.

Check Sheets. The ***check sheet*** (not to be confused with "check list") is a data gathering tool generally used in the preliminary stages of the study of a problem. The operator running a process (for example, the machine operator) is often given the responsibility for recording the data on the check sheet, and the data are often recorded in the form of simple check marks.

Example 4 Check Sheet Application

For the dimensional data in the frequency distribution of Table 2, suppose we wanted to see if there were any differences between the three shifts that are responsible for making the parts. A check sheet has been designed for this purpose, and data have been collected. Analyze the data.

Solution: The check sheet is illustrated in Table 3. The data include the shift on which each dimensional value was produced (shifts are identified simply as 1, 2, and 3). The data in a check sheet are usually recorded as a function of time periods (days, weeks, months), as in our table.

It is clear from the data that the third shift is responsible for much of the variability in the data. Further analysis, shown in Table 4, substantiates this finding. This should lead to an investigation to determine the causes of the greater variability on the third shift, with appropriate corrective action to address the problem.

We also note from Table 4 that the average daily production rate for the third shift is somewhat below the daily rate for the other two shifts. The third shift seems to be a problem that demands management attention. ■

Check sheets can take many different forms, depending on the problem situation and the ingenuity of the analyst. The form should be designed to allow some interpretation of results directly from the raw data, although subsequent data analysis may be necessary to recognize trends, diagnose the problem, or identify areas of further study.

Defect Concentration Diagrams. The defect concentration diagram is a graphical method that has been found to be useful in analyzing the causes of product or part defects. It is a drawing of the product (or other item of interest), with all relevant views displayed,

TABLE 3 Check Sheet Using Data from Table 2 Recorded According to Shift on Which Parts Were Made

Range of Dimension	May 5	May 6	May 7	May 8	May 9	Weekly Totals
1.975 ≤ x < 1.980			3			1
1.980 ≤ x < 1.985		2		3	3	3
1.985 ≤ x < 1.990	1	3	3	1	3	5
1.990 ≤ x < 1.995	1 2	11 2 3	1 2	1 2	1 22	13
1.995 ≤ x < 2.000	11 222 3	11 22 3	111 222 3	11 222 3	11 22 3	29
2.000 ≤ x < 2.005	11 22 3	11 22 3	111 22 3	11 222 3	111 22	27
2.005 ≤ x < 2.010	1 2 3	1 2 3	22 3	1 33	1 2 3	15
2.010 ≤ x < 2.015	3	3	3		3	4
2.015 ≤ x < 2.020	3			3		2
2.020 ≤ x < 2.025	3					1
Total parts/day	20	20	21	20	19	100

TABLE 4 Summary of Data from Check Sheet of Table 3 Showing Frequency of Each Shift in Each Dimension Ranges

Range of Dimension	Shift 1	Shift 2	Shift 3	Totals
1.975 ≤ x < 1.980			1	1
1.980 ≤ x < 1.985		1	2	3
1.985 ≤ x < 1.990	2		3	5
1.990 ≤ x < 1.995	6	6	1	13
1.995 ≤ x < 2.000	11	13	5	29
2.000 ≤ x < 2.005	12	11	4	27
2.005 ≤ x < 2.010	4	5	6	15
2.010 ≤ x < 2.015			4	4
2.015 ≤ x < 2.020			2	2
2.020 ≤ x < 2.025			1	1
Weekly total parts/shift	35	36	29	100
Average daily parts/shift	7.0	7.2	5.8	

onto which the various types of defects or other problems of interest have been sketched at the locations where they each occurred. By analyzing the defect types and corresponding locations, it may be possible to identify the underlying causes of the defects.

Montgomery [11] describes a case study involving the final assembly of refrigerators that were plagued by surface defects. A defect concentration diagram (Figure 6) was utilized to analyze the problem. The defects were clearly shown to be concentrated around the middle section of the refrigerator. Upon investigation, it was learned that a belt was wrapped around each unit for material handling purposes. It became evident that the defects were caused by the belt, and corrective action was taken to improve the handling method.

Scatter Diagrams. In many industrial problems involving manufacturing operations, it is useful to identify a possible relationship that exists between two process variables. The scatter diagram is helpful in this regard. A ***scatter diagram*** is an *x-y* plot of the data taken of the two variables of interest, as illustrated in Figure 7. The data

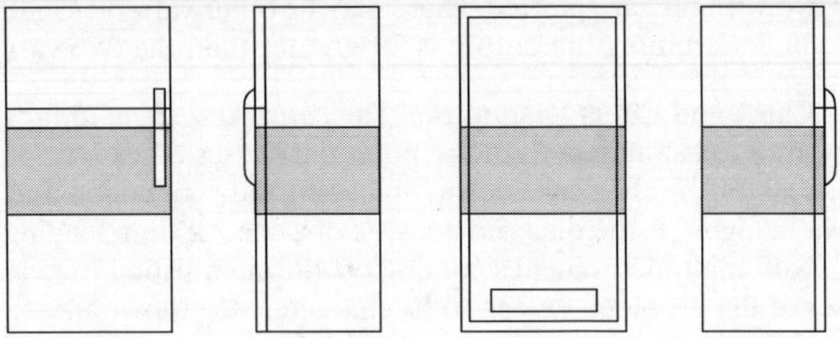

Figure 6 Defect concentration diagram showing four views of refrigerator with locations of surface defects indicated in shaded areas.

are plotted as pairs; for each x_i value, there is a corresponding y_i value. The shape of the data points considered in aggregate often reveals a pattern or relationship between the two variables. For example, the scatter diagram in Figure 7 indicates that a negative correlation exists between cobalt content and wear resistance of a cemented carbide cutting tool. As cobalt content increases, wear resistance decreases.

One must be circumspect in using scatter diagrams and in extrapolating the trends that might be indicated by the data. For instance, it might be inferred from our diagram that a cemented carbide tool with zero cobalt content would possess the highest wear resistance of all. However, cobalt serves as an essential binder in the pressing and sintering process used to fabricate cemented carbide tools, and a minimum level of cobalt is necessary to hold the tungsten carbide particles together in the final product. There are other reasons why caution is recommended in the use of the scatter diagram, since

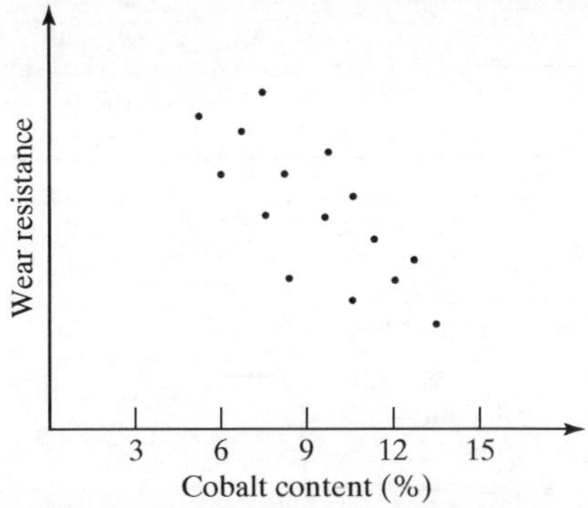

Figure 7 Scatter diagram showing the effect of cobalt binder content on wear resistance of a cemented carbide cutting tool insert.

only two variables are plotted. There may be other variables in the process whose importance in determining the output is far greater than the two variables displayed.

Cause and Effect Diagrams. The ***cause and effect diagram*** is a graphical-tabular chart used to list and analyze the potential causes of a given problem. It is not really a statistical tool, in the sense of the preceding data collection and analysis techniques. As shown in Figure 8, the diagram consists of a central stem leading to the effect (the problem), with multiple branches coming off the stem listing the various groups of possible causes of the problem. Owing to its characteristic appearance, the cause and effect diagram is also known as a ***fishbone diagram***. In application, cause and effect diagrams are often developed by worker teams who study operational problems. The diagram provides a graphical means for discussing and analyzing a problem and listing its possible causes in an organized and understandable way. Members of the team collectively identify the branches of the diagram (causes of the problem) and then attempt to determine which causes are most consequential and how to take corrective action against them.

As a starting point in identifying the causes of the problem (the main branches in the fishbone diagram), six general categories of causes are often used because they are the factors that affect performance of most production and service processes. Called the 5Ms and 1P [4], they are as follows:

1. *Machines.* This refers to the equipment and tooling used in the process.
2. *Materials.* These are the starting materials in the process.

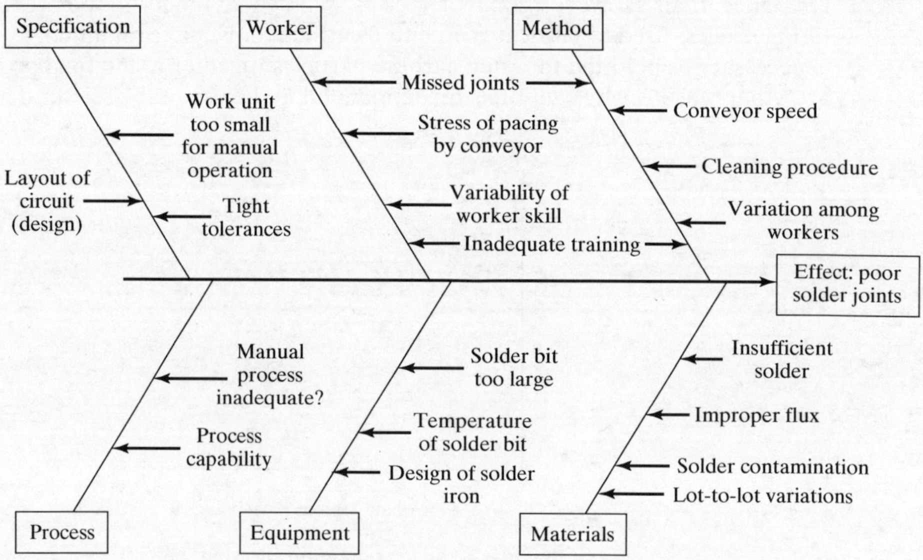

Figure 8 Cause and effect diagram for a manual soldering operation. The diagram indicates the effect (the problem is poor solder joints) at the end of the arrow and the possible causes are listed on the branches leading toward the effect.

3. *Methods.* This refers to the procedures, sequence of activities, motions, and other aspects of the method used in the process.
4. *Mother Nature.* This is a pseudonym for environmental factors such as air temperature and humidity that might affect the process.
5. *Measurement.* This relates to the validity and accuracy of the data collection procedures.
6. *People.* This is the human factor. Does the worker bring the necessary skills to the process?

During construction of the fishbone diagram, more specific causes and issues are listed on the smaller branches within each of these six categories as the analysis team pursues a solution to the problem.

4 METHODS ENGINEERING AND AUTOMATION

The issue of automation arises frequently in methods engineering. The analysis of an operation may lead to the conclusion that an automated or semiautomated work system is preferable to performing a task manually. However, a certain caution and respect must be observed in applying automation technologies. In this section, we offer three approaches for dealing with automation projects in methods engineering: (1) the USA Principle, (2) ten strategies for automation, and (3) an automation migration strategy.

4.1 USA Principle

The USA principle is a commonsense approach to automation projects. Similar procedures have been suggested in the manufacturing and automation trade literature, but none have a more captivating title than this one. USA stands for three steps in the analysis and design procedure:

1. *Understand* the existing process.
2. *Simplify* the process.
3. *Automate* the process.

Described in [10], the approach is so general that it is applicable to nearly any automation project. One might argue that the USA principle is basically an abbreviated version of the methods engineering approach (Section 2.1).

The purpose of the first step in the USA principle is to understand the current process in all of its details. What are the inputs? What are the outputs? What exactly happens to the work unit between input and output? What is the function of the process? How does it add value to the product? What are the upstream and downstream operations in the production sequence and can they be combined with the process under consideration?

Some of the basic charting tools used in methods engineering are useful in this step. Applying these kinds of tools to the existing process provides a model of the process that can be analyzed and searched for weaknesses and opportunities. The number of steps in the process, the number and placement of inspections, the number of moves and delays experienced by the work unit, and the time spent in storage can be determined from these charting techniques.

Mathematical models of the process may also be useful to indicate relationships between input parameters and output variables. What are the important output variables? How are these output variables affected by inputs to the process, such as raw material properties, process settings, operating parameters, and environmental conditions? This information may be valuable in identifying what output variables need to be measured for feedback purposes and in formulating algorithms for automatic process control.

Once the existing process is understood, then the search begins for ways to simplify the process (step 2). This often involves a checklist of questions about the existing process. What is the purpose of this operation or this transport? Is that operation necessary? Can this step be eliminated? Is the most appropriate technology being used in this process? How can this step be simplified? Are there unnecessary steps in the process that might be eliminated without detracting from the function? These are basic questions in a methods engineering study.

Some of the ten strategies for automation (Section 4.2) may be used to simplify the process. Can steps be combined? Can steps be performed simultaneously? Can steps be integrated into a manually operated production line? Simplifying the process may lead to the conclusion that automation is not necessary, thus saving the significant investment cost that would be entailed.

When the process has been reduced to its simplest form, then automation can be considered (step 3). The possible forms of automation include those listed in the ten strategies discussed in the following section. An automation migration strategy (Section 4.3) might be implemented for a new product that has yet to prove itself.

4.2 Ten Strategies for Automation

The USA Principle is a good first step in any automation evaluation project. As suggested previously, it may turn out that automation is unnecessary or cannot be cost justified after the process has been simplified. If automation seems a feasible solution to improving productivity, quality, or another measure of performance, then the following ten strategies provide a road map to search for these improvements.[13] Although we refer to them as strategies for automation, some of them are applicable whether the process is a candidate for automation or just simplification.

1. *Specialization of operations.* Analogous to the concept of labor specialization for improving labor productivity, this strategy involves the use of special-purpose equipment designed to perform one operation with the greatest possible efficiency.
2. *Combined operations.* Production almost always occurs as a sequence of operations. Complex parts may require dozens, or even hundreds, of processing steps.

[13]These ten strategies were first published in my book *Automation, Production Systems, and Computer-Aided Manufacturing* (Prentice Hall, 1980). They seem as relevant and appropriate today as they did in 1980.

The strategy of combined operations involves reducing the number of distinct workstations through which the work units must be routed. This is accomplished by performing more than one operation at a given workstation, thereby reducing the number of separate workstations needed.

3. *Simultaneous operations.* A logical extension of the combined operations strategy is to simultaneously perform the operations that are combined at one workstation. In effect, two or more operations are performed at the same time on the same work unit, thus reducing total processing time.
4. *Integration of operations.* This strategy involves linking several workstations together into a single integrated mechanism using automated work handling devices to achieve continuous work flow. With an integrated sequence of workstations, several work units can be processed simultaneously (one at each station), thereby increasing the overall output of the system.
5. *Increased flexibility.* This strategy attempts to achieve maximum utilization of human and equipment resources for low and medium volume situations by using the same resources for a variety of work units. It involves the use of the flexible automation concepts that are implemented using computer systems.
6. *Improved material handling and storage.* The use of automated material handling and storage systems is a great opportunity to reduce nonproductive time. Typical benefits include reduced work-in-process and shorter lead times. In information service operations, the counterpart is a the use of advanced database and data processing technologies.
7. *On-line inspection.* Inspection for quality is traditionally performed after the process. This means that any poor quality product or service has already been completed by the time it is inspected. Incorporating inspection into the process permits corrections during the process. This brings the overall quality level closer to the nominal specifications intended by the designer.
8. *Process control and optimization.* This includes a wide range of control schemes intended to operate individual processes and associated equipment more efficiently. By using this strategy, the individual process times can be reduced and quality improved.
9. *Plant operations control.* Whereas the previous strategy is concerned with control of the individual process, this strategy is concerned with control at the plant level. It attempts to manage and coordinate the aggregate operations in the plant more efficiently. Its implementation usually involves a high level of computer networking within the facility.
10. *Computer integrated manufacturing (CIM).* Taking the previous strategy one level higher, we have the integration of factory operations with engineering design and the business functions of the firm. CIM involves extensive use of computer applications, computer databases, and computer networking throughout the enterprise.

The ten strategies constitute a checklist of the possibilities for improving the work system, through automation or simplification. They should not be considered as mutually exclusive. For many situations, multiple strategies can be implemented in one improvement project.

4.3 Automation Migration Strategy

Because of competitive pressures in the marketplace, a company often needs to introduce a new product in the shortest possible time. The easiest and least expensive way to accomplish this objective is to design a manual production method, using a sequence of workstations operating independently. The tooling for a manual method can be fabricated quickly and at low cost. If more than a single set of workstations is required to make the product in sufficient quantities, as is often the case, then the manual cell is replicated as many times as needed to meet the demand. If the product turns out to be successful and high demand is anticipated in the future, it makes sense for the company to automate production. The improvements are often carried out in phases. Many companies have an ***automation migration strategy***—a formalized plan for evolving the manufacturing systems used to produce new products as demand grows. The following phases are included in the typical automation migration strategy:

Phase 1: ***Manual production*** using single station manned cells operating independently. This is used for introduction of the new product for reasons mentioned above: quick and low-cost tooling to get started.

Phase 2: ***Automated production*** using single station automated cells operating independently. As demand for the product grows and it becomes clear that automation can be justified, the single stations are automated to reduce labor and increase production rate. Work units are still moved between workstations manually.

Phase 3: ***Automated integrated production*** using a multistation automated system with serial operations and automated transfer of work units between stations. When the company is certain that the product will be produced in mass quantities and for several years, then integration of the single station automated cells is warranted to further reduce labor and increase production rate.

This strategy is illustrated in Figure 9. Details of the automation migration strategy vary from company to company, depending on the types of products they make and the processes they perform. But well-managed companies have policies like this one. There are several advantages to such a strategy:

- It allows introduction of the new product in the shortest possible time, since production cells based on manual workstations are the easiest to design and implement.
- It allows automation to be introduced gradually (in planned phases), as demand for the product grows, engineering changes in the product are made, and time is allowed to do a thorough design job on the automated manufacturing system.
- It avoids the commitment to a high level of automation from the start, since there is always a risk that demand for the product will not justify it.

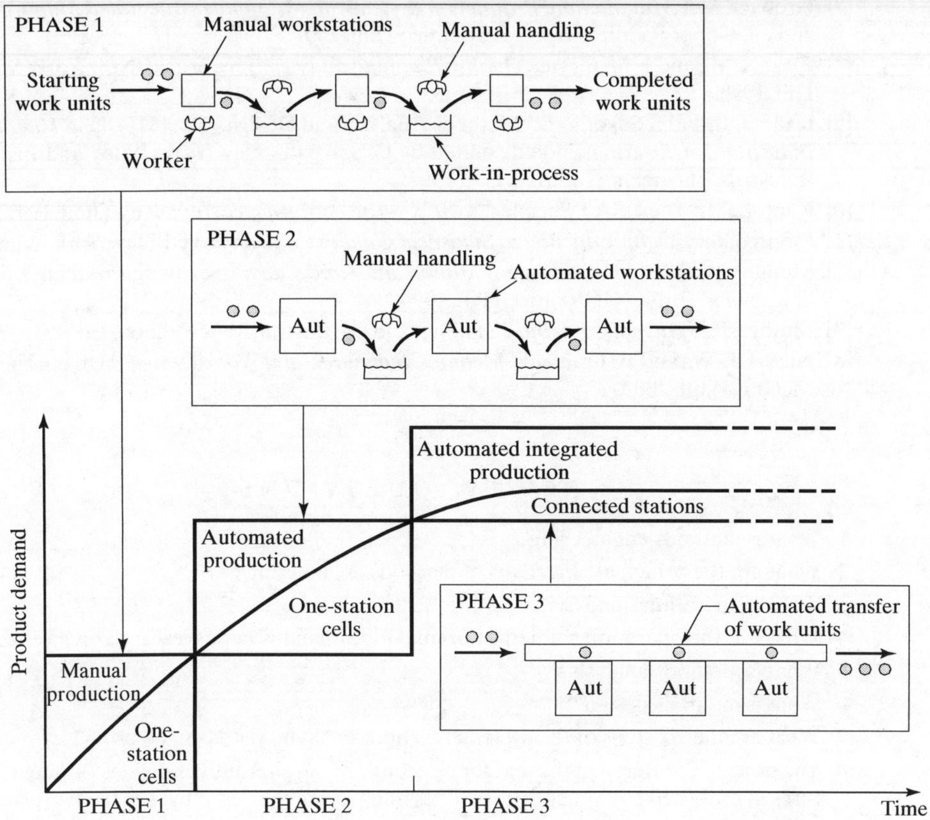

Figure 9 The three phases of a typical automation migration strategy: (1) manual production with single independent workstations, (2) automated production stations with manual handling between stations, and (3) automated integrated production with automated handling between stations.

REFERENCES

[1] Aft, L. S. *Work Measurement and Methods Improvement.* New York: Wiley, 2000.

[2] Akiyama, M., and H. Kamata. "Method Engineering and Workplace Design." Pp.4. 3–4.20 in *Maynard's Industrial Engineering Handbook*, 5th ed., edited by K. Zandin. New York: McGraw-Hill, 2001.

[3] Barnes, R. M. *Motion and Time Study: Design and Measurement of Work.* 7th ed. New York: Wiley, 1980.

[4] Eckes, G. *Six Sigma for Everyone.* Hoboken, NJ: Wiley, 2003.

[5] Geitgey, D. C. "Operation Analysis." Pp. 3.23–3.40 in *Maynard's Industrial Engineering Handbook*, 4th ed., edited by W. K. Hodson. New York: McGraw-Hill, 1992.

[6] Groover, M., M. Weiss, R. Nagel, and N. Odrey. *Industrial Robotics: Technology, Programming,and Applications.* New York: McGraw-Hill, 1986.

[7] Groover, M. P. *Automation, Production Systems, and Computer Integrated Manufacturing*. 2nd ed. Upper Saddle River, NJ: Prentice Hall, 2001.
[8] Juran, J. M., and F. M. Gryna. *Quality Planning and Analysis*. 3rd ed. New York: McGraw-Hill, 1993.
[9] Kadota, T., and S. Sakamoto. "Methods Analysis and Design." Pp. 1415–45 in *Handbook of Industrial Engineering*, 2nd ed., edited by G. Salvendy. New York: Wiley and Institute of Industrial Engineers, Norcross, GA, 1992.
[10] Kapp, K. M. "The USA Principle." *APICS—The Performance Advantage* (June 1997): 62–66.
[11] Montgomery, D. *Introduction to Statistical Quality Control*. 3rd ed. New York: Wiley, 1996.
[12] Mundel, M. E., and D. L. Danner. *Motion and Time Study: Improving Productivity*. 7th ed. Englewood Cliffs, NJ: Prentice Hall, 1994.
[13] Muther, R. *Systematic Layout Planning*. 2nd ed. Boston, MA: Cahners Books, 1973.
[14] Niebel, B. W., and A. Freivalds. *Methods, Standards, and Work Design*. 11th ed. New York: McGraw-Hill, 2003.

REVIEW QUESTIONS

1 What is methods engineering?

2 What are the principal objectives of methods engineering?

3 What is operations analysis?

4 What was the operation studied by Frank Gilbreth in his initial research on motion study?

5 What is methods analysis?

6 What is methods design?

7 What are the six steps of the systematic approach in methods engineering?

8 The procedure offered in the text for selecting among alternatives divides the technical features of proposed equipment alternatives into two categories. What are the two categories?

9 What is a histogram?

10 What is a Pareto chart?

11 What is a check sheet?

12 What is a defect concentration diagram?

13 What is a scatter diagram?

14 What is a cause and effect diagram?

15 What does "USA" stand for in the USA principle?

16 What are the three phases in the automation migration strategy?

17 Why would a company want to use manual production methods instead of automated methods at the beginning of production of a new product?

PROBLEMS

1 A factory has 10 departments, all of which have quality problems leading to delays in shipping products to customers. A breakdown of the number of quality problems for each department (listed alphabetically) is as follows: (1) assembly, 16; (2) final packaging, 9; (3) finishing, 37; (4) forging, 73; (5) foundry, 362; (6) machine shop, 294; (7) plastic molding, 120; (8) receiving inspection, 124; (9) sheet metalworking, 86; and (10) tool-making, 42.

(a) Construct a Pareto chart for this data. (b) Assuming that all quality problems are of equal value, in which department would you start to take corrective action to reduce the quality problems? (c) Determine the percentage of total quality problems that are attributable to the two departments (20% of the departments) with the most quality problems.

2 Using your answer to part (c) of the preceding problem, (a) determine the parameter A in equation (1) representing the Pareto cumulative distribution. Use 20% of the departments as the x value in your computations. (b) Construct the idealized Pareto chart based on your answer to part (a) and discuss the comparison between this idealized chart and the actual data in the previous problem. Use a spreadsheet program to calculate the data for part (b).

3 Assume that 75% of the sales in a retail company are accounted for by 25% of the customers. (a) Determine the parameter A in the Pareto cumulative distribution equation. (b) Given that the relationship is valid for the remaining sales, how much of the sales value is accounted for by 50% of the customers?

4 The inventory policy of a retail company is to hold only the highest sales volume items in its distribution center and to ship the remaining lower sales volume items direct from the respective manufacturers to its stores. This policy is intended to reduce transportation costs. Total annual sales of the company are $1 billion. It is known that half of this amount is accounted for by only 15% of the items. In addition, it is assumed that equation (1) in the text can be used to model the Pareto cumulative distribution. (a) If the company wants to stock the top selling 35% of the items in the distribution center, what is the expected value of these items in terms of annual sales? (b) On the other hand, if the company wants to stock only those items accounting for the top 75% of annual sales, what proportion of the items corresponds to this sales volume?

5 The marketing research department for the Stitch Clothing Company has determined that 22% of the items stocked account for 70% of the dollar sales. A typical outlet store carries 1000 items. The items accounting for the top 60% of sales are replenished from the company's distribution center. The rest are shipped directly from the supplier (manufacturer) to the stores. How many items are represented by the top 60%?

6 Consider some process or procedure with which you are familiar that manifests some chronic problem. Develop a cause and effect diagram that identifies the possible causes of the problem. This is a project that lends itself to a team activity.

Charting and Diagramming Techniques for Operations Analysis

Charting and diagramming techniques are useful for analyzing a work process because they graphically illustrate and summarize the activities in that process. Several charting and diagramming techniques include:

- Network diagrams for depicting work flow in sequential operations
- From-To charts for indicating material flows and/or distances among workstations or departments
- Precedence diagrams for assembly line balancing
- Gantt charts and network diagrams for scheduling projects

This chapter discusses the important charting and diagramming techniques used in methods engineering and operations analysis.

1 OVERVIEW OF CHARTING AND DIAGRAMMING TECHNIQUES

Charting and diagramming techniques are intended to graphically display relationships among the various entities included in the graphic. Objectives in using charts and diagrams to study work include the following:

1. To permit work processes to be communicated and comprehended more readily
2. To allow the use of algorithms specifically designed for the particular diagramming technique
3. To divide a given work process into its constituent elements for analysis purposes
4. To provide a structure in the search for improvements
5. To represent a proposed new work process or method

In this chapter, the charting and diagramming techniques for operations analysis are classified into three categories: (1) network diagrams, (2) traditional industrial engineering charts and diagrams, and (3) block diagrams and process maps.

How does the analyst create the chart or diagram for the process of interest? Any of four methods or combinations thereof can be used to develop a description of the work process that is ultimately used to create the graphic:

- *The analyst is intimately familiar with the process.* In this case, the analyst works in the area and already knows how the process works. The analyst develops a graphic of the process and asks others who are also familiar with it to review it.
- *The analyst observes and records information about the process.* The analyst spends the time necessary to observe and understand the process, develops a chart or diagram of the process, and asks others familiar with it to react to it.
- *One-on-one interviews of those familiar with the process.* The analyst conducts a series of one-on-one interviews of the people who are intimately familiar with the process. A graphical depiction of the process is developed based on the interviews and subjected to review by the interviewees.
- *Group interviews of those familiar with the process.* The analyst asks those who understand the process to participate in a group meeting and describe it. A skilled facilitator may be used to elicit input from the participants. The analyst records the discussion of the meeting and develops a graphical model of the process. The analyst then asks the participants to review it. The advantage of a group meeting is that the participants can challenge each other, thus ultimately developing a more accurate picture of the actual process.

Once the chart or diagram is created, how is it analyzed? Again, there is more than one approach:

- *Algorithmic.* The specific algorithm for the particular diagram is used. Examples include line balancing algorithms for assembly lines and critical path methods for project scheduling.
- *Checklists.* In this case, the analyst reviews a series of general questions to assess whether they can be applied to the particular problem of interest. We offer a number of these checklist questions in Section 3.

- *Brainstorming.* This is a group or team activity in which participants contribute recommendations about potential improvements in the process.
- *Separating value-added and non-value-added operations.* This approach attempts to distinguish between those steps in the process that actually add value to the product or service from the customer's viewpoint and those that do not. ***Value-added steps*** are operations that (1) the customer considers important and (2) physically change the product or service. Potential non-value-added operations include rework, delays, unnecessary inspections, and unnecessary moves.

2 NETWORK DIAGRAMS

A ***network diagram*** consists of (1) nodes representing operations, work elements, or other entities and (2) arrows connecting the nodes indicating relationships among the nodes. When used in the context of work systems analysis, the arrows usually indicate either direction of work flow between nodes or precedence order among them, and the nodes represent work activities (e.g., operations, work elements, tasks).

The network diagram is used to model work flow between operations. In this case, the nodes are processing operations and the arrows indicate the sequence in which the operations are performed and the direction of work transport. A network diagram is used to model the precedence order in which work elements must be performed in assembly operations. Called a precedence diagram, nodes represent the assembly work elements, and arrows indicate the sequence in which the elements must be performed. Critical path method (CPM) and program evaluation and review technique (PERT) diagrams are network diagrams used to schedule the work activities in a project. The methods for analyzing the various network diagrams differ for the different applications, but the same basic format is used in constructing the diagrams.

For network diagrams with two-way flows between nodes (e.g., materials moving in both directions between two departments), the maximum number of arrows is given by

$$\text{Maximum number of arrows possible} = n(n - 1) \tag{1}$$

where n = number of nodes in the diagram. For network diagrams containing only one-way arrows (e.g., arrows indicating precedence order of work elements or activities), the maximum possible number of arrows between nodes in the network is given by the following:

$$\text{Maximum number of arrows possible} = \frac{n(n - 1)}{2} \tag{2}$$

Most network diagrams have fewer than the maximum values given by these equations.

3 TRADITIONAL INDUSTRIAL ENGINEERING CHARTING AND DIAGRAMMING TECHNIQUES

The charts and diagrams discussed in this section are commonly used to analyze an existing operation, sequence of operations, or other work activity for the purpose of making improvements. The underlying assumption is that by examining the work situation in detail, and subjecting the details to critical scrutiny, improvements can be found more readily than through macroscopic examination. The possible improvements include reducing cycle time and cost, eliminating unnecessary steps, mitigating safety hazards, and improving product quality. In addition to analyzing existing operations, the charts and diagrams can also be used to present proposals for new ways of accomplishing the same operations, or to design new operations that have never been implemented before.

There are many charting and diagramming techniques that have been developed over the years within the discipline of industrial engineering. For purposes of organization, we classify them into the following four major categories: (1) operation charts, (2) process charts, (3) flow diagrams, and (4) activity charts.[1] Each of these techniques provides a graphical and symbolic means of visualizing the work situation for better understanding of its scope and details. The differences relate to the levels of detail and how the work situation is represented graphically. Also, within a given category there may be variations in format and symbols depending on the subject of the analysis, for example, whether the purpose of the analysis is to study a material or to study a human worker.

In addition to these four categories of charting and diagramming techniques, the Gantt chart is a charting tool associated with traditional industrial engineering that is used in production control and project scheduling.

3.1 Operation Charts

The ***operation chart*** is a graphical and symbolic representation of the operations used to produce a product. There are two types of operations in an operation chart: (1) processing and assembly operations, and (2) inspection operations. The operation chart can also be used to analyze the steps involved in the delivery of a service, but this application of the chart is far less common. As shown in Figure 1, the operation chart consists of a series of vertical stems, each one depicting the sequence of operations and inspections performed on a given component of the product. The operation chart uses only two symbols (for operation and inspection), which are defined in Table 1. At the top of each stem is the starting material or purchased part, and the steps performed on it are indicated by symbol and brief description. The time to accomplish the operation (e.g., standard time) is also sometimes included. As each component is completed, it is assembled to other components toward the right. The column at the far right usually represents the base part or chassis of the assembly. It is the component to which all other parts in the chart are joined.

Developing the detailed listing of operations for the components and their assembly into the final entity (e.g., product, subassembly) is only the first step in the operation chart analysis. The second step involves examination of the chart to discover possible

[1]There is considerable variation in some of the terminology among different authors, and we have attempted to rationalize and abbreviate the terms. Where appropriate, we identify the alternative names of the charts.

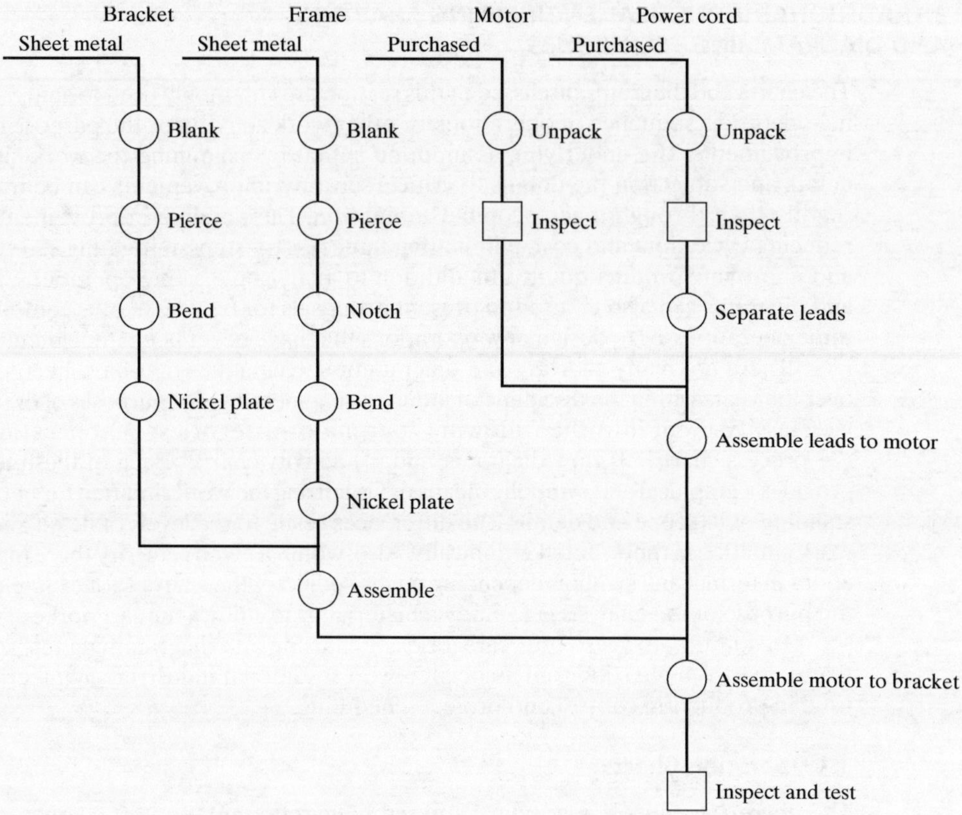

Figure 1 An operation chart for the subassembly of a product.

TABLE 1 Symbols Used in Operation Charts

Symbol	Letter	Description
○	O	***Processing or assembly operation***. Processing operations consist of changing the shape, properties, or surface of a material or workpart. Assembly operations join two or more parts to form an assembly.
□	I	***Inspection operation.*** An inspector checks the material, workpart, or assembly for quality or quantity.

improvements. Because the focus of the operation chart is on the materials of a product and the operations performed on them, the examination step consists of a questioning procedure aimed at the materials and operations. A systematic approach includes questions such as those offered in the checklist of Table 2. The third step in the use of the operation chart for an existing work situation is to develop proposals for improvement based on the results of the questioning procedure.

TABLE 2 Checklist of Questions Used to Analyze an Operation Chart

Questions related to material

What alternative starting material could be used (e.g., plastic rather than metal)?
Would a design change allow the part to be purchased as a standard commercially available item?
Could the functions of several separate components be combined into one component through a design change?
Make or buy decision: should this part be produced in our own factory or purchased from an outside vendor?

Question related to processing or assembly operations

What is the purpose of each processing operation?
Is the processing operation necessary?
Can operations be eliminated, combined, or simplified?
Is the operation time too high?
Could the processing operation be automated?
Could a different joining method be used for assembly (e.g., snap fit rather than threaded fasteners to save time)?

Questions related to inspection operations

What is the purpose of the inspection operation?
Is the inspection operation necessary?
Can the inspection operation be combined with the preceding processing or assembly operation?
If the operation is performed 100%, could it be performed on a sampling basis to reduce inspection time?
Could the inspection operation be automated?

3.2 Process Charts

A ***process chart*** is a graphical and symbolic representation of the processing activities performed on something or by somebody. The chart consists of a vertical list of the steps performed on or by the work entity using various symbols to represent operations, inspections, moves, delays, and other activities. The principal types of process chart are: (1) the ***flow process chart***, used to analyze a material or workpiece being processed, (2) the ***worker process chart***, used to analyze a worker performing a process, and (3) the ***form process chart***, used to analyze the processing of paperwork forms. These charts are described in the following sections.

Flow Process Chart. The flow process chart uses five symbols, as defined in Table 3 to detail the work performed on a material or work part as it is being processed through a sequence of operations and other activities.[2] Either iconic symbols or letter symbols can be used in constructing the chart, depending on the analyst's preference. The characteristic features of the flow process chart are shown in Figure 2. Alternative formats are possible, such as the standardized form shown in Figure 3.

The operation and inspection symbols are sometimes combined if the processing step includes a processing operation combined with an inspection at the same workstation—for example, a worker buffing a part and periodically checking its luster. In this case, the symbol consists of a circle inside a square, with the diameter of the circle equal to the side of the square.[3] Significantly more detail about the steps required to process a material

[2]Other names for the flow process chart include process chart-product analysis [7].
[3]The reverse of this format is also used in the charting literature, in which a square is positioned inside a circle to represent the combination of operation and inspection.

TABLE 3 Symbols Used in the Flow Process Chart

Symbol[a]	Letter	Description
○	O	***Operation***, usually a processing operation performed on the material at one location or workstation in which the physical shape or chemical characteristics of the material are changed. Assembly operations are unusual in a flow process chart.
□	I	***Inspection***, either to check for quality or quantity, performed at a single location or workstation.
→	M	***Move*** that involves transport of the material from one location to another, but not including moves within an operation at a workstation.
D	D	***Delay*** that occurs when the material does not or cannot proceed to the next activity—for example, a material waiting to be processed at a workstation, but other materials are ahead of it.
▽	S	***Storage*** in which the material is kept in a protected location to prevent unauthorized removal. Storage usually involves the use of a requisition to withdraw from storage, whereas a delay does not involve such a transaction.

[a]Based on symbols developed by the American Society of Mechanical Engineers (ASME). A simple arrow (→) has been substituted for the ASME move symbol (⇒) for ease of drawing.

is provided in the flow process chart than in the operation chart. Consequently, this charting technique is used to study only a single material or work part rather than the multiple components of an assembly. For each symbol, a brief description of the work activity is listed in the flow process chart. In addition, the chart also indicates the distances for move activities and times for the other activities. The time values may be especially relevant for operations, inspections, delays, and storages.

As in the operation chart, the flow process chart is examined for possible improvements and savings. However, the emphasis in the questioning procedure is expanded beyond the coverage of the operation chart because the details in the flow process chart include more types of activities. In addition to the questions shown in Table 2, current questions focus on moves, delays, and storages. Table 4 indicates the types of question that the methods analyst would want to ask. (For completeness, we have included questions from Table 2 in this checklist for the flow process chart.)

Worker Process Chart. The ***worker process chart*** is used to analyze the activities of a human worker as he or she performs a task that requires movement around a facility.[4] The symbols are virtually the same as those appearing in Table 3, but they are interpreted in terms of what the human worker does rather than what is done to a material. Table 5 summarizes the interpretations. The storage activity is difficult to interpret in the context of human work activity, so it is omitted. Analysis of the worker process chart in the search for improvements involves the same kinds of questions as in the flow process chart, only in the context of the worker performing the task of interest.

Form Process Chart. The ***form process chart*** is used to analyze the flow of paperwork forms and office procedures that normally involve the processing of documents.

[4]Alternative names for the worker process chart include process chart-person analysis [7].

Flow Process Chart					
Part No. 459011	Material: Steel C1045 forging	Description: Forgings processed in batches of 20			
Seq.	Activity Description	Symbol	Time	Distance	Analysis Notes
1	Forgings transported from forge shop	→		300 m	Forklift truck
2	Inspection of incoming forgings	□	1 hr		
3	Forgings moved and placed in storage	→		75 m	Hand truck
4	Storage	∇	7 days		Factory warehouse
5	Forgings retrieved from storage	→		75 m	Hand truck
6	Transport to machine shop	→		180 m	Forklift truck
7	Move to milling machine	→		20 m	Hand truck
8	Delay in queue for milling machine	D	5 hr		
9	Milling operation (roughing and finishing)	O	8 min/pc		Milling Machine No. 573
10	Move to drill press	→		20 m	Hand truck
11	Delay in queue for drill press	D	2 hr		
12	Drilling and tapping operations (6 holes)	O	3 min/pc		CNC Drill Press No. 226
13	Delay waiting for inspection	D	4 hr		
14	Inspection for machining operations	□	0.2 hr		
15	Delay waiting for transport to cleaning	D	3 hr		
16	Transport to finishing department	→		75 m	Forklift truck
17	Move to cleaning operation	→		10 m	Hand truck
18	Delay in queue for cleaning operation	D	30 min		
19	Cleaning operation (all parts in batch)	O	10 min		Solvent clean tank
20	Move to nickel plate operation	→		15 m	Hand truck
21	Delay in queue for nickel plate operation	D	45 min		
22	Nickel plate operation (all parts in batch)	O	20 min		Electroplating tank
23	Delay waiting for transport to storage	D	30 min		
24	Transport to storage	→		200 m	Forklift truck
25	Storage awaiting assembly	∇			Factory warehouse

Figure 2 A flow process chart used to detail the steps in the processing of a material. In the example shown, the material is a forging, and its processing consists of several machining operations, cleaning, and electroplating, but much of its time is spent in transport, delays, and storage.

Activities that occur in form processing require a change in the interpretation of the symbol. Additional symbols are also sometimes used to cover activities that are not associated with process charts for materials and workers. Symbols that can be used for the form process chart are presented and defined in Table 6.

Date:	Flow Process Chart				Page ___ of ___
Analyst:	Approval:	Summary of Activities			
Job:	Part No:	Activity (symbols)	Count	Time	Distances
Material:		Operations (○, O)			
Description:		Inspections (□ , I)			
		Moves (→, M)			
		Delays (D, D)			
		Storages (∇, S)			

Seq.	Activity Description	Symbol	Time	Distance	Analysis Notes
1					
2					
3					
4					
5					
6					

Figure 3 A standardized form for the flow process chart that can be readily created using word processing software.

3.3 Flow Diagrams

The ***flow diagram*** is a drawing of the facility layout but with the addition of lines representing movement of materials or workers to specific locations in the facility. Arrows are used on the lines to indicate the direction of movement. The flow diagram is often used in conjunction with a process chart, especially when movement of the material, worker, or form is a major factor in the analysis. An example of a flow diagram for a setup worker is presented in Figure 4. When used in connection with a process chart, the operations, inspections, delays, and storages at specific locations in the layout can be identified by numbers that are referenced to the activity numbers in the process chart.

The flow diagram reveals problems in the work flow that may not readily be identified using the process chart alone. For example, if the work flow involves considerable backtracking, this can be seen in the flow diagram whereas it is indicated only as distances in the process chart. Other work flow problems may include excessive travel, possible traffic congestion, points where delays typically occur, and inefficient layout of workstations.

3.4 Activity Charts

An ***activity chart*** is a listing of the work activities of one or more subjects (e.g., workers, machines) plotted against a time scale to indicate graphically how much time is

TABLE 4 Checklist of Questions Used to Analyze a Flow Process Chart

Questions related to material

What alternative starting material could be used (e.g., plastic rather than metal)?
Would a design change allow the part to be purchased as a standard commercially available item?
Could the functions of several separate components be combined into one component through a design change?
Make or buy decision: should this part be produced in our own factory or purchased from an outside vendor?

Question related to processing operations

What is the purpose of each processing operation?
Is the processing operation necessary?
Can operations be eliminated, combined, or simplified?
Is the operation time too high?
Could the processing operation be automated?
Where else could this operation be performed to reduce move distances?

Questions related to inspection operations

What is the purpose of the inspection operation?
Is the inspection operation necessary?
Can the inspection operation be combined with the preceding processing operation?
If the operation is performed 100%, could it be performed on a sampling basis to reduce inspection time?
Could the inspection operation be automated?

Questions relating to moves

How can moves be shortened or eliminated by combining or eliminating operations?
Can the parts or materials be collected into larger unit loads to increase efficiency in material handling?
What material handling equipment is used to transport materials? Can the level of mechanization be increased (e.g., using forklift trucks rather than manually pushed dollies)?
Can the operation sequence be modified to reduce distances traveled?

Questions relating to delays

What is the reason for the delay? Can the reason be eliminated?
Is the delay avoidable?
Why can't the material be started immediately at the next operation?

Questions relating to storage

Is the storage necessary?
Why can't the material be moved immediately to the next operation?
Can just-in-time delivery be used to eliminate the storage (e.g., can the material received from the supplier be moved immediately to the first operation after delivery rather than into storage)?

spent on each activity. The usual format is to provide brief descriptions of the activities against a vertical time scale, as shown in Figure 5 for a single worker performing a repetitive work cycle. Instead of using symbols for the work activities, as in the other charting and diagramming techniques described previously, the activities are indicated by vertical lines or bars. When bars are used, they are shaded or colored to indicate

TABLE 5 Symbols Used in the Worker Process Chart

Symbol	Letter	Description
○	O	***Operation*** performed by a worker at a single location or workstation. The operation may involve movements of materials within the workstation.
□	I	***Inspection***, either to check for quality or quantity, performed by a worker at a single location or workstation.
→	M	***Move*** in which the worker moves from one location to another as a regular element required in the task. It does not include moves within a workstation.
D	D	***Delay*** of the worker. Worker is forced by the situation to wait (e.g., waiting for an elevator). The waiting may involve moving, but the move is not a regular element required in the task (e.g., worker goes to the coffee machine while waiting for the elevator).

TABLE 6 Symbols Used in the Form Process Chart

Symbol	Letter	Description
◎	C	***Creation*** of the form (circle in a circle). This symbol is used for the origination of the form, when the form is first initiated.
○	O	***Operation*** performed on the form at a single location or workstation. The operation may involve calculations, data entries, filling out forms, folding, photocopying, stapling, assembling multiple forms into one document, etc.
□	I	***Inspection*** to read information from the form or check for correctness performed at a single location or workstation.
→	M	***Movement*** of the form from one location to another by mail or human carrier.
D	D	***Delay*** of the form. Form is waiting to be worked on, located in an in-basket or similar location other than a storage file.
▽	S	***Storage*** in a file, normally in a file cabinet or other organized filing system. This usually involves storage for a considerable time period, rather than a temporary delay.
X	X	***Disposal*** of the form. The form or a copy is destroyed.

the kind of activity being performed. Figure 6 indicates some possible shading and color conventions.[5]

Activity charts usually have more than one time scale. In Figure 5 two time scales are used, one for cumulative time during the work cycle and the second to indicate the time taken for each work activity. When activity charts are used to track several participants working together, the general name of the chart is a ***multiple-activity chart***, which consists of multiple columns, one for each participant. In this case, one time scale marks cumulative time during the cycle and a separate time scale indicates activity times for each of the columns.

There are a number of work situations in which the multiple-activity chart is useful for analysis purposes. Because the situations involve multiple entities working together, a common objective of using the chart is to analyze how the workload is coordinated and

[5]There seems to be significant variation in shading and color conventions among different experts and authors, and users are at liberty to develop their own conventions or color schemes to suit the purposes of their respective studies.

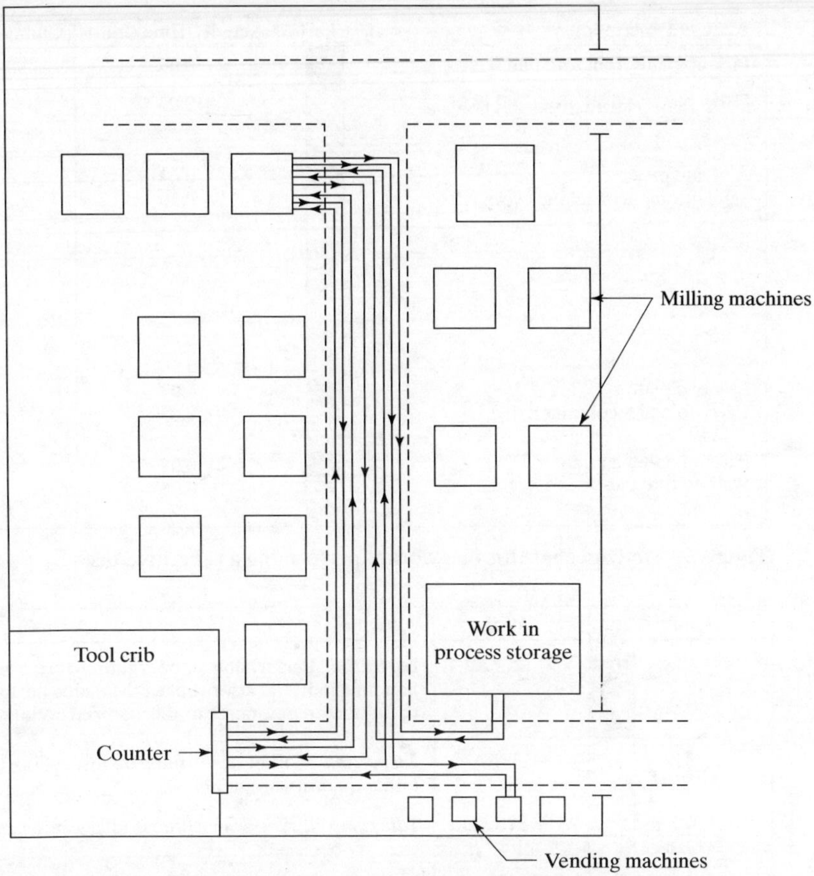

Figure 4 Flow diagram for a worker setting up a milling machine in the milling department. Note the large number of trips back and forth between the milling machine and the tool crib, which suggests that the setup worker's task might be made more efficient if all of the items needed for the setup were collected in one trip.

shared among them. The following is a listing of the major types of multiple-activity charts:

- *Right-hand/left-hand activity chart.* This chart details the contributions of the right and left hands of one worker performing a task that is highly repetitive. The task is usually performed at a single workplace, and so the chart is sometimes referred to as a ***workplace activity chart***. Figure 7 illustrates a right-hand/left-hand activity chart for a task in which the worker is using his left hand as a workholder while his right hand performs nearly all of the activities. A methods analyst would seek to install a fixture to hold the work unit during the operation

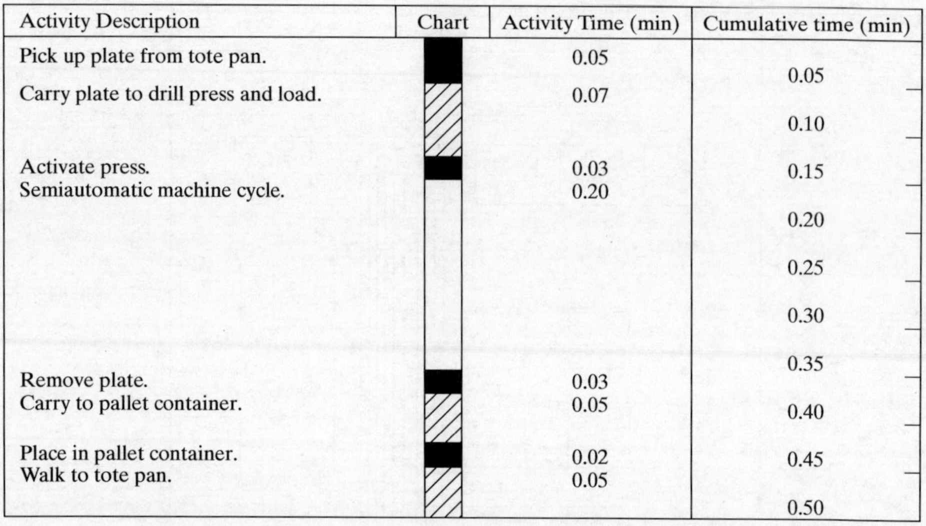

Figure 5 Activity chart for one worker performing a repetitive task.

Shading	Color	Activity
Black	Blue	***Operation***: Performing an operation. Worker operating on or handling material at workplace. Machine performing an operation on automatic or mechanized cycle.
Gray	Yellow	***Inspection***: Worker performing an inspection, to check for either quantity or quality.
White (blank)	White (blank)	***Idle time***: Worker or machine is idle, waiting, or stopped.
Diagonal lines	Green	***Moving***: Worker walking outside immediate workplace (e.g., to fetch tools or materials).
Horizontal lines	Red	***Holding***: Worker holding an object in fixed position without performing any work on it.

Figure 6 Shading formats for activity charts.

and to achieve a more even balance of the workload between the right and left hands.

- *Worker-machine activity chart.* As the name indicates, this chart shows how the work elements and associated times are allocated between a worker and a machine for the repetitive cycle of a worker-machine system. Like the right-hand/left-hand activity chart, it consists of two main columns, one for the worker and the other for the machine. The worker-machine activity chart can often help to identify opportunities for cycle time improvement, such as the replacement of external work elements by internal elements, where the worker and machine perform parallel rather than sequential activities.

Left Hand	Time (min)	Right Hand	Cumulative time (min)
Pick up board	0.08		0.08
Hold board	0.06	Pick up peg and insert	0.14
Hold board	0.06	Pick up peg and insert	0.20
Hold board	0.06	Pick up peg and insert	0.26
Hold board	0.06	Pick up peg and insert	0.32
Hold board	0.06	Pick up peg and insert	0.38
Hold board	0.06	Pick up peg and insert	0.44
Hold board	0.06	Pick up peg and insert	0.50
Hold board	0.06	Pick up peg and insert	0.56
Put assembly in tote pan	0.06		0.62

Figure 7 Right-hand/left-hand activity chart.

Worker	Time (min)	Machine 1	Time	Machine 2	Time	Cumulative time (min)
Walks to machine 1	0.2					
Services machine 1	0.3	Idle	0.3			0.5
Walks to machine 2	0.2	Automatic cycle				
Services machine 2	0.3			Idle	0.3	1.0
				Automatic cycle		
	0.5					1.5
Walks to machine 1	0.2		1.2			
Services machine 1	0.3	Idle	0.3			2.0
Walks to machine 2	0.2	Automatic cycle			1.2	
Services machine 2	0.3			Idle	0.3	2.5
Idle				Automatic cycle		
	0.5					3.0
Walks to machine 1	0.2		1.2			
Services machine 1	0.3	Idle	0.3			3.5
Walks to machine 2	0.2	Automatic cycle			1.2	
Services machine 2	0.3			Idle	0.3	4.0

Figure 8 Worker-multimachine activity chart.

- *Worker-multimachine activity chart.* This chart is similar to the preceding except that the worker is responsible for more than one machine, and a work cycle must be developed that minimizes or eliminates ***machine interference*** (when one machine must wait for service because the worker is currently servicing another machine). Figure 8 illustrates the worker-multimachine activity chart for two machines. We have previously referred to this worker-multimachine arrangement as a ***machine cluster***.
- *Gang activity chart.* Other names include ***gang chart*** and ***multiworker activity chart***. This chart tracks the activities of two or more workers performing together as a team. Work situations involving the activities of a team or crew are often somewhat complex. The purpose of the activity chart analysis is to better coordinate the activities and balance the workload among the workers.

4 BLOCK DIAGRAMS AND PROCESS MAPS

Several additional diagramming techniques are available to show the detailed steps and work flow in a given process. They utilize labeled blocks and other objects, connected by arrows, to indicate processes and their interrelationships. In this section, we describe two types of diagramming techniques: block diagrams and process maps.

4.1 Block Diagrams

Block diagrams are commonly applied in linear control theory to portray the relationships among components of a physical system or process. A simple example is illustrated in Figure 9. In control system applications, arrows represent the flow of signals or variables between blocks, and blocks contain transfer functions that define how the input signals are mathematically transformed into output signals. A transfer function is the ratio of the output signal to the input signal.[6] For example, the variable y in Figure 9 equals the variable x_3 multiplied by the transfer function B.

In addition to blocks and arrows, two other operations are possible in block diagrams. First, two or more separate variables can be summed algebraically using a summing node, indicated by the circle enclosing a summation symbol in Figure 9. Thus, the variable x_2 is equal to x_1 minus z. Second, any given signal can be used as an input to more than one block. In Figure 9, the variable x_3 is used as an input to blocks B and C. The operation is called a takeoff point, shown in the diagram as a large dot between blocks A and B.

In linear control theory and other physical system applications, a form of algebra (called "block diagram algebra") can be used to reduce a complex block diagram to a single block containing the input/output relationship for the entire system. Thus, a block diagram is useful for developing the input/output functions of the individual components of a control system and then analyzing the diagram to determine overall system performance.

Our applications of block diagrams in this book deal with systems that tend to be more subjective and operations oriented. In general, our systems do not lend themselves to the mathematical treatment by which physical systems can be analyzed. Nevertheless, the block diagram format is a powerful means of depicting the signal flows and interrelationships

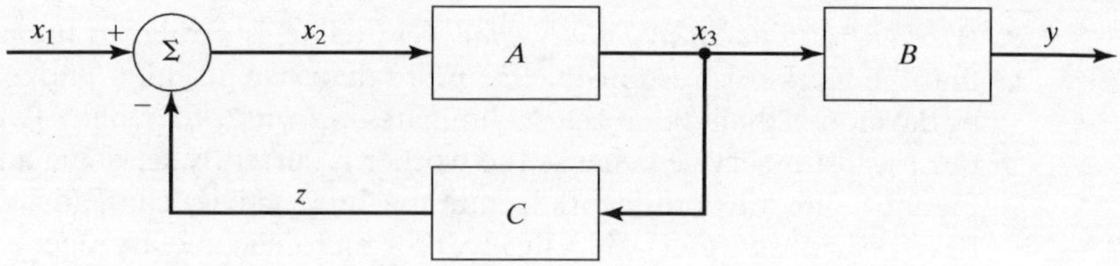

Figure 9 Block diagram of a feedback control system.

[6]To be more precise, the transfer function is the ratio of the Laplace transform of the output variable to the Laplace transform of the input variable, given that all initial conditions are zero.

among components in complex systems that are related to work. We use them frequently throughout this text.[7] In addition, block diagrams have clearly influenced the development of other diagramming techniques in operations analysis, such as process maps.

4.2 Process Maps

Process mapping techniques have been widely applied to business processes. They are also applicable to production, logistics, and service operations. As in other diagramming and charting techniques, process maps provide a detailed picture of the process or system of interest that is helpful for communicating and understanding by those involved in the operations analysis study.

There are several forms of process maps. The basic process map is a block diagram that shows the steps in the process of interest. A ***process*** is defined as a sequence of tasks or activities that add value to one or more inputs to produce outputs. The inputs and outputs may be materials, products, information, services, or other form. The process must consist of more than one step, and the steps are linked together in a logical way. The process has a beginning point and an ending point, and its purpose in the organization is to provide something of value to its customers.

Block symbols used in the basic process map are shown in Figure 10, and an example of their arrangement in a process map is illustrated in Figure 11. The block for

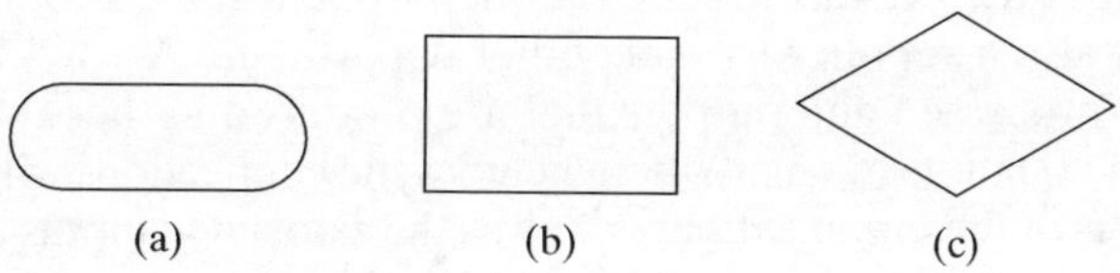

Figure 10 Symbols in the basic process map: (a) beginning/ending point of the process, (b) task or activity step, and (c) decision point. Brief labels or names are written in the various blocks to identify them.

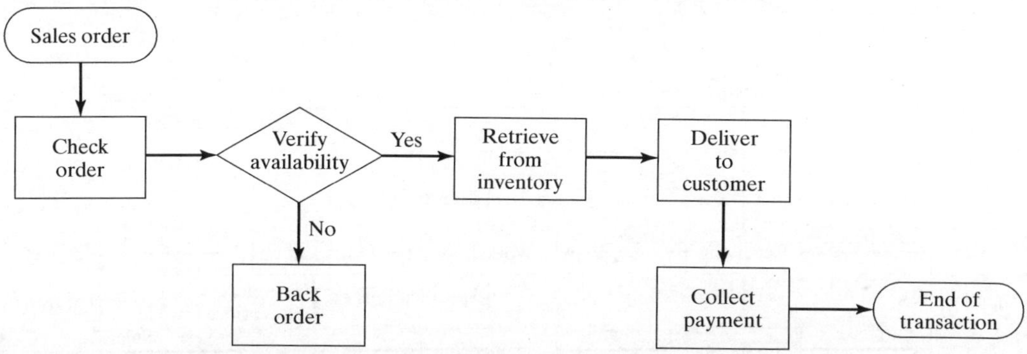

Figure 11 An example of a basic process map.

[7]The author's preference for block diagrams may derive from his educational origins in mechanical engineering.

the beginning point of the process is a racetrack oval. It is the boundary between the process under study and the activities that occur outside the process under study. The same symbol and interpretation apply to the end of the process. Rectangular blocks are used to symbolize tasks or activity steps in the process. Decision points are diamond-shaped blocks. Labels in the blocks identify what each step and decision point does, as suggested in Figure 11. Arrows are used to indicate the sequence of the steps and the flow of the work.

Process mapping can be accomplished at various levels of detail. A ***high-level process map*** depicts a macroscopic view of the process of interest and includes only the most important steps in the process. Each step in the high-level map consists of tasks or work elements, which can be examined in greater detail to create a ***low-level process map*** for that step, also called a ***detailed process map***. When this is done, the blocks in the high-level map are shadowed or otherwise highlighted to indicate that the lower-level process map exists. In some cases, more than two levels of process maps may be developed for processes requiring such detail.

Alternative forms of process maps include relationship maps and cross-functional process maps [4]. A ***relationship map*** is a block diagram that shows the input-output connections among the departments or other functional components of an organization. The map consists of blocks that represent the departments and arrows to show the flow of work. A relationship map illustrates the pairs of supplier-customer relationships throughout the organization. Every department is a customer of another department, and it is also a supplier to some other department. Arrows indicate the flow of inputs that are processed and outputs that are produced in these supplier-customer relationships. The relationship map often includes the connections with external suppliers and/or customers of the organization, as well as the associated inputs and outputs. Figure 12 illustrates a relationship map for a custom workshop.

A ***cross-functional process map*** is a block diagram that shows how the steps of a process are accomplished by the various departments or other functional groups that contribute to it. As shown in Figure 13, the departments are listed in rows separated by dashed lines. This format causes the cross-functional process map to also be known as

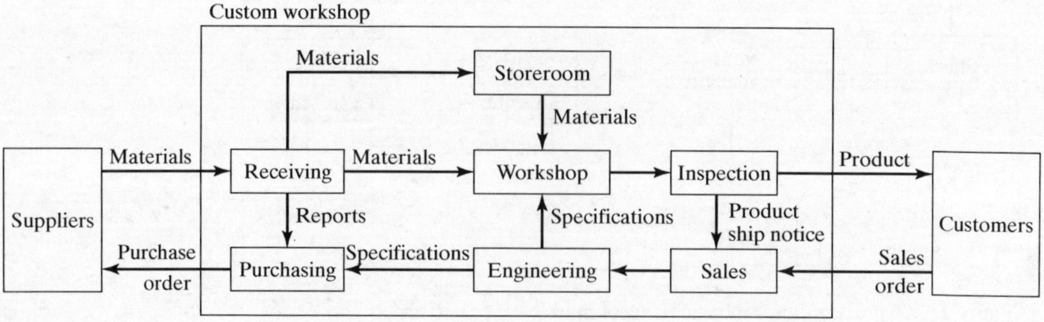

Figure 12 Relationship map for a custom workshop.

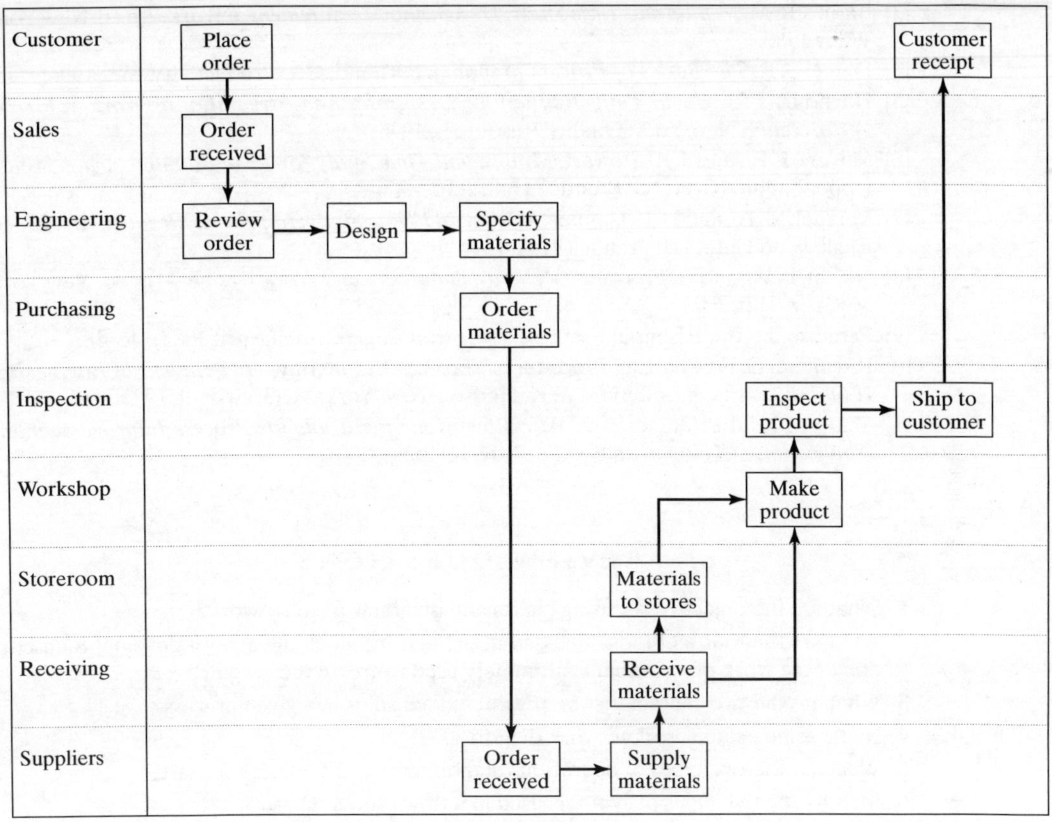

Figure 13 A cross-functional process map for a custom workshop.

the ***swim-lane chart***. Rectangular blocks represent activity steps in the process, and diamond-shaped blocks represent decision points. Arrows indicate the inputs and outputs for each block, as well as the sequence of steps.

The cross-functional process map differs from the relationship map by showing the blocks as process steps (work activities), whereas the relationship map uses blocks to represent departments. The difference between the cross-functional process map and the basic process map is the use of rows (swim lanes) to show where the process steps are accomplished. In the basic process map, the process steps do not indicate in what department the work is done.

REFERENCES

[1] Aft, L. S. *Work Measurement and Methods Improvement*. New York: Wiley, 2000.

[2] ANSI Standard Z94.0-1989. *Industrial Engineering Terminology*. Norcross, GA: Industrial Engineering and Management Press, Institute of Industrial Engineers, 1989.

[3] Barnes, R. M. *Motion and Time Study: Design and Measurement of Work*. 7th ed. New York: Wiley 1980.

[4] Damelio, R. *The Basics of Process Mapping*. Portland, OR: Productivity, Inc., 1996.

[5] Harbour, J. L. *Cycle Time Reduction: Designing and Streamlining Work for High Performance*. New York: Quality Resources, 1996.

[6] Meyers, F. E., and J. R. Stewart. *Motion and Time Study for Lean Manufacturing*. 3rd ed. Upper Saddle River, NJ: Prentice Hall, 2002.

[7] Mundel, M. E., and D. L. Danner. *Motion and Time Study: Improving Productivity*. 7th ed. Englewood Cliffs, NJ: Prentice Hall, 1994.

[8] Niebel, B. W., and A. Freivalds. *Methods, Standards, and Work Design*. 11th ed. New York: McGraw-Hill, 2003.

[9] Paradiso, J. "The Essential Process." *Industrial Engineering* (April 2003): 46–48.

[10] Raymond, G. F. "Charting Procedures." Pp. 3.3–3.22 in *Maynard's Industrial Engineering Handbook*. 4th ed., edited by W. K. Hodson. New York: McGraw-Hill, 1992.

[11] Sharp, A., and P. McDermott. *Workflow Modeling: Tools for Process Improvement and Application Development*. Boston: Artech House, 2001.

REVIEW QUESTIONS

1 What are the objectives of using charts and diagrams to study work?

2 What are the four methods indicated in the text by which the analyst develops a description of the work process that is ultimately used to create the graphic?

3 What are the two characteristics of value-added steps in a given process?

4 Name some examples of network diagrams.

5 What are the two types of operations diagrammed in an operation chart?

6 Identify the five types of symbols used in a flow process chart.

7 Name the three types of process chart described in the text, and identify the application area for each.

8 What is a flow diagram?

9 What are some of the problem areas that can be identified using a flow diagram?

10 What is an activity chart?

11 Identify some of the types of multiple activity charts.

12 What are the three block symbols used in a basic process map?

PROBLEMS

Traditional Industrial Engineering Charting and Diagramming Techniques

1 A motorist experienced a flat tire on the driver side rear wheel of his car and went through the following procedure to replace the flat tire with the spare. The tire change occurred in the middle of the day in his own driveway about 20 ft in front of his garage. He first secured the other three wheels of the car with six bricks from his garage to prevent the vehicle from rolling (two trips back and forth to the garage). He then took out the jack, crank, and lug nut wrench from the trunk of the car, and read over the attached instructions for operating the jack. He removed the spare tire from the trunk and placed it near the rear left wheel.

Next, he proceeded to position the jack under the car at the recommended support beam on the car frame. He began to turn the crank to elevate the car. After the left rear portion of the car was lifted a few inches, but before the flat tire was lifted from the driveway surface, he used the lug nut wrench to loosen the five lug nuts securing the tire to the wheel hub. He then returned to the task of elevating the car, turning the jack crank until the flat tire was completely off the driveway surface. The next step was to remove the loosened lug nuts, placing them in a nearby position within reach. The flat tire was then removed and lifted into the trunk. The motorist moved the spare tire into position and lifted it onto the five studs protruding from the wheel hub. He reached for the five lug nuts, one at a time, placing them onto the studs and rotating them until finger tight. The lug nut wrench was used to tighten the five nuts. With the tire secure, he proceeded to lower the car by cranking the jack down slowly until the spare tire supported the car. For good measure, he again tightened the five lug nuts now that the car was securely on the ground. He collected the hardware, put it back into the trunk, and removed the bricks from the other three wheels and put them back into his garage. Document this tire changing procedure using a worker process chart.

2 With reference to the tire changing procedure of the previous problem, develop the steps of changing a tire, as they would be accomplished in an automotive tire center, where the worker has access to a hydraulic car lift and pneumatic lug nut wrench instead of the manual tools used by the motorist in his driveway. Document your improved tire changing procedure using a worker process chart.

3 A foundry uses the following steps in its procedure for high production of investment casting process: (1) Produce wax patterns by injection molding. (2) Transport wax patterns to an assembly work area where they are manually assembled to a wax sprue forming a pattern tree. The entire tree is made of wax. (3) Move pattern tree to a separate room where the tree is coated with a thin layer of refractory material. (4) In the same room, coat tree with successive layers of refractory material to make it a rigid structure that will become the mold for casting. (5) Move tree to a furnace room, where it should be held in an inverted position and heated to melt the wax out of the mold cavities. With the wax removed, the rigid structure is now a multiple-cavity mold with runners leading to each cavity from the sprue cavity. (6) In the same furnace room, heat the mold to a high temperature to ensure that all contaminants are removed from the mold. (7) With the mold still heated at an elevated temperature and in an upright orientation pour the molten metal into the sprue; metal will flow through the runners to each cavity. (8) After the metal cools and solidifies move the assemblage to a finishing room; the mold can be broken away from the cast metal and the parts separated from the runners and sprue. Assignment: (a) Develop the flow process chart for this casting process. (b) Based on your flow process chart, what are some changes in the investment casting procedure that you would recommend?

4 A supplier of machined components for industrial machinery (e.g., power tools, pumps, motors, compressors) operates a factory that includes a forge shop, machine shop, and finishing department. Many of the parts produced by the company are fabricated through these three departments. Because of this, the factory is laid out as three large square rooms, arranged in-line to form a rectangle with an aspect ratio of three-to-one. Each room is 200 ft by 200 ft. The rectangle runs from north to south, with the forge shop on the south end and the finishing department on the north end. Large doors are located on the south wall for work entering the factory and on the north wall for finished products exiting the factory. For one part of particular interest here, the raw material is a steel billet that is purchased from a steel wholesale supplier. The billets arrive in pallet loads of 100 billets at the shipping and receiving department, which is a building that is 35 ft by 50 ft located

25 ft from the south wall door of the factory. The shipping and receiving department inspects the parts and sends them by forklift truck to be stored in the company's warehouse that is located in another building 500 ft away from the factory in a southerly direction. The warehouse is 200 ft by 200 ft with its entrance door on the north wall. When a production order for the part is received, a factory forklift truck is dispatched to the warehouse to retrieve the billets. The forklift truck must wait while the warehouse crew locates the billets in storage, takes a pallet out of storage using the same type of forklift truck, and delivers the pallet to the dock where it is transferred to the factory forklift. The pallet is then brought back to the factory and delivered to the forge shop. The billets must wait their turn in the production schedule before being pressed into the desired shape by one of the forge presses. From the forge shop, the parts are moved to the machine shop where they are machined on two different machine tools, a milling machine and a drill press. From the machine shop, the parts travel to the finishing department for painting and baking (to cure the paint). From the finishing department, the parts are moved back to the machine shop, where additional milling is accomplished to provide two machined metal surfaces that will mate with other components in the final product. The parts are then moved to the shipping and receiving department for shipment to the customer. Develop the (a) flow process chart and (b) flow diagram for the process, using the centroid of each department to estimate distances between departments. (c) Based on your flow process chart, what are some changes in the production process that you would recommend? (d) Develop a revised procedure for the production process, documenting your revision in the form of a new flow process chart.

5 The Calm Seas Cruise Ship Line wants to analyze its passenger laundry operation. A typical cruise ship of the line is 850 ft in length and has 600 passenger cabins located on four decks. For every occupied cabin during a cruise, the cabin stewards retrieve the bed linens (sheets and pillowcases) and towels (washcloths, hand towels, and bath towels) when they make up the rooms each day. Each steward is responsible for 15 cabins. The steward separates the bed linens from the towels, putting them into two separate laundry bags. Because of the large size of each bag, the two bags are separately hand-carried to the laundry department, which is located on one of the lower decks. Depending on which deck and deck section a steward serves, the travel distance ranges from several hundred feet to more than a thousand feet, plus several flights of stairs. In the laundry department, the bags are emptied, making sure that the bed linens are not mixed with the towels during laundering. The two categories of laundry are washed separately in large washing machines, using a different wash cycle for each category. After washing, the linens and towels are dried in tumble dryers located on the same deck about 100 ft away, and then they are folded and stacked. They are then moved in stacks to the ironing department, which is located on the deck immediately above the laundry department, where they are separated and individually ironed in large flat ironers. After ironing, they are folded and stacked. From the ironing department they are transported to either of two main storerooms, located fore and aft on one of the main passenger decks for access on the following day by the cabin stewards in making up the rooms. (a) Construct a flow process chart of the laundry operation, using the bed linens and towels as the subject material in the analysis. Estimate distances moved but ignore operation times. (b) Based on your flow process chart, what are some changes in the laundry operation that you would recommend? (c) Develop a revised procedure for the laundry operation, documenting your revision in the form of a new flow process chart.

6 Given the information and data in previous problem, the cruise ship line wants to analyze the work activities of a cabin steward in its passenger laundry operation. Do not consider all of the activities that are performed in cleaning and making over a passenger cabin

(vacuuming, making beds, collecting towels and linens, etc.) as separate operations. Instead, consider making up a room and collecting the laundry in each room as one operation. The focus of the analysis is on the work activities of a cabin steward that relate to the laundry operation. (a) Construct a worker process chart to analyze the duties of the steward that are related to the ship's laundry operation. (b) Based on your worker process chart, what are some changes that you would recommend? (c) Develop a revised procedure for the laundry operation, documenting your revision in the form of a new worker process chart.

7 The Purchasing Department is required to use the following paperwork procedure for each purchase order (PO) related to a company production order. The purchase order is the legal document used by the company to order raw materials and parts from vendors in specified quantities and to guarantee payment to the vendors upon delivery of the items ordered. The purchase order procedure is triggered by the release of a production order that has been authorized by top management for one of the company's regular products. The production order indicates what product is to be produced, how many units, and when it is to be completed. To produce the product, the raw materials and component parts must be ordered in the correct quantities from suppliers (vendors). To initiate the purchase order procedure, a purchasing agent in the Purchasing Department fills out a blank purchase requisition form for each raw material or component part, obtaining the quantity information from the bill of materials for the product. The purchase requisition is an internal company document used to obtain approvals by several departments that are responsible for the product and/or its production. The purchase requisition is sent first to the Design Engineering Department where it is checked for any engineering changes that may have been made to the item ordered. The requisition is then sent from Design Engineering to the Manufacturing Engineering Department, which checks to make sure that a valid route sheet exists for the item. The route sheet is the process plan that indicates how the item is to be processed in the factory. From Manufacturing Engineering, the requisition is sent to the Production Control Department, which checks the requisition to make sure the quantity information and delivery date agrees with the production order. At each of these departments, the signature of the department manager is required in addition to the regular department employee who performed the check. It takes an average of three days in each department to obtain the necessary checks and approvals. After approval by Production Control, the purchase requisition is returned to the Purchasing Department, where it is used as the authorization to prepare the actual purchase order that will be sent to the vendor. The information on the purchase requisition is transcribed onto a blank purchase order form by the originating purchasing agent, and the PO is then signed by the manager of the Purchasing Department and mailed to the vendor. Each PO is sent in a separate envelope by first class mail, even though there are many vendors receiving more than one purchase order from the company. (a) Construct a form process chart for the current purchase order procedure. (b) Based on your form process chart, what are some changes that you would recommend? (c) Develop a revised purchase order procedure, documenting your revision in a new form process chart.

8 Consider the allocation of time between the right hand and left hand in the activity chart shown in Figure 7 in the text. (a) If the workplace were redesigned using a workholding fixture, and the worker were trained to use both hands simultaneously to perform the task, construct a right-hand/left-hand activity chart for the revised method, estimating the amounts of time for each step in the method. (b) What is the percent reduction in cycle time?

9 The repetitive work cycle in a worker-machine system consists of the work elements and associated times given in the table below. As the table shows, all of the operator's elements are external to the machine time. (a) Construct a worker-machine activity chart for this work cycle. (b) Can some of the worker's elements be made internal to the machine cycle? If so, construct a worker-machine activity chart for the revised work cycle. What is the approximate cycle time for the revised cycle?

Sequence	Work Element Description	Worker Time (min)	Machine Time (min)
1	Worker walks to tote pan containing raw stock	0.13	(idle)
2	Worker picks up raw work part and transports it to machine	0.23	(idle)
3	Worker loads part into machine and engages machine semiautomatic cycle	0.12	(idle)
4	Machine semiautomatic cycle	(idle)	0.75
5	Worker unloads finished part from machine	0.10	(idle)
6	Worker transports finished part and deposits into tote pan	0.15	(idle)
Totals		0.73	0.75

Case Problem: Flow Process Chart and Flow Diagram

10 A company produces machinery for industry. Many of the company's products are made in large quantities. This case problem deals with the mechanism plate for one of these machinery products, shown in Figure P10(a). The mechanism plate is a major part in the machine, serving as the backbone of the product. Most of the internal components and subassemblies are fastened to this plate. In the finished product, the plate is completely enclosed within the machine. The mechanism plate is the most expensive part in the product and is the source of numerous quality problems as well. Similar mechanism plates are used on many of the products, and their methods of production are similar, so any improvements made to the subject plate will apply to the other plates as well.

As is typical in batch production, the manufacturing lead time of the mechanism plate (time between release of the order and its completion) is quite long. Since other parts are being processed at the same time in the plant, there are delays in front of each production station as batches of mechanism plates wait their turn in the queues at these stations. Mechanism plates take an average of 18 weeks to complete, once a production order has been released. No information is available about how this time is distributed among the different production steps. In addition, the castings may remain in the warehouse prior to production for as much as 4 months. The following description summarizes the sequence of steps used to fabricate the mechanism plate. Figure P10(b) and (c) show floor layouts for the two stories of the factory building. Key areas and departments relating to the mechanism plate production are indicated in the description and on the floor layouts by numbers in parentheses.

The mechanism plate is a sand casting, supplied by a foundry located 20 miles away. It is made of cast iron and is very heavy, constituting fully one-third the total weight of the product. The designer selected cast iron because of its inherent rigidity and vibration damping characteristics. However, because it is a large flat part, the casting is subject to warping.

The castings are shipped to the company in batches of 50 to 100 units and inspected twice:(1) prior to being stored in the plant warehouse and (2) when an order is placed for

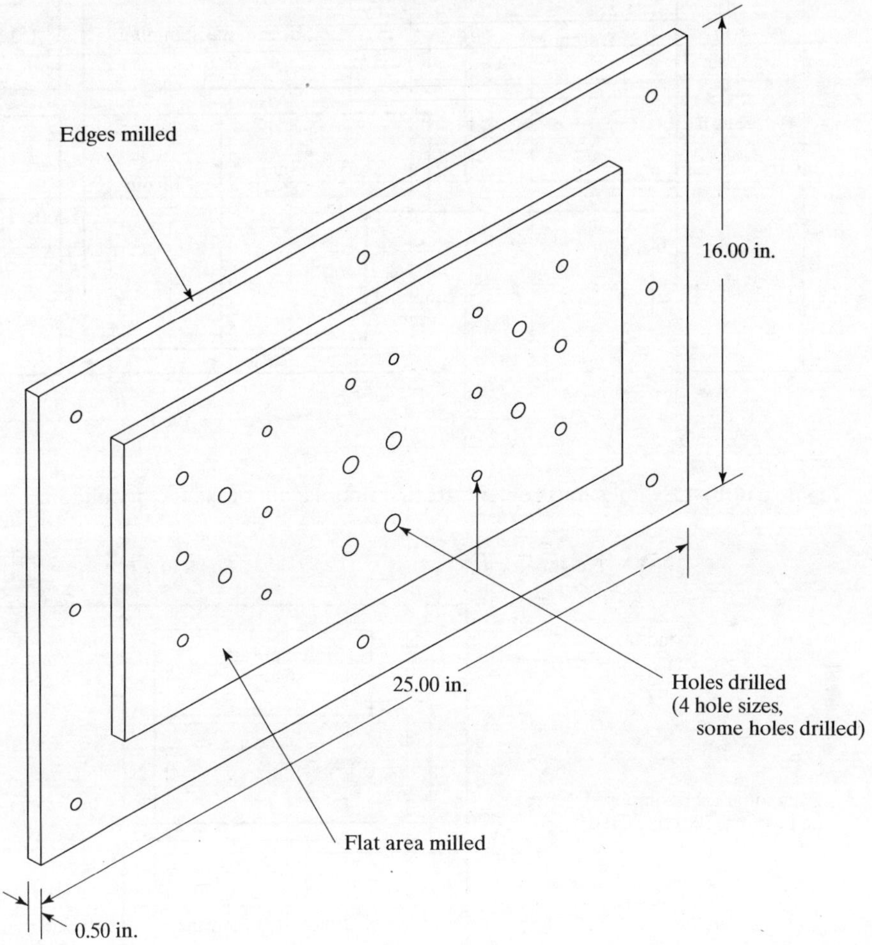

Part name: Mechanism Plate	Casting tol: +/−0.075 in.	Drawn by: M.P.G.
Material: Cast Iron sand casting	Machining tol: +/−0.010 in.	Date: Jan21/99

Figure p10a Exhibits for Problem 10: mechanism plate.

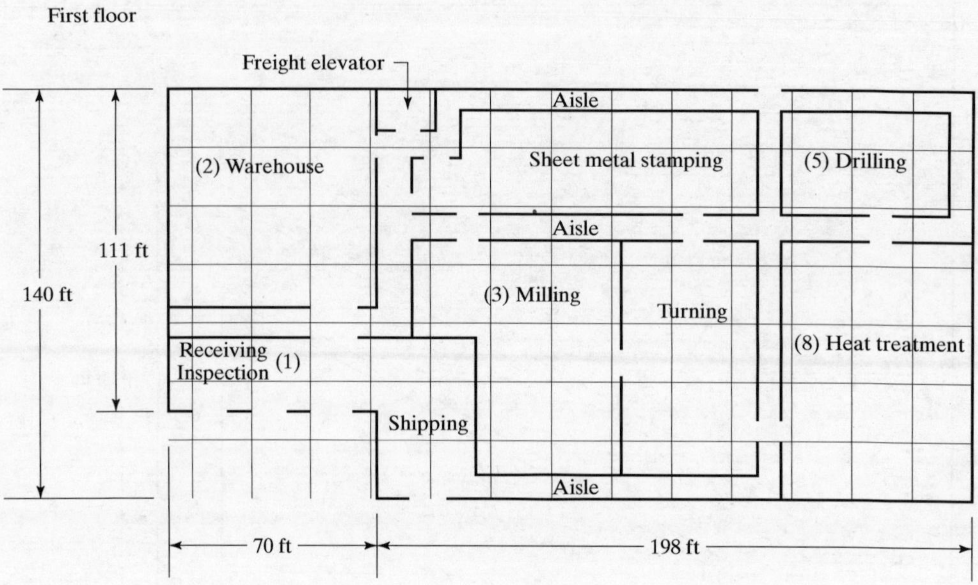

Figure p10(b) Exhibits for Problem 10: first floor layout of the factory building

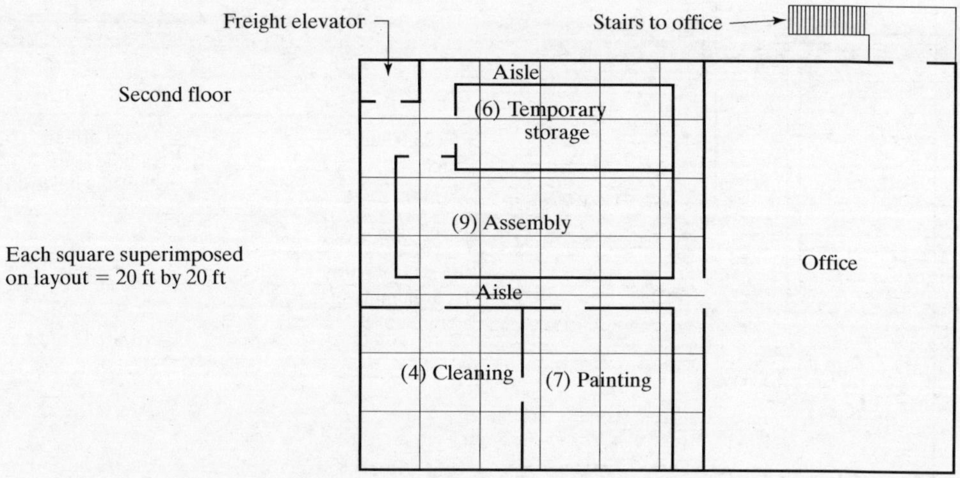

Figure p10(c) Exhibits for Problem 10: second floor layout.

their release to production. Production lot sizes are usually 5 to 10 parts. When the castings are picked from the warehouse for an order, the first step is to send them to a local firm (5 miles away) that specializes in sand blasting (which the company is not currently set up to do). This treatment dislodges any sand imbedded in the surface that is left over from the mold, removes rust that has occurred during storage, and smoothes the surface. The plates are then returned to the company warehouse.

The parts are then processed through a series of machining operations, the first and second of which are in the milling department (3). The first milling operation is face milling to make one side of the plate flat and smooth to accept the components that are to be attached. This is accomplished in one setup on a large milling machine in the mill department. The second milling requires a separate setup, and this operation makes the edges of the casting smooth and straight.

As the second milling operation is completed on each part, it is moved individually to the chemical cleaning department (4) to be cleaned and pickled. The cleaning is performed by human workers using cloth wipers soaked with chemical solvents. The purpose of the cleaning is to remove cutting fluids from machining. Pickling is then performed in open tanks filled with relatively dilute acid which etches the cast iron. The pickling brightens the surface texture of the machined surface of the casting. Owing to the size of the casting, each part must be separately dipped into the tank. The parts are then individually returned back to the machining area (drilling department) to reconstitute the batch.

The next step involves a series of hole drilling operations in the drilling department (5). These holes are used to attach the various brackets and components to the plate. This is performed on four different upright drill presses, organized according to drill size. There are four different hole sizes in the plate. After drilling, two of the hole sizes are tapped in the same department (5), using two additional drill presses. After drilling and tapping, the plates are returned to the cleaning department (4) for cleaning and pickling. Again, they must be dipped separately and moved individually to a temporary storage area (6) near the assembly department (9).

The plates are stored in the temporary storage area (6) until the other components that are to be assembled have been collected. When all of the components have been collected, the mechanism plate is sent to the painting department (7). The painting is needed to provide a protective coating and for appearance reasons. The operation is performed by human workers using paintbrushes to work the paint into the rough texture of the sand cast surface. Two coats are applied in this way, with a five hour low temperature baking operation following each coating. The baking ovens are located in the heat treatment department (8) at the rear of the factory. As many as five plates can be baked at one time.

After the final bake, the mechanism plates rejoin the other components in the temporary storage area (6). A "kit" of components is then made up, which consists of one mechanism plate and a set of all the components that are to be assembled to it. The kit is then sent to the assembly department (9), where the subassembly is completed. A total of 75 parts, including fasteners, are attached to the plate. Each mechanism plate subassembly is put together at a single workstation. When finished, it is put back into temporary storage (6) to await final assembly into the machinery product.

Assignment: (a) Prepare a flow process chart showing the operations, moves, delays, etc., in the current process. (b) Summarize the flow process chart by determining the number of operations and moves, the total distances moved, and delays, etc. (c) Construct a flow diagram of the path followed by the mechanism plate during its manufacture. (d) Develop a list of possible improvements that might be made in the production of the mechanism plate. (e) Develop a proposed improved method based on your answers to (a), (b), (c), and (d), and document your proposed new method by means of a flow process chart. (f) Summarize the flow process chart for the proposed method, indicating the number of operations and moves, the total distances traveled, and delays, etc. Show how this method is an improvement over the current method in terms of these statistics. (g) Consider the issue of plant layout in more detail. What changes in the overall layout of the plant would you make to improve the efficiency of mechanism plate production?

Process Mapping

11 Develop a basic process map for the cruise ship laundry operation described in Problem 5. What recommendations can you make for improving the operation?

12 Develop a relationship map for the machinery components factory described in Problem 4.

13 Develop a cross-functional process map for the Purchasing Department and other departments described in Problem 7. What recommendations can you make for improving the paperwork flow?

Motion Study and Work Design

This chapter focuses on the traditional industrial engineering topics of motion study and work design. ***Motion study*** involves the analysis of the basic hand, arm, and body movements of workers as they perform work.[1] ***Work design*** involves the methods and motions used to perform a task. This design includes the workplace layout and environment as well as the tooling and equipment (e.g., workholders, fixtures, hand tools, portable power tools, and machine tools). In short, work design is the design of the work system. The traditional approaches in motion study and work design are based on the findings of researchers such as Frank and Lillian Gilbreth in the early part of the twentieth century. The approaches also include common sense "principles of motion economy" that are used to simplify and improve the efficiency and effectiveness of manual work. Today, these principles are widely used not only by industrial engineers but also by workers themselves who in recent years are increasingly being given greater responsibility for designing their own work methods.

Work design is commonly associated with manual work, the type of work done in production and logistics. In recent decades, with the growth of service industries,

[1]The definition of motion study developed by the Employee and Industrial Relations Committee [ANSI Standard Z94.13-1989] is the following: "The study of the basic manual movements and procedures associated with the accomplishment of work. Historically associated with the Gilbreths (Frank and Lillian), in contrast to time study, associated with Taylor (Frederick)."

greater attention has been focused on the design of work procedures and environments in those industries. To the extent that service operations usually involve a manual component, the general principles that apply to manual work are applicable to service and office work as well. In addition, work design principles dealing with worker comfort, workplace layout, and equipment operation apply just as well to service and office work as they do to manual tasks.

The traditional approaches in motion study and work design were developed before the advent of ergonomics and human factors, which are also applied in the design of work.

1 BASIC MOTION ELEMENTS AND WORK ANALYSIS

As indicated in the pyramidal structure of work, any manual task is composed of work elements, and the work elements can be further subdivided into basic motion elements. In this section, we define the basic motion elements and how they can be used to analyze work.

1.1 Therbligs

Frank Gilbreth was the first to catalog the basic motion elements. He called each motion a ***therblig*** (Gilbreth spelled backward except for the "th"). A list of Gilbreth's 17 therbligs is presented in Table 1 along with the letter symbol he used for each as well as a brief description. Therbligs are the basic building blocks of virtually all manual work performed at a single workplace and consisting primarily of hand motions. Therbligs are relatively few in number, but they are performed over and over, often in very similar sequences, during a given task. For example, a common hand motion sequence in repetitive assembly work is to reach for a part in the work area, grasp it, move and position it, and then release it. This sequence may be repeated many times in a work cycle, depending on how many parts are assembled in the cycle. Therbligs include mental elements as well as physical elements. With some modification, these basic motion elements are used today in a number of work measurement systems, such as Methods-Time Measurement (MTM) and the Maynard Operation Sequence Technique (MOST).

The therbligs in a manual task can be classified in several ways that are useful in analyzing the work cycle. One possible classification is shown in Table 2, in which therbligs are classified (1) as to their physical or mental emphasis and (2) whether they are effective or ineffective. Methods analysis at the therblig level seeks to eliminate or reduce ineffective therbligs.

1.2 Work Analysis Using Therbligs

Each therblig represents time and energy expended by a worker to perform a task. If the task is repetitive, of relatively short duration, and will be performed many times, it may be appropriate to analyze the therbligs that make up the work cycle as part of the

TABLE 1 Gilbreth's Seventeen Therbligs

Therblig	Letter Symbol	Description
Transport empty	TE	Reaching for an object with empty hand; for example, reach for a part prior to grasping and moving the part. Today, we commonly refer to the transport empty motion element as a "reach."
Grasp	G	Grasping an object by contacting and closing the fingers of the active hand about the object until control has been achieved.
Transport loaded	TL	Moving an object using a hand motion; for example, moving a part from one location to another at a workstation. Today, we commonly refer to a transport loaded motion element as a "move."
Hold	H	Holding an object; for example, holding an object with one hand while the other hand performs some operation on it.
Release load	RL	Releasing control of an object, typically by opening the fingers that held it and breaking contact with the object.
Preposition	PP	Positioning and/or orienting an object for the next operation and relative to an approximate location; for example, lining up a pin next to a hole for insertion into the hole. Preposition usually follows transport loaded.
Position	P	Positioning and/or orienting an object in the defined location that is intended for it. Position is generally performed during transport loaded; for example, moving a pin toward a hole and simultaneously lining it up in preparation for insertion into the hole.
Use	U	Manipulating and/or applying a tool in the intended way during the course of working, usually on an object; for example, using a screwdriver to turn a threaded fastener or using a pen to sign one's name.
Assemble	A	Joining two parts together to form an assembled entity; for example, using a threaded fastener to assemble two mating parts by hand.
Disassemble	DA	Separating multiple components that were previously joined in some way; for example, unfastening two parts held together by a threaded fastener.
Search	Sh	Attempting to find an object using the eyes or hand, concluding when the object is found.
Select	St	Choosing among several objects in a group, usually involving hand-eye coordination, and concluding when the hand has located the selected object.
Plan	Pn	Deciding on a course of action, usually consisting of short pause or hesitation in the motions of the hands and/or body.
Inspect	I	Determining the quality or characteristics of an object using the eyes and/or other senses.
Unavoidable delay	UD	Waiting due to factors beyond the control of the worker and included in the work cycle; for example, waiting for a machine to complete its feed motion.
Avoidable delay	AD	Waiting that is within the worker's control, causing idleness that is not included in the regular work cycle; for example, the worker opening a pack of chewing gum.
Rest	R	Resting to overcome fatigue, consisting of a pause in the motions of the hands and/or body during the work cycle or between cycles.

work design process. The term ***micromotion analysis*** is sometimes used for this type of analysis. For example, the activities of the right and left hands when performing a manual task can be specified in terms of therbligs. Figure 1 illustrates this kind of analysis for

TABLE 2 Classification of Therbligs

	Effective Therbligs	Ineffective Therbligs
Physical basic motion elements	Transport empty (TE) Grasp (G) Transport loaded (TL) Release load (RL) Use (U) Assemble (A) Disassemble (DA)	Hold (H) Preposition (PP)
Physical and mental basic motion elements		Position (P) Search (Sh) Select (St)
Mental basic elements	Inspect (I)	Plan (Pn)
Delay elements	Rest (R)	Unavoidable delay (UD) Avoidable delay (AD)

Source: Adapted from a classification in [7].

Sequence	Left hand	Therbligs		Right hand	Cumulative Time (min)
1	Reach for board	TE	AD	Idle	
2	Grasp board	G	AD	Idle	
3	Transport board	TL	AD	Idle	
4	Position board	PP	AD	Idle	0.08
5	Hold board	H	TE	Reach for peg	
6	Hold board	H	G	Grasp peg	
7	Hold board	H	TL	Transport peg to board	
8	Hold board	H	P	Position peg in hole	
9	Hold board	H	R	Release peg	0.14
10	Hold board	H	TE	Reach for peg	
11	Hold board	H	G	Grasp peg	
12	Hold board	H	TL	Transport peg to board	
13	Hold board	H	P	Position peg in hole	
14	Hold board	H	R	Release peg	0.20

Figure 1 Right-hand/left-hand activity chart where therbligs are used to define the work cycle. Only the first two cycles of the right hand are shown here.

the same task that is described in the right-hand/left-hand activity chart. The following general objectives are involved in micromotion analysis:[2]

- Eliminate therbligs that are ineffective if possible; for example, eliminate the need to search for parts or tools by positioning them in a known and fixed location in the workplace.

[2]The list of objectives is based largely on a list of basic principles in [11, p. 398].

- Avoid the use of a hand for holding parts; use a workholder instead.
- Combine therbligs where possible; for example, perform right-hand and left-hand motions simultaneously.
- Simplify the overall method; for example, resequence therbligs in the cycle.
- Reduce the time required for the motion; for example, shorten distances of therbligs such as transport empty and transport loaded.

As in the analysis associated with the various charting techniques, checklists are useful in micromotion analysis. Table 3 presents a checklist of questions and suggestions for possible improvements for each therblig.

2 PRINCIPLES OF MOTION ECONOMY AND WORK DESIGN

The principles of motion economy have been developed over many years of practical experience in work design. They are guidelines that can be used to help determine the work method, workplace layout, tools, and equipment that will maximize the efficiency and minimize the fatigue of the worker. Most of the guidelines are based on common sense. Many are derived from the preceding therblig analysis and will be recognizable to those who have studied Table 3. The reader might question why it is even necessary to state these principles, since some of them seem so obvious. The answers to that question can be found in factories, warehouses, offices, and other workplaces around the world in the many instances where these principles are violated.

The principles of motion economy can be organized into three categories: (1) principles related to the use of the human body, (2) principles related to workplace arrangement, and (3) principles related to the design of tooling and equipment.[3] Our coverage is based on this organization.

2.1 Principles Related to the Use of the Human Body

The principles of motion economy that are related to the use of the human body can be used to design the most appropriate methods and motions of the human worker in performing a given task. They are most applicable to manual work, either repetitive or nonrepetitive.

1. ***Both hands should be fully utilized.*** The natural tendency of most people is to use their preferred hand (right hand for right-handed people and left hand for left-handed people) to accomplish most of the work. The other hand is relegated to a minor role, such as holding the object, while the preferred hand works on it. This first principle states that both hands should be used as equally as possible.
2. ***The two hands should begin and end their motions at the same time.*** This principle follows from the first. To implement, it is sometimes necessary to design the method so that the work is evenly divided between the right-hand side and the left-hand side of the workplace. In this case, the division of work should be organized according to the following principle.

[3]This is a classification suggested by Barnes [4]. Sources for the principles discussed in this section include [1], [4], [9], [11], and [13].

TABLE 3 Micromotion Analysis Checklist for Possible Improvements

Therblig	Questions and Suggestions
Transport empty (TE)	Minimize number of parts in the product to reduce frequency of TE and TL.
	Minimize reach distance required.
	Use parts bins that have easy access.
	Can abrupt changes in direction of movement of body member be eliminated or minimized?
	Locate parts and tools used most frequently near their respective points of use.
	Minimize requirements for hand-eye coordination during reach.
	Can right and left hands be used simultaneously to accomplish two transport empty motions?
Grasp (G)	Use parts bins that have easy access.
	Use workholders that have fast release mechanism. For example, screw type vises are time consuming to operate, while pneumatic clamps are fast-acting.
	Locate parts and tools in known locations to save time in searching.
	Can right and left hands be used simultaneously to accomplish two grasp motions?
	Avoid transfer of objects from one hand to the other.
	Design parts that do not tangle.
Transport loaded (TL)	Can parts be slid across work surface rather than carried above work surface? This usually saves time.
	Can abrupt changes in direction of movement of body member be eliminated or minimized?
	Design parts and tools to be as lightweight as possible to save move time.
	Minimize number of parts in the product to reduce frequency of TE and TL.
	Minimize move distance required.
	Locate parts and tools used most frequently near their respective points of use.
	Minimize requirements for hand-eye coordination during movement.
	Can right and left hands be used simultaneously to accomplish two transport loaded motions?
Hold (H)	This is considered an ineffective therblig. Can it be eliminated?
	Can a workholding device (e.g., fixture, jig, vise, clamp) be used instead of holding by hand?
	Can friction, an adhesive, or a mechanical stop be used instead of holding by hand?
	If holding by hand cannot be eliminated, can an armrest be provided?
Release load (RL)	Is it possible to release the object by dropping it (e.g., into a chute)?
	Is the delivery point (e.g., bin, workholder) designed for ease of release of the object?
	Minimize requirements for hand-eye coordination during release.
Preposition (PP)	This is considered an ineffective therblig. Can it be eliminated?
	Can symmetry of prepositioning be increased? For example, it is easier to preposition a round shaft relative to a round hole than a square shaft relative to a square hole because of increased symmetry of the fit.
	Can a guide be designed to facilitate prepositioning?
	Can an armrest be used to steady the hand during prepositioning?
	Design parts and tools to be as lightweight as possible to save prepositioning time.
	Make sure object is grasped properly to facilitate prepositioning.
Position (P)	This is considered an ineffective therblig. Can it be eliminated?
	Can symmetry of positioning be increased? For example, it is easier to position a round shaft relative to a round hole than a square shaft relative to a square hole because of increased symmetry of the fit.
	Can a guide be designed to facilitate positioning?
	Can an armrest be used to steady the hand during positioning?
	Can tools be suspended from overhead to avoid positioning?
	Design parts and tools to be as lightweight as possible to save positioning time.
	Make sure object is grasped properly to facilitate positioning.
Use (U)	Can a more efficient hand tool be designed to reduce the time of the use motion?
	Can a portable power tool be devised to reduce the time of the use motion?

Therblig	Questions and Suggestions
	The part should be held in a workholder during the use motion.
	Can a jig be designed to guide the use of the tool? A ***jig*** is a special workholder that has a mechanism for guiding the tool.
	Can a mechanized or automated operation be used to eliminate the need for the use motion?
Assemble (A)	Can a hand tool be designed to reduce the time required for the assembly motion?
	Can a portable power tool be devised to reduce the time of the assembly motion?
	The base part or existing subassembly should be positioned in a workholder during the assembly motion.
	Can the product be designed with fewer components to minimize assembly time?
	Design the product for automated assembly to eliminate the need for manual assembly.
Disassemble (DA)	Can a hand tool be designed to reduce the time required for the disassembly motion?
	Can a portable power tool be devised to reduce the time required for the disassembly motion?
	The base part or existing subassembly should be positioned in a workholder during the disassembly motion.
Search (Sh)	This is considered an ineffective therblig. Can it be eliminated?
	Make sure lighting is adequate to facilitate searching.
	Can parts be fed from magazines or chutes to avoid searching?
	Locate tools in known positions in the workplace to facilitate searching; for example, suspend tools from overhead.
	Can different parts be made with different colors to facilitate searching?
Select (St)	This is considered an ineffective therblig. Can it be eliminated?
	Use parts bins that have easy access.
	Make sure lighting is adequate to facilitate selecting.
	Can parts be fed from magazines or chutes for one-at-a-time selection?
	Can different parts be made with different colors to facilitate searching?
Plan (Pn)	This is considered an ineffective therblig. Can it be eliminated?
	Remove the need for the worker to decide on a course of action that causes hesitation in the work cycle.
Inspect (I)	Make sure lighting is adequate to facilitate the inspection procedure.
	Minimize the number of characteristics to inspect. Only the key characteristics of the part should be inspected. Time should not be wasted inspecting unimportant characteristics.
	Can the object be inspected using gauges instead of actually measuring the characteristics of interest? Gauging takes less time than measuring.
	Can inspection be combined with another operation so it is not performed separately?
	Can inspection be automated (e.g., machine vision) to eliminate the need for a worker to accomplish it (e.g., visually)?
	Can multiple but separate inspection steps be combined into one inspection?
Unavoidable delay (UD)	This is considered an ineffective therblig. Can it be eliminated?
	Eliminate the reason for the delay. For example, can the machine speed be increased to reduce the machine cycle time?
	Can external work elements be made into internal work elements to fill up the delay time with useful work activities?
Avoidable delay (AD)	This is considered an ineffective therblig. Can it be eliminated?
	Eliminate the reason for the delay.
	Provide incentives for the worker to minimize delay time.
Rest (R)	Reduce metabolic load on worker through the use of machines and tools to minimize need for rest breaks.
	Improvements in methods and motions through analysis of previous therbligs should reduce need for rest breaks.

Source: Adapted from checklists in [4], [11], and other sources.

3. ***The motions of the hands and arms should be symmetrical and simultaneous.*** This will minimize the amount of hand-eye coordination required by the worker. And since both hands are doing the same movements at the same time, less concentration will be required than if the two hands had to perform different and independent motions. It should be noted that not all tasks can be organized according to this principle. If this is the case, then the principle that follows next is applicable.
4. ***The work should be designed to emphasize the worker's preferred hand.*** The preferred hand is faster, stronger, and more dexterous. If the work to be done cannot be allocated evenly between the two hands, then the method should take advantage of the worker's best hand. For example, work units should enter the workplace on the side of the worker's preferred hand and exit the workplace on the opposite side. The reason is that greater hand-eye coordination is required to initially acquire the work unit, so the worker should use the preferred hand for this element. Releasing the work unit at the end of the cycle requires less coordination.
5. ***The worker's two hands should never be idle at the same time.*** The work method should be designed to avoid periods when neither hand is working. It may not be possible to completely balance the workload between the right and left hands, but it should be possible to avoid having both hands idle at the same time. The exception to this principle is during rest breaks. The work cycle of a worker-machine system may also be an exception, if the worker is responsible for monitoring the machine during its automatic cycle, and monitoring involves using the worker's cognitive senses rather than the hands. If machine monitoring is not required, then internal work elements should be assigned to the worker during the automatic cycle.

The central theme of these first five principles is the use of two hands and the allocation of work between them. Barnes [4] cites the results of a study done at the University of Iowa in which a right-handed worker performed a relatively simple manual task consisting of reaching, selecting, grasping, transporting, and releasing small parts. The task was accomplished using two different containers for the parts: a rectangular bin and a bin with tray (the bin with tray making it easier to perform the select and grasp elements). The worker performed the work cycle with each container using (1) only the right hand, (2) only the left hand, and (3) both hands performing symmetrical and simultaneous motions. The results of the study are presented in Table 4. The normalized times are simply the percentage values of the left hand and both hands using the right- hand time as the base. As expected, the right-handed worker was able to complete the work cycle in the shortest time using the right hand. Also as expected, the work cycle

TABLE 4 Study Results of a Task Performed One-Handed and Two-Handed

	Rectangular Bin			Bin with Tray		
	Right Hand	Left Hand	Both Hands	Right Hand	Left Hand	Both Hands
Time to perform	1.04 sec	1.10 sec	1.48 sec	0.81 sec	0.91 sec	1.07 sec
Normalized time	100%	106%	142%	100%	112%	132%

Source: [4].

using both hands took the longest time. However, two parts were completed using both hands, so the time per part for each tray type is one-half the value shown. Accordingly, using both hands was the most productive method.

The next five principles of motion economy attempt to utilize the laws of physics to assist in the use of the hands and arms while working.

6. ***The method should consist of smooth continuous curved motions rather than straight-line motions with abrupt changes in direction.*** It takes less time to move through a sequence of smooth continuous curved paths than through a sequence of straight paths that are opposite in direction, even though the actual total distance of the curved paths may be longer (since the shortest distance between two points is a straight line). This is especially true when an object is being moved and the mass of the object affects the motions. The reason behind this principle is that the straight-line path sequence includes start and stop actions (accelerations and decelerations) that consume the worker's time and energy. Motions consisting of smooth continuous curves minimize the lost time in starts and stops.
7. ***Momentum should be used to facilitate the task wherever possible.*** When carpenters strike a nail with a hammer, they are using ***momentum***, which can be defined as mass times velocity. Imagine trying to apply a static force to press the nail into the wood. Not all work situations provide an opportunity to use momentum as a carpenter uses a hammer, but if the opportunity is present, exploit it. The previous principle dealing with smooth continuous curved motions illustrates a beneficial use of momentum (i.e., conservation of momentum) to make a task easier.
8. ***The method should take advantage of gravity instead of opposing it.*** Less time and energy are required to move a heavy object from a higher elevation to a lower elevation than to move the object upward. The principle is usually implemented by proper layout and arrangement of the workplace, and so it is often associated with the workplace arrangement principles of motion economy.
9. ***The method should achieve a natural rhythm of the motions involved.*** Rhythm refers to motions that have a regular recurrence and flow from one to the next. Basically, the worker learns the rhythm and performs the motions without thinking, much like the natural and instinctive motion pattern that occurs in walking.
10. ***The lowest classification of hand and arm motions should be used.*** The five classifications of hand and arm motions are presented in Table 5. With each lower classification, the worker can perform the hand and arm motion more quickly and with less effort. Therefore, the work method should be composed of motions at

TABLE 5 Five Classifications of Hand and Arm Motions

Classification	Defined as:
1	Finger motions only
2	Finger and wrist motions
3	Finger, wrist, and forearm motions
4	Finger, wrist, forearm, and upper arm motions
5	Finger, wrist, forearm, upper arm, and shoulder motions

the lowest classification level possible. This can often be accomplished by locating parts and tools as close together as possible in the workplace.

The two remaining human body principles of motion economy are recommendations for using body members other than the hands and arms.

11. ***Minimize eye focus and eye travel activities***. In work situations where hand-eye coordination is required, the eyes are used to direct the actions of the hands. ***Eye focus*** occurs when the eye must adjust to a change in viewing distance—for example, from 25 in. to 10 in. with little or no change in line of sight. ***Eye travel*** occurs when the eye must adjust to a line-of-sight change—for example, from one location in the workplace to another, but the distances from the eyes are the same. Since eye focus and eye travel each take time, it is desirable to minimize the need for the worker to make these adjustments as much as possible. This can be accomplished by minimizing the distances between objects (e.g., parts and tools) that are used in the workplace.
12. ***The method should be designed to utilize the worker's feet and legs when appropriate***. The legs are stronger than the arms, although the feet are not as dexterous as the hands. The work method can sometimes be designed to take advantage of the greater strength of the legs, for example, in lifting tasks.

2.2 Principles Related to Workplace Arrangement

The principles of motion economy in this section are directed at the design of the workplace—for example, the layout of the workstation and the arrangement of tools and parts in it. The first three principles deal with the immediate work area and contribute to a natural rhythm in the work cycle. The other principles cover the use of gravity and the general conditions of the workplace.

1. ***Tools and materials should be located in fixed positions within the work area.*** As the saying goes, "a place for everything, and everything in its place." The worker eventually learns the fixed locations, allowing him or her to reach for the object without wasting time looking and searching.
2. ***Tools and materials should be located close to where they are used.*** This helps to minimize the distances the worker must move (travel empty and travel loaded) in the workplace. In addition, any equipment controls should also be located in close proximity. This guideline usually refers to a normal and maximum working area, as shown in Figure 2 and clarified further in Table 6. It is generally desirable to keep the parts and tools used in the work method within the normal working area, as defined for each hand and both hands working together. If the method requires the worker to move beyond the maximum working area, then the worker must move more than just the arms and hands. This expends additional energy, takes more time, and ultimately contributes to greater worker fatigue.
3. ***Tools and materials should be placed in locations that are consistent with the sequence of work elements in the work cycle***. Items should be arranged in a logical pattern that matches the sequence of work elements. Those items that are

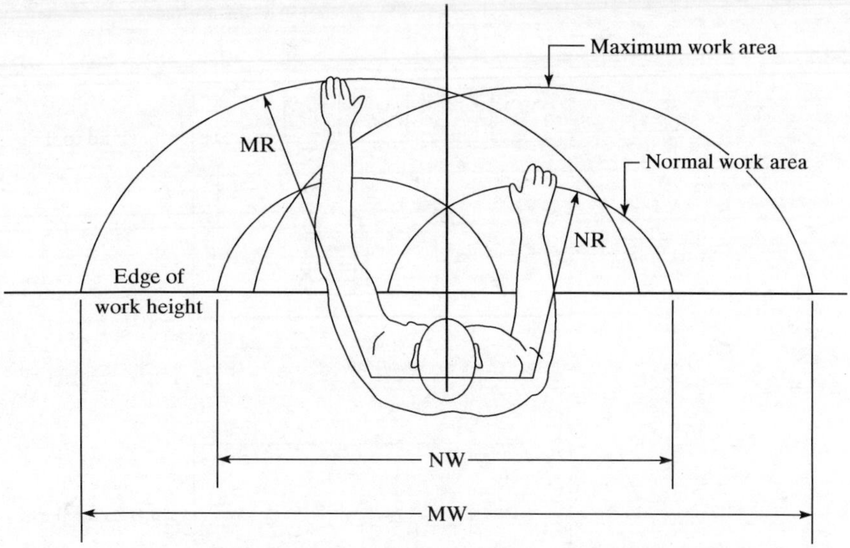

Figure 2 Normal and maximum working areas in the workplace. See Table 6 for working area dimensions of average male and female workers. (Adapted from [4]. Original source was R. Farley, "Some Principles of Methods and Motion Study as Used in Development Work," *General Motors Engineering Journal* 2, no. 6: 20–25.)

TABLE 6 Normal and Maximum Working Area Dimensions in Figure 2

Symbol in Figure 2	Dimension in Working Area for Worker Seated at Worktable	Male Worker [cm (in)]	Female Worker [cm (in)]
NR	Normal radius of arm reach	39 (15.5)	36 (14.0)
MR	Maximum radius of arm reach	67 (26.5)	60 (23.5)
NW	Normal width of arm reach	109 (43.0)	102 (40.0)
MW	Maximum width of arm reach	163 (64.0)	147 (58.0)

used first in the cycle should be on one side of the work area, the items used next should be next to the first, and so on, until the last items are obtained on the other side of the work area. The alternative to this sequential arrangement is to locate items randomly about the work area. This increases the amount of searching required and detracts from the rhythm of the work cycle.

Figure 3 shows the top view of a workplace layout that illustrates these first three principles. Note that the layout in (b) locates bins in a more accessible pattern that is consistent with the sequence of work elements.

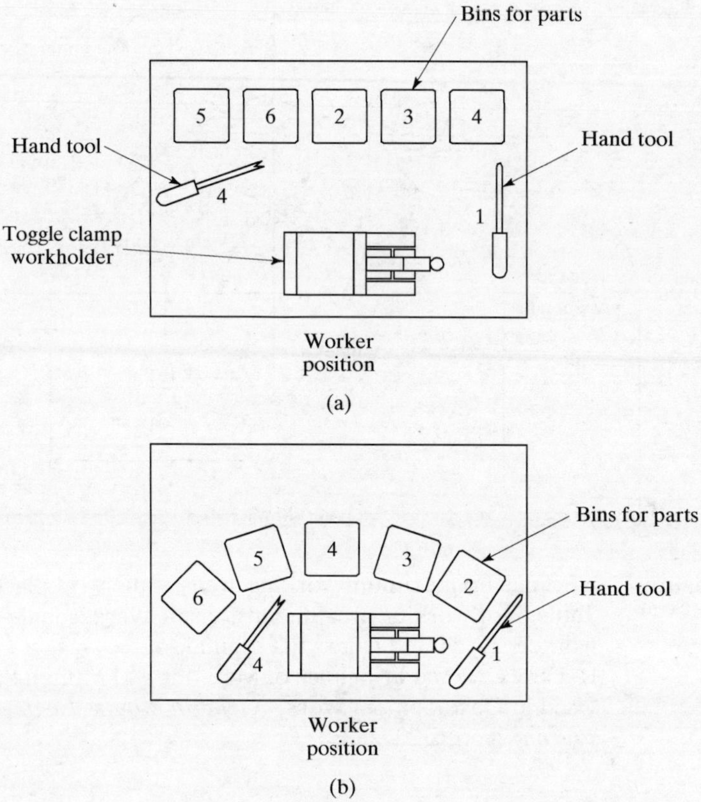

Figure 3 Two workplace layouts. The layout in (b) illustrates principles of good workplace arrangement while the one in (a) does not. Numbers indicate sequence of work elements in relation to locations of hand tools and parts bins.

4. ***Gravity feed bins should be used to deliver small parts and fasteners***. A gravity feed bin is a container that uses gravity to move the items in it to a convenient access point for the worker. One possible design is shown in Figure 4(a). It generally allows for quicker acquisition of an item than a conventional rectangular tray shown in Figure 4(b).
5. ***Gravity drop chutes should be used for completed work units where appropriate***. The drop chutes should lead to a container adjacent to the worktable. The entrance to the gravity chute should be located near the normal work area, permitting the worker to dispose of the finished work unit quickly and conveniently. There are obvious limitations on the use of gravity chutes. They are most appropriate for lightweight work units that are not fragile.

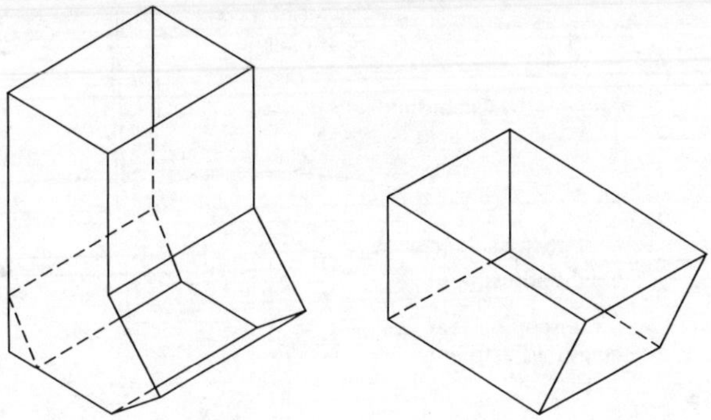

Figure 4 Two types of bins used for small parts and fasteners in the workplace: (a) gravity feed bin and (b) conventional rectangular bin.

6. ***Adequate illumination must be provided for the workplace.*** The issue of illumination is normally associated with ergonomics. However, illumination has long been known to be an important factor in work design, well before ergonomics and human factors became a field of study in the scientific and engineering community. Illumination is especially important in visual inspection tasks. Adequate illumination means not only enough light on the work area; it also refers to color, absence of glare, contrast among items in the field of view, and the location of the light source(s). Other aspects of workplace environment are also important, such as noise and temperature.
7. ***A proper chair should be provided for the worker.*** This usually means an adjustable chair that can be fitted to the size of the worker. The adjustments usually include seat height and back height. Both the seat and back are padded. Many adjustable chairs also provide a means of increasing and decreasing the amount of back support. The chair height should be in proper relationship with the work height. An adjustable chair for the workplace is shown in Figure 5.

2.3 Principles Related to the Design of Tooling and Equipment

The principles of motion economy in this section are helpful for designing special tools and controls on equipment used in the workplace.

1. ***Workholding devices should be designed for the task; a worker's hand should not be used as a workholder.*** A mechanical workholder with a fast-acting clamp permits the work unit to be loaded quickly and frees both hands to work on the task productively. Typically, the workholder must be custom-designed for the

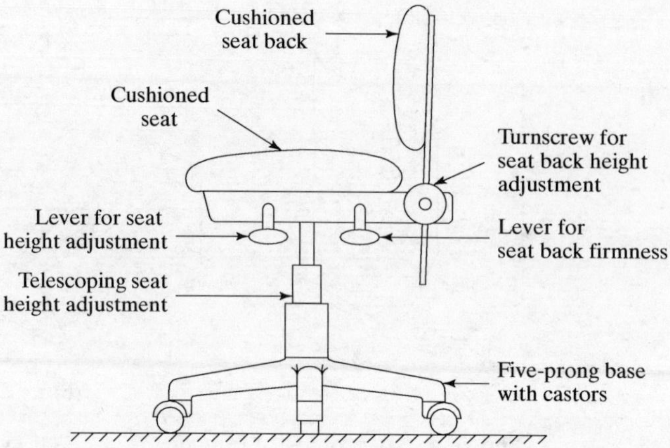

Figure 5 An adjustable chair for the workplace. The adjustments provide comfortable seating related to the size of the worker and the work height.

work part processed in the task. A conventional vise is not recommended for a repetitive work cycle because of its slow-acting screw clamping mechanism.

2. ***The hands should be relieved of work elements that can be performed by the feet.*** Foot pedal controls can be provided instead of hand controls to operate certain types of equipment. Sewing machines and church organs are two examples in which foot pedals are used as integral components in the operation of the equipment. As our examples suggest, training is often required for the operator to become proficient in the use of the foot pedals.
3. ***Multiple tooling functions should be combined into one tool whenever possible.*** Many of the common hand tools and implements exhibit this principle. The head of a claw hammer is designed for both striking and pulling nails. Nearly all pencils are designed for both writing and erasing. Less time is usually required to reposition such a double-function tool than to put one tool down and pick another one up.
4. ***Multiple operations should be performed simultaneously rather than sequentially whenever possible.*** A work cycle is usually conceptualized as a sequence of work elements or steps. The steps are performed one after the other by the worker and/or machine. In some cases, the work method can be designed so that the steps are accomplished at the same time rather than sequentially. Special tooling and processes can often be designed to simultaneously accomplish the multiple operations. Examples include the following:

   - Pneumatically powered, multiple-spindle lug nut runner used to attach wheels to the car in automobile final assembly plants
   - Multiple-spindle drill presses to drill holes in printed circuit boards
   - Wave soldering in electronics assembly to solder all connections on a printed circuit board simultaneously.

5. ***Where feasible, an operation should be performed on multiple parts simultaneously.*** This usually applies to cases involving the use of a powered tool such as a machine tool. A good example is the drilling of holes in a printed circuit board (PCB). The PCBs are stacked three or four thick, and a numerically controlled drill press drills each hole through the entire stack in one feed motion.
6. ***Equipment controls should be designed for operator convenience and error avoidance.*** Equipment controls include dials, cranks, levers, switches, push buttons, and other devices that regulate the operation of the equipment. All of the controls needed by the operator should be located within easy reach, so as to minimize the body motions required to access and actuate them. In addition, the controls should be designed to be mistake-proof, so that the operator does not cause an equipment action that is different from the one intended.
7. ***Hand tools and portable powered tools should be designed for operator comfort and convenience.*** For example, the tools should have handles or grips that are slightly compressible so that they can be held and used comfortably for the duration of the shift. The location of the handle or grip relative to the working end of the tool should be designed for maximum operator safety, convenience, and utility of the tool. If possible, the tool should accommodate both right-handed and left-handed workers.
8. ***Manual operations should be mechanized or automated wherever economically and technologically feasible.***[4] Mechanized or automated equipment and tooling that are designed for the specific operation will almost always outperform a human worker in terms of speed, repeatability, and accuracy. This results in higher production rates and better quality products. The economic feasibility depends on the quantities to be produced. In general, higher quantities are more likely to justify the investment in mechanization and automation. The technological feasibility relates to the time and difficulty involved in mechanizing or automating a given operation. The time issue is the amount of time required to design and build an automated machine. It may take more than a year before the equipment can be installed, but the company must begin production right away on a product with a short life cycle. The difficulty issue refers to problems such as (1) physical access to the work location, (2) adjustments required in the task, (3) requirements of manual dexterity, and (4) demands on hand-eye coordination.

REFERENCES

[1] Aft, L. S. *Work Measurement and Methods Improvement*. New York: Wiley, 2000.

[2] Akiyama, M., and H. Kamata. "Method Engineering and Workplace Design." Pp. 4.3–4.20 in *Maynard's Industrial Engineering Handbook*, 5th ed., edited by K. Zandin. New York: McGraw-Hill, 2001.

[4]***Mechanization*** refers to the use of machinery, usually powered machinery, in place of human (or animal) labor. A human is usually required to operate and/or oversee the machinery. ***Automation*** refers to the use of powered equipment that operates under its own control and without human assistance or oversight.

[3] ANSI Standard Z94.0-1989. *Industrial Engineering Terminology*, Norcross, GA: Industrial Engineering and Management Press, Institute of Industrial Engineers, 1989.

[4] Barnes, R. M. *Motion and Time Study: Design and Measurement of Work*. 7th ed. New York: Wiley, 1980.

[5] Becker, F., and F. Steele. *Workplace by Design*. San Francisco: Jossey-Bass, 1995.

[6] Gilbreth, F. B. *Motion Study*. New York: Van Nostrand, 1911.

[7] Kadota, T., and S. Sakamoto. "Methods Analysis and Design." Pp. 1415–45 in *Handbook of Industrial Engineering*, 2nd ed., edited by G. Salvendy. New York: Wiley, and Institute of Industrial Engineers, Norcross, GA, 1992.

[8] Kanawaty, G., ed. *Introduction to Work Study*. 4th ed. Geneva, Switzerland: International Labour Office, 1992.

[9] Konz, S., and S. Johnson. *Work Design: Industrial Ergonomics*. 5th ed. Scottsdale, AZ: Holcomb Hathaway Publishers, 2000.

[10] Meyers, F. E., and J. R. Stewart. *Motion and Time Study for Lean Manufacturing*. 3rd ed. Upper Saddle River, NJ: Prentice Hall, 2002.

[11] Mundel, M. E., and D. L. Danner. *Motion and Time Study: Improving Productivity*. 7th ed. Englewood Cliffs, NJ: Prentice Hall, 1994.

[12] Nadler, G. *Work Design*. Homewood, IL: Irwin, 1963.

[13] Niebel, B. W., and A. Freivalds. *Methods, Standards, and Work Design*. 10th ed. New York: McGraw-Hill, 1999.

REVIEW QUESTIONS

1 What is motion study?

2 What is work design?

3 What is a therblig?

4 Identify some of the ineffective therbligs.

5 What is the term sometimes used for the kind of analysis involving therbligs in a task?

6 What are the general objectives of micromotion analysis?

7 Name some of the principles of motion economy that deal with the use of the two hands.

8 Why are smooth continuous curved motions better than straight-line motions when performing manual work?

9 What is the lowest classification of hand and arm motions?

10 What is the difference between eye focus and eye travel?

11 What advantage does the use of the legs have over the use of the arms?

12 What is a gravity feed bin and what is its advantage over a simple tray?

13 What are the desirable adjustments on a chair designed for the workplace?

14 Why are multiple-function tools better than separate tools for each function?

PROBLEMS

Therbligs

1 A plumber, kneeling on the floor next to the sink, reached for the monkey wrench in his toolbox, pushing around a few other tools before grasping the wrench and picking it up.

He then moved it to the pipe beneath the sink, positioned it onto the pipe fitting, and turned the fitting one-third of a rotation to loosen it. Once loose, he put down the wrench and continued turning by hand. Four rotations were required before the fitting was free of the mating pipe threads, during which he had to grasp and regrasp the fitting ten times due to the limited rotation ability of his own wrist. Write a list of the therbligs that comprise this motion sequence and label each basic motion with a brief description.

2 A secretary reached for the envelope with her right hand, picked it up and exchanged it to her left hand. She then reached for the letter opener with her right hand, picked it up, positioned the blade under the sealed lid of the envelope, and proceeded to slit the top of the envelope open. Still holding the envelope in her left hand, she laid the letter opener aside, and reached into the envelope with her right hand, pulled out the document, and began to read. Write a list of the therbligs that comprise this motion sequence and label each basic motion with a brief description.

3 A grocery store checkout clerk picked up the item from the checkout counter and moved it across the bar code scanner. Immediately, the scanner audibly responded that it had successfully identified and recorded the item. Since this was the only item the customer had brought into the checkout lane, the clerk punched one of the buttons on the cash register to print out the sales slip. While the register printed, the checkout clerk placed the item into an open plastic bag in front of him, picked up and closed the bag, and handed it to the customer. Write a list of the therbligs that comprise this motion sequence and label each basic motion with a brief description.

4 Sitting at her desk, a writer reached for a mechanical pencil, picked it up, positioned it, and then began to write on a pad of paper. After finishing one sentence, she lifted the pencil, and read the sentence. She then put the pencil aside and reached for the rectangular eraser nearby. Grasping and positioning it, she erased one of the words in the sentence. Write a list of the therbligs that comprise this motion sequence and label each basic motion with a brief description.

5 For the previous problem, identify some areas for possible study that might improve the method, indicating the nature of the improvement that might result.

6 A worker reached for a small part a short distance away in the workplace, picked up the part, and placed it in a vise. The worker then rotated the screw handle of the vise three turns to hold the part between the vise jaws. In rotating the screw handle, he had to grasp and regrasp the handle six times due to the limited rotation ability of his own wrist. On the final turn, he applied additional torque to tighten the vise. Write a list of the therbligs that comprise this motion sequence and label each basic motion with a brief description.

7 For the previous problem, identify some areas for possible study that might improve the method, indicating the nature of the improvement that might result.

8 An assembly worker reached for an Allen wrench in the workplace, hesitating momentarily while searching for the correct size from the group of Allen wrenches that were available. Finding the correct size, she picked it up and positioned it into the hexagonal socket of a screw that had previously been hand-turned into a threaded hole in the work unit. She then twirled the Allen wrench handle with one continuous finger and wrist motion until the screw had been rotated seven turns. At this point she gripped the Allen wrench handle with her hand and tightened the screw the last quarter turn. Write a list of the therbligs that comprise this motion sequence and label each basic motion with a brief description.

9 For the previous problem, identify some areas for possible study that might improve the method, indicating the nature of the improvement that might result.

Principles of Motion Economy

10 Charles Dickens was working well into the night, writing with his quill on one piece of paper after the next, the only light provided by the lone candle in front of him on the desk. (a) Identify some of the principles of motion economy that seem to be violated by Dickens' method of working and workplace. (b) Make recommendations for improving the work method and workplace.

11 An assembly worker is performing a repetitive manual task consisting of inserting 8 plastic pegs into 8 holes in a flat wooden board. A slight interference fit is involved in each insertion. Each work cycle consists of her picking up a board from the stack of boards located on the left side of the worktable (about 15 in. away from center, where they were placed by a material-handling worker), performing the 8 insertions, and then placing the assembled board into a rack that is next to the starting stack. Her first step in the work cycle is to reach for the top board in the stack with her right hand, pick it up, and exchange it to the left hand. While holding the board in her left hand, she picks up the pegs from a tray about 10 in. away in front of her with her right hand and inserts them into the holes in the board, one peg at a time. The rack holding the completed boards has a capacity of six assemblies. When the rack is full, the worker gets up from her worktable, picks up the loaded rack, carries it to a pallet located on the floor 3 ft away from the workplace, and places it onto the pallet. The pallet only holds four racks on one layer. A material-handling worker riding in a forklift truck must periodically take the pallet away and replace it with an empty pallet. Because of delays by the material-handling worker, the assembly worker is occasionally forced to stop working and wait for the pallet exchange to occur. (a) Identify some of the principles of motion economy that are violated in this work cycle. (b) What recommendations for improvement would you make?

12 Sitting in front of her all-wooden desk in her all-wooden chair, a writer reached for her wooden pencil, picked it up, positioned it, and then began to write on the pad of paper. After finishing one sentence, she lifted the pencil, and read the sentence. She then put the pencil aside and reached for the eraser nearby. Grasping and positioning it, she erased one of the words in the sentence. She then laid the eraser aside, picked the pencil up, made a correction, and continued writing. Periodically, she would repeat this sequence of writing, erasing, correcting, and then continuing to write. After working in this way for about two hours, she went and took a nap. (a) Identify some of the principles of motion economy that are violated in this work sequence. (b) What recommendations for improvement would you make?

13 The Calm Seas Cruise Ship Line wants to analyze the method used by its stewards to clean each of the passenger cabins on its ships. The current method used by a steward to clean one cabin is the following. First the steward knocks on the cabin door with his right hand to determine if the room is empty. Hearing no response, the steward reaches for the master key in his pocket, unlocks the door, opens it slightly and yells "housekeeping." If there is still no answer, he walks into the room to look around. After looking around, he goes back out into the hallway, and pushes his cart into the room. He then goes back into the hallway for his vacuum cleaner and carries it into the room. His first cleaning step is to vacuum the room and adjoining bathroom. He then strips the bed linen, puts it into the hamper on his cart, goes back into the hallway and walks down to the closet where the fresh bed linens are kept. He picks out a set of linen, carries them back to the room, and proceeds to make the bed. Next, he walks into the bathroom, picks up the used towels and carries them out to the cart hamper. He then goes back into the hallway and walks down to the same closet as before to obtain fresh towels for the room. He brings the towels back and places them onto racks in the bathroom. From his cart, he obtains fresh soap items for the bathroom. His final cleaning step is to pick up any trash items that may have been left in the room by the passengers. (a) Identify some of the principles of motion economy that are violated in this method. (b) Besides the principles of motion economy, what other deficiencies in the method can you identify? (c) What recommendations for improvement in the method would you make?

Facility Layout Planning and Design

The term ***facility layout*** refers to the size and shape of a facility as well as the relative locations and shapes of the functional areas (e.g., departments), equipment, workstations, storage spaces, aisles, and common areas (e.g., restrooms, cafeteria) in it. The term ***plant layout*** is also used, often synonymously with facility layout, but it suggests a more limited planning scope focused on production plants. While planning and design of production plants is an important application in facility layout, it is certainly not the only application. Facility layout includes all types of facilities: warehouses, distribution centers, office buildings, retail establishments, hospitals, and so on. Facility layout planning and design are concerned with the problems of laying out a new facility and making changes in an existing facility. These are important industrial engineering problems because their solutions affect the performance of the work systems in the facility.

The layout of a facility is an important factor in determining the overall efficiency and effectiveness of the production or service operations that are performed in it. A poor layout can result in inefficient work flows, unhappy workers, unsafe working conditions, and a diminished capacity to carry out the operational mission of the facility. A well-designed layout tends to avoid these pitfalls and to satisfy the following objectives of layout planning:

- Efficient movement of materials and people
- Logical work flow and minimum travel distances between operations
- Efficient utilization of space
- Safety and satisfaction of workers and others who use the facility
- Flexibility to meet changing future requirements
- Advancing the operational mission of the facility.

In this chapter, we discuss the various types of facility layouts and the techniques used to solve facility layout problems. We begin with a discussion of the three principal types of layouts used in production plants.

1 TYPES OF PRODUCTION PLANT LAYOUTS

There are three basic types of layouts, most commonly associated with production plants and therefore referred to as plant layouts: (1) process layout, (2) product layout, and (3) fixed-position layout. In addition, there are hybrids of the three basic types (Section 1.4) and there are other types of layouts associated with nonproduction operations such as storage and service (Section 2).

The reason for the different types of production layouts is that there are different types of production. Two important factors by which to distinguish types of production are production quantity and product variety symbolized by Q and P respectively. ***Production quantity*** refers to the number of units of a given part or product that the facility produces annually. We can distinguish three ranges of production quantity: (1) ***low production***, in which the quantities range between 1 and 100 units per year, (2) ***medium production***, in which the annual range is 100 to 10,000 units, and (3) ***high production***, in which the annual range is 10,000 to millions of units. The boundaries between the three ranges are somewhat arbitrary (author's judgment), and these boundaries may shift by an order of different magnitude, depending on industry and product type.

Product variety refers to the different product designs or types that are produced in a plant. Different products have different shapes, sizes, and styles; they perform different functions; they are sometimes intended for different markets; some have more components than others; and so forth. The number of different product types made each year can be counted. When the number of product types made in the factory is high, this indicates high product variety.

There tends to be an inverse correlation between product variety and production quantity in terms of plant operations. When product variety is high, production quantity tends to be low; and vice versa. The relationship is depicted in Figure 1. Manufacturing plants tend to specialize in a combination of production quantity and product variety that lies somewhere inside the diagonal band in Figure 1. In general, a given factory tends to be limited to the product variety value that is correlated with that production

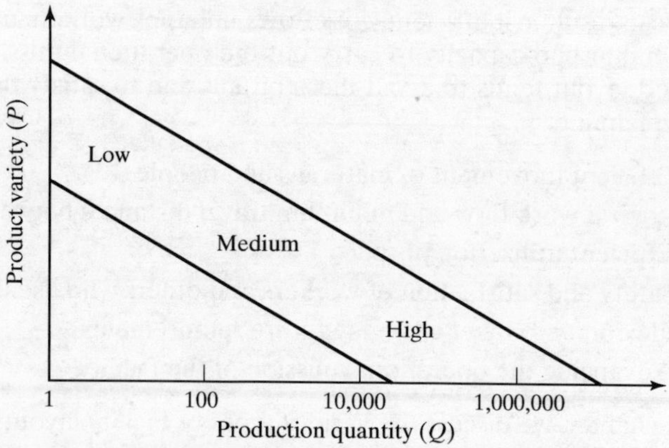

Figure 1 Relationship between product variety (P) and production quantity (Q) in discrete product manufacturing.

quantity. It has been found that certain types of plant layout are suited to certain combinations of production quantity and product variety. The sections that follow describe the three basic layout types and how they correlate with these two parameters.

1.1 Process Layouts

The distinguishing feature of a ***process layout*** is that the equipment is arranged according to function. Accordingly, the term ***functional layout*** is also used for this layout type. In a plant that does machining, the different types of machine tools are in different departments. There is a lathe department, a milling department, a drilling department, and so on, as depicted in Figure 2. The process layout is most suited to low and medium production quantities where the product variety is medium to high. In this type of production, different parts or products are processed through different operation sequences in batches, and the process layout accommodates these differences by allowing each batch of parts to follow its own routing through the departments. Some batches start their processing in the milling department, while others begin in the lathe department or drilling or some other department. There is no common work-flow path through the plant that is followed by all work units. Each part type must be transported from one operation to the next in its own unique sequence, and this generally means a considerable material-handling effort in the plant to move parts. It also means high work-in-process inventory in a process layout. The material-handling equipment must be able to deal with the variations in routing, and forklift trucks are common equipment in process layouts.

The process layout is noted for its flexibility and versatility. It can deal with a variety of different operations and operation sequences for different part and product designs. The equipment found in process layout plants is general purpose. It can be adapted to a variety of different operations and setups, but skill is required of the machine operators to make the adaptations. Because of the variety and requirements of the work,

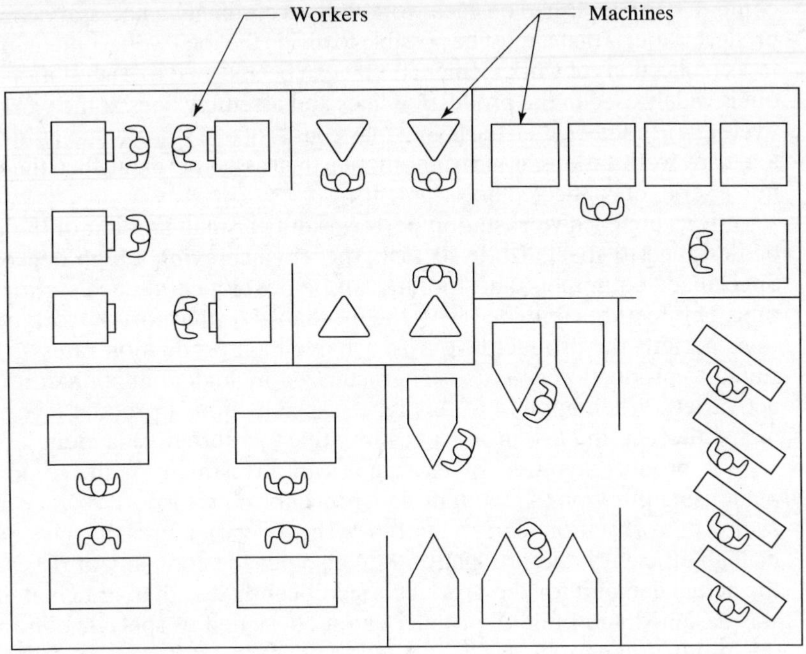

Figure 2 Process layout.

the workforce consists of skilled workers who are well paid. The price of versatility is low efficiency. Production rates tend to be reduced because of the need to frequently change over the equipment setups.

1.2 Product Layouts

In a ***product layout***, the workstations and equipment are located along the line of flow of the work units, as depicted in Figure 3. The work units are typically moved along the flow line by a powered conveyor. At each workstation, a small amount of the total work

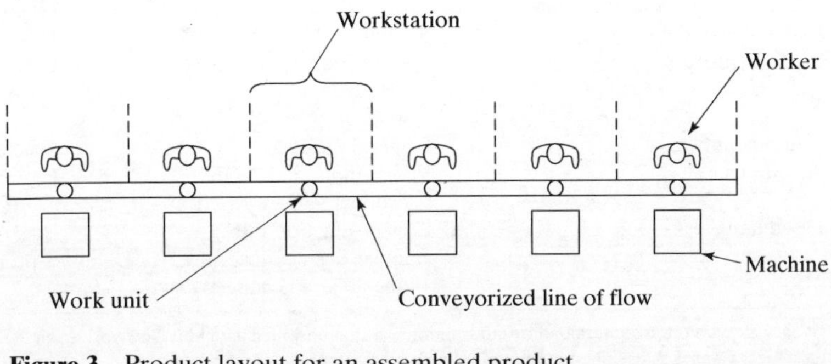

Figure 3 Product layout for an assembled product.

content is accomplished on each work unit. Accordingly, a necessary condition for using a product layout is that it must be possible to divide the total work content into relatively small tasks (collections of work elements) that can be assigned to each station. The product layout is widely used in the production lines and assembly lines. If the workstations are relatively few in number, then the layout may consist of one straight line, as in our figure. If there are many workstations, as in an automobile final assembly plant, then the layout is arranged into a series of connected line segments.

Because each workstation performs only a small amount of the total work, it can be designed to specialize in its task, thereby achieving a high degree of proficiency. Specialized equipment and tooling can be developed at each station to reduce cycle time. This feature combined with the mechanized transport of work units between stations permits the product layout to achieve high production rates. It is therefore best suited to production situations characterized by high annual quantities and low product variety. When applied to this type of production, a product layout is noted for its high efficiency and low product cost relative to alternative layouts.

A product layout involves a significant investment by the company that builds a plant using this type of layout design. Mechanized transport of work units and specialization of workstations carry a high cost. These very features that give the product layout its high efficiency and production rate also put the company at risk if it turns out that the actual demand for the product is significantly less than anticipated when the plant was designed and built. A product layout, designed to specialize in the production of one product, cannot be easily adapted to produce a different product. Accordingly, the disadvantage of a product layout is that its specialized equipment and arrangement may become obsolete when demand for the product runs out. The automotive companies must deal with this issue every time they change car models. Major revisions and investments may be required to change over the plant for the new model.

The process layout and product layout are often compared, even though they are intended for quite different production situations. Table 1 summarizes the features and differences.

TABLE 1 Comparison of Process Layout and Product Layout

Comparison Feature	Process Layout	Product Layout
Annual production quantities	Low or medium	High
Product variety	High	Low
Production rate and efficiency	Low	High
Labor skill and wage rate[a]	Skilled, higher wage rates	Unskilled, lower wage rates
Work-in-process	Batch production usually results in high work-in-process	Lower work-in-process, one work unit per workstation
Equipment type	General purpose	Special purpose
Advantages	Versatility to deal with product variety	High production rate, high efficiency
Disadvantages	Low production rates, low efficiency, lost time due to setup changeovers	Risk of obsolescence, limited product variety

[a]Wage rates are often confounded by labor unions, so that unskilled assembly line workers in the automotive industry may earn higher wages than skilled nonunion workers in machine shops and foundries.

1.3 Fixed-Position Layouts

A ***fixed-position layout*** is one in which the product remains in one location in the plant during its fabrication, and the equipment and workers are brought to the product to work on it. This kind of arrangement is shown in Figure 4. As the figure suggests, the reason for keeping the product in the same location is because it is large and heavy, and therefore difficult to transport inside the facility. It is easier to move the processing equipment to the product than to move the product to the equipment. Examples of such products include ships, large aircraft, railway locomotives, and heavy machinery. Production quantities for each item are usually low, and product variety is high.

The kind of work performed on products made in a fixed-position layout typically includes a large proportion of assembly operations. Component parts are often manufactured elsewhere, usually in process layout plants, and then brought in for final assembly to the product. Because of the high assembly content and low product quantities, much manual labor is involved. The type of equipment used in the fabrication and assembly operations tends to be mobile or portable.

1.4 Hybrid Layouts

There are two hybrids of the three basic types of layouts: (1) cellular, which tries to combine the best features of process and product layouts, and (2) combinations of fixed-position layouts and process or product layouts.

Cellular Layouts. Although product variety was identified as a quantitative parameter (the number of different product types made by the plant or company), this parameter is much less exact than production quantity because details on how much the designs differ is not captured simply by the number of different designs. Differences between an air conditioner and an automobile are far greater than between an air conditioner and a heat pump. Products can be different, but the extent of the differences may be small or great. The automotive industry provides some examples to illustrate this point. Each of the U.S. automotive companies produces cars with two or three different

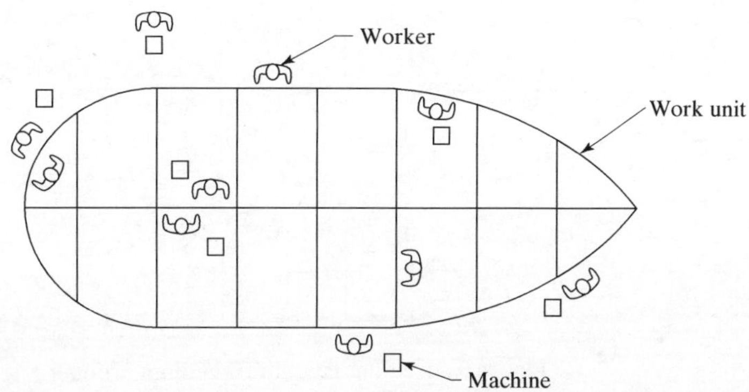

Figure 4 Fixed-position layout for a large fabricated product.

nameplates in the same assembly plant, although the body styles and other design features are nearly the same. In different plants, the same auto company builds heavy trucks. Let us use the terms "hard" and "soft" to describe these differences in product variety. ***Hard product variety*** is when the products differ substantially. In an assembled product, hard variety is characterized by a low proportion of common parts among the products; in many cases, there are no common parts. The difference between a car and a heavy truck is hard. ***Soft product variety*** is when there are only small differences between products, such as the differences between car models made on the same production line. There is a high proportion of common parts among assembled products whose variety is soft. The variety between different product types tends to be hard variety. The variety between different models within the same product type tends to be soft.

Product layouts can be designed to accommodate assembled products characterized by soft variety. It is common practice in the automotive industry to design final assembly plants with the capability to cope with minor product variations. Cars coming off the line have differences in options and trim representing several levels and/or models and sometimes different nameplates of the same basic car design. An assembly line capable of producing multiple models of the same basic product is called a ***mixed-model assembly line***, which is arranged as a product layout.

When the product variety is greater than soft but softer than hard, and the production quantities are in the medium range, then an alternative to the product layout must be used. The traditional approach to layout design would be to use batch production and arrange the plant as a process layout. The problem with batch production is the lost time between batches due to setup changes. Given this combination of production parameters (medium product variety and medium production quantities), it is sometimes possible to organize the work around a ***cellular layout***, depicted in Figure 5. In this layout design, the work units flow between workstations, roughly as in a production line, but each workstation is equipped to deal with a variety of part or product styles without the need for time-consuming changeovers. In effect a cellular layout can be thought of as a combination of product and process layouts. It attempts to combine the efficiency of a product layout with the versatility of a process layout.

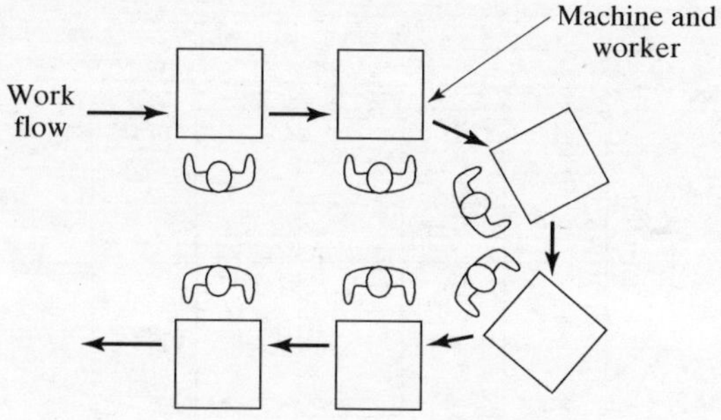

Figure 5 Cellular layout for medium product variety and medium production quantities.

It achieves neither objective perfectly, but it is more efficient than a process layout and more versatile than a product layout.

The cellular layout is associated with a type of production called ***cellular manufacturing***, in which the workstations and equipment are configured into cells consisting of several workstations that are tooled to make families of similar parts or products without the need to make drastic changes in the setup for each different work unit. Cellular manufacturing relies on the principles of ***group technology***—a manufacturing philosophy in which similar parts (or products) are identified and grouped together to take advantage of their similarities in design and production.

Combinations of Fixed-Position Layout and Process or Product Layout. In a pure fixed-position layout, the product remains in the same location throughout its fabrication. In practice, large products such as aircraft and ships are not built all at one location. The actual work arrangements are hybrids of either fixed-position layout and process layout (for ships), or fixed-position layout and product layout (for aircraft).

A shipyard is an example of a combination of fixed-position and process layouts. Depending on the sizes of the ships produced, one shipyard may complete only a few ships per year, and the fabrication time of one ship may be several years. Shipyards are laid out more or less as process layouts, with fabrication departments organized by function; for example, a cutting department that performs flame cutting of large steel plates, a forming department that shapes the plates to form the hull components, and a welding department where the components are brought to fabricate modules of the ship. There may be multiple departments of a given type, each specializing in a certain category of operations. Movement of materials is by forklift or similar large industrial truck for components and welded sections below a certain tonnage limit, and large-capacity cranes are used to move the larger pieces and the completed modules. Because of its large size, each module is built at a single location (fixed-position layout) in the welding department. When each module is completed, it is moved into position near the water so the completed ship can be lowered and floated (as the reader may have guessed, shipyards are located next to a body of water). In this final location, each module is welded to other modules to gradually assemble the complete ship, one module at a time. The key characteristic for success of this final fabrication procedure is that the shapes of each hull module must match its mating module at their connections. If the hull sections do not align with each other, it is a major problem.

The final assembly plant for large commercial aircraft can be considered to be a combination of fixed-position layout and product layout. An example of such a facility is Boeing's plant in Everett, Washington, which produces 747 and 777 models. The main assembly building at the Everett plant has one of the largest interior volumes of any building in the world. In the final assembly area, the plane is assembled, not all at one location but gradually in stages, moving the partially assembled aircraft through a series of workstations where workers who specialize in certain tasks are grouped. At the first station, assembly of the fuselage is initiated, and then the work progresses at the following stations, building the fuselage and adding internal fittings (e.g., seats, galleys, restrooms, etc.), attaching the wings and tail sections, and finally installing the engines. At each station, the organization of work is around a fixed-position layout. The plane spends several days at each location. Industrial trucks are used to move it from one station to the next, as in the operation of a product layout.

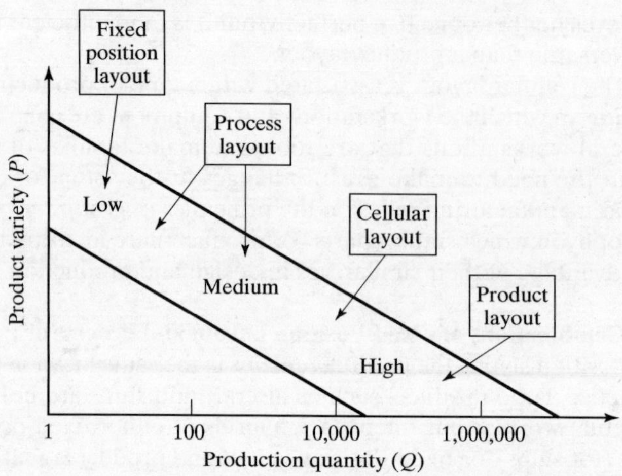

Figure 6 Types of plant layout used for different levels of production quantity (Q) and product variety (P).

1.5 Plant Layout Applications

A manufacturing company attempts to organize its plants in the most efficient way to satisfy the particular mission of each plant. The result is that we have the various plant layout types, each intended for its type of production. Figure 6 summarizes the appropriate applications for most of the production plant layouts we have discussed, using annual production quantity and product variety as the parameters that define the application.

2 OTHER TYPES OF LAYOUTS

Just as different plant layouts are used for different types of production, there are additional layout types used for operations other than production. We briefly identify some of these other layout types in this section.

2.1 Warehouse Layouts

A ***warehouse*** is a facility for storing merchandise, commodities, or other items. The layout of a warehouse must be planned for the principal function of a warehouse, which is storage. However, storage is not the only function, and consideration must be given to other functions that also occur in a warehouse facility. The four main warehouse functions are (1) receiving, (2) storing, (3) order picking, and (4) shipping. These same functions occur at all storage facilities, including distribution centers, factory storerooms, and tool cribs. In addition to the four functions, the facility may also be required to perform additional services, such as preparing special labeling and packaging to satisfy particular customer requirements.

While most of the volumetric space in a storage facility is devoted to storage, areas for the other functions must also be planned. One of the important decisions in warehouse layout design is where to locate the receiving and shipping functions. The obvious answer is that they must be located against an exterior wall of the building, and access must be provided to the transportation infrastructure (e.g., highway, rail line, seaport, airport). But should the two functions be combined at one location or separated? Figure 7 illustrates the two alternatives. The advantages of centralizing receiving and shipping at one location include (1) sharing of personnel and material-handling equipment; (2) sharing of docks and docking space; for example, if at a particular time of day, there are more incoming trucks than departing trucks, some of the docks normally used for shipping can be used for receiving; and (3) facilitating ***cross-docking***, which refers to the immediate transfer of received materials to shipping without being entered into storage. The incoming materials from suppliers are shipped to customers without the steps of storing and order picking.

The advantages of separating or decentralizing the two functions of receiving and shipping include the following: (1) reduced congestion in the dock areas, (2) reduced risk of confusing incoming loads with outgoing materials, and (3) the layout can be designed to provide a flow-through of materials, from receiving to storage to shipping, as indicated in Figure 7(b).

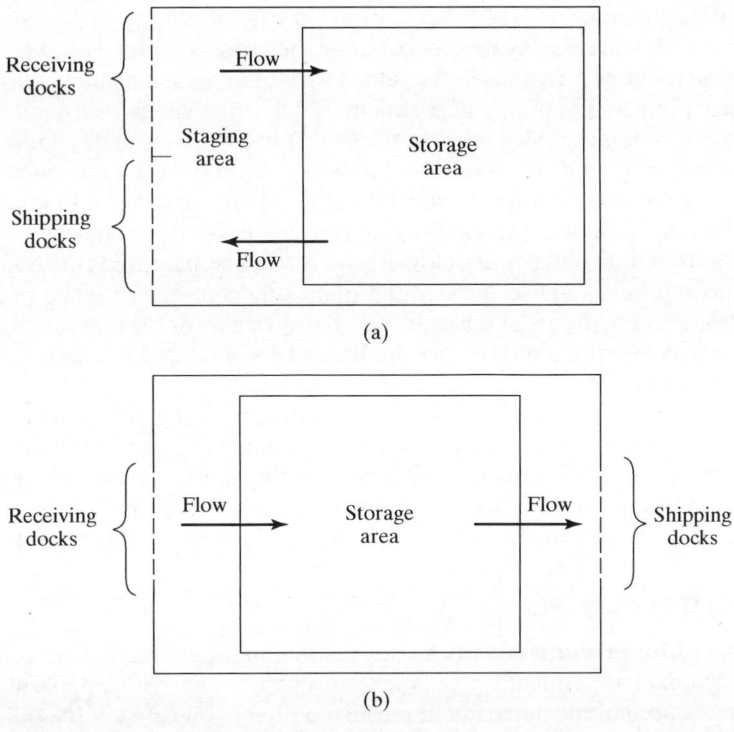

Figure 7 Warehouse layouts: (a) centralized receiving and shipping in a single dock area and (b) decentralized receiving and shipping to achieve a flow-through in the storage facility.

2.2 Project Layouts

A ***project layout*** usually applies to a construction project, in which the appropriate work teams and equipment for the type of project have been brought to the construction site. The layout is temporary because the project has a scheduled completion date. The product of the project (e.g., the structure) will remain at the site, but the workers and equipment will vacate upon the project's completion. The project layout has similarities with the fixed-position layout. In a fixed-position layout, the product is large and heavy and difficult to move; in a project layout, the product is large and heavy and cannot be moved. In both layouts, the workers and equipment are brought to the product. The difference between them is that when the product is completed in a fixed-position layout, it is transported away from the site and the workers and equipment remain, whereas when the product is completed in a project layout, the workers and equipment are transported away from the site and the product remains.

2.3 Service Facility Layouts

Each type of service has its own layout requirements for best achieving its mission and interacting with its customers. Our purpose here is to provide a brief overview of the facility layout issues. In Section 2.4, we provide a separate discussion of the layout issues in office planning.

Most service layouts are based on the process layout. For organizations that accomplish multiple functions in the same facility, the personnel and equipment are organized according to function or department. A department store is a good example of a process layout in retail service operations. While the objectives in designing a process layout for manufacturing are to minimize the flow of materials, the analogous objectives in a service organization are related to the flow of information and people (e.g., workers and customers). In most cases, the goal is to minimize the distances traveled by paperwork (information) and people. However, in retail merchandising, the objective is to maximize the exposure of customers to the items on display in order to promote greater sales. Accordingly, the aisles designed into the store layout for customers to travel are not necessarily the shortest distances but instead are intended to exhibit as much merchandise as possible.

Another aspect of facility design in service organizations is aesthetics. Although not as important a consideration in a manufacturing or warehouse facility, the general appearance and ambiance of a service facility must be pleasant for those who work in it and for its customers. An important aspect of a service is that the customer experiences it. Pleasant surroundings promote a more satisfying customer experience.

2.4 Office Layouts

An ***office layout*** is usually an approximation of a process layout in the sense that the personnel are typically grouped according to functions or departments. The personnel in the accounting department are all together in one area of the office building; the purchasing department personnel are in another area, and so on, depending on what functions occupy the building. Within each department, a work-flow pattern usually exists

TABLE 2 Office Space Guidelines for Various Positions in the Organization

Position in Organization	Office Area	Position in Organization	Office Area
Top-level executives	425 sq ft	Modular workstation	100 sq ft
Middle-level executives	350 sq ft	Conference room	25 sq ft/person
Supervisors	200 sq ft	Reception room	35 sq ft/person
Office employees	75–100 sq ft		

Source: [4].

and can be used to determine the proper placement of personnel and their offices or desks. To give an obvious example, the executive secretary of a vice president should be located near the VP's office, not down the hall. The flow of work among departments should also be used to decide their locations in the building. For example, the data processing and accounting departments should be near each other because of the work flow and communication that occurs between them. Noisemaking departments, such as printing and duplicating, should be located near each other but away from departments that require a noise-free environment, such as functions that accomplish creative work. Executive officers of the organization should be located away from heavily traveled areas. There are usually status issues that place their offices in more secluded regions of the building, such as the upper floors of a multistory office building.

One of the office layout decisions that must be made in the beginning stages of planning an office complex is whether to use a traditional walled office layout or an open office concept. The walled office layout is characterized by many private offices with permanent walls defining each floor plan of the building. The arrangement and locations of offices are based on the hierarchical structure of the organization, where exterior corner offices reflect a higher rank or position than internal offices. The size of the office also indicates position and importance, as indicated by the recommendations listed in Table 2.

Trends in office layout design tend to favor the open office concept, and more office buildings are being constructed or renovated today based on this design approach. The ***open office concept*** means that the office layout consists of large open areas in which modular furniture and partitions rather than permanent walls are used to designate and separate workstations. The workers in each area are organized to promote efficient work flow. Function-oriented workstations are often used in place of conventional desks in open offices. Several advantages are given for using the open office concept rather than permanent walled offices [4]: (1) lower construction costs for buildings based on the open office concept, (2) easier supervision of employees, (3) flexibility in making periodic changes in office layout that may be required, (4) better control of heating, cooling, and lighting, and (5) improved communications among employees.

3 SYSTEMATIC LAYOUT PLANNING

In this section we discuss ***systematic layout planning*** (SLP), an approach to plant layout design developed by Richard Muther [2,3]. There are other approaches to plant layout planning, but this one is the most widely used. SLP is most applicable to process

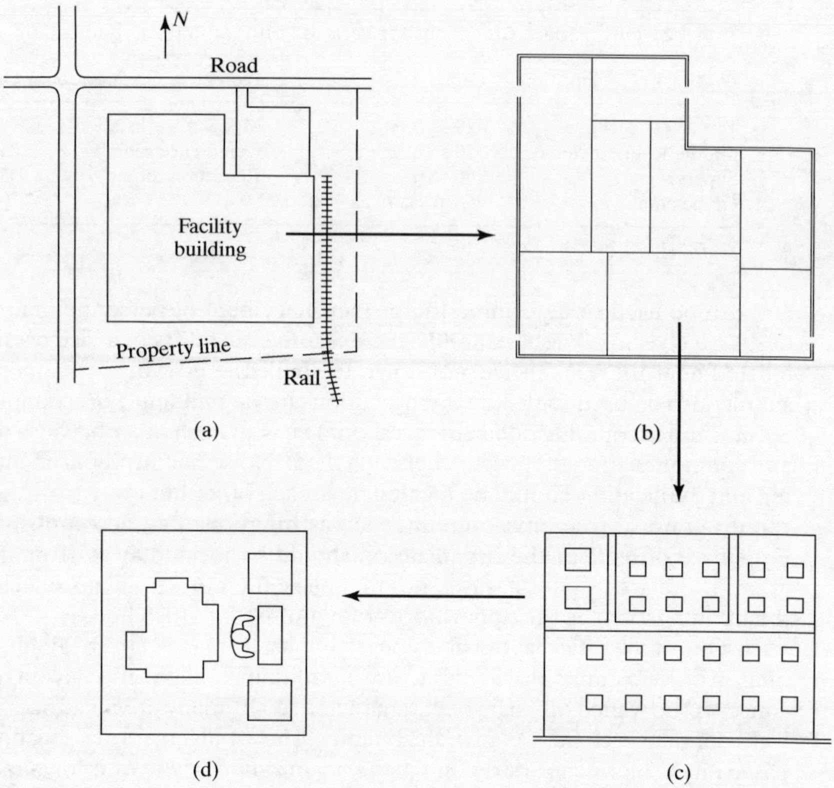

Figure 8 Types of plant layout: (a) site layout, (b) block layout, (c) detailed layout, and (d) workstation layout.

layouts, but the initial definition and analysis steps in the procedure must be performed for any type of layout. Process layouts are widely used in the manufacturing industry, and many other facilities are also based on the process layout type (e.g., department stores, offices). In Section 3.1, the SLP procedure is applied to the design of process layouts. In Section 3.2, SLP is adapted for product layouts.

Before discussing SLP and its application to process layouts, it should be noted that there are several levels of detail in plant layout designs, as illustrated in Figure 8: (a) ***site layout***, which shows how the building will be located on the property, indicating position and orientation relative to roads and rail sidings; (b) ***block layout***, which shows the arrangement and sizes of departments in the building (c) ***detailed layout***, which shows how workstations and equipment are arranged in each department, and (d) ***workstation layout***, which indicates the locations of equipment, workbench, work-in-process inventory, and worker floor space for each workstation type.

3.1 Design of Process Layouts

Systematic layout planning is most appropriate for designing a new plant (a so-called "green field" facility), and it assumes that the plant location has already been decided. The following steps in SLP are identified in the context of a production plant design:[1]

1. Determine requirements and collect data.
2. Analyze material flows.
3. Define activity relationships and develop activity relationship chart.
4. Construct activity relationship diagram.
5. Determine space requirements.
6. Construct space relationship diagram.
7. Make adjustments and add allowances.
8. Develop block layout.
9. Develop detailed layout.

Step 1. Determine Requirements and Collect Data. Each plant layout problem is unique in the sense that it is being planned to satisfy a unique set of specifications: (1) a specific product or set of products, (2) a particular set of manufacturing and/or assembly processes, and (3) specified quantities of the parts and products to be produced. Rarely if ever will two production plants have exactly the same specifications. The first step in planning a plant layout is to determine the specified requirements for the plant. Muther refers to these as P-Q-R-S-T requirements, where each letter stands for the following requirement:

P—product
Q—quantity
R—routing
S—supporting services
T—time issues

To design a plant, we must know what products and/or parts (P) are to be produced and how many units of each (Q) are to be made. The product and part information is usually known in advance, although changes are likely during the life of the facility. If the plant will produce parts only (no final assembled products), then the general characteristics of the parts must be known. Product information includes starting materials, part and product designs, bills of material, and other documentation available from the product design department. The quantity information is more problematic, because that number depends on the demand for the product, and for a new product the demand can only be estimated. Nevertheless, the plant must be built to have a certain production capacity, so the quantity requirements must be specified. The P-Q data can be displayed

[1]The steps in SLP listed here are slightly modified from those published in [2], and some of the terms we use are different to be consistent with the rest of our terminology. We have attempted to retain the basic approach developed by Muther.

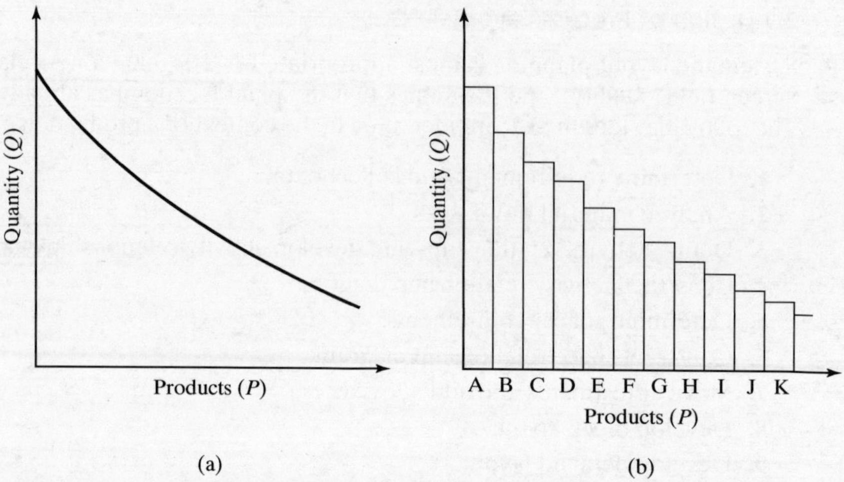

Figure 9 The P-Q curve shown in (a) is actually a Pareto chart shown in (b).

on a P-Q curve, as shown in Figure 9. (This is not the same as the P and Q data shown earlier in Figure 1.) The P-Q curve shown in Figure 9 (a) is actually a Pareto chart (Figure 9 b), in which the products are arranged along the *x*-axis in the order of their annual production quantities.

The shape of the P-Q curve provides information about the type of plant that will be required. For example the P-Q curve shown in Figure 10 (a) requires a process layout because product variety is high and quantities are medium. The P-Q curve shown in

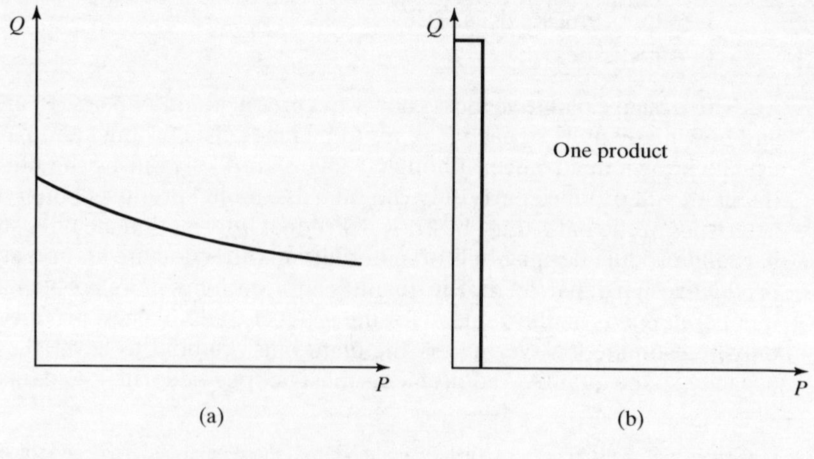

Figure 10 Two P-Q curves indicating (a) a process layout and (b) a product layout.

Figure 10 (b) indicates that one product dominates production, and so a more specialized layout dedicated to that product is required, probably a product layout.

The requirements related to routing (R) must next be considered. Through what manufacturing processes will the products and/or parts be routed? In effect this requirement specifies the manufacturing processes that will be conducted in the plant. The sequence of operations for each part can be used to plan the arrangement of the equipment and their corresponding departments. Routing data can be obtained from a ***route sheet***, a production document that lists the operations and machines that are used to process a given part or product. Such a list indicates the sequence of machines that the part must visit during its processing, and thus it provides the routing of the part in the plant. The routing data combined with the quantity data are used to determine how many of each type of processing equipment will be needed.

The requirements for supporting services (S) will involve additional provisions that must be included in the facility but are not related directly to the product or its manufacture. Such services include utilities (e.g., electrical, water, heating, ventilation, air conditioning), restrooms, locker rooms, cafeteria (if one is to be included), offices, and so on. Storage areas are sometimes included among the S data, or they may be included as integral components in the routing data. Supporting services often require a significant proportion of the total plant area and must be given adequate consideration.

The requirements for time issues (T) are related to the operation of the facility as well as the schedule to design the layout and construct the building. Time issues related to plant operations include how many shifts the plant will operate. Will it operate one 8-hour shift and five days per week, or will it operate on a 24/7 schedule? If the plant performs hot processing operations (e.g., casting, molding, heat treating), then it may have to run 24 hours per day to avoid the cost of heating up the equipment each day. In other cases, management must decide the hours of operation, which will affect plant size and equipment requirements. Theoretically, a plant that operates three shifts per day needs only one-third the floor space and one-third the number of pieces of equipment as a plant that runs one shift per day.

The P-Q-R-S-T data provide the basis for making design decisions and calculations in the later steps of the systematic layout planning procedure.

Step 2. Analyze Material Flows. In a process layout, material handling and material flows are important issues because of the cost and inefficiencies involved. A production facility designed around a process layout is typically a job shop or a batch production plant. The staff required to move and store materials in the plant is usually a significant proportion of the total manpower, and the handling operations are characterized by delays that can adversely affect production. Analysis of material flows is an important step in the planning procedure.[2]

The tools and techniques used in the analysis of material flows in systematic layout planning involve charting techniques covered in earlier chapters:

- Operation charts for indicating sequence of processing, assembly, and inspection operations of a product

[2]To stress the point, Muther states: "Flow-of-materials analysis is the heart of layout planning whenever movement of materials is a major portion of the process" [2, p. 4–1].

TABLE 3 A Part Routing Matrix

Part	A	B	C	D	E	F	G	H	I
Weekly Quantities	50	25	30	5	18	66	55	78	15
1. Cut (power saw)	1	1		1			1	1	
2. Turn (lathe)	2	2	1						
3. Face (lathe)		3	2						
4. Drill (drill press)	3		3	3		3	4	3	2
5. Tap (drill press)			4	4		4			3
6. Slab mill (milling machine)				2		1		2	
7. Face mill (milling machine)					1	2	2		1
8. Bore (boring mill)					2		3		4
9. Grind (surface grinder)				5	3	5		4	
10. Grind (cylindrical grinder)	4								
11. Grind (centerless grinder)			5						
12. Clean (cleaning station)	5	4	6	6	4		5		5

- Flow process charts for indicating the processing operations and other details in the production of single entities (e.g., parts)
- From-To charts for indicating quantities and directions of material flows between workstations and departments

In situations where there are multiple parts or products, as is typical of a process layout plant, a simple way of tabulating the part processing data is to use a ***part routing matrix***, shown in Table 3. In this matrix, parts (or products) are listed along the top row (letters in Table 3). For each part, the weekly (or other time period) quantities are shown in the second row. Starting in the third row, all of the processing operations to be performed in the plant are listed in the left-hand column, and the entries for each part indicate which operations are used to process the part and the sequence in which the operations are performed on it. Accordingly, the part routing matrix indicates the usage of all manufacturing operations that will be needed in the plant. The matrix can be used to develop a From-To chart indicating the flow of materials in the plant.

Step 3. Define Activity Relationships and Develop Activity Relationship Chart. Material flows are an important component in deciding the activity relationships among different departments or functions that will be located in the facility.[3] ***Activity relationships*** indicate the relative need to place activities or departments in close proximity to each other. The activity relationships are defined by closeness ratings that are assigned to pairs of departments. The value of a closeness rating is often determined directly from the amount of material that flows between two departments. The six closeness ratings used in systematic layout planning are defined in Table 4. There are two reasons for using closeness ratings rather than the numerical data: (1) visualizing and

[3]The word "activity" usually refers to departments that are or will be located in the facility. The word may also refer to functions, work centers, operations, or groups of operations for which there is a need to define activity relationships.

TABLE 4 Closeness Ratings in Systematic Layout Planning

Closeness Rating	Definition
A	Absolutely necessary for departments to be next to each other
E	Especially important
I	Important
O	Ordinary
U	Unimportant
X	Undesirable for the departments to be located near each other

interpreting large amounts of quantitative material flow data is a difficult process and (2) the closeness ratings are sometimes based on factors other than material flows.

Among the factors that determine the closeness rating for pairs of departments, material flow is the most important, at least for departments between which material flow occurs. But other factors may affect the decision to assign a particular value of closeness rating. For pairs of departments between which no materials flow, one or more of these other factors may be the only reason for assigning a given closeness rating. The following factors are included (based largely on a list in Muther [2]):

1. Material flow
2. Need for contact between personnel
3. Use of the same equipment
4. Sharing of common records
5. Sharing of supervision or technical support staff
6. Use of the same utilities
7. High noise level
8. Emission of fumes, odors, etc.

Note that some of the factors (7 and 8) are reasons for separating a given department from others. In some cases, it is undesirable for departments to be located next to each other, so an "X" closeness rating should be assigned. Departments such as drop forging (high noise level) and painting (emission of fumes) are likely to be in this category.

The ***activity relationship chart*** is a tabular means of displaying the closeness ratings among all pairs of activities or departments. The usual format for the activity relationship chart is illustrated in Figure 11. In each cell representing the intersection of two departments, the letter code for the closeness rating is inserted in the top half of the cell, and the reason(s) for assigning the rating is inserted in the bottom half, using numerical codes such as the list of factors given above. Although Muther devised the form of the activity relationship chart shown in Figure 11, a more traditional tabular format can also be used, as illustrated in Table 5.

In many cases, the main reason for a particular closeness rating is material flow. The numerical values of material flow—for example, those listed in a From-To chart—must be converted into a corresponding letter code. One possible way of making this conversion

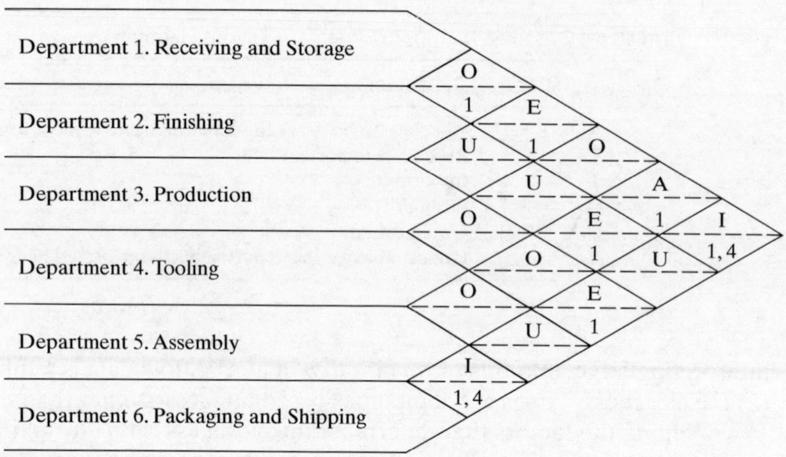

Figure 11 Activity relationship chart.

TABLE 5 Tabular Format for the Activity Relationship Chart.[a]

	Departments					
To:	1	2	3	4	5	6
From: 1	—	O	E	O	A	I
2	1	—	U	U	E	U
3	1		—	O	O	E
4				—	O	U
5	1	1			—	I
6	1, 4		1		1, 4	—

[a]Closeness ratings are shown above the main diagonal and reasons for assigning the closeness ratings are shown below the main diagonal.

is to find the highest value of material flow between two departments and divide by 4 to obtain four ranges of material flow values. All values of material flow in the highest range are converted to an "A" closeness rating, the values in the next range are converted to an "E" rating, and so on. The "U" closeness rating is assigned to pairs of departments between which there is no material flow. The following example illustrates the procedure.

Example 1 Converting Material Flows to Closeness Ratings

The anticipated material flows between six production departments are given in the From-To chart shown in Table 6. The six departments are (1) receiving and storage, (2) finishing, (3) production, (4) tooling, (5) assembly, and (6) packaging and shipping. The values in the

TABLE 6 From-To Chart Showing Material Flows and Directions in Example 1

	Departments					
To:	1	2	3	4	5	6
From: 1	—	27		15	110	
2		—			42	
3	82		—			74
4			21	—	30	
5	10	26	8		—	53
6	49					—

TABLE 7 Flow-Between Chart Showing Total Material Flows Between Departments in Example 1

	Departments					
Between	1	2	3	4	5	6
1	—	27	82	15	120	49
2		—			68	
3			—	21	8	74
4				—	30	
5					—	53
6						—

table indicate the number of unit loads that must be moved per day and their direction. Convert the material flows to closeness ratings and show them in an activity relationship chart.

Solution: The first step is to aggregate the data in the From-To chart into the cells located above the main diagonal to create a ***flow-between chart***. For example, the flow from departments 1 to 5 is added to the flow from 5 to 1 to determine the total material flow between those two departments. The flow-between chart for our data is shown in Table 7. The highest value in the flow-between chart is 120 between departments 1 and 5. Dividing this value by 4 gives the following ranges on which to base closeness ratings: 0 through 30 is rated "O," 31 through 60 is rated "I," 61 through 90 is rated "E," and 91 through 120 is rated "A." The resulting activity relationship chart is shown in Figure 11. ■

Step 4. Construct Activity Relationship Diagram. The ***activity relationship diagram*** is a graphical means of displaying the closeness ratings among pairs of activities. It uses blocks (or nodes) to represent the activities, and the blocks are connected by lines indicating the closeness ratings. The closeness ratings in the diagram are identified either by color or by number of lines and type of lines. Muther recommends the color and line conventions listed in Table 8 [3]. An initial iteration of the activity relationship diagram for the departments in Example 1 is shown in Figure 12. Also included in Table 8 (last column

TABLE 8 Closeness Rating Conventions in the Activity Relationship Diagram

Closeness Rating	Definition	Color Code	Line Code	Numerical Value
A	Absolutely necessary	Red	////	4
E	Especially important	Orange	///	3
I	Important	Green	//	2
O	Ordinary	Blue	/	1
U	Unimportant	(no line)	(no line)	0
X	Undesirable	Brown	﹏﹏	−5

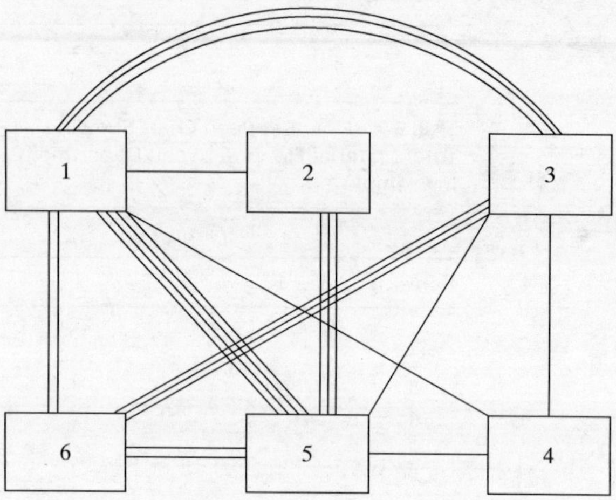

Figure 12 First iteration of an activity relationship diagram for Example 1.

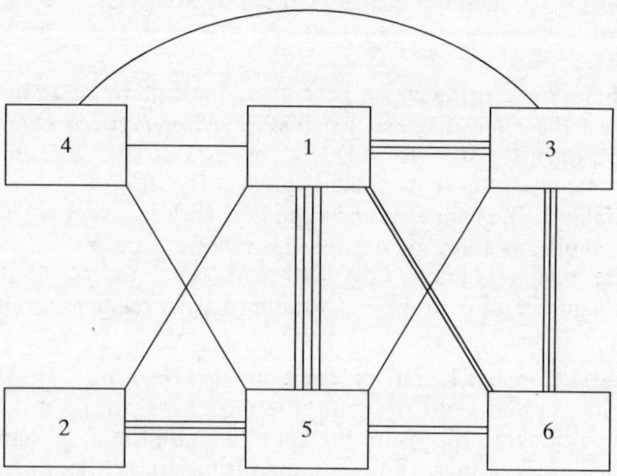

Figure 13 An improved activity relationship diagram for Example 1.

on right) are numerical values that can be used to assess the quality of a given layout during the development of the final block layout during step 8 in the SLP procedure.

It is useful to try to improve on the starting activity relationship diagram, by rearranging the blocks so as to place departments with high closeness ratings near each other. Also, an attempt should be made to separate any departments with "X" ratings. Several iterations may be required to obtain a satisfactory arrangement. Figure 13 shows one possible arrangement of blocks that seems to be an improvement over the original diagram in Figure 12.

Step 5. Determine Space Requirements. The blocks in the activity relationship diagram provide no indication of the relative sizes of the departments. All blocks in the diagram are the same size. The fifth step in systematic layout planning is to determine the space requirements of each department. This can be done using the following procedure:

1. List all of the workstation types that will be located in each department. A workstation includes the worker and any equipment associated with the work. In a machine shop, there will be a variety of workstation types, such as milling, drilling, turning, and so on. Within each category, there may be further subdivisions that are appropriate. Let i = a subscript that will be used to identify each workstation type. All workstations of a given type i are virtually identical in terms of space requirements.
2. Determine the floor space requirement for each workstation type. This may be based on an existing workstation of similar type or by designing a new workstation layout for each type. The floor area so determined must include floor space for equipment, worker(s), work-in-process inventory at the station, and so forth. Access to the machinery for maintenance must also be provided. Let A_i = floor space required for workstation type i.
3. Determine the number of workstations of each type that will be required. This can be done by the methods based on total workload divided by the available time per workstation. Letting n_i = the number of workstations of type i that are required,

$$n_i = \text{Minimum Integer} \geq \frac{WL_i}{AT_i} \tag{1}$$

where WL_i = total workload that must be accomplished in a certain period (e.g., per week, month, year), expressed in hours of work per period; and AT_i = available time at the workstation in the same period. This calculation is likely to result in an n_i value ending with a decimal fraction, and the value should be rounded up to the next integer, since it is not possible to have a fractional workstation.

4. If the workload for a given workstation type i consists of multiple part or product types, then the following summation process can be used:

$$WL_i = \sum_j Q_{ij} T_{cij} \tag{2}$$

where Q_{ij} = quantity of part type j that is processed on workstation type i in the period of interest, and T_{cij} = the average cycle time of part type j that is processed on workstation type i during the period of interest. If setup time is not apportioned in the value of T_{cij}, then the workload associated with setups must be included in the value of WL_i. And other factors may also have to be included in the workload and available time determinations, such as worker efficiency, reliability, and scrap rate.

5. Determine the total area required for each workstation type. This is found by multiplying the number of workstations by the area for each workstation; that is,

$$TA_i = n_i A_i \tag{3}$$

where TA_i = total area required for all workstations of type i.

6. Determine the total area in each department by summing the areas for all of the workstation types included in that department.

$$DA_k = \sum_{i \epsilon k} TA_i \tag{4}$$

where DA_k = area of department k, and the summation process is carried out over all workstation types (i) that are included in department k.

Example 2 Determination of Floor Space Requirements

Four types of workstations will be included in department 1. The floor area for each type (in square meters), workloads per week, and available times per week are given in the table below. Determine the total area required for these four workstation types.

Workstation Type	Area per Workstation (m^2)	Workload per Week (hr)	Available Time per Week (hr)
1	16	262	38
2	20	123	36
3	15	244	38
4	25	89	37

Solution: For workstation type 1, the number of workstations required is calculated as

$$n_1 = \frac{262}{38} = 6.89$$

which is rounded up to 7 workstations.

The total area required for workstations of type 1 is

$$TA_1 = 7(16\ m^2) = 112\ m^2$$

The values for the other workstations are calculated in the table below. We can see that the computations represent an ideal application for spreadsheet software.

i	A_i (m^2)	WL_i (hr)	AT_i (hr)	n_i	Integer n_i	TA_i (m^2)
1	16	262	38	6.89	7	122
2	20	123	36	3.42	4	80
3	15	184	38	4.84	5	75
4	24	98	35	2.80	3	72

The total area required by four workstation types (DA_1) is 349 m^2. ■

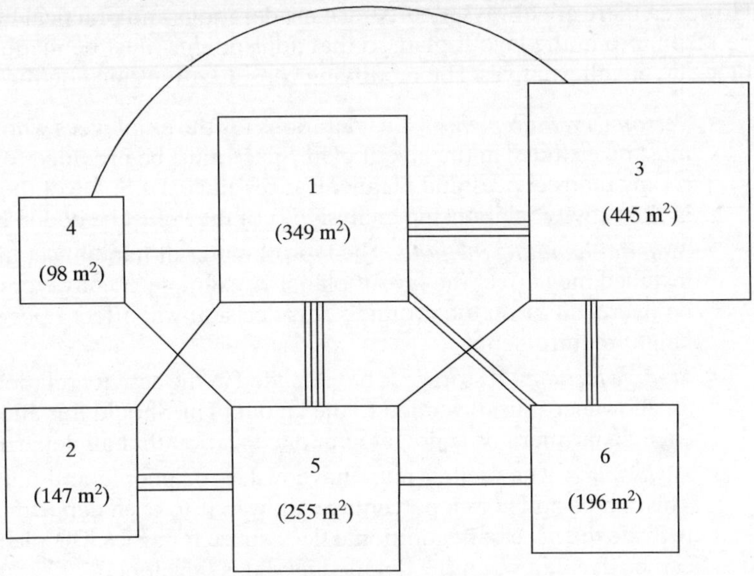

Figure 14 Space relationship diagram for Example 3.

Step 6. Construct Space Relationship Diagram. The ***space relationship diagram*** is an extension of the activity relationship diagram in which the blocks representing departments are now assigned areas that are proportional to the areas computed in the previous space determination step. The shapes of the blocks may be changed as appropriate in developing this diagram, but their basic positions remain the same as they were in the last iteration of the previous activity relationship diagram from step 4.

Example 3 Space Relationship Diagram

Assume that the total areas have been determined for the six departments in Example 1. The total area values for each department are listed in the table below. Construct the space relationship diagram for this data.

Department (k)	1	2	3	4	5	6
Total area (DA_k)	349 m^2	147 m^2	445 m^2	98 m^2	255 m^2	196 m^2

Solution: The space relationship diagram is shown in Figure 14. It takes the previous activity relationship diagram in Figure 13 and adjusts the relative sizes of the blocks in accordance with the DA_k values in the table. ■

Step 7. Make Adjustments and Add Allowances. If the lines connecting the blocks in the space relationship diagram are removed and the blocks are moved together so that their borders are contiguous and some of the shapes are adjusted, we would have a block layout. It could be argued that the resulting layout is optimum in the sense that its development is based directly on the activity relationships and space determinations.

However, there are always modifying considerations and practical limitations that must be taken into in the layout plan, so that adjustments must be made before developing block layout alternatives. The modifying considerations include the following:

- *Personnel requirements.* Considerations for the employees who work in the facility must be included in the layout plan. Space must be provided for rest rooms, locker rooms, food services, and plant entrances and exits. Some of these may be included in the activity relationship analysis. If not they must be added here.
- *Material-handling methods.* The type of material-handling equipment that is to be installed may affect the layout plan. For example, if conveyors are used, will they be overhead or on the ground? This decision will affect floor space and building height requirements.
- *Storage facilities.* If storage is not included in the activity relationship analysis, then an allowance must be added to the layout plan. Should this allowance be added to each department or aggregated in one location that all departments will use?
- *Aisle space.* The facility must have aisles for people and materials to move in. This can be added as a percentage allowance to each department area in order to provide the necessary additional floor space for aisles. The placement of the aisles can be decided when the detailed layout is developed.
- *Offices.* If a department is to have an office for clerical and supervisory staff, then office space must be added to the department total.
- *Building features.* These considerations include ceiling height, floor load capability, support column locations, walls, and doors, any of which may affect the layout plan.
- *Site conditions.* The exterior of the facility is considered here. The placement and direction of the building on the property, provision for parking space, and landscaping are included.

In addition to these modifying considerations, there are sure to be practical limitations that the layout planner must deal with. The limitations that may affect the layout design include the following:

- *Budget.* There is a budget that has been established for designing and constructing the facility, and this may impose a limitation on the size of the building. In general, construction costs are proportional to the amount of floor space in the structure.
- *Building codes.* The facility must be constructed according to the local building codes. This may affect the placement of the building on the property as well as structural and utility details.
- *Safety requirements.* The facility must be a safe place to work. Some safety requirements are included in the building codes. Other requirements are included in the Occupational Safety and Health Act of 1970.
- *Existing building.* If the layout is to be implemented in an existing building, then the shape and size of building will be a limitation on the layout design.

The modifying considerations and practical limitations must be factored into the layout plan, as the SLP procedure transitions from space relationship diagram to block layout.

Step 8. Develop Block Layout. The recommended approach in designing the block layout is to develop several alternatives, all based on the space relationship diagram but using different shapes and tweaking the positions of the departments. The shapes can be rectangles with various aspect ratios (including one-to-one) or nonrectangular, perhaps approximating the shape of the space relationship diagram. Two alternative block layouts for our example problem are illustrated in Figure 15.

The final solution to any design problem always reflects a compromise between competing objectives, modifying considerations, and practical limitations that must be taken into account. So it is with plant layout design. To select the best compromise, the various alternatives must be evaluated, and those layouts that fail the evaluation process are either eliminated or revised to create a new alternative for evaluation.

To evaluate the alternatives, a procedure such as "selecting among alternatives" might be useful. This is a systematic evaluation approach that leads up to a final "winner." Managers participating in the decision process would probably be comfortable with this procedure because of its combination of subjective and objective evaluations.

Quantitative methods are also available to score a given block layout. Here we present a method based on adjacency scores, in which the closeness ratings (A, E, I, O, U, and X) are converted into their corresponding numerical values (4, 3, 2, 1, 0, and -5,

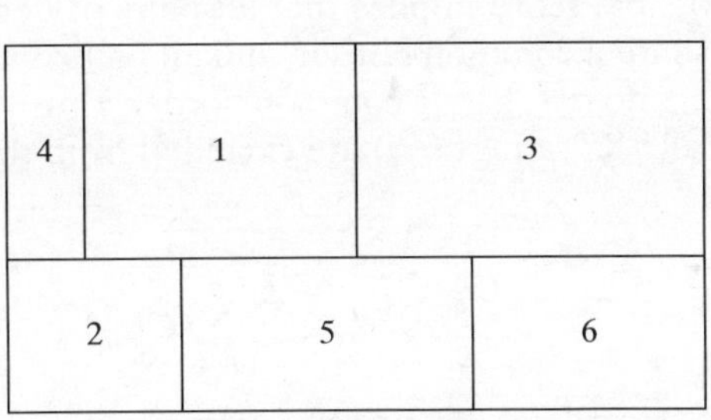

(a)

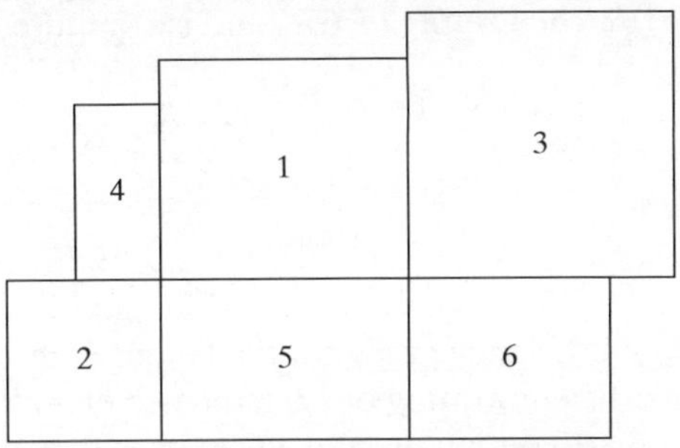

(b)

Figure 15 Two block layouts for Example 3: (a) rectangular and (b) approximating the space relationship diagram in Figure 14.

as in Table 8). The ***adjacency score*** (AS) is computed by summing the numerical closeness rating values for all contacting pairs of blocks. Stating this mathematically, let x_{ij} represent an adjacency variable indicating whether departments i and j are in contact at their borders. If department i shares a common border with department j, then $x_{ij} = 1$; but if department i does not share a common border with department j, then $x_{ij} = 0$. Departments contacting only at their corners do not count as sharing a common border ($x_{ij} = 0$). The adjacency variable is used in the following equation to compute the adjacency score:

$$AS = \sum_{i=1}^{n}\sum_{j=1}^{n} x_{ij}(CR_{ij}) \tag{5}$$

where AS = adjacency score for the layout of interest; x_{ij} = adjacency variable, either 0 or 1; and CR_{ij} = numerical value of the closeness rating between department i and department j. Depending on the success of the process of positioning the departments according to their closeness ratings, better layouts will have higher layout ratings.

The value of AS can be compared to the maximum possible adjacency score that the layout can have (AS_{max}), which is the sum of all closeness ratings between departments excluding any negative values associated with "X" closeness ratings. This maximum possible score implies that all pairs of departments that have positive closeness ratings share a common border, and all pairs of departments that have negative closeness ratings do not share a common border. Thus, AS_{max} consists of only positive closeness ratings; all "X" ratings (–5) are excluded from the summation. We can define AS_{max} as follows:

$$AS_{max} = \sum_{i=1}^{n}\sum_{j=1}^{n} (CR_{ij}^{+}) \tag{6}$$

where $CR_{ij}^{+} = CR_{ij}$ if $CR_{ij} > 0$ and $CR_{ij}^{+} = 0$ if $CR_{ij} \leq 0$.

The ratio of the adjacency score and the maximum possible adjacency score is called the ***layout efficiency rating*** (LER) and is computed as follows:

$$LER = \frac{As}{As_{max}} = \frac{\sum_{i=1}^{n}\sum_{j=1}^{n} x_{ij}(CR_{ij})}{\sum_{i=1}^{n}\sum_{j=1}^{n} (CR_{ij}^{+})} \tag{7}$$

where LER = layout efficiency rating for the layout of interest, and the other terms are defined above. An efficiency rating of 1.0 indicates that all department pairs with positive closeness ratings are contiguous, and any pairs with negative closeness rating are not contiguous. As we have defined the efficiency rating in equation (7), LER can take on negative values if the adjacency score AS is dominated by "X" ratings between contacting departments.

Using either the adjacency score or the efficiency rating to compare alternative layouts, the alternative with the highest score is the winner. The following example demonstrates the scoring procedure.

Example 4 Adjacency Scores and Layout Efficiency Ratings

Determine the adjacency score and layout efficiency rating for the block layout in Figure 15 (a), using the closeness ratings for Example 1 given in Table 5 and the numerical values in Table 8.

Solution: For the layout in Figure 15 (a),

$$AS = CR_{12} + CR_{13} + CR_{14} + CR_{15} + CR_{25} + CR_{35} + CR_{36} + CR_{56}$$
$$= 1 + 3 + 1 + 4 + 3 + 1 + 3 + 2 = 18$$

$$AS_{max} = CR_{12} + CR_{13} + CR_{14} + CR_{15} + CR_{16} + CR_{25}$$
$$+ CR_{34} + CR_{35} + CR_{36} + CR_{45} + CR_{56}$$
$$= 1 + 3 + 1 + 4 + 2 + 3 + 1 + 1 + 3 + 1 + 2 = 22$$

$$LER = \frac{18}{22} = 0.818$$

■

Step 9. Develop Detailed Layout. The detailed layout is the final step in the SLP procedure. It involves filling in the block layout with the details of how each department will be arranged, as indicated in Figure 8. The details include locations and areas for workstations and equipment, aisles, department offices, storage areas, and so on. Designing the detailed layout provides a check on the decisions and calculations that were made in planning the block layout. If the details do nct fit into the department areas in the block layout, or if there is space left over in a department after the details are added, then corrections to those department areas and/or shapes must be made. Material flows, people movement, and the flow relationships with neighboring departments should all be considered when laying out a given department. For example, the aisles in a department must line up with the aisles in adjacent departments.

The detailed layout is the model that will be used by all stakeholders to visualize the new facility, including the executives who must authorize the investment in it. The layout will also serve as the basis for the architecture and structure of the building. The detailed layout must allow all parties to be able to visualize how the plant will look and operate. Presentation of the layout is important. Alternative presentation methods include: (1) drawings similar to those in some of our figures, (2) templates and layout boards that allow equipment pieces to be moved if desired, (3) three-dimensional physical models, using miniature models of equipment on a poster board drawing of the layout, and (4) computer-aided design (CAD) models, which can be manipulated to show various views and enlargements.

3.2 Design of Product Layouts

For planning purposes, a product layout can be considered to be one large department whose function is to accomplish the step-by-step production of the product. The product is usually an assembly, and the layout is an assembly line. In cases where there is more than one department the layout for each department can be designed more or less independently as long as the line-of-flow is consistent at the connection points from one department to the next. For example, an automobile final assembly plant is usually organized into three main departments: (1) body shop, (2) paint shop, and (3) general assembly (or trim-chassis-final, as some car companies call it). The body shop is where the sheet metal panels are spot welded together to form the car body. The paint shop is where the car body is painted. And the general assembly department is where all of the remaining assembly work is accomplished, adding the engine, transmission, wheels, windows, seats, dashboard, and all other subassemblies and components. Each department is organized as a production line. The departments are planned separately, but the design efforts are coordinated with regard to cycle time, joining of the flow line between departments, and budgets.

To apply the systematic layout planning procedure for a product layout, the starting point is the P-Q-R-S-T data. The plant will be designed to produce a specific product at a specified annual production rate. The production and assembly processes and their sequence must be known. Support services must be provided. And the number of shifts per week must be decided.

At this point in the layout planning procedure, the details of the production or assembly operations at each workstation must be specified. This is properly done by developing a list of work elements for the total work content (the total amount of work that will be accomplished on the production line per work unit), determining the times for those work elements, and allocating the elements to workers using one of the line balancing algorithms. In addition, the number of workers that will be assigned to each station must be decided. For large products such as automobiles and trucks, it makes sense to use more than one worker in each station. In these cases, the number of stations may be significantly fewer than the number of workers, thus conserving real estate. Based on these calculations and decisions, the total number of manual workstations on the line is determined:

$$n_m = \text{Minimum Integer} \geq \frac{T_{wc}}{E_r E_b M T_c} \tag{8}$$

where n_m = number of manual workstations; T_{wc} = total work content time, min; E_r = repositioning efficiency; E_b = line balancing efficiency, M = manning level, average number of workers per station; and T_c = cycle time of the line, min. In addition, the number of automated workstations ($M = 0$) must be included in the station count to obtain the total:

$$n = n_m + n_a \tag{9}$$

where n = total number of workstations, n_m = number of manual stations, and n_a = number of automated stations.

Each workstation takes up a certain amount of floor space that depends on the design of the station. As in the development of the process layout, a layout must be planned for each workstation to perform the particular set of work elements allocated to that station. If we assume that the floor shape of each workstation is rectangular, with length L_s along the line of flow and width W_s, then the area of the station is $A_s = L_s W_s$.

The total length of the production line is then the sum of the station lengths, and the total working area of the line is the sum of the station areas. That is,

$$L = \sum_{i=1}^{n} L_{si} \tag{10}$$

and

$$A = \sum_{i=1}^{n} A_{si} \tag{11}$$

where L = line length, L_{si} = length of station i, A = working area of the line, and A_{si} = area of station i.

To this area must be added allowances for aisles, storage areas to supply the line with parts, and space to satisfy personnel requirements and other factors among the modifying considerations in step 7 of the SLP procedure.

REFERENCES

[1] Hanna, S. R., and S. Konz. *Facility Design and Engineering*, 3rd ed. Scottsdale, AZ: Holcomb Hathaway Publishers, 2004.

[2] Muther, R. *Systematic Layout Planning*. 2nd ed. New York: Van Nostrand Reinhold, 1973.

[3] Muther, R. "Plant Layout". Pp 13.35–13.73 in *Maynard's Industrial Engineering Handbook*, 4th ed., edited by W. K. Hodson. New York: McGraw-Hill, 1992.

[4] Quible, Z. K. *Administrative Office Management*. 7th ed. Upper Saddle River, NJ: Prentice Hall, 2001.

[5] Russell, R. S., and B. W. Taylor III. *Operations Management*. 4th ed., Upper Saddle River, NJ: Prentice Hall, 2003.

[6] Tompkins, J. "Facilities Size, Location and Layout." Pp 1465–501 in *Handbook of Industrial Engineering*, 3rd ed. edited by G. Salvendy New York: Wiley Institute of Industrial Engineers, Norcross, GA, 2001.

[7] Tompkins, J. A., J. A. White, Y. A. Bozer, and J. M. A. Tanchoco. *Facilities Planning*. 3rd ed. New York: Wiley, 2003.

[8] Wrennall, W. "Facilities Layout and Design." Pp 8.21–8.62 in *Maynard's Industrial Engineering Handbook*, 5th ed. edited by K. Zandin New York: McGraw-Hill, 2001.

REVIEW QUESTIONS

1 Define the term *facility layout*.

2 What are the objectives in layout planning?

3 What is the difference between a process layout and a product layout?

4 What are some of the principal advantages of a process layout over a product layout?

5 What are some of the principal advantages of a product layout over a process layout?

6 What is a fixed-position layout?

7 Identify the typical application areas of the three basic layout types in terms of production quantity and product variety.

8 What is a cellular layout?

9 What are the similarities and differences between a construction project layout and a fixed-position layout?

10 What is the difference between the traditional office layout and the open office concept?

11 What are the differences between a site layout, a block layout, and a detailed layout?

12 In systematic layout planning, what are the P-Q-R-S-T data requirements? Specifically, what do P, Q, R, S, and T stand for?

13 What are some of the charting techniques used to analyze material flows?

14 What do the closeness ratings A, E, I, O, and U mean?

15 Identify some of the factors that may influence the assignment of a particular closeness rating to a pair of departments.

16 What is an activity relationship chart?

17 What is an activity relationship diagram?

18 What is a space relationship diagram?

19 What are some of the modifying considerations that are likely to influence the layout design?

20 What are some of the practical limitations that may influence the layout design?

PROBLEMS

Activity Relationship Charts

1 A factory has five production departments: M (milling), D (drilling), T (turning), G (grinding), and F (finishing). Products are routed for processing through these departments in the quantities and sequences indicated in the table below. (a) Based on these data, construct the From-To chart. (b) Develop the activity relationship chart for these five departments, given that the From-To chart is the only basis for it.

Product	Quantities per Day	Sequence
1	25	M-D-G
2	5	T-G-F
3	10	T-F
4	50	D-M-D-G-F
5	25	M-T-F
6	15	M-G

2 A college office building has five departments: A (accounting office), B (bursar's office), C (credit department), D (data processing department), and E (educational support services). Paper forms are routed for processing through these departments in the quantities and sequences indicated in the table below. (a) Based on these data, construct the From-To chart. (b) Develop the activity relationship chart for these five departments, given that the From-To chart is the only basis for it.

Product	Quantities per Day	Sequence
1	20	A-B-D
2	13	B-E-A
3	10	E-C
4	30	D-A-B-D
5	25	A-C-E-B
6	18	C-B-E-D-A

3 A manufacturing plant has six production departments: M (milling), D (drilling), T (turning), G (grinding), F (finishing), and A (assembly). Products are routed for processing through these departments in the quantities and sequences indicated in the table below. (a) Construct the From-To chart for the data. (b) Develop the activity relationship chart for the six departments, given that the From-To chart is the only basis for it.

Product	Quantities per Day	Sequence
1	40	M-D-F-A
2	50	T-G-F
3	20	T-D-F
4	60	G-F-A
5	70	M-D-M-G-F
6	30	T-M-F-A
7	10	M-T-G

Workstation and Area Requirements

4 Two alternative plant layout designs are being proposed for the production of a new product. The production will consist exclusively of labor-intensive assembly. The first alternative is a 300,000 sq ft building (single-story) and will use a one-shift operation. The second alternative is a 100,000 sq ft building (single-story) and will use a three-shift operation. Under these assumptions, the production capacities of the two plants will theoretically be equal. Compare the two alternatives in terms of the following criteria: (a) construction costs, (b) flexibility to adapt to the ups and downs in product demand, (c) labor availability, (d) work flow and material handling.

5 A certain type of machine will be used to produce three products: A, B, and C. Sales forecasts for these products are 52,000, 65,000, and 70,000 units/year, respectively. Production rates for the three products are, respectively, 12, 15, and 10 pc/hr; and scrap rates are, respectively, 5%, 7%, and 9%. The plant will operate 50 weeks/year, 10 shifts/week, and 8 hr/shift. It is anticipated that production machines of this type will be down for repairs on average 10% of the time. (a) How many machines will be required to meet demand? (b) If each machine requires a floor area of 30 m^2, and there is a 25% aisle allowance that must be added to the total machine space, what is the total plant area that must be planned for these three new products?

6 Future production requirements in a machine shop call for several automatic bar machines to be acquired to produce three new parts (A, B, and C) that have been added to the product line. Annual demand and machining cycle times for the three parts are given in the table below. The machine shop operates one 8-hour shift for 250 days per year. The machines are expected to be 95% reliable, and the scrap rate is 3%. (a) How many automatic bar machines will be required to meet the specified annual demand for the three new parts? (b) If each bar machine requires a floor area of 175 ft^2, and there is a 30% aisle allowance that must be added to the total machine space, what is the total machine shop area that must be added for the three parts?

Part	Annual Demand	Machining Cycle Time (min)
A	25,000	5.0
B	40,000	7.0
C	50,000	10.0

7 A one-product plant will operate 250 days per year using a single 8-hour shift each day. Sales requirements are 100,000 units per year. The product consists of two major components: A and B (one of each component goes into each unit of product). The operations required to produce each component are given in the table below, as are the associated production time and scrap rates. Proportion uptime is expected to be 90% during each 8-hour shift. Determine how many machines are required of each type, assuming that a product layout will be used, and therefore that no machine will be shared between operations, thus eliminating the need for setup changes.

Component	Operation	Machine	Production time (min/pc)	Scrap Rate (%)
A	1	Lathe	7.0	3
A	2	Milling machine	10.0	5
B	3	Lathe	5.0	3
B	4	Milling machine	13.0	6
B	5	Drill	4.0	4

8 A machine shop must acquire several CNC horizontal milling machines to produce three new parts (A, B, and C) that have been added to the shop's product line. Annual demand, machining cycle times, and scrap rates for the parts are given in the table below. The machine shop operates two 8-hour shifts for 250 days/year. The machines are expected to be 90% reliable. (a) How many CNC milling machines will be required to meet the specified annual demand for the three new parts? (b) If each CNC machine requires a floor area of 350 ft^2, and there is a 30% allowance that must be added to the total machine space for aisles and parts storage, what is the total shop area that must be planned?

Part	Annual Demand	Machining Cycle Time (min)	Scrap Rate (%)
A	30,000	15.0	5
B	40,000	8.0	8
C	50,000	10.0	3

9 A factory has just signed a contract with one if its best customers to produce 40,000 units of a certain part annually. The part will be made on a processing machine designed specifically for the part. The machine costs $200,000, and its reliability (availability) is estimated at 95%. The standard time for each unit is 16.5 min. The plant normally operates one shift (40 hours/week, 50 weeks/year). Assume scrap rate is 2% and worker efficiency is 100%. (a) How many machines will be needed to meet production requirements? (b) If the plant were to operate a second shift (40 hours/week, 50 weeks/year) just for production of this part, and direct labor cost for the operation is $10/hour, how much money would the company save by reducing the number of machines required?

10 A plastic injection molding plant will be built to produce 6 million molded parts per year. The plant will run three 8-hour shifts/day, 5 days/week, 50 weeks/year. For planning purposes, the average order size is 5000 moldings, average changeover time between orders is 6 hr, and average molding cycle time per part is 30 sec. Assume scrap rate is 2%, and average uptime proportion (reliability) per molding machine is 97%, which applies to both run time and changeover time. (a) How many molding machines are required in the new plant? (b) If each molding machine requires a floor area of 300 ft^2, and there is a 35% allowance that must be added to the total machine space for aisles and work-in-process, what is the total plant area that must be planned?

11 A plastic thermoforming plant will be built to produce 5.5 million parts per year. The plant will run two 8-hour shifts/day, 5 days/week, 50 weeks/year. For planning purposes, the average batch size is 2000 thermoformed parts, average changeover time between batches is 1.5 hr, and average thermoforming cycle time per part is 60 sec. Production workers perform both setups and production runs. Assume scrap rate is 2%, and average uptime proportion (reliability) per thermoforming machine = 90%, which applies to both run time and changeover time. The number of production workers in the plant each shift is equal to the number of machines. In addition to production workers, supervisors and material-handling workers add 20% more personnel each shift. Each thermoforming machine requires a floor space 15 ft wide by 18 ft long. Additional space requirements in the facility include (1) aisle space allowance of 30% added to the total area required for machines, (2) storage for raw materials and finished parts of 2000 sq ft, (3) rest rooms and locker space, for which 10 sq ft is allowed per employee in the plant, (4) office space of 500 sq ft, and (5) utility space of 250 sq ft. What is the total area of the thermoforming plant, not counting the area taken up by walls?

12 A small company that specializes in converting pickup trucks into rear-cabin vehicles has just received a long-term contract and must expand. Heretofore, the conversion jobs were customized and performed in a garage. Now a larger building must be occupied, and the operations must be managed more like a production plant. Three models will be produced: A, B, and C. Annual quantities for the three models are as follows: A, 700; B, 400; and C, 250. Conversion times are as follows: A, 20 hr; B, 30 hr; and C, 40 hr. Defect rates are as follows: A, 11%; B, 7%; and C, 8%. Work teams of three workers each will accomplish the conversions. Each work team will require a space of 350 sq ft in the plant. Reliability (availability) and worker efficiency of the work teams are expected to be 95% and 90%, respectively. Although the defect rates are given, no truck is permitted to leave the plant with any quality defects. Accordingly, all of the defects must be corrected, and the average time to correct the defect is 25% of the initial conversion time. The same work teams will accomplish this rework. (a) If the plant is run as a one shift (2000 hr/year) operation, how many work teams will be required? (b) If the total floor space in the building must include additional space for aisles and offices, and the allowance that is added to the working space is 30%, what is the total area of the building?

13 A final assembly plant for a certain automobile model is to have a capacity of 225,000 units annually. The plant will operate 50 weeks/year, 2 shifts/day, 5 days/week, and 7.5 hr/shift. It will be divided into three departments: (1) body shop, (2) paint shop, (3) general assembly department. The body shop welds the car bodies using robots, and the paint shop coats the bodies. Both of these departments are highly automated. General assembly has no automation. There are 15.0 hr of direct labor content on each car in this third department, where cars are transported through workstations by a continuous conveyor. Determine (a) hourly production rate of the plant and (b) number of workers and workstations required in general assembly if no automated stations are used, the average manning level is 2.5, balancing efficiency is 90%, proportion uptime is 95%, and a repositioning time of 0.15 min is allowed for each worker. (c) If each workstation in the general assembly department is 7.2 m long (parallel to the work flow) and 9.1 m wide, determine the length of the production line and the elapsed time a car spends in the department. (d) If an aisle allowance of 20% is added to the area occupied by the actual production line, find the total area in the department.

Adjacency Scores

14 Determine the adjacency score and layout efficiency rating for the block layout in Figure 15(b), using the closeness ratings for Example 1 given in Table 5 and the numerical values in Table 8.

15 Determine the layout efficiency rating for the block layout shown below, given the closeness ratings between pairs of departments in the table at the right of the layout. Use the numerical values for closeness ratings in Table 8.

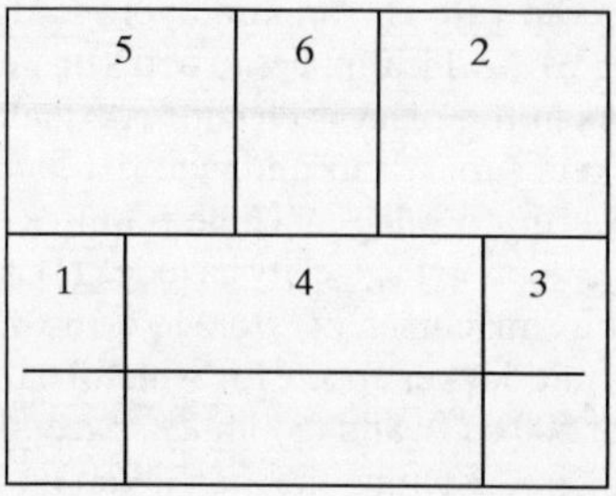

	To	1	2	3	4	5	6
From	1	—	O	E	I	O	U
	2		—	X	I	U	U
	3			—	I	A	U
	4				—	A	E
	5					—	U
	6						—

16 In the preceding problem, what changes in the locations of the departments can be made to improve the layout efficiency rating? All departments must retain their current shape and orientation in the layout, but departments can be relocated within the existing building shape.

17 The block layout shown below consists of seven departments, all of equal size at 100 ft on a side (department area = 10,000 sq ft). The table on the right indicates the closeness ratings between the seven departments. (a) Determine the layout efficiency rating for the current layout. (b) You have been asked to improve the efficiency rating by rearranging departments. Determine a revised layout that obtains a layout efficiency rating of 1.0, given that the building shape must remain the same, but the departments can be moved around within the building.

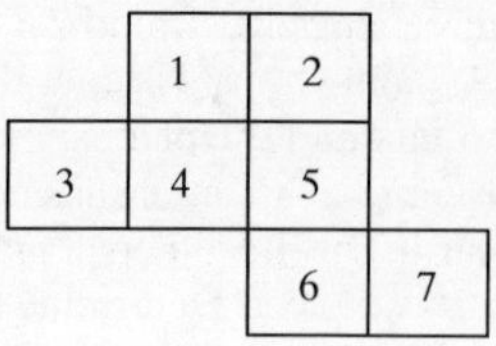

	To	1	2	3	4	5	6	7
From	1	—	O	U	U	I	U	U
	2		—	O	U	U	U	U
	3			—	U	A	U	E
	4				—	U	U	U
	5					—	U	U
	6						—	A
	7							—

Case Problem: Process Layout

18 Landlubber Ultramarine (LU) is a manufacturer of metal products for the maritime industry. Its product line is highly regarded by the leisure boat industry. However, its manufacturing plant is in need of modernization. The current facility is an old dilapidated building on the south side of town. LU is considering the construction of a new plant, and you have been called in to participate in the layout planning of the new facility. Principal manufacturing processes performed in the new LU plant will be sand casting, sheet metal stamping, machining, and mechanical assembly. These are very similar to the current processes and so reliable data are available on operation times, material flows, and other aspects of the plant operations.

The new plant will consist of 10 departments, including the corporate office. It will operate one 8-hour shift/day, 5 days/week. Because of equipment downtime, operator breaks, etc., each work center is expected to operate only 7.5 hr/shift. The plant is shut down 2 weeks/year for vacation.

The exhibits below provide the necessary data for completing a block layout design for the plant. From the information provided together with your engineering judgment, you should submit the following as your solution to this problem: (a) Activity relationship chart based on the From-To chart, other data provided, and your own judgment. (b) Activity relationship diagram, which should locate the 10 departments into the most logical arrangement. (c) Table showing calculated values of numbers of work cells, work cell areas for each work cell type, department areas, and numbers of workers of each type (e.g., production workers, supervisors, material-handling workers, etc.). The table should indicate the total areas of departments, grand total area in the plant, and number of workers in the plant. Use a spreadsheet program to make the computations. (d) Space relationship diagram, showing how the floor space of each department is determined. (e) Block layout for the plant; do not include details of machine and equipment locations within departments except for the following:

- Show locations of aisles in the plant. All materials and parts will be moved by forklift trucks in these aisles.
- Show locations of worker locker and washroom facilities.
- Show the overall dimensions for the building on the drawing.

(f) A brief report detailing your procedure and justifying your design. Use a word processor to prepare your report.

State any assumptions and show the computations you must make to solve the problem.

Exhibit A: LU Departments

Dept. No.	Name and Brief Description
1	*Foundry*: Pattern and core making, mold-making, pouring, trimming and cleaning.
2	*Forming Department*: Forging and extrusion.
3	*Machine Shop*: Turning, milling, drilling, and other machining operations.
4	*Finishing Department*: Cleaning, plating, and painting of metal parts before assembly.
5	*Assembly Department*: Assembling products for shipment. Electronics subassemblies used in the product are not made at LU but are purchased from a vendor and assembled here. Individual operators assemble the products; no assembly lines are used due to the variety of products and small lot sizes produced.
6	*Packaging and Shipping*: Packing products and shipping them to the company's distribution outlets.
7	*Tool, Mold, and Die Shop*: Making patterns for Dept. 1, dies for Dept. 2, fixtures for Dept. 3, and assembly tools and workholders for Dept. 5. This department includes a tool crib mainly used by Dept. 3.

(continued)

Table (*continued*)

Dept. No.	Name and Brief Description
8	*Receiving and Receiving Inspection*: Receiving and inspecting of all materials and supplies shipped to LU.
9	*Storage Department*: Storing of raw materials and some finished product. Work-in-process (WIP) is stored on the shop floor.
10	*Office*: Work area for company officers, personnel, accounting, sales, and other business functions.

Exhibit B: From-To Chart Between LU Departments, Forklift Truckloads/Week

To Dept.	1	2	3	4	5	6	7	8	9
From Dept. 1	—	0	180	12	0	0	8	0	21
2	0	—	25	238	0	0	9	0	15
3	0	2	—	90	15	22	6	0	30
4	2	1	4	—	300	45	0	0	33
5	0	0	2	3	—	250	2	0	41
6	0	0	0	0	0	—	0	0	18
7	50	14	30	3	9	0	—	0	0
8	30	126	92	11	237	8	5	—	350
9	160	68	120	0	60	12	9	0	—

Notes: (a) Trips to and from the office (Dept. 10) are not included in the chart. (b) Only trips in which materials are moved are counted here. Return trips or trips in which no materials are moved are not included in the From-To chart. This is why the number of trips "to" a department may not equal the number of trips "from." (c) All trips are made by forklift trucks that are the only mechanized materials-handling equipment used by the company. (d) Numbers in the chart represent average trips per week. Only current products are included in the data. Future product flow is expected to be similar. (e) The finishing department (Dept. 4) should be segregated from other departments to the extent possible because of fumes and odors.

Exhibit C: Production Rates, Demand Rates, and Scrap Allowances for Current and Anticipated Future Business

Process	Operation Time	Annual Demand	Scrap Rate (%)
Dept. 1			
Core making	8.0 min/part	30,000 parts	5
Mold making	6.0 min/part	55,000 parts	5
Melting and pouring	1.0 hr/50 parts	55,000 parts	2
Cooling	4.0 hr/50 parts	55,000 parts	0
Mold removal	1.0 min/part	55,000 parts	7
Trimming and cleaning	1.5 min/part	55,000 parts	4
Dept. 2			
Forging	1.5 min/part	200,000 parts	10
Extrusion	3.0 min/part	300,000 parts	10
Dept. 3			
Turning	10.0 min/part	35,000 parts	3
Drilling	2.0 min/part	40,000 parts	2
Milling	15.0 min/part	42,000 parts	4
Sawing	3.0 min/part	25,000 parts	6
Dept. 4			
Cleaning	5.0 min/40 parts	450,000 parts	0
Electroplating	10.0 min/40 parts	300,000 parts	4
Painting	3.0 min/part	150,000 parts	6

Process	Operation Time	Annual Demand	Scrap Rate (%)
Dept. 5			
Assembly	40 min/product	45,000 products	0
Dept. 6			
Packaging	4.0 min/product	45,000 products	0
Dept. 7			
Boring	60 min/tool	1000 tools	0
Turning	20 min/tool	700 tools	0
Drilling	15 min/tool	2500 tools	0
Milling	45 min/tool	2000 tools	0
Shaping	15 min/tool	100 tools	0
Miscellaneous	20 min/tool	3000 tools	0

Notes: (a) Operation times are average standard time values in minutes, rounded to the nearest minute, and include an allowance for setup times. (b) Annual demand rates apply for the current and anticipated future product mixes.

Exhibit D: Production and Support Space Requirements

Department	Process	Facility type	Space
1. Foundry	Core making	Sand box	4 m × 5 m
	Mold making	Sand box	3 m × 5 m
	Melting	Melting furnace	5 m × 5 m
	Cooling	Cooling bays	7 m × 8 m
	Mold removal	Sand box	4 m × 5 m
	Trimming and cleaning	Bench	3 m × 5 m
2. Forming	Forging	Forging press	6 m × 8 m
	Extrusion	Extrusion press	5 m × 7 m
3. Machine Shop	Turning	Lathe	4 m × 8 m
	Drilling	Drill press	4 m × 5 m
	Milling	Milling machine	4 m × 5 m
	Sawing	Saw	2 m × 4 m
4. Finishing	Cleaning	Cleaning tank	2 m × 8 m
	Electroplating	Electroplating tank	3 m × 10 m
	Painting	Painting booth	6 m × 5 m
5. Assembly	Assembly	Assembly bench	3 m × 5 m
6. Packaging and Shipping	Packaging	Packaging bench	4 m × 5 m
7. Tool, Mold, and Die Shop	Boring	Boring machine	5 m × 8 m
	Turning	Lathe	4 m × 8 m
	Drilling	Drill press	4 m × 3 m
	Milling	Milling machine	5 m × 5 m
	Shaping	Shaper	3 m × 5 m
	Miscellaneous	Bench	4 m × 4 m

Notes: (a) Space indicated represents dimensions of area needed per machine or work center. To obtain the total area in the department needed for this work center type, multiply by the (closest larger integer) number of work centers. (b) Each operating department (Depts. 1, 2, 3, 4, and 5) should be provided with an enclosed supervisor's office to afford desk space for the supervisor, department secretary, and files. This space should be 100 sq m. (c) In Depts. 1 through 5, temporary storage space for work-in-process should be provided: 120 sq m in each department. (d) Although precise dimensions are given in the "space" column, the shape of the workspace is somewhat flexible so long as the total area is provided. (e) One production worker per cell unless otherwise noted. (f) Number of material-handling workers = 20% of production workers.

Exhibit E: Nonproduction Space Requirements

Dept.	Description and Space Requirements
7	Tool crib should be allotted 300 sq m.
8	Receiving/receiving inspection should be allotted 500 sq m.
9	Storage Room should be allotted 1000 sq m.
10	Office space should be provided as follows:

Activity Space	Area (sq m)
Lobby	50
Main offices	1000
Sales offices	100
Secretarial/typing pool	60
Restrooms	100
Hallways	20% of above total

Notes: (a) The storage room (Dept. 9) should be located adjacent to the receiving and receiving inspection department (Dept. 8) for easy access. (b) Receiving (Dept. 8) and packaging and shipping (Dept. 6) should each be provided with at least one truck dock. (c) Except for a modest provision in the storage room (Dept. 9), the inventory of finished product is to be maintained at the company's distribution center. (d) Aisles for forklift trucks between departments are to be 3 m wide throughout (to allow for two-way travel). To allow for this extra aisle space, add 25% to each operating department (Depts. 1 through 7). (e) Allowance for lavatories, washroom and lockers for the labor force should be approx. 3 sq. m. per worker on day shift. The space provided for lavatories, washroom, and lockers should be in two rooms (for men and women). The rooms should be next to each other and centrally located in the plant if possible. (f) No provision is to be made for food service for the employees. Vending machines are to be located outside the locker room. (g) Supervisor-to-worker ratio in the factory is 1:15. Number of clerical staff per supervisor is one.

Introduction to Work Measurement

Time is important in work systems because of its economic significance. Most workers are paid for the time they are on the job. The labor content to produce a product or deliver a service is often a major determinant of the cost of the product or service. For any organization to operate efficiently and effectively, it is critical to know how much time should be required to accomplish a given amount of work. For the reader's amusement, a list of quotations and sayings about time is compiled in Table 1.

The terms *time study* and *work measurement* are often used interchangeably. Both are concerned with how much time it should take to complete a unit of work. ***Work measurement*** refers to a set of four techniques that are concerned with the evaluation of a task in terms of the time that should be allowed for an average human worker to perform that task: (1) direct time study, (2) predetermined motion time systems, (3) standard data systems, and (4) work sampling, an alternative work measurement technique in which statistical measures are determined about how workers allocate their time among

TABLE 1 Quotations and Sayings About Time

Time flies when you're having fun.
Take care of the minutes, and the hours will take care of themselves. (Lord Chesterfield)
Time heals all things—except leaky faucets.
Those who kill time eventually mourn the corpse.
Time changes with age: in youth, time marches on; in middle age, time flies; and in old age, time runs out.
All things come to him who waits, except the precious time lost while waiting.
Some people count time, others make time count.

Source: Compiled from E. Esar, *20,000 Quips and Quotes* (New York: Barnes and Noble 1995) and other sources.

multiple activities. The task that is measured is usually a repetitive work cycle. The objective of these work measurement techniques is to determine a ***standard time*** for the task.

Because of its emphasis on time, work measurement is often called time study. However, in modern usage and in our coverage in this text, time study has a slightly broader meaning. Whereas work measurement is generally focused on human work effort, ***time study*** refers to all of the ways in which time is investigated and analyzed in work situations, whether the work is accomplished by human workers or automated systems. For example, in an automated work system in which a human worker periodically attends to the system but is not present every cycle, it is still important to know the automatic cycle time. Time study also includes the learning curve phenomenon, which is not usually included in the definition of work measurement.

Here, we discuss the various techniques used to measure work and other job activities of human workers. Time is an important variable used to evaluate performance in the variety of work systems. In manual work, worker-machine systems, assembly lines, logistics work, service operations, and projects, time is the common factor that determines performance. In this chapter, we provide an overview of work measurement, the basic definitions and principles that apply to all of the techniques, and the issues that are faced in their application.

1 TIME STANDARDS AND HOW THEY ARE DETERMINED

Most workers are paid on the basis of time. The common work shift is 8 hours per day, and the worker is paid an hourly rate for those 8 hours. Several questions may be asked by a worker's employer: How much work did the worker accomplish in those 8 hours? Has the worker done a fair day's work? Time standards provide a way to answer these questions.1 The most meaningful and useful measure of work is the amount of time it takes to accomplish it. Time is objective. It is quantifiable. People understand time.

[1]The terms *time standard* and *standard time* are used interchangeably and synonymously in this text. Other terms for time standards include *work standards* and *labor standards*.

The ***standard time*** for a given task is the amount of time that should be allowed for an average worker to process one work unit using the standard method and working at a normal pace. The standard time includes some additional time, called the ***allowance***, to provide for the worker's personal needs, fatigue, and unavoidable delays during the shift. The standard time is sometimes referred to as the ***allowed time***, because it indicates how much time is allowed the worker to process each work unit so that by the end of the shift a fair day's workload has been accomplished, despite the various interruptions that may occur.

How does an organization know whether it needs time standards for its operations? The following characteristics are typical of industrial situations in which time standards would be beneficial:

- *Low productivity.* If the current level of productivity is low, then there are significant opportunities for improvement.
- *Repeat orders.* Once the time standard is set during the first order, the same standard can be used for successive orders.
- *Long production runs.* A long production run means that the time invested to set the standard is apportioned over more parts, thus reducing the average cost of work measurement.
- *Repetitive work cycles.* Work measurement can be justified more readily when the work cycle is highly repetitive.
- *Short cycle times.* Short work cycles require less time to set standards.

When accurately determined, time standards serve the following important functions and applications in an organization:

- They define a "fair day's work." If the quantity of work units completed by a worker, when multiplied by their respective standard times, adds up to the number of hours in the shift, then the worker has put in a fair day's work.
- They provide a means of converting the workload to be produced into the staffing and equipment resources needed to accomplish the workload. They help to determine manpower requirements and capacity limitations.
- They provide an objective way to compare alternative methods for accomplishing the same task.
- They provide a basis for wage incentives and for evaluating worker performance.
- They provide time data for production planning and scheduling, cost estimating, material requirements planning, and other management functions that depend on accurate task time data.

1.1 Methods to Determine Time Standards

There are several methods by which "standard times" can be established for a task. They vary in terms of the accuracy and reliability of the values that are derived from them

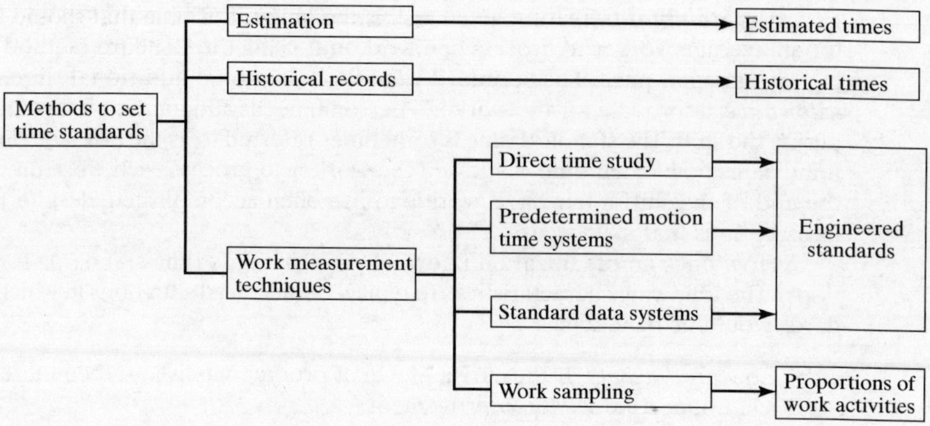

Figure 1 Classification of methods to determine time standards.

and in the amount of time required to apply them. The following methods can be used to determine time standards, as shown in Figure 1:

- *Estimation.* In this method, the department foreman or other person familiar with the jobs performed in the department is asked to judge how much time should be allowed for the given task. Because this method depends on the estimator's judgment, it is the least accurate of the techniques for determining time standards.[2] On the other hand, it is better than making no estimate of the time and simply assigning a worker to the task with no accountability.
- *Historical records of previous production runs.* In this method, the actual times and production quantities from records of previous identical or similar job orders are used to determine the time standards. Most companies require workers to submit time records (e.g., "time cards") indicating the time spent on orders or jobs and the quantities of parts turned in against that time. From these records a calculation is made to determine the average time per part, and this can be used as a "time standard" for the next order. Historical records are an improvement over estimates because they represent actual times for amounts of work completed. Their limitation is that they do not include any indication of the efficiency with which the work was accomplished.
- *Work measurement techniques.* These are the four techniques identified in the chapter introduction: direct time study, predetermined motion time systems, standard data systems, and work sampling. These techniques are described in Section 1.2.

The work measurement techniques are more time consuming to implement, but they are more accurate than estimation or historical records. It is the author's opinion that task time values determined by estimation or historical records should not even be called "time standards." They should be called "estimated times" and "historical times," respectively, and in fact they are sometimes identified by these names.

[2]The issue of accuracy in work measurement is discussed in Section 4.1.

Among the four work measurement techniques, work sampling should be differentiated from the other three. The primary purpose of work sampling is to determine proportions of time spent in various categories of work activity using randomized observations of the subjects of interest. On the other hand, the principal purpose of direct time study, predetermined motion time systems, and standard data systems is to establish time standards. Standards set by these three techniques are sometimes referred to as ***engineered standards***, because (1) they are based on measured time values that have been adjusted for worker performance, and (2) some effort has been made to determine the best method to accomplish the task. Although work sampling can be used to determine time standards, the technique is not as reliable because of statistical errors, and no attempt is made to improve the method by which the work is accomplished.

1.2 Work Measurement Techniques

The four work measurement techniques are described briefly in the following sections. In the pyramidal structure of work, a task consists of work elements, and how each work element consists of basic motion elements. The various work measurement techniques measure work at different levels of this task hierarchy. Figure 2 shows the correspondence between the task hierarchy and work measurement techniques.

Direct Time Study. Direct time study (DTS) involves direct observation of a task using a stopwatch or other chronometric device to record the time taken to accomplish the task. The task is usually divided into work elements and each work element is timed separately. While observing the worker, the time study analyst evaluates the worker's performance (pace), and a record of this pace is attached to each work element time. This evaluation of the worker's pace is called ***performance rating***. The observed time is multiplied by the performance rating to obtain the ***normal time*** for the element or the task:[3]

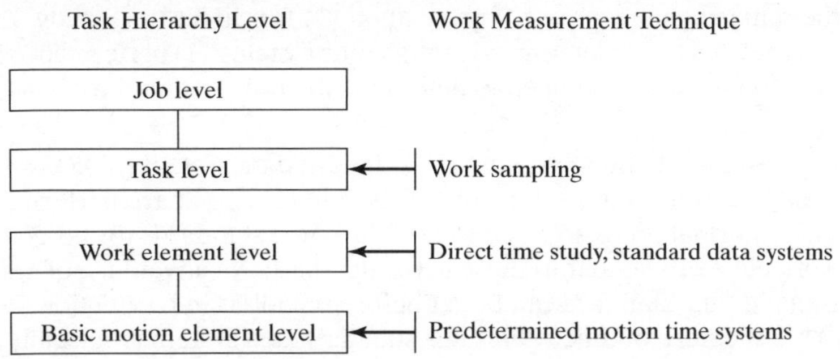

Figure 2 How the work measurement techniques correspond to different levels in the general task hierarchy.

[3]Some time study analysts attach an overall performance rating to the entire task while others prefer to rate the worker's performance during each work element.

$$T_n = T_{obs}(PR) \tag{1}$$

where T_n = normal time (the time required by a worker working at 100% pace for one cycle), min; T_{obs} = observed time, min; and PR = performance rating of the worker's pace observed by an analyst, usually recorded as a percentage during the observation but applied as a decimal fraction in the equation. If the task is repetitive, several work cycles are observed and the normalized time values are averaged to improve statistical accuracy.

To determine the standard time for the task, an allowance is added to the normal time to provide for personal time, fatigue, and delays. The calculation of the standard time is summarized in the following equation:

$$T_{std} = T_n(1 + A_{pfd}) \tag{2}$$

where T_{std} = standard time, min.; T_n = normal time, min.; and A_{pfd} = allowance factor for personal time, fatigue, and delays (PFD). The PFD allowance is explained in Section 3.1.

Predetermined Motion Time Systems. A predetermined motion time system (PMTS) relies on a database of basic motion elements (therbligs) such as reach, grasp, and move that are common to nearly all manual industrial tasks. Associated with each motion element is a set of normal times, whose values depend on the conditions under which the motion element was performed. For example, the normal time for a reach depends on the distance reached. Longer distances take more time. The normal time for a move depends on the distance moved and the weight of the object being moved. And so on.

To use a predetermined motion time system to set a standard time for a given task, the analyst lists all of the basic motion elements that comprise the task, noting their respective conditions, and retrieves the normal time for each element from the database. The normal times for the motion elements are then summed to obtain the normal time for the task. Finally, the standard time is calculated by adding a PFD allowance. This final step is the same as that expressed by equation (2) for direct time study. There are two advantages related to predetermined motion time systems: (1) performance rating is not required and (2) they can be applied to determine the time standard for a task before production.

Standard Data Systems. A standard data system (SDS) is a compilation of normal time values for work elements used in tasks that are performed in a given facility. These normal times are used to establish time standards for tasks that are composed of work elements similar to those in the database. An advantage of a standard data system is that a time standard can be set before the job is in production.

The normal time values in a standard data system are usually compiled from previous direct time studies, but they may be based on predetermined motion time data, work sampling data, or even historical time records. Large amounts of data are generally required to compile the database, and the work elements are performed under different work variables that may affect their normal time values. Accordingly, the normal time for a given element is a function of the work variable(s), and this functionality must be included in the database in the form of tables, charts, or mathematical equations.

To use a standard data system, the analyst first identifies the work elements that make up the task together with the values of the work variables respectively for each element. He or she then accesses the database to find the normal time for each element. The work element values are summed to determine the normal time for the task. As in the other work measurement techniques, an allowance is added to the normal time to compute the standard time.

Work Sampling. Work sampling uses random sampling techniques to study work situations so that the proportions of time spent in different activities can be estimated with a defined degree of statistical accuracy. Examples of the activities in a work sampling study might include setting up for production, producing parts, machine idle, and so on. The activities must be defined specifically for the work situation that the study is intended to address. The capability to include multiple subjects (e.g., workers, machines) in the study is one of the advantages of work sampling. Direct time study and predetermined motion time systems are generally limited to one worker for each study. A large number of observations over an extended period of time are usually made in a work sampling study in order to achieve the desired level of statistical accuracy. The period of the study must be representative of the activities normally performed by the subjects, and the observations must be made at random times in order to minimize bias; for example, if the workers knew when the observations would be made, it might influence their behavior.

The objectives in a work sampling study may be to measure machine utilization in a plant or to determine an appropriate allowance factor for use in setting standards in direct time study. The objective is not always to determine time standards. But when used to establish standards, the statistical errors inherent in the sampling procedure cause the "time standards" to be less accurate than those obtained by the other work measurement techniques.

Computerized Work Measurement. The purpose of work measurement and time standards is to improve the productivity of the workers who perform the value-adding tasks of the organization. But work measurement itself can be very time-consuming for the analysts who do it. A number of hardware and software products have been introduced commercially to improve the productivity of the analysts who perform work measurement. These products reduce the amount of time required by the analyst to set a time standard. Thus fewer analysts can set more standards.

Computerized products have been developed for all four of the work measurement techniques: direct time study, predetermined motion time systems, standard data systems, and work sampling. They make use of the ubiquitous personal computer (PC) as well as portable devices such as personal digital assistants (PDAs). In general, these products reduce the time and effort to perform work measurement by means of the following conveniences:

- Facilitating the collection of data at the work site in direct time study and work sampling
- Automatically performing the routine computations that previously had to be performed by the analyst

- Organizing the time standards files and databases
- Retrieving data from databases in predetermined motion time systems and standard data systems
- Assisting in the preparation of the documentation required in work measurement (e.g., methods descriptions, reports).

2 PREREQUISITES FOR VALID TIME STANDARDS

The time to perform one work cycle of a given manual task depends on the worker (his or her physical size and strength, as well as mental abilities), the worker's pace, the method used (hand and body motions, tooling, equipment, and work environment), and the work unit. As a prerequisite for establishing a standard time for a task, all of these factors must be standardized. The standardized factors are the following:

- The task is performed by an ***average worker***
- The worker's pace represents ***standard performance***
- The worker uses the ***standard method***
- The task is performed on a ***standard work unit*** that is defined before and after processing.

Establishing these definitions for the task is a requirement for setting a valid time standard, as depicted in Figure 3. And the definitions must be fully documented for future reference. If any of the factors change in future replications of the task, then it can be argued that the previously determined time standard is no longer valid. The only exception is the worker. Different workers are all expected to work by the same definition of standard time, whether they represent the "average worker" or not.

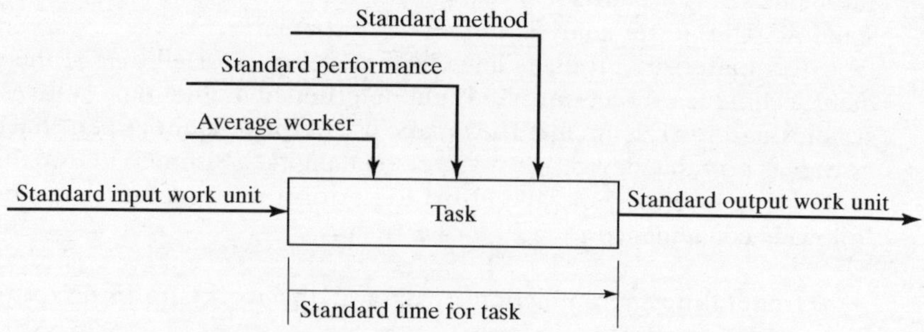

Figure 3 Model indicating the factors that must be standardized before a standard time can be set for a task.

2.1 Average Worker and Standard Performance

For the purpose of defining standard time, an ***average worker*** is a person who is representative of those who perform tasks similar to the task being measured. If similar tasks are performed mostly by men, and gender makes a difference in the ability to perform the task, then the average worker should be defined as a male. If performed mostly by women, then average worker means a female worker. Sometimes men are better suited to certain types of work, and sometimes women are better suited. In addition, the average worker is assumed to have learned the task and is practiced and proficient at it. He or she is well into the learning curve and is capable of performing the task consistently throughout the shift, which includes occasional rest breaks as befits the work situation.

To accomplish the task in the standard time, the average worker works at standard performance. Performance refers to the rate or speed with which a worker does the task. It is the pace of working. ***Standard performance*** is a pace of working that can be maintained by the average worker throughout an entire work shift without harmful effects on the worker's health or physical well-being. The work shift is usually considered to be an 8-hour workday during which the worker is allowed periodic rest breaks and may experience other interruptions. Standard performance is a pace the worker can achieve day after day. It is the normal pace of an average worker trained to perform the given task.

Several benchmarks of "standard performance" have been developed over the years. Two of the most popular are the following:

- Walking at 3 miles per hour (or 4.82 km per hour) on level flat ground
- Dealing four hands of cards from a 52 card deck in exactly 30 seconds.

The term ***normal performance*** is often used in place of standard performance. Basically, the two terms mean the same thing. Normal performance is 100% pace while the worker is working, while standard performance is 100% performance but with the proviso that periodic breaks are taken and other delays are likely to occur during the shift. A worker could not maintain 100% pace for 8 hours straight (imagine walking at 3 miles per hour for 8 straight hours, 24 miles, without an occasional rest stop). However, with periodic breaks a worker is able to work at 100% pace when he or she is working (with occasional rest breaks amounting to total of an hour or so, walking 24 miles in a day can be readily accomplished by a person who has trained for it[4]).

When an individual work cycle is performed at 100% performance, the time taken is the ***normal time*** for the cycle. The normal time is less than the standard time because the normal time does not include an allowance for time losses during the shift. When this allowance is added to the normal time, we have the ***standard time***. This is captured concisely in our equation for standard time, equation (2):

$$T_{std} = T_n (1 + A_{pfd})$$

[4]There are many accounts during the American Civil War (1861–1865) of entire armies marching distances more than 24 miles per day over terrain that was hardly flat and level.

The allowance factor A_{pfd} is intended to provide for the average time losses for personal needs, fatigue, and delays that occur during the shift. The allowance factor must be determined for the particular task or category of work to which it is applied. If the work is physically demanding, then a greater allowance factor must be provided for rest breaks. Allowances are discussed in Section 3.

Worker performance varies among individual workers. The variations occur due to age, sex, size and physical strength, physical conditioning, skill and aptitude for the task, experience and training, and motivation. For large numbers of workers, studies have shown that worker performance is normally distributed, and the ratio of the highest performing and lowest performing worker ranges between about 2.3 to 1.[5] The results (hypothetical) are presented in Figure 4. Worker performance in these studies is usually indicated by the hourly or daily production rate for a representative manual task.

It is common industrial practice to define standard performance as a pace that can be readily attained by the majority of workers. The companies (and unions representing the workers) want most workers to be able to achieve the standard performance fairly easily, so they define standard to be a performance that is less than the average in Figure 4. This is an additional condition on our preceding definition of standard performance. A typical multiplier is 1.30, although some companies prefer not to use a multiplier at all (in effect, the value of the multiplier for these companies is 1.0). A multiplier of 1.30 means that an average worker should be able to work at a pace that is 130% of the defined standard pace. This standard pace is sometimes referred to as ***day work pace***.

The production rate is equivalent to the reciprocal of the time to complete the task. Thus, for an output of 100 pieces per day (480 min) at average performance, the average task time would be 4.80 min (480 min/100 pc). Using a multiplier of 1.30 to define standard performance, this means that 100 pc/day is 130% of standard performance, and the corresponding standard time is therefore 4.80 (1.30) = 6.24 min, or a daily production rate of 77 pc. These values can be seen in Figure 5, a revision of our

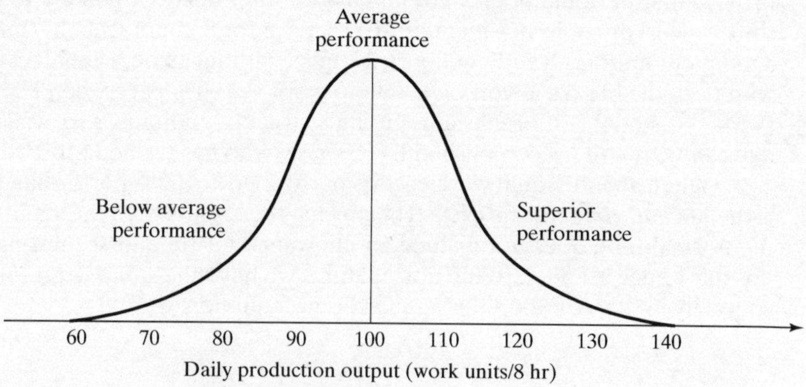

Figure 4 Distribution of performance (daily production output) for large numbers of workers.

[5]Several studies are cited in [8].

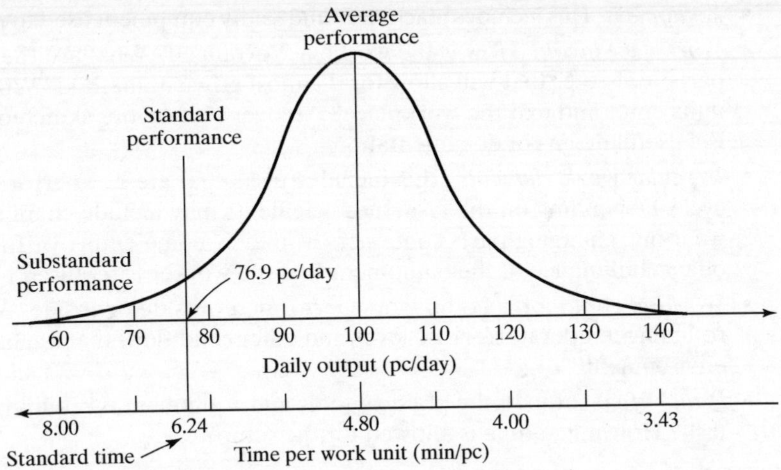

Figure 5 Distribution of performance and task time for large numbers of workers, indicating how standard time is typically defined as a time that can be readily achieved by most workers.

previous performance distribution. Accordingly, we can define ***standard performance*** in common industrial practice to be the pace of working at which the standard time for the task is 130% (or some other multiple, depending on company policy) of the mean time that can be maintained throughout an entire work shift by an average worker without harmful effects on the worker's health or physical well-being.

2.2 Standard Method

The ***standard method*** is the procedure that has been determined to be the optimum method for processing a work unit. The standard method satisfies the "one best method principle." It is the procedure that is the safest, quickest, most productive, and least stressful to the worker. It is constrained only by the practical conditions and economic limitations of the particular work environment. If the task is loading coal into a furnace in a steel mill, it is impractical and uneconomical to perform such work in a clean, air-conditioned environment that is void of safety hazards.

The standard method should include the following details about how a task is performed:

- *Procedure (actions and motions) used by the worker.* This is best described by listing the work elements that comprise the work cycle. The predetermined time systems provide a natural means for doing this because they list the basic motions that comprise the procedure. For direct time study and standard data systems, the procedure must be included in the statement of the standard method.
- *Tools.* This includes hand tools and portable power tools, fixtures, and gauges used in the procedure.

- *Equipment.* This includes machinery and safety equipment used to perform the task.
- *Workplace layout.* How is the workplace arranged? What are the locations of the parts, tools, etc., that will allow for the most efficient method? Where do the work units enter and exit the workplace? An overhead layout sketch of the workplace is a useful means of documentation.
- *Irregular work elements.* This includes tasks that are not performed every work cycle. Depending on the task, these elements may include changing tools as they wear out, changing parts containers as they become empty or full, and any periodic maintenance of the equipment that the worker is required to perform.
- *Working conditions.* Is the work performed outside or inside? What is the surrounding temperature, noise level, and other conditions that might affect the work environment?
- *Setup.* What setup of the physical tools and equipment is required to perform the task? How much time is allowed for the setup?

All of these factors should be thoroughly documented in a written statement of the standard method. At some future time, when the task is performed again after a long delay, the document will provide an invaluable and timesaving description of the task for which the time standard applies. If there is some dispute about the standard method or the standard time, the written statement will be a useful resource in resolving the dispute. Good documentation, a burden to prepare, is a blessing to practitioners.

2.3 Standard Input and Output Work Units

Most tasks involve a process or action performed on a work unit. The state or condition of the work unit is altered in some way by the task. Value is added to the work unit by performing the task on it (at least we hope so). The time required to accomplish the task is likely to depend on the condition of the input work unit. Therefore this condition must be specified as completely as possible in the standard method statement. Similarly, the condition of the output work unit must be specified. Exactly what changes have been made in the work unit as a result of the task performed on it? What is the final state of the completed work unit?

The starting and completed work units are usually easy to define in production because they deal with objects being processed. The status or condition of the starting work unit is usually defined explicitly by engineering documents that can be referenced in the standard method statement. The completed work unit is specified by similar documents. If an actual work part does not conform to these specifications, either before or after processing, then this nonconformance may necessitate a deviation from the standard method. For example, if a starting sand casting has too much metal to be machined due to variations or errors in the casting process, an additional machining pass across the surface may be required, which will take more time. This condition can be determined by comparing the actual part dimensions with those specified in the engineering drawing. If inspection reveals that the incoming part from the foundry is oversized beyond the tolerance, so that an extra machining pass is required, then additional time must be allowed for the extra pass (and the foundry should be notified to take corrective action for future deliveries).

In service work, the input and output work units are usually more difficult to define. However, most service tasks consist of a standard approach or method, which is the best procedure to accomplish the task. And the standard method may also have a "standard time" associated with it. An example is the routine automotive repair work performed in a car dealer's service department. Changing motor oil, replacing the oil filter, rotating four tires, and state inspection are all pretty standard jobs. For a given car model, each of these tasks has a standard method and a standard time. You can sometimes find the standard time on your bill from the service department.

3 ALLOWANCES IN TIME STANDARDS

In all of the work measurement techniques, the normal time is adjusted by an allowance factor to obtain the standard time. Allowances are used because there will be periods during the regular work shift when the worker is not working. The purpose of the allowance factor is to compensate for this lost time by providing a small increment of "allowance time" in each cycle. This way, even with the time losses, the operator will still be able to complete a fair day's work during the hours of the shift.

3.1 Accounting for Lost Time in the Workplace

There are various reasons why people do not work continuously during a regular shift. Some of the interruptions are work-related while others are not. Table 2 lists some typical causes of interruptions that occur in industrial work.

There is no denying that these interruptions occur during the work shift, and there is no denying that allowance time in some form should be provided to deal with them. The question is how much should be allowed, and how should it be provided to the worker. Companies address the allowance issue using two basic approaches, often in combination: (1) scheduled break periods during the shift and (2) a PFD allowance added to the normal time.

Scheduled Break Periods. Scheduled breaks are planned periods set aside during the shift as break time from work. Lunch breaks (or supper break for evening and night shifts) are almost always handled this way. Many companies treat rest breaks the same

TABLE 2 Typical Causes of Interruptions in the Workplace

Causes of Work-Related Interruptions	Reasons for Nonwork Related Interruptions
Machine breakdowns or malfunctions	Personal needs (e.g., restroom interruption)
Waiting for materials, parts, or other items necessary to proceed with work	Talking to coworkers about matters unrelated to work
Receiving instructions from foreman	Lunch break
Talking to coworkers about job-related matters	Smoke break
Waiting at a tool crib for the attendant to deliver a tool	Beverage break
Rest breaks to overcome fatigue for physiologically demanding work	Personal telephone call
Cleaning up at the end of the shift	

way. There is a specified rest break in the morning and one in the afternoon. The duration of these breaks is typically 5 to 15 minutes. All workers take their breaks during these specified times, and the workers are paid during these breaks.

In this approach, the shift is scheduled with breaks to divide the work day into periods of roughly equal length. For example, the day shift begins at 8:00 A.M. and ends at 4:30 P.M. There is a 15-minute rest break in midmorning, a lunch break from noon to 12:30 P.M., and another 15-minute rest break in midafternoon. Accordingly, the shift lasts 8.5 hours, which includes 8 hours of paid time (clock time).

The PFD Allowance. In this approach, an appropriate value of the ***personal time, fatigue, and delay*** (PFD) allowance factor (A_{pfd}) is determined for use in converting the normal time into the standard time. It results in extra time prorated in the time standard to compensate for the interruptions experienced by the worker during the shift, both work related and non-work related. Some companies include rest breaks in the allowance rather than using a scheduled break time for everyone as described above.

Personal time includes restroom breaks, phone calls, water fountain visits, and similar interruptions of a personal nature. A typical allowance for this category of interruption is 5%. A larger value would be appropriate if the work environment is hot and uncomfortable, and a lower value would be used for very favorable working conditions.

The ***fatigue*** or ***rest*** allowance is intended to compensate the worker for time that must be taken to overcome fatigue due to work-related stresses and conditions. For example, if the work is physiologically very demanding and the worker expends significant metabolic energy in performing it, then relaxation time should be allowed periodically for the body to recover. Some of the factors that cause fatigue in human workers are listed in Table 3. The allowance for fatigue for a given task is often determined by a combination of (1) the rest formulas and (2) negotiation between labor and management. The rest formulas provide a more or less scientific basis to make the determination. In practice, rest allowances are often the result of negotiated agreements between workers, perhaps represented by their union, and company management. An allowance of 5% is typical for fatigue in light and medium work. For heavy work it may be much higher, perhaps 20% or more.

Delays are unavoidable interruptions from work that occur at random times during the day. They usually refer to work-related events, such as, some of the interruptions listed in Table 2. It should be mentioned that work delays associated with a worker's personal needs (e.g., a sudden urge for a cigarette break) should not be counted in this

TABLE 3 Factors Causing Fatigue in Workers

Physical Factors	Mental and Cognitive Factors	Environmental and Work Factors
Standing	Concentration and attention	Poor lighting
Abnormal body position	Mental strain	Noise
Use of force	Monotony and tediousness	Fumes
Expenditure of muscular energy	Eyestrain	Heat
		Atmospheric conditions

Source: Adapted from a publication by the International Labour Office, *Introduction to Work Study* (1964) and other sources, as cited in [1].

category of interruption, since they are already included in the personal needs category. The delay category is generally reserved for delays that are ultimately the responsibility of management. For example, a machine breakdown may seem like a random occurrence, but management is responsible for the maintenance of the machine so that breakdowns are avoided. Other examples include waiting for parts or tools, waiting for an elevator, and waiting for the foreman's instructions. In general, these kinds of work-related delays must be controlled by company management. Certainly the worker is not responsible.

Determining the delay allowance is more challenging than determining allowances for personal needs or fatigue. There are traditions and/or formulas, often adjusted by negotiations, for determining these other allowances. But delays are usually random events that vary from day to day, and determining an allowance factor to account for them boils down to a problem of collecting data in the workplace so that an average lost-time value can be found. Two techniques are used to collect the data: (1) intensive observation over several days and (2) work sampling. Of the two methods, work sampling is usually preferred for several reasons: (1) it can be conducted over a longer period of time (e.g., weeks instead of days), so the plant activity observed is more likely to represent normal operations; (2) it can include a much larger scope of plant operations, because the observer is not limited to one location; (3) it does not require continuous observation, so it is more comfortable for workers and observer; and (4) statistical measures can be calculated to assess the accuracy of the results derived from the data.

The three allowances for personal needs, fatigue, and delays are then combined into a single allowance factor, which we symbolize A_{pfd}.

3.2 Other Types of Allowances

In addition to the PFD allowance factor, there are other reasons for adding allowances to the standard time of a task. They are not as common as the PFD allowance, but in some work situations they are quite appropriate. These other allowances are applied in addition to A_{pfd}, not as a substitute for it.

Contingency Allowances. The contingencies for which these allowances are provided are usually because of some kind of problem with the task or the production equipment used to perform it. Some examples of these problems are listed in Table 4. The

TABLE 4 Examples of Problems for Which Contingency Allowances Might Be Provided

Problem Area	Problems and Examples
Materials or parts	Starting materials or parts are out of specification, and extra time is needed to correct the nonconformance (e.g., oversized casting that requires an extra machining pass or slower feed rate).
Process	The manufacturing process is not in statistical control (too much variability), and additional time is required to inspect every piece rather than inspect on a sampling basis.
Equipment	Equipment is malfunctioning or breaking down more frequently than what is provided by the unavoidable delay factor, and additional time is needed to compensate the worker to make adjustments, lubricate the machine more frequently, or other extra task(s) not included in the standard time.

problems are beyond what is covered by the regular PFD allowance, and so an additional allowance is provided. Contingency allowances should not be greater than 5% [1]. The problems that contingency allowances are intended to address should not occur in the first place, but if they occur, the problem itself should be solved. Contingency allowances may be needed on a temporary basis to keep production going, but the long-term solution is to fix the underlying problem.

Policy Allowances. These allowances are intended to cover special work situations that are usually associated with a wage incentive system. An example is the ***machine allowance*** that is added to the machine-paced portion of a work cycle in the operation of a worker-machine system. The machine allowance provides an opportunity for the worker to maintain a high rate of earnings even though he or she has control over only a portion of the cycle. It is company policy that the worker be given this opportunity. The application of the machine allowance to compute the standard time is as follows:

$$T_{std} = T_{nw}(1 + A_{pfd}) + T_m(1 + A_m) \tag{3}$$

where T_{nw} = normal time of the worker during the worker-controlled portion of the cycle, min; A_{pfd} = PFD allowance; T_m = machine cycle time, min; and A_m = machine allowance. If company policy does not recognize the need for a separate machine allowance when computing the time standard, then either $A_m = 0$ or it is set equal to the value of the PFD allowance. The following example illustrates the way the worker benefits from a machine allowance.

Example 1 Use of Machine Allowance in a Wage Incentive Plan

A wage incentive plan pays workers a daily wage at a rate of \$15.00/hr multiplied by the number of standard hours accomplished during the shift. One worker-machine task in the plant includes worker-paced elements totaling a normal time of 1.00 min and machine-paced elements with a time of 3.00 min. The PFD allowance is 15%. Determine the standard time for the task given that (a) $A_m = 0$ and (b) $A_m = 30\%$. (c) What does a worker earn for the day under each policy if he or she produces 115 parts that day?

Solution: **(a)** $T_{std} = 1.00\,(1 + 0.15) + 3.00\,(1 + 0) = 1.15 + 3.00 = 4.15$ min.

(b) $T_{std} = 1.00\,(1 + 0.15) + 3.00\,(1 + 0.30) = 1.15 + 3.90 = 5.05$ min.

(c) For the standard of 4.15 min, the number of standard hours is H_{std} = 115(4.15)/60 = 7.95 hr and the worker's earnings would be \$15.00 (7.95) = \$119.25.[6]

For T_{std} = 5.05 min, H_{std} = 115(5.05)/60 = 9.68 hr and the worker's earnings would be \$15.00(9.68) = \$145.19.

Comment: Which is fair? A PFD allowance of 15% equates to a lost time per day of 62.6 min in an 8-hour shift, which leaves an actual working time of 417.4 min. Of this time, machine time took 115 cycles x 3.00 min/cycle = 345 min, which leaves 417.4 – 345 = 72.4

[6]Most incentive plans pay a guaranteed base rate, so the worker's wage for the day would be 8(\$15.00) = \$120.00.

min for worker time. Given that 115 cycles were completed by the worker, his performance during the worker-paced portion of the cycle must have been 115(1.00)/72.4 = 1.59 = 159%.

Certainly this level of performance would seem to merit some bonus above the base rate of $15/hr. The standard time in (a), T_{std} = 4.15 min, does not even pay the worker $15/hr (unless there is a guaranteed base rate, see footnote). The standard time in (b), T_{std} = 5.05 min, does earn a respectable bonus of $30.19. The worker's efficiency is 9.68/8.0 = 1.21 or 121%.

The other side of the argument is that the worker has free time for 345 min during the shift (because this is machine cycle time), so why should he or she be paid a premium bonus for the entire shift for only working 72.4 min of total shift time? This is a difficult issue, one on which common interest can often be found by both labor and management in keeping the machinery operating as high a proportion of time as possible (a win-win situation for both labor and management). Labor wins by earning higher bonuses. Management wins by using the equipment more efficiently. ■

Other types of policy allowances include ***training allowances*** for workers whose responsibilities include teaching other workers their jobs, and ***learning allowances*** for workers who are learning a new job or new employees who are just beginning work. In nearly all of the situations covered by policy allowances, a worker's earnings would be adversely affected if the allowances were not applied. Workers would be reluctant to train others or to learn new jobs unless some form of compensation were provided to cover the losses in earnings they would otherwise suffer for doing so. If a wage incentive plan is not used, there is less reason to have policy allowances since the worker's wage is not affected. The reason they are called policy allowances is because they are based on company policy, rather than any time interruptions actually experienced during the work shift.

4 ACCURACY, PRECISION, AND APPLICATION SPEED RATIO IN WORK MEASUREMENT

Work measurement is a measurement process. There are similarities and differences between the measurement of work and the measurement of physical variables in science and technology. Let us begin by defining measurement as it is applied in the physical sciences. ***Measurement*** is a procedure in which an unknown quantity is compared to a known standard, using an accepted and consistent system of units. The measurement provides a numerical value of the quantity of interest, within certain limits of accuracy and precision. All measurement systems are based on seven basic physical quantities: (1) length, (2) mass, (3) time, (4) electrical current, (5) temperature, (6) luminous intensity, and (7) matter. All other physical quantities (e.g., area, volume, velocity, force, electrical voltage) are derived from these seven basic quantities.

Time is one of the seven basic physical quantities, and time is the common quantity of interest in the measurement of work. The standard unit for time is the second.[7] Although time standards in work measurement often use alternative units (e.g., minutes, hours), they all can be related back to seconds.

[7]The ***second*** is defined in the System International as the "duration of 9,192,631,770 cycles of the radiation associated with a change in energy level of the cesium atom."

Three important attributes of a measurement system are accuracy, precision, and speed of response. These attributes are discussed in the following sections, and comparisons are made between the measurement of quantities in science and the measurement of work.

4.1 Accuracy and Precision

Measurement ***accuracy*** is the degree to which the measured value agrees with the true value of the quantity of interest. The measurement system is accurate if it is free of ***systematic errors***, which are positive or negative deviations from the true value that are consistent from measurement to measurement.

Measurement ***precision*** refers to the repeatability of the measurement system. High precision means that the random errors in the measurement procedure are small. It is generally assumed that random errors follow a normal statistical distribution with mean (μ) equal to zero and standard deviation (σ) indicating the amount of dispersion in the measured data. The normal distribution has well-defined properties, one of which is that 99.73% of the population is included within $\pm 3\sigma$, and this is often used as a quantitative indicator of the measurement system's precision.

The distinction between accuracy and precision is depicted in the three normal distributions of Figure 6. In distribution (a), the random errors in the measurement are large (large variance), which indicates that the precision is low, but the mean value agrees with the true value of the variable of interest, which indicates perfect accuracy. In (b), the random errors are low (high precision), but the measured value differs from the true value (low accuracy). In (c), we have high accuracy and high precision.

Accuracy and precision are important in work measurement, but these terms that are so readily applied to physical measurements are fraught with difficulty when applied to the measurement of work, especially direct time study. Accuracy is concerned with closeness to the true value, but how can that definition be applied to the time that should be allowed a worker to perform a given task? What is the true value of a task time? Measurement is a procedure in which an unknown quantity is compared to a known standard. In work measurement, there is no way to make that comparison because the closest that we can come to a known standard is in the minds of the time study analysts.

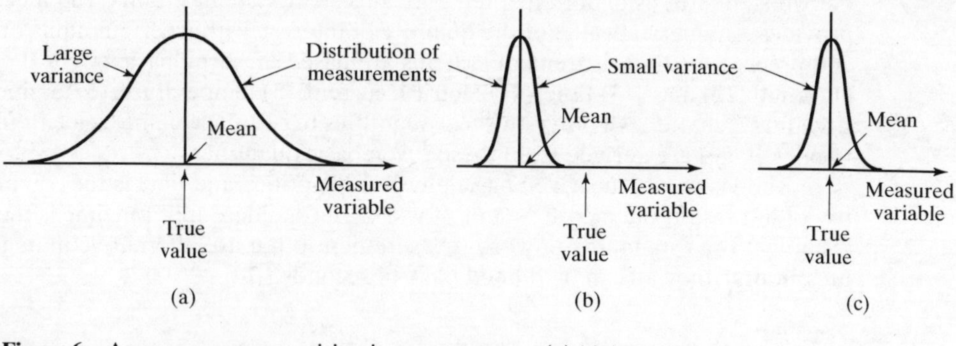

Figure 6 Accuracy versus precision in measurement: (a) high accuracy but low precision, (b) low accuracy but high precision, and (c) high accuracy and high precision.

And that standard is not based on time; it is based on a definition of performance (the organization's definition of standard performance). The issue becomes more confounded in direct time study because of performance rating. The time study analyst records the observed time of a given work element and then applies a performance rating to that time in order to align the observed time with the analyst's concept of standard performance.[8] We must conclude that accuracy in work measurement is elusive because it is impossible to scientifically determine the true value of the quantity of interest.

Although there are difficulties in determining accuracy in work measurement, the precision of the time standard resulting from a work measurement study can be determined, and this is sometimes used as a pseudonym for accuracy. The precision of the time standard is determined at a certain reliability level. For example, we state that the standard time for the task is 4.00 min, and that we are 95% certain that the actual time is within ± 5% of that time. In other words, in 95 out of 100 time studies performed on the task, the resulting standard time values will lie between 3.80 min and 4.20 min. This is analogous to confidence intervals in statistics, and we make use of them in Chapter 13 to determine how many cycles must be observed in direct time study in order to achieve a known level of reliability and precision in the time standard. The term ***consistency*** also applies here, and it refers to the variations in standard time values among different time study analysts who study the same task. Good consistency means small variations in the resulting time standards by different analysts. The term ***precision*** refers to the expected variability within a single time study or the time standard resulting from that study.

The relative accuracies of the various methods of determining time standards are of interest. These are summarized in Figure 7. Estimation is likely to be the least accurate because it is not based on any actual data or measurement. It relies solely on the estimator's judgment, which may not be very good. By comparison, historical records provide hard data on the average time required for the previous production order, and that is generally an improvement over judgment. Nevertheless, the accuracy of the record is sometimes questionable. Were the parts counted correctly, or did workers inflate

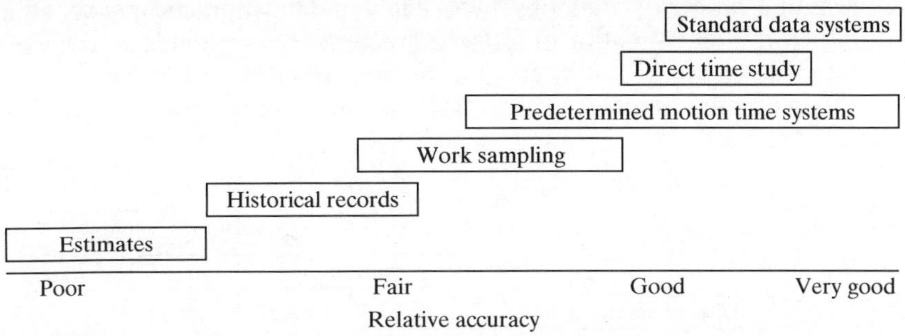

Figure 7 Methods of determining time standards ranked by relative accuracy.

[8]Mitchell Fein, a leading industrial engineering consultant for many years, made the following observation about direct time study: "No other measurement system which tests data for statistical validity alters the observed data" [4].

numbers to make themselves look more productive? Did the time sheet provide an accurate accounting of time spent on the particular order, or was other work done and charged to this order? How long did the setup take for this order? Although historical records are likely to be more accurate than pure estimation, they suffer from the fact that they are not based on a measurement of the actual work; instead, they are based on measures of the work output and the time that was recorded for that output.

In terms of relative accuracy, the work measurement techniques are more accurate than estimation or historical records. Of the four work measurement techniques, work sampling is not as accurate for determining time standards as the other three techniques. This due to (1) the statistical errors that result from the sampling process and (2) the absence of any attempt to analyze and improve the method used in the task.

4.2 Application Speed Ratio

Accuracy and precision are not the only criteria in selecting a work measurement technique. The amount of time required to perform the work measurement procedure is also important. In other measurements, the ***speed of response*** refers to the lag between the time when the measuring device is applied and when the measured value is available to the user. We would like to obtain our measurement of the variable of interest as quickly as possible, whether we are measuring a physical variable in science or a task time in a work situation.

In work measurement, the related term is ***application speed ratio***, which is the ratio of the time required to determine a time standard relative to the standard time itself. For example, an application speed ratio of 100 means that it takes 100 min of analyst time to determine a 1.0-min time standard. In general there is an inverse relationship between application speed ratio and "accuracy." Methods for setting time standards that can be applied quickly tend to be less accurate than those that take more time to apply.

The time required to perform any of the work measurement techniques is significantly greater than the time required to estimate a task time or to compute the task time from historical records. If accuracy of the task time is not important, or if the work consists of a variety of "odd jobs," where it would be impractical to set a time standard for each job, then estimation or historical records are preferable as a way of developing the time values. Figure 8 indicates the relative application speeds of the various methods for setting time standards. The PMT systems have a large range of application speeds

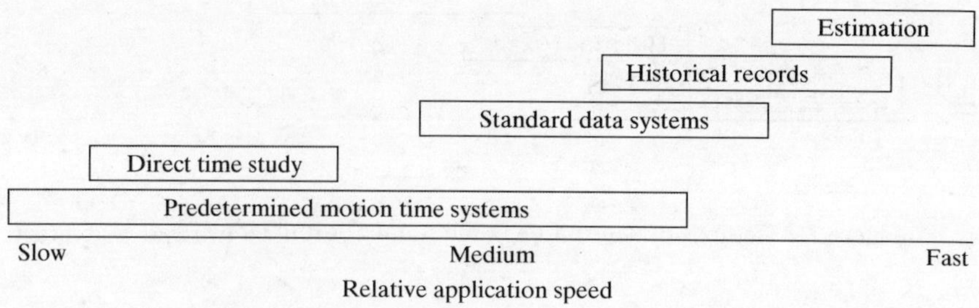

Figure 8 Methods of determining time standards ranked by relative application speed.

because of the variety of systems available, some of which are very accurate but very time consuming, while others are less accurate and take less time. The application speeds for standard data systems and historical records are relatively fast, but these systems require a substantial investment of time to develop before they are operational. Work sampling is omitted from the chart because it requires an extended period of data collection before standards can be determined.

REFERENCES

[1] Allerton, L. J. "Allowances." Pp. 5.101–119 in *Maynard's Industrial Engineering Handbook*, 5th ed., edited by K. Zandin. New York: McGraw-Hill, 2001.

[2] Barnes, R. M. *Motion and Time Study: Design and Measurement of Work*. 7th ed. New York: Wiley, 1980.

[3] Bishop, G. "Purpose and Justification of Engineered Labor Standards." Pp. 5.23–40 in *Maynard's Industrial Engineering Handbook*, 5th ed., K. Zandin. New York: McGraw-Hill, 2001.

[4] Fein, M. "How 'Reliability,' 'Precision,' and 'Accuracy' Refer to Use of Work Measurement Data." Pp. 30–37 in *Work Measurement, Principles and Practice*, edited by R. L. Shell. Norcross, GA: Industrial Engineering and Management Press, 1986.

[5] Hancock, W. M., and Bayha, F. H. "The Learning Curve." Pp. 1585–98 in *Handbook of Industrial Engineering*, 2nd ed., edited by Gavrial Salvendy. New York: Wiley; Institute of Industrial Engineers, Norcross, GA, 1992.

[7] Konz, S. "Time Standards." Pp. 1391–408 in *Handbook of Industrial Engineering*, 3rd ed., edited by Gavrial Salvendy. New York: Wiley; Institute of Industrial Engineers, Norcross, GA, 2001.

[8] Mundel, M. E., and D. L. Danner. *Motion and Time Study: Improving Productivity*. 7th ed. Englewood Cliffs, NJ: Prentice Hall, 1994.

[9] Niebel, B. W., and A. Freivalds. *Methods, Standards, and Work Design*. 10th ed. New York: McGraw-Hill, 1999.

[10] Panico, J. A. "Work Standards: Establishment, Documentation, Usage, and Maintenance." Pp. 1549–84 in *Handbook of Industrial Engineering*, 2nd ed., edited by Gavrial Salvendy. New York: Wiley; Institute of Industrial Engineers, Norcross, GA, 1992.

[11] Sellie, C. N. "Predetermined Motion-Time Systems and the Development and Use of Standard Data." Pp. 1639–98 in *Handbook of Industrial Engineering*, 2nd ed., edited by Gavrial Salvendy. New York: Wiley; Institute of Industrial Engineers, Norcross, GA, 1992.

[12] Smith, G. S., "Developing Engineered Labor Standards." Pp. 5.73–100. *Maynard's Industrial Engineering Handbook*, 5th ed., edited by K. Zandin. New York: McGraw-Hill 2001.

[13] Zandin, K. B., *MOST Work Measurement Systems*. 3rd ed. New York: Marcel Dekker, 2003.

REVIEW QUESTIONS

1 What is the standard time for a task? Provide a definition.

2 What are some of the characteristics typical of industrial situations in which time standards would be beneficial?

3 What are the functions and applications of accurately established time standards in an organization?

4 Identify the three basic methods to determine time standards.
5 What are the four basic work measurement techniques?
6 What is the difference between the normal time and the standard time for a task?
7 How does computerized work measurement reduce the time and effort of the time study analyst?
8 What are the prerequisites for valid time standards?
9 Identify the two common benchmarks of standard performance that are often used.
10 What are the details that should be included when defining the standard method?
11 What is a PFD allowance in time standards?
12 What are some of the reasons why workers experience lost time during a work shift?
13 What is a contingency allowance?
14 What is the difference between accuracy and precision in a measurement system?
15 Why is accuracy an elusive quality in work measurement?
16 What is precision in work measurement?
17 What is consistency in work measurement?
18 What is the application speed ratio in work measurement?

PROBLEMS

Determining Time Standards

1 The average observed time for a repetitive work cycle in a direct time study was 3.27 min. The worker was performance rated by an analyst at 90%. The company uses a PFD allowance factor of 13%. What is the standard time for this task?

2 A time study analyst observed a repetitive work cycle performed by a worker and then studied the task using a predetermined motion time system. During the observation, the analyst made a record of the work elements. He also made a note of the worker's performance and rated it as 85%. Back in the office, the analyst listed the basic motion elements for the task and retrieved from his computer the corresponding normal time values. The sum of the normal times for the basic motion elements was 1.38 min. The company uses a PFD allowance factor of 15%. Determine the standard time for the task.

3 The ABC Company uses a standard data system to set time standards. One of the time study analysts listed the three work elements for a new task to be performed in the shop and then determined the normal time values to be 0.73 min, 2.56 min, and 1.01 min. The company uses a PFD allowance factor of 16%. Determine the standard time for the task.

Allowances

4 In the ABC machine shop, workers punch in at 8:00 A.M. and punch out at 4:30 P.M. The labor-management agreement allows 30 min for lunch, which is not counted as part of the 8-hour shift. In determining the allowance for computing time standards, two 15 min breaks are provided (personal time and fatigue), one in the morning and one in the afternoon; and 20 min have been negotiated as lost time due to supervisor interruptions and equipment malfunctions. What PFD allowance factor should be added to the normalized time to account for these losses in the computation of a standard time, so that if workers work at standard performance, they will produce exactly 8 standard hours?

5 In the WS&FP plant, workers punch in at 8:00 A.M. and punch out at 5:00 P.M. The labor-management agreement allows 1 hour for lunch, which is not counted as part of the 8-hour shift. In determining the allowance for computing time standards, two 12 min breaks are included (personal time and fatigue), one in the morning and one in the afternoon; and 35 min are included as lost time due to interruptions and delays. What PFD allowance factor should be added to the normalized time to account for these losses in the computation of a standard time, so that if workers work at standard performance, they will earn exactly 8 standard hours?

6 Determine the PFD allowance to be used for computing time standards in the following situation. Second shift workers punch in at 3:30 P.M. and punch out at 12:00 midnight. They are provided 30 min for supper at 6:00 P.M., which is not counted as part of the 8-hour shift. For purposes of determining the allowance, 30 min of break time (personal time and fatigue) are allowed each worker. In addition, the plant allows 35 min for lost time due to unavoidable delays. What should the PFD allowance factor be?

7 The work shift at the ABC Company runs from 7:30 A.M. to 4:15 P.M. with a 45 min break for lunch from 11:30 to 12:15 P.M. that does not count as part of the work shift (workers are not paid for this time). The company provides two 12-min rest breaks during working hours (paid time), one in the morning and one in the afternoon. The company also allows 25 min per day for personal needs (paid time). In addition, a work sampling study has shown that on average, unavoidable delays in the plant result in 20 min lost time per worker per day (paid time). Determine the PFD allowance factor for the following two management policies on allowances: (a) the two 12-min breaks are both scheduled breaks that all workers take at the same time and (b) the two 12-min breaks are included in the allowance factor so that workers can take their breaks whenever they please.

Direct Time Study

Direct time study, also known as ***stopwatch time study,*** involves the direct and continuous observation of a task using a stopwatch or other timekeeping device to record the time taken to accomplish a task.[1] While observing and recording the time, an appraisal of the worker's performance level is made. These data are then used to compute a standard time for the task, adding an allowance for personal time, fatigue, and delays.

Direct time study was the first work measurement technique to be used, dating back to around 1883. It is inextricably connected with the origins of industrial engineering. Computerized techniques have improved the accuracy and application speed of direct time study as well as the database management functions that support it.

The use of direct time study is most appropriate for tasks that involve a repetitive work cycle, at least a portion of which is manual. This kind of work is common in

[1]The Work Measurement and Methods Standards Committee (ANSI Standard Z94.11-1989) defines time study as follows: "A work measurement technique consisting of careful time measurement of the task with a time measuring instrument, adjusted for any observed variation from normal effort or pace and to allow adequate time for such items as foreign elements, unavoidable or machine delays, rest to overcome fatigue, and personal needs. Learning or progress effects may also be considered. If the task is of sufficient length, it is normally broken down into short, relatively homogeneous work elements, each of which is treated separately as well as in combination with the rest."

batch and mass manufacturing. Also, standards for routine office work can often be established using direct time study. Performing a direct time study is time-consuming and is therefore best justified when the job will have a relatively long production run, and/or there will be repeated orders in the future. A limitation of this work measurement technique is that it cannot be used to set a time standard prior to the start of production.

1 DIRECT TIME STUDY PROCEDURE

The procedure for determining the standard time for a task using direct time study can be summarized in the following five steps:

1. Define and document the standard method.
2. Divide the task into work elements.
3. Time the work elements to obtain the observed time for the task.
4. Evaluate the worker's pace relative to standard performance, a procedure called ***performance rating***. This is used to determine the normal time. Steps 3 and 4 are accomplished simultaneously.
5. Apply an allowance to the normal time to compute the standard time.

Steps 1 and 2 are preliminary steps before actual timing begins, during which the analyst becomes familiar with the task and attempts to improve the work procedure before defining the standard method. In steps 3 and 4, several work cycles are timed, each one performance rated independently. Finally, the values collected in steps 3 and 4 are averaged to determine the normalized time. An appropriate allowance factor for the kind of work involved is then added to compute the standard time for the task. Let us examine each of the steps in more detail.

1.1 Define and Document the Standard Method

Before defining and documenting the standard method, a methods engineering study should be undertaken to ensure that the standard method obeys the "one best method" principle—the best method that can be devised under the present economic and technological circumstances. All of the steps in the method should be defined. Any special tools, gauges, or equipment that can improve the task should be designed and included in the method. If there are irregular elements in the work cycle, the frequency with which these elements are to be performed should be stated explicitly. If the labor-management climate in the facility allows, the worker's advice and opinion should be sought in developing the standard method. Once the standard method has been defined, it should be difficult or impossible for the operator to make further improvements.

The standard method should be thoroughly documented. The company should have forms and/or checklists to make certain that all information about the method is included. An example of a methods description form is shown in Figure 1. The documentation should enumerate details about the procedure (hand and body motions), tools, equipment and the machine settings used for the equipment (e.g., feeds and speeds

Date	**Standard Method Description for Direct Time Study**		Page of
Operation	Dept.	Part No.	
Machine	Analyst		
Methods Improvements (check if implemented)	Sketch of Workplace:		

Work Element No. and Description with Machine Parameters for Machine Cycles	Freq.	Tools and Gauges

Additional Notes

Figure 1 Form for documenting the standard method.

on machine tools), workplace layout, irregular work elements, working conditions, and setup. If there is a work unit associated with the task, then it should also be specified, both its starting and its completed conditions. A videotape (or other video medium) of the standard method can also be made as part of the documentation. This is especially helpful for complex tasks in which details of the method are difficult to explain in writing.

There are several reasons why thorough documentation of the standard method is important:

- *Batch production*. If the task is associated with batch production, then it is likely to be repeated at some time in the future. The time lapse may be significant between the previous batch and the next batch. A different worker may be assigned to perform the task on the next batch. The statement of the standard method provides the worker and the foreman with a complete description of the task and the procedure for doing it, as well as any tooling or equipment needed. This avoids "reinventing the wheel."
- *Methods improvement by the operator*. At some future time, the operator may discover a way to improve the method.[2] A question then arises: Should the methods improvement be incorporated into a new standard method (which would require a change in the standard time), or should the operator be allowed to benefit from the improvement without formally changing the standard method? The typical labor-management contract only allows for retiming the task if it can be demonstrated that a real change in the method has been made. If the operator has indeed made a methods improvement, this can be identified by comparing the method in use with the standard method description.
- *Disputes about the method*. If the operator complains that the standard for the task is too tight, or there is some other reason for a dispute about the standard method, documentation of the standard method can be used to settle the dispute.[3] Perhaps the operator is using a less efficient method than the standard method, or a certain hand tool that should be used in the operation has been neglected. These problems can be addressed by reference to the standard method documentation.
- *Data for standard data system*. Time standards developed by direct time study are sometimes used in standard data systems. Good documentation of the standard method, especially regarding the work elements and associated normal times, is essential in developing the database for a standard data system.

[2]This possibility seems at odds with the fact that the one best method has already been devised and has been defined as the standard method. However, the intelligence and ingenuity of the worker should not be underestimated. It must be acknowledged that the worker may be able to figure out some motion shortcut or hand tool or other gimmick that reduces the time for the work cycle, even though the work cycle has been subjected to a thorough methods study.

[3]A "tight" standard means that the standard time is too short, making it difficult or impossible to accomplish the task within the time standard. A "loose" standard is one in which the time is relatively long, making it easy to achieve a high worker efficiency.

1.2 Divide the Task into Work Elements

Any task can be divided into work elements. A ***work element*** is a series of motion activities that are logically grouped together because they have a unified purpose in the task. The description of the standard method can be organized into work elements suitable for use in direct time study. Indeed, the most natural way to describe the standard method is often as a list of work elements. Some practical guidelines for defining work elements in direct time study are presented in Table 1. An important reason for defining the

TABLE 1 Guidelines for Defining the Work Elements in Direct Time Study

Guideline	Explanation and Examples
Each work element should consist of a logical group of motion elements.	The work element should have a unified purpose, such as reaching for an object and moving it to a new location (e.g., reach, grasp, move, and place). There would be no purpose in separating the reach from the move motions since they both involve the same object.
Beginning point of one element should be end point of preceding element.	There should be no gap between one element and the next in the task sequence. Otherwise, the time of the gap is omitted from the recorded total time.
Each element should have a readily identifiable end point.	A readily identifiable end point can be easily detected during the study. It can often be anticipated to allow reading of the watch more conveniently. An audible sound, such as the actuation of a pneumatic device, provides a readily identifiable end point.
Work elements should not be too long.	If a work element is very long (i.e., several minutes), it should probably be divided into multiple elements that are timed separately. Machine semiautomatic cycle time is an exception. Some machine cycles can take several minutes and should be identified as one element.
Work elements should not be too short.	A practical lower limit in direct time study is around 3 sec. Below this, reading accuracy may suffer. If a video camera is used for timing purposes, shorter elements may be possible.
Irregular work elements should be identified and distinguished from regular elements.	Irregular elements are work elements that do not occur every cycle. The frequency with which they should be performed must be noted. The time(s) for the irregular element(s) are prorated across the regular work cycle when the standard time is computed.
Manual elements should be separated from machine elements.	Manual elements depend on the operator's performance (pace) and therefore vary over time. Machine elements are generally constant values that depend on machine settings. Once the settings are established, the actuation time shows no perceptible variation.
Internal elements should be separated from external elements.	Internal elements are performed by the operator during the machine cycle. In most cases, they do not affect the overall work cycle time. External elements are performed outside of the machine cycle. They contribute to the overall work cycle time.

Source: Adapted from guidelines in [13] and other sources.

work elements is that the worker may exhibit different performance levels on different elements. Accordingly, these performance levels are rated and recorded separately by the time study analyst.

1.3 Time the Work Elements

Once the work elements have been defined, the analyst is ready to collect data. The time data are usually recorded on a time study form, similar to the one shown in Figure 2. Space is provided for a listing of the work elements, which can be referenced to the more complete standard method documentation. Each element should be timed over several cycles to obtain a reliable average, and the form is designed for recording multiple cycles of the task. The appropriate number of cycles can be determined using the statistical techniques described in Section 2. For the convenience of the analyst, the time study form is usually held in a special clipboard that also holds the stopwatch used in the study.

There are several pieces of equipment that can be used to record the times for the work cycles. We describe the products in Section 4. The traditional instrument in direct time study is the stopwatch, which is usually calibrated in decimal minutes. There are two principal methods for using a stopwatch in direct time study: (1) snapback timing method and (2) continuous timing method. In the ***snapback timing method***, the watch is started at the beginning of every work element by snapping it back to zero at the end of the previous element. The reader must therefore note and record the final time for that element just as the watch is being zeroed. (Most stopwatches, especially electronic watches, have features that facilitate this reading.) In the ***continuous timing method***, the watch is zeroed at the beginning of the first cycle and allowed to run continuously throughout the duration of the study. The analyst records the running time on the stopwatch at the end of each respective element. Some analysts prefer to adapt the continuous method by zeroing at the beginning of each work cycle, so that the starting time of any given work cycle is always zero. This facilitates cycle-to-cycle comparisons during the study.

There are two advantages to the snapback method: (1) the analyst can readily see how the element times vary from one cycle to the next, and (2) no subtraction is necessary, as in the continuous timing method, to obtain individual element times. The advantages of the continuous method include the following: (1) when the clock is continuously running, elements are not as easily omitted by mistake, (2) regular and irregular elements can be more readily distinguished, and (3) not as much manipulation of the stopwatch is required as in the snapback method.

1.4 Rate the Worker's Performance

While observing and recording the time data, the analyst must simultaneously observe the performance of the worker and rate this performance relative to the definition of standard performance used by the organization. Other terms for performance include pace, speed, effort, and tempo. Standard performance is given a rating of 100%. A performance rating greater than 100% means that the worker's performance is better than standard (which results in a shorter observed work cycle time), and less than 100% means poorer performance than standard (and a longer observed time).

Date	**Direct Time Study Observation Form**		Page of
Operation		Dept.	Part No.
Machine			Tooling
Worker			Worker No.
Analyst	Start Time	Finish Time	Elapsed Time

Work Elements, Machine Settings, and Observations				Cycle No. (regular elements)										
Element Number and Description	Feed	Speed		1	2	3	4	5	6	7	8	9	10	Avg T_n
1			T_{obs}											
			PR											
			T_n											
2			T_{obs}											
			PR											
			T_n											
3			T_{obs}											
			PR											
			T_n											
4			T_{obs}											
			PR											
			T_n											
5			T_{obs}											
			PR											
			T_n											
6			T_{obs}											
			PR											
			T_n											
7			T_{obs}											
			PR											
			T_n											
8			T_{obs}											
			PR											
			T_n											
						Normal time = Sum of T_n (regular work elements)								

Irregular Element and Description	Freq	T_0	T_f	PR	T_n	**Calculation of Standard Time T_{std}**	
A						Sum of T_n (regular work elements)	
B						Sum of freq x T_n (irregular elements)	
C						Total T_n per cycle	
D						PFD allowance A_{pfd}	
E						Standard time $T_{std} = T_n(1 + A_{pfd})$	

Additional Notes

Figure 2 Direct time study form.

The observed time is subsequently multiplied by the performance rating to obtain the ***normal time*** (other names include ***normalized time*** and ***base time***) for the element or cycle. The calculation is summarized in the following equation:

$$T_n = T_{obs}(PR) \tag{1}$$

where T_n = normal time, min; T_{obs} = observed time, min; and PR = performance rating, usually expressed as a percentage but used in the equation as a decimal fraction. The symbols T_n and T_{obs} can be used to represent individual work elements or the entire work cycle, depending on how the data are taken and recorded.

Performance rating is the most difficult and controversial step in direct time study. The reason is that it requires the judgment of the analyst to assess the value of PR. The analyst's judgment of standard performance may differ from that of the worker who is being observed. It is in the worker's interest and advantage to be rated at a high performance level during the study, because that will mean that the normal time and ultimately the standard time for the task will be longer (resulting in a looser standard). Thus, it will be easier for the worker to achieve a higher efficiency level as the job continues. This is especially important to the worker if he or she is paid on a wage incentive plan. We consider performance rating and the issues surrounding it in Section 3.

1.5 Apply Allowance to Compute Standard Time

To obtain the standard time for the task, a PFD allowance is added to the normal time, as calculated in the following equation:

$$T_{std} = T_n(1 + A_{pfd}) \tag{2}$$

where T_{std} = standard time, min; T_n = normal time, min; and A_{pfd} = allowance factor for personal time, fatigue, and delays. This is often expressed as a percentage but used as a decimal fraction in our equation. The function of the allowance factor is to inflate the value of the standard time relative to the normal time in order to account for the various reasons why the operator loses time during the work shift. The allowance factor represents an average for the type of work, equipment, and conditions under which the operator works. Some days the worker may lose more time, other days less time, than what is provided by the allowance factor. In the long run it is intended to average out to a realistic value.

Example 1 Determining a Standard Time for Pure Manual Work

A direct time study was taken on a manual work cycle using the snapback timing method. The regular work cycle consisted of three elements, identified as a, b, and c in the following table. Element d is an irregular element performed every 5 cycles. Observed times and performance ratings of the elements are also given. Determine (a) the normal time and (b) the standard time for the work cycle, using an allowance factor of 15%.

Work Element	a	b	c	d
Observed time	0.56 min	0.25 min	0.50 min	1.10 min
Performance rating	100%	80%	110%	100%

Solution **(a)** The normal time for the cycle is obtained by multiplying the observed element times by their respective performance ratings and summing. In the case of element *d*, this normal time is prorated over 5 cycles.

$$T_n = 0.56(1.00) + 0.25(0.80) + 0.50(1.10) + 1.10(1.00)/5$$

$$= 0.56 + 0.20 + 0.55 + 0.22 = 1.53 \text{ min}$$

(b) The standard time is computed by adding the allowance.

$$T_{std} = 1.53(1 + 0.15) = 1.76 \text{ min.}$$

■

If the task includes a machine cycle, then company policy may provide for a machine allowance factor to be included in the standard time computation. The standard time equation becomes

$$T_{std} = T_{nw}(1+A_{pfd})+T_m(1+A_m) \quad (3)$$

where T_{nw} = normal time of the worker external elements, min; T_m = machine cycle time, min; A_m = machine allowance factor; and the other terms have the same meanings as before. If the company does not include a separate machine allowance, then $A_m = 0$ in the equation, or it uses the regular allowance A_{pfd}. Equation (3) assumes that there are no internal elements in the cycle. If the work cycle includes internal elements, then it must be determined whether the sum of the worker internal elements or the machine cycle time is larger in order to determine the normal time and the standard time.

Example 2 Determining a Standard Time for a Task That Includes a Machine Cycle

The snapback timing method was used in a direct time study of a task that includes a machine cycle. Elements *a*, *b*, *c*, and *d* are performed by the operator, and element *m* is a machine semi-automatic cycle. Element *b* is an internal element performed simultaneously with element *m*, and element *d* is an irregular element performed once every 15 cycles. Observed times and performance ratings are given in the table below. The PFD allowance factor is 15%, and the machine allowance is 20%. Determine (a) the normal time and (b) the standard time for the work cycle.

Worker element	*a*	*b*	*c*	*d*
Observed time, manual	0.22 min	0.65 min	0.47 min	0.75 min
Performance rating	100%	80%	100%	100%
Machine element		*m*		
Observed time, machine	(idle)	1.56 min	(idle)	(idle)

Solution **(a)** The normal time must take account of which element, *b* or *m*, has the larger value. Also, element *d* must be prorated across 15 cycles.

$$T_n = 0.22(1.00) + \text{Max}\{0.65(0.80), 1.56\} + 0.47(1.00) + 0.75(1.00)/15$$
$$= 0.22 + 1.56 + 0.47 + 0.05 = 2.30 \text{ min}$$

(b) The same comparison between elements *b* and *m* must be made in computing the standard time.

$$T_{std} = (0.22 + 0.47 + 0.05)(1 + 0.15)$$
$$+ \text{Max}\{0.52(1 + 0.15), 1.56(1 + 0.20)\}$$
$$= 0.85 + 1.87 = 2.72 \text{ min}$$

■

2 NUMBER OF WORK CYCLES TO BE TIMED

One of the practical issues in taking a time study is determining how many work cycles should be timed. The reason this issue arises is that there is statistical variation in the times of respective elements from one work cycle to the next. Direct time study involves a sampling procedure, and the objective is to determine a value for the population work element time as accurately as is possible and practical. As we increase the sample size, we expect the accuracy of the estimate to improve. On the other hand, increasing the sample size also increases the cost of taking the time study. It seems reasonable to try to find a balance between these competing factors.

There is inherent variability in any human activity, and performing manual work is a human activity. Work element times vary from cycle to cycle because of the following reasons:

- Variations in hand and body motions
- Variations in the placement and location of parts and tools used in the cycle
- Variations in the quality of the starting work units (e.g., a plastic molded part with flash that must be trimmed)
- Mistakes by operator (e.g., operator accidentally drops the work part)
- Errors in timing the work elements by the analyst
- Variations in worker pace

All of these variations are manifested in the work element times recorded for the cycle. Performance rating is supposed to compensate for the last item, variations in worker pace. However, because performance rating requires judgment by the analyst, that also introduces error and variation.

For analysis purposes, we assume that the observed work element times are normally distributed about the true value of the work element time. For practical purposes, we identify the longest work element in the cycle, or the most critical element (the one in whose accuracy we are most interested), as the element to focus on. Let us call this element time T_e. Our objective is to be able to identify the true value of T_e within a certain confidence interval. For example, we might state that we want to be 95% confident that the true value of T_e lies within $\pm 10\%$ of the observed average value of the element time. Let us identify the average value simply as $\bar{x}$. This is illustrated in Figure 3, which shows the distribution of observed time values taken during the time study.

The area under the normal curve between $\pm 10\%$ of $\bar{x}$ represents the probability that the true value of element time T_e lies within $\pm 10\%$ of $\bar{x}$. The general statement of the confidence interval can be expressed as follows:

$$\Pr\left(T_e \text{ lies within } \bar{x} \pm z_{\alpha/2} \frac{\sigma}{\sqrt{n}} \right) = (1 - \alpha) \tag{4}$$

where $z_{\alpha/2}$ = standard normal variate, s = standard deviation of the population element time, n = sample size, and (1 − a) = confidence level. The term $z_{\alpha/2} \frac{\sigma}{\sqrt{n}}$ is made equal to our desired interval size (e.g., $\pm 10\%$ of $\bar{x}$), and we solve for the value of n, the number of work cycles to time.

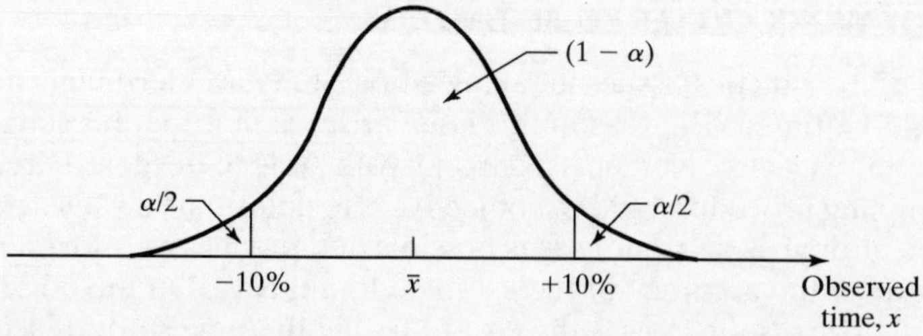

Figure 3 Distribution of observed element times in a direct time study.

There are two difficulties with the preceding analysis: (1) we do not know the population standard deviation s and (2) the sample size n that we are usually dealing with is relatively small. The standard deviation must be estimated from the sample itself, just as the mean $\bar{x}$ must be determined from the sample. The value of the sample standard deviation is given by

$$s = \sqrt{\frac{\Sigma(x-\bar{x})^2}{n-1}} \tag{5}$$

where s = sample standard deviation, x = individual values of the observed times collected during the study, and the other terms have previously been defined. Because the sample size n is usually small (e.g., less than 30), the sample values are distributed according to the student t rather than the normal distribution.

Taking these adjustments into account, we can make the following confidence interval statement to replace equation (4):

$$\Pr\left(T_e \text{ lies within } \bar{x} \pm t_{\alpha/2}\frac{s}{\sqrt{n}}\right) = (1-\alpha) \tag{6}$$

Our objective is to find the value of sample size n that will satisfy our specification of α and interval size for the values of $\bar{x}$ and s that have been determined from the data collected. Let us express the interval size in more general terms:

$$\text{Interval size} = \bar{x} \pm k\bar{x}$$

where k = a proportion that specifies the interval size (e.g., k = 10% or 0.10). We will set that equal to $\bar{x} \pm t_{\alpha/2}\frac{s}{\sqrt{n}}$, from which the following can be established:

$$k\bar{x} = t_{\alpha/2}\frac{s}{\sqrt{n}} \tag{7}$$

Rearranging and solving for n, we have

$$n = \left(\frac{t_{\alpha/2}s}{k\bar{x}}\right)^2 \tag{8}$$

where values of $t_{\alpha/2}$ can be found in the Appendix: Statistical Tables.

Example 3 Determining the Number of Work Cycles to Be Timed

A time study analyst has collected 10 readings on a particular work element of interest and would like to consider how many more cycles to time. Based on the sample, the mean time for the element is $\bar{x} = 0.40$ min and the sample standard deviation $s = 0.07$ min. At a 95% confidence level, how many cycles should be timed to ensure the actual element time is within ±10% of the mean?

Solution: We have $10 - 1 = 9$ degrees of freedom in the t distribution, so the value of $t_{\alpha/2}$ at the 95% confidence level ($\alpha/2 = 0.025$) is 2.262. Using equation (8), we obtain

$$n = \left(\frac{2.262(0.07)}{0.10(0.40)}\right)^2 = 15.7$$

This should be rounded up to 16 cycles total. Since 10 cycles have already been timed, the analyst needs data from 6 more work cycles. ■

The time study analyst may wish to turn the problem around; that is, to determine the size of the confidence interval at a certain desired confidence level, given that the observed times have already been recorded for a completed time study. This can be done using equation (8) but rearranging to solve for k.

Notwithstanding the preceding statistical approach, the problem of determining how many work cycles should be timed often boils down to the practical issue of how much time can we afford to spend doing the time study. Certain observations are germane here:

- The statistical accuracy of the time data increases when more observations are taken. The equations tell us that. If the task being studied is an important one in the factory operations, then more time should be spent on the time study to ensure the highest possible accuracy of the standard. More time should be spent studying high production operations than low production operations.
- Shorter work cycles allow more cycles to be timed during the study. For work cycles under 1 minute, 30 or more cycles are practical. For longer work cycles, fewer cycles can be included. For work cycles of 30 minutes, it may only be practical to observe six work cycles (which is 3 hours or more of time study observation).
- It is a judgment call by the time study department as to the appropriate number of work cycles to be timed. The judgment attempts to balance the desire for statistical accuracy against the cost of the time study.

3 PERFORMANCE RATING

Performance rating, also called ***performance leveling***, is the step in direct time study in which the analyst observes the worker's performance and records a value representing that performance relative to the analyst's concept of standard performance. A number of different performance rating methods have been proposed over the years, but the simplest and most common method is based on speed or pace.[4] It is sometimes referred to as speed rating. The other methods are rarely used today.

As its name indicates, ***speed rating*** involves rating the operator's pace of working relative to the concept of standard performance. A rating greater than 100% means that the worker is working faster than standard pace, and less than 100% means the worker is slower than standard. Pace is the only factor that is rated. However, pace depends on the type of work involved. To rate the operator's pace, the analyst must use judgment that is based on previous training and experience in rating similar work. An analyst who is experienced in machine shop time studies would find this experience of limited value if suddenly faced with the job of conducting time studies in a garment factory. The concept of standard performance is different for different kinds of work. Standard performance for a highly repetitive manual assembly task in which the cycle time is 1 minute should be defined differently than standard performance in a design prototype modeling shop in which the worker must apply technical skill and artistic talent to the job. And within a given category of work, some tasks are more difficult than others. Accordingly, the analyst must observe two aspects of the work scene during performance rating: (1) the degree of difficulty of the task and what 100% pace would be for that task, and (2) the subject worker's pace relative to the concept of 100% pace.

Let us examine these two aspects of performance using one of our accepted definitions of standard performance, walking at 3 miles/hr (4.83 km/hr). This is a 20-minute mile. The more complete definition is walking at 3 miles/hr on level flat ground, using 27-inch steps.[5] Also, it is assumed that the walker carries no load. If any of these conditions are not satisfied (i.e., level ground, 27-inch steps, no load), then it represents a change in the degree of difficulty, and so the definition of 100% performance might need adjusting. For example, walking uphill on a 3% slope might have a standard pace of only 2.5 miles/hr. But if the conditions of the definition are satisfied, so that standard performance is 3 miles/hr, then an individual's walking speed can be measured to assess his or her performance rating relative to this standard. In fact, walking is a situation where we can very precisely determine performance level if we assume that performance level is directly proportional to the speed of the walker. For example, suppose the walker is able to complete 1 mile in 18 min (0.30 hr) instead of 20. This is a speed of 3.33 miles/hr (1 mile ÷ 0.3 hr). Compared to 3.0 miles/hr, the performance level is 111%. We do not necessarily know that the walker's performance was a constant 111% (3.33 miles/hr) throughout the entire mile, but we know that on average it was 111%.

Unfortunately, very few work situations lend themselves to such a precise measurement of performance. Thus, performance rating comes down to a matter of the analyst judging the worker's pace relative to his or her concept of standard performance for the type of work involved. Direct time study is not the only instance where judgment is used to rate people. There are many areas of human activity in which judgments are used by experts to decide the relative performance of subjects, and the expert's judgments are readily accepted. Table 2 presents a list of activities in which judges rate the

[4]For the interested reader, the other performance rating methods are described in [14].

[5]This definition was apparently proposed by Ralph Presgrave, one of the early workers in time and motion study.

TABLE 2 Activities in Which Trained and Experienced Judges Rate the Contestants

Human Activities That Are Judged	Other Activities That Are Judged
Figure skating	Dog shows
Diving events	Farm shows
Gymnastics	Gourmet food contests
Bodybuilding contests	Art contests
Beauty contests	High school science fair contests
Umpire calling balls and strikes behind home plate in a baseball game	Grading of (college) freshman English essays

contestants, often reducing the judgment to a numerical score. Just as in these other areas, time study analysts must be trained and become practiced in performance rating. Training is accomplished through the use of training films (videotapes) that show scenes of workers performing various kinds of industrial tasks at a variety of performance levels. The workers' pace in these scenes have been performance rated by experts, so that a trainee can judge each scene and compare his or her ratings with those of the experts. On-the-job practice is obtained by accompanying experienced analysts during actual time studies.

Depending on the type of work and length of the work cycle, the analyst must decide whether to rate the performance of individual elements (called ***elemental rating***) or to rate the entire cycle (***overall rating***). If the work cycle is relatively short (e.g., less than a minute) and the work content is similar throughout the cycle, then convenience may favor rating the entire cycle. If the cycle is longer and involves different kinds of work elements, on which the operator exhibits different pace levels, then elemental rating is more appropriate.

Operator selection can influence the performance rating procedure. The pace observed by the analyst depends to some extent on the worker's skill, experience, exertion level, and attitude toward time study. If there is more than one worker performing the same task that is to be time studied, then it is in the analyst's interest to select a skilled worker who is familiar with the job (has had time to learn the task) and who accepts time study as a necessary management tool. Such workers are usually willing to cooperate with the time study analyst, even to the extent that they will attempt to work at a pace consistent with the company's definition of standard performance, thus relieving the analyst of being forced to attach a rating that is significantly different from 100%. It has been found that when the subject performs at a pace that is within about 15% of standard, the resulting standard time value is much more likely to be fair and accurate and accepted by the worker. If the subject's performance during observation deviates significantly from standard, not only does this make life more difficult for the analyst, it increases the likelihood that the standard will not be an accurate measure of the task.

Potential difficulties are encountered in performance rating because a potential conflict of interest exists between the subject worker and the time study analyst. It is always in the worker's interest for the performance rating to be high due to its effect on the computation of standard time. Notwithstanding the difficulties, we can identify the following characteristics of a well-implemented performance rating system:

- *Consistency among tasks.* The performance rating system should provide consistent ratings from one task to another. A worker who is able to perform at 125% efficiency on one task should be able to achieve the same efficiency level on any other task. The performance rating used to establish the normal time is a key factor in obtaining this consistency among tasks.
- *Consistency among analysts.* The performance rating for a task should not depend on which time study analyst does the rating. Consistency within a group of time study analysts can be measured using the deviations of individual *PR* values about the group average. Niebel and Freivalds indicate that a deviation of $\pm5\%$ is considered adequate [14]. Proper initial training and periodic refresher training for the analysts in a company should provide this level of consistency.
- *Easily understood.* The rating system should be easy to explain by the analyst and simple to understand by the worker.
- *Related to standard performance.* The company should have a well-defined concept of standard performance. To the extent possible, this concept should be documented for reference by workers. Time study analysts should apply this definition when performance rating a task.
- *Machine-paced elements rated at 100%.* The operator has no control over machine-paced elements and therefore deserves no performance rating for these elements. Any adjustment for machine-cycle elements should be done using a machine allowance when computing the standard time.
- *Performance rating recorded during observation of task.* The performance should not be rated and recorded afterward.
- *Worker notification.* At the conclusion of the time study observation session, the analyst should inform the worker of the performance rating that was observed. This sets a proper tone for the relationship between the two people. It puts pressure on the analyst to be as fair as possible in the rating process, and it allows the worker to express agreement or disagreement with the rating.

4 TIME STUDY EQUIPMENT

In direct time study, the analyst directly observes the task as a worker performs it. The equipment used by the analyst ranges from simple to sophisticated. In our coverage we divide the range into three categories: (1) traditional time study using a stopwatch, (2) video camera to record the observation on tape, and (3) computerized time study techniques.

4.1 Stopwatch Time Study

The traditional equipment used in direct time study consists of a stopwatch and a time study form on which to record the times during observation. There are alternatives to the stopwatch, such as a wristwatch or wall clock, but the proper professional instrument

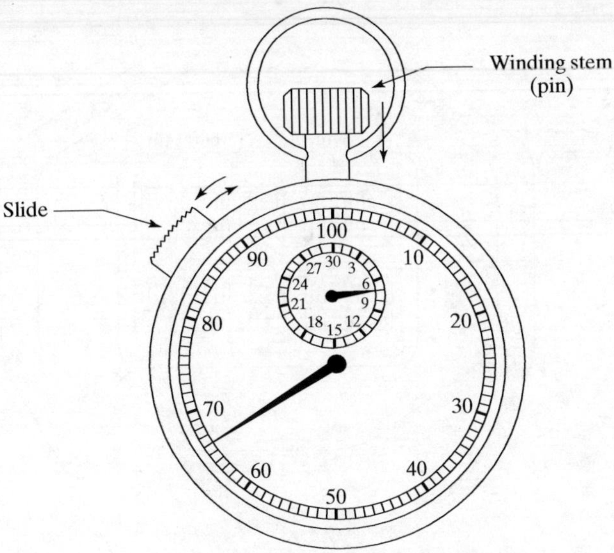

Figure 4 Mechanical stopwatch calibrated in decimal minutes (0.01 min) on the large dial. The small dial reads up to 30 minutes. Depressing the pin (also used as the winding stem) zeros the watch. The slide is used to start and stop the timing of individual work elements.

is a stopwatch. The time study form is usually held on a clipboard, which is designed to hold the stopwatch as well. Following the observation, the collected time data are analyzed and a time standard is calculated for the task.

Stopwatches can be classified as mechanical or electronic. ***Mechanical stopwatches*** have the familiar round face with one or more rotating hands, as shown in Figure 4. They are designed to be held in the time study clipboard or the palm of one's hand so the fingers can actuate the pin and slide at the top. Mechanical stopwatches are not a recent development. They have been used for time study since the late 1800s. Modern stopwatches for time study are typically graduated in one of three time measurement scales: (1) decimal minutes, shown in Figure 4, (2) decimal hours, and (3) TMUs (Time Measurement Units); 1 TMU = 0.00001 hr or 0.036 sec). The reason for having different scales is that different organizations have adopted different units to express their time standards. Decimal minute watches seem to be the most common, decimal hours less common, and TMUs are sometimes used because they are usually the time units in certain predetermined motion time systems.

Electronic stopwatches (Figure 5) provide a digital display of the time; otherwise their operating features are similar to those of mechanical watches. They have largely replaced mechanical stopwatches in time study for several compelling reasons. Because they display a digital readout, they are easier to read than the graduated mechanical dial, especially if the mechanical hand is moving. Because they are easier to read, reading errors occur less frequently. They are lighter in weight and generally less

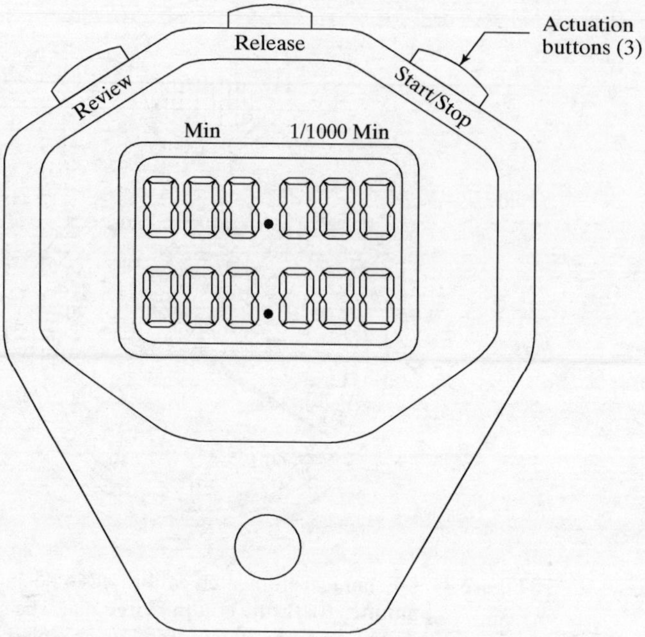

Figure 5 Electronic stopwatch with LED read-out, that can be used for continuous or snapback timing methods.

susceptible to damage when dropped or otherwise abused. Electronic watches are also more accurate and precise, which allows them to be used to read shorter work elements more conveniently. Some electronic watches can be switched back and forth between different time scales, unlike their mechanical counterparts. They can be used for either the continuous timing mode or the snapback mode. Finally, electronic stopwatches are less expensive than mechanical stopwatches.

The direct time study observation form (Figure 2) provides space for the analyst to record the observed times and the performance rating of the operator. Either the continuous timing method or the snapback method can be used. Observed times for multiple work cycles can be entered on the form.

4.2 Video Cameras

Video cameras have become a familiar piece of electronic equipment not only to consumers but to time study analysts as well. They are useful in direct time study because they provide a complete visual and audio record of the method used by the worker. The method is captured in much greater detail than the analyst can observe with the naked eye or is willing to include in any written documentation of the method. The tape also provides an accurate record of the times taken by each work element (accurate to 1/30 sec based on a frame-to-frame frequency of 30 Hz in the United States, or 1/25 sec based on 25 Hz in Europe). The tape can be subsequently played and replayed (in slow motion if desired) to analyze the method, perhaps uncovering possible improvements in the task. Work element times can be analyzed for cycle-to-cycle variations. Operator performance can be rated in a much more relaxed and objective setting than what is possible in the shop floor environment. And finally, a standard time can be determined for the task from the tape.

Later, if a dispute arises about the standard time, the method, or the performance rating, the tape can be viewed to help settle the dispute, perhaps avoiding a formal grievance. If the operator wants to watch his own work performance, perhaps to decide whether he agrees with the rating, this can be accommodated. The tape can be used for training purposes for new time study analysts. The videotape provides an objective and accurate record of the worker performing the task using the method for which the time standard was determined.

Video cameras can be used for a variety of work situations in motion and time study: short repetitive work cycles, long cycles with variable elements, worker-machine systems, crews of workers, and several workers working independently but captured in the field of vision of the camera.[6]

REFERENCES

[1] Aft, L. S. *Work Measurement and Methods Improvement.* New York: Wiley, 2000.

[2] Aft, L. S. "Measurement of Work." Pp. 5.3–5.22 in *Maynard's Industrial Engineering Handbook*, 5th ed., edited by K. Zandin. New York: McGraw-Hill, 2001.

[3] ANSI Standard Z94.0-1989, *Industrial Engineering Terminology*. Norcross, GA: Industrial Engineering and Management Press, Institute of Industrial Engineers, 1989.

[4] Barnes, R. M. *Motion and Time Study: Design and Measurement of Work*. 7th ed. New York: Wiley, 1980.

[5] Bishop, G. "Purpose and Justification of Engineered Labor Standards." Pp. 5.23–5.40 in *Maynard's Industrial Engineering Handbook*, 5th ed., edited by K. Zandin. New York: McGraw-Hill, 2001.

[6] Jay, T. A. *Time Study*. Poole, England: Blandford Press, 1981.

[7] Kanawaty, G., ed. *Introduction to Work Study*. 4th ed. Geneva, Switzerland: International Labour Office, 1992.

[8] Karger, D. W., and F. H. Bayha. *Engineered Work Measurement.* New York: Industrial Press Inc., 1987.

[9] Konz, S., and S. Johnson. *Work Design: Industrial Ergonomics*. 5th ed. Scottsdale, AZ: Holcomb Hathaway Publishers, 2000.

[10] Konz, S. "Time Standards." Pp. 1391–408 in *Handbook of Industrial Engineering*, 3rd ed., edited by G. Salvendy. New York: Wiley; Institute of Industrial Engineers, Norcross, GA, 2001.

[11] Matias, A. C. "Work Measurement: Principles and Techniques." Pp. 1409–462 in *Handbook of Industrial Engineering*, 3rd ed., edited by G. Salvendy. New York: Wiley; Institute of Industrial Engineers, Norcross, GA, 2001.

[12] Meyers, F. E., and J. R. Stewart. *Motion and Time Study for Lean Manufacturing*. 3rd ed. Upper Saddle River, NJ: Prentice Hall, 2002.

[13] Mundel, M. E., and D. L. Danner. *Motion and Time Study: Improving Productivity*. 7th ed. Englewood Cliffs, NJ: Prentice Hall, 1994.

[14] Niebel, B. W., and A. Freivalds. *Methods, Standards, and Work Design*. 11th ed. New York: McGraw-Hill, 2003.

[6]Most of the items in this list were suggested by [13].

[15] Polk, E. J. *Methods Analysis and Work Measurement.* New York: McGraw-Hill, 1984.
[16] Sellie, C. N. "Stopwatch Time Study." Pp. 17.21–17.46 in *Maynard's Industrial Engineering Handbook*, 5th ed., edited by K. Zandin. New York: McGraw-Hill, 2001.
[17] Smith, G. L., Jr. *Work Measurement: A Systems Approach.* Columbus, OH: Grid Publishing, 1978.

REVIEW QUESTIONS

1 Define direct time study.

2 Identify the five steps in the direct time study procedure.

3 Why is it so important to define and document the standard method as precisely and thoroughly as possible?

4 What is the snapback timing method when using a stopwatch during direct time study?

5 What is the continuous timing method when using a stopwatch during direct time study?

6 Why is performance rating a necessary step in direct time study?

7 Why is an allowance added to the normal time to compute the standard time?

8 What are some of the causes of variability in the observed work element times that occur from cycle to cycle?

9 Why is the student t distribution rather than the normal distribution used in the calculation of the number of work cycles to be timed?

10 What is the difference between elemental performance rating and overall performance rating?

11 What are the characteristics of a well-implemented performance rating system?

12 What are the advantages of electronic stopwatches compared to mechanical stopwatches?

PROBLEMS

Note: Some of the problems in this set require the use of parameters and equations.

Determining Standard Times for Pure Manual Tasks

1 The observed average time in a direct time study was 2.40 min for a repetitive work cycle. The worker's performance was rated at 110% on all cycles. The personal time, fatigue, and delay (PFD) allowance for this work is 12%. Determine (a) the normal time and (b) the standard time for the cycle.

2 The observed element times and performance ratings collected in a direct time study are indicated in the table below. The snapback timing method was used. The PFD allowance in the plant is 14%. All elements are regular elements in the work cycle. Determine (a) the normal time and (b) the standard time for the cycle.

Work element	*a*	*b*	*c*	*d*
Observed time (min)	0.22	0.41	0.30	0.37
Performance rating(%)	90	120	100	90

3 The standard time is to be established for a manual work cycle by direct time study. The observed time for the cycle averaged 4.80 min. The worker's performance was rated at 90% on all cycles observed. After eight cycles, the worker must exchange parts containers, which took 1.60 min, rated at 120%. The PFD allowance for this class of work is 15%. Determine (a) the normal time, (b) the standard time for the cycle, and (c) the worker's efficiency if the worker produces 123 work units during an 8-hour shift.

4 The snapback timing method was used to obtain the average times and performance ratings for work elements in a manual repetitive task. (See table below). All elements are worker-controlled and were performance rated at 80%. Element *e* is an irregular element performed every five cycles. A 15% allowance for personal time, fatigue, and delays is applied to the cycle. Determine (a) the normal time and (b) the standard time for this cycle. If the worker's performance during actual production is 120% on all manual elements for 7 actual hours worked on an 8-hour shift, (c) how many units will be produced and (d) what is the worker's efficiency?

Work element	*a*	*b*	*c*	*d*	*e*
Observed time (min)	0.32	0.85	0.48	0.55	1.50

5 The continuous timing method is used to direct time study a manual task cycle consisting of four elements: *a*, *b*, *c*, and *d*. Two parts are produced each cycle. Element *d* is an irregular element performed once every six cycles. All elements were performance rated at 90%. The PFD allowance is 11%. Determine (a) the normalized time for the cycle, (b) the standard time per part, (c) the worker's efficiency if the worker completes 844 parts in an 8-hour shift during which she works 7 hours and 10 min.

Element	*a*	*b*	*c*	*d*
Observed time (min)	0.35	0.60	0.86	1.46

6 The readings in the table below were taken by the snapback timing method of direct time study to produce a certain subassembly. The task was performance rated at 85%. In addition to the above regular elements, an irregular element must be included in the standard: each rack holds 20 mechanism plates and has universal wheels for easy movement. After completing 20 subassemblies, the operator must move the rack (which now holds the subassemblies) to the aisle and then move a new empty rack into position at the workstation. This irregular element was timed at 2.90 min and the operator was performance rated at 80%. The PFD allowance is 15%. Determine (a) the normalized time for the cycle, (b) the standard time, and (c) the number of parts produced by the operator, if he or she works at standard performance for a total of 6 hr and 57 min during the shift.

Element and Description	Observed Time (min)
1. Pick up mechanism plate from rack and place in fixture.	0.42
2. Assemble motor and fasteners to front side of plate.	0.28
3. Move to other side of plate.	0.11
4. Assemble two brackets to plate.	0.56
5. Assemble hub mechanism to brackets.	0.33
6. Remove plate from fixture and place in rack.	0.40

7 The time and performance rating values in the table below were obtained using the snapback timing method on the work elements in a certain manual repetitive task. All elements are worker-controlled and were performance rated at 85%. Element *e* is an irregular element performed every five cycles. A 15% PFD allowance is applied to the cycle. Determine (a) the normal time and (b) the standard time for this cycle. If the worker's performance during actual production is 125% on all manual elements for 7 actual hours worked on an 8-hour shift, (c) how many units will be produced and (d) what is the worker's efficiency?

Work element	*a*	*b*	*c*	*d*	*e*
Observed time (min)	0.61	0.42	0.76	0.55	1.10

Determining Standard Times for Worker-Machine Tasks

8 The snapback timing method was used to obtain average times for work elements in one work cycle. The times are given in the table below. Element *d* is a machine-controlled element and the time is constant. Elements *a*, *b*, *c*, *e*, and *f* are operator-controlled and were performance rated at 80%; however, elements *e* and *f* are performed during the machine-controlled element *d*. The machine allowance is zero (no extra time is added to the machine cycle), and the PFD allowance is 14%. Determine (a) the normal time for the cycle and (b) the standard time for the cycle.

Element	*a*	*b*	*c*	*d*	*e*	*f*
Observed time (min)	0.24	0.30	0.17	0.76	0.26	0.14

9 The continuous timing method in direct time study was used to obtain the element times for a worker-machine task as indicated in the table below. Element *c* is a machine-controlled element and the time is constant. Elements *a*, *b*, *d*, *e*, and *f* are operator-controlled and external to the machine cycle, and they were performance rated at 80%. If the machine allowance is 25%, and the worker PFD allowance is 15%, determine (a) the normal time, (b) the standard time for the cycle, and (c) the worker's efficiency if the worker completes 360 work units working 7.2 hr on an 8-hour shift.

Element	*a*	*b*	*c*	*d*	*e*	*f*
Observed time (min)	0.18	0.30	0.88	1.12	1.55	1.80

10 A worker-machine cycle is direct time studied using the continuous timing method. One part is produced each cycle. The cycle consists of five elements: *a*, *b*, *c*, *d*, and *e*. Elements *a*, *c*, *d*, and *e* are manual elements, external to machine element *b*. Every 16 cycles the worker must replace the parts container, which was observed to take 2.0 min during the time study. All worker elements were performance rated at 80%. The PFD allowance is 16%, and the machine allowance is 20%. Determine (a) the normalized time for the cycle, (b) the standard time per part, and (c) the worker's efficiency if the worker completes 220 parts in an 8-hour shift during which he or she works 7 hr and 12 min.

Element	Description	Cumulative Observed Time (min)
a	Worker loads machine and starts automatic cycle.	0.25
b	Machine is engaged in automatic cycle.	1.50
c	Worker unloads machine.	1.75
d	Worker files part to size.	2.30
e	Worker deposits part in container.	2.40

11 In the preceding problem, a recommendation has been submitted for elements *d* and *e* to be performed as internal elements (accomplished simultaneously) with machine element *b*. The worker would file the part from the previous cycle and deposit it in the container while the current part is being processed in the machine automatic cycle. Performance rating and allowances are the same as in the previous problem. Determine (a) the normal time for the cycle, (b) the standard time per part, and (c) the number of parts that will be produced if the worker's efficiency is 115% and he works a total of 7 hr and 12 min during an 8-hour shift.

12 The snapback method was used to time study a worker-machine cycle consisting of elements *a*, *b*, and *c*. Elements *a* and *b* are worker-controlled and were performance rated at 100% during the time study. Element *c* is machine-controlled. Elements *b* and *c* are performed simultaneously. The PFD allowance is 12% and the machine allowance is 10%. One work piece is produced each cycle. Determine (a) the normal time, (b) the standard time for the cycle. (c) the number of pieces completed if the worker works 7 hr and 10 min during an 8-hour shift, and his performance level is 135%.

Element	*a*	*b*	*c*
Observed time (min)	1.25	0.90	0.80

13 The snapback timing method in direct time study was used to obtain the times for a worker-machine task. The recorded times are listed in the table below. Element *c* is a machine-controlled element and the time is constant. Elements *a*, *b*, and *d* are operator-controlled and were performance rated at 90%. Elements *a* and *b* are external to machine-controlled element *c*. Element *d* is internal to the machine element. The machine allowance is zero, and the PFD allowance is 13%. Determine (a) the normal time and (b) the standard time for the cycle. The worker's actual time spent working during an 8-hour shift was 7.08 hours, and he produced 420 units of output during this time. Determine (c) the worker's performance during the operator-controlled portions of the cycle and (d) the worker's efficiency during this shift.

Element	*a*	*b*	*c*	*d*
Observed time (min)	0.34	0.25	0.68	0.45

14 The table below lists the average work element times obtained in a direct time study using the snapback timing method. Elements *a* and *b* are operator-controlled. Element *c* is a machine-controlled element and its time is constant. Element *d* is a worker-controlled irregular element performed every five cycles. Elements *a*, *b* and *d* were performance rated at 80%. The worker is idle during element *c*, and the machine is idle during elements *a*, *b*, and *d*. One product unit is produced each cycle. To compute the standard, no machine allowance is applied to element *c*, and a 15% PFD allowance is applied to elements *a*, *b*, and *d*. (a) Determine the standard time for this cycle. (b) If the worker produces 220 units on an 8-hour shift during which 7.5 hours were actually worked, what was the worker's efficiency? (c) For the 220 units in (b), what was the worker's performance during the operator-paced portion of the cycle?

Element	*a*	*b*	*c*	*d*
Observed time (min)	0.60	0.45	1.50	0.75

15 The continuous timing method in direct time study was used to obtain the times for a worker-machine task as indicated in the table below. Element *c* is a machine-controlled element and the time is constant. Elements *a*, *b*, *d*, *e*, and *f* are operator-controlled and were performance rated at 95%; they are all external elements performed in sequence with machine element *c*. The machine allowance is 30%, and the PFD allowance is 15%. Determine (a) the normal time and (b) standard time for the cycle. (c) If the operator works at 100% of standard performance in production and one part is produced each cycle, how many parts are produced if the total time worked during an 8-hour day is 7.25 hours? (d) For the number of parts computed in (c), what is the worker's efficiency for this shift?

Element	*a*	*b*	*c*	*d*	*e*	*f*
Observed time (min)	0.22	0.40	1.08	1.29	1.75	2.10

16 The snapback timing method was used to obtain average time and performance rating values for the work elements in a certain repetitive task. The values are given in the table below. Elements *a*, *b*, and *c* are worker-controlled. Element *d* is a machine-controlled element and its time is the same each cycle (N.A. means performance rating is not applicable). Element *c* is performed while the machine is performing its cycle (element *d*). Element *e* is a worker-controlled irregular element performed every six cycles. The machine is idle during elements *a*, *b*, and *e*. Four product units are produced each cycle. The machine allowance is zero, and a 15% PFD allowance is applied to the manual portion of the cycle. Determine (a) the normal time and (b) the standard time for this cycle. If the worker's performance during actual production is 140% on all manual elements for 7 actual hours worked on an 8-hour shift, determine (c) how many units will be produced and (d) what the worker's efficiency will be.

Work Element	*a*	*b*	*c*	*d*	*e*
Observed time (min)	0.65	0.50	0.50	0.55	1.14
Performance rating (%)	90	100	120	N.A.	80

17 The continuous timing method was used to obtain the times for a worker-machine task. Only one cycle was timed. The observed time data are recorded in the table below. Elements *a*, *b*, *c*, and *e* are worker-controlled elements. Element *d* is machine controlled. Elements *a*, *b*, and *e* are external to the machine-controlled element, while element *c* is internal. There are no irregular elements. All worker-controlled elements were performance rated at 80%. The PFD allowance is 15% and the machine allowance is 20%. Determine (a) the normal time and (b) standard time for the cycle. (c) If worker efficiency is 100%, how many units will be produced in one 9-hour shift? (d) If the actual time worked during the shift is 7.56 hours, and the worker performance is 120%, how many units would be produced?

Worker element (min)	*a* (0.65)	*b* (1.80)	*c* (4.25)	*e* (5.45)
Machine element (min)			*d* (4.00)	

18 The continuous stopwatch timing method was used to obtain the observed times for a worker-machine task. Only one cycle was timed. The data are recorded in the table below. The times listed indicate the stopwatch reading at the end of the element. Elements *a*, *b*, and *d* are worker-controlled elements. Element *c* is machine controlled. Elements *a* and *d* are external to the machine-controlled element, while element *b* is internal. Every four cycles, there is an irregular worker element that takes 1.32 min rated at 100% performance. For determining the standard time, the PFD allowance is 15% and the machine allowance is 30%. Determine (a) the normal time and (b) standard time for the cycle. (c) If worker efficiency is 100%, how many units will be produced in one 8-hour shift? (d) If the actual time worked during the shift is 6.86 hours, and the worker performance is 125%, how many units will be produced?

Worker Element	Description of Worker Element	Time (min)	Performance Rating (%)	Machine Element	Description of Machine Element	Time (min)
a	Acquire workpart from tray, cut to size, and load into machine	1.24	100	(idle)		
b	Enter machine settings for next cycle	4.24	120	*c*	Automatic cycle controlled by machine settings entered in previous cycle	4.54
d	Unload machine and place part on conveyor	5.09	80	(idle)		

19 The snapback timing method in direct time study was used to obtain the times for a worker-machine task. The recorded times are listed in the table below. Element *d* is a machine-controlled element and the time is constant. Elements *a*, *b*, *c*, *e*, and *f* are operator-controlled and were performance rated at 90%. Element *f* is an irregular element, performed every five cycles. The operator-controlled elements are all external to machine-controlled element *d*. The machine allowance is zero, and the PFD allowance is 13%. Determine (a) the normalized time for the cycle and (b) the standard time for the cycle. The worker's actual time spent working during an 8-hour shift was 7.08 hours, and he produced 400 units of output during this time. Determine (c) the worker's performance during the operator-controlled portions of the cycle and (d) the worker's efficiency during this shift.

Element	*a*	*b*	*c*	*d*	*e*	*f*
Observed time (min)	0.14	0.25	0.18	0.45	0.20	0.62

20 For a worker-machine task, the continuous-timing method was used to obtain the times indicated in the table below. Element *c* is a machine-controlled element and the time is constant. Elements *a*, *b*, *d*, and *e* are operator-controlled and were performance rated at 100%; however, element *d* is performed during the machine-controlled element *c*. The machine allowance is 16%, and the PFD allowance is 16%. Determine (a) the normal time and (b) standard time for the cycle. (c) If the operator works at 140% of standard performance in production and two parts are produced each cycle, how many parts are produced if the total time worked during an 8-hour day is 7.4 hours? (d) For the number of parts computed in (c), what is the worker's efficiency for this shift?

Element	*a*	*b*	*c*	*d*	*e*
Observed time (min)	0.30	0.65	1.65	1.90	2.50

21 For a certain repetitive task, the snapback timing method was used to obtain the average work element times and performance ratings listed in the table below. Elements *a*, *b*, and *c* are worker-controlled. Element *d* is a machine-controlled element and its time is the same each cycle (N.A. means performance rating is not applicable). Element *c* is performed while the machine is performing its cycle (element *d*). Element *e* is a worker-controlled irregular element performed every six cycles. The machine is idle during elements *a*, *b*, and *e*. One part is produced each cycle. The machine allowance is 15%, and a 15% PFD allowance is applied to the manual portion of the cycle. Determine (a) the normal time and (b) the standard time for this cycle. If the worker's performance during actual production is 130% on all manual elements for 7.3 actual hours worked on an 8-hour shift, (c) how many units will be produced and (d) what is the worker's efficiency?

Work Element	*a*	*b*	*c*	*d*	*e*
Observed time (min)	0.47	0.58	0.70	0.75	2.10
Performance rating (%)	90	80	110	N.A.	85

22 The work element times for a repetitive work cycle are listed in the table below, as determined in a direct time study using the snapback timing method. Elements *a* and *b* are operator-controlled. Element *c* is a machine-controlled element and its time is constant. Element *d* is a worker-controlled irregular element performed every 10 cycles. Elements *a* and *b* were performance rated at 90%, and element *d* was performance rated at 75%. The worker is idle during element *c*, and the machine is idle during elements *a*, *b*, and *d*. One product unit is produced each cycle. No special allowance is added to the machine cycle time (element *c*), but a 15% allowance factor is applied to the total cycle time. (a) Determine the standard time for this cycle. If the worker produced 190 units on an 8-hour shift during which 7 hours are actually worked, (b) what was the worker's efficiency, and (c) what was his performance during the operator-paced portion of the cycle?

Work element	*a*	*b*	*c*	*d*
Observed time (min)	0.75	0.30	1.62	1.05

Number of Cycles

23 Seven cycles have been observed during a direct time study. The mean for the largest element time is 0.85 min, and the corresponding sample standard deviation *s* is 0.15 min, which was also the largest. If the analyst wants to be 95% confident that the mean of the sample was within ±0.10% of the true mean, how many more observations should be taken?

24 Nine cycles have been observed during a time study. The mean for the largest element time is 0.80 min, and the corresponding sample standard deviation *s* is 0.15 min, which was also the largest. If the analyst wants to be 95% confident that the mean of the sample was within ±0.10 min of the true mean, how many more observations should be taken?

25 Six cycles have been observed in a direct time study. The mean for the largest element time is 0.82 min, and the corresponding sample standard deviation *s* is 0.11 min, which was also the largest. If the analyst wants to be 95% confident that the mean of the sample was within ±0.10 min of the true mean, how many more observations should be taken?

26 Ten cycles have been observed during a direct time study. The mean time for the longest element was 0.65 min, and the standard deviation calculated on the same data was

0.10 min. If the analyst wants to be 95% confident that the mean of the sample was within ±8% of the true mean, how many more observations should be taken?

27 Six cycles have been observed during direct time study. The mean time for the longest element was 0.82 min, and the standard deviation calculated on the same data was 0.13 min. If the analyst wants to be 90% confident that the mean of the sample was within ±0.06 min of the true mean, how many more observations should be taken?

28 Six cycles have been observed during a direct time study. The mean for the largest element time is 1.00 min, and the corresponding sample standard deviation s is 0.10 min. (a) Based on these data, what is the 90% confidence interval on the 1.0 min element time? (b) If the analyst wants to be 90% confident that the mean of the sample was within ±10% of the true mean, how many more observations should be taken?

29 A total of 9 cycles has been observed during a direct time study. The mean for the largest element time is 1.30 min, and the corresponding sample standard deviation s is 0.20 min. (a) Based on these data, what is the 95% confidence interval on the 1.30 min element time? (b) If the analyst wants to be 98% confident that the mean of the sample was within ±5% of the true mean, how many more observations should be taken?

Performance Rating

30 One of the traditional definitions of standard performance is a person walking at 3.0 miles per hour. Given this, what is the performance rating of a long-distance runner who breaks the four-minute mile?

31 In 1982, the winner of the Boston Marathon was Alberto Salazar, whose time was 2 hr, 23 min and 3.2 sec. The marathon race covers 26 miles and 385 yards. Given that one of the traditional definitions of standard performance is a person walking at 3.0 miles per hour, what was Salazar's performance rating in the race?

Predetermined Motion Time Systems

The controversial step in direct time study is performance rating. It is based on a judgment by the time study analyst, and there is always room for disagreement between the worker doing the task and the analyst evaluating the worker's pace. An alternative to direct time study that does not include the performance-rating step, at least not directly, is the family of work measurement techniques known as predetermined motion time systems.

A ***predetermined motion time system*** (PMTS), also called a ***predetermined time system***, is a database of basic motion elements and their associated normal time values, together with a set of procedures for applying the data to analyze manual tasks and establish standard times for the tasks.[1] The PMTS database is most readily conceptualized as a set of tables listing time values that correspond to the basic motion elements, the lowest level in our hierarchy of manual work activity. They include motions such as reach, grasp, move, and release. The time required to perform these basic motions usually depends on certain work variables. For example, the time to reach for an

[1]The Work Measurement and Methods Standards Committee (ANSI Standard Z94.11-1989) defines a predetermined motion time system as follows: "An organized body of information, procedures, techniques, and motion times employed in the study and evaluation of manual work elements. The system is expressed in terms of the motions used, their general and specific nature, the conditions under which they occur, and their previously determined performance times."

object increases with the distance of the reach, among other factors. The time to move an object depends on its weight and the distance it is moved. The normal time values in the database have been determined based on extensive research of manual work activity, usually consisting of frame-by-frame analysis of motion pictures of the activity.

In this chapter we provide a general discussion of predetermined motion time systems, which were first identified around 1925 (Historical Note 1). We then examine two important examples of these systems: methods-time measurement (MTM) and the Maynard Operation Sequence Technique (MOST).

HISTORICAL NOTE 1 PREDETERMINED MOTION TIME SYSTEMS

The notion that manual work consists of basic motion elements is attributed to Frank B. Gilbreth, who was a pioneer in the subject of motion study. His studies resulted in the first methodical classification of motion elements, which he called ***therbligs*** (Gilbreth spelled backwards—well, almost). The 17 therbligs consist mostly of arm and hand motions.

Asa B. Segur is credited with developing the first commercial predetermined motion time system, called Motion-Time Analysis (MTA). Segur was aware of Gilbreth's classification scheme for basic motion elements, and MTA's 17 basic motion elements agree closely with Gilbreth's 17 therbligs. Segur began the development of MTA in 1922 by analyzing motion picture films taken during World War I of operators performing factory tasks. The films were originally intended for use as training materials for blind and otherwise handicapped workers, but Segur constructed his system of motions and times from them. Supposedly for commercial reasons, he limited public access to MTA, and this is one of the reasons why his system is no longer used. However, his work influenced those who followed him in developing other predetermined motion time systems.

One of these analysts was Joseph H. Quick, who developed the Work-Factor system between 1934 and 1938. The system was based on the analysis of large numbers of motion picture films, snapshots, stroboscopic lighting techniques, and stopwatch studies taken of many different kinds of industrial operations. Among Quick's contributions in PMTS research were his studies involving cognitive work, such as visual inspection and similar technical labor.

Harold B. Maynard stands as one of the more important figures in the development of predetermined motion time systems. He is largely responsible for the Methods-Time Measurement (MTM) system, and the Pittsburgh-based consulting firm of H. B. Maynard and Company bears his name. In 1946, Maynard began development of MTM with colleagues G. J. Stegemerten and J. L. Schwab under the sponsorship of the Westinghouse Electric Company. Their study began by analyzing movies of drilling operations and relating the work patterns to therbligs. The therblig classification was found to be wanting in some respects, and many of the basic motion elements were revised, renamed, or removed. MTM became the most successful and widely used first level PMTS after its release in 1948. The MTM database of motion elements was used in the development of many higher-level systems, including those in the MTM family (see Table 5 later in this chapter).

Other individuals who should be mentioned for their efforts in developing PMT systems include G. B. Bailey and R. Presgrave, who developed Basic Motion Timestudy in 1950; R. M. Crossan and H. W. Nance, who developed Master Standard Data in the late 1950s; and G. C. Heyde, who developed the Modular Arrangement of Predetermined Time Standards (MODAPT) in the mid 1960s.

Kjell B. Zandin is largely responsible for the development of the Maynard Operation Sequence Technique (MOST). Starting in the late 1960s, he led a group at the Swedish Division of H. B. Maynard & Company in studying applications of MTM. It was observed that there were similarities in the motion patterns and MTM sequences of many manual operations. This ultimately resulted in the definition of three principal motion groups, which were called sequence models in the MOST system. MOST was first introduced in Sweden in 1972 and in the United States in 1974. Today, it is one of the most widely used PMT systems.

Subsequent further development of predetermined motion time systems has been in the computerization of several of these systems as commercial products. Examples include MOST for Windows and MTM-LINK.

1 OVERVIEW OF PREDETERMINED MOTION TIME SYSTEMS

This section provides a general introduction to PMT systems. First, we discuss the usual procedure in applying a predetermined motion time system to a task. One of the significant advantages of a PMTS is that it can be used to determine a standard time for a task before that task is in production. It can also be used to set a standard for an existing task. We then indicate the differences among PMT systems and how they can be classified.

1.1 The PMTS Procedure

All PMT systems are applied using the same general procedure. The differences are in the details. To apply a predetermined motion time system to a task, the analyst must accomplish the following steps:

1. Synthesize the method that would be used by a worker to perform the task (or analyze the method that is being used by a worker in an existing task). The method is described in terms of the basic motions comprising the task, based on a defined workplace layout and set of tools (if tools are used).[2]
2. Retrieve the normal time value for each motion element, based on the work variables and conditions under which the element will be (is) performed. Sum the normal times for all motion elements to determine the normal time for the task.

[2]Different predetermined motion time systems have different basic motion definitions, and the analyst must describe the method using the definitions and conventions of the particular system.

3. Evaluate the method to make improvements by eliminating motions, reducing distances, introducing special tools, using simultaneous right and left hand motions, and so on. The objective of this evaluation is to reduce the normal time. The evaluation process is facilitated by the detailed listing of basic motion elements and corresponding time values.
4. Apply allowances to the normal time to determine the standard time for the task.

If the emphasis in the application is methods improvement, then step 4 may be omitted. If the emphasis is setting a time standard, then step 4 is required.

The basic time values in PMT systems do not include any allowances, so the user organization must add an allowance for personal time, fatigue, and delays according to its policies on allowances. This is step 4 in our PMTS procedure outlined above. The following equation is the usual way in which allowances are applied to determine the time standard for a task:

$$T_{std} = T_n(1 + A_{pfd}) \tag{1}$$

where T_{std} = standard time, min; T_n = normal time, which is the sum of the basic motion time values that make up the task (step 2 with possible adjustments resulting from step 3 in the PMTS procedure), min; and A_{pfd} = PFD allowance factor.

A performance rating step is not necessary in a predetermined motion time system, because the basic motion times are already rated at standard (100%) performance. However, different PMT systems use different definitions of standard performance. MTM and MOST use the definition of "daywork" standard performance. If the organization using either of these systems defines standard performance differently, then a universal adjustment must be made to all time values in the database to bring these data into agreement with the organization's definition.

Similarly, for predetermined motion time systems other than MTM or MOST, an adjustment in all data values may be necessary to achieve agreement with the organization's definition of standard performance. For example, Motion Time Analysis (MTA) time values were determined based on a faster working pace, and therefore the basic motion times are less than MTM times by about 20%. Therefore, if a company were to use the MTA system but wanted to set standards using the "daywork" as the standard performance level, then all of the MTA times must be multiplied by 125%.

1.2 PMTS Levels and Generations

There is a variety of predetermined motion time systems. Although we might think that the basic motions of the human body should be the same in all PMT systems, some PMT systems combine basic motions into larger motion elements. Thus, we have various levels of PMT systems. First-level systems use the basic motion elements (e.g., reach, grasp), while higher-level systems combine several basic motion elements into ***motion aggregates***, combined motion sequences that are commonly used in work situations. For example, the basic motions ***reach*** and ***grasp*** might be combined into one element called

get for use in a higher-level PMT system. This motion aggregate would be common in assembly work, for example.

First-level PMT systems tend to be very detailed, with body motions differentiated very precisely in their databases. For example, ***reach*** and ***grasp*** are typically distinguished as two separate motion elements, even though they are commonly carried out as one smooth arm and hand movement. The times for the basic motions tend to be very short, sometimes much less than a second. Higher-level systems use condensed databases, with fewer body motions contained in the tables and longer time values for each motion sequence. The tables are simplified, with fewer work variables that must be identified about the task by the analyst.

Chronologically, first-level PMT systems were the first to be developed, and then second- and higher-level systems were subsequently constructed based on the first-level systems. Because of this chronological development of the systems, the level of the system usually corresponds to the ***generation*** of the system. First-level PMT systems are called first generation systems, and the subsequent systems are second and third generations. For example, MTM-1 is first generation. MTM-2 is second generation and is based on MTM-1. MTM-3 is a third generation MTM system.

Methods descriptions in first-level systems consist of long lists of elements, and the time to determine a standard for the task is long (high application speed ratio). For example, using MTM-1, a first-level system, the time to set a standard is a factor of about 250 compared to the duration of the task time [7]. For a task of 1 minute, it takes over 4 hours of analyst time to establish the standard time. Higher-level PMT systems require less application time due to their use of elements that combine basic motions. For example, MTM-2 is a higher-level system that is based on MTM-1, and the time to set a standard is a factor of 100 compared to the task time. The cost of this greater convenience is that the accuracy of higher-level systems tends to be less than for a first-level system. The general characteristics of PMT system levels are summarized in Table 1.

More than 50 predetermined motion time systems have been developed over the years. Most of these systems are no longer used. Table 2 provides a brief description of the major PMT systems that were developed, with an emphasis on those that are commercially important today. The most widely used systems today are based on MTM. Section 2 discusses MTM, both the first-level system (MTM-1) and some of its higher-level versions. Section 3 discusses MOST, a widely used higher-level PMTS based on MTM.

TABLE 1 Characteristics of PMT System Levels

Characteristic	First-Level PMTS	Higher-Level PMTS
Accuracy	Most accurate	Less accurate
Application time	Much time to set standard	Less time to set standard
Suited to specific types of tasks	Highly repetitive	Repetitive or batch
Cycle times	Short cycle (e.g., 1 min)	Longer cycle times feasible
Motion elements	Basic motions	Aggregates of basic motions
Methods description	Very detailed	Less detailed, easier to apply
Flexibility of application	Highest flexibility	Less flexibility

TABLE 2 Summary of Predetermined Motion Time Systems

Motion-Time Analysis (MTA): A first-level system developed by A. B. Segur in the mid- and late 1920s. Its primary importance today stems from the fact that it was the first PMTS to be developed and applied. Today it is seldom used if at all. There are 17 basic motion elements in MTA, involving one or more body movements. The elements are classified as positive (considered useful to the task), negative (motions that should be reduced or eliminated), or either (might be positive or negative).

Work-Factor (WF): A first-level PMTS developed by J. H. Quick, W. J. Shea, and R. E. Koehler in the mid-1930s, with applications starting in 1938. It is still used today and at least one simplified version has been developed to reduce application time. Coverage includes both factory and office work.

Methods-Time Measurement (MTM): Developed by H. B. Maynard, G. J. Stegemerten, and J. L. Schwab in the mid-1940s. The original MTM was a generic, first-level system published as a book in 1948. Today, that original PMTS is known as MTM-1, and several higher-level and specific PMT systems have been developed based on MTM-1. We describe the MTM family in Section 2.

Basic Motion Timestudy (BMT): Developed by R. Presgrave, G. B. Bailey, and J. A. Lowden in the early 1950s. Its initial applications were in 1952, and it was published in book form in 1958. It is considered a first-level system, but some of its motion elements are combinations of therbligs. At least one second-level PMTS has been developed based on BMT.

Master Standard Data (MSD): One of the first second-level systems. It is based on MTM-1 and was developed in Canada by R. M. Crossan and H. W. Nance in the late 1950s (published as a book in 1962) to reduce the analyst's time needed to set a time standard for manual production operations with fewer than 100,000 cycles per year. Its coverage emphasizes reach-grasp-move-release motions that are common in such operations.

Maynard Operation Sequence Technique (MOST): Developed by K. B. Zandin and others at the Swedish Division of H. B. Maynard Company as a higher-level PTMS based on MTM-1 and MTM-2. Its coverage emphasizes production operations and material handling. We describe MOST in Section 3.

Modular Arrangement of Predetermined Time Standards (MODAPTS): A second-level PTMS developed by C. Heyde and others in Australia during the mid-1960s. It is based on MSD, MTM-1, and MTM-2. The basic motion element in MODAPTS is a finger movement, and other body motions are expressed in terms of this element. Coverage includes production operations and material handling, with a special version covering office work.

Source: Compiled from [1], [7], and other sources.

2 METHODS-TIME MEASUREMENT

Methods-Time Measurement (MTM) is a PMTS that can be used to analyze the method for performing a given task and to set a time standard for the task. MTM is defined by its developers as follows [4]:

> Methods-Time Measurement is a procedure which analyzes any manual operation or method into the basic motions required to perform it and assigns to each motion a predetermined time standard which is determined by the nature of the motion and the conditions under which it is made.

The hyphenation of "Methods-Time" was intended by its developers to emphasize the important connection between the basic motions used to perform a task and the time values associated with these motions. MTM is an analysis tool by which the method for a task is divided into its component elements to determine if any methods improvements can be made (step 3 in the PMTS procedure). Only after this analysis should a standard time be established.

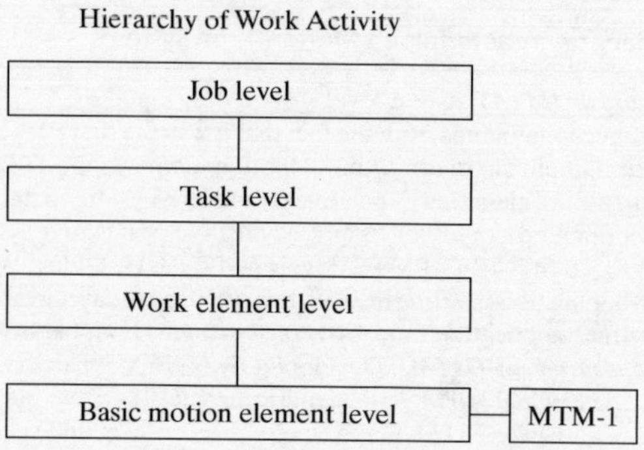

Figure 1 The position of MTM motion elements in our work hierarchy.

MTM is actually a family of predetermined motion time systems. The original MTM is now called MTM-1. It is the first-level PMTS upon which all of the other MTM systems are based. We describe MTM-1 in Section 2.1. Other versions of MTM are briefly discussed in Section 2.2. Training in the members of the MTM PMTS family is available through the MTM Association, located in Des Plaines, Illinois.[3]

2.1 MTM-1

In our hierarchy of work activity, MTM-1 operates at the basic motion element level, as illustrated in Figure 1. Most of the MTM-1 basic motions involve hand and arm movements, although elements are also provided for eye, leg, foot, and body actions. Many of the basic motions correspond to the original therbligs as developed by Frank Gilbreth. However, the definitions of these basic motions have been adjusted to conform to the needs of MTM, and new elements not included among the original therbligs have been added.

Time units in MTM are called TMUs (time measurement units). MTM was developed by studying motion pictures of work activity, and the time units for MTM were originally defined as the time per frame of motion picture film. This proved awkward, and the TMU is now defined as follows:

$$1 \text{ TMU} = 0.00001 \text{ hr} = 0.0006 \text{ min} = 0.036 \text{ sec}$$

Conversely, there are 100,000 TMUs in 1 hr, 1667 TMUs in 1 min, and 27.8 TMUs in 1 sec.

Table 3 defines the MTM-1 motion elements, and Table 4 presents a tabulation of their time values. As with other PMT systems, the analyst must describe the task in terms of these basic motion elements, taking note of the work variables that influence the element time and accounting for simultaneous right-hand and left-hand motions,

[3]MTM Association, 1111 East Touhy Avenue, Des Plaines, IL 60018; their Web site can be accessed at www.mtm.org.

TABLE 3 Summary of MTM-1 Motion Elements

Motion Element (Symbol) and Description

Reach (R): A basic motion element involving movement of the hand or fingers. Its purpose is to move the hand or finger to a new destination. The corresponding therblig is "transport empty." If the hand is holding something during the motion, it is still classified as a reach if its primary purpose is to reposition the hand or fingers and not to move the object—for example, reaching for an object while holding a cigarette. Reach depends on two work variables: (1) the distance moved and (2) the case under which the reach is performed. The case refers to such factors as whether the reach is toward an object in a known location or the object is jumbled amongst other objects and must be searched out. The five cases are identified in Table 4 (a), which provides time values as a function of distance and case. If the hand is in motion before and/or after the reach, then the time is reduced slightly, as indicated in the table under "hand in motion" for cases A and B. The complete symbol for a given reach element in MTM-1 includes the distance and the case (e.g., R10C).

Grasp (G): A motion element used by the fingers and hand to gain control of one or more objects. It is commonly employed as a prerequisite motion for performing the next basic motion, which is likely to be a move—for example, grasping an object prior to moving it. There are five categories of grasp: (1) pickup, (2) regrasp, (3) transfer, (4) select, and (5) contact. Within the pickup and select categories, there are several cases that must be distinguished. Table 4 (b) defines the various categories and cases and lists the times for them. The complete symbol for a grasp includes category and case (e.g., G1C3).

Move (M): A hand or finger motion whose primary purpose is to relocate an object. The corresponding therblig is "transport loaded." The move element includes pushing or sliding an object across a surface, so long as the hand controls the object. Move depends on three work variables: (1) the weight of the object being moved, (2) the distance of the move, and (3) the case under which the move is performed. There are three cases, as described in Table 4 (c). The weight variable is divided into classes, and the user selects the next higher weight given in the table for the object weight in the given application. The complete symbol for move includes the distance, case, and weight—for example, M6B10 symbolizes a move of 6 in. under case B for an object weight of 10 lb. The following formula must be used to determine the TMU value from Table 4 (c):

$$\text{TMU} = \text{Constant} + \text{Factor} \times (\text{TMU value from table})$$

where Constant is the constant value from the table for the object weight in the application, TMU; Factor is the factor value from the table for the object weight; and (TMU value from table) is the TMU value from the table for the corresponding distance of the move and the move case. For example, given the symbol M6B10, the formula would be used as follows:

$$\text{TMU} = 3.9 + 1.11(8.9) = 13.8 \text{ TMU (about } {}^{1}\!/_{2} \text{ sec)}$$

Position (P): A relatively short hand motion (no greater than 1 in.) employed to align, orient, or engage one object relative to another. It is usually preceded by a move. ***Align*** refers to the relative positioning of longitudinal axes of the objects; ***orient*** refers to the relative positioning of rotational axes of the objects; and ***engage*** refers to the insertion of one object into the other following either an alignment or an orientation. Accordingly, the position element may occur several times together depending on the number of separate positioning moves required. The work variables that affect the time for a position motion are the following: (1) pressure required to achieve the fit, (2) symmetry of the objects, and (3) ease of handling. Pressure to achieve fit is divided into three categories: loose (class 1), close (class 2), and exact (class 3). Symmetry is also divided into three categories: symmetrical (S)—for example, a round peg in a round hole; nonsymmetrical (NS)—for example, a key inserted into a lock; and semisymmetrical (SS), which is any case between S and NS. Ease of handling is simply divided into easy (E) and difficult (D). The categories are listed in Table 4 (d) along with the time to perform the element. The complete symbol for a position includes the three work variables (e.g., P3NSD).

Release (RL): A hand and finger motion element whose purpose is to surrender control of an object. There are only two cases of release: (1) the fingers open to effect the release and (2) contact release with no finger motion. The complete symbol for release identifies the case (e.g., RL1 or RL2). Times are given in Table 4 (e).

Disengage (D): A hand and finger motion that causes the separation of two objects from one another, where the objects were previously held together by some force. Thus, disengagement breaks the force, resulting in a recoil action by the hand. The work variables that affect the time of a disengage motion are (1) class of fit and (2) ease of handling. Classes

(*continued*)

TABLE 3 *(continued)*

Motion Element (Symbol) and Description
of fit are loose (slight effort required, class 1), close (normal effort, class 2), and tight (considerable effort, class 3). Ease of handling is either easy (E) or difficult (D). The disengage symbol indicates the two variables (e.g., D3E). Times are given in Table 4 (f).
Turn (T): A basic motion element that involves rotation of the hand and wrist about the long axis of the forearm. The hand can either be holding an object (e.g., turning a dial on a machine) or empty. Turn depends on two work variables: (1) the degrees of turn and (2) resistance to the turn. Table 4 (g) lists the time values as a function of these factors. The maximum turn in the table is 180°, which is imposed by the anatomical structure of the elbow and forearm. Resistance to turn is indicated by force of resistance, divided into three categories in the table. The complete symbol for turn includes both variables; for example, T90L symbolizes a turn of 90° and a large resisting force.
Apply pressure (AP): An MTM-1 element that involves the application of force, but the force results in little or no movement. The force is usually applied by the hand and/or fingers, but the element applies to a force applied by any body member. There are two categories of apply pressure: (1) apply pressure alone (APA) and (2) apply pressure preceded by a regrasp (APB). Time values for these two cases are given in Table 4 (h).
Eye travel (ET), **eye focus (EF)**, and **reading**: Basic eye usage motions that are important enablers for performing manual work. However, the effect of the eyes during a motion element is usually accounted for in the tabulated TMU values. For example, a reach motion that requires greater hand-eye coordination takes longer; for example, compare Case C and Case A in Table 4 (a). On the other hand, there are situations when eye travel and/or eye focus are prerequisites for subsequent motions. In these cases, they must be counted as separate basic elements. Times for the two basic eye usage motions are given in Table 4 (i). In addition, MTM-1 uses a normal time for reading text as 5.05 TMUs per word. Thus, reading a 200 word paragraph would be allowed 1010 TMUs (about 36 sec).
Body, leg, and foot motions: Additional basic motions that involve moving the body, one or both legs, and/or one or both feet. The motions include walking, bending, stooping, standing from a seated position, and sitting from a standing position. These activities are distinct from those performed at a workbench, most likely with the worker in a sitting position. These elements and others are identified in Table 4 (j), together with their symbols and normal times.
Simultaneous motions: Basic motion elements that are performed at the same time. In general, it is desirable for more than one body member to be moving simultaneously. For example, it is desirable for both the right hand and left hand to be active during the task, not only sequentially but also simultaneously. When basic motion elements can be combined simultaneously, the time required for the combination is the greater of the two parallel motions. This is called the "limiting principle," which was first proposed by the original developers of MTM (Maynard, Stegemerten, and Schwab, Historical Note 1). Certain combinations of motions are more difficult to perform simultaneously than others. The degrees of difficulty can be classified as follows: (1) easy to perform simultaneously, (2) can be performed simultaneously with practice, and (3) difficult to perform simultaneously. Table 4 (k) indicates the degree of difficulty for various combinations of basic motion elements. In degrees of difficulty (1) and (2), the limiting principle applies, assuming sufficient practice is allowed for the worker in (2). In degree of difficulty (3), both times should be added.

internal elements when the task involves operation of a machine, and other special circumstances. The analyst then retrieves the time for each basic motion element and sums the times to obtain the normal time for the task. Since the MTM time values do not include any allowances, the analyst must add the proper allowance according to company policy for the type of work being measured. Having stated this, we are obligated to mention that MTM-1 should not be used in industrial work measurement applications until the analyst has received proper training in the technique.

2.2 Other MTM Systems

Additional members of the MTM family have been introduced to satisfy various user needs. Several functional systems have been developed for specific work situations such as clerical activity, machine shop work, and electronic testing. Also, second- and third-level

TABLE 4 (a) Normal Time Values for MTM-1 Motion Element: **Reach** (R)

Distance		Time in TMU				Hand in Motion		Case and Description
cm	inches	A	B	C or D	E	A	B	
< 2.0	< 0.75	2.0	2.0	2.0	2.0	1.6	1.6	**A** Reach to object in fixed location, or to object in other hand or on which other hand rests.
2.5	1	2.5	2.5	3.6	2.4	2.3	2.3	
5.1	2	4.0	4.0	5.9	3.8	3.5	2.7	
7.6	3	5.3	5.3	7.3	5.3	4.5	3.6	**B** Reach to single object in location that may vary slightly from cycle to cycle.
10.1	4	6.1	6.4	8.4	6.8	4.9	4.3	
12.5	5	6.5	7.8	9.4	7.4	5.3	5.0	
15.2	6	7.0	8.6	10.1	8.0	5.7	5.7	
17.8	7	7.4	9.3	10.8	8.7	6.1	6.5	**C** Reach to object jumbled with other objects in a group so that search and select occur.
20.3	8	7.9	10.1	11.5	9.3	6.5	7.2	
22.9	9	8.3	10.8	12.2	9.9	6.9	7.9	
25.4	10	8.7	11.5	12.9	10.5	7.3	8.6	
30.5	12	9.6	12.9	14.2	11.8	8.1	10.1	**D** Reach to a very small object or where accurate grasp is required.
35.6	14	10.5	14.4	15.6	13.0	8.9	11.5	
40.6	16	11.4	15.8	17.0	14.2	9.7	12.9	
45.7	18	12.3	17.2	18.4	15.5	10.5	14.4	
50.8	20	13.1	18.6	19.8	16.7	11.3	15.8	**E** Reach to indefinite location to get hand in position for body balance or next motion or out the way.
55.9	22	14.0	20.1	21.2	18.0	12.1	17.3	
61.0	24	14.9	21.5	22.5	19.2	12.9	18.8	
66.0	26	15.8	22.9	23.9	20.4	13.7	20.2	
71.1	28	16.7	24.4	25.3	21.7	14.5	21.7	
76.2	30	17.5	25.8	26.7	22.9	15.3	23.2	
Additional		0.4	0.7	0.7	0.6	TMU per 2.54 cm > 76 cm (per 1.0 in > 30 in.)		

TABLE 4 (b) Normal Time Values for MTM-1 Motion Element: **Grasp** (G)

Type of Grasp	Case	Time, TMU	Description and Object Dimensions	
Pickup	1A	2.0	Any size object, by itself	
	1B	3.5	Object very small or lying close against a flat surface	
	1C1	7.3	Interference with grasp on bottom and one side of cylindrical object	Diameter > 1.3 cm (0.5 in.)
	1C2	8.7		Diameter 0.6 to 1.3 cm (0.25 to 0.5 in.)
	1C3	10.8		Diameter < 0.6 cm (0.25 in.)
Regrasp	2	5.6	Change grasp without relinquishing control	
Transfer	3	5.6	Control transferred from one hand to other	
Select	4A	7.3	Object jumbled with other objects so that search and select occur	Size larger than 2.5 × 2.5 × 2.5 cm (1 × 1 × 1 in.)
	4B	9.1		0.6 × .6 × .3 cm (.25 × .25 × .12 in) to 2.5 × 2.5 × 2.5 cm (1 × 1 × 1 in.)
	4C	12.9		Size smaller than .6 × .6 × .3 cm (.25 × .25 × .12 in.)
Contact	5	0	Contact, sliding, or hook grasp	

TABLE 4 (c) Normal Time Values for MTM-1 Motion Element: **Move** (M)

Distance		Time in TMU				Weight	Formula Parameters		Case and Description
					Hand in motion	up to			
cm	inches	A	B	C	B	kg (lb)	Constant	Factor	
< 2.0	< 0.75	2.0	2.0	2.0	1.7				**A** Move object to other hand or against stop.
2.5	1	2.5	2.9	3.4	2.3	1.1 (2.5)	0	1.00	
5.1	2	3.6	4.6	5.2	2.9				
7.6	3	4.9	5.7	6.7	3.6	3.4 (7.5)	2.2	1.06	
10.1	4	6.1	6.9	8.0	4.3				**B** Move object to approximate or indefinite location.
12.5	5	7.3	8.0	9.2	5.0	5.7 (12.5)	3.9	1.11	
15.2	6	8.1	8.9	10.3	5.7				
17.8	7	8.9	9.7	11.1	6.5	7.9 (17.5)	5.6	1.17	
20.3	8	9.7	10.6	11.8	7.2				
22.9	9	10.5	11.5	12.7	7.9	10.2 (22.5)	7.4	1.22	**C** Move object to exact location.
25.4	10	11.3	12.2	13.5	8.6				
30.5	12	12.9	13.4	15.2	10.0	12.5 (27.5)	9.1	1.28	
35.6	14	14.4	14.6	16.9	11.4				
40.6	16	16.0	15.8	18.7	12.8	14.7 (32.5)	10.8	1.33	
45.7	18	17.6	17.0	20.4	14.2				
50.8	20	19.2	18.2	22.1	15.6	17.0 (37.5)	12.5	1.39	
55.9	22	20.8	19.4	23.8	17.0				
61.0	24	22.4	20.6	25.5	18.4	19.3 (42.5)	14.3	1.44	
66.0	26	24.0	21.8	27.3	19.8				
71.1	28	25.5	23.1	29.0	21.2	21.5 (47.5)	16.0	1.50	
76.2	30	27.1	24.3	30.7	22.7				
Additional		0.8	0.6	0.85	TMU per 2.54 cm > 76 cm (per 1.0 in. > 30 in.)				

TABLE 4 (d) Normal Time Values for MTM-1 Motion Element: **Position** (P)

			Time in TMU	
Class	Description of Fit	Symmetry	Easy to Handle	Difficult to Handle
1	Loose (no pressure required)	S	5.6	11.2
		SS	9.1	14.7
		NS	10.4	16.0
2	Close (light pressure required)	S	16.2	21.8
		SS	19.7	25.3
		NS	21.0	26.6
3	Exact (heavy pressure required)	S	43.0	48.6
		SS	46.5	52.1
		NS	47.8	53.4

Key: S = symmetrical, SS = semi-symmetrical, NS = nonsymmetrical.

TABLE 4 (e) Normal Time Values for MTM-1 Motion Element: **Release** (RL)

Case	Time in TMU	Description
1	2.0	Normal release performed by opening fingers as an independent motion
2	0	Contact release with no finger motion

TABLE 4 (f) Normal Time Values for MTM-1 Motion Element: **Disengage** (D)

			Time in TMU	
Class	Description of Fit	Height of Recoil	Easy to Handle	Difficult to Handle
1	Loose (very slight effort, blends with subsequent move)	Up to 2.5 cm (1 in)	4.0	5.7
2	Close (normal effort, slight recoil) (1 to 5 in)	2.5 to 12.7 cm	7.5	11.8
3	Tight (considerable effort, hand recoils markedly)	12.7 to 30 cm (5 to 12 in)	22.9	34.7

TABLE 4 (g) Normal Time Values for MTM-1 Motion Element: **Turn** (T)

	Time in TMU for Degrees Turned										
Weight, kg (lb)	30°	45°	60°	75°	90°	105°	120°	135°	150°	165°	180°
Small, up to 0.9 (2)	2.8	3.5	4.1	4.8	5.4	6.1	6.8	7.4	8.1	8.7	9.4
Medium, 1 to 4.5 (2 to 10)	4.4	5.5	6.5	7.5	8.5	9.6	10.6	11.6	12.7	13.7	14.8
Large, 4.5 to 16 (10 to 35)	8.4	10.5	12.3	14.4	16.2	18.3	20.4	22.2	24.3	26.1	28.2

TABLE 4 (h) Normal Time Values for MTM-1 Motion Element: **Apply Pressure** (AP)

Symbol	Time in TMU	Description
APA	10.6	Apply pressure alone
APB	16.2	Apply pressure preceded by regrasp

TABLE 4 (i) Normal Time Values for MTM-1 Motion Element: **Eye Travel** (ET) and **Eye Focus** (EF)

Eye motion	Symbol	Time in TMU	Key to Symbols
Eye travel	ET	$\frac{15.2L}{D}$	L = distance between points from and to which eye travels, D = perpendicular distance from the eye to the line of travel. Maximum time allowed = 20 TMU
Eye focus	EF	7.3	
Reading	(none)	$5.05N$	N = number of words read (330 words/min)

TABLE 4 (j) Normal Time Values for MTM-1 Motion Element: **Body, leg,** and **foot motions** (various symbols given in table)

Motion	Symbol	Time in TMU	Description and Conditions
Sit	SIT	34.7	From standing position
Stand	STD	43.4	From seated position
Turn body	TBC1	18.6	Turn body 45° to 90°, Case 1 – Lagging foot not aligned with leading foot
Turn body	TBC2	37.2	Turn body 45° to 90°, Case 2 – Lagging foot aligned with leading foot
Bend	B	29.0	Bend body forward so hands can reach knees
Stoop	S	29.0	Stoop body forward so hands can reach floor
Arise	AB	31.9	Arise from bent position
Arise	AS	31.9	Arise from stooped position
Kneel	KOK	29.0	Kneel on one knee
Kneel	KBK	69.4	Kneel on both knees
Arise	AKOK	31.9	Arise from kneeling position on one knee
Arise	AKBK	76.7	Arise from kneeling position on both knees
Walk	W*X*FT	5.3 per ft	Walking in ft of distance, X = distance in ft
Walk	W*N*P	15.0/pace	Walking in number of paces, N = number of paces
Walk	W*N*PO	17.0/pace	Walking in number of paces with weight or obstruction, N = number of paces
Leg motion	LM6	7.1	Move leg up to 6 in. any direction
Leg motion	LM*X*	$7.1 + 1.2(X\text{-}6)$	Move leg more than 6 in. any direction, where X = distance of movement
Foot motion	FM	8.5	Foot moves up to 4 in. hinged at ankle
Foot motion	FMP	19.1	Foot moves up to 4 in. hinged at ankle, apply heavy pressure with leg muscles

TABLE 4 (k) MTM-1 Simultaneous Hand and Arm Motion Elements

Motion of One Hand		Reach			Grasp			Move			Position			Disengage	
Motion of other hand	Case or Class	A E	B	C D	1A 2 5	1B 1C	4	A Bm[a]	B	C	1S	1SS 2S	1NS 2SS 2NS	1E 1D	2
Reach	A, E	1	1	1	1	1	1	1	1	2	1	1	2	1	1
	B	1	1	1	1	1	2	1	1	2	2	2	3	1	1
	C, D	1	1	1	1	2	3	2	2	3	3	3	3	2	3
Grasp	1A, 2, 5	1	1	1	1	1	1	1	1	1	1	1	3	1	3
	1B, 1C	1	1	2	1	3	2	1	1	2	3	3	3	3	3
	4	1	2	3	1	2	3	1	2	3	3	3	3	3	3
Move	A	1	1	2	1	1	1	1	1	1	1	1	2	1	1
	B	1	1	2	1	1	2	1	1	1	2	2	3	1	1
	C	2	2	3	1	2	3	1	1	2	3	3	3	2	3
Position	1S	1	2	3	1	3	3	1	2	3	2	3	3	3	3
	1SS,2S	1	2	3	1	3	3	1	2	3	3	3	3	3	3
	1NS, 2SS,2NS	2	3	3	3	3	3	2	3	3	3	3	3	3	3
Disengage	1E,1D	1	1	2	1	3	3	1	1	2	3	3	3	1	1
	2	1	1	3	3	3	3	1	1	3	3	3	3	1	1

[a]Bm is Case B with hand in motion.

(continued)

TABLE 4 (k) *(continued)*

Key: The cell numbers indicate the degree of difficulty when motions are performed simultaneously. 1 = Easy to perform simultaneously. Use the longest motion element time. 2 = Can be performed simultaneously with practice. Use the longest motion element time. 3 = Difficult to perform simultaneously. Add the times of the two simultaneous motion elements.
Assumptions: All Reach, Grasp, and Move motions are performed within the area of normal vision. In the Position and Disengage motion elements, objects are assumed easy to handle. In general, the degree of difficulty increases if these assumptions are violated.
Motions not included in the table: Turn: normally degree of difficulty = 1 except when Turn is controlled or with Disengage. Position Class 3: degree of difficulty = 3. Disengage Class 3: normally degree of difficulty = 3. Release: degree of difficulty = 1.

TABLE 5 Members of the MTM Family of Predetermined Motion Time Systems

MTM-1: The first level MTM, in which basic motion elements are used to describe, analyze, and determine the normal time for a manual task. The MTM-1 motion elements and associated times are listed in Table 3 and 4. MTM-1 is best suited to high production operations with relatively short cycle times. The analyst time required to apply MTM-1 is about 250 times the task cycle time.

MTM-2: A second-level MTM system, in which the basic motion elements are combined into motion aggregates in order to reduce the analyst's time to apply the technique. MTM-2 consists of 11 motions and motion aggregates, called *motion categories*. The two most important MTM-2 categories are GET, which combines Reach, Grasp, and Release; and PUT, which combines Move and Position. MTM-2 is suited to operations that are not highly repetitive and the cycle times are greater than 1 min. The analyst time required to apply MTM-2 is about 100 times the task cycle time.

MTM-3: A third-level MTM system designed to further reduce the analyst's time to set a time standard but at some sacrifice in accuracy. MTM-3 has only four motion categories: (1) Handle, (2) Transport, (3) Step and foot motions, and (4) Bend and arise. Tasks that include additional elements, such as eye movements, should not be analyzed using MTM-3. The analyst time required to apply MTM-3 is about 35 times the task cycle time.

MTM-UAS: A third-level MTM system that is suited to applications in batch production. It includes seven basic motion categories: (1) Get and place, (2) Place, (3) Handle tool, (4) Operate, (5) Motion cycles, (6) Body motions, and (7) Visual control. Additional second-level standard data in MTM-UAS cover activities such as fastening, marking, packing, and assembling. The analyst time required to apply MTM-UAS is about 30 times the task cycle time.

MTM-MEK:A third-level system intended for work measurement applications in small lot production with long cycle times and other tasks performed infrequently. Time standards are usually not established in these work situations by conventional time study because the cost of setting the standard is too high. MTM-MEK can be used for these cases and the analyst time is about 5 to 15 times the cycle time.

MTM-HC: A functional PMTS designed for work activities found in the health-care industry. It is described as a standard database by the MTM Association.

MTM-C: A functional MTM system used for work measurement applications of clerical work activity, such as typing or keypunching, filing, reading, and writing. It was developed by an association of banking and other service industries. There are two levels of MTM-C: MTM-C1 and MTM-C2. The difference is that MTM-C1 emphasizes precision and motion detail in its applications, while MTM-C2 emphasizes speed of application. The analyst time to apply MTM-C1 is about 125 times the task cycle time, and about 75 times for MTM-C2.

MTM-V: A functional standard data system developed using MTM-1 for work measurement in machine tool operation. Its work elements include handling of work parts, operating a machine tool and other equipment (e.g., cranes,

(continued)

TABLE 5 *(continued)*

fixtures, chucks), and setting up a job for production. The analyst time required to apply MTM-V is about 10 times the task cycle time.

MTM-TE: A functional standard data system designed for work measurement in electronic testing applications. Its work elements cover both manual and mental activities.

MTM-M: A functional MTM system for measuring assembly work that is performed under a stereoscopic microscope.

Source: Estimates of analyst time to apply the various MTM systems are based on [7].

systems are available to reduce the time required to develop time standards. Finally, several computerized systems have been developed based on MTM. Table 5 lists many of these MTM systems with a brief description of each. Readers interested in learning more about the other MTM systems can consult the coverage provided in [6] or the MTM Web site at www.mtm.org.

3 MAYNARD OPERATION SEQUENCE TECHNIQUE

The Maynard Operation Sequence Technique (MOST) is a high-level predetermined motion time system that is based on MTM. It uses the same time units as in MTM: the TMU (time measurement unit), which is 0.00001 hr. MOST is a product of H. B. Maynard and Company, an educational and consulting firm located in Pittsburgh, Pennsylvania.[4] The basic version of MOST, which is now referred to as Basic MOST, was developed at Maynard's Swedish Division around 1967 under the direction of Kjell Zandin (Historical Note 1). Section 3.1, describes the Basic MOST package. Several additional versions of MOST have been developed since Basic MOST was introduced, and these are summarized in Section 3.2. Section 3.3 describes a computerized version of MOST.

3.1 Basic MOST

The focus of Basic MOST is on work activity involving the movement of objects. In fact, the majority of industrial manual work does involve moving objects (e.g., parts, tools) from one location to another in the workplace. The underlying premise of Basic MOST is that the movement of objects consists of a pattern of body motions and actions that is nearly the same for all moves. Only the details of the pattern differ, depending on the object being moved and the circumstances of the work activity. Consistent with this premise, Basic MOST uses motion aggregates (collections of basic motion elements) that are concerned with moving things. The motion aggregates are called ***activity sequence models*** in Basic MOST. In our hierarchy of work activity, an activity sequence model is either at the same level as a work element, or slightly below. Depending on how a work element is defined for a given task, it may include one or more activity sequence models. Rarely would a work element be defined as less than a complete activity sequence model. The relationships are indicated in Figure 2.

[4]MOST is a registered trademark of H. B. Maynard and Company, Inc.

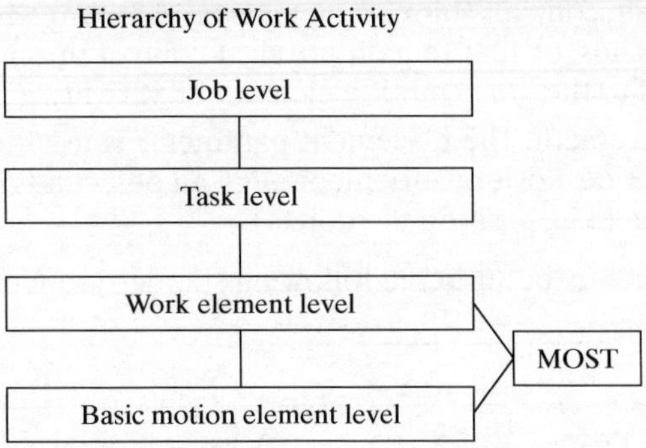

Figure 2 The position of the Basic MOST activity sequence model in our work hierarchy.

There are three activity sequence models in Basic MOST, each of which consists of a standard sequence of actions:

- *General move.* This sequence model is used when an object is moved freely through space from one location to the next (e.g., picking something up from the floor and placing it on a table).
- *Controlled move.* This sequence model is used when an object is moved while it remains in contact with a surface (e.g., sliding the object along the surface) or the object is attached to some other object during its movement (e.g., moving a lever on a machine).
- *Tool use.* This sequence model applies to the use of a hand tool (e.g., a hammer or screwdriver).

The actions in an activity sequence model, called ***sequence model parameters*** in Basic MOST, are similar to basic motion elements in MTM, but there is not a one-to-one correspondence. Some parameters map directly into MTM basic motions, while others are unique to Basic MOST. Let us examine the three sequence models and indicate the standard sequence of model parameters for each.[5]

General Move. The General Move sequence is applicable when an object is moved through the air from one location to another. There are four parameters (actions) in the General Move, symbolized by letters of the alphabet:

A—Action distance, usually horizontal. This parameter is used to describe movements of the fingers, hands, or feet (e.g., walking). The movement can be performed either loaded or unloaded.

B—Body motion, usually vertical. This parameter defines vertical body motions and actions (e.g., sitting, standing up).

[5]Once again, we must caution against the application of MOST without proper training. Guidelines can be obtained from H. B. Maynard & Company in Pittsburgh, Pennsylvania; their Web site can be accessed at www.hbmaynard.com.

G—Gain control. This parameter is used for any manual actions involving the fingers, hands, or feet to gain physical control of one or more objects. It is closely related to the grasp motion element in MTM (e.g., grasp the object).

P—Placement. The placement parameter is used to describe the action involved to lay aside, position, orient, or align an object after it has been moved to the new location (e.g., position the object).

These parameters occur in the following standard sequence in the General Move:

A	B	G	A	B	P	A
Action distance	Body motion	Grasp	Action distance	Body motion	Placement	Action distance

where the first three parameters (A B G) represent basic motions to ***get*** an object, the next three parameters (A B P) represent motions to ***put*** or move the object to a new location, and the final parameter (A) applies to any motions at the end of the sequence, such as ***return*** to original position.

To complete the activity sequence model, each parameter is assigned a numerical value in the form of a subscript or index number that represents the time to accomplish that action. The value of the index number depends on the type of action, its motion content, and the conditions under which it is performed. Table 6 lists the parameters and possible circumstances for the action, together with the corresponding values of the index numbers. When the index values have been entered for all parameters, the time for the sequence model is determined by summing the index values and multiplying by 10 to obtain the total TMUs. The procedure is illustrated in the following example.

Example 1 General Move

Develop the activity sequence model and determine the normal time for the following work activity: A worker walks 5 steps, picks up a small part from the floor, returns to his original position, and places the part on his worktable.

Solution: Referring to Table 6, the indexed activity sequence model for this work activity would be the following:

$$A_{10} B_6 G_1 A_{10} B_0 P_1 A_0$$

where A_{10} = walk 5 steps, B_6 = bend and arise, G_1=gain control of small part, A_{10} = walk back to original position, B_0 = no body motion, P_1 = lay aside part on table, and A_0 = no motion. The sum of the index values is 28. Multiplying by 10, we have 280 TMUs (about 10 sec). ■

The General Move is the most common way in which materials are moved and is therefore the most frequently used activity sequence model in Basic MOST. Approximately half of all manual work occurs as General Moves. For assembly work and material handling, the proportion is higher. For machine shop work, the proportion is lower.

TABLE 6 MOST Parameters and Index Values for the General Move Activity Sequence Model

General Move activity sequence model = **A B G A B P A**				
Index	**A** = Action distance	**B** = Body motion	**G** = Gain control	**P** = Placement
0	Close ≤ 5 cm (2 in.)			Hold, Toss
1	Within reach (but > 2 in.)		Grasp light object using one or two hands	Lay aside Loose fit
3	1 or 2 steps	Bend and arise with 50% occurrence	Grasp object that is heavy, or obstructed, or hidden, or interlocked	Adjustments, light pressure, double placement
6	3 or 4 steps	Bend and arise with 100% occurrence		Position with care, or precision, of blind, or obstructed, or heavy pressure
10	5, 6, or 7 steps	Sit or stand		
16	8, 9, or 10 steps	Through door, or Climb on or off, or Stand and bend, or Bend and sit		

Controlled Move. The Controlled Move sequence model is used when an object is moved through a path that is somehow constrained. The object cannot be freely moved through the air. This situation arises when an object is slid across a surface or when the object is attached to something else and it can be moved only through a controlled path. The second case is commonly encountered in the operation of machinery, and the move involves a lever, crank, switch button, or similar entity that is attached to the machinery. The parameters in the Controlled Move include the A, B, and G parameters from the General Move. In addition, three new parameters are introduced:

M—Move, controlled. This parameter is used to describe any manual body motions required to move an object over a controlled path.

X—Process time. Since the Controlled Move can include the operation of machinery, there is often a process time associated with the machinery (e.g., time to turn the workpiece in a lathe). No manual motions are included in this parameter.

I—Align. This parameter is used when manual motions are performed at the end of the controlled move to align objects.

These parameters occur in the following standard sequence in the Controlled Move:

A	B	G	M	X	I	A
Action distance	Body motion	Grasp	Move, controlled	Process time	Align	Action distance

where the first three parameters (A B G) are the basic motions to ***get*** an object, the next three parameters (M X I) represent moving or actuating the object followed by a process time and alignment, and the final parameter (A) provides for a possible ***return*** at the end of the sequence.

TABLE 7 MOST Parameters and Index Values for the Controlled Move Activity Sequence Model

Controlled Move activity sequence model = **A B G M X I A**				
Index	**M** = Move, controlled	**X** = Process time[a]		**I** = Alignment
		Seconds	Minutes	
1	Push, pull, pivot: button, switch, knob ($\leq$ 12 in.)	0.5	0.01	Align to one point
3	Push and pull, turn, open, seat, shift, press: resistance encountered, or high control required, or 2 stages of control ($\leq$ 12 in.); 1 crank of lever.	1.5	0.02	Align to 2 points, Close align ($\leq$ 4 in.)
6	Open and shut, operate, push or pull: with 1 or 2 steps ($>$ 12 in.); 3 cranks of lever.	2.5	0.04	Align to 2 points, Close align ($>$ 4 in.)
10	Manipulate, maneuver, push, or pull with 3, 4, or 5 steps; 6 cranks of lever.	4.5	0.07	Precision align
16	Push or pull with 6, 7, 8, or 9 steps included; 11 cranks of lever.	7.0	0.11	High precision align

[a]For process times longer than those listed in the table, the actual process time in seconds can be multiplied by 2.78 and rounded to the next higher value to obtain the index for the X parameter.

Index values are applied to each parameter as in the General Move. The same A, B, and G index values from Table 6 apply to the Controlled Move. Table 7 lists the index values for the M, X, and I parameters used exclusively for the Controlled Move.

Example 2 Controlled Move

Develop the activity sequence model and determine the normal time for the following work activity: A worker takes 2 steps, grasps the waist-level feed lever on the lathe, pulls up the lever approximately 15 cm to engage the feed. The process time to turn the part is 25 sec. There is no alignment and no action by the worker at the end of the process time.

Solution: Referring to Tables 6 and 7, and multiplying the 25 sec process time by 2.78 to obtain a value of 69.5 for the X parameter (rounded up to 70), we obtain the following indexed activity sequence model for this work activity:

$$A_3\ B_0\ G_1\ M_1\ X_{70}\ I_0\ A_0$$

where A_3 = take 2 steps, B_0 = no body motion, G_1 = gains control of lever, M_1 = pull the lever up 15 cm, X_{70} = process time of 25 sec, I_0 = no alignment, and A_0 = no motion. The sum of the index values is 75. Multiplying by 10, we have 750 TMUs (about 27 sec). The lathe process time accounts for all but 2 sec of the activity sequence. ■

Tool Use. The Tool Use sequence model applies to the variety of work situations that involve the use of a hand tool. Hand tools covered by this model include screwdrivers, ratchets, hammers, scissors, knives, various kinds of wrenches, and common measuring instruments. When a worker's hand is used to perform a motion such as turning a screw, Tool Use is employed. The sequence model also covers writing, marking, reading, thinking, and inspecting. The parameters in the Tool Use sequence include A, B, G, and

P that were previously used in the General Move and Controlled Move. Only one new parameter is included in Tool Use, and that refers to the specific action that applies to the tool being used in the activity sequence. The possible parameters include the following:

F—Fasten. This parameter is used to describe any fastening motion that is performed with the fingers, hand, or a tool such as a screwdriver or wrench.

L—Loosen. This parameter is similar to Fasten, except the objective is to unfasten or disassemble an object.

C—Cut. The Cut parameter describes the manual actions required to slice, slit, or otherwise separate an object. Common tools for cutting include knives, scissors, and pliers.

S—Surface treat. This parameter is used for applying a coating to the surface of an object (e.g., using a brush) or to remove a material from the surface (e.g., wiping the surface).

M—Measure. The use of measuring instruments (e.g., linear scales, calipers, micrometers) or gauges is modeled by this parameter.

R—Record. The manual actions involving the use of a pen, pencil, or other marking tool to record data are covered by this parameter.

T—Think. This parameter models the visual and mental activities required to read or inspect an object.

Only one of these parameters is included in the standard sequence for the Tool Use activity sequence model. Its placement in the sequence model is indicated by the asterisk (*) in the following:

ABGABP*ABPA

where the first three parameters (A B G) are the motions to ***get*** the tool, the next three parameters (A B P) ***put*** or place the tool into position, * is the tool use code (F, L, C, S, M, R, or T), the next three parameters (A B P) ***put*** the tool aside, and the final parameter (A) is to provide for the worker to ***return*** to some previous position. Table 8 (a) and (b) list the index values for the Tool Use parameters.

Example 3 Tool Use

Develop the activity sequence model and determine the normal time for the following work activity: A worker picks up a screw from his worktable, positions it into a threaded hole, and turns it three spins with his fingers. He then picks up a screwdriver from the worktable, positions it on the head of the screw, fastens the screw with six turns, and lays the screwdriver aside.

Solution: This requires two activity sequence models, corresponding to the two sentences of the work description. The first model is developed as follows:

$$A_1\ B_0\ G_1\ A_1\ B_0\ P_3\ F_6\ A_0\ B_0\ P_0\ A_0$$

TABLE 8 (a) MOST Parameters and Index Values for Tool Use—Fasten and Loosen

Fasten or Loosen = **F** or **L**

Index	Finger Action	Wrist Action				Arm Action					Tool Action	Index
	Fingers, Screw-driver	Hand, Screw-driver, Ratchet, T-wrench	Wrench, Allen key	Wrench, Allen key, Ratchet	Hand, Hammer	Ratchet	T-wrench, 2 hands	Wrench, Allen key	Wrench, Allen key, Ratchet	Hand, Hammer	Power wrench	
	Spins	Turns	Strokes	Cranks	Taps	Turns	Turns	Strokes	Cranks	Strikes	Diameter	
1	1	—	—	—	1	—	—	—	—	—	—	**1**
3	2	1	1	1	3	1	—	1	—	1	6 mm (1/4 in.)	**3**
6	3	3	2	3	6	2	1	—	1	3	25 mm (1 in.)	**6**
10	8	5	3	5	10	4	—	2	2	5		**10**
16	16	9	5	8	16	6	3	3	3	8		**16**
24	25	13	8	11	23	9	6	4	5	12		**24**
32	35	17	10	15	30	12	8	6	6	16		**32**
42	47	23	13	20	39	15	11	8	8	21		**42**
54	61	29	17	25	50	20	15	10	11	27		**54**

TABLE 8 (b) Parameters and Index Values for Tool Use—Cut (C), Surface treat (S), Measure (M), Record (R), and Think (T)

	Cut = **C**				Surface Treat = **S**			Measure = **M**	Record = **R**		Think = **T**				
	Cutoff	Secure	Cut	Slice	Air clean	Brush clean	Wipe	Measure	Write		Mark	Inspect	Read		
	Pliers		Scissors	Knife	Nozzle	Brush	Cloth	Measuring Tool	Pen/Pencil		Marker	Eyes, fingers	Eyes		
Index	Wire		Cuts	Slices	.1 m^2 (1 ft^2)	.1 m^2 (1 ft^2)	.1 m^2 (1 ft^2)		Digits	Words	Digits	Points	Digits, single words	Text	Index
1		Grip	1						1		Check	1	1	3	**1**
3	Soft		2	1			1/2		2		1 Scribe line	3	3	8	**3**
6	Medium	Twist Form loop	4		1 Spot cavity	1			4	1	2	5 Feel for heat	6	15	**6**
10	Hard		7	3			1	Profile gauge	6		3	9 Feel defect	12	24	**10**
16		Secure cotter pin	11	4	3	2	2	Fixed scale, Caliper	9	2	5	14		38	**16**
24 **32**			15 20	6 9	4 7	3 5	 5	Feeler gauge Steel tape, Depth micrometer	13 18	3 4	7 10	19 26		54 72	**24** **32**
42			27	11	10	7	7	OD micrometer	23	5	13	34		94	**42**
54			33					ID micrometer	29	7	16	42		119	**54**

where $A_1 B_0 G_1$ = pick up screw from worktable, $A_1 B_0 P_3$ = position screw into threaded hole, F_6 = turn screw three spins with fingers, and $A_0 B_0 P_0 A_0$ = no motions. The second activity sequence model is the following:

$$A_1 B_0 G_1 A_1 B_0 P_3 F_{10} A_1 B_0 P_1 A_0$$

where $A_1 B_0 G_1$ = pick up screwdriver from worktable, $A_1 B_0 P_3$ = position screwdriver on screw head, F_{10} = turn screwdriver six turns, $A_1 B_0 P_1$ = lay screwdriver aside, and A_0 = no motion.

The sum of the index values is 12 for the first model and 18 for the second, a total of 30. Multiplying by 10, we have 300 TMUs (about 10.8 sec). ■

3.2 Additional Versions of MOST

In addition to Basic MOST, several additional versions of MOST are available for other application characteristics. These are described in Table 9. A description of Basic MOST is included for comparison purposes.

3.3 MOST for Windows

Keeping up with trends in work measurement, H. B. Maynard and Company has developed a computerized version of MOST, called MOST for Windows. Depending on the application, MOST for Windows allows the user to analyze a given work situation by any of the three MOST analysis techniques: (1) Basic MOST, (2) Maxi MOST, or (3) Mini

TABLE 9 Other Versions of MOST Work Measurement Packages

Basic MOST: A system designed for manual work that involves the movement of objects. It is intended for applications in which the work cycle is performed more than 150 times per week but less than 1500 times per week. A typical cycle time for Basic MOST is 30 sec to 3 min. As described in Section 3.1, Basic MOST uses three activity sequence models: (1) General Move, (2) Controlled Move, and (3) Tool Use. The analyst time required to apply Basic MOST is about 10 times the task cycle time.

Maxi MOST: A system developed for applications in which the work cycle is performed fewer than 150 times per week and there are variations in the cycle. Task times of several hours can be analyzed using this version. Examples of work activity that can be analyzed by Maxi MOST include setup tasks and heavy assembly. Maxi MOST consists of five activity sequence models: (1) part handling, (2) tool/equipment use, (3) machine handling, (4) transport with powered crane, and (5) transport with wheeled truck. The analyst time required to apply Maxi MOST is 3 to 5 times the task cycle time.

Mini MOST: A system developed for operations in which the work cycle is highly repetitive and performed more than 1500 times per week. For a 40-hour week, this translates to a cycle time of 1.6 min or less. However, cycle times analyzed by Mini MOST are usually much less than this. Mini MOST consists of two activity sequence models: (1) General Move and (2) Controlled Move. The analyst time required to apply Mini MOST is about 25 times the task cycle time.

Clerical MOST: A system similar to Basic MOST but designed for clerical work activity. In addition to the three basic activity sequence models in Basic MOST (General Move, Controlled Move, and Tool Use), there is an additional model for equipment use. The format of the model is the same as Tool Use, except that additional parameters are available for actions involving the operation of office equipment.

Source: Estimates of analyst time to apply the MOST versions are based on [9].

MOST (Table 9). Other alternatives are also available. The analyst can use action distances (the A parameter in Basic MOST) and body motions (the B parameter) that are based on data about the layout of the workplace, rather than determining and inputting the index values directly.

Among the other options, MOST for Windows includes two modules that can be called by the analyst:

- *Quick MOST.* This feature permits the user to select among multiple possible work methods that might be applied to the given application. The method description, activity sequence model, and associated normal time are immediately provided by Quick MOST, where editing can be performed by the analyst if needed. The selection list of work methods is based on data of industrial applications compiled by Maynard. The user can add additional work methods representing the company's unique applications if desired.
- *Direct MOST.* This MOST for Windows feature automatically generates a description of the work method based on data provided about the work situation. The module allows the analyst to override or edit the automatically generated work method description when appropriate. Parameter index values are automatically developed by Direct MOST when the analyst selects rules that have been developed for MOST applications. These rules are available to the user through drop-down menus, or by specification of workplace objects and locations.

The following are the benefits and advantages reported by Maynard for users of MOST for Windows: (1) A complete methods description is provided. (2) Nonproductive work elements are identified during the analysis so that they can be eliminated from the standard method. (3) MOST for Windows is a simple and easy-to-use work measurement technique. (4) Developing time standards by MOST for Windows is efficient and accurate. (5) Database search capabilities are provided.

REFERENCES

[1] Barnes, R. M. *Motion and Time Study: Design and Measurement of Work.* 7th ed. New York: Wiley, 1980.

[2] Karger, D. W., and F. H. Bayha. *Engineered Work Measurement.* 4th ed. New York: Industrial Press, 1987.

[3] Konz, S., and S. Johnson. *Work Design: Industrial Ergonomics*. 5th ed. Holcomb Hathaway Publishers, Scottsdale AZ, 2000.

[4] Maynard, H. B., G. J. Stegemerten.and J. L. Schwab. *Methods-Time Measurement.* New York: McGraw-Hill, 1948.

[5] Mundel, M. E., and D. L. Danner. *Motion and Time Study: Improving Productivity*. 7th ed. Englewood Cliffs, NJ: Prentice Hall, 1994.

[6] Niebel, B. W., and A. Freivalds. *Methods, Standards, and Work Design.* 11th ed. New York: McGraw-Hill, 2003.

[7] Sellie, C. N. "Predetermined Motion-Time Systems and the Development and Use of Standard Data." Pp. 1639–98 in *Handbook of Industrial Engineering.* 2nd ed., edited by Gavrial Salvendy. New York: Wiley; Institute of Industrial Engineers, 1992.

[8] Smith, G. L., Jr. *Work Measurement: A Systems Approach*. Columbus, OH: Grid Publishing, 1978.

[9] Zandin, K. *MOST Work Measurement Systems*. 3rd ed. New York: Marcel Dekker, 2003.

REVIEW QUESTIONS

1 Define *predetermined motion time system*.

2 What are the steps in applying a predetermined motion time system?

3 What is the difference between a first-level PMTS and a higher-level PMTS?

4 What is a motion aggregate in a higher-level PMTS?

5 Compare the advantages of a higher-level PMTS and a first-level PMTS.

6 What is the unit of time used in methods-time measurement?

7 What does the acronym MOST stand for?

8 What is the primary focus of MOST in terms of type of work activity?

9 What are the motion aggregates in MOST called?

10 What is the difference between General Move and Controlled Move in MOST?

PROBLEMS

MTM-1

1 A worker seated at a table performs a REACH. The sought-after object is jumbled with other objects in a tote pan, and the distance of the reach is 18 in. Determine the MTM-1 symbol and normal time in TMUs for this motion element.

2 An assembly worker standing at a workbench performs a MOVE. The object being moved weighs 10 lb. It is moved to an exact location a distance of 20 in. Determine the MTM-1 symbol and normal time in TMUs for this motion element.

3 An office worker sitting at a desk performs a MOVE. The moved object is a file weighing less than 1 lb. The distance is an approximate location 14 in. away from the starting point. Determine the MTM-1 symbol and normal time in TMUs for this motion element.

4 A mechanic performs two POSITION elements in sequence. The first requires an alignment along longitudinal axes of the objects, and the second requires an orientation of their rotational axes. Both elements can be classified as close fits with no symmetry, and the objects are easy to handle. (a) Determine the MTM-1 symbols and normal times in TMUs for these motion elements. (b) What is the total time for both elements in seconds?

5 What is the MTM-1 normal time in TMUs that should be allowed an operator who must read an instruction set before proceeding to perform a processing task, in which the instruction document contains 150 words? How many seconds is this?

6 In performing a certain manual task, a worker must walk a distance of 30 ft (one way) as one of the elements. (a) What is the MTM-1 normal time in TMUs that should be allowed for the element? (b) What is this walking time in seconds?

7 For safety reasons, a worker's eye travel time in a certain operation must be separated from the manual elements that follow. The distance the worker's eyes must travel is 20 in. The perpendicular distance from her eyes to the line of travel is 2 ft. No refocus is required. What is the MTM-1 normal time in TMUs that should be allowed for the eye travel element?

8 A work element in a manual assembly task consists of the following MTM-1 elements: (1) R16C, (2) G4A, (3) M10B5, (4) RL1, (5) R14B, (6) G1B, (7) M8C3, (8) P1NSE, and (9) RL1. (a) Determine the normal times in TMUs for these motion elements. (b) What is the total time for this work element in seconds?

9 A work element in a machine maintenance operation consists of the following MTM-1 elements: (1) W5P, i.e., walk 5 paces, (2) B, i.e., bend (3) R14B, (4) G1A, (5) AB, i.e., arise from bend, (6) W5P, (6) M12B2, (7) P1SSE, (8) RL1. (a) Determine the normal times in TMUs for these motion elements. (b) What is the total time for this work element in seconds?

MOST

10 Develop the activity sequence model and determine the normal time for the following work activity: A worker walks 3 steps, picks up a screwdriver from the floor, returns to his original position, and places the screwdriver on his worktable.

11 Develop the activity sequence model and determine the normal time for the following work activity: A clerk walks 8 steps, bends and picks up a file folder from the floor, places it on the counter within reach at that location, and then returns to her original location.

12 Develop the activity sequence model or models and determine the normal time for the following work activity: An assembly worker obtains 4 bolts in one hand from a bin located 10 in. away on his worktable and puts one bolt each into four holes in the bracket within easy reach in front of him.

13 Develop the activity sequence model and determine the normal time for the following work activity: A machinist standing in front of his milling machine grasps the waist level feed lever on the machine, and rotates the lever 1 crank to engage the feed. The process time to mill the part is 50 sec. There is no alignment and no action by the worker at the end of the process time.

14 Develop the activity sequence model and determine the normal time for the following work activity: A material-handling worker grasps a carton weighing 20 lb on a counter and slides it along the countertop a distance of 2 ft.

15 Develop the activity sequence model and determine the normal time for the following work activity: A drill press operator reaches 20 cm (8 in.) and pulls the feed lever down to engage the feed motion, which takes 12 sec.

16 Develop the activity sequence model and determine the normal time for the following work activity: A worker walks three steps, picks up a screw from his worktable, walks back to his initial location, positions the screw into a threaded hole, and turns it 5 spins with his fingers.

17 Develop the activity sequence model and determine the normal time for the following work activity: A worker picks up a screwdriver within reach from his worktable, positions it onto the head of a screw, fastens the screw with 6 turns, and lays the screwdriver aside.

18 Develop the activity sequence model and determine the normal time for the following work activity: An assembly worker on a production line obtains an Allen key within reach, positions it 15 cm (6 in.) onto a bolt head, cranks it 7 times to seat the bolt, and then sets the key aside.

19 Express the MTM-1 motion elements in Problem 8 as one or more MOST activity sequence models with index numbers. (a) Determine the normal times in TMUs for these activity sequence models. (b) What is the total time for this (these) activity sequence model(s) in seconds? (c) How do the MOST normal times compare with the normal times from MTM-1?

20 Express the MTM-1 motion elements in Problem 9 as one or more MOST activity sequence models with index numbers. (a) Determine the normal times in TMUs for these activity sequence models. (b) What is the total time for this (these) activity sequence model(s) in sec? (c) How do the MOST normal times compare with the normal times from MTM-1?

21 A work element in a worker-machine cycle has been reduced to the following two MOST activity sequence models:

$$A_3 B_{10} G_3 A_6 B_{10} P_3 A_3$$

$$A_3 B_0 G_1 M_1 X_T I_0 A_3$$

In the second sequence model, the process time is known to be 9.3 sec. This value must be converted to the correct index value, symbolized by the subscript T for the X parameter in the second sequence model. (a) What is the correct value of T? (b) Determine the normal time in seconds that would be allocated for this work element.

Miscellaneous

22 The normal time for walking in MTM-1 is 5.3 TMU/ft distance. (a) Using this value, determine the amount of time in minutes that would be required to walk 1 mile (5280 ft). (b) How does this compare with the traditional benchmark of standard performance of walking at 3 miles/hr?

23 The normal time for walking in MOST is 6.9 TMU/ft distance.[6] (a) Using this value, determine the amount of time in minutes that would be required to walk 1 mile (5280 ft). (b) How does this compare with the traditional benchmark of standard performance of walking at 3 miles/hr?

[6]Based on tabulated values in [9, p. 35].

Standard Data Systems

A ***standard data system*** (SDS) in work measurement is a database of normal time values, usually organized by work elements, that can be used to establish time standards for tasks composed of work elements similar to those in the database.[1] The normal time values for the work elements are usually compiled from previous direct time studies (DTS). Unlike those previous time studies, it is not necessary to directly observe the task in order to set a time standard using a standard data system. Accordingly, standards can be determined for a task before the job is running.

When using a standard data system, the analyst lists the work elements that would be required for a new task, specifying the details and parameters that will affect the time to accomplish the element. For example, the weight of the work unit is likely to affect

[1]The Work Measurement and Methods Standards Committee (ANSI Standard Z94.12-1989) defines standard data as follows: "A structured collection of normal time values for work elements codified in tabular or graphical form. The data are used as a basis for determining time standards on work similar to that from which the data were collected without additional time studies."

its handling time, and the dimensions of a metal part will affect its machining time. Taking the unique details and parameters of the work situation into account, the analyst retrieves the normal time for each element from the database, adds them to determine the normal time for the task, and includes the appropriate allowance factor to compute the time standard. The database provides normal times rather than standard times because the allowance factor may change over time, or different allowance factors may apply for different types of jobs or machines.

Although the element times in an SDS are most commonly based on direct time studies, other data can also be used, including work element times based on predetermined motion time systems (PMTS), work sampling, historical records, and time estimates. The accuracy requirements that will be demanded of the system usually determine the source of the starting data. If accuracy is important, then previous direct time studies or predetermined motion time systems should be the source of the normal time data. For instance, if the system will be used in conjunction with a wage incentive system, then the time values should be engineered standards. If only rough estimates of the task times are required of the standard data system, then the source of the data can be work sampling studies, historical records, or estimates. Appropriate applications for less accurate standard data systems include workload estimation, production scheduling, and decisions on staffing levels.

When a predetermined motion time system is used to develop times for a standard data system, it is for either of the following purposes: (1) to supplement the database of direct time study values because some of those data are missing, or (2) to develop the SDS database of work element normal times from the basic motion element times in the PMTS. This second purpose is distinguished from the conventional application of a PMTS, which is to determine the normal times for tasks. When used to develop a standard data system, the function of the PMTS is to determine normal times for work elements that will reside in the SDS database. Relating this distinction to our hierarchy of work activity SDS data consist of work elements, while PMTS data consist of basic motion elements. The elements in an SDS are referred to by the term ***macroscopic***, while the PMTS elements are called ***microscopic***. The relationships are illustrated in Figure 1.

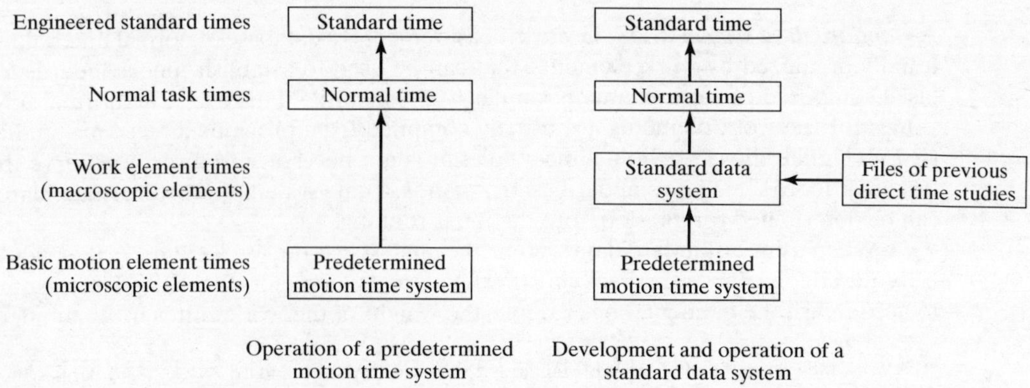

Figure 1 The relationships between a predetermined motion time system and a standard data system in setting time standards.

A standard data system is most suited for the following general characteristics and requirements of work situations:

- *Similarity in tasks.* If the tasks performed in a given work facility are similar, and there are many such tasks, then a standard data system is probably a more efficient way to set standards than direct time study. Similarity of tasks is characteristic of nearly all work facilities, because each facility tends to focus on a certain type of product or service, and the range of tasks required to deliver that product or service is limited to some extent. Machine shops and other batch production facilities are usually good candidates for SDS because the tasks are similar.
- *Batch production.* Standard data systems are best suited for medium production of batches. Very short cycle, highly repetitive operations are not suited to an SDS due to the need for detail and accuracy [3].
- *Large number of standards to be set.* Standard data systems are suited to the setting of a relative large number of standards. If the number of standards to be established per week is greater than the available analysts are capable of setting by direct time study or a predetermined motion time system, then an SDS would help to alleviate this problem. On the other hand, if only a few time standards are needed per week, then the investment cost of developing an SDS may be difficult to justify.
- *Need to set standards before production.* Direct time study requires direct observation of the task in order to set a standard. This means that the job must already be in production. With a standard data system, the standard can be established before the job is running.

1 USING A STANDARD DATA SYSTEM

The purpose of a standard data system is to establish a time standard for a new task. In using the SDS, the analyst should first make sure the new task is included within the coverage of the system. The term ***coverage*** refers to the family of tasks for which the SDS is applicable. A standard data system is not a universal system. It is designed for a limited range of tasks. One of the potential problems with an SDS is that it may be applied to tasks for which it is not designed. The task family coverage should be clearly stated in the SDS documentation.

1.1 Steps in Using an SDS

Assuming the coverage requirement is satisfied, the analyst would proceed through the following steps to determine a time standard for a new task:

1. *Analyze the new task and divide into work elements.* The work elements in the new task should correspond to elements in the SDS database. The analyst must distinguish between different types of elements, such as setup versus production elements, constant versus variable elements, and other differences among elements (Section 3).

2. *Access database to determine normal times for work elements.* Using the database provided in the SDS (Section 1.2), the analyst determines the normal time for each work element in the new task, distinguishing between setup, if applicable, and production cycle.

3. *Add element normal times to obtain task normal time.* Again, setup and production tasks are computed separately. The sum of the setup element times is equal to the setup normal time, $T_{n\text{-}su}$. The sum of the production element times is equal to the production cycle normal time, T_n. In the case of the production cycle, the analyst must distinguish any internal elements in the case of machine cycles. These must be excluded from the calculation, as in direct time study, if the total internal time is less than the machine time.

4. *Compute standard times for setup and production cycle.* The standard time for setup includes an allowance factor. The following equation to compute the standard time for setup is applicable:

$$T_{std\text{-}su} = T_{n\text{-}su}(1 + A_{pfd}) \tag{1}$$

where $T_{std\text{-}su}$ = standard time for setup, min; $T_{n\text{-}su}$ = normal time for setup, min; and A_{pfd} = allowance factor for personal time, fatigue, and delays. To compute the standard time for the production cycle, we must distinguish whether the work cycle includes a machine cycle. For manual work with no machine cycle, the following equation is applicable:

$$T_{std} = T_n(1 + A_{pfd}) \tag{2}$$

For a worker-machine system that includes machine time, the following equation is applicable:

$$T_{std} = T_{nw}(1 + A_{pfd}) + T_m(1 + A_m) \tag{3}$$

where A_m = machine allowance factor. It should be noted that different PFD allowance factors (A_{pfd}) might be used for setup and production.

1.2 The SDS Database

The SDS database contains the work element normal times for the types of tasks accomplished in a facility. It is a catalog of normal time values, organized to allow the analyst to access the values that correspond to work elements performed under various conditions and parameters. Let us call these conditions and parameters the ***work variables***, which refer to factors such as the work unit characteristics, the task parameters, and the working conditions that affect the normal time of the element. The analyst must identify the values of these work variables that apply to the element being considered. Different work variables are applicable to different types of elements, and the number of applicable work variables for a given element may range from none (a constant element time) to three or more (for convenience, the number should be kept to the minimum necessary to satisfy accuracy requirements of the system). Once these values have been established, the analyst can retrieve the work element normal time value that corresponds to the relevant work variable values.

A variety of different database formats can be used for a standard data system. The most common formats are charts, tables, mathematical formulas, worksheets, and computerized databases and retrieval systems. These are discussed in the sections that follow.

Charts. A ***chart*** is a graphical plot that indicates the value of the normal time (dependent variable) as a function of one or more work variables (independent variables). The simplest case is one work variable. For two work variables, a family of plots can be used to indicate the normal time on a single graph. Figure 2 illustrates these two cases. For three work variables, multiple graphs are needed.

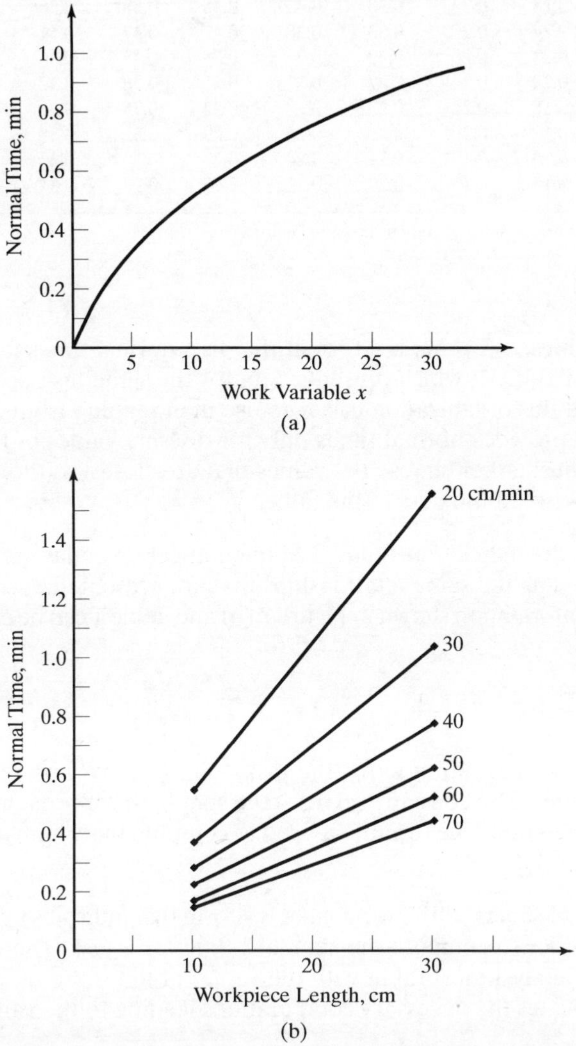

Figure 2 Chart format for determining the normal time in a standard data system: (a) one work variable and (b) two work variables.

TABLE 1 Table Format for Determining Normal Time (decimal min) in a Standard Data System.[a]

Feed Rate (cm/min)	Workpiece Length (cm) 10	12	14	16	18	20	22	24	26	28	30
20	0.55	0.65	0.75	0.85	0.95	1.05	1.15	1.25	1.35	1.45	1.55
25	0.44	0.52	0.60	0.68	0.76	0.84	0.92	1.00	1.08	1.16	1.24
30	0.37	0.43	0.50	0.57	0.63	0.70	0.77	0.83	0.90	0.97	1.03
35	0.31	0.37	0.43	0.49	0.54	0.60	0.66	0.71	0.77	0.83	0.89
40	0.28	0.33	0.38	0.43	0.48	0.53	0.58	0.63	0.68	0.73	0.78
45	0.24	0.29	0.33	0.38	0.42	0.47	0.51	0.56	0.60	0.64	0.69
50	0.22	0.26	0.30	0.34	0.38	0.42	0.46	0.50	0.54	0.58	0.62
55	0.20	0.24	0.27	0.31	0.35	0.38	0.42	0.45	0.49	0.53	0.56
60	0.18	0.22	0.25	0.28	0.32	0.35	0.38	0.42	0.45	0.48	0.52
65	0.17	0.20	0.23	0.26	0.29	0.32	0.35	0.38	0.42	0.45	0.48
70	0.16	0.19	0.21	0.24	0.27	0.30	0.33	0.36	0.39	0.41	0.44
75	0.15	0.17	0.20	0.23	0.25	0.28	0.31	0.33	0.36	0.39	0.41

[a]This table presents data for the same operation shown in Figure 2 (b).

Tables. A ***table*** is a format that lists normal times in a tabular arrangement, as shown in Table 1, which presents data for the same task as in Figure 2 (b). Some analysts find this organization easier to use than reading from a chart. The trouble with it is that it provides normal times only for discrete values of the work variables, and the reader must either choose the values that are closest to those in the new task, or interpolate between the data in the table.

Mathematical Formulas. Mathematical formulas are often a more concise way of expressing the same relationships that are presented in charts and tables. For example, the information shown in Figure 2 (b) and Table 1 can be summarized in the following equation:

$$T_n = \frac{1+L}{f_r} \tag{4}$$

where T_n = normal time for the task, min; L = workpiece length, cm; and f_r = feed rate, cm/min. The constant 1 (cm) is the sum of the approach and overtravel allowances in the operation. The formula is used to compute machining time in a turning operation (Section 4.1).

Worksheets. The worksheet is a form that indicates the steps the analyst must follow in order to compute the standard time for a task. The worksheet includes blanks that the analyst must fill in with the values of the work variables in the task. The form also indicates the necessary computations leading to the value of the normal time.

Computerized Database and Retrieval Systems. A computerized database and retrieval system is the modern format for a standard data system, combining the formats described above into a single database that can be organized around one of the available spreadsheet packages, such as Excel. Its use is similar to that of a worksheet. The user enters the values of the work variables that apply to the new task. The computer retrieves or calculates the normal times from a database that uses a combination of constant values and mathematical formulas. The system then computes the normal time for the task.

2 DEVELOPING A STANDARD DATA SYSTEM

A standard data system is almost always custom-engineered and developed for the facility that will use the system. Because each plant's products, production methods, and policies, including its policy on time standards, tend to be unique, a standard data system developed for one company cannot be readily migrated to another company. The general steps in an SDS development project are outlined in Table 2.

TABLE 2 Recommended Steps in Developing a Standard Data System

1. ***Define the objectives of the system.*** When undertaking a major project such as the development of a standard data system, it is always useful to prepare a written statement of the objectives. What is expected of the system when it is completed? What tools will be developed to allow analysts to set time standards? What are the accuracy requirements? Formal answers to these kinds of questions help to structure the project, reduce ambiguities that may arise and can later be referenced to assess whether the project was successful.
2. ***Define the coverage of the system.*** A standard data system is not a universal system capable of setting standards for all tasks. It is designed for a limited range of tasks. The family of tasks or group of task families in the plant that will be covered by the system must be defined.
3. ***Obtain work element normal time data.*** Direct time studies are the most common data source for developing an SDS. The data should include all types of tasks within the defined coverage. The normal times for work elements that make up these tasks must be extracted from the DTS data. An alternative to DTS data is to develop work element normal times using a predetermined motion time system.
4. ***Classify work elements.*** Setup elements must be distinguished from production (or repetitive) elements. Constant elements must be distinguished from variable elements. And so forth. The various categories and distinctions are discussed in Section 3.
5. ***Analyze data to determine element normal times.*** For constant elements, compute the average normal time. For variable elements, determine the work variables that affect the normal times and develop relationships that allow the normal times to be predicted depending on the values of the work variables. Different approaches are used for different element categories.
6. ***Develop database to predict normal times.*** This is the database that will be used by the analyst to retrieve the normal time for a new task. It is a catalog of normal time values. The database format can range from charts to computerized systems (Section 1.2). Multiple formats may be combined in one system because the best method to determine a normal time may differ for different types of work elements.
7. **Prepare documentation.** The standard data system documentation should describe each step in the development project. Most importantly, it must provide a user's manual that will allow an analyst to apply the SDS to determine time standards.

Source: Compiled and summarized from several sources, including [1], [3], [8], [11], and other sources.

3 WORK ELEMENT CLASSIFICATION IN STANDARD DATA SYSTEMS

The database in a standard data system is organized by work elements. When the user retrieves a particular work element in the system, a normal time corresponding to that element is provided to the user. Different categories of work elements must be distinguished in an SDS, similar to the way different work element types must be distinguished in direct time study. Classification of work elements is even more important in a standard data system because the normal time is a predicted value rather than an observed value, as in direct time study. The method by which it is predicted depends on the type of element. The classification of work elements in a standard data system must account for differences between the following element types:

- ***Setup*** and ***production*** elements
- ***Constant*** and ***variable*** elements
- ***Worker-paced*** and ***machine*** elements
- ***Regular*** and ***irregular*** elements
- ***Internal*** and ***external*** elements

3.1 Setup and Production Elements

The first distinction is between setup elements and production elements. Standard data systems are frequently applied in batch production, in which a batch of one part or product style is produced, after which the equipment is changed over to produce a batch of a different part or product style. Most manufacturing operations involve batch production (e.g., parts, books, apparel, machines). The quantities in each batch vary, typically ranging from several units to several thousand units. The changeover between production runs takes time. Called the ***setup time*** or ***changeover time***, it is the time required to change the physical arrangement of the workplace, to replace the tooling, and to reprogram or reset the equipment to get ready for the next batch. This is lost production time, a disadvantage of batch production. ***Setup elements*** in a standard data system are those associated with the activities required to accomplish the changeover.

Production elements are associated with the processing of work units. They occur in the regular work cycle, with perhaps an occasional irregular element thrown in. One work unit is produced each cycle (in most cases). If a machine is involved, its elements are included in the work cycle. As in direct time study, internal and external elements must be distinguished.

The key point here is that setup elements occur once per batch, while production elements occur once per work unit. Therefore, total time for the batch is given by

$$T_b = T_{su} + QT_c \tag{5}$$

where T_b = total batch time, T_{su} = setup time (sum of setup elements), Q = quantity of units in the batch, and T_c = cycle time (sum of production elements) per work unit. The standard data system is designed to provide normal times for T_{su} and T_c; that is, the SDS provides $T_{n\text{-}su}$ as the value for T_{su} and T_n as the value for T_c. These values are then used to compute the corresponding standard times for the job.

3.2 Constant and Variable Elements

A second consideration in our classification of work elements is the difference between constant elements and variable elements. Setup and production elements can be either type. ***Constant elements*** have the same time value in all time studies. Any variations from one job to the next are random and are generally accounted for by variations in operator performance and/or analyst timing of the element among different time studies. The following are typical examples of constant elements:

- *Replace cutting tool in tool post.* On a given lathe, equipped with standard tool post, the time to change the cutting tool should be a constant value regardless of work part style.
- *Dial telephone number of customer.* Using a touch-tone phone, the time to dial up a customer should be constant, given the worker has ready access to the number.[2]
- *Push two buttons to initiate press stroke.* In this case, the worker operates some type of press (e.g., stamping press, forge press, printing press), and the time each cycle to actuate the press requires the worker to press two buttons, one with each hand. For a given press, this time should be a constant regardless of the work unit.

For each of these examples and for any other work elements believed to be constant, there will be observable random variations in the time study data among occurrences, at least for those elements that are operator-paced. The analyst must perform a statistical analysis to ensure that randomness is the only reason for the variation. Otherwise, a search for the factor(s) responsible for the variation must be undertaken.

Variable elements have the same basic motion patterns and the same basic function from one job to the next, but the normal time varies because of differences in work variable values. There is a causal relationship between these work variables and the normal time to perform the element. There will also be random variations in the time, just as in constant elements, but the distinguishing feature of a variable element is that its normal time depends on the job characteristics. Examples of variable elements include the following:

- *Keypunch address.* This office task is used to compile lists of customers, students, etc. and involves entering data from some source into a computer file. Defining one work element as each name and address, the time required depends on (1) the source (e.g., another list, telephone interview), (2) the number of lines and (3) the total number of characters in the name and address. The skill of the typist will also affect the time, but this is taken into account by the definition of standard performance.

[2]If an old-fashioned rotary dial phone is used, the time to dial depended on the individual digits in the telephone number. Higher digits and zero took longer because of the longer return rotation of the phone dial.

- *Fetch kit of components for assembly.* In this case, the work element involves walking from a given workstation in the factory to the storage crib to withdraw a kit of parts for assembly (the kit has been prepared in advance) and returning to the workstation. The normal time depends on the distance between the station location and the storage crib. Longer walking distances take more time. Another factor that may influence the time is the size of the component kit (a larger kit with more parts may increase the walking time, or may require two trips).
- *Load workpiece into lathe and tighten chuck.* The size and weight of the work part will affect the time required to load it. Heavier parts take more time. If the part is too heavy for the operator, a hoist is required, which takes still more time. The type of chuck (e.g., self-centering versus independent tightening of jaws) also has a significant effect.
- *Turn workpiece in one pass.* This follows the loading element in the preceding example. This is a machine-paced element whose time depends on (1) the feed and cutting speed of the lathe, and (2) the length and diameter of the workpiece.

In the case of variable elements, the job of the analyst is twofold: (1) identify the factors and features of the element and/or work unit upon which the normal time to perform it depends, and (2) determine the exact nature of the relationship so that it can be used as a predictive model of future performance.

3.3 Operator-Paced and Machine-Controlled Elements

Operator-paced elements are manual elements, perhaps involving the use of a tool or other implement. They include both setup and production elements, and they can be constant or variable. Our previous examples include both types. Whether constant or variable, they contain unavoidable random variations that are characteristic of any human manual activity. With constant elements, random variations are the only cause of the observed differences in element times that occurred during the original time studies. With variable elements, there are one or more causal factors that affect the observed times of the work elements, and it is the job of the system developer to determine what these factors are and how to best include them in the standard data system.

Machine-controlled elements are usually variable, and the variables upon which machine time depends are the operating parameters of the machine and the characteristics of the work unit. Once these parameters and characteristics are established, the element time can be determined with great accuracy and precision. One of our previous examples indicates the parameters of the machine and the characteristics of the work unit that determine machine time:

- *Turn workpiece in one pass.* In this machine-controlled element time the operating parameters of the machine are feed and speed and the workpiece characteristics are its length and diameter.

In Section 4, we examine some common manufacturing processes and the methods by which machine time can be determined for them.

3.4 Other Work Element Differences

Other distinctions in work elements that must be considered in designing and using a standard data system include regular versus irregular elements and whether the element is internal or external. These terms have the same meanings as in direct time study. A ***regular element*** occurs at least once every work cycle, and it can be constant or variable, operator paced or machine controlled. By definition regular elements are always production elements and not setup. An ***irregular element*** occurs less frequently than once per work cycle. Its time is prorated in the regular cycle time to arrive at a standard.

External and internal elements must be distinguished in the standard data system. The distinction is most closely associated with a regular production cycle that involves a machine-controlled element rather than the initial setup of the machine. ***External elements*** are those performed in series with the machine time. They are therefore included in the calculation of the normal time for the work cycle. ***Internal elements*** are performed in parallel with the machine time. As long as the total time of the internal elements is less than the machine cycle, then they do not count in determining the normal time for the work cycle.

3.5 Work Cycle Standard Data

Instead of breaking a given task into work elements and then analyzing the times for each work element separately, it may be appropriate under some circumstances to study the whole task as a single entity [11]. There are several work situations in which this aggregating approach may be applicable: (1) the individual work elements that make up the task are highly variable, (2) the elements are difficult to separate or identify, (3) the task consists of many elements, (4) there are many elements that are similar, and (5) the standards determined by the system will not be used for wage incentive purposes but may be used to evaluate and compare worker performance. The following examples illustrate this approach:

- *Checkout of customer at supermarket counter.* In this example, we are considering the entire task rather than a single work element within the task. The obvious factors that determine the checkout time include (1) the number of items selected by the customer, (2) the types of items selected, e.g., proportion of boxed goods versus produce, (3) whether checking out involves bar codes or manual entry of item price, (4) the method by which the customer pays (e.g., cash or credit card), and (5) whether the clerk must also bag the customer's items, or there is a separate helper who does the bagging.
- *Prepare legal document for submission to client.* This task involves taking a standard document form (e.g., last will and testament) that resides on a PC word processor file in a lawyer's office, and filling in the blanks and otherwise altering the document to fit the needs of a particular client. The time required for a paralegal assistant to accomplish the task depends on factors such as (1) the number of pages in the starting standard form, (2) the number of active clauses in the document, and (3) the number of items that must be filled in, added to, or deleted from the document, based on the handwritten notes taken by the lawyer during the client interview.

- *Time to proofread a document.* The number of pages to proofread is an obvious parameter that affects task time in this example. Other factors include line spacing (single-spaced, double-spaced, etc.), font size, type of text (technical versus nontechnical).

Developing standard data for the entire task rather than dividing it into work elements is a shortcut that is likely to have certain advantages: (1) saves time for the system developer, (2) results in a simpler predictive model that is much easier to use by the analyst, and (3) may be just as accurate for setting standards as a system based on dividing the task into elements.

4 ANALYSIS OF MACHINE-CONTROLLED ELEMENT TIMES

For worker-machine systems the standard method often includes a machine cycle, in which the equipment runs under its own control for a certain length of time. Examples of machine cycles include the following:

- *Power feed motion of a machine tool* (e.g., lathe, drill press, milling machine). Once activated by the worker, the machine operates in a mechanized mode according to feed and speed settings that have been established for the operation.
- *Semiautomatic cycle of a machine.* The machine cycle is determined by a part program that is executed under computer numerical control (CNC) or a similar programmable controller. The operator's responsibility consists of loading and unloading the machine each work cycle, periodically changing tools, and monitoring the operation.
- *Fully automated cycle.* The machine operates under program control for extended periods of time that are greater than one work cycle. The operator periodically attends to the machine, perhaps loading and unloading a work part storage unit, changing tools, and so forth. In this case, the operator may not be required to be present at the machine 100% of the time. In other cases, the worker may be responsible for continuously monitoring the machine to ensure high utilization.

For these situations, the time taken by the machine cycle can be measured or calculated with high accuracy, given the machine settings and the parameters of the part program. These settings and parameters should be included in the standard method documentation. During production, the operator is obligated to run the machine using these settings. If not, then the standard method is not being followed and the time standard for the task is not valid.

In the following sections, we explain the calculation of machine times for the most common machining operations: (1) turning, (2) drilling, and (3) milling. For these operations, the relationships to compute machine time are well established. They are classified as metal removal processes, in which excess metal is removed from a starting workpiece by means of a sharp cutting tool so that the remaining part has the desired geometry. Similar expressions can usually be developed for other mechanized or automated processes.

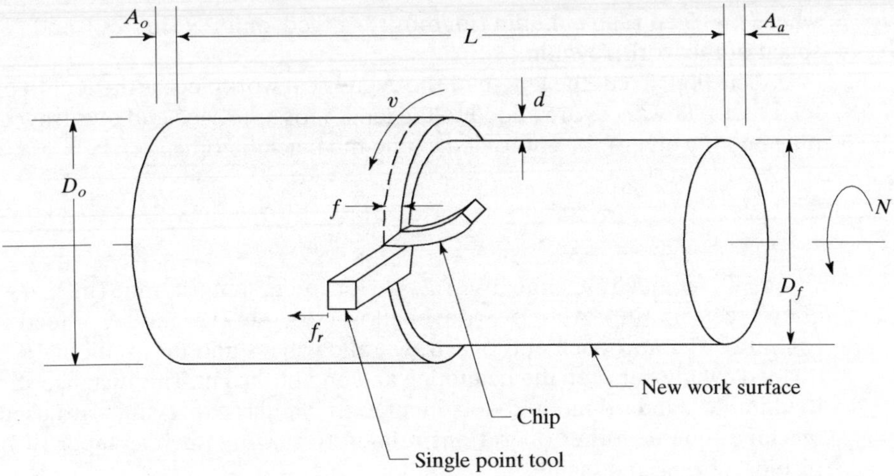

Key: D_o = staring diameter, D_f = final diameter, L = length, v = cutting speed, f = feed, d = depth of cut, f_r = feed rate, N = rotational speed, A = approach allowance, and A_o = overtravel allowance.

Figure 3 Turning operation.

4.1 Turning

Turning is a machining operation in which a single point cutting tool is used to remove metal from the surface of a rotating cylindrical work piece by feeding the tool linearly in a direction parallel to the axis of rotation, as shown in Figure 3. Turning is traditionally performed on ***lathe***. The specified operating parameters (called ***cutting conditions*** in machining) are cutting speed (surface speed at the original work diameter), feed (tool travel distance per revolution of the workpiece), and depth of cut below the original work surface.

Although cutting speed is specified in the cutting conditions, this must be converted to the corresponding machine setting, which is the rotational speed of the lathe spindle (the spindle drives the workpiece). The following equation is used for this purpose:

$$N = \frac{v}{\pi D_o} \tag{6}$$

where N = spindle rotational speed, rev/min; v = cutting speed, m/min (ft/min); and D_o = original diameter of the workpiece, m (ft). The feed in turning is generally expressed as mm/rev (in./rev), which is the second machine setting required to compute machine time. This feed is converted to a linear feed rate in mm/min (in./min) as follows:

$$f_r = Nf \tag{7}$$

where f_r = feed rate, mm/min (in./min); f = feed, mm/rev (in./rev); and N = rotational speed of the work, rev/min.[3]

The time to cut the length of the cylindrical workpiece is the length divided by the feed rate. Allowances are added to the length for approach and overtravel at the beginning and the end of the cut to determine the machine time.

$$T_m = \frac{A_a + L + A_o}{f_r} \tag{8}$$

where T_m = machine time, min; L = workpiece length, mm (in.); A_a = approach allowance, mm (in.); A_o = overtravel allowance, mm (in.); and f_r = feed rate, mm/min (in./min). The approach and overtravel allowances add up to about 10 mm (0.4 in.), divided evenly between the beginning and end of the cut. This distance should be specified in the standard method documentation. Similar expressions are used to compute machine time for other operations related to turning, such as taper turning, contour turning, boring, and facing.[4]

4.2 Drilling

Drilling is a machining operation that creates a round hole in a workpiece, using a rotating drill bit. The usual drill bit is a ***twist drill***, and the machine tool is a ***drill press***. The cutting speed in a drilling operation is the outside surface speed of the drill bit, even though virtually all of the actual cutting is done by the sharp cutting edges at the end of the drill, where the relative speed between tool and work is lower. As in turning, the machine setting on a drill press is rotational speed, so surface speed must be converted as follows:

$$N = \frac{v}{\pi D} \tag{9}$$

where N = rotational speed of the drill bit, rev/min; v = cutting speed, m/min (ft/min); and D = drill diameter, m (ft). The feed in drilling is specified in units of linear travel distance per revolution (as in turning), so it must be converted to a feed rate:

$$f_r = Nf \tag{10}$$

where f_r = feed rate of the drill into the work, mm/min (in./min), and f = feed, mm/rev (in./rev), and N = rotational speed of the drill, rev/min.

A drilled hole is classified as either a ***through hole***, which means the drill bit passes through the work and exits on the opposite side; or a ***blind hole***, which means the drill bit does not pass through the work. The two cases are illustrated in Figure 4 (a) and (b) respectively. For a through hole, an approach allowance must be added to the

[3]Recommended cutting conditions (speeds and feeds) can be found in various handbooks such as *Machinery's Handbook* [4].

[4]These machining operations and others discussed here are described in most manufacturing processes textbooks, among which we recommend [5].

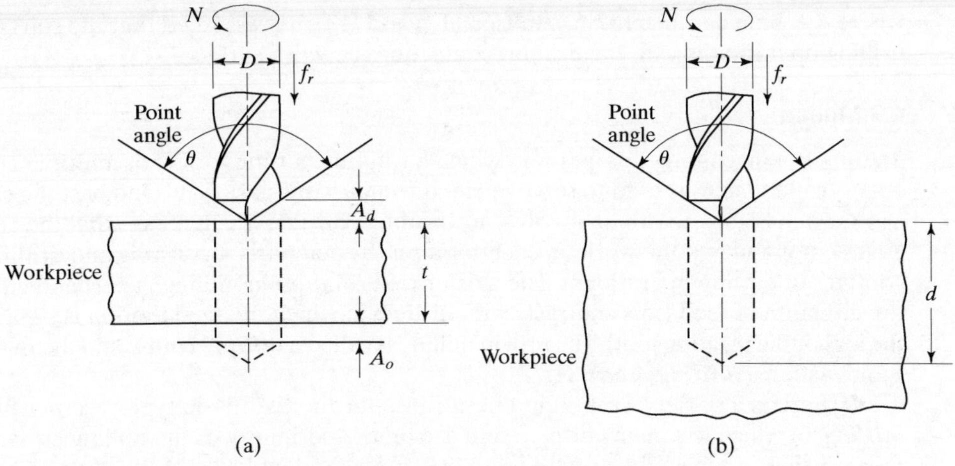

Figure 4 Drilling operation (a) through hole and (b) blind hole.

thickness of the work in order to obtain the total travel distance of the drill bit. The approach allowance depends on the point angle on the drill bit, as defined in our drawings, and can be calculated as follows:

$$A_d = 0.5D \tan\left[90^\circ - \frac{\theta}{2}\right] \tag{11}$$

where A_d = allowance to reach full diameter, mm (in.); D = drill diameter, mm (in.); and θ = drill point angle, degrees. A typical value for drill point angle is 118°. Once the drill bit breaks through on the other side of the piece, it is allowed to overtravel by a short distance to clear the hole. The machine time for a through hole is then determined from the following equation:

$$T_m = \frac{A_d + t + A_o}{f_r} \tag{12}$$

where T_m = machine time, min; A_d = allowance to reach full diameter, mm (in.); t = work thickness, mm (in); and A_o = overtravel allowance, mm (in.).

For a blind hole, in which hole depth is defined as in Figure 4 (b), no approach allowance is needed, and the machine time can be computed as the depth divided by the feed rate:

$$T_m = \frac{d}{f_r} \tag{13}$$

where d = hole depth, mm (in.). In Eqs. (12) and (13), it is assumed that the start of the drilling operation is with the drill bit contacting the work surface.

4.3 Milling

Milling is a machining operation in which a rotating cutting tool with multiple cutting edges (called ***teeth***) is used to remove metal from a work part that is fed past the cutter, as shown in Figure 5. Milling involves interrupted cutting, which means that the cutting edges enter and exit the work on each rotation (by comparison, turning and drilling are continuous cutting operations). The axis of tool rotation in milling is perpendicular to the direction of feed (this contrasts with drilling in which the feed motion is parallel to the axis of the rotating tool). The tool in milling is called a ***milling cutter***, and the machine tool is called a ***milling machine***.

There is a variety of milling operations, but the two basic types are ***peripheral milling***, in which the main cutting teeth are on the periphery of the milling cutter; and ***face milling***, in which the cutting teeth are on the end and side of the cutter. The two types are shown in Figure 5 (a) and (b). In either case, the specified cutting speed is the surface speed at the outside diameter of the cutter. This must be converted to a machine setting, which is the spindle rotational speed:

$$N = \frac{v}{\pi D} \tag{14}$$

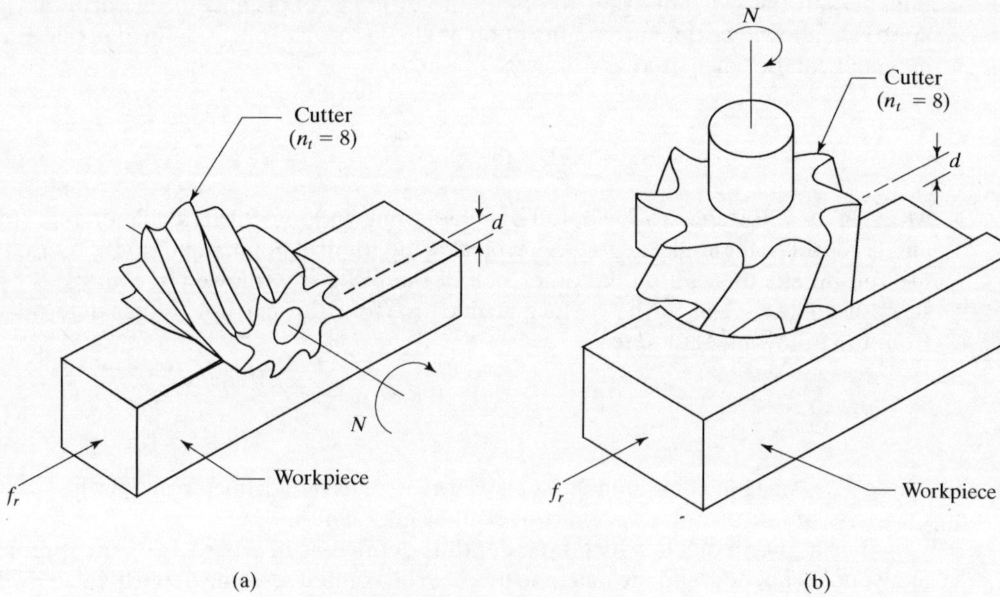

Key: f_r = feed rate, N = rotational speed or cutter, d = depth of cut, and n_t = number of teeth on cutter.

Figure 5 Milling operations: (a) peripheral milling and (b) face milling.

where N = rotation speed of milling cutter, rev/min; v = cutting speed, m/min (ft/min); and D = diameter of cutter, m (ft). The feed in milling, also called the ***chip load***, is the size of the cut taken by each tooth of the cutter. This is converted into feed rate as follows:

$$f_r = N n_t f \tag{15}$$

where n_t = number of teeth on milling cutter; f = feed (chip load), mm (in.); and the other terms have the same meaning as before.

Peripheral Milling. To determine the machine time in peripheral milling, an approach distance must be added to the length of the workpiece to allow the cutter to reach full depth. This approach distance is illustrated in Figure 6 and can be computed from the following equation:

$$A_d = \sqrt{d(D-d)} \tag{16}$$

where A_d = distance to reach full depth, mm (in.); d = depth of cut, mm (in.); and D = cutter diameter, mm (in.).

In addition to this distance to reach full depth there are also added the customary approach and overtravel allowances. Thus machine time for peripheral milling is determined as follows:

$$T_m = \frac{A_a + A_d + L + A_o}{f_r} \tag{17}$$

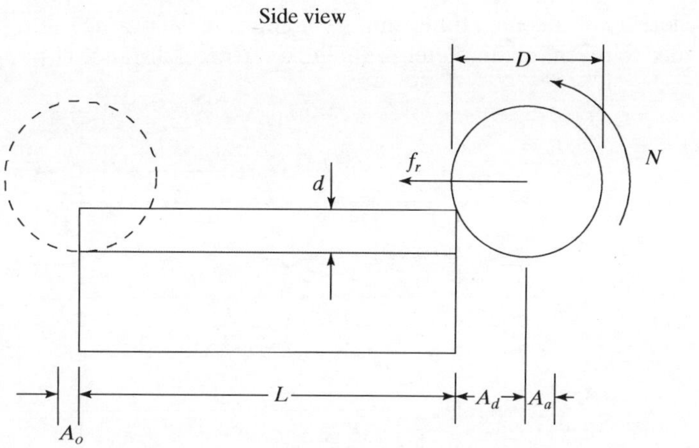

Key: D = cutter diameter, N = cutter rotational speed, f_r = feed rate, L = workpiece length, d = depth of cut, A_d = distance to reach full depth, A_a = approach allowance, and A_o = overtravel allowance.

Figure 6 Peripheral milling showing the approach distance required by the cutter to reach full depth.

where T_m = machine time, min; A_a = approach allowance, mm (in.); A_d = allowance distance to reach full depth, mm (in.); L = workpiece length, mm (in.); A_o = overtravel allowance, mm (in.); and f_r = feed rate, mm/min (in./min). The allowances for approach and overtravel are usually kept as small as possible, perhaps $A_a + A_o$ = 10 to 15 mm (0.4 to 0.6 in.). The values should be specified in the standard method since they affect the machine time.

Face Milling. For face milling, we will consider the situation in which the cutter is centered over a rectangular workpiece and the workpiece is wider than the cutter diameter, as shown in Figure 7. Other geometries are also possible, and we explore some of these in our end-of-chapter problems. To the length of the workpiece must be added an approach distance to allow the cutter to reach full diameter into the work. In addition, an overtravel distance must be provided to allow the cutter to move completely past the workpiece. These distances are the same and can be computed as

$$A_d = \frac{D}{2} \tag{18}$$

where A_d = allowance distance to reach full diameter, mm (in.); and D = cutter diameter, mm (in.).

In addition to the approach and overtravel distances to allow for cutter diameter we need the usual allowances A_a and A_o. Machine time for face milling can now be determined:

$$T_m = \frac{A_a + 2A_d + L + A_o}{f_r} \tag{19}$$

where T_m = machine time, min; A_a = approach allowance, mm (in.); A_d = approach distance to reach full diameter (equal to overtravel distance to pass completely beyond the

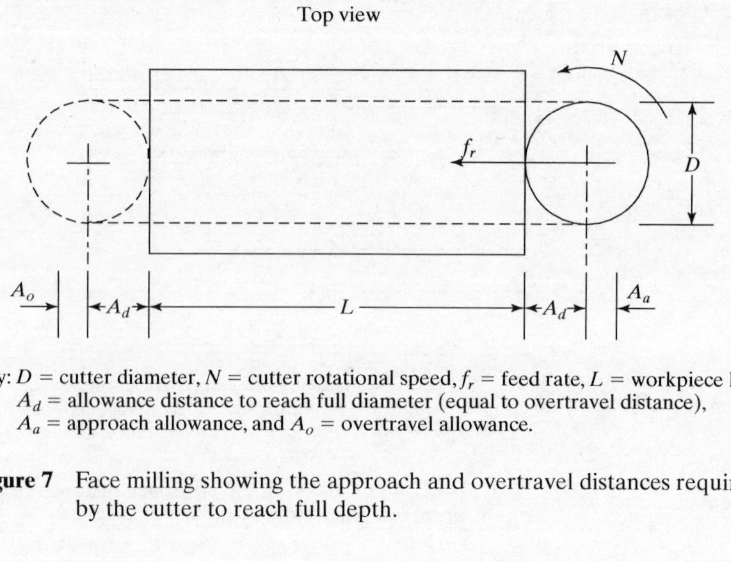

Key: D = cutter diameter, N = cutter rotational speed, f_r = feed rate, L = workpiece length, A_d = allowance distance to reach full diameter (equal to overtravel distance), A_a = approach allowance, and A_o = overtravel allowance.

Figure 7 Face milling showing the approach and overtravel distances required by the cutter to reach full depth.

work), mm (in.); L = workpiece length, mm (in.); A_o = overtravel allowance, mm (in.); and f_r = feed rate, mm/min (in./min). Our previous comments about minimizing A_a and A_o and documenting the values in the standard method also apply here.

5 SDS ADVANTAGES AND DISADVANTAGES

Developing a standard data system requires considerable time and effort by the plant or company. In this section, we summarize the advantages and disadvantages of this type of system.

Advantages

- *Productivity in setting standards.* The time required to set a time standard using a standard data system is considerably less than the time required using direct time study. One estimate is that the productivity improvement is a factor of five [9]. Thus, more standards can be established with fewer analysts.
- *Cost savings.* If a plant has a large number of time standards that must be set, then a standard data system may be economically justified by the cost savings of the analysts who would otherwise have to take direct time studies to set the standards.
- *Setting standards before production.* The time standard can be set prior to the start of the job using a standard data system. This is not possible with direct time study due to its requirement for direct observation.
- *Avoids the need for performance rating.* The performance rating has already been factored into the normal time data used to develop the SDS. If the SDS data consist of the original time studies, they were normalized in the performance rating step. If the SDS data are based on a predetermined motion time system, these are normalized values.
- *Consistency in the standards.* Standards set by a standard data system are based on more data because they represent an average of many time studies from similar tasks. Any single standard set by direct time study may be slightly high or low, due to differences or errors in operator pace, performance rating, stopwatch readings, and so forth. Using a standard data system tends to smooth these high and low values to produce a more consistent standard.
- *Inputs to other information systems.* Because standards can be set beforehand, the time values can be used as inputs to other planning and scheduling programs, such as product cost estimating, computer-assisted process planning, material requirements planning (MRP), and enterprise resource planning (ERP). Indeed, a modern, well-designed standard data system is itself a module in the company's computerized information system, enabling automatic communication of time standards to the other modules in that larger system.

Disadvantages and Limitations

- *High investment cost.* As mentioned, developing a standard data system involves considerable time and effort. The company must be sure that the investment will be justified. If the number of standards to be set by the SDS is relatively low, then the system is not likely to be cost-effective.

- *Source of data.* Because the database for the SDS is compiled from previous time studies, the company must have a sufficient file of these studies in order to undertake development of a standard data system. It must also have confidence in the validity of the original data. If the original time standards are systematically biased, either high or low, then the standards set by the standard data system will be likewise biased.
- *Methods descriptions.* Use of a standard data system does not eliminate the need for documentation of a standard method for each task. Although written descriptions may exist for the work elements in the original study, these descriptions will surely differ in detail and language. New standard method descriptions may have to be developed for use with the SDS.
- *Risk of improper applications.* A standard data system is designed with a certain scope of coverage in mind. It is developed from data for a defined family of tasks and its applications are limited to setting time standards for new tasks in that same family. One of the risks in the application of an SDS is that it will be used to set standards for tasks outside of that family.

REFERENCES

[1] Aft, L. S. *Work Measurement and Methods Improvement*. New York: Wiley, 2000.

[2] ANSI Standard Z94.0-1989. *Industrial Engineering Terminology*. Norcross, GA: Industrial Engineering and Management Press, Institute of Industrial Engineers. 1989.

[3] Connors, J. "Standard Data Concepts and Development." Pp. 5.41–5.72 in *Maynard's Industrial Engineering Handbook*. 5th ed. edited by K. Zandin. New York: McGraw-Hill, 2001.

[4] Green, R. E., ed. *Machinery's Handbook*. 25th ed. New York: Industrial Press, 1996.

[5] Groover, M. P. *Fundamentals of Modern Manufacturing: Materials, Processes, and Systems*, 3rd ed. Hoboken, NJ: Wiley, 2007.

[6] *Machining Data Handbook*. 3rd ed. Cincinnati, OH: Machinability Data Center, 1980.

[7] Meyers F. E., and J. R. Stewart, *Motion and Time Study for Lean Manufacturing*, 3rd ed. Prentice Hall, Upper Saddle River, N. J., 2002.

[8] Mundel, M. E., and D.L. Danner, *Motion and Time Study*, 7th ed. Prentice Hall, Upper Saddle River, N. J., 1994.

[9] Niebel, B. W., and A. Freivalds. *Methods, Standards, and Work Design*. 11th ed. WCB New York: McGraw-Hill, 2003.

[10] Sellie, C. N., "Predetermined Motion-Time Systems and the Development and Use of Standard Data." Pp. 1639–98. *Handbook of Industrial Engineering*, 2nd ed. edited by Gavrial Salvendy. New York: Wiley, Institute of Industrial Engineers, 1992.

[11] Smith, G. L., Jr. *Work Measurement: A Systems Approach*. Columbus, OH: Grid Publishing, 1978.

REVIEW QUESTIONS

1 What is a standard data system?

2 Which work measurement techniques should be used as the source of the data in a standard data system if accuracy of the standards is important?

3 What are the general characteristics and requirements of work situations for which a standard data system is most suited?

4 Identify the steps in using a standard data system.

5 What are the database formats commonly used in a standard data system?

6 Identify the different work element classifications encountered in standard data systems for work measurement.

7 What are the advantages of a standard data system that is based on determining the normal time for an entire work cycle rather than individual work elements?

8 What are some of the disadvantages and limitations of standard data systems and the reasons that a company might not want to develop such a system?

PROBLEMS

Developing Time Formulas

(The problems in this group do not require the use of statistical methods for their solution.)

1 A parcel delivery service makes deliveries by truck within a metropolitan area from its headquarters. Each morning, trucks are assigned to delivery routes in various sectors of the city. You have been asked to develop a formula to compute how long it takes to complete a route. At the beginning of the day, the following factors are known: (1) the total number of deliveries Q to be made during the route, and (2) the total length L of the day's route (miles), including the return trip back to headquarters. An average driving speed of 20 miles/hr is assumed. The time allowed to walk the parcel to the addressee in the building while the truck is stopped at the delivery address and then return to the truck after the delivery is $T = 4.0$ min. (a) Develop a formula to compute the total time TT in minutes required to complete the route based on the information given above. Express the formula in a way that would be most convenient for clerical people to use. (b) Using your formula, compute the total time to complete a route consisting of 37 deliveries and 117 miles.

2 This problem is intentionally omitted from this text

3 In the previous problem, weight is a work variable that affects the normal time to perform the MOVE element. It is treated in the MTM table only at discrete values. Again, consider case A. (a) Derive an equation that expresses the normal time (in TMUs) to move an object that weighs w lb as a function of move distance x. In other words, include the weight of the object as a work variable in your equation. (b) Check your equation using a distance of $x = 20$ in. and an object weight of 17.5 lb to see how closely it agrees with the tabulated value.

4 A self-employed friend who operates a lawn mowing service wants to develop a formula for estimating how much time it takes to mow a lawn. The times for elements required for each lawn-mowing job are given in the table below. The lawn mower cuts a swath that is 18 in. wide. One turn is required at the end of each swath. On average, 600 sq ft of lawn clippings fill one bushel. (a) Construct a formula that will give the estimated time for cutting

rectangular lawns of various dimensions. (b) Use the formula to compute the allowed time for cutting and trimming a lot that is 75 ft by 100 ft. (c) Is it more economical to cut the swath in the long dimension or the short dimension? Why? (d) What methods improvements can you recommend to reduce the estimated time to mow a lawn?

Work Element Description	Element Time
Unload mower and other equipment from truck	7.5 min/job
Lubricate equipment (once per 5 jobs)	3.5 min/job
Cutting grass	0.005 min/linear ft
Turn mower for return cut	0.20 min/turn
Rake grass clippings	0.010 min/sq ft
Gather, carry, and dump clippings in truck	3.0 min/bushel
Return equipment to truck and load	6.0 min/job

5 Standard time data are to be developed for the drilling department. The parts routed through the department have different numbers of holes and different depths of holes. All drilling operations have the same cycle, consisting of (1) load, (2) drill, and (3) unload. The time for the load and unload steps depend on the size and weight of the part (size is closely correlated to weight). The time for drilling depends on the numbers of holes and the depths of the holes. For a given part, the depths of all holes are the same. The data in the table below have been collected by direct time study and represent normalized times. (a) Develop a formula to set standard times for future drilling operations. (b) Using your formula, what is the standard time for drilling a part weighing 10.2 lb with 6 holes each of depth 1.5 in.?

Part Loading and Unloading

Part Weight (lb)	Time to Load (min)	Time to Unload (min)
2.0	0.52	0.25
5.3	0.69	0.35
15.8	1.21	0.66
7.5	0.79	0.41

Drilling Operation

Number of Holes	Depths of Holes (in.)	Time to Drill (min)
4	1.0	1.00
8	1.2	2.25
2	1.5	0.65
4	2.0	1.60
8	0.5	1.40
15	0.8	3.30

REGRESSION ANALYSIS

(The problems in this group require the use of statistical methods for their solution. Regression analysis using a spreadsheet package such as Excel is recommended.)

6 The sawing department in a woodworking plant is attempting to develop a formula to compute the standard time for one of its operations. The operation involves cutting irregular contours out of one-half inch plywood using a band saw. Data have been collected from previous time studies indicating the observed time and performance rating for a variety of sawing contours. The observed times include piece loading time just before cutting begins.

It is hypothesized that the sawing time is closely correlated with the length of the saw cut, and length data (to the nearest half-inch) have been collected from the original engineering drawings for these jobs to test this hypothesis. All of these data are presented in the table below. (a) Plot the data on linear graph paper, and determine the corresponding formula to compute the standard time for a job, given that the length of the cutting contour is known and the PFD allowance factor is 15%. (b) Test the formula by computing the standard time for a job in which the cut length is 75.0 in.

Length, L (in.)	Observed Time, T_{obs} (min)	Performance Rating (%)
127.5	8.84	90
73.5	4.56	100
152.0	11.75	85
89.5	5.91	105
44.0	2.97	110
61	3.81	90
68.5	6.14	80
83.5	5.16	100
29.0	1.99	105
57.5	4.07	100

7 Solve the preceding problem but use regression analysis in part (a) to develop the formula to compute standard time.

8 A telephone calling center performs two types of solicitations: (1) donations and (2) sales. The center wants to determine how much time on average a caller spends on each type of solicitation. The issue is complicated by the fact that some calls get busy signals, some go unanswered, and some last for less than one minute, which is interpreted to mean that the recipient is not interested or hangs up the receiver. The center's telephone computer system monitors several factors, including these various categories of calls. The callers must do their own dialing of telephone numbers from purchased lists of potential donors and sales prospects. The computer monitoring system tracks and compiles the following statistics for each hour: (1) number of donation calls, (2) number of sales calls, (3) number of calls resulting in busy signals, (4) number of calls that went unanswered, and (5) number of calls in which the conversations were terminated by the recipient within one minute. These values are listed in the table below in addition to other data. Determine the average time spent in each of the five categories of phone calls. Time = total time on telephone for all callers working, w = number of workers (callers) working continuously during the hour, X_1 = number of donation calls, X_2 = number of sales calls, X_3 number of calls with busy signals, X_4 number of unanswered calls, and X_5 number of calls terminated by the recipient within 1 min. Each period in the table is 1 hr.

Period	Time (min)	w	X_1	X_2	X_3	X_4	X_5
1	247.6	5	36	10	24	14	30
2	203.8	4	0	27	12	21	21
3	316.9	6	0	46	23	18	13
4	369.2	7	64	7	36	34	44
5	276.3	5	54	0	21	31	31
6	315.9	6	22	25	30	35	41
7	219.2	4	34	9	11	13	15
8	315.7	6	42	16	35	25	13

(continued)

Table (*continued*)

Period	Time (min)	w	X_1	X_2	X_3	X_4	X_5
9	372.5	7	34	28	36	28	35
10	250.8	5	51	0	29	29	20
11	264.2	5	29	15	21	25	30
12	288.3	6	31	16	41	36	25
13	305.2	6	70	0	20	11	7
14	214.4	4	12	25	17	13	8
15	252.4	5	0	34	38	29	11

9 The sales order department supplements its regular office staff by using temporary workers from a local agency to fill in during busy periods.[5] The function of the department is to process various types of customer sales orders. Processing involves some paperwork and some computer interaction, the amounts and proportions varying for different order categories. The sales orders are of the following types: (1) regular sales orders, (2) rush orders, (3) back orders, (4) change orders, and (5) cancellation orders. Each type requires a different amount of time on average, and the time per order within a type is a variable. The company would like to know how much time it has taken to process each type, and it would like to develop an equation to estimate its daily staffing requirements for a known daily number of orders to be processed for each different type. Historical data are presented in the table below indicating daily staff hours in the order department, together with the number of orders processed of the five types. (a) Develop an equation to compute the total daily staff hours that will be required to complete given numbers of each order type. The company knows at least one day in advance how many orders the department must process the following day. (b) Determine the average amount of time spent on each order type. (c) Using your equation from (a), determine the total number of staff hours required for the following numbers of orders: regular sales orders = 160, rush orders = 30, back orders = 15, change orders = 10, and cancellation orders = 20. Given this number, how many temporary people will be needed, assuming that there are 6 regular staff workers in the department and that the length of the shift is 8 hours?

Workers, w	Total Time (hr)	Regular Orders (#)	Rush Orders (#)	Back Orders (#)	Change Orders (#)	Cancellations (#)
6	48	130	19	11	35	32
7	56	169	23	13	25	28
6	48	182	5	10	16	15
8	64	214	18	20	18	19
8	64	220	19	17	14	24
9	72	236	25	24	12	30
10	80	252	35	27	16	21
7	56	169	27	17	13	18
6	48	125	28	18	19	20
6	48	118	33	16	17	25

10 The manager of a plate steel fabricator plant wants to develop a standard data system to estimate the time required to arc weld the plates together to form the welded assembly. The

[5]This problem was suggested by an industrial case study that W. J. Rishardson performed and documented in his book *Cost improvement, Work Sampling, and Short Interval Scheduling* (Reston Publishers, Reston, Virginia, 1976, pp. 220–24). The data in our problem have been simplified.

standard data system will be based on the use of a mathematical formula in which the arc welding time depends on three variables in the job: (1) the length of the weld path, (2) the plate thickness, and (3) the number of parts in the welded assembly. For a given assembly, the plate thickness would be the same for all parts. Because the plant specializes in low carbon plate steel, the welding voltage, current, and other machine settings are constant for all jobs to be included in the coverage of this standard data system. The data that have been collected from previous direct time studies are presented in the table below. (a) Use regression analysis to derive an equation that relates welding time to these work variables. Let T = the welding time, min; L = length of weld path, m; t = plate thickness, mm; and n_p = number of parts in the welded assembly. (b) Test your equation with the following values: L = 5.0 m, t = 8 mm, and n_p = 6 parts.

Length, L (m)	Thickness, t (mm)	Number of Parts, n_p	Welding Time, T (min)
0.68	6	2	2.47
3.26	8	5	10.85
1.45	6	3	5.21
2.10	10	7	8.69
2.66	6	4	8.71
4.75	6	8	16.35
0.81	10	3	3.30
1.82	8	4	7.01
1.49	8	5	5.61
2.05	6	4	6.99
3.79	6	2	10.56
2.92	8	3	9.65
4.22	10	7	14.65
3.66	10	5	12.45
1.78	8	4	6.61

Machine Cycle Times

11 A turning operation will be used to reduce the diameter of a cylindrical workpiece from 180 mm to 172 mm. The workpiece is 750 mm long. Cutting conditions are as follows: cutting speed = 175 m/min, feed = 0.3 mm/rev, and depth of cut = 4.0 mm. Determine the time to complete one turning pass along the entire length if the approach and overtravel allowances are each 5 mm (total = 10 mm).

12 In a turning operation the starting workpiece is 900 mm long and 300 mm in diameter. It is to be turned to a diameter of 292 mm for a distance of 568 mm to form a "step" in the workpiece. Cutting conditions are as follows: cutting speed = 200 m/min, feed = 0.25 mm/rev, and depth of cut = 4.0 mm. Due to the large size of the piece, the approach allowance is to 7.5 mm. Determine the time to complete the turning pass.

13 A cylindrical workpiece has a 6.0 in. diameter and is 30 in. long. It is to be turned in an engine lathe at the following cutting conditions: cutting speed = 400 ft/min, feed = 0.015 in./rev, and depth of cut = 0.150 in. Determine the time to complete one turning pass if the approach and overtravel allowances are each 0.25 in. (total = 0.50 in.).

14 A blind hole with a diameter of 18.0 mm is to be drilled in an aluminum casting to a depth of 72 mm. The point angle of the drill is 118°. Cutting conditions are as follows: cutting speed = 40 m/min and feed = 0.10 mm/rev. If machining time begins as soon as the drill makes contact with the work, how much time will the drilling operation take?

15 A through hole with a diameter of 20.0 mm is to be drilled through a steel plate that is 50 mm thick. Cutting conditions are as follows: cutting speed = 25 m/min, feed = 0.08 mm/rev, and the point angle of the drill = 118°. If machining time begins as soon as the drill makes contact with the work, how much time will the drilling operation take?

16 A drilling operation is to be performed on a cast iron workpiece to form a through hole that will be subsequently tapped. The hole diameter is 0.50 in., and the material thickness is 1.25 in. The point angle of the drill is 118°. Cutting conditions are as follows: cutting speed = 50 ft/min and feed = 0.003 in./rev. How long will the drilling operation take? Assume the process time begins when the drill bit makes initial contact with the work surface.

17 A peripheral milling operation is to be performed on a rectangular workpiece that is 500 mm long and 125 mm wide. The milling cutter is 100 mm in diameter and has six cutting edges (teeth). It is 150 mm long and is oriented in the milling machine so that it overhangs the workpiece on both sides. Cutting conditions are as follows: cutting speed = 75 m/min, chip load = 0.2 mm/tooth, and depth of cut = 4 mm. Determine the machine cycle time if the approach and overtravel allowances are each 5 mm (total = 10 mm).

18 A face milling operation is to be performed on a rectangular workpiece that is 500 mm long and 250 mm wide. The milling cutter is 85 mm in diameter and has 12 cutting teeth. The workpiece is fed through the cutter as shown in Figure 7 in the text at a depth of 2.5 mm. Cutting conditions are as follows: cutting speed = 100 m/min and chip load = 0.10 mm/tooth. Determine the machine cycle time if the approach and overtravel allowances are each 5 mm (total = 10 mm).

19 A rectangular workpiece that is 500 mm long is machined in a face milling operation using a milling cutter that is 80 mm in diameter and has 10 cutting teeth. The workpiece is fed through the cutter, as shown in Figure P19 so that the width of the swath is 20 mm on one side of the work. The depth of cut is 2.5 mm. Cutting conditions are as follows: cutting speed = 75 m/min and chip load = 0.08 mm/tooth. (a) Derive an equation to determine the approach and overtravel distances to reach full cutter engagement. (b) Using your equation, determine the machine cycle time if the approach and overtravel allowances are each 5 mm (total = 10 mm).

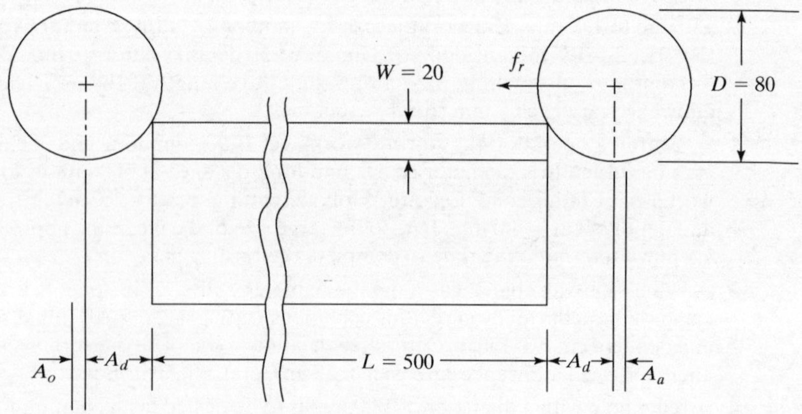

Figure P19 Face milling operation in Problem 19.

20 A peripheral milling operation will be used to cut a rectangular workpiece that is 20.0 in. long and 3.5 in. wide. The diameter of the milling cutter is 4.0 in., its length is 5.0 in., and it has 6 cutting edges (teeth). The cutter is oriented so that it overhangs the workpiece on both sides. Cutting conditions are as follows: cutting speed = 125 ft/min, chip load = 0.05 in./tooth, and depth of cut = 0.100 in. Determine the machine cycle time if the approach and over-travel allowances are each 0.25 in. (total = 0.50 in.).

21 A face milling operation will be used to cut a rectangular workpiece that is 18.5 in. long and 6.0 in. wide. The diameter of the milling cutter is 3.0 in. and it has 10 cutting teeth. The workpiece is fed through the cutter as shown in Figure 7 in the text at a depth of 0.075 in. Cutting conditions are as follows: cutting speed = 300 ft/min and chip load = 0.004 in./tooth. Determine the machine cycle time if the approach and overtravel allowances are each 0.25 in. (total = 0.50 in.).

Work Sampling

The statistical technique for determining the proportions of time spent by subjects (e.g., workers, machines) in various defined categories of activity (e.g., setting up a machine, producing parts, idle) is known as ***work sampling***.[1] In a work sampling study, a large number of observations are made of the subjects over an extended period of time, and statistical inferences are drawn about the proportion of time in each activity category based on the proportion of observations in that category. For statistical accuracy, the observations must be taken at random times during the period of the study, and the period must be representative of the types of activities performed by the subjects.

The following general characteristics of work situations are particularly well-suited for work sampling:

- *Sufficient time available to perform the study.* A work sampling study usually requires a substantial period of time to complete. There must be enough time available (e.g., several weeks or more) to conduct the study.
- *Multiple subjects.* Work sampling is commonly used to study the activities of multiple subjects rather than one subject.

[1]The Work Measurement and Methods Standards Subcommittee (ANSI Standard Z94.11-1989) defines work sampling as follows: "An application of random sampling techniques to the study of work activities so that the proportions of time devoted to different elements of work can be estimated with a given degree of statistical validity."

- *Long cycle times.* The jobs covered in the study have relatively long cycle times.
- *Nonrepetitive work cycles.* The work is not highly repetitive. The jobs consist of various tasks rather than a single repetitive task. However, it must be possible to classify the work activities into a distinct number of categories.

For highly repetitive jobs with short cycle times performed by one worker, and for those jobs requiring an immediate measurement of a task, an alternative work measurement technique, such as direct time study, standard data, or predetermined motion time system, is preferred over work sampling.

As its name suggests, work sampling is usually applied in work situations. However, its applications are not limited to the work environment. It can be applied in any situation where one or more subjects are engaged in two or more different categories of activity at different times. Other names used for work sampling, some of them accounting for these broader application opportunities, include ***activity sampling***, ***occurrence sampling***, and ***ratio delay study***. The originator of the technique, L. H. C. Tippett, used the term ***snap reading method***, meaning that the individual observations of the subjects are made quickly and without prior warning (Historical Note 1).

HISTORICAL NOTE 1 WORK SAMPLING

The technique of work sampling was introduced by L. H. C. Tippett, a statistician who was studying textile factories in England in 1927. Tippett was doing surveys of loom operations, attempting to ascertain the durations of and reasons for stoppages (downtime). At the beginning of his studies, he used a stopwatch to measure the times, but the practical limits of this method only allowed him to observe up to four looms at a time. He felt he should include a much larger number of looms in his survey in order to obtain reliable statistics about the problem. One day a weaving manager mentioned to Tippett that he could tell at a glance whether a loom was working or not, simply by the actions of the weaver who was tending the loom. If the worker was bending over his loom making repairs, the loom was down. If the worker was just watching the loom, it was running. The light immediately clicked on in Tippett's mind. He realized that a snapshot of a given loom could be taken and its status (working or not working) could be classified in that instant. If not working, the cause of the stoppage could be determined. All of the looms in the factory could be surveyed in one tour through the building. Over a period of time, multiple tours would permit multiple samples to be gathered on the looms. On reflection, he concluded that the proportion of looms observed running during a given period of time was equal to the proportion of time that they ran. Similarly, the downtime proportion was equal to the proportion of looms stopped during the same period. Because of the way the data-gathering technique worked, taking "snapshots" throughout the work area, Tippett called it the "snap reading method."

The snap reading method was introduced into the United States in 1941 by R. L. Morrow, a professor at New York University, who changed the name of the technique to "ratio delay study," because he saw its primary application to be in the sampling of delays during production. The name "work sampling" was later coined by C. L. Brisley and H. L. Waddell in an article that appeared in *Factory Management and Maintenance* magazine in 1952.

1 HOW WORK SAMPLING WORKS

The following example illustrates a common application that demonstrates how work sampling works.

Example 1 Work Sampling to Study Machine Utilization

A total of 500 observations were made at random times during a one-week period (a total of 40 hours) in the automatic lathe section. The subjects consisted of 10 identical machines. In each observation, the activity of the machine was identified and classified into one of three categories: (1) being set up, (2) running production, or (3) idle. The number of observations in each category is summarized in the table below. Estimate how many hours per week an average machine spent in each of the three categories.

Category	Number of Observations
(1) Being set up	75
(2) Running production	300
(3) Machine idle	125
	500

Solution: The proportion of observations spent in the setup is 75/500 = 0.15, the proportion spent in production is 300/500 = 0.60, and the proportion spent idle is 125/500 = 0.25. Based on a 40-hour week, these proportions convert into the hourly values per week for each machine given in the table below.

Category	Proportion of Observations	Hours per Category
(1) Being set up	0.15	6
(2) Running production	0.60	24
(3) Machine idle	0.25	10
	1.00	40

■

Work sampling can be applied in a variety of situations. Some of the more common applications are to determine the following:

- *Machine utilization.* This is the application in Example 1. How is the time of a machine allocated among setup, production, downtime, and other activities or nonactivities?
- *Worker utilization.* This is basically the same as the machine utilization application, except that the subjects are workers instead of machines. How do workers spend their time among various categories of activity (or nonactivity)?
- *Allowances for time standards.* Any properly set time standard has an allowance built into its value to cover personal time, fatigue, and delays. Work sampling can be used to assess the delay components of the allowance, such as machine malfunctions and downtime, and/or other interruptions in the normal work routine. In fact, the name "ratio delay study" was used by Morrow for the technique because he saw this as the principal application (Historical Note 1).

- *Average unit time.* If the number of units produced or serviced during the course of the work sampling study is known, the average time taken per unit can be determined.
- *Time standards.* In certain work situations, usually involving indirect labor and office work, standard time values can be determined by work sampling. Owing to limitations in statistical accuracy, standards set by work sampling should not be used for incentive pay work.

2 STATISTICAL BASIS OF WORK SAMPLING

The statistical basis of work sampling is the binomial distribution, in which the parameter p in the binomial distribution equals the true proportion of time spent engaged in a given activity category of interest. There are usually multiple activity categories, as in Example 1, so we identify the different proportions by subscript. Let us use the subscript k; thus we have $p_1, p_2, \ldots, p_k, \ldots p_K$ proportions for K different activity categories. The sum of the proportions must equal unity.

The binomial distribution is often approximated by the normal distribution for computational convenience. In general, the accuracy of the normal approximation is quite sufficient due to the large number of observations in a typical work sampling study. In the normal approximation of the binomial distribution, the mean μ and standard deviation σ are defined as follows:

$$\mu = np \tag{1}$$

$$\sigma = \sqrt{np(1-p)} \tag{2}$$

wwhere n = total number of observations.

These parameters are converted back to proportional values by dividing by the number of observations:

$$p = \frac{\mu}{n} = \frac{np}{n} \tag{3}$$

$$\sigma_p = \frac{\sqrt{np(1-p)}}{n} = \sqrt{\frac{p(1-p)}{n}} \tag{4}$$

where σ_p = standard deviation of the proportion p.

In a sampling study, we let $\hat{p}$ = the proportion of the total number of observations devoted to an activity category of interest. The proportion $\hat{p}$ is our estimate of the true value of the population proportion p. We would like it to be a good estimate of the true value, which means that it is absent of bias and it has a low variance. A ***biased estimate*** is one that tends to consistently differ from the true value, either because the estimating method is somehow flawed or the variable being estimated is influenced by the act of observing it. For example, if human subjects could anticipate when the work sampling observer were coming, they might be inclined to adjust their behavior in response. This would bias the estimates of activity category proportions. Bias in $\hat{p}$ is reduced or eliminated by randomizing the observation times, so the human subjects cannot anticipate the arrival of the observer. A ***low variance*** means that if the variable of interest is measured multiple times, all of the measured values will be close together. The variance is the squared value of the standard deviation (variance = σ_p^2). As indicated by equation (4), the standard deviation (and therefore the variance) is reduced by increasing the number of observations ***n***.

2.1 Confidence Intervals in Work Sampling

We expect $\hat{p}$ to be close to p, but it is not likely to be exactly equal due to statistical error. Our problem is to estimate p within a defined error range at a given confidence level. The general statement of a confidence interval for our situation in the standard normal distribution can be expressed as follows with reference to Figure 1:

$$\Pr\left(-z_{\alpha/2} < \frac{\hat{p} - p}{\hat{\sigma}_p} < +z_{\alpha/2} \right) = 1 - \alpha \tag{5}$$

where $\hat{\sigma}_p$ = calculated value of the proportion standard deviation, equation (4), based on the estimated proportion $\hat{p}$. Rearranging,

$$\Pr(\hat{p} - z_{\alpha/2}\hat{\sigma}_p < p < \hat{p} + z_{\alpha/2}\hat{\sigma}_p) = 1 - \alpha \tag{6}$$

Stating equation (6) in words, the probability that the actual value of p lies between $\hat{p} - z_{\alpha/2}\,\hat{\sigma}_p$ and $\hat{p} + z_{\alpha/2}\,\hat{\sigma}_p$ is $(1 - \alpha)$. Expressing this as a confidence interval, the value of p lies between $\hat{p} - z_{\alpha/2}\,\hat{\sigma}_p$ and $\hat{p} + z_{\alpha/2}\,\hat{\sigma}_p$ at a confidence level of $(1 - \alpha)$. Typical confidence levels used in work sampling are 90%, in which case $z_{\alpha/2} = 1.65$, and 95%, in which case $z_{\alpha/2} = 1.96$. Other confidence levels and corresponding $z_{\alpha/2}$ values can be found in tables of the standard normal distribution.

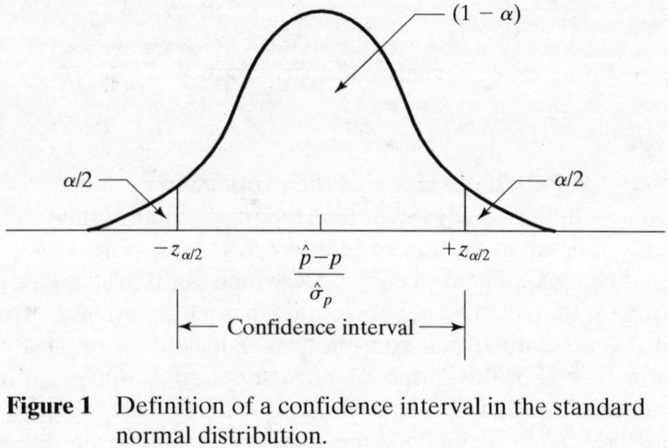

Figure 1 Definition of a confidence interval in the standard normal distribution.

Example 2 Confidence Interval in Work Sampling

Determine the 95% confidence interval for the proportion of time spent setting up the machines, category (1), in Example 1.

Solution: From the solution of Example 1, we know that the proportion of time spent setting up machines is $\hat{p} = 0.15$. Computing the standard deviation using equation (4), given that there are a total of 500 observations ($n = 500$),

$$\hat{\sigma}_p = \sqrt{\frac{0.15(1 - 0.15)}{500}} = 0.01597$$

For the 95% confidence level, the corresponding $z_{\alpha/2} = 1.96$; thus

$$\hat{p} - z_{\alpha/2}\,\hat{\sigma}_p = 0.15-1.96(0.01597) = 0.15 - 0.01313 = 0.1187$$

and

$$\hat{p} + z_{\alpha/2}\,\hat{\sigma}_p = 015 + 1.96(0.01597) = 0.15 + 0.013 = 0.1813$$

Accordingly, we can state that at the 95% confidence level, the true value of the setup time proportion lies between 0.1187 and 0.1813. ■

2.2 Determining Number of Observations Required

The statistical errors in work sampling can be reduced by increasing the number of observations. That is, the accuracy and precision of our estimate of a given proportion of interest p can be increased, and the limits of the confidence interval around it can be narrowed, by increasing n. One might argue that we should increase n to a very large value in order to achieve near perfect accuracy in our estimate of p, but increasing n takes more time and costs more. It is possible to balance these opposing issues, accuracy versus time and cost, by determining how many observations are required to achieve a given confidence interval about the estimate of p.

The confidence interval must first be defined, which requires decisions about the following two parameters:

1. The confidence level, $1 - \alpha$. Corresponding to the confidence level, we can determine $z_{\alpha/2}$ from a table of values of the standard normal variate.
2. The half-width of the confidence interval, defined as the desired acceptable deviation from the value of p. Let us define this interval parameter as c (think of c as a tolerance about p). It is a proportion, same as p. Thus we can state the confidence interval as $p \pm c$, displayed graphically in Figure 2.

Note in our figure that the value of c corresponds to $z_{\alpha/2}\,\hat{\sigma}_p$. That is,

$$c = z_{\alpha/2}\,\hat{\sigma}_p \tag{7}$$

Therefore, based on our defined values of $z_{\alpha/2}$ and c, we can determine the associated value of $\hat{\sigma}_p$ that achieves the desired confidence interval:

$$\hat{\sigma}_p = \frac{c}{z_{\alpha/2}} \tag{8}$$

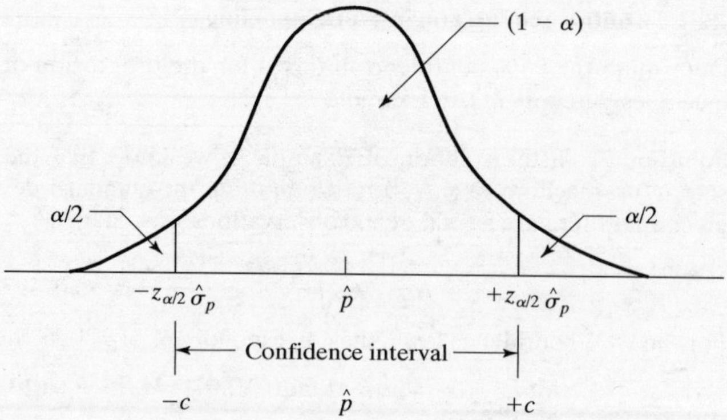

Figure 2 Confidence interval superimposed on the normal distribution, with $(1 - \alpha)$ and $Z_{\alpha/2}$ defined.

Next, we take note of equation (4), which defines $\hat{\sigma}_p$ in the binomial distribution. Squaring both sides of equation (4) and rearranging the terms, we obtain n as a function of $\hat{p}$ and $\hat{\sigma}_p$.

$$n = \frac{\hat{p}(1 - \hat{p})}{\hat{\sigma}_p^2} \tag{9}$$

where $\hat{\sigma}_p$ has the value determined from equation (8).

Example 3 Determining the Number of Observations Required

In the context of our previous examples, determine how many observations will be required to estimate the proportion of time used to set up the 10 machines in the automatic lathe section. The confidence interval must be within $\pm$ 0.03 of the true proportion, which the foreman initially estimates to be $\hat{p} = 0.20$. A 95% confidence level will be used.

Solution: At the 95% confidence level, $z_{\alpha/2} = 1.96$. The confidence interval is 0.20 ± 0.03, so the half-width of the interval c is 0.03. From Equation (8),

$$\hat{\sigma}_p = 0.03/1.96 = 0.0153$$

Using this value in equation (9), we obtain the required number of observations:

$$n = \frac{0.20(1 - 0.20)}{(0.0153)^2} = 683.5, \text{ rounded up to 684 observations.}$$ ■

Equations (8) and (9) can be combined to compute n in one step rather than the two steps used in Example 3:

$$n = \frac{(z_{\alpha/2})^2 \hat{p}\,(1 - \hat{p}\,)}{c^2} \tag{10}$$

After taking the computed number of observations, if it turns out that the value of $\hat{p}$ is different than the estimated value used to compute n (as it probably will be), then n should be recomputed. If the recomputed n is greater than the original value, then the indicated additional number of observations must be taken in order to maintain the desired confidence level. If the new value of n is less than the original, it means that the confidence level is greater than the specified level, or that the confidence interval is narrower than the original.

2.3 Determining Average Task Times and Standard Times

Average task times and standard times can be determined using work sampling. However, time standards established by work sampling are not as accurate as those set by direct time study, standard data, or predetermined time systems. In particular, standards determined by work sampling are not appropriate for wage incentive plans. Given this caveat, work sampling can be used when other more accurate work measurement techniques are not practical—for example, when the length of time required to use one of the more accurate techniques would be excessive.

Let us first consider how average task times can be determined, and then how standard times are set. The difference is that an average task time is simply how much time was required to complete an average work unit, with no consideration of the worker's performance during the work. Setting a standard by work sampling requires the observer not only to correctly classify the activity category during the observation but also to simultaneously rate the worker's performance. In either case, the quantity of work units completed during the duration of the work sampling study must be counted.

Determining Average Task Times. In a work sampling study, the average task time for a given work category is determined by first computing the total time associated with that category and then dividing by the total count of work units produced during this time. The calculation is summarized in the following equation:

$$T_{ci} = \frac{p_i(TT)}{Q_i} \tag{11}$$

where T_{ci} = average task time (average cycle time for task i), hr or min; p_i = proportion of observations associated with the work category of interest; TT = total time of work sampling study, hr or min; and Q_i = total quantity of work units associated with the work category of interest that are completed during the total time.

Example 4 Determining Average Task Times in Work Sampling

Suppose in Example 1 that a total of 1572 work units were completed by the 10 machines and that a total of 23 setups were accomplished during the 5-day period. Determine (a) the average task time per work unit during production and (b) the average setup time.

Solution: Let us first compute the total time of the work sampling study. The duration of the study was 40 hr, but there were 10 machines (subjects), so the total time is 40 hr × 10 machines:

$$TT = (40 \text{ hr})(10 \text{ machines}) = 400 \text{ hr}$$

(a) The 1572 work units are associated with the "running production" category, whose proportion $\hat{p} = 0.60$.

$$T_c = \frac{0.60(400)}{1572} = 0.1527 \text{ hr} = 9.16 \text{ min}$$

(b) The 23 setups are associated with "being set up," whose proportion $\hat{p} = 0.15$.

$$T_{su} = \frac{0.15(400)}{23} = 2.609 \text{ hr} = 156.52 \text{ min/setup}$$

■

The computed times in this example may be of limited value. For example, it is unlikely that the 1572 work units are all the same. Given that there were 23 setups performed during the observation period, this means that there were 23 different batches produced, each batch probably being of a different part design. Different part designs require different processing sequences, and the associated machining times are no doubt different. Similarly, the setups for the different part designs were different too, and so the setup times were different. Although we must recognize these limitations in the work sampling results, the study has nevertheless provided information that may be useful. We now know that the average setup time per batch is 2.609 hr, and the average cycle time per part is 9.16 min. Are these times reasonable? The foreman may be able to make a judgment that 2.609 hours is much longer than it should take to set up an automatic lathe for the types of parts made in this shop.

Determining Time Standards. For repetitive, well-defined tasks in which the task times are relative short cycle (no more than a few minutes), direct time study, predetermined time systems, or standard data systems are the recommended work measurement techniques. These kinds of tasks are usually performed by direct labor. Work sampling would not normally be used for these work situations. Where work sampling is most appropriate for setting time standards is on indirect labor activities, clerical office work, and similar work situations in which the units of work may be common but there is inherent variability in the tasks required to process them. The variability may be due to irregular elements in the task, adjustments or testing, mental analysis or diagnosis that may be needed before proceeding with the work, and so forth. A good candidate for work sampling might be repair work on digital cameras and other products returned to the factory. The returned cameras are similar, perhaps differing slightly in model features, and the nature of the defect or malfunction may differ among them, so that the repair work varies to some extent from camera to camera. Also, cameras may be only one of several products that the workers are responsible for repairing. So each repair worker's time is shared among several different types of product. In this kind of situation, work sampling would be useful for providing management with data on the amount of time, on average, that should be allowed for each work unit.

For the work sampling study to be most useful in setting time standards, there must be some homogeneity in the work units for which the standard is set. Repairing digital cameras must be distinguished from repair work on the other products. Each different product type must be identified as a separate activity category, and a separate count of the different products must be recorded, so that a standard can be determined for each type. It is true that there will be variations in repair work within a given product category, but the differences between product categories would typically be much more significant, and the standard times should reflect this fact. This was not done in Example 4 in which there were 23 different part designs, each requiring its own machining cycle time. Trying to use the overall average time for each of these different part designs would be a gross and unfair simplification. We certainly would not want to use the average time for any kind of worker incentive system. The workers would all choose the easier work units that take less time than the average.

When the purpose of the work sampling study is to set time standards, the analyst must rate the performance of the worker during each observation, in addition to identifying the category of activity. Performance rating is especially challenging in work sampling because the observer has only a brief moment to make the judgment. It is almost like trying to judge the speed of an automobile in a photograph. Notwithstanding the difficulty, some judgment about the pace or effort level of the worker is required in order for the resulting time standard to be consistent with the company's definition of normal performance. Of course, if the activity category is nonwork (e.g., idle, away from workstation), then no performance rating is required.

Determining a standard time from a work sampling study is similar to finding the preceding average task time, except that the performance rating must be factored in and the appropriate allowance must be added. The normalized time can be determined as follows:

$$T_{ni} = \frac{p_i(TT)(\overline{PR_i})}{Q_i} \tag{12}$$

where T_{ni} = normal time for work unit associated with activity category i, min; $\overline{PR}_i$ = average value of the performance ratings for ail observations in category i, expressed as a decimal fraction; and the other parameters have the same meaning as before. The standard time includes the allowance

$$T_{stdi} = T_{ni}(1 + A_{pfd}) \tag{13}$$

where T_{stdi} = the standard time for work unit i, min; and A_{pfd} = allowance for personal time, fatigue, and unavoidable delays.

3 APPLICATION ISSUES IN WORK SAMPLING

Each work sampling study is different. It must be custom-designed for the specific problem it is intended to address. However, the general steps in the design process have been developed by practitioners over many years, and their recommendations are summarized in Table 1. Let us consider the following implementation issues in this section: (1) defining the activity categories, (2) work sampling forms, and (3) scheduling the observation times.

TABLE 1 Recommended Steps in Conducting a Work Sampling Study

1. ***Define the objective(s) of study.*** What is the problem to be studied? Why is work sampling the appropriate technique to study the problem? What is the desired information that will be realized from the study? Formal answers to these kinds of questions help to structure the study, reduce ambiguities, and define expectations.
2. ***Define the subjects to be studied.*** If the study involves the activities of workers, which specific workers are to be studied? If the study involves machines, which specific machines will be included?
3. ***Define the output measure(s).*** This applies to situations in which an average task time or time standard will be established by means of the work sampling study. In a factory, what are the parts or products that relate to the activities performed by the subjects in the study? In an office work situation, what are the bills, or claims, or other documents that are being processed by the subjects? If the objective of the work sampling study is to determine a time per unit of output, the output units will have to be counted. If the work sampling study has other objectives, then defining an output measure may not be necessary.
4. ***Define the activity categories.*** These are the defined states of the subjects that will be identified during the study. If the study includes output measures, the activity categories must correlate with these outputs. But additional categories will likely be included also, such as "idle," "waiting for work," and "downtime." Some of the issues in defining the activity categories are discussed in Section 3.1.
5. ***Design the study.*** Design of the work sampling study includes the following steps and decisions: (a) Design the forms that will be used to record the observations (Section 3.2). (b) Determine how many observations will be required. This is likely to involve the types of decisions and calculations discussed in Section 2.2. (c) Decide on the number of days or shifts to be included in the study. It is important that the period covered by the study is representative of the usual activities engaged in by the subjects. (d) Schedule the observations. What are the randomized times when the observations will be made (Section 3.3), and what are the routes the observers will follow to make the observations? (e) Determine the number of observers needed.
6. ***Identify the observers who will do the sampling.*** The likely candidates include the industrial engineer in charge of the work sampling study, technicians who are assigned to this industrial engineer, and first-line supervisors in charge of the subject workers. An alternative approach is to use ***self-observation*** where the subjects themselves record the data, using a buzzer in the work area or beepers for workers located remotely. The problem with this technique is the risk that bias will be introduced into the results. Training will be required for whoever is assigned to be an observer. Typical training would include making sure the observers understand the objective(s), introduction to the principles of sampling and statistics, practice in identifying the activity categories, and understanding the importance of making the observations at the appointed times. If the study requires performance ratings to be made by the observer, then special training in this function must be provided.
7. ***Announce the study.*** All those who will be affected by the study should be informed about it. This includes obtaining the approval of the supervisor of the subject population. In particular, the subjects who will be observed are owed an explanation about the study and its objectives. This announcement step is of critical importance. Work sampling studies have failed because workers were not properly informed and their support was not obtained. Only novices and fools would be tempted to perform a secret work sampling study and expect the results to be taken seriously.
8. ***Make the observations.*** Make all observations according to the schedule. Record the data, and summarize the data each day. At the beginning, before collecting the data, it may be appropriate to conduct a trial study over a one- to three-day period. This will help to work out any "bugs" in the study, such as difficulties in classifying activity categories or recognizing and dealing with biases, or it may lead to a revision in the length of the full study or the number of observations required. Some or all of the data in this initial trial period may need to be discarded if problems exist.
9. ***After completing the study, analyze and present the results.*** Prepare a report that summarizes and analyzes all data. Make recommendations if appropriate.

Source: Compiled and summarized from several sources, including [1], [3], [10], and [11].

3.1 Defining the Activity Categories

The activity categories are the states of the subjects that the observer must be able to identify and classify during the snapshot observation. They must be defined so as to be consistent with the objectives of the study, immediately recognizable by the observer, and mutually exclusive (with each category being distinguishable from the others). If the work sampling study includes consideration of output measures, some of the activity categories will correlate with these outputs. For example, if three different outputs are being counted in the study, then three activity categories must be defined that correspond to the processing of these outputs. Additional categories such as "idle," "waiting for work," "resting," and "downtime" are also likely to be defined. The activity categories must be defined for the specific study being conducted.

For improved statistical accuracy and to simplify the data collection during the study itself, it is helpful to limit the number of defined activity categories to 10 or fewer. Fewer categories will result in higher average values of $\hat{p}_k$, which will reduce variances and improve confidence levels. This will also make the observer's task more manageable when recording data, since there will be fewer choices about the state of the subject. This is likely to mean less confusion and fewer mistakes in classifying the observed state. On the other hand, if the objectives of the study call for more categories to be defined, then this need may take precedence over statistical accuracy and observer convenience. For example, in a machine utilization study, is it sufficient to use just a single activity category for "machine idle," or will it be more informative to identify the reason for the machine being idle by including categories such as "downtime due to breakdown," "waiting for work," and "no scheduled work"? These additional categories will mean some analysis is required by the observer to distinguish between them, and it may lead to mistakes in classification. The designer of the work sampling study must thus find an appropriate compromise between these competing issues.

Two examples of possible activity categories for various types of work are presented in Table 2 and Table 3. Again, it should be noted that the categories must be defined with reference to the objectives of a particular work sampling study and that these tables are intended to be instructional more than representative of actual studies.

TABLE 2 Possible Activity Categories for a Work Sampling Study on Machinists in a Small Lot Job Shop

Category	Description
1. Plan	Worker is studying engineering drawing in preparation for new job.
2. Setup	Worker is setting up machine tool for new job.
3. Run production	Worker is running machine tool in production of parts.
4. Cleanup	Worker is cleaning up machine tool and immediate work area.
5. Wait	Worker is waiting for materials, tools, instructions from foreman, etc.
6. Personal	Worker is taking personal time, rest break, or coffee break, conversing with coworker.
7. Away	Worker is not at machine, not in sight.

Source: Based on an example in [10].

TABLE 3 Possible Activity Categories for a Work Sampling Study on Office Workers

Category	Description
1. Keypunching at computer terminal	Each desk is equipped with a personal computer. Worker is involved with the operation of a computer.
2. Writing at desk	Worker is filling out paper forms, or engaged in similar paperwork.
3. Filing	Worker is at central file area, performing either storage or retrieval tasks.
4. Telephone	Worker is using telephone.
5. Walking	Worker is walking within office area.
6. Conversing	Worker is conversing with coworker, supervisor, or customer in office.
7. Personal	Worker is taking personal time, rest break, coffee break, etc.
8. Away	Worker is not at desk, not in office.

3.2 Work Sampling Forms

The forms used to make the observations in a work sampling study must be designed specifically for the given study. The reason for this is that each study is different from all others in activity categories, subjects, total number of observations, and time period over which the study will be made. The observation form must be custom-designed to accommodate the parameters of the specific study. Objectives in the design problem are to make the form easy and convenient to use, conducive to making snap readings of the subject(s) and quickly recording the data. An example (hypothetical, based on the categories in Table 3) of such a form is presented in Figure 3. Forms similar to this can be readily prepared using word processing software.

3.3 Scheduling Observation Times

The total number of observations in a work sampling study is usually large. Several thousand is not unusual. The number must ultimately be reduced to a schedule of observations: At what times during the study period should the observer make the rounds to observe the subjects?

Preparing a Schedule of Randomized Observation Times. Observation times in a work sampling study must be randomized in order to improve the statistical accuracy of the data and to reduce the bias that might be introduced by the subjects if they could anticipate the observation times and modify their activities accordingly. There are various ways in which randomization can be accomplished. One possibility is to randomize the times throughout the entire study period. Using Example 1 to illustrate, since there are 10 subject machines that must be observed each round, the 500 observations reduces to a total of 500/10 = 50 rounds during the one-week period. The times for these 50 rounds could be randomized throughout the 5 days. This means that, on average, there would be 10 rounds per day. However, due to randomization, there would probably not be exactly 10 rounds each day. Some days would have more, other days fewer.

An alternative for scheduling observation times is to use the principle of ***sampling stratification***, a technique in which the total number of observations is divided into a

Date	Work Sampling Data Collection Form	Page of
Period of Study	Activity Category (AC)	
Observer	1. Keypunch	5. Walking
Department	2. Writing	6. Conversation
Notes:	3. Filing	7. Personal
	4. Telephone	8. Away

	Subjects											
Observation Date and Time	Smith		Jones		Wang		Schneider		Kim		Kowalski	
	AC	PR	AC	PR	AC	PR	AC	PR	AC	PR	AC	PR

Key: AC = activity category, PR = performance rating.

Figure 3 Work sampling observation form designed for recording the category number and performance rating of the subject.

specified number of time periods (e.g., days, half-days, hours) so that there are an equal number of samples taken in each period. For our machine utilization example, stratification means that instead of randomizing the observation times throughout the entire 5-day period, we make exactly 10 observation rounds each day. Within each day, the 10 observation times would be randomized. This is stratifying the observations by days and randomizing within days. This could be taken a step further, so that we take 5 observations each half-day (e.g., 5 in the morning and 5 in the afternoon). In this case we are stratifying by half-days and randomizing within half-days. Stratification has been found to reduce the variance in the estimated proportions in a work sampling study [8]. In addition, it is probably more convenient for observers to use stratified sampling. They know that each day or half-day (or other time period), a certain number of observation rounds must be made. It adds an element of structure to the study. The degree to which the sampling times are stratified is a decision that must be made by the designer of the work sampling study.

The actual procedure of randomizing the times can be accomplished through the use of any of the following sources of random numbers: (1) handbooks or textbooks that contain tables of random numbers, (2) pseudo-random number generators available in various spreadsheet software packages, (3) pseudo-random number generators programmed into some handheld scientific and engineering calculators, and (4) the last three or four digits of the numbers listed in the white pages of telephone directories. Whatever the source, the random numbers are converted to clock times during the time period of interest (e.g., shift) and then resequenced into chronological order (spread sheet sort routines could be used to reorder the starting sequence of random numbers). Using three digit numbers, the random number 248 converts to 2:48 p.m. Certain numbers would have to be discarded, for example 275 would be discarded because 2:75 is not a time. Other adjustments must be made to accommodate the given shift, as seen in the following example.

Example 5 Generation of Random Observation Times for Work Sampling

For the machine utilization example, generate the schedule of 10 observation times for the first day. The shift hours are 8:00 A.M. to noon, then 1:00 P.M. to 5:00 P.M.

Solution: A set of three digit numbers were randomly generated from a uniform distribution between 1 and 999 using Excel (seed number = 193). The first 18 numbers generated were as follows: 021, 542, 865, 804, 023, 488, 587, 743, 570, 722, 308, 118, 431, 465, 337, 605, 229, 325. Conversion of these numbers into clock times is accomplished using the following rules: (1) numbers with first digits = 8, 9, 1, 2, 3, and 4 are read directly as the clock hour, (2) numbers with first digits = 0 and 6 are read as clock hours 10 and 11, respectively, (3) numbers with first digits = 5 and 7 are discarded, (4) numbers with second digits 6 through 9 are discarded. The results of the conversion are presented in Table 4. The converted times are then resequenced into chronological order to yield the following schedule of observation times for the first day: in the morning: 8:04, 10:21, 10:23, and 11:05; and in the afternoon: 1:18, 2:29, 3:08, 3:25, 3:37, and 4:31.

TABLE 4 Conversion of Random Numbers into Observation Times in Example 5

Random Number	Conversion to Clock Time	Random Number	Conversion to Clock Time	Random Number	Conversion to Clock Time
021	10:21	587	Discarded	431	4:31
542	Discarded	743	Discarded	465	Discarded
865	Discarded	570	Discarded	337	3:37
804	8:04	722	Discarded	605	11:05
023	10:23	308	3:08	229	2:29
488	Discarded	118	1:18	325	3:25

■

Personal Digital Assistants and Random Time Beepers. Considerable effort can be devoted to the task of preparing the schedule of random observation times for a work sampling study, as Example 5 suggests (imagine a schedule for 10 weeks). Once the schedule is developed, a second problem is ensuring that the observations are taken at the specified times during the study. A supposed advantage of work sampling is that the analyst can be taking care of other duties while the work sampling study is going on. But if the analyst must always be watching the clock to make sure that the next sampling moment is not missed, the other duties cannot be given the full attention that they deserve.

Commercial devices are available to address these problems. We mention two such devices here that can be used in work sampling studies: the personal digital assistant (PDA) and the JD-7 Random Reminder. Let us mention their application in the context of developing and implementing a schedule of random observation times. PDAs are small personal computers that can be conveniently carried on one's person. The JD-7 Random Reminder, marketed by Divilbiss Electronics, Ltd., is a lightweight box that can be clipped to one's belt and worn throughout the day. Devices of this type can be programmed to serve the following two functions in work sampling:

- *Random times.* Random time devices can determine the random times during the period of the study at which the observer should commence a round of observations. The user sets a sampling rate parameter on the device, and the sampling times are automatically determined. Sampling time interval settings can range from several minutes to several hours.
- *Beeper.* With the sampling rate set, the device provides either an audible beep lasting for one second or a vibrating signal lasting for several seconds, depending on the preference of the user.

3.4 Advantages and Disadvantages of Work Sampling

Work sampling is a powerful tool of work measurement, but it is not without its limitations. In this section, we list the advantages and disadvantages, compiled with the assistance of some of the original practitioners of this technique [3] and [5].

Advantages

- Operations and activities that are impractical or too costly to measure by continuous observation (e.g., direct time study) can be measured using work sampling.
- Multiple subjects (e.g., crews) can be included in a single work sampling study. Other work measurement techniques must be used one worker at a time.
- It usually requires less time and lower cost to perform a work sampling study than to acquire the same amount of information through direct continuous observation.
- In work sampling, observations are taken over a long period of time, thus reducing the risk of short-time aberrations in the work routine of the subjects. Also, techniques are available (i.e., control charts) by which these aberrations can be identified and excluded from the study results.
- Training requirements to perform a work sampling study are generally less than for direct time study or predetermined time systems.
- Performing a work sampling study tends to be less tiresome and tedious on the observer than continuous observation.
- Being a subject in a work sampling study tends to be less demanding, since the observations are made quickly at random times rather than over a long continuous period. Some people are not comfortable being watched continuously for a long time.

Disadvantages and Limitations

- For setting time standards, work sampling is not as accurate as other work measurement techniques, such as direct time study and predetermined time systems. Because of its lack of accuracy, time standards set by work sampling should not be used for an incentive payment plan.
- Work sampling is usually not practical or economical for studying a single subject.
- If the subjects in a work sampling study are separated geographically by significant distances, the observer may spend too much time walking between them. This is not a productive use of the observer's time. In addition, it may allow workers at the beginning of the observer's tour to alert workers at the end of the tour that the observer is coming, with the possible risk that they would adjust their activities and bias the results of the study.
- Work sampling provides less detailed information about the work elements of a task than direct time study or predetermined time systems.
- Since work sampling is usually performed on multiple subjects, it tends to average their activities; thus differences in each individual's activities may be missed by the study.
- Because work sampling is based on statistical theory, workers and their supervisors may not understand the technique as readily as they understand direct time study. Consequently, worker acceptance of the study and its results could be a problem.
- A work sampling study does not normally include detailed documentation of the methods used by the workers. If methods changes are subsequently made, it may be difficult to determine whether the results of the study are still valid.
- As in so many fields of study, the behavior of subjects may be influenced by the act of observing them. If this occurs in work sampling, the results of the study can become biased, perhaps leading to incorrect conclusions and inappropriate recommendations.

REFERENCES

[1] Aft, L. S. *Work Measurement and Methods Improvement*. New York: Wiley, 2000.

[2] ANSI Standard Z94.0-1989. *Industrial Engineering Terminology*. Norcross, GA: Industrial Engineering and Management Press, Institute of Industrial Engineers, 1989.

[3] Barnes, R. M. *Work Sampling*. 2nd ed. New York: Wiley, 1957.

[4] Brisley, C. L. "Work Sampling and Group Timing Technique." Pp 17.47–17.64 in *Maynard's Industrial Engineering Handbook*, 5th ed., edited by K. Zandin. New York: McGraw-Hill, 2001.

[5] Heiland, R. E., and W. J. Richardson. *Work Sampling*. New York: McGraw-Hill, 1957.

[6] Konz, S., and S. Johnson. *Work Design: Industrial Ergonomics*. 5th ed. Scottsdale, AZ: Holcomb Hathaway Publishers, 2000.

[7] Matias, A. C. "Work Measurement: Principles and Techniques." Pp 1409–62 in *Handbook of Industrial Engineering*, 3rd ed., edited by G. Salvendy. New York: Wiley; Institute of Industrial Engineers, Norcross, GA, 2001.

[8] Moder, J. J. "Selection of Work Sampling Observation Times: Part 1—Stratified Sampling." *AIIE Transactions*. 12, no. 1 (March 1980) 23–31.

[9] Niebel, B. W., and A. Freivalds. *Methods, Standards, and Work Design*. 11th ed. New York: McGraw-Hill, 2003.

[10] Pape, E. S. "Work Sampling." Pp 1699–721 in *Handbook of Industrial Engineering*, 2nd ed., edited by G. Salvendy. New York: Wiley; Institute of Industrial Engineers, Norcross, GA, 1992.

[11] Richardson, W. J. *Cost Improvement, Work Sampling and Short Interval Scheduling*. Reston, VA: Prentice Hall, 1976.

REVIEW QUESTIONS

1 Define work sampling.

2 What are the characteristics of work situations for which work sampling is most suited?

3 What are some of the common applications of work sampling?

4 What is a biased estimate in work sampling?

5 On what kinds of jobs or tasks is work sampling an appropriate technique for setting time standards?

6 What is meant by the term sampling stratification?

7 Name three advantages of work sampling.

8 Name three disadvantages and limitations of work sampling.

PROBLEMS

1 For the data in Example 1, determine a 90% confidence interval for the proportion of time spent running production, category (2).

2 The personal time, fatigue, and delay (PFD) allowance is to be determined in the machine shop area. If it is estimated that the proportion of time per day is spent in these three categories (personal time, fatigue, and delay are grouped together to obtain one proportion) is 0.12, determine how many observations would be required to be 95% confident that the estimated proportion is within $\pm$ 0.02 of the true proportion.

3 This problem uses the context and data from Examples 1 and 3 in the text. After taking 684 observations (as computed in Example 3), the observed proportion was found to be $\hat{p} = 0.15$ (as in Example 1), instead of 0.20 as the foreman had originally estimated. Recompute the number of observations required for this new proportion, and if the value is less than 684, determine (a) the new confidence level that is obtained from 684 observations and (b) the new value of c, the half-width of the confidence interval at the original confidence level of 95%.

4 The foreman in the welding department wanted to know what value of allowance to use for a particular section of the shop. A work sampling study was authorized. Only two activity categories were considered: (1) welding and other productive work, and (2) personal time, rest breaks, and delays. Over a four-week period (40 hours/week), 125 observations were made at random times. Each observation captured the category of activity of each of eight welders in the shop section of interest. Results indicated that category 2 constituted 33% of the total observations. (a) Define the limits of a 96% confidence interval for activity 2. (b) If a total of 725 work units were produced during the 4 weeks, and all category 1 activities were devoted to producing these units, what was the average time spent on each unit?

5 A work sampling study was performed during a 3-hour final exam to determine the proportion of time that students spend using a calculator. There were 70 students taking the exam. A total of five observations were taken of each student at random times during the 3 hours. Of the total observations taken, 77 of the observations found the students using their calculators. (a) Form a 90% confidence interval on the proportion of time students spend using their calculators during an exam. (b) How many observations must be taken for the analyst to be 95% confident that the estimate of proportion of time a student uses a calculator is within $\pm 3\%$ of the true proportion?

6 The Chief Industrial Engineer in the production department wanted to know what value of PFD allowance to use for a particular section of the shop. A work sampling study was authorized. Only three activity categories were considered: (1) production work, (2) personal time, rest breaks, and delays, and (3) other activities. Over a 4-week period (40 hours/week), 100 observations were made at random times. Each observation captured the category of activity of each of 22 production workers in the shop section of interest. Results indicated that category 2 constituted 19% of the total observations. (a) Define the limits of a 95% confidence interval for activity 2. (b) If a total of 522 work units were produced during the 4 weeks, and the 1540 observations in category 1 were all devoted to producing these units, what was the average time spent on each unit?

7 A work sampling study is to be performed on an insurance office staff consisting of 15 persons to see how much time they spend processing claims. The duration of the study is 20 days, 8 hours per day. Processing claims is only one of the activities done by the staff members. The office manager estimates that the proportion of time processing claims is 0.20. (a) At the 95% confidence level, how many observations are required if the upper and lower confidence limits are 0.16 and 0.24? (b) Regardless of your answer to (a), assume that a total of 1200 observations were taken, and staff members were processing claims in 300 of those observations. Construct a 98% confidence interval for the true proportion of time processing claims. (c) Records for the period of the study indicate that 335 claims were processed. Estimate the average time per claim processed. (d) Determine a standard for processing claims, but express the standard in terms of the number of claims processed per day (8 hr) per person. Assume a 100% performance rating and that no allowance factor is to be included in the standard.

8 A work sampling study is to be performed on an office pool consisting of 10 persons to see how much time they spend on the telephone. The duration of the study is to be 22 days, 7hr/day. All calls are local. Using the phone is only one of the activities that members of the pool accomplish. The supervisor estimates that 25% of the workers' time is spent on the phone. (a) At the 95% confidence level, how many observations are required if the lower and upper limits on the confidence interval are 0.20 and 0.30. (b) Regardless of your answer to (a), assume that 200 observations were taken on each of the 10 workers (2000 observations total), and members of the office pool were using the telephone in 590 of these observations. Construct a 95% confidence interval for the true proportion of time on the telephone. (c) Phone records indicate that 3894 phone calls (incoming and outgoing) were made during the observation period. Estimate the average time per phone call.

9 The shop foreman has estimated that the proportion of time the machines in her department are idle is a mere 10%. On the basis of this estimate, a work sampling study is to be performed. (a) If we want a 95% confidence level that the true value of the proportion idle time is within $\pm 2.5\%$ of this 10% (that is, the confidence interval runs from 7.5% to 12.5%), how many observations must be taken? (b) Suppose after the study is taken with the number of observations from part (a), the proportion of observations is actually 15% rather than

10%. What is the range of the 95% confidence interval in this case? (c) How many more observations need to be taken to achieve a confidence interval of 15% ± 2.5%?

10 A work sampling study has been performed on a college sorority to determine how much time the women spend at their desks reading homework assignments. The sorority consists of 30 women. The duration of the study was 4 weeks, 7 days/week, between the hours of 7:00 A.M. and 11:00 P.M. each day. It is assumed that no reading was done before 7:00 A.M. or after 11:00 P.M., since the sorority members observe a very strict work ethic code. Five observations were taken at random times each day, and each observation included all 30 women. Out of all the observations, a total of 1344 observations found the women reading homework assignments at their desks. (a) Construct a 95% confidence interval for the true proportion of time spent reading homework assignments. (b) What is the average time per day that each woman spends reading homework assignments? (c) If the women in the sorority collectively completed a total of 513 reading assignments during the observation period, how many hours did each assignment take, on average?

11 A work sampling study is to be performed on the art department in a publishing company. The department consists of 22 artists who work at computer graphics workstations developing line drawings based on authors' rough sketches. The duration of the study is 15 days, 7 hr/day. Line drawings are the main activity performed by the artists, but not the only activity. The supervisor of the department estimates that the proportion of time spent making line drawings is 75% of each artist's day. (a) At the 95% confidence level, how many observations are required if the lower and upper confidence limits are 0.72 and 0.78, respectively? (b) Regardless of your answer in part (a), assume that a total of 1000 observations were actually taken, and artists were making line drawings in 680 of those observations. Construct a 97.5% confidence interval for the true proportion of time making line drawings. (c) Records for the period of the study indicate that 5240 line drawings were completed. Estimate the average time per line drawing. (d) Determine the standard time for one line drawing, given that the average performance rating for the artists was observed to be 90%, and the allowance for personal time, fatigue, and delays is 15%.

12 A work sampling study was performed on the day-shift maintenance department in a power generating station. The day shift consists of four repair persons, each of whom works independently to repair equipment when it breaks down. A total of 800 observations (200 observations per repair person) were taken during a 4-week period (160 total hours of station operation). The observations were classified into one of the following categories: (1) maintenance person repairing equipment, or (2) maintenance person idle. There were a total of 432 observations in category 1. It is known that 83 equipment repairs were made during the 4 weeks. (a) How many more observations would be required, if any, to be 90% confident that the true proportion of category 1 activity is within ±0.03 of the proportion indicated by the observations? Also, determine (b) the average time it takes a repair person to repair a piece of broken equipment, and (c) how many hours of idle time per week is experienced by each repair person, on average.

13 A work sampling study was performed on 12 assembly workers in a small electronics final assembly plant. Various products are made in small lot sizes, and it would not be cost effective to direct time study every job. However, the jobs can be distinguished on the basis of the size of the starting printed circuit board (PCB), and it is believed that work sampling might provide estimates of the average time per board size. There are three different PCB sizes: A (large), B (medium), and C (small). The study was carried out over a 5-week period (25 eight-hour days or 200 working hours). Observations were taken at random times four times each day for 25 days, for a planned total of 1200 observations ($4 \times 25 \times 12$). However, due to worker absences, 60 observations were omitted (15 worker-day absences). Results of the study are presented in the table below. (a) What is the mean assembly time per product unit for each of the three PCB sizes? (b) For the C size PCB assembly, construct a 96% confidence interval about the mean assembly time per product.

Category of Activity	A Assembly	B Assembly	C Assembly	Miscellaneous
Number of observations	228	285	456	171
Number of units completed	610	1127	3025	(none)

14 A work sampling study was performed on four account executives in a stockbroker's office. Virtually all sales in the office are made through telephone solicitations. A total of 500 observations were made over a period of 1 week (7 hr/day, 5 days/week). The categories of activity and number of observations per category were as follows: (1) telephone calls, 164; (2) filing and sorting, 150; (3) reading and research, 101; (4) personal and nonproductive time, 85. Total sales during this period were $525,000, on which the office earned a commission of 4.0%. (a) Construct a 97% confidence interval on the proportion of time on the telephone during the 1-week period. (b) Estimate how many hours were spent on the phone by the four account executives during this period. (c) The office is considering hiring a clerk at $800/week to do the filing and sorting (category 2). This would reduce the time taken by the account executives on these activities by 7 hr/day. It is anticipated that all of these extra 7 hr would be spent on phone calls to increase sales. If sales level (in dollars) has been found to be proportional to time on the telephone, will the increase in commissions pay for the clerk? Compute the estimated net increase or decrease in weekly revenues from hiring the clerk.

15 A work sampling study was performed on 15 social workers in a county government office. The social workers handle three types of cases: A, single parents; B, foster parents; and C, juvenile delinquents. The purpose of the work sampling study was to determine estimates of the average time per case for each case type. In addition to the three case types, two additional activity categories were included in the study: D, traveling between cases; and E, other (miscellaneous) activities. The study was carried out over a 5-week period (25 eight-hour days or 200 working hours). Observations were taken at random times four times each day for 25 days, for a planned total of 1500 observations ($4 \times 25 \times 15$). Social workers were provided with cell phones so they could be contacted if they were not in the office building. Because of worker absences, 72 observations were omitted (18 worker-days of absences). The results of the study are presented in the table below. (a) What is the mean time per case for each of the three case types? (b) What is the average travel time spent on a case? (c) For the C type cases, construct a 92.5% confidence interval about the mean case time.

Category of Activity	A Cases	B Cases	C Cases	D Transport	E Other
Number of observations	314	272	350	388	104
Number of cases completed	439	725	273	(none)	(none)

Computerized Work Measurement and Standards Maintenance

Using the work measurement techniques in the traditional way (without a computer) can be very time consuming for an analyst. Determining a time standard for a task using MTM-1 requires about 250 minutes for each minute of the task itself. Although other work measurement techniques require less application time, one must nevertheless acknowledge that work measurement is a costly overhead function for an organization. Since the 1960s, efforts have been underway to develop computerized systems to augment and automate the work measurement function or portions of it.

Computer systems can be applied to each of the four work measurement techniques: (1) direct time study (DTS), (2) predetermined motion time systems (PMTS), (3) standard data systems (SDS), and (4) work sampling. Direct time study and work sampling are work measurement techniques that require the analyst to be present during the study. In DTS, the analyst must be at the work site to observe and time the worker performing the task. In work sampling, the analyst (or an agent of the analyst, such as an analyst's assistant, technician, or foreman) must take the tours to observe and classify the activity categories of the subjects. A limitation of both techniques is that time standards cannot be established before the job is running. This limitation does not apply to predetermined motion time systems and standard data systems. The current trend in computerized work measurement seems to favor PMTS and SDS approaches, often used in combination. Future systems are likely to employ some form of artificial intelligence to more fully automate the work measurement function.

In this chapter we discuss all of these computerized systems: DTS and work sampling in Section 1, PMTS and SDS in Section 2, and the use of expert systems (a branch of artificial intelligence) in Section 3. In addition, the maintenance of time standards is an important function in work measurement, and this topic is discussed in Section 4. A modern standards maintenance system is implemented by computer.

Work measurement is certainly not the only engineering problem area that has been subjected to computerization. It joins a long list of problem areas requiring solution techniques that can either be augmented by means of a computer or would be infeasible without a computer. Examples of these other engineering areas include finite element modeling, analysis of variance, regression analysis, mathematical programming, discrete-event simulation, and numerical control part programming. The objective in computerized work measurement systems is similar to the objectives in these other areas: to reduce the manual and clerical content of the problem solving technique by performing the tedious and time-consuming computational chores. The creative problem-solving and design components of the technique still require the expertise of an analyst or engineer.

1 COMPUTER SYSTEMS FOR DIRECT TIME STUDY AND WORK SAMPLING

In direct time study and work sampling, the analyst is required to be present at the work site to observe the workers. Computerized tools must take this requirement into account by providing more convenient ways to prepare for and record data during the study than when the techniques are accomplished in conventional (noncomputerized) ways.

1.1 Computerized Tools for Direct Time Study

The conventional procedure for determining a time standard in direct time study consists of the following steps:

1. Define and document the standard method.
2. Divide the task into work elements.
3. Time the work elements to obtain the observed time for the task.
4. Rate the worker's performance to determine the normalized time.
5. Apply allowances to compute the standard time.

When this procedure is applied without computer assistance, several hours of analyst time may be required to establish a standard time for a task of only a few minutes duration. Steps 1 and 2 still require an experienced time study analyst who is familiar with the type of work activity. The documentation of the standard method may be aided by the use of a word processor, but the creative mental effort of the analyst is essential in

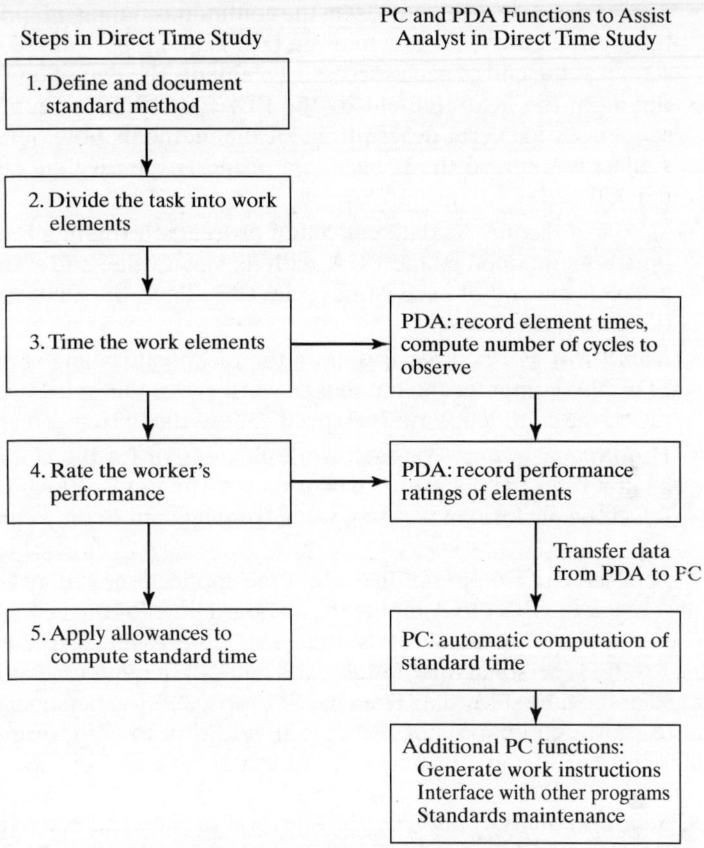

Figure 1 Steps in direct time study and how personal computers and personal digital assistants can be applied.

methods definition and work element identification. The opportunities for computer assistance in direct time study occur in steps 3, 4, and 5, as illustrated in Figure 1.

Collecting and Recording the Data. Steps 3 and 4 are performed simultaneously. Timing the work elements and rating the worker's performance require a portable device that can be conveniently held and used at the site of the job. The handheld personal digital assistant (PDA) is a product that satisfies this requirement. Programmed with time study software, the analyst uses the PDA in the following ways while observing the task:

- *Work element descriptions.* The analyst enters brief descriptions of the work elements comprising the task cycle into the PDA. These are abbreviations of the elements defined in the standard method and are used for identification purposes during the observation.

- *Timing the work elements.* Using the continuous timing method, the analyst records the work element times while the task is being performed by tapping the PDA screen at the end of each successive element. The end of one element initiates the timing of the next element by the PDA. The PDA screen displays a revolving sequence of several descriptions of the elements now being performed by the subject worker, so the analyst can properly identify the current work element being timed.
- *Statistical record.* As data collection proceeds, a running record of each element time is maintained by the PDA, with its mean value and standard deviation computed at the end of each work cycle. This allows the analyst to track these statistics during the study.
- *Number of work cycles.* Based on the mean values and standard deviations, the PDA also computes the number of work cycles that must be observed in order to satisfy the confidence interval specifications that have been entered by the analyst.
- *Performance rating.* For each work element, or for the complete work cycle, the analyst rates the operator's performance. The PDA software allows the analyst to select the performance rating value from a menu to the nearest 5%.

Analysis and Computations. In some applications, it may be appropriate for the analyst to use the PDA to compute the standard time for the task (step 5), so the worker can be informed immediately of its value. This requires the analyst to enter the allowance value for PFD (personal time, fatigue, and delays). In other cases, the analyst may prefer to transfer the time study data from the PDA to a desktop personal computer to perform a more thorough analysis of the data in addition to computing the time standard. The opportunities and advantages of using a PC in step 5 include the following:

- *Statistical analysis and charting.* Several of the DTS software products facilitate the transfer of time study data to a spreadsheet package such as Microsoft Excel, thus permitting the powerful statistical analysis features of such packages to be employed in the analysis and display of the data. For example, it is helpful for the data to be exhibited in the form of a histogram so that outliers can be identified and discarded from the computation of the standard time.
- *Standard time computation.* The value of the time standard is automatically computed, based on the value of PFD allowance that has been entered for the category of task. The standard time can be expressed in various time units, such as decimal hours or decimal minutes. Most time study software products also calculate additional measures, such as normal time and anticipated hourly production rate at standard performance.
- *Generation of work instructions.* Documentation for the task includes a description of the standard method. This can be converted into detailed instructions for operators performing the task. Work drawings and part prints can also be included in this shop documentation.
- *Interface to other programs.* The methods and standards residing in the computer database are a component in the organization's management information system. The time standards can be exported to other components in the information system,

such as material requirements planning (MRP), manufacturing resource planning (MRPII), computer-aided process planning (CAPP), machine loading, and production scheduling.

- *Standards maintenance.* This file management module provides storage and maintenance capabilities for the standards and related documentation. Standards maintenance is discussed in Section 4.

1.2 Computerized Tools for Work Sampling

The procedure in a work sampling study consists of the following steps:

1. Define the objectives of the work sampling study.
2. Define the subjects to be studied.
3. Define the output measures.[1]
4. Define the activity categories.
5. Design the study, which includes (a) determining how many observations will be required to achieve the desired statistical accuracy and (b) developing a schedule of random times when the observations will be made.
6. Identify the observers.
7. Announce the study.
8. Make the observations (collect the data).
9. Analyze and report results.

As in direct time study, some of these steps can be simplified using the computer and related digital devices, while other steps require the creative judgment of the analyst in charge of the study. Steps 1 through 4 are design steps that must be accomplished by an analyst who is familiar with the work activities to be studied and the work sampling technique. Step 5 involves computations, and these can be accomplished much more rapidly and without the likelihood of human error by the computer. Steps 6 and 7 involve human resources decisions and educational activities. These steps cannot be automated; the analyst must perform them. Steps 8 and 9 require active human participation, but there are also opportunities for computer assistance in these steps. The steps in a work sampling study and the opportunities for using PCs and PDAs are illustrated in Figure 2.

Computations During Work Sampling Design. Work sampling software is commercially available to perform virtually all of the preliminary calculations that are required during the design of a work sampling study. Typical capabilities of these products include the following:

- *Number of observations.* For this computation, the analyst must specify the confidence level, the confidence interval, and an estimate of the proportion of the activity category of greatest interest. Several alternatives can be easily evaluated

[1]Output measures are the work units that are produced as a result of certain work activity categories. Not all work sampling studies include collection of output measure data. When output measures are included in a work sampling study, it is possible to determine the average time or standard time per work unit.

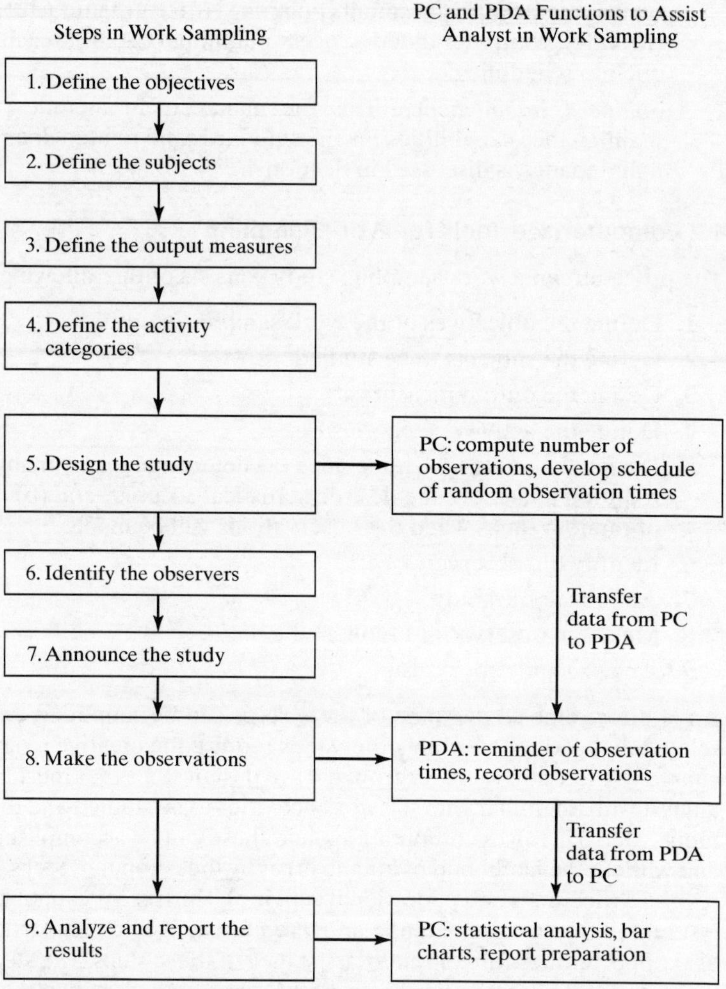

Figure 2 The steps in a work sampling study and the opportunities for using PCs and PDAs.

on the computer, so that the analyst can balance the requirements of statistical accuracy against the cost of taking a larger number of observations.

- *Schedule of randomized times.* Determining this schedule is time-consuming and tedious when done manually. Computerizing the procedure reduces the task to nothing. In the typical software application, the analyst must enter several specifications that are taken into account in the calculations: (1) the number of observations in the study, (2) the number of subjects, (3) the period of the study, and (4) the shift schedule (clock times at the beginning and ending of the shift and any scheduled breaks during the shift). The computer prepares a daily schedule of random times when the tours should be taken to make the observations. If the analyst identifies multiple possible routes, they are included in the schedule, and their occurrences are randomized.

Making the Observations. In a traditional work sampling study, making the observations is a paper and pencil activity. This procedure can be simplified by means of a PDA that has been programmed with work sampling software. There are several typical features and applications of the PDA during the observation phase of the study

- *Using a random beeper.* The PDA can be programmed to provide an audible beeping sound when the scheduled time comes to take an observation tour. Instead of the observer constantly watching the clock while waiting for the next sampling time, the beeper alerts the observer when that time has arrived. As an alternative to using a PDA, a specialized device called the JD-7 Random Reminder, marketed by Devilbiss Electronics, is available. It clips onto one's belt and provides either an audible beeping sound or a vibratory signal to the user.
- *Recording the observation data.* The PDA must initially be programmed to accept the identification codes for the subjects and activity categories in the study. Then, while making the observation rounds, the observer enters the appropriate codes as he or she comes upon each subject. The data are stored for subsequent analysis.
- *Uploading to a desktop or notebook PC.* Use of the PDA allows the observation data to be uploaded directly to a PC rather than entered manually by keyboard if taken by paper and pencil. Uploading can be accomplished at the end of the work sampling study or while the study is in progress. Transferring data to the PC during the study allows the use of day-by-day and cumulative charting techniques and other means of tracking the ongoing study.

Analysis and Reporting of Results. Assuming that the observation data are uploaded to a PC, a wide range of analysis and report-writing capabilities can be used to perform a statistical analysis and prepare the final report. The basic information derived from the study consists of the proportions (or percentages) of each activity category. The activity categories are often presented in a table that lists them in descending order of their relative proportions. The significance of the proportions may be emphasized by using one or more of the following techniques:

- Use bar charts to graphically illustrate the relative percentages.
- Combine activity categories into broader classes that distinguish, for example, productive work activity versus nonproductive activity.
- Express the proportions as hours of time or dollars spent per week or per year, which would highlight the significance of the results more than proportions.
- Chart the day-by-day observation data on a time chart, which would be useful to indicate variations in the daily proportions or to show trends in the data.

2 COMPUTERIZED SYSTEMS BASED ON PREDETERMINED MOTION TIMES AND STANDARD DATA

Although computerized tools are useful in direct time study and work sampling, the techniques themselves suffer the disadvantage of requiring the analyst to be present during the study. As a consequence, a time standard cannot be set by direct time study for a job until the job is in production. Although a work sampling study often has objectives other than setting standards, when it is used to set time standards, those standards cannot be computed until after the work sampling study is completed.

The ideal computerized work measurement system would include a means of setting the standard for a task in advance. Among the conventional work measurement techniques, predetermined motion time systems (PMTS) and standard data systems (SDS) allow time standards to be set beforehand. Accordingly, the ideal computerized system is likely to include one or both (more likely both) of these two measurement techniques as the core of the system. Some of today's commercially available systems are based on this approach.

As our chapter title suggests, the ideal computerized work measurement system should actually serve two principal functions:

- *Work measurement.* The system should have the capability to set a time standard for a task before the task is running, and it should be capable of preparing the required documentation that accompanies the standard (e.g., methods description).
- *Standards database.* The system should include a database for time standards that have already been established, and it should provide for the maintenance of those standards.

Let us discuss the desirable features of a computerized system that provides these two functions. They are discussed separately in the following sections, even though they are integrated in the same system and each must interact with the other to accomplish its function.

2.1 The Work Measurement Function

The work measurement function in a computerized PMTS or SDS still requires the knowledge and expertise of an analyst. The relationship between the analyst and the computer is synergistic. Each enables the other to accomplish the work measurement function. Let us examine the complimentary roles of the two participants. The analyst brings analytical skills, experience with the work situation, and good judgment to accomplish the following responsibilities:

- Definine the standard method (e.g., attempt to determine the "one best method").
- Decide what special tools, fixtures, and gauges might be required to make the task easier.
- Define and evaluate the work variables that affect element times in the task.
- Retrieve data from the database on element times.
- Interact with the system, exploiting its features and capabilities to develop the time standard and accompanying documentation.

Most of these responsibilities are the same as those in a conventional SDS or PMTS. They require the expert judgment of an analyst who is familiar with the tasks being measured and the work environment in which they are performed.

The job of a PC in implementing the work measurement function is to perform the routine computations and facilitate the retrieval of data needed by the analyst. The steps in work measurement using a PMTS or SDS and the role played by a computer in the system are shown in Figure 3. Let us discuss the features and issues that are associated with these activities.

Automatic Computations. Work measurement is one of the two primary functions of the computerized system. It should perform all of the calculations necessary to determine the time standard for a given task, thus relieving the analyst of this burden and possibly avoiding errors in the calculations. Assuming that the system is either a PMTS or an SDS, or a combination of the two, the computer-assisted analyst would define the method and select the motion elements to be included, and the PC would sum the element times and apply the appropriate allowance factor to arrive

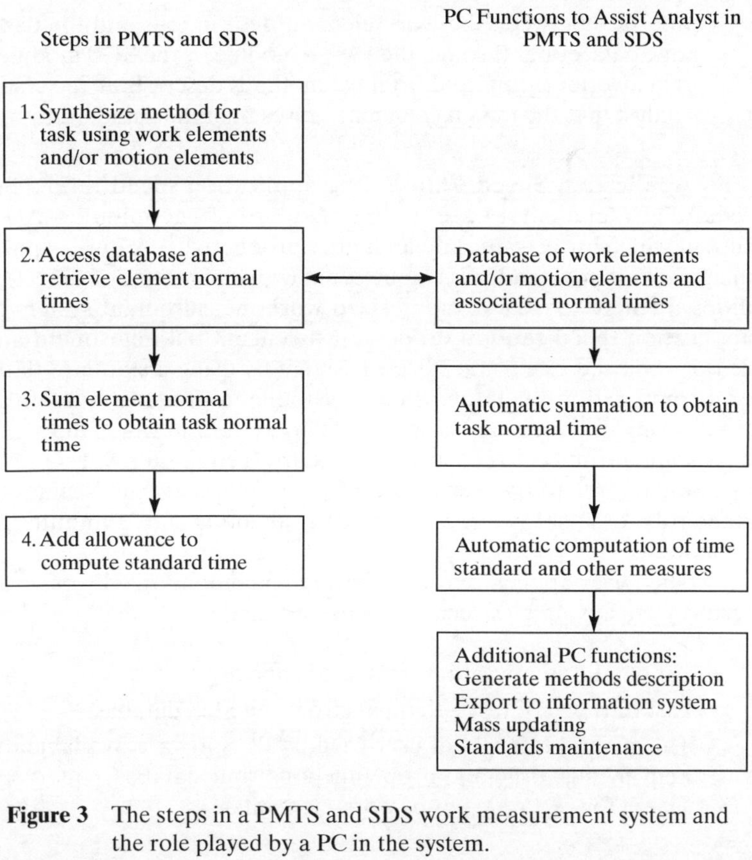

Figure 3 The steps in a PMTS and SDS work measurement system and the role played by a PC in the system.

at the time standard. Other calculated values, such as the normal time, manual and machine times, allowance time per cycle, and production rate, would be included in the documentation.

If the SDS uses mathematical formulas to determine work element values, the system should have the capacity to accept new equations, alter existing equations, or delete formulas that are no longer required. The analyst is responsible for entering the applicable work variable values in the formulas.

Generation of Methods Description. The documentation for any time standard must include a description of the standard method. The standard time is valid only for the standard method. This description is used as the instructions for the worker performing the task and the foreman in charge of the department. The computerized work measurement system should provide features to facilitate the generation of this description. There are several possibilities:

- A library of generic work element descriptions that can be readily retrieved, edited, and combined to fit the method description for the specific task of interest.
- Easy entry of new descriptions into the library.
- Interface between the work element descriptions and the database of elemental time data, either through the PMTS module or the SDS module. If a work element is inadvertently omitted from the methods description, the system should alert the analyst that the missing element causes the time standard to be inconsistent.

Application Speed Ratio. The application speed ratio—the amount of time required by an analyst to set a time standard of one minute—is a productivity measure in which lower values mean higher productivity. A lower application speed ratio means that more standards can be set in a given amount of time. Compared to its traditional counterpart, a computerized work measurement system must have a lower application speed ratio in order to justify its initial investment and operating costs. This is achieved in a computerized system by using a standard data system approach or a combination of standard data system and predetermined motion time system. When compared to a manual standard data system, in which the analyst refers to tables, charts, and formulas to construct a standard, a computerized standard data system can be applied three to five times faster [3]. This comparison assumes that the number of standards to be set is large, so that the advantages of computerization can be fully exploited.

The lower application speed ratio in a computerized work measurement system results from advantages such as the following:

- Automatic computations (discussed above)
- Fast retrieval of work elements from the SDS database
- The general features of user-friendly PC software available today, such as icons, help menus, drag-and-drop functions, and database query commands (e.g., to search for certain types of work elements).

2.2 The Standards Database Function

The second principal function of the computerized work measurement system is to serve as a database for existing time standards and to provide for the maintenance of those standards. The features and issues associated with the database function are discussed in the following sections.

Storage and Retrieval Capabilities. The database contains existing standards and the work elements that comprise these standards. It should be designed as a centralized data system, with access permitted by qualified users through their desktop PCs. Network technologies allow users from different plant locations to access the same database. This avoids differences in time standards for the same tasks performed at different plants. The database should have adequate capabilities for entering new standards and supporting documentation, and the data should be coded to allow for ease of finding and retrieving needed information.

Mass Updating Capabilities. Mass updating refers to situations in which a certain group of standards needs to be updated as a result of a change in the tasks to which those standards apply. The change may involve a product design change, methods improvement, new tooling, introduction of new equipment, a change in the allowance factor, or other reasons. If these updates were made manually by pulling all of the files for the standards and making the changes, this would be a very time-consuming chore, depending on how many standards are affected. The computerized system should possess mass updating capabilities that would allow these types of changes in the standards to be made in a matter of minutes rather than hours or days.

Data Export Features. Time standards are an important component in an organization's management information system. The time standards database should be available to other components in the information system that require time data to perform their respective functions. These other components include product cost estimating, computer-aided process planning (CAPP), material requirements planning (MRP), manufacturing resource planning (MRP-II), enterprise resource planning (ERP), production scheduling, and shop floor control. The standards database should include mechanisms for sharing data with other modules that require it.

Standards Maintenance. The purpose of a standards maintenance program is to make sure that the existing time standards in the database are periodically reviewed and updated if necessary. This purpose is most readily accomplished within the context of a computerized database. We discuss the issues in standards maintenance more thoroughly in Section 4.

3 WORK MEASUREMENT BASED ON EXPERT SYSTEMS

The next generation of computerized work measurement systems is likely to use expert systems technology. Several systems based on this technology have already been developed, including AutoMOST by H. B. Maynard and Company and Quick-LINK by the

MTM Association. An ***expert system*** is a computer program that is capable of solving complex problems that normally require a human with years of education and experience. Work measurement fits within the scope of this definition because a good time study analyst must have training and years of experience.

Three ingredients are required in a computerized work measurement system that is fully automated using expert systems technology:

1. Knowledge base of an expert time study analyst
2. Computer-compatible description of the task for which the time standard is to be set
3. Capability to apply the knowledge base to a given task description to set a standard.

The ***knowledge base*** contains (1) the technical knowledge about the tasks to be studied and (2) the logic used by a successful time study analyst to set a standard. Technical knowledge and logic are normally captured through a series of interviews of one or more experts who are knowledgeable in the problem area. The knowledge and logic constitute a set of rules used by the analyst, which are used to solve a work measurement problem. These rules must be coded into a computer program.

The second ingredient involves developing a way to describe the task that can be understood by the computer system. The computer-compatible description must contain all of the information needed to determine the time standard for the task. This information includes the sequence of work elements or motion elements, distances moved and other work variables, tooling used, and other details. The codes used in predetermined motion time systems such as MTM-1 and MOST represent one possible approach to the problem of developing this kind of description. However, those codes are normally determined by an expert human analyst who has had years of experience using the PMTS. The objective of using a computerized expert system is to eliminate the need for the human expert. The problem can be addressed by means of an interactive approach in which a nonexpert user of the system would be guided through an interview process to arrive at the appropriate description of the task.

The third ingredient in an expert system for work measurement is the capability to apply the knowledge base (first ingredient) to a given task description (second ingredient) in order to determine the standard time for the task. In other words, the expert system uses its knowledge and logic to solve a specific work measurement problem. This problem-solving procedure is called the ***inference engine***, in the terminology of expert systems.

The benefits of a computerized work measurement expert system are based on the ability of such a system to transfer the expert analyst's knowledge to other staff members who do not possess the expert's experience and who would presumably be paid at salary levels below that of the expert, thus reducing the average cost of standards development and maintenance. The application speed of setting a standard would also be increased, further reducing the overhead cost of the work measurement function. Another benefit cited by suppliers of these systems is that the human expert's time can now be devoted to other important functions that require creative analysis, such as identifying and implementing methods and process improvements in the organization.

4 MAINTENANCE OF TIME STANDARDS

A time standard for a task applies only to the standard method used when the standard was set. If the method actually used by a worker in production differs from the standard method, then the time standard is no longer valid. The actual method will be less productive than the standard method or it will be more productive. In either case, some form of corrective action should be taken.

If the actual method used by the worker is less productive than the standard method, then the worker will have difficulty making 100% efficiency. This is usually a case of improper instructions or lack of training given to the worker. It is likely to be discovered because the worker complains that he or she cannot keep up with the standard, or by the foreman observing that the standard method is not being used. The corrective action in this case is to provide the proper instructions and training about the standard method to the worker and to make sure that the standard method is used. In rare cases (we hope), the standard time is too "tight" for the standard method, and the corrective action should be to revise the standard.

The other alternative is that the actual method used by the worker is more productive than the standard method, which means that the required time to perform the task is less than that reflected in the normal and standard times. This case is usually more difficult to identify and rectify because the worker may try to conceal the method improvement to keep the advantage that has been gained by it. The original standard method was supposed to be the "one best way" to perform the task. However, the time study analyst is only human, and it may be that an opportunity for an improvement was overlooked. The ingenuity and creativity of the worker to discover the oversight should not be underestimated. The possible improvements that might be made by a worker include the following:

- The worker improvises a special tool or makes a change in an existing tool that shaves time from one of the work elements.
- The workplace layout is revised, which reduces the time to move things during the task.
- Manual elements that were external to the machine time are made internal elements.
- Work elements that were listed in the standard method as being accomplished sequentially by one hand are instead accomplished simultaneously using both hands.
- The worker changes the machine settings (e.g., speeds and feeds on a milling machine) to reduce the machine cycle time.

These surreptitious changes made by the worker are not the only reasons why the actual method may differ from the standard method. Other changes affecting the task time are legitimate and official changes that may be overlooked in the standards updating process. They include the following:

- Engineering changes in the design of the product or its parts that affect processing or assembly time
- A new, faster production machine that replaces the machine used when the standard was set
- An improved workholding fixture with fast-acting pneumatic clamp that replaces the screw-actuated clamp used when the standard was set

Any of these changes, surreptitious or legitimate, are potentially beneficial to the organization because they can have the effect of improving productivity, reducing costs, and increasing its competitiveness. However, for the benefits to be realized, the change in the method must be accompanied by a corresponding change in the time standard. Sometimes the improvements are small and each one by itself would have only a negligible effect on the time. These are sometimes referred to as ***creeping changes***. Although each change may be insignificant, a succession of creeping changes can ultimately have a significant effect on the validity of the time standard for the task.

The purpose of a standards maintenance program is to protect the validity of the time standards by periodically reviewing the tasks and updating the standards for those tasks that have been affected by methods improvements or other changes. Implementing a standards maintenance program involves conducting periodic audits of existing standards to determine whether they are still valid. The auditing procedure consists of observing the task as it is being performed and comparing the actual method being used against the description of the standard method. The methods comparison is usually accomplished work element by work element. A thorough audit should also include a review of machine speeds and feeds, changes in equipment or tooling, engineering changes in the product, frequency of irregular elements, and other factors that may affect the time to perform the task. If a discrepancy is found between the actual method and the standard method, then the improvements should be incorporated into the standard method, and the standard time should be updated. Updating rules are sometimes agreed upon between management and the union representing the workers. For example, the parties may agree that when an improvement is discovered, only the work element or elements that are affected by the improvement can be restudied, so that the unaffected elements remain as they are. Another example is the ***5% rule***, which means that unless the standard time is affected by more than 5%, it remains as is.

The frequency with which standards should be audited depends on the relative importance of the tasks. The more important the task, the more frequently it should be audited. Table 1 lists a possible auditing schedule recommended by Niebel [2] that is based on the annual number of hours devoted to the task.

The consequence of having no standards maintenance program or a poorly implemented standards maintenance program is that the standards are gradually eroded over time, which means that the disparity between the standard time and the actual time

TABLE 1 Recommended Frequency for Auditing Standards

Standard Hours per Year (Standard Time × Number of Pieces Processed)	Frequency of Audit
More than 700 hr	6 months
Less than 700 hr but more than 100 hr	1 year
Less than 100 hr but more than 50 hr	2 years
Less than 50 hr	3 years

Source: [2].

required to perform a given task increases with each passing year. Standards erosion results in the following problems for the organization:

- Labor productivity is reduced, because the workers limit their own output in order to avoid a reduction in the time standard for the task.
- Incentive earnings escalate if the organization uses an incentive system.
- Labor costs rise.
- Estimates of workload and the scheduling of work become inaccurate.
- The organization suffers a loss in its competitive edge.

REFERENCES

[1] Mundel, M. E., and D. L. Danner. *Motion and Time Study: Improving Productivity*. 7th ed. Englewood Cliffs, NJ: Prentice Hall, 1994.

[2] Niebel, B. W. "Time Study." Pp. 1599–38 in *Handbook of Industrial Engineering*, edited by G. Salvendy. New York: Wiley; Institute of Industrial Engineers, Norcross, GA, 1992.

[3] Peretin, J., and G. S. Smith. "Computerized Labor Standards." Pp. 5.121–32 in *Maynard's Industrial Engineering Handbook*, 5th ed., edited by K. Zandin. New York: McGraw-Hill, 2001.

[4] Sellie, C. N. "Predetermined Motion-Time Systems and the Development and Use of Standard Data." Pp. 1639–98 in *Handbook of Industrial Engineering*, 2nd ed., edited by G. Salvendy. New York: Wiley; Institute of Industrial Engineers, Norcross, GA, 1992.

[5] Zandin, K. B. "MOST Work Measurement Systems." Pp. 65–82 in *Maynard's Industrial Engineering Handbook*, 5th ed., edited by K. B. Zandin. New York: McGraw-Hill, 2001.

REVIEW QUESTIONS

1 What is the objective of computerizing portions of the various work measurement procedures?

2 What are the five steps in the conventional time study procedure, and in which of those steps are there opportunities for computer assistance?

3 How are personal digital assistants (PDAs) used in direct time study?

4 How are personal computers (PCs) used in direct time study?

5 How can PCs and PDAs be used in a work sampling study?

6 What are the two principal functions of an ideal computerized work measurement system that is based on a predetermined motion time system and/or a standard data system?

7 What is the computer's job in implementing the work measurement function in an ideal computerized work measurement system that is based on a predetermined motion time system and/or a standard data system?

8 What is the computer's job in implementing the standards database function in an ideal computerized work measurement system that is based on a predetermined motion time system and/or a standard data system?

9 What are the three ingredients required in a computerized work measurement system that is fully automated using expert systems technology?

10 What is the typical reason that a worker may have difficulty making 100% efficiency on a task for which a time standard has been set?

11 What are some of the possible improvements that a worker might make to devise a method that is more productive than the standard method?

12 What is meant by the term creeping changes (in work methods)?

13 What is the function of a standard maintenance program?

14 What are the problems that result from standards erosion over time—that is, time standards that become less and less valid over time due to creeping changes and surreptitious methods improvements made by the worker?

Learning Curves

A phenomenon associated with virtually all repetitive work is the learning curve. First observed and studied in the aircraft industry during the 1930s, the ***learning curve phenomenon*** refers to the reduction in cycle time that occurs in a repetitive work activity as the number of cycles increases.[1] The learning curve is an important topic in our coverage of time study.

Learning curves are easiest to visualize in terms of an individual worker who performs a manual task. When the worker accomplishes the task over and over, the time required for each successive work cycle decreases as he or she learns the task. As the saying goes: "practice makes perfect." At first the learning effect is rapid, and the cycle time decreases significantly.

[1]The Employee and Industrial Relations Subcommittee (ANSI Standard Z94.13-1989) defines the learning curve as follows (in part): "A graph or mathematical formula plotting the course of production during a period in which an employee is learning a job; the vertical axis plots a measure of proficiency while the horizontal axis represents some measure of practice or experience (time)."

As more and more cycles are completed, the reduction in cycle time becomes less and less. The learning effect occurs at a diminishing rate as the number of repetitions increases.

Although the learning curve phenomenon is easiest to envision for an individual worker, the same kind of improvement occurs in the repetitive operations of worker teams and larger work organizations, even entire enterprises. The learning curve effect is inherent in any work system that continues to seek improvement in its operations. Alternative terms are sometimes used for organizational learning and technological improvements. These terms include ***manufacturing progress function*** and ***experience curve***.

The learning curve phenomenon is not limited to the cycle time of a repetitive operation. It can also be used to estimate the reduction in product cost over time as the number of units increases. One might reason that this follows directly from the reduction in cycle time because the unit cost depends largely on the unit time (e.g., hourly direct labor rate applied to the unit time). However, unit cost includes other factors such as material cost and product design. It has been found that these factors can also be improved over time to reduce unit product cost, further sustaining the learning curve effect. In addition to unit time and unit cost, learning curve analysis has also been applied to product quality, occupational safety, contract administration, pricing strategies, and other areas.

The standard time for a given task or operation can be referred to as a constant and the actual cycle time for the task as a variable that is affected by operator performance (pace) and other factors. We also see that one of those other factors, and an important one indeed, is the learning curve phenomenon.

1 LEARNING CURVE THEORY

According to learning curve theory, there is a constant learning rate that applies to a given repetitive task. The ***learning rate*** is defined as the proportion by which the dependent variable, usually task time, is multiplied every time the number of task cycles or work units doubles. The doubling effect in learning curve theory can be seen in the hypothetical plot of cycle time versus number of cycles shown in Figure 1. If the time to accomplish the first work unit is 10 hours, and the learning rate is 80%, then the time to accomplish the second work unit is 0.80 of the time for the first, the time to accomplish the fourth unit is 0.80 of the time for the second, the time to accomplish the eighth unit is 0.80 of the time for the fourth, and so on. Between these points in the plot, the cycle times decrease gradually and predictably.

A closely related term is the ***rate of improvement***, defined as the proportion by which the dependent variable is reduced every time the number of units doubles. The rate of improvement is the complement of the learning rate; that is,

$$IR = 1 - LR \tag{1}$$

where IR = improvement rate expressed as a decimal fraction, and LR = learning rate, also expressed as a decimal fraction. A learning rate of 0.80 means that the rate of improvement is 0.20 every time the number of cycles doubles. Although decimal fractions are used to represent the LR and IR rate in our equations, their values are often expressed as percentages. Thus, a learning rate of 80% is equivalent to an improvement rate of 20%.

Different learning rates are associated with different types of tasks, and different workers have different learning capabilities that affect the learning rate of an individual

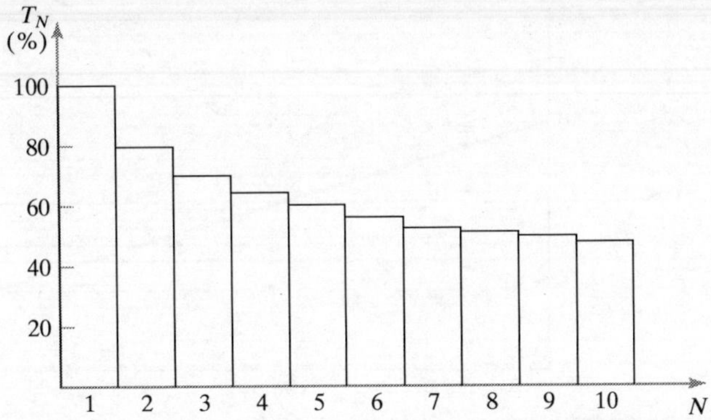

Figure 1 The learning curve phenomenon for a learning rate of 80%. Key: T_N = time for the Nth unit

operation. As a practical matter, values of learning rate range from about 60% to less than 100%. A learning rate of 60% indicates a very rapid reduction in task time, with progression toward a zero time in just a few doublings of the number of cycles. There are very few instances in industry where a learning rate as low as 60% has been observed. A learning rate of 100% implies no learning.[2] Finally, a learning rate higher than 100% implies a loss of learning. One would think loss of learning is unlikely, at least over the long run. Some typical values of learning rate for various industries and types of tasks are presented in Section 3.1.

When the data of Figure 1 are plotted on log-log coordinates, the plot yields a straight line with slope m, as shown in Figure 2. The relationship can be represented mathematically by the equation

$$y = kx^m \tag{2}$$

where y is the dependent variable (in the case of learning curves, this is usually the time or cost of a task cycle or work unit); k = a constant representing the value of the dependent variable for the first work unit; x = number of work units completed (the independent variable), and m = an exponent corresponding to the learning rate.

For learning rates less than 1.0, m is a negative value, and so the slope is negative as seen in Figure 2. For the 80% learning rate in Figure 2, $m = -0.322$. In general, the slope m can be determined from the learning rate using the following equation:

$$m = \frac{ln(LR)}{ln2} \tag{3}$$

where LR = learning rate expressed as a decimal fraction (e.g., 80% = 0.80). The natural logarithm in the denominator takes into account the fact that the learning rate applies every time the number of cycles is doubled.

[2]The incongruity in learning curve terminology, to which the reader must become accustomed, is that a higher value of learning rate (value of LR closer to one) means slower learning in the task or operation, and a lower value means faster learning.

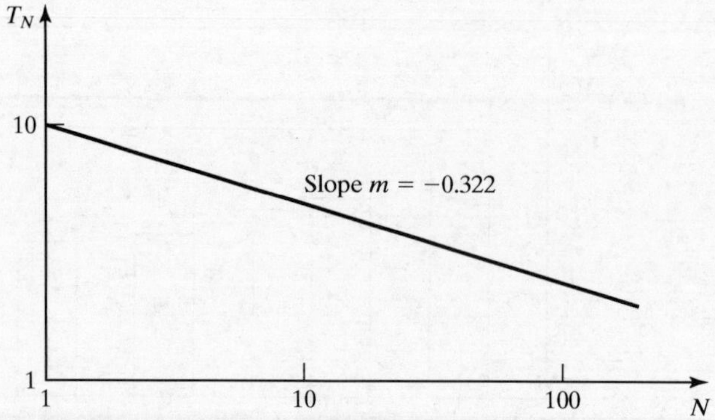

Figure 2 The learning curve data of Figure 1 plotted on log-log coordinates.

If the slope of the learning curve is known, then the corresponding learning rate can be determined by rearranging equation (3) and solving for LR.

$$LR = 2^m \tag{4}$$

where LR is expressed as a decimal fraction. This can be converted to a percentage value by multiplying by 100.

Because equation (2) plots as a straight line in log-log coordinates, it is often referred to as the ***log-linear model*** in learning curve theory. The two most widely used learning curve models are based on the log-linear equation form. They are called the Crawford model and the Wright model, after the aircraft industry researchers who developed them (Historical Note 1). The difference between them is the definition of the y term (dependent variable) in equation (2).

HISTORICAL NOTE 1 DEVELOPMENT OF LEARNING CURVE THEORY

Learning curve theory traces its roots to the seminal paper by T. P. Wright, "Factors Affecting the Cost of Airplanes," which was published in a 1936 issue of the ***Journal of Aeronautical Sciences***. The general effect of the learning curve had been observed before Wright's work, but it was he who described it mathematically. He defined the learning rate as "the factor by which the average labor cost in any quantity shall be multiplied in order to determine the average labor cost for a quantity of twice that number of airplanes [13]." Basically, he was defining the Wright version of the log-linear model in learning curve theory.

The other important log-linear model of the learning curve is attributed to J. R. Crawford, who prepared an in-house training manual for the Lockheed Aircraft Corporation titled ***Learning Curve, Ship Curve, Ratios, Related Data*** (unfortunately, no date is given). The difference in the models is that Crawford used unit cost (time) as the dependent variable in his equation, whereas Wright used the average cost (i.e., the cumulative average cost).

1.1 The Crawford Model

The Crawford model is the most widely used learning curve model in industry today.[3] It has attained this standing because it is relatively simple to apply and it accurately reflects the effects of learning that occur in many industrial situations. It is sometimes called the unit time (or unit cost) model because the dependent variable is the unit time associated with the Nth work cycle. Given the time required to perform the first work cycle and the learning rate, the expected time to perform the Nth work cycle can be calculated by the Crawford model as follows:

$$T_N = T_1 N^m \tag{5}$$

where T_N = unit time for the Nth work cycle, T_1 = time for the first work cycle, N = number of the work cycle in the repetitive sequence, and m = an exponent that is determined from the learning rate according to equation (3).

Example 1 Computation of T_N Using the Crawford Model

How long will it take to complete the 20th work unit of a task for a learning rate of 80%, given that the time for the first unit is 10 hr?

Solution: Given that $T_1 = 10$ hr and $LR = 0.80$, we first compute the value of m.

$$m = \frac{ln(0.80)}{ln2} = -0.32193$$

Using equation (5), we have

$$T_{20} = 10(20)^{-0.32193} = 10(0.3812) = 3.81 \text{ hr}$$

To reinforce the result obtained here, we note that the doubling effect has occurred four times at the 16th work unit. That is, $T_{16} = 10(0.80)(0.80)(0.80)(0.80) = 4.096$ hr. The 20th cycle is just a few more cycles, so we would expect its value to be close to but less than that of the 16th cycle. ■

It is often desirable to know not only the unit time of the Nth work unit, as in the example above, but also the ***total cumulative time*** for all N work units. For example, this information might be useful in bidding on a batch of N work units for a prospective customer. With the Crawford model, this can be determined exactly by the following summing procedure:

$$TT_N = T_1 \sum_{i=1}^{N} i^m \tag{6}$$

where TT_N = total cumulative time for N work units, i = an intermediate variable for the summing procedure, and the other terms have been defined previously.

[3]Delionback [4] indicates that approximately 92% of all firms use the Crawford model (presumably based on a survey of companies that use learning curves).

Unfortunately, the summing process required in equation (6) is tedious, especially for large values of N. An approximation equation is available, based on integrating a continuous function of the equation $y = kx^m$ over the number of units to be summed:

$$E(TT_N) = T_1\left(\frac{(N + 0.5)^{m+1} - (0.5)^{m+1}}{m + 1}\right) \tag{7}$$

where $E(TT_N)$ = the estimated value of TT_N, and the other symbols have been defined above.

Example 2 Cumulative Total Times for the Crawford Model

Determine the cumulative total time to complete the 20 work units in Example 1 using (a) the exact equation, equation (6) and (b) the approximation equation, equation (7).

Solution **(a)** Summing the unit times for units 1 through 20 using equation (6), we obtain

$$\begin{aligned} TT_{20} &= 10(1 + .800 + .7021 + 0.640 + 0.5956 + \ldots + 0.3812) \\ &= 104.85 \text{ hr} \end{aligned}$$

(b) Using the approximation equation, we obtain

$$E(TT_{20}) = 10\left(\frac{(20 + 0.5)^{1-0.32193} - (0.5)^{1-0.32193}}{1 - 0.32193}\right) = 105.12 \text{ hr}$$

This is a difference (error from the correct value of TT_{20}) of only 0.258%, probably good enough for most applications, given the randomness that is usually associated with time data of this kind.

Several observations can be made about the magnitude of the error associated with the approximation formula [12]. First, the size of the error is greater for steeper slopes (lower values of learning rate). Second, the accuracy of the approximation equation is better over large numbers of units (high values of N). Third, the greatest errors are associated with the earlier units, especially the first, second, and third units ($N = 1, 2$, and 3).

Equation (7) is a special case of the more general situation of summing between any two N values in the sequence, say between N_1, the lower value in the sequence, and N_2, the upper value in the sequence ($N_2 > N_1$). The sum of unit times between N_1 and N_2 can be approximated by the equation

$$E(TT_{N_1,N_2}) = E(TT_{N_2}) - E(TT_{N_1}) = T_1\left(\frac{(N_2 + 0.5)^{m+1} - (N_1 - 0.5)^{m+1}}{m + 1}\right) \tag{8}$$

where $E(TT_{N_1, N_2})$ = cumulative total time to complete units N_1 through N_2, inclusively, and the other terms have already been defined.

Example 3 Cumulative Total Times for Two Batches

The customer in Example 2 wants the 20 units produced in two separate batches of 10 units each, and the two batches are to be priced separately, taking into account the effect of the learning progression.

Solution: Whatever the pricing policy the supplier uses, total cumulative times must be determined for the first 10 units (units 1 through 10) and the second 10 units (units 11 through 20). For the first batch, equation (7) can be used:

$$E(TT_{10}) = 10\left(\frac{(10 + 0.5)^{1-0.32193} - (0.5)^{1-0.32193}}{1 - 0.32193}\right) = 63.42 \text{ hr}$$

For units 11 through 20, equation. (8) is used:

$$E(TT_{11,20}) = 10\left(\frac{(20 + 0.5)^{1-0.32193} - (11 - 0.5)^{1-0.32193}}{1 - 0.32193}\right) = 41.70 \text{ hr}$$

Note that the sums are equal to the total time for units 1 through 20 that we obtained in Example 2. ■

The final variable of interest in the Crawford model is the ***cumulative average time***—that is, the average time per work unit over a given total number of units. For the range from 1 through N units, the cumulative average time is given by

$$\overline{T}_N = \frac{TT_N}{N} \tag{9}$$

where $\overline{T}_N$ = the cumulative average time per unit, and TT_N = the total cumulative time to complete units 1 through N. The approximation $E(TT_N)$ from equation (7) can be substituted for TT_N when its computation would be too laborious.

Example 4 Cumulative Average Time with the Crawford Model

Use the Crawford model to compute the cumulative average time per work unit for the 20 units of the previous examples.

Solution: Given the total cumulative time for the 20 units from Example 2, the average cumulative time is simply

$$\overline{T}_{20} = \frac{104.85}{20} = 5.24 \text{ hr}$$ ■

When the range of interest is from N_1 to N_2, inclusively, then the computation can be accomplished using the following equation:

$$\overline{T}_{N_1,N_2} = \frac{TT_{N_2} - TT_{N_1-1}}{N_2 - N_1 + 1} \tag{10}$$

where $\overline{T}_{N_1,N_2}$ = cumulative average time for the range from N_1 through N_2, inclusively; TT_{N_2} = total cumulative time from the first unit through unit N_2; and TT_{N_1-1} = total cumulative time from the first unit through unit $N_1 - 1$.

1.2 The Wright Model

The Wright learning curve model was the first log-linear formula to be published. For many years it was the most widely used before being overtaken by the Crawford model. The difference between them is that the Wright model uses the cumulative average time as the dependent variable in the basic equation, whereas the Crawford model uses the unit time as the dependent variable. Thus, the Wright equation is given by

$$\overline{T}_N = T_1 N^m \tag{11}$$

where $\overline{T}_N$ = cumulative average time per unit, T_1 = time to complete the first work u (same value as in the Crawford equation), N = number of work units over which the cumulative average applies, and m = exponent related to the learning rate using equation (3).

In Section 1.3, we take a closer look at the differences between the Crawford and Wright models. For now, it is instructive to note that in the Crawford model, the unit time plots as a straight line on a log-log graph, whereas in the Wright model, the cumulative average time plots as a straight line on a log-log graph.

The total cumulative time for N units in the Wright learning curve model can be determined by either of two equations. First, since the cumulative average time is determined in the basic log-linear equation, equation (11), then the total cumulative time for N work units is simply N multiplied by $\overline{T}_N$. That is,

$$TT_N = N\overline{T}_N \tag{12}$$

where TT_N = total cumulative time for N work units. The alternative equation, which permits computation in one step instead of first finding $\overline{T}_N$ and then multiplying by N, is the following:

$$TT_N = T_1 N^{m+1} \tag{13}$$

The unit time in the Wright model is determined as the difference between successive total cumulative times for the N value of interest. That is,

$$T_N = TT_N - TT_{N-1} \tag{14}$$

where TT_N and TT_{N-1} are computed by either equations (12) or (13).

Example 5 Computation of $\overline{T}_N$, TT_N, and T_N Using the Wright Model

For the same parameter values of T_1 = 10 hr and LR = 80% used in the Crawford model of the previous examples, compute (a) $\overline{T}_N$, (b) TT_N, and (c) T_N for N = 20 using the Wright model.

Solution: To begin, we need the value of the slope m in the log-linear model. Using equation (3) for T_1 = 10 and LR = 0.80, we have

$$m = \frac{ln(0.80)}{ln 2} = -0.32193$$

This is the same value that we determined for the Crawford model in Example 1. No surprise: same equation, same value. However, in the Wright model, the dependent variable is the cumulate average time.

(a) Using equation (11), we have

$$\overline{T}_{20} = 10(20)^{-0.32193} = 10(0.3812) = 3.812 \text{ hr}$$

Again, we obtain the same value. Only now it is the cumulative average time rather than the unit time.

(b) The total cumulative time TT_N is determined by equation (12):

$$TT_{20} = 20(3.812) = 76.24 \text{ hr}$$

If we check this value against equation (13), we obtain

$$TT_{20} = 10(20)^{1-0.32193} = 10(20)^{0.67807} = 10(7.62416) = 76.24 \text{ hr}$$

(c) The unit time for the 20th unit is the difference in total cumulative times between the 20th and 19th units. We have TT_{20}; we need TT_{19}.

$$TT_{19} = 10(19)^{1-0.32193} = 10(19)^{0.67807} = 10(7.36354) = 73.64 \text{ hr}$$

The unit time $T_{20} = 76.24 - 73.64 = 2.60$ hr. ■

1.3 Comparison of the Crawford and Wright Models

Several comparisons of the Crawford and Wright learning curve models can be made from our example problems. The computed values are listed in Table 1. The first comparison is that the unit time value calculated by the Crawford model is the same as the cumulative average time by the Wright model. This is the basic difference between these two log-linear models, and all other differences follow directly from this fact. All of the values calculated by the Crawford model are larger than their counterparts from the Wright model. The cumulative average time for either model is always greater than the unit time because the average includes unit time values for lower values of N, and these time values are larger.

A further comparison is shown in Figure 3, which shows the values of T_N, TT_N, and $\overline{T}_N$ for the two models plotted on the same log-log graph for the learning curve parameters we have been using ($T_1 = 10.0$ and $LR = 80\%$). The unit time values (T_N) in the Crawford model coincide with the cumulative average time values ($\overline{T}_N$) in the Wright model, and the plot is a straight line in log-log coordinates. In both models, lines representing the unit time values are always lower than the cumulative average times, due to the averaging process. For the Crawford model, the lines representing the total cumulative times and average cumulative times are nonlinear. For the Wright model, the total cumulative time plot is linear in a log-log graph, whereas the unit time plot is nonlinear but tends toward being straight and parallel to the average cumulative time line for higher values of N.

TABLE 1 Comparison of Crawford and Wright Learning Curve Models for Example Problems

Model	T_1	LR	T_{20}	TT_{20}	$\overline{T}_{20}$
Crawford model	10.0	80%	3.81	104.85	5.24
Wright model	10.0	80%	2.60	76.24	3.81

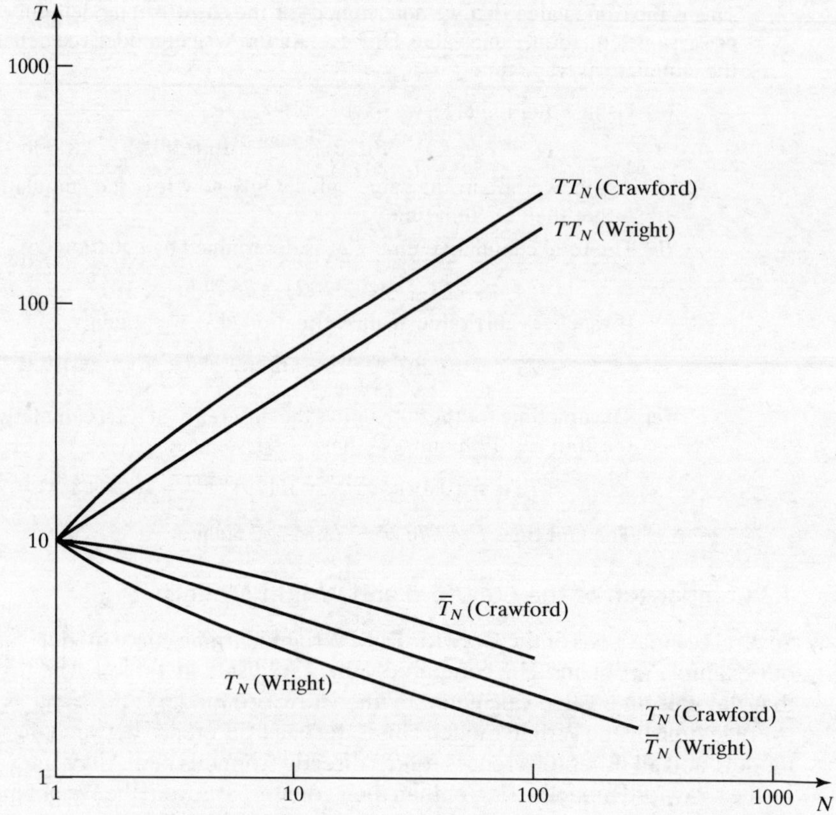

Figure 3 Unit times (T_N), total cumulative times (TT_N), and average cumulative times ($\overline{T}_N$) in the Crawford and Wright models for parameter values of $T_1 = 10$ and $LR = 80\%$.

Actual learning curve plots based on data collected in industry rarely exhibit the mathematical perfection that we see in our calculated values. There are random variations from a straight line when the data are plotted on log-log paper. In some cases, a log-linear model turns out not to be the best model to use, and several alternatives to the log-linear formula are explored in some of our references [2, 11, 12]. The trouble with the alternative learning curve equations is that they have more complex forms and require the valuation of more parameters than the log-linear model. A significant advantage of the log-linear model is its simplicity. It consists of only two parameters:

1. The time (or cost) associated with the first unit T_1.
2. The slope m, from which the learning rate LR can be deduced. Conversely, if the learning rate LR is known, the slope m can be determined.

Most learning curve analysts favor the log-linear form. Then the question arises: Which model should be used in a given industrial situation, Crawford or Wright? Probably the best answer to this question is whichever model best fits the data, if actual data are available. In some cases, owing to the time variations from one unit to the next, it is possible to fit either model (Crawford or Wright) to the data. The selection often reduces to the preference of the analyst. As indicated, most learning curve practitioners prefer the Crawford model, which emphasizes the task time of each individual work unit. In applications where averages are important, the Wright model may be advantageous.

A word of caution is in order here. We cannot determine the learning rate using one model and then apply that learning rate to the other model. An inference we can draw from Figure 3 is that, for the same set of data, the Wright model leads to a higher value of learning rate than the Crawford model. The following example proves the point.

Example 6 Crawford Model Versus Wright Model for the Same Data

We are given only that the time for the first unit T_1 is 10 hr and that the total cumulative time TT_{20} is 100 hr for 20 units. Determine the learning rate for (a) the Crawford model and (b) the Wright model.

Solution **(a)** Using our approximation formula for TT_N for the Crawford model, equation (7), and given that $N = 20$, we can set up the following equation:

$$E(TT_{20}) = 10\left(\frac{(20.5)^{m+1} - (0.5)^{m+1}}{m+1}\right) = 100$$

This requires a trial-and-error solution to determine the value of m, from which we can determine the learning rate LR. After several iterations, the value converges to $m = -0.3488$. Now using equation (4), $LR = 0.785$ or 78.5%.

(b) Using equation (13), the learning rate can be determined directly for the Wright model. For the given data,

$$100 = 10(20)^{m+1} \quad \text{or} \quad 10 = (20)^{m+1}$$
$$(m + 1)\, ln(20) = 2.9957(m + 1) = ln(10) = 2.30259$$
$$m + 1 = 2.30259/2.9957 = 0.7686$$
$$m = -0.23137$$
$$LR = 2^{-0.23137} = 0.852 \text{ or } 85.2\%$$

■

2 WHY THE LEARNING CURVE OCCURS

There are many reasons that can be given to explain why the learning curve occurs. It is appropriate to distinguish between the contributions to learning made by the worker and those made by the larger organization.

The worker's contributions are limited to those aspects of the work cycle that he or she can control. How is the worker able to reduce the cycle time as the number of work units increases? Here are some answers:

- The worker becomes familiar with the task; he or she "learns" the task.
- The worker makes fewer mistakes as the task is repeated.

- The worker's hand and body motions become more efficient, and a rhythm and pattern are developed in the work cycle.
- Minor adjustments are made in the workplace layout to reduce the distances moved.
- There are fewer delays that interrupt the operation.

The worker is not the only reason why the learning curve occurs for a given operation or product. The larger organization also contributes to improvement in ways beyond the control of the worker to effect reductions in cycle time. Its contributions also help to sustain the learning curve phenomenon. The term ***continuous improvement*** is sometimes used to refer to the constant search for ways to reduce cycle time and cost and to improve quality and effectiveness. Possible contributions to learning by the organization may include the following:

- Methods improvements by the industrial engineering department or other group whose objective is cost reduction
- Fine-tuning of machinery and tooling to eliminate delays and determine optimum operating conditions
- Development of special tooling that facilitates performing the task
- Technological improvements in processes, tooling, and machinery
- Product design improvements that make the product easier to make
- Improved quality of incoming materials so that variations and exceptions are reduced
- Management learning, such as better planning and scheduling

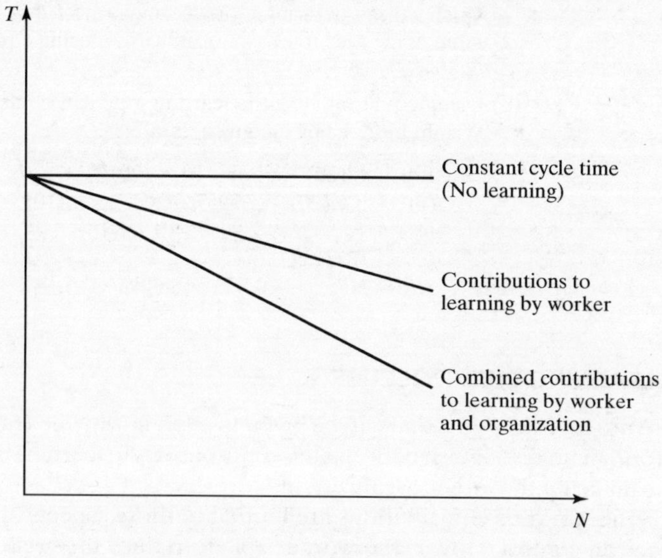

Figure 4 Contributions to the learning curve by the worker and the organization (log-log plot). The relative proportions are not to scale and will vary for different situations.

- Improved logistical support for the operation, such as minimizing delays due to lack of raw materials
- Better motivation of workers

Some of these improvements cause step function reductions in the cycle time; for example, the introduction of a new machine that performs at a faster cycle rate than the machine it replaces. Viewed in the long run, these step changes are part of the learning curve effect.

Contributions to the learning curve by the worker and the organization are illustrated in Figure 4. The horizontal line indicates the constant cycle time that would represent no learning in the operation. The intermediate sloping line indicates the contribution to learning by the worker only, and the bottom sloping line indicates the combined contributions of the worker and the organization.

3 DETERMINING THE LEARNING RATE

In practical applications of learning curve theory, the analyst must have accurate information that describes the learning behavior of the subjects being considered (e.g., the workers, worker teams, departments, products, or industries). For the log-linear learning curve, the most important information is the learning rate LR, from which the learning curve slope m in the basic Crawford or Wright equation can be readily calculated. Of course, the unit time of the first unit T_1 is also an important factor. Its value and the slope completely define the log-linear equation. However, the value of T_1 depends on the particular task or product of interest. For example, the value of T_1 for an entire product made of machined components would be much larger than T_1 for one component part in the product, but their learning rates would probably be quite similar. The learning rate LR is a more generic parameter. It will be our primary focus in the discussion that follows.

There are two ways to obtain the learning rate for a given application: (1) use industry averages and (2) analyze data from the actual application or very similar applications. Sometimes the values so obtained must be adjusted for factors such as interruptions in production or contributions of multiple departments whose learning rates are different. We examine these adjustments in Section 4.

3.1 Industry Averages

Some typical values of learning rate for the Crawford model are listed in Table 2 for types of work and industry categories. Industry learning rates tend to be composites of the different types of work accomplished in a particular industry. Other factors also affect these rates, such as the influences of management, labor unions, cultures, and customs within a given company or industry.

3.2 Using Data from the Application

Given that actual data are available from the application, the learning rate can be determined in several ways. We discuss the following methods here: (1) observing the doubling effect, (2) finding the slope from any two observations that do not possess the doubling effect, and (3) regression analysis using multiple observations.

TABLE 2 Typical Learning Rates (Crawford Model) for Various Types of Work and Industry Categories

Type of Work	Learning Rate (%)	Industry Category	Learning Rate (%)
Assembly, electrical harness	85	Aerospace	85
Assembly, electronics	85	Complex machine tools	75 to 85
Assembly, mechanical	84	Construction	70 to 90
Assembly of prototypes	65	Electronics manufacturing, repetitive	90 to 95
Clerical operations, repetitive	75–85	Machine shop, repetitive	90 to 95
Inspection	86	Punch press operations, repetitive	90 to 95
Machining, repetitive	90	Purchased parts	85 to 88
Sheet metal work	90	Raw materials	93 to 96
Welding	85–90	Shipbuilding	80 to 85

Sources: Compiled from [4, 8, 11, 12].

Observing the Doubling Effect. The learning rate is defined as the reduction in cycle time when the number of units doubles. Accordingly, the simplest way to estimate the learning rate for the Crawford model is to take the ratio of the unit time for the second unit as compared to the unit time for the first unit. That is,

$$LR = \frac{T_2}{T_1} \tag{15}$$

where LR = learning rate, T_2 = unit time for the second unit, and T_1 = unit time for the first unit.

The same estimating procedure can be applied every time the number of units doubles—that is, units 2 and 4, or units 4 and 8, or units 5 and 10, and so on. In general,

$$LR = \frac{T_{2N}}{T_N} \tag{16}$$

where N is any unit number, and $2N$ is double that number. The same basic approach can be used for the Wright model, except the values used in the ratio are the cumulative average times rather than the unit times.

Finding the Slope from Any Two Observations. If data are not available to observe the doubling effect in unit time values, any two values can be used to determine the slope of the learning curve, and from the slope the learning rate can be found. For the log-linear equation, the data must be transformed by taking the logarithms for any two sets of N and T_N values. The slope is then calculated for the Crawford model using the following equation:

$$m = \frac{lnT_{N_2} - lnT_{N_1}}{ln(N_2) - ln(N_1)} \tag{17}$$

where m = learning curve slope, and T_{N_2} and T_{N_1} are the unit times for units N_2 and N_1, respectively. In our equation, we have used the natural logarithms of the data, but base 10 logarithms can also be used. A similar approach can be applied to the Wright model, only using cumulative average times rather than unit times.

Once the slope is determined, then the learning rate can be determined using equation (4), which is repeated here: $LR = 2^m$.

Regression Analysis Using Multiple Observations. The trouble with the two preceding methods is that both are based on only two observations. There are bound to be statistical variations in learning curve data, and these methods do not average these variations. When multiple data values are available, least squares curve-fitting procedures, or regression analysis, can be used to determine the parameters m and T_1 of the learning curve equation. Because the form of the equation is log-linear, the data must be transformed to their logarithmic values, using either natural logarithms or logs to the base 10. Statistical curve-fitting procedures are available in commercial spreadsheet software such as Microsoft Excel, and these procedures will not be included in our coverage.

A simpler alternative to using least-squares techniques is to plot the data on log-log paper and determine the slope by fitting a straight line through the data by eye. The slope must be determined by measuring the rise over the run using a linear scale or ruler.

4 FACTORS AFFECTING THE LEARNING CURVE

The type of work being accomplished and the industry category are not the only factors that affect the learning rate. The other factors that may influence its value and the general behavior of the learning curve are discussed in this section.

4.1 Learning in Worker-Machine Systems

It is reasonable to believe that when a work cycle consists of a worker-controlled portion and a machine-controlled portion, the worker's manual portion will be affected by the learning curve phenomenon, but the machine's portion will not because it operates on a constant cycle time. Accordingly, the overall learning rate in the task will be greater (the rate of improvement will be less) than for a task that is entirely worker-controlled. There is evidence to support this belief. When the learning rates for different types of work and industries in Table 2 are compared, we find that the types of operations that contain a higher proportion of machine involvement (e.g., machining, punch press operations) have higher learning rates than those that are more manual (e.g., assembly, clerical, fabricating complex machine tools, construction).

An estimate of the learning rate for a worker-machine system can be based on the relative proportions of time that the worker and machine contribute to the entire cycle. That is,

$$LR_{w-m} = p_w LR_w + p_m LR_m \tag{18}$$

where LR_{w-m} = learning rate of worker-machine system; p_w = proportion of cycle time controlled by worker; LR_w = learning rate associated with worker, p_m = proportion of the cycle time controlled by machine; and LR_m = learning rate associated with machine, assumed to be 100% ($LR_m = 1.0$ in the equation). The values of p_w and p_m can be readily determined from the operation, although these values will change over time as learning occurs. The difficulty comes in deciding the appropriate value of the worker's learning rate LR_w. A value of 70% has been proposed as representative of the learning rate in pure manual labor [12].[4]

The assumption that no learning occurs in the machine-controlled portion of the cycle ($LR_m = 1.0$) should be challenged. There are various opportunities for machine cycle time reduction, depending on the type of operation and the level of automation that is possible. For example, in a machining operation such as turning, the use of a more advanced tool material (e.g., a coated carbide to replace a conventional cemented carbide) would permit faster cutting speeds with a corresponding reduction in the machining cycle time. And the use of a CNC turning center to replace an engine lathe might allow some of the nonproductive steps in the cycle to be reduced or eliminated.[5]

4.2 Composite Learning Curve

The ***composite learning curve*** refers to the situation in which a learning rate is to be determined for a large entity of work, such as an entire product, and this learning rate is a function of the learning rates of the various types of work that contribute to its completion. How should the learning rates of the contributing work categories be combined to determine the composite learning rate?

One approach is to compute a weighted average similar to the procedure used above for the worker-machine system. This method is described in [11] and is attributed to McCampbell and McQueen.[6] The approach reduces to the following formula:

$$LR_c = \sum_i p_i LR_i \tag{19}$$

where LR_c = composite learning rate, p_i = proportion of work content contributed by work category i, LR_i = learning rate associated with work category i, and the summation process is carried out over all of the work categories that produce the product (or other work entity). Of course, the p_i values must sum to 1.0.

Rougher estimating methods have been proposed for composite learning. An example is the set of benchmark values presented in Table 3 for various proportions of assembly work and machine work that make up the product.

[4]The proposed value is given in the context of discussing a method published by E. B. Cochran in *Planning Production Costs: Using the Improvement Curve* (Chandler Publishing, San Francisco, 1968) and should probably be attributed to him rather than Teplitz.

[5]CNC stands for computer numerical control, "a form of (computer-controlled) automation in which the mechanical actions of a piece of equipment are controlled by a program containing coded alphanumerical data" [6].

[6]E. W. McCampbell and C. W. McQueen, "Cost Estimating from the Learning Curve," *Aero Digest*, 73 (1956):36.

TABLE 3 Composite Learning Rates for Various Combinations of Assembly Labor and Machine Labor

Proportion of Assembly Labor (%)	Proportion of Machine Labor (%)	Composite Learning Rate (%)
75	25	80
50	50	85
25	75	90

Source: T. G. Vayda, "How to Use the Learning Curve for Planning and Control," *Cost and Management* (July-August 1972): 28, cited in [2].

4.3 Interruptions in the Learning Curve

The learning curve effect is often disrupted by breaks in production. Some of the many possible reasons for interruptions include the following: (1) batch production, in which a given part or product is manufactured in a specified order quantity and there is a time delay (e.g., weeks, months, years) before the next order for the same part or product is received, (2) labor strikes, (3) vacations, either of individual workers or an entire plant, and (4) raw material shortages.

Such interruptions in continuous production are likely to cause a loss in the progression of learning that would otherwise be maintained had the interruption not occurred. The learning loss, known as ***remission***, shows itself as an upward step in the cycle time when production is resumed after the break, as illustrated in Figure 5. Loss of learning may occur during production interruptions for the following reasons: (1) the worker

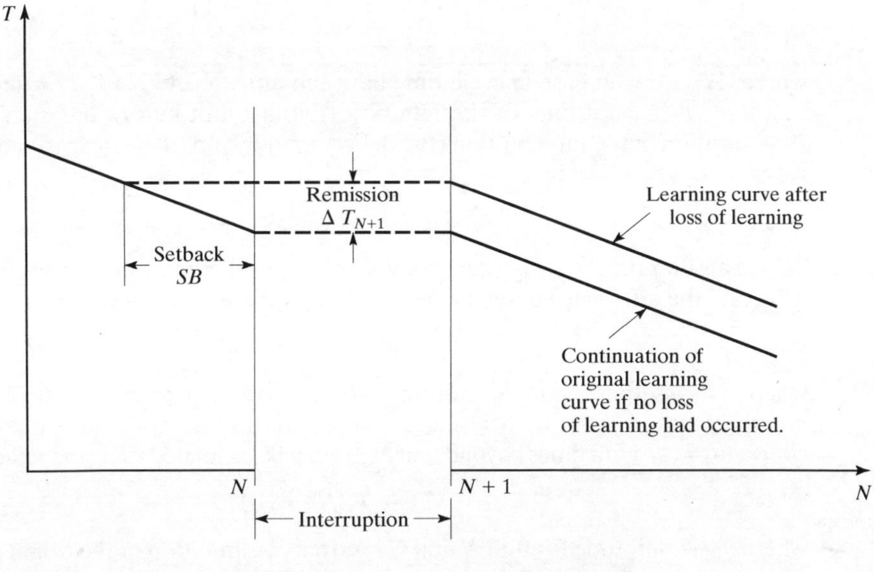

Figure 5 Loss of learning due to an interruption in production.

actually forgets some or all of what had been learned prior to the interruption, (2) new workers are substituted for workers previously assigned to perform the task, (3) the standard method description for the task is lost, (4) the supervisor forgets the subtle tricks not included in the standard method description that made the task more efficient when it ran before, (5) the special tooling that was designed for the task is lost or forgotten, and (6) the workplace is not as efficiently laid out as before.

With reference to Figure 5, ***remission*** in the learning curve is defined as the increase in cycle time between units N and $N + 1$. Associated with remission is the ***setback***, defined as the number of units lost along the N scale—that is, the difference between $N+1$ and the number corresponding to the work unit whose cycle time is equal to T_{N+1}. A key question remains: How can we estimate the magnitudes of the remission and setback, as well as the behavior of the learning curve after unit $N + 1$ for a given situation?

Smith [11] proposes a simple method for answering this question, based on his experience in industrial applications of the learning curve phenomenon. The method assumes that time is the single most important factor in learning loss and that the duration of the interruption is the only variable that influences remission and setback. Two additional assumptions about the effect of the duration are then made. First, if the duration of the interruption exceeds 12 months, then resuming production after the break would be the same as starting over for the first time. In other words, T_{N+1} is equal to the original T_1. Second, if the duration of the interruption is less than one month, there is no appreciable learning loss and therefore no effect on remission. The learning curve picks up exactly from where it left off before the break. If we apply these assumptions, the remission (increase in cycle time following an interruption in production) can be predicted by means of the following formula:

$$\Delta T_{N+1} = (T_1 - T_N)\left(\frac{D - 1}{11}\right) \tag{20}$$

where ΔT_{N+1} = increase in cycle time between units N and $N+1$; T_1 = unit time of the first unit; T_N = unit time of the Nth unit (the last unit before the interruption); and D = duration of the interruption (the delay) rounded up to the nearest month. Thus, the value of T_{N+1} is given by

$$T_{N+1} = T_N + \Delta T_{N+1} \tag{21}$$

This unit time T_{N+1} is equal (or very close) to the unit time for an earlier unit, call it N_e, and the difference between $N+1$ and N_e is the setback. Expressed as an equation,

$$SB = (N + 1) - N_e \tag{22}$$

where SB = setback, number of units; $N + 1$ = number of the first unit following the interruption; and N_e = number of unit prior to interruption whose unit time is equal to (or closest to) T_{N+1}. Unit times beyond unit $N + 1$ can be estimated using the setback as follows:

$$T_N = T_1(N - SB)^m \tag{23}$$

where T_N = unit time for unit N and N is now a continuation of the original units count; T_1 = unit time for original first unit; and SB = setback, defined by equation (22).

Similar adjustments can be made using the setback SB to estimate the total cumulative times TT_N and average cumulative times $\overline{T}_N$.

Example 7 Predicting the Effects of an Interruption in Production

A part is to be produced in batches. The first unit of production takes 10 hours to complete and the learning rate for this type of part is known to be 80% (Crawford model). The first order is for 30 units. The second order is expected in 4 months for another 30 units. Determine (a) the cycle time for the first unit in the second batch, (b) the setback, and (c) the total time to produce the second batch compared to the total time to produce that batch if no interruption had occurred.

Solution **(a)** To apply equation (21), we need the value of T_{30}, the last unit in the first batch of 30. We know from previous examples that the slope m corresponding to an 80% learning rate is $m = -0.32193$:

$$T_{30} = 10(30)^{-0.32193} = 10(0.33456) = 3.35 \text{ hr}$$

$$\text{The remission } \Delta T_{31} = (10 - 3.35)\left(\frac{4-1}{11}\right) = 6.65(0.273) = 1.81 \text{ hr}$$

$$T_{31} = 3.35 + 1.81 = 5.16 \text{ hr}$$

(b) To determine the setback, we must find the number corresponding to the previous work unit whose cycle time is equal to 5.16 hr. We can use the Crawford log-linear equation to solve for N:

$$5.16 = 10\,(N)^{-0.32193}$$
$$(N)^{-0.32193} = 0.516$$
$$-0.32193\, ln\,(N) = ln\,(0.516) = -0.66165$$
$$ln(N) = 2.0553$$
$$N = 7.81$$

which is rounded up to unit 8. This is a setback of 31 − 8 or 23 work units.

(c) The total cumulative time to produce the second batch is calculated using the approximation equation but including the effect of setback.

$$E(TT_{31,60}) = 10\left(\frac{(60.5-23)^{0.67807} - (30.5-23)^{0.67807}}{0.67807}\right) = 10(11.438) = 114.38 \text{ hr}$$

If the 4-month interruption had not occurred but instead units 31 through 60 had been a continuation of the previous production run, then the total cumulative time would have been the following:

$$E(TT_{31,60}) = 10\left(\frac{(60.5)^{0.67807} - (30.5)^{0.67807}}{0.67807}\right) = 10(8.848) = 88.48 \text{ hr}$$

According to our calculations, the interruption of 4 months has caused an increase in total production time of 114.38 − 88.48 = 25.9 hr. ■

4.4 Other Factors that Affect the Learning Curve

The following additional factors have been found to influence the behavior of the learning curve in industrial practice: (1) product complexity, (2) preproduction planning, (3) labor turnover, and (4) the plateau model.

Product complexity is measured by factors such as the number of components in a final assembly or the direct labor time content in fabricating the product. Greater product complexity has been found to provide more opportunities for learning, and this tends to be reflected in higher values of first unit time or cost and steeper learning slopes (lower learning rates and higher rates of improvement). In general, if the time to complete the first unit (T_1) is high, either due to product complexity or perhaps because a somewhat casual effort was devoted to the first unit of production, then there exist greater opportunities to reduce the production times of subsequent units.

The converse is also true. If the amount of ***preproduction planning*** prior to the first unit is high, then T_1 will be depressed, and the slope m will be flatter. Preproduction planning includes the following kinds of activities:

- *Tooling.* Production tools, fixtures, jigs, and gauges designed to facilitate the production operation and reduce cycle time.
- *Machine selection.* Choosing the most appropriate production equipment for the operation.
- *Methods analysis.* Industrial engineering studies of the tasks to be performed to try to find the most efficient method.
- *Product design.* Efforts in design for manufacture (DFM) and design for assembly (DFA) to develop a product design that will be easier to produce.
- *Worker training.* Training of workers in the tasks they will perform prior to actual production.
- *Scheduling and logistics support.* Making sure that parts and materials are available at the start of production.

When greater attention is paid to preproduction planning by the organization, there are fewer opportunities for later reductions in unit times. Accordingly, the first unit time and cost are lower, and the learning rate LR is higher (flatter slope m).

Labor turnover, bringing in new workers to replace workers who have retired or moved to other jobs, disrups learning. This is reflected in the learning curve as lower rates of improvement and higher values of learning rate. When workers are moved to new jobs, whatever improvements they had brought to their tasks tend to be lost, and new workers must start the learning process all over again. Also, the experienced workers who do not move spend more time teaching the new workers and less time continuing the learning curve progression.

The ***plateau model*** refers to the sometimes-held belief that learning eventually ceases, resulting in the learning curve shape shown in Figure 6. In the plateau model, there are two phases that occur in the plot of cycle time (or other dependent variable) and number of units: (1) start-up phase, during which learning progresses according to a log-linear or similar function, and (2) steady-state phase, in which no further improvement

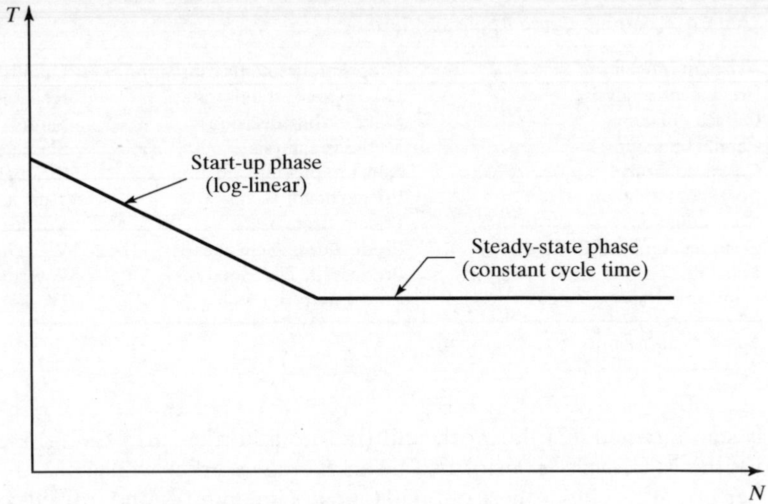

Figure 6 The plateau learning curve model.

in the dependent variable occurs. In the steady-state phase, the curve flattens out, perhaps suddenly as we have depicted in our figure, or more gradually, as if approaching some asymptotic limit. Various propositions have been offered to explain the plateau phenomenon [12]: (1) in a worker-machine system, the worker is finally limited from further improvement by the speed of the equipment, (2) workers are able to achieve a rate of production that is greater than standard performance, and there is no incentive for them to work faster, (3) management is unwilling or unable to invest in newer and more productive technology that would sustain the learning curve progression, and (4) management does not believe the learning curve can continue indefinitely, and this becomes a self-fulfilling prophecy.

5 LEARNING CURVE APPLICATIONS

There are many work situations in which the learning curve phenomenon can be applied. It is doubtful that all of the opportunities for its application have been realized at this point in the study of this phenomenon. More applications are sure to be found in the future. To demonstrate the wide applicability of learning curves, we have compiled a general list of application areas in Table 4. Our end-of-chapter problem set also provides an instructive survey of the many potential applications of learning curves.

6 TIME STANDARDS VERSUS THE LEARNING CURVE

It may seem that there is a fundamental contradiction between the learning curve phenomenon and time standards. The time standard for a given work cycle is a constant value that is defined under the following conditions: (1) the method used by the worker

TABLE 4 Learning Curve Application Areas

Accident prevention	Labor requirements estimating	Quality control
Break-even analysis	Labor (time) standards	Reliability analysis
Capacity planning	Make-or-buy decisions	Safety
Capital budgeting	Methods analysis	Shop performance analysis
Cost accounting	New product introduction	Strategic planning
Cost estimating	Pricing negotiations	Time and motion studies
Cost reduction	Pricing strategies	Vendor selection
Contract administration	Product design changes	Wage incentives
Economic order quantity analysis	Product life cycle analysis	Warranty maintenance
Failure analysis	Productivity analysis	Worker performance analysis

Source: Compiled from [2, 11, 12, and 13].

is standardized, (2) the work unit (before and after processing) is standardized, and (3) the work cycle is performed by an average worker whose pace is equal to standard performance. Under these defined (and documented) standardized conditions, the standard time is a constant. By contrast, the learning curve indicates that the actual time for the work cycle will decrease over time, according to a constant learning rate every time the number of units doubles. How can a constant value (the standard time) be reconciled with the decreases in cycle time predicted by the learning curve?

First, let us recognize that although the standard time is a constant, the actual cycle time for a given manual task is a variable whose value changes from one cycle to the next. One of the reasons for the variation is because the worker learns the task, thus becoming more proficient at doing it and gradually reducing the cycle time as the number of repetitions increases. This is predicted by the learning curve. As long as there are no changes in the standard method or the standard work unit, it seems fair to give credit to the worker for any reductions in cycle time that result from the improvement of his or her own skill, effort, pace, consistency, and other attributes associated with learning the job. Let the worker reap the benefits of this learning process, including any rewards that may come from superior performance, such as incentive pay bonuses.

However, if the reductions in cycle time result from changes in the method or work unit, such as the use of a better tool or a new machine to perform the task or a redesign of the part that makes it easier to produce, then these changes require a revision in the definition of standard method and/or work unit, which in turn calls for a new time standard. These kinds of changes are usually made by industrial or manufacturing engineering in the case of methods and product design engineering in the case of the work unit. In the end, the method and work unit for a given task are the responsibility of management, and establishing a new time standard is justified when improvements are made in these input factors of the work cycle. By making methods improvements and product design changes, and then revising the corresponding time standards for the affected operations, management is perpetuating the learning curve effect.

Of course, the technicality of who is responsible becomes an issue when methods changes are made by the worker without notifying management or the supporting staff engineering departments (changes in work unit are more difficult for the worker to make, because of the more detailed specifications and drawings used in product design).

The worker has surreptitiously found a way to improve the method (that is, to "beat the system") and does not want to share the discovery with the larger organization. This is especially a problem when the worker's pay is based on a wage incentive plan. Trying to decide what's fair in this case is a matter of viewpoint. The worker may feel that he or she is entitled to whatever benefit (and incentive bonus) results from the improvement by right of being its inventor. However, the fact is that the time standard, and any incentive bonus based on it, is no longer valid because the standard method is no longer used in the task. It does not matter whether the change in method was made by the worker or a staff support department. The method has changed, and so too must the time standard. Perhaps a suggestion system, in which the worker is rewarded for recommending methods improvements in the task, is a way to deal with this difficult matter of who is responsible for a methods improvement.

The second issue that is germane to this discussion of time standards versus learning curves is concerned with the following question: Given that we acknowledge the existence of the learning curve, at what value of N should the time standard be set? Surely the worker must be given ample opportunity to learn the work cycle before his or her performance is measured against the time standard for it. In addition, the quantity of the production run is important in answering this question. The term ***standard reference quantity*** (SRQ) should be introduced here; it is the discrete quantity of production (e.g., 10, 100, 1000 units) for which the standard time for the task is applicable. It is the production quantity for which the standard is valid. If the actual quantity of production is different from the SRQ, then an adjustment in the standard should be made to reflect the difference. The situation is illustrated in Figure 7. If the actual production quantity differs from the SRQ, then the standard time is adjusted by the ratio on the vertical axis corresponding to the actual quantity to reflect the learning curve effect. It should be mentioned that not all companies bother to make this adjustment in setting time standards.

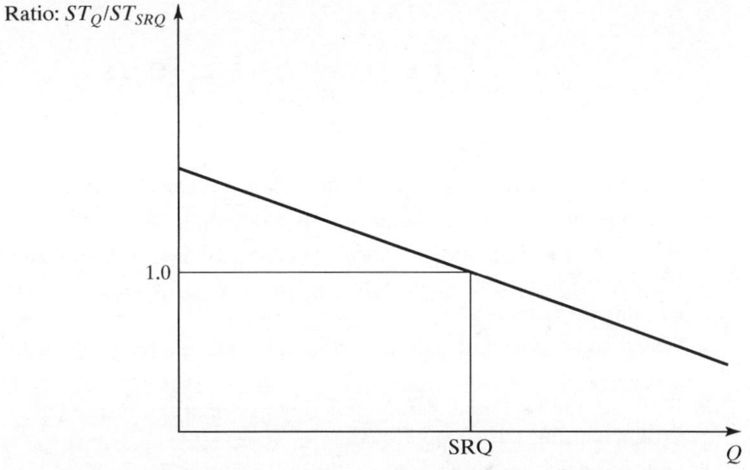

Figure 7 The standard reference quantity (SRQ) for a hypothetical work cycle (log-log plot).

REFERENCES

[1] ANSI Standard Z94.0-1989. *Industrial Engineering Terminology*. Norcross, GA: Industrial Engineering and Management Press, Institute of Industrial Engineers, 1989.

[2] Belkaoui, A. *The Learning Curve: A Management Accounting Tool*. Westport, CT: Quorum Books, 1986.

[3] Chase R., and N. Aquilano, *Production and Operations Management*. 5th ed. Homewood, IL: Irwin, 1989.

[4] Delionback, L. M. "Learning Curves and Progress Functions." Pp. 157–81 in *Cost Estimator's Reference Manual*, edited by R. D. Stewart and R. M. Wyskida. New York: Wiley, 1987.

[5] Engwall, R. L. "Learning Curves." Pp. 5.145–5.161 in *Maynard's Industrial Engineering Handbook*, 4th ed., edited by W. K. Hodson. New York: McGraw-Hill, 1992.

[6] Groover, M. P. *Fundamentals of Modern Manufacturing: Materials, Process, and Systems*. 3rd ed. New York: Wiley, 2007.

[7] Hancock, W. M., and F. H. Bayha. "The Learning Curve." Pp. 1585–98 in *Handbook of Industrial Engineering*. 2nd ed., edited by G. Salvendy. New York: Wiley; Institute of Industrial Engineers, Norcross, GA, 1992.

[8] Konz, S., and S. Johnson. *Work Design: Industrial Ergonomics*. 5th ed. Scottsdale, AZ: Holcomb Hathaway Publishers, 2000.

[9] Niebel, B. W., "Time Study." Pp. 1599–638 in *Handbook of Industrial Engineering*, 2nd ed., edited by G. Salvendy. New York: Wiley; Institute of Industrial Engineers, Norcross, GA, 1992.

[10] Niebel, B.W., and A. Freivalds. *Methods, Standards, and Work Design*. 11th ed. New York: McGraw-Hill, 2003.

[11] Smith, J. *Learning Curve for Cost Control*. Norcross, GA: Industrial Engineering and Management Press, Institute of Industrial Engineers, 1989.

[12] Teplitz, C. J. *The Learning Curve Workbook*. New York: Quorum Books, 1991.

[13] Wright, T. P. "Factors Affecting the Cost of Airplanes," *Journal of Aeronautical Sciences* 3 (1936): 122–128.

[14] Yelle, L. E. "The Learning Curve: Historical Review and Comprehensive Survey." *Decision Sciences* 10(1979): 302–28.

REVIEW QUESTIONS

1 Describe the learning curve phenomenon.

2 Define the term *learning rate*.

3 What is the rate of improvement and how is it related to the learning rate?

4 Which value of learning rate means faster learning, 75% or 90%?

5 Why is the basic equation in learning curve theory, $y = kx^m$, called a log-linear model?

6 What is the basic difference between the Crawford equation and the Wright equation in learning curve theory?

7 Why does the cumulative average time always have a higher value than the unit time in the log-linear equation?

8 What are the two basic parameters that are required to use either the Crawford or the Wright learning curve equations?

9 How is the worker able to reduce the cycle time as the number of work units increases?

10 How is the larger organization able to reduce the cycle time as the number of work units increases?

11 What are the two ways to obtain the value of the learning rate for a given application?

12 What is the simplest way to estimate the learning rate based on actual data?

13 Why is it reasonable to believe that the learning rate for a worker-machine system will be higher than for pure manual work?

14 What is a composite learning curve?

15 What is remission when used in the context of an interruption in the learning curve?

16 How does product complexity affect the learning curve?

17 What is the likely effect of greater preproduction planning on the first unit time T_1 and the slope m in the log-linear learning curve?

18 What is the plateau model in learning curve terminology?

19 What does the term *standard reference quantity* mean in the context of learning curves?

PROBLEMS

Learning Curve Theory

1 In a mechanical assembly operation, the first work unit required 7.83 min to complete and the learning rate for mechanical assembly is 84% in the Crawford model. Using this learning curve model, determine the unit times to produce (a) the second unit, (b) the 10th unit, and (c) the 100th unit. (d) What are the total cumulative time and the average cumulative time for the 100 units?

2 In a certain manual operation, the first work unit required 7.83 min to complete and the learning rate is known to be 84% in the Wright model. Using this learning curve model, determine the average cumulative times to produce (a) the second unit, (b) the 10th unit, and (c) the 100th unit. (d) Find the total cumulative time for the 100 units and the unit time for the 100th unit.

3 The unit time for the first unit of production is 72 hr and the total cumulative time for 50 units is 2347 hr. Determine the learning rate for (a) the Crawford learning curve model and (b) the Wright learning curve model.

4 A metal fabrication shop would like to know what the learning rate is for a certain section of the plant that makes welded assemblies. In one case study, a total of four assemblies were completed. Records were kept for units 1 and 4, and the times were 60 hr and 48.6 hr, respectively. Unfortunately, the times for units 2 and 3 were lost. Use the Crawford learning curve model to determine the learning rate indicated by the data.

5 A worker produces 13 parts during the first day on a new job, and the first part takes 46 min (unit time). On the second day, the worker produces 20 parts, and the 20th part on the second day takes 18 min. Using the Crawford learning curve model, determine (a) the learning rate and (b) the total cumulative time to produce all 33 parts.

6 A welder produces 7 welded assemblies during the first day on a new job, and the seventh assembly takes 45 min (unit time). The worker produces 10 welded assemblies on the second day, and the 10th assembly on the second day takes 30 min. Given this information, (a) what is the learning rate percentage and (b) what is the total cumulative time to produce all 17 welded assemblies? Use the Crawford learning curve model.

7 Four units of a welded steel product have been completed and are being shipped to the customer by 18-wheeler tractor-trailer. The same worker welded all units. The total time to complete all four units was 100 hr. If the learning rate applicable to the fabrication of products of this type is known to be 84%, what were the unit times for each of the four units? Use the Crawford learning curve model.

8 Solve the previous problem but use the Wright learning curve model instead of the Crawford model.

9 A new commercial aircraft is being produced by Penn Airplane Company. Records indicate that the first unit of the new plane required 100,000 hrs (unit time) to complete, and a cumulative total of 534,591 hrs had been spent by the time the eighth aircraft was completed. Assuming a constant learning rate was in effect, determine (a) the learning rate percentage, and (b) the most likely unit time required to build the 20th airplane. Use the Crawford learning curve model.

10 Solve the previous problem but use the Wright learning curve model instead of the Crawford model.

11 Fifty units of a special pump product are scheduled to be made for a Middle Eastern country to move water across the desert. A team of four workers will make the pumps, and they have already produced three units. Time records for the first unit were not kept; however, the second and third units took 15.0 hr and 13.4 hr, respectively. Using the Crawford learning curve model, determine (a) the percent learning rate, (b) the most likely time it took to do the first unit, and (c) how long it will take to complete the entire quantity of 50 units if the learning rate continues.

12 An assembled product is built by 10 workers who coordinate their tasks. A total of 100 units will be made. Time records indicate that the 10 workers took a total of 95 hrs (unit time) to complete the first unit of the product. Times to complete the second and third units of work are not available; however, the fourth work unit took 71 hr to complete. Determine (a) the learning rate percentage and (b) the most likely times required to complete the second and third units. (c) If the learning rate continues, how long will it take to complete the 100th unit? (d) What is the expected total time that will be expended by the ten workers on all 100 units?

13 A new product will be produced in the factory by six workers, each contributing to its total work content. A total of 500 units will be made. Time records indicate that the six workers took a total of 8.25 hr (unit time) to complete the first unit of the product. The time to complete the second unit of work is not available; however, the third work unit took 6.50 hr to complete. Using the Crawford learning curve model, determine (a) the learning rate percentage, (b) the most likely time it took to do the second unit, and (c) how long it will take to complete the last unit (500th unit) if the learning rate continues,? (d) What is the expected total cumulative time to complete all 500 units?

Interruptions in Learning

14 An assembled product is to be made in batches. The first unit of production takes 92.7 min to complete and the learning rate for this type of part is known to be 85% in the Crawford learning curve model. The first batch was for 100 units. The second order is expected in 6 months for another 100 units. Determine (a) the cycle time for the first unit in the second batch, (b) the setback, and (c) the total time to produce the second batch compared with the total time to produce that batch if no interruption had occurred.

Learning Curve Applications

15 A firm specializes in customizing vans and trucks for its clients. For a certain order for five customized vans, it took 90 hours to remake the first unit, but time records were not kept for the other four vehicles. The firm knows that a learning rate of 82% is typical for its jobs.

(a) If the firm charges $40/hr, how much should it charge the client for this order? (b) If labor cost is $20/hr and average materials cost per van is $800, how much profit did the firm realize on the five units? (c) On the other hand, if the firm prices the first job at cost (labor cost and materials) plus 15%, and makes its profit on the remaining models on the basis of the learning curve effect, what is the firm's total profit for all five vans? Use the Crawford learning curve model.

16 An automobile-customizing firm makes alterations on new cars to satisfy individual requirements of its clients. Jobs include customizing of cars for police and fire departments, limousine fleets, etc. For a certain order for four customized cars, it took 100 hr to remake the first unit, but time cards were lost for the remaining three vehicles. However, the firm knows that a learning rate of 80% is typical for its jobs. If the firm charges $30/hr, how much should it charge the client for this order? Use the Crawford learning curve model.

17 A team of workers produced a total of 12 special processing machines for a large pharmaceutical company. Unfortunately, time records were documented for only the 12th unit, and the labor hours expended on this unit totaled 137 hr. Although the firm did not record the labor hours for the previous 11 units, it knows from past experience that a learning rate of 86% is typical for worker teams producing machines of this general type. The cost of component parts per machine is $3000, and the labor cost is $18/hr. In setting the price for the 12 machines, the policy is to charge $35 per labor hour and to mark up the component parts cost by 20%. (a) How much should the pharmaceutical company be charged for the 12 machines? (b) How much profit was realized on the 12 machines? Use the Crawford learning curve model.

18 The learning curve phenomenon is one of the reasons why an assembly line with n stations is capable of out-producing n single workstations, where each single station does the entire work content of the job. Consider the case of a product whose theoretical work content time for the first unit is 20 min. The effect of an 85% learning rate is to be compared for two cases, using the Crawford learning curve model:

- Ten single workstations, each doing the entire assembly task
- One perfectly balanced 10-station assembly line, where each station does 2.0 minutes of the total work content.

For the 1000th unit produced, determine the rate of production of (a) the 10 single workstations, and (b) the 10-station assembly line. Use the Crawford learning curve model.

19 An important customer is considering the ABC Company as a contractor for an assembly job to produce 500 units of a certain subassembly that is used on one of its products. The customer will let the contract to ABC for an average cumulative time of 10 hr per unit at an allowed labor rate that is attractive to ABC. The customer has provided two sets of component parts for the subassembly for analysis of the job. After a minimum of preplanning, ABC sets up a trial assembly workstation and its assembly team is able to complete the first unit in 27.4 hr and the second unit in 21.8 hr. Using the Wright learning curve model, evaluate whether the terms of the contract are favorable to ABC.

20 Solve the previous problem but use the Crawford learning curve model instead of the Wright model.

21 The ABC Company uses a screening test for job applicants in its assembly department. Since the typical assembly work in the department is batch assembly in quantities between 10 and 100 units per batch, the screening test requires the applicant to achieve a unit time of 15 min on the tenth unit for a certain assembly task that has been designed specifically for the test. However, although this is the test that all concerned parties in the company have agreed to, it has been decided that requiring the worker to perform 10 repetitions of the assembly task would be too time-consuming, not only for the applicant but for ABC personnel as well. An alternative test has been proposed in which the applicant would perform only two cycles of the test assembly task, and the results would be analyzed to determine if the applicant is likely to be capable of finishing the tenth cycle in 15 min. Determine which of the following applicants passes the screening test: (a) an applicant who finishes the first and second units in 40.0 min and 30.4 min, respectively, or (b) an applicant who finishes the first and second units in 29.0 min and 23.5 min, respectively. Use the Crawford learning curve model in your analysis.

Lean Production

In this chapter, we examine several additional approaches related to methods engineering. These approaches are aimed at increasing productivity, reducing cost, improving quality, and solving problems in the operations of an organization. These objectives are basically the same as those in methods engineering. In many ways, the topics discussed here are adaptations and modifications of the previous methods engineering techniques and principles. However, these alternative approaches are of more recent vintage than the traditional methods engineering programs, and they represent a more contemporary view of work and the social environment in which it is performed. One of the distinguishing characteristics of this current view is that the active participation of the worker should be enlisted in the improvement activities. The new approaches can be presented in two ways: (1) lean production, a highly efficient production system developed at Toyota Motors in Japan, and (2) Six Sigma, a quality improvement procedure that seeks perfection.

Lean production means doing more work with fewer resources. It is an adaptation of mass production in which work is accomplished in less time, smaller space, with fewer workers and less equipment, and yet achieving higher quality levels in the final product. Lean production also means giving customers what they want and satisfying or surpassing their expectations. Lean production is based on the way manufacturing operations were organized at the Toyota Motors Company in Japan during the 1980s. Toyota had pioneered a system of production that was quite different from the mass production techniques used by automobile companies in the United States and Europe. The Toyota Production System, as it was called before the term "lean" was applied to it, began to evolve in the 1950s to cope with the realities of Japan's postwar economy (e.g., a much smaller domestic auto market than in the United States or Europe and a scarcity of Japanese investment capital for plant and equipment). To deal with these challenges, Toyota developed a production system that could produce a variety of car models with fewer quality problems, lower inventory levels, smaller manufacturing lot sizes for the parts used in the cars, and reduced lead times to produce the cars. Development of the Toyota Production System was led by Taiichi Ohno (Historical Note 1). In this chapter, we examine the methods used at Toyota that have come to be called lean production.

HISTORICAL NOTE 1 LEAN PRODUCTION

The person credited with developing the Toyota Production System is Taiichi Ohno (1912–1990), an engineer and executive at Toyota Motors. In the post–World War II period, the Japanese automotive industry had to basically start over. Ohno visited a U.S. auto plant to learn American production methods. However, the car market in Japan was much smaller than its U.S. counterpart, so a Japanese plant could not afford the large production runs and huge work-in-process inventories that were common in the United States. Ohno knew that Toyota's plants needed to be more flexible. Also, space was (and is) very precious in Japan. These conditions, as well as Ohno's aversion to waste in any form (***muda***, as the Japanese call it), motivated him to develop some of the basic ideas and procedures that have come to be known as lean production. He and his colleagues then proceeded to perfect these ideas and procedures over the next several decades, including just-in-time production and the ***kanban*** system of production control, production leveling, setup time reduction, quality circles, and dedicated adherence to quality control.

Ohno himself did not coin the term "lean production" to describe the collection of methods and systems used at Toyota to improve production efficiency. In fact, he titled his book ***The Toyota Production System: Beyond Large-Scale Production*** [13]. The term "lean production" was coined by researchers at Massachusetts Institute of Technology to describe the activities and programs that seemed to explain Toyota's success in the efficiency with which they produced cars and the quality of the cars they produced. In an MIT research project that came to be known as the International Motor Vehicle Program (IMVP), a survey was conducted of 87 automobile assembly plants throughout the world. The research was popularized by the book ***The Machine that Changed the World*** [23]. In the subtitle of the book was the term "lean production."

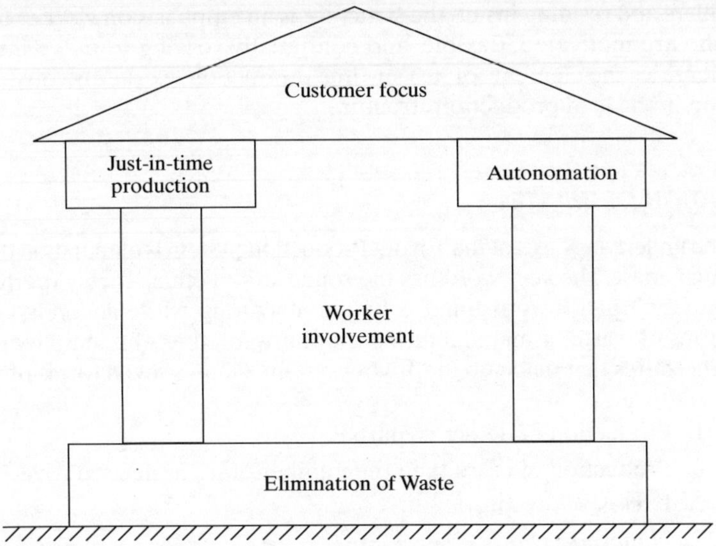

Figure 1 The structure of a lean production system.

TABLE 1 The Elements of Just-in-Time Production, Worker Involvement, and Autonomation in the Lean Production Structure

Just-in-Time Production	Worker Involvement	Autonomation
Pull system of production control using kanbans	Continuous improvement (kaizen)	Stop the process when something goes wrong (e.g., production of defects)
Setup time reduction for smaller batch sizes	Quality circles	Prevention of overproduction
Production leveling	Visual management	Error prevention and mistake proofing
On-time deliveries	The 5S system	Total productive maintenance for reliable equipment
Zero defects	Standardized work procedures	
Flexible workers	Participation in total productive maintenance by workers	

The ingredients of a lean production system are shown in the structure in Figure 1.[1] At the base of the structure is the foundation of the Toyota system: elimination of waste in production operations. Taiichi Ohno was driven to reduce waste at Toyota. Standing on the foundation are two pillars: (1) just-in-time production and (2) autonomation (automation with a human touch).[2] The two pillars support a roof that symbolizes a focus on the customer. The goal of lean production is customer satisfaction. Between the two

[1]Various forms of the "lean structure" have appeared in the literature. We believe the one shown here is representative.

[2]Taiichi Ohno describes just-in-time and autonomation as the two pillars needed to support the Toyota production system [13].

pillars and residing inside the structure is an emphasis on worker involvement: workers who are motivated, flexible, and continually striving to make improvements. Table 1 identifies the elements of just-in-time production, worker involvement, and autonomation in the lean production structure.

1 ELIMINATION OF WASTE

The underlying basis of the Toyota Production System is elimination of waste—called ***muda*** in Japanese. The very word has the sound of something messy (perhaps because it begins with the English word "mud"). In manufacturing, waste abounds. Ohno identified seven forms of waste in manufacturing that he wanted to eliminate by means of the various procedures that made up the Toyota system. Ohno's seven forms of waste are as follows:

1. Production of defective parts
2. Production of more than the number of items needed (overproduction)
3. Excessive inventories
4. Unnecessary processing steps
5. Unnecessary movement of people
6. Unnecessary transport and handling of materials
7. Workers waiting.

1.1 Production of Defective Parts

Eliminating production of defective parts (waste form 1) requires a quality control system that achieves perfect first-time quality. In the area of quality control, the Toyota production system was in sharp contrast with the traditional QC systems used in mass production. In mass production, quality control is typically defined in terms of an acceptable quality level (AQL), which means that a certain minimum level of fraction defects is sufficient, even satisfactory. In lean production, by contrast, perfect quality is required. The just-in-time delivery discipline used in lean production necessitates a zero defects level in parts quality, because if the part delivered to the downstream workstation is defective, production is forced to stop. There is little or no inventory in a lean system to act as a buffer. In mass production, inventory buffers are used just in case these quality problems occur. The defective work units are simply taken off the line and replaced with acceptable units. However, the problem is that such a policy tends to perpetuate the cause of the poor quality. Therefore, defective parts continue to be produced. In lean production, a single defect draws attention to the quality problem, forcing corrective action and a permanent solution. Workers inspect their own production, minimizing the delivery of defects to the downstream production station.

1.2 Overproduction and Excessive Inventories

Overproduction (waste form 2) and excessive inventories (waste form 3) are correlated. Producing more parts than necessary means that there are leftover parts that must be stored. Of all of the forms of muda, Ohno believed that the "greatest waste of all is excess inventory."[3] Overproduction and excess inventories generate increased costs in the following areas:

- Warehousing (building, lighting and heating, maintenance)
- Storage equipment (pallets, rack systems, forklifts)
- Additional workers to maintain and manage the extra inventory
- Additional workers to make the parts that were overproduced
- Other production costs (raw materials, machinery, power, maintenance) to make the parts that were overproduced and stored
- Interest payments to finance all of the above.

The kanban system (Section 2.1) for just-in-time production provides a control mechanism at each workstation to produce only the minimum quantity of parts needed to feed the next process in the sequence. In so doing, it limits the amount of inventory that is allowed to accumulate between operations.

1.3 Other Forms of Waste

Waste forms 4 through 7 all represent inefficient use of resources. Most of these inefficiencies can be corrected through the use of good methods engineering and layout planning. Good equipment maintenance (total productive maintenance, Section 3.3) helps to reduce machine downtime that causes waiting time for workers.

Unnecessary Processing Steps. Unnecessary processing steps mean that energy is being expended by the worker and/or machine to accomplish work that adds no value to the product. An example of this waste form is a product that is designed with features that serve no useful function to the customer, and yet time and cost are consumed to create those features. Another reason for unnecessary processing steps is that the processing method for the given task has not been well designed. Perhaps no work design has occurred at all. Consequently, the method used for the task includes wasted hand and body motions, unnecessary work elements, inappropriate hand tools, inefficient production equipment, poor ergonomics, and safety hazards.

Unnecessary Movement of Workers and Materials. The movement of people and materials is a necessary activity in manufacturing. Body motions and walking are necessary and natural elements of the work cycle for most workers, and materials must be transported from operation to operation during their processing. It is when the movement of workers or materials is done unnecessarily and without adding value to the

[3]Ohno [13].

product that waste occurs. The following reasons explain why people and materials are sometimes moved unnecessarily:

- *Inefficient workplace layout.* Tools and parts are randomly organized in the work space, so that workers must search for what they need and use inefficient motion patterns to complete their tasks.
- *Inefficient plant layout.* Workstations are not arranged along the line of flow of the processing sequence.
- *Improper material-handling method.* For example, manual-handling methods are used instead of mechanized or automated equipment.
- *Improper spacing of production machines.* Greater distances mean longer transit times between machines.
- *Larger equipment than necessary for the task.* Larger machines need larger access space and greater distances between machines.
- *Conventional batch production.* In batch production, changeovers are required between batches that result in downtime during which nothing is produced.

Workers Waiting. The seventh form of muda is workers waiting. When workers are forced to wait, it means that no work (either value-adding or non–value-adding) is being performed. There is a variety of reasons why workers are sometimes forced to wait:

- Materials have not been delivered to the workstation.
- The assembly line has stopped.
- A machine has to be repaired.
- A machine is being serviced by the setup crew.
- A machine is performing its automatic processing cycle on a work part.

2 JUST-IN-TIME PRODUCTION

Just-in-time (JIT) production systems were developed to minimize inventories, especially work-in-process. Excessive WIP is seen in the Toyota Production System as waste that should be minimized or eliminated. The ideal ***just-in-time production system*** produces and delivers exactly the required number of each component to the downstream operation in the manufacturing sequence at the exact moment when that component is needed. Each component is delivered "just in time." This delivery discipline minimizes WIP and manufacturing lead time as well as the space and money invested in WIP. In the Toyota Production System, the just-in-time discipline was applied not only to its own production operations but to supplier delivery operations as well.

While the development of JIT production systems is attributed to Toyota, many U.S. firms have also adopted the just-in-time philosophy. Other terms are sometimes applied to the American practice of JIT to suggest differences with the Japanese practice. For example, ***continuous flow manufacturing*** is a widely used term in the United States that denotes a just-in-time style of production operations in which work parts are processed and transported directly to the next workstation one unit at a time. Each process is completed just before the next process in the sequence begins. In effect, this is JIT with a batch size of one work unit. Prior to JIT, the traditional U.S. practice might be described as a "just-in-case" philosophy—that is, to hold large in-process inventories to cope with production problems such as late deliveries of components, machine breakdowns, defective components, and wildcat strikes.

The just-in-time production discipline has shown itself to be very effective in high-volume repetitive operations, such as those found in the automotive industry [12]. The potential for WIP accumulation in this type of manufacturing is significant, due to the large quantities of products made and the large numbers of components per product.

The principal objective of JIT is to reduce inventories. However, inventory reduction cannot simply be mandated to happen. Three requisites must be in place for a just-in-time production system to operate successfully: (1) a pull system of production control, (2) setup time reduction for smaller batch sizes, and (3) stable and reliable production operations.

2.1 Pull System of Production Control

JIT is based on a ***pull system*** of production control, in which the order to make and deliver parts at each workstation in the production sequence comes from the downstream station that uses those parts. When the supply of parts at a given workstation is about to be exhausted, that station orders the upstream station to replenish the supply. Only upon receipt of this order is the upstream station authorized to produce the needed parts. When this procedure is repeated at each workstation throughout the plant, it has the effect of pulling parts through the production system. By comparison, in a ***push system*** of production control, parts at each workstation are produced irrespective of the immediate need for those parts at its respective downstream station. In effect, this production discipline pushes parts through the plant. The risk in a push system is that more parts get produced in the factory than it can handle, resulting in large queues of work in front of machines. The machines are unable to keep up with arriving work, and the factory becomes overloaded with work-in-process inventory. The difference between push and pull systems of production control is illustrated in Figure 2.

The Toyota Production System implemented its pull system by means of kanbans. The word *kanban* (pronounced kahn-bahn) means "card" in Japanese. The ***Kanban system*** of production control is based on the use of cards that authorize (1) parts production and (2) parts delivery in the plant. Thus, there are two types of kanbans: (1) production kanbans, and (2) transport kanbans. A ***production kanban*** (P-kanban) authorizes the upstream station to produce a batch of parts. As parts are produced, they are placed in containers, so the batch quantity is just sufficient to fill the container. Production of more than this quantity of parts is not allowed in the kanban system. A ***transport kanban*** (T-kanban) authorizes transport of the container of parts to the downstream station.

The operation of a kanban system is illustrated in Figure 3. The workstations shown in the figure (station i and station $i + 1$) are only two in a sequence of multiple stations upstream and downstream. The flow of work is from station i (the upstream station)

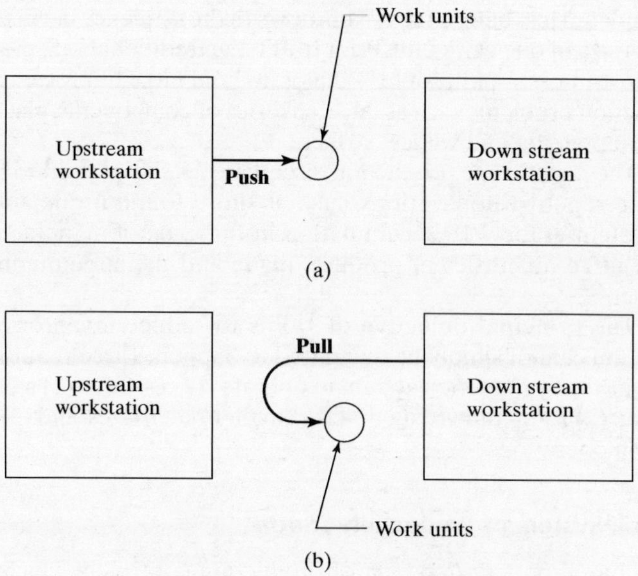

Figure 2 The difference between push and pull systems of production control: (a) push system, in which upstream stations push work to downstream stations and (b) pull system, in which downstream stations pull work from upstream stations.

to station $i + 1$ (the downstream station). The sequence of steps in the kanban pull system is as follows (our numbering sequence is coordinated with Figure 3):

1. Station $i + 1$ removes the next P-kanban from the dispatching rack. This P-kanban authorizes it to process a container of part b. A material handling worker removes the T-kanban from the incoming container of part b and takes it back to station i.
2. At station i, the material-handling worker finds the container of part b, removes the P-kanban and replaces it with the T-kanban. He then puts the P-kanban in the dispatching rack at station i.
3. The container of part b that was at station i is moved to station $i + 1$, as authorized by the T-kanban. The P-kanban for part b at station i authorizes station i to process a new container of part b, but it must wait its turn in the rack for the other P-kanbans ahead of it. Scheduling of work at each station is determined by the order in which the production kanbans are placed in the dispatching rack. Meanwhile, processing of the b parts at station $i + 1$ has been completed and that station removes the next P-kanban from the dispatching rack and begins processing that container of parts (it happens to be part d as indicated in the figure).

As mentioned, stations i and $i + 1$ are only two adjacent stations in a longer sequence. All other pairs of upstream and downstream stations operate according to the

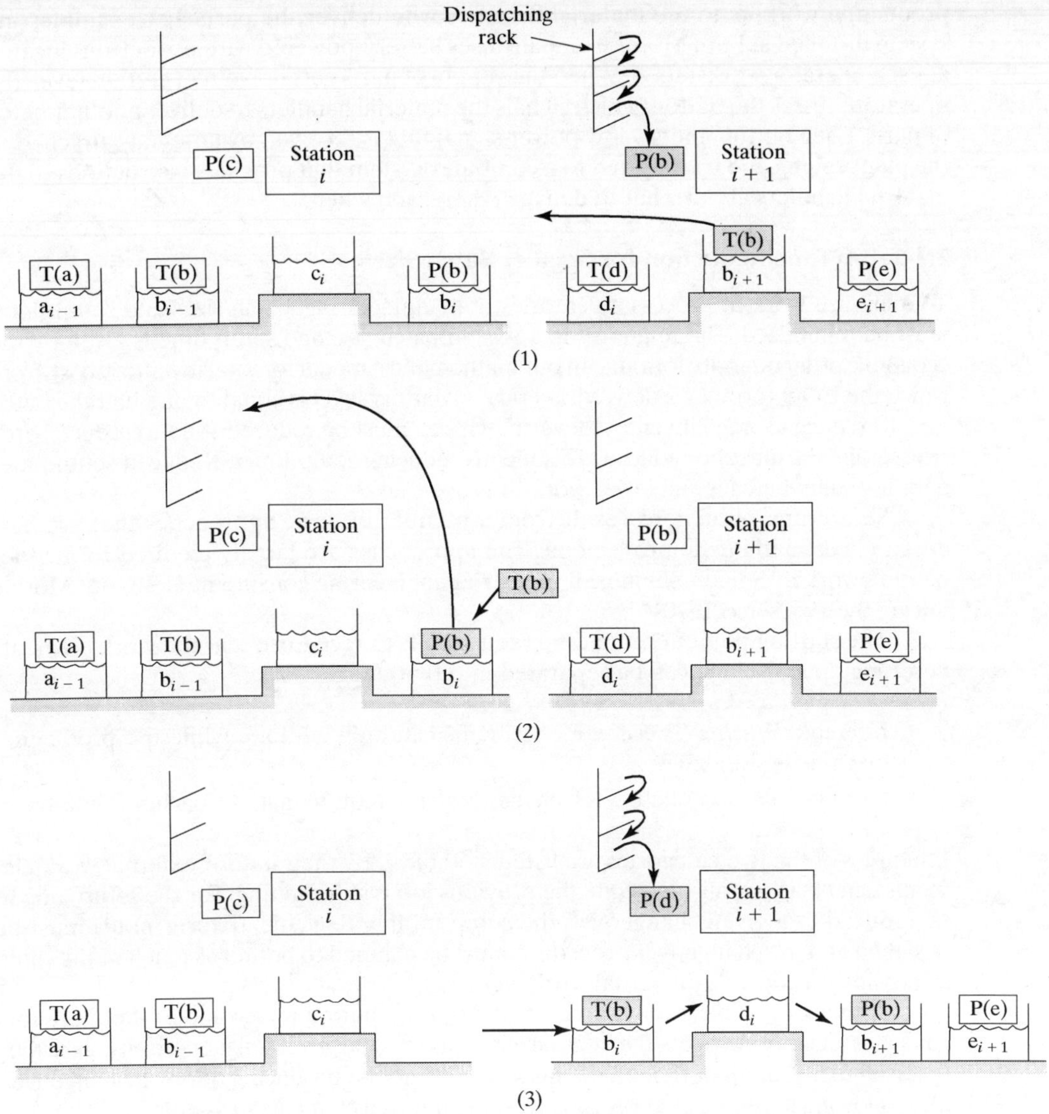

Figure 3 Operation of a kanban system between workstations (see description of steps in the text).

same kanban pull system. This production control system avoids unnecessary paperwork. The kanban cards are used over and over again instead of generating new production and transport orders every cycle. Although considerable labor is involved in material handling (moving cards and containers between stations), this is claimed to promote teamwork and cooperation among workers.

Today's kanban installations in the automotive industry rely on modern communications technologies rather than cards [6]. These electronic kanban systems connect production workers to the material handlers who deliver the parts. For example, one system installed at Ford Motor Company uses battery-powered wireless buttons located at each operator workstation. When the supply of parts gets down to a certain level, the operator presses the button, which signals the material handlers to deliver another batch of parts. Each button emits a low power signal that is received by antennas attached to the plant ceiling and transmitted to a computer system that provides instructions to the material handlers about what to deliver, where, and when.

2.2 Setup Time Reduction for Smaller Batch Sizes

To minimize work-in-process inventories in manufacturing, batch sizes and setup times must be minimized. The relationship between batch size and setup time is given by the economic order quantity formula. In our mathematical model for total inventory cost, from which the EOQ formula is derived, average inventory level is equal to one-half the batch size. To reduce average inventory level, batch size must be reduced. And to reduce batch size, setup cost must be reduced. This means reducing setup times. Reduced setup times permit smaller batches and lower work-in-process levels.

Setup time reductions result from a number of basic approaches that are best described as methods improvements. The approaches are largely credited to the pioneering work of Shigeo Shingo, an industrial engineering consultant at Toyota Motors during the 1960s and 1970s.[4]

The starting point in setup time reduction is to recognize that the work elements in setting up a machine can be separated into two categories:

- *Internal elements.* These work elements can only be done while the production machine is stopped.
- *External elements.* These work elements do not require that the machine be stopped.

Examples of the two categories are listed in Table 2. By their nature, external work elements can be accomplished while the previous job is still running. For the setup time to be reduced in a given changeover, the setup tooling (e.g., die, fixture, mold) must be designed and the changeover procedure must be planned to permit as much of the setup as possible to consist of external work elements.

Although it is desirable to reduce the times required to accomplish both internal and external work elements, the internal elements must be given a higher priority, since they determine the length of time that a machine will not be producing during a changeover. The following approaches apply mostly to the internal elements in a setup:

- Use time and motion study and methods improvements to reduce the sum of the internal work elements to the minimum possible time.
- Use two workers working in parallel to accomplish the setup, rather than one worker working alone. This approach is not applicable to all changeover situations,

[4]They have been documented in [4], [12], [18], [19], and [22]. The approaches can be applied to virtually all batch production situations, but their applications in the automotive industry have emphasized pressworking and machining operations, owing to their widespread use in this industry.

TABLE 2 Examples of Internal and External Work Elements During a Production Setup or Changeover

Internal Work Elements	External Work Elements
Removing tooling (e.g., dies, molds, fixtures) used in previous production job from machine	Retrieving tooling for next job from tool storage
Positioning and attaching tooling for next job in machine	Assembling tooling components next to machine (if tooling consists of separate pieces that must be assembled)
Making final adjustments and alignments of tooling	Reading engineering drawings regarding new setup
Trying out the setup and making trial parts	Reprogramming machine for next job (e.g., downloading part program for new part)

TABLE 3 Examples of Setup Reductions in Japanese and U.S. Industries

Industry	Equipment Type	Setup Time Before Reduction	Setup Time After Reduction	Reduction (%)
Japanese automotive	1000 ton press	4 hr	3 min	98.7
Japanese diesel	Transfer line	9.3 hr	9 min	98.4
U.S. power tool	Punch press	2 hr	3 min	97.5
Japanese automotive	Machine tool	6 hr	10 min	97.2
U.S. electric appliance	45 ton press	50 min	2 min	96.0

Source: [21].

but where it is applicable, it theoretically reduces the downtime to one-half the time required for one worker.

- Eliminate or minimize adjustments in the setup. Adjustments are time-consuming.
- Use quick-acting fasteners instead of bolts and nuts where possible.
- When bolts and nuts must be used with washers, use U-shaped instead of O-shaped washers. A U-shaped washer can be inserted between the parts to be clamped without completely disassembling the nut from the bolt. To add an O-shaped washer, the nut must be removed from the bolt.
- Design modular fixtures consisting of a base unit plus insert tooling that can be quickly changed for each new part style. The base unit remains attached to the production machine, so that only the insert tooling must be changed.

Although methods for reducing setup time were pioneered by the Japanese, U.S. firms have also adopted these methods. Results of the efforts are sometimes dramatic. Table 3 presents some examples of setup reductions in Japanese and U.S. industries reported by Suzaki [21].

The economic impact of setup time reduction in a production operation can be assessed using the economic order quantity equations.

Example 1 Effect of Setup Reduction on EOQ and Inventory Cost

Let us determine the effect on economic batch size and total inventory costs of reducing setup time given the following information: annual demand = 15,000 pc/yr, unit cost = \$20, holding cost rate = 18%/yr, setup time = 5 hr, and cost of downtime during setup = \$150/hr. Suppose it were possible to reduce setup time from 5 hr to 5 min (this kind of reduction is not so far-fetched, given the data in Table 3). Determine (a) the economic order quantity and (b) total inventory cost for this new situation.

Solution: First, recall the results of the earlier example. Setup cost C_{su} = (5 hr)(\$150/hr) = \$750 and holding cost C_h = 0.18(\$20) = \$3.60. Using these values, the economic order quantity was computed as

$$EOQ = \sqrt{\frac{2(15{,}000)(750)}{3.60}} = 2500 \text{ units}$$

The corresponding total inventory costs are computed as

$$TIC = 0.5(2500)(3.60) + 750(15{,}000/2500) = \$9000$$

(a) Reducing the setup time to 5 min reduces the setup cost to C_{su} = (5/60 hr)(\$150) = \$12.50. Holding cost remains the same, and the new economic order quantity is

$$EOQ = \sqrt{\frac{2(15{,}000)(12.50)}{3.60}} = 323 \text{ units}$$

This is a significant reduction from the 2500-piece batch size when setup time was 5 hr.

(b) Total inventory costs are also reduced, as follows:

$$TIC = 0.5(323)(3.60) + 12.50(15{,}000/323) = \$1161$$

This is an 87% cost reduction from the previous value. ■

2.3 Stable and Reliable Production Operations

Other requirements for a successful JIT production system include (1) production leveling, (2) on-time delivery, (3) defect-free components and materials, (4) reliable production equipment, (5) a workforce that is capable, committed, and cooperative, and (6) a dependable supplier base.

Production Leveling. If production is to flow as smoothly as possible, there must be minimum perturbations from the fixed schedule. Perturbations in downstream operations tend to be magnified in upstream operations. A 10% change in final assembly is often amplified into a 50% change in parts production operations, due to overtime, unscheduled setups, variations from normal work procedures, and other exceptions. By maintaining a constant master production schedule over time, smooth workflow is achieved and disturbances in production are minimized.

The trouble is that demand for the final product is not constant. Accordingly, the production system must adjust to the ups and downs of the marketplace using ***production***

leveling, which means distributing the changes in product mix and quantity as evenly as possible over time. Production leveling can be accomplished using the following approaches [5]:

- Authorizing overtime during busy periods
- Using finished product inventories to absorb daily ups and downs in demand
- Adjusting the cycle times of the production operations
- Producing in small batch sizes that are enabled by setup time reduction techniques. In the ideal, the batch size is reduced to one. Instead of producing parts A and B according to a schedule that looks like this:

  AAAAAAAAAABBBBBBBBBB,

  the parts are instead scheduled like this:

  ABABABABABABABABABAB.

The benefits of production leveling include greater responsiveness to changes in product demand, shorter lead times, smaller in-process and finished goods inventories, and regularity in the workload of production workers.

On-Time Deliveries, Zero Defects, and Reliable Production Equipment. Just-in-time production requires near perfection in on-time delivery, parts quality, and equipment reliability. Owing to the small lot sizes used in JIT, parts must be delivered before stock-outs occur at downstream stations. Otherwise, these stations are starved for work and production is forced to stop.

JIT requires high quality in every aspect of production. If parts are produced with quality defects, they cannot be used in subsequent processing or assembly stations, thus interrupting work at those stations and possibly stopping production. Such a severe penalty motivates a discipline of very high quality levels (zero defects) in parts fabrication. Workers are trained to inspect their own output to make sure it is right before it goes to the next operation. In effect, this means controlling quality during production rather than relying on inspectors to discover the defects later.

JIT also requires highly reliable production equipment. Low work-in-process leaves little room for equipment stoppages. Machine breakdowns cannot be tolerated in a JIT production system. The equipment must be "designed for reliability," and the plant that operates the equipment must employ total productive maintenance.

Workforce and Supplier Base. Workers in a just-in-time production system must be cooperative, committed, and cross-trained. Small batch sizes mean that workers must be willing and able to perform a variety of tasks and to produce a variety of part styles at their workstations. As indicated above, they must be inspectors as well as production workers in order to ensure the quality of their own output. They must be able to deal with minor technical problems that may be experienced with the production equipment, so that major breakdowns are avoided.

The suppliers of raw materials and components to the company must be held to the same standards of on-time delivery, zero defects, and other JIT requirements as the company itself. New policies such as the following are required for JIT for dealing with vendors:

- Reducing the total number of suppliers, thus allowing the remaining suppliers to do more business
- Entering into long-term agreements and partnerships with suppliers, so that suppliers do not have to worry about competitively bidding for every order
- Establishing quality and delivery standards and selecting suppliers on the basis of their capacity to meet these standards
- Placing employees into supplier plants to help those suppliers develop their own JIT systems
- Selecting parts suppliers that are located near the company's final assembly plant to reduce transportation and delivery problems.

3 AUTONOMATION

Appearing at first glance to be a misspelling of "automation" ***autonomation*** has been defined by Taiichi Ohno as "automation with a human touch" [13].[5] The notion is that the machines operate autonomously as long as they are functioning properly. When they do not function properly—for example, when they produce a defective part—they are designed to stop immediately. Another aspect of autonomation is that the machines and processes are designed to prevent errors, to be mistake-proof. Finally, machines in the Toyota Production System must be reliable, which requires an effective maintenance program. Three aspects of autonomation are discussed in this section: (1) stopping the process automatically when something is wrong, (2) error prevention, and (3) total productive maintenance.

3.1 Stopping the Process

Much of autonomation is embodied in the Japanese word ***jidoka***, which refers to machines that are designed to stop automatically when something goes wrong, such as a defective part being processed. Production machines in Toyota plants are equipped with automatic stop devices that activate when a defective work unit is produced.[6] Therefore, when a machine stops, it draws attention to the problem, requiring corrective action to be taken to avoid recurrences. Adjustments must be made to fix the machine, thereby eliminating or reducing subsequent defects and improving overall quality of the final product.

In addition to its quality control function, autonomation also refers to machines that are controlled to stop production when the required quantity (the batch size) has been completed, thus preventing overproduction (one of the seven forms of muda).

[5]An alternative definition of autonomation is "automation with a human mind" [12].

[6]The origins of ***jidoka*** in the Toyota Production System can be traced to Ohno's work experience early in his career in the textile industry, where the weaving machines were equipped with automatic stopping mechanisms that shut down the looms when abnormal operating conditions occurred. He implemented the idea at Toyota.

Although autonomation is often applied to automated production machines, it can also be used with manual operations as well. In either case, it consists of the following control devices: (1) a sensor to detect abnormal operation that would result in a quality defect, (2) a device to count the number of parts that have been produced, and (3) a means to stop the machine or production line when abnormal operation is detected or the required batch quantity has been completed.

The alternative to autonomation is when a production machine is not equipped with these control mechanisms and continues to operate abnormally, possibly completing an entire batch of defective parts before the quality problem is even noticed, or producing more parts than the quantity required at the downstream workstation. To avoid such a calamity in a plant that does not have automatic stop mechanisms on its machines, each machine must have a worker in continuous attendance to monitor its operation. Machines equipped with autonomation do not require a worker to be present all the time when it is functioning correctly. Only when it stops must the worker attend to it. This allows one worker to oversee the operation of multiple machines, thereby improving worker productivity significantly.

Because workers are called upon to service multiple machines, and the machines are frequently of different types, the workers must be willing and able to develop a greater variety of skills than those who are responsible for only a single machine type. The net effect of more versatile workers is that the plant becomes more flexible in its ability to shift workers around among machines and jobs to respond to changes in workload mix.

At Toyota, the jidoka concept is extended to its final assembly lines. Workers are empowered to stop the assembly line when a quality problem is discovered, using pull cords located at regular intervals along the line. Downtime on final assembly lines in the automotive industry is expensive. Managers desperately want to avoid it. They accomplish this by making sure that the quality problems that cause it are eliminated. Pressure is applied on the parts fabrication departments and suppliers to keep parts and subassemblies that are defective out of the final assembly area.

3.2 Error Prevention

This aspect of autonomation is derived from two Japanese words: ***poka***, which means error, and ***yoke***, which means prevention. Together, ***poka-yoke*** refers to the prevention of errors through the use of low cost devices that detect and/or prevent them. The poka-yoke concept was developed by Shigeo Shingo, who also did pioneering work in setup time reduction (Section 2.2). The use of poka-yoke devices relieves the worker of constantly monitoring the process for errors that might cause defective parts or other undesirable consequences (e.g., unsafe working conditions, omitting a processing step).

Mistakes in manufacturing are common, and they often result in the production of defects. Examples include the following:

- Omission of processing steps, such as neglecting to spray lubricant on a mold cavity to prevent sticking of the molded part
- Incorrectly locating a work part in a fixture
- Using the wrong tool (for example, using the wrong cutting tool material for a given work material)

- Not aligning jigs and fixtures properly on the machine tool table (which could result in the entire batch of parts being processed incorrectly)
- Neglecting to add a component part in an assembly

When a poka-yoke identifies that an error or other exception has occurred, it responds in either or both of the following ways:

- *Stops the process.* The mechanized or automated cycle is stopped when a problem is detected in the operation of a production machine. For example, a limit switch installed in a workholder detects that the workpiece is incorrectly located and is interlocked with the milling machine to prevent the process from starting.
- *Provides an alert.* This response provides an audible or visible warning signal that an error has occurred. This signal alerts the operator and perhaps other workers and supervisors about the problem. The use of andon boards (Section 4.2) is a means of implementing this type of response.

3.3 Total Productive Maintenance

Production equipment in the Toyota Production System must be highly reliable. The just-in-time delivery system cannot tolerate machine breakdowns, since there is little buffer stock between workstations to keep upstream and downstream stations producing when the middle station stops. Lean production requires an equipment maintenance program that minimizes machine breakdowns. ***Total productive maintenance*** (TPM) is a coordinated group of activities whose objective is to minimize production losses due to equipment failures, malfunctions, and low utilization through the participation of workers at all levels of the organization. Worker teams are formed to solve maintenance problems (such as the kaizen projects, discussed in Section 4.1). Workers who operate equipment are assigned the routine tasks of inspecting, cleaning, and lubricating their machines. This leaves the regular maintenance workers with time to perform the more demanding technical duties, such as emergency maintenance, preventive maintenance, and predictive maintenance (see definitions in Table 4). In TPM, the goal is zero breakdowns.

TABLE 4 Some Maintenance Definitions

Term	Definition
Emergency maintenance	Repairing equipment that has broken down and returning it to operating condition. Action must be taken immediately to correct the malfunction. Also known as reactive maintenance.
Preventive maintenance	Performing routine repairs on equipment (e.g., replacement of key components) to prevent and avoid breakdowns.
Predictive maintenance	Anticipating equipment malfunctions before they occur based on computerized machine monitoring, machine operator being attentive to the way the machine is running, historical data, and other predictive techniques.
Total productive maintenance	Integration of preventive and predictive maintenance to avoid emergency maintenance.

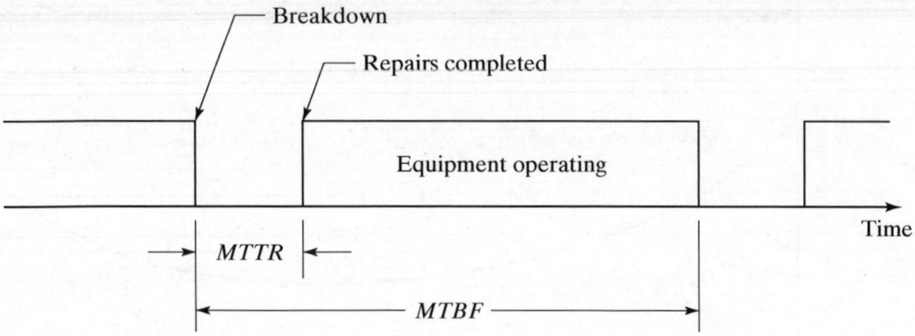

Figure 4 Time scale showing MTBF and MTTR for a piece of machine that breaks down occasionally.

The traditional measure of machine reliability is ***availability***, which is the proportion of the total desired operating time that the machine is actually available and operating.[7] To be more precise, availability is defined in terms of two other reliability measures: ***mean time between failures*** (*MTBF*) and ***mean time to repair*** (*MTTR*). *MTBF* indicates the average length of time the piece of equipment runs between breakdowns. *MTTR* indicates the average time required to service the equipment and put it back into operation after a breakdown occurs. *MTBF* and *MTTR* are illustrated in Figure 4. Using these terms, ***availability*** is defined as follows:

$$A = \frac{MTBF - MTTR}{MTBF} \tag{1}$$

where A = availability, $MTBF$ = mean time between failures, hr; and $MTTR$ = mean time to repair, hr. Availability is typically expressed as a percentage. When a piece of equipment is brand new (and being debugged), and later when it begins to age, its availability tends to be lower. This results in a typical U-shaped curve for availability as a function of time over the life of the equipment, as shown in Figure 5.

There are other reasons besides breakdowns that might cause a piece of production equipment to operate at less than its full capability. Such reasons include low equipment utilization, production of defective parts, and operating at less than the machine's designed speed.

Utilization refers to the amount of output of a production machine during a given time period (e.g., week) relative to its capacity during that same period. This can be expressed as an equation,

$$U = \frac{Q}{PC} \tag{2}$$

where U = utilization of the facility; Q = actual quantity produced by the facility during a given time period—for instance, pc/wk; and PC = production capacity for the same period, pc/wk. Utilization can also be measured as the number of hours of productive

[7]Availability is similar to line efficiency or uptime proportion.

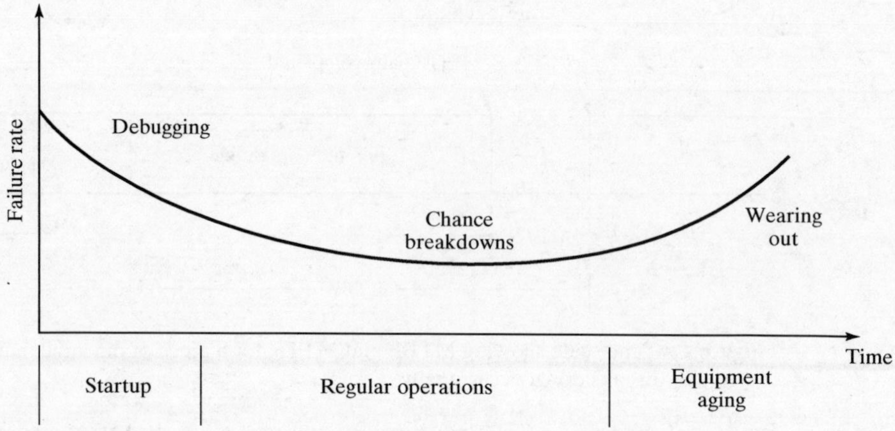

Figure 5 Typical U-shaped availability curve for a piece of equipment during its life.

operation relative to the total number of hours the machine is available. Reasons for poor machine utilization include poor scheduling of work, machine starved for work by upstream operation, downtime due to setups and changeovers between production batches, worker absenteeism, and low demand for the type of process performed by the machine. Utilization can be assessed for a single machine, an entire plant, or any other productive resource (e.g., labor). It is often expressed as a percentage (e.g., the plant is operating at 83% of capacity).

Production of defective parts may be due to incorrect machine settings, inaccurate adjustments in the setup, or improper tooling. All of these reasons are related to equipment maintenance problems. Additional reasons for producing defects that may not be related to equipment problems include defective starting materials and human error. The ***fraction defect rate*** is defined as the proportion of defective parts that are produced in a given process. The yield of an individual process is defined as

$$Y = 1 - q \tag{3}$$

where Y = process yield (ratio of conforming parts produced to total parts processed).

Finally, running the equipment at less than its designed speed also reduces its ***operating capability***, which is the ratio of the actual operating speed divided by the designed speed of the machine, symbolized as r_{os}.

All of these factors can be combined as follows to obtain a measure of the overall equipment effectiveness:

$$OEE = AUYr_{os} \tag{4}$$

where OEE = overall equipment effectiveness, A = availability, U = utilization, Y = process yield, and r_{os} = operating capability. The objective of total productive maintenance is to make OEE as close as possible to unity (100%).

4 WORKER INVOLVEMENT

Between the two pillars of lean production in Figure 1 are workers who are motivated and flexible and who participate in continuous improvement. Our discussion of worker involvement in the lean production system consists of three topics: (1) continuous improvement, (2) visual management and 5S, and (3) standardized work procedures.

4.1 Continuous Improvement

In the context of lean production, the Japanese word ***kaizen*** means continuous improvement of production operations. Kaizen is usually implemented by means of worker teams, sometimes called ***quality circles***,[8] which are organized to address specific problems that have been identified in the workplace. The teams address not only quality problems but also problems relating to productivity, cost, safety, maintenance, and other areas of interest to the organization. The term ***kaizen circle*** is also used, suggesting the broader range of issues that are usually involved in team activities.

Kaizen is a process that attempts to involve all workers as well as their supervisors and managers. Workers often are members of more than one kaizen circle. Although a principal purpose of organizing workers into teams is to solve problems in production, there are other less obvious but also important objectives. Kaizen circles encourage a an individual sense of responsibility, allow workers to gain acceptance and recognition among colleagues, and improve workers' technical skills [12].

Kaizen is applied on a problem-by-problem basis by worker teams. The team is constituted to deal with a specific problem. As mentioned above, the problem may relate to any of various areas of concern to the organization (e.g., quality, productivity, maintenance). Team members are selected according to their knowledge and expertise in the problem area and may be drawn from various departments. They serve part-time on a project team in addition to fulfilling their regular operational duties. On completion of the project, the team is disbanded. The usual expectation is that the team will meet two to four times per month, and each meeting will last about an hour.

The steps in each project depend on the type of problem being addressed. Details of the approaches recommended by different authors also vary [10, 15, 16]. Basically, the approach is the same as our systematic approach in methods engineering.

4.2 Visual Management and 5S

The principle behind ***visual management*** is that the status of the work situation should be evident just by looking at it.[9] If something is wrong, this condition should be obvious to the observer, so that corrective action can be taken immediately. Also called the ***visual workplace***, the principle applies to the entire plant environment. Objects that obstruct the view inside the plant are not allowed, making the entire interior space visible. The buildup of work-in-process is limited to a specified height (e.g., five feet). Thus, the visual workplace provides visibility throughout the plant and encourages continuous improvement and good housekeeping.

[8]The terms ***quality control circle*** and ***QC circle*** have also been used for these teams [9, 12].

[9]This is what statistician L. Tippett discovered in England during the 1920s while he was studying downtime of loom operations. The discovery resulted in the development of work sampling.

The use of kanbans in just-in-time production systems can be considered an example of visual management. The kanbans provide a visual mechanism for authorizing production and transportation of parts within the plant.

An important means of implementing visual management involves the use of an ***andon board***, a light panel positioned above a workstation or production line that is used to indicate its operating status. Its operation is commonly associated with the pull cords along a production line that permit a worker to stop the line. If a problem occurs, such as a line stoppage, the andon board identifies where the problem is and the nature of the problem. Different colored lights are often used to indicate the status of the operation. For example, a green light indicates normal operation, yellow means a worker has a problem and is calling for help, and red shows that the line has stopped. Other color codes may be used to indicate the end of a production run, shortage of materials, the need for a machine setup, and so on.

The visual workplace principle can also be applied in worker training. It includes the use of photographs, drawings, and diagrams to document work instructions, as opposed to lengthy text that is void of illustrations. "A picture is worth a thousand words" can be a powerful training tool for workers. In many cases, an actual example of the work part is used to convey the desired message; for example, examples of good parts and defective parts are shown to teach inspectors in quality control.

A means of involving workers in the visual workplace is a system called ***5S***, a set of procedures that is used to organize work areas in the plant. The name represents the first letters of five Japanese words as they would be spelled in English: ***seiri*** (sort), ***seiton*** (set in order), ***seiso*** (shine), ***seiketsu*** (standardize), and ***shitsuke*** (sustain).

The steps in 5S, briefly described in Table 5, provide an additional means of implementing visual management to provide a clean, orderly, and visible work environment that promotes high morale among workers and encourages continuous improvement. The steps are usually carried out by worker teams, and the 5S system must be a continuing process to sustain the accomplishments that have been made.

TABLE 5 The Five Steps in the 5S System

1. ***Sort.*** Sort things in the workplace; in particular, identify the items that are not used and dispose of them. This eliminates the clutter that usually accumulates in a workplace after many years.
2. ***Set in order.*** Organize the items remaining in the work area after sorting according to frequency of use, and provide easy access to those items that are most often needed.
3. ***Shine.*** Clean the work area and inspect it to make sure that everything is in its proper place. The alternative S-words for this step are "sweep" and "scrub," which may also be required in the work area.
4. ***Standardize.*** Document the standard locations for items in the workplace. For example, use a "shadow board" for hand tools, in which the outline of the tool is painted on the board to indicate where it belongs. Looking at the shadow board, workers can immediately tell whether a tool is present and where to return it.
5. ***Sustain.*** Establish a plan for sustaining the gains made in the previous four steps, and assign individual responsibilities to team members for maintaining a clean and orderly work environment. Make workers responsible for taking care of the equipment they operate, which includes cleaning and performing minor maintenance tasks.

Source: [5] and [14].

4.3 Standardized Work Procedures

Standardized work procedures are established in the Toyota Production System, using approaches that are similar to the traditional methods engineering techniques. And time study is used to determine the length of time that should be taken to complete a given work cycle. However, there are differences in the Toyota approach to the development of standard methods and standard times, and these differences are emphasized in the discussion that follows. The following objectives are part of the standardized work procedures at Toyota:

- Maintain high productivity—that is, accomplish the required amount of production using the fewest possible number of workers.
- Balance the workload among all processes.
- Minimize the amount of work-in-process in the production sequence.

In the Toyota Production System, a standardized work procedure for a given task has three components [13]: (1) cycle time, (2) work sequence, and (3) standard work-in-process quantity. These components are documented using forms that emphasize Toyota's unique manufacturing procedures. The forms are sometimes quite different from those used in traditional methods engineering and work measurement.

Cycle Time and Takt Time. The ***cycle time*** is the actual time it takes to complete a task. This time is established using stopwatch time study. Closely related to the cycle time is the ***takt time***, the reciprocal of the demand rate for a given product or part, adjusted for the available shift time in the factory ("takt" is a German word meaning cadence or pace). For a given product or part,

$$T_{takt} = \frac{EOT}{Q_{dd}} \tag{5}$$

where T_{takt} = takt time, EOT = effective daily operating time, and Q_{dd} = daily quantity of units demanded. The effective daily operating time is the shift hours worked each day, without subtracting any allowances for delays, breakdowns, or other sources of lost time. The daily quantity of units demanded is the monthly demand for the item divided by the number of working days in the month, without increasing the quantity to allow for defective units that might be produced. The reason why the effective daily operating time is not adjusted for lost time and the daily quantity is not adjusted for defects is to draw attention to these deficiencies so that corrective action will be taken to minimize or eliminate them.

Example 2 Takt Time

The monthly demand for a certain part is 10,000 units. There are 22 working days in the month. The plant operates two shifts, each with an effective operating time of 440 min. Determine the takt time for this part.

Solution: With two shifts, the effective daily operating time is 2(440 min) = 880 min. The daily quantity of units demanded is 10,000/22 = 454.5 pc/day.

$$T_{takt} = 880/454.5 = 1.94 \text{ min}$$

The takt time provides a specification based on demand for the part or product. In the Toyota Production System, the work must be designed so that the operation cycle time is synchronized with the takt time. This is accomplished through planning of the work sequence and standardizing the work-in-process quantity.

Work Sequence. The ***work sequence*** defines the order of work elements or operations performed by a given worker in accomplishing an assigned task. For a worker performing a repetitive work cycle at a single machine, it indicates the actions that need to be carried out, such as pick up the work part, load it into the machine, engage the feed, and unload the completed part at the end of the cycle. For a multifunction worker responsible for several machines, each with its own semiautomatic cycle, the work sequence describes what must be done at each machine and the order in which the machines must be attended. Pictures and drawings are often included (the visual workplace, Section 4.2) to show the proper use of hand tools and other aspects of the work routine such as safety practices and correct ergonomic posture.

For the multimachine situation, the work sequence is documented by means of the standard operations routine sheet, as shown in Figure 6. This form lists the machines that must be visited by the worker during each work cycle. A horizontal time scale indicates how long each operation should take, a solid line for the worker and dashed lines for the machines, and squiggly, nearly vertical lines are used to depict the worker walking between machines. The time lines show how well the machine cycle times are matched to the work routine performed by the worker each cycle.

Most production parts require more than one process (see sequential operations). It is not unusual for a dozen or more processing steps to be required to complete a part. The cycle time for a given process may be different from the takt time, which is based on the demand for the item produced in the task, not the requirements of the task itself. In the Toyota system, attempts are made to organize the work in such a way that the cycle time for each processing step is equal to the takt time for the part. By matching the cycle times with the takt time, all of the processes in the sequence are balanced, and the amount of work-in-process is minimized.

How can the work to produce a given part be organized so that the cycle time for each processing step is equal to the takt time? In the Toyota Production System, the

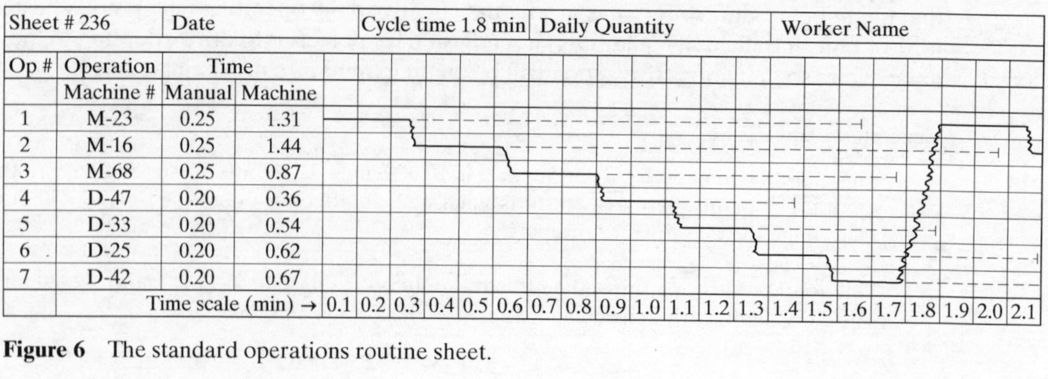

Figure 6 The standard operations routine sheet.

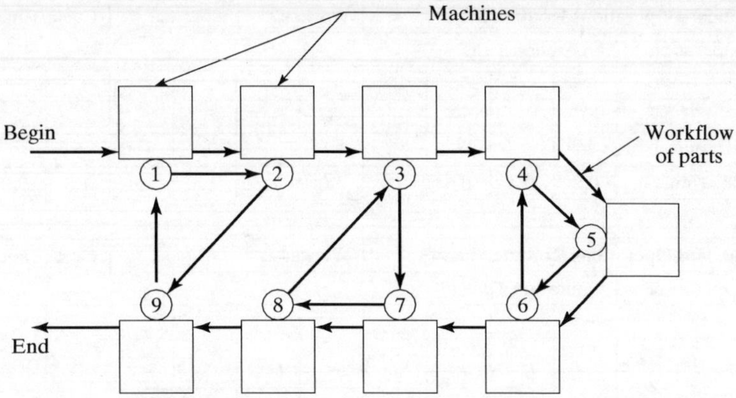

Figure 7 Cell layout with three workers performing nine operations. Operations are indicated by numbers in circles. The first worker performs operations 1, 2, and 9; the second worker performs operations 3, 7, and 8; and the third worker performs operations 4, 5, and 6.

tasks are integrated into work cells. At Toyota, a ***work cell*** is a group of workers and processing stations that are physically arranged in sequential order so that parts can be produced in small batches, in many cases one at a time. The cells are typically U-shaped rather than straight to promote comradeship among the workers and to achieve continuous flow of work in the cell. An example of a work cell layout and the operations performed in it by three workers is shown in Figure 7.[10] A total of nine operations are performed by the three workers, as depicted by the arrows in the figure. The corresponding standard operations routine sheets are illustrated in Figure 8. The total workload is balanced among the workers and the operations are allocated so the corresponding cycle times are equal to the takt time for the part produced in the cell.

Standard Work-in-Process Quantity. ***Work-in-process*** (*WIP*) is the quantity of work parts that have been started in the production sequence but are not yet completed. *WIP* consists of both the parts that are currently being processed (e.g., parts that are fixtured in the machines) as well as those that are between processing steps (e.g., parts waiting to be loaded into machines). WIP does not include parts that have been completed, nor does it include the starting raw materials.

In the Toyota Production System, the standard work-in-process quantity is the minimum number of parts necessary to avoid situations where workers are waiting. For example, if the first worker in Figure 7 had only one work part for machines 1 and 2, he would have to wait for machine 1 to finish its cycle before moving the part to machine 2. But if there were two work parts, one in front of each machine, then he could load the first machine and move immediately to load the second machine without waiting for the first machine to finish.

[10]Based on an example in [12].

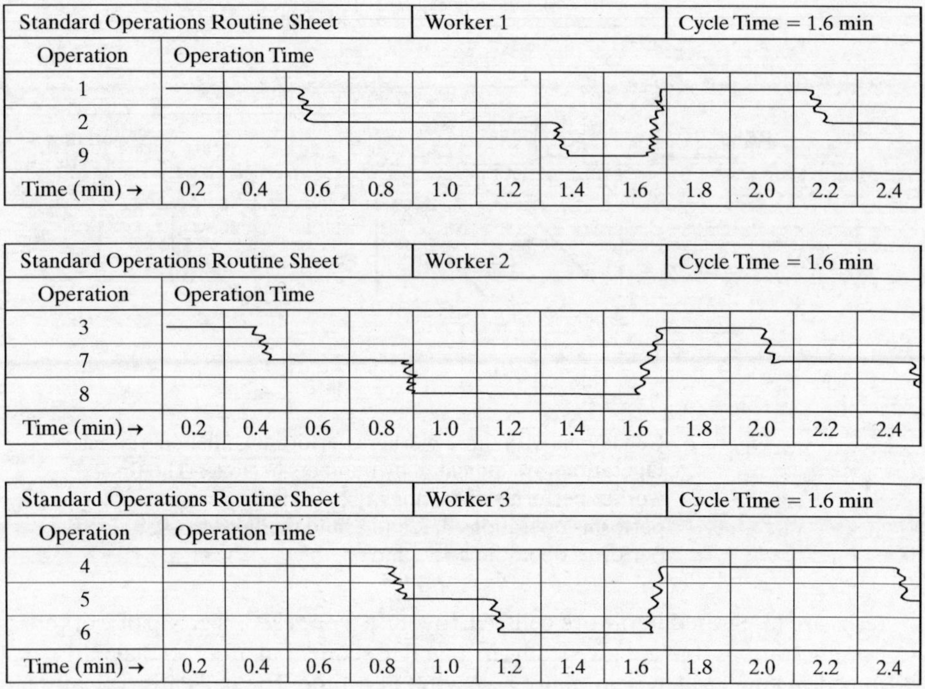

Figure 8 The standard operations routine sheets for the three workers in Figure 7.

REFERENCES

[1] Bodek, N. "Quick and Easy Kaizen." *IIE Solutions.* (July 2002): 43–45.

[2] Box, G. E. P., and N. R. Draper. *Evolutionary Operation*. New York: Wiley, 1969.

[3] Brecker, J. "Leaning Toward Six Sigma." Paper presented at a meeting of East Coast Region 3 Conference, Society of Manufacturing Engineers, Bethlehem, Pa., October 10–11, 2003.

[4] Claunch, J. W. *Setup Time Reduction.* Inc., Chicago: Irwin, 1996.

[5] Dennis, P. *Lean Production Simplified*. New York: Productivity Press, 2002.

[6] "Ford's Electronic Kanban Makes Replenishment Easy." *Lean Manufacturing Advisor.* 5, no. 5 (October 2003): 6–7.

[7] Groover, M. P. *Automation, Production Systems, and Computer Integrated Manufacturing.* 2nd ed. Upper Saddle River, NJ: Prentice Hall, 2001.

[8] Hirai, Y. "Continuous Improvement (*Kaizen*)." Pp. 4.21–4.32 in *Maynard's Industrial Engineering Handbook.* 5th ed. edited by K. Zandin. New York: McGraw-Hill, 2001.

[9] Imai, M. *Kaizen, The Key to Japan's Competitive Success.* New York: McGraw-Hill 1986.

[10] Juran, J. M., and F. M. Gryna. *Quality Planning and Analysis*. 3rd ed. New York: McGraw-Hill, 1993.

[11] Monden, Y., and H. Aigbedo, "Just-in-time and Kanban Scheduling." Pp. 9.63–9.86 in *Maynard's Industrial Engineering Handbook*, 5th ed. edited by K. Zandin. New York: McGraw-Hill, 2001.

[12] Monden, Y. *Toyota Production System*. Norcross, GA: Industrial Engineering and Management Press, Institute of Industrial Engineers, 1983.

[13] Ohno, T. *Toyota Production System, Beyond Large-Scale Production*. New York: Productivity Press, 1988; Original Japanese edition published by Diamond, Inc., Tokyo, 1978.

[14] Peterson, J., and R. Smith. *The 5S Pocket Guide*. Portland, OR: Productivity Press, 1998.

[15] Pyzdek, T., and R. W. Berger. *Quality Engineering Handbook*. New York: Marcel Dekker; ASQC Quality Press, Milwaukee, WI, 1992.

[16] Robison, J. "Integrate Quality Cost Concepts into Team's Problem-Solving Efforts." *Quality Progress* (March 1997): 25–30.

[17] Schonberger, R. *Japanese Manufacturing Techniques: Nine Hidden Lessons in Simplicity*. New York: Free Press, Division of Macmillan Publishing, 1982.

[18] Sekine, K., and K. Arai. *Kaizen for Quick Changeover*. Cambridge, MA: Productivity Press, 1987.

[19] Shingo, S. *Study of Toyota Production System from Industrial Engineering Viewpoint—Development of Non-Stock Production*. Nikkan Kogyo Shinbun Sha, 1980.

[20] Shirahama, S. "Setup Time Reduction." Pp. 4.57–4.80 in *Maynard's Industrial Engineering Handbook*. 5th ed. edited by K. Zandin. New York: McGraw-Hill, 2001.

[21] Suzaki, K. *The New Manufacturing Challenge: Techniques for Continuous Improvement*. New York: Free Press, 1987.

[22] Veilleux, R. F., and L. W. Petro. *Tool and Manufacturing Engineers Handbook*. 4th ed. Vol. 5, *Manufacturing Management*. Dearborn, MI: Society of Manufacturing Engineers, 1988.

[23] Womack, K., D. Jones, and D. Roos. *The Machine that Changed the World*. Cambridge, MA: MIT Press, 1990.

REVIEW QUESTIONS

1 Define lean production.

2 Name the two pillars of the Toyota Production System.

3 What is the Japanese word for waste?

4 Name the seven forms of waste in production, as identified by Taiichi Ohno.

5 What is meant by the term *just-in-time production system*?

6 What is the objective of a just-in-time production system?

7 What is the difference between a push system and a pull system in production control?

8 What is a kanban? What are the two types of kanban?

9 What is the basic starting point in a study to reduce setup time?

10 What does production leveling mean?

11 How is production leveling accomplished?

12 What does autonomation mean?

13 What does total productive maintenance mean?

14 What is availability as a reliability measure and how is it determined?

15 What does the Japanese word "kaizen" mean?

16 What is a quality circle?

17 What is visual management?

18 What is an andon board?

19 What is the 5S system?

20 What is takt time?

21 What are standardized work procedures in the Toyota Production System?

PROBLEMS

Setup Time Reduction

1 A stamping plant supplies sheet metal parts to a final assembly plant in the automotive industry. The following data are values representative of the parts made at the plant. Annual demand is 150,000 pc (for each part produced). Average cost per piece is $18 and holding cost is 20% of piece cost. Changeover (setup) time for the presses is 5 hr and the cost of downtime on any given press is $200/hr. Determine (a) the economic batch size and (b) the total annual inventory cost for the data. If the changeover time for the presses could be reduced to 10 min, determine (c) the economic batch size and (d) the total annual inventory cost.

2 A supplier of parts to an assembly plant in the household appliance industry is required to make deliveries on a just-in-time basis (daily). For one of the parts that must be delivered, the daily requirement is 200 parts, 5 days/week, 52 weeks/year. However, the supplier cannot afford to make just 200 parts each day; it must produce in larger batch sizes and maintain an inventory of parts from which 200 units are withdrawn for shipment each day. Cost per piece is $20 and holding cost is 24% of piece cost. Changeover time for the production machine used to produce the part is 2 hr and the cost of downtime on this machine is $250/hr. Determine (a) the economic batch size and (b) the total annual inventory cost for the data. The supplier hopes to reduce the batch size from the value determined in part (a) to 200 units, consistent with the daily quantity delivered to the appliance assembly plant. (c) Determine the changeover time that would allow the economic batch size in stamping to be 200 pieces. (d) What is the corresponding total annual inventory cost for this batch size, assuming the changeover time in part (c) can be realized?

3 Monthly usage rate for a certain part is 15,000 units. The part is produced in batches and its manufacturing costs are estimated to be $7.40. Holding cost is 20% of piece cost. Currently the production equipment used to produce this part is also used to produce 19 other parts with similar usage and cost data (assume the data to be identical for purposes of this problem). Changeover time between batches of the different parts is now 4.0 hr, and cost of downtime on the equipment is $275/hr. A proposal has been submitted to fabricate a fast-acting slide mechanism that will permit the changeovers to be completed in just 5.0 min. Cost to fabricate and install the slide mechanism is $150,000. (a) Is this cost justified by the savings in total annual inventory cost that would be achieved by reducing the economic batch quantity from its current value based on a 4-hour setup to the new value based on a 5-minute setup? (b) How many months of savings are required to pay off the $150,000 investment?

4 An injection-molding machine is used to produce 25 different plastic molded parts in a typical year. Annual demand for a typical part is 20,000 units. Each part is made out of a different plastic (the differences are in type of plastic and color). Because of the differences, changeover time between parts is significant, averaging 5 hr to (1) change molds and (2) purge the previous plastic from the injection barrel. One setup person normally does these two activities sequentially. A proposal has been made to separate the tasks and use two setup persons working simultaneously. In that case, the mold can be changed in 1.5 hr and purging takes 3.5 hr. Thus, the total downtime per changeover will be reduced to 3.5 hr from the previous 5 hr. Downtime on the injection-molding machine is $200/hr. Labor cost for setup time is $20/hr. Average cost of a plastic molded part is $2.50, and holding cost is 24% annually. For the 5-hour setup, determine (a) the economic batch quantity, (b) the total number of hours per year that the injection-molding machine is down for changeovers, and (c) the annual inventory cost. For the 3.5-hour setup, determine (d) the economic batch quantity, (e) the total number of hours per year that the injection-molding machine is down for changeovers, and (f) the annual inventory cost.

5 Solve the previous problem, but assume that a second proposal has been made to reduce the purging time of 3.5 hr during a changeover to less than 1.5 hr by sequencing the batches of parts so as to reduce the differences in plastic type and color between one part and the next. In the ideal, the same plastic can be used for all parts, thus eliminating the necessity to purge the injection barrel between batches. Thus, the limiting task in changing over the machine is the mold change time, which is 1.5 hr. For the 1.5-hour setup, determine (a) the economic batch quantity, (b) the total number of hours per year that the injection-molding machine is down for changeovers, and (c) the annual inventory cost.

Availability, Utilization, and Fraction Defect Rate

6 Data have been collected on the malfunctions and breakdowns that have caused line stoppages on a certain automated production line. Based on these data, the mean time between failures is 4.37 hr, and the mean time to repair is 24.1 min. Determine the availability of this line.

7 An automated guided vehicle system (AGVS) has been installed recently in a production warehouse. The company that supplied the AGVS claims that its system is very reliable and has an availability of 95%. In the first week of operation, the mean time between malfunctions that caused downtime averaged 12.3 hr/vehicle. On average, how long was each vehicle out of service if the supplier's claim of 95% availability is correct?

8 Three automatic screw machines are dedicated to the production of a certain high-demand fastener. The machines operate 40 hr/week and each machine produces at a rate of 73.2 parts/hr when producing. (a) How many parts can the three machines produce each week at full capacity? (b) If, during a particular week of interest, the three machines actually produced 7514 parts, how many hours of downtime did the three machines experience? (c) In part (b), if 9.25 hr are known to have been due to equipment malfunctions, what was the utilization of the three machines (due to reasons other than reliability problems)?

9 A certain production machine has an availability of 97%, and its utilization is 92%. The fraction defect rate of the parts made on the machine is 0.025, and it operates at only 85% of its rated speed. What is the overall equipment effectiveness of this machine?

Takt Time and Cycle Time

10 The weekly demand for a certain part is 950 units. The plant operates 5 days/week, with an effective operating time of 440 min/day. Determine the takt time for this part.

11 The monthly usage for a component supplied to an appliance assembly plant is 5000 parts. There are 21 working days in the month and the effective operating time of the plant is 450 min/day. Currently, the defect rate for the component is 2.2%, and the equipment used to produce the part is down for repairs an average of 22 min/day. Determine the takt time for this part.

12 The monthly demand for a part produced for an automotive final assembly plant is 16,000 units. There are 20 working days in February and the effective operating time of the plant is 900 min/day (two shifts). The fraction defect rate for the component is 0.017, and the automated machine that produces the part has an availability of 96%. Determine the takt time for this part.

Six Sigma and Other Quality Programs

Customers pay much more attention to the quality of the products and services they buy today than they did a few decades ago. They tend to select goods and services that provide greater customer satisfaction, commonly associated with higher quality. As a result, producers and service providers are forced to pay more attention to quality. In general, firms that maintain high quality in their products and services are more successful commercially.

Webster's New World Dictionary defines ***quality*** as "the degree of excellence which a thing possesses," or "the features that make something what it is." Juran and Gryna summarized it as "quality is customer satisfaction" [10]. The definition offered by the American Society for Quality (ASQ) is "the totality of features and characteristics of a product or service that bear on its ability to satisfy given needs" [5]. The meaning of quality cannot be captured easily in a simple short statement. One approach is to identify the attributes that determine the quality. For manufactured products, Garvin proposes eight dimensions of quality [6], which are defined in Table 1.

In this chapter, we discuss the quality-oriented improvement programs. The current leading program is Six Sigma, which is the main focus of this chapter. We also briefly describe several other quality programs, including statistical process control, total quality management, quality function deployment, and ISO 9000 (the international standard for quality systems).

TABLE 1 Dimensions that Determine Product Quality

1. ***Performance.*** Totality of the product's operating characteristics. In an automobile, performance attributes include acceleration, top speed, braking distance, steering and handling, and ride.
2. ***Features.*** Special characteristics and options that are often intended to distinguish the product from its competitors. In a television, these features might include a larger viewing screen and "picture-in-picture."
3. ***Aesthetic appeal.*** Usually, the appearance of a product. How pleasing is the product to the senses, especially the visual sense? A car's body style, front grille treatment, and color influence the aesthetic appeal of the car for the customer.
4. ***Conformance.*** The degree to which the product's appearance and function conform to preestablished standards. The term ***workmanship*** is often applicable here. In an automobile, conformance includes the body's fit and finish, and the absence of squeaks and rattles.
5. ***Reliability.*** The degree to which a product is always available for the customer over an extended period before final failure. In a car, it is the quality factor that allows the car to be started in cold weather and the absence of maintenance and repair visits to the dealer.
6. ***Durability.*** The ability of a product and its components to last a long time despite heavy use. Signs of durability in a car include a motor that continues to run for well over 100,000 miles, a body that does not rust, a dashboard that does not crack, and upholstery fabric that does not wear out after many years of use.
7. ***Serviceability.*** The ease with which a product is serviced and maintained. Many products have become so complicated that the owner cannot do the servicing and must take the product back to the original dealer for service. Accordingly, serviceability includes such factors as the courtesy and promptness of the service provided by the dealer.
8. ***Perceived quality.*** A subjective and intangible factor that may include the customer's perception (whether correct or not) of several of the preceding dimensions. Perceived quality is often influenced by advertising, brand recognition, and the reputation of the company making the product.

Source: Adapted from [6].

1 OVERVIEW AND STATISTICAL BASIS OF SIX SIGMA

Six Sigma is the name of a quality-focused program that utilizes worker teams to accomplish projects aimed at improving an organization's operational performance. The first Six Sigma program was implemented at Motorola Corporation (Historical Note 1). The name Six Sigma is derived from the normal statistical distribution, in which the Greek letter sigma (σ) is the standard deviation or measure of dispersion in a normal population. In the normal distribution, six sigma implies near perfection in a process, and that is the goal of a Six Sigma program. To operate at the six sigma level over the long term, a process must be capable of producing no more than 3.4 defects per million, where a defect refers to anything that is outside of customer specifications. Six Sigma projects can be applied to any manufacturing, service, or business processes that affect the satisfaction of both internal and external customers. There is a strong emphasis on the customer and customer satisfaction in Six Sigma.

HISTORICAL NOTE 1 SIX SIGMA

The seeds for Six Sigma were planted in the late 1970s, when Dr. Mikel Harry, an engineer at Motorola Corporation, began to experiment with the use of statistical analysis to solve problems in the company's Government Electronics Group (GEG). The thrust of his work was that increases in process variations reduce the likelihood of meeting customer requirements, resulting in lower customer satisfaction. Using his methods, Motorola's GEG was able to design and produce products in less time and at lower cost than previously possible.

Encouraged by then CEO Robert Galvin, Dr. Harry worked on formulating an approach to apply his problem-solving and change-management methods throughout the company. This culminated in the paper "The Strategic Vision for Accelerating Six Sigma Within Motorola." He was subsequently named head of the Motorola Six Sigma Research Institute. Interestingly, credit for coining the term "six sigma" was given to Motorola engineer Bill Smith in 1986.

In 1988, Motorola was the winner of the Malcolm Baldrige Quality Award, the prestigious national award for quality in corporate America. Motorola gives much of the credit for winning the award to its Six Sigma Program.

CEO Galvin had become an enthusiastic believer in Six Sigma, as it gradually showed impressive results in his company's performance. In the early 1990s, he was presenting speeches on the subject. Other companies began to listen. In 1991, Lawrence Bossidy became the chief executive at Allied Signal and began implementing Six Sigma. Within a few years, his company was reaping the benefits in millions of dollars in savings and in improved customer relations. In 1995, the CEO of General Electric, Jack Welch, was playing golf with Bossidy and inquired about the success that Allied Signal was enjoying. By the end of that year, GE had decided that Six Sigma should be a corporate-wide program. Since then, General Electric has probably been the most successful user of Six Sigma, with documented savings measured in billions of dollars.

The general goals of Six Sigma and the projects that are performed under its banner can be summarized as follows:

- Better customer satisfaction
- High quality products and services
- Reduced defects
- Improved process capability through reduction in process variations
- Continuous improvement
- Cost reduction through more effective and efficient processes

Worker teams who participate in a Six Sigma project are trained in the use of statistical and problem-solving tools as well as project management techniques to define, measure, analyze, and make improvements in the operations of the organization by eliminating defects and variability in its processes. The teams are empowered by management, whose responsibility is to identify the important problems in the processes of the organization and to sponsor the teams to address those problems.

A central concept of Six Sigma is that defects in a given process can be measured and quantified. Once quantified, the underlying causes of the defects can be identified, and corrective action can be taken to fix the causes and eliminate the defects. The results of the improvement effort can be seen using the same measurement procedures to make

TABLE 2 Sigma Levels and Corresponding Defects per Million, Fraction Defect Rate, and Yield in a Six Sigma Program

Sigma Level (σ)	Defects per Million (DPM)	Fraction Defect Rate q	Yield Y (%)
6	3.4	0.0000034	99.99966
5	233	0.000233	99.977
4	6,210	0.00621	99.38
3	66,807	0.0668	93.32
2.5	158,655	0.1587	84.13
2	308,538	0.3085	69.15
1.5	500,000	0.5000	50
1	691,462	0.6915	30.85

a before-and-after comparison. The comparison is often expressed in terms of sigma level. For example, the process was originally operating at the 3-sigma level, but now it is operating at the 5-sigma level. In terms of defect levels, this means that the process was previously producing 66,807 defects/million and now it is producing only 233 defects/million. Various other sigma levels and corresponding defects per million (DPM) and other measures are listed in Table 2. A more complete listing of sigma levels and associated measures is presented in Chapter Appendix.

The traditional metric for good process quality is $\pm 3\sigma$ (three sigma level). If a process is stable and in statistical control for a given output variable of interest, and this output is normally distributed, then 99.73% of the process output will be within the range defined by $\pm 3\sigma$. This situation is illustrated in Figure 1. It means that there will be 0.27% (0.135% in each tail) of the output that lies beyond these limits, or 2700 parts/million produced.

Let us compare this with a process that operates at the six-sigma level. Under the same assumptions as before (normally distributed stable process in statistical control), the proportion of the output that lies within the range $\pm 6\sigma$ is 99.9999998%, which corresponds to a defect rate of only 0.002 defects/million. This situation is illustrated in Figure 2.

The reader has probably noticed that this defect rate does not match the rate associated with Six Sigma in Table 2. The rate shown in the table is 3.4 defects/million, which corresponds to a yield of 99.99966%. Why is there a difference? Which is correct?

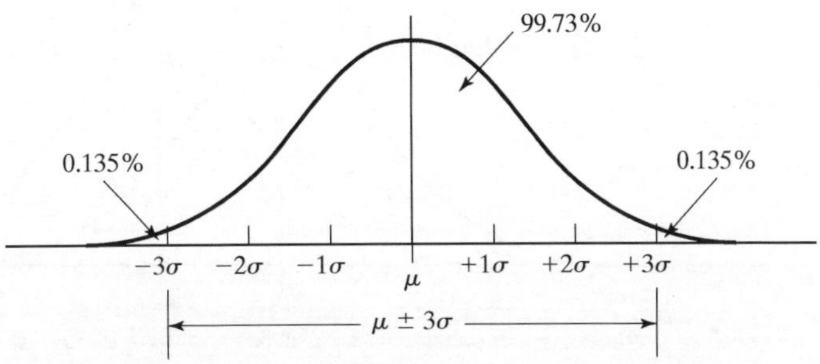

Figure 1 Normal distribution of process output variable, showing the $\pm 3\sigma$ limits.

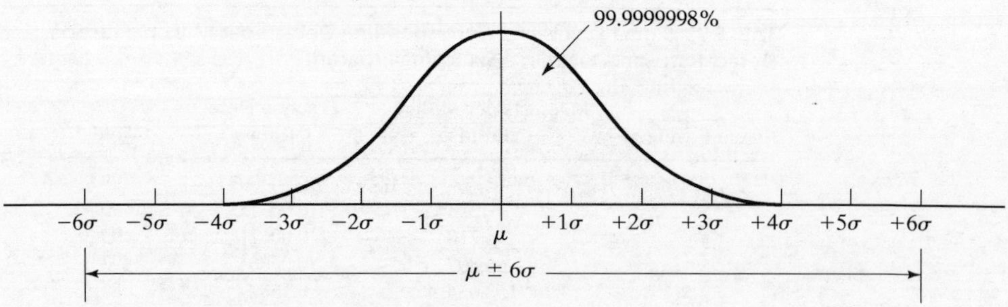

Figure 2 Normal distribution of process output variable, showing the $\pm 6\sigma$ limits.

If we look up the proportion of the population that lies within $\pm 6\sigma$ in a standard normal probability table (if we can find a table that goes that high), we would find that 99.9999998% is the correct value, not 99.99966%. Admittedly, it does not seem like much of a difference when the yields are compared. But the difference between 0.002 defects/million and 3.4 defects/million is significant.

The explanation for this anomaly is that when the engineers at Motorola devised the Six Sigma standard, they considered processes that operate over the long run. And processes over the long run tend to deviate from the original process mean. While data are collected from a process over a relatively short period of time (e.g., a few weeks or months) to determine the mean and standard deviation, the same process may run for years. During the long-term operation of that process, its mean will likely undergo shifts to the right or left. To compensate for these likely shifts, Motorola selected to use 1.5σ as the magnitude of the shift, while leaving the original $\pm 6\sigma$ limits in place for the process. The effect of this shift is shown in Figure 3. Accordingly, when 6σ is used in Six Sigma, it really refers to 4.5σ in the normal probability tables.

Some reinforcement of this alteration of the normal probability tables can be seen in Table 2 in the line for 1.5σ. A shift in the process mean of 1.5σ moves the distribution to a new center located at 1.5σ in the previous distribution. With the mean located at this new position, 50% of the population is located to the right of the mean, and this corresponds to the 1.5σ for the old distribution as given in Table 2. Other lines in the table can be compared with the standard normal probability values in the same way.

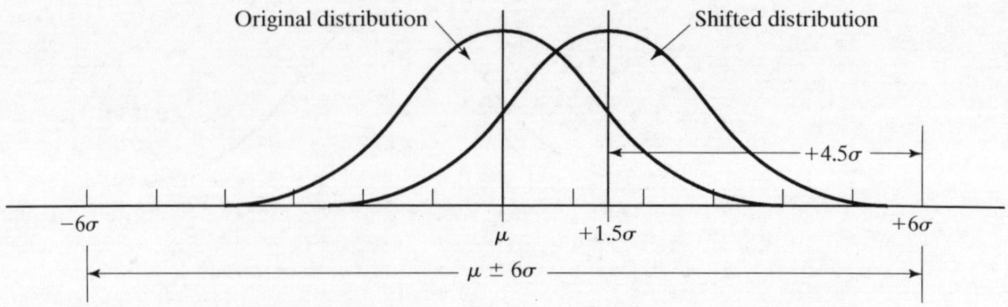

Figure 3 Normal distribution shift by a distance of 1.5σ from the original mean.

So, now we have discovered that Six Sigma really means 4.5 sigma, due to the 1.5σ shift. Perhaps Motorola should have named their quality program 4.5 Sigma. No, it just doesn't have the same impact.

2 THE SIX SIGMA DMAIC PROCEDURE

Six Sigma teams use a problem-solving approach called DMAIC, sometimes pronounced "duh-may-ick." It consists of five steps:

1. ***Define*** the project goals and customer requirements.
2. ***Measure*** the process to assess its current performance.
3. ***Analyze*** the process and determine root causes of variations and defects.
4. ***Improve*** the process by reducing variations and defects.
5. ***Control*** the future process performance by institutionalizing the improvements.

These are the basic steps in an improvement procedure intended for existing processes that are currently operating at low sigma levels and need improvement. DMAIC provides the worker team with a systematic and data-driven approach for solving an identified problem. It is a roadmap that guides the team toward improvement in the process of interest. Although the approach seems very sequential (e.g., step 1, then step 2, and so on), an iterative implementation of DMAIC is sometimes required. For example, in the analyze step (step 3), the team may discover that it did not collect the right data in the measure step (step 2). Therefore, it must iterate the previous step to correct the deficiency.

The reader will no doubt notice the similarities between the DMAIC approach and our systematic approach in methods engineering, which is based on the more general scientific method. Solving problems requires a systematic approach that is quite universal in its progression. The exact tools and techniques must be selected based on the details of the problem. And the details are always different, which is why ingenuity and creativity of the team using the approach is required. As the saying goes, "the devil is in the details." In the following sections, the five steps of the DMAIC approach are described and the typical tools that might be applied in each step are identified.

2.1 Define

The define step in DMAIC can be divided into the following phases: (1) organizing the project team, (2) providing it with a charter (the problem to solve), (3) identifying the customers served by the process, and (4) developing a high-level process map.

Organizing the Project Team. Members of the project team are selected on the basis of their knowledge of the problem area and other skills. The team members, at least some of them, have had Six Sigma training. Some of the team members are the workers who operate the process of interest. Team leaders in a Six Sigma project are called ***black belts***; they are the project managers. They have had detailed training in the entire range of Six Sigma problem-solving techniques. Assisting them are ***green belts***, other team members who have been trained in some Six Sigma techniques. Providing technical resources and serving as consultants and mentors for the black belts are ***master black belts***. Master black belts are generally full-time positions, and they are selected for their teaching aptitudes, quantitative skills, and experience in Six Sigma.

Participating in the formation of a Six Sigma project team is an individual known in Six Sigma terminology as the ***champion***, who is typically a member of management. The champion is often the owner of the process, and the process needs improvement.

Providing a Charter. The charter is the documentation that justifies the project to be undertaken by the Six Sigma team. Much of the substance of the charter is provided by the champion, the one with the problem. The charter documentation usually includes the following:

- It describes the problem and the background of the problem. What is wrong with the process? How long has the problem existed? How does the process currently operate, and how should it be operating? An attempt is made to define the problem in quantitative terms.
- It defines the objectives of the project. What should the project team be able to accomplish within a certain time frame, say six months? What will be the benefits of the project?
- It defines the scope of the project. What areas should the project team focus on and what areas should be avoided?
- It establishes the business case for solving the problem. How is the project justified in economic terms? What is the potential return by accomplishing the project? Why is this problem more important than other problems?
- It determines a schedule for the project. What are the logical milestones in the project? These are often defined in terms of the five steps in the DMAIC procedure. When should the define step be completed? How many weeks should the measure step take? And so forth.

Identifying the Customers. Every process serves customers. The output of the process (e.g., the product or part produced or the service delivered) has one or more customers. Otherwise, there would be no need for the process. It would be an unnecessary operation (one of the seven forms of waste in lean production). Customers are the recipients of the process output and are directly affected by its quality, either advantageously or adversely. Customers have needs and requirements that must be satisfied or exceeded. An important function in the define step is to identify exactly who are the customers of the process and what are their requirements.

Of particular interest in identifying the customers is to determine those characteristics of the process output that are critical to quality (CTQ) from a customer's viewpoint. The CTQ characteristics are the features or elements of the process and its output that directly impact the customer's perception of quality. Typical CTQ characteristics include the reliability of a product (e.g., automobile, appliance, lawn mower) or the timeliness of a service (e.g., fast food restaurant, repair shop, plumber). Identifying the CTQ characteristics allows the Six Sigma team to focus on what's important and not to dissipate its energy on unimportant issues.

Developing a High-Level Process Map. The final task in the define step is to develop a high-level process map. Process mapping is one of the variety of graphical techniques that can be used to depict the sequence of steps that operate on the inputs to the process and produce the output. Process mapping is the preferred technique in a Six Sigma project because it can be used to portray the process at various levels of detail. In the define step, when the improvement project is just getting underway, it is appropriate to visualize the process at a high level, without the details that will be examined in subsequent steps. The process map developed here should include the suppliers, inputs, process, outputs, and customers (SIPOC in Six Sigma terminology).

In addition to the high-level viewpoint, the process map should also be an "as is" picture of the current process, without any attempt to make improvements. Viewing the status quo process map may very well provide leads that will result in improvements. The "as is" process map provides a benchmark against which to compare the subsequent improvements.

2.2 Measure

The measure step in DMAIC can be divided into the following phases: (1) creating a data collection plan, (2) implementing the plan by collecting the data, and (3) measuring the current sigma level of the process. Assessing the sigma level of the current process is useful for making later comparisons after improvements have been added.

Creating a Data Collection Plan. The first phase in creating a data collection plan is deciding what should be measured. This decision should be made with reference to the process map and the critical-to-quality (CTQ) characteristics developed in the define step. The measurements can be classified into three categories:

- *Input measures.* These are variables related to the process inputs, which are provided by its suppliers. What are the important quality measures to assess the performance of the suppliers?
- *Process measures.* These are the internal variables of the process itself. In general, they deal with efficiency measures such as cycle time and waiting time, and quality measures such as dimensional variables and fraction defect rate.
- *Output measures.* These are the measures seen by the customer. They indicate how well customer requirements and expectations are being satisfied. They are functionally related to the input measures and process measures.

Once the decision on what to measure has been made, it is usually necessary to design data collection forms for the project. Every Six Sigma project is different, and different types of data must be collected for each of them. There are several issues related to the design of the data collection form:

- *Type of data.* The two basic types of data are discrete and continuous. ***Discrete data*** include binary data (e.g., on/off, defective/nondefective) and counts (e.g., number of parts produced per hour, number of defects per car). ***Continuous data***, also called ***variable data***, refer to measures that exist over a continuum of values, and any value within the continuum is possible. Examples include time, temperature, and length (e.g., part dimensional data). Different forms are usually required for the various data types.

- *Amount of data to collect.* How much data should be collected to satisfy the needs of the project? Requirements for accuracy and completeness must be balanced against the need to use resources efficiently and complete the project in a timely manner.
- *Sampling intervals.* How frequently should data be collected? The accepted practice is to collect data at random rather than regular intervals.
- *Time period to collect the data.* How long should the data collection phase last? The period should be representative of normal operations.

Collecting the Data. The second phase in the measure step is to implement the planning phase by collecting the data. Adjustments in the data collection plan are sometimes required by problems encountered in the collection procedure. The problems may be related to occurrences or variables in the process that were not anticipated in the planning phase (e.g., identification of an important variable that was previously overlooked) or design of the data collection forms (e.g., no space on the form to note unusual events). To recognize these problems and take the appropriate corrective actions, an important rule of data collection in a Six Sigma project is for the team itself to be involved in the data collection and not to delegate the task to others [16].

Measuring the Current Sigma Level. After data collection has been completed, the team is in a position to analyze the current sigma level of the "as-is" process. This provides a starting point for making improvements and measuring their effects on the process. It allows a before-and-after comparison. The first step in assessing the current sigma level of the process is to determine the number of defects per million. That value is then converted to the corresponding sigma level using Table 2 or Chapter Appendix at end of this chapter.

There are several alternative measures of defects per million that can be used in a Six Sigma program. The most appropriate measure is probably the ***defects per million opportunities*** ($DPMO$), which refers to the fact that there may be more than one opportunity for defects to occur in each unit. Thus the number of opportunities takes into account the complexity of the product or service so that entirely different types of products and services can be compared on the same sigma scale. Defects per million opportunities is calculated as:

$$DPMO = 1{,}000{,}000 \frac{N_d}{N_u N_o} \tag{1}$$

where $DPMO$ = defects per million opportunities, N_d = number of defects, N_u = number of units in the population of interest, and N_o = number of opportunities for a defect per unit. The factor 1,000,000 converts the proportion into defects per million.

Other common measures include defects per million (DPM) and defective units per million ($DUPM$). ***Defects per million*** measures all of the defects encountered in the population, and there is more than one opportunity for a defect per defective unit.

$$DPM = 1{,}000{,}000 \frac{N_d}{N_u} \tag{2}$$

Defective units per million is the count of defective units in the population of interest, and a defective unit may contain more than one defect.

$$DUPM = 1{,}000{,}000\frac{N_{du}}{N_u} \tag{3}$$

where N_{du} = number of defective units. The following example illustrates the procedure for determining *DPMO, DPM*, and *DUPM*, as well as the corresponding sigma levels.

Example 1 Determining the Sigma Level of a Process

A refrigerator final assembly plant inspects its completed products for 37 features that are considered critical-to-quality (CTQ). During the previous three-month period, a total of 31,487 refrigerators were produced, among which 1690 had defects of the 37 CTQ features, and a total of 902 refrigerators had one or more defects. Determine (a) the defects per million opportunities and corresponding sigma level, (b) defects per million and corresponding sigma level, (c) defective units per million and corresponding sigma level.

Solution: Summarizing the data, $N_o = 37$ defect opportunities per product, $N_u = 31{,}487$ products units, $N_d = 1690$ defects, and $N_{du} = 902$ defective units.

(a) $DPMO = 1{,}000{,}000\dfrac{1690}{31{,}487(37)} = 1451$ defects per million opportunities.

This corresponds to the 4.5 sigma level.

(b) $DPM = 1{,}000{,}000\dfrac{1690}{31{,}487} = 53{,}673$ defects per million.

This corresponds to the 3.1 sigma level.

(c) $DUPM = 1{,}000{,}000\dfrac{902}{31{,}487} = 28{,}647$ defective units per million

This corresponds to the 3.4 sigma level. ■

2.3 Analyze

The analyze step in DMAIC can be divided into the following phases: (1) basic data analysis, (2) process analysis, and (3) root cause analysis. The analyze step is a bridge between measure (step 2) and improve (step 4). Analyze takes the data collected in step 2 and, through the analysis performed on the data, provides a quantitative basis for developing improvements in step 4. The analyze phase seeks to identify where the improvement opportunities are located.

Basic Data Analysis. The purpose of the basic data analysis is to present the collected data in a way that lends itself to making inferences. This usually means graphical displays of the data. The displays have different forms depending on whether the data are discrete or continuous.

For discrete data, appropriate ways to graphically display the data include histograms, Pareto charts, pie charts, and defect concentration diagrams. For continuous data, some of these same techniques can sometimes be used by first classifying the continuous data into discrete categories, which can then be displayed using discrete charting tools such as the histogram, Pareto chart, and pie chart. For dealing with the continuous data in its more natural form, check sheets and scatter diagrams are more suitable.

Additional statistical analysis tools often used for data analysis include regression analysis (least-squares analysis), analysis of variance, and hypothesis testing. Readers who have taken a course in statistical analysis should be familiar with these methods.

Process Analysis. Process analysis is concerned with interpreting the results of the basic data analysis and developing a more detailed picture of the way the process operates and what is wrong with it. The more detailed picture usually includes a series of process maps that focus on the individual steps in the high-level process map created earlier in the define step (step 1 in DMAIC). The low-level process maps are useful in better understanding the inner workings of the process. The Six Sigma team progresses through a process analysis by asking questions such as the following:

- What are the value-adding steps in the process?
- What are the non–value-adding but necessary steps?
- What are the steps that add no value and could be eliminated?
- What are the steps that generate variations, deviations, and errors in the process?
- Which steps are efficient and which steps are inefficient (in terms of time, labor, equipment, materials, and other resources)? The inefficient steps merit further scrutiny.
- Why is so much waiting required in this process?
- Why is so much material handling required?

The reader will note that these kinds of questions are similar to those asked during a traditional methods engineering study. The difference here is that the Six Sigma team is asking them rather than the methods engineer. Worker involvement can be a powerful motivator for improvement.

Root Cause Analysis. Root cause analysis attempts to identify the significant factors that affect process performance. The situation can be depicted using the following general equation:

$$y = f(x_1, x_2, \ldots, x_i, \ldots x_n) \tag{4}$$

where y = some output variable of interest in the project (e.g., some quality feature of importance to the customer); and $x_1, x_2, \ldots, x_i, \ldots x_n$ are the independent variables in the process that may affect the output variable. The value of y is a function of the values of x_i. In root cause analysis, the team attempts to determine which of the x_i variables are most important and how they influence y. In all likelihood, there are more than one y variables of interest. For each y, there is likely to be a different set of x_i variables.

Root cause analysis consists of the following phases: (1) brainstorming of hypotheses, (2) eliminating the unlikely hypotheses, and (3) validating the hypotheses. In general, ***brainstorming*** is a group problem-solving activity that consists of group members spontaneously contributing ideas on a subject of mutual interest. The cause and effect diagram is a tool that is sometimes used to focus thoughts in brainstorming.

The guidelines for successful brainstorming include: (1) all ideas are accepted, none are rejected; (2) all ideas are documented; (3) new ideas are only generated, not discussed or evaluated yet; and (4) everyone participates.

At the end of the brainstorming phase, there is a long list of hypotheses, some of which are less likely to be valid than others. There is a priority of worthiness among the hypotheses. The elimination phase begins. The team must use its collective wisdom and knowledge of the process to identify which hypotheses are highest on the priority list and which ones should be eliminated from further consideration. During this phase, the various ideas are questioned, clarified, and discussed but not criticized. The list of hypotheses is reduced from a large number to a much smaller number. The important x_i variables are identified, and the relationships of $y = f(x)$ are conjectured.

The final phase of root cause analysis is concerned with validating the reduced list of hypotheses. It involves testing these hypotheses and determining the mathematical relationship for $y = f(x_1, x_2, \ldots, x_i, \ldots, x_n)$. Scatter diagrams can be especially useful in determining the shape of the relationship and the form of the mathematical model for the process. In some cases, additional data must be collected on particular variables that have been identified as significant. Designed experiments may be required to ensure that the desired information is extracted from the data collection procedure in the most efficient way.

2.4 Improve

The improve step of DMAIC consists of the following phases: (1) generation of alternative improvements, (2) analysis and prioritization of alternative improvements, and (3) implementation of improvements.

Generation of Alternative Improvements. The preceding root cause analysis should indicate the areas in which potential improvements and problem solutions are likely to be found. The Six Sigma team uses brainstorming sessions to generate and refine the alternatives. The search is for improvements and solutions that will reduce defects, increase customer satisfaction, improve the quality of the product or service, reduce variation, and increase process efficiency.

Analysis and Prioritization. In all likelihood, the generation of improvement opportunities has resulted in more alternatives than can be feasibly implemented. At this point the alternatives must be analyzed and prioritized, and those alternatives that are deemed impractical must be discarded. Techniques that can be used to analyze the alternatives include (1) process mapping and (2) failure mode and effect analysis (FMEA).

The process map developed during this phase is a "should be" description of the process. It incorporates the potential improvements and solutions into the current process to allow visualization and provide graphical documentation of how it would work after the changes have been made. This allows the proposed improvements to be analyzed and refined prior to implementation.

A ***failure mode and effect analysis*** (FMEA) is a systematic technique used in quality engineering to identify potential ways in which a process or product can fail and to assess the risk and severity of the failure. It is a technique sometimes used in Six Sigma projects. FMEA combines nontechnical and technical approaches in the analysis procedure. Nontechnical approaches include brainstorming, consideration of past experiences, and subjective judgment. Technical approaches include risk analysis and reliability theory. FMEA considers the following factors:

1. *Possible failure mode.* What is the type of failure or malfunction? Examples include a short circuit in an electrical component or a stress failure of a structural component.
2. *Occurrence.* How frequently does each failure mode occur? A scale is used to rate occurrence. The scale ranges from "remote" (failure is unlikely, ranking = 1) to "very high" (failure is almost inevitable, ranking = 10).
3. *Potential effects of failure.* These effects are usually customer oriented. What will the customer experience if a given failure occurs? Examples include inability to use the product, physical injury, and loss of life.
4. *Severity.* This is an assessment of the seriousness of the effect of the failure. How severe is the effect on the customer? A scale is typically used to rate severity, ranging from "no effect" (ranking = 1) to "very hazardous with no warning" (ranking = 10).
5. *Detection.* How difficult is it to detect an impendent failure before it occurs? The alternatives range from "almost certain detection" (ranking = 1) to "absolute uncertainty" (ranking = 10).

Three of these factors (occurrence, severity, and detection) are then combined into a ***risk priority number***, which is the product of the rankings of the three factors. That is,

$$RPN = OSD \tag{5}$$

where RPN = risk priority number, O = occurrence rank number, S = severity rank number, and D = detection rank number. Those failure modes with the highest RPN merit the most attention. In FMEA, corrective actions must be proposed and analyzed to determine how the risk factors (O, S, and D) can be reduced from their present values, thereby reducing the RPN. Examples of possible corrective actions might include design changes, alternative materials for the application, emphasis on training to reduce a hazard, and mistake proofing devices (poka-yoke from lean production). A more complete treatment of failure mode and effect analysis is presented in [2] and other texts on quality management.

Following analysis, the alternative improvements must be prioritized. Two systematic approaches can be used to prioritize the alternatives:

- *Pareto priority index.* This approach, described in [10], is based on Pareto analysis and can be used to evaluate and prioritize alternatives that have costs and expected savings. The index is defined as

$$PPI = \frac{E(S)}{CT} \tag{6}$$

where PPI = Pareto priority index; $E(S)$ = expected savings from the improvement, which equals anticipated savings multiplied by the probability of success; C = cost of project; and T = time to complete, years. The candidates with the highest PPI values are selected for study.

- *Criteria matrix.* This is a tabular listing of the alternatives and the criteria by which they will be evaluated. The criteria are divided into two categories: (1) must criteria and (2) desirable features. Alternatives that do not satisfy the must criteria are eliminated. The remaining alternatives are then evaluated by a scoring scheme against the desirable features.

Implementation of Improvements. Having prioritized the proposed improvements, the next phase in the DMAIC improve step is implementation. The priority list of proposed improvements determines where to start. Implementation can proceed one proposal at a time or in groups of proposals, depending on how the proposed changes relate to each other. For example, if the changes in the process required by two different proposals are very similar, it may make sense to implement both at the same time, even though one proposal occupies a much higher priority than the other. Also, if the objectives of the project are to achieve a certain level of overall improvement in the process that is deemed sufficient, then it may not be necessary to implement all of the proposals on the list.

To determine the overall process improvement, the same quality performance measurements should be made as in the original sigma level assessment (Example 1). This will provide the project team with a before-and-after comparison to gauge the effect of the various changes.

2.5 Control

Sometimes when process improvements are made, they are gradually discarded and the improvement benefits erode over time. This phenomenon occurs for a variety of reasons:

- Human resistance to change
- Familiarity and comfort associated with the former method
- Absence of standard procedures detailing the new method
- Inadequate monitoring of process performance
- Lack of attention by supervisory personnel.

The purpose of the control step in DMAIC is to avoid this potential erosion and to maintain the improved performance that was achieved through implementation of the proposed changes. The control step consists of the following actions: (1) develop a control plan, (2) transfer responsibility back to original owner and disband the Six Sigma team.

Development of a Control Plan. The final task of the Six Sigma team is to document the results of the project and develop a control plan that will sustain the improvements that have been made in the process. The control plan documentation establishes the ***standard operating procedure*** (SOP) for the improved process. It should address issues and questions such as the following:

- Details of the process control relationships. This refers to the various $y = f(x_i)$ relationships that have been developed by the Six Sigma team. These relationships indicate how control of the process is achieved and which variables (x_i) are important to achieve it.

- What input variables must be measured and monitored?
- What process variables must be measured and monitored?
- What output variables must be measured and monitored?
- Who is responsible for these measurements?
- What are the corrective action procedures that should be followed in the event that something goes wrong in the process?
- What institutional procedures must be established to maintain the improvements?
- What are the worker training requirements to sustain the improvements?

Transferring Responsibility and Disbanding the Team. The Six Sigma team has been actively involved in the operation of the process for an extended period of time by now. Their work is nearly complete. One of their final actions is to turn whatever responsibility they had for operating the process back to its original owner (e.g., the champion). They must make sure that the owner understands the control plan and that it will be continuously implemented.

Once responsibility reverts back to the original owner, the team is no longer needed. It is therefore disbanded, and the black belt is assigned to a new team and the next project.

3 OTHER QUALITY PROGRAMS

Six Sigma is the latest in a list of quality programs that have been developed over the years. The starting points for most of these programs were in the late 1970s and early to mid-1980s, although their statistical underpinnings have much earlier origins. The principal quality-related programs being used today other than Six Sigma DMAIC are briefly described in this section. These programs are described more thoroughly in several of the references listed at the end of this chapter [2, 5, 7, 11, 12, 13, and 18]. Much of the following discussion is extracted from [8].

Statistical Process Control (SPC). ***Statistical process control*** (SPC) involves the use of various methods to measure and analyze a process. SPC is applicable to both manufacturing and nonmanufacturing situations, but most of the applications are in manufacturing. The overall objectives of SPC are as follows: (1) improve the quality of the process output, (2) reduce process variability and achieve process stability, and (3) solve processing problems. Most of the methods used in SPC are basic statistical techniques such as histograms, Pareto charts, check sheets, and other data gathering and analysis tools. There are also nontechnical aspects in the implementation of statistical process control. To be successful, SPC must include a commitment to quality that pervades the organization from senior top management to the starting worker on the production line.

Total Quality Management. ***Total quality management*** (TQM) and Six Sigma are quite similar in their emphasis on management involvement, the team approach, and the list of tools that are employed. It has been argued that Six Sigma is really an extension of TQM in which the objective is to establish a defined target for quality—and that target is six sigma [7]. The tools in Six Sigma and TQM include the statistical techniques associated with statistical process control.

Total quality management denotes a management approach that pursues three main objectives: (1) achieving customer satisfaction, (2) encouraging involvement of the entire workforce, and (3) continuous improvement. The focus in TQM is on the customer and customer satisfaction. Products are designed and manufactured with this quality focus. Juran's definition, "quality is customer satisfaction," defines the requirement for any product. The product features must be established to achieve customer satisfaction. The product must be free of defects. Included in the customer focus is the notion that there are internal customers as well as external customers. The final assembly department is the customer of the parts production departments. The engineer is the customer of the technical staff support group. And so forth.

Employee involvement in TQM runs throughout the organization. It extends from the top through all levels below. The important influence that product design has on product quality is recognized. Decisions made in product design directly impact the quality that can be achieved in manufacturing. In production, the viewpoint is that inspecting the product after it is made is not good enough. Quality must be built into the product. Production workers must inspect their own work and not rely on the inspection department to find their mistakes. Quality is the job of everyone in the organization. It even extends outside the immediate organization to the suppliers.

High product quality is a process of continuous improvement. It is a never-ending chase to design better products and then to manufacture them better. The team project approach for continuous improvement and problem solving used in TQM and Six Sigma is similar to kaizen circles in lean production.

Taguchi Methods in Quality Engineering. The term ***quality engineering*** encompasses a broad range of activities whose aim is to ensure that a product's quality characteristics are at their nominal or target values. The field owes much to Genichi Taguchi, who has had an important influence on its development, especially in the design area—both product design and process design. Among Taguchi's contributions are the following techniques:

- *Robust design.* The objective in robust design is to develop products and processes in which the function and performance are relatively insensitive to variations. In product design, robustness means that the product can maintain consistent performance with minimal disturbance due to variations in uncontrollable factors in its operating environment. In process design, robustness means that the process continues to produce good product with minimal effect from uncontrollable variations in raw materials and manufacturing processes.
- *Taguchi loss function.* This technique applies to tolerance design. Loss occurs when a product's functional characteristic differs from its nominal or target value. When the dimension of a component deviates from its nominal value, the component's function is adversely affected. Even small deviations cause some loss in function. The loss increases at an accelerating rate as the deviation grows, according to the Taguchi loss function. At some level of deviation, the loss is prohibitive, and this level identifies one possible way to specify the tolerance limit for the dimension.

Quality Function Deployment. As applied to product design, the objective of ***quality function deployment*** (QFD) is to design products that will satisfy or exceed customer requirements. Of course, any product design project has this aim, but the approach is often very informal and unsystematic. QFD uses a formal and systematic procedure for defining customer desires and requirements, and interpreting them in terms of product features and process characteristics. In a QFD analysis, a series of interconnected matrices are developed to establish the relationships between customer requirements and the technical features of a proposed new product. The matrices represent a progression of phases in the QFD analysis, in which customer requirements are first translated into product features, then into manufacturing process requirements, and finally into quality procedures for controlling the manufacturing operations.

Design for Six Sigma. The majority of the companies using Six Sigma employ the DMAIC procedure to improve current processes and solve existing problems. A few companies are also using an approach to design that is based on Six Sigma concepts. It is called Design for Six Sigma (DFSS). Design in this context refers to the development and design of new products, processes, and services, with the objective of designing and manufacturing to a quality level that will achieve only 3.4 defects per million in the new products, processes, and services.

Although the objective in DFSS is clear (six sigma quality level), the methodology of Design for Six Sigma is not nearly so universally recognized and accepted as DMAIC is for addressing existing processes. Different consultants, authors, and user companies tout their own individual approaches to DFSS, and there are differences in these approaches. In general, the common theme is an emphasis on the customer and the critical-to-quality (CTQ) characteristics that are important to the customer. As with the tools used in the Six Sigma DMAIC methodology, the various approaches in Design for Six Sigma borrow techniques from other quality initiatives. Examples include failure mode and effect analysis (Section 2.4), Taguchi methods, and quality function deployment.

ISO 9000. ISO 9000 is a set of international standards on quality developed by the International Organization for Standardization (ISO), based in Geneva, Switzerland, and representing virtually all industrialized nations. ISO 9000 establishes standards for the systems and procedures used by a facility that affect the quality of the products and services produced by the facility. It is not a standard for the products or services themselves. ISO 9000 includes a glossary of quality terms, guidelines for selecting and using the various standards, models for quality systems, and guidelines for auditing quality systems.

The ISO standards are generic rather than industry-specific. They are applicable to any facility producing any product and/or providing any service, no matter what the market. As mentioned, the focus of the standards is on the facility's quality system rather than its products or services. A ***quality system*** is defined as "the organizational structure, responsibilities, procedures, processes, and resources needed to implement quality management."[1] ISO 9000 is concerned with the set of activities undertaken by a facility to ensure that its output provides customer satisfaction. It does not specify methods or procedures for achieving customer satisfaction; instead it describes concepts and objectives for achieving it.

[1]From ISO 8402.

ISO 9000 can be applied in a facility in two ways. The first is to implement the standards or selected portions of the standards simply for the sake of improving the firm's quality systems. Improving the procedures and systems for delivering high quality products and services is a worthwhile accomplishment, whether or not formal recognition is awarded. The second way to apply ISO 9000 is to become registered. ISO 9000 registration not only improves the facility's quality systems, but it also provides formal certification that the facility meets the requirements of the standard. A significant benefit of certification is that it qualifies the facility for business partnerships with companies that require ISO 9000 registration. This is especially important for firms doing business in the European Community, where certain products are classified as regulated and ISO 9000 registration is required for companies making these products as well as their suppliers.

REFERENCES

[1] Basu, R. "Six Sigma to Fit Sigma." *IIE Solutions* (July 2001): 28–33.

[2] Besterfield, D. H., C. Besterfield-Michna, G. H. Besterfield, and M. Besterfield-Sacre. *Total Quality Management*. 3rd ed. Upper Saddle River, NJ: Prentice Hall, 2003.

[3] Crosby, P. B. *Quality Is Free*. New York: McGraw-Hill, 1979.

[4] Eckes, G. *Six Sigma for Everyone*. Hoboken, NJ: Wiley, 2003.

[5] Evans, J. R., and W. M. Lindsay. *The Management and Control of Quality*. 3rd ed. St. Paul, MN: West Publishing, 1996.

[6] Garvin, D. A. "Competing on the Eight Dimensions of Quality." *Harvard Business Review* (June 1987): 101–109.

[7] Goetsch, D. L., and S. B. Davis. *Introduction to Total Quality*. 2nd ed. Upper Saddle River, NJ: Prentice Hall, 1997.

[8] Groover, M. P. *Automation, Production Systems, and Computer Integrated Manufacturing*. 2nd ed. Upper Saddle River, NJ: Prentice Hall, 2001.

[9] Jing, G. G., and L. Ning. "Claiming Six Sigma." *Industrial Engineer* (February 2004): 37–39.

[10] Juran, J. M., and F. M. Gryna. *Quality Planning and Analysis*. 3rd ed. New York: McGraw-Hill, 1993.

[11] Lochner, R. H., and J. E. Matar. *Designing for Quality.* White Plains, NY: Quality Resources; American Society for Quality Control, Milwaukee, WI, 1990.

[12] Montgomery, D. *Introduction to Statistical Quality Control*. 3rd ed. New York: Wiley, 1996.

[13] Peace, G. S. *Taguchi Methods*, Reading, MA: Addison-Wesley, 1993.

[14] Pyzdek, T., and R. W. Berger. *Quality Engineering Handbook*. New York: Marcel Dekker; ASQC Quality Press, Milwaukee, WI, 1992.

[15] Robison, J. "Integrate Quality Cost Concepts into Team's Problem-Solving Efforts." *Quality Progress* (March 1997): 25–30.

[16] Stamatis, D. H. *Six Sigma Fundamentals—A Complete Guide to the System, Methods, and Tools*. New York: Productivity Press, 2004.

[17] Summers, D. C. S. *Quality*. Upper Saddle River, NJ: Prentice Hall, 1997.

[18] Taguchi, G., E. A. Elsayed, and T. C. Hsiang. *Quality Engineering in Production Systems*. New York: McGraw-Hill, 1989.

[19] Titus, R. "Total Quality Six Sigma Overview." Slide presentation, Lehigh University, Bethlehem, PA, May 2003.

REVIEW QUESTIONS

1 Eight dimensions of product quality are identified in the text. Name four of these dimensions.
2 What is Six Sigma?
3 What are the general goals of Six Sigma?
4 Why does 6σ in Six Sigma really mean 4.5σ?
5 What does DMAIC stand for?
6 What is the define step in DMAIC? What is accomplished during the define step?
7 What are master black belts in the Six Sigma hierarchy?
8 What is a CTQ characteristic?
9 What is the measure step in DMAIC?
10 Why is defects per million (*DPM*) not necessarily the same as defects per million opportunities (*DPMO*)?
11 What is the analyze step in DMAIC?
12 What is root cause analysis?
13 What is the improve step in DMAIC?
14 What is failure mode and effect analysis?
15 What are the three factors in FMEA that determine the risk priority number?
16 What is the control step in DMAIC?
17 What other quality program is very similar to Six Sigma?
18 What are the three main objectives of total quality management?
19 What do the terms external customer and internal customer mean?
20 What is a robust design in Taguchi's quality engineering?
21 What is quality function deployment (QFD)?
22 What is ISO 9000?

PROBLEMS

Determining Sigma Level

1 A garment manufacturer produces 22 different coat styles, and every year new coat styles are introduced and old styles are discarded. Whatever the style, the final inspection department checks each coat before it leaves the factory for nine features that are considered critical-to-quality (CTQ) characteristics for customer satisfaction. The inspection report for last month indicated that a total of 366 deficiencies of the nine features were found among 8240 coats produced. Determine (a) defects per million opportunities and (b) sigma level for the manufacturer's production performance.

2 A next-day parcel delivery service uses sigma level to determine the quality of its delivery service. The CTQ characteristics of interest are (1) accuracy, (2) timeliness, and (3) damage. Accuracy refers to whether the parcel was delivered to the correct address. Timeliness refers to whether the parcel was actually delivered on the following day. Damage refers to whether the parcel was damaged during transit. Over a two-week period, a total of 352,476 parcels were delivered. Of this number, 216 were reported as being delivered to the wrong address, 818 were late deliveries (delivered the second day or later), and 17 parcels were reported as damaged. Determine (a) defects per million opportunities and (b) sigma level

of the parcel delivery service's performance. (c) Is there any correlation among the CTQ statistics?

3 A producer of cell phones checks each phone prior to packaging, using seven CTQ characteristics that are deemed important to customers. Last year, out of 205,438 phones produced by the company, a total of 578 phones had at least one defect, and the total number of defects among these 578 phones was 1692. Determine (a) the number of defects per million opportunities and corresponding sigma level, (b) the number of defects per million and corresponding sigma level, and (c) the number of defective units per million and corresponding sigma level.

4 The inspection department in an automobile final assembly plant checks cars coming off the line against 85 features that are considered CTQ characteristics for customer satisfaction. During a one-month period, a total of 16,578 cars were produced. For those cars, a total of 1989 defects of various types were found, and the total number of cars that had one or more defects was 512. Determine (a) the number of defects per million opportunities and corresponding sigma level, (b) the number of defects per million and corresponding sigma level, and (c) the number of defective units per million and corresponding sigma level.

5 A pizza delivery shop wants to determine its service quality using sigma level as the metric. There are three CTQ characteristics for which the shop tracks data: (1) delivery window, (2) order accuracy, and (3) temperature of pizza. Delivery window refers to the company's policy to deliver the pizza to the customer within 30 minutes of the telephone order. Order accuracy means delivering exactly what the customer ordered. The third CTQ characteristic is measured using a thermometer that is inserted into the pizza delivery box. Over a seven-day period, the data in the table below were collected. Determine (a) defects per million opportunities and (b) sigma level of the delivery shop's performance. (c) Is there any correlation among the CTQ characteristics? (d) Can you make any recommendations to improve service performance?

Day	Number of Orders	Number of Delivery Window Defects	Number of Order Accuracy Defects	Number of Temperature Defects
1	35	1	0	3
2	26	0	0	1
3	41	2	2	4
4	19	0	0	0
5	23	0	0	2
6	29	0	0	1
7	31	2	0	3

6 A digital camera maker produces three different models: (1) base model, (2) zoom model, and (3) zoom model with extra memory. Data for the three models are shown in the table below. The three models have been on the market for one year, and the first year's sales are given in the table. Also given are CTQ characteristics and total defects that have been tabulated for the products sold. Higher model numbers have more CTQ characteristics (opportunities for defects) because they are more complex. The category of total defects refers to the total number of defects of all CTQ characteristics for each model. For each of the three models, determine (a) the number of defects per million opportunities and corresponding sigma level, (b) the number of defects per million and corresponding sigma level, and (c) the number of defective units per million and corresponding sigma level. (d) Does any one model seem to be produced at a higher quality level than the others? (e) Determine aggregate values for *DPMO*, *DPM*, and *DUPM* and their corresponding sigma levels for all models made by the camera maker.

Model	Annual Sales	CTQ Characteristics	Number of Defective Cameras	Total Number of Defects
1	62,347	16	127	282
2	31,593	23	109	429
3	18,662	29	84	551

7 An airline wants to rate its service quality level. The following CTQ characteristics are to be used to assess quality: (1) on-time departures, (2) on-time arrivals, (3) missed connections, (4) cancelled flights, (5) overbooked flights, (6) lost luggage, and (7) miscellaneous passenger complaints (complaints regarding items 1 through 6 are not included). Data for these characteristics have been collected each month and are shown below for a recent six-month period. Also shown is the number of flights for each month. (a) Determine defects per million opportunities and corresponding sigma level of the airline's performance. (b) Are there any correlations among the CTQ statistics? (c) Are there any other issues or problems related to the data or the categories of data? (d) Do you recommend that any of the CTQ characteristics be omitted in the calculations. If so, which ones and why? (e) What CTQ characteristics must the airline devote more attention to in order to improve its service quality sigma level?

Month	March	April	May	June	July	August
Total flights	4562	4467	4588	4451	4602	4623
On-time departures	4520	4424	4577	4428	4578	4601
On-time arrivals	4518	4425	4578	4428	4573	4599
Missed connections	15	20	5	11	10	8
Cancelled flights	0	0	0	1	0	1
Overbooked flights	5	7	4	6	7	8
Lost luggage	122	99	84	90	102	143
Misc. passenger complaints	28	32	37	19	25	41

Failure Mode And Effect Analysis

8 A failure mode and effect analysis was performed on a product that will be produced by an equipment company. The analysis resulted in the identification of eight possible failure modes. For each mode an assessment was made of the occurrence frequency, potential effects, severity, and difficulty of detection. These assessments are listed in the table below. The table lists ranking numbers for occurrence, severity, and detection. (a) Which failure mode is the most important to analyze and determine possible corrective actions to avoid it? (b) Develop a list of failure modes according to risk priority. (c) Which failure mode(s) seem to be unimportant according to the analysis?

Failure Mode	Occurrence	Potential Effects	Severity	Detection
Electric shock	2	Potential death to user	10	7
Casing fracture	1	Inability to use	8	9
Finger pinch	3	Loss of fingers	9	8
Motor failure	1	Inability to use	8	7
Transmission failure	2	Inability to use	8	6
Mechanism binding	4	Reduced utility	6	8
Sharp edges on casing	10	Injuries to user	9	1
Premature actuation	3	Injuries to user	9	7

Chapter Appendix

Sigma Levels, Defects per Million, Fraction Defect Rate, and Yield in a Six Sigma Program

Sigma Level (σ)	Defects per Million[a]	Fraction Defect Rate q	Yield Y (%)
6.0	3.4	0.0000034	99.99966
5.9	5.4	0.0000054	99.99946
5.8	8.5	0.0000085	99.99915
5.7	13.4	0.0000134	99.99866
5.6	21	0.000021	99.9979
5.5	32	0.000032	99.9968
5.4	48	0.000048	99.9952
5.3	72	0.000072	99.9928
5.2	108	0.000108	99.9892
5.1	159	0.000159	99.9841
5.0	233	0.000233	99.9770
4.9	337	0.000337	99.9663
4.8	483	0.000483	99.9517
4.7	687	0.000687	99.9313
4.6	968	0.000968	99.9032
4.5	1,350	0.001350	99.865
4.4	1,866	0.001866	99.813
4.3	2,555	0.002555	99.745
4.2	3,467	0.003467	99.653
4.1	4,661	0.004661	99.534
4.0	6,210	0.006210	99.379

Sigma Level (σ)	Defects per Million[a]	Fraction Defect Rate q	Yield Y (%)
3.9	8,198	0.008198	99.18
3.8	10,724	0.01072	98.93
3.7	13,903	0.01390	98.61
3.6	17,864	0.01768	98.23
3.5	22,750	0.02275	97.73
3.4	28,716	0.02872	97.13
3.3	35,930	0.03590	96.41
3.2	44,565	0.04457	95.54
3.1	54,799	0.05480	94.52
3.0	66,807	0.06681	93.32
2.9	80,757	0.08076	91.92
2.8	96,801	0.09680	90.32
2.7	115,070	0.11507	88.49
2.6	135,666	0.13567	86.43
2.5	158,655	0.15866	84.13
2.4	184,060	0.18406	81.59
2.3	211,855	0.2118	78.82
2.2	241,964	0.2420	75.80
2.1	274,253	0.2743	72.57
2.0	308,538	0.3085	69.15
1.9	344,578	0.3446	65.54
1.8	382,089	0.3821	61.79
1.7	420,740	0.4207	57.93
1.6	460,172	0.4602	53.98
1.5	500,000	0.5000	50
1.4	539,828	0.5398	46.02
1.3	579,260	0.5793	42.07
1.2	617,911	0.6179	38.21
1.1	655,422	0.6554	34.46
1.0	691,462	0.6915	30.85

Source: Compiled from [4], Appendix.

[a]Can be used for defects per million *DPM*, defects per million opportunities *DPMO*, or defective units per million DUPM.

Introduction to Ergonomics and Human Factors

Ergonomics is an applied scientific discipline that is concerned with how humans interact with the tools and equipment they use while performing tasks and other activities.[1] A common focus of ergonomics is the interface between humans and equipment—for example, the controls, displays, and other devices that are used by workers to operate the equipment. Our primary interest is on the activities that humans perform while working. These work activities impose a continuum of physical and cognitive demands on the human worker, as represented by the scale in Figure 1. In fact, most human activities require a combination of physical and cognitive exertions. Ergonomics is also concerned with the physical and social environment in which the tasks and activities are performed and how humans and machines interact with the environment. The word is derived from two Greek words, *ergon*, meaning work, and *nomos*, meaning rules or laws.[2] Combined, the words mean (roughly) the study of work. A professional whose practice is primarily focused on ergonomics is called an ***ergonomist.***

A term frequently used in place of ergonomics is ***human factors.*** Until recently, this term was most commonly used in the United States, while "ergonomics" was the

[1]The Work Measurement and Methods Standards Subcommittee (ANSI Standard Z94.12-1989) defines ergonomics as follows: "The application of a body of knowledge (life sciences, physical science, engineering, etc.) dealing with the interactions between man and the total working environment, such as atmosphere, heat, light and sound, as well as all tools and equipment of the workplace."

[2]The word ***ergonomics*** entered the English language in 1949. It was coined by British scientist K. F. H. Murrell, although it had been used first by Polish scientist W. Jastrzebowski in an 1857 newspaper article.

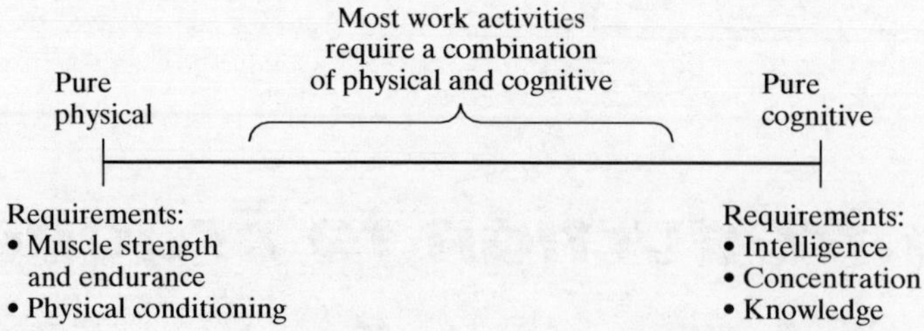

Figure 1 Continuum of physical and cognitive demands that work activities impose on humans. Based on a figure in [13].

preferred term in Europe.[3] Today it is generally accepted that ergonomics and human factors are synonymous (Historical Note 1). If there was a difference in these terms, the difference was that ergonomics emphasized work physiology and anthropometry,[4] while human factors emphasized experimental psychology and systems engineering [7]. Also, the interest and applications in European ergonomics was more on industrial work systems, while the interest and applications in human factors in the United States was more on military systems.

HISTORICAL NOTE 1 HISTORY OF ERGONOMICS

Ergonomics as an identified field of study can be traced back to around 1945, although some of the motivating influences precede this date. One of the most important was no doubt the scientific management movement, or ***Taylorism***,[5] with its emphasis on task planning, motion and time study, and worker efficiency. Critics have argued that Taylorism created industrial jobs that were simplistic and repetitive, and that it dehumanized labor. On the other hand, it made possible an industrial system in the United States that was the most productive in the world. And it focused attention on work as an area of study and research. Included in the scientific management movement were the pioneering studies of Frank and Lillian Gilbreth in the area of motion study, which has been referred to as "one of the forerunners" of human factors [15].

In the early 1900s, there was considerable effort in industry devoted to the selection of workers for a given job. This was called "fitting the man to the job" (FMJ). The idea was to choose from the pool of job applicants those individuals who were best suited to the requirements of the position on the basis of their physical and/or mental

[3]It is of interest to note that the Human Factors Society in the United States changed its name in 1992 to include the word ergonomics. The society is now called the Human Factors and Ergonomics Society.
[4]These terms are defined in Section 3.
[5]Named after Frederick W. Taylor, the father of scientific management.

aptitudes. Psychological testing was often used in the selection process when intelligence and personality were among the job requirements.

Studies carried out in the late 1920s at the Hawthorne Works of Western Electric Company near Chicago drew attention to the importance of social factors in the workplace. The Hawthorne experiments as they came to be known represented the beginning of interest in "human relations" research.

Finally, another important influence leading up to ergonomics was the growth in the use of machinery and mechanization between 1900 and 1945. The automobile industry was the significant growth industry at the beginning of this period, and the production of cars was enabled by mechanized machine tools and conveyorized assembly lines. In the 1930s, World War II forced nations to develop modern production technologies to meet the demand for munitions. Although the United States did not officially enter the war until the end of 1941, it was supplying weapons to its future allies during the 1930s.

Recognition of an emerging discipline related to humans working with machines crystallized around the end of World War II. It was called *ergonomics* in Europe and *human factors* in the United States. The war had witnessed a dramatic increase in the technological complexity and sophistication of weapons systems, such as aircraft, artillery, tanks, radar, and sonar. Significant problems were sometimes encountered in the operation of this equipment by humans, with loss of life too often the result. These problems only increased with the new jet aircraft that were being developed after the war. There was a need to deal with a new problem area known as *human–machine systems*. The interest in the United States was on aircraft and other weapons systems, and human factors research was frequently associated with "knobs and dials" between 1945 and 1960. The Human Factors Society was established in the United States in 1957.

Meanwhile, the field of ergonomics was starting in Britain. K. F. H. Murrell, an early contributor in the field, is credited with giving the discipline its name in 1949. The emphasis of ergonomics in Europe was on industrial work systems, including equipment and workspace design used in such systems. In 1950, British researchers met to discuss a new professional society to represent the discipline, and the name Ergonomics Research Society was adopted in that year (the name was later shortened to Ergonomics Society).

By the 1960s, the space age had arrived and the computer industry had begun its growth spurt. In the United States, human factors started to be applied outside of the military. The National Aeronautics and Space Administration (NASA) had been established in 1958 for the exploration of space, and human factors were quickly identified as a concern in manned space flight. Industrial applications of human factors also grew during the decades following 1960, to design both work systems and consumer products. A human factors group was established in the early 1960s at Eastman Kodak Company, the first company to form such a department.

Between 1980 and the present, interest in ergonomics and human factors has continued to grow, motivated on the one hand by advances in computer and automation technologies and on the other hand by several disasters that have highlighted the critical importance of the human in the operation of advanced human–machine systems.

In a computer system, the computer is the machine with which the human interacts. Human factors research has focused on the human-computer interface and the effective exchange and processing of information between these components. Several textbooks have been written on this subject, including two that are listed among our references [4, 6].

Since 1979, the following significant human-related disasters have contributed to public awareness about the importance of ergonomics and human factors:

- Three Mile Island nuclear power plant accident (near Harrisburg, Pennsylvania, March 1979)
- Bhopal pesticide plant, Union Carbide Company (Bhopal, India, December 1984)
- *Challenger* space shuttle (above Cape Kennedy, Florida, January 1986)
- Chernobyl nuclear power plant explosion (Kiev, Ukraine, April 1986)
- *Exxon Valdez* oil spill (Prince William Sound, Alaska, March 1989)
- *Columbia* space shuttle (over Texas, February 2003).

Many of these disasters were the result of human errors, sometimes caused by inadequate attention to ergonomics and human factors in system design and system management, and other times caused by flaws in decisions by humans.

This chapter provides an overview of the field of ergonomics and human factors, including its history and main topical areas. It then focuses on the human–machine system, an important model in the application of ergonomics.

1 OVERVIEW OF ERGONOMICS

In this section, we discuss the objectives and applications of ergonomics, and how the field has evolved into an important area in work design that attempts to adapt the task to the worker's capabilities.

1.1 Objectives and Applications of Ergonomics

The main objective of ergonomics is to improve the performance of systems consisting of people and equipment. Such systems are often referred to as human–machine systems (Section 2), although the word *machine* includes a variety of objects that are not normally thought of as machines—for example, aircraft, appliances, automobiles, chairs, computers, hand tools, and sports equipment. Better performance of human–machine systems in an ergonomics context means the following:

- Greater ease of interaction between the user and the equipment
- Avoidance of errors and mistakes by the user
- Greater comfort and satisfaction in the use of the equipment

- Reduced stress and fatigue while using the equipment
- Greater efficiency and productivity
- Safer operation of the equipment
- Avoidance of accidents and injuries.

These objectives are similar to those in methods engineering. Methods engineering and ergonomics are closely related and their general objectives are the same: (1) to improve the performance of existing systems and (2) to design new systems for optimum performance. Whereas methods engineering emphasizes issues such as efficiency, cost reduction, and elimination of waste, ergonomics emphasizes the human aspects such as comfort and safety and the interactions that occur between the human, the equipment, and the environment.

Ergonomics has a wide variety of applications, nearly all of which can be classified into two main areas:

- *Work system design.* This area is concerned with the interaction between worker and the equipment used in the workplace. Objectives include safety, accident avoidance, and related performance attributes. Work system design includes consideration of factors related to the work environment such as lighting and noise levels.
- *Product design.* This area deals with the design of products that are safer, more comfortable, and more user-friendly and mistake-proof. In addition to providing greater customer satisfaction by means of these kinds of features, an issue in product design is product liability lawsuits and their avoidance through consideration of ergonomics.

In our treatment of ergonomics here, the focus is on work systems, which in fact overlap with product design in the sense that work systems usually include equipment, and equipment is designed and fabricated by companies that are selling it as a product. A production machine is a product that must be designed with ergonomics in mind if it is to operate productively and safely.

1.2 Fitting the Job to the Person

A common employment practice prior to ergonomics was based on a philosophy called "fitting the person to the job" (FPJ), which recommended that workers be selected on the basis of their mental aptitudes and physical characteristics for a particular job opening.[6] Psychometric testing (e.g., tests for intelligence and personality characteristics) had begun to be used following World War I in the hiring process to improve productivity by trying to identify workers who had the right psychometric capabilities for the particular job. A worker's physical attributes were also used in the selection process for jobs requiring characteristics such as size and strength. The FPJ approach is still considered among the eligibility factors for certain positions in many hiring situations today; for example, firefighters must meet physical endurance requirements and

[6]The original term used was "fitting the man to the job" (FMJ). To observe modern gender-neutral language conventions, we have changed the name to "fitting the person to the job" (FPJ).

candidates seeking to become military pilots must meet height requirements. Educational qualifications are also widely used in selecting employees for certain positions such as engineering and public school teaching, and professional certification is required for many occupations, including medical doctors, dentists, and lawyers. All of these examples represent situations in which mental, physical, and/or educational requisites are used to ensure that the person is qualified for a given job.

The ergonomics approach is diametrically opposite of FPJ. The philosophy in ergonomics is "fitting the job to the person" (FJP)—that is, designing the job so that nearly any member of the workforce can perform it. There are several factors that explain why the new philosophy has evolved and now occupies a position that operates in parallel with and sometimes supersedes the FPJ approach: (1) changes in worker skill requirements, (2) demographic changes, and (3) social and political changes.

In the early decades of the 1900s, the general skill requirements for many jobs were much lower than today and there were many applicants, including many young people, for those low-skilled positions. Companies could be much more selective when hiring their workers. Today, the skill requirements of employment are much higher. Whereas the work in earlier times was largely physical and clerical, today it involves the operation of machinery and computers. The equipment is often sophisticated, and the work processes are complex. The average age of the available workforce is older than in the early 1900s. Companies are often faced with a smaller pool of applicants to choose from, and they cannot afford to be as choosy. They must hire from the pool those who are qualified but not necessarily optimal in the FPJ sense. Training must be provided, and the work itself must be designed to be readily understood so that the necessary amount of training can be minimized and workers can be productive as soon as possible after employment begins.

One significant manifestation of the demographic changes in employment has been the increase in the number of working women in the latter half of the twentieth century. More women have been entering the workforce in positions heretofore dominated by male workers. Women have been hired as assembly line workers and machine operators, and they have attended college in growing numbers to occupy positions as engineers and managers. Table 1 provides some statistical data to show the demographic changes that have taken place between 1930 and 2000.

At the same time that these changes in skill requirements and demographics were occurring, social and political pressures were effecting changes in cultural attitudes and government regulations. Equal opportunities legislation was enacted to prevent discrimination on the basis of race, gender, and age. Laws were enacted at the state and

TABLE 1 Changes in U.S. Population and Workforce Between 1930 and 2000

	1930	2000
Total population in the United States	123 million	281 million
Life expectancy	60 years	77 years
Median age	27 years	35 years
Number of people aged 65 and over	7 million	35 million
Proportion of women in the labor force	22%	61%

Source: U.S. Census Bureau. (www.census.gov/pubinfo/www/1930_factsheet.html, March 28, 2002.)

federal levels to mandate that physically handicapped persons be provided with access ramps and other conveniences at public facilities and in transportation. Hiring of the handicapped was encouraged. In some cases, organizations went beyond the legislation by pursuing proactive policies on the hiring of minorities and the handicapped.

2 HUMAN–MACHINE SYSTEMS

Worker–machine systems, from an operational perspective, can focus on issues such as the kind of work done and the time factors involved. In this section, we consider the same basic work systems but from an ergonomics viewpoint. The basic model in ergonomics is the ***human–machine system***, defined as a combination of humans and equipment interacting to achieve some desired result. The number of humans can range from one to many, and the type and amount of equipment can range from a single hand tool to a complex and sophisticated collection of machines and computers. The desired result achieved by the system refers to its purpose and/or function—for example, to produce a product or provide a service. A human–machine system can have multiple objectives—for example, to produce a product, to contribute to the profit of the organization, and to provide a safe and comfortable workplace.

Human–machine systems can be classified into three basic categories [15]:

1. *Manual systems.* This system involves a person using some hand tool or other nonpowered implement to perform an activity. An example is a farmer using a pitchfork to load hay into a wagon.
2. *Mechanical systems.* This system refers to one or more humans using powered equipment to accomplish some job. The typical case is that the equipment provides the mechanical power for the job, and the function of the human(s) is to control the equipment. An example is a farmer driving a tractor to harvest a crop.
3. *Automated systems.* This system involves the performance of a job with a minimum of human attention. The truth is that automated systems do require occasional human attention, for purposes of maintenance and repair, reprogramming, or loading and unloading of parts from a production machine. In addition, humans are required to design and install automated systems. Thus, even automated systems are human–machine systems.

A key feature of a human–machine system is that interactions occur between the humans and machines, as depicted in Figure 2. The human controls the machine operation, and the machine displays its actions. The display may consist of the operator simply observing the operation, or it may involve some sort of display device such as a television monitor. Whatever the case, the human senses the operation, processes the sensed information, and performs actions on the machine controls that regulate its operation. The interactions consist of a cycle of activities accomplished by the human and the machine. The interactions occur in an environment—both physical and social—that may influence system performance. For example, poor lighting may impede a worker's ability to perform an inspection task; an unfriendly supervisor may reduce a worker's motivation to work.

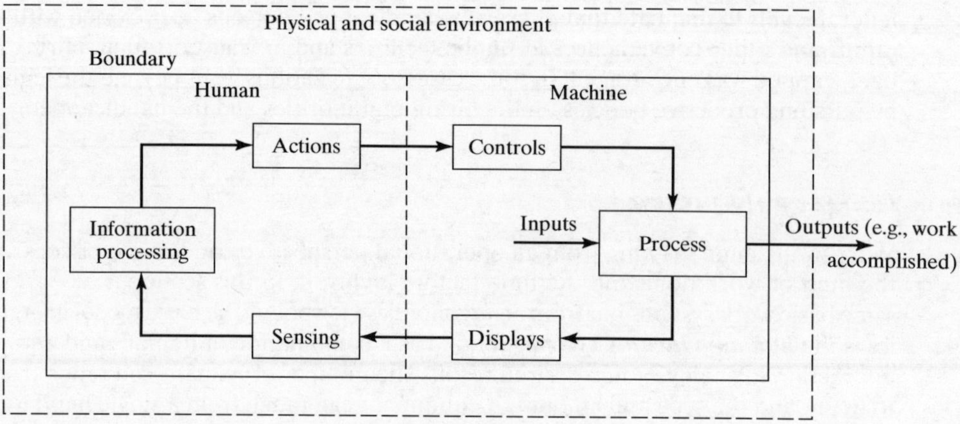

Figure 2 Block diagram model of the interactions in a human–machine system.

From an ergonomics design viewpoint, a human–machine system has boundaries, as shown in Figure 2, that define what components are included within the scope of the system for purposes of analysis and design. Most systems are components of a larger system. There is a systems hierarchy. A worker–machine production cell is one component in the larger production department, which is only one of many departments in the company. The ergonomist must decide where to draw the boundaries of the human– machine system of interest. The boundaries separate the human–machine system from its environment.

The two main components of a human–machine system are the human and the equipment. In turn, the human and the machine have components that must be considered in the context of the interactions occurring between them. The third component is the environment, which interacts with the human-machine system. The ergonomic objective is to optimize the performance of the system by making the interactions between the human and the equipment as seamless as possible while the system operates in its environment.

Human Components. As suggested by the model of the human–machine system in Figure 2, the human components of interest are those that perform three functions: (1) sensing the operation, (2) information processing, and (3) actions. The corresponding human components are the following:

1. *Human senses.* The five basic human senses are vision, hearing, touch, taste, and smell. They are the sensors by which humans are able to be aware of where they are and what is happening around them. Vision and hearing are the most important in ergonomics, although the others are sometimes useful—for example, sensing that a machine is running too hot or that it is emitting noxious fumes. People use a combination of their senses in many of their activities. For example, when we eat a meal at a fine restaurant, we enjoy not only its taste but also the visual presentation of the food and its aroma.

2. *Human brain.* The human brain can be considered as a data- and information-processing unit, analogous in some ways to the operation of a computer. It receives data through the human senses as well as feedback from the joints and muscles of the body (data entry). It stores the data in memory (computer storage). It operates on the data (as in the operation of a computer's central processing unit) by thinking, planning, calculating, solving problems, and making decisions about what actions to take. These thought processes include both reflex and cognitive activities (low-level and high-level software). The decisions are communicated to and executed by the human effectors (computer peripherals).
3. *Human effectors.* An effector is a body part such as a muscle or group of muscles that actuates in response to some stimulus. The principal human effectors in the human–machine system are the fingers, hands, feet, and voice. These are supported by the musculoskeletal system of the body, and the stimulus is provided by the information processing occurring in the human brain.

These human components operate in a coordinated fashion and interact with the machine components in the human–machine system.

Machine Components. As indicated previously, the machine in the human–machine system can range from a simple hand tool to a complex and sophisticated system of equipment. The typical model in ergonomics is one in which the interactions between the human and the machine are directly coupled. The following are three common examples:

- A worker using a shovel to dig a hole in the ground. The digger maintains continuous control over the shovel, using arm and body strength to manipulate it and accomplish the hole-digging activity.
- A person driving a car. The driver continuously steers the car using the steering wheel and controls its speed using the throttle pedal, and the car provides feedback such as direction, speed data, and engine rpm. The connections between the car and driver are tangible as the car moves down the road.
- A student writing a term paper on a PC. The student types in the text using the alphanumeric keyboard, and the computer responds by displaying the text on the monitor and identifying spelling and grammar errors.

In other cases, the coupling is less direct and the interactions are less tangible, as in the following two examples:

- A worker monitoring the operation of an automated chemical process on a computer terminal. The automated process proceeds without human intervention. The worker's function is to make sure that each process variable remains within a defined tolerance of its target value and to take some action (directly interact with the process) only if the tolerance is exceeded or some other exception occurs.
- A researcher using the Internet to search for articles on a topic of interest. The researcher enters keywords about the topic, and a search engine looks on the

Internet to find Web sites that provide links with the keywords. The search engine is guided by its own software, independent of any further input from the researcher.

As Figure 2 indicates, there are three principal components of the machine in the human–machine system:

1. *The process.* The process refers to the function or operation performed by the human–machine system, such as digging a hole, driving a car, writing a term paper, performing a chemical process automatically, or searching the Internet.
2. *Displays.* For processes that are simple and the worker participates directly, the display function is accomplished by the worker observing the process as it is being performed. No additional display of information is needed. For example, the worker digging a hole sees the depth and shape of the hole as each shovelful is removed and proceeds with digging until the proper hole size has been achieved. For processes that are more mechanized and automated, there is a greater need for artificial displays to allow the human to see and understand what is going on. Driving a car requires a combination of natural and artificial displays. The driver receives input about the process directly by observing how the car is tracking the road ahead and indirectly by observing the speedometer and other dashboard gauges. Highly automated processes like the chemical process in our example require the worker to obtain the necessary information entirely from the display monitor because the process itself cannot be directly observed.
3. *Controls.* The human interacts with the equipment using machine controls that can be operated by the human effectors, usually the fingers and hands. When the equipment is simple (e.g., a hand tool), the controls often consist of one of the equipment components. In our example of a worker digging a hole, the handle of the shovel is the only control that is manipulated by the worker. As the machine becomes more complex, the controls tend to be more remote from the actual operation performed by the human–machine system. Examples of these remote controls include the steering wheel of an automobile, the alphanumeric keyboard of a personal computer, the foot pedals of a church organ, and the levers on an engine lathe for feed and speed.

Environmental Components. A human–machine system operates in an environment that includes two components:

- *Physical environment.* The physical environment includes the immediate area of the human–machine system, separated from the system by a defined boundary in Figure 2. Components of the physical environment usually include the location and surrounding lighting, noise, temperature, and humidity. These environmental factors can affect the performance of the human–machine system and are of interest to the ergonomist. For example, the workspace of a fighter aircraft is its cockpit, which imposes severe limitations on the freedom of movement of the pilot. The many controls of the aircraft must be located within easy reach of the pilot.

- *Social environment.* Work serves a social function. It is a chance for workers to meet and interact with other people. The primary work interactions are job-related, but social interactions occur also. The social environment at work is determined by coworkers and colleagues, immediate supervisors, organizational culture, and the work organization. The work organization consists of factors such as whether workers work alone or in teams, the required pace of the work, and whether the pace is set by the worker or by a machine.

3 TOPIC AREAS IN ERGONOMICS

As an academic subject, ergonomics has a breadth and depth that are much greater than we can do justice to in the space we have allocated to the subject in this text. For the interested reader, there are a number of good textbooks listed among our references as well as a handbook devoted to the subject. In our coverage, we emphasize the following topics.

Physical Ergonomics. Many work activities require physical exertion. The term *manual labor* is often used to refer to these activities. ***Physical ergonomics*** is mostly about manual labor. It is concerned with (1) how the human body functions during physical exertion and (2) how the physical dimensions of the body affect the capabilities of the worker. These two areas are related to the sciences of human physiology and anthropometry.

Physiology is the branch of biology that deals with the vital processes carried out by living organisms and how their constituent tissues and cells function. Our interest in physiology is directed at how the human muscles function during work activities. There are strength and endurance limitations of the muscles that must be considered in the design of manual work. The energy expenditure that is required in the activity must be in balance with the capacity of the body's cardiovascular and respiratory systems. Rest periods must be allowed for work periods involving strenuous physical output. There are guidelines and formulas that can be used to determine the appropriate rest periods for work of a given physical energy expenditure.

Anthropometry is the branch of anthropology that is concerned with the physical dimensions and other data related to the human body, such as height, reach, and weight. The data for a given dimension is normally distributed for a defined population (e.g., heights of females living in Northern Europe), but there are differences in these dimensions between defined populations (e.g., males versus females living in Northern Europe). There are several ergonomic design principles that relate to anthropometric data. One widely applied principle is "design for extreme individuals," which recommends that the designed entity should accommodate virtually all of the user population. For example, doorways should be designed for very tall people, even though the vast majority of users who pass through them are not very tall.

Cognitive Ergonomics. Most work activities also include cognitive elements as well as physical elements. Even manual labor usually requires some cognitive effort. Human activities with a high cognitive component include thinking, reading, speaking, learning, problem solving, and decision making. ***Cognitive ergonomics*** is concerned with the capabilities and limitations of the human brain and sensory system while performing activities that include a significant amount of information processing. It is the ergonomics area that considers how the human brain receives information from the environment, processes that information, and determines appropriate responses and actions. The human cognitive processes include the following components:

- *Sensory system.* This system consists of the five senses—vision, hearing, touch, smell, and taste—that are activated by external stimuli, such as sights and sounds. The vast majority of human information input is by sight and hearing.
- *Perception.* This is the stage of cognition that follows the sensing of external stimuli. It occurs when the human mind becomes aware of the sensation and interprets it based on previous experience and knowledge.
- *Memory.* Human memory consists of two main components: working memory and long-term memory. Working memory is temporary memory that holds a limited amount of information while being processed. It transfers information to and retrieves information from long-term memory, which is the warehouse of one's knowledge and experiences.
- *Response selection and execution.* This is the cognitive process of figuring out what actions are needed in the light of information perceived through the sensory system and processed through working memory and long-term memory.

The functions and operations of these components are not described completely here, nor are the number of ergonomic design guidelines that are derived from an understanding of them.

The Physical Work Environment. As noted in Figure 2, work is performed in an environment that includes both physical and social aspects. The physical work environment can be classified into the following components: (1) the visual environment, (2) the auditory environment, and (3) the climate.

The ***visual environment*** is what the worker sees while working. Most of the information input perceived by the worker is through visual stimuli. The important factor enabling the proper functioning of a worker's sense of vision is lighting. The term that describes how well things can be seen is ***visibility***. The visibility of tools, materials, and other items in the workplace depends on lighting levels, brightness contrast, color, and glare. The job of the ergonomist is to determine the optimum illumination levels for the task and to implement other design details in the workplace (e.g., types of lamps, colors, glare reduction) in order to achieve the best possible visual environment.

The ***auditory environment*** is what the worker hears while working. Much of the information input received by the worker is through the sense of hearing. Auditory information input is the second most important after visual in most work situations. Included in the auditory environment is ***noise***, which can be defined as sound that is undesired and possibly harmful to a worker's sense of hearing. The possible effects of noise range from minor distraction to major deafness. The most important factors about noise in terms of its effects on humans are (1) intensity, perceived as loudness, and (2) duration of exposure. The Occupational Safety and Health Administration has established permissible noise levels that define the duration of exposures allowed for various intensity levels. Employers must make provisions to control noise in the workplace through various administrative and engineering approaches.

The ***climate*** is what the worker feels while working. Climate in the workplace environment is defined by four primary variables: (1) air temperature, (2) humidity, (3) air movement, and (4) radiation from surrounding objects (e.g., machines that operate at elevated temperatures and radiate heat). To a limited extent, the human body can compensate for variations in the normal body temperature of 35°C (98.6°F) through such mechanisms as perspiration when body temperature is above normal and shivering when body temperature is below normal. However, the climatic conditions that cause heat stress and cold stress often require interventions beyond the body's natural responses. The interventions include proper clothing for the conditions, frequent rest breaks, and heating and air conditioning of the facility.

Occupational Safety and Health. Every year in the United States, approximately 5000 lives are lost due to occupational injuries, and about 50,000 lives are lost due to work-related diseases and illnesses. Occupational safety and health constitute an important national issue that affects virtually every person who works. Several government agencies have been established to address the issue. The following federal agencies were established with the enactment of the Occupational Safety and Health Act in 1971:

- Occupational Safety and Health Administration (OSHA), whose responsibilities include enforcing the provisions of OSHAct, implementing safety and health programs, and setting occupational safety and health standards.
- National Institute for Occupational Safety and Health (NIOSH), whose responsibility is to engage in research, training, and education in the area of occupational safety and health.

The topics of occupational safety and occupational health are certainly related, but distinctions can be made between them. ***Occupational safety*** is concerned with the avoidance of industrial accidents, which are one-time events that can cause injury or fatality. The occupational safety objective in ergonomics is to understand how and why accidents, injuries, and fatalities occur and to take the necessary steps to prevent them. ***Occupational health*** is concerned with avoiding diseases and disorders that are caused by workers being exposed to hazardous materials or conditions in the workplace. These diseases and disorders do not generally occur immediately upon exposure. Instead they tend to develop after prolonged periods of exposure to the materials or conditions. The effects of the exposure are cumulative and may take years before symptoms reveal the onset of the malady.

REFERENCES

[1] ANSI Standard Z94.0-1989. *Industrial Engineering Terminology.* Norcross, GA: Industrial Engineering and Management Press, Institute of Industrial Engineers, 1989.

[2] Bridger, R. S. *Introduction to Ergonomics.* 2nd ed. London: Taylor and Francis, 2003.

[3] Czaja, S. J. "Systems Design and Evaluation." Pp. 16–40 in *Handbook of Human Factors and Ergonomics*, 2nd ed., edited by G. Salvendy. New York: Wiley, 1997.

[4] Dix, A. J., J. E. Finlay, G. D. Abowd, and R. Beale. *Human-Computer Interaction.* 2nd ed. London: Prentice Hall Europe, 1998.

[5] Eastman Kodak Company, Human Factors Section. *Ergonomic Design for People at Work*, Vol. 1, edited by S. Rodgers and E. Eggleton. Belmont, CA: Lifetime Learning Publications, 1983.

[6] Eberts, R. E. *User Interface Design.* Englewood Cliffs, NJ: Prentice Hall, 1994.

[7] Helander, M. G. "The Human Factors Profession." Pp. 3–16 in *Handbook of Human Factors and Ergonomics*, 2nd ed., edited by G. Salvendy. New York: Wiley, 1997.

[8] Konz, S., and S. Johnson. *Work Design, Industrial Ergonomics.* 5th ed. Scottsdale, AZ: Holcomb Hathaway Publishers, 2000.

[9] Kroemer, K. H. E., H. B. Kroemer, and K. E. Kroemer-Elbert. *Ergonomics: How to Design for Ease and Efficiency*. Upper Saddle River, NJ: Prentice Hall, 1994.

[10] Niebel, B. W., and A. Freivalds. *Methods, Standards, and Work Design.* 11th ed. New York: WCB McGraw-Hill, 2003.

[11] Phillips, C. A. *Human Factors Engineering.* New York: Wiley, 2000.

[12] Pulat, B. M. *Fundamentals of Industrial Ergonomics.* Upper Saddle River, NJ: Prentice Hall, 1992.

[13] Pulat, B. M., and D. C. Alexander, eds. *Industrial Ergonomics Case Studies.* Norcross, GA: Industrial Engineering and Management Press, Institute of Industrial Engineers, 1991.

[14] Salvendy, G., ed. *Handbook of Human Factors and Ergonomics.* 2nd ed. New York: Wiley, 1997.

[15] Sanders, M. S., and E. J. McCormick. *Human Factors in Engineering Design.* 7th ed. New York: McGraw-Hill, 1993.

[16] Smith, S. "Elements of Effective Ergonomics." *Industrial Engineering* (January 2003): 49–52.

[17] Wickens, C. D., J. Lee, Y. Liu, and S. Becker. *An Introduction to Human Factors Engineering.* 2nd ed. Upper Saddle River, NJ: Pearson/Prentice Hall, 2004.

REVIEW QUESTIONS

1 Define the word *ergonomics*.

2 What are some of the objectives and benefits of ergonomics as applied to human–machine systems?

3 Ergonomics has two main application areas. Identify and briefly describe them.

4 What is meant by the work philosophy "fitting the person to the job?"

5 What is a human–machine system?

6 What are the three basic categories of human–machine systems?

7 What are the basic functions performed by humans in the human–machine system?

8 What are the three components of the human that correspond to the three functions?

9 What are the principal components of the machine in the human–machine system, as indicated in the diagram of the system?

10 Briefly describe the physical environment and the social environment in which the human–machine system operates.

11 Define physical ergonomics as this term is used in the text.

12 What is anthropometry?

13 Define cognitive ergonomics as the term is used in the text.

14 What are the three main components of the physical work environment?

15 What is the difference between occupational safety and occupational health, as these terms are distinguished in the text?

Physical Ergonomics: Work Physiology and Anthropometry

A large number of occupations require workers to expend physical energy to perform their jobs. Manual labor is a primary work activity in industries such as construction, agriculture, mining, manufacturing, and logistics. These work situations include a significant amount of lifting, carrying, and other manual handling tasks involving tools, parts, packages, materials, and containers. This chapter is concerned with ***physical ergonomics***—how the human body responds to physical work activity (work physiology) and how the physical dimensions of the human body affect the capabilities of a worker (anthropometry).

We begin with a general discussion of human physiology. ***Physiology*** is a branch of biology that is concerned with the vital processes of living organisms and the functioning of their constituent tissues and cells. The living organisms of interest here are humans and in particular the way their muscles function. The relationship between human physiology and work is then established and discussed. The chapter concludes with an introduction to ***anthropometry***, which deals with the physical dimensions of the human body. Physiology and anthropometry are key topics in ergonomics.

1 HUMAN PHYSIOLOGY

The human musculoskeletal system is the primary actuator for performing physical labor and other activities requiring force and motion. It is composed of the muscles and bones in the body, and the tissues connecting them. Energy to perform physical activity is provided by metabolism. In this section, the metabolic processes of the human muscles are described and how they obtain the nutrients and oxygen to function. First, we briefly describe the skeletal component of the musculoskeletal system.

The normal human body contains 206 bones. The bones and their joints provide the structure of the musculoskeletal system. The various bones have different functions. The function of some bones is to provide protection of vital organs. Principal examples are the skull that protects the brain and the rib cage that protects the lungs, heart, and liver. Most of the other bones provide a framework for physical activity, such as the bones in the arms and legs. The bones in the body are connected to each other at their joints by means of ligaments. Joints for body movement are of three principal types: (1) ball-and-socket, such as the shoulder and hip joints, (2) pivot joints, such as the elbow and knee, and (3) hinge joints, such as the wrist and ankle. Of interest in the context of work physiology is that ball-and-socket joints can apply forces that are greater than those applied by pivot joints, which in turn can apply greater forces than hinge joints.

1.1 Muscle Activity and Metabolism

The muscles in the human body are of three types: (1) cardiac muscle, (2) smooth muscle, and (3) skeletal muscle. Cardiac muscle is heart muscle that performs the pumping function for the cardiovascular system. Smooth muscles are found in the intestines and blood vessels. In the intestines, they accomplish peristalsis that is essential for food digestion; and in the blood vessels, they serve in the regulation of blood flow and blood pressure.

Skeletal Muscles. Our main interest is in the skeletal muscles, which provide the power for force and motion in the musculoskeletal system. The skeletal muscles are a flesh tissue composed of bundles of long cells that contract when energized to produce forces and motions around the joints. The larger the cross section of the bundle, the greater the forces it can produce. There are approximately 400 skeletal muscles in the human musculoskeletal system, organized in pairs on the right and left sides of the body. The muscles account for about 40 percent of human body weight [17]. Each muscle consists of multiple bundles of cells surrounded by connective tissue. Blood vessels and nerves are distributed throughout the connective tissue to deliver fuel to the muscles and to provide feedback on their condition. Skeletal muscles are connected to bones by ***tendons***, which consist of a tough fibrous tissue that transmits the forces and motions exerted by muscle contraction through the skeletal framework.

A skeletal muscle functions by contracting between the bones to which it is attached. Contraction occurs when the muscle is activated in response to impulses from the body's central nervous system. These impulses may be voluntary (e.g., based on

TABLE 1 Equivalencies of the Kilocalorie (kcal) and Kilocalorie per Minute (kcal/min)

Energy	Energy Rate
1 kcal = 1000 cal	1 kcal/min = 1000 cal/min
1 kcal = 4.186 kJ = 4186 J = 4186 Nm	1 kcal/min = 4186 J/min = 4186 Nm/min
1 kcal = 3.968 Btu	1 kcal/min = 69.77 J/s = 69.77 W
1 kcal = 3087.4 ft-lb	1 kcal/min = 3087.4 ft-lb/min = 0.09356 hp

Key to abbreviations: kcal = kilocalorie; cal = calorie; kJ = kilojoule; J = joule; Nm = newton-meter; Btu = British thermal unit; ft-lb = foot-pound; W = watt; hp = horsepower.

an intentional signal from the brain to swing into action) or involuntary (e.g., reflex action). Muscle contraction does not necessarily mean that the muscle has become shorter. Contraction refers to the physiological condition of the muscle when it is activated. There are three types of muscle contractions: (1) ***concentric muscle contraction***, in which the muscle becomes shorter when it contracts; (2) ***eccentric muscle contraction***, in which the muscle elongates when it contracts; and (3) ***isometric muscle contraction***, in which the muscle length stays the same when it contracts [3].

Skeletal muscles in the human body are organized in pairs acting in opposite directions about the joints that are moved by them. The biceps and triceps muscles in the upper arm are examples. To open the elbow joint as if to straighten the arm, the triceps muscle becomes shorter while the biceps muscle becomes longer. To close the angle of the elbow joint, the biceps muscle reduces in length while the triceps muscle elongates. To hold a 10-lb dumbbell in a fixed position, both muscles contract isometrically. Simultaneous and coordinated contraction of the multiple muscle pairs in these different ways allows the human body to regulate strength and motion during physical activity.

Muscle contraction is enabled by the conversion of chemical energy into mechanical energy. The conversion process is called ***metabolism***, which refers to the sum of the biochemical reactions that occur in the cells of a living organism to (1) provide energy for vital processes and activities and (2) assimilate new organic material into the body. Metabolism can be viewed as an energy rate process—that is, the amount of energy per unit time at which chemical energy contained in food is converted into mechanical energy and the formation of new organic matter. The common measure of energy used in ergonomics is the kcal,[1] and the corresponding measure for energy rate is the kcal/min. The kcal and kcal/min can be converted to other measures of energy and energy rate by means of the equivalencies given in Table 1.

Types of Metabolism. The minimum amount of energy used by the human body when it is resting and there is no digestive activity is called ***basal metabolism***. It is the energy used only to sustain the vital circulatory and respiratory functions. It is measured as the ***basal metabolic rate***, defined as the rate at which heat is given off by an awake,

[1]One ***kilocalorie*** (abbreviated ***kcal***) is defined as the amount of heat required to raise the temperature of 1 kilogram of water by one degree Celsius at a pressure of 1 atmosphere. It is also known as the large calorie to distinguish it from the calorie, which is the heat required to raise one gram of water by 1 degree Celsius. The kilocalorie or large calorie is also the measure commonly used for the energy-producing value in food when metabolized by the body. We usually refer to it simply as the calorie.

resting human in a warm location at least 12 hours after eating. Other forms of metabolism are ***activity metabolism***, which is the energy associated with physical activity such as sports and manual work, and ***digestive metabolism***, which is the energy used for digestion. The total metabolic rate in the human body during the course of a day is the sum of the three types:

$$TMR_d = BMR_d + AMR_d + DMR_d \tag{1}$$

where TMR_d = total daily metabolic rate, kcal/day; BMR_d = daily basal metabolic rate, kcal/day; AMR_d = daily activity metabolic rate, kcal/day; and DMR_d = daily digestive metabolic rate, kcal/day.

The basal metabolic rate of an individual depends on the person's weight, gender, and age, as well as other factors such as heredity and percentage of body fat. For our purposes, we will use the following values for weight and gender, and then apply an age correction to these values. Note that the values are hourly rates (BMR_h):

- For a 20-year-old male, BMR_h/kg = 1.0 kcal/hr per kg of body weight
- For a 20-year-old female, BMR_h/kg = 0.9 kcal/hr per kg of body weight

As a person ages, his or her basal metabolism rate declines slowly, so the age correction is simply to subtract 2% from the preceding values for each decade above 20 years (we ignore people significantly younger than 20 because they are not in the workforce).

Example 1 Daily Basal Metabolism Rate

Determine the daily basal metabolism rate for a 35-year-old woman who weighs 130 lb.

Solution: The hourly basal metabolism rate must be adjusted for the woman's age. Given that she is 1.5 decades older than 20 years, the age correction is 1.5(0.02) = 0.03. The adjusted BMR_h/kg value is 0.9(1 – 0.03) = 0.873 kcal/hr per kg of body weight. Her weight of 130 lb must be converted to kilograms using the equivalency that 1 kg = 2.2 lb. Thus, her weight = 59 kg. For 24 hours,

$$BMR_d = 0.873(59)(24) = 1238 \text{ kcal}$$

This can be converted to an equivalent BMR value per minute by dividing by the number of minutes in a 24-hour period = 24(60) = 1440 min/day.

$$BMR_m = 1238/1440 = 0.86 \text{ kcal/min}$$ ■

Energy rates associated with activity metabolism are discussed in the context of work requirements in Section 2. The daily rate of digestive metabolism is estimated to be about 10% of the combined rate of basal and activity metabolism [12]. That is,

$$DMR_d = 0.1(BMR_d + AMR_d) \tag{2}$$

Biochemical Reactions in Metabolism. Let us consider the process by which the human body converts food into muscle activity. The source of chemical energy for metabolism is the foods that are ingested and digested by the body. The primary food nutrients that provide energy for muscle activity are carbohydrates, proteins, and

TABLE 2 Three Basic Nutrients in Foods, with Calorie Contents, Functions in Body, and Common Food Sources

Nutrient	Energy	Functions in Body	Common Food Sources
Carbohydrates	4 kcal/gram	Energy source for muscles, brain, nervous system, and red blood cells Helps regulate fat metabolism	Fruits, fruit juices, milk Bread, rice, potato, pasta Sugar, syrup, honey, jelly
Proteins	4 kcal/gram	Body tissue growth and maintenance Hormone, enzyme, and antibody production Body temperature regulation	Meat, poultry, fish, cheese Beans, peas, soybeans, lentils, nuts
Lipids (fats)	9 kcal/gram	Energy source for body Surrounds and cushions vital organs Helps maintain body temperature Essential in making vitamins A, D, E, and K available to body	Butter, cheese, whole milk Fatty meats (bacon, ham) Fast foods (hamburgers, fried chicken, fries, pizza, ice cream)

Source: J. S. Armentraut, *The Professional Chef's Techniques of Healthy Cooking*, 2nd ed., The Culinary Institute of America. (New York: Wiley, 2000).

TABLE 3 Energy (kcal) Contents of Common Foods

Food (Portion)	Calories (kcal)	Food (Portion)	Calories (kcal)
Meats and fish:		Fast food:	
Roast beef, lean and fat (6 oz)	420	Hamburger (1/4 lb)	530
Tenderloin steak (8 oz)	450	Cheeseburger (large)	610
Pork loin chop (6 oz)	330	Fried chicken (breast)	370
Ham, lean and fat (6 oz)	500	Pizza, cheese (12 in.)	900
Chicken breast, roasted (6 oz)	330	Pizza, pepperoni (12 in.)	1100
Tuna, canned in oil (6 oz)	380	French fries (6 oz)	360
Tuna, canned in water (6 oz)	200	Sundae, hot fudge (regular)	290
Vegetables and fruits:		Beverages:	
Baked beans (4 oz)	75	Water (12 fl oz)	0
Peas, canned (4 oz)	85	Cola (12 fl oz)	150
Lettuce (1 cup)	15	Orange juice (8 fl oz)	105
Beets (4 oz)	35	Wine, Chardonnay, white, dry (6 fl oz)	135
Potato, boiled (4 oz)	80	Wine, Merlot, red, dry (6 fl oz)	140
Tomato (medium sized)	20	Wine, Port, ruby, sweet (6 fl oz)	275
Apple (medium)	60	Beer, regular (12 fl oz)	140
Banana (medium)	80	Beer, light (12 fl oz)	110

Source: www.annecollins.com/calories/protein-calories.htm

lipids (fats). The energy contents (kcal/gram) of these nutrients are indicated in Table 2, along with their functions in the human body and common food sources for them. Table 3 lists the energy contents (kcal) of common foods we eat. The liberation of chemical energy from these foods begins in the digestive tract where large food molecules are reconstructed into smaller molecules that can be used in metabolism. Carbohydrates are organic compounds that have the general chemical formula $C_x(H_2O)_y$ and are transformed into two simpler sugars: glucose ($C_6H_{12}O_6$) and glycogen $(C_6H_{10}O_5)_x$.

Glycogen is stored in the muscles and changed into glucose as needed. Proteins are broken down into amino acids (organic acids containing an amino group NH_2 and a carboxyl group COOH). Lipids include fats and are converted into fatty acids (e.g., acetic acid, $C_2H_4O_2$) and glycerol ($C_3H_8O_3$).

Carbohydrates are the primary source of muscle energy, converted by digestion into glucose and glycogen. Let us follow the trail of glucose as it is processed for muscle strength and action. In the metabolic process, glucose is reacted with oxygen to form carbon dioxide and water, and energy is released in the process. The series of chemical reactions can be summarized as follows:

$$C_6H_{12}O_6 + 6O_2 \rightarrow 6CO_2 + 6H_2O + \text{energy} \tag{3}$$

The immediate energy requirements for muscle contraction are provided by two phosphate compounds that are stored in the living muscle tissue: ATP, which stands for adenosine triphosphate ($C_{10}H_{16}N_5P_3O_{13}$), and CP, which stands for creatine phosphate ($C_4H_{10}N_3PO_5$). In the case of ATP, energy is made available to the cell by hydrolysis, in which one of the triphosphate bonds is broken to form ADP (adenosine diphosphate, $C_{10}H_{15}N_5P_2O_{10}$). This can be conceptualized by the following reaction [9]:

$$\text{ATP} + H_2O \rightarrow \text{ADP} + \text{energy} \tag{4}$$

This is the energy used for muscular contraction. In order for the muscle cells to continue to be supplied with energy, the ADP must be converted back to ATP. This is accomplished by three possible mechanisms, one of which involves the CP in the cell according to the following reaction [9]:

$$\text{ADP} + \text{CP} + \text{energy} \rightarrow \text{ATP} \tag{5}$$

Thus, CP acts as a backup energy source by reacting with the ADP to replenish the supply of ATP for continued muscle activity.

The use of CP in the reaction of equation (5) is the fastest way to produce ATP. However, the energy-generating capacity of CP is limited. For sustained muscular activity, alternative ways of producing ATP must be used. These alternatives involve reactions known as ***glycolysis***, in which glucose is broken down into pyruvic acid ($C_3H_4O_3$) and energy is released and used to form ATP molecules. If sufficient amounts of oxygen are available, then the pyruvic acid is oxidized to form carbon dioxide and water as in equation (3), and the process is referred to as ***aerobic glycolysis*** (also called ***aerobic metabolism***). However, glycolysis can take place without oxygen, in which case it is called ***anaerobic glycolysis***, and the products of the reaction are different from those in the aerobic process. If insufficient oxygen is provided, then the pyruvic acid is converted to lactic acid ($C_3H_6O_3$). There are two important differences in these alternative forms of glycolysis:

1. Aerobic glycolysis produces about 20 times the amount of energy compared to the anaerobic reaction. This energy is then used to increase the amounts of ATP and creatine phosphate available for continued muscle activity.
2. Accumulation of lactic acid in the muscle tissue resulting from anaerobic glycolysis is a principal cause of muscle fatigue, weakness, and possible pain. These conditions ultimately limit the amount of activity that the muscle can continue to perform.

1.2 Cardiovascular and Respiratory Systems

Our discussion of metabolism and glycolysis indicates that the delivery of oxygen is a key factor in the efficient liberation of energy from glucose for muscle activity. Oxygen is captured from the air by the respiratory system, and delivery of oxygen, glucose, and other nutrients to the muscle cells and organs is accomplished by the cardiovascular system. A model of these two systems and how they interact in the human body is illustrated in Figure 1.

Delivery of oxygen, glucose, and other nutrients to the muscle tissue and organs is accomplished by the ***cardiovascular system***, which consists of the heart, arteries, veins, and capillaries. Our primary interest is in the fluid circulated in the cardiovascular system: blood. Blood consists of plasma plus three types of blood cells. Plasma constitutes about 55% of the total blood volume and is about 90% water. The other 45% of the total volume consists of (1) red blood cells, (2) white blood cells, and (3) platelets. Red blood cells are of most interest here because they carry oxygen to the muscle cells and carbon dioxide away. White blood cells fight infections in the body, and platelets assist in blood clotting.

The heart is the pump that drives the circulation of blood throughout the body. The arteries, veins, and capillaries act as a closed loop transportation system that carries the materials for the biochemical reactions in equation (3). The arteries convey blood carrying oxygen and nutrients to the muscles and organs, and the veins move blood containing waste products and carbon dioxide back through the heart. The capillaries are very small blood vessels connecting the arteries and veins. They form a network that permeates the body tissue and enables the exchange of nutrients and wastes between the blood and tissue. The capillary walls are semipermeable membranes only a few microns thick that allow oxygen and glucose molecules to diffuse from the blood to the tissue while molecules of

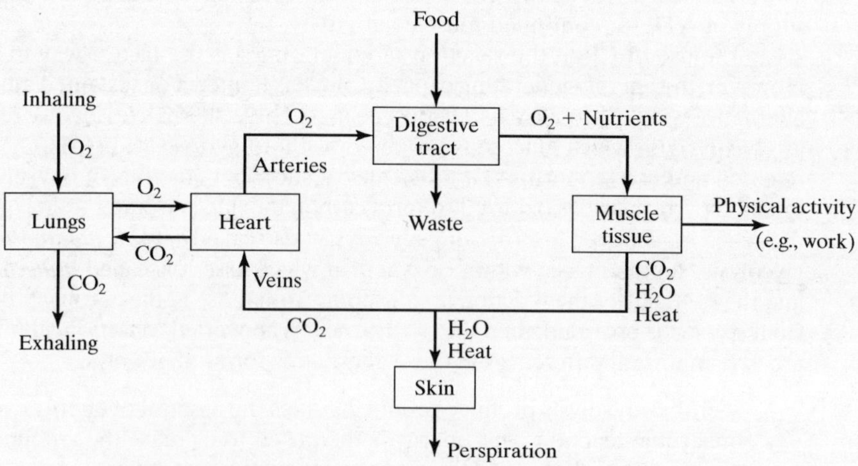

Figure 1 The major components of the respiratory and cardiovascular systems and how they work together to transport materials necessary for metabolism.

carbon dioxide, water, and other waste products diffuse into the blood to be transported to the lungs, kidneys, and liver through which they are removed from the body.

The lungs are of particular interest in metabolism because they are the source of the oxygen used by the muscle cells. They also exhaust carbon dioxide from the body. The lungs are primary components of the human ***respiratory system***, which includes the nasal cavity (nose) and the air passageway between it and the lungs. The passageway extends from the neck into the chest where it connects to the right and left main bronchi leading into the lungs. The bronchi divide and subdivide into increasingly smaller passageways, culminating in microscopic ***alveoli***, which are the air-containing cells of the lungs. Although small, they are numerous, between 200 million and 600 million and providing 70 to 90 m^2 (750 to 970 ft^2) of surface area in an adult human for O_2/CO_2 exchange [9]. The alveolar tissue in the lungs is permeated with capillaries that provide for the exchange of gases in the blood being circulated in them. Oxygen contained in the air inhaled into the lungs is diffused into the blood, which flows back to the heart and is pumped throughout the body. Carbon dioxide in the blood returning from the body is diffused in the opposite direction and ultimately exhaled from the lungs.

When the physical demands on the human body increase because of greater muscle activity, the respiratory system and cardiovascular system must work harder. The body must breathe heavier to oxygenate more blood through the lungs, and the heart must beat faster to distribute the greater amounts of oxygenated blood to the muscle tissue and return the waste products to be expelled. Blood pressure increases. Proportionately more blood is distributed to the muscles when they are engaged in moderate to heavy physical activity.[2]

In addition to the mechanical actions accomplished by the muscles, body heat is produced. The process of converting the chemical energy contained in the nutrients into mechanical energy manifested in muscle activity is far from 100% efficient, and most of the energy produced in the biochemical reaction in equation (3) is in the form of heat.[3] The body perspires to dissipate the excess heat produced by the increased muscle activity. Thus, greater oxygen consumption, faster heart rate, and perspiration are three principal reactions of the human body to increased physical activity. Oxygen consumption and heart rate can be measured while a person is working and are frequently used in ergonomics research to assess the level of strain on the human body due to physical (and/or mental) exertion.

2 MUSCULAR EFFORT AND WORK PHYSIOLOGY

In manual work situations, as well as athletics and other human physical activities, the muscles of the body must expend energy and apply forces to perform the activity. The capacity of the body to use energy and apply forces depends on the following:

1. The capacity of the cardiovascular and respiratory systems to deliver the required fuel and oxygen to the muscles for energy generation and to carry away waste products.

[2]When the body is resting, about 15% to 20% of the blood flow is distributed to the muscles. In heavy work 70% to 75% is distributed [2].

[3]Estimates of the amount of energy converted by the muscles into heat include (1) 80% or more [3, p. 193] and (2) approximately 70% [15, p. 229].

2. Muscle strength and endurance (muscle endurance is dependent largely on cardiovascular and respiratory limitations and the buildup of lactic acid and other waste products in the muscles).
3. Ability to maintain the proper heat balance within the body.

This section is organized around these three capacities.

2.1 Cardiovascular/Respiratory Capacity and Energy Expenditure

The rate of oxygen consumed by the body is proportional to the heart rate, at least in the steady state. Several research studies have demonstrated this proportionality, as reported in [2] and [14]. Furthermore, the amount of oxygen consumed by humans engaged in physical activity is approximately proportional to the quantity of energy expended. An energy expenditure of 4.8 kcal requires an average of 1 liter of oxygen to be consumed by the human body [12]. As the physical activity becomes more strenuous, the energy expenditure increases, and so does the heart rate and oxygen consumption. Figure 2 illustrates how these measures are related to several subjective categories of work activity.

Energy Expenditure Rates. Every type of physical activity requires a certain rate of energy expenditure when performed at a steady pace. These energy expenditure rates are sometimes referred to as the physiological cost of the activity to the human body and

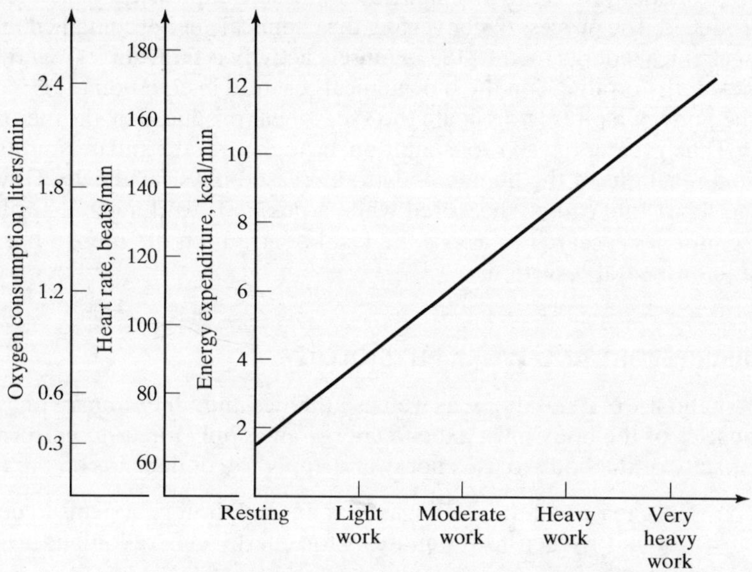

Figure 2 Energy expenditure, heart rate, and oxygen consumption for several subjective categories of work activity for a male worker in good physical condition. From American Industrial Hygiene Association, as reported in [15].

can be expressed in kilocalories per minute. Estimates of energy rate requirements for a variety of activities, including manual work tasks, are compiled in Table 4. To perform these physical activities, the human body must generate energy at a comparable rate in the form of basal and activity metabolism. This can be expressed as the following equation:

$$ER_m = BMR_m + AMR_m \tag{6}$$

where ER_m = energy expenditure rate of the activity, kcal/min; and $BMR_m + AMR_m$ = sum of basal and activity metabolic rates, kcal/min. Thus, the daily total metabolic rate of the body can be determined by (1) summing the energy expenditure rates multiplied by the respective times during which they apply in a given 24-hour period, and then (2) adding the digestive metabolic rate. The metabolic rate while sleeping is assumed to equal the basal metabolic rate, and the digestive metabolic rate is given by equation (2).

The energy expenditure rates in Table 4 are assumed to be for a person who weighs 72 kg (160 lb). If a person's weight differs from 72 kg (160 lb), then an adjustment should be made by multiplying the *ER* value in the table by the ratio *W*/72 if the weight is given in kg (or *W*/160 if the weight is given in lb), where W = the person's body weight. The following example illustrates the calculation of daily total metabolic rate.

Example 2 Daily Total Metabolic Rate for Various Activities

The 35-year old female worker in Example 1 expends energy during various times of the day as follows: (1) sleeps for 8 hr, (2) walks to and from work for 1 hr at an assumed pace of 4.5 km/hr, (3) stands for 2 hr, (4) performs soldering work while seated for 6 hr, (5) watches TV and rests for 7 hr. Determine her total metabolic rate for the 24-hour period.

TABLE 4 Physiological Costs (Energy Expenditure Rate, ER_m) for Various Physical Activities, Including Physical Work Activities

Physical Activities Other Than Manual Labor	Energy Expenditure Rate (ER_m)	Physical Work Activities	Energy Expenditure Rate (ER_m)
Sleeping	BMR_m	Office work, seated	1.6 kcal/min
Resting (seated)	1.5 kcal/min	Office work, standing	1.8 kcal/min
Standing (not walking)	2.2 kcal/min	Light assembly work, seated	2.2 kcal/min
Walking at 3 km/hr (1.9 mi/hr)	2.8 kcal/min	Soldering tasks while seated	2.7 kcal/min
Walking at 4.5 km/hr (2.8 mi/hr)	4.0 kcal/min	Cleaning windows	3.1 kcal/min
Walking at 6 km/hr (3.7 mi/hr)	5.2 kcal/min	Bricklaying	4.0 kcal/min
Climbing stairs at 100 steps/min	13.7 kcal/min	Sawing wood manually	6.8 kcal/min
Jogging at 7.2 km/hr (4.5 mi/hr)	7.5 kcal/min	Chopping wood	8.0 kcal/min
Running at 12 km/hr (7.5 mi/hr)	12.7 kcal/min	Mowing lawn (push mower)	8.3 kcal/min
Cycling at 16 km/hr (10 mi/hr)	5.2 kcal/min	Shoveling loads of 7 kg (15 lb)	8.5 kcal/min
		Climbing stairs with 8 kg (17 lb) load	9.0 kcal/min
		Climbing steep stairs with 10 kg (22 lb)	16.2 kcal/min

Source: Compiled from [2, 6, 9]; H. W. Vos, "Physiological Workloads in Different Body Postures, While Working Near to, or Below Ground Level," *Ergonomics* 16, no. 6 (1973): 817–28; R. Passmore and U. Durnin, "Human Energy Expenditure," *Physiological Reviews* 35 (1955): 83–89, as summarized in [12]; O. Edholm, *The Biology of Work* (New York: McGraw-Hill, 1967); and [5] as summarized in [15].

Solution: From the previous example, we know her basal metabolic rate is 0.86 kcal/min. The calculation of TMR_d is summarized in the table below. TMR_d = 2330 kcal for the 24-hour period, using ER_m values from Table 4.

Activity	Time (min)	ER_m (kcal/min)	Weight Factor	Total Energy (kcal)
Sleeping	480	0.86	(no correction)	413
Walking	60	4.0	130/160 = 0.81	194
Standing	120	2.2	130/160 = 0.81	214
Soldering work	360	2.7	130/160 = 0.81	787
Other activities	420	1.5	130/160 = 0.81	510
	1440		$BMR_d + AMR_d =$	2118
Digestive metabolism			$0.10(BMR_d + AMR_d) =$	212
			$TMR_d =$	2330 kcal

■

There are times when the demand for energy by the muscles is greater than what can be supplied by the reactions summarized in equation (3). This imbalance between energy supply and demand occurs at the beginning of physical activity after the body has been at rest. There is a time lag of several minutes before the body can respond to the increased need for oxygen through increased cardiovascular and respiratory activity. Compensating for the imbalance, at least on a temporary basis, is the energy that has been stored in the muscle cells in the form of ATP and CP. The glycolysis during these first few minutes of activity is anaerobic, and as the muscles continue to work even though insufficient oxygen is available, a condition called oxygen debt occurs. ***Oxygen debt*** is the difference between the amount of oxygen needed by the muscles during muscular activity and the amount that is supplied. This debt must be paid back when muscle activity is discontinued. The effect is illustrated in Figure 3. When work stops and a rest break begins, the breathing and heart rate do not immediately return to their previous lower levels. Instead, breathing remains heavy and the heart continues to pump greater amounts of oxygenated blood so that the muscles can replenish their stored energy supplies and decompose any accumulated lactic acid produced during anaerobic glycolysis.

Recommended Limits of Energy Expenditure. For the physical well-being of a worker, it is important that the worker's energy expenditure rate and heart rate be kept within reasonable limits over the course of a shift. A number of recommendations have been proposed in the ergonomics literature. For an 8-hour shift, Table 5 lists guidelines reported in [12],[4] which are representative. The guideline values assume that the male and female workers are in good physical condition.

[4]Pulat's guidelines are based on recommendations in F. H. Bonjer, "Actual Energy Expenditure in Relation to Physical Working Capacity," *Ergonomics* 5 (1962): 467–70, and L. Brouha, *Physiology in Industry* (New York: Pergamon Press, 1960).

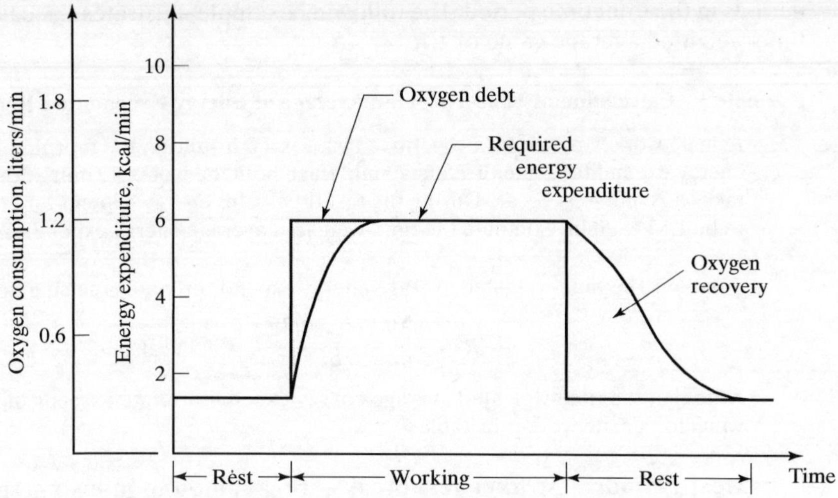

Figure 3 Oxygen debt accumulated at the beginning of work activity, which must be repaid when the activity stops.

TABLE 5 Recommended Guidelines for Energy Expenditure and Heart Rate for an 8-hour Work Shift

Physiological Measure	Male Worker	Female Worker
Energy expenditure rate of the physical activity (maximum time-weighted average during shift) $\overline{ER}_m$	5.0 kcal/min	4.0 kcal/min
Energy expenditure of the physical activity for the entire 8-hr shift	2400 kcal	1920 kcal
Heart rate (maximum time-weighted average during shift) $\overline{HR}_m$	120 beats/min	110 beats/min

Source: [12].

The values of energy expenditure rate and heart rate in Table 5 are time-weighted average values during the shift, which means that there may be periods when these values are exceeded so long as they are averaged with other periods at lower energy expenditure rates that are long enough to compensate for those high values. The following equation can be used to compute the time-weighted average energy expenditure rates during a time period of interest:

$$\overline{ER} = \frac{\sum_i T_i(ER_i)}{\sum_i T_i} \tag{7}$$

where $\overline{ER}$ = time-weighted average energy expenditure rate, kcal/min; T_i = duration of time period i during total time period of interest, min; and ER_i = energy expenditure rate during time period i; and the summation is carried out over all of the individual periods in the total time period. The following example illustrates the calculation of the time-weighted average value of $\overline{ER}$.

Example 3 Calculation of Time-Weighted Average of Energy Expenditure Rates

A male worker performs a repetitive task for 4.0 hr during the morning that requires an energy expenditure rate of 7.5 kcal/min. Each hour, he works 40 min at this task and then takes a 20-min rest break. During the rest breaks, his energy expenditure rate is estimated to be 1.5 kcal/min. Compute the time-weighted average energy expenditure rate.

Solution: The time-weighted average energy expenditure rate is calculated as follows:

$$\overline{ER} = \frac{40(7.5) + 20(1.5)}{60} = 5.5 \text{ kcal/min}$$

Note that the time-weighted average energy expenditure rate exceeds the recommended value for a male worker in Table 5. ■

Rest Periods. Worker rest breaks are common in industry. They should be included and paid for by the employer as regular work time. In most situations rest breaks are of relatively short duration, lasting from 5 to 20 min, according to the U.S. Department of Labor.[5] Rest breaks are often included in the allowance factor that is built into the time standard for a task. On the other hand, meal periods (e.g., lunch breaks) do not count as rest breaks, and they are not included in the time standard or paid for as work time. Usually 30 min or more are sufficient for a meal period, during which the worker is completely relieved from duty.

Rest breaks of short duration (i.e., 5 to 20 min) are appropriate when the energy expenditure rates of the work are less than or equal to recommended values such as those given in Table 5 (5 kcal/min for men and 4 kcal/min for women). In work situations where the energy expenditure rates are greater than the recommended values, longer rest periods must be provided to allow the body to recover from fatigue. The rest periods at low energy expenditure rates time-averaged with the higher ER values while working provide a way of keeping the total energy expenditures during the shift within acceptable bounds. Various methods have been proposed for determining the appropriate length of rest periods. One common approach is based on the energy expenditure time-averaging equation. Starting with equation (7), the following formula can be derived:

$$T_{rst} = \frac{T_{wrk}(ER_{wrk} - \overline{ER})}{(\overline{ER} - ER_{rst})} \tag{8}$$

where T_{rst} = rest time, min; T_{wrk} = working time (how much time the worker spends actually working), min; ER_{wrk} = energy expenditure rate associated with the physical activity, kcal/min (typical values given in Table 4); $\overline{ER}$ = average or standard acceptable energy expenditure rate (as suggested in Table 5, $\overline{ER}$ = 5 kcal/min for male workers and 4 kcal/min for female workers); and ER_{rst} = metabolic rate of worker while resting, which is slightly above the basal metabolic rate (ER_{rst} = 1.5 kcal/min from Table 4). This form of equation was suggested in [11] and is frequently cited in the ergonomics literature.

[5]Code of Federal Regulations pertaining to the U.S. Department of Labor, Title 29, CFR 785.18.

Example 4 Determining the Appropriate Rest Period for a Given Work Time

A male worker performs physical labor that has an energy expenditure rate of 8.2 kcal/min for 20 min. How long a rest break should the worker be allowed at the end of this work period?

Solution: From Table 5, the recommended average energy expenditure rate is 5.0 kcal/min; the expenditure rate while the worker rests is 1.5 kcal/min, according to Table 4. Using equation (8), the appropriate duration of the rest break is determined as follows:

$$T_{rst} = \frac{20(8.2 - 5.0)}{(5.0 - 1.5)} = 18.29 \text{ min}$$ ■

An alternative form of the rest period equation can also be derived. It uses the total time TT rather than the actual work time T_{wrk}. This formula can be stated as follows:

$$T_{rst} = \frac{TT(ER_{wrk} - \overline{ER})}{(ER_{wrk} - ER_{rst})} \quad (9)$$

where $TT = T_{wrk} + T_{rst}$ = total time that includes both work time and rest time, min. For example, the total time might be the number of hours in the shift.

Example 5 Determining the Appropriate Rest Proportion for an 8-hour Shift

A male worker performs hard physical labor interspersed with rest breaks for fatigue during an 8-hour shift. The physical work has an energy expenditure rate of 8.2 kcal/min. (a) How should the 8-hour shift be divided between work periods and rest breaks? (b) Is this division consistent with the rest period value computed in previous Example 4? (c) As a check, is the time-weighted average energy expenditure rate for the shift within the recommended 5 kcal/min?

Solution (a) Using the recommended average energy expenditure rate of 5.0 kcal/min and the rest break expenditure rate of 1.5 kcal/min, the proportion of total time that should be devoted to rest breaks is

$$\text{Rest proportion} = \frac{8.2 - 5.0}{8.2 - 1.5} = 0.4776 = 47.76\%$$

This leaves 0.5224 or 52.24% of the shift as working time. Of the 8-hour shift, rest time accounts for $0.4776(8.0) = 3.821$ hr, and work time accounts for $0.5224(8.0) = 4.179$ hr.

(b) The total work-rest time cycle in Example 4 is $TT = 20.0 + 18.29 = 38.29$ min. The proportion of rest time to total time is

$$\frac{18.29}{38.29} = 0.4777$$

This is the same proportion (within round-off error) calculated in part (a). Therefore, the division between work and rest is consistent with the rest period value computed in Example 4.

(c) The time-weighted average energy expenditure rate during the 8-hour shift is

$$\overline{ER} = \frac{4.179(8.2) + 3.82(1.5)}{4.179 + 3.821} = \frac{34.678 + 5.7315}{8.0} = 5.0 \text{ kcal/min}$$ ■

The scheduling of the work-rest cycles during the shift is an important consideration. In Example 5, the purpose of rest breaks would be subverted if the worker were forced to work continuously for 4.179 hr and then rest for the remaining 3.821 hr of the shift. The worker would experience extreme fatigue if he had to labor at an energy expenditure rate of 8.2 kcal/min for 4.179 hr. Few workers would be willing or able to endure such a work period. The purpose of a rest break is to recover from muscle fatigue, increased heart rate, and the buildup of lactic acid in the muscle cells. In general, short work-rest cycles improve the body's capability for physiological recovery, the shorter the better. The heart rate and lactic acid buildup during the heavy physical activity are less when the work periods are shorter, and recovery from fatigue occurs more quickly. Thus, in Example 4, a 20-minute work period followed by an 18.29-minute rest break would probably be too long a cycle. Working 2 min at 8.2 kcal/min and then resting for 1.8 min would be far preferable, both for physiological comfort and the efficiency with which the worker performs his job.

Of course, the physiological well-being of the worker must sometimes be balanced against the scheduling demands of the job. If the job operates on a 5-minute cycle, the worker may be required to perform at an increased energy expenditure rate for that entire time, and then take a rest break of 4.6 min. Physical training may be required to increase the worker's stamina during the work periods, and short rest pauses of a few seconds each may be necessary during the cycle for the worker to continue at the required pace for the full 5 min.

2.2 Muscle Strength and Endurance

In addition to energy considerations in the operation of human muscles, strength is also a factor in many physical activities, including manual work. In the context of muscle capacity, ***strength*** is defined as the maximum torque that a given muscle or muscle group can exert voluntarily about the skeletal joint that it spans [9]. Strength is also defined in terms of the maximum force that can be applied by the muscle or muscle group under specified conditions, and force is usually more convenient to measure than torque. There are two basic conditions under which strength is measured, corresponding to the two basic types of muscle activity:

1. *Static strength.* Measured by the human subject applying as high a force as possible against an immovable object. To avoid muscle fatigue, the duration of the applied force is short, lasting only a few seconds. The measured value is influenced by joint type (e.g., arms, legs), joint angle, motivation of the human subject, and other factors.
2. *Dynamic strength.* Tested under conditions that involve changes in joint angles and motion speed. Instantaneous values of force are measured at various joint configurations during the motion pattern. Dynamic strength is affected by the speed of the motion pattern, with higher strength values being associated with slower speeds.

TABLE 6 Comparison of Static and Dynamic Muscular Activities

	Static Muscular Activity	Dynamic Muscular Activity
Description	Sustained contraction.	Rhythmic contraction and relaxation.
Examples	Holding a part in a static position. Squeezing a pair of pliers.	Cranking a pump handle. Turning a screwdriver.
Physiological effect	Reduced blood flow to tissue restricts oxygen supply and waste removal. Lactic acid is generated. Metabolism is anaerobic.	Adequate blood flow allows oxygen supply and waste removal needs to be satisfied. Metabolism is aerobic.

Owing to differences in the required measurement apparatus, static strength is more easily assessed than dynamic strength, and most of the available data on human strength are in terms of static strength. Yet, most work activities involve dynamic muscle effort, and dynamic effort is physiologically less costly to the muscles than static effort. A comparison of static and dynamic muscular activities is summarized in Table 6.

Factors Affecting Strength. There are significant variations in strength among individuals. The differences in measured static strength between the strongest and weakest workers in a given industrial population can be as much as 8 to 1 [4]. There are many factors that explain such a wide range in human physical strength. Among them are the following personal characteristics of the worker: (1) size (e.g., height, body weight, build), (2) physical conditioning, (3) gender, and (4) age.

Certainly the size and physical conditioning of the worker are key factors. Size does matter. A 32-year-old male worker who is 6-ft, 2-in. tall, weighs 190 lb, and exercises regularly is bound to be stronger than a 5-ft, 6-in. worker of the same age who weighs 130 lb and does little else other than watch TV during his nonworking hours. Physical exercise can increase strength by as much as 50% [12].

In comparing the strengths of male and female workers, it comes as no surprise that male workers are stronger. A rule of thumb that is frequently cited in the ergonomics literature is that the average strength of females is 67% (two-thirds) the average strength of males over the various muscle groups that are normally tested in the body.[6] However, there is considerable variation from this average for specific muscle groups, as well as within the male and female distributions. Thus, the male and female distributions overlap one another, and many women are stronger than many men.

Age is also a factor in strength capability. Strength achieves a maximum level in humans when they are 23 to 35 years old. It decreases slowly until the mid-forties and then decreases more rapidly thereafter. In the mid-fifties average strength is about 80% of its peak, and in the mid-seventies it is about 60% of its peak [15].

Endurance. Muscle ***endurance*** is defined as the capability to maintain an applied force over time. The term is most readily explained in the context of a static force. The ability of a person to maintain his or her maximum static force lasts only a short time.

[6]The original source of this rule of thumb seems to be J. Roebuck, K. Kroemer, and W. Thomson, *Engineering Anthropometry Methods* (New York: Wiley Interscience, 1975).

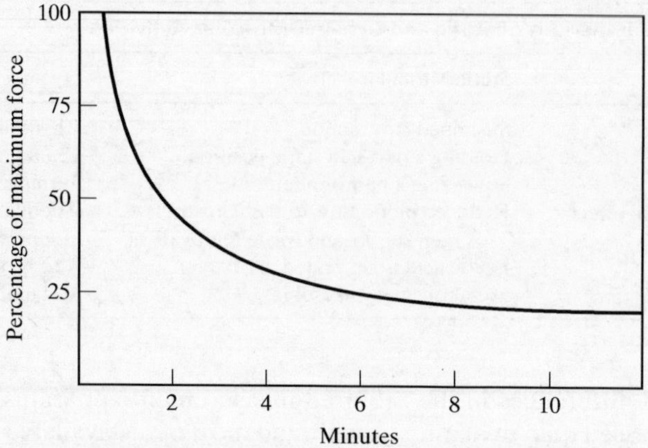

Figure 4 Strength endurance: general relationship between the maximum force capability that can be applied by a person as a function of time. Based on a figure in [9].

The general relationship between force capability and time is indicated in Figure 4. The plot suggests that after 8 or 10 min, a person can apply only about 23% of the maximum static force that could be achieved at the start of the test, due to the onset of muscle fatigue. This finding is important in the design of work methods because a worker cannot be expected to grip an object continuously at a high force level for an extended period of time. The general rule is to use a mechanical workholder rather than require the worker to perform that function. If the task requires the worker to maintain a static force for several minutes, that force should be significantly less than the worker's maximum capacity.

A somewhat similar relationship occurs in dynamic muscle activity, in which the individual is required to apply forces during a repetitive motion cycle. Muscle fatigue gradually causes the applied dynamic force to decline over time, but the decline is slower than in the case of an applied static force, and a sustainable bottom level is reached that is higher than the 23% observed in Figure 4 for static forces. The difference is that dynamic muscular activity is physiologically better for the muscle cells than applying a static force.

2.3 Thermal Balance and Thermoregulation

The third factor affecting the capacity of the human body to perform physical work is its ability to maintain a proper thermal balance. If body temperature rises too far above its normal level or falls too far below this level, body function is impaired.

For our discussion of thermal balance, the human body can be considered to consist of a core surrounded by a shell. The shell is perhaps 2.5 mm (1 in.) thick or less and consists of skin and the flesh immediately beneath it. The core consists of the organs in the body, such as the heart, liver, lungs, stomach, and intestines. The brain should also be included, although it confounds the core-in-shell model somewhat. The brain, liver, heart, and working muscles are the primary generators of heat within the body. The muscles function to convert the food and oxygen into mechanical output, but the conversion process is only 20% to 30% efficient, and the remainder of the energy is in the form of heat. The heat is transferred from the core (organs and muscles) to the shell (skin) by blood flowing in the cardiovascular system. Blood is mostly water, which has ideal thermal properties for this purpose (high volumetric specific heat and thermal conductivity). At the shell, perspiration is produced by sweat glands in the skin and then evaporated to the atmosphere. Evaporation extracts heat from the body. Convection and radiation also contribute to the heat loss if the surrounding temperatures are lower than skin temperature.

Body temperature in the core is controlled by a complex thermoregulation system that attempts to maintain a set point value of approximately 37°C (98.6°F). Body core temperatures that increase or decrease significantly from this value mean trouble. Core temperatures above 38°C (100.4°F) tend to reduce physiological performance; temperatures above 40°C (104°F) tend to be disabling; and temperatures above 42°C (107.6°F) are likely to cause death. Lower than normal body temperatures are called ***hypothermia*** and can also have severe consequences if the deviation becomes too great. Below about 35°C (95°F), central nervous system coordination is reduced, and the person becomes apathetic. Below 32°C (90°F), the muscles become rigid, and the person loses consciousness. Below about 30°C (86°F), there is severe cardiovascular stress. Death occurs when body temperature drops to around 27°C (86°F). The shell temperature is not required to stay within the close limits of the normal core temperature and may differ significantly in cold or hot climates.

The body's thermoregulation system maintains body temperature within the narrow range about normal by achieving a thermal balance with the environment. This thermal balance involves heat exchange between the body and the environment that can be expressed in the following equation:

$$\Delta HC = M - E \pm R \pm C - W \tag{10}$$

where ΔHC = net change in heat content in the body (heat gained or lost), M = metabolic energy produced, E = heat lost through perspiration and evaporation, R = radiant heat loss or gain, C = heat loss or gain by convection, and W = work performed by the body. Appropriate units in the equation are kcal or kJ or other energy units. Although equation (10) is not practical for actual calculations, it is a useful conceptual model for discussing how body temperature is regulated.

Assessing the terms on the right-hand-side of equation (10), metabolism (M) is always a positive term because of the heat generation that accompanies the biochemical reactions associated with it. Evaporation (E) is always a negative term (as indicated by the minus sign) because of the heat of vaporization required to convert perspiration (mostly water) to vapor. Much of that heat is extracted from the body. Radiation (R) can be positive or negative, depending on whether the body is cooler or warmer than its surroundings. Convection (C) involves the transfer of heat by the flow of fluid (e.g., air) past the surface of an object. Convection can be positive or negative in equation (10).

If the body skin is warmer than the surrounding air flowing in contact with it, hcat will be transferred away from the body. If the air is warmer than the skin, heat will be transferred into the body by convection. Finally, the work energy term (W) will always require energy expenditure and thus will be a negative term in the equation.

When ΔHC = zero in the heat exchange equation, it means that the body is in thermal balance with its environment. When ΔHC is positive or negative, it means there is a net heat gain or loss that translates into an increase or decrease in body core temperature, with the potentially dire consequences described above. The thermal regulation system tries to compensate for deviations from normal temperature by increasing heat generation when body temperature drops below normal and by expelling heat from the body when its temperature is above normal. Control strategies are guided by equation (10). There are three automatic mechanisms used by the body to try to regulate body temperature [15]: (1) sweating to increase heat losses by evaporation, (2) shivering to increase heat generation by metabolism, and (3) constricting or dilating blood vessels to reduce or increase blood flow.

In addition, a person experiencing a net heat gain or loss is likely to take a variety of conscious actions to mitigate the effect: (1) wearing lighter clothing in warm weather, (2) moving out of the sunlight and into the shade in hot weather, (3) adding more layers of clothing in cold and windy weather, (4) exercising the body in cold weather to increase body heat, and (5) moving into the sunlight in cold weather for radiant heat.

3 ANTHROPOMETRY

Anthropometry is an empirical science that is concerned with the physical measurements of the human body, such as height, range of joint movements, and weight. The word is derived from the Greek words ***anthropos*** (man) and ***metron*** (to measure). Anthropometry is usually considered a branch of anthropology.[7] Strength characteristics are also sometimes included in the scope of anthropometry.

3.1 Anthropometric Variables and Data

A considerable amount of anthropometric data has been collected and published over the years, despite the significant expense in finding statistically representative subjects from the population, performing the measurements, and compiling the data. A very small amount of such data is summarized in this section. More complete tables of data are available in several of our references [3, 9, 12, and 16]. The types of anthropometric variables and the methods of measurement have been standardized to some degree by the International Organization for Standardization (ISO). Table 7 presents a subset of these variables to give the reader a sense of the kinds of body dimensions that are measured in anthropometry. A number of these dimensions are illustrated in Figure 5.

[7]***Anthropology*** is the scientific study of humans, especially in relation to origins, racial classifications, physical and cultural characteristics and differences, and social relationships.

TABLE 7 Selected Anthropometric Variables and Methods of Measurement (ISO/DIS 7230)

Anthropometric Variable	Definition and Method of Measurement
Stature (height)	Standing height, vertical distance between floor and highest part of head with subject standing erect, feet together, and heels, buttocks, shoulders, and back of head against a vertical surface.
Eye height	Vertical distance between floor and inner eye corner, with subject standing as in the preceding.
Shoulder height	Vertical distance between floor and outer upper point of the shoulder blade, with subject standing as in the preceding.
Elbow height	Vertical distance between floor and lowest bony point of elbow, with upper arm hanging freely and elbow flexed at 90 degrees, with subject standing as in the preceding.
Sitting height	Sitting erect, vertical distance between horizontal sitting surface and highest part of head, with subject sitting against a vertical surface, thighs fully supported and lower legs hanging freely.
Sitting eye height	Vertical distance between horizontal sitting surface and inner eye corner, with subject sitting as in the preceding.
Sitting shoulder height	Vertical distance between horizontal sitting surface and outer upper point of the shoulder blade, with subject sitting as in the preceding.
Shoulder breadth	Horizontal distance between right and left outer upper points of the shoulder blades.
Knee height	Vertical distance between floor and upper surface of thigh, with knees bent 90 degrees.
Hand length	Distance between tip of middle finger and most distal point of styloid process of radius with hand outstretched.
Foot length	Maximum distance between back of heel and tip of longest toe.
Head length	Distance along a straight line between glabella (smooth prominence on the forehead between the eyebrows) and rearmost point of the skull.
Head breadth	Maximum breadth of head above ears.
Head circumference	Maximum circumference around head over glabella (smooth prominence on the forehead between the eyebrows) and rearmost point of the skull.
Forward reach	Maximum distance between a vertical wall against which subject presses shoulder blades and grip axis of hand.
Waist circumference	Trunk circumference in region of navel.
Body weight	Subject standing still on weighing scale.

Human Variability. One of the significant issues in the collection and application of anthropometric data is human variability. Differences in body dimensions exist among people because of ethnicity, nationality, heredity, diet, health, sex, age, and living conditions. To illustrate some of these differences, height data are compiled in Table 8 for adult males and females from selected geographical regions of the world. Height differences between males and females average around 12 cm (4.7 in.) for the regions covered by the data. The standard deviation in these data averages approximately 6.5 cm (2.5 in.) for males and 5.9 cm (2.3 in.) for females, so the males versus female differences are significant. Height differences are also significant among different regions of the world, with Northern Europeans at the upper end of the range and Southern Indians and Southeast Asians at the lower end.

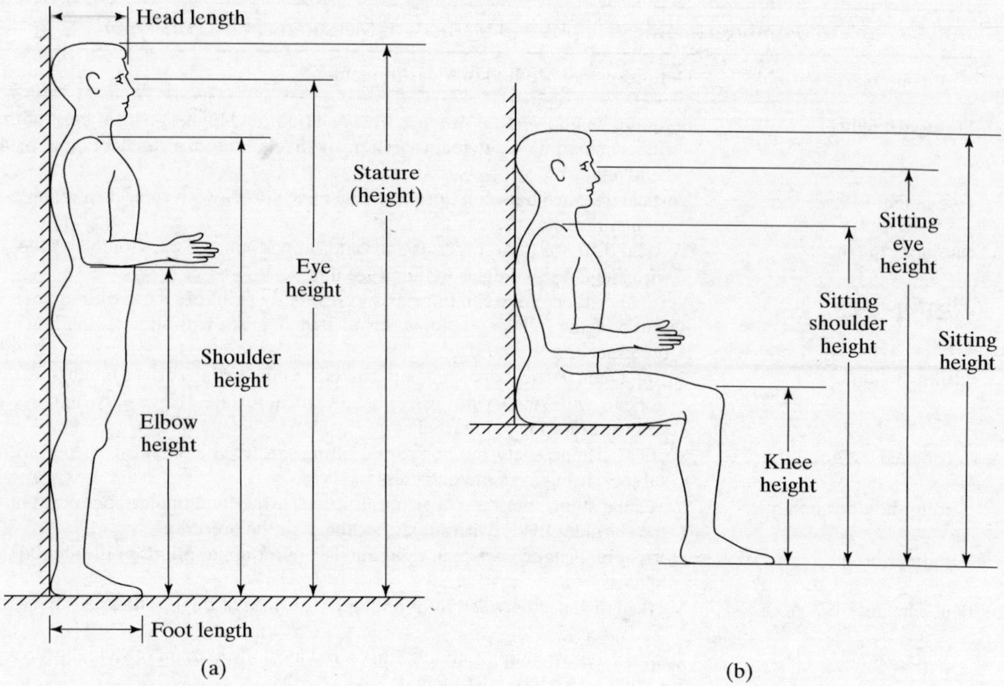

Figure 5 Static dimensions of several anthropometric variables: (a) subject standing and (b) subject sitting.

TABLE 8 Statures (Standing Heights) of Male and Female Adults from Selected Geographical Regions of the World

	Males		Females	
Region	Centimeters	Inches	Centimeters	Inches
North America	179	70.5	165	65.0
Northern Europe	181	71.3	169	66.5
Central Europe	177	69.7	166	65.4
Southeastern Europe	173	68.1	162	63.8
India, North	167	65.7	154	60.6
India, South	162	63.8	150	59.1
Japan	172	67.7	159	62.6
Southeast Asia	163	64.2	153	60.2
Australia (European)	177	69.7	167	65.7
Africa, North	169	66.5	161	63.4
Africa, West	167	65.7	153	60.2

Source: Based on data in H. W. Juergens, I. A. Aune, and U. Pieper, *International Data on Anthropometry* (Geneva, Switzerland: International Labor Office, 1990), as reported in [9].

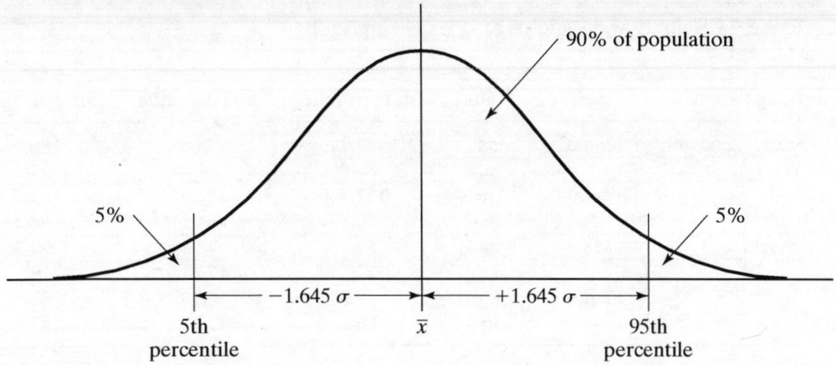

Figure 6 The normal distribution of a given anthropometric variable of interest. The 5th and 95th percentile points in the distribution include the middle 90% of the population.

The Normal Distribution in Anthropometric Data. It has been found that anthropometric data compiled from a homogenous population usually follow a normal distribution.[8] Anthropometric data are usually published not only to list mean values (as in Table 8 on adult heights) but also to reveal the dispersion in the distribution. This is done by indicating (1) percentile limits on the variable, for example, the 5th and 95th percentiles and/or (2) the standard deviation that applies to the distribution of the specific anthropometric variable. As indicated in Figure 6, the 5th and 95th percentile points in the distribution include the middle 90% of the population. These percentile points are related to a certain number of standard deviations away from the mean of the distribution—for example, ±1.645 standard deviations for the 5th and 95th percentiles. The 50th percentile point is the mean of the distribution. Values of height and weight of U.S. civilian adults are compiled in Table 9. Values at the 5th, 50th, and 95th percentiles are given, as well as the standard deviation. The reader will observe that the mean values (50th percentile point) in the height data in this table do not agree perfectly with the data from a different source compiled in Table 8. This discrepancy highlights one of the problems in the collection of anthropometric data.

Body Weight. Estimated weight data for adult males and females in the United States are presented in Table 9 [9]. There is a rough correlation between body height and body weight, but a person's ancestry, build, eating habits, and amount of exercise cause a significant variation in this relationship. Obesity is emerging as a serious health problem in the United States in the early part of the 21st century due to the abundant eating opportunities enjoyed by most Americans and the sedentary lifestyles that many have adopted.

Metrics have been established to assess whether an individual is within a reasonable weight range for his or her height or is overweight or obese. One of these metrics is

[8]A homogeneous population is one in which the members of the population have similar characteristics. For example, males and females would be distinguished and not grouped in the same population.

TABLE 9 Heights and Weights of U.S. Civilian Adults

Body Parameter	Sex	Units	5th Percentile	50th Percentile	95th Percentile	Standard Deviation
Standing height	Male	cm	164.7	175.6	186.7	6.68
		in.	64.8	69.1	73.5	2.63
	Female	cm	152.7	162.9	173.7	6.36
		in.	60.1	64.1	68.4	2.50
Weight	Male	kg	57.7	78.5	99.3	12.6
		lb	127	173	219	27.8
	Female	kg	39.2	62.0	84.8	13.8
		lb	86	137	187	30.4

Source: Based on data in C. C. Gordon et al., *1988 Anthropometric Survey of U. S. Army Personnel: Summary Statistics Interim Report* (Natick, MA: 1989), U. S. Army Natick Research, Development and Engineering Center, as reported in [9]. Data for 5th and 95th percentiles and standard deviations are estimated based on K. H. E. Kroemer, "Engineering Anthropometry: Designing the Workplace to Fit the Human," Proceedings, Annual Conference of American Institute of Industrial Engineers, Norcross, GA 1981, pp. 119–26, as reported in [9].

TABLE 10 Interpretation of Body Mass Index Values

BMI value	$BMI < 18.5$	$18.5 \le BMI < 25$	$25 \le BMI < 30$	$30 \le BMI < 40$	$BMI \ge 40$
Interpretation	Underweight	Ideal	Overweight	Obese	Morbidly obese

the ***body mass index***, adopted by the U.S. Department of Agriculture in 1990. The index is based on one's weight and height and can be calculated using the following formula:

$$BMI = \frac{W}{h^2} \tag{11}$$

where BMI = body mass index (no units necessary, although technically, the units are kg/m^2); W = body weight, kg; and h = standing height, m. The units are important in the terms on the right side of the equation to properly interpret the BMI value. The formula can be adapted to the U.S. Customary System of units by multiplying by 703; that is,

$$BMI = \frac{703W}{h^2} \tag{12}$$

where W = body weight, lb; and h = standing height, in. The interpretations of the BMI calculation are given in Table 10.

3.2 Anthropometric Design Principles and Applications

Several principles and guidelines have been developed for applying anthropometric data in design [3, 12, and 15]. These principles are briefly discussed in this section and examples of applications are given. Although different principles are applicable in different design situations, the common theme in these principles is designing for the user population.

Design for Extreme Individuals. This principle makes use of the statistical nature of available anthropometric data by attempting to develop a design (e.g., product, workplace) that can accommodate nearly all users. In many design problems, there is a limiting dimension or feature that restricts usage by some individuals—for example, the height of a doorway into a room in a building. If the height of the doorway were designed for the average person (50th percentile), then its height would be 175.6 cm (5 ft, 9.1 in.) to accommodate the mean height of a male, according to data in Table 9. Perhaps a small clearance would be added. Unfortunately, 50% of the male population would not be able to pass through the doorway without stooping. Using the principle of designing for extreme individuals, the doorway height would be selected to accommodate some upper percentile, such as the 95th percentile. Height data for males at the 95th percentile are listed in Table 9 as 186.7 cm (6 ft, 1.5 in.). Adding a clearance, the doorway would be designed with a height of 195 cm (6 ft, 5 in.) or higher. In fact, most household doorways are designed with a height of around 205 cm (81 in.), which means they can accommodate well over 95% of the male population. There will still be individuals who have to duck when passing through the opening (e.g., tall professional basketball players).

The doorway design is an example of ***designing for the maximum*** anthropometric dimension. Other examples of designing for the maximum include automobile door openings, mattress sizes, escape hatches in military vehicles (e.g., tanks), elevations of overhead conveyors and other equipment suspended from the ceiling in a factory, and strength of a support rung in a ladder.

The opposite situation is ***designing for the minimum*** anthropometric dimension, in which the design feature must accommodate the 5th (or other lower end) percentile. Examples of designing for the minimum body dimensions include heights of kitchen cabinets, locations of levers and dials on equipment, and weights of portable power tools.

Design for Adjustability. In many cases, products are designed so that certain features can be adjusted in order to accommodate a wide range of users' anthropometric dimensions. Examples of adjustable product features include automobile driver seats, adjustable steering wheel in an automobile, office chairs, worktable heights, tilt angles of computer monitors, lawnmower handle heights, and bicycle handlebars.

Designing for adjustability allows virtually all users to make the necessary adjustments in the equipment to suit their particular body dimensions. The usual practice in these cases is to design the adjustment feature to include a certain specified range, such as the 5th to the 95th percentile. If the products are intended for both male and female users, then the appropriate range would be between the 5th percentile for females up to the 95th percentile for males. Because of the overlap in body dimensions between the male and female distributions, this range covers more than 90% of the combined population. It reaches below the 5th percentile for males and beyond the 95th percentile for females.

Design for the Average User. There are certain situations where the principles of design for extreme individuals and design for adjustability are not appropriate. The notion of extreme individuals is not applicable to the design problem, and designing adjustable features into the product is either impossible or cost prohibitive. In these cases, the compromise is to design for the average user (50th percentile point). Examples of designing for the average user include stair heights in stairways of buildings, seats in high school football stadiums, sofas and chairs, heights of checkout counters at supermarkets, and lengths of shovel handles.

One final comment that should be included in our discussion of this principle is that no person exists whose every body dimension is "average" (at the 50th percentile point). There is no such thing as the all-around average person. It's like saying that the average family has 2.3 children. No family has 2.3 children. When using anthropometric data, if only one body dimension is important (e.g., height), then individuals can be found who match that average. But as the number of body dimensions required in the design problem increases, it becomes less likely that any individual will be average in all of those dimensions. Although body dimensions are correlated (e.g., standing height is correlated with body weight), the correlation is often far from perfect. Designing for the average user is a somewhat hypothetical design strategy.

Designing Different Sizes for Different Users. In some product situations, the only way to adequately accommodate the user population is for the same product to be made available in different sizes. Important examples of these situations are clothing, shoes, and desks and chairs for students in elementary schools (kindergarten through eighth grade).

In the case of clothing, different body dimensions are important for different articles of clothing. For shirts, the important dimensions include neck, chest, and waist circumferences, forward reach (arm length), and wrist circumference (for long sleeve shirts). For trousers, the dimensions include waist girth, hip breadth, crotch height, and leg length. And so on for overcoats, underwear, hats, and shoes. Anthropometric data are available for all body dimensions that are used by the clothing industry to design garments in different sizes. The problem for the individual garment companies is to decide which sizes and how many sizes to produce. Sizing systems for clothing divide the population into subgroups, each of which is assumed to have the same body dimensions so that a garment in that size category will fit everyone in that group. In other words, within each subgroup, the guiding principle is "design for the average user." In actual practice, fitting problems arise because of the lack of correlation between different body dimensions. Some producers attempt to deal with the fitting problem by making a wide range of size alternatives available. Table 11 shows a list of the available sizes for men's suit coats from a mail-order retail-clothing store. Imagine the inventory problems. The challenge in the garment industry is to find the right balance between satisfying customer needs and keeping production and inventory costs in check.

TABLE 11 Men's Suit Coat Sizes Available from a Mail-Order Retail-Clothing Store

Coat Sizes	37	38	39	40	42	44	46	48	50	52	54	56	58	60
Short (under 5′8″)	x	x	x	x	x	x								
Regular (5′8″ to 5′11″)	x	x	x	x	x	x	x	x	x	x	x	x	x	x
Long (6′ to 6′3″)				x	x	x	x	x	x	x	x	x	x	x
Extra long (over 6′3″)					x	x	x	x	x	x	x	x		
Portly short (under 5′8″)					x	x	x	x						
Portly regular (5′8″ to 5′11″)					x	x	x	x	x	x				

REFERENCES

[1] Astrand, P. O., and K. Rodahl. *Textbook of Work Physiology*. 3rd ed. New York: McGraw-Hill, 1986.

[2] Astrand, P. O., K. Rodahl, H. A. Dahl, and S. B. Stromme. *Textbook of Work Physiology*. 4th ed. Champaign, IL: Human Kinetics, 2003.

[3] Bridger, R. S. *Introduction to Ergonomics*. 2nd ed. London: Taylor and Francis, 2003.

[4] Chaffin, D., and G. Andersson. *Occupational Biomechanics*. 2nd ed. New York: Wiley 1991.

[5] Grandjean, E. *Fitting the Task to the Man*. 4th ed. London: Taylor and Francis, 1988.

[6] Gross, C. M., J. C. Banaag, R. S. Goonetilleke, and K. K. Menon. "Manufacturing Ergonomics." Pp. 8.3–8.43 in *Maynard's Industrial Engineering Handbook*, 4th ed., edited by W. K. Hodson. New York: McGraw-Hill, 1992.

[7] Karwowski, W., and D. Rodrick. "Physical Tasks: Analysis, Design, and Operation." Pp. 1041–110 in *Handbook of Industrial Engineering*, 3rd ed., edited by G. Salvendy. New York: Wiley, 2001.

[8] Kroemer, K. H. E. "Engineering Anthropometry." Pp. 219–32 in *Handbook of Human Factors and Ergonomics*, 2nd ed., edited by G. Salvendy. New York: Wiley, 1997.

[9] Kroemer, K. H. E., H. B. Kroemer, and K. E. Kroemer-Elbert. *Ergonomics: How to Design for Ease and Efficiency*. Upper Saddle River, NJ: Prentice Hall, 1994.

[10] Marras, W. S. "Biomechanics of the Human Body." Pp. 233–67 in *Handbook of Human Factors and Ergonomics*, 2nd ed., edited by G. Salvendy. New York: Wiley, 1997.

[11] Murrell, K. *Human Performance in Industry*. New York: Reinhold, 1965.

[12] Pulat, B. M. *Fundamentals of Industrial Ergonomics*. Upper Saddle River, NJ: Prentice Hall, 1992.

[13] Rodgers, S. H. "Work Physiology—Fatigue and Recovery." Pp. 268–97 in *Handbook of Human Factors and Ergonomics*, 2nd ed., edited by G. Salvendy, New York: Wiley, 1997.

[14] Rodahl, K. *The Physiology of Work*. London: Taylor and Francis, 1989.

[15] Sanders, M. S., and E. J. McCormick. *Human Factors in Engineering Design*. 7th ed. New York: McGraw-Hill, 1993.

[16] Weimer, J. *Handbook of Ergonomic and Human Factors Tables*. Englewood Cliffs, NJ: Prentice Hall, 1993.

[17] Wickens, C. D., J. Lee, Y. Liu, and S. G. Becker. *An Introduction to Human Factors Engineering*. 2nd ed. Upper Saddle River, NJ: Pearson/Prentice Hall, 2004.

REVIEW QUESTIONS

1 Define physiology.

2 How many bones are there in the normal human body?

3 What are the three principal types of joints associated with body movement in the human body?

4 What are the three types of muscles in the human body?

5 Name and briefly define the three types of muscle contraction.

6 Define metabolism.

7 What are the three types of metabolism?

8 What are the three primary food types that provide energy for the human body?

9 The capacity of the body to use energy and apply forces depends on what three capabilities?

10 What is meant by the term *oxygen debt*?
11 How should rest breaks intended to relieve workers from muscle fatigue be scheduled?
12 Why is dynamic muscular activity better for the muscles than static muscular activity?
13 What are the primary factors that affect human muscle strength?
14 What is muscle endurance?
15 What is hypothermia?
16 What are some of the automatic mechanisms that the body uses to regulate its temperature?
17 Define anthropometry.
18 What is the body mass index and what does its value indicate?
19 Give some examples of the anthropometric principle "design for extreme individuals."
20 When is the anthropometric principle "design for the average user" appropriate?

PROBLEMS

Calorie Contents in Foods

1 A 10.75-oz can (net weight) of condensed chicken noodle soup is mixed with an equal part of water to make 2.5 servings. Each serving contains 890 mg of sodium (in salt), 1.5 g of fat, 8 g of carbohydrate (including 1 g of sugars), and 3 g of protein. Use the energy data in Table 2 to determine the number of calories (kcal) in each serving.

2 A 3-oz package of dry soup ingredients is mixed with boiling water to make one serving of cheddar cheese and noodle soup. The mix contains 1190 mg of sodium (in salt), 16 g of fat, 38 g of carbohydrate (including 1 g of sugars), and 7 g of protein. Use the energy data in Table 2 to determine the number of calories (kcal) in the serving.

3 A 19-oz can (net weight) of lentil soup contains 1540 mg of sodium (in salt), 2 g of fat, 48 g of carbohydrate (including 10 g of sugars), and 16 g of protein. There are two servings per can. Use the energy data in Table 2 to determine the number of calories (kcal) in each serving.

4 Consider a 15-oz can (net weight) of cheese ravioli in tomato and meat sauce. The label on the can states that it makes two servings. Each serving contains 1060 mg of sodium (in salt), 7 g of fat, 36 g of carbohydrate (including 5 g of sugars), and 9 g of protein. A teenage boy eats the entire contents for lunch. Use the energy data in Table 2 to determine the number of calories (kcal) he has consumed.

5 A 15.5-oz can (net weight) of corn makes 3.5 servings. Each serving contains 310 mg of sodium (in salt), 1 g of fat, 16 g of carbohydrate (including 6 g of sugars), and 2 g of protein. Use the energy data in Table 2 to determine the number of calories (kcal) in the can.

Metabolism and Energy Expenditure

6 A worker is 40 years old and weighs 160 lb. He sleeps 8 hr each night during which time his average energy expenditure rate is assumed to be at the basal metabolic rate. The physical requirements of his job result in an average energy expenditure rate of 4 kcal/min over the 8-hour shift. During his remaining nonworking, nonsleeping hours, his activity level results in an energy expenditure rate that averages 1.7 kcal/min. His digestive metabolism is assumed to be 10% of the total of his basal and activity metabolic rates over the 24-hour period of the day. What is his daily total metabolic rate?

7 A female worker eats three meals each day that are nutritionally well balanced. She sleeps 8 hr each night, and her average energy expenditure rate while sleeping is assumed to be her basal metabolic rate. Her job consists of office work as follows during the 8-hour shift (percentages based on time): 10% walking (assume 2.8 miles/hr), 25% standing, and 65% seated. During the 8 hr when she is not working, her activities consist of the following: resting, 7.0 hr; jogging, 30 min; and standing, 30 min. Her digestive metabolism is assumed to be 10% of the total of her basal and activity metabolic rates over the 24 hr of the day. The woman is 30 years old and weighs 125 lb. What is her required daily calorie intake for the three meals if it must be perfectly balanced with her energy expenditure for the day? Use Table 4 for the required energy expenditure rates.

8 A male worker consumes food containing a total of 3500 calories (3500 kcal) each day. He is 60 years old and weighs 200 lb. He sleeps 8 hr each night, and his average energy expenditure rate while sleeping is assumed to be his basal metabolic rate. When he is not working or sleeping, his energy expenditure rate averages 1.7 kcal/min (no correction for weight). What must be his average energy expenditure rate (kcal/min) for the 8 hr he works, if it is perfectly balanced with his food calorie intake? His digestive metabolism is assumed to be 10% of the total of his basal and activity metabolic rates over 24 hr.

9 Using the two energy expenditure rates for jogging and running in Table 4, (a) extrapolate from these two values to determine how much energy is consumed by a long-distance runner who completes a 1-mile race in 4 min. Assume the runner weighs 160 lb. (b) Estimate how much oxygen the runner consumes during the 4 min.

10 Using the two energy expenditure rates for jogging and running in Table 4, extrapolate from these values to determine how much energy is consumed by a sprinter who runs a 100-meter dash in 10 sec. Assume the sprinter weighs 160 lb.

11 A marathon race has a distance of 26 miles and 385 yards. A very good time for a marathon race is 2 hr, 30 min. (a) Using the two energy expenditure rates for jogging and running in Table 4, extrapolate from these two values to determine how much energy is consumed by a long-distance runner who completes the marathon in this time. Assume that the runner weighs 160 lb. (b) What is the total amount of energy expended by the runner during the race? (c) Estimate how much oxygen the runner consumes during the race.

Time-Weighted Average Energy Expenditure and Rest Periods

12 Starting with the definition of the time-weighted average energy expenditure rate in equation (7), derive the first rest time formula, equation (8).

13 Starting with the definition of the time-weighted average energy expenditure rate in equation (7), together with the equation $TT = T_{wrk} + T_{rst}$, derive the second rest time formula, equation (9).

14 A male worker performs a task during the 4 hr of the morning that has an energy expenditure rate of 6.0 kcal/min. Determine how much of this 4-hour period should be allowed for rest breaks. The energy expenditure rate during the rest breaks is 1.5 min. Use a maximum time-weighted average energy expenditure rate of 5.0 kcal/min as the standard or recommended level.

15 Solve the previous problem except for a female worker. Use a maximum time-weighted average energy expenditure rate of 4.0 kcal/min as the standard or recommended level.

16 A male worker starts his shift at 8:00 A.M. He works at a machine for 110 min during the morning, takes a 20-min break before working another 110 min, and then breaks for lunch. The lunch period is 30 min. His afternoon routine is the same. He works for 110 min, takes a 20-min break, and then completes his shift working until 4:30 P.M. During the work periods, his energy expenditure rate is 6.5 kcal/min. During the rest breaks, his energy expenditure rate is 1.5 kcal/min. (a) Compute the time-weighted average energy expenditure rate. (b) Using a maximum time-weighted average energy expenditure rate of 5.0 kcal/min as the standard or recommended level, what is the appropriate amount of rest time during the 4-hour morning and afternoon work periods?

17 A female worker performs a repetitive task that takes 25 min. Her energy expenditure rate while performing the task is 6.3 kcal/min. How much of a rest break should she take at the end of each cycle? Use a maximum time-weighted average energy expenditure rate of 4.0 kcal/min as the standard or recommended level.

18 A male worker performs a repetitive task with a 12-min work cycle. During each cycle, his energy expenditure rate is 7.8 kcal/min for 20% of the time and 5.6 kcal/min for the remaining 80%. How much of a rest break should be allowed at the end of each work cycle if he must work 4.0 hr in the morning and 4.0 hr in the afternoon? Use a maximum time-weighted average energy expenditure rate of 5.0 kcal/min as the standard or recommended level.

Body Mass Index

19 Compute the body mass index of a person who weighs 77 kg and stands 175 cm tall. How would this person be classified using the BMI classification?

20 Compute the body mass index of a person who weighs 190 lb and is 5 ft, 9 in. tall. How would this person be classified using the BMI classification?

21 Show how equation B* from the footnote below is derived from equation A** (also below) using the following conversion factors:

$$1 \text{ lb} = 0.4536 \text{ kg} \quad \text{and} \quad 1 \text{ in.} = 0.0254 \text{ m}$$

22 A man is 6 ft tall and weighs 200 lb. How much weight must he lose to be classified as "ideal" rather than "overweight"?

* $SPL_{twa} = 16.61 \log_{10} (ND/100) + 90$

** $EWT = 35.74 + 0.6215\, T_a - 35.75\, v^{0.16} + 0.4275\, T_a (v^{0.16})$

Cognitive Ergonomics: The Human Sensory System and Information Processing

Most human activities contain cognitive components as well as physical components. Physical ergonomics is concerned with the physical capabilities and limitations of the human body while performing an activity. It considers

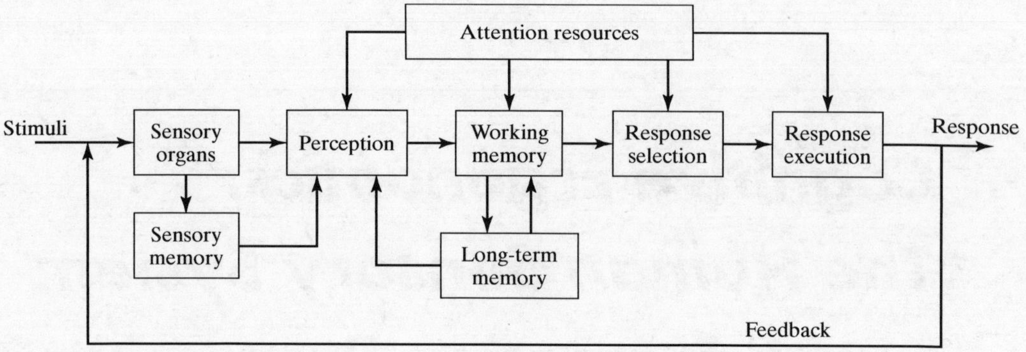

Figure 1 A model of human information processing. Adapted from [11].

the response of the human body to the physical aspects of work. In this chapter we discuss ***cognitive ergonomics***, which is concerned with the capabilities and limitations of the human brain and sensory system while performing activities that have a significant information processing content. Cognitive activities include reading, writing, listening, speaking, thinking, learning, planning, designing, calculating, problem solving, diagnosing, decision making, and interacting with a computer.

Cognitive ergonomics has become increasingly important relative to physical ergonomics because of several trends in industry and technology:

- Growth in the service industry sector of the economy relative to the manufacturing sector. Service work has a high content of information processing and interacting with other humans.
- Increased use of mechanization and automation in physical tasks, requiring workers to monitor and control processes that were previously performed manually.
- Increased use of technologically sophisticated equipment that is cognitively more challenging to operate, maintain, and repair.

Cognitive ergonomics considers how the human mind perceives its environment and processes information. Figure 1 presents a useful model that reveals how these cognitive functions are performed. It is a sequential model in which an external stimulus is received by the human sensory system (e.g., eyes, ears), the mind perceives the stimulus, and responds to it using attention resources interacting with short-term and long-term memory. In this chapter, we use this information-processing model as a framework for our discussion of topics in cognitive ergonomics.

1 THE HUMAN SENSORY SYSTEM

A human receives stimuli from sources of energy both external and internal to the body. Some of these stimuli are sensed by ***receptors***, the body's sensory organs. Receptors that sense external stimuli are called ***exteroceptors*** and are associated with the five human senses: (1) vision, (2) hearing, (3) touch, (4) smell, and (5) taste. The two most important exteroceptors are the eyes and ears for seeing and hearing. It is estimated that about 80% of human information input is by means of vision, and about 15% to 19% of the input is by means of hearing [9]. Sensory receptors that are excited by stimuli arising from within the body are called ***proprioceptors***. These receptors are located in muscles, tendons, and joints in the body. Our principal focus in this chapter is on the exteroceptive sensory organs.

1.1 Vision

Vision is the most important of the five basic human senses. The eye is stimulated by light, which is electromagnetic radiant energy that lies within the visible spectrum. The visible spectrum covers only a very narrow band in the total range of electromagnetic radiation, as shown in Figure 2. Electromagnetic radiation is commonly characterized by its wavelength. In the visible range, the wavelength determines the color or ***hue*** of the light. It ranges from about 400 nm (1 nm = 10^{-9} m), which is observed as blue-violet, to about 700 nm, which is observed as red. The brightness of the light, called ***luminous intensity***, is determined by the amplitude of the radiation.

Anatomy and Operation of the Eye. The eye is approximately spherical, with a diameter of about 2.5 cm (1.0 in.). The anatomy of the eyeball is shown in Figure 3. The eyeball is protected by a tough outer shell, called the ***sclera***, and filled with ***vitreous humor***, a transparent jellylike fluid that maintains the eyeball's spherical shape. The sclera includes a modified region at the front of the eyeball, called the ***cornea***. The cornea is a transparent and protective covering. It is the eyeball's window. The cornea is more curved than the rest of the eyeball, and this curvature functions to bend and focus the light entering the eye. Light rays forming an image enter the eyeball through the cornea. The light passes through the ***pupil***, which is the contractible aperture in the ***iris***. The pupil regulates the amount of light passing into the lens. It dilates in low light and constricts in bright light. The light passes through the ***lens***, which adjusts its shape to focus the image on the retina at the back surface of the eyeball. For distance vision, the lens becomes flatter to increase its focal length; and for close-up vision, the lens becomes rounder and thicker to reduce its focal length.[1] This capacity of the lens to make these focusing adjustments is called ***accommodation***.

The ***retina*** is a layer of nerve tissue consisting of millions of light receptors. These photosensitive cells are of two types, called cones and rods because of their respective shapes under a high-powered microscope. The ***cones*** are highly sensitive to bright light and are used for daylight vision (e.g., sunlight). The ***rods*** are sensitive in low levels of illumination and are used for night vision (e.g., moonlight). Combinations of rod and cone photoreceptors are used for light levels between bright and dark.

The retina has two regions: the fovea and the optic disk. Much of the image is focused on the fovea region of the retina. The ***fovea*** has a high concentration of cones and is therefore the region of greatest visual sharpness under good lighting conditions.

[1]Certain vision disorders are associated with a reduced capability of the lens to adjust its shape. Farsightedness, or ***hyperopia***, is when the lens has difficulty focusing on objects that are close (the image comes to focus behind the retina). Older readers commonly experience this condition and must use reading glasses. The opposite condition is nearsightedness, or ***myopia***, when the lens has difficulty focusing on objects that are far away (the image comes to focus in front of the retina).

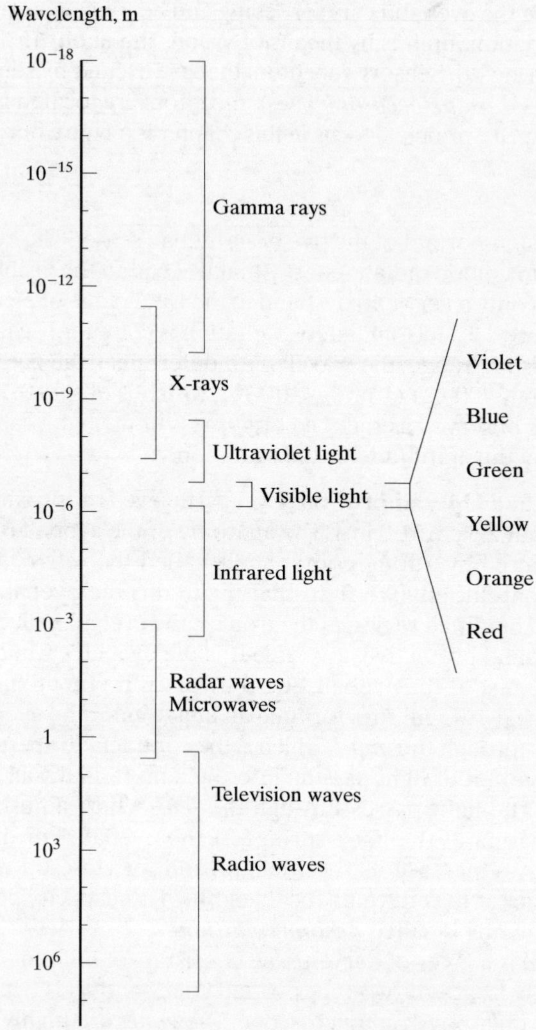

Figure 2 The electromagnetic radiation spectrum, with the visible range enlarged.

By comparison, the density of rods is low in the fovea region but much higher around 20 degrees away from the fovea. This is why humans can see a given object at nighttime better when they look slightly away from the location of the object. This causes the image of the object to project onto the rod receptors, which are more sensitive under very low lighting conditions. The ***optic disk*** is the region of the retina where the optic nerve is located. The ***optic nerve*** transmits the image focused on the retina to the visual centers of the brain for interpretation. The optic disk itself is absent of photoreceptors and is therefore a blind spot on the retina.

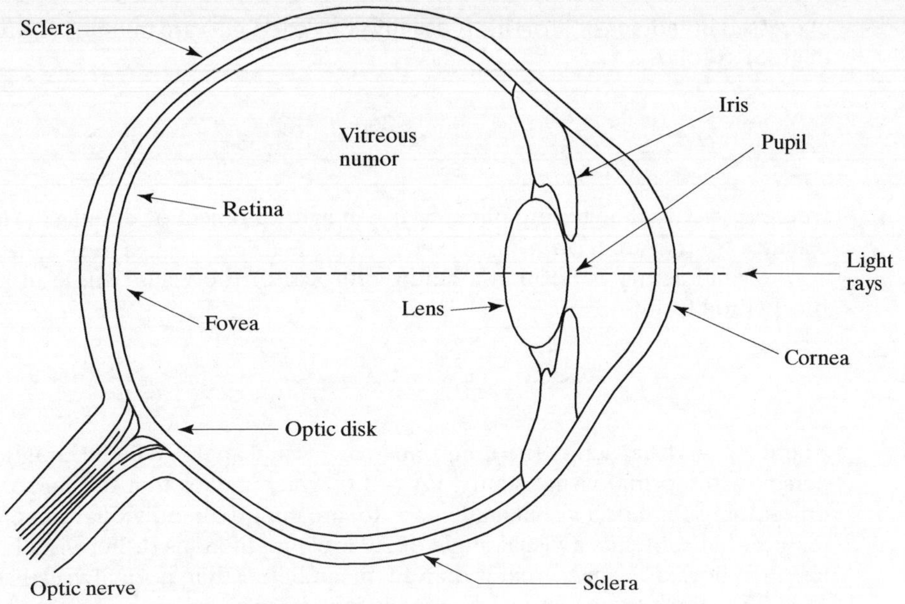

Figure 3 Anatomy of the eyeball.

Visual Performance. There are several measures of human visual performance that should be mentioned in our discussion of the eyes. These performance measures affect an individual's capacity to function effectively in many job situations. In this section, we discuss visual acuity, depth perception, color discrimination, and adaptation.

Visual acuity is the capability to discriminate small objects or fine details. It depends mainly on the accommodation of the eyes. The common measure of visual acuity is ***minimum separable acuity***, which refers to the smallest feature that can be detected by the eye. This is usually defined in terms of the visual angle α_v subtended at the eye by the smallest distinguishable detail, as illustrated in Figure 4. For small angles, α_v is determined simply as the height of the detail divided by its distance from the eye,

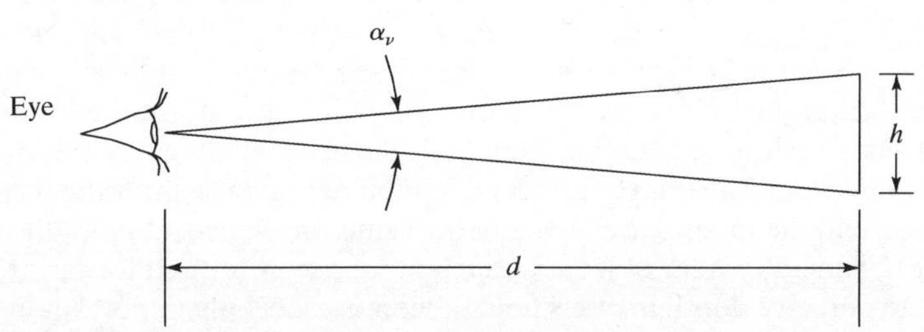

Figure 4 Visual angle α_v subtended by an object of height h at a distance d from the eye.

expressed in radians of arc. This is usually converted into arc minutes (1 arc min = 1/60 degree) as follows:

$$\alpha_v = 60\frac{360}{2\pi}\frac{h}{d} = 3438\frac{h}{d} \quad (1)$$

where α_v = visual angle, arc minutes; h = height of object or detail, cm (in.); and d = distance from eye, cm (in.).

Visual acuity is defined as the reciprocal of the visual angle in arc minutes. In equation form,

$$VA = \frac{1}{a_v} \quad (2)$$

where VA = visual acuity (no units), and α_v = visual angle given by equation (1). For a person with normal visual acuity, VA = 1.0, which means that the person can see an object that subtends a visual angle α_v = 1.0 arc min. If an individual can only discern a feature that subtends a visual angle of 2.0 arc min, then his or her visual acuity is 0.5, less than normal. Values greater than 1.0 mean better than normal visual acuity.

There are various standard methods for testing visual acuity. The common method used by ophthalmologists during eye examinations is based on the ***Snellen chart***, which consists of rows of alphabetical letters against a bright white background located a certain distance away from the patient. The usual distance is 6 m (20 ft). The patient is asked to identify the letters as their sizes become increasingly smaller, and accordingly as the subtended angle made by them also becomes smaller. The row of letters on which the patient begins to misread the letters is used as the measure of acuity. ***Snellen acuity*** is expressed as a ratio, for example, 20/40 (6/12 in the metric system). Normal vision is 20/20, which corresponds to a visual angle of 1 arc min at 20 ft and a visual acuity value of 1.0. An individual with 20/40 vision has below normal vision and can just read letters at 20 ft that a person with normal vision can read at 40 ft. Similarly, 20/15 is better than normal vision and means that the individual can read letters at 20 ft that a normal person can read at 15 ft. Of course, the two eyes of a patient may have different Snellen acuity scores, which is why the ophthalmologist usually tests the eyes separately. A person whose better eye is worse than 20/200 (after correction with glasses) is defined as legally blind [3].

Depth perception is a form of visual acuity called ***stereoscopic acuity***, which is the capability to perceive depth in one's field of view. This is made possible by the fact that a person sees an object with two eyes that are separated by a few inches. Thus, each eye sees a slightly different view of the object. The brain integrates and interprets the two images to estimate the approximate distance of the object relative to its surroundings in the view field. The images projected on the two retinas differ the most for objects that are close, and the images are virtually the same for objects at great distances. Thus, estimating distances of near objects is much more accurate than for far away objects. The ability to perceive depth in one's field of view is especially important in tasks such as driving a truck, operating a crane, and firing artillery shells at a distant enemy position.

Color discrimination is enabled by the cones in the retina, which are the photoreceptor cells that are sensitive to light. Rod-type cells are not color sensitive, and that is why people cannot distinguish colors at very low illumination levels. Cone receptors are of three types, differentiated by the presence of one of three types of color-discriminating pigments. Certain cones are sensitive to red colors, others to green, and the remaining ones to blue. Thus, a red object would stimulate the red receptors but not the blue and green receptors. Colors other than red, blue, and green would stimulate combinations of receptors in relative strengths so that the combined sensation could be interpreted by the brain to identify the color. For example, a yellow object would stimulate the red and green receptors but not the blue.

In good lighting, a person with normal color vision can discriminate among hundreds of different colors. However, a significant number of people are afflicted by various forms of color blindness. It is estimated that between 15% and 20% of the population is color blind [9]. People who can see only various shades of gray but no colors are called ***monochromats***. Instances of complete color blindness (***monochromatism***) are rare. More common are conditions where the eyes lack sensitivity to one of the three colors (red, green, or blue), due to a deficiency in the corresponding type of cone receptors. People who are partially color blind in this way are called ***dichromats*** (they are sensitive to only two colors), and the condition is called ***dichromatism***.

Color discrimination is important in everyday living and in many work activities. In everyday living, color perception adds to the pleasure of observing nature, watching television, and most other common visual activities. Drivers who are color-blind may create hazards to themselves and others by their inability to correctly interpret the colors of traffic lights. This problem is reduced by standardizing traffic lights so that the red light is always in the top position. Job activities that require good color discrimination include driving a vehicle (e.g., truck, bus, taxicab), visual inspection, production work in which color displays are used (e.g. andon boards), and color matching of paints.

In vision terms, ***adaptation*** refers to the ability to adapt to changes in light levels. There are two situations of interest. ***Dark adaptation*** means adapting from a brightly illuminated environment to a dark environment, and ***light adaptation*** means adapting from a dark environment to a bright one. Light adaptation occurs relatively quickly, with complete adaptation in about 1 min. Dark adaptation takes much longer (about 30 min) and involves a changeover from the use of cones to rods, followed by gradual adjustments in the rods to maximize their sensitivity to the low illumination levels.

1.2 Hearing

Hearing is the process of perceiving sound. It is the sensation that is stimulated by acoustic waves, which are pressure oscillations in an elastic medium such as air. Mechanical energy is being transmitted through the air by these pressure oscillations. A simple sound-generating source produces the sinusoidal air pressure oscillations illustrated in Figure 5. An example of such a source is a tuning fork, whose vibrating surfaces generate a pure tone that is transmitted through the air. The plot shows the positive and negative variations (compression and rarefaction) about ambient air pressure that are caused by the sound source.

A pure tone, such as that shown in Figure 5, is characterized by two physical attributes: (1) frequency, which is perceived in hearing as the pitch of the sound, and

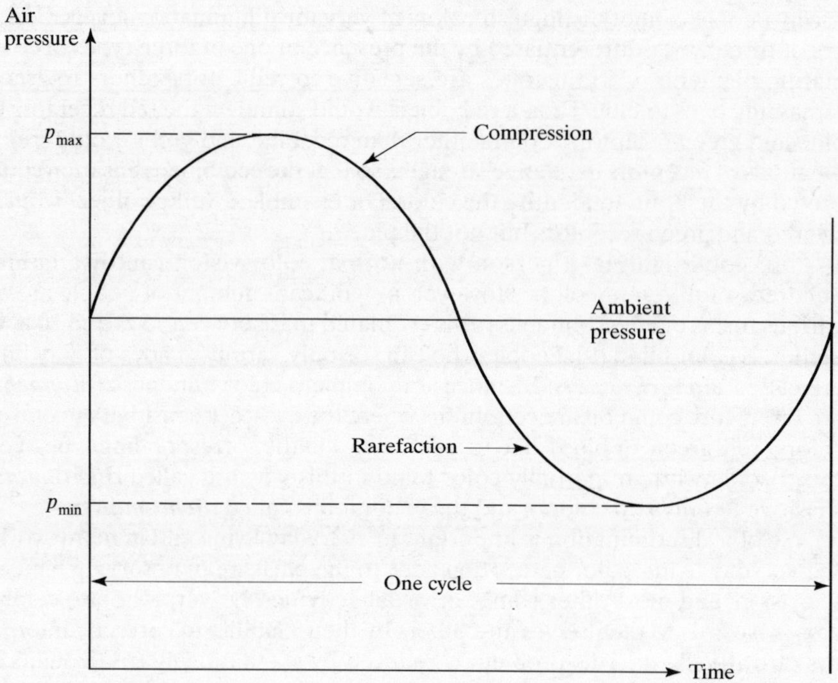

Figure 5 The sinusoidal pressure oscillations of a simple sound-generating source.

(2) intensity, which is perceived by the listener as loudness. The ***frequency*** of a pure tone is the number of cycles per second or hertz (abbreviated Hz), where the duration of one cycle is shown in Figure 5. The ear of a young person (e.g., 17 years old) can perceive sounds in the range of about 20 to 20,000 Hz. To give the reader a perspective, middle C of a properly tuned piano generates a tone of 263 Hz.

The ***intensity*** of the sound relates to the amplitude ($p_{max} - p_{min}$), of the oscillations in Figure 5 and the two terms intensity and amplitude are often used interchangeably. Sound intensity is measured as pressure, such as newton per square meter (N/m^2) or pascal (Pa). However, the range of sound pressures is so large (from the threshold of human hearing at about 0.00002 N/m^2 to the upper limit of hearing at about 20 N/m^2) that a logarithmic scale is used to achieve a more convenient and comprehensible measure of sound intensity. This logarithmic measure of sound intensity is called the ***sound pressure level*** (SPL), expressed in units of decibels (dB):

$$SPL = 20 \log_{10}\left(\frac{p_s}{p_r}\right) \quad (3)$$

where SPL = sound pressure level, dB; p_s = the sound pressure from the source, N/m^2; and p_r = the reference sound pressure, N/m^2. As indicated in the equation and by definition, the decibel is a unit of measure equal to 20 times the logarithm of the ratio of a given sound pressure level to a reference sound pressure level. The usual reference level is the threshold of hearing, taken to be 0.00002 N/m^2. To account for the positive and negative oscillations about the average atmospheric pressure value, the sound pressure is averaged using the root-mean-square (rms) technique.

Example 1 Sound Pressure Level

What is the decibel level (SPL) of a single tone sound that has a frequency of 1000 Hz and a pressure of 2.4 N/m^2?

Solution: Sound intensity is unaffected by the frequency (although the perception of loudness may be affected by the pitch of the source), so our computations do not include consideration of the 1000 Hz. Using equation (3), we obtain the following:

$$SPL = 20 \log_{10} \frac{2.4}{0.0002} = 20 \log_{10} 120{,}000 = 20(5.079) = 101.6 \text{ dB} \qquad \blacksquare$$

Most sounds are more complex than single tones and include multiple frequencies and intensities. Sound sources are vibrating surfaces such as the strings of a violin, the diaphragm of an acoustical loudspeaker, or the human vocal cords. Sound is also produced by turbulent fluid flow such as a howling wind, a roaring surf, or a policeman's whistle. A sound containing multiple frequencies and intensities can be plotted as a continuous power spectrum, as in Figure 6, which indicates power level for the various frequencies that make up the sound. The power level of a sound is the square of its amplitude.

The intensity of a sound diminishes as the distance from the source increases. Thus, sound intensity is measured from the listener's perspective. It is not a power measurement of the sound source. The physical relationship is that the intensity of a sound wave varies inversely as the square of the distance from the source. For example, a person listening to someone talk at a distance of 15 cm (6 in.) hears an intensity level of about 80 dB, while that same listener hears only about 65 dB from a distance of 100 cm

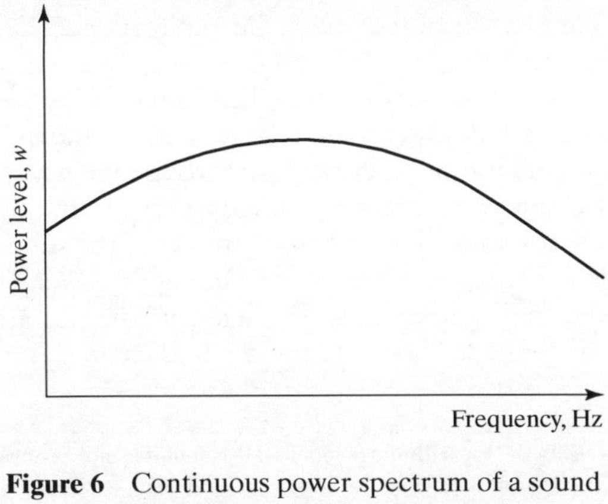

Figure 6 Continuous power spectrum of a sound consisting of multiple frequencies.

TABLE 1 Some Sounds and Their Corresponding Decibel Levels at Given Distances

Sound	Sound Pressure Level (dB)	Sound	Sound Pressure Level (dB)
Threshold of hearing	0	Talking at 15 cm (6 in)	80
Normal breathing	10	Milling machine at 1 m (3 ft)	90
Soft whispering at 1 m (3 ft)	20	Powered lawn mower at 1 m (3 ft)	100
Loud whispering at 1 m (3 ft)	30	Riveting machine at 1 m (3 ft)	110
Library environment	40	Jet engine at 60 m (200 ft)	120
Quiet restaurant environment	50	Loud siren at 30 m (100 ft)	130
Room air conditioner at 3 m (10 ft)	60	Jet engine at 30 m (100 ft)	140
Freight train at 30 m (100 ft)	70		

Source: Compiled from [1, 3, 7, 10, and 11].

(40 in.).[2] Table 1 gives some examples of sound intensities for various types of sounds and distances.

Although sound intensity is a ratio measure, as indicated in equation (3), the decibel scale allows one sound to be compared to another sound as a difference rather than a multiple. For example, the fire alarm buzzer in a building can be said to be 25 dB more intense (louder) than the background noise in the building. Similarly, the earplugs used by workers in a foundry can be said to reduce the noise level by 12 dB. Loss of hearing can also be assessed using this scale, and a person who is partially deaf, perhaps due to exposure to intense sound over an extended period, can be said to have a 20 dB hearing loss.

Anatomy and Operation of the Ears. The ear is a transducer. Its basic function is to transform the mechanical energy of received sound waves into electrical nerve signals that are transmitted to the brain for interpretation. To accomplish this function, the ear consists of three primary components: the outer ear, the middle ear, and the inner ear, as illustrated in Figure 7.

The outer ear consists of the pinna, the auditory canal, and the eardrum. The ***pinna*** is the external ear, consisting largely of cartilaginous tissue, whose purpose is to collect the variations in air pressure caused by sound. The pinna's irregular shape, combined with the fact that there are two ears, also provides some sense of the direction from which a sound is coming. The incoming sound is channeled through the ***auditory canal*** to the eardrum. The ***eardrum***, also called the ***tympanic membrane***, is a thin membrane that vibrates in response to sound. It serves to mechanically transmit the sound to the middle ear.

The middle ear consists of three small bones or ***ossicles***, called the hammer, anvil, and stirrup due to their geometries (the scientific names are the ***malleus***, ***incus***, and ***stapes***, respectively). The purpose of this ossicular chain is to mechanically transmit and

[2]Another reason for using the logarithmic decibel scale is that it is more consistent with a human's perception of loudness levels. The loudness levels of a person talking from a distance of 6 in. versus the same person talking from 40 in. does not seem to be that much different, but the sound pressures received at those two distances is almost an order of magnitude different.

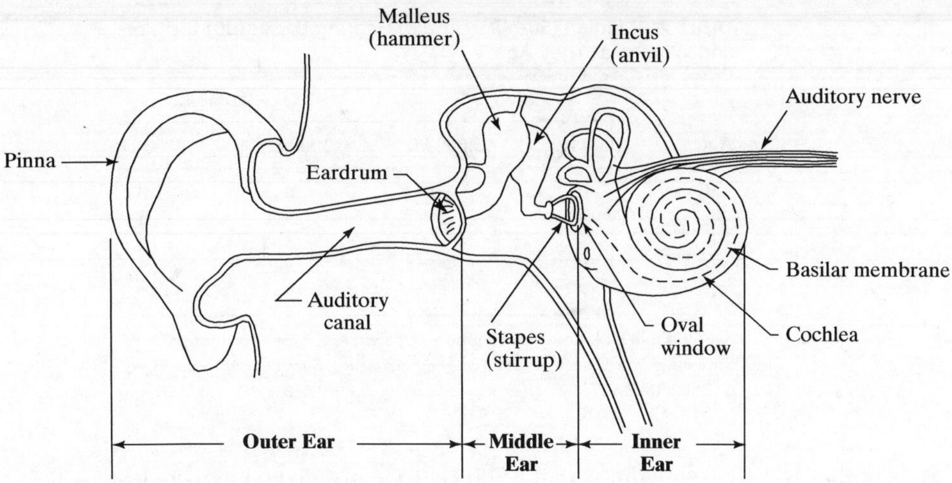

Figure 7 Anatomy of the human ear.

amplify the vibrations of the eardrum to the oval window of the inner ear. Because of the relatively large size of the eardrum and the mechanical leveraging applied by the ossicular chain, the sound energy is amplified about 20 times as it reaches the inner ear. In addition to the three bones, the middle ear also includes two small muscles that contract in response to intense noises. This contraction is called the ***aural reflex***, and it reduces the energy transmission to the inner ear, thus helping to protect it against harmfully loud noises.

The inner ear is a spiral-shaped organ called the ***cochlea*** that begins at the oval window. The organ is filled with fluid. The mechanical action of the stapes on the oval window causes the fluid to be vibrated, and this vibration is transmitted to the ***basilar membrane***, a thin membrane running the length of the organ. In turn, the basilar membrane stimulates sensory hair cells along its length, which send neural impulses to the brain through the ***auditory nerve***. Different sensory cells are responsive to different frequencies, and this allows the brain to make an approximate interpretation of pitch.

Auditory Performance. Certain analogies exist between the hearing and visual senses. In purely physical terms, sound intensity is analogous to luminous intensity, and sound frequency is analogous to hue. Humans perceive sound intensity as loudness, and frequency is interpreted as pitch. Thus, in comparing the human senses of hearing and sight, loudness is similar to brightness, and pitch is similar to color. In the following paragraphs we discuss some of the performance characteristics associated with hearing, as we did earlier for vision.

As stated earlier, humans with normal hearing can perceive sound frequencies in the approximate range 20 Hz to 20,000 Hz when they are young. However, humans have different auditory sensitivities to different frequencies. Low frequencies (below about 300 Hz) are not heard as well as high frequencies (in the range 1000 Hz to 5000 Hz).

TABLE 2 Median (50th Percentile) Hearing Losses (dB) for Men and Women as They Age

	Men		Women	
Age	1000 Hz	4000 Hz	1000 Hz	4000 Hz
20	0	0	0	0
40	3	8	3	5
50	6	17	5	10
60	9	27	8	15
70	16	43	13	25

Source: From [10], based on the following paper: K. Kryter, "Presbycusis, Sociocusis, and Nosocusis," *Journal of the Acoustical Society of America* 73, no. 6 (1983): 1897–917.

Another way of saying this is that a 300 Hz tone at a given intensity level will not seem as loud to the human listener as a 3000 Hz tone of the same intensity level. Maximum sensitivity is in the range 3000 Hz to 4000 Hz.

Pitch is the qualitative perception of a sound that depends mainly on its frequency. As frequency increases, pitch increases also. One's sense of pitch is also affected by the loudness of the sound. For a 3000 Hz tone, the pitch remains relatively constant over a wide range of intensity levels. However, for tones lower than 3000 Hz, pitch is reduced as the intensity of the tone increases. That is, the pitch seems lower as the sound becomes louder, although the frequency remains the same. Similarly, for tones higher than 3000 Hz, pitch seems to increase for louder tones, even though the frequency is actually the same.

The aging process takes its toll on hearing, just as it does on vision and so many other human capabilities. Normal hearing loss due to aging is called ***presbycusis***. A related source of auditory decline is ***sociocusis***, which is hearing loss due to everyday sounds such as television and traffic noises. These sources are nonoccupational. The hearing loss due to these maladies affects the sensitivities to higher frequencies more than to lower frequencies. And human males are more afflicted with the declines than females. Table 2 compares the hearing losses for men and women at various ages for two different frequencies. The hearing losses compiled in the table also include the effects of ***nosocusis***, which is hearing loss due to pathological effects.

1.3 The Other Sensory Receptors

Vision and hearing are the most important human sensory receptors for occupation, avocation, and recreation. Together, they account for 95% or more of the information input to the human brain. The other human exteroceptors are the senses of touch, smell, and taste. The sense of taste, however much it adds to the pleasures of eating, is rarely applicable in the workplace except during the lunch hour.[3] Accordingly, we omit coverage of this sense in the following discussion.

[3]Exceptions exist. The sense of taste is certainly important in the restaurant business.

The sense of touch, or ***tactile sense***, is excited by receptors that are in the skin, and for this reason, the more general term is ***cutaneous sense***. The nerve receptors in the skin are sensitive to several types of stimuli, including pressure (which comes closest to the tactile sense), temperature (hot and cold), and pain (which might derive from either of the previous two types or from an injury). In the workplace the tactile sense is used in tasks such as inspection (e.g., inspecting for surface roughness or sharp burrs), part handling, hand tool manipulation, and operating controls using switches and dials. In these applications it is usually an auxiliary sense applied in conjunction with vision. Its functionality is more than auxiliary for people with serious vision impairments.

The sense of smell, also called the ***olfactory sense***, derives from sensory cells located in each nostril that are stimulated by vapor molecules in the air. These receptor cells contain olfactory hairs that actually perform the sensing function. For a substance to have an odor, it must be sufficiently volatile to release molecules into the air that can be inhaled through the nasal cavity. Most of these substances are organic compounds. The sense of smell is not generally useful in the workplace, except in the operations of the food industry and other industries producing olfactory products (e.g., perfumes). In some instances, the sense of smell may alert a worker to an abnormal condition, such as something burning or a machine producing hazardous odors.

2 PERCEPTION

In our model of human information processing in Figure 1, perception is the stage that follows the sensing of some external stimuli by the human sensory system. ***Perception*** refers to the stage of cognition in which the human becomes aware of the sensation caused by the stimuli and interprets it in the light of his or her experience and knowledge. During perception, the sensed stimuli are given meaning and significance. The following examples illustrate perception in human information processing:

- The operator of a production machine in a factory sees the blinking yellow light suddenly switch on, indicating that the supply of raw material is almost exhausted. The yellow light is the stimulus that is sensed. The perception is the need to resupply more raw materials to the machine.
- The driver of a car hears the honking of the truck close behind her on an interstate highway. The honking is the stimulus that is sensed. The perception is that the truck is dangerously close.
- The welder smells the odor of garlic in the air. The odor is the stimulus that is sensed. The perception is that acetylene is escaping from its container, with the imminent danger of an explosion when combined with oxygen in the air.[4]
- The salesperson looks up and sees a customer waiting for service. The sight of the customer is the stimulus that is sensed. The perception is the need to provide the service.

[4]Acetylene (C_2H_2) is a colorless, odorless gas that is highly flammable when mixed with oxygen. During its production it is given a characteristic garlic odor for safety reasons.

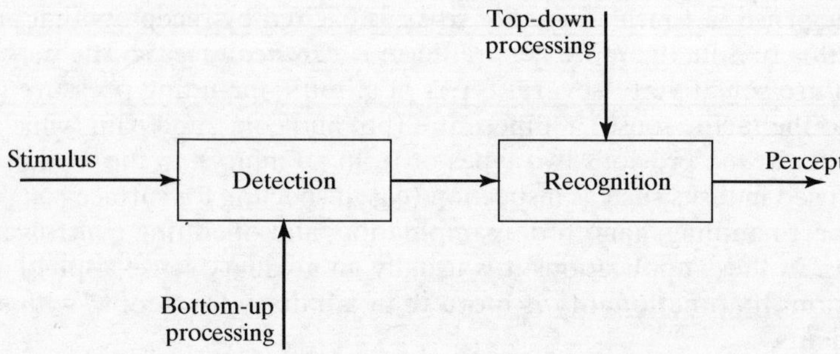

Figure 8 The two steps of perception: detection and recognition.

Our definition and examples suggest that perception consists of detection and recognition, as illustrated in the sequence shown in Figure 8. Detection occurs when the human becomes aware of the presence of the stimulus. Recognition occurs when the human comprehends that the stimulus has been encountered before and is able to relate it to prior experience.

Detection means becoming aware of the stimulus of interest, which may be mixed in with many other stimuli. It is a process of discovery, but no interpretation of the stimulus has yet occurred. ***Recognition*** means interpreting the meaning of the stimulus by identifying it in the context of previous experience. Recognition follows detection, as in Figure 8, although the time lag between the two may be so small that the two steps seem to occur simultaneously. Consider the following examples:

- A person walking along the street sees an animal in the neighbor's yard and recognizes it immediately as a large dog (simultaneous detection and recognition). Identifying the breed may be delayed by a few seconds.
- An office worker is startled by the sudden blare of an alarm siren in the building (detection), but it takes a few moments to properly identify it as a fire alarm (recognition).
- A student is reading a physics textbook, moving his eyes across the page in a succession of fast movements and fixations (detection), trying to extract meaning out of each sentence (recognition), and attempting to derive understanding out of each paragraph (comprehension).

The detection step in perception involves the sensing of stimuli, and therefore detection emphasizes the use of the human sensory organs. Recognition involves the interpretation of the sensed stimuli, and the emphasis is therefore on the use of the brain. The distinction between detection as a sensory process and recognition as a cerebral process in the perception stage of human information processing can be explained using the concept of bottom-up and top-down processing [11]. These terms are used in our model of perception in Figure 8, and we now explain them.

Bottom-up processing refers to the stimulation of the senses by external sources. It is the human information processing that responds to all of the sights and sounds and other stimuli in the outside world. Bottom-up processing is concerned with the detection step in perception. By contrast, ***top-down processing*** refers to the information processing activities of perception that are based on a human's knowledge, experience, and expectations. As such, it is concerned with the recognition step in perception. It also depends on motivation, one's ability to concentrate on a given stimulus in order to interpret it.

Bottom-up processing is concerned with the actual stimulus, while top-down processing provides the added dimension of our previous experience with similar or identical stimuli. These previous experiences create expectancies that facilitate the recognition step. Perception is usually a combination of bottom-up and top-down processing. Deficiencies in the actual stimulus during bottom-up processing can often be compensated for during top-down processing. For example, if a machine operator were reading the instruction manual for a new piece of equipment in the factory and came across the sentence "When a red light flashes on the control panel, turn the machine . . ." (through a printing error, the last word in the sentence is missing), he would be able to infer that the missing word is "off" based on the context of the sentence and his expectancy. The operator is able to make up for the deficiency in the actual stimulus (the missing word) through his knowledge and experience with previous similar machines.[5]

Different people have different experiences and expectancies, and this means that the same stimulus may be interpreted differently by them. Two medical doctors may review the symptoms of a sick patient and arrive at different diagnoses about the affliction. This is known to happen, and it is why it is important to get a second opinion in serious cases.

3 ATTENTION RESOURCES

Attention resources occupy an important position in our model of human information processing in Figure 1. As the diagram indicates, attention resources act upon nearly all stages of cognition as a driver of these stages. ***Attention*** means keeping one's mind on something. It involves mental concentration and the readiness for such concentration. In cognitive ergonomics, several types of attention can be distinguished: (1) selective attention, (2) focused attention, (3) divided attention, (4) sustained attention, and finally lack of attention, sometimes caused by boredom.

Selective Attention. ***Selective attention*** refers to the situation in which a person is required to monitor multiple sources of information in order to perceive irregularities or opportunities. It involves filtering out certain channels of information that are at least temporarily extraneous in order to focus on one channel that is deemed important, and then rotating attention to other channels in turn. Humans are inherently multichannel beings in that they have multiple sensory organs (e.g., eyes, ears, nose) and each one is capable of responding to multiple stimuli. Examples of selective attention include the following:

- A pilot scanning the airplane's instrument panel, looking for readings that would explain the plane's erratic behavior
- A driver periodically checking the gauges and dials on the dashboard while watching the road ahead
- A football quarterback watching the opposing team's defensive line for weaknesses that might be exploited in the next play.

[5]This example is based on an example in [11].

In a task involving selective attention, the individual must select which channels to give attention to and which channels to ignore (at least temporarily). Factors that influence this selection process include expectancy, salience, and value. ***Expectancy*** means that if a person expects a certain channel to provide the required information, he or she is more likely to pay more attention to that channel. The pilot in the preceding example is more likely to look at the instrument dial that is expected to change during a given maneuver such as a landing procedure. ***Salience*** refers to stimuli that stand out among the rest of the channels; they grab your attention. The truck horn in an earlier example was a salient stimulus. Finally, the ***value*** of the information acquired by means of a given input channel is likely to bias its selection. If the channel usually provides no useful information, less attention will be paid to it. Conversely, if the input channel is deemed important, more attention will be paid to it. When driving a car, viewing the road and vehicles ahead is a much more important input channel than the gasoline gauge in the dash panel.

Focused Attention. As in selective attention, tasks involving ***focused attention*** force the individual to cope with multiple input channels, but the difference is that the person must focus on only one channel for a sustained period of time and exclude all of the other stimuli. The person attends to the one stimulus (or a small number of stimuli) and is not distracted by the others, which can be considered as noise. Examples of focused attention include the following:

- Having a conversation with one friend in a crowded room full of people who are also talking
- Having a conversation with two friends in a crowded room full of people who are also talking
- Reading a book in an airport lobby while many other activities are going on in the area
- A fighter pilot landing his airplane on the deck of an aircraft carrier during rough seas.

Factors affecting one's ability to focus attention on a single stimulus include proximity, separation of the sources, and background noise. ***Proximity*** refers to the physical distance of the stimulus source from the person trying to focus attention. It is easier to pay attention to someone when they are speaking right next to you. ***Separation*** of the sources means that the stimuli are arriving from distinctly different directions. It is easier to focus attention on the source that is facing you rather than someone located in your peripheral vision. The intensity of the ***background noise*** will affect one's ability to focus on the channel of interest. The more noise (e.g., visual clutter, auditory noise), the less one can concentrate on the desired stimulus.

Divided Attention. In ***divided attention***, there are again multiple stimuli present, but the difference here is that multiple tasks must be performed together. The term ***time-sharing*** is sometimes used for this type of situation. Divided attention does not necessarily mean that the tasks are performed simultaneously, although that sometimes happens. In many cases, the individual performing the multiple tasks accomplishes them sequentially, switching back and forth among them. Examples of divided attention include the following:

- Driving a car while having a conversation with the passenger in the car
- Driving a car while talking to someone on a cell phone
- Trying to do income taxes while watching television
- A machine operator attending several machines in a machine cluster.

The important issue in divided attention is that performance on at least one of the tasks is likely to be adversely affected because the person is trying to accomplish more than one task. The following recommendations address this issue, to improve performance in divided attention situations: (1) minimize the number of input information channels, (2) reduce the level of difficulty of the tasks, and (3) reduce the similarity of the tasks in terms of demands on input channels, mental processing, and output requirements [10].

Sustained Attention. ***Sustained attention***, also known as ***vigilance***, involves a situation in which an individual must watch for a signal of interest over a relatively long period of time, and it is important to avoid missing the signal. False alarms should also be avoided, but the situations are usually such that a much higher penalty is paid for missed signals. Examples of sustained attention include the following:

- An inspector looking for defective products moving along a conveyor line on their way to packaging
- A radar operator on a U.S. Navy cruiser monitoring a radar screen for incoming enemy aircraft or missiles
- Security guards observing a bank of TV monitors showing scenes of various locations in a building and looking out for intruders
- A parent waiting up for a teenage son on his first night out with the family car.

Numerous studies of vigilance have shown a decline in the performance of detection tasks as time proceeds. Called the ***vigilance decrement***, it affects both the speed and accuracy of signal detection as time on the job proceeds. Laboratory studies have shown that the frequency of missed signals increases significantly after only one-half hour [9]. The following recommendations have been made to improve performance in tasks requiring sustained attention: (1) rotate the workers every 30 min or so, (2) increase the intensity of the incoming signal, if that is technological feasible, (3) provide periodic feedback on performance to the workers, (4) emphasize the importance of the monitoring task and the consequences of misses, and (5) provide optimal environmental conditions (illumination, temperature, etc.) for the workers [9, 10].

Lack of Attention and Boredom. ***Lack of attention*** means not concentrating on the task. It results in a diminished state of readiness to perform the task. It is usually caused by ***boredom***—the state of being weary and restless due to lack of interest. (It is hoped that the reader will not be in this state as he or she reads this text.) Factors that lead to boredom on the job include the following [9]: (1) short cycle times, (2) low requirements for body movements, (3) warm environment, (4) lack of contact with coworkers, (5) low motivation, and (6) low lighting levels in the workplace.

4 MEMORY

The memory system occupies three blocks in our model of the human information processing system in Figure 1: (1) sensory memory, (2) working memory, and (3) long-term memory. ***Sensory memory*** is associated with the human sensory channels, mainly sight and hearing. The vision and the auditory sensory channels each have a very short-term storage unit that retains a representation of the stimulus after the actual stimulus stops. The other sensory channels may also have similar memory units as well. The vision sensory memory is called ***iconic storage***, and the hearing sensory memory is called ***echoic storage***. The iconic representation lasts only about one second, and the echoic representation lasts but a few seconds. After that the sensory information disappears unless it is encoded and processed into working memory, which requires the utilization of attention resources. Iconic storage and echoic storage operate autonomously. They do not require the worker's attention.

Working memory is temporary storage that holds a limited amount of information, including information from sensory memory, while it is being processed. It also serves as a conduit to long-term memory. ***Long-term memory*** is the warehouse for all of the retained knowledge and experiences that have been accumulated over one's lifetime.

4.1 Working Memory

According to one plausible model, working memory consists of three primary components: (1) a central executive component, (2) a visuospatial sketchpad, and (3) a phonological loop.[6] The ***central executive component*** coordinates the activities of the other two components as information is being processed, and it also interacts with long-term memory, entering items into storage and retrieving items from storage. The ***visuospatial sketchpad*** operates with visual and spatial information while it is being processed in working memory, and the ***phonological loop*** works with verbal and acoustical information in working memory. This information enters working memory either through the visual and auditory sensory channels or from long-term memory.

Attention resources are required to keep an information item active in working memory, such as the rehearsal of a telephone number either vocally or subvocally until the number has been dialed. The item is then forgotten forever unless entered into long-term memory. A crossover sometimes occurs between the visuospatial sketchpad and the phonological loop. For example, when given driving directions to get to a desired destination, we may convert those verbal directions into a spatial form that will be easier to remember.

The number of images, sounds, and ideas that can be processed at one time in working memory is limited, and the length of time that the information items can be kept active is also limited. In addition, the amount of attention required and the similarity of the information items being processed are key performance factors in the operation of working memory. Thus, we have four factors to discuss: (1) capacity, (2) the time factor, (3) attention resources, and (4) similarity of information items.

[6]The model of working memory is described in [11] and attributed to A. D. Baddeley, *Working Memory* (New York: Oxford University Press, 1986).

Capacity of Working Memory. The upper limit on the number of information items that can be processed at one time in working memory is about seven plus or minus two (7 ± 2).[7] An information item is defined as a ***chunk***, which is an information entity that the mind works with as a unit. The unit can be a single digit or it can be a much larger grouping of digits or other data forms that can be stored in memory as a single item. When a chunk is retrieved, say from long-term memory, it is recalled in its entirety, as if it were one item. Consider the following string of ten digits: 6107584030. Surely, remembering this number in working memory would be difficult. It contains 10 chunks of data, which exceeds the magic number of 7 ± 2. However, if that number is recognized as a telephone number and formatted as the telephone number 610-758-4030, the number of chunks is reduced considerably, and the number becomes easier to remember. The area code is 610, and certainly people who live in this area code know it. The exchange is 758, which is one of a limited number of exchange numbers in area code 610. It happens to be the exchange for Lehigh University. So, for someone who knows area code 610 and is familiar with the 758 exchange, the 10-digit number reduces to six chunks: (610)-(758)-4-0-3-0. For callers outside of area code 610, they need to remember to dial 1 first (1-610-758-4030), a fact that can be retrieved from long-term memory just before telephoning.

The same kind of chunking applies to letter and word sequences. Instead of reading the individual letters in a word, the word becomes a chunk, and when combined with other words in a long sentence, several words taken together become a chunk, and finally the sentence can be interpreted because, even though it may consist of more than 100 letters, the reader does not read the sentence as letters, but rather as words and collections of words that are chunked into units that can be managed within the limitations of working memory. This also explains why short sentences are easier to read and interpret, and why a reader must sometimes go back to the beginning of a long sentence and reread it in order to make sense of it. Readers may have experienced this problem in this paragraph.

The Time Factor. Working memory is also called ***short-term memory***, because the information contained in working memory gradually declines in strength as time proceeds. Nearly everyone has had the experience of being introduced to someone and after just a few moments the name has been forgotten. In order to avoid this decay that is characteristic of working memory, the information must be periodically refreshed. This is readily conceptualized as rehearsing the information chunks when the chunks are phonological. A person repeats the sequence of chunks subvocally in order to keep them in working memory. For visual and spatial chunks, the refresh process is analogous and sometimes involves the translation of visual chunks into verbal form. For example, we see a telephone number in the directory, but we convert that number into its vocal counterpart in order to remember it. On the other hand, at an art museum, there is no way of converting a beautiful painting into a verbal equivalent. It must be remembered, however faithfully, in its visual form.

[7]This finding is attributed to G. A. Miller, "The Magical Number of Seven Plus or Minus Two: Some Limits on Our Capacity for Processing Information," *Psychological Review* 63 (1956): 81–97.

Attention Resources and Similarity. Attention resources are required during the operations of working memory. As more chunks of information are being processed, more resources are required. Attention resources are needed during the refresh cycle (e.g., rehearsal), and they are needed for transfer of information to long-term memory. If the resources are diverted, the refresh cycle is interrupted, and the decay of information in working memory accelerates. For example, if a person is interrupted while dialing a strange telephone number, it is likely that the number will be lost from working memory, or if it is not lost, that the person will forget which digit was completed prior to the interruption.

Diversions can be auditory or visual. In our model of working memory, verbal diversions are more disruptive of the phonetic loop, and visual diversions are more disruptive of the visuospatial sketch pad [11]. Auditory diversions seem to be more generally disruptive on the operations of working memory than visual distractions. Many people find music to be a significant distraction when they are trying to perform even simple tasks that require working memory, such as reading.

The similarity of the information chunks being processed affects working memory performance. Chunks that are similar are more difficult to process and decay at a faster rate, especially when the sequence of the chunks is important. This observation seems most applicable in the phonetic loop. For example, the string of alphanumeric characters T G 3 E D B is likely to be more difficult to maintain in working memory than the sequence T K 5 L N O, because the sounds in the first sequence are so similar.

4.2 Long-Term Memory

Much of the information that is processed in working memory is transferred to and retrieved from long-term memory. Of course, as our description of working memory suggests, a good deal of what is processed never makes it to long-term memory. The information contained in long-term memory consists of semantic codes, in which the individual items are given meaning and are organized into symbolic structures and associations. The structures and associations have been developed through learning and experience, and their organization allows for new information to be added. One possible model of long-term memory is that of a semantic network, as illustrated in Figure 9. This model emphasizes the associative nature of its contents, almost like a family tree.

Semantic memory is predominantly used to store facts, figures, and other information that relates to general knowledge about the world as well as specific knowledge such as that related to one's work. Long-term memory also includes ***episodic memory***, which refers to memory of important events and episodes in one's life, such as the death of one's parent.

The real value of long-term memory is demonstrated when information items must be retrieved from it. The ease with which items can be retrieved from long-term memory depends largely on the strength of the item and the associations it has with other items in memory [11]. The strength of a given item depends on the frequency with which it is used (e.g., retrieved and processed) and how recently it was last used. The higher the frequency and recency of use, the easier it is to retrieve. We have little difficulty remembering the names of the people we live with, because we see them all the time (high frequency and recency). We have a more difficult time remembering the names of people we rarely see and it has been years since we last saw them (low frequency and recency).

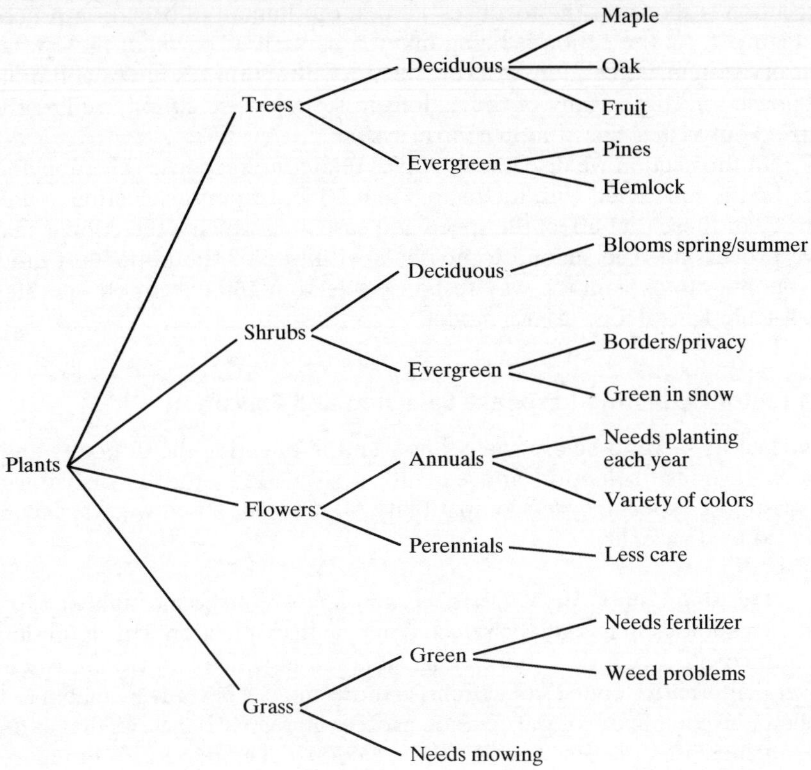

Figure 9 One possible model of long-term memory as a semantic network.

5 RESPONSE SELECTION AND EXECUTION

Response selection is the cognitive process of figuring out what actions to take, if any, in the light of information perceived through the sensory channels (bottom-up processing) and information stored in long-term memory (top-down processing). If action is deemed necessary, it may take several forms (e.g., moving the hands, walking, talking, or combinations), usually executed by the human effectors (fingers, hands, feet, and voice). The actions can be passive. For example, a person is reading a novel and the only action is to continue reading. Response selection is accomplished in working memory as a series of information-processing transformations. The capability to perform these transformations is limited by the capacity of working memory as well as the time factor. Only a small number of chunks of information (facts, figures, images, and ideas) can be managed by working memory at one time, and the chunks decay with time unless focus is maintained by attention resources.

Response execution means carrying out the action. It involves both cognitive and physical elements. The cognitive element is concerned with coordinating the actions of the musculoskeletal system, and the physical element deals with expending the necessary strength and energy to accomplish the action. An important feature of response execution is shown as the feedback loop in our human information processing model in Figure 1. As the action is being taken, it is verified through the operations of the sensory system, perception, working memory, attention resources and motivation, and response selection. Many of the actions in response execution are largely automatic, carried out as in a closed-loop control system.

In this section we discuss two topics related to response selection and execution. The first is concerned with the factors that affect response selection and execution, in particular those that affect the speed and ease with which a selection is made in cognitive processing. The second topic deals with one of the important models used in ergonomics to explain the way response selection and execution operates, called the Skill-Rule-Knowledge (SRK) model.

5.1 Factors Affecting Response Selection and Execution

Five factors seem to be especially important in affecting the difficulty and speed with which response selection and execution is carried out: (1) decision complexity, (2) response expectancy, (3) compatibility, (4) the tradeoff between speed and accuracy, and (5) feedback [11].

Decision Complexity. ***Decision complexity*** refers to the number of possible alternative responses that could be selected in response selection. The definition fits readily into the context of a decision-making situation in which a person must decide among several alternative courses of action. As more choices become available to the decision maker, the complexity of the decision process increases. It follows that as decision complexity increases, the time to make the selection will increase. This time is referred to as the ***reaction time***, which can be modeled by a relationship known as the Hick-Hyman law of reaction time:[8]

$$RT = a + b \operatorname{Log}_2 N \tag{4}$$

where RT = reaction time, N = number of possible choices to select among, and a and b are constants whose values can be determined empirically for a given situation. To establish the Hick-Hyman relationship, the subject is shown a cue to which he or she must provide a corresponding response. As the number of possible cues (and the number of corresponding responses) increases, the choice-reaction time also increases, but not as a linear function. Instead, the function is logarithmic. Log to the base 2 is used to be consistent with the binary digit system, which is used in information theory. When $N = 1$, meaning there is no choice, but only a single stimulus to respond to (e.g., a light flashing on), the reaction time is called the ***simple reaction time***. This is the time needed by the human information processing system to sense the stimulus and for the signal to pass through perception, working memory, response selection and execution, and engagement of the effector (e.g., press a button with one's finger). The simple reaction time is

[8]W. E. Hick, "On the Rate of Gain of Information," *Quarterly Journal of Experimental Psychology* 4 (1952): 11–26; and R. Hyman, "Stimulus Information as a Determinant of Reaction Time," *Journal of Experimental Psychology* 45 (1953): 423–32.

indicated by the value of the parameter a in the Hick-Hyman equation. Typical values of a are well under 1 sec.

Response Expectancy. ***Expectancy*** refers to the fact that humans can process information they are expecting much faster than they can process information they are not expecting. Similarly, humans can select a response that they expect to choose much more quickly and accurately than one that is unexpected. For example, if a machine operator is required to press a start button at the beginning of every semiautomatic work cycle in response to a green light on the machine's control panel, the operator's reaction time will be very rapid and accurate. However, if all of a sudden, the red light turns on instead of the green light (perhaps indicating a malfunction), the operator's response selection will be more difficult because the red light was unexpected. Both the time to respond and the probability of error will be greater.

Compatibility. ***Compatibility*** in human information processing refers to the relationship between a stimulus and the expected consequence of a given response to that stimulus. Thus, compatibility and expectancy are closely related. For example, when flipping on a wall switch for a ceiling light, our expectation is that flipping the switch toggle to the up position will turn the light on, and flipping it down will turn it off. Response compatibility means that when a person must select a response, the possible actions should be consistent with the person's expectations. Controls designed with good compatibility offer the following benefits: (1) faster learning by the user, (2) faster reaction times, (3) reduced errors, and (4) higher user satisfaction.

Three types of compatibility can be distinguished, all of which are relevant in response selection and execution: (1) conceptual, (2) spatial, and (3) movement [10]. ***Conceptual compatibility*** is concerned with the associations people have between codes and symbols and the things they are supposed to represent. For example, for a given program (e.g., word processor), the icons at the top of the computer monitor screen are designed to identify the operation that is performed when the cursor is clicked on that icon. Another example is the octagonal stop sign at a road intersection.

Spatial compatibility is concerned with the physical arrangement of controls (e.g., dials, switches) and their corresponding labels. Figure 10 shows two possible arrangements of displays and their control dials. Which arrangement is more spatially compatible?

Movement compatibility refers to the relationship between moving a control in a certain direction and the expected result that will occur due to that movement. The light switch example illustrates movement compatibility. We expect the light to go on when we flip the switch up. When we rotate a control dial clockwise, we expect the variable that is controlled by it to increase. For example, to increase the sound volume on a radio, we turn the volume dial clockwise.

Speed-Accuracy Trade-off. The ***speed-accuracy trade-off*** refers to the fact that in most situations of response selection and execution, the faster a person selects a response, the more likely it is that an error will be made. There is a negative correlation between speed and accuracy, and a proper balance must be achieved between these two performance measures for the given response situation. If very high accuracy is required

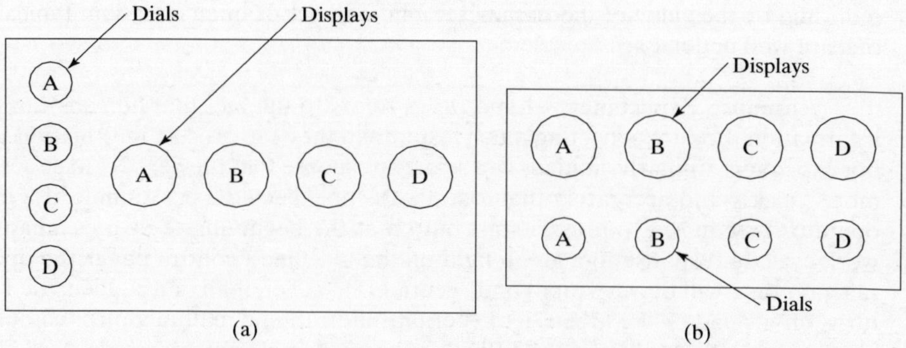

Figure 10 Two alternative arrangements of displays and their controls. The arrangement in (b) is more intuitive (better spatial compatibility) than the one in (a).

in the application, then enough time must be allowed for the person to select the correct response. For example, an air-traffic controller must be allowed sufficient time to make sure mistakes are avoided.

Feedback. In the human information-processing model of Figure 1, the feedback loop allows a person to see and/or hear the effect of his or her actions. Feedback is important in response selection and execution because it provides verification and reinforcement of the response action that was taken. The time delay between the response action and the feedback should be as small as possible. Otherwise, the individual cannot directly confirm that the response action had the desired effect.

5.2 Skill-Rule-Knowledge Model

The Skill-Rule-Knowledge (SRK) model was first proposed by Rasmussen in 1983 and is widely cited in the ergonomics and human factors literature.[9] The SRK model identifies three types of performance or behavior: (1) skill-based, (2) rule-based, and (3) knowledge-based. The three categories refer to types of cognitive processing that are performed in executing various kinds of tasks, and it also takes into account the level of experience possessed by the person performing a given task. Situations in which skill-based and rule-based behavior are exhibited tend to be routine, whereas situations in which knowledge-based behavior is exhibited tend to be nonroutine.

Skill-based behavior occurs when a person has gained a high degree of familiarity and proficiency in a task (or other activity), to the point where the task can be performed automatically and subconsciously. It is usually a task with significant manual content. Attention resources required for skill-based activities are minimal because the motion pattern is automatic. Examples of skill-based tasks and activities include walking, riding a bicycle, performing a repetitive one-minute work cycle on an assembly line, and loading and unloading a production machine that operates on a semiautomatic cycle and produces the same part over and over.

[9] J. Rasmussen, "Skills, Rules, and Knowledge: Signals, Signs, and Symbols, and Other Distinctions in Human Performance Models," *IEEE Transactions on Systems, Man, and Cybernetics* 13, no. 3 (1983): 257–67.

Rule-based behavior occurs when a person performs a task according to a set of rules or instructions. Greater demands are made on attention resources in tasks characterized by rule-based behavior because the rules or guidelines have to be consciously followed. When a person is learning a new task but has not yet mastered it, his or her actions tend to be guided by rule-based behavior. Examples of rule-based behavior include following a checklist when starting up a chemical process, setting up a fixture on a milling machine, performing blood tests in a medical clinic, following a recipe to prepare a dessert, and performing a new repetitive task according to the recommended procedure. In the case of repetitive tasks, once the task has been fully learned, the behavior transitions from rule-based to skill-based.

Knowledge-based behavior refers to tasks and activities that require a high degree of cognitive processing because the situations are unfamiliar and cannot be dealt with using rules or past experience. A person manifesting this type of behavior must define objectives, evaluate alternatives, and mentally analyze or physically test the consequences of the alternatives. Examples of knowledge-based behavior include designing a mechanical component for a machine, diagnosing a medical patient's symptoms, solving a complex mathematical problem, analyzing the results of a scientific experiment, and identifying the cause of a quality problem in a production operation.

There are sometimes job situations in which more than one type of behavior is applied, such as for different tasks of the same job. A worker can sometimes be guided by rules to perform certain tasks, and at other times knowledge and analysis must be used to solve unfamiliar new problems. In addition, a worker may begin a task using rule-based behavior and gradually convert to skill-based behavior once that job has been thoroughly learned. In some cases, all three types of behavior can be exhibited in the same job. For example, a skilled machinist may be assigned a routine batch production job that has been run in the shop before but never by this machinist. The job must first be set up, which requires rule-based behavior (e.g., reading instructions, obtaining the proper tools, and affixing them to the machine according to the instructions). Then the parts are produced, which requires a skill-based behavior once the work cycle pattern has been learned (the machinist has performed many similar jobs in the past, and the work quickly becomes routine). Finally, the surface finish on the part begins to deteriorate during production, and the machinist must analyze the situation to determine what course of action should be taken to correct the problem (knowledge-based behavior).

6 COMMON COGNITIVE TASKS

In this section, we examine three important and somewhat overlapping categories of information-processing tasks that are commonly encountered in cognitive work: (1) decision making, (2) planning, and (3) problem solving.

6.1 Decision Making

Decision making is the cognitive operation in which a person makes a judgment to select one alternative over other possible alternatives in order to achieve some objective or satisfy some criteria. Decision making is a central activity in human information processing because it is an integral part of so many other cognitive processes, such as planning, designing, problem solving, and troubleshooting. The typical decision-making situation consists of the following elements: (1) one alternative must be selected from among multiple options, (2) some information is available about the options, (3) the time frame within which the decision must be made is relatively long, and (4) there is uncertainty about the options and their outcomes [11]. Decision making is distinguished from a ***choice reaction***, which refers to a judgment that must be made quickly and often reflexively—for example, choosing to depress the brake pedal because the car in front is too close. The time frame in decision making is longer.

The output of the decision-making process is a decision. Decisions can be classified as good or bad, correct or incorrect, and optimal or suboptimal. Oftentimes these classifications cannot be assigned until long after a decision has been made, and it can be seen whether the selected alternative did in fact achieve the objective that was sought after. The ergonomic interest in decision making is to better understand the mental process by which decisions are made and to provide tools and guidelines that will increase a person's chances of making good decisions and minimize the chances of making bad decisions.

Models of decision making can be divided into two categories: (1) rational and (2) descriptive. Rational decision-making models are based on classical decision theory founded in economics and statistics. They represent logical approaches to decision making, but people often do not make decisions based strictly on logic. Descriptive models try to represent the behavioral aspects of decision making.

Rational Decision Models. In ***rational decision models***, the emphasis is on logically or quantitatively determining the optimal alternative among the various options. They are also called ***normative decision models*** because they represent decision making the way people should accomplish it, not necessarily the way people actually do accomplish it. Rational decision-making models use multiattribute utility theory, in which an overall value is calculated for each alternative based on the scores of various attributes that are used to judge the alternatives. The overall value is calculated using the formula

$$V_i = \sum_{j=1}^{n} u_j a_{ij} \tag{5}$$

where V_i = overall value of alternative i, u_j = utility or weighting factor for attribute j; a_{ij} = score of attribute j for alternative i; and n = number of attributes used as decision criteria. The logical decision is to select the alternative with the highest V_i.

Rational decision models can also be used to compute the expected values of a set of alternatives by multiplying the payoff for each outcome by the respective probability of that outcome and then subtracting the cost of the alternative (if applicable). That is,

$$E(V_i) = p_i P_i - C_i \tag{6}$$

where $E(V_i)$ = expected value of alternative i; p_i = probability of the alternative becoming the outcome; P_i = the payoff value of the alternative; and C_i = cost of the alternative, if an investment was made when that alternative was selected. The alternative with the highest expected value is the choice of the rational decision maker.

Example 2 Decision Making Using Expected Values

The state lottery is now worth \$20 million. A ticket to enter costs \$1.00. The chances of one ticket winning the lottery are 1 in 700 million. A person wants to buy 5 tickets. Should he? What is the rational decision using expected values?

Solution: The two alternatives are (a) keep the \$5.00 and (b) buy 5 tickets with a potential \$20 million payoff.

(a) The first alternative has an expected value of zero. As the saying goes, "nothing ventured, nothing gained."
(b) The expected value of the second alternative is calculated as follows:

$$E(V_i) = 5\left(\frac{1}{700{,}000{,}000}\right)(\$20{,}000{,}000) - \$5.00 = \$0.143 - \$5.00 = -\$4.86$$

A rational decision maker would not take a chance on a state lottery ticket. ■

Descriptive Decision Models. The trouble with rational decision models is that people often do not make decisions according to that model. Our lottery ticket buyer in Example 2 loses money by purchasing state lottery tickets, but he keeps on doing it, hoping for his lucky day. Because people do not always obey the structure of rational decision making, other models have been developed that attempt to explain the way people actually do make decisions. These models are termed descriptive (as opposed to quantitative, which characterizes the rational decision models). Descriptive decision models emphasize the cognitive and behavioral aspects of human decision making. These models recognize that people often make decisions using ***heuristics***—approaches guided by rules-of-thumb and simplifications rather than detailed analysis. The following techniques are some of the heuristics that people use in decision making:

- *Satisficing.* In this heuristic, the decision maker considers a series of options until one is found that is satisfactory. That alternative is then selected because finding a better alternative is not worth the additional effort. The term ***satisficing*** is derived from "satisfactory decision," and the concept is attributed to H. Simon.[10] Given the limitations of working memory, and perhaps the need to make a decision within a limited time frame, satisficing is a practical and reasonable way for people to make decisions.
- *Anchoring heuristic.* People tend to give more weight to information obtained early in the decision-making process. Thus, the final decision is influenced more by early information that anchors the process than by information obtained subsequently.
- *Availability heuristic.* People are more likely to retrieve from long-term memory a hypothesis that has been used recently or frequently. It is readily available and

[10] H. A. Simon, *Models of Man* (New York: Wiley 1957).

the first thing that comes to mind, and it is therefore assumed to be a reasonable hypothesis for making a decision or solving a problem.

- *Representativeness heuristic.* In this heuristic, a person makes a decision about a given entity because it appears to fit the mind's prototype of that entity. The entity is representative of the prototype. For example, if we are asked to decide if a certain individual (whom we do not know) is a construction worker or a librarian, our decision would be influenced by the person's appearance relative to how we perceive the appearance of a construction worker and a librarian.

More complete descriptions of these and other heurstics are given in [4] and [11]. Heuristics are often used as a matter of convenience, but there are other situations in which people are forced to make decisions quickly under adverse dynamic conditions, and they must be guided by heuristics combined with their skill and experience. Examples of people that sometimes find themselves in these kinds of situations include surgeons operating in emergency surgery, firefighters fighting a major forest fire, newspaper production editors getting ready to go to press, police officers engaged in pursuit of a crime suspect, and college students nearing the end of a one hour quiz that is too long.

6.2 Planning

Planning is the mental process of devising a detailed method for doing or making something. Developed before something must be done, planning is an important information-processing activity because so many human endeavors must be planned: vacations, careers, weddings, meetings, and projects, to name a few. Related cognitive activities include scheduling, designing, scheming, and plotting. They all require the planner to envision the realization of a desired goal or objective.

Planning is accomplished using two cognitive processes, sometimes in combination [12]. The first involves the use of ***scripts*** that have been developed of typical sequences of events based on previous experience and saved in long-term memory. The planner recalls the previous plan, perhaps making adjustments to account for differences in the present situation, and adopts it. For example, professional wedding planners use this kind of routine planning approach. The cast of characters, ceremonies, and venues may change, but not the basic steps leading up to and concluding the marital union.

The second cognitive process used in planning is ***mental simulation***, in which the planner must mentally develop the steps in the method and imagine what would happen if those steps were followed. Mental simulation is required when the planning situation cannot be reduced to a script. For example, planning the next moves in a chess game requires mental simulation. The chess player must imagine what the opponent will do in response to various board moves that might be made.

Planning can make significant demands on a person's working memory, especially when mental simulation is used in the process. Consequently, people tend to be easily distracted when the planning activity is purely mental (no planning aids). Also, people seem to plan over the short term rather than the long term. This requires fewer resources in working memory, and everyone knows that any plan becomes less certain as time increases into the future. As in other cognitive activities, much of the mental workload in planning can be relieved by the use of ***planning aids***—techniques for constructing and/or graphically representing the plan. Planning aids can be as simple as a sketchpad or as sophisticated as a computer simulation. Planning aids are also useful for documenting and visualizing the steps in the plan. Planning techniques discussed in this text include Gantt charts and critical path networks.

6.3 Problem Solving

A ***problem*** is a question or issue that has been raised for solution or consideration. The solution may require mathematical calculations, brainstorming, analysis, diagnosis, evaluation of alternatives, creative design work, or combinations of these cognitive activities. Problem solving requires attention resources directed at the interaction between information stored in long-term memory and operations carried out in working memory. It must also utilize the sensory and perception functions in an iterative process of seeking an answer to the question. Thus, most problem-solving tasks engage all of the functions in the human information-processing cycle of Figure 1.

Cognitive tasks related to problem solving include ***diagnosis*** and ***troubleshooting*** [12]. In fact, diagnosis and troubleshooting are often required steps in problem solving. Diagnosis and troubleshooting both involve an investigation and analysis of the cause of a problem or situation. Diagnosis results in the identification of the cause, as in the medical diagnosis of a disease based on a patient's symptoms. Troubleshooting implies not only the identification of the cause but also its repair or resolution, as in troubleshooting an automobile engine or mediating a diplomatic dispute. In the case of a diagnosis, repair or other corrective action is not necessarily included. For example, one doctor may provide a diagnosis but refer the patient to another doctor for a second opinion that includes recommending a cure.

Problems have a technical context, which refers to the field of expertise needed to solve the problem. A chemical engineering problem requires a different approach and the use of different solution techniques than a problem in accounting. Problems also possess a degree of difficulty. Easy problems require less mental effort to solve than difficult ones. Degree of difficulty refers to attributes such as the uniqueness of the problem, number of steps required in its solution, and technical complexity (e.g., a chemical process consisting of five reactions is likely to be more complex than one involving a single reaction).

A first step in problem solving is to realize that certain pieces of information are relevant to the solution of the problem and other pieces of information are irrelevant. A good problem solver is able to distinguish between the two categories. In Example 1, where sound pressure p_s in N/m^2 is converted to sound pressure level SPL in decibels, the frequency of the sound is irrelevant. It does not enter the computations.

Different problems require different approaches for their solution. The approaches can be related to our Skill-Rule-Knowledge model described in Section 5.2. In some cases, the problem solver is able to relate the problem to previous experiences with similar problems, so that solving the new problem is a matter of recalling from long-term memory the solutions that worked with those previous problems. For example, a dentist has seen a type of tooth infection many times before and has prescribed a particular antibiotic that has worked nearly every time to relieve the symptoms. For the current patient experiencing those same symptoms, the dentist immediately jumps to the solution of prescribing the same antibiotic. In effect, the dentist has exhibited skill-based behavior to solve the problem.

In slightly more difficult problems, the problem solver may not be able to conclude the answer based on pattern matching with previous experience. Instead, a procedure must be followed (rule-based behavior) that will lead to the answer. The dentist in the previous example wants to know the location of the infection. The patient is able to identify the general location of the discomfort but not the exact tooth. The standard procedure for the dentist to follow is to take an X-ray of the area to pinpoint the infected tooth so that a root canal can be performed.

Finally, problems at the highest degree of difficulty are less likely to lend themselves to a skill-based approach, and a purely rule-based approach may not be applicable either. In these cases, a knowledge-based approach or a combination of rule-based and knowledge-based approaches is needed. The problem solver is confronted with a situation that is unfamiliar and must rely on his or her expertise and understanding of the problem's technical context stored in long-term memory (knowledge-based behavior) combined with a general problem-solving approach (rule-based behavior). These kinds of problem situations are common in medical diagnosis, scientific research, engineering design, industrial management, creative writing, and final exams in college. Returning to our dentist example, the patient has a swollen lower jaw and discomfort that is consistent with an infected tooth. However, an X-ray of the area reveals no darkened mass that would identify the infected tooth. The dentist is faced with a problem that is uncharacteristic of those he has treated before. It may not even be a dental problem at all. Determining a course of action requires consideration of several alternatives, including referral of the patient to a medical doctor.[11]

Problems requiring a knowledge-based approach are especially demanding of cognitive resources—in particular, working memory. Because the capacity of working memory is limited to about seven "chunks" of information at one time, and in problem solving the chunks tend to be complex so as to reduce the number that can be managed simultaneously, it is useful for the problem solver to use some form of external memory aid. A memory aid can be as simple as a sketchpad to record the details of the problem and capture the progression of ideas and computations. The problem solver is often aided by sketching a model to represent the problem—for example, a network diagram showing the sequence of steps in a process and their relationships. This relieves working memory and activates the visual sense in the problem-solving exercise.

Problems do occur with the problem-solving process. The principal difficulties and biases encountered during problem solving, troubleshooting, and diagnosis are described in [1] and [11]. These are summarized in the following list:

- *Cognitive tunneling.* This is a bias associated with troubleshooting and diagnosis. It is when the expert identifies one hypothesis to answer the question and stays focused on it to the exclusion of other possible explanations. He or she seeks out evidence to confirm the chosen hypothesis but overlooks or ignores clues that might disprove it.
- *One solution fixation.* Analogous to cognitive tunneling in troubleshooting and diagnosis, this problem occurs when a person chooses one solution for a problem and sticks with that solution even though it may not be succeeding.

[11] I am indebted to my dentist, Dr. Eric J. Marsh, Allentown, Pennsylvania, for his technical advice in devising these dental examples while he was working on my teeth (an instance of divided attention, Section 3).

- *Stuck in a loop.* This problem occurs when the problem solver continues to repeat a sequence of actions that have no result except to lead back to the starting point of the problem.
- *Inability to think ahead.* This problem occurs in situations that require multiple solution steps or the consideration of multiple alternatives, which causes the working memory of the problem solver to become overloaded. The person is unable to think ahead more than a few steps.

7 DESIGN GUIDELINES FOR COGNITIVE WORK

Our coverage of the human information-processing system in this chapter has already revealed a number of guidelines that can be used in cognitive work situations. For example, the concept of compatibility (Section 5.1) is useful in the design of controls for an operation. We want the controls to be located in logical positions relative to the operation (spatial compatibility), and we want the actuation of the controls to be consistent with the operator's expectations (movement compatibility). In this final section we explore some of the other design guidelines that should be followed in work design. Our coverage is organized according to the principal phases of human information processing in Figure 1. Additional coverage of these guidelines can be found in some of the textbooks listed in our references; for example, see [9], [10], and [11].

7.1 Guidelines for Sensory Reception and Perception

The design guidelines and principles that follow are intended to support the human information-processing stages of sensory reception and perception.

- *Selection of sensory modality.* As noted earlier, humans receive 95% or more of their information by means of the visual and hearing sensory modes. In many situations, the question arises whether it is better to present information by means of a visual or an auditory stimulus. Some guidelines on selecting the sensory modality are presented in Table 3. The other sensory modes (e.g., touch) are not usually considered except in special cases (e.g., blind people). As a general rule, it is better to present warning messages using both visual and audible stimuli. If only

TABLE 3 Guidelines for Selecting Visual or Auditory Presentation Modes

When to Use Visual Presentation	When to Use Auditory Presentation
Message is long.	Message is short.
Message is complex.	Message is simple.
Message will be referred to later.	Message requires immediate action.
Environment is noisy.	Location is either very bright or very dark.
Person receiving the message is expected to remain in one location.	Person receiving the message is expected to be moving around.

Source: Complied from [9] and [10]. Original source is B. H. Deatherage, "Auditory and Other Sensory Forms of Information Presentation," *Human Engineering Guide to Equipment Design*, edited by H. P. Van Cott and R. G. Kinkade (Washington, DC: U.S. Government Printing Office, 1972).

one stimulus can be used as a warning message, then the auditory mode is more effective in alerting people.

- *Standardization.* Standardization is an accepted principle in nearly all design situations. In ergonomics design, it means having similar devices operate the same way. A person can work at one machine and then relocate to another machine and that second machine has the same kinds of controls. Other examples of standardization include color-coding of electrical wiring, labeling of hazardous substances, and laying out all of a company's department stores the same way so that when store managers are relocated, they do not have to learn an entirely new layout. In sensory reception, standardization means the use of standard symbols and codes for displays, standardized paperwork forms within an organization, and standard icons for computer programs.
- *Redundancy.* It is sometimes important to present information using more than one sensory mode. The combination of visual and auditory modes for warning messages is a good example. Police and fire department vehicles that use sirens and flashing lights are examples. A machine operator is more likely to be alerted that something is wrong with his machine through the use of both visual and auditory warnings.
- *Graphical displays.* Information presented graphically (e.g., photographs, bar graphs, pie charts) is usually more effective than the same information presented in the form of text. In the Toyota Production System, work instructions are documented using a combination of written instructions and pictures (e.g., photographs of various kinds of defects that the machine operator should watch out for).
- *Stimulus variation.* It is often useful to provide variable stimuli rather than stimuli that are constant and continuous [5]. Thus, a flashing light on a control panel is more likely to grab an operator's attention than a continuous light that went on while the operator was looking away. Sirens that sound intermittently or vary in tone are more effective warnings than continuous, monotone sirens.

7.2 Guidelines for Working Memory

Most of the following design guidelines are aimed at mitigating the limitations of working memory (e.g., capacity and the time factor). They are compiled mostly from [11].

- *Minimize demands on working memory.* This is a general rule that means designing the mental workload so as to minimize the number of alphanumeric items that must be kept in working memory and the length of time they must be retained. A manufacturing company could implement this rule by adopting a part number system with fewer digits—for example, using a five-digit number instead of a seven-digit number. People in the company would have a much easier time working with these smaller numbers.
- *Exploit chunking.* Working memory is limited to processing seven or so chunks of information at one time. A chunk is one piece of information that has meaning. It is not limited to a single digit or character. Given the way working memory manages chunks, there are several ways in which chunking can be used: (1) formulate

meaningful sequences out of a string of alphanumeric characters, so that the string can be retained as one chunk—for example, the emergency number 911, which is sufficiently familiar to people that it is retained as a single chunk; (2) favor the use of letters over numbers because they are more likely to have meaning; (3) limit the chunk size to three or four characters.

- *Provide reminders for sequential operations.* This guideline is intended for work cycles consisting of multiple steps, during which the worker might become distracted and forget which steps have been completed. Most of us have found ourselves saying "now, where was I?" when we were interrupted in the middle of doing something. Implementing this guideline means providing some form of visual feedback to help operators remember which step they are working on.
- *Maintain congruence in written instructions.* Instructions should be written in simple, easily understood sentences in order to avoid mistakes in following them. In addition, it is important that the sequence in which instructions are presented is the same as the order in which they must be carried out. For example, the instruction "Do A; then do B" is easier to follow than "Do B after doing A" because the instruction sequence is consistent with steps in the task.

7.3 Guidelines for Long-Term Memory

In nonrepetitive and batch operations, as well as emergency situations, workers are often required to remember facts and procedures that are retrieved from long-term memory, when they must perform a task that was last performed months or years before. The following guidelines (compiled mostly from [11]) are intended to avoid problems that might be encountered due to the limitations of long-term memory:

- *Increase the frequency and recency of using information stored in long-term memory.* Retrieval of specific pieces of information from long-term memory is aided by increasing the frequency and recency with which it is recalled. There are several ways this guideline can be implemented: (1) having drills to recall emergency procedures, (2) holding regular and frequent training sessions, and (3) standardizing procedures in batch operations so that all jobs consist of similar steps or approaches.
- *Use memory aids.* For tasks that are performed infrequently or where it is important that steps in the task be carried out in the correct order and that none be omitted, the use of written instructions rather than reliance on memory should be required. Memory aids can take the form of a paper document or computerized instructions.

REFERENCES

[1] Bridger, R. S. *Introduction to Ergonomics*. 2nd ed. London: Taylor and Francis, 2003.

[2] Drury, C. G. "Inspection Performance." Pp. 2282–314 in *Handbook of Industrial Engineering*. 2nd ed., edited by G. Salvendy. New York: Wiley 1992.

[3] Kroemer, K. H. E., H. B. Kroemer, and K. E. Kroemer-Elbert. *Ergonomics: How to Design for Ease and Efficiency*. Upper Saddle River, NJ: Prentice Hall, 1994.

[4] Lehto, M. R. "Decision Making." Pp. 1202–48 in *Handbook of Human Factors and Ergonomics*. 2nd ed., edited by G. Salvendy. New York: Wiley 1997.

[5] MacLeod, D. "Cognitive Ergonomics." *Industrial Engineer*. (March 2004) 26–30.

[6] Marmaras, N., and T. Kontogiannis. "Cognitive Tasks." Pp. 1013–41 in *Handbook of Industrial Engineering*. 3rd ed., edited by G. Salvendy. New York: Wiley, 2001.

[7] Niebel, B. W., and A. Freivalds. *Method, Standards, and Work Design*. 11th ed. New York: McGraw-Hill, 2003.

[8] Proctor, R. W., and J. D. Proctor. "Sensation and Perception." Pp. 43–88 in *Handbook of Human Factors and Ergonomics*. 2nd ed., edited by G. Salvendy. New York: Wiley 1997.

[9] Pulat, B. M. *Fundamentals of Industrial Ergonomics*. Upper Saddle River, NJ: Prentice Hall, 1992.

[10] Sanders, M. S., and E. J. McCormick. *Human Factors in Engineering Design*. 7th ed. New York: McGraw-Hill, 1993.

[11] Wickens, C. D., J. Lee, Y. Liu, and S. G. Becker. *An Introduction to Human Factors Engineering*. 2nd ed. Upper Saddle River, NJ: Pearson/Prentice Hall, 2004.

[12] Wickens, C. D., and C. Melody Carswell. "Information Processing." Pp. 89–129 in *Handbook of Human Factors and Ergonomics*. 2nd ed., edited by G. Salvendy. New York: Wiley 1997.

REVIEW QUESTIONS

1 What is cognitive ergonomics?

2 Identify some of the common cognitive activities that humans engage in.

3 Why is cognitive ergonomics becoming increasingly important relative to physical ergonomics?

4 What is an exteroceptor?

5 Name the five human senses.

6 What is the component of the eye through which light rays enter the eyeball?

7 What is the retina in the eyeball?

8 Define visual acuity.

9 What is monochromatism?

10 A pure sound tone is characterized by what two attributes?

11 Why was the logarithmic decibel scale developed for measuring sound intensity?

12 What is the common name for the tympanic membrane?

13 What is the aural reflex?

14 What is the normal hearing range of humans in Hz?

15 Why is the tactile sense also referred to as the cutaneous sense.

16 What are the two steps in perception, as described in the text?

17 What do the terms *bottom-up processing* and *top-down processing* mean?

18 What is the difference between selective attention and focused attention?

19 What is the meaning of the term *sustained attention*? What is another name for it?

20 What are the three types of memory in the information-processing model?

21 What is a chunk of information, as the term is used in regard to working memory?

22 What is the difference between semantic memory and episodic memory as these terms are used in the context of long-term memory?

23 What is response selection?
24 What is compatibility in human information processing?
25 In the Skill-Rule-Knowledge model, what is the difference between skill-based and rule-based behavior?
26 What is the difference between rational decision models and descriptive decision models in decision theory?
27 What are the two cognitive processes used in planning something?
28 What is cognitive tunneling?

PROBLEMS

Vision and Hearing

1 An individual is capable of detecting a small object that is 20 mm high at a distance of 35 m. Determine the visual angle subtended by the object and the visual acuity of the individual.
2 A person with normal vision has a visual acuity of 1.0. What is the size of the smallest feature that can be distinguished by this person at a distance of 100 yd?
3 A sharpshooter with better than normal vision has a visual acuity of 1.8. What is the size of the smallest target that can be distinguished by this person at a distance of 300 yd?
4 What is the decibel level (SPL) of a sound that has a pressure of 0.75 Pa?
5 What is the pressure level (N/m^2) corresponding to a sound intensity $SPL = 90$ dB?
6 A passing train produces a sound intensity of 1.3 N/m^2 to a person standing 10 m away from the track. (a) Determine the sound pressure level (SPL in dB) of this pressure. (b) If the person were standing 20 m away rather than 10 m, what would the sound pressure level (dB) be?
7 A sound is measured at a distance of 20 ft to have a decibel level of 100 dB. What would the decibel level be at a distance of 100 ft?

Decision Models

8 A small manufacturing company wants to select the best machine tool based on three criteria: (1) productivity, (2) cost, and (3) maintenance. Productivity is considered the most important criterion and is given a weighting factor of 8; cost is weighted 6, and maintenance is weighted 4. The company's industrial engineer on the project has evaluated four models (A, B, C, and D) and has compiled their respective scores for each attribute, as shown in the table below. Which machine tool should be selected based on the multiattribute decision model?

	Weighting Factor		
Alternative	Productivity (8)	Cost (6)	Maintenance (4)
A	7	5	8
B	8	4	6
C	4	8	5
D	7	6	7

9 An investor has $100,000 to invest in several alternative ventures. The investor's plan is to sell the investment at the end of 1 year and make a profit. Venture A costs $75,000, and there is a 50% chance that it can be sold for $150,000 at the end of 1 year; otherwise it will be sold at cost. Venture B costs $90,000, and there is a 35% chance that it can be sold for $200,000 at the end of 1 year; otherwise it will be sold at a loss (selling price = $60,000). Venture C costs $140,000, and there is a 25% chance that it can be sold for $300,000 at the end of 1 year, and a 40% chance that it can be sold for $200,000 at the end of 1 year; otherwise it will be sold at cost. Which of the three ventures should be selected?

The Physical Work Environment

Whether work is physical or cognitive, it is performed in an environment. The general model of the human-machine system operates in an environment that includes both physical and social aspects. In this chapter we examine the physical aspects—in particular, the lighting, noise, and climate surrounding the workplace. By making the physical components of the work environment as comfortable and undistracting as possible, better job satisfaction and greater productivity are encouraged.

1 THE VISUAL ENVIRONMENT AND LIGHTING

About 80 percent of the information input to the human brain comes from visual stimuli. We also introduced some of the physical concepts about light as a source of stimulation for the sense of sight. In this section, we discuss the visual environment at work and how lighting can improve it.

1.1 The Physics of Light

Light is electromagnetic radiant energy within the visible spectrum between ultraviolet and infrared. The branch of optical physics that is concerned with the measurement of light is called ***photometry***. An instrument that measures light is called a ***photometer***. The ergonomic interest in photometry is to provide the proper levels of lighting and contrasts among objects in a workplace or other environment. In particular, a photometer measures the luminous intensity that is emitted by a source of light or reflected from the surface of an object. The basic quantity in photometry is ***luminous flux***—the rate at which light energy is emitted in all directions from a light source. It is the power of the light source (power is a rate quantity). Luminous flux is measured in units of ***lumens*** (lm).[1]

A closely related term is ***luminous intensity***, which is the luminous flux emitted in a given direction. Specifically, luminous intensity is the luminous flux (power of the light) radiated per unit solid angle, and its unit of measure is the ***candela*** (cd). The lumen and the candela are both units of light power. One candela is equal to 1 lumen (lm) per unit solid angle. The ***steradian*** is the unit of measure of a solid angle (analogous to the radian for a plane circle). One steradian is equal to the solid angle subtended at the center of a sphere of unit radius by the unit area on its surface. This is illustrated in Figure 1, which shows a point source of light at the center of the sphere and the cone shape of one steradian that intersects the surface of the sphere to create an area of 1 sq m. The point source radiates isotropically (uniformly in all directions). Since the total area of a sphere is given by $4\pi r^2$, then the area of a sphere of unit radius $= 4\pi = 12.566$. Thus, there are 4π steradians about the center of a sphere (analogous to 2π radians about the center of

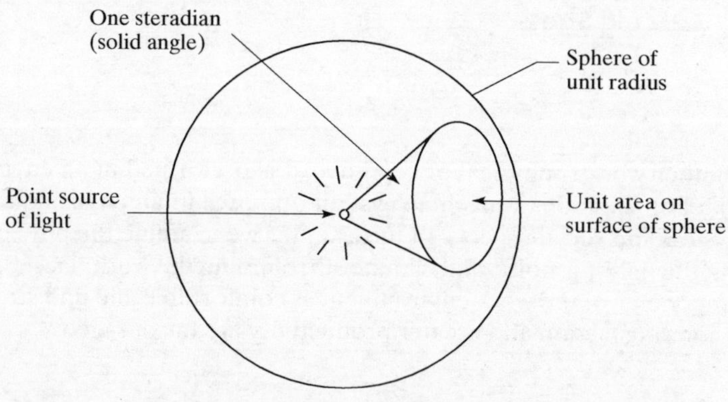

Figure 1 A point source of light at the center of a sphere of unit radius. Also shown is a solid angle of 1 steradian, which intersects the surface of the sphere to create an area of 1 sq m.

[1]To give the reader a sense of the power magnitude, it takes 683 lumens to equal one Watt at a wavelength of 555 Nm (yellow-green), which is the wavelength of maximum sensitivity of the human eye.

a plane circle). In terms of luminous intensity and luminous flux, a 1 cd point source of light radiates a total of 12.566 lm. Also, a 1 cd point source radiates 1 lm per steradian. These facts can be reduced to the following equation:

$$F = 4\pi I \tag{1}$$

where F = light flux, lm; and I = source intensity, cd.

In practice, there is no such thing as an isotropic point source of light. Luminous flux radiates from a real light source with different intensities in different directions. Using a photometer, light measurements can be taken from a particular direction relative to the source to determine the luminous flux emanating in that direction.

The amount of light shining on a surface is called the ***illuminance*** (the term ***illumination*** is also used), which is the amount of luminous flux per unit area of the surface. Its unit of measure is the lux (lx). One ***lux*** is equal to 1 lumen per square meter; that is, 1 lx = 1 lm/sq m. In equation form,

$$E = \frac{F}{A} \tag{2}$$

where E = illuminance, lx; F = luminous flux, lm; and A = area of illuminated surface, sq m.

Illuminance decreases as the distance from the light source increases. The reduction is proportional to the square of the distance, as expressed in the following:

$$E = \frac{I}{d^2} \tag{3}$$

where E = illuminance, lx; I = luminous intensity of light source, cd; and d = distance of surface from source, m. This equation assumes that the surface is perpendicular to the line of the distance between source and surface, as illustrated in Figure 2 (a).

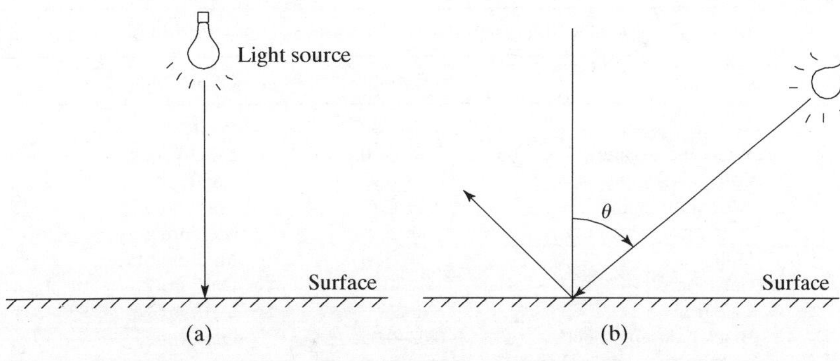

Figure 2 Angle of incidence defined for equations (3) and (4): (a) $\theta = 0$ and (b) incident light is at an angle θ, where θ = angle of incidence.

If the angle of incidence is other than perpendicular, as shown in Figure 2 (b), then the illuminance must take the angle of incidence into account and is determined as follows:

$$E = \frac{I}{d^2}\cos\theta \tag{4}$$

where θ = angle of incidence in Figure 2 (b). Note that when $\theta = 0$, $\cos\theta = 1$, and equation (4) reduces to equation (3).

When light shines on a surface, some of the light is absorbed into the surface, and some of it is reflected from the surface. In addition, for materials that are translucent (e.g., glass), some of the light is transmitted through the material. The light that is reflected from an object is what allows humans to visually perceive it. The amount of light reflected from the surface is called ***luminance***, and its units of measure are candelas per square meter (cd/sq m). The luminance of a surface depends not only on the amount of light shining on it (illuminance) but also on the color and texture of the surface. The proportion of light reflected from the surface to the light striking it is the property of the surface known as reflectance. Specifically, reflectance is defined in the SI system of units as follows:

$$R = \frac{\pi L}{E} \quad \text{or} \quad L = \frac{RE}{\pi} \tag{5}$$

where R = reflectance (a dimensionless fraction); L = luminance, cd/sq m; and E = illuminance, lx. The π term in the numerator is a conversion factor to account for the difference in units between luminance and illuminance. Some typical values of reflectance are listed for different types of surfaces and paint colors in Table 1. Some typical values of illuminance and luminance for various lighting situations are presented in Table 2.

TABLE 1 Typical Reflectance Values for Various Objects and Paint Colors

Object	Reflectance	Paint Color	Reflectance
Mirrored glass	0.80–0.90	White	0.85
White matte paint	0.75–0.90	Light yellow	0.75
Porcelain enamel	0.60–0.90	Light green	0.65
Aluminum paint	0.60–0.70	Light blue	0.55
Newsprint	0.55	Medium gray	0.55
Dull brass	0.35	Medium blue	0.35
Cardboard	0.30	Dark gray	0.30
Cast iron	0.25	Dark brown	0.10
Black painted object	0.03–0.05	Dark blue	0.08

Source: From [5] for reflectance values of objects; from [7] for reflectance values of colors.

TABLE 2 Some Typical Values of Illuminance and Luminance for Various Lighting Situations

Lighting Situation	Illuminance on Surface (lm/m^2)	Type of surface	Luminance of Surface (cd/m^2)
Clear summer sky[a]	150,000	Grass	2,900
Overcast summer sky[a]	16,000	Grass	300
Office work	500	White paper	120
Good street lighting	10	Concrete road surface	1.0
Moonlight	0.5	Asphalt road surface	0.01

Source: From [2].
[a]Northern temperate zone.

Example 1 Light from an Isotropic Source

An isotropic light source has an intensity of 50 cd. Located 3 m away is a wall that has a reflectance of 0.65. Calculate (a) the total luminous flux emanating from the light source, (b) the illuminance of the wall, and (c) the luminance emitted by the reflected light.

Solution **(a)** The total luminous flux emanating from the light source is

$$F = 4\pi I = 4\pi(50 \text{ cd}) = 628 \text{ lm}$$

(b) The illuminance on the wall is

$$E = \frac{I}{d^2} = \frac{50}{3^2} = 5.55 \text{ lx}$$

(c) The reflected light can be determined using equation (5), the equation defining reflectance.

$$L = \frac{ER}{\pi} = \frac{5.55(0.65)}{\pi} = 1.15 \text{ cd/m}^2$$ ■

1.2 Visibility

The visibility of tools, materials, and equipment features is important in most work situations. ***Visibility*** refers to the relative possibility of being seen under the prevailing conditions of lighting, distance, and related factors. In this section, we discuss the important factors that affect visibility and visual performance.

Recommended Illumination Levels. The most important factor for good visibility is the amount of light shining on the object—the level of illumination in the work area. Recommended illumination levels have been developed by the Illuminating Engineering Society of North America.[2] Some of these recommendations have been adapted for our

[2]J. Kaufman and J. Christensen, eds., *IES Lighting Handbook* (New York: Illuminating Engineering Society of North America, 1984).

TABLE 3 Recommended Interior Illumination Levels for Various Activities and Work Situations

Category	Areas and Activities	Illumination Level, Lux
A	Public areas with dark surroundings	35
B	Where general lighting in area is required	75
C	Where visual tasks are performed occasionally	150
D	Where visual tasks of high contrast and/or large size are performed	350
E	Where visual tasks of medium contrast and/or small size are performed	750
F	Where visual tasks of low contrast and/or very small size are performed	1,500
G	Where visual tasks of low contrast and/or very small size are performed over extended periods	3,500
H	Where very prolonged and exacting visual tasks are performed	7,500
I	Where very special visual tasks involving very low contrast and small objects are performed	15,000

Source: Adapted from Illuminating Engineering Society of North America.

TABLE 4 Adjustments to Recommended Illumination Levels: Weighting Factors for Task and Worker Characteristics, and Adjustment Multiplier

(a) Weighting Factors	−1	0	+1	(b) Algebraic Sum	Adjustment to Illumination Level
Worker age	Under 40	40–55	Over 55	−2 or −3	Multiply by 0.7
Speed and accuracy required	Unimportant	Important	Critical	−1 or 0 or +1	Multiply by 1.0
Reflectance of task background	70–100%	30–70%	0–30%	+2 or +3	Multiply by 1.3

Source: Based on the recommendations of the Illuminating Engineering Society of North America.

coverage and are presented in Table 3. Lighting systems to achieve the recommended illumination levels are discussed in Section 1.3.

These recommended levels are intended for persons aged 40 to 55 working under specified conditions of reflectance and speed/accuracy requirements. For a given work situation of interest, if the worker's age or the actual conditions in the workplace differ from the specified conditions, then adjustments must be made in the recommended illumination levels. The three adjustment criteria are indicated in Table 4(a): (1) worker age, (2) speed and accuracy requirements, and (3) reflectance of task background. For each criterion, a weighting factor is applied (−1, 0, or +1), depending on the worker and task characteristics. The three weighting factors are then summed algebraically, and an adjustment is made to the recommended illumination level as indicated in Table 4(b).

Example 2 Recommended Illumination Level

A factory workplace has a reflectance of only 25% for a task that is performed by a 45-year-old female worker. The task includes visual elements involving small objects. Speed and accuracy requirements are judged to be critical. What is the recommended illumination level?

Solution: The work situation best fits into category E, in which the recommended illumination level is 750 lx from Table 3.

Taking into account the worker's age, speed and accuracy requirements, and reflectance, the weighting factors from Table 4(a) are 0, +1, and +1, respectively, for a total of +2. Based on Table 4(b), we multiply the base illumination level of 750 lx by 1.3. Thus the recommended illumination level is 1.3(750) = 975 lx. ■

Other Factors Affecting Visibility and Visual Performance. In addition to illumination level, other factors that affect visibility and visual performance include visual angle, brightness contrast, color, and glare. ***Visual angle*** is defined as the angle subtended at the eye by the smallest distinguishable detail. For small angles, it is the height of the detail divided by its distance from the eye, converted to arc minutes:

$$\alpha_v = 3438 \frac{h}{d} \tag{6}$$

where α_v = visual angle, arc min (1 arc min = 1/60 degree); h = height of object or detail, cm (in); and d = distance from eye, cm (in.). The visual angle can be increased by increasing the size of the object (increasing h) or by bringing it closer (decreasing d). These effects are often achieved by using microscopes and similar magnifying instruments.

Brightness contrast is the relative luminance between an object and its background. It is defined by the following equation:

$$BC = \frac{L_{max} - L_{min}}{L_{max}} \tag{7}$$

where BC = brightness contrast (no units); L_{max} = luminance of brighter surface, cd/m^2; and L_{min} = luminance of darker surface, cd/m^2. Increasing brightness contrast increases visibility. High contrast can be achieved either by a dark object against a light background or by a light object against a dark background.

Color is normally characterized by its hue, which is the attribute of a color that allows it to be classified as red, green, or blue, or something intermediate between any pair of these primary colors. Hue is determined primarily by the dominant wavelength of the light waves emitted by an object. Basically, color and hue are synonyms. The human eye is more sensitive to certain colors than to others, as indicated in Figure 3. This color sensitivity can sometimes be exploited in the design of a task requiring visual performance.

Other attributes of color are brightness and strength [2]. ***Brightness*** indicates the extent to which the color reflects illuminance. Light colors reflect more light than dark colors, and this fact can be used to establish a desired level of contrast between objects in the workplace. Basically, the brightness of an object refers to its luminance, which depends on the amount of light illuminating it and the reflectance of its surface.

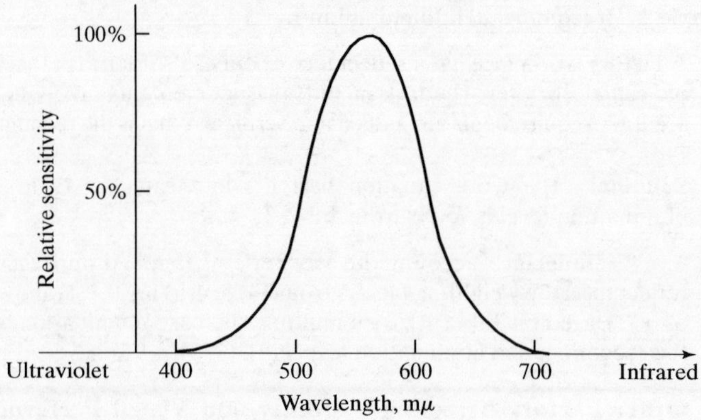

Figure 3 Color sensitivity of the human eye.

The ***strength*** of the color indicates how it is positioned on a scale between pale and vivid. Pale means lack of color and whitish, such as a pale yellow. Vivid means intense and striking, such as a vivid red.

Color can be used to enhance the environmental conditions and comfort level of the workplace. Also, certain colors are associated with certain common meanings or circumstances. For example, red means danger (e.g., stop signs, stop traffic lights, fire alarm boxes, emergency stop buttons on equipment), yellow means caution (e.g., caution traffic light, aisles in buildings), and green means safety (e.g., proceed traffic light, first-aid equipment).

Glare is defined as a harsh, uncomfortably bright light in the field of vision. The bright light may be a source of light or a reflected light from an object. In any case, the brightness is greater than what the eyes have adapted to, causing annoyance and possible loss of visual performance. Three levels of glare can be distinguished, based on their effects on the observer: (1) discomfort glare, in which the observer is annoyed but not necessarily inhibited from performing a visual task; (2) disability glare, in which the observer is annoyed and visual performance is reduced; and (3) blinding glare, in which the glare is temporarily blinding to the observer [9].

1.3 Lighting Systems

The ergonomic objective is to provide the proper amount of lighting for the task. This is accomplished by designing an appropriate lighting system, one that gives sufficient but not too much light for the task at hand. Two terms of interest are lamps and luminaires. The term ***lamp*** refers to a single artificial source of light (e.g., an incandescent lamp). A ***luminaire*** is a complete lighting unit, including one or more lamps, reflectors and/or other pieces of apparatus to distribute the light, and a means to connect it to a power supply.

Lamps. Lamps can be classified into two basic types: (1) incandescent lamps and (2) discharge lamps. ***Incandescent lamps*** operate by electrically heating a filament that produces radiant energy, some of which is in the visible spectrum. The common material

TABLE 5 Characteristics of Selected Lamp Types

Lamp Type	Luminous Efficacy (lm/W)	Lamp Life (hr)	Color Rendering (CRI)	Typical Applications
Incandescent (tungsten)	10–20	750–2000	97–100	Residential
Fluorescent	60–110	9000–20,000	50–95	Commercial
High-pressure mercury (vapor)	30–60	16,000–24,000	15–50	Industrial, agriculture
High-pressure mercury (halide)	50–110	3000–20,000	65–95	Industrial, commercial
High-pressure sodium	60–140	10,000–24,000	20–70	Industrial, road

Source: Compiled from [2] and other sources.

for the filament is tungsten. ***Discharge lamps*** produce light by means of an electric discharge in a gas. Discharge lamps are generally more complicated (and expensive) because they require special controls to provide the conditions under which the discharge is initiated and sustained. The most common discharge lamp is the fluorescent lamp, usually in the form of a glass tube whose inner surface is coated with fluorescent material and which contains mercury vapor whose bombardment by electrons causes light emission.

The following characteristics about lamps are important in lighting design: (1) luminous efficacy, (2) lamp life, and (3) color rendering. Luminous efficacy and lamp life are economic considerations, and color rendering is a quality feature. Typical values of these characteristics for various types of lamps along with common applications of each are presented in Table 5.

Luminous efficacy refers to the efficiency of the lamp—that is, its capacity to convert electrical power into luminous power. The measure of efficacy is lumens per watt (lm/W). ***Lamp life*** is how long the type of lamp is expected to last, expressed in hours. Note that there are variations and trade-offs within a given type. For example, a long-life incandescent bulb lasts longer than a conventional incandescent bulb, but its light output (lm) is lower during that life.

Color rendering refers to the lamp's capability to illuminate objects in their true colors. Lamp types vary in this capability. The issue is important for tasks in which colors must be identified or compared. The most widely used measure for color rendering is the ***color rendering index*** (CRI). The highest CRI score is 100, which is obtained in daylight. As the CRI score of a given lamp type decreases, this indicates a reduction in the lamp's color rendering capability. Unfortunately, there is somewhat of a negative correlation between CRI and luminous efficacy, as shown by the data in Table 5. An incandescent lamp gives very good color rendering, but its efficiency is quite poor.

Luminaires. Luminaires consist of one or more lamps, together with the other hardware components needed to complete the lighting unit. Multiple luminaires are usually required to make up a complete lighting system for a room in a facility. Modern lighting systems often include controls to alter the lighting levels, depending on time of day and function of the room. For example, less artificial light may be needed on a sunny day when there is plenty of natural light entering through the windows.

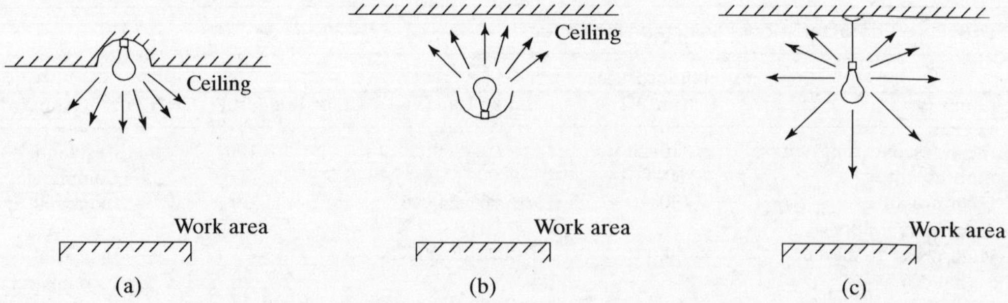

Figure 4 Types of luminaires: (a) direct lighting, (b) indirect lighting, and (c) combination of direct and indirect lighting.

Luminaires can be classified according to the proportions of light that are emitted above or below the fixture itself. Three major categories are illustrated in Figure 4. Direct lighting shines downward, providing high direct illumination of the work area. However, glare may be a problem. Indirect lighting shines on the ceiling. Because the ceiling is usually a color with a high reflectance (e.g., white), most of the light is reflected downward and diffused to reduce glare.

2 THE AUDITORY ENVIRONMENT AND NOISE

Auditory stimuli are the second most important means by which humans receive information. Together, visual and sound stimuli account for 95% or more of a person's information input. However, in addition to its information value, the auditory environment often includes ***noise***, which can be defined simply as unwanted sound. In this section, we discuss the auditory environment, with particular attention to noise.

2.1 The Effects of Noise on Humans

The possible effects of noise on a human being are both physiological and psychological. The effects include (1) distraction, (2) negative emotions such as annoyance, frustration, anger, and fear, (3) interference with conversation, thinking, and other cognitive processes, (4) interference with sleeping, (5) temporary hearing loss, and (6) permanent hearing loss.

Noise Factors that Affect Humans. The two physical attributes of sound are frequency, which is perceived by the listener as pitch, and intensity, which is perceived as loudness. Noise is characterized by the same attributes. In assessing the potentially negative effects of noise on human performance, intensity is the more important of the two. Industrial noise is usually ***broadband***, meaning that it is composed of a wide range of frequencies, so the importance of frequency is reduced.

In addition to intensity, the elapsed time of the exposure to the noise is also important. Increased duration of exposure to a loud noise increases the risk of hearing damage. Thus, we have two factors that are of primary concern in assessing the effects of noise on the human worker: (1) ***intensity*** of the noise and (2) ***duration of exposure*** to the noise source.

Intensity and duration of exposure can both be measured. In the case of a continuous noise of constant intensity, duration is simply a time measurement. Sound intensity is measured using a ***sound level meter***, which is basically a sound pressure meter that converts the reading to decibels. Most meters are equipped to allow the user to set one of several different scales when taking a sound pressure measurement. The two most important scales are designated A and C by the American National Standards Institute (ANSI). The difference between them is that they electronically weight certain frequencies of the sound pressure signal differently. The A-scale is weighted to approximate the hearing response of the human ear, and for this reason it is the most commonly used scale and the one used by the Occupational Safety and Health Agency to establish noise level standards. The decibel units for the A-scale are dBA. The C-scale is intended to weight all frequencies the same.

Another factor that characterizes noise is whether the sound is continuous or noncontinuous. Continuous noise has a fairly constant intensity over time, such as the collection of sounds that would be produced by the steady operation of machinery in a factory. Noncontinuous noise varies in intensity over time. It includes the following categories: (1) intermittent noise, such as machinery that operates with an on-off cycle, (2) impact noise, as in the operation of a drop forge hammer, and (3) impulse noise, as created by gunfire [9].

Physiological Effects of Noise. When a person is exposed to a sudden loud noise (e.g., impulse noise), the reaction is called ***startle response***, which causes spontaneous muscle contractions (e.g., clenching of fists), blinking or closing the eyes, and head-jerk movements [3, 9]. Other physiological effects include slower and heavier breathing, variations in heartbeat rate, and dilation of eye pupils. Startle response occurs quickly, and its symptoms dissipate rapidly. Upon repeated exposure to the same noise burst, the magnitude of the response becomes less and less severe. Startle response causes distraction and disruption of a person's current activity, and although its physiological effects are transient, it can elicit annoyance and other negative emotions.

Of particular concern in ergonomics is hearing loss due to noise, which can be classified into three types: (1) temporary threshold shift, (2) noise-induced permanent threshold shift, and (3) acoustic trauma [4]. ***Temporary threshold shift*** (TTS) is a hearing impairment of relative short duration (e.g., minutes or hours). The effect is reversible so that full hearing capability is gradually restored. The term threshold shift refers to the amount of hearing loss, measured in decibels. For example, a person may suffer a 20 dB threshold shift (hearing loss) 2 minutes after being exposed to a loud noise over a certain period of time. As time proceeds, the dB loss gradually decreases until hearing is fully recovered (threshold shift = 0 dB). The amount of threshold shift in TTS increases as the intensity and duration of the noise is increased.

Noise-induced permanent threshold shift (NIPTS)[3] is a hearing loss that is not reversible. Full hearing is never recovered. NIPTS results from long-term exposure to

[3]The simpler term permanent threshold shift (PTS) is also used. However, a permanent hearing loss can occur due to reasons other than noise. For example, presbycusis is a permanent hearing loss (threshold shift) that results from the aging process. The term noise-induced permanent threshold shift clarifies that the reason for the hearing loss is noise.

noise levels above about 90 dB. The damage takes place in the cochlea of the inner ear, which contains the microscopic auditory hair cells. High-intensity noise exposure over extended periods of time gradually destroys these sensory cells. The net effect of the permanent damage is a threshold shift expressed in decibels. Thus, NIPTS does not imply complete deafness; it means a reduction in auditory capability. The amount of hearing loss depends on the intensity level, and it varies among individuals.

The third type of hearing loss is ***acoustic trauma***, caused by a single exposure to a very high intensity noise of short duration, such as that which results from an impact or impulse noise like a gunshot or explosion. Depending on the intensity of the noise, the hearing loss can be temporary or permanent.

2.2 Permissible Noise Levels

Noise level standards set by the Occupational Safety and Health Administration are designed to avoid the hearing loss effects discussed above. The standards specify the permissible duration of exposure for each of various sound pressure levels using the dBA scale. A partial listing of the standards is presented in Table 6. The values indicate that a continuous sound pressure level of 80 dBA is acceptable and requires no abatement steps. A value of 85 dBA is customarily used as the threshold level at which employers should begin to take action to control the noise. A sound pressure level of 90 dBA must be limited to 8 hours of exposure, and any level above 90 means that noise abatement procedures of some kind are required (Section 2.3).

For sound pressure levels not given in Table 6, the permissible duration of exposure for a given sound level can be calculated using the following equation:

$$T_{pde} = \frac{8}{2^{0.2(SPL-90)}} \tag{8}$$

where T_{pde} = permissible duration of exposure, hr; and SPL = sound pressure level, dBA.

It is not uncommon for a worker to be simultaneously exposed to several different noise sources, each with its own sound intensity. The combined effect of these sources, expressed as an equivalent sound pressure level, can be obtained using the following equation:

$$SPL_{tot} = 10 \log_{10} \sum_i 10^{0.1 SPL_i} \tag{9}$$

where SPL_{tot} = total sound pressure level of multiple noise sources, dBA; SPL_i = sound pressure level of noise source i, dBA; and i = a subscript to distinguish different sources.

TABLE 6 Permissible Exposure Durations for Various Sound Pressure Levels (OSHA Standard)

Sound Pressure Level	Daily Duration	Sound Pressure Level	Daily Duration
80 dBA	32 hr	95 dBA	4 hr
85 dBA	16 hr	100 dBA	2 hr
90 dBA	8 hr	105 dBA	1 hr
92 dBA	6 hr	110 dBA	30 min

Example 3 Total Sound Pressure Level of Two Noise Sources

A worker is exposed to two noise sources, one at 87 dBA and the other at 89 dBA. Determine (a) the total sound pressure level of the two sources and (b) the permissible duration of exposure for this sound pressure level.

Solution **(a)** The calculation of total sound pressure level is made as follows:

$$SPL_{tot} = 10 \log (10^{8.7} + 10^{8.9}) = 10 \log_{10} (501{,}187{,}234 + 794{,}328{,}235)$$

$$= 10 \log_{10} (1{,}295{,}515{,}469) = 10(9.112) = 91.12 \text{ dBA}$$

(b) The permissible duration of exposure for this sound pressure level is determined as follows:

$$T_{pde} = \frac{8}{2^{0.2(91.12-90)}} = \frac{8}{2^{0.224}} = \frac{8}{1.168} = 6.85\text{hr}$$

Comment: Note in part (a) that although neither of the two noise sources exceeds the OSHA standard of 90 dBA, their combined effect does exceed the standard. Part (b) indicates the allowable duration of exposure to this combination of noise sources. ■

Another common situation is for a worker to be exposed to several different noise sources (with different sound pressure levels) for different durations throughout a given workday. The combined effect of these different sound intensities can be summarized in the term ***noise dose***—a percentage value that combines several noise components into one measure, such that any value above 100% exceeds the OSHA permissible limit. A noise dose value that is less than or equal to 100 is acceptable. The noise dose is calculated as follows:

$$ND = 100 \sum_j T_{exj}/T_{pdej} \tag{10}$$

where ND = noise dose; T_{exj} = exposure time at a given sound pressure level during period j, hr; T_{pdej} = permissible duration of exposure at the given sound pressure level, hr; and the summation is carried out over all periods during the shift.

The calculated value of noise dose can be converted to a ***time-weighted average sound pressure level*** (SPL_{twa}). This corresponds to the constant value of sound pressure level that is equivalent to the collection of intensities to which the worker is exposed during the workday. The time-weighted average sound pressure level is calculated from the noise dose as follows:

$$SPL_{twa} = 16.61 \log_{10}(ND/100) + 90 \tag{11}$$

where SPL_{twa} = time-weighted average sound pressure level, dBA; and ND = noise dose computed from equation (10).

Example 4 Noise Dose and Time-Weighted Average Sound Pressure Level

During an 8-hour shift, a worker is exposed to 85 dBA for 5 hr and 92 dBA for 3 hr. Determine (a) the noise dose for these two exposures and (b) the time-weighted average sound pressure level for the 8-hour day.

Solution **(a)** According to Table 6, the permissible duration for the 85 dBA exposure is 16 hr, and the permissible duration for the 92 dBA exposure is 6 hr. The noise dose is computed using equation (10) as follows:

$$ND = 100\left(\frac{5}{16} + \frac{3}{6}\right) = 100(0.3125 + 0.50) = 81.25$$

This is well below the limit of 100%.

(b) The time-weighted average sound pressure level for the 8-hour day is determined using equation (11):

$$SPL_{twa} = 16.61 \log_{10}(81.25/100) + 90 = 16.61 \log_{10}(0.8125) + 90$$
$$= 16.61(-0.090177) + 90 = 90 - 1.5 = 88.5 \text{ dBA}$$

■

Although the noise dose computation in equation (10) is straightforward, the task of obtaining the necessary data to make the calculation may be inconvenient if the worker is exposed to a variety of noise levels during the shift. For example, if the worker's job requires moving about the facility and encountering many different noise levels, compiling the sound intensity levels (SPL_j) and exposure times (T_{exj}) at each location would be cumbersome. This problem can be addressed by a ***noise dose meter***, which is a portable and inexpensive version of a sound level meter but is designed to measure the accumulated noise dose during the shift. The noise dose meter can be worn by a worker to assess the *ND* value for that worker throughout the work day.

2.3 Noise Control

Given the existence of a noise problem in a given facility, two general approaches can be pursued to address the problem: (1) administrative controls and (2) engineering controls.

Administrative Controls to Avoid Hearing Damage. Administrative controls are directed at managing the exposure durations (T_{exj}) for employees who work in noisy environments by scheduling the exposure times to achieve a total noise dose less than 100%. The scheduling involves balancing the times spent in noisy environments against offsetting times spent in quiet environments, as indicated by the noise dose equation, equation (10).

Another form of administrative control involves education and training of workers about the potential hazards of intense noise and the importance of using the engineering controls that have been installed for noise abatement. Although the importance of administrative noise control must not be minimized, it is generally agreed that the more desirable and potentially more effective approach is through engineering controls.

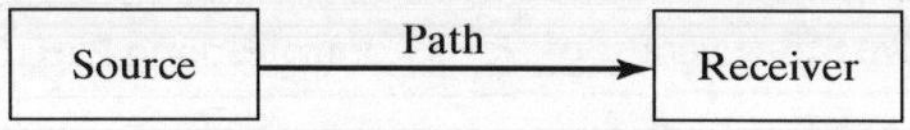

Figure 5 The source-path-receiver viewpoint in the design of engineering controls for noise abatement.

Engineering Controls for Noise Abatement. Engineering controls involve various techniques and approaches that can be implemented to reduce noise intensity levels in the work environment. The viewpoint taken in the design of engineering controls for noise abatement is that there are three regions where the noise level can be reduced: (1) at the source, (2) at the receiver, and (3) along the path between the source and the receiver. This source-path-receiver viewpoint is illustrated in Figure 5.

Noise control at the source involves redesigning the machine or process that generates the noise. Reducing the noise level emanating from the source is usually the most effective approach to abatement, but also it is usually the most difficult and expensive approach. The machine or process has been designed to accomplish a given function, and that function may be inherently noisy. Examples of inherently noisy machines include jackhammers, riveting machines, forge hammers, and stamping presses. It is difficult to design these machines for quieter operation without impairing their productivity. Some suggestions for engineering noise controls at the source are listed in Table 7.

Engineering controls at the receiver means providing ear protection for the worker who is located in a noisy environment. The types of ear protection equipment include earplugs, earmuffs, and helmets. Earplugs are made of pliable material (e.g., foamed polymer) that can be fitted into the auditory canal (outer ear passage) to reduce the sound that reaches the middle ear and inner ear mechanisms. Earmuffs cover the complete outer ear to reduce noise. Helmets fit over the head and ears, in some cases completely enclosing the head (e.g., space helmet). Earplugs and earmuffs are often

TABLE 7 Possible Engineering Controls at Source of Noise

Machine or Process	Engineering Control at Source
Fans and blowers	Increase the size of the fan or blower so that it moves the same amount of fluid (e.g., air) at lower rotational speed. This generally reduces noise output.
Pneumatic tools	Substitute hydraulic or electric drive motors that operate more quietly.
Vibrating machinery	Provide better balancing of the components. Such noise often results from an imbalance of rotating members.
Vibrating machinery	Use resilient couplings and mountings for vibrating mechanisms to dampen the vibrations and isolate them from surrounding machine components.
Impact equipment such as stamping presses and forge hammers	Move the equipment onto rubber mounts to reduce the transmission, if possible. The impact noise of this kind of equipment is often partially transmitted through the floor of the plant.

Source: Compiled from [3, 7].

TABLE 8 Relative Effectiveness of Noise Controls Along Path Between Source and Receiver

Type of Noise Control Along Path	Threshold Shift (dBA)
Original noisy machine with no controls	0 dBA
Vibration isolators between machine and floor	2 dBA
Baffle between machine and receiver	5 dBA
Rigid sealed enclosure around the machine	20–25 dBA
Rigid sealed enclosure plus vibration isolators	30–35 dBA
Enclosure with absorption material plus vibration isolators	40–45 dBA
Double-walled enclosure with absorption material plus vibration isolators	60–80 dBA

Source: Compiled from [4].

combined to increase the protection level over either one alone. All of these ear protection controls are considered less satisfactory than engineering controls at the source. One of the reasons for this is the occasional lack of worker compliance in using them.

The third application area for noise abatement using engineering controls is along the path between the source and the receiver. The approach includes implementation of the following means of separating the source from the receiver: enclosures that surround the noise source, barriers to transmission (e.g., baffles located between source and receiver), vibration isolators (e.g., rubber mounts between the machine and the floor), and sound absorbing materials (e.g., porous materials such as felt, carpets, draperies, and curtains) to reduce reverberation of the noise in the room. The relative effectiveness of these noise controls that separate the source from the receiver can be seen in the data listed in Table 8. The noise reduction is expressed as threshold shift in decibels (dBA).

3 CLIMATE CONTROL IN THE WORK ENVIRONMENT

The climate in the work environment is an important factor in determining the physical comfort of workers, and their comfort affects job satisfaction and performance. Although the word climate usually refers to outside weather conditions, our current interest is in the climatic conditions that are encountered in the workplace environment, whether it is indoors or outdoors. There are four primary variables that define climate: (1) air temperature, (2) humidity, usually taken as relative humidity, (3) air movement, and (4) radiation from surrounding objects, including the sun. The most comfortable working environment (sometimes called the ***comfort zone***) seems to be in the temperature range between 19°C and 26°C (66°F and 79°F) at a relative humidity of 50% and slow air movement of about 0.2 m/s (0.64 ft/sec) [8].

The four variables strongly affect not only the comfort level of workers, but also their physical well-being. The heat balance and thermoregulation mechanisms that operate to control temperature in the human body can have debilitating and sometimes fatal consequences that occur when the body temperature deviates from its normal value of 37°C (98.6°F). In the current section, we discuss interventions that can be introduced to protect the worker from environmental conditions that might cause body temperatures to rise above or fall below normal (heat stress and cold stress, respectively).

3.1 Heat Stress

Hot working environments occur naturally in many manual jobs in foundries (e.g., metal casting), boiler operations (e.g., steam and power generation), basic metals industries (e.g., iron- and steelmaking, aluminum production), hot working of metals (e.g., hot forging, hot rolling), heat treatment of metals and glass, certain chemical operations, and outdoor construction in the summertime. These are the most common jobs in which heat stress is a problem.

Heat stress occurs when the body takes in and/or produces more heat than it gives off, thus raising the core body temperature according to the thermal balance equation. That equation indicates that body temperature can increase due to various combinations of high air temperature (which reduces convection heat loss), high humidity (which reduces evaporation from sweating), high radiation heat input, high energy expenditure (due to physical workload), and high metabolism. In fact, metabolism increases as body temperature rises. The metabolic rate increases about 10% for every 1°C rise in body temperature. The increase in metabolic rate generates additional body heat, further raising the body temperature. The potential result is an out-of-control cycle that feeds on itself and can be fatal.

Depending on severity, heat stress can result in the following forms of illness: (1) ***heat rash***, (also known as ***miliaria***) in which areas of the skin erupt into red or white bumps due to inflammation of the sweat glands; (2) ***heat cramps***, which are spasms of the muscles used in manual work (or other physical activity) and associated with low salt due to sweating; (3) ***heat exhaustion***, which is also associated with low salt and whose symptoms include weakness in the muscles, nausea, dizziness, and fainting; and (4) ***heatstroke***, which is a serious failure of the body's thermal regulatory system characterized by high fever, dry skin, collapse, and sometimes convulsions and coma [9]. Heatstroke is the most severe of these illnesses; in extreme cases, death can occur.

There are various approaches that can be used to reduce the incidence of heat stress in the work environment. It should first be mentioned that the body's cardiovascular system and sweat glands operate to relieve heat stress. The cardiovascular response is to dilate the blood vessels in the skin and to increase the heart rate, which together have the effect of increasing blood flow from the heated internal regions of the body to the external skin areas. Perspiration produced in the sweat glands removes heat by evaporation. Additional approaches must often be implemented to assist the body in reducing or relieving heat stress. A list of these approaches, which include both administrative and engineering controls, is compiled in Table 9.

3.2 Cold Stress

In a hot environment, a breeze is a blessing, because it removes heat from the body by evaporation of sweat and possibly convection (if the air temperature is cooler than skin temperature). In a cold environment, a breeze also removes heat from the body (mostly by convection and radiation), but this heat removal can cause a drop in body temperature to levels that are physiologically harmful. The combination of air temperature and air movement is captured in the ***windchill index*** (also called the ***windchill factor***), which provides an estimate of the cooling effect of moving air on exposed skin. The index is

TABLE 9 Techniques for Reducing or Relieving Heat Stress

Administrative Controls	Engineering Controls
Encourage workers to drink water, and provide adequate supplies or sources of drinking water.	Provide air conditioning of the workplace, where feasible.
Provide training in work procedures for hot environments and first-aid techniques.	Provide fans to increase air circulation and facilitate removal of heat by evaporation of sweat.
Establish a buddy system. Encourage workers to watch out for each other while working in hot environments.	Reduce humidity with dehumidifiers, which in hot, muggy environments will increase comfort level.
Allow for frequent rest breaks in cool environments.	Shield radiant heat sources in the workplace.
Limit work times in the hot environment.	Provide protective equipment, including vests that are cooled by water, air, or ice.
Reduce rate of working.	Redesign tasks to reduce energy expenditure levels. This might involve introduction of mechanized equipment such as hoists.
Schedule outdoor work during cooler times of the day (e.g., early morning).	
Allow for heat acclimatization. Workers become physically acclimated to working in a hot environment after about 2 weeks of exposure.	

Source: Compiled from [3] and [9].

most commonly expressed as the ***equivalent windchill temperature***, which indicates how a given combination of actual air temperature and wind velocity would feel as a calm air temperature. As wind velocity increases at a given actual air temperature, the effect is that the equivalent windchill temperature gets colder and colder. In November 2001, the U.S. National Weather Service and the Meteorological Services of Canada (the Canadian equivalent of the NWS) adopted the following formula for determining the equivalent windchill temperature based on the actual air temperature and the wind velocity:

$$EWT = 35.74 + 0.6215\,T_a - 35.75\,v^{0.16} + 0.4275\,T_a(v^{0.16}) \quad (12)$$

where EWT = equivalent windchill temperature, °F; T_a = actual air temperature, °F; and v = wind velocity, miles/hr. This formula is based on the U.S. Customary System of units. To convert to the International System of units, one should note that (temperature in °F) = 1.8 (temperature in °C) + 32°F, and (wind speed in miles/hr) = 1.60934(wind speed in km/h). Table 10 presents a selection of equivalent windchill temperatures for various combinations of actual air temperature and wind speed.

Cold work environments are associated with various job situations such as those in poorly heated buildings, in refrigerated warehouses (cold storage), and in construction and other types of outdoor work in the wintertime. These are commonly the jobs in which cold stress is a problem.

Cold stress occurs when the body gives off more heat than it takes in and/or produces, thus lowering the core body temperature in the thermal balance equation. The physiological responses to a reduced body temperature are vasoconstriction and shivering. ***Vasoconstriction*** is a narrowing of the blood vessels in the skin, especially in the extremities (e.g., fingers and toes). This serves to keep warm blood

TABLE 10 Equivalent Windchill Temperatures for Various Combinations of Actual Air Temperature and Wind Velocity

Wind Speed, km/h (miles/hr)	Actual Air Temperature, °C (°F)					
	−1 (30)	−7 (20)	−12 (10)	−18 (0)	−23 (−10)	−29 (−20)
Calm 0 (0)	−1 (30)	−7 (20)	−12 (10)	−18 (0)	−23 (−10)	−29 (−20)
16 (10)	−6 (21)	−13 (9)	−20 (−4)	−27 (−16)	−33 (−28)	−41 (−41)
32 (20)	−8 (17)	−16 (4)	−23 (−9)	−30 (−22)	−37 (−35)	−44 (−48)
48 (30)	−9 (15)	−17 (1)	−24 (−12)	−32 (−26)	−39 (−39)	−47 (−53)
64 (40)	−11 (13)	−18 (−1)	−26 (−15)	−34 (−29)	−42 (−43)	−49 (−57)

Source: Adapted from National Weather Service, based on the revised formula adopted in November 2001.

away from these areas that are exposed to the cold, and the reduced blood flow increases the insulating capacity of the skin. Consequently, the extremities quickly lose heat to the surrounding air and become significantly colder than the core body temperature. ***Shivering*** consists of a rapid quivering or shaking of the muscles, which increases metabolism to generate body heat.

These physiological responses are of limited value in extremely cold environments, and the two conditions associated with severe cold stress are frostbite and hypothermia. ***Frostbite*** occurs when the tissue freezes and ice crystals form in the tissue cells. It most commonly occurs in the hands and feet. In the extreme, frostbite can lead to gangrene in the affected extremities. With regard to the equivalent windchill temperature values compiled in Table 10, it should be noted that frostbite occurs in 15 min or less at windchill values of −28°C (−18°F) or lower.

Hypothermia occurs when the core body temperature is at or below 35°C (95°F), which results in diminished physical and mental capacity.

A combination of measures is available to help the body resist frostbite, hypothermia, and the general physical discomfort associated with a cold working environment. A list of these measures is compiled in Table 11. Many of these approaches are counterparts of the techniques used to address heat stress.

One of the most effective controls for reducing or relieving cold stress is the most obvious: proper clothing. Clothing provides insulation of the body from the cold environment, reducing convection and radiation losses. In general, the insulation value of clothing is proportional to its thickness. Type of fabric (e.g., wool, cotton) is less important than thickness. The insulating qualities derive from the air that is captured within the weave of the fabric.

An important principle in dressing for cold environments is ***layering***, which consists of the use of multiple layers of clothing to achieve the appropriate level of insulation against the cold. The proper application of the layering principle in the work environment is to use a number of thin layers rather than one or two thick layers. In this way, clothing layers can be added or subtracted (1) to achieve a proper balance between the environment and the metabolic heat production of the work activity and (2) to avoid sweating.

TABLE 11 Techniques for Reducing or Relieving Cold Stress

Administrative Controls	Engineering Controls
Provide training in work procedures for cold environments and first-aid techniques.	Provide proper heating of the building, space heaters when the entire building cannot be feasibly heated, use of radiant heat sources in the workplace.
Establish a buddy system. Encourage workers to watch out for each other while working in cold environments.	Proper clothing.
Limit work times in the cold environment.	Establish rewarming rooms, a warm facility where workers can go to recover body warmth after exposure to extremely cold environments.
Schedule outdoor work during warmer times of the day (e.g., during sunshine hours).	Provide gloves. Gloves help to keep the hands warm, but they may impede dexterity.
Allow for cold acclimatization. Acclimation to cold does not seem to be as effective as heat acclimatization.	Provide partial gloves, which leave portions of the fingers exposed to improve dexterity.
Allow frequent breaks to warm hands.	
Rotate jobs.	

Source: Compiled mostly from [8] and [9].

REFERENCES

[1] Bensel, C. K., and W. R. Santee. "Climate and Clothing." Pp. 909–34 in *Handbook of Human Factors and Ergonomics* 2nd ed., edited by G. Salvendy. New York: Wiley, 1997.

[2] Boyce, P. R. "Illumination." Pp. 858–90 in *Handbook of Human Factors and Ergonomics*. 2nd ed., edited by G. Salvendy. New York: Wiley, 1997.

[3] Bridger, R. S. *Introduction to Ergonomics*. 2nd ed. London: Taylor and Francis, 2003.

[4] Crocker, M. J. "Noise." Pp. 790–827 in *Handbook of Human Factors and Ergonomics*. 2nd ed., edited by G. Salvendy. New York: Wiley, 1997.

[5] Konz, S., and S. Johnson. *Work Design, Industrial Ergonomics*. 5th ed. Scottsdale, AZ: Holcomb Hathaway Publishers, 2000.

[6] Kroemer, K. H. E., H. B. Kroemer, and K. E. Kroemer-Elbert. *Ergonomics: How to Design for Ease and Efficiency*. Upper Saddle River, NJ: Prentice Hall, 1994.

[7] Niebel, B. W., and A. Freivalds. *Methods, Standards, and Work Design*. 11th ed. New York: McGraw-Hill, 2003.

[8] Pulat, B. M. *Fundamentals of Industrial Ergonomics*. Upper Saddle River, NJ: Prentice Hall, 1992.

[9] Sanders, M. S., and E. J. McCormick. *Human Factors in Engineering Design*. 7th ed. New York: McGraw-Hill, 1993.

[10] Wickens, C. D., J. Lee, Y. Liu, and S. G. Becker. *An Introduction to Human Factors Engineering*. 2nd ed. Upper Saddle River, NJ: Pearson/Prentice Hall, 2004.

REVIEW QUESTIONS

1 What does the word *photometry* mean?

2 What is luminous flux and what are its units of measure?

3 What is the difference between illuminance and luminance?

4 What does the term *visibility* mean?

5 What is brightness contrast?

6 What are the two basic types of lamps?

7 What does the term *luminous efficacy* mean?

8 In the auditory sense, what is noise?

9 What are some of the effects of noise on humans?

10 What are the two factors of primary concern in assessing the effects of noise on human workers?

11 What is noise-induced permanent threshold shift?

12 What is the difference between administrative controls and engineering controls in avoiding hearing damage?

13 What are some of the ways of reducing the noise along the path between the source and the receiver?

14 What are the four primary variables that define climate?

15 What is heat stress?

16 What are some of the illnesses that can result from heat stress?

17 What is cold stress?

18 What are the two physiological responses to cold stress of the human body?

19 What are some of the administrative controls for reducing or relieving cold stress?

20 What is meant by the term *layering* in dressing for cold environments?

PROBLEMS

Visual Environment and Lighting

1 An isotropic light source has an intensity of 100 cd. Located 5 m away is a wall that has a reflectance of 0.75. Calculate (a) the total luminous flux emanating from the light source, (b) the illuminance of the wall, and (c) the luminance emitted by the reflected light.

2 An isotropic light source has an intensity of 250 cd. Located 3 m away is an object whose surface has a reflectance of 0.35. Calculate (a) the total luminous flux emanating from the light source, (b) the illuminance of the surface of the object, and (c) the luminance emitted by the reflected light.

3 A ceiling lamp (assume a point source of light) has a luminous intensity of 200 cd and its distance above an office desk is 1.5 m. It provides direct lighting of the desk surface, which is medium gray and has a reflectance of 0.55. The worksheets being processed are white (reflectance = 0.80) with black lettering (reflectance = 0.08). The average size of the lettering is 2.5 mm, and the worker's eyes are about 300 mm away from the worksheets. Determine (a) the illuminance striking the desk surface, (b) the luminance of the desk surface, (c) the contrast between the worksheets and the lettering, and (d) the visual angle subtended by the lettering as seen by the worker.

4 A light source (assume a point source of light) with a luminous intensity of 160 cd is suspended 600 mm above an inspection worktable, thus providing direct lighting of the worktable surface, which is light gray in color, with a reflectance of 75%. The work parts being inspected are dark brown, with a reflectance of 12%, and circular in shape, with a diameter of 25 mm. A machine vision camera is located 450 mm away from the work parts during the inspection procedure. Determine (a) the illuminance striking the table surface, (b) the luminance of the table surface, (c) the contrast between the workparts and the table surface, and (d) the visual angle of the part as it is seen by the camera.

5 A workplace has a reflectance of 75%, and the work is performed by a man whose age is 60 years. The contrast between the objects in the workplace and the background is medium. The task involves assembly work requiring good hand-eye coordination. The speed and accuracy requirement is critical. What is the recommended illumination level for this task?

6 A worker is filling out a report at a workbench illuminated by a 200-cd source located 750 mm overhead. The report form is white paper (85% reflectance), and the inspector is writing with black ink (10% reflectance). Determine (a) the illumination on the form, (b) luminance of the form, and (c) contrast in the writing task. (d) Assuming that a worker is 35 years old and that speed and accuracy are important but not critical, is the illumination for this task sufficient? If not, what illumination level is required?

7 An office room is currently illuminated by ten 75-watt incandescent lamps, each having a luminous efficacy of 15 lumens/watt. A proposal has been submitted to replace the incandescent lighting with a sufficient number of fluorescent lamps to provide the same light flux in the room. The fluorescent lamps are 40 watts and have a luminous efficacy of 80 lumens/watt. (a) Determine the number of fluorescent lamps that would provide the same or slightly greater illuminance as the incandescent lights. (b) Compare the daily electric power costs of the two lighting systems if they operated 12 hours per day and electrical power cost is 7 cents per kW-hr.

8 The inspection department in a factory is currently illuminated by eight overhead incandescent lamps with reflectors. Each lamp is 100 watts and has a luminous efficacy of 16 lumens/watt. It is proposed that the incandescent lighting be replaced with three fluorescent lamps rated at 40 watts. The luminous efficacy of each fluorescent lamp is 85 lumens/watt. Compare (a) the illuminance levels and (b) annual electricity costs of the two alternatives, given that they will operate three shifts (24 hr/day), 250 days/year, and power cost is 6.5 cents per kW-hr. (c) Each incandescent lamp has a lamp life of 1500 hr and costs $0.60. Each fluorescent lamp has a lamp life of 15,000 hr and costs $6.00. Determine the annual cost of lamps for the two alternatives.

Auditory Environment and Noise

9 A worker is exposed to two noise sources, one at 86 dBA and the other at 90 dBA. Determine (a) the total sound pressure level of the two sources and (b) the permissible duration of exposure for this sound pressure level.

10 During an 8-hour shift, a worker is exposed to 85 dBA for 4 hours and 95 dBA for 4 hours. Determine (a) the noise dose for these two exposures and (b) the time-weighted average sound pressure level for the 8-hour day.

11 During a given work shift of 8 hours, a worker is exposed to two coexisting sources of noise for 5 hours, one at 85 dBA and the other at 88 dBA. For the remaining 3 hours, he is exposed to one noise source of 92 dBA. Determine whether this exposure level exceeds the OSHA permissible noise exposures.

12 During a given work shift of 8 hours, a worker is exposed to two coexisting sources of noise for 3 hours, one at 87 dBA and the other at 89 dBA. For the remaining 5 hours, he is exposed to one noise source of 90 dBA. Determine whether this exposure level exceeds the OSHA permissible noise exposures.

13 During a given work shift of 8 hours, a worker is exposed to three coexisting sources of noise for 6 hours, one at 80 dBA, another at 85 dBA, and the third at 90 dBA. For the remaining 2 hours, he is exposed to one noise source of 95 dBA. Determine (a) the noise dose of this exposure level, (b) the time-weighted average sound pressure level, and (c) whether this exposure level exceeds the OSHA permissible noise exposures.

14 A worker is exposed to two coexisting sources of noise during the first 4 hours of an 8-hour work shift, one at 86 dBA and the other at 88 dBA. During the other 4 hours, he is exposed to one noise source of 92 dBA. Determine (a) the noise dose of these three sources and (b) the time-weighted average sound pressure level. (c) What are some steps that management might take to reduce the noise exposure level of the worker? Name three.

15 A worker is currently exposed to two coexisting sources of noise during an 8-hour work shift, one at 83 dBA and the other at 86 dBA. The noise results from two production machines that are near the worker. Management wants to install a third production machine that will expose the worker to an additional noise source of 92 dBA. Determine (a) the noise dose of these three sources and (b) the time-weighted average sound pressure level. (c) Management realizes that the third noise source (from the third machine) must be reduced to satisfy OSHA standards. Determine to what dBA level must the noise level of the third machine be reduced in order to satisfy OSHA noise dose requirements. (d) What are some steps that management might take to reduce the noise exposure level of the worker if the third machine is installed? Name three.

16 A worker is currently exposed to two coexisting sources of noise during an 8-hour work shift, one at 85 dBA and the other at 87 dBA. The noise results from two turbines located near the worker. A proposal has been made to install a third turbine that will expose the worker to an additional noise source of 91 dBA, but only for 2 hours of the 8-hour shift. (a) Determine the noise dose of these three noise sources. (b) The noise level from the third turbine must be reduced to satisfy OSHA standards. To what dBA level must the noise level of the third turbine be reduced in order to satisfy OSHA noise dose requirements?

Climate

17 Determine the equivalent windchill temperature in degrees Fahrenheit if the actual air temperature is 35°F and the wind is blowing at 15 miles/hr.

18 On a cold day in January in Fairbanks, Alaska, the actual air temperature is minus 30°F, the wind velocity is 25 miles/hr, and it is dark outside. Determine the equivalent windchill temperature in degrees Fahrenheit.

19 Compute the equivalent windchill temperature in degrees centigrade for a location in the Austrian Alps where the actual air temperature is minus 5°C and the wind is blowing at 25 km/h.

Occupational Safety and Health

One of the important goals of ergonomics and human factors is to provide a safe workplace. Safety and a healthful working environment are not only desirable social objectives; they are also a significant cost issue for industry and government. Consider the following:[1]

- Each day, an average of 16 workers die from injuries that occurred while working. This amounts to approximately 5000 lives lost per year due to occupational injuries.
- These deaths and injuries are estimated to cost society more than $100 billion per year, not to mention the personal upheavals and tragedies inflicted upon the families involved.
- Each day, an average of 9000 workers in the United States suffer injuries on the job. This amounts to nearly 5 million workers per year.
- The number of workdays lost due to occupational injuries is between 50 million and 100 million per year.
- Each day, an average of 137 workers die from work-related diseases. This adds up to approximately 50,000 lives lost per year due to occupational illnesses.

[1]Compiled from Web sites for Bureau of Labor Statistics (www.bls.gov), Occupational Safety and Health Administration (www.osha.gov), and National Institute for Occupational Safety and Health (www.cdc.gov/niosh), based on 2002 data.

Although occupational safety and occupational health are related topics, they should be distinguished. ***Occupational safety*** is concerned with the avoidance of industrial accidents and in particular accidents that cause injury or fatality. These accidents are one-time events. The goal in ergonomics is to understand how and why they occur and to undertake steps to prevent them. ***Occupational health*** is concerned with avoiding diseases and disorders that are induced by exposures to materials or conditions in the workplace. These sicknesses and ailments do not generally occur immediately but instead develop after prolonged periods of exposure to the materials or conditions. The effects of the exposure are cumulative.

Our chapter begins with a discussion of industrial accidents and injuries: what causes them, and what steps can be taken to reduce their frequency and severity. The second section deals with disorders and diseases that result from exposures in the workplace. Next we review the important laws that have been enacted in the area of industrial safety and health. The federal agency that is most directly concerned with industrial safety and health is the Occupational Safety and Health Administration (OSHA). Finally, we define some of the measurements that are used to compile statistics about occupational safety and health.

1 INDUSTRIAL ACCIDENTS AND INJURIES

An ***industrial accident*** is an unexpected and unintentional event that disrupts work procedures and has the potential to cause damage to property and injury or death to workers. To be classified as an accident, the event does not have to actually cause damage, injury, or death; it only has to have the potential for these consequences. The objective of an occupational safety program is to reduce the incidence of accidents by reducing the hazards that precipitate them. A ***hazard*** is a condition or set of conditions that has the potential for causing an accident or other harmful outcome. The ***danger*** posed by a hazard is the relative exposure or liability to injury, death, and/or damage from that hazard. For example, a railroad crossing is a hazard, but it poses little danger so long as the crossing signal works and drivers pay attention to the signal.

Industrial accidents can cause injuries that are fatal or nonfatal. The Bureau of Labor Statistics maintains statistical records on occupational injuries, illnesses, and fatalities. The rates vary according to industry. A representative listing of fatal and nonfatal injury rates in the United States is compiled in Table 1. In Section 2, we provide a list of industrial illnesses. It should be noted that the statistics in these tables include only private industries (only private industries are covered by OSHA), and so it excludes government occupations, some of which are inherently dangerous (e.g., police, firefighters, military).

The causes of fatal and nonfatal injuries can be identified and classified, and the Bureau of Labor Statistics compiles statistics on the causes. Table 2 lists the major causes. Ranking at the top of the list are transportation incidents (e.g., highway accidents causing death or injury) that occurred during employment. So much industrial commerce involves transportation. Also note that homicides and suicides are high on the list. These are fatal injuries that occurred during work.

TABLE 1 Private Industry Categories with Frequencies of Fatal and Nonfatal Injuries

Industries in Order of Frequency of Fatal Injuries	Fatal Injuries per 100,000 Workers	Industries in Order of Frequency of Nonfatal Injuries	Nonfatal Injuries per 100 Workers
Mining	23.5	Construction	6.9
Agriculture	22.7	Manufacturing	6.4
Construction	12.2	Agriculture	6.0
Transportation	11.3	Transportation	5.8
Manufacturing	3.1	Wholesale, retail trade	5.1
Wholesale, retail trade	2.4	Services	4.3
Services	1.7	Mining	3.8
Finance, insurance, real estate	1.0	Finance, insurance, real estate	1.5

Source: Bureau of Labor Statistics (www.bls.gov), based on 2002 data.

TABLE 2 Causes and Exposures of Fatal and Nonfatal Injuries

Transportation incidents (e.g., collisions)
Overexertion (e.g., back problems from lifting)
Assaults and violent acts (includes homicides and suicides)
Contact with objects and equipment (e.g., struck by objects, compression)
Falls
Exposure to harmful substances and environments (electric shock, temperature extremes, hazardous substances)
Fires and explosions

Why do industrial accidents occur? Three factors are commonly identified in the ergonomics literature as the primary reasons:

- *Human errors.* These factors relate to the worker or workers who are responsible for the operation and make mistakes that are sometimes the direct cause of an industrial accident.
- *Job factors.* This category refers to the kinds of tasks, methods, materials, equipment, and so on that are used in the operation. Some jobs are more dangerous than others.
- *Environmental conditions.* The environment includes lighting, noise, temperature, and other conditions that surround the operation. For example, the dim lighting in a plant made it difficult for a worker to see the obstacle in his path, and he tripped and broke his ankle.

These factors often act in combination, so that the cause of an accident cannot be isolated to a single reason.

In addition to these primary factors, there are organizational variables and management policies that influence the likelihood that an accident will occur in a given company. For example, if management shows little regard for safety in the plant, the company's workforce may develop a culture that disregards hazards, thus increasing the probability of accidents. A model that depicts all of these factors is shown in Figure 1.

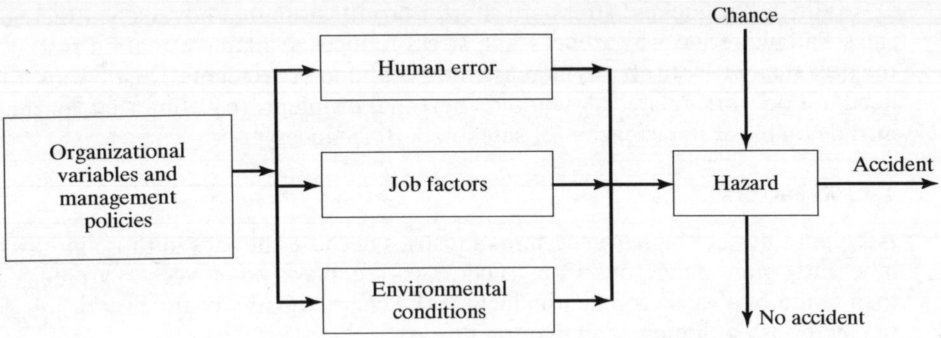

Figure 1 A model depicting the possible factors that contribute to industrial accidents.

1.1 Human Error and Accidents

Human error is often identified as the cause of an industrial accident. In fact, human error probably plays a role in the various other factors identified in Figure 1 that ultimately contribute to an industrial accident. In the preceding example on environmental conditions, the plant engineer who neglected to bring the lighting in the plant up to an acceptable level caused the conditions that resulted in the worker breaking his ankle. Based on this kind of reasoning, it could be argued that all accidents are caused by human error, either directly or indirectly.

In the context of industrial accidents, ***human error*** can be defined as an improper and/or inadvertent human act or decision that has the effect or the potential to reduce effectiveness or safety in the workplace. Human errors can be classified as (1) errors of omission and (2) errors of commission. ***Errors of omission*** occur when a worker fails to take some action that is called for. For example, a home improvement contractor forgets to turn off the circuit breaker to the section of the house that he is rewiring and experiences an electrical shock (defined in Section 1.2). ***Errors of commission*** occur when a worker takes an action that is incorrect. For example, the same home improvement contractor remembers to turn off the circuit breaker, but he switches off the wrong circuit, causing him to suffer an electrical shock.

Among the factors that correlate with accident rates are (1) age, (2) time on the job, (3) fatigue, and (4) stress [9]. Age is a significant factor. Young persons have higher accident rates according to research studies. One can speculate that as people become more mature, they become more cautious and conservative, and their propensity for risk-taking decreases. The net effect is a reduction in accident rates. Contrasting with this trend, however, is that accident rates increase for the elderly, at least in work that requires a high level of physical and cognitive capacity.

Time on the job also correlates with accident rate. A high proportion of industrial accidents occur within the first three years of employment on a new job, with the rate peaking at two to three months [9]. This is explained by the fact that the new worker has completed whatever training program was provided but is still lacking in the experience needed to adequately recognize hazards and select optimal responses.

Finally, fatigue and stress are shorter-term factors that adversely affect accident rates. Fatigue reduces awareness, and stress reduces available attention resources for the task at hand. Both effects increase the likelihood of accidents. The reasons for stress need not be work-related. A worker's personal problems (e.g., financial, marital) may intrude on his or her capacity for safe job performance.

1.2 Job Factors

Accident rates are higher in certain industries because the jobs in those industries are inherently more dangerous. Construction work exposes employees to greater dangers than real estate work. Job factors include the characteristics of the task or job, such as the methods, equipment, and materials used.

Methods. The methods used in a job may be manual, mechanized, or automated, or there may be combinations of these categories for certain tasks. If completely manual, the job may require a high physical workload that leads to physical fatigue, a result that increases the likelihood of human error and accidents. Material handling represents a significant proportion of manual labor tasks in industry (e.g., moving cartons in warehouses, loading and unloading production machines, handling materials at a construction site), and it accounts for a large fraction of occupational accidents and injuries. Common injuries in material handling include (1) musculoskeletal strains and sprains resulting from lifting loads that are too heavy, (2) fractures and bruises caused by loads being dropped and similar mishaps, and (3) lacerations and bruises resulting from efforts to dislodge items in storage and cutting of packaging materials used for items in storage [2].

Mechanized and automated methods can often be used to mitigate the accident and injury rates due to manual material-handling tasks. These methods include the use of powered forklift trucks, conveyors, and cranes. However, material handling by machine carries its own risks. Forklift trucks are driven by humans, and humans commit errors. Aside from the bad driver issues, there are problems with loads not being centered on the forks, overloading, loads stacked too high, and so on. Conveyor systems provide an efficient method to move large amounts of materials in factories, warehouses, and distribution centers. Common causes of conveyor injuries include pinch points between moving and stationary components of the conveyor, loads jamming, loads falling from the conveyor, and workers falling as they try to cross the conveyor. Cranes are used for lifting and moving large loads in a facility, and hazards often arise simply because the loads are heavy. As the vice president of a crane company once said at a material-handling meeting, "We stand behind our product, but we don't stand beneath it."

Equipment. The equipment used by a worker can be the source of hazards in a job. The machine component often plays its role in the worker-machine system through its capacity to apply greater forces and power than a human can apply. The capacity for high forces and power gives rise to equipment hazards. These hazards can be classified into three categories: (1) electrical hazards, (2) mechanical hazards, and (3) temperature hazards.

TABLE 3 Common Effects on Human Body of Various Current Levels for a 1-Second Duration

Current Level (amps)	Effect on Human Body
0.001	Faint tingling sensation.
0.005	Slight shock felt that is disturbing but not painful. Most individuals can let go.
0.006–0.025	Painful shock with loss of muscular control. At the lower end of this range is the "let-go" current level, above which the individual is unable to voluntarily let go of the contact.
0.050–0.150	Extreme pain, respiratory arrest, muscular convulsions, and possible death.
1	Heart fibrillation (lack of rhythmic pumping action), severe muscular convulsions, and death likely.
10	Severe burns, cardiac arrest, and probable death.

Source: Controlling Electrical Hazards, OSHA Publication 3075, U.S. Department of Labor, Washington, DC, 1986.

TABLE 4 Techniques for Reducing Electrical Hazards

Insulate electrical circuits using materials that are suitable for the voltage and conditions (e.g., temperature, humidity, chemicals).
Isolate indoor electrical installations of more than 600 volts so that unqualified personnel cannot gain access (e.g., lock-controlled rooms or screens, elevation above the floor).
Provide proper grounding of equipment to provide a low-resistance path to the earth so that higher than normal voltages will avoid using the human body to complete the circuit to ground.
Use fuses and circuit breakers to limit excessive current flow.
Use appropriate personal protective equipment and clothing.
De-energize electrical equipment before performing maintenance.

Source: Compiled from [2].

Electrical hazards arise because of ***electrical shock***, which is the discharge of electricity through the body that causes a sudden stimulation of the nerves and possible convulsive contraction of the muscles.[2] An electrical shock occurs when the body is part of an electrical circuit, and current passes through the circuit. The severity of the shock usually depends on the level of current, its duration, and the path of the current between the contact points of the body with the circuit. Table 3 describes the common effects on the human body of various current levels for a 1-second duration, where the path of the current is from the hand to the foot. It should be noted that these reactions vary for different individuals. Burns are the most common injury from electrical shock. Electrical burns are caused by (1) current passing through the body tissue, (2) electrical arcs and flashes, (3) contact with hot surfaces of overheated electrical components, and (4) burning clothing caused by electrical contact or arcing. Electrical shock sometimes induces secondary injuries due to involuntary muscle contractions. These muscle contractions can cause falls and impact injuries due to body reactions. Table 4 presents a list of actions that can be taken to reduce or prevent electrical shock hazards.

[2]Much of this section on electrical hazards is based on *Controlling Electrical Hazards*, OSHA Publication 3075, U.S. Department of Labor, Washington, DC, 1986.

Mechanical hazards arise due to the mechanical motions and forces applied by equipment components. Equipment producing these motions and forces include rotating machinery (e.g., lathes, motors, turbines), shearing equipment (e.g., power shears, brake presses), presses (e.g., press forges, stamping presses, injection molding machines), and impact equipment (e.g., stamping presses, forge hammers). The power generated by these kinds of equipment creates the conditions under which accidents can occur. If we add the potential for human error to the mix, there is an increased risk of fatalities and injuries such as scrapes, cuts, lacerations, broken bones, severed limbs, crushed body parts, and eye loss. Table 5 presents various means by which mechanical hazards are reduced.

The category of temperature hazards includes equipment that is too hot or too cold, but it does not include fire hazards, which are generally associated with the materials used in the job rather than equipment. However, it should be noted that fires are sometimes initiated by electrical problems in equipment, resulting in so-called "electrical fires." Equipment that normally operates at elevated temperatures includes processes such as arc welding, oxyfuel welding, brazing, soldering, heat treatment, flame cutting, metal casting, plastic molding, and glassworking. Burns are the obvious types of injuries that occur with equipment that operates hot. Cryogenic equipment operates at temperatures that are well below freezing, and human physical contact with the cold surfaces or materials (e.g., liquid nitrogen) used in the processes causes skin damage.

Materials. Many industries use materials in their normal operations that are classified as hazardous—that present health or safety hazards to workers, the facility in which they are used, or the environment. Materials that cause such hazards to humans can be classified into three categories: (1) corrosive materials, (2) toxic or irritant materials, and (3) flammable materials [5].

Corrosive materials are usually acidic or caustic substances that can burn or damage human tissue. Exposure can occur due to skin contact or inhalation.

Toxic or irritant materials are poisons that disrupt the normal body processes. They include liquids, gases, and solids. ***Toxicology*** is the science that studies poisons and their effects and problems. There are more than 50,000 known toxic substances. Their effects depend on the concentration of the toxic chemical, and in some instances the effects do not manifest themselves for years. Effects may include (1) cancerous tumors and other tumors, (2) embryo damage, (3) irritation of the skin, eyes, or respiratory tract, (4) reduction in mental alertness, (5) altered behavior, (6) general decline in health, (7) reduction in sexual function, and (8) other short-term or long-term illnesses [6].

TABLE 5 Techniques and Devices for Reducing Mechanical Hazards

Design a machine so that its dangerous working parts are not accessible to operators.
Surround the entire machine with enclosures that isolate it from workers.
Use machine guards to enclose certain operations if enclosures for the entire machine are not feasible.
Install interlocks for doors that open to the operation, so that only when the doors are closed can the operating cycle proceed.
Place emergency stop buttons within easy reach of the operator.
Use two-hand start buttons that require both hands to begin the machine cycle. This ensures that both hands are out of the operation area of the machine.

Source: Compiled from [2].

There are three ways in which toxic substances can enter the body: (1) inhalation, (2) absorption, and (3) ingestion. Inhalation is the most rapid entry mode, and since the respiratory and circulatory systems are so closely associated in the lungs, inhaled toxic materials are readily transported throughout the body. Absorption through the skin is less common than inhalation because the epidermis resists absorption, especially through the palms of the hands, where the skin is thicker. Finally, ingestion of toxic materials is also less common because humans tend to exercise reasonable judgments about the things they eat and drink.

Flammable materials are those that present hazards of fire or explosion. Three ingredients are needed to ignite a flammable material: (1) an oxidizer, (2) heat, and (3) a chain chemical reaction. Preventing ignition of flammable materials means denying them of these conditions. There are several ways to remove these conditions: (1) separating the flammable material from the oxidizer, (2) quenching, and/or (3) inhibiting the chain chemical reaction. Table 6 describes the four classes of fires, based on the fuel involved. Different firefighting approaches are required for the each class.

1.3 Environmental Conditions

Environmental conditions are those factors in the immediate surroundings of an operation. They include (1) physical factors and (2) social or psychological factors. Table 7 organizes these environmental factors according to this distinction. If environmental factors are found to adversely affect workers, they will play a role in increasing the risk of industrial accidents.

TABLE 6 Four Classes of Fires

Class	Description
Class A	Burning of solid materials such as wood, coal, and paper.
Class B	Burning of gases or liquids that require vaporization for combustion.
Class C	Class A or B fires involving electrical equipment.
Class D	Burning of easily oxidized metals such as magnesium, titanium, or aluminum.

TABLE 7 Environmental Factors that May Affect the Likelihood of Industrial Accidents

Physical Environmental Factors	Social/Psychological Environmental Factors
Lighting	Management policies and practices
Noise	Social and cultural norms
Temperature and humidity	Morale
Vibration	Training and instruction
Airborne pollutants	Incentives
Fire hazards	Safety programs in place
Radiation hazards	
Conditions that increase the likelihood of falls	

Source: Based on a table in [9].

TABLE 8 Some Common Cumulative Trauma and Other Occupational Disorders

Disorder	Description
Carpal tunnel syndrome	Inflammation of the tendons in the carpal tunnel (in the wrist) resulting in compression of the median nerve, causing pain, swelling, and numbness.
Bursitis	Inflammation of the bursa, which are pouches containing fluid that reduce friction in the joints.
Tendonitis	Inflammation of certain tendons resulting from excessive use.
Trigger finger	Condition in which the person can curl the finger but is unable to straighten it out, except passively.
Neuritis	Inflammation of the nerve in a body member such as the hand.
Lower-back disorders	Condition of the lower back muscles and skeleton causing pain and accounting for a high proportion of all nonfatal occupational injuries. It is estimated that the jobs of as many as 30% of workers in the United States require tasks that risk lower-back disorders.

Source: Compiled from [6] and [8].

2 OCCUPATIONAL DISORDERS AND DISEASES

The injuries and fatalities discussed in the previous section are one-time events or ***single-incident traumas***. Sometimes, the injury or health problem is one that results from a cumulative condition. These types of disorders, which may take years before their effects are evident, are called ***cumulative trauma disorders*** (CTDs). They are also known as repetitive-motion disorders because they are caused by repeated use of certain tendons and nerves, such as those in the fingers, wrist, forearm, upper arm, and shoulder. Occupations in which these body members are used repeatedly and in which CTDs are common include manual assembly with short cycle times, garment sewing, packaging, wiring, and carpentry [6]. In these kinds of manual operations, there are several causal factors leading to cumulative trauma disorders: (1) highly repetitive activity, (2) unnatural joint postures, and (3) application of forces through hinge joints. A list of cumulative trauma disorders is compiled in Table 8.

Occupational diseases usually result from exposure to a substance over an extended period of time. In some cases, the onset of the disease is delayed for many years. Some of these maladies are discussed in the context of toxic substances in Section 1.2. The more common occupational diseases are identified and briefly described in Table 9.

3 OCCUPATIONAL SAFETY AND HEALTH LAWS AND AGENCIES

This section focuses on the important legislation that has been enacted to promote safer and more healthful conditions in the workplace. In most cases, the laws have created governmental agencies to promulgate and enforce the policies and standards established by the legislation. Before these laws and agencies came into being, it is generally acknowledged that working conditions were neither safe nor healthful in many industries throughout the world. The two most important pieces of legislation enacted into law in the United States are (1) the various state workers' compensation laws and (2) the Occupational Safety and Health Act (OSHAct), a federal law.

TABLE 9 Some Common Occupational Diseases

Disease	Description
Allergic and irritant dermatitis	Various occupational skin diseases caused by contact with toxic or irritant substances. Accounts for 15% to 20% of all reported occupational diseases.
Asthma and chronic obstructive pulmonary disease	Various diseases related to the airway and breathing. The number of workers in the United States who are exposed to substances that cause airway diseases is believed to exceed 20 million.
Fertility and pregnancy abnormalities	Adverse effects on the reproductive organs of both males and females caused by chemicals in the workplace.
Infectious diseases	Such diseases include tuberculosis, hepatitis B and C, and human immunodeficiency virus (HIV). Most at risk are health-care workers, social service workers, corrections personnel, and laboratory workers who work with infectious substances.
Asbestosis	An occupational lung disease that causes progressive shortness of breath. It results from exposure to asbestos, a common insulation material whose use has been discontinued due to this illness.
Byssinosis	An occupational lung disease that causes chest tightness, coughing, and airway obstruction. It results from exposure to cotton and similar materials used in the textile industry.
Silicosis	An occupational lung disease that inhibits breathing. It results from exposure to silica that is associated with work in foundries, mines, and facilities that work with stone, clay, and glass.
Coal miners' pneumoconiosis	An occupational lung disease that causes fibrosis and emphysema. It results from exposure to coal dust and is estimated to afflict nearly 5% of all coal miners. A common form of the disease is called "black lung disease."
Lung cancer	An occupational lung disease that results from exposure to materials such as chromates, arsenic, asbestos, chloroethers, ionizing radiation, nickel, and certain hydrocarbon compounds.
Other occupational cancers	Various cancers suspected of being caused at least in part to exposure to materials in the workplace. Types of cancers include liver, kidney, bladder, nasal cavity, larynx, bone, and leukemia.

Source: Compiled from [8].

3.1 Workers' Compensation Laws

The first workers' compensation law was enacted in Prussia in 1884 [3].[3] In the United States, these types of laws were introduced by individual states, the first being Montana in 1909 and New York in 1910. By 1915, 30 states had passed similar legislation. Today, all 50 states have workers' compensation laws. In addition, the federal government, the District of Columbia, Puerto Rico, U.S. Virgin Islands, and Guam have such laws. About 80% of all U.S. workers are covered by these laws [3].

Although the legislation varies by state or other government body, the general objectives of workers' compensation laws can be stated as follows: (1) to provide prompt and

[3]This Prussian compensation law applied only to railroad employees.

reasonable income and medical benefits to work accident victims or income benefits to their families (in the case of the victim's death), (2) to reduce court workloads, costs, and delays from personal-injury lawsuits, (3) to eliminate fees to lawyers in these lawsuit cases, and (4) to encourage employer interest in occupational safety and health. On this last objective, employers have not only a social interest in the welfare of their employees but also an economic interest, because companies must either pay insurance premiums for coverage or demonstrate that they have the financial resources to be self-insured.

Three conditions must be satisfied in order for a worker to receive benefits under workers' compensation: (1) the injury must have been caused through an industrial accident, (2) it must have arisen from the worker's employment, and (3) it must have occurred during the course of that employment.

The alternative to workers' compensation would be litigation filed by each accident victim or their survivors. In order for these lawsuits to succeed, the plaintiff (victim or survivor) would have to prove negligence or maliciousness on the part of the employer. As we have seen in our discussion of the factors that are generally involved in an accident, the worker often contributes to the accident through human error. Workers' compensation avoids the legal requirement of proving fault because it is based on the doctrine of strict liability, which relieves the victim of the burden of proving negligence (similar to "no-fault" automobile insurance). If the worker is injured or killed in an industrial accident, there will be compensation regardless of whose fault it was. Because the cost of accidents is ultimately borne by the employers, there is an economic incentive for them to prevent accidents and to provide safe working conditions.

3.2 Occupational Safety and Health Act

The Occupational Safety and Health Act (OSHAct), also known as the Williams-Steiger Act, was signed into law in late 1970 and became effective in April 1971. The purpose of the law is (1) to ensure so far as possible that every working man and woman will be provided with safe and healthful working conditions and (2) to preserve the nation's human resources.

Not all workers are covered by the OSHAct. Specific exclusions include state and local government employees, self-employed persons, farms on which only immediate family members work, and workplaces covered by other federal laws (e.g., mines are covered by the Federal Mine Safety Act of 1977, whose provisions are similar to those in OSHAct). Also, employers of 10 or fewer workers are exempted from the record-keeping requirements except under circumstances that warrant such records.

The Occupational Safety and Health Act created several new agencies within various departments of the federal government: (1) the Occupational Safety and Health Administration (OSHA), which enforces the provisions of the act, (2) the Occupational Safety and Health Review Commission (OSHRC), which reviews citations and proposed penalties when employers or employees contest enforcement actions of OSHA, and (3) the National Institute for Occupational Safety and Health (NIOSH), which engages in research, training, and education in the area of occupational safety and health. In addition, the Bureau of Labor Statistics (a previously existing federal agency) was charged with the responsibility for conducting statistical surveys related to occupational injuries and illnesses. Let us briefly discuss each of the new agencies.

Occupational Safety and Health Administration. OSHA was established within the U.S. Department of Labor to enforce the OSHAct. The responsibilities of OSHA include the following:

- Implement safety and health programs.
- Establish mandatory occupational safety and health standards.
- Enforce the standards in industry by conducting inspections and assessing penalties (or taking other legal actions) for violations.
- Define responsibilities and rights for employers and employees to promote better safety and health conditions.
- Maintain a reporting system and database of occupational injuries and illnesses.
- Work with states in the development and support of state occupational safety and health programs.

One of the mechanisms by which OSHA carries out its enforcement function is on-site inspections. The law provides that an OSHA compliance officer must be given access to a facility upon presentation of proper credentials to the facility's person in charge. Most inspections are conducted with no advance notice. At the start of an inspection, the employer is requested to designate an employer representative to accompany the OSHA agent. An employee representative (e.g., an authorized union member) also has the opportunity to participate in the inspection process. At the end of the inspection, the compliance officer meets with the employer and reports any violations and other findings. These findings are subsequently communicated to an OSHA area director who determines any citations and penalties that will be imposed. The six categories of OSHA violations are presented in Table 10.

TABLE 10 OSHA Violation Categories and Penalties

Violation Type	Description and Possible Penalty
No penalty	Conditions that have no immediate effect on safety and health (e.g., adequate numbers of toilets for men and women). No penalty.
Nonserious violation	Conditions that impact safety and health, although the hazards are unlikely to cause serious injury or death. Possible penalty: $7,000.
Serious violation	Hazardous conditions in which the probability of serious injury or death is significant and employer should have known about it. Mandatory penalty: $7,000 for each violation.
Willful violation	Hazardous conditions that are known to employer and yet employer has made no meaningful effort to correct. Possible penalty: $70,000 for each violation. If a worker death has occurred, employer risks imprisonment.
Repeat violation	The same violation occurs on a subsequent inspection. Possible penalty: $70,000 for each repeated violation.
Imminent danger	Hazardous conditions in which the danger of serious injury or death is high either imminently or before normal corrective measures can be taken. The OSHA compliance officer can order the operation to be stopped or the entire plant to be shut down.

Source: [5].

Occupational Safety and Health Review Commission. The Occupational Safety and Health Review Commission (OSHRC) is a three-member quasi-judicial panel that is responsible for holding hearings and reviewing alleged violations of OSHA standards and the penalties for these violations. The actions of the panel are typically initiated by employers who are contesting the violations that have been cited by an OSHA compliance officer. The panel has the power to assess penalties and order corrective actions to be taken by violators. The three members of OSHRC are appointed by the president of the United States.

National Institute for Occupational Safety and Health. The National Institute for Occupational Safety and Health (NIOSH) is an institute that was established within the U.S. Department of Health and Human Resources by the OSHAct to conduct research and make recommendations for the prevention of work-related injuries and illnesses.[4] Its objective is to help ensure safe and healthful working conditions by engaging in research and providing information, education, and training in the area of occupational safety and health. The major objectives of NIOSH can be summarized as follows:[5] (1) conduct research to reduce work-related injuries and illnesses, (2) promote safe and healthful workplaces, through standards, recommendations, and interventions, and (3) improve global workplace safety and health through collaborations in the international community.

In 1996, NIOSH and more than 500 partner organizations created the National Occupational Research Agenda (NORA) to establish a framework for research in the area of occupational safety and health. A total of 21 priority research areas have been identified by NORA, including topics such as traumatic injury, asthma and chronic pulmonary disease, and hearing loss.

4 SAFETY AND HEALTH PERFORMANCE METRICS

The Occupational Safety and Health Act mandated that all employers with 11 or more employees maintain records on work-related cases of injury, illness, and fatality. OSHA distinguishes three types of recordable cases:[6]

1. *Fatalities*. All work-related fatalities must be reported even though there may be a time lapse between the injury and the death.
2. *Lost workday cases*. These are nonfatal injuries or illnesses involving either days away from work or days of restricted work activity.
3. *Cases not resulting in fatality or lost workdays*. These are nonfatal injuries or illnesses that do not involve days away from work.

A recordable case must meet the following criteria:

1. It must involve a death, injury, or illness to an employee.
2. It must result from work.

[4]At the time the OSHAct was enacted, the Department of Health and Human Resources was called the Department of Health, Education, and Welfare.

[5]Much of this information has been obtained from the NIOSH Web site (www.cdc.gov/niosh).

[6]The information and definitions used in this section were obtained from the OSHA Web site (www.osha.gov).

3. It must result in at least one of the following:
   a. Medical treatment beyond first aid
   b. Loss of consciousness
   c. Restriction of work or motion
   d. Transfer to another job

Cases that do not meet these criteria do not need to be entered into the records.

OSHA statistical records emphasize two aspects of work-related injuries, illnesses, and fatalities: (1) incidence rates and (2) severity rates.

Incidence Rates. Incidence rates are a means of quantifying how many incidents of a certain kind (e.g., injuries, illnesses, fatalities) occurred during a given time period (e.g., one calendar year). The measurement makes adjustments for company size and employee exposure time. It is based on the exposure of 100 full-time employees (40 hr/week, 50 weeks/year), and may be interpreted as a percentage of employees who have been injured and/or become ill in one year. It is calculated as follows:

$$IR = \frac{200{,}000 N_{rc}}{H_{je}} \tag{1}$$

where IR = incidence rate, N_{rc} = number of recordable cases of a given category of interest (e.g., number of injuries, number of injuries due to a certain cause, number of illnesses) during the period of interest, and H_{je} = worker hours of job exposure during the same period. H_{je} is determined as the sum of the hours on the job for all workers in the facility or other unit of interest. The constant of 200,000 is obtained from 100 employees working 40 hr/week for 50 weeks/year: 100(40)(50) = 200,000.

Severity Rates. The severity rate tracks the number of workdays lost due to illnesses or injuries. The number of lost workdays is used as the measure of the seriousness of the injury or illness, which is the purpose of the severity rate. It uses the same base as the incidence rate (100 employees working 40 hr/week for 50 weeks/year), and so it can be interpreted as the number of lost workdays per year per 100 employees.

$$SR = \frac{200{,}000\ N_{lwd}}{H_{je}} \tag{2}$$

where SR = severity rate, N_{lwd} = number of lost workdays during the period of interest, and H_{je} = worker hours of job exposure during the period. The number of lost workdays is defined as the number of days, consecutive or not, that the employee was away from work or restricted in his or her work activities due to the injury or illness. The number of lost workdays does not include the day of the injury or the onset of the illness.

A related metric is the average severity, which provides an average measure of the severity of all injuries at a given facility. It is determined as the number of lost workdays divided by the number of recordable cases, which is also equal to the severity rate divided by the incidence rate. That is,

$$AS = \frac{N_{lwd}}{N_{rc}} = \frac{SR}{IR} \tag{3}$$

where AS = average severity, and the other terms are defined above.

Another measure of severity is the number of lost workdays for those cases in which workdays were lost. This is calculated as follows:

$$ADAW = \frac{N_{lwd}}{N_{clwd}} \tag{4}$$

where $ADAW$ = average days away from work, N_{lwd} = number of lost workdays, and N_{clwd} = number of cases involving lost workdays.

Example 1 Safety Performance Metrics

A company's safety records for the most recent year contain the following data: 932 workers each worked an average of 1934 hr (job exposure hours); 43 injury cases occurred, none of which were fatal; of the 43 injuries, 17 were cases in which lost workdays occurred and a total of 457 workdays were lost. For these injuries, determine (a) incidence rate, (b) severity rate, (c) average severity, and (d) average days away from work.

Solution **(a)** Total worker hours of job exposure $H_{je} = 932(1934) = 1{,}802{,}488$ hours.

$$\text{Incidence rate } IR = \frac{200{,}000(43)}{1{,}802{,}488} = 4.77 \text{ injuries per 100 workers}$$

(b) $$\text{Severity rate } SR = \frac{200{,}000(457)}{1{,}802{,}488} = 50.7 \text{ lost workdays per 100 workers.}$$

(c) $$\text{Average severity } AS = \frac{457}{43} = 10.6 \text{ lost workdays per recordable case.}$$

(d) $$\text{Average days away from work } ADAW = \frac{457}{17} = 26.9 \text{ lost workdays per}$$

case in which lost workdays occurred. ■

REFERENCES

[1] Asfahl, C. R. *Industrial Safety and Health Management*. 5th ed. Upper Saddle River, NJ: Pearson/Prentice Hall, 2004.

[2] Bloswick, D. S., and R. Sesek. "Occupational Safety Management and Engineering." Pp. 6.171–6.204 in *Maynard's Industrial Engineering Handbook*. 5th ed., edited by K. B. Zandin. New York: McGraw-Hill, 2001.

[3] Hammer, W., and D. Price. *Occupational Safety Management and Engineering*. 5th ed. Upper Saddle River, NJ: Prentice Hall, 2001.

[4] Konz, S., and S. Johnson, *Work Design: Industrial Ergonomics*. 5th ed. Scottsdale, AZ: Holcomb Hathaway Publishers, 2000.

[5] Niebel, B. W., and A. Freivalds. *Method, Standards, and Work Design*. 11th ed. New York: McGraw-Hill, 2003.

[6] Pulat, B. M. *Fundamentals of Industrial Ergonomics*. Upper Saddle River, NJ: Prentice Hall, 1992.

[7] Sanders, M. S., and E. J. McCormick. *Human Factors in Engineering Design*. 7th ed. New York: McGraw-Hill, 1993.

[8] Smith, M. J., P. Carayon, and B-T. Karsh. "Design for Occupational Safety and Health." Pp. 1156–91 in *Handbook of Industrial Engineering*. 3rd ed., edited by G. Salvendy. New York: Wiley, 2001.

[9] Wickens, C. D., J. Lee, Y. Liu, and S. G. Becker. *An Introduction to Human Factors Engineering*. 2nd ed. Upper Saddle River, NJ: Pearson/Prentice Hall, 2004.

REVIEW QUESTIONS

1 What is the difference between occupational safety and occupation health?

2 What is an industrial accident?

3 What are some of the industries in which the frequency of fatal injuries is high? Name two.

4 What are some of the industries in which the frequency of nonfatal injuries is high? Name two.

5 What are some of the most important causes of fatal and nonfatal injuries? Name three.

6 What are the three factors that are commonly identified as reasons why industrial accidents occur?

7 What are the two basic categories of human error? Briefly define each category.

8 Electrical shock is included in the category of job factors involving equipment problems. What is electrical shock?

9 What are the three categories of materials that cause safety or health hazards to humans?

10 What is the difference between single-incident traumas and cumulative trauma disorders?

11 What are the general objectives of workers' compensation laws?

12 What are the three conditions that must be satisfied for a worker to receive benefits under workers' compensation?

13 What are the responsibilities of the Occupational Safety and Health Administration (OSHA)?

14 What are the responsibilities of the National Institute for Occupational Safety and Health (NIOSH)?

15 What are the two aspects of work-related injuries, illnesses, and fatalities that are emphasized in OSHA statistical records?

PROBLEMS

1 The following injury data have been compiled during the most recent year for a construction contracting company: 137 workers worked an average of 2354 hr (job exposure hours); 22 injury cases occurred; no fatalities; of the 22 injuries, 12 were cases in which lost workdays occurred; a total of 129 workdays were lost. For these injuries, determine (a) incidence rate, (b) severity rate, (c) average severity, and (d) average days away from work. (e) How does this company's incidence rate compare with the rest of the construction industry, as shown in Table 1?

2 A distribution center's injury statistics for the most recent year are as follows: 528 workers worked an average of 1979 hr (job exposure hours); 42 injury cases occurred; 1 fatality; of the 42 injuries, 18 were cases in which lost workdays occurred; a total of 537 workdays were lost. For these injuries, determine (a) incidence rates for fatal and nonfatal injuries, (b) severity rate for nonfatal injuries, (c) average severity, and (d) average days away from work. (e) How does this distribution center's incidence rates compare with the rest of the wholesale and retail trade industry, as shown in Table 1?

3 An automobile final assembly plant has compiled the following statistics on injuries sustained in the plant during the most recent calendar year: 1892 workers worked an average of 2160 hr (job exposure hours); 127 injury cases occurred; 1 fatality; of the 127 injuries, 55 were cases in which lost workdays occurred; a total of 173 workdays were lost. For these injuries, determine (a) incidence rates for fatal and nonfatal injuries, (b) severity rate for nonfatal injuries, (c) average severity, and (d) average days away from work. (e) How does this plant's incidence rates compare with the rest of the manufacturing industry, as shown in Table 1?

4 Based on the statistical data in Table 1 for the mining industry, how many fatal and nonfatal injuries can be expected for a mining company that employs 12,628 workers?

Work Organization

Management consists of planning, organizing, controlling, and directing the human, physical, and financial resources of an organization to achieve its objectives. In general, management achieves the organizational objectives by working through others. Managers supervise subordinates. There are several traditional functions related to management:

- *Planning.* Managers must establish objectives and policies for their organizational units and must figure out how to achieve the objectives and administer the policies.
- *Organizing.* Managers must determine the structure and staffing of their organizational units in the manner that best executes the plan for achieving the organizational objectives and conducting the day-to-day activities of their units.
- *Controlling.* Managers must devise control mechanisms that will enable them to coordinate the actions of subordinates and measure their performance relative to the organizational objectives.
- *Leading.* Managers must optimize the performance of their subordinates by coaching, mentoring, training, and motivating them. In short, managers must exercise leadership.

This chapter focuses on the organizational function of work management—in particular, on organizational principles and structures. The common theme is human resources: how to create an organization in which workers can do their jobs most effectively and efficiently, how to motivate them, how to determine the worth of their jobs, how to evaluate their performance, and how to reward them for jobs well done.

1 ORGANIZATION PRINCIPLES

An ***organization*** is an administrative and functional association of people that is established for the purpose of assigning work to individuals and groups in order to achieve defined objectives.[1] Organizations of some form occur in nearly all collections of people who have been brought together to pursue some objective or set of objectives. Different organizations have different objectives, and so their organizational designs differ. The starting point in organizational design is the objective or set of objectives of the organization. The objectives must be defined first, and then the work required to achieve these objectives must be determined. The work must then be divided into tasks and functions, and then job positions can be identified based on these tasks and functions. Next, the job positions can be organized into administrative units, with a supervisor in charge of each unit. These units are then arranged into higher-level administrative units, and so on. The resulting organization structure assumes the shape of a pyramid, with a single individual at the top (e.g., the chief executive officer) in charge of the entire enterprise.

In order for an organization to operate successfully, its design and management must follow certain principles. We organize them into two categories in this section: (1) principles of organization structure and (2) principles of organization administration. The structure principles deal with the form of the organization, while the administration principles are concerned with its function. The distinction between the two categories is admittedly subtle.

1.1 Principles of Organization Structure

In this section, we discuss the following principles that relate to the structure of the organization: (1) specialization, (2) departmentalization, and (3) span of supervision.

Specialization and Departmentalization. ***Specialization*** is the process of directing one's efforts and skills to a specific task or function. It follows from the division of labor principle in economics and is based on the learning curve effect . Although the total work of the organization may be complex, it can be divided into relatively simple tasks and functions. According to the specialization principle, job positions are assigned to each of those individual tasks and functions. The workers in those positions quickly become expert at performing their jobs, and the organization benefits from the resulting efficiencies. Advantages and disadvantages of specialization to management and labor are listed in Table 1.

Departmentalization is the process of organizing positions with similar tasks and functions into separate administrative units (i.e., departments). The departmentalization principle follows directly from the specialization principle. When positions have

[1]The Organization Planning and Theory Committee (ANSI Standard Z94.9-1989) has defined *organization* as follows: (1) The classification or groupings of the activities of an enterprise for the purpose of administering them. Division of work to be done into defined tasks along with the assignment of these tasks to individuals or groups of individuals qualified for their efficient accomplishment. (2) Determining the necessary activities and positions within an enterprise, department, or group, arranging them into the best functional relationships, clearly defining the authority, responsibilities, and duties of each, and assigning them to individuals so that the available effort can be effectively and systematically applied and coordinated.

TABLE 1 Advantages and Disadvantages of Labor Specialization

Advantages to Management	Disadvantages to Management
High productivity due to task simplicity and repetitiveness Ease of recruitment and rapid training of workers due to minimum skill requirements Lower wage rates due to minimum skill requirements Good control over workloads and work flow Increased organizational flexibility because workers can be transferred between tasks that can be learned quickly	Quality control is a potential problem since responsibility for the product or service is distributed among many workers, each responsible for only a small part of the total Possible worker dissatisfaction, resulting in labor turnover, absenteeism, grievances, and other labor problems
Advantages to Labor	**Disadvantages to Labor**
Little or no educational requirements needed to get the job Ease of training due to task simplicity and repetitiveness For some workers, the simplicity and repetitiveness of the work is satisfying	Boredom due to task simplicity and repetitiveness Little personal gratification from tasks in which the worker makes a very small contribution to the total product or service Possible frustration due to lack of control over work pace Possibility of muscle fatigue and cumulative trauma disorders due to repetitive use of the same muscle groups Little opportunity to demonstrate initiative Little opportunity to advance to a better position

Source: Compiled mostly from [6].

been organized according to specialization, it is reasonable to group similar positions into departments. The grouping is usually based on one of the following factors [5]:

- *Purpose.* This refers to the output of the department, such as its product or service. A company may have three different product lines, with a separate division being responsible for each line.
- *Function.* This refers to the type of work that is performed in the department. Machine tool operators are grouped into the machining department, punch press operators are located in the stamping department, and so on. Each type of production process is treated as a distinct function.
- *Place.* This refers to the geographical location where the work is performed. The organization may have one office in New York and another in Chicago. It makes sense for each office to operate independently, at least to some extent.
- *Clientele.* This refers to the type of clients or customers for whom the work is performed. The organization may sell its products in both industrial markets and consumer markets, and separate sales organizations must be used to address the unique characteristics of each market.

The use of departmentalization in organizational design provides identity and clarity of an administrative unit's mission. It distinguishes one department's mission from the missions of other departments. The potential downside of departmentalization is that it creates separations among administrative units (sometimes referred to as *silos*) that may inhibit cooperation among them in pursuit of the larger organizational objectives. Also, departmentalization can be taken too far, as the following example illustrates.

Example 1 Too Much Departmentalization

A manufacturing firm wants to have specialized departments that are organized by (1) product, (2) function, (3) location, and (4) customer. There are five major product lines, each with its own organization. There are six functions: (1) design engineering, (2) sales, (3) parts production, (4) assembly, (5) inspection, and (6) logistics. The firm currently has four geographical locations, each considered strategic to its global ambitions. In addition, there are three customer categories: (1) the general public, (2) government, and (3) industry. If the firm were to departmentalize along all of these divisions, how many departments would be needed?

Solution: If the departmentalization requirements of each product line, function, location, and customer category were satisfied, the required number of departments would be determined as follows:

$$\text{Total number of departments} = 5 \times 6 \times 4 \times 3 = 360 \text{ departments}$$ ■

Span of Supervision. The ***span of supervision*** (also called ***span of control*** and ***span of management***) refers to the number of subordinates under a given supervisor or manager. Any supervisor is limited in the number of subordinates that he or she can adequately manage, and so the question is: what should the optimum number be? Some experts have speculated that the optimum span of supervision is between four and eight subordinates. Yet, in some organizations the span of control is much greater than eight, at least on average, while in others it is less than four. The following factors influence the span of control:

- *Level in the organization.* First-line supervisors generally have a greater number of workers reporting to them than the number of vice presidents who report to the president. The terms ***span of operating control*** and ***span of executive control*** are used to distinguish these cases.
- *Capabilities of the supervisor.* The management aptitudes and interpersonal skills of the supervisor have an effect on the number of subordinates that he or she can manage. The supervisor's willingness to delegate and to appoint assistants affects the span of control. Some individuals are better managers and can handle the workload of more workers.
- *Capabilities of the subordinates.* If the subordinates know their jobs and the decisions they must make are routine, then less time is required by the supervisor in policy-making decisions and exceptions, and a high span of supervision is appropriate.
- *Employee turnover rate.* If turnover rate is high, then the supervisor must spend more time training new hires, and a low span of supervision is necessary.

- *Complexity of problems and issues.* Difficult problems and complex issues take more time to resolve, and this reduces the span of supervision.
- *Nonsupervisory duties.* If the supervisor's job includes many nonsupervisory duties, such as keeping records and writing reports, then not as much time is available for supervising the subordinates.

An organization's policy regarding span of supervision affects the number of layers of management in its pyramidal structure. Wide spans create flatter organizations (fewer layers of management) while narrower spans create taller structures (more layers). This can have a significant effect on the organization's payroll costs, because managers are paid relatively well compared to workers at the bottom layer. The higher they are in the organization, the higher their salaries are. The following example illustrates the effect.

Example 2 Effects of Span of Supervision for Two Companies

The organization structures of companies A and B are to be compared. (Both structures are assumed to be pure pyramids.[2]) In Company A, three vice presidents report to the president at the top of the organization, and 10 workers report to each foreman at the operating level. In between, the span of supervision is five at all intermediate levels. In company B, five vice presidents report to the president at the top of the organization, 20 workers report to each foreman at the operating level and the span of supervision is 10 at all intermediate levels. Each organization employs 100,000 direct labor personnel. At the lowest level, each worker is paid $16,000 annually, foremen are paid 50% more than workers, and at each level above, the salary increment is 50% more than subordinates, all the way up to the president. For each company, determine (a) the number of layers of management, (b) the number of supervisory, management, and executive personnel, and (c) the total payroll costs for these personnel.

Solution **(a)** The numbers of individuals at each level in the organization for the two companies are listed in Table 2. These values are determined by starting with the 100,000 workers (at the bottom of the table) and dividing by the foreman's span of supervision to find the number of foremen. The same process is repeated for each level above. As the table indicates, Company B has a much flatter organization, with two fewer layers of management. Company A has seven layers of management, including foremen, while Company B has five.

(b) The total number of supervisory, management, and executive personnel for company A adds up to 12,500. For Company B, the corresponding number is 5556.

(c) Payroll costs for these personnel are figured for Company A in Table 3 (a) and for Company B in Table 3 (b). The salary for each level is 50% greater than the level below, starting with the foremen, who earn 50% more than the $16,000 earned by the line workers. Note that the payroll costs for Company A are nearly three times those of Company B. This is due not only to the increased number of management layers, but also because of the salary inflations that occur at the higher levels of management.

[2]The pure pyramid is characteristic of the line organization structure, discussed in Section 2.1.

TABLE 2 Numbers of Employees at Each Level in Example 2

Company A			Company B		
Title	Span of Supervision	Employees	Title	Span of Supervision	Employees
President	3	1			
Vice presidents	5	3			
Assistant Vice presidents	5	16	President	5	1
Senior managers	5	80	Vice presidents	10	5
Managers	5	400	Managers	10	50
Supervisors	5	2000	Supervisors	10	500
Foremen	10	10,000	Foremen	20	5,000
Workers		100,000	Workers		100,000

TABLE 3 Payroll Costs for Supervisory, Management, and Executive Personnel in Example 2

	Title	Number	Salary	Payroll Cost	Total Payroll Cost
(a) Company A	President	1	$273,375	$273,375	
	Vice presidents	3	$182,250	546,750	
	Assistant Vice presidents	16	$121,500	1,944,000	
	Senior managers	80	$81,000	6,480,000	
	Managers	400	$54,000	21,600,000	
	Supervisors	2000	$36,000	72,000,000	
	Foremen	10,000	$24,000	240,000,000	$342,844,125
(b) Company B	President	1	$121,500	$121,500	
	Vice presidents	5	$81,000	405,000	
	Managers	50	$54,000	2,700,000	
	Supervisors	500	$36,000	18,000,000	
	Foremen	5,000	$24,000	120,000,000	$141,226,500

■

The number of management levels required in a pure pyramidal organization consisting of a certain number of line workers at the base of the pyramid can be determined using a more direct calculation than the approach used in Table 2. To make the computation, the values of span of supervision must be given for the foreman level and for all levels above the foremen (assumed the same for all levels above foreman). The equation for this calculation is the following:

$$L = \frac{\ln w - \ln SS_f}{\ln SS_m} + 1 \qquad (1)$$

where L = number of levels of supervision and management in the organization, w = number of line workers, SS_f = span of supervision at the foreman's level, and SS_m = span of supervision at the managers' level (all levels above the foremen). The following example compares the calculated values based on equation (1) with the results shown earlier in Example 2.

Example 3 Determining the Number of Management Levels in Two Companies

Using the data in Example 2 and equation (1), determine the number of management levels in Companies A and B.

Solution: For Company A, w = 100,000 line workers, $SS_f = 10$ and $SS_m = 5$.

$$L = \frac{\ln 100{,}000 - \ln 10}{\ln 5} + 1 = \frac{11.513 - 2.303}{1.61} + 1 = 6.72$$

which is rounded up to seven layers of supervision and management.

For Company B, w = 100,000 line workers, $SS_f = 20$ and $SS_m = 10$.

$$L = \frac{\ln 100{,}000 - \ln 20}{\ln 10} + 1 = \frac{11.513 - 2.996}{2.303} + 1 = 4.70$$

which is rounded up to five layers of supervision and management.

Comment: The reason the calculated values are not integers and are slightly less than the values obtained in previous Example 2 is because the spans of supervision at the very tops of the two organizations are less than SS_m for the other levels. Nevertheless, equation (1) provides a nice shortcut for calculating the number of layers in an organization. ■

1.2 Principles of Organization Administration

In this category of organization principles we have (1) unity of command, (2) delegation of responsibility and authority, and (3) equality of responsibility and authority. They are all concerned with who is in charge and who makes the decisions.

Unity of Command. ***Unity of command*** means that one person is in charge of each administrative unit at each level of the pyramid, including one person at the very top of the pyramid. That person at the top has overall authority and responsibility for the entire organization. The same principle applies at levels below the top, so that everyone reports to one person (e.g., supervisor, manager, vice president, and president). Everyone knows whom to report to, and everyone above the bottom level knows who reports to him or her. According to the unity of command principle, no worker should report to more than one boss.

With unity of command, there should be no confusion about who is responsible for which activities, who gives the orders, and who must obey the orders. Unity of command is the foundation for the hierarchy of authority and responsibility in the organization. It establishes the ***chain of command***, which is the sequence of supervisor/subordinate relationships that runs from the top to the bottom of the organization.

Delegation of Responsibility and Authority. In an organizational context, ***responsibility*** means that an individual member of an organization has an obligation to perform the assigned tasks and functions to the best of his or her ability. The member has a responsibility to the organization and is accountable to his or her direct supervisor for those tasks and functions. ***Authority*** means that a member of the organization has been given official power to utilize certain organizational resources such as personnel and equipment in the discharge of his or her responsibilities. The authority gives that person the right to take actions, make decisions, and give directions to subordinates within the scope of the assigned responsibilities.

The individual at the top of the pyramid is the one ultimately responsible for the success of the organization. But that individual cannot be personally responsible for everything. He or she cannot make all of the decisions that need to be made. Some responsibilities and decision-making authority must be delegated to executives at the next level below the top. And those executives must delegate some of their responsibilities and authority to managers at the third level, and so on, down to the base of the pyramid where the real work of the organization is accomplished.

When responsibility is delegated to a subordinate, it does not mean that the person who delegated it is relieved of it. It just means that the person has entrusted a subordinate to accomplish the actual work assignment. For example, a foreman is responsible for the production output in his or her department, but the actual production work is delegated to the operators in the department. The foreman is still responsible for getting the work done in the eyes of his or her manager. If the operators do not get the work done, they have failed their responsibility to the foreman, but the foreman has failed his or her responsibility to the manager.

At what level should decisions be made in the organization? The general guideline is that decisions should be made at levels as low as possible in the organization, given that the decision makers at those levels are provided with sufficient knowledge and information to make good decisions. This means that some decisions should be made at the very lowest levels of the organization. Today, we call this ***worker empowerment***. When this guideline is followed, it frees the supervisors at the next higher level from having to make decisions that would be regarded as routine for that higher level. It avoids ***micromanagement***, which occurs when the supervisor feels obligated to get involved in all of the day-to-day details of his or her department and to make all of the corresponding decisions that must be made.

What constitutes a routine decision? A ***routine decision*** is one for which rules have been formulated to guide the decision maker, and as long as the situation fits the rules, then the decision is more or less automatic. The problems occur when the situation does not fit the available decision rules. Let us consider two of these nonroutine decision-making situations.

The first nonroutine situation is one that requires a ***policy-making decision***—a decision that must be made without the guidance of established rules. Instead the decision requires the formulation of rules and policies that are consistent with organizational objectives. This is contrasted with an ***operating decision***—a decision that must be made according to established rules, procedures, and policies, and it is usually associated with situations that occur regularly or repetitively. At any given level in an organization, most decision-making situations can be classified into one of these two categories. When the situation requires an operating decision, then it is made at the given level. The authority to make operating decisions at this level is called ***operating authority***. When the situation requires a policy-making decision, it is made at some level above that has ***policy-making authority*** at that level. An operating decision is a routine decision; a policy-making decision is not. For example, suppose a company policy stated that an employee shall be dismissed if he or she is absent from work 10 days in one calendar year. Thus, when a particular worker missed his tenth day of work within the first four months of the year, the supervisor fired that worker in accordance with stated company policy. The decision to establish the policy was made at some higher level in the organization. The supervisor made a routine operating decision.

The second nonroutine decision-making situation is one that involves an exception from the normal operating authority, and therefore the decision is not a routine one. These cases require the application of the ***exception principle***, which states that when the circumstances of the situation are not covered by the normal decision-making rules in effect at the given level of the organization, the decision should be made at the next higher level. Going back to our example of the supervisor who made the operating decision to fire the worker who had missed 10 days of work, suppose the worker in question happens to be the son of the company president. Understandably, the supervisor might feel uncomfortable with firing the boss's son. To avoid the dilemma, he might invoke the exception principle and pass the dismissal decision up the chain of command to some higher level.

Equality of Responsibility and Authority. Both the responsibility and the authority for a given position are documented in the position's job description. The responsibility is often spelled out more precisely than the authority. The person filling the position is sometimes expected to use his or her ingenuity to carry out the responsibilities. Responsibility and authority are delegated from above by one's immediate superior.

The principle of equality of responsibility and authority states that when a position is delegated a responsibility, the position should also be delegated a commensurate level of authority to discharge that responsibility. More concisely, the responsibility and authority of a position must be equal. A worker cannot be given a responsibility without being given the means to carry it out. If a department supervisor is made responsible for increasing production output, then he or she must also be given a corresponding increase in resources to achieve the production increase. The supervisor must be allowed to authorize overtime for production workers or to hire and train new workers.

2 ORGANIZATION STRUCTURES

Over the years, various organizational structures have been developed. In nearly all cases, the structural form is customized to meet the particular needs and objectives of the individual organization. Because the needs and objectives often evolve over time, the organizational structure also evolves. The organization itself and its structure are dynamic. For example, the structure is influenced by changes in the membership of the organization, especially those individuals who are in positions of authority. In this section, we discuss the various types of organization structure, distinguishing between (1) traditional organization structures and (2) new organization forms and trends.

2.1 Traditional Organization Structures

Two basic types of traditional organization structure can be recognized: (1) line organization and (2) line and staff organization. Of historical interest is an additional structure called the *functional organization*, which was developed by Frederick W. Taylor in the late 1800s. We discuss this in Historical Note 1.

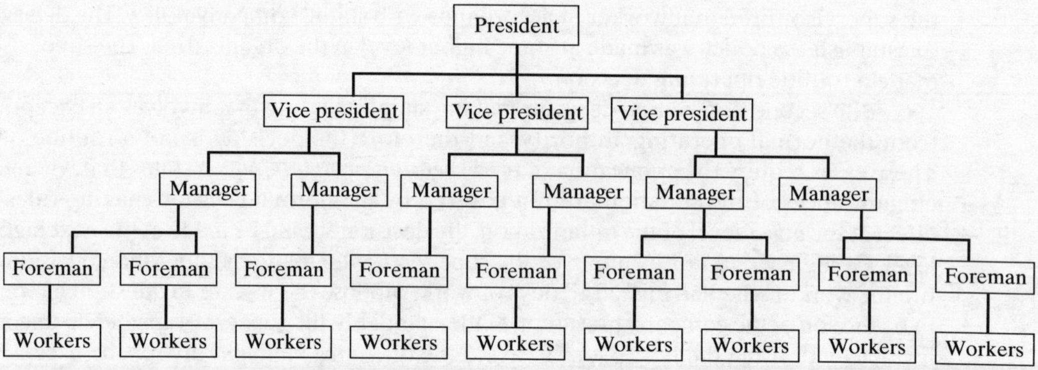

Figure 1 Line organization structure.

Line Organization The ***line organization*** is the oldest organizational form, having originated with the armies of ancient cultures. It has a simple pyramidal structure that is characterized by a direct chain of command extending from the top of the organization to the bottom, as illustrated in Figure 1. The workers at the lowest level of the pyramid are all involved in the operations of the organization. No staff or advisory positions exist in a pure line organization.

The principal advantage of a line organization is the clarity of its reporting structure. It obeys the unity-of-command principle very clearly. Each first-level worker reports to a single supervisor, each supervisor reports to a single manager, and so on up to the top of the pyramid. If a question or problem arises, there is one person at the next higher level to go to for the answer. That individual does not have to consult with staff advisors, so decisions can be made more quickly in a line organization. If the decision is correct, then the credit goes to the decision maker. If the decision is bad, it is difficult for the decision maker to duck the blame. Buck-passing is discouraged by the visibility of the line structure. Also, the absence of staff personnel means the absence of overhead salaries associated with them, so the line organization can operate at lower cost than one burdened with these expenses.

The problem with the pure line organization, at least in a modern enterprise, is that certain staff-type functions have to be performed within each stem of the structure. Workers must be hired (and maybe fired), they must be trained, the work must be planned and scheduled, payrolls must be met, and so on. The direct supervisors of the departments must perform these duties, and those individuals cannot be expert in all of the specialty functions, nor do they have the time to perform them. Thus, without staff assistants, the supervisors, managers, and others in the upper levels of the organization become overworked and underachieving. Some of the auxiliary tasks are not done or are done quickly and poorly.

Because of these problems encountered in the pure line organization, this type of structure is rare except in small organizations such as companies just getting started or family businesses. In other words, it is uncommon except when the pyramid has only one or two layers above the base level. A line structure is impractical in enterprises of any significant size because of all the specialty and advisory functions that must be accomplished (e.g., recruiting, training, planning and scheduling, accounting, and so on). To address these additional chores that must be performed, two alternative structures evolved, one called the *functional organization* and the other the *line and staff organization*. The functional organization has not stood the test of time and is not used today. It is nevertheless of interest because (1) Frederick W. Taylor was the person who proposed it (and installed it in at least two factories), and (2) it can be argued that it was the genesis of the line and staff organization. The functional organization is described in Historical Note 1, and the line and staff structure is discussed in the section that follows.

HISTORICAL NOTE 1 FUNCTIONAL ORGANIZATION

Functional organization was first developed during the 1880s, a period when the line organization was the principal way of managing a factory but its limitations were apparent. Frederick W. Taylor reasoned that because line foremen could not be specialists in all of the functional areas required to manage factory operations, these areas should be assigned to eight different foremen who would each specialize in one area. Thus, each foreman supervised the workers in his specialty,[3] and each worker had eight bosses. The functional organization (also called ***functional foremanship***) is depicted in Figure 2. Taylor implemented the functional organization at Midvale Steel Company in Philadelphia around 1888, and there is evidence that he also installed this type of organizational structure around 1899 at the Bethlehem Iron Works (which became Bethlehem Steel Company in 1903) [19].

As indicated in Figure 2, the eight foremen were divided into two groups (four foremen each), one group in charge of planning and clerical functions and the other in charge of production and performance functions.[4] The job titles and basic duties of the eight foreman are listed in Table 4. The main advantage of functional foremanship was that it brought expertise to the specialty functions that were required in a factory. Taylor also claimed that functional organization eliminated one-man control of operations and promoted cooperation.

The following disadvantages of functional foremanship far outweighed the advantages: (1) the structure violated the unity of command principle because each worker had to report to eight bosses, who sometimes gave conflicting instructions; (2) when something went wrong, it was difficult to determine which boss was responsible; (3) coordination was difficult because there was no one person in charge; and (4) although the structure might have developed good specialists, it did not develop good general managers.

[3]Please excuse the lapse in using "his" rather than "his or her". At the time that Taylor was implementing his functional organization, women forepersons were rare if they existed at all in the kinds of factories where Taylor worked (e.g., machine shops).

[4]Peter Drucker, a well-known business author, has observed that "to have discovered that planning is different from doing was one of Taylor's most valuable insights"; see Peter F. Drucker, *The Practice of Management* (New York: Harper, 1954).

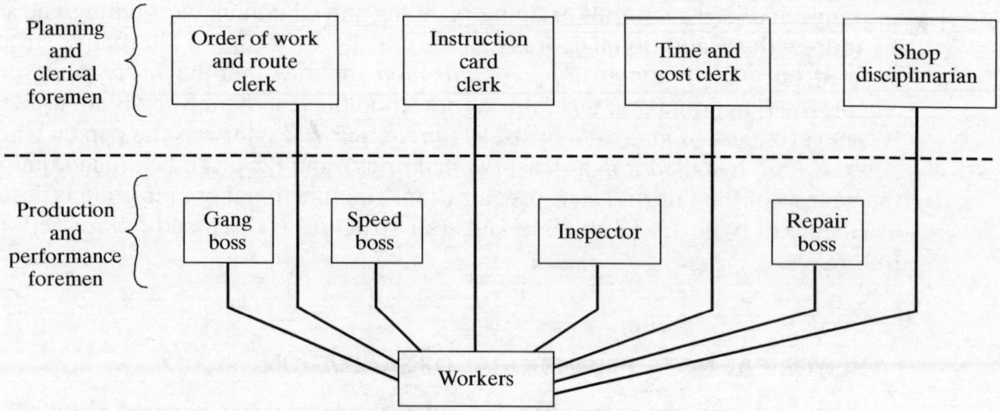

Figure 2 Taylor's functional organization.

TABLE 4 The Foreman in Taylor's Functional Organization

Planning and Clerical Foremen
Order of work and route clerk. Decide and plan the order in which the work is to be done.
Instruction card clerk. Provide instructions on tools, materials, piece rates, and similar information.
Time and cost clerk. Record data on actual times and costs.
Shop disciplinarian. Keep records of each worker's merits and misdeeds; hire and fire workers.
Production and Performance Foremen
Gang boss. Set up the machines and move work parts between machines.
Speed boss. Specify speeds and feeds for the machine tools.
Inspector. Maintain quality control.
Repair boss. Maintain and repair machines.

Line and Staff Organization. As an organization grows, the need to accomplish specialty functions grows also. The pure line organization is no longer adequate to satisfy this need. A new organization form is required, and the line and staff organization evolved out of the line structure, with likely influence from Taylor's functional foremanship. A ***line and staff organization*** is basically a line organization with staff positions added at various levels to provide specialized knowledge. Its form is illustrated in Figure 3. The line components of the line and staff structure maintain the chain of command, while the staff positions bring expertise to technical problems and administrative functions. Individuals in the line structure at levels above the operations level can focus on managing, while individuals in the staff structure can focus on the auxiliary functions that are required to run the enterprise.

At the bottom of the line portion of the line and staff pyramid are the operations personnel or line workers—the people who make the product or deliver the service. They are usually grouped into departments (e.g., machining, painting, assembly). The staff workers are also organized into departments (e.g., production planning, payroll, manufacturing engineering), and these departments usually have a pyramidal structure similar to the conventional line organization. The departments have first-line staff personnel who are supervised

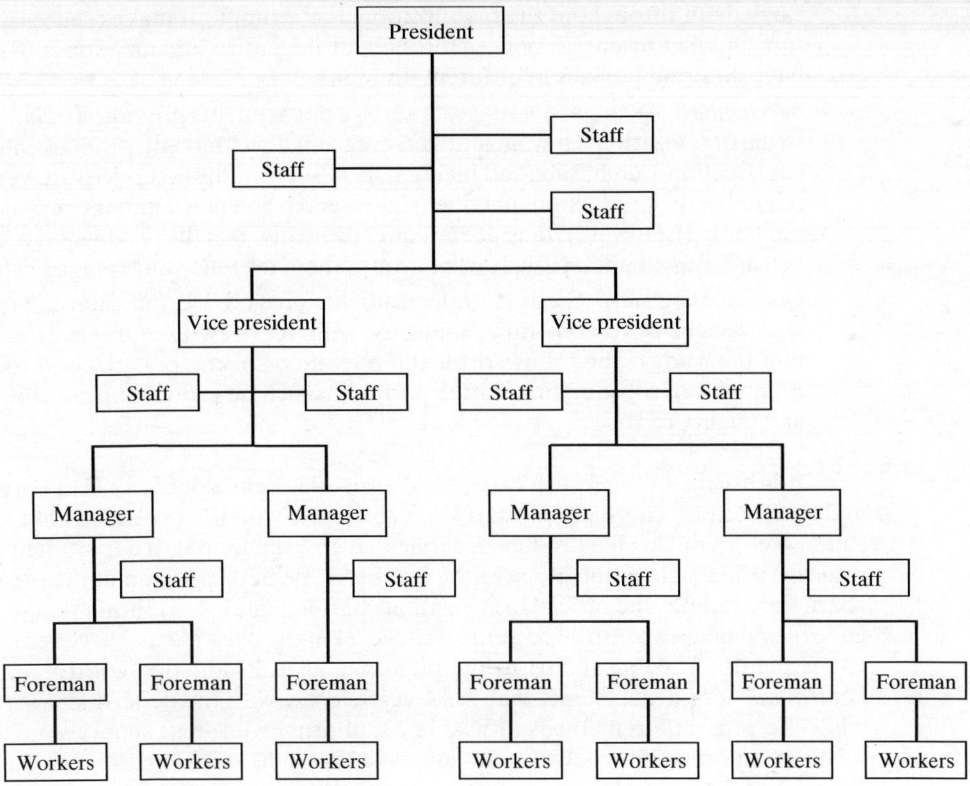

Figure 3 Line and staff organization structure.

by managers, and these managers may very well report to higher-level managers in the same functional staff area. The question is: what do staff workers do that distinguishes them from operating personnel? A simple and general answer can be provided: "Lines do; staffs advise. Line officers say 'do'; staff officers say 'if and when you do, do it this way.'"[5]

Although this statement is a good summary of the difference between line and staff, the reality is somewhat more complicated than the dichotomy between doing and advising. Many staff departments have broader responsibilities than simply advising, and their responsibilities sometimes overlap those of the line organization. Staff functions in an organization can be classified into the following four categories [1]:

- *Advisory staff.* This category includes specialty functions in which the line managers and executives who must make decisions need guidance. The advisory staff provides the advice, but the line personnel make the decisions. Advisory staff functions include legal, public relations, and economics.
- *Control staff.* These departments include accounting, budgeting, human resources, and other groups that are given the authority to make sure their functions are

[5]Quoted from [13].

carried out throughout the organization. For example, it makes sense to have the same human resources polices throughout the entire organization rather than to have different policies in different divisions.

- *Service staff.* As the name suggests, service departments provide specialty services to the organization. They include research and development, product engineering, construction, purchasing, and maintenance. Some of these services are very closely related to the production function (e.g., research and development, product design, purchasing). However, they are not directly involved in the production of the product, and this characteristic is what groups them into the staff category.
- *Coordinating staff.* These staff departments give advice, but their advice carries such weight as to constitute authority, with very few exceptions. It is essential that their advice be followed for the operations of the organization to succeed. Examples of coordinating staff departments include production control, logistics, and quality control.

It is usually in the fourth category that overlaps and conflicts occur between line and staff, because coordinating staff work so closely with the operations of the organization (i.e., producing the product or service). A coordinating staff department normally achieves its de facto authority over the line by virtue of its position in the organization chart. For example, the official organization chart in Figure 4 (a) shows that production control and quality control are at the same level in the pyramid as the general foreman of the factory. They all report to the plant manager. Production control and quality control are staff departments that work very closely with the department supervisors, while the general foreman has official line authority over those supervisors. There are no direct reporting lines between the supervisors and the staff departments. But because the rank of the general foremen is the same as the two staff departments in the organization chart, and because the plant manager has delegated the responsibilities of production control and quality control to those respective staff departments, this gives

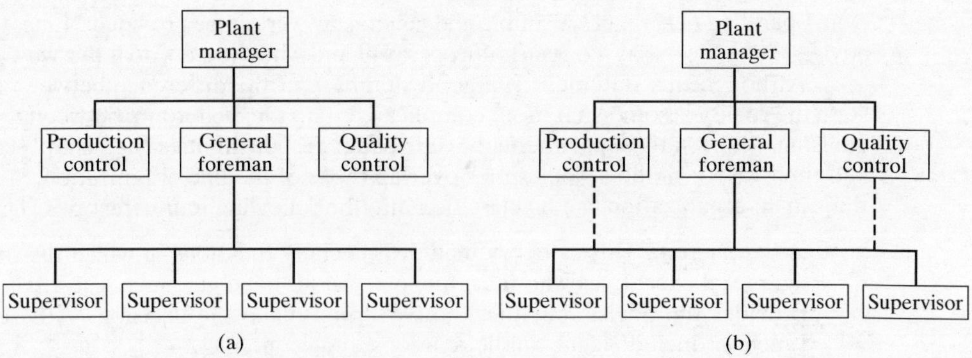

Figure 4 Organization charts for a factory: (a) the official chart and (b) the de facto authority possessed by production control and quality control as indicated by the dashed lines.

those departments authority over the line. If a department supervisor decides to disobey the production schedule, he or she will ultimately have to answer to the plant manager. In effect, the organization chart in Figure 4 (b) that shows the dashed lines indicating the de facto authority of the two staff departments over the factory gives a more accurate picture of the factory organization.

Although the line and staff organization is a big improvement over the pure line structure, it is not without faults. There are several potential disadvantages to this type of organization:

- *Who's in charge?* The line officers are officially in charge, but the staff personnel often carry significant authority that can sometimes lead to confusion and conflict.
- *Too many bosses.* In effect, the authority delegated to the staff departments means that the department supervisors must take instructions from multiple bosses. It is not as bad as in the functional organization, but it can be troublesome.
- *Conflicting instructions.* In the organization chart in Figure 4 (b), what if the staff departments gave conflicting instructions to the factory? For example, production control tells the supervisor to ship the product to the customer, but quality control tells the same supervisor not to ship because of a quality problem.

2.2 New Organization Forms and Trends

The line and staff organization structure is widely applied in business and industry, the military, and government. Other forms of organizing have also developed, and these are generally overlaid on the line and staff structure. In this section, we discuss matrix organizations and virtual organizations. Here we examine the matrix organization in detail.

Matrix Organizations. There are occasions in the management of an organization when a number of individuals from different departments must be grouped into an organizational unit that is separate from the regular line and staff structure. The individuals in the unit may include both line and staff functions. Examples of these organizational units include committees and project teams. The resulting overall form is known as a ***matrix organization***—a two-dimensional structure consisting of horizontal lines intended to pursue special assignments superimposed on the traditional vertical lines of the line and staff organization. The matrix organizational structure is depicted in Figure 5. The special assignments may involve projects, committee duties, and other activities that are not part of the organization's line operations or staff functions.

In Figure 5, the traditional functions of the line and staff organization are listed along the top of the chart, and the special assignments (e.g., projects and committees) are listed vertically at the side. The vertical lines in the chart indicate resources available in the line and staff organization, and horizontal lines indicate the possible need for resources in the project or committee. At the intersection points, a circle means that resources from the given function are needed, and absence of a circle means that resources from that function are not required. Note that different projects and committees need different types of resources.

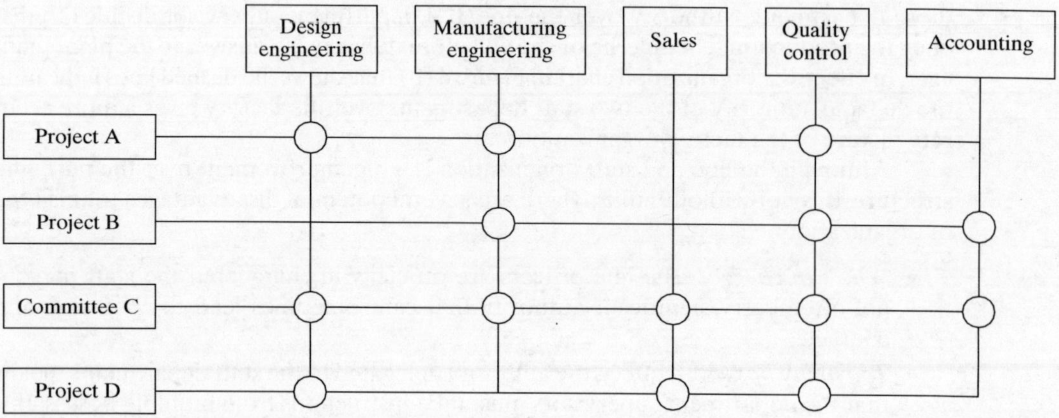

Figure 5 Matrix organization structure.

Special assignments can be temporary or permanent. As indicated above, projects and committees are two common situations giving rise to the need for a matrix organization. By definition, projects are temporary undertakings, and so the assignment of workers to a project is temporary. When the project is completed, the workers are assigned to other projects or return to their regular duties in the line and staff organization.

A ***committee*** is a group of people selected to consider, investigate, take action on, or report on some matter of interest. The selection process may consist of self-nominating, or others with an interest in the matter may nominate the members. Typical reasons and purposes to form a committee include the following:

- *Advisory.* This type of committee is created to advise a decision maker on issues, problems, and/or policies. The purpose is to synthesize the best thinking of several persons, thus leading to a better final decision.
- *Discussion.* A committee can be a discussion group, formed to be a sounding board for a supervisor on his or her decisions and policies. The feedback is an aid to the supervisor in future decisions, and the committee members feel a sense of participation in the management process.
- *Coordination.* Committees are often formed of individuals from several different departments in the organization to ensure that the interests of those functions are all satisfied. Committee members are responsible for representing their respective functions and reporting back the findings or decisions of the committee to their departments.
- *Investigative.* A committee may be formed to investigate some event such as an accident, to determine its cause, and to report the committee findings.

Committees can be temporary (***ad hoc committees***) or permanent (***standing committees***). Advisory, discussion, and coordination committees can be either category (temporary to address a particular problem or permanent to deal with continuing operations). Investigative committees are usually ad hoc because they deal with one-time events.

The matrix organization structure has the following advantages: (1) it focuses attention and resources on the special assignment, which otherwise may become lost in the day-to-day operations of the organization; and (2) it collects the specific expert knowledge required for the special assignment into one organizational unit. The disadvantages include the following: (1) project or committee members must report to two bosses: their regular supervisors and the project team leader or committee chairman; (2) performance appraisal of team members becomes complicated by the dual roles of the workers; and (3) line and staff supervisors may somehow have to find the resources to do the work of the subordinate who has been assigned to the project or committee.

Virtual Organizations. A virtual organization is one that extends beyond the boundaries of a single enterprise. It is a way of combining the best resources of multiple enterprises. A ***virtual organization*** (also known as ***virtual enterprise*** and ***virtual corporation***) is a temporary partnership of resources (e.g., personnel, production capability, market access) from separate organizations intended to exploit a temporary market opportunity or achieve some other objective. The separate organizations are usually different companies, in some cases firms that normally compete with each other. Once the market opportunity is passed or the objective is achieved, the virtual organization is dissolved. In such a partnership, resources are shared among the partners, and benefits (profits) are also shared.

In some respects, the concept of the virtual organization is an extension of ***outsourcing***—the practice engaged in by a company of contracting to an outside firm work that is traditionally accomplished by the company itself. In outsourcing, the company has a strictly business relationship with the outside firm, and the relationship consists of paying for services rendered. In a virtual organization, a partnership is created in which the participants are co-equal rather than buyer-seller.

The formation of a virtual enterprise has the following potential benefits: (1) it may provide access to resources and technologies that are not available in any single organization, (2) it may provide access to new markets and distribution channels, (3) it is likely to reduce product development time because it utilizes resources that already exist (although in some other company) rather than require one company to have all of the resources itself, and (4) it accelerates technology transfer. Some of the guidelines and potential problems associated with virtual organizations are listed in Table 5.

TABLE 5 Guidelines for Virtual Organizations and Problems that Can Occur with Them

Guidelines	Marry well. Choose the right partners for good reasons.
	Play fair. The virtual organization should be a "win-win" opportunity for all participants.
	Put your best people into these relationships.
	Define the objectives.
	Build a common infrastructure.
Problems	Legal issues, such as protection of intellectual property rights currently owned by one of the participants.
	Difficulties evaluating each participant's contribution, so profits can be equitably shared.
	Reluctance of companies to share proprietary information.
	Potential loss of competitive advantage by sharing knowledge.

REFERENCES

[1] Amrine, H. T., J. A. Ritchey, and C. L. Moodie. *Manufacturing Organization and Management*. 5th ed. Englewood Cliffs, NJ: Prentice-Hall, 1987.

[2] Bethel, L. L., F. S. Atwater, G. H. E. Smith, and H. A. Stackman Jr. *Industrial Organization and Management*. New York: McGraw-Hill, 1962.

[3] Blanchard, B. S. *Engineering Organization and Management*. Englewood Cliffs, NJ: Prentice Hall, 1976.

[4] Broom, H. N. *Production Management*. Homewood, IL: Irwin, 1962.

[5] Carzo, R. Jr., and J. N. Yanouzas. *Formal Organizations: A Systems Approach*. Homewood, IL: Irwin, 1967.

[6] Chase, R., N. Aquilano, and R. Jacobs. *Operations Management for Competitive Advantage*. New York: McGraw-Hill, 2001.

[7] Dvir, T., and Y. Berson. "Leadership, Motivation, and Strategic Resource Management." Pp. 841–67 in *Handbook of Industrial Engineering*, 3rd ed., edited by G. Salvendy. New York: Wiley, 2001.

[8] Eastman Kodak Company, Human Factors Section. *Ergonomic Design for People at Work*, Vol. I, edited by S. Rodgers and E. Eggleton. Belmont, CA: Lifetime Learning Publications, 1983.

[9] Eden, D., and S. Globerson. "Financial and Nonfinancial Motivation." Pp. 817–44 in *Handbook of Industrial Engineering*, 2nd ed., edited by G. Salvendy. New York: Wiley, 1992.

[10] Flippo, E. B. *Principles of Personnel Management*. New York: McGraw-Hill, 1961.

[11] George, C. S. Jr. *Management in Industry*. 2nd ed. Englewood Cliffs, NJ: Prentice-Hall, 1964.

[12] Monks, J. G. *Operations Management, Theory and Problems*. New York: McGraw-Hill, 1977.

[13] Moore, F. G. *Manufacturing Management*, 3rd ed. Homewood, IL: Irwin, 1961.

[14] Moore, F. G., and T. E. Hendrick. *Production/Operations Management*. 7th ed. Homewood, IL: Irwin, 1977.

[15] Russell, R. S., and B. W. Taylor III. *Operations Management*, 4th ed. Upper Saddle River, NJ: Prentice Hall, 2003.

[16] Scott, W. G., T. R. Mitchell, and P. H. Birnbaum. *Organization Theory: A Structural and Behavioral Analysis*. 4th ed. Homewood, IL: Irwin, 1981.

[17] Scott, W. G., and T. R. Mitchell. *Organization Theory: A Structural and Behavioral Analysis*. Homewood, IL: Irwin, 1972.

[18] Veilleux, R. F., and L. W. Petro, eds. *Tool and Manufacturing Engineers Handbook*. 4th ed., Vol. 5: *Manufacturing Management*. Dearborn, MI: Society of Manufacturing Engineers, 1988.

[19] Wredge, C. D., and R. G. Greenwood. *Frederick W. Taylor, The Father of Scientific Management: Myth and Reality*. Burr Ridge, IL: Irwin Professional Publishing, 1991.

REVIEW QUESTIONS

1 Define management.

2 What are the four functions of management?

3 What is an organization?

4 What is the specialization principle?

5 What is meant by span of supervision?

6 What are the factors that determine the span of supervision?

7 What does unity of command mean?

8 What is the difference between responsibility and authority in an organization?

9 What is the difference between an operating decision and a policy-making decision?

10 What is the main advantage of a pure line organization?

11 What is a line and staff organization?

12 What are the four categories of staff functions in a line and staff organization?

13 What is a matrix organization?

14 What is the difference between an ad hoc committee and a standing committee?

15 What is a virtual organization?

PROBLEMS

1 In a company's line organization, six vice presidents report to the chief executive officer, seven managers report to each vice president, eight supervisors report to each manager, and 14 workers report to each foreman. Determine (a) the number of workers and (b) the total number of employees in the line organization.

2 In the line portion of a company's line and staff organization, four vice presidents report to the chief executive officer, five managers report to each vice president, six supervisors report to each manager, and 10 direct labor workers report to each foreman. In the staff portion of the organization, five staff personnel report to the president, four staff report to each vice president, three staff report to each manager, and two staff report to each foreman. Determine (a) the number of direct labor workers, (b) the total number of staff personnel, and (c) the total number of employees in the organization.

3 In a firm's line organization, 20 workers report to each foreman at the operating level. Above foremen there are four levels of management (five levels total, including the president at the top). The company employs 80,000 direct labor personnel. What is the average span of supervision in the intermediate management levels?

4 The Department of Transportation in the state government employs 12,000 workers at the lowest level of its line organization. The span of supervision is 10 at the foreman's level and five at all levels of management above foremen. Determine the total number of management levels in the department.

5 An army division has 16,000 foot soldiers. The span of supervision at the sergeant's level is 15. If there are five ranks above sergeant in the division's organization, what is the average span of supervision above sergeant?

6 A certain federal government agency employs 90,000 workers at the lowest level of its line organization. There are six layers of management in the agency. If the span of supervision above the level of foreman is six, what is the span of supervision at the foremen's level?

7 In the line organization of a company, 15 workers report to each foreman at the operating level. In between, the span of supervision is around seven at most other levels. The company employs 90,000 direct labor personnel. At the lowest level, each worker is paid $15,000 annually, foremen are paid 45% more than workers, and at each level above, the salary increment is 45% more than subordinates, all the way up to the president. Determine (a) the number of layers of management, (b) the number of supervisory, management, and executive personnel, and (c) total wage and salary costs for the company's line organization.

Worker Motivation and the Social Organization at Work

What motivates people to work? Certainly one of the motivators is money. People have to earn a living in order to live. There are other factors of a nonmonetary nature that affect worker motivation. In this chapter, we examine several motivation theories and how they apply to work situations. We also discuss the social aspects of the work environment and how worker behavior is affected by this social organization.

1 MOTIVATION AND JOB SATISFACTION

In order to succeed, an organization requires more than just the membership of the individuals who belong to it. It requires the active participation of motivated contributors. ***Motivation for work*** means that an employee is willing to devote effort and energy in productive activity. Motivated workers apply themselves. They want to be effective. They take initiative and show responsibility. They want to improve the methods and processes by which their work is accomplished and to contribute to their organization's goals and objectives.

The topic of worker motivation is of considerable interest to the managers of an organization simply because motivated workers are more productive. Motivated workers tend to have greater job satisfaction, and this benefits other employees and creates a more favorable social environment in the workplace. In this section we discuss (1) some of the theories that have been advanced about work motivation, (2) the conclusions that can be drawn from these theories, and (3) job satisfaction and morale.

1.1 Motivation Theories

Behavioral scientists and social psychologists have developed a number of theories about what motivates people, and these theories contain seeds that can be sowed in the workplace. In the following discussion, we cover the following traditional motivation theories: (1) Maslow's needs gratification theory, (2) Herzberg's dual factor theory, and (3) McGregor's Theory X and Theory Y.

Maslow's Needs Gratification Theory. The needs gratification theory was introduced by Abraham Maslow in the early 1940s.[1] Other social researchers have added to the theory, but Maslow's needs hierarchy remains the best-known treatment. The theory proposes that humans attempt to satisfy five basic needs, briefly described in Table 1. These needs are arranged in a hierarchical order, such that if an individual is able to satisfy the lower level needs, then those needs will no longer be motivators, and he or she will seek to satisfy the higher order needs.

The needs hierarchy is a motivational progression that applies to people who are healthy, normal, and living in a developed society. In general, such a society satisfies the lower-level needs (physiological needs, safety, and security), and therefore, these needs are not motivators. Having satisfied the lower-level needs, people are then motivated to satisfy the higher-level needs through friendships and social interactions, seeking esteem, being creative, and getting ahead in the world.

It should be acknowledged that different individuals respond differently to the various motivators. Some people are quite content to satisfy third- and fourth-level needs—that is, to have family and friends and to work proficiently at a routine job that provides a steady income. Other people are more ambitious; they are driven to climb the corporate ladder to top positions in their organizations or to achieve a scientific breakthrough in their fields of research.

TABLE 1 Maslow's Needs Hierarchy

1. ***Physiological needs.*** The needs of the human body, such as thirst, hunger, sleep, activity, and sex; if these needs are not satisfied, they remain as primary motivators.
2. ***Safety and security.*** The need to be safe and secure, and to be protected against danger.
3. ***Love and esteem by others.*** The social needs which include the desire to obtain the love and friendship of others, to be appreciated and respected by others, and to belong to groups.
4. ***Self-esteem.*** The need for self-esteem and self-respect; it is the desire to be worthy in one's own mind.
5. ***Self-actualization.*** The need to find self-fulfillment, to achieve one's full potential, and to become all that one is capable of; it motivates the individual toward self-improvement, self-development, self-expression, and similar ambitions.

[1]A. H. Maslow, "A Theory of Human Motivation," *Psychological Review* (July 1943): Vol. 50, No. 4, pp 370–396. The theory is also described in Maslow's book, *Motivation and Personality* (New York: Harper, 1954).

TABLE 2 Herzberg's Extrinsic and Intrinsic Factors

Extrinsic Factors (Dissatisfiers)	Intrinsic Factors (Satisfiers)
Wages or salary, including fringe benefits	Achievement and personal satisfaction in accomplishing a task or project
Wage and salary increases	Recognition (e.g., receiving an award for a job achievement)
Company policies and procedures	The work itself (e.g., the job content and whether it is personally satisfying to the worker)
Competence of supervision	Responsibility for one's own work
Interpersonal relations with colleagues at work (e.g., supervisors, peers, subordinates)	Responsibility for other workers
Working conditions, physical surroundings, size of one's office	Advancement (e.g., promotion to a higher level)
Status in the organization	Growth (e.g., learning new skills)
Job security	
Personal life (because personal factors can affect job satisfaction)	

Herzberg's Dual Factor Theory. Frederick Herzberg advocated an alternative theory of work motivation. Based on his study of nearly 1700 employees, he proposed that two types of factors motivate people: extrinsic factors and intrinsic factors.[2] ***Extrinsic factors*** are those that originate from outside the actual work content and potentially result in job dissatisfaction. Herzberg called them *dissatisfiers*. ***Intrinsic factors*** are those that relate to the nature and content of the work itself. They are the basis for job satisfaction and are called *satisfiers*. Table 2 lists examples of the two categories that form his dual factor theory. If the extrinsic factors in a person's job lie below some level that represents an acceptable level to the individual, then he or she becomes dissatisfied. On the other hand, if these factors are above the acceptable level, they do not necessarily result in job satisfaction; they just avoid job dissatisfaction. Job satisfaction is derived from increments in the intrinsic factors—for example, achieving completion of an important project or advancing to a higher position in the organization. Absence of these factors does not result in job dissatisfaction; it just inhibits job satisfaction.

Theory X and Theory Y. Douglas McGregor's theory consists of two alternative models or assumptions about worker behavior: one that represents a very negative view of workers (Theory X) while the other represents a very positive view (Theory Y).[3] The characteristics of the two models are described in Table 3. In the years following the publication of McGregor's book *The Human Side of Enterprise*, Theory X and Theory Y were credited with profoundly changing the way supervisors and managers perceived their subordinates and in how work should be organized and workers administered. Theory X presents a set of assumptions about workers that may have been quite valid for the late 1800s and early 1900s. Frederick W. Taylor would probably have endorsed Theory X. On the other hand, Theory Y seems a better description of workers in the latter half of the twentieth century and the early twenty-first century. Workers today would have difficulty being supervised according to Theory X. We can see the

[2]F. Herzberg, *Work and the Nature of Man* (Cleveland, OH: World Publishing, 1966).
[3]D. McGregor, *The Human Side of Enterprise* (New York: McGraw-Hill, 1962).

TABLE 3 McGregor's Theory X and Theory Y

Theory X	Theory Y
The average human has an inherent aversion toward work and will avoid it if at all possible.	Expenditure of physical energy and mental effort in work is as natural as resting or playing.
Because of this aversion to work, workers must be coerced, threatened, and directed in order to motivate them to work.	Workers will exercise self-direction and self-control when they are pursuing objectives to which they are committed.
The average worker is of limited ability and intellectual capacity.	Commitment to objectives by workers depends on the rewards associated with achieving the objectives.
The average worker avoids responsibility.	The average human can learn not only to accept responsibility but also to seek it.
The average worker prefers to be told what to do.	Creativity, imagination, ingenuity, and intellectual potential are widely distributed in the general population.
The average human seeks security above all.	The intellectual potential of the average human is only partially utilized in most job situations.

applications of Theory Y in the use of self-managed work teams, quality circles and kaizen circles, Six Sigma project teams, the matrix organization structure and modern approaches to performance appraisal.

1.2 Conclusions on Worker Motivation

At the risk of overgeneralizing from the theories of worker motivation discussed above, we can conclude that people respond to two general types of motivations: positive motivation and negative motivation. In ***positive motivation***, a manager attempts to affect the behavior of workers by holding out the promise of gains and rewards that are tangible (e.g., money, bonuses, salary increases) or intangible (e.g., recognition, friendship). In ***negative motivation***, the manager tries to influence the behavior of employees through the use of threats or fear. Again, the consequences can be tangible (e.g., job loss, a demotion with less pay) or intangible (e.g., holding back recognition, loss of friendship). Supervisors and managers tend to use both types of motivation on their subordinates, although the contemporary human resources view is that positive motivation is more likely to result in greater productivity and higher morale over the long term. Nevertheless, there is always an implicit power that a supervisor holds over a subordinate that elicits a negative motivational influence. Most supervisors have the authority to fire a subordinate even though they rarely and reluctantly exercise that authority.

The traditional theories seem to discount the motivating effect of money: wages and salaries. A fundamental assumption in economics is that human behavior is guided by self-interest based on financial gain. Most managers firmly believe that money is a powerful motivator. This belief is based on their observations of people in general, their subordinates in particular, and their own personal feelings about money. Even people who already possess significant wealth are almost always motivated to seek greater wealth, sometimes with drives that far exceed those of the average worker. Managers and executives earning six- and seven-figure salaries are often paid performance bonuses by their companies, and their ambitions and expectations are to receive still more money the following year.

Let us attempt to reconcile this belief in the motivating effect of money with some of the traditional theories of motivation. In the case of Maslow's needs hierarchy, although physiological needs, safety, and security are not expressed in monetary terms by Maslow, money is nevertheless the means by which these needs are satisfied in a modern industrial society. People are motivated to work in order to achieve satisfaction of these basic needs. The extraordinary monetary ambitions of wealthy individuals described above suggest perhaps the existence of a sixth level in Maslow's hierarchy, one that is beyond self-actualization and concerned simply with obtaining wealth for its own sake. Trying to reconcile the wealth-acquisition ambitions with Herzberg's hypothesis about extrinsic factors, we can only surmise that people who earn high salaries have a very high standard regarding the acceptable salary level that avoids dissatisfaction. Although they achieve salary levels far above the average, they firmly believe that they are worth at least that much.

1.3 Job Satisfaction and Morale

Highly motivated workers are usually satisfied with their jobs and exhibit high morale. ***Job satisfaction*** refers to the mental state of contentment with one's work and work situation. It is a contentment felt by an individual worker: "I feel good about my job. I like the work I do." ***Morale*** is a mental and emotional sense of common purpose felt by a group about the tasks that lie ahead. It is an esprit de corps that reflects a confidence about the future: "We can succeed, despite the hardships that lie before us." Morale is closely related to teamwork and team spirit. Job satisfaction is more of an individual feeling, while morale tends to be a group emotion.

Factors Affecting Job Satisfaction and Morale. The factors that determine job satisfaction are suggested by Herzberg's theory dealing with satisfiers and dissatisfiers. Job satisfaction results from intrinsic factors such as personal achievement, recognition, work content of the job, responsibility, advancement, and growth (Table 2). These factors tend to have a positive effect on job satisfaction when they are present but do not necessarily lead to job dissatisfaction if they are not present. Causes of job dissatisfaction tend to correlate with the extrinsic factors in Herzberg's theory. They include poor relationships with supervisors and coworkers, poor company policies, ineffective management, poor working conditions, and low wages or salaries. Reversing the direction of these factors from negative to positive will not necessarily turn job dissatisfaction into job satisfaction, according to Herzberg's theory, but it may provide a work situation in which intrinsic factors have a positive influence on job satisfaction.

One of the most important determinants of job satisfaction of an employee and the general morale of a worker group is the direct supervisor. A good supervisor can elicit the intrinsic factors that cause job satisfaction and mollify the extrinsic factors that cause job dissatisfaction. A supervisor who exhibits good leadership and technical authority can educe high morale from the group or department. The typical traits of good supervisors and managers are listed in Table 4. Through these traits, supervisors and managers earn the respect of their subordinates.

TABLE 4 Typical Traits of Good Supervisors and Managers

They treat their subordinates with fairness, consistency, and respect.
They take a personal interest in their subordinates; they are understanding of subordinates' personal problems.
They readily recommend their subordinates for promotions, job upgrades, awards, and other forms of recognition.
They communicate with their subordinates, informing them of upcoming changes and challenges, and soliciting the subordinates' ideas and opinions.
They make sure that subordinates are provided with the required tools, materials, and resources for the subordinates to do their jobs.
They are technically knowledgeable about their subordinates' jobs; if the subordinate has a problem or issue, the supervisor knows how to deal with it.
They know how to delegate, and they avoid micromanaging.
They know and enforce standard procedures, safety rules, and company policy.
They are able to convey the objectives of the organization, so that subordinates feel that they are stakeholders, not just employees.

A survey taken of 589 workers in the United States in August 2004 indicated that a majority is satisfied with their jobs.[4] About half responded that they are "very satisfied" with their jobs, and seven in ten said they are paid fairly. White-collar workers (e.g., professionals and executives) are more likely to say that their work is interesting, while blue-collar workers are least likely to say their jobs are interesting. Women are more likely to respond that they felt their work is important than men.

Individual workers can be satisfied or dissatisfied with their jobs, or they can have neutral feelings about it. And they can collectively be of high morale or low morale, or there can be an absence of this feeling. There is usually, but not always, a correlation between job satisfaction and morale in a group or organization. If a person feels good about his or her job, this attitude radiates positively on coworkers and has an uplifting effect on group morale. Table 5 describes signs of job satisfaction and dissatisfaction and high and low employee morale.

TABLE 5 Job Satisfaction and Dissatisfaction and High and Low Employee Morale

Signs of Job Satisfaction and High Morale	Signs of Job Dissatisfaction and Low Morale
High productivity	Low productivity and high costs
High quality of products and services	Poor quality of products and services
A good safety record	High accident and injury rates
Respect for company property and policies	Poor housekeeping, sabotage of company property
Low labor turnover	High labor turnover
Low absenteeism	High absentee rates

[4]W. Lester, "A Majority of Americans Find Satisfaction in Their Work," *The Morning Call* (September 2004, p. D3).

Job Enlargement, Job Enrichment, and Job Rotation. When jobs are specialized, the work content is simple and the task time is short. Although there are many advantages to specialization (e.g., high efficiency and productivity), it is often viewed negatively by the workers who specialize. Job satisfaction can be adversely affected because tasks that have been specialized tend to be routine, boring, unappealing, unchallenging, and unrewarding.

Job enlargement and job enrichment represent efforts to reverse these adverse characteristics. The terms are especially applicable to manual, repetitive tasks. They are attempts to make the work less routine and more interesting by expanding the scope of the job to include more activities and/or greater responsibilities. ***Job enlargement*** refers to a horizontal increase in the number of activities included in the work, where the activities still consist of the same basic type as before. If a worker's previous job was to attach two components to the base plate of a 10-piece subassembly, and the job scope was expanded so that the worker now puts the entire subassembly together, that would represent a case of job enlargement. The worker now has the satisfaction of completing the whole subassembly rather than simply doing a small portion of the work. The job is now more interesting because of the variety of tasks that comprise it.

Job enrichment refers to a vertical increase in the work content associated with the job, which means that the worker assumes greater responsibility for planning the work content and for inspecting the resulting work unit. Suppose a worker's current job is simply to load parts into a milling machine, engage the feed, and unload the finished piece at the end of each cycle. Someone else sets the machine up for the production batch, and someone else inspects the finished pieces in the batch. If the scope of the job is now increased so that the worker is responsible for setting up the machine and inspecting the completed parts in addition to the actual production, this would be an example of job enrichment. As in job enlargement, the worker now performs a greater variety of tasks, but the tasks deal with activities that are traditionally accomplished by other specialists, such as setup personnel, foremen, and inspectors. Because the scope of a given job is often increased both horizontally and vertically, the term *job enrichment* is commonly used to cover both categories of change.

Another way to increase the variety of tasks in a worker's job is through ***job rotation***, a situation in which a worker is trained to perform several different tasks but each task is a relatively simple one of the type associated with job specialization. An example of job rotation would be when a worker on an assembly line is trained to perform the specialized tasks at several different stations on the line and is assigned to each of those stations at different times of the day or on different days. The term ***cross training*** is used for the situation in which a worker is trained to perform multiple tasks. When a worker has the opportunity to perform a variety of tasks rather than just one single task, the job becomes more interesting. Being proficient at several different tasks probably increases a worker's sense of self-esteem.

Figure 1 depicts graphically the key features of job specialization, enlargement, enrichment, and rotation.

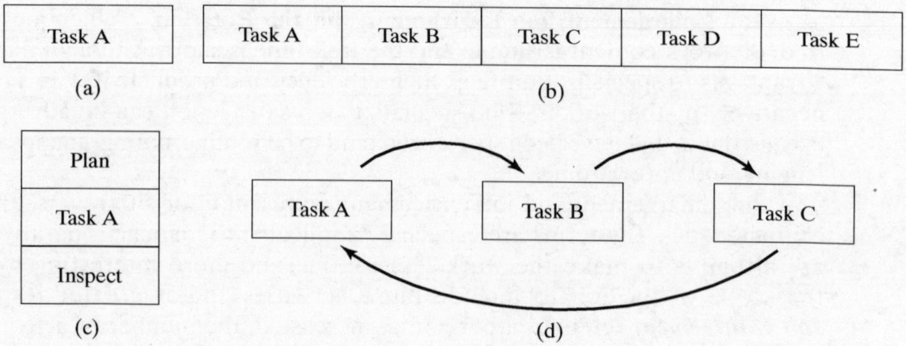

Figure 1 Graphical depictions of (a) job specialization, (b) job enlargement, (c) job enrichment, and (d) job rotation.

2 THE SOCIAL ORGANIZATION AT WORK

Work serves an important social function. People go to their jobs; they work with other people, socialize, make new friends, and establish relationships that often transcend the workplace. Work is a time away from home and family (unless the person works at home) that allows for interactions with other individuals who are similarly away. It provides a change of environment and a respite from what otherwise might be too much time spent with the same family members.

Humans have a desire to associate with members of the same species, to belong to a group, and to be accepted by that group on a social basis. This is a need that appears in Maslow's needs hierarchy, and it is also an intrinsic factor in Herzberg's theory. It has been argued that this human need for association is probably a stronger motivator than the individual self-interest based on financial gain assumed by most economists and managers.[5] One of the pioneering research studies to identify the importance of the social or informal aspects of organizational behavior was conducted starting in 1924 and continuing into the 1930s at the Hawthorne Works of Western Electric Company near Chicago, Illinois.[6] The experiments, which came to be known as the ***Hawthorne studies***, are described in Historical Note 1. The initial objective of the experiments was to determine the effect of lighting on productivity. However, lighting and other physical changes made in the workplace environment were discovered to be much less important in affecting productivity than the feelings, attitudes, and relationships of the workers. The social aspects of the organization were demonstrated to be powerful influences on the motivation and performance of workers.

[5]Elton Mayo, *The Social Problems of an Industrial Civilization* (Boston, MA: Harvard Business School, 1945).

[6]The Western Electric Company was the manufacturing division of AT&T Corporation when AT&T was the telephone monopoly in the United States. After the breakup of AT&T in 1984, Western Electric was separated from the parent corporation and became AT&T Technologies. The company renamed itself Lucent Technologies in 1996.

HISTORICAL NOTE 1 THE HAWTHORNE STUDIES

The Western Electric Company was a manufacturer of telephone equipment and a part of the AT&T Corporation. In 1924, in collaboration with the National Research Council and several psychologists, the company initiated a series of experiments to discover the effect of lighting on production output and worker fatigue. Later, the scope of the study was expanded to include other factors, such as changes in shift hours, introduction of rest breaks of different durations and periodicities, and provision of refreshments during the breaks. The investigation continued for about eight years and included an interview phase that covered about 21,000 employees.

In one of the main physical experiments, two groups of workers were used as the subjects: a control group and a test group. The changes in lighting and other factors were implemented in the test group but not in the control group. The surprising result was that both groups substantially increased their production outputs and that the changes in work methods had little effect. Output increased in the control group because of the competitive challenge. Those workers wanted to demonstrate that they were as productive as the workers in the test group. The researchers concluded that worker attitude is an important determinant of productivity. Workers who participated in the experiments, whether in the control group or the test group, were made to feel important because they had become the focus of attention of the research scientists as well as company management. The workers themselves became interested in the experiments and believed it was to their own advantage to increase production. Their work had a purpose. The social function of work had been united with the production function to create a work system that increased productivity. The social work environment thus emerged as an important factor.

The formal principles and structures of organizations include the chain of command, departmental functions, spans of supervision, and other features of the organization. This chapter focuses on the informal structures of organizations—the many personal and social relationships that exist among workers who are distributed throughout the various departments of the organization. These relationships are often the real basis for getting things done. They form a social organization that affects members and their ***behavior***—the manner in which they conduct themselves, usually in response to environmental stimuli. Behavior is guided by certain rules that are instinctive or have been learned. Our interest is in the behavior of the members of a work organization while they are at work. Members of an organization behave according to its formal rules, but their behavior is also influenced by informal norms that are social in nature. Thus, an individual member exhibits (1) formal behavior in the formal organization and (2) informal behavior in the social organization.

Formal behavior means that members conduct themselves according to standards that have been established by the formal organization. These standards are documented in the official policies and operating procedures of the organization, and they also include undocumented rules that are learned as the accepted ways in which the organization and its members accomplish their business. The formal organization and its rules governing formal behavior are very much oriented toward the objectives to be achieved. The following examples illustrate how formal behavior is involved in performing the work of the organization:

- A professor submitting grades of students in a course according to the specified procedure of the university
- A surgeon using a standard surgical procedure to perform a gall bladder operation
- A priest presenting a sermon to the congregation at Sunday mass
- A clerk requisitioning office supplies for a department
- A salesperson explaining the operation and features of a dishwasher to a customer in an appliance store
- A production worker following the standard method to perform a task
- A production worker reporting up the chain of command about a quality problem experienced in performing a task

Formal behavior may include social elements. For example, the surgeon may spend time with the patient before the surgical procedure explaining what is going to happen and discussing the prognosis. The priest may inject some humor into his sermon in order to keep the attention of the parishioners. And the salesperson may feel it is in the interest of the sale to exchange pleasantries with the customer during the initial encounter. These extra elements are social, but they may be very important steps in achieving the work objectives of the organization.

Informal behavior refers to behavior that is not prescribed by the documented and undocumented policies, procedures, and rules of the formal organization. It is behavior that has a social orientation. Informal behavior may be work-oriented or purely social. Work-oriented informal behavior is socially directed behavior that is consistent with and/or pursuant to the objectives of the organization. The following examples illustrate work-oriented informal behavior:

- A professor temporarily taking over the course load of another professor who is away at a conference
- A production worker giving advice to another worker who is having difficulty keeping up with the pace of a task
- A car salesperson completing a sale for another salesperson when the other salesperson's spouse arrives unexpectedly

These examples represent favors granted by one coworker to another that are not included in the job descriptions of the respective positions. In fact, some acts of work-oriented informal behavior may even violate the rules of the formal organization. For example, the production worker who is having trouble keeping up with his or her task should seek help from the supervisor, not a fellow production worker.

Purely social behavior in the workplace is behavior that is not related to work accomplishment. The following examples illustrate this type of behavior:

- A foreman stopping by a production operation to ask the worker how her sick mother is doing

- Two office workers chatting about the baseball game last night white waiting for an elevator
- A car salesman telling a joke to another salesman while waiting for customers to arrive in the dealer showroom.

Both work-oriented and purely social behavior in the workplace are unintended in the official view of the formal organization. While work-oriented informal behavior supports the work purpose, purely social behavior is extraneous to work. Yet the social organization and its associated behavior exist in the formal organization whether it is unintended or not. A certain amount of pure socializing may in fact be beneficial to the operations of the organization because it helps to build strong personal relationships among members, which will likely increase individual motivation, job satisfaction, and morale. In addition, the social organization establishes a framework for cooperation among members, which facilitates the procedures of the formal organization. Accordingly, purely social behavior is tolerated and even encouraged by the formal organization, so long as limits are placed on the time that members engage in it. When these limits are exceeded, responsible supervisors must intervene and represent the interests of the organization by warning the errant employees.

Just as the formal organization establishes rules that attempt to regulate the behavior of members, the social organization also has rules that have a similar objective. The social rules are based on culture, customs, ethnicity, morality, age, gender, and shared beliefs. The formal rules and the social rules often reinforce each other. Physical abuse of one employee by another is against company policy, and there is a commonly held norm in most social cultures that frowns on physical abuse. Violators are subject to reprimand or dismissal in the formal organization, and they may be subjected to social penalties in the informal organization, such as ostracism or disassociation. Either form of sanction is undesirable to the individual, which serves to regulate behavior against physical abuse.

In some cases, the formal rules are at odds with the social rules. The formal rules are designed to encourage greater productivity and efficiency in the pursuit of the organization's objectives. The socially oriented rules of the informal organization may favor other objectives when increased productivity and efficiency are seen as threats to the individual workers. For example, job security is an important shared belief among workers. It is understandably part of their social norm. If increased productivity, which means greater output with fewer workers, is thought to result in layoffs, then the affected workers may resist the methods changes that would increase productivity.

REFERENCES

[1] Amrine, H. T., J. A. Ritchey, and C. L. Moodie. *Manufacturing Organization and Management*. 5th ed. Englewood Cliffs, NJ: Prentice-Hall, 1987.

[2] Bridger, R. S. *Introduction to Ergonomics*. 2nd ed. London: Taylor and Francis, 2003.

[3] Dvir, T., and Y. Berson. "Leadership, Motivation, and Strategic Resource Management." Pp. 841–67 in *Handbook of Industrial Engineering*, 3rd ed., edited by G. Salvendy. New York: Wiley, 2001.

[4] Eden, D., and S. Globerson. "Financial and Nonfinancial Motivation." Pp 817–844 in *Handbook of Industrial Engineering*, 2nd ed., edited by G. Salvendy New York: Wiley, 1992.

[5] Fay, C. H., M. A. Thompson, and D. Knight, eds. *The Executive Handbook on Compensation*. New York: Free Press, 2001.

[6] Mylan, T. A., and T. M Schmidt. "Involvement, Empowerment, and Motivation." Pp. 2.85–2.99 in *Maynard's Industrial Engineering Handbook*, 5th ed., edited by K. B. Zandin. New York, McGraw-Hill, 2001.

[7] Niebel, B. W., and A. Freivalds. *Methods, Standards, and Work Design*. 11th ed. New York: McGraw-Hill, 2003.

[8] Wickens, C. D., J. Lee, Y. Liu, and S. Becker. *An Introduction to Human Factors Engineering*. 2nd ed. Upper Saddle River, NJ: Pearson/Prentice Hall, 2004.

REVIEW QUESTIONS

1 What does motivation for work mean?

2 What is Maslow's needs gratification theory of worker motivation?

3 What are the physiological needs in Maslow's needs gratification theory?

4 What does self-actualization mean in Maslow's needs gratification theory?

5 What is the difference between extrinsic factors and intrinsic factors in Herzberg's dual factor theory of work motivation?

6 What are some examples of extrinsic factors in Herzberg's dual factor theory of work motivation? Name three.

7 What are some examples of intrinsic factors in Herzberg's dual factor theory of work motivation? Name three.

8 What is McGregor's Theory X–Theory Y?

9 What do the terms *positive motivation* and *negative motivation* mean?

10 Define job satisfaction.

11 What is job enlargement?

12 What is job enrichment?

13 What was the original objective of the Hawthorne studies?

14 What was the significant finding of the Hawthorne studies?

15 An individual member exhibits (1) formal behavior in the formal organization and (2) informal behavior in the social organization. What is the meaning of these two forms of behavior?

Job Evaluation and Performance Appraisal

One of the important questions faced by the management of any organization is how much to pay each employee. The appropriate answer is that an employee's pay level should be based on (1) the type of job the employee holds and (2) how well the employee performs that job. Certain jobs have more value to the organization, and certain employees make greater contributions to the organization. ***Job evaluation*** is a systematic method for assessing the relative values of jobs in an organization and for determining an appropriate wage or salary structure for those jobs.[1] The focus is on the jobs and not the persons holding those jobs. Assessing the relative contributions and merits of the individuals holding the jobs is called ***performance appraisal***.[2] This chapter is concerned with these two topics in human resources management: job evaluation, which deals with the work, and performance appraisal, which deals with the worker.

[1]The Employee and Labor Relations Committee (ANSI Standard Z94.13-1989) defines job evaluation as follows: "The evaluation or rating of jobs to determine their position in a job hierarchy. The evaluation may be achieved through the assignment of points or the use of some other systematic rating method for essential job requirements such as skill, experience, and responsibility. Job evaluation is widely used in the establishment of wage rate structures and in the elimination of wage inequalities. It is always applied to jobs rather than the qualities of individuals in the job."
[2]The Employee and Labor Relations Committee (ANSI Standard Z94.13-1989) defines performance appraisal as follows: "Supervisory or peer analysis of work performance. May be made in connection with wage and salary review, promotion, transfer, or employee training."

1 JOB EVALUATION

Job evaluation is a procedure for determining the value of a given job relative to other jobs in the same organization. A ***job*** is defined as the collection of tasks, duties, and responsibilities that are assigned to one or more persons whose work is at the same level and of the same nature. Job evaluation is a formal procedure based on three principles:

1. Job evaluation determines the relative values of jobs, not their absolute values.
2. The evaluation procedure is concerned with the job, not the person holding the job.
3. The results of job evaluation represent only one factor in the decision about the appropriate pay level for a given job.

Other factors in the pay level decision include the laws of supply and demand that operate in the labor market and the organization's philosophy and policy regarding the average levels of its own pay scales relative to those of other employers in the region.

The job evaluation process can be a major undertaking for an organization, requiring the commitment of significant resources in time and money. The decision to perform such a process is made at the top of the chain-of-command. Most organizations with more than a few dozen employees elect to use a formal job evaluation for the following reasons:

- The organization desires to have an equitable wage structure as part of its wage and salary policy.
- The organization wants a wage structure that can be defended against claims of unfairness, favoritism, and gender or age bias. The federal Equal Pay Act of 1963 mandates "equal pay for equal work."
- The organization's current wage structure is no longer consistent with the jobs accomplished because the nature of the work done by the organization has changed significantly since the current wage structure was installed.
- The organization's pay levels are not competitive, at least in certain types of positions, as evidenced by a high employee turnover rate and problems in recruiting new employees. The organization wants to become more competitive but it wants to use a rational approach in making the necessary pay level adjustments.
- The organization is changing its compensation system (e.g., moving from a direct wage incentive plan to a gain-sharing plan), and a sound wage structure is a prerequisite for making the change.

Once the decision to conduct the job evaluation has been made, two additional decisions are required: (1) which jobs should be included in the study and (2) who should perform the study?

Deciding which jobs to evaluate is not a trivial matter. Most organizations consist of various categories of employees whose functions entail entirely different kinds of work. Production workers perform jobs that are completely different from the jobs performed in the front office. The usual practice in job evaluation is to select for study a group whose jobs are fairly homogenous. For instance, the procedure would be concerned only with the production workers, so that the study could be custom-designed for that group, with job classifications defined for the type of production work done in the facility.

The next decision involves the selection of the individuals who will conduct the study. There are two basic choices: to hire a consulting firm that specializes in job evaluation or to use internal staff, such as members of the human resources department. The consulting firm can be contracted either to accomplish the entire procedure itself or to provide expert advice and assistance to the internal staff that performs the actual study. There are clear advantages to having internal staff involved: (1) they know their own organization and the jobs in it better than an outside firm, (2) employee acceptance is likely to be greater when internal people are doing the study, and (3) although the job evaluation itself is a once-and-done process, the resulting wage structure is permanent (at least for the foreseeable future), and internal staff must administer and maintain it. In any case, the following steps usually take place in a job evaluation:

1. Analyze each job, leading to a set of job descriptions for all positions.
2. Determine the relative worth of the jobs using one of the available job evaluation methods.
3. Establish a wage structure for the jobs.

Our discussion in the following sections is organized around these three steps.

1.1 Job Analysis

Job analysis is the process of obtaining and documenting all of the relevant information about a specific job, such as tasks performed, responsibilities assumed, and skills and knowledge required.[3] The documentation that results from a job analysis is called a ***job description***, which is a written statement about the job, including its identification (e.g., job title), duties and responsibilities, qualifications required for the position, and working conditions. The typical contents of a job description are presented in Table 1.

For purposes of job evaluation, the information contained in a job description is used for determining the worth of each job relative to other jobs in the organization. In addition, a job description has other applications apart from job evaluation:

- It documents the precise duties of the position. Thus, the expectations of the position are known to the jobholder. It also indicates the limits of the required duties. For example, if a worker is requested to perform a task that is outside the scope of duties in the description, the worker has the right to decline the request.
- It identifies the qualifications (e.g., education level, skills, experience) required in employee recruitment and selection.
- It indicates what training may be required of the jobholder.
- It serves as basic information during employee performance appraisal.

[3]The Employee and Labor Relations Committee (ANSI Standard Z94.13-1989) defines job analysis as follows: "Systematic study of a job (or position) leading to a detailed specification of qualifications and performance requirements for purposes of wage (or salary) administration, employee selection or training, determination of skill transfer opportunity, comparison or consolidation of jobs or organization design."

TABLE 1 Typical Contents of a Job Description

Job title. An identification of the position. Examples include "machine tool operator," "laboratory technician," and "supervisor of assembly department."

Summary of duties. A concise description (e.g., one or two sentences) that indicates the general nature of the duties and tasks performed in the position. For example, "The position consists of operating various production machine tools in the machine shop."

Detailed statement of duties. A list of specific tasks required of the position. For example, the statement might list the specific equipment included within the duties and what additional tasks are involved, such as setting up the machine and minor maintenance responsibilities.

Qualifications required. A description of the technical skills, education, training, previous experience, and physical qualifications needed in the position.

Responsibilities. A statement of the nature of the responsibilities assumed in the position, such as safety, budgetary, and supervisory concerns.

Working conditions. A description of the physical working conditions encountered in the position. Is the work performed indoors or outdoors? What are the hazards?

Relationship to other jobs. Identification of the direct supervisor (by title, not person), subordinates if any, promotion opportunities, and relationships with coworkers.

Job analysis requires considerable time, not only by the human resources staff involved in the study, but also by current jobholders and their supervisors. The time is required to gather the information, analyze it, and process it into the proper job description format. For the jobholder, it is an intrusive process because its purpose is to explore what workers actually do in their jobs, and what they do may be at odds with what they should be doing. It also attempts to determine allocations of their time to the various activities that comprise their workload. The sources of data used in job analysis may include questionnaires, interviews with the jobholder, current job descriptions, and direct observation of the job being performed. This kind of investigation may be uncomfortable and worrisome for the employee who does not know how the results of the study will affect his or her position and pay.

1.2 Job Evaluation Methods

When the job analysis step has been completed and the job descriptions are available, the value of each job is determined using one of the available job evaluation methods or an adaptation of these methods. Job evaluation methods are often distinguished as qualitative or quantitative. Qualitative methods tend to compare jobs by examining the whole job, whereas quantitative methods analyze the various component factors in the job and assign numerical scores to these factors to indicate their relative values. In our coverage, we describe four methods: (1) job ranking method, (2) job classification method, (3) factor comparison method, and (4) point-factor method. The first two methods are qualitative, and the third and fourth are quantitative.

Job Ranking Method. The job ranking method is a simple qualitative evaluation technique that requires the least amount of time to complete. In the ranking procedure, jobs are ranked in order of increasing value by the judgment of the evaluators and then organized into a hierarchy of job grades. Various approaches can be used to arrive at the ranking, depending on the number of jobs to be evaluated, the structure of the organization, and the preferences of the evaluators. For medium and larger organizations

TABLE 2 Summary of the Paired Comparison Technique Applied to Seven Jobs

Job	Number of Times Rated Higher	Job Ranking
General machine operator	4	3
Material handler	0	7 (lowest)
Tool and die maker	6	1 (highest)
Drill press operator	1	6
Milling machine operator	3	4
Lathe operator	2	5
Machine setup person	5	2

with multiple departments, the starting point is usually for the jobs within each department to be ranked separately by groups of staff personnel familiar with the work done in the respective department. Once this task is completed, comparisons across departments are made to determine job rankings for the larger organization. This must be done by a group of evaluators who understand the jobs in the different departments.

One technique often used in the job ranking process is ***paired comparisons***, in which all of the jobs are compared two at a time to identify which of each pair is of greater value. The advantage of this technique is that it requires only two jobs to be compared at a time, thus simplifying each decision for the evaluator. The disadvantage of paired comparisons is exhibited when there are many such comparisons to be made. The number of comparisons can be determined as follows:

$$\text{Number of paired comparisons} = \frac{n\,(n-1)}{2} \tag{1}$$

where n = the number of jobs to be compared. For 10 jobs, the number of paired comparisons is 45, but for 20 jobs, the comparisons number 190.

Table 2 shows a possible outcome of the paired comparisons technique for seven jobs that were evaluated. The second column indicates the number of times that each job was rated as more important when compared at random with one other job in the list. The job with the highest score (i.e., number of times it was rated first) is ranked as the highest value, the next highest score is ranked second, and so on. The completed rankings are shown in the third column. After the rankings across departments have been completed, the jobs must be arranged into job grades. Wage ranges are subsequently assigned to these grades.

The advantages of the job ranking method are (1) its simplicity, which means it does not require a staff that is sophisticated in job evaluation techniques, and (2) the fact that it can be completed in a relatively short period. Its disadvantages are (1) its subjectivity and (2) lack of analytical rigor, which sometimes results in a wage structure that is more difficult to defend against claims of inequity.

Job Classification Method. Like the job ranking method, the job classification method is a qualitative approach that ranks jobs into grades. The difference is that the job grades are defined in advance rather than after the ranking process, as in job ranking. This preliminary definition of job grades has given rise to several other names for the job classification method, including the ***grade description method*** and ***predetermined grading***. Once the grade descriptions are defined, evaluators then decide into which grade each job should be classified, using the job descriptions as the basis for classification.

The most difficult step in the job classification method is preparing the set of job grade descriptions. An organization can either develop its own grade descriptions or it can save itself from this chore by purchasing one of several commercially available prepackaged grading systems. If it develops its own job grade descriptions, two key issues must be considered: (1) the number of grades to be included and (2) the type of wording to be used.

The number of grades required in the job classification method depends on the type of organization and the number of different jobs. This number typically ranges between 5 and 15, although as many as 30 have been used [3]. The most well known implementation of the job classification method is the U.S. Civil Service Commission, which uses 18 job grades (GS-1 through GS-18) in its General Schedule for white-collar positions in the federal government.

The wording of the descriptions should include key words and job factors that will subsequently permit evaluators to slot a variety of job descriptions into the corresponding grades. For example, the Civil Service Commission uses eight job factors: (1) difficulty and variety of work, (2) degree of supervision received or exercised by jobholder, (3) judgment, (4) originality, (5) type and purpose of official contacts, (6) responsibility, (7) experience, and (8) knowledge. The language used in the descriptions must be sufficiently general that job descriptions from diverse technical fields (e.g., engineering, accounting, legal) can all be classified. At the lowest job grade, the descriptions often include phrases such as "simple routine tasks are performed," "little experience is required," "much supervision is needed," and so on. At higher job grades, the phrases are more likely to be "tasks require analysis," "at least five years of experience is required," and "little supervision is needed."

Advantages of the job classification method are similar to those of the job ranking method: (1) simplicity and (2) relative speed of implementation. In addition, the job classification method is considered more objective and precise than the job ranking method due to the preexistence of job grade descriptions. The two methods share the disadvantage of subjectivity. Other disadvantages are unique to the job classification method: (1) the difficulties in developing the job grade definitions or finding a commercial package that is a good match with the organization's job hierarchy, and (2) ambiguity in assigning jobs to grades when certain factors of the job seem to fit one grade but other factors fit a different grade.

Factor Comparison Method. The factor comparison method is based on the premise that all jobs contain certain universal factors that can be compared separately for each job in order to evaluate the total worth of the job. The following universal factors are commonly accepted: (1) skill, (2) mental demands, (3) physical demands, (4) responsibility, and (5) working conditions. Based on comparison of these factors for a given job, a dollar value of each factor is determined, so that the sum of the dollar values for all factors is the dollar value of the job (i.e., the wage rate or salary). Even though some judgments are required during the evaluation procedure, the factor comparison method is considered to be more objective than the preceding methods, and it is a quantitative method because of the dollar calculations that are required.

TABLE 3 The Ranking of Benchmark Jobs in the Five Universal Factors

Job Title	Skill	Mental Demands	Physical Demands	Responsibility	Working Conditions
Machinist	1	1	4	1	3
Assembler	2	2	3	2	4
Material handler	3	3	2	3	2
Laborer	4	4	1	4	1

Source: Based on an example in [3].

The factor comparison method requires the selection of ***benchmark jobs*** (also known as ***key jobs***)—jobs that serve as reference points from which other jobs can be compared. One of the selection criteria for these benchmark jobs is that they are paid at rates that the evaluators can agree are appropriate and fair levels. The benchmark jobs should cover a wide range of wage rates and a diverse mixture of job factors.

The first step in the factor comparison method is to rank the benchmark jobs for each factor. This can be accomplished by means of a simple ranking or by using paired comparisons. Table 3 shows one possible ranking of four benchmark jobs in a factory for each of the five factors.

The second step is to determine for each benchmark job the dollar amount of the wage rate that should be allocated to each universal factor. Even though it involves dollar amounts, this is a subjective process that requires judgment by the evaluators. Table 4 shows how this step might turn out for the four job titles in the previous table. For each job title, the sum of the dollar amounts for each universal factor is equal to the wage rate for that job title.

The final step in the factor comparison method is to use the same two steps described above for all of the nonbenchmark jobs in the organization. The other jobs must be ranked in terms of the five universal factors together with the benchmark jobs, and then dollar amounts for each factor must be assigned for these other jobs in a manner consistent with the benchmark jobs. Table 5 shows how the final wage rate determinations might look for a subset of the jobs in the factory.

The following advantages are usually attributed to the factor comparison method: (1) it is customized for the organization, (2) it uses wages rates from the existing organization as benchmarks against which to compare the other jobs, and (3) it includes the establishment of the wage structure as an integral part of the method, whereas this is a required follow-on step in the other job evaluation methods. The following disadvantages

TABLE 4 Allocation of Wage Rates to Each Universal Factor for the Benchmark Jobs

Job Title	Wage Rate ($/hr)	Skill	Mental Demands	Physical Demands	Responsibility	Working Conditions
Machinist	$20.00	7.00	5.50	2.50	3.50	1.50
Assembler	$17.00	6.00	4.00	3.00	2.50	1.50
Material handler	$15.00	3.00	2.50	6.00	1.50	2.00
Laborer	$12.00	1.50	1.00	6.00	1.00	2.50

Source: Based on an example in [3].

TABLE 5 Allocation of Wage Rates to Each Universal Factor for Other Jobs

Job Title	Skill	Mental Demands	Physical Demands	Responsibility	Working Conditions	Wage Rate ($/hr)
Machinist	7.00	5.50	2.50	3.50	1.50	$20.00
Quality inspector	5.00	6.00	2.00	3.50	1.50	$18.00
Assembler	6.00	4.00	3.00	2.50	1.50	$17.00
Punch operator	5.00	3.50	3.00	2.50	2.00	$16.00
Material handler	3.00	2.50	6.00	1.50	2.00	$15.00
Storage clerk	3.00	3.00	4.00	2.00	2.00	$14.00
Laborer	1.50	1.00	6.00	1.00	2.50	$12.00
Janitor	1.00	1.00	5.00	1.00	2.00	$10.00

Source: Based on an example in [3].

and issues are attributed to the factor comparison method: (1) there may be wage inequities in the benchmark jobs, (2) the method is difficult for the rank and file to understand because of its complexity, and (3) despite its claim of objectivity, some judgment is required in the apportionment of dollar amounts to universal factors for each job.

Point-Factor Method. The point-factor method, also called the ***point rating method*** or simply the ***point method***, assigns point values to the individual factors that make up a given job, and then sums the points to obtain a total score for the job. The scores of all jobs are then organized into a job hierarchy based on their scores. These scores are used to establish the wage structure for the organization. The point-factor method is the most widely used job evaluation system in industry. Its appeal lies in its quantitative approach, apparent objectivity, and adaptability to the needs of the individual organization.

The first step in the point-factor method is selection of the list of factors that are to be used to evaluate the jobs. Staff within the organization can develop these factors or they can be adopted and adapted from commercially available point-factor systems. Commonly selected factors are skill, effort, responsibility, and working conditions.[4] These factors are then divided into subfactors that are relevant to the main factor, and a scale is developed that is arranged into "degrees" that apply to the subfactor. Table 6 lists the main factors and subfactors used in the point-factor system developed by the National Electrical Manufacturers' Association (NEMA). The table also shows the scale of degrees associated with each subfactor. The degrees specify the different levels or qualifications for the subfactor. For example, the experience subfactor might be divided into the following degrees: (1) 0 to 3 months, (2) 3 months to 1 year, (3) 1 year to 3 years, and (4) over 3 years. As another example, the education subfactor might be divided into the following degrees: (1) high school diploma, (2) associate degree or two-year technical school, (3) four-year bachelor's degree, (4) master's degree, and (5) doctoral degree. As our examples illustrate, the number of degrees can vary for different subfactors. The commercial systems include rather comprehensive definitions of the factors, subfactors, and degrees. An organization would have to develop these definitions itself if it were to devise its own point-factor system.

[4]Note that these factors are similar to those used in the factor comparison method, except that mental demands and physical demands have been combined into the single factor of effort.

TABLE 6 Factors and Subfactors in the Point-Factor System of the National Electrical Manufacturers' Association

		Degrees				
Factor	Subfactor	1	2	3	4	5
Skill	1. Education					
	2. Experience					
	3. Initiative and ingenuity					
Effort	4. Physical demand					
	5. Mental/visual demand					
Responsibility	6. Equipment or process					
	7. Material or product					
	8. Safety of others					
	9. Work of others					
Job conditions	10. Working conditions					
	11. Hazards					

The next step in the point-factor method is to assign total weighting values to the job subfactors and to divide the weighting values into point scores that are allocated to each degree for each subfactor. For instance, the education subfactor might be assigned a total weighting value of 70 points, while the experience subfactor might be assigned 110 points. These total weights would then be allocated among the degrees according to some mathematical progression. For example, one possible allocation is to simply divide the total weighting value by the number of degrees, and use that as the score for the first degree, two times that value for the second degree, and so on. This is the procedure used to construct the point scores for degrees in Table 7, which is an enhancement of our

TABLE 7 Factors and Subfactors in the Point-Factor System of the National Electrical Manufacturers' Association

		Degrees and Points				
Factor	Subfactor	1	2	3	4	5
Skill	1. Education	14	28	42	56	70
	2. Experience	22	44	66	88	110
	3. Initiative and ingenuity	14	28	42	56	70
Effort	4. Physical demand	10	20	30	40	50
	5. Mental/visual demand	5	10	15	20	25
Responsibility	6. Equipment or process	5	10	15	20	25
	7. Material or product	5	10	15	20	25
	8. Safety of others	5	10	15	20	25
	9. Work of others	5	10	15	20	25
Job conditions	10. Working conditions	10	20	30	40	50
	11. Hazards	5	10	15	20	25

previous table. All subfactors havc five degrees in this table, and the point score for degree 5 is the maximum possible score that can be assigned to that subfactor. Note that the lowest possible total score is the sum of the degree 1 scores (100 points), and the highest possible score is the sum of the degree 5 scores (500 points).

Thus far in our description of the point-factor method, we have covered only the setup of the job evaluation system. Now that the system has been set up, the process of rating the jobs can begin. Rating the jobs consists of three steps: (1) determining the degree for each subfactor for each job based on job descriptions, (2) assigning the point score for each subfactor according to its degree, and (3) summing the point scores for all subfactors to obtain a total for each job. The following example illustrates the rating procedure.

Example 1 Job Evaluation Using the Point-Factor System

A particular job was evaluated to be first degree in subfactors 1, 2, 5, 9, and 11; second degree in subfactors 3, 6, 7, 8, and 10; and fourth degree in subfactor 4. What is the total point score for the job based on the scores in Table 7?

Solution: The solution is shown in Table 8. Summing the point scores across the third row, we have a total point score of 169. ■

Once the total scores have been determined for each job, all jobs can be listed in numerical order and classified into job grades based on those scores. One possible list of 10 job grades, matched against ranges of total scores, is shown in Table 9. Wage rates can then be determined for each of these job grades.

Some of the advantages of the point-factor system have already been mentioned: (1) The system is quantitative, (2) it is objective, and (3) it is adaptable to the needs of the individual organization. There are also additional advantages: (4) the system permits job comparisons to be readily made across multiple departments and functions, and (5) because it is so widely used by so many companies, comparisons can also be made among companies and industries. The point-factor system has the following disadvantages: (1) it is complicated and therefore not as readily understood by employees

TABLE 8 Solution to Example 1

Subfactor	1	2	3	4	5	6	7	8	9	10	11	
Degree	1	1	2	4	1	2	2	2	1	2	1	
Point score	14	22	28	40	5	10	10	10	5	20	5	Total = 169

TABLE 9 Job Grades for Given Point Score Ranges

Job Grade	Total Score Range	Job Grade	Total Score Range
1	100–140	6	301–340
2	141–180	7	341–380
3	181–220	8	381–420
4	221–260	9	421–460
5	261–300	10	461–500

as other job rating systems and (2) it potentially requires a significant amount of time to construct the system of factors, subfactors, and the degrees associated with them.

1.3 Establishing the Wage Structure

Certainly one of the major objectives of job evaluation within an organization is to establish an appropriate ***wage structure***—a pay schedule that indicates the wage rates that are paid for different job grades, including any wage range within a given job grade. Based on the evaluation methods discussed in Section 1.2, the jobs are now organized into grades. If the factor comparison method of job evaluation is used, then the wage structure is an outcome of that method. If any of the other methods are used, then establishing the wage structure is a separate process that is based on job grades.

Factors that Affect the Wage Structure. The wage structure of an organization reflects the decisions made about its pay policy regarding several factors that are illustrated in Figure 1. Let us discuss these factors with reference to this figure:

- *Slope of the wage structure.* The slope of the wage structure indicates the pay differential between high and low job grades. The difference is indicated in Figure 1 (a). A steep slope means a large pay difference between the highest and lowest job grades. A shallow slope means smaller pay differences between job grades.
- *Wage range for each job grade.* The common practice in organizations is to incorporate a range of wages into each grade of the structure. This is illustrated in Figure 1 (b), and the absence of a wage range is shown in Figure 1 (c).
- *Width of the wage range.* If wage ranges are elected, how wide should they be? An argument in favor of wide ranges is that they permit more frequent and/or larger pay increases within a given grade, which may have a beneficial effect on worker morale. These increases may be based on merit or seniority or a combination of these two factors.
- *Overlapping wage ranges.* Wide wage ranges usually mean overlapping ranges. Figure 1 (d) shows overlapping wage ranges, whereas Figure 1 (b) shows no overlap between adjacent grades. Overlapping wage ranges means that the highest paid worker in a lower grade earns more than the lowest grade worker in the next job grade. This can be awkward.

There are additional policy factors that can influence the design of an organization's wage structure, but the ones covered here provide a good introduction.

An organization's wage structure is also affected by external factors—namely, the laws of supply and demand existing in the community where the organization is located and in the industry to which it belongs. If the wage rates for certain job grades or the general pay level of the organization's employees are low relative to these external markets, there will be difficulties with employee turnover and the recruitment of replacement workers. Policy decisions are usually made, either formally or informally, in each organization to pay (1) at or near the average in the community or industry, (2) above average wages, or (3) below average wages [7]. Most companies elect to pay at or near the average of the community. The stated policy reads something like this: "Our policy is to pay competitive wage rates."

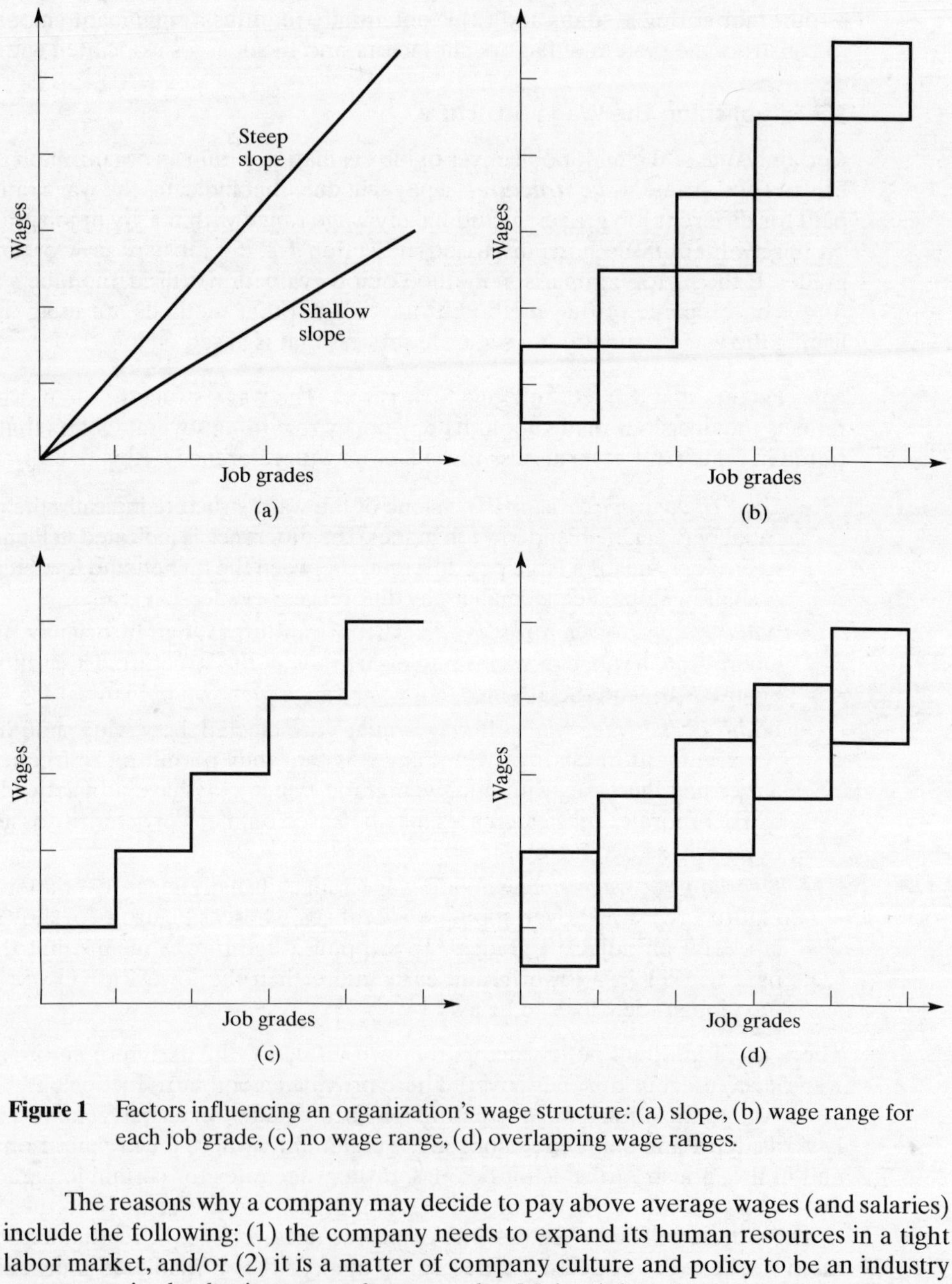

Figure 1 Factors influencing an organization's wage structure: (a) slope, (b) wage range for each job grade, (c) no wage range, (d) overlapping wage ranges.

The reasons why a company may decide to pay above average wages (and salaries) include the following: (1) the company needs to expand its human resources in a tight labor market, and/or (2) it is a matter of company culture and policy to be an industry or community leader in terms of wage scales. Maintaining above average wages and salaries carries certain risks. Paying higher wages is no guarantee that an organization's workers will be more productive than those of its competitors, but the costs of its products and services will be higher because its employees are more highly compensated.

Accordingly, the company may find itself at a competitive disadvantage in terms of the prices of its products and services. Its customers are not going to care about its benevolent wage policies.

There are several reasons why a company or other organization may decide to pay below average rates: (1) the management (who may be the owners of the business) are greedy and are willing to endure the problems associated with lower than average pay scales (e.g., high employee turnover, absenteeism, difficulties in recruiting), (2) the company is young and cannot afford to pay anything more than below average wages, and/or (3) the company is faced with significant competitive pressures and/or financial difficulties that force it to pay below average rates in order to survive.

Implementation and Administration Issues. Once the wage structure has been established, it is likely that the current wages of some employees will be found to be below the lower limit of the wage range for their job grades, while other employees earn wages that are above the upper limit of the range for their grades. Common practice in compensation administration is to increase the current rate of the employees who are below the lower limit up to the newly established minimum. The difference between the current rate and the new lower limit is called the employee's ***green circle rate***. One might be tempted to conclude that it would have been better to leave well enough alone and not conduct the job study in the first place, because to correct all of the green circle rates will involve a significant cost to the organization. However, the appropriate view is that one of the purposes of the job study was to correct just this kind of inequity.

What are more difficult to correct are ***red circle rates***, which occur when an employee's wage rate is above the upper limit of the wage range for his or her job grade. Job evaluation studies are usually launched with the stated proviso that no employee's wage will be cut as a result of the study. When red circle rates are revealed after the job study is completed, the organization can address the difference in several possible ways. One approach is to leave the individual's rate at its current level until periodic increases in the upper limit of the range catch up (this may take several years). Another approach is to transfer the employee to a higher job grade, in which his or her wage will lie within the range for that grade. Still another approach is to offer the overpaid workers a buyout in exchange for correcting their red circle rates. In the present context, a ***buyout*** is a lump sum amount that is equivalent to the extra money that would have been earned by the worker during some fixed time into the future (e.g., one or two years).

No matter how well the processes of job evaluation and establishing the pay rates are accomplished, the wage structure may become outmoded over a period of years if it is not properly administered and maintained. The type of work done by the organization may evolve, and accordingly the duties and responsibilities within some of the job grades may change. New equipment and processes may be installed, which require new job grades within the existing wage structure. The average cost of living in the community may increase, forcing the organization to make general wage adjustments in all employees' base rates, called ***cost of living adjustments*** (COLA). Or perhaps the laws of supply and demand in the labor market cause certain job grades to become priced above the average rates paid by the wage structure, and the organization must respond by violating its own wage structure for those job classifications.

2 PERFORMANCE APPRAISAL

Job evaluation is concerned with evaluating the position; in the ideal situation, it has nothing to do with the person in the job. By contrast, performance appraisal is concerned with evaluating the person holding the job. ***Performance appraisal*** (PA) is the process by which an employee is periodically evaluated relative to his or her accomplishments and contributions to the organization. Other names for performance appraisal include ***merit rating***, ***performance rating***, and ***performance evaluation***. PA can be a stressful process for both the evaluator (e.g., the supervisor) and the employee being evaluated, depending on how skillful the evaluator is at communicating the results of the appraisal and how receptive the employee is to feedback on his or her performance.

The performance appraisal process can be done informally or formally. Most large- and medium-sized organizations, and even many small organizations, utilize a formal PA process in their human resources management. In the process, employees are reviewed annually or semiannually by their supervisors in a structured interaction that includes both documented reports and face-to-face interviews. Formal appraisals are preferred over informal ones because they bring greater objectivity, fairness, accuracy, and legal defensibility to the process. In a formal process, the performance of the subordinate is reviewed and discussed with the supervisor, strengths and weaknesses of the employee are identified, and future work objectives and skill enhancements are examined. If done properly, performance appraisal is beneficial to both the employee and the organization. The employee is motivated to achieve better performance, and the organization benefits accordingly.

Organizations use performance appraisals for the following reasons, which often differ for different organizations:

- To provide feedback to the employee on his or her work performance
- To establish links between the goals of the organization and the goals of the employee
- To determine merit pay increases (in addition, there may be cost of living adjustments, which are not based on performance appraisal)
- To indicate training and skill-enhancement needs of employees
- To identify high performing individuals who may be candidates for promotions, advancements, and transfers
- To identify workers who are in need of counseling (both personal and work-related)
- To identify poor performing workers who should be laid off, if layoffs become necessary
- To identify very poor performers who should be terminated.

The techniques and procedures for accomplishing the performance appraisal process vary widely from one organization to the next. They are often customized for each organization, especially regarding the documentation. The documentation is important because it often serves a legal function. For example, if an employee is dismissed on the grounds of poor performance, he or she may take legal action against the employer for reinstatement or damages (or both). If it subsequently turns out in court proceedings that the employee has a human resources file containing PA reports indicating nothing but good or excellent performance, then it becomes difficult to justify dismissal for poor performance. How does

Quantity of work (volume of work regularly produced, speed and consistency of output)

____ Almost always exceeds standards; exceptionally productive.
____ Regularly produces more than required.
____ Volume of work is satisfactory; equals job standards.
____ Quite often does not meet standards.
____ Almost never meets standard output.

(a)

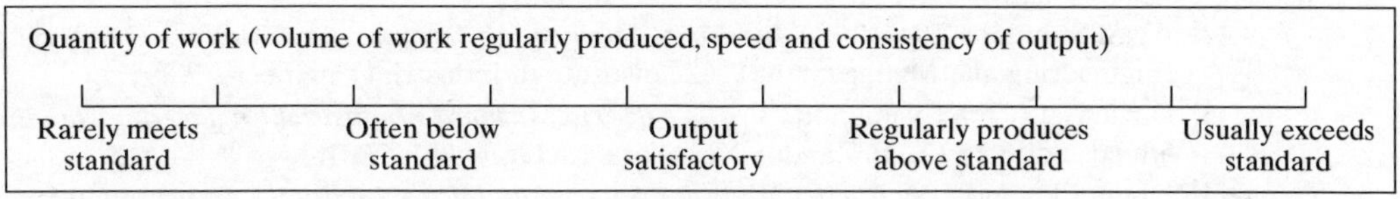

(b)

Figure 2 Documentation methods in performance appraisal: (a) checklist and (b) graphical rating scale.

this kind of situation happen? One of the reasons is that the supervisor found it easier to give good evaluations than to confront the subordinate about his or her work deficiencies.

The following techniques are used in performance appraisal, in particular those regarding the documentation part of the process:

- *Checklists.* The evaluator is requested to check from a list of performance attributes those that apply to the employee. The lists are usually organized by category (e.g., skill, quantity of work), and the evaluator must check off the terms that best describe the employee's contribution (e.g., "exhibits great skill," "regularly produces above standard output"). An example of the checklist format is illustrated in Figure 2 (a).
- *Graphical rating scales.* Each performance attribute is accompanied by a linear scale ranging from low performance to excellent performance, and the evaluator must mark the scale at the point that describes the employee's performance. An example of a graphical rating scale is illustrated in Figure 2 (b).
- *Simple ranking.* The supervisor is required to rank order his or her subordinates from highest performer to lowest performer. This is often challenging for the supervisor, especially if there are many subordinates. To facilitate the task, the ranking process is sometimes organized so that workers are grouped into quartiles of performance.
- *Essays.* The evaluator writes a paragraph or two detailing the worker's performance. The essay may be combined with one of the preceding methods.

Formal performance appraisal procedures date from around World War II. Prior to that time, most appraisals were informal. The formal procedures have evolved and are still evolving. PA systems have traditionally emphasized uniform procedures narrowly focused on an employee's past performance and based on supervisory input only [5]. Current trends include the following: (1) aligning the performance appraisal process with the strategic objectives of the organization, which means more customization of the PA procedures, (2) using multiple evaluators, including use of self-evaluation and evaluation of supervisors by subordinates, and (3) paying greater attention to future development of the employee rather than past performance.

REFERENCES

[1] Amrine, H. T., J. A. Ritchey, and C. L. Moodie. *Manufacturing Organization and Management.* 5th ed. Englewood Cliffs, NJ: Prentice-Hall, 1987.

[2] ANSI Standard Z94.0-1989. *Industrial Engineering Terminology.* Norcross, GA: Industrial Engineering and Management Press, Institute of Industrial Engineers, 1989.

[3] Davic, N. D. "Job Evaluation." Pp. 7.17–7.39 in *Maynard's Industrial Engineering Handbook*, 5th ed., edited by K. B. Zandin. New York: McGraw-Hill, 2001.

[4] Dunn, J. D., and F. M. Rachel. *Wage and Salary Administration: Total Compensation Systems.* New York: McGraw-Hill, 1971.

[5] Dvir, T., and Y. Berson. "Leadership, Motivation, and Strategic Resource Management." Pp. 841–67 in *Handbook of Industrial Engineering*, 3rd ed., edited by G. Salvendy. New York: Wiley, 2001.

[6] Hannon, J. M., J. M. Newman, G. T. Milkovich, and J. T. Brakefield. "Job Evaluation in Organizations." Pp. 899–919 in *Handbook of Industrial Engineering*, 3rd ed., edited by G. Salvendy. New York: Wiley, 2001.

[7] Matkov, G. J., and D. I. Danner. "Job Evaluation." Pp. 8.83–8.126 in *Maynard's Industrial Engineering Handbook*, 4th ed., edited by W. K. Hodson. New York: McGraw-Hill, 1991.

[8] Nethersell, G. "The Role of Job Measurement and Work Assessment." Pp. 138–49 in *The Executive Handbook on Compensation*, edited by C. H. Fay, M. A. Thompson, and D. Knight. New York: Free Press, 2001.

[9] Archer North and Associates, www.performance-appraisal.com. 2003.

REVIEW QUESTIONS

1 What is job evaluation?

2 What are the reasons why an organization performs a job evaluation? Name three.

3 What is job analysis?

4 Describe the job ranking method of job evaluation.

5 What is the paired comparisons technique for ranking items such as jobs?

6 Describe the job classification method of job evaluation.

7 Describe the factor comparison method of job evaluation.

8 Describe the point-factor method of job evaluation.

9 What are the advantages of the point-factor method of job evaluation?

10 What is a wage structure?

11 What is a green circle rate in wage administration?

12 What is performance appraisal?

13 What are some of the reasons for an organization to use performance appraisals in human resources management? Name three.

14 Identify two current trends in performance appraisal.

Compensation Systems

Employers have a reasonable expectation that their employees will each accomplish a fair day's work. In return, employees expect to be fairly compensated. They expect to be paid at a rate that is commensurate with their qualifications and the effort they invest in their jobs. This is an equality cycle of a fair day's pay for a fair day's work.

In this chapter we discuss the other part of the equality cycle: how organizations pay their employees. An employer's ***compensation system*** consists of the various forms of financial rewards and fringe benefits that are provided to employees in return for their services. An individual's total compensation commonly includes the following components: (1) base pay, (2) variable pay, and (3) fringe benefits. The absolute and relative values of these components vary for different employers and they vary for different employees within a given organization.

1 OVERVIEW OF COMPENSATION SYSTEMS

The pay component of a compensation system can be based on either or both of two attributes of the service provided by an employee: (1) the time served by the individual in the service of the employer and (2) some measure of the individual's performance while providing the service to the employer. Thus, we can identify two basic types of pay systems:

1. *Time-based pay systems*, in which the employee is paid for the time worked.
2. *Incentivized pay systems*, in which pay is based on the amount of work accomplished or some other measure of performance.

These basic pay systems are represented by the continuum in Figure 1, in which the extremes of the continuum are 100% time-based pay systems on one end and 100% incentivized systems at the other end. In a 100% time-based system, the worker is paid only for time-worked, and no part of the pay is based on performance. Whether the worker's performance on the job is good or bad, it has no effect on the earnings received, at least not in the short run. In a 100% incentivized system, the worker is paid only for his or her performance, and there is no time-based pay component. No matter how much time the worker puts into the job, there is no direct compensation for this time. Examples of these extremes are presented in Table 1.

Many pay systems are actually combinations of time-based and incentivized systems. The pay earned by the employee is a function of both time-based pay and performance. The proportions of the two components vary. In some cases, the payment system

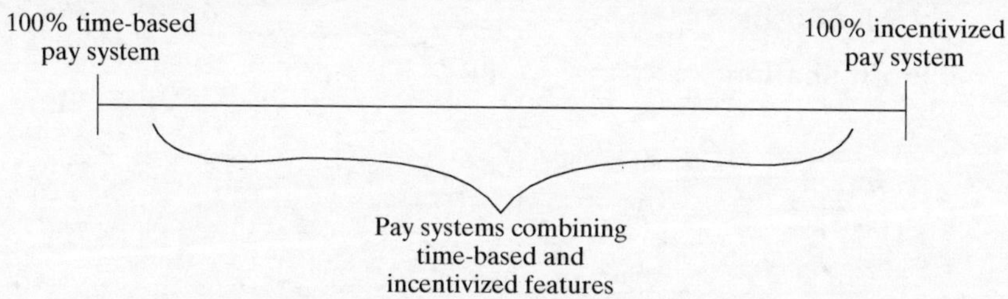

Figure 1 Continuum of pay systems.

TABLE 1 Examples of 100% Time-Based Pay Systems and 100% Incentivized systems

100% Time-Based Pay Systems	100% Incentivized Systems
Production worker who monitors an automatic production machine. The worker must periodically load and unload the machine and check for product quality.	Production worker working on a piecework system in which he or she is paid only for the number of pieces turned in at the end of the shift.
Salesperson working on salary only (no commission) who takes orders at a sales counter.	Salesperson working on commission only (no salary), in which he or she is paid in proportion to the dollar value of sales.
Security guard in a building on the night shift who watches a bank of closed-circuit television monitors.	A professional golfer who derives his or her income entirely from success in tournament competition.

is very close to a 100% time-based system, but there is usually some incentive to perform well, even if only to maintain one's employment. More commonly, an employee is motivated by the desire to advance to a higher position or job classification in the organization. And with that advancement, he or she will earn more money. Examples of employees who are paid on the basis of these combinations of time-based and incentivized systems include the following:

- A salesperson who is paid a base salary plus commission for sales dollars above a defined minimum level.
- A production worker who earns an hourly wage and also receives a bonus that is proportional to his or her individual output, so long as the output is above a standard quantity.
- A manager who earns a regular salary and is also paid a bonus for achieving defined goals of the organization.

As indicated in our chapter introduction, a worker's total compensation usually consists of base pay, variable pay, and fringe benefits. The ***base pay*** is the wage or salary that is paid to the employee on a regular basis, such as weekly or monthly. This is commonly a time-based pay component. Its amount is generally determined by specific factors: (1) the value of the job within the organization, (2) the value of the individual to the organization, and (3) the laws of supply and demand that operate in the local labor market. Most organizations have a formal base-pay structure that establishes the various pay levels for different types of jobs. The base-pay structure usually includes a ***base pay progression***, which is a series of increases within each job classification that depends on factors such as length of service to the organization and the merits of the individual.

In addition to the base pay level and its progression over time, the compensation system may include a ***variable pay*** component that is usually based on some measure of performance of either the individual worker or groups of workers (e.g., worker teams). Variable pay is usually an incentivized pay system. It is normally thought of as a bonus, such as a bonus for a production worker's high output or for an executive's success in managing a company division.

Incentivized pay systems can be classified in several ways. One classification distinguishes between the direct and indirect wage incentive systems. ***Direct incentive systems*** pay workers a bonus that is in direct proportion to their output, so long as the output exceeds some minimum threshold value. ***Indirect incentive systems*** pay workers a bonus, but the bonus is not directly tied to output; instead, it is based on some other measure of performance, such as improvements in productivity or the profits of the company. The terms *gain sharing* and *profit sharing* are used for two important categories of these indirect incentive systems. Direct incentive systems are discussed in Section 3. Gain sharing and profit sharing are discussed in Sections 4 and 5, respectively. Another way to distinguish incentivized systems is whether they are individual incentives or group incentives. Piecework is normally an individual incentive system, while gain sharing and profit sharing are group incentives.

The third component in total compensation is the package of ***fringe benefits***—employment benefits that have monetary value to the employee and are an expense to

TABLE 2 Common Fringe Benefits Offered by Employers

Social Security and Medicare. These benefits are mandated by federal law. They are government-operated insurance programs to which employers and employees must both contribute. They provide retirement and other benefits.

Workers' compensation. This provides benefits to workers who are disabled by occupational injury or illness. It is mandated by state law.

Disability insurance. The employer pays disability insurance premiums for coverage that will benefit the employee if the employee becomes disabled for any work or non–work-related reason. It is additional insurance beyond workers' compensation.

Medical benefits/medical insurance. Typical coverage includes employees and their immediate family members being reimbursed for medical and hospital expenses by the employer or through insurance paid by employer. Plans are often co-pay, in which the employee shares in the cost of the medical coverage. Medical benefits can also include vision care.

Prescription drug benefit. This benefit is similar to a medical benefits package. Employees and their immediate family members are reimbursed for prescription drug costs by the employer or through insurance paid by employer. A co-pay feature is common.

Paid vacation. The employee is eligible for paid vacation time. The length of the vacation time is usually dependent on the years of service with the organization (e.g., two weeks vacation after one year of service, three weeks after five years, and so on).

Paid holidays. Employees are paid for a certain number of holidays throughout the year.

Dental insurance. This coverage is similar to the medical benefit, but co-pay and limits usually apply. For example, cleanings and examinations are 100% covered, fillings are 80% covered, dental prosthetics and orthodontics are 50% covered. Orthodontics have a limit (e.g., $1000).

Pension plan. The employer agrees to provide a pension to employee upon retirement, either by direct payment by the employer or through contributions to a pension plan that accumulates for the benefit of the employee.

Life insurance. The employer pays life insurance premiums for coverage that will benefit family members of employee.

Tuition reimbursement. The employer reimburses the employee for tuition costs of attending courses at local colleges and universities. Usually, the course must have some relevance to the employee's job.

Stock or stock options. The company offers employees eligibility to acquire company stock, either by some matching formula (e.g., employer agrees to match shares purchased by employee up to some limit) or through options to buy stock at beneficial prices.

Discounts on products. Consumer products companies and retailers often offer a discount to employees to purchase products at a specified discount below regular prices.

the employer but do not affect the employee's financial pay.[1] A list of common fringe benefits offered by employers is presented in Table 2. Of course, the mix of fringe benefits and their details differ among organizations, and some employers provide no fringe benefits beyond those required by law. Employers operating illegally usually offer even less.

2 TIME-BASED PAY SYSTEMS

In a ***time-based pay system***, the employee is paid at a specified rate of pay for his or her time. These systems are divided into two categories: (1) ***hourly pay*** systems, in which the employee is paid at an hourly rate for the amount of time worked, and (2) ***salary*** systems,

[1]According to a March 2004 survey taken by the Bureau of Labor Statistics, fringe benefits accounted for 29.0% of total compensation costs to U.S. nonfarm businesses and state and local governments.

in which the employee is paid a fixed amount at regular intervals for his or her services. In popular usage, hourly pay is referred to as a wage. As a generalization, wages are typically associated with blue-collar workers, while salaries are associated with white-collar workers.

2.1 Hourly Pay Systems

Hourly pay plans are very common. In our coverage we distinguish between (1) conventional hourly pay systems, in which workers are paid an hourly rate for hours worked, and (2) measured day work, in which workers are paid an hourly rate but their work output is measured using time standards.

Conventional Hourly Pay Systems. In conventional hourly pay systems, the worker is paid an hourly rate, but there is no direct measure taken of the amount of work accomplished. The worker is simply paid for the number of hours worked. The term ***day work*** is sometimes used for these positions. They include both full-time and part-time jobs. Workers typically covered by hourly pay plans include production and construction workers, material handlers, food services employees, many government employees, and retail sales personnel. There are several reasons for paying on an hourly basis:

- Time standards are not feasible for the work performed. For example, the work consists of a various odd jobs, as is often the case in construction work and material handling.
- The work requires interactions with people, and these interactions occur on an intermittent and/or random basis (e.g., retail sales personnel).
- The work consists of active periods and nonactive periods, but the worker is paid during both periods (e.g., maintenance and repair personnel in a factory, municipal firefighters).
- The job involves tending a machine that operates on an automatic cycle, and there is little or no correlation between the worker's effort and the resulting output. An incentive pay system would not increase productivity.

Workers paid an hourly wage rate are usually nonexempt employees, while salaried workers are usually exempt. The ***exempt*** status means that the employee is exempt from certain provisions of the Fair Labor Standards Act of 1938 and similar state laws—specifically that the employee is not paid at a time-and-a-half rate for hours worked above 40 during a fixed work week. Employers are required by law to pay nonexempt workers at the higher rate for hours in excess of 40 per week.

A worker's wage in a day work payment plan is simply the hourly rate multiplied by the number of hours worked during the pay period. That is,

$$W = R_{hr}H_w \tag{1}$$

where W = wage for the period, assumed to be 1 week, \$/week; R_{hr} = hourly rate, \$/hr; and H_w = hours worked per week. This assumes that the worker is nonexempt and the number of hours worked does not exceed 40 per week. If the hours exceed 40, then overtime must be figured into the wage computation by adding one-half the regular hourly rate for every hour above 40:

$$W = R_{hr}H_w + 0.5\,R_{hr}(H_w - 40) \tag{2}$$

The hourly rates paid by an organization in a day work system depend on a number of factors: (1) laws of supply and demand that operate in the local labor market, (2) job classification of the position, (3) quantity and quality of the work accomplished by the employee, (4) skill, training, and experience of the worker, (5) length of service to the organization, and (6) compensation policies of the organization.

Measured Day Work. ***Measured day work*** is an hourly pay system in which time standards are used to measure the amount of work accomplished by each employee. Work measurement and time standards are used by management for labor staffing, production planning, work scheduling, cost estimating, and other time standards applications, but not for direct wage incentives. The workers are paid on an hourly basis. However, a worker efficiency index is calculated for each employee covered by the system, based on the standard hours accomplished relative to clock hours worked. This index can be used by supervision to evaluate workers and to establish goals for them. In some applications, the index values are posted in the department, allowing each worker to know how well he or she is performing relative to other workers. Such posting tends to have a motivational effect even if there is no direct relationship to wages earned.

Measured day work was introduced in the 1930s when direct incentive systems such as piecework and standard hour plans were widely used (Section 3.1). Labor unions opposed incentive systems, and measured day work represented a compromise between a regular hourly pay system and an incentive pay system. In the first installations of measured day work, the worker efficiency index was used to determine each worker's base pay rate. Adjustments were made in the hourly wage rate at three-month intervals. This was quite satisfactory to the workers as long as they could achieve good index numbers. They knew exactly what they were earning for the hours worked, and it reduced the stress of working under a direct incentive system. However, problems arose when the workers did not achieve good index numbers. This meant that the worker's earnings were reduced for the next three months, which was not a prospect to be happy about. As a consequence of this kind of issue, the base rate adjustment was eventually dropped from the measured day work system. Today, measured day work is strictly an hourly pay system, with the measurements used for the management and control purposes as discussed above.

2.2 Salary Systems

Salaried positions are almost always classified as exempt, and compensation occurs at regular intervals: weekly, biweekly, or monthly. Exempt employees are expected to spend a certain number of hours per week on the job (e.g., 40) and to maintain a regular work schedule (e.g., 8:00 A.M. to 5:00 P.M. with a one-hour lunch break). However, many exempt employees are professional or managerial, and they are expected to put in the amount of time necessary to get the job done, even if that time sometimes exceeds 40 hours per week. Contrasting with this potential drawback, many exempt positions allow flexibility in the work-shift schedule. For example, if there is a need to take personal time off during the regular workday, this is allowed without requiring the approval of supervision and without being docked for the lost time in one's paycheck. In general, nonexempt workers do not enjoy this privilege.

Positions usually falling within the exempt category are executive, managerial, administrative, and professional employees, and salespersons who sell outside the employer's place of business (e.g., a traveling salesman). Some of the criteria used to classify an employee as exempt include the following: (1) high earnings level, (2) supervision of workforce, (3) work requiring the exercise of discretion and independent judgment, and (4) job qualifications requiring advanced knowledge in the given field of science or learning.

If an organization is found liable of incorrectly classifying an employee as exempt, penalties will be imposed. There have been cases in which employers have taken advantage of workers by granting them management titles (exempt positions) and then obligating them to work 60 or more hours per week at relatively low salaries. Lawsuits have been filed and won against some of these organizations, requiring them to pay back overtime wages and punitive damages.

In general, the salary paid to a salaried employee depends on factors such as the following: (1) the technical or business domain involved (e.g., accounting, legal, engineering), (2) knowledge and experience in the domain, (3) education level of the employee, (4) level of responsibility of the employee in the organization, (5) previous achievements of the employee, and (6) compensation policies of the organization.

In addition, the laws of supply and demand operate in the salaried labor market. In some cases, when demand for professional staff is strong, companies needing to hire new college graduates are forced to increase their starting salaries for entry-level positions at a rate that is faster than the annual increases awarded to current employees. This has sometimes created the awkward situation in which new hires with no experience start at higher salaries than employees who have worked several years for the organization. To avoid this anomaly, some companies offer signing bonuses in lieu of abnormally high starting salaries. A signing bonus of several thousand dollars provides a strong inducement for the individual to accept the position, but it allows the company to maintain a rational pay structure for its current employees.

3 DIRECT WAGE INCENTIVE SYSTEMS

An issue that arises with time-based pay systems, in particular hourly pay plans, is that there is no direct relationship between a worker's output and the wage earned. The hourly compensation system provides little or no motivation for high effort and performance on the job. In this arrangement, a worker who produces half as much as another worker doing the same job earns the same hourly pay. To deal with this issue, incentive pay systems have been developed. A ***direct incentive system*** pays a wage or salary that increases as the work output increases. Workers receive higher pay for greater output. Because greater output usually requires a greater level of effort by the employee, an incentive system provides a motivation for the employee to work harder. The following are some examples of direct incentive pay systems:

- Piece rate systems, in which a production worker is paid in proportion to his or her output
- Sales commissions, in which the salesperson is paid in proportion to the amount that he or she sells
- Management bonus plans, in which the manager of a department receives a bonus in direct relation to the output of the department

Direct incentive pay systems can be divided into two basic categories: (1) individual incentives and (2) group incentives. Our coverage in this section is organized around this classification. We then discuss why incentive systems have not always operated in practice as effectively as they were expected to operate in theory.

3.1 Individual Wage Incentive Plans

An ***individual wage incentive plan*** pays each worker according to his or her individual output. It is a direct incentive system because of the direct relationship between wage and output. Individual wage incentive systems have been widely used in the manufacturing industries, but their applications have fallen off in recent years in the United States. We divide the production-oriented individual incentive systems into the following categories: (1) piecework, (2) standard hour plans, and (3) bonus-sharing plans. We also discuss sales incentive plans, which operate the same way.

Piecework. The most basic of the individual incentive pay systems is ***piecework*** (also called ***piece rate***) in which the worker is paid a fixed rate per unit of work accomplished. The wage earned by the worker is determined as follows:

$$W = R_u Q \tag{3}$$

where W = wage earned by worker during pay period of interest, \$/period (e.g., day, week); R_u = unit rate per piece, \$/pc; and Q = quantity of work units completed during period, pc.

Piecework systems were widely used prior to World War II. They were easy for the worker to understand and easy for the plant to administer, as long as the rates remained stable. But when the general wage levels of the workers increased, it meant that the plant had to make adjustments in all of the piece rates to reflect the wage increases. This was a monumental chore. Another disadvantage of piecework is that it does not provide the worker a ***guaranteed base rate***—a minimum daily rate (based on an hourly rate) paid to the worker regardless of the quantity of work units produced. The absence of a guaranteed base rate is in conflict with federal minimum wage laws, which require a minimum hourly rate for workers. After World War II, piecework systems were largely abandoned in favor of incentive systems based on time standards.[2]

[2]It should be noted that incentive plans based on time standards are sometimes incorrectly referred to as piecework or piece rate systems. To be technically correct, one should use the term *piecework* (or *piece rate*) only when the wage is based on a fixed rate per unit of work (e.g., dollars per piece).

An observation about piece rate systems should be noted here. Most companies selling products and services operate under an economic system that is basically piecework. Their revenues are in direct proportion to the prices of their products or services and how many they sell. If they do not sell their products and services, they do not earn revenues. There is no guaranteed base rate for a commercial company.

Standard Hour Plan. A ***standard hour plan*** operates like a piecework system, but the rate per piece is a time rate rather than a dollar rate (or other currency), and the time rate is established by work measurement. The worker is paid an hourly rate multiplied by the number of standard hours accomplished during the pay period. The worker's wage for an eight-hour shift is determined as follows:

$$W = R_{hr}H_{std} \text{ if } H_{std} > H_{sh} \tag{4a}$$

and

$$W = R_{hr}H_{sh} \text{ if } H_{std} \leq H_{sh} \tag{4b}$$

where W = wage earned during shift (or other period of interest), \$; R_{hr} = hourly rate, \$/hr; H_{std} = number of standard hours completed during shift (or other period), hr; and H_{sh} = number of hours in shift (or other period), hr.

Equation (4a) applies when the worker's output exceeds standard, in which case the worker earns a ***bonus***—an amount above and beyond the regular hourly wage. Its value in the standard hour plan is determined as follows:

$$B = R_{hr}(H_{std} - H_{sh}) \tag{5}$$

where B = bonus, \$; and the other terms are defined above. Equation (4b) applies when the worker's output is less than or equal to the standard output. In effect, equation (4b) provides the guaranteed base rate.

The number of standard hours in the preceding equations is calculated by the formula: $H_{std} = QT_{std}$ where Q = quantity of work units completed during the period of interest, pc; and T_{std} = time standard for one work unit, hr/unit. If the standard time is expressed in minutes, as is normally the case, then it must be converted to hours for consistency of units. If the worker works on several jobs during the pay period, then the work accomplished would have to be summed over those jobs (the total of QT_{std} for all jobs completed during the period).

The relationships between wages and output for the piecework and standard hour plans are illustrated in Figure 2. As long as the worker's output is greater than standard, the wage increases in direct proportion to his or her output (one-for-one). In piecework, if the output is less than standard, the wage is still proportional to output (the diagonal line to the left of standard output). In the standard hour plan, if the output is less than standard, the guaranteed base rate kicks in (the horizontal line to the left of standard output).

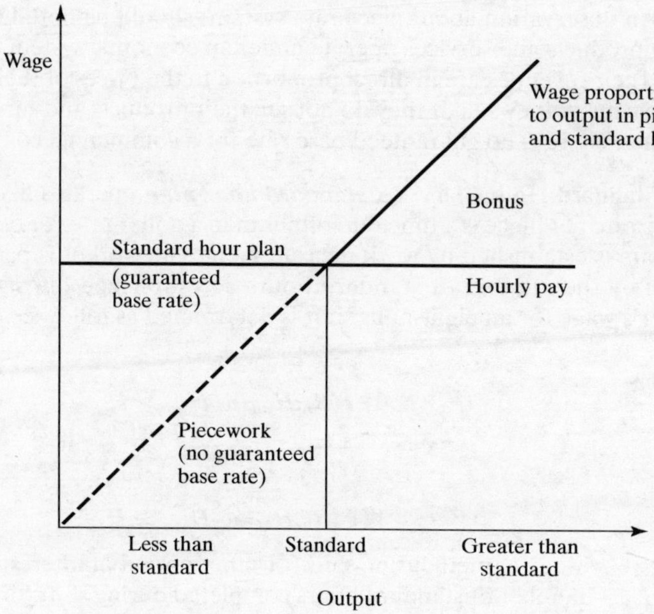

Figure 2 Relationship between wages and output for piecework, standard hour plan, and hourly pay.

Example 1 Standard Hour Plan

A worker is paid weekly, but his wage is calculated on a daily basis. In one three-day period, he worked on the same job, which had a time standard of 5.0 min/work unit. The worker is paid a rate of \$10.00/hr in a standard hour plan that has a guaranteed base rate. Determine (a) the worker's wages, (b) his bonus if one is earned, and (c) the direct labor cost per work unit to the company for each of the three days if he produced 88 work units on the first day, 96 units on the second day, and 110 units on the third day.

Solution **(a)** Note that the standard output for this job is 480 min (8 hr × 60 min/hr) ÷ 5.0 min/work unit; that is, Q_{std} = 96 units/day. On the first day, the worker produced only 88 units, which is less than standard. Therefore, he is paid the guaranteed base rate for the first day.

$$W_1 = \$10(8.0) = \$80/\text{day}$$

On the second day, he produced 96 units, which is equal to the standard output.

$$W_2 = \$10(8.0) = \$80/\text{day}$$

On the third day, the output was 110 units, and the wage under the standard hour plan is calculated as follows:

$$H_{std} = 110(5/60) = 9.167 \text{ hr}$$
$$W_3 = \$10(9.167) = \$91.67/\text{day}$$

(b) The worker earns no bonus on the first and second days because his output was either below or equal to the standard output quantity ($B_1 = B_2 = 0$). On the third day,

$$B_3 = \$10(9.167 - 8.0) = \$11.67$$

(c) The direct labor costs per work unit to the company for each of the three days is determined by dividing the labor cost by the number of units produced. Thus,

$$C_{pc1} = \$80.00/88 = \$0.909/\text{pc}$$
$$C_{pc2} = \$80.00/96 = \$0.833/\text{pc}$$
$$C_{pc3} = \$91.67/110 = \$0.833/\text{pc}$$

Comment: Note that the direct labor cost to the company is increased when the worker's output is below standard. It is therefore in the company's best interest to try to encourage high worker efficiency through good training, supervision, maintenance of equipment (if equipment is involved in the task), and scheduling of work (e.g., making sure that the worker does not run out of raw materials and other necessities of the task).

Also note that when the worker's output is greater than standard, the company's direct labor cost per unit does not increase in the standard hour plan. The worker earns a higher wage, but the company does not pay more per work unit produced. If one recognizes that in addition to direct labor costs, there are overhead costs that remain constant regardless of the quantity produced, it is clear that these fixed costs can be spread out over a larger quantity as output increases. Therefore, total unit costs (direct labor plus overhead) are reduced as output is increased above standard. ■

Bonus-Sharing Plans. In a standard hour plan, the worker receives the entire bonus earned for output greater than standard. As indicated in Figure 2, the earnings are directly proportional to the increased output on a one-for-one basis, just like a piece-work system. Several incentive plans have been developed in which the worker receives only a portion of the bonus. In this type of pay scheme, called a ***bonus-sharing plan***, the worker's wage as a function of output is shown in Figure 3. The remainder of the bonus is shared with either (1) the company or (2) supervision (e.g., foremen) and/or indirect workers such as setup and maintenance employees.

The wage in a bonus-sharing plan is based on the proportion of the bonus that is received by the worker. The formula can be expressed as

$$W = R_{hr}H_{sh} + pR_{hr}(H_{std} - H_{sh}) \tag{6}$$

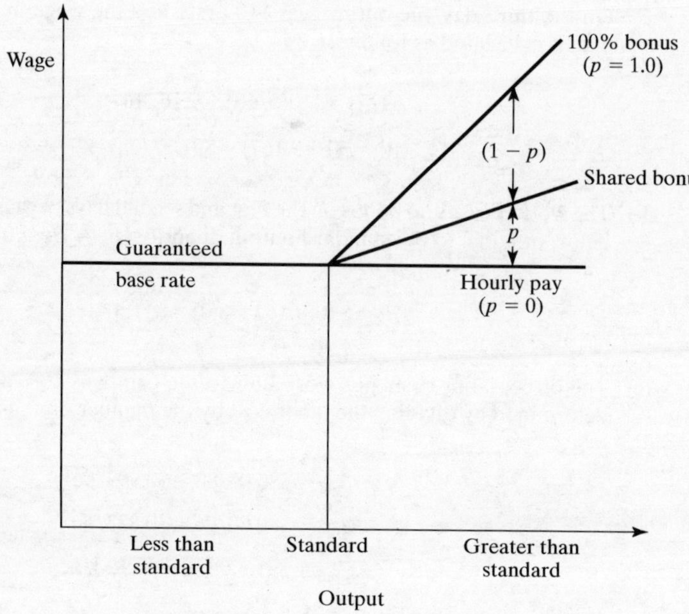

Figure 3 The relationship between wage and output in a bonus-sharing plan.

where W = wage per period, \$/period; R_{hr} = hourly rate, \$/hr; H_{sh} = number of shift hours in period, hr/period; H_{std} = number of standard hours accomplished during period, hr/period; and p = proportion of total bonus that is received by worker. Thus, the worker's bonus in a bonus-sharing plan is given by the second term in equation (6); that is,

$$B = pR_{hr}(H_{std} - H_{sh}) \tag{7}$$

Typical values of p range between 0.25 and 0.50. If the value of p in equation (6) equals 1.0, then the bonus-sharing plan reduces to a standard hour plan, as expressed by equation (4). If $p = 0$, then equation (6) reduces to an hourly pay system.

In a modern bonus-sharing plan, there is a guaranteed base rate. If the number of standard hours accomplished is less than or equal to the shift hours—that is, if $(H_{std} - H_{sh}) \leq 0$ in equation (6)—then only the first term is used to compute the wage $(W = R_{hr}H_{sh})$.

Since p represents the proportion of the bonus received by the worker, $(1 - p)$ is the proportion that is shared with others (e.g., the company or supervisors). The shared amount of each individual worker's bonus is therefore given by the following:

$$SB = (1 - p)R_{hr}(H_{std} - H_{sh}) \tag{8}$$

where SB = shared bonus, \$; and the other terms are defined previously.

Example 2 Bonus-Sharing Plan

Using the data in Example 1, determine (a) the worker's wages, (b) his bonus if one is earned, and (c) the direct labor cost per work unit to the company under a bonus-sharing plan in which the proportion of the bonus received by the worker is 0.50 (called a 50-50 sharing plan). The pay plan features a guaranteed base rate. Recall that the time standard is 5.0 min/work unit, and the hourly rate is $10.00/hr. The worker produced 88 work units on the first day, 96 units on the second day, and 110 units on the third day.

Solution **(a)** The standard output is 96 work units per day, as determined in the previous example. On the first day, the worker produced 88 units. Since this is less than standard, the guaranteed base rate applies.

$$W_1 = 8(\$10) = \$80/\text{day}$$

On the second day, when 96 units are produced,

$$W_2 = 8(\$10) = \$80/\text{day}$$

On the third day, the output is 110 units, and the wage is calculated as

$$H_{std} = 110(5/60) = 9.167 \text{ hr}$$

$$W_3 = \$10(8.0) + 0.50(\$10)(9.167 - 8.0) = \$80.00 + 5.83 = \$85.83$$

(b) As in the previous example, $B_1 = B_2 = 0$. Only on the third day is a bonus earned:

$$B_3 = 0.50(\$10)(9.167 - 8.0) = \$5.83$$

(c) The direct labor cost per work unit to the company for each of the three days is again determined by dividing the wage by the number of units produced. Thus,

$$C_{pc1} = \$80.00/88 = \$0.909/\text{pc}$$

$$C_{pc2} = \$80.00/96 = \$0.833/\text{pc}$$

$$C_{pc3} = \$85.83/110 = \$0.780/\text{pc}$$

Comment: The direct labor cost per unit follows the same pattern as before when the worker's output is equal to or below standard. However, in a bonus-sharing plan, the direct labor cost continues to be reduced as the worker's output increases above standard. Why? Because the worker is receiving half of the total bonus and the difference is a cost saving to the company. ■

Two examples of bonus-sharing plans are the Halsey premium plan and the Bedaux point system. The ***Halsey premium plan*** is one of the oldest bonus-sharing pay schemes; it was instituted in the late 1800s in production factories before direct time study was widely practiced. Piecework systems were in widespread use. In many cases, standards were loose, and workers were able to produce 200% and 300% above standard. Although production pay scales were very low at that time, the prevailing management attitude was that bonuses of this magnitude were exorbitant and must be limited. The Halsey plan helped to "curb those runaway piece rates." A typical proportion received by workers was one-third ($p = 0.333$).

Halsey-type plans are still used, but they are based on time standards instead of piece rates, and they are not necessarily referred to as Halsey plans. They are described as consisting of two parts: (1) an hourly rate, which is a time-based pay rate, and (2) an incentive rate, which is based on output accomplished expressed as standard hours. Several of our end-of-chapter problems address this issue.

The ***Bedaux point system***, developed by Charles Bedaux in 1916, uses a payment formula that fits the model of equation (6). For his wage payment scheme, Bedaux defined a standard unit of work (which he called a "B") as "one minute composed of relative proportions of work and rest as indicated by the whole job." In other words, a "B" is one standard minute with a personal time, fatigue, and delay (PFD) allowance built in. It is really no different than other standard measures of work that are based on time units. In the Bedaux system, the typical value of the sharing proportion was $p = 0.75$. Instead of sharing the other 25% with the company, as in most other bonus-sharing systems, the bonus goes into a pool that is shared with supervisors and indirect workers (e.g., maintenance and setup workers). The reasoning behind this is that these other workers are not usually eligible to earn output-based bonuses because their job performance does not depend on traditional work unit measures. Their success comes in supporting the regular production workers so that these workers can increase output. Accordingly, it seems fair and reasonable for the production workers to share their bonuses with the support workers.

Sales Incentive Plans. A ***sales incentive plan*** is a payment system designed to motivate sales personnel to achieve increased sales of the company's products. Sales incentives are not appropriate for all sales situations, such as those involving the following kinds of characteristics: (1) the salesperson simply takes orders, (2) the selling activity involves a long sales cycle, and (3) the sales process requires the complex involvement of several parties, and it is difficult to assess the relative contributions of the parties [4]. These situations are suited to a compensation package based on salary only. In some organizations, sales management may use sales contests and/or recognition programs as incentives for salaried sales people.

Sales incentives are appropriate when the selling process requires the following: (1) independence of action to consummate the sale, (2) the selling activity involves a short sales cycle, and (3) a high degree of persuasion is required. When a sales incentive plan is deemed appropriate, the type of plan must be decided. The following are the basic types of sales incentive plans:

- *Commission only.* This plan links the salesperson's compensation to sales performance during designated periods (e.g., weeks, months). No salary is included in the pay package. Sales performance can be measured in various ways, depending on what sales objectives are important to the company. Common performance measures are sales dollar volume, number of units sold, and dollars of profit made by the company. The pay of the salesperson is directly proportional to the performance measure. In commission-only plans, a personal pool may be established for the salesperson that serves to smooth the ups and downs of the marketplace. Deposits are made from the individual's pay in periods of high sales, so that money will be available for withdrawal during periods of low sales.

- *Base salary plus commission.* This is a combination plan consisting of a portion that is a guaranteed base salary and a portion that is commission. The ***incentive mix*** is the ratio of base salary to incentive pay. For example, a 60/40 incentive mix means 60% of the salesperson's earnings come from the base salary, and 40% represent the incentive opportunity. The sum of the two portions equals 100% at some defined sales target level. This is the expected level of sales for the salesperson. If sales exceed this target, then pay is greater than 100%. If sales are below this target, then pay is less than 100%.
- *Base salary plus bonus.* This plan guarantees the salesperson a base rate plus a bonus if a defined performance quota is achieved or exceeded. The sales quota might be expressed as a dollar volume or some other measure that is meaningful to the company. If the sales quota is met, the bonus is paid; otherwise it is not. Accordingly, a sales bonus is different from a sales commission in that it is not directly proportional to sales. The bonus can be paid as a fixed dollar amount or as a percentage of base salary.

Sales incentive plans that operate on commission only are effectively piecework systems, and those that are base salary plus commission are analogous to bonus-sharing plans.

3.2 Group Incentive Plans

A group incentive plan pays each member of a group or team the same bonus percentage, and that amount is based on the output of the group. The plan is based on direct incentive systems because the amount of the bonus is directly proportional to the output of the group. Wages within the group may vary according to job classification, but the computed bonus is based on the same differential between actual output and standard output. We include in this category only plans that operate like individual incentive pay plans. The difference is that they cover worker teams rather than individuals. Not included are gain-sharing plans (Section 4) and profit-sharing plans (Section 5), which are group plans but do not pay out in proportion to output in the same direct way as conventional wage-incentive plans.

In group incentive plans, several workers must operate as a team, and the output of the team depends on the effort of each team member. Each worker's wage is based on the output of the group. Worker teams have become an important way of managing work, and with them the importance of group incentive systems has increased. Examples of worker teams that might be covered by a group incentive system include members of a production department or work unit (e.g., production work teams operating a single piece of equipment), work cells, workers on an assembly line, material-handling workers in a facility, and ship crews. The common theme in these examples is that the output of the group reflects the combined (and often synergistic) efforts of its members rather than a summation of the individual member's outputs. Another similarity among the examples is that the team members are usually in close physical proximity.

There are advantages and disadvantages of group incentive systems relative to individual incentives [3, 15]. In general, the following advantages are found in a group incentive system:

- Group plans are easier to install and administer than individual plans. Because the output of the group is measured, no assignment of outputs to individual workers is needed. The output is applied to the entire group. Also, all workers in the group receive the same bonus percentage. Record keeping is simplified.
- Fewer supervisory personnel may be needed. The team may be self-managed which means that traditional supervisors are not needed at all.
- Success of the group requires cooperation and teamwork, and this requirement encourages that behavior within the group.
- Workers jockeying to get the easier jobs (e.g., those jobs with loose standards) is minimized. This eliminates variances in wages among group members, which is sometimes a source of personnel problems in traditional individual incentive plans.

There are also drawbacks and disadvantages related to group incentive systems:

- No attention is paid to individual performance, at least not officially. In general, there are no standards for individual tasks within the group (which contributes to the advantage of easier installation and administration mentioned above). However, this can result in personnel problems within the group when some team members loaf.
- Group incentive pay systems do not provide as much of an incentive for greater individual effort as individual incentive systems. That is, group incentive systems do not motivate workers as much as individual incentive systems.

3.3 Management of Incentive Systems

Direct incentive plans do not always operate as well as intended by those who implement them. In this section, we consider this problem area by discussing two management issues related to incentive systems: (1) why direct incentive plans sometimes fail and (2) success factors in the implementation and operation of a direct incentive system.

There are two basic objectives of a direct incentive system: (1) to increase productivity for the organization that sponsors it and (2) to increase earnings for the workers who participate in it. Achieving these two objectives provides a mutual interest in the success of the incentive system by both management and workers. An incentive system, whether individual or group, is supposed to be a "win-win" arrangement. However, if the system increases workers' earnings but does not increase productivity, then it is a cost burden to the organization. And if the system increases productivity but does not increase workers' earnings, then it is of no benefit to the workers. Achieving a win-win arrangement for management and labor turns out to be more elusive than one would think.

Why Wage Incentive Plans Sometimes Fail. In principle, wage incentive systems seem to offer much promise to motivate workers toward higher levels of effort, which will in turn generate greater output and productivity. The problem is that workers are sometimes motivated not only to put forth greater effort but also to find ways to circumvent and convolute the polices and spirit of the incentive system—to try to "beat the system." Supervision and management often contribute to this problem by not fulfilling their basic responsibility of dutifully administering the incentive system and the workers covered by it. The following factors identify some of the reasons why incentive systems sometimes fail. These reasons apply mainly to individual incentive systems, which are supposed to have a strong motivational effect but which sometimes motivate a darker side of human behavior.

- *Conflicting objectives.* Although the basic objective of an incentive system is to reward both the organization and the workers, workers may be tempted to take a narrower view. Their interest is to maximize their own wages, and any attention to benefits for the organization is secondary at most. The objectives of the worker are therefore not the same as those of the organization. The organizational objectives include higher productivity, better quality, lower labor costs, greater customer satisfaction, improved profits, and so on. The workers may not care much about these organizational objectives. The structure of the incentive system motivates and rewards higher individual output, and that is what workers focus on.
- *Penalties for increasing productivity.* Workers have sometimes been penalized for increasing productivity. Such increases mean that the same amount of work can be accomplished in fewer hours and/or with fewer workers. This may have the following consequences for workers: (1) less overtime, which means less money, (2) worker displacements to less desirable jobs, and (3) layoffs. None of these consequences are beneficial from the worker's viewpoint. Workers may therefore restrict their own output to avoid them, which is opposed to the basic goal of the incentive system.
- *Emphasis on physical effort.* Incentive systems encourage increased output that is accomplished through increased physical effort, which may mean working harder but not necessarily smarter. The payment structure of the incentive system is based on worker output while using a standard method. Output is measured as piece count multiplied by the time standard per piece. Any change in the method mandates a change in the time standard. Therefore, the emphasis of the incentive system is to reward the worker for greater effort and speed. It does not reward the worker for making changes in the method. Methods improvements (working smarter) may be a more fruitful source of productivity increases than greater physical effort (working harder).
- *Standards eroding over time.* Through gradual improvements over several years, the time standards for at least some jobs become loose, allowing the worker to increase output and earnings. Why do the standards become loose? There are many reasons, most of them related to the operation of the learning curve. The learning curve manifests itself in two ways. The first is that the worker learns the task and becomes more proficient and efficient at performing it, thus completing

it in less and less time. These gains represent a valid outcome of the incentive system and are consistent with the purpose of the system. The worker should be rewarded for these gains. The second way in which the learning curve can occur is that the worker makes unofficial changes in the method, developing tricks and tweaks and tools of which supervision is either unaware or permissive. These are methods changes, and if their effects are significant, then a restudy of the task is warranted with a resulting adjustment in the time standard. If no updates are made to account for the changes, the standard gradually becomes loose, yielding great rewards for the worker and marginal benefits for the organization. Mindful of the likelihood that high bonuses will focus attention on their jobs and that revised time standards will be set, workers sometimes elect to limit their own output to levels that will avoid retiming of their jobs. Of course, this is inconsistent with the goal of the incentive system.

- *Mixing day work and incentive work.* Problems arise when incentive work and day work occur in the same plant. Some employees work on incentive while others are on day work, and one group earns more money (usually the incentive group), provoking jealousy from the other group. Another possible mixing occurs when someone works part of the shift on incentive and the rest of the shift at an hourly rate. One of the problems with this mixing of the two pay systems is that it may be difficult to obtain an accurate accounting of how much time was spent in each category. An inaccurate accounting of these times might unfairly inflate a worker's earnings to the disadvantage of the company. Another problem is that workers prefer to work on the incentive system because they can earn more money than they earn on day work if all they receive on day work is the base hourly rate with no bonus. This puts pressure on management to provide some inducement for them to perform day work when nonincentive tasks must be performed (e.g., machine setups, maintenance, training new workers). An inducement often agreed to by management is to pay a worker performing day work at his or her ***average earned rate***, which is the average rate that he or she receives when working on incentive. This means that the worker enjoys the higher pay rate, but there is no motivation to get the job done in the shortest possible time.

Incentive Plan Success Factors. What are the conditions that must be satisfied in order for the two objectives of a direct incentive plan (increased productivity for the company and increased earnings for the workers) to be achieved? Although there are no guarantees of success, the following conditions usually allow an incentive pay system to operate successfully:

- *Clearly defined and documented incentive plan.* The incentive plan (how it works, how workers are paid, etc.) should be completely specified and written in plain language (not legalese). The policy statement should cover all possible work situations, indicating which tasks are covered by incentive and which ones are not. There should be no ambiguities or loopholes. A clearly defined and documented incentive policy will reduce the chances of employees "beating the system" or of supervision acceding to its occurrence.

- *Easy to understand plan.* The incentive plan should be easy for the worker to understand. It should be a straightforward matter for the worker to compute his or her earnings based on the plan.
- *Plan stability.* The plan should not be in a state of constant flux, with management making periodic adjustments. Making changes is likely to make the workers suspicious and resentful when the changes are disadvantageous to them.
- *Training of workers.* Employees working on incentive must be trained. Two areas of worker training are important: (1) the philosophy of the incentive system and how it operates and (2) the standard method to be used by the worker in each particular job.
- *Link between effort and output.* There must be a direct relationship between the worker's effort and output. It must be possible for the worker's output to be increased through his or her increased effort and performance. If the nature of the job does not allow this relationship to exist, then the job should not be covered by the incentive plan.
- *Measurable output.* The worker's output must be measurable. If the amount of work accomplished by the worker cannot be accurately measured, then there is no basis for accurately determining the worker's additional earnings (his or her bonus). In general, measurable output means (1) accurate time standards that are maintained and (2) accurate accounting of work units completed and the amount of time to complete them.
- *Accurate time standards.* Time standards for tasks must be accurately established. This means using engineered work measurement techniques (direct time study, predetermined motion time systems, and standard data systems). Without accurate standards, some standards will turn out to be loose while others are tight, leading to inequities in earnings among workers. Workers will zealously compete for the easy-money jobs, and they will shun the difficult jobs.
- *Maintenance of time standards.* The time standards must not be allowed to erode over time. When changes in work methods are made, the time standards must be adjusted accordingly.

When these conditions are satisfied, the incentive system is more likely to function properly to provide the sponsoring company with higher productivity, lower costs, good employee morale, high product quality, and a more secure competitive position in its industry.

4 GAIN SHARING

Because of the problems sometimes encountered in the implementation and administration of direct wage incentive plans, many companies have implemented alternative systems by which to motivate employees and to reward them for their efforts. They are sometimes referred to as indirect incentive plans because there is not a direct relationship between production output and wages. The alternatives fall into two categories: (1) gain sharing, which is discussed in this section, and (2) profit sharing, which is discussed in Section 5.

A ***gain-sharing plan*** is an indirect group incentive system in which employees are encouraged to make improvements that increase productivity and reduce cost, and the company shares the benefits of those improvements with the employees in the form of a periodic bonus. It might be argued that gain sharing represents an evolutionary development of direct wage incentives. In this evolved system, employees are motivated not only to work harder but also to work smarter, unlike a direct wage incentive plan in which the emphasis is on working harder. In gain sharing, workers share their process knowledge, recommend methods changes, suggest cost reductions, solve operating problems, improve product quality, and so on, all of which contribute to productivity increases for the company. In fact, gain-sharing plans are sometimes called ***productivity sharing plans*** because of their emphasis on productivity improvement. In return for their involvement in productivity improvement, employees share in the gains achieved.

The most familiar gain-sharing plans today are (1) the Scanlon plan, (2) the Rucker plan, and (3) Improshare. The main difference between them is the formula used to calculate the cash bonus. In addition, many companies have developed their own custom-designed gain-sharing plans, plucking features from the three plans we cover here, and adding their own twists to fit their unique circumstances. The trend in industry seems to be in the direction of these customized gain-sharing plans.

4.1 Scanlon Plan

The ***Scanlon plan*** was the first formalized plan in the gain-sharing category. It was developed around 1935 by Joseph Scanlon, a union representative at a steel mill on the verge of financial failure. To try to save the company (and the jobs of his union members), he collaborated with the mill's management by drawing out the ideas of the workers on how to improve operations. The collaboration went well. The mill survived for the next 20 years, at which time another company acquired it. The steelworkers union was so impressed with Scanlon's success that they asked him to use the same approach to save other steel companies in distress (and the union jobs in those companies).

The Scanlon plan covers all employees at a particular location. A philosophy of cooperation permeates the organization, and the workers are involved in "production committees" that develop recommendations for improvement.[3] The formula for computing the bonus is based on the ratio of payroll costs in a defined base period to net sales for the same period. This base ratio is summarized as follows:

$$SBR = \frac{PC_b}{NS_b} \tag{9}$$

where SBR = Scanlon base ratio, PC_b = payroll costs for base period, which consists of total wages plus fringe benefits, and NS_b = net sales for same base period, which is actual sales less returns and shipping costs. Adjustments to net sales are also made for any increases or decreases in inventories. The ratio SBR defines the baseline against which improvements will be compared.

[3]The reader will note similarities between these "production committees" and the other improvement teams.

Once the plan is in operation, the actual payroll costs in a given period (usually 3 months) are compared against the base ratio multiplied by net sales. If actual payroll costs are lower, then the bonus is the calculated difference. That is,

$$B_i = SBR\,(NS_i) - PC_i \tag{10}$$

where B_i = bonus for period i, SBR = base ratio determined by equation (9), NS_i = net sales in period i; and PC_i = payroll costs in period i. If the calculated bonus value is positive, it means that savings have been realized. If negative, it means that costs have increased and there is no bonus to be shared.

The allocation of the bonus is a decision the company must make. A typical allocation is for the company and the employees to share the bonus on a 50-50 basis. The employees' share is then divided into a portion that is distributed in cash immediately (typically 75% of the employees' share) and a portion (the remaining 25%) that is deposited into a reserve pool in case of future negative bonuses. If any money is left in the pool at the end of the year, it is distributed to the workers. The following example illustrates the operation of the Scanlon plan bonus formula.

Example 3 Scanlon Gain-Sharing plan

In a two-year base period used to determine the base ratio for the Scanlon plan in a small company, net sales totaled \$24,000,000, payroll costs were \$7,200,000, and other production costs (e.g., raw materials, supplies, power) added up to \$14,000,000. In a subsequent 3-month period when the plan was in operation and several productivity improvements had been made, net sales amounted to \$3,500,000 and payroll costs were \$960,000. Determine (a) the base ratio for the Scanlon plan, (b) the amount of the bonus in the 3-month period if a bonus is deserved, and (c) the cash amount distributed immediately to employees.

Solution **(a)** The base ratio for the Scanlon plan is $SBR = \dfrac{7{,}200{,}000}{24{,}000{,}000} = 0.30$

(b) The bonus is deserved if the calculated value in equation (10) is positive.

$$B_i = 0.30(3{,}500{,}000) - 960{,}000 = 1{,}050{,}000 - 960{,}000 = \$90{,}000.$$

(c) The \$90,000 is divided 50-50 between the company and the employees, leaving \$45,000 for the employees. Of this amount 75% is distributed immediately as a cash payment. Thus, the cash amount distributed to employees is 0.75(45,000), or \$33,750. ■

4.2 Rucker Plan

The ***Rucker plan*** was developed around 1948 by Allen Rucker. Its features are similar to those of the Scanlon plan, encouraging cooperation between management and labor. It uses suggestion committees, called "Rucker committees," and determines a bonus based on productivity improvements. A different feature of the Rucker plan is that it compares payroll costs against a value-added quantity rather than net sales. The value-added quantity is supposed to represent the dollar value added by labor to the product during a given period (e.g., 1 month or 3 months). It is calculated as net sales less production costs other than labor costs. A base ratio is calculated as payroll costs divided by this value-added quantity for some designated base period.

$$RBR = \frac{PC_b}{VA_b} \tag{11}$$

where RBR = Rucker base ratio; PC_b = payroll costs for base period, which consists of total wages plus fringe benefits; and VA_b = value-added quantity for same base period. This ratio represents the labor cost per dollar of value added to the product by labor. Later, in operation of the plan, the base ratio is used to compute the bonus as follows:

$$B_i = RBR\,(VA_i) - PC_i \tag{12}$$

where B_i = bonus for period i; BR_b = Rucker base ratio; VA_i = value added by labor in period i; and PC_i = payroll costs in period i. If the bonus is positive, then savings have occurred. Otherwise, costs have increased relative to the base period and no bonus is available.

Distribution of the bonus is similar to the procedure followed in the Scanlon plan. It is shared between the company and employees (e.g., a 50-50 ratio), and a percentage of the employees' share (e.g., 25%) is put into a reserve pool while the remainder is distributed as cash. The reserve pool is used to offset negative bonuses during future periods.

Example 4 Rucker Gain-Sharing Plan

Using the same basic data given in Example 3, assume that during a two-year base period, net sales are \$24,000,000, payroll costs are \$7,200,000, and other production costs are \$14,000,000. In a later 3-month period when the Rucker plan was in operation and productivity improvements had been made, net sales are \$3,500,000, payroll costs are \$960,000, and other production costs are \$2,000,000. Determine (a) the base ratio for the Rucker plan, (b) the amount of the bonus in the 3-month period if a bonus is deserved, and (c) the cash amount distributed immediately to employees.

Solution **(a)** With net sales of \$24 million and other production costs of \$14 million, the difference is the amount of value added to the product by labor.

$$VA_b = \$24,000,000 - \$14,000,000 = \$10,000,000$$

Using the payroll cost of \$7.2 million, the base ratio is

$$RBR = \frac{7,200,000}{10,000,000} = 0.72$$

Thus, the labor cost per dollar of value added to the product by labor is 72 cents.

(b) To calculate the bonus, we first need the value-added amount:

$$VA_i = 3,500,000 - 2,000,000 = \$1,500,000$$

$$B_i = 0.72(1,500,000) - 960,000 = 1,080,000 - 960,000 = \$120,000$$

(c) The \$120,000 is divided 50-50 between the company and the employees, leaving \$60,000 for the employees. Of this amount 75% is distributed immediately as a cash payment. Thus, the cash amount distributed to employees is 0.75(60,000), or \$45,000. ■

4.3 Improshare

Improshare—which stands for "improved productivity through sharing"—is a gain-sharing plan that was developed by Mitchell Fein and introduced in 1974. It advocates the same kind of cooperation and involvement as the Scanlon and Rucker gain-sharing plans. Its basic departure from these other plans is that it measures labor hours rather than dollars (sales and costs) to determine the bonus that is paid to employees. There are two strong arguments in favor of using hours over financial data in a gain-sharing plan: (1) hourly data are easier for employees to understand than financial data, so an incentive system based on hourly data is easier to understand; and (2) many of the factors that affect financial data are not related to productivity improvement, so changes in cost factors could either overstate or obscure productivity increases. In order to make proper use of the labor hour data, Improshare requires time standards that are set by an engineered work measurement system.

The base ratio in Improshare is called the *base productivity factor* (*BPF*). The *BPF* is determined as the total standard hours of all production employees for all of the products completed during a designated base period, divided by the total employee hours in the facility in the same period. The standard hours is determined by first summing the standard times for all of the tasks that went into the production of each product completed during the period, and then summing these times to obtain a total standard hours for all products completed. This is consistent with our previous terminology relating to standard hours:

$$TH_{std(b)} = \sum_j Q_j \Sigma T_{stdj} \tag{13}$$

where $TH_{std(b)}$ = total standard hours completed in base period, hr; Q_j = quantity of product j completed during base period, pc; and ΣT_{stdj} = sum of standard times for all tasks required to produce those products. Total employee hours include all of the production workers plus all of the supervisory, indirect, and support personnel. Although this second group does not directly make product, it may nevertheless influence productivity and is included in the base productivity factor, which is calculated as follows:

$$BPF = \frac{TEH_b}{TH_{std(b)}} \tag{14}$$

where BPF = base productivity factor; TEH_b = total employee hours in base period, hr; and $TH_{std(b)}$ = total standard hours completed during same period, hr. Once the *BPF* is established, it is used to determine the labor hour savings, or gain to the company from any productivity improvements. The labor hour savings is the actual hours required to complete products during a given period (e.g., a week or month) subtracted from the number of hours that would have been required in the base period:

$$LHS_i = BPF(TH_{std(i)}) - TEH_i \tag{15}$$

where LHS_i = labor hour savings for period i, hr; BPF = base productivity factor, $TH_{std(i)}$ = total standard hours during period i, hr; and TEH_i = total employee hours during period i, hr. Half of the labor hour savings are used to determine a cash incentive bonus that is paid to the employees. The following example illustrates the calculations in Improshare.

Example 5 Improshare

During the base period, a total of 90,000 standard hours were required to complete a mixture of products, while employee hours during the same period totaled 144,000. These values were used to determine the base productivity factor. Later, during one particular month of interest, standard hours totaled 12,000 and employee hours totaled 17,500. Determine (a) the base productivity factor, (b) the labor hour savings to the company during the month of interest, and (c) the incentive bonus that is paid to the employees.

Solution **(a)** $BPF = \dfrac{144{,}000}{90{,}000} = 1.60$

(b) $LHS_i = 1.60(12{,}000) - 17{,}500 = 19{,}200 - 17{,}500 = 1{,}700$ hr

(c) Half of the labor hour savings are used to determine the incentive bonus for the employees (1700/2 = 850 hr). The incentive bonus is determined as a percentage rate above the total employee hours.

Incentive bonus rate = 850/17,500 = 0.0486 = 4.86%

This percentage would be applied as a cash payment to each employee's paycheck. ■

5 PROFIT SHARING

Profit sharing is just what it sounds like—an arrangement in which a company pays to its employees a share of its profits. Usually, all employees are included in the coverage. A profit-sharing plan is an indirect group incentive system because sharing the profits serves to motivate employees toward greater service to the company, and yet the bonus they receive is not directly related to their own output.

Although the details of profit-sharing plans differ among companies, three basic types can be identified: (1) cash plans, (2) deferred plans, and (3) combinations of cash and deferred plans. In ***cash plans***, the profit bonus is paid to employees soon after profits are determined. Each employee receives his or her share in the form of check or company stock. The payment frequency is usually annually or quarterly, consistent with accounting schedules. In ***deferred plans***, the profit share is credited to an employee account that is withdrawn at retirement or some other specified circumstance, such as severance, death, or disability. In some cases, withdrawals are allowed during employment. Finally, ***combination plans*** pay part of the profit share as cash and the remainder is deferred.

The size of the share received by each employee depends on company policy. Some companies pay all employees the same amount, in the belief that this is the most egalitarian way for the company to share its prosperity with employees. Of course, eligible employees must have attained a certain length of company service. These types of profit-sharing systems seem to be rare.

In most profit-sharing plans, the following factors are used to determine the size of the share received by individual employees:

- *Annual salary level.* The profit share is proportional to the employee's annual wage or salary level.
- *Length of company service.* Companies often give higher profit bonuses to employees who have been with the company more than a certain number of years. The length of service is typically factored into the share determination as follows: the size of the share is proportional to years of service up to some point (e.g., 5 years of service) after which it levels off.
- *Proportion of total profit allocated to profit sharing.* A company is unlikely to distribute all of its profits to the employees because stockholders' interests have to be also considered. Deciding what proportion of the profit to distribute to employees is made at the very top of the chain of command in the organization.
- *Size of the profit.* In order for a profit-sharing plan to pay out, the company must make a profit. If there is no profit, then there is nothing to share with employees.

A profit-sharing plan tends to instill a sense of partnership between employees and their company. They feel that they have a stake in the business. Profit sharing is an attractive benefit for recruiting purposes, and employee turnover is usually lower at companies with these plans. On the other hand, profit sharing is not without problems. First, the motivational value toward higher individual performance is not as strong as it is with traditional direct wage incentives. The worker cannot perceive a clear relationship between performance and the bonus received. And there is no built-in mechanism for worker involvement and cooperation as there is with a gain-sharing plan. Finally, if the company does not make a profit, then there is nothing to share. Employees may come to expect and rely on the extra money each year, and they may feel a sense of betrayal by the company's lack of financial success when profits are low or negative. The inability of the company to make a profit may be due to economic conditions that are beyond the control of individual employees and company management.

REFERENCES

[1] Amrine, H. T., J. A. Ritchey, and C. L. Moodie. *Manufacturing Organization and Management.* 5th ed. Englewood Cliffs, NJ: Prentice-Hall, 1987.

[2] Barnes, R. M. *Motion and Time Study: Design and Measurement of Work.* 7th ed. New York: Wiley, 1980.

[3] Celley, A. F. "Conventional Wage Incentives," Pp. 6.17–6.42 in *Maynard's Industrial Engineering Handbook,* 4th ed., edited by W. K. Hodson. New York: McGraw-Hill, 1992.

[4] Colletti, J. A., and D. J. Cichelli. "Increasing Sales-Force Effectiveness Through the Compensation Plan." Pp. 290–303 in *The Compensation Handbook,* 3rd ed., edited by M. L. Rock and L. A. Berger. New York: McGraw-Hill, 1991.

[5] Dantico, J. A., and R. Greene. "Compensation Administration." Pp. 7.79–7.96 in *Maynard's Industrial Engineering Handbook*, 5th ed., edited by K. B. Zandin. New York: McGraw-Hill, 2001.

[6] Dunn, J. D., and F. M. Rachel. *Wage and Salary Administration: Total Compensation Systems.* New York: McGraw-Hill 1971.

[7] Eden, D., and S. Globerson. "Financial and Nonfinancial Motivation." Pp. 817–844 in *Handbook of Industrial Engineering*, 2nd ed., edited by G. Salvendy. New York: Wiley 1992.

[8] Fay, C. H., M. A. Thompson, and D. Knight, eds. *The Executive Handbook on Compensation,* New York: Free Press, 2001.

[9] Fein, M. *Rational Approaches to Raising Productivity*, Monograph Series No. 5, Work Measurement and Methods Engineering Division. Norcross, GA: American Institute of Industrial Engineers, 1974.

[10] Fein, M., "Improshare: A Technique for Sharing Productivity Gains with Employees." Pp. 158–175 in *The Compensation Handbook*, 3rd ed., edited by M. L. Rock and L. A. Berger. New York: McGraw-Hill, 1991.

[11] Gardner, D. L., "Lean Organization Pay Design." Pp. 7.41–7.50 in *Maynard's Industrial Engineering Handbook*, 5th ed., edited by K. B. Zandin. New York: McGraw-Hill, 2001.

[12] Gerhart, B., and S. L. Rynes. *Compensation: Theory, Evidence, and Strategic Implications.* Thousand Oaks, CA: Sage Publications, 2003.

[13] Graham-Moore, B. "Gainsharing." Pp. 527–38 in *The Executive Handbook on Compensation,* edited by C. H. Fay, M. A. Thompson, and D. Knight. New York, Free Press, 2001.

[14] Kuh, L. M. "Measured Daywork." Pp. 6.3–6.15 in *Maynard's Industrial Engineering Handbook*, 4th ed., edited by W. K. Hodson. New York: McGraw-Hill, 1992.

[15] Niebel, B. W., and A. Freivalds. *Methods, Standards, and Work Design.* 11th ed., New York: McGraw-Hill, 2003.

[16] Ross, T. L., and R. A. Ross. "Gain Sharing: Sharing Improved Performance." Pp. 176–89 in *The Compensation Handbook*, 3rd ed., edited by M. L. Rock and L. A. Berger. New York: McGraw-Hill, 1991.

[17] Wallace, M. C. III, and M. J. Wallace Jr. "Performance-Based Compensation: Designing Total Rewards to Drive Performance." pp. 7.3–7.16 in *Maynard's Industrial Engineering Handbook*, 5th ed., edited by K. B. Zandin. New York: McGraw-Hill, 2001.

[18] Weiss, R. M. "Gain Sharing." Pp. 6.43–6.59 in *Maynard's Industrial Engineering Handbook,* 4th ed., edited by W. K. Hodson. New York: McGraw-Hill, 1992.

[19] Weiss, R. M. "Reengineering Production Incentive Plans," Pp. 7.51–7.64 in *Maynard's Industrial Engineering Handbook*, 5th ed., edited by K. B. Zandin. New York: McGraw-Hill, 2001.

REVIEW QUESTIONS

1 What are the three components of an individual's total compensation?

2 What are the two basic types of pay systems?

3 What is the base pay in an employee's compensation package?

4 What is meant by the term *base pay progression*?

5 What is the variable pay in an employee's compensation package?

6 Define fringe benefits.

7 What are the two categories of time-based pay systems?

8 What does the term *exempt* mean in the context of pay systems?

9 Define measured day work.

10 What is a direct wage incentive system?

11 What is the difference between a piecework system and a standard hour plan?

12 What is meant by the expression *guaranteed base rate*?

13 Under what kind of selling circumstances is a sales incentive system appropriate?

14 What are the two basic objectives of a direct incentive system?

15 What are some of the reasons why direct incentive plans sometimes fail?

16 What is a gain-sharing plan?

17 The Scanlon and Rucker gain-sharing plans use financial measures in their bonus-sharing formula, while Improshare uses labor hours. What are the two main advantages of using labor hours instead of financial data in a gain-sharing plan?

18 What are the three basic types of profit-sharing plans?

PROBLEMS

Time-Based Pay Systems

1 An hourly pay system uses a rate of \$12.40/hr. The regular workweek is 40 hours, Monday through Friday. All workers are nonexempt. There is no paid sick day benefit. Determine the weekly wage under the following circumstances: (a) the employee worked 32 hours during the week and called in sick on Friday, (b) the employee worked 45 hours during the week, including 5 hours overtime on Wednesday evening, and (c) the employee was absent on Monday, but worked 8 hours each day for the remaining 4 days of the week and then worked 6 hours on Saturday.

2 Solve the previous problem except that all workers are exempt and are paid a weekly salary. Also, the company has a paid sick day policy that covers up to 10 sick days per year.

Direct Incentive Pay Systems

3 A time standard of 0.25 min has been set in a stamping operation. The plant uses a standard hour plan at \$10/hr with a daily guarantee of 8 hours pay minimum. Determine the daily earnings of a worker whose daily output for two days is (a) 1800 pieces and (b) 2200 pieces.

4 On two consecutive 8-hour days, a worker produced 167 units and 132 units, respectively, on a job whose standard time is 3.55 min. His hourly rate is \$9.00/hr. Compute his earnings for the two days under the following wage payment plans: (a) daywork, (b) standard hour plan with guaranteed base rate, and (c) bonus-sharing plan with $p = 0.75$. Assume that the bonus-sharing plan has a guaranteed base rate.

5 A worker's base rate is \$10.00/hr, and he works on a job whose standard time is 6.00 min/pc. Standard output per day for this job is 80 units. Compute his earnings for a given day under the following circumstances: (a) his output is 90 units and the incentive plan is a standard hour plan with guaranteed base rate, (b) his output is 75 units and the plan is a standard hour plan with no guaranteed base rate, (c) his output is 90 units and the incentive plan is a Bedaux Point System with $p = 0.65$. Assume that the standard is expressed as 6.0 B-points/pc, and that the plan has a guaranteed base rate.

6 In a certain repetitive manual operation, the standard time is 2.50 min/work unit and the worker's base rate is \$9.00/hr. The plant's policy is to pay workers a weekly wage for their weekly output. During one 40-hour workweek, the daily output in work units was 200, 230, 180, 220, and 240 for the 5 days. Determine the worker's wage for the week under the following payment plans: (a) day rate, (b) standard hour plan with guaranteed base rate, and (c) bonus-sharing plan where bonus sharing factor $p = 0.35$. Finally, assume the same plan as (b) except the worker is paid daily (8 hours/day) for his daily output. (d) What are his weekly earnings?

7 A machine shop uses a wage payment system that is a combination of a daywork plan (hourly pay) and a standard hour plan. The day work portion pays an hourly rate of \$4.50, while the standard hour portion pays a rate of \$5.50/hr. During a particular 8-hour shift, a worker produced 92 units on a task in which the standard time is 6.00 min. (a) How much did the worker earn during the day? (b) Show that this plan is the same as a Halsey-type bonus-sharing plan, and determine the bonus sharing factor p and the hourly rate that should be used.

8 A local steel foundry uses a wage payment system that is a combination of an hourly pay and a standard hour plan. The hourly pay portion pays a rate of \$6.00/hr worked, while the standard hour portion pays a rate of \$10.00/standard hr earned. During a particular 8-hour shift, a worker produced 120 units on a task in which the standard time is 5.00 min. (a) How much did the worker earn during the day? (b) Show that this plan is the same as a Halsey plan, and determine the bonus sharing factor p and the hourly rate that should be used.

9 A 50-50 bonus sharing plan guarantees a base rate of \$11.00/hr. The standard time per work unit for a given task is 2.0 min. On three consecutive days, the worker's efficiencies were 70%, 100%, and 130% of standard. For each day, determine (a) the worker's wage for the 8-hour shift and (b) the direct labor cost per work unit.

10 A worker is paid weekly, but her wage is calculated on a daily basis. In three days of interest she worked on the same job, which had a time standard of 4.0 min/work unit. The worker is paid a rate of \$14.00/hr in a standard hour plan that has a guaranteed base rate. Determine (a) the worker's wages and (b) the direct labor costs per work unit to the company for each of the three days if she produced 110 work units on the first day, 125 units on the second day, and 145 units on the third day.

11 Solve the previous problem but assume that the plan is a bonus-sharing plan in which the worker's bonus-sharing proportion is 0.40.

12 A wage payment system is described as a combination of day work (hourly pay) and a standard hour plan. The day work portion pays an hourly rate of \$8.40, while the standard hour portion pays a rate of \$3.60/hr. During a particular 8-hour shift, a worker produced 57 units on a task in which the standard time is 10.00 min. (a) How much did the worker earn during the day? (b) Show that this plan is the same as a Halsey plan, and determine the bonus sharing factor p and the hourly rate that should be used. Using this hourly rate, determine how much the worker would earn in (c) a 50-50 bonus sharing plan and (d) a standard hour plan. What is the labor cost per piece to the company under each of the three incentive plans: (e) the Halsey plan in (b), (f) the 50-50 plan in (c), and (g) the standard hour plan in (d)?

13 In a bonus-sharing plan, a worker gets 65% of the bonus earned. The plan has a guaranteed base rate of \$12.50/hr for the regular 8-hour shift. The wage is computed daily and paid weekly. Company policy allows 10 paid sick days per calendar year at the guaranteed base rate. In the first full week of January, a worker named Sam called in sick on Monday and Tuesday. On Wednesday, Thursday, and Friday of the same week, Sam produced 150 pieces, 180 pieces, and 193 pieces, respectively, on a job whose standard time per piece was

3.00 min. (a) What was the worker's gross wage that week? (b) What was the average cost per piece to the company for the pieces produced by Sam that week?

Gain-Sharing Plans

14 A Scanlon plan used a two-year base period several years ago to compute the base ratio. During that period, total sales amounted to \$125 million, and total employee payroll costs were \$55 million. The plan operates with the following features: it pays quarterly; there is no reserve pool; all bonus monies above the ratio are shared between the workers and the firm; sharing is 75% to workers and 25% to firm; and a negative bonus amount is absorbed by the company. Under this plan, determine the amount of the bonus and how it was shared during the last two quarters of the previous year: (a) third quarter during which sales were \$18 million and payroll costs were \$7 million; (b) fourth quarter during which sales were \$20 million and payroll costs were \$9 million.

15 A Scanlon plan with the following features was established three years ago at the Lifelong Uniform Company: payments are made annually based on productivity improvements in the preceding year; there is no reserve pool; all bonus monies above the ratio are shared between the workers and LU, with 60% going to workers and 40% to LU; and any negative bonus amount is absorbed by LU. Two years ago a total bonus was paid to the workers of \$1,200,000 based on net sales of \$75,000,000. One year ago a total bonus was paid to the workers of \$2,040,000 based on net sales of \$80,000,000. Payroll costs for both years were the same. If net sales for the current year are projected to be \$83,000,000, and payroll costs are expected to increase by 5%, what will the workers' expected bonus be? The hourly base rate paid to the workers remained the same throughout the period of interest in this problem.

16 A Rucker plan used a two-year base period three years ago to compute the base ratio. During that period, total sales amounted to \$152 million, total employee payroll costs were \$55 million, and other production costs were \$67 million. The plan has the following features: it pays quarterly; there is a reserve pool of 25% to offset negative gains; sharing is 50% to workers and 50% to firm. Under this plan, determine the amount of the bonus and how it was shared during the last two quarters of last year: (a) third quarter during which sales were \$25 million, payroll costs were \$8.8 million, and other production costs were \$10.7 million; (b) fourth quarter during which sales were \$32 million, payroll costs were \$11.2 million, and other production costs were \$14.1 million.

17 During the base period in the implementation of an Improshare system, a total of 118,000 standard hours were required to complete a mixture of products, while the total employee hours during the same period totaled 197,000 hr. These values were used to determine the base productivity factor. Later, during one particular month of interest, the total standard hours were 16,300 hr and the total employee hours were 22,700 hr. Determine (a) the base productivity factor, (b) the labor hour savings to the company during the month of interest, and (c) the incentive bonus percentage that is paid to the employees.

Appendix

TABLE 1 Standard Normal Distribution

z	0.00	0.01	0.02	0.03	0.04	0.05	0.06	0.07	0.08	0.09
0.00	0.5000	0.5040	0.5080	0.5120	0.5160	0.5199	0.5239	0.5279	0.5319	0.5359
0.10	0.5398	0.5438	0.5478	0.5517	0.5557	0.5596	0.5636	0.5675	0.5714	0.5753
0.20	0.5793	0.5832	0.5871	0.5910	0.5948	0.5987	0.6026	0.6064	0.6103	0.6141
0.30	0.6179	0.6217	0.6255	0.6293	0.6331	0.6368	0.6406	0.6443	0.6480	0.6517
0.40	0.6554	0.6591	0.6628	0.6664	0.6700	0.6736	0.6772	0.6808	0.6844	0.6879
0.50	0.6915	0.6950	0.6985	0.7019	0.7054	0.7088	0.7123	0.7157	0.7190	0.7224
0.60	0.7257	0.7291	0.7324	0.7357	0.7389	0.7422	0.7454	0.7486	0.7517	0.7549
0.70	0.7580	0.7611	0.7642	0.7673	0.7704	0.7734	0.7764	0.7794	0.7823	0.7852
0.80	0.7881	0.7910	0.7939	0.7967	0.7995	0.8023	0.8051	0.8078	0.8106	0.8133
0.90	0.8159	0.8186	0.8212	0.8238	0.8264	0.8289	0.8315	0.8340	0.8365	0.8389
1.00	0.8413	0.8438	0.8461	0.8485	0.8508	0.8531	0.8554	0.8577	0.8599	0.8621
1.10	0.8643	0.8665	0.8686	0.8708	0.8729	0.8749	0.8770	0.8790	0.8810	0.8830
1.20	0.8849	0.8869	0.8888	0.8907	0.8925	0.8944	0.8962	0.8980	0.8997	0.9015
1.30	0.9032	0.9049	0.9066	0.9082	0.9099	0.9115	0.9131	0.9147	0.9162	0.9177
1.40	0.9192	0.9207	0.9222	0.9236	0.9251	0.9265	0.9279	0.9292	0.9306	0.9319
1.50	0.9332	0.9345	0.9357	0.9370	0.9382	0.9394	0.9406	0.9418	0.9429	0.9441
1.60	0.9452	0.9463	0.9474	0.9484	0.9495	0.9505	0.9515	0.9525	0.9535	0.9545
1.70	0.9554	0.9564	0.9573	0.9582	0.9591	0.9599	0.9608	0.9616	0.9625	0.9633
1.80	0.9641	0.9649	0.9656	0.9664	0.9671	0.9678	0.9686	0.9693	0.9699	0.9706
1.90	0.9713	0.9719	0.9726	0.9732	0.9738	0.9744	0.9750	0.9756	0.9761	0.9767
2.00	0.9772	0.9778	0.9783	0.9788	0.9793	0.9798	0.9803	0.9808	0.9812	0.9817
2.10	0.9821	0.9826	0.9830	0.9834	0.9838	0.9842	0.9846	0.9850	0.9854	0.9857
2.20	0.9861	0.9864	0.9868	0.9871	0.9875	0.9878	0.9881	0.9884	0.9887	0.9890
2.30	0.9893	0.9896	0.9898	0.9901	0.9904	0.9906	0.9909	0.9911	0.9913	0.9916
2.40	0.9918	0.9920	0.9922	0.9925	0.9927	0.9929	0.9931	0.9932	0.9934	0.9936
2.50	0.9938	0.9940	0.9941	0.9943	0.9945	0.9946	0.9948	0.9949	0.9951	0.9952
2.60	0.9953	0.9955	0.9956	0.9957	0.9959	0.9960	0.9961	0.9962	0.9963	0.9964
2.70	0.9965	0.9966	0.9967	0.9968	0.9969	0.9970	0.9971	0.9972	0.9973	0.9974
2.80	0.9974	0.9975	0.9976	0.9977	0.9977	0.9978	0.9979	0.9979	0.9980	0.9981
2.90	0.9981	0.9982	0.9982	0.9983	0.9984	0.9984	0.9985	0.9985	0.9986	0.9986
3.00	0.9987	0.9987	0.9987	0.9988	0.9988	0.9989	0.9989	0.9989	0.9990	0.9990
3.10	0.9990	0.9991	0.9991	0.9991	0.9992	0.9992	0.9992	0.9992	0.9993	0.9993
3.20	0.9993	0.9993	0.9994	0.9994	0.9994	0.9994	0.9994	0.9995	0.9995	0.9995
3.30	0.9995	0.9995	0.9995	0.9996	0.9996	0.9996	0.9996	0.9996	0.9996	0.9997
3.40	0.9997	0.9997	0.9997	0.9997	0.9997	0.9997	0.9997	0.9997	0.9997	0.9998
3.50	0.9998	0.9998	0.9998	0.9998	0.9998	0.9998	0.9998	0.9998	0.9998	0.9998

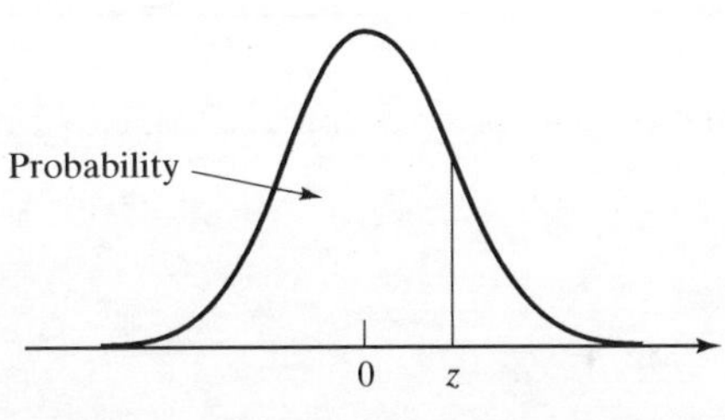

Acknowledgement is given to Prof. Emeritus John W. Adams, who developed the table using Excel.

TABLE 2 Student *t* Distribution

dof	$\alpha = 0.10$	$\alpha = 0.05$	$\alpha = 0.025$	$\alpha = 0.01$	$\alpha = 0.005$
1	3.078	6.314	12.706	31.821	63.657
2	1.886	2.920	4.303	6.965	9.925
3	1.638	2.353	3.182	4.541	5.841
4	1.533	2.132	2.776	3.747	4.604
5	1.476	2.015	2.571	3.365	4.032
6	1.440	1.943	2.447	3.143	3.707
7	1.415	1.895	2.365	2.998	3.499
8	1.397	1.860	2.306	2.896	3.355
9	1.383	1.833	2.262	2.821	3.250
10	1.372	1.812	2.228	2.764	3.169
11	1.363	1.796	2.201	2.718	3.106
12	1.356	1.782	2.179	2.681	3.055
13	1.350	1.771	2.160	2.650	3.012
14	1.345	1.761	2.145	2.624	2.977
15	1.341	1.753	2.131	2.602	2.947
16	1.337	1.746	2.120	2.583	2.921
17	1.333	1.740	2.110	2.567	2.898
18	1.330	1.734	2.101	2.552	2.878
19	1.328	1.729	2.093	2.539	2.861
20	1.325	1.725	2.086	2.528	2.845
21	1.323	1.721	2.080	2.518	2.831
22	1.321	1.717	2.074	2.508	2.819
23	1.319	1.714	2.069	2.500	2.807
24	1.318	1.711	2.064	2.492	2.797
25	1.316	1.708	2.060	2.485	2.787
26	1.315	1.706	2.056	2.479	2.779
27	1.314	1.703	2.052	2.473	2.771
28	1.313	1.701	2.048	2.467	2.763
29	1.311	1.699	2.045	2.462	2.756
inf	1.282	1.645	1.960	2.326	2.576

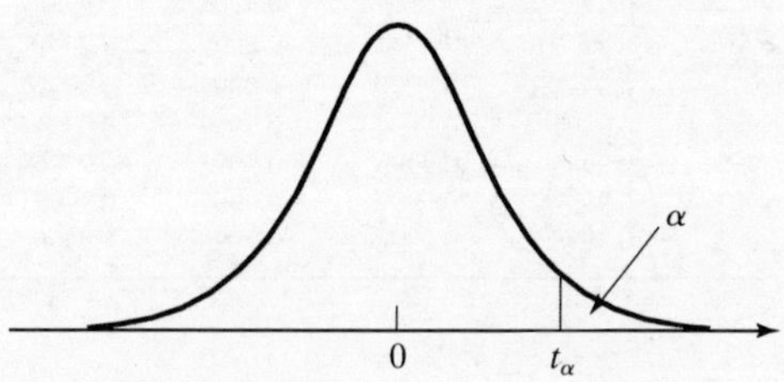

Acknowledgement is given to Prof. Emeritus John W. Adams, who developed the table using Excel.

Index

Page references followed by "f" indicate illustrated figures or photographs; followed by "t" indicates a table.

D

Q

R

S